Alison B

Alison Balter's
Mastering Microsoft® Office
Access 2007
Development

SAMS | 800 East 96th Street, Indianapolis, Indiana 46240 USA

Alison Balter's Mastering Microsoft® Office Access 2007 Development

Copyright © 2007 by Sams Publishing

All rights reserved. No part of this book shall be reproduced, stored in a retrieval system, or transmitted by any means, electronic, mechanical, photocopying, recording, or otherwise, without written permission from the publisher. No patent liability is assumed with respect to the use of the information contained herein. Although every precaution has been taken in the preparation of this book, the publisher and author assume no responsibility for errors or omissions. Nor is any liability assumed for damages resulting from the use of the information contained herein.

10-Digit International Standard Book Number: 0-672-32932-8

13-Digit International Standard Book Number: 978-0-672-32932-6

Library of Congress Cataloging-in-Publication Data

Balter, Alison.

  [Mastering Microsoft Office Access 2007 development]

  Alison Balter's mastering Microsoft Office Access 2007 development / Alison Balter.

      p. cm.

  ISBN 0-672-32932-8

  1. Microsoft Access. 2. Database management. I. Title. II. Title: Mastering Microsoft Office Access 2007 developmentment.

QA76.9.D3B3255 2007

005.75'65—dc22

                                        2007009580

Printed in the United States of America

Fifth Printing: August 2011

Trademarks

All terms mentioned in this book that are known to be trademarks or service marks have been appropriately capitalized. Sams Publishing cannot attest to the accuracy of this information. Use of a term in this book should not be regarded as affecting the validity of any trademark or service mark.

Warning and Disclaimer

Every effort has been made to make this book as complete and as accurate as possible, but no warranty or fitness is implied. The information provided is on an "as is" basis.

Bulk Sales

Sams Publishing offers excellent discounts on this book when ordered in quantity for bulk purchases or special sales. For more information, please contact

  U.S. Corporate and Government Sales
  1-800-382-3419
  corpsales@pearsontechgroup.com

For sales outside of the U.S., please contact

  International Sales
  international@pearsoned.com

Associate Publisher
Greg Wiegand

Acquisitions Editor
Loretta Yates

Development Editor
Kevin Howard

Managing Editor
Gina Kanouse

Project Editor
George E. Nedeff

Copy Editor
Chuck Hutchinson

Indexer
Lisa Stumpf

Proofreader
Karen A. Gill

Technical Editor
Todd Meister

Publishing Coordinator
Cindy Teeters

Multimedia Developer
Dan Scherf

Book Designer
Gary Adair

Composition
Nonie Ratcliff and Bumpy Design

 This Book Is Safari Enabled

The Safari® Enabled icon on the cover of your favorite technology book means the book is available through Safari Bookshelf. When you buy this book, you get free access to the online edition for 45 days. Safari Bookshelf is an electronic reference library that lets you easily search thousands of technical books, find code samples, download chapters, and access technical information whenever and wherever you need it.

To gain 45-day Safari Enabled access to this book

  ▶ Go to http://www.quepublishing.com/safarienabled.

  ▶ Complete the brief registration form.

  ▶ Enter the coupon code J7LG-RQLN-USDF-7ZNB-JUF5. If you have difficulty registering on Safari Bookshelf or accessing the online edition, please email customer-service@safaribooksonline.com.

Contents at a Glance

*The following appendixes are available for download
at www.samspublishing.com/title/0672329328.*

Table of Contents

Part II   What to Do When Things Don't Go as Planned

16   Debugging: Your Key to Successful Development   727

*The following appendixes are available for download
at www.samspublishing.com/title/0672329328.*

About the Author

Alison Balter is the president of InfoTechnology Partners, Inc., a computer consulting firm based in the rural Santa Rosa Valley Area, close to Camarillo, California. Alison is a highly experienced independent trainer and consultant specializing in Windows applications training and development. During her 23 years in the computer industry, she has trained and consulted with many corporations and government agencies. Since Alison founded InfoTechnology Partners, Inc. (formerly Marina Consulting Group) in 1990, its client base has expanded to include major corporations and government agencies such as Shell Oil, Accenture, Northrop, the U.S. Drug Enforcement Administration, Prudential Insurance, Transamerica Insurance, Fox Broadcasting, the U.S. Navy, and others.

InfoTechnology Partners, Inc., is a Microsoft Certified Partner, and Alison is a Microsoft Certified Professional. Alison was one of the first professionals in the computer industry to become a Microsoft Certified Solutions Developer.

Alison is a partner in the multimedia training company Blast Through Learning, Inc., and is the author of more than 300 internationally marketed computer training videos and CD-ROMs, including 18 Access 2000 videos, 35 Access 2002 videos, and 15 Access 2003 videos. These videos and CD-ROMs are available through Alison's company, InfoTechnology Partners, Inc. Alison travels throughout North America, giving training seminars on Microsoft Access, Visual Studio .NET, Microsoft SQL Server, and Visual Basic for Applications. She is also featured in several live satellite television broadcasts for National Technological University.

Alison is a regular contributing columnist for *Access/Office/VB Advisor* as well as other computer publications. She is also a regular on the Access, Visual Studio .NET, SQL Server, and Visual Basic national speaker circuits. She was one of four speakers on the Visual Basic 4.0 and 5.0 World Tours seminar series cosponsored by Application Developers Training Company and Microsoft.

Alison is also author of 14 books published by Sams Publishing: *Alison Balter's Mastering Access 95 Development, Alison Balter's Mastering Access 97 Development, Alison Balter's Mastering Access 2000 Development, Alison Balter's Mastering Access 2002 Desktop Development, Alison Balter's Mastering Access 2002 Enterprise Development, Alison Balter's Mastering Microsoft Access Office 2003, Teach Yourself Microsoft Office Access 2003 in 24 Hours, Access Office 2003 in a Snap, Alison Balter's Mastering Access 2007 Development*, a power user book on Microsoft Access 2007, three e-books on Microsoft Access 2007, and *Teach Yourself SQL Express 2005 in 24 Hours*. Alison is a coauthor of 3 Access books published by Sams Publishing: *Essential Access 95, Access 95 Unleashed*, and *Access 97 Unleashed*.

An active participant in many user groups and other organizations, Alison is a past president of the Independent Computer Consultants Association of Los Angeles and of the Los Angeles Clipper Users' Group. She is currently immediate past president of the Ventura County Professional Women's Network.

On a personal note, Alison keeps herself busy horseback riding, skiing, ice skating, running, lifting weights, hiking, traveling, and dancing. She most enjoys spending time with her husband, Dan, their daughter, Alexis, their son, Brendan, and their golden retriever, Brandy.

Alison's firm, InfoTechnology Partners, Inc., is available for consulting work and onsite training in Microsoft Access, Visual Studio .NET, Visual Basic, and SQL Server, as well as for Windows Server 2003, Windows 2000, Windows NT, Windows 98, Windows XP, PC networking, and Microsoft Exchange Server. You can contact Alison by email at Alison@InfoTech-Partners.com, or visit the InfoTechnology Partners website at http://www.InfoTech-Partners.com.

Dedication

I dedicate this book to my husband, Dan, my daughter, Alexis, my son, Brendan, my parents, Charlotte and Bob, and my real father, Herman. Dan, you are my partner in life and the wind beneath my wings. You are a true partner in every sense of the word. I am so lucky to be traveling the path of life with such a spectacular person. Alexis, you are the sweet little girl that I always dreamed of. You are everything that I could have ever wanted and so very much more. You make every one of my days a happy one! Brendan, you are the one who keeps me on my toes. There is never a dull moment with you around. I wish I had just a small portion of your energy. I thank you for the endless laughter that you bring to our family and for reminding me about all the important things in life. Mom and Dad, without all that you do to help out with life's chores, the completion of this book could never have been possible. Words cannot express my gratitude!

Herman, I credit my ability to soar in such a technical field to you. I hope that I inherited just a small part of your intelligence, wit, and fortitude. I am sorry that you did not live to see this accomplishment. I hope that you can see my work and that you are proud of it. I also hope that in some way you share in the joy that Dan, Alexis, and Brendan bring to me.

Finally, I want to thank God for giving me the gift of gab, a wonderful career, an incredible husband, two beautiful children, a spectacular area to live in, a very special home, and an awesome life. Through your grace, I am truly blessed.

Acknowledgments

Writing a book is a monumental task. Without the support and understanding of those close to me, my dreams for this book would have never come to fruition. Special thanks go to the following special people who helped to make this book possible and, more importantly, who give my life meaning:

Dan Balter (my incredible husband), for his ongoing support, love, encouragement, friendship, and, as usual, patience with me while I wrote this book. Dan, words cannot adequately express the love and appreciation that I feel for all that you are and all that you do for me. You treat me like a princess! Thank you for being the phenomenal person you are, and thank you for loving me for who I am and for supporting me during the difficult times. I enjoy not only sharing our career successes, but even more I enjoy sharing the life of our beautiful children, Alexis and Brendan. I look forward to continuing to reach highs we never dreamed of. There is no one I'd rather spend forever with than you.

Alexis Balter (my precious daughter and dynamite dancer, actress, and ice skater), for giving life a special meaning. Your intelligence, compassion, caring, and perceptiveness are far beyond your years. Alexis, you make all my hard work worth it. No matter how bad my day, when I look at you, sunshine fills my life. You are the most special gift that anyone has ever given me. Finally, thanks for being my walking partner. I love the conversations that we have as we walk many miles each day.

Brendan Balter (my adorable son and little actor and athlete), for showing me the power of persistence. Brendan, you are small, but, boy, are you mighty! I have never seen such tenacity and fortitude in such a little person. Your imagination and creativity are amazing! Thank you for your sweetness, your sensitivity, and your unconditional love. Most of all, thank you for reminding me how important it is to have a sense of humor.

Charlotte and Bob Roman (Mom and Dad), for believing in me and sharing in both the good times and the bad. Mom and Dad, without your special love and support, I never would have become who I am today. Without all your help, I could never get everything done. Words can never express how much I appreciate all that you do!

Al Ludington, for helping me to slow down and experience the shades of gray in the world. You somehow walk the fine line between being there and setting limits, between comforting me and confronting me. Words cannot express how much your unconditional love means to me. Thanks for always being there for me and for showing me that a beautiful mind is not such a bad thing after all.

Herb and Maureen Balter (my honorary mom and dad), for being such a wonderful mother-in-law and father-in-law. Although our paths were rocky at the beginning, I want you to know how special you are to me. I appreciate your acceptance and your warmth. I also appreciate all you have done for Dan and me. I am grateful to have you in my life.

Sue Terry, for being the most wonderful best friend anyone could possibly have. You inspire me with your music, your love, your friendship, and your faith in God. Whenever I am having a bad day, I picture you singing "Dear God" or "Make Me Whole," and suddenly my day gets better. Thank you for the gift of friendship.

Roz, Ron, and Charlie Carriere, for supporting my endeavors and for encouraging me to pursue my writing. It means a lot to know that you guys are proud of me for what I do. I enjoy our times together as a family. Charlie, have a great time at Yale.

Steven Chait, for being a special brother. I want you to know how much you mean to me. When I was a little girl, I was told about your gift for writing. You may not know this, but my desire to write started as a little girl, wanting to be like her big brother. Now that we're adults, I see how many ways we truly are alike.

Sonia Aguilar, for being the best nanny that anyone could ever dream of having. You are a person far too special to describe in words. Although you are no longer part of our daily lives, Alexis and Brendan will love you always. I appreciate the beautiful foundation that you gave them during their key developmental years. You are an amazing model of love, kindness, and charity.

Greggory Peck from Blast Through Learning, for your contribution to my success in this industry. I believe that the opportunities you gave me early on have helped me reach a level in this industry that would have been much more difficult for me to reach on my own. Most of all, Greggory, thanks for your love and friendship. I love you, bro!

Nicole Phelps, for being a great office manager. Thanks for making my day-to-day work life easier. Although you are my office manager, you are much more than that. You are a friend, and you are like a little sister to me. You are a very special person and deserve the best in life. Don't ever forget how special you are!

Scott Barker, for helping me to manage my heavy schedule and for being a special friend. On a work level, I can't express how much you help me. You treat my clients as I would and have a work ethic beyond reproach. On a personal level, you, Diana, and your family are all great friends. My children adore your family, and Dan and I adore you and Diana. Thanks for being in our lives.

Reverend Molly, for advancing me spiritually in ways that I can't even describe. You are an amazing woman and are my mentor. I love you dearly. Thanks also to all of my church friends: Ed, Robin, Gayle, Gail, Greg, Ivette, Sharon, Heather, Jim, Sheryl, John, Rick, Janie, Sherri, Mildred, Opal, Sue, Mary, Terri, Susan, Beth, and all of the people I am forgetting to mention, for all of your love and support.

Diane Dennis, Shell Forman, Ann Sookikian, Bob Hess, Anne Weiderweber, Norbert Foigelman, Chris Sabihon, and all the other wonderful friends that I have in my life. Diane, you have been my soul mate in life since we were four! Shell, my special "sister," I am lucky to have such a special friend as you. Ann, although I haven't known you for very long, you are a very special friend in my life. Bob, you are always there when we need you, and somehow manage to keep a smile on your face. Anne, you are a wonderful friend, walking partner, and confidante. Norbert, you are a very special friend to me and to my family. Chris, you are not only a special friend, but you have had an important impact on my spiritual path in life!

¡Gaby Ayar gracias por todo! ¡Tú eres una amiga perfecta! Queiro que tengas una vida perfecta. ¡Te amo mucho!

Ellen McCrea, Chuck Hinkle, Diane Buehre, Dan Buffington, Silas Raymond, Philip Ochoa, and all the other special clients and work associates that I have in my life. Although all of you started out as work associates, I feel that our relationship goes much deeper than that. I am *very* lucky to have people in my work life like you. Thank you all for your patience with my schedule as I wrote this book.

Loretta Yates, George Nedeff, Todd Meister, and Kevin Howard, for making my experience with Sams a positive one. Loretta, I can't tell you how much I have enjoyed working with you over the past several years. You are very easy to work with, and I enjoy the personal relationship that we have developed as well. I look forward to working together for years to come. George, Todd, and Kevin, I know that you all worked very hard to ensure that this book came out on time and with the best quality possible. Without you, this book wouldn't have happened. I have *really* enjoyed working with *all* of you over these past several months. I appreciate your thoughtfulness and your sensitivity to my schedule and commitments outside this book. It is nice to work with people who appreciate me as a person, not just as an author.

We Want to Hear from You!

As the reader of this book, *you* are our most important critic and commentator. We value your opinion and want to know what we're doing right, what we could do better, what areas you'd like to see us publish in, and any other words of wisdom you're willing to pass our way.

As an associate publisher for Sams Publishing, I welcome your comments. You can email or write me directly to let me know what you did or didn't like about this book—as well as what we can do to make our books better.

Please note that I cannot help you with technical problems related to the topic of this book. We do have a User Services group, however, where I will forward specific technical questions related to the book.

When you write, please be sure to include this book's title and author as well as your name, email address, and phone number. I will carefully review your comments and share them with the author and editors who worked on the book.

Email: feedback@quepublishing.com

Mail: Greg Wiegand
          Associate Publisher
          Sams Publishing
          800 East 96th Street
          Indianapolis, IN 46240 USA

Reader Services

Visit our website and register this book at www.samspublishing.com/register for convenient access to any updates, downloads, or errata that might be available for this book.

Introduction

$\mathbf{M}$any excellent books about Access are available, so why write another one? In talking to the many students I meet in my travels around the country, I have heard one common complaint. Instead of the several great books available for the user community or the host of wonderful books available to expert Access developers, my students yearn for a book targeted toward the intermediate-to-advanced developer. They yearn for a book that starts at the beginning, ensures that they have no gaps in their knowledge, and takes them through some of the most advanced aspects of Access development. Along the way, they want to acquire volumes of practical code that they can easily port into their own applications. In addition, developers of all levels need to transition to Access 2007, which is dramatically different from its predecessors. I wrote *Alison Balter's Mastering Microsoft Office Access 2007 Development* with those requests and objectives in mind.

This book begins by providing you with an introduction to Access development. It alerts you to the types of applications that you can develop in Access and introduces you to the components of an Access application. After you understand what an Access application is and when it is appropriate to develop one, you will explore the steps involved in building an actual Access application. The book covers several strategies before you build the first application component. This ensures that you, as the developer of the application, are aware of the design issues that might affect you in your particular environment.

After you have discovered the overall picture, you will be ready to venture into the specific details of each object within an Access database. Chapters 2 through 6 cover the basics of tables, relationships, queries, forms, and reports. The intent of these chapters is to provide you with an approach to developing these database objects from a developer's perspective. Although this text starts at the beginning, it provides many tips, tricks, and caveats not readily apparent from the documentation or from books targeted toward end users.

When you have a strong foundation of knowing how to build tables, queries, forms, and reports, you will be ready to plunge full-force into the process of building applications. Chapter 7 covers the process of using macros as part of the application-building process. Although macros were not a choice for serious developers in the past, the new embedded macros, error handling, and the inclusion of variables in macros make them a more viable solution for at least part of your applications. Chapters 8 and 9 provide you with an extremely strong grasp of the Visual Basic for Applications (VBA) language. Once again, starting with the basics, the book takes you gently through some of the most complex intricacies of the VBA language and Access object model. The text provides you with many practical examples to ensure that you thoroughly digest each topic.

Chapters 10 through 12 provide you with an advanced discussion of forms, reports, and queries. By the time you reach this point in the book, you should be familiar with all the basics of creating database objects. These chapters combine the basics of table, query, form, and report design with the VBA and object techniques covered in Chapters 8 and 9. The power techniques covered in Chapters 10 through 12 provide you with the expertise that you need to design the most complex types of forms, reports, and queries required by your applications.

After you cover the basics, you will be ready to delve into more advanced techniques. Chapter 13 covers advanced VBA techniques. It is followed by an in-depth discussion of class modules in Chapter 14. The chapter includes many practical examples of how and why to utilize class modules.

Before you ride through the frontier of the many intricacies of the Access development environment, one basic topic remains. Chapter 15 introduces you to ActiveX Data Objects. You will see how you can move away from bound objects, manipulating the data within your database using code.

Unfortunately, things don't always go as planned. No matter what your level of expertise, you will often find yourself stumped over a piece of code and looking for answers. Chapter 16 shows you how to effectively employ the debugger to solve any coding problem you might run into. Even after your application has been thoroughly debugged, you still must provide a responsible means of handling errors within your applications. Chapter 17 shows you everything you must know to implement error handling. Included in the text and on the sample code CD-ROM is a generic error handler that you can easily build into any of your own applications.

Even the fanciest of applications will not please its users if it is sluggish. Chapter 18 covers optimization—that is, all the techniques you should incorporate into your programming code to ensure that your application runs as efficiently as possible.

With the foundation provided by the first 18 chapters, you will be ready to move into the richer and more complex aspects of the VBA language and the Access development environment. Chapters 19 through 22 cover the basics of developing applications for a multi-user or a client/server environment. You can explore locking strategies, ways to interact with non-native Access file formats, and the alternatives for designing client/server applications, including designing them with Microsoft SharePoint.

As an Access developer, you realize your world is not limited to just Access. To be effective and productive as an Access developer, you must know how to interact with other applications and how to use ActiveX controls, libraries, menu add-ins, wizards, and builders to assist you with the application development process. Chapters 23 through 28 cover ribbons, automation, the Windows API, and library and add-in techniques, and provide an introduction to Access and the Internet. After reading these chapters, you will understand how to employ the use of external objects and functionality to add richness to your applications without too much effort on your part.

Having reached the final part of the book, you will be ready to put the final polish on your application. Chapters 29 through 31 cover security, documentation, and database maintenance. You will learn how to properly secure your application so that you do not in any way compromise the investment you have put into the application development process. You will also learn how easy but necessary it is to properly document and maintain your application.

The Access development environment is robust and exciting. With the keys to deliver all that it offers, you can produce applications that provide much satisfaction as well as many financial rewards. After poring over this hands-on guide and keeping it nearby for handy reference, you too can become masterful at Access 2007 development. This book is dedicated to demonstrating how you can fulfill the promise of making Access 2007 perform up to its lofty capabilities. As you will see, you have the ability to really make Access 2007 shine in the everyday world!

Conventions Used in This Book

The people at Sams Publishing have spent many years developing and publishing computer books designed for ease of use and containing the most up-to-date information available. With that experience, we've learned what features help you the most. Look for these features throughout the book to help enhance your learning experience and get the most out of Access 2007.

▶ Screen messages, code listings, and command samples appear in monospace type.

▶ Terms that are defined in the text appear in italics. *Italics* are sometimes used for emphasis, too.

▶ In code lines, placeholders for variables are indicated by using *italic monospace type*.

▶ With VBA, Access 97 and higher, the line continuation character is an underscore.

TIP

Tips give you advice on quick or overlooked procedures, including shortcuts.

NOTE

Notes present useful or interesting information that isn't necessarily essential to the current discussion, but might augment your understanding with background material or advice relating to the topic.

CAUTION

Cautions warn you about potential problems a procedure might cause, unexpected results, or mistakes that could prove costly.

PART I

The Basics of Access Development

IN THIS PART

CHAPTER 1

Access as a Development Tool

Why This Chapter Is Important

In talking to users and developers, I find that Access is a very misunderstood product. Many people think that it is just a toy for managers or secretaries wanting to play with data. Others feel that it is a serious developer product intended for no one but experienced application developers. This chapter dispels the myths of Access. It helps you decipher what Access is and what it isn't. After reading the chapter, you will know when Access is the tool for you, and when it makes sense to explore other products.

What Types of Applications Can You Develop in Access?

I often find myself explaining exactly what types of applications you can build with Microsoft Access. Access offers a variety of features for different database needs. You can use it to develop six general types of applications:

▶ Personal applications

▶ Small business applications

▶ Departmental applications

▶ Corporationwide applications

▶ As a front end for enterprisewide client/server applications

▶ Intranet/Internet applications

Access as a Development Platform for Personal Applications

At its most basic level, you can use Access to develop simple personal database-management systems. I caution people against this idea, though. People who buy Access hoping to automate everything from their wine collections to their home finances are often disappointed. The problem is that Access is deceptively easy to use. Its wonderful built-in wizards make Access look like a product that anyone can use. After answering a series of questions, you have finished application switchboards, data entry screens, reports, and the underlying tables that support them. In fact, when Microsoft first released Access, many people asked whether I was concerned that my business as a computer programmer and trainer would diminish because Access seemed to let absolutely anyone write a database application. Although it's true that you can produce the simplest of Access applications without any thought of design and without writing a single line of code, most applications require at least some designing and custom code.

As long as you're satisfied with a wizard-generated personal application with only minor modifications, no problems should occur. It's when you want to substantially customize a personal application that problems can happen.

Access as a Development Platform for Small Business Applications

Access is an excellent platform for developing an application that can run a small business. Its wizards let developers quickly and easily build the application's foundation. The ability to build code modules enables developers to create code libraries of reusable functions, and the ability to add code behind forms and reports enables them to create powerful custom forms and reports.

The main limitation of using Access for developing a custom small business application is the time and money involved in the development process. Many people use Access wizards to begin the development process but find they need to customize their application in ways they can't accomplish on their own. Small business owners often experience this problem on an even greater scale. The demands of a small business application are usually much higher than those of a personal application. Many doctors, attorneys, and other professionals have called me in after they reached a dead end in the development process. They're always dismayed at how much money it will cost to make their application usable.

Access as a Development Platform for Departmental Applications

Access is perfect for developing applications for departments in large corporations. It's relatively easy to upgrade departmental users to the appropriate hardware; for example, it's much easier to buy additional RAM for 15 users than it is for 4,000! Furthermore, Access's performance is adequate for most departmental applications without the need for client/server technology. Finally, most departments in large corporations have the development budgets to produce well-designed applications.

Fortunately, most departments usually have a PC guru who is more than happy to help design forms and reports. This gives the department a sense of ownership because they have contributed to the development of their application. It also makes my life as a developer much easier. I can focus on the hard-core development issues, leaving some of the form and report design tasks to the local talent.

Access as a Development Platform for Corporationwide Applications

Although Access might be best suited for departmental applications, you can also use it to produce applications that you distribute throughout the organization. How successful this endeavor is depends on the corporation. There's a limit to the number of users that can concurrently share an Access application while maintaining acceptable performance, and there's also a limit to the number of records that each table can contain without a significant performance drop. These numbers vary depending on factors such as the following:

► How much traffic already exists on the network?

► How much RAM and how many processors does the server have?

► How is the server already being used? For example, are applications such as Microsoft Office being loaded from the server or from local workstations?

► What types of tasks are the users of the application performing? Are they querying, entering data, running reports, and so on?

► Where are Access and your Access application run from, the server or the workstation?

► What network operating system is in place?

My general rule of thumb for an Access application that's not client/server-based is that poor performance generally results with more than 10–15 concurrent users and more than 100,000 records. Remember, these numbers vary immensely depending on the factors mentioned, as well as on the definition of acceptable performance by you and your users. The basics of when to move to a client/server database are covered in Chapter 22, "Developing Multiuser and Enterprise Applications." I cover additional details about this topic in a separate book, *Alison Balter's Mastering Access 2002 Client/Server Development*, also published by Sams.

Developers often misunderstand what Access is and what it isn't when it comes to being a client/server database platform. People often ask me, "Isn't Access a 'client/server' database?" The answer is that Access is an unusual product because it's a file server application out of the box, but it can act as a front end to a client/server database. In case you're lost, here's an explanation: If you buy Access and develop an application that stores the data on a file server in an Access database, the workstation performs all data processing. This means that every time the user runs a query or report, the file server returns all the data to the workstation. The workstation machine then runs the query and displays the results in a datasheet or on a report. This process generates a significant amount of network traffic, particularly if multiple users are running reports and queries at the same time on large Access tables. In fact, such operations can bring the entire network to a crawl.

Access as a Front End for Enterprisewide Client/Server Applications

A client/server database, such as Microsoft SQL Server or Oracle, processes queries on the server machine and returns results to the workstation. The server software itself can't display data to the user, so this is where Access comes to the rescue. Acting as a front end, Access can display the data retrieved from the database server in reports, datasheets, or forms. If the user updates the data in an Access form, the workstation sends the update to the back-end database. You can accomplish this process either by linking to these external databases so that they appear to both you and the user as Access tables, or by using techniques that access client/server data directly.

Because Access 2007 ships with an integrated data store (the SQL Server 2005 Express Database Engine), you can develop a client/server application on the desktop and then easily deploy it to an enterprise SQL Server database. Chapter 22 briefly covers the alternatives and techniques for developing client/server applications. *Alison Balter's Mastering Access 2002 Client/Server Development* provides details on how to develop Access projects.

When you reduce the volume of network traffic by moving the processing of queries to the back end, Access becomes a much more powerful development solution. It can handle huge volumes of data and a large number of concurrent users. The main issues usually faced by developers who want to deploy such a wide-scale Access application are the following:

▶ The variety of operating systems used by each user

▶ Difficulties with deployment

▶ The method by which each user is connected to the application and data

▶ The type of hardware each user has

Although processing of queries in a client/server application is done at the server, which significantly reduces network traffic, the application itself still must reside in the memory of each user's PC. This means that each client machine must be capable of running the appropriate operating system and the correct version of Access. Even when the correct operating system and version of Access are in place, your problems are not over. Dynamic link library (DLL) conflicts often result in difficult-to-diagnose errors and idiosyncrasies in an Access application. Furthermore, Access is not the best solution for disconnected users who must access an application and its data over the Internet. Finally, Access 2007 is hardware hungry! The hardware requirements for an Access application are covered later in this chapter. The bottom line is that, before you decide to deploy a wide-scale Access application, you need to know the hardware and software configurations of all your system's users. You must also decide whether the desktop support required for the typical Access application is feasible given the number of people who will use the system that you are building.

Access as a Development Platform for Intranet/Internet Applications

Using data access pages, you can publish your database objects as static or dynamic HTML pages. Static pages are standard HTML you can view in any browser. Access 2000 introduced the capability to create XML data and schema documents from Jet or SQL Server structures and data. You can also import data and data structures into Access from XML documents. You can accomplish this either using code or via the user interface.

> **NOTE**
>
> This book provides coverage of Internet-related features, such as working with HTML and XML files.

Access as a Scalable Product

One of Access's biggest strong points is its scalability. You can scale an application that begins as a small business application running on a standalone machine to an enterprisewide client/server application. If you design your application properly, you can accomplish the scaling process with little to no rewriting of your application. This feature makes Access an excellent choice for growing businesses, as well as for applications you are testing at a departmental level with the idea that you might eventually distribute them corporationwide.

The great thing about Access is that, even acting as both the front end and back end with data stored on a file server in Access tables, it provides excellent security and the capability to establish database rules previously available only on back-end databases. You can apply referential integrity rules at the database level, ensuring that, for example, users do not enter orders for customers who don't exist. You can enforce data validation rules at either a field or record level, maintaining the integrity of the data in your database. In other words, many of the features previously available only on high-end database servers are now available by using Access's own proprietary data storage format.

What Exactly Is a Database?

The term *database* means different things to different people. For many years, in the world of xBase (dBASE, FoxPro, CA-Clipper), *database* was used to describe a collection of fields and records. (Access refers to this type of collection as a *table*.) In a client/server environment, *database* refers to all the data, schema, indexes, rules, triggers, and stored procedures associated with a system. In Access terms, a database is a collection of all the tables, queries, forms, data access pages, reports, macros, and modules that compose a complete system.

Getting to Know the Database Objects

As mentioned previously, tables, queries, forms, reports, macros, and modules combine to comprise an Access database. Each of these objects has a special function. An Access application also includes several miscellaneous objects, including relationships, database properties, and import/export specifications. With these objects, you can create a powerful, user-friendly, integrated application. Figure 1.1 shows the Access application window. Notice the categories of objects listed in the Navigation Pane. The following sections take you on a tour of the objects that make up an Access database.

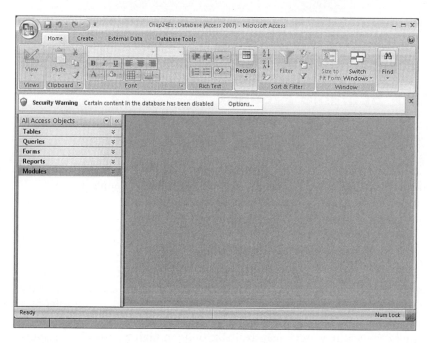

FIGURE 1.1   The Navigation Pane displays categories for each type of database object.

Tables: A Repository for Your Data

Tables are the starting point for your application. Whether your data is stored in an Access database or you are referencing external data by using linked tables, all the other objects in your database either directly or indirectly reference your tables.

To view all the tables that are contained in the open database, select Tables from the Navigation Pane drop-down, as shown in Figure 1.2. (Note that you won't see any hidden tables unless you have checked the Hidden Objects check box in the Navigation Options dialog box, as shown in Figure 1.3.) If you want to view the data in a table, double-click the name of the table you want to view.

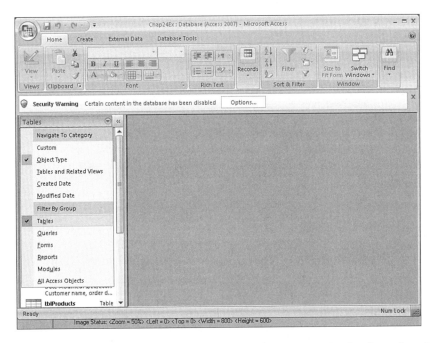

FIGURE 1.2   To view all tables, select Tables from the Navigation Pane drop-down.

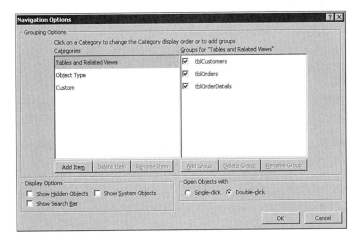

FIGURE 1.3   The Navigation Options dialog box allows you to show hidden tables.

Access displays the table's data in a datasheet, which includes all the table's fields and records (see Figure 1.4). Note that I have collapsed the Navigation Pane so that you get a better view of the table (described later in this chapter). You can modify many of the datasheet's attributes and even search for and filter data from within the datasheet. If the table is related to another table (such as the Northwind Customers and Orders tables), you can also expand and collapse the subdatasheet to view data stored in child tables.

This book does not cover these techniques. You can find them in the Access user manual or any introductory Access book, such as *Sams Teach Yourself Microsoft Office Access 2007 in 24 Hours*.

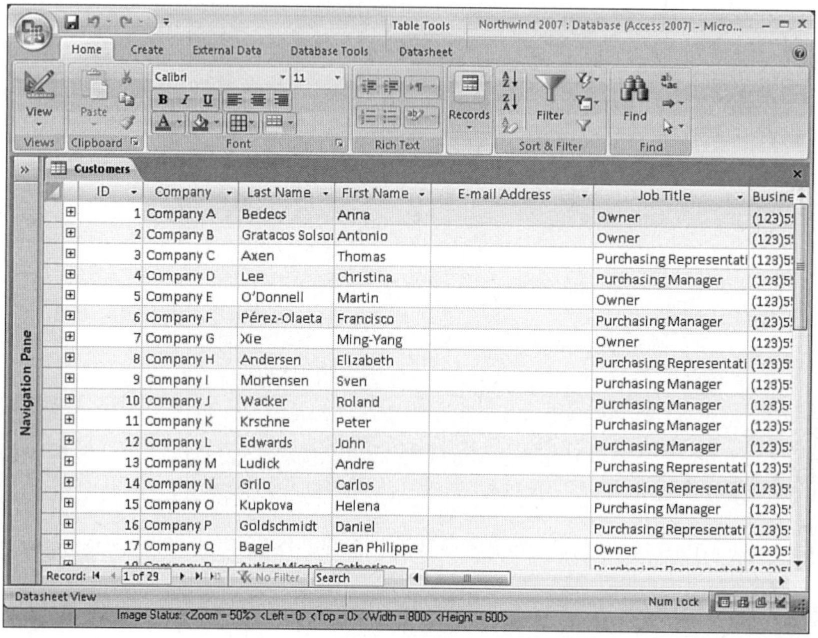

FIGURE 1.4   The Datasheet view of the Customers table in the Northwind database includes all the table's fields and records.

As a developer, you most often want to view the table's design, which is the blueprint or template for the table. To view a table's design, click the View icon on the home page of the ribbon while the table is open (see Figure 1.5). In Design view, you can view or modify all the field names, data types, and field and table properties. Access gives you the power and flexibility you need to customize the design of your tables. Chapter 2, "What Every Developer Needs to Know About Databases and Tables," covers these topics.

Relationships: Tying the Tables Together

To properly maintain your data's integrity and ease the process of working with other objects in the database, you must define relationships among the tables in your database. You accomplish this by using the Relationships window. To view the Relationships window, click to select the Database Tools tab. Then select the Relationships button in the Show/Hide group. The Relationships window appears, as shown in Figure 1.6.

In this window, you can view and maintain the relationships in the database. If you or a fellow developer has set up some relationships, but you don't see any in the Relationships window, select the All Relationships button in the Relationships group on the Design tab to unhide any hidden tables and relationships.

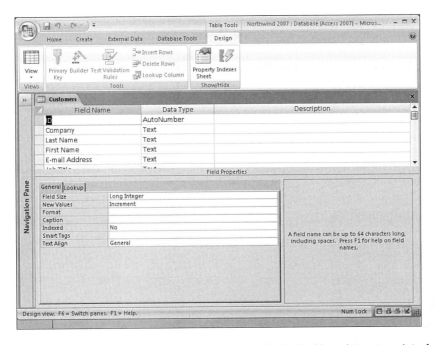

FIGURE 1.5   The design of the Customers table is the blueprint or template for the table.

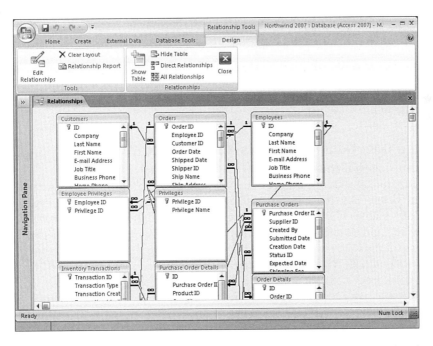

FIGURE 1.6   The Relationships window is the place where you view and maintain the relation-ships in the database.

Notice that many of the relationships in Figure 1.6 have a join line between tables with a number 1 and an infinity symbol (∞). This indicates a one-to-many relationship between the tables. If you double-click the join line, the Edit Relationships dialog box opens (see Figure 1.7). In this dialog box, you can specify the exact nature of the relationship between tables. The relationship between Customers and Orders, for example, is a one-to-many relationship with referential integrity enforced. This means that the user cannot add orders for customers who don't exist. Notice that the check box to Cascade Update Related Fields is not checked. This means that the user cannot update the CustomerID of a customer in the Customers table. Because Cascade Delete Related Records is not checked, the user cannot delete customers from the Customers table if they have corresponding orders in the Orders table.

FIGURE 1.7   The Edit Relationships dialog box lets you specify the nature of the relationship between tables.

Chapter 3, "Relationships: Your Key to Data Integrity," extensively covers the process of defining and maintaining relationships. It also covers the basics of relational database design. For now, remember that you should establish relationships both conceptually and literally as early in the design process as possible. They are integral to successfully designing and implementing your application.

Queries: Stored Questions or Actions You Apply to Your Data

Queries in Access are powerful and multifaceted. Select queries enable you to view, summarize, and perform calculations on the data in your tables. Action queries let you add to, update, and delete table data. To run a query, select Queries from the Navigation drop-down and then double-click the query you want to run, or right-click to select the query you want to run and then click Open. When you run a select query, a datasheet appears, containing all the fields specified in the query and all the records meeting the query's criteria (see Figure 1.8). When you run an action query, Access runs the specified action, such as making a new table or appending data to an existing table. In general, you can update the data in a query result because the result of a query is actually a dynamic set of records, called a *dynaset*, based on your tables' data.

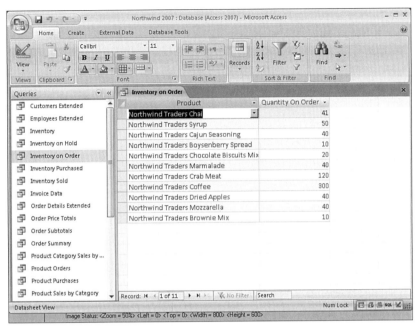

FIGURE 1.8   When you run the Inventory on Order query, a datasheet appears, containing all the fields specified in the query and all the records meeting the query's criteria.

When you store a query, only its definition, layout or formatting properties, and datasheet are actually stored in the database. Access offers an intuitive, user-friendly tool for you to design your queries. Figure 1.9 shows the Query Design window. To open this window, select Queries from the Navigation pane drop-down, choose the query you want to modify, and right-click and select Design. The query pictured in the figure selects data from Purchase Orders, Purchase Orders Status, and Purchase Price Totals tables and queries. (Note that you can base queries on tables and on other queries.) It displays the Creation Date, Supplier ID, Shipping Fee, Taxes, and several other fields from the Purchase Orders table, the Status from the Purchase Order Status table, and the Sub Total expression from the Purchase Price Totals query. Chapter 4, "What Every Developer Needs to Know About Query Basics," and Chapter 12, "Advanced Query Techniques," both cover queries. Because queries are the foundation for most forms and reports, I cover them throughout this book as they apply to other objects in the database.

Forms: A Means of Displaying, Modifying, and Adding Data

Although you can enter and modify data in a table's Datasheet view, you can't control the user's actions very well; likewise, you can't do much to facilitate the data entry process. This is where forms come in. Access forms can take on many traits, and they're very flexible and powerful.

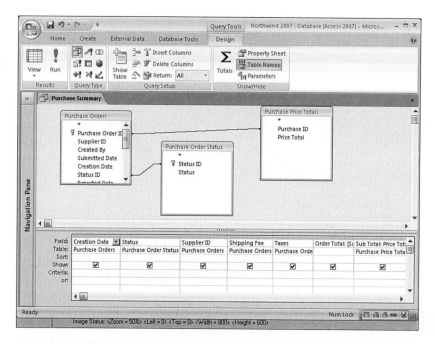

FIGURE 1.9   The design of this query displays data from the Purchase Orders and Purchase Order Status tables and the Purchase Price Totals query.

To view any form, select Forms from the Navigation Pane. Then double-click the form you want to view, or right-click the form you want to view and click Open. Figure 1.10 illustrates a form in Form view. This form is actually four forms in one: one main form and three subforms. The main form displays information from the Orders table, and the subforms display information from the Order Details table and the Orders table. As the user moves from order to order, the form displays the orders details associated with that order. When the user clicks to select the Shipping Information and Payment Information tabs, she can see additional information about that order.

As with tables and queries, you can also view forms in Design view. To view the design of a form, right-click the Form from within the Navigation Pane and select Design. Figure 1.11 shows the Order Details form in Design view. Notice the three subforms within the main form. Chapter 5, "What Every Developer Needs to Know About Forms," and Chapter 10, "Advanced Form Techniques," officially cover forms. I also cover forms throughout this text as they apply to other examples of building an application.

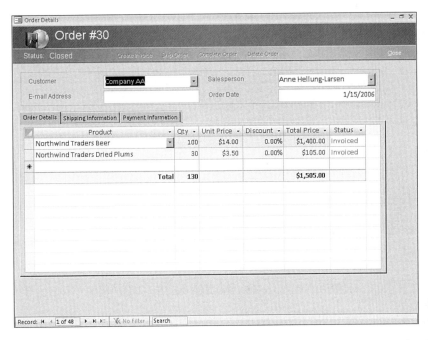

FIGURE 1.10   The Order Details form includes customer, order, and order detail information.

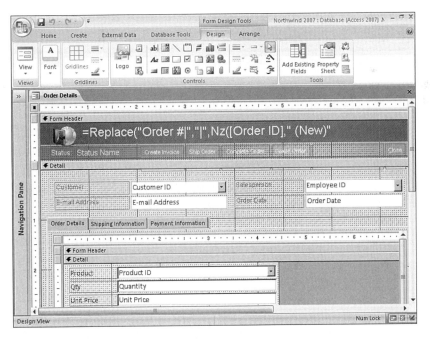

FIGURE 1.11   The design of the Order Details form shows three subforms.

Reports: Turning Data into Information

Forms enable you to enter and edit information, but with reports, you can display information, usually to a printer. Figure 1.12 shows a report in preview mode. To preview any report, right-click the report in the Navigation Pane and select Print Preview, or double-click the report you want to preview. Notice the colors in the report, as well as other details, such as the shaded area for the column headings. Like forms, reports can be elaborate and exciting, yet can contain valuable information.

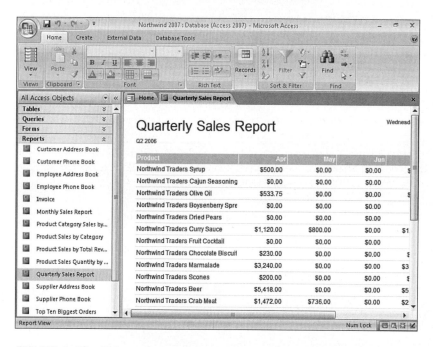

FIGURE 1.12   This preview of the Quarterly Sales Report displays information in the report.

If you haven't guessed yet, you can view reports in Design view, as shown in Figure 1.11. To view the design of any report, right-click the report in the Navigation Pane and select Design View. Figure 1.12 illustrates a report with many sections; in the figure you can see a Report Header, Page Header, Detail section, Page Footer, and Report Footer—just a few of the many sections available on a report. Just as a form can contain subforms, a report can contain subreports. Chapter 6, "What Every Developer Needs to Know About Reports," and Chapter 11, "Advanced Report Techniques," cover reports. I also cover them throughout the book as they apply to other examples.

Macros: A Means of Automating Your System

Macros in Access aren't like the macros in other Office products. You can't record them, as you can in Microsoft Word or Excel, and Access does not save them as Visual Basic for Applications (VBA) code. With Access macros, you can perform most of the tasks that you can manually perform from the keyboard, menus, and toolbars. Macros enable you to build logic into your application flow.

Available in Microsoft Office Access 2007 are *embedded* macros. Instead of appearing in the Navigation Pane as a separate object, an embedded macro is part of the object to which it is associated. When you modify an embedded macro, it does not affect any other macros or objects in the database. Because you can prevent embedded macros from performing certain potentially unsafe operations, they are trusted. (Macros, including embedded macros, are covered in Chapter 7, "What Are Macros, and When Do You Need Them?")

To run a macro, select Macros from the Navigation Pane, right-click the macro you want to run, and then click Run. Access then executes the actions in the macro. To view a macro's design, right-click the macro in the Navigation Pane and select Design View. The macro pictured in Figure 1.13 has four columns. The first column enables you to specify a condition. The action in the macro's second column won't execute unless the condition for that action evaluates to True. The third column shows you the arguments for that line of the macro, and the fourth column lets you document the macro. In the bottom half of the Macro Design window, you specify the arguments that apply to the selected action. In Figure 1.13, the selected action is OpenForm, which accepts six arguments: Form Name, View, Filter Name, Where Condition, Data Mode, and WindowMode.

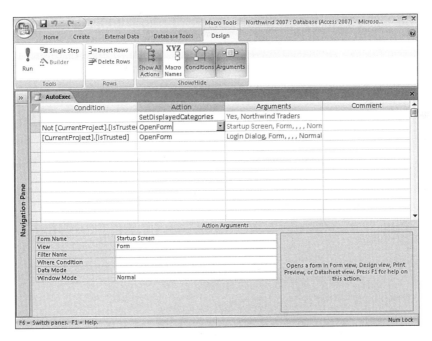

FIGURE 1.13   The design of the AutoExec macro contains conditions, actions, arguments, and comments.

Modules: The Foundation to the Application Development Process

Modules, the foundation of any application, let you create libraries of functions that you can use throughout your application. You usually include subroutines and functions in the modules that you build. Functions always return a value; subroutines do not. By using code modules, you can do the following:

▶ Perform error handling

▶ Declare and use variables

▶ Loop through and manipulate recordsets

▶ Call Windows API and other library functions

▶ Create and modify system objects, such as tables and queries

▶ Perform transaction processing

▶ Perform many functions not available with macros

▶ Test and debug complex processes

▶ Create library databases

These are just a few of the tasks you can accomplish with modules. To view the design of an existing module, right-click the module you want to modify in the Navigation Pane and click Design View to open the Module Design window (see Figure 1.14). The global code module in Figure 1.14 contains a General Declarations section and five functions. The function that is visible is called CreateInvoice. Chapter 8, "VBA: An Introduction," and Chapter 13, "Advanced VBA Techniques," discuss modules and VBA, respectively. I also cover modules and VBA extensively throughout this book.

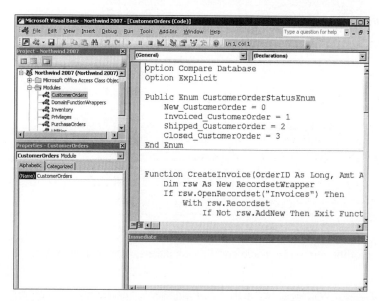

FIGURE 1.14   The global code module in Design view shows the General Declarations section and CreateInvoice function.

Object Naming Conventions

Finding a set of naming conventions—and sticking to it—is one of the keys to successful development in Access or any other programming language. When you're choosing a set of naming conventions, look for three characteristics:

- ▶ Ease of use
- ▶ Readability
- ▶ Acceptance in the developer community

The naming conventions that I use in this book were derived from the Leszynski/Reddick naming conventions that were prominent in Access versions 1.x and 2.0. These standards were adopted and used extensively by the development community and can be found in most good development books and magazine articles written in the past few years. These conventions give you an easy-to-use, consistent methodology for naming the objects in all these environments.

Appendix A, "Naming Conventions," is available for download at www.samspublishing.com and includes a summarized version of the conventions for naming objects. I'll be using them throughout the book and highlighting certain aspects of them as they apply to each chapter.

Hardware Requirements

One of the downsides of Access is the number of hardware resources it requires. The requirements for a developer are different from those for an end user, so I have broken the system requirements into two parts. As you read through these requirements, be sure to note actual versus recommended requirements.

What Hardware Does Microsoft Office Access 2007 Require?

According to Microsoft documentation, these are the *official* minimum requirements to run Microsoft Access 2007:

- ▶ 500 megahertz (MHz) processor or higher
- ▶ Windows XP with Service Pack 2, Windows 2003 with Service Pack 1, or a later operating system, such as Windows Vista.
- ▶ 256 megabytes (MB) RAM or higher
- ▶ 1.5 gigabytes (GB) of hard disk space (some will be freed after the original download package is removed from the hard drive
- ▶ 1024×768 or higher resolution
- ▶ CD-ROM or DVD drive
- ▶ A pointing device

The bottom line for hardware is the more, the better. You just can't have enough memory or hard drive capacity. The more you have, the happier you will be using Access.

How Do I Get Started Developing an Access Application?

Many developers believe that because Access is such a rapid application development environment, there's absolutely no need for system analysis or design when creating an application. I couldn't disagree more. As mentioned earlier in this chapter, Access applications are deceptively easy to create, but without proper planning, they can become a disaster.

Task Analysis

The first step in the development process is *task analysis*, or considering each and every process that occurs during the user's workday—a cumbersome but necessary task. When I started working for a large corporation as a mainframe programmer, I was required to carefully follow a task analysis checklist. I had to find out what each user of the system did to complete her daily tasks, document each procedure, determine the flow of each task to the next, relate each task of each user to her other tasks as well as to the tasks of every other user of the system, and tie each task to corporate objectives. In this day and age of rapid application development and changing technology, task analysis in the development process seems to have gone out the window. I maintain that if you don't take the required care to complete this process at least at some level, you will have to rewrite large parts of the application.

Data Analysis and Design

After you have analyzed and documented all the tasks involved in the system, you're ready to work on the data analysis and design phase of your application. In this phase, you must identify each piece of information needed to complete each task. You must assign these data elements to subjects, and each subject will become a separate table in your database. For example, a subject might be a client; every data element relating to that client—the name, address, phone, credit limit, and any other pertinent information—would become fields within the client table.

You should determine the following for each data element:

- Appropriate data type
- Required size
- Validation rules

You should also determine whether you will allow the user to update each data element and whether it's entered or calculated; then you can figure out whether you have properly normalized your table structures.

Normalization Made Easy

Normalization is a fancy term for the process of testing your table design against a series of rules that ensure that your application will operate as efficiently as possible. These rules are based on set theory and were originally proposed by Dr. E. F. Codd. Although you could spend years studying normalization, its main objective is an application that runs efficiently with as little data manipulation and coding as possible. Chapter 3 covers normalization and database design in detail. For now, here are six of the basic normalization rules:

1. Fields should be *atomic*—that is, each piece of data should be broken down as much as possible. For example, instead of creating a field called Name, you would create two fields: one for the first name and the other for the last name. This method makes the data much easier to work with. If you need to sort or search by first name separately from the last name, for example, you can do so without extra effort.

2. Each record should contain a unique identifier so that you have a way of safely identifying the record. For example, if you're changing customer information, you can make sure you're changing the information associated with the correct customer. We refer to this unique identifier as a primary key.

3. The *primary key* is a field or fields that uniquely identify the record. Sometimes you can assign a natural primary key. For example, the Social Security number in an employee table should serve to uniquely identify that employee to the system. At other times, you might need to create a primary key. Because two customers could have the same name, for example, the customer name might not uniquely identify the customer to the system. You might need to create a field that would contain a unique identifier for the customer, such as a customer ID.

4. A primary key should be short, stable, and simple. *Short* means it should be small (not a 50-character field). A Long Integer is perfect as a primary key. *Stable* means the primary key should be a field whose value rarely, if ever, changes. For example, although a customer ID would rarely change, a company name is much more likely to change. *Simple* means it should be easy for a user to work with.

5. Every field in a table should supply additional information about the record that the primary key serves to identify. For example, every field in the customer table describes the customer with a particular customer ID.

6. Information in the table shouldn't appear in more than one place. For example, a particular customer name shouldn't appear in more than one record.

Take a look at an example. The datasheet shown in Figure 1.15 is an example of a table that hasn't been normalized. Notice that the CustInfo field is repeated for each order, so if the customer address changes, it has to be changed in every order assigned to that customer. In other words, the CustInfo field is not atomic. If you want to sort by city, you're out of luck, because the city is in the middle of the CustInfo field. If the name of an inventory item changes, you need to make the change in every record where that inventory item was ordered. Probably the worst problem in this example involves items ordered. With this design, you must create four fields for each item the customer orders: name, supplier, quantity, and price. This design would make it extremely difficult to build sales reports and other reports your users need to effectively run the business.

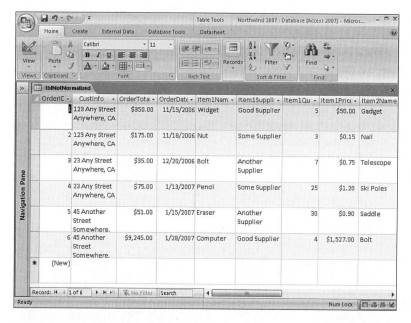

FIGURE 1.15   This table hasn't been normalized.

Figure 1.16 shows the same data normalized. Notice that I've broken it out into several different tables: tblCustomers, tblOrders, tblOrderDetails, and tblSuppliers. The tblCustomers table contains data that relates only to a specific customer.

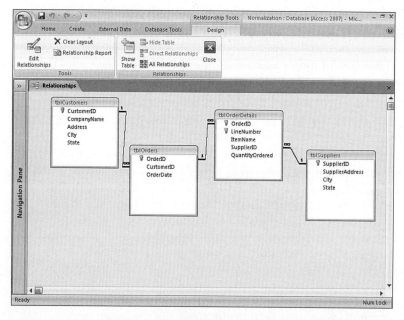

FIGURE 1.16   The data has been normalized into four separate tables.

I have uniquely identified each record by a contrived `CustID` field, which I use to relate the orders table, `tblOrders`, to `tblCustomers`. The `tblOrders` table contains only information that applies to the entire order, rather than to a particular item that the customer ordered. This table contains the `CustID` of the customer who placed the order and the date of the order, and I've related it to the `tblOrderDetails` table based on the `OrderID`. The `tblOrderDetails` table holds information about each item ordered for a particular `OrderID`.

There's no limit to the potential number of items that the user can place on an order. The user can add as many items to the order as needed, simply by adding more records to the `tblOrderDetails` table. Finally, I placed the supplier information in a separate table, `tblSuppliers`, so that if any of the supplier information changes, the user has to change it in only one place.

Prototyping

Although the task analysis and data analysis phases of application development haven't changed much since the days of mainframes, the prototyping phase has changed. In working with mainframes or DOS-based languages, it was important to develop detailed specifications for each screen and report. I remember requiring users to sign off on every screen and report. Even a change such as moving a field on a screen meant a change order and approval for additional hours. After the user signed off on the screen and report specifications, the programmers would go off for days and work arduously to develop each screen and report. They would return to the user after many months only to hear that everything was wrong. This meant the developer had to go back to the drawing board and spend many additional hours before the user could once again review the application.

The process is quite different now. As soon as you have outlined the tasks and the data analysis is complete, the developer can design the tables and establish relationships among them. The form and report prototype process can then begin. Rather than the developer going off for weeks or months before having further interaction with the user, the developer needs only a few days, using the Access wizards, to quickly develop form prototypes.

Testing

As far as testing goes, you just can't do enough. I recommend that, if your application is going to be run in Windows 2000, Windows 2003, Windows XP, and Windows Vista, you test in all environments. I also suggest you test your application extensively on the lowest common denominator piece of hardware; the application might run great on your machine but show unacceptable performance on your users' machines.

Testing your application both in pieces and as an integrated application usually helps. Recruit several people to test your application and make sure they range from the most savvy of users to the least computer-adept person you can find. These different types of users will probably find completely different sets of problems. Most importantly, make sure you're not the only tester of your application, because you're the least likely person to find errors in your own programs.

Implementation

Your application is finally ready to go out into the world, or at least you hope so! Distribute your application to a subset of your users and make sure they know they're performing the test case. Make them feel honored to participate as the first users of the system, but warn them that problems might occur, and it's their responsibility to make you aware of them. If you distribute your application on a wide-scale basis and it doesn't operate exactly as it should, regaining the confidence of your users will be difficult. That's why it is so important to roll out your application slowly.

Maintenance

Because Access is such a rapid application-development environment, the maintenance period tends to be much more extended than the one for a mainframe or DOS-based application. Users are much more demanding; the more you give them, the more they want. For a consultant, this is great. Just don't get into a fixed-bid situation. Because of the scope of the application changing, you could very well end up on the losing end of that deal.

There are three categories of maintenance activities: bug fixes, specification changes, and frills. You need to handle bug fixes as quickly as possible. The implications of specification changes need to be clearly explained to the user, including the time and cost involved in making the requested changes. As far as frills go, try to involve the users as much as possible in adding frills by teaching them how to enhance forms and reports and by making the application as flexible and user-defined as possible. Of course, the final objective of any application is a happy group of productive users.

What's New in Access 2007?

Access 2007 sports a plethora of new features, all worth taking a look at. Although Microsoft targeted many of the new features to the end user, there are many other useful enhancements in the product. The following sections provide an overview of the new features. I cover each feature in more detail in the appropriate chapter of this book.

What's New in the User Interface?

The user interface in Microsoft Office Access 2007 has been redesigned from the ground up. Microsoft made this design change to help you find the commands that you need, when you need them. Many features that previously were buried deep within Access's menu structure are now easily accessible. From the moment you launch Microsoft Office Access 2007 to the time you exit the application, your user experience will be very different from that of Access 2003, or any of the previous versions of Microsoft Access.

When you launch Access 2007, the screen appears as shown in Figure 1.17. Here, you can opt to create a new blank database, open a recently used database, open other existing databases, or create a new database from a template. If you select Blank Database, Access prompts you for the name and location of the database, as shown in Figure 1.18. When you click Create, the screen appears as shown in Figure 1.19.

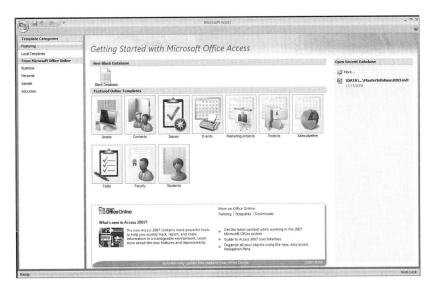

FIGURE 1.17   The Access 2007 desktop looks quite different from that of its predecessors.

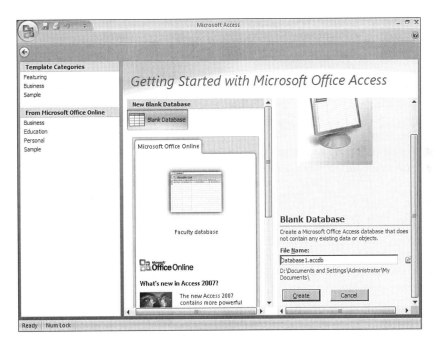

FIGURE 1.18   You must select a name and a location for the database.

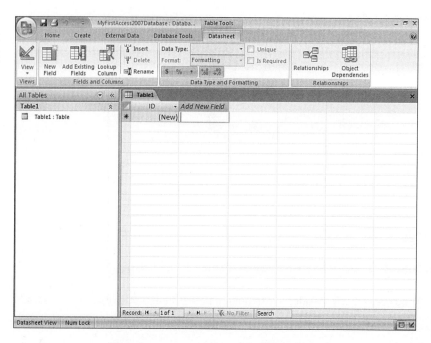

FIGURE 1.19   Access 2007 includes a new tabbed interface.

Notice that Microsoft Office Access 2007 provides you with a tabbed interface (see Figure 1.19). When you create a new blank database, Access 2007 provides you with a new datasheet so that you can create the first table contained in the database. You can use this technique to create a table, or you can create a table in Design view. Notice that underneath the tabs is what looks like a fancy toolbar. Microsoft refers to this toolbar as the *ribbon*. The next section ("Getting to Know the Ribbon") goes into the details of the ribbon. In the sections that follow, we'll look at each tab available in Microsoft Office Access 2007.

Getting to Know the Ribbon

The ribbon is the area at the top of the program window; it replaces menus and toolbars. Using the ribbon, you can choose the category of commands with which you want to work. The ribbon contains command tabs and contextual command tabs. The following sections cover both types of tabs.

Exploring the Command Tabs

When you launch Microsoft Office Access 2007, you are presented with a tabbed interface. The tabs displayed include Home, Create, External Data, Database Tools, and Datasheet. This section explores the details of each tab.

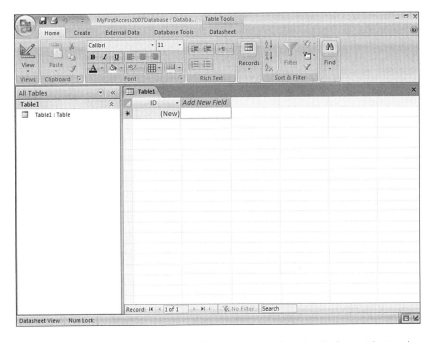

FIGURE 1.20   The Home tab enables you to perform basic formatting and record-oriented tasks.

The first tab is the Home tab (see Figure 1.20). It enables you to perform the following types of functions:

- ▶ Switch between views (datasheet and design)
- ▶ Cut, copy, and paste
- ▶ Format text (add bold or underline, change the font, and so on)
- ▶ Work with rich text (bulleted lists and numbered lists)
- ▶ Work with records (save, total, spell check, and so on)
- ▶ Sort and filter data
- ▶ Locate data meeting specific criteria

The second tab is the Create tab (see Figure 1.21). It enables you to perform the following types of functions:

- ▶ Create tables, table templates, and SharePoint lists
- ▶ Create various types of forms
- ▶ Create various types of reports
- ▶ Create queries and macros

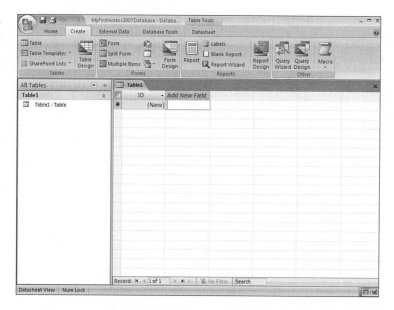

FIGURE 1.21   The Create tab enables you to create database objects.

The third tab is the External Data tab (see Figure 1.22). This tab enables you to perform the following types of tasks:

- ▶ Process saved imports and exports
- ▶ Interface with other Access databases, as well as with Excel spreadsheets, SharePoint lists, text files, XML files, and other databases such as Open Database Connectivity (ODBC) databases
- ▶ Create and manage email

The fourth tab is called the Database Tools tab (see Figure 1.23). It enables you to do the following:

- ▶ Launch the Visual Basic editor
- ▶ Work with macros
- ▶ Work with relationships and object dependencies
- ▶ Perform analysis tasks
- ▶ Interface with SQL Server
- ▶ Work with linked tables
- ▶ Manage switchboards
- ▶ Encrypt databases
- ▶ Work with add-ins
- ▶ Compile your database

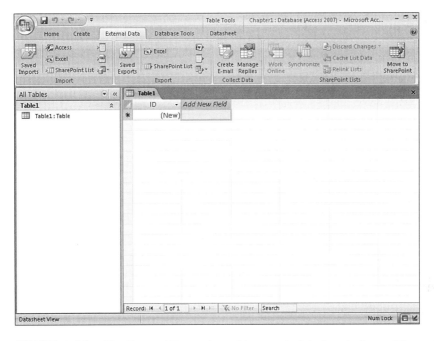

FIGURE 1.22   The External Data tab enables you to interface between Microsoft Office Access 2007 and other applications, such as Excel and SharePoint.

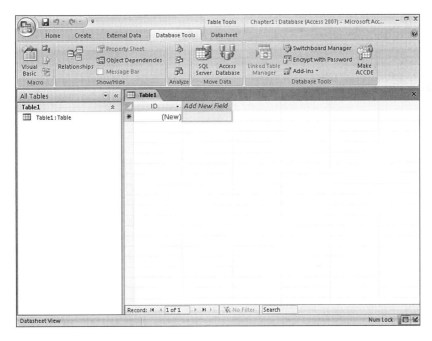

FIGURE 1.23   The Database Tools tab enables you to perform miscellaneous database-related tasks.

Exploring the Contextual Command Tabs

Other tabs are contextual and therefore vary depending on what you are doing. For example, when you first create a new database, Access assumes that your first task will be to create a new table. It places you in Datasheet view, and the Datasheet tab appears (see Figure 1.24). This tab enables you to perform all tasks relating to the process of working with a datasheet. These tasks include working with fields and columns, modifying the data type and formatting associated with a column, and working with relationships. I cover each context-sensitive tab as appropriate within this shortcut.

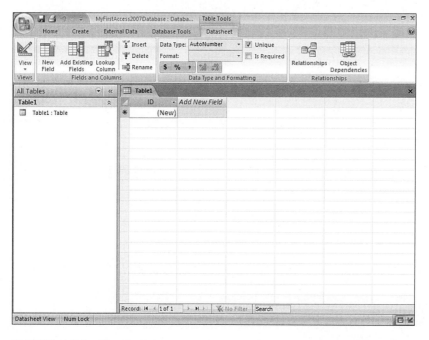

FIGURE 1.24   The Datasheet tab is a contextual tab, available while you are working in Datasheet view.

Utilizing the Gallery

The gallery is a control that displays a choice visually so that you can see the results you will get. The idea is to allow you to browse and see what Microsoft Office Access 2007 can do. Figure 1.25 provides an example. As you can see, when you click the arrow on the right side of the Gridlines button, a gallery appears showing you how each result will appear. This feature makes it easy for you to confidently make your selection from the options available.

Working with the Quick Access Toolbar

The Quick Access toolbar is a single standard toolbar that appears at the top of the ribbon and provides single-click access to commands such as Save and Undo. Notice the Save, Print, and Undo buttons in Figure 1.26. These buttons are all on the Quick Access toolbar; you can easily access them at any time. You can customize the Quick Access toolbar to include the commands that you use most often. You also can modify the placement and size of the toolbar. As you can see, the small toolbar appears above the command tabs. To change the placement of the Quick Access toolbar, simply right-click the toolbar and select Show Quick Access Toolbar Below the Ribbon. The toolbar appears below the ribbon (see Figure 1.27).

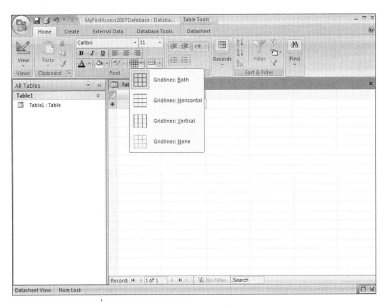

FIGURE 1.25   The gallery gives you a preview of the effect that the selected choice will make.

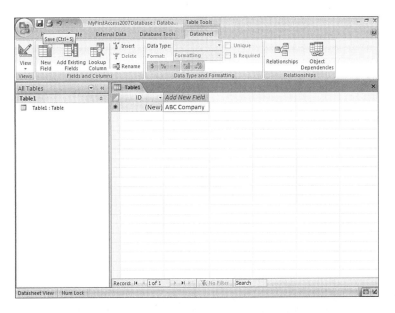

FIGURE 1.26   The Quick Access toolbar enables you to easily access commonly used commands.

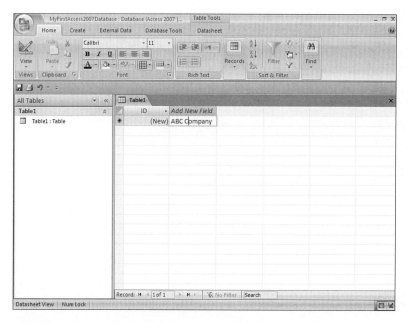

FIGURE 1.27   You can place the Quick Access toolbar under the ribbon.

Working with the Microsoft Office Access Button

The Microsoft Office Access button appears in the upper-left corner of the application window. When you click the Microsoft Office Access button, a menu appears (see Figure 1.28). Using the menu, you can perform the following tasks:

- ▶ Create new databases

- ▶ Open existing databases

- ▶ Save changes to the current object

- ▶ Use the Save As menu to save to other Access file formats as well as to a web server or to a PDF or XPS file

- ▶ Print or print preview

- ▶ Manage databases by compacting and repairing them, backing them up, and working with Database properties

- ▶ Email your databases to other people

- ▶ Close the current database

Ribbon Tips and Tricks

You can use the same keyboard shortcuts with Microsoft Office Access 2007 that you could with previous versions of Access. This means that you can perform many of the commonly used features (such as Save) using the keyboard shortcuts that you are familiar with. When you hover your mouse pointer over the ribbon on a button that is associated with a keyboard shortcut, the shortcut appears as a ToolTip (see Figure 1.29).

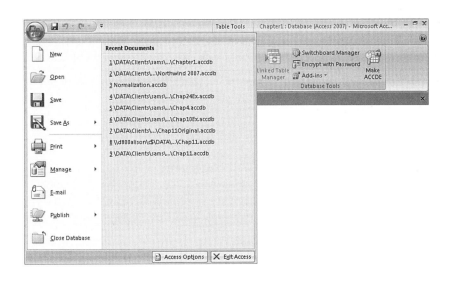

FIGURE 1.28   The Microsoft Office Access button provides a menu necessary to perform commonly used commands.

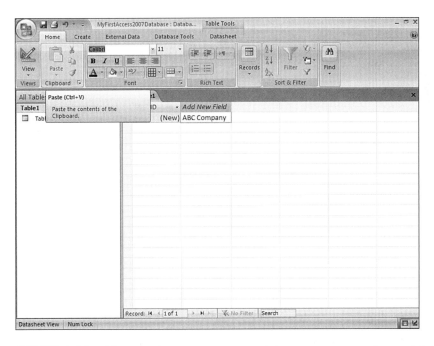

FIGURE 1.29   When you hover your mouse pointer over a command associated with a keyboard shortcut, the shortcut appears as a ToolTip.

Another way in which you can identify keyboard shortcuts is to press your Alt key while on a particular tab. All the Alt key shortcuts appear as small indicators (see Figure 1.30). For example, when you press Alt with the Home tab active, you can see that Alt+F will access the Microsoft Office Access button.

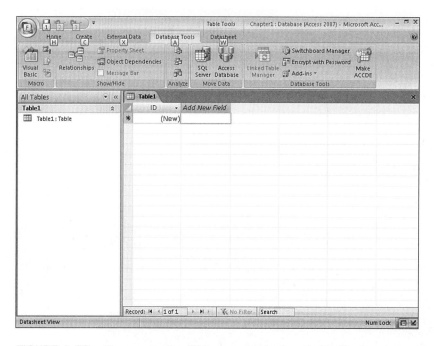

FIGURE 1.30   If you press the Alt key on your keyboard, the Alt shortcuts appear as small indicators.

Sometimes you are going to want extra screen real estate and will want to collapse the ribbon so that only the active command tab appears. Microsoft Office Access 2007 makes this quite easy. To collapse the ribbon, double-click the active command tab. Your application window appears as in Figure 1.31. To open it again, simply click the tab you want to activate.

Customizing the Quick Access Toolbar

As mentioned in the section "Working with the Quick Access Toolbar," you can customize the Quick Access toolbar. To do so, right-click the toolbar; a context-sensitive menu appears (see Figure 1.32). Select Customize Quick Access Toolbar. The Access Options dialog box appears with the Customization page selected (see Figure 1.33). The following steps show you how to customize the Quick Access toolbar:

1. Use the Choose Commands From drop-down list to select the category of commands from which you want to choose. For example, in Figure 1.34, the Create commands are selected.

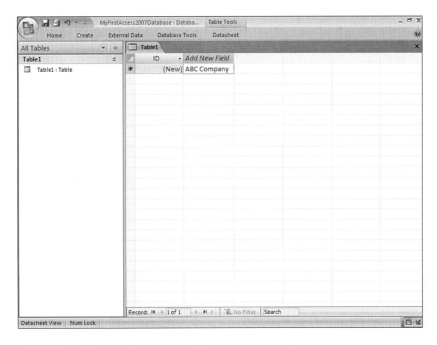

FIGURE 1.31   Double-click the ribbon to collapse it.

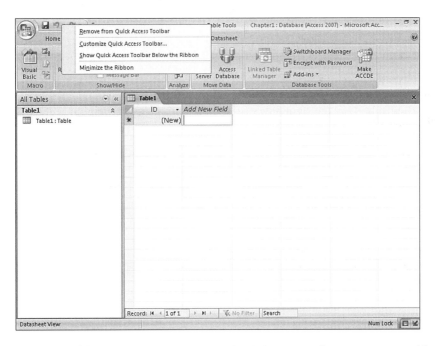

FIGURE 1.32   When you right-click the Quick Access toolbar, a context-sensitive menu appears.

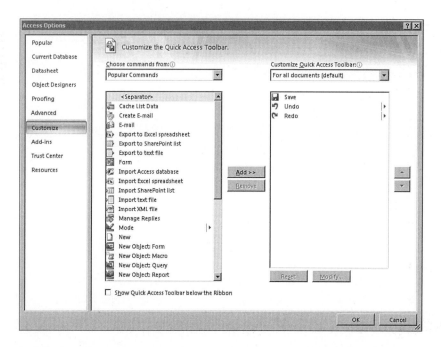

FIGURE 1.33   The Customization page of the Access Options dialog box enables you to customize the Quick Access toolbar.

2. Use the Customize Quick Access Toolbar drop-down list to determine whether your changes will apply for all documents (databases) or for only the specific document that you are working with.

3. Select a command from the list box on the left side of the dialog box and click Add to add it to the list box on the right side of the dialog box. For example, in Figure 1.34, the Blank Form command has been added from the Create Tab options.

4. Use the up and down arrows on the right side of the dialog box to move the command up or down within the list of existing commands.

5. After you add all the desired commands, click OK to complete the process. The Quick Access toolbar now appears with the icons associated with the commands that you added to the toolbar (see Figure 1.35).

TIP

If you want to reset the Quick Access toolbar to its default state, click the Reset button on the Customization page of the Access Options dialog box.

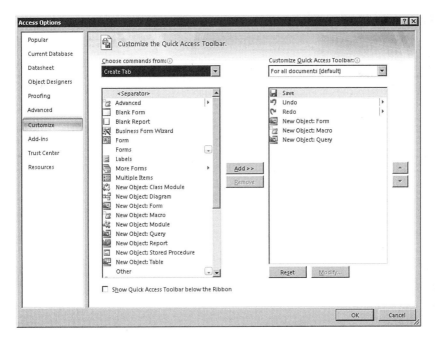

FIGURE 1.34 After you select Add, the command appears in the list box on the right side of the dialog box.

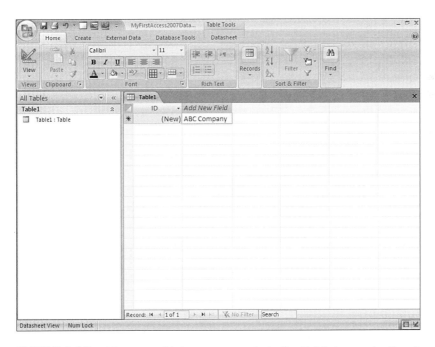

FIGURE 1.35 After you add three commands to the Quick Access toolbar, they appear next to the existing toolbar buttons.

Getting to Know the Navigation Pane

Microsoft has replaced the Database window with the Navigation Pane. The Navigation Pane contains the names of all the objects in your database, including the forms, reports, pages, macros, and modules that compose your database. In Figure 1.36, you can see that the Contacts database is composed of one table, one query, two forms, and two reports.

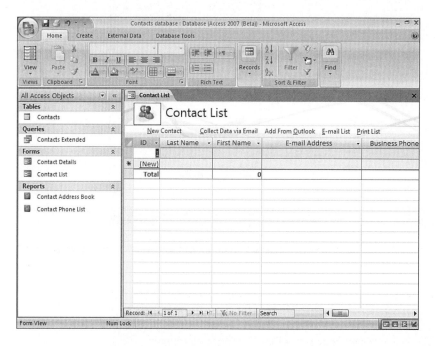

FIGURE 1.36   The Navigation Pane enables you to select and work with the appropriate database object.

Applying a command to a database object is easy; simply right-click the object, and a context-sensitive menu appears. For example, the context-sensitive menu associated with the Contacts table enables you to open, design, import, export, delete, and perform other important functionality necessary when administering a table (see Figure 1.37). Another example is the context-sensitive menu that appears when you right-click a form. Notice in Figure 1.38 that the options for a form are quite different from those for a table. They include the ability to work with the form in various views; to export, rename, and delete the form; as well as to view form properties.

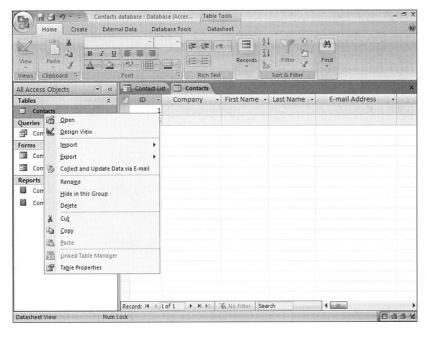

FIGURE 1.37   After you right-click a table, the context-sensitive menu enables you to perform functionality associated with a table.

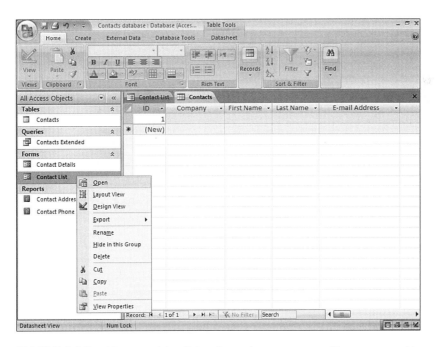

FIGURE 1.38   After you right-click a form, the context-sensitive menu enables you to perform functionality associated with a form.

Working with Tabbed Documents

In Microsoft Office Access 2003, all open documents (forms, reports, and so on) appeared on the taskbar. Microsoft has replaced this paradigm with that of tabbed documents. When you have open forms, reports, and other objects, they appear as tabs on the ribbon (see Figure 1.39). You can easily move from object to object by simply clicking each tab. Notice in Figure 1.39 that three objects are open: Contact List, Contacts Extended, and Contact Address Book. The Contact List form is currently the active tab.

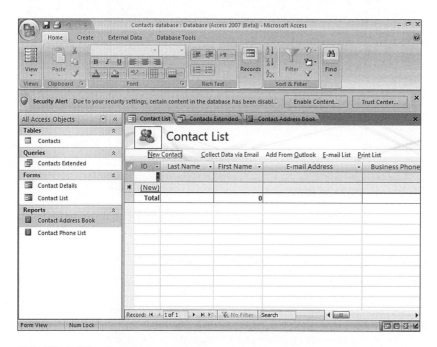

FIGURE 1.39   Each open document appears as a tab on the ribbon.

Showing or Hiding Document Tabs

If you prefer the older style of either viewing only one object at a time or of overlapping windows that appear on the taskbar, you can change the behavior of Access by using Access Options. Follow these steps to view only one object at a time:

1. Click the Microsoft Office button.

2. Select Access Options (see Figure 1.40). The Access Options dialog box appears.

3. Click Current Database. Your screen should appear as in Figure 1.41.

4. In the Application Options section, click Display Document Tabs to deselect it.

5. Click OK to close the dialog box. You will receive a message indicating that you must close and reopen the current database for the specified option to take effect.

1

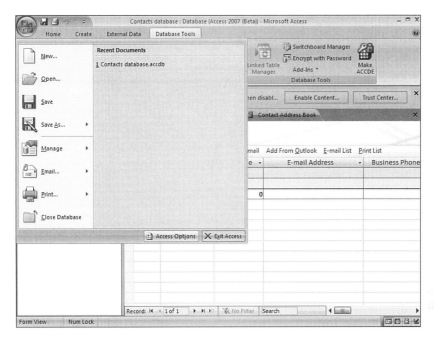

FIGURE 1.40   Access Options enables you to modify the behavior of Access and specific databases.

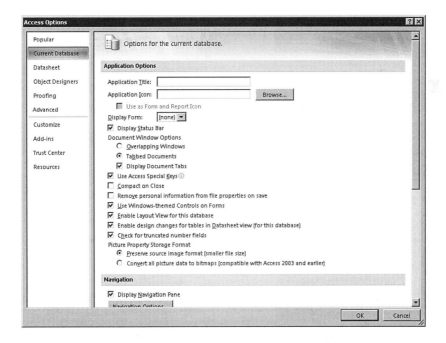

FIGURE 1.41   The Current Database options affect the behavior of a specific database.

6. Close and reopen the database to see the changes take effect. Your screen should now appear as in Figure 1.42. Notice that no tabs appear under the ribbon.

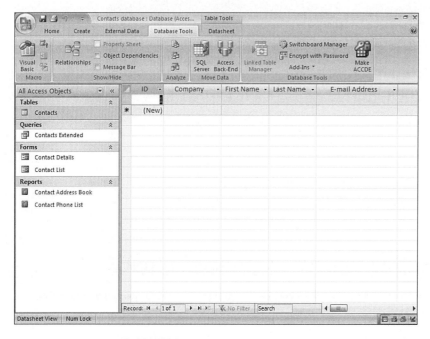

FIGURE 1.42   After you close and reopen the database, no tabs appear under the ribbon.

Displaying Overlapping Windows

Another option is to display overlapping windows. Here are the steps involved:

1. Click the Microsoft Office button.

2. Select Access Options. The Access Options dialog box appears.

3. Click Current Database.

4. Click Overlapping Windows to select it.

5. Click OK to close the dialog box.

6. Close and reopen the database to see the changes take effect. Your screen should now appear as in Figure 1.43. Notice that no tabs appear under the ribbon.

NOTE

The Display Documents Tabs setting is a per-database setting. You must modify this setting for each database. New databases created using Access 2007 show document tabs by default. Databases created in earlier versions of Access use overlapping windows by default.

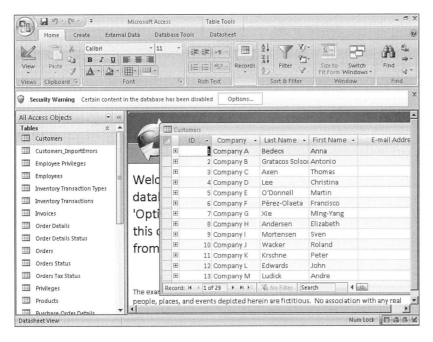

FIGURE 1.43   After you close and reopen the database, you can see each object as an over-lapping window.

Exploring the New Status Bar

The status bar in Microsoft Office Access 2007 is similar to that of earlier versions of Access but sports some new features. In addition to showing status messages, property hints, progress indicators, and other features familiar to earlier versions of Access, the new status bar enables you to modify the current view and to zoom. It also provides rich right-click functionality.

You can quickly and easily modify the view you are working with by simply clicking the appropriate tool in the lower-right corner of the status bar (see Figure 1.44). For example, when a form is open, you can switch among Form view, Datasheet view, Layout view, and Design view. When a table is open, you can switch among Datasheet view, PivotTable view, PivotChart view, and Design view.

Another feature of the new status bar is the capability to adjust the zoom level to zoom in or out. You do this by using the slider on the status bar.

Finally, the new status bar provides a host of commands that are available when you right-click it. Notice in Figure 1.45 that you can perform commands such as changing the Caps Lock setting, the Num Lock setting, and whether the data is filtered. You simply click to select or deselect the appropriate setting.

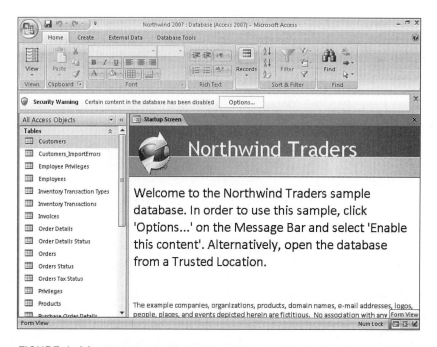

FIGURE 1.44   You can modify the view that you are working with by clicking the appropriate tool on the status bar.

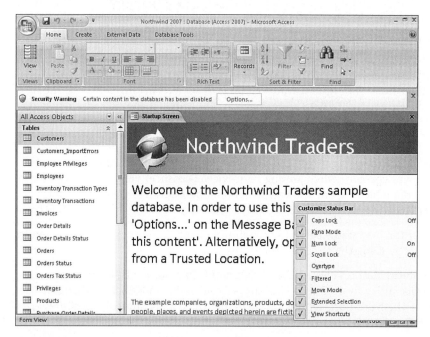

FIGURE 1.45   When you right-click on the status bar, you can perform many commands.

Showing or Hiding the Status Bar

Microsoft Office Access 2007 gives you the option of hiding or showing the status bar. The following are the steps you must take to change the visibility of the status bar:

1. Click the Microsoft Office button.

2. Select Access Options. The Access Options dialog box appears.

3. Click Current Database.

4. Click within the Application Options section to deselect Display Status Bar.

5. Click OK to close the dialog box.

6. Close and reopen the database. The status bar should no longer be visible (see Figure 1.46).

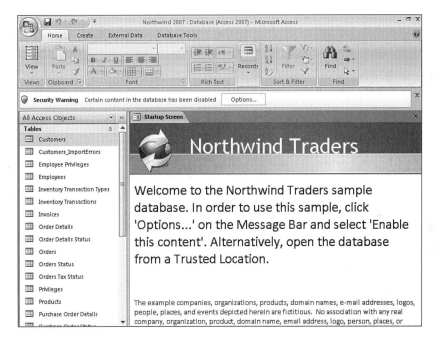

FIGURE 1.46   After you close and reopen the database, the status bar no longer appears.

Working with the Mini Toolbar

Microsoft Office Access 2007 offers many text formatting features. In earlier versions of Access, formatting text required using a menu or displaying the formatting toolbar. The mini toolbar enables you to easily access formatting features without having to use menus or display a toolbar. Here's how:

1. Select the text you want to change. (The text must be in a memo field using the rich text feature.) The mini toolbar appears above the selected text (see Figure 1.47).

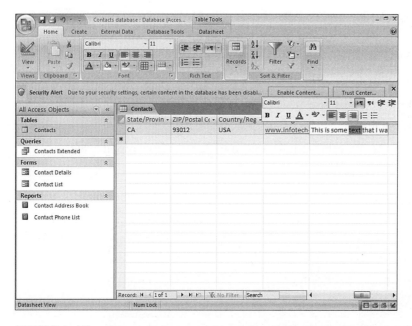

FIGURE 1.47   After you select text, the mini toolbar appears above the selected text.

2. Click to select the appropriate formatting options (for example, bold).

3. Move your mouse pointer away from the mini toolbar. The mini toolbar fades away, and the text appears with the selected formatting (see Figure 1.48).

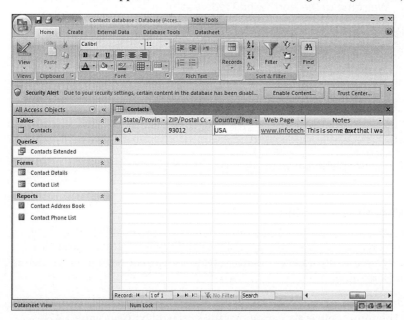

FIGURE 1.48   Notice that the word *text* in the Notes field is bold and italic.

> **NOTE**
>
> If you don't want to apply formatting to a selection, simply move your mouse pointer a few pixels away from the toolbar, and the mini toolbar disappears.

> **NOTE**
>
> You can apply formatting only in specific situations, such as within a Memo field where the Text Format property is set to Rich Text.

What's New with Forms?

The number of new features available with forms in Access 2007 is so vast that I will provide an overview here and then will supply the details in Chapter 5. The features new to forms include the following:

- ▶ The ability to quickly create a form with Quick Create

- ▶ A new view called Layout view

- ▶ The ability to work with Stacked and Tabular layouts

- ▶ Split forms

- ▶ Alternating background colors

- ▶ New filtering features for form data

What's New with Reports?

Reports also sport a plethora of new features. Many of the features are similar to those provided for reports. They include the following:

- ▶ The ability to create a report with Quick Create

- ▶ A new view called Layout view

- ▶ The ability to work with Stacked and Tabular layouts

- ▶ New Group, Sort, and Totals features

The Exciting World of Pivot Tables and Pivot Charts

Access 2002, 2003, and 2007 enable the user to view any table, query, or form in PivotTable or PivotChart view. Pivot tables and pivot charts enable users to easily perform rather complex data analyses. This means that you can perform many of the data analysis tasks once left to Microsoft Excel directly within Microsoft Access. Pivot tables and pivot charts are available in subforms as well, and you can programmatically react to the events that they raise.

Other New Features Found in Access 2007

Microsoft Office Access 2007 includes greatly improved importing and exporting features. For example, you can now export to PDF and XPS fields. You can also save your importing and exporting specifications so that you can reuse them later. I cover these features in Chapter 20, "Using External Data."

Microsoft Office Access 2007 is tightly integrated with Microsoft Office Outlook 2007. You can both collect and update data using Microsoft Office Outlook 2007. When you use the new Data Collection feature, Microsoft Office Access 2007 can automatically create a Microsoft Office InfoPath 2007 or HTML form. It can then embed that form in an email message. You can then send it to selected Outlook contacts or even to contacts stored in an Access database. When the recipient fills out the form and returns it, you can seamlessly store the resulting data in your Microsoft Office Access 2007 database.

In addition, Microsoft has completely revamped security in Microsoft Office Access 2007. The User Security model has been completely eliminated in Access 2007, unless you keep your database in the old Access file format (.mdb or .mde) and that database already has user-level security applied. In other words, if you open a database created in an earlier version of Access and that database already has security applied, Access 2007 will support user-level security for that database. If you convert a database created in an earlier version of Access to the Access 2007 file format, Access 2007 will strip all user-level security settings from the database, and Access 2007 security will apply. You will learn much more about security in Chapter 31, "Database Security Made Easy."

What Happened to Replication?

Replication is not supported in Microsoft Office Access 2007, unless you keep your database in the old Access file format. If you open an existing .mdb file where replication has already been implemented, the replication will be supported. You can also use Access 2007 to replicate a database created in an earlier version of Access, as long as you do not convert that database to the new file format.

You will not be able to convert a replicated database to the Access 2007 file format. However, there is a solution, which involves manually re-creating the database in the Access 2007 file format. You should do this *only* if you feel that the benefits afforded by the Access 2007 file format outweigh the benefit received from replication. If you do decide to manually re-create the database, you must first make sure that all hidden and system objects are available. Then do the following:

1. Open the replica that you want to convert using the same version of Access in which you created it.

2. Select Tools, Options.

3. Click the View tab. The Options dialog box appears, as in Figure 1.49.

4. In the Show section, select Hidden Objects and System Objects.

5. Click OK to apply your settings and close the Options dialog box.

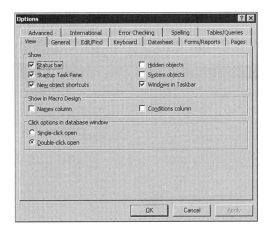

FIGURE 1.49   The Options dialog box allows you to view hidden and system objects.

Re-Creating the Database

Next, you must manually re-create the database. Here's how:

1. Create a blank Access 2007 database and open it.

2. Close the table called Table1 without saving it.

3. Click the External Data tab (see Figure 1.50).

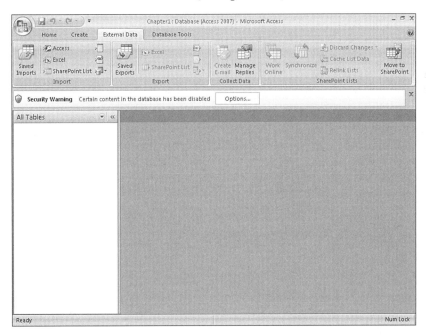

FIGURE 1.50   You use the External Data tab to import and export data.

4. In the Import group, select Access. The Get External Data – Access Database dialog box appears (see Figure 1.51).

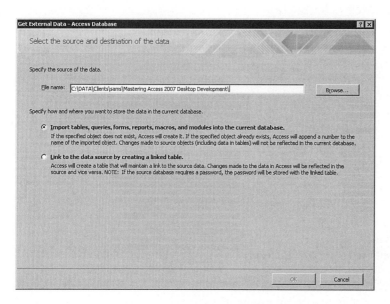

FIGURE 1.51   The Get External Data – Access Database dialog box prompts you to locate the database whose objects you are importing.

5. Browse to locate the replicated database, and then click Open.

6. In the Get External Data – Access Database dialog box, click Import Tables, Queries, Forms, Reports, Macros, and Modules into the Current Database and then click OK. The Import Objects dialog box appears (see Figure 1.52).

FIGURE 1.52   The Import Objects dialog box prompts you to select the objects you want to import.

7. Click to select the objects that you want to import into the new database. If you want to import all objects, click Select All on each tab. *Do not* select any tables. You will handle them separately.

8. Access prompts you to save your import steps. If you want to do so, click the Save Import Steps check box, enter the required information (see Figure 1.53), and then click Save Import.

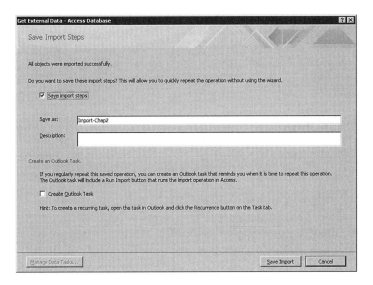

FIGURE 1.53   Select Save Import if you plan to perform the import process again at a later time.

9. Open the replicated database in Access 2007.

10. Make sure that the s_GUID, s_Lineage, and s_Generation fields are visible. To do this, right-click the top of the Navigation Pane and select Navigation Options. The Navigation Options dialog box appears (see Figure 1.54).

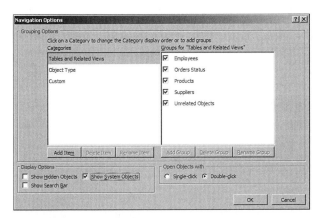

FIGURE 1.54   Use the Navigation Options dialog box to indicate that you want to display system objects.

11. Select Show System Objects in the Display Options section. Click OK to close the dialog box.

12. Create a Make Table query for each table in the database. The Make Table query will take all the data in the old table and create a table in the new database with the same data. If the s_GUID is a primary key that acts as a foreign key in other tables, you must include the s_GUID field in the new table. There is no need to copy the s_Lineage and s_Generation fields to the new table.

13. Run the Make Table queries. This will create the tables in the new database. It's important to note that the new table will not inherit any of the field properties, and it will not inherit the primary key setting from the original table.

14. In the new database, create the same index and primary key used in the replica's tables.

15. Create the necessary relationships for each table in the new database.

16. Save your new database.

What Happened to ADP Files?

Access Data Project (ADP) is also no longer supported in Microsoft Office Access 2007, again unless you keep your database in the old Access file format. Although supported with the old Access file format, it is probably best that you do not do any new development with ADP files. If you have existing ADP files that are currently meeting your business needs, you don't need to rewrite them at this time. If you decide at some point to make major changes to those existing applications, that is when you should consider moving them to the new `.accdb` or `.accde` file format and rewriting their functionality as necessary to take advantage of the new features available in Microsoft Office Access 2007 and eliminating the features specific to ADP files.

Additional Tips and Tricks

There are a few additional tips and tricks that you should be aware of when working with Microsoft Office Access 2007. They include advanced Navigation Pane techniques and the process of working with multi-valued fields. The following sections discuss each of these topics in detail.

Advanced Navigation Pane Techniques

Microsoft Office Access 2007 sports some wonderful Navigation Pane techniques that you should be aware of. These include the capability to create custom categories and groups, show or hide the groups or objects in a category, and remove and restore objects in custom groups. Let's start with the process of creating custom categories. Here are the steps involved:

1. Right-click the menu at the top of the Navigation Pane. A cascading menu appears (see Figure 1.55).

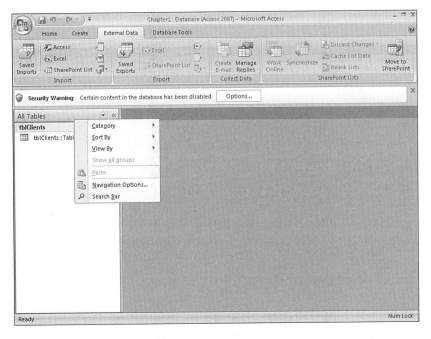

FIGURE 1.55   A cascading menu enables you to control the behavior of the Navigation Pane.

2. Select Navigation Options. The Navigation Options dialog box appears (see Figure 1.56).

3. Click Add Item to add a category. Your dialog box appears as in Figure 1.57.

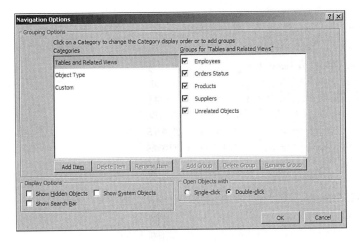

FIGURE 1.56   The Navigation Options dialog box enables you to manipulate important features of the Navigation Pane.

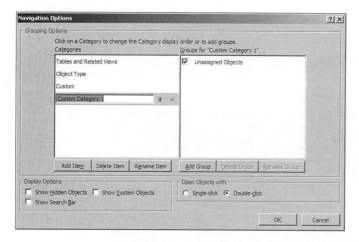

FIGURE 1.57   You can easily add a category to the Navigation Pane.

4. Type the name of the new category.

5. Use the up and down arrows to move the category up or down in the list.

6. Click OK to close the dialog box. If you left-click the Navigation Pane menu, you
    will see your new category in the list (see Figure 1.58).

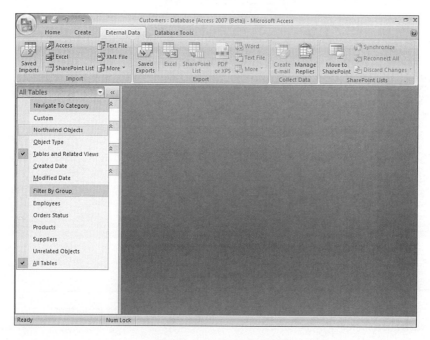

FIGURE 1.58   After you create a custom category, you will see it in the list of available
categories.

Adding Custom Groups to the Category

After you have created a custom category, you will want to add custom groups to it. Here are the steps involved:

1. Right-click the menu at the top of the Navigation Pane and select Navigation Options. The Navigation Options dialog box appears.

2. Click to select the category to which you want to add groups. In Figure 1.59, Northwind Objects is selected.

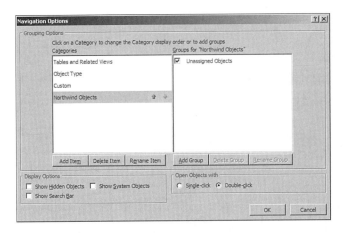

FIGURE 1.59   Select the category to which you want to add groups.

3. Click the Add Group command button. A new group appears.

4. Type the name of the new group.

5. Continue adding new groups to the category. When you are finished, the Navigation Options dialog box should appear as in Figure 1.60.

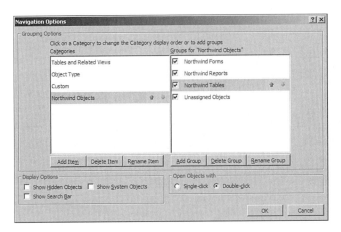

FIGURE 1.60   After you add groups, they appear in the dialog box.

6. Click OK to close the dialog box. The groups now appear within the category (see Figure 1.61).

NOTE

You can create a maximum of 10 custom categories. Of course, you can rename or delete categories at any time.

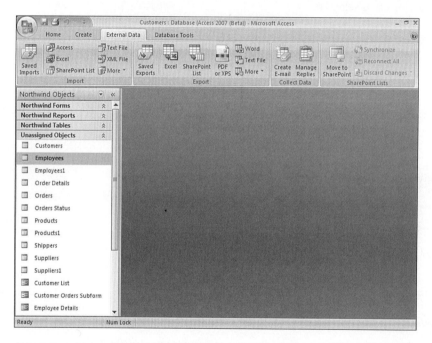

FIGURE 1.61   After you close the dialog box, the new groups appear within the category.

Adding Objects to Custom Groups

You are now ready to add objects to your custom groups. Here's how:

1. Click to select the category to which you want to add the new objects.

2. In the Unassigned Objects group, select the objects you want to include in your custom group and then move them to the group. You can drag the items individually; hold down the Ctrl key and click and drag multiple items; or right-click one of the selected items, point to Add to Group, and then click the name of the custom group. Regardless of the method, Access adds the objects to the designated group.

NOTE

When you add a database object from the Unassigned Objects group to a custom group, you are creating a shortcut to the object. If you remove the object from the custom group, you are not removing the object. Instead, you are removing the shortcut contained in the custom group.

Hiding the Unassigned Objects Group

After you have added all your objects to custom groups, you might want to hide the Unassigned Objects group. The process is quite simple:

1. Right-click the menu at the top of the Navigation Pane and select Navigation Options. The Navigation Options dialog box appears.

2. Click to select a category (for example, Northwind Objects).

3. In the Groups for *Category* pane (see Figure 1.62), click to clear the Unassigned Objects check box.

4. Click OK to close the dialog box. The Unassigned Objects group no longer appears (see Figure 1.63).

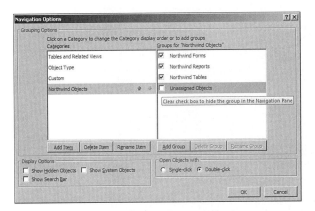

FIGURE 1.62   Click to clear the Unassigned Objects check box.

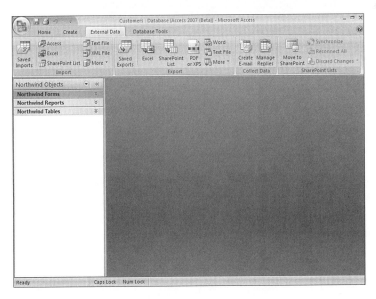

FIGURE 1.63   The Unassigned Objects group no longer appears.

Creating a New Custom Group Containing an Object Found in an Existing Group

Another trick is to create a new custom group containing an object found in an existing group. To complete this process, you must have a custom category and group containing at least one item. Here's the process:

1. Use the Navigation Pane to view the object you want to place in the new group.

2. Right-click the object and select Add to Group, New Group (see Figure 1.64). A new group appears in the Navigation Pane (see Figure 1.65).

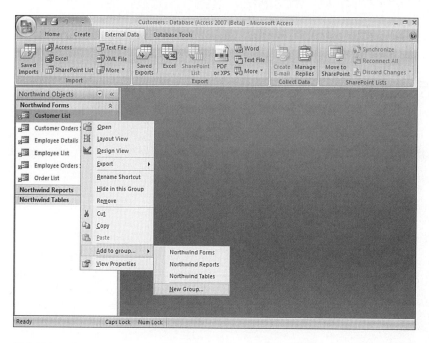

FIGURE 1.64   You can right-click an object and immediately add it to a new group.

3. Enter a name for the new group.

4. Notice that the object you selected appears in the new group. Drag additional short-cuts to the group as desired.

In addition to what you have learned thus far, you can also show or hide the groups and objects in a category. In fact, you can show or hide some or all of the groups in a custom category and some or all of the objects in a group. There are some important points to remember:

▶ You can hide an object either via the Navigation Pane or via a property of the object itself.

▶ You can completely hide objects or groups, or you can simply disable them.

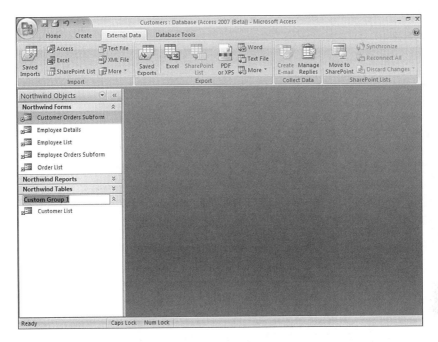

FIGURE 1.65   The new group appears in the Navigation Pane.

Completing the Process

Now that you know the details of showing or hiding groups and objects in a category, here's how you finish the process. To hide a group in a category, simply right-click the title bar of the group that you want to hide and then select Hide from the context-sensitive menu. To restore a hidden group to a category, follow these steps:

1. Right-click the menu bar at the top of the Navigation Pane and select Navigation Options.

2. Click to select the category containing the hidden object.

3. In the Groups for *Category* list, click to select the check box next to the hidden group.

4. Click OK. The group should now appear in the Navigation Pane.

Hiding an Object in Its Parent Group

At times you will want to hide an object in its parent group. All you need to do is right-click the specific object that you want to hide and then select Hide. If you want to hide an object from all categories and groups, follow these steps:

1. Right-click the object that you want to hide and select View Properties. The Properties dialog box appears (see Figure 1.66).

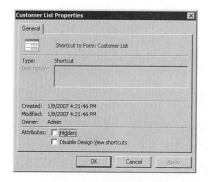

FIGURE 1.66   You use the Properties dialog box to hide an object.

2. Click the Hidden check box.

3. Click OK. You will no longer see the object in the Navigation Pane.

Restoring a Hidden Object

You are probably wondering how to restore an object after it is hidden. Here's how:

1. Right-click the menu at the top of the Navigation Pane and select Navigation Options from the shortcut menu.

2. Under Display Options, click Show Hidden Objects.

3. Click OK to close the dialog box and return to the Navigation Pane. The Navigation Pane shows all hidden objects as dimmed (see Figure 1.67).

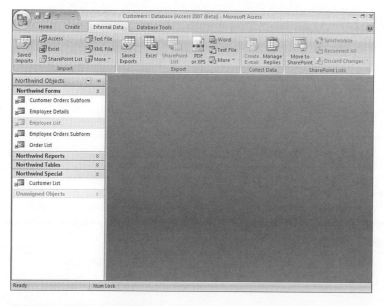

FIGURE 1.67   The Navigation Pane shows all hidden objects as dimmed.

4. If you hid the object from its parent group and category, right-click the object and select Unhide. If you used the `Hidden` property to hide the object from all categories and groups, right-click the object, select View Properties, and then clear the Hidden check box.

You can easily add, remove, or rename an object in a custom group. If you want to delete an item from a custom group, simply right-click the object and select Delete. This action does not remove the object from the database; it simply removes the shortcut from the custom group. The object will appear in the list of Unassigned Objects. You can then add that object to another group. First, you must display the Unassigned Objects group. Then click and drag the object to the appropriate group. Finally, if you want to rename an object, simply right-click it and select Rename Shortcut. Type the new name for the shortcut and press Enter.

Creating Multi-valued Fields

Another new feature available in Microsoft Office Access 2007 is the new multi-valued field. As its name implies, a *multi-valued field* is a field that holds multiple values. You can use this to represent a relationship between two tables. For example, an order table can have a multi-valued field for the employee associated with the order, if that order can be associated with multiple employees. When you use the drop-down list in the order to select an employee, the list appears with check boxes. You can select multiple items in the list and then click OK to close the list (see Figure 1.68).

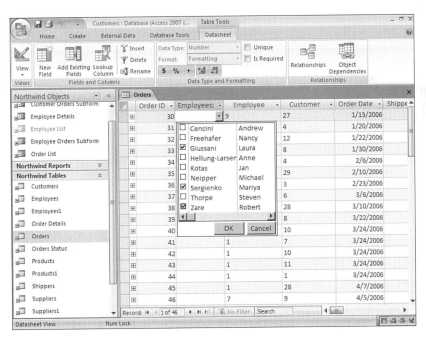

FIGURE 1.68   You can easily select multiple items in a multi-valued field.

Multi-valued fields are appropriate for specific situations. One of those situations is when you are using Microsoft Office Access 2007 to interface with data stored in Microsoft Windows SharePoint 2007, and that list contains a field that uses one of the multi-valued field types available in Windows SharePoint Services. Another situation is when you want to purposely simplify the database design. Although this seems counter to basic database design principles, it helps to understand that the Microsoft Office 2007 database engine does not actually store the multiple values in a single field. It uses system tables to build the relationship and then visually brings the data back together for the user. If you think about it, you will realize that the relationship between the tables is actually a many-to-many relationship. In this example, an order can be associated with multiple employees, and each employee can be associated with multiple orders.

Multi-valued fields allow Microsoft Office Access 2007 and SharePoint 2007 to be tightly integrated because using multi-valued fields in Access supports the equivalent field type in SharePoint Services. This means that when you link to a SharePoint list containing a multi-valued data type, Access creates a multi-valued data type locally. When you export an Access table to SharePoint, multi-valued fields seamlessly port to SharePoint. In fact, when you move an entire Access database to SharePoint, all the tables containing multi-valued fields become field types available in Windows SharePoint Services.

You might still be wondering when it is appropriate to use multi-valued fields. The following are some guidelines:

- When you want to link to a SharePoint list
- When you plan to export an Access table to a SharePoint site
- When you plan to move an Access database to a SharePoint site
- When you want to store a multi-valued selection from a *small* list of choices

CAUTION

Do not use multi-valued fields if you plan to upsize your data to Microsoft SQL Server because SQL Server does not support multi-valued fields. Therefore, when you upsize an Access database to SQL Server, the upsizing process will convert the multi-valued field to an ntext (memo) field containing a delimited list of values.

Now that you know when you will want to create a multi-valued field, take a look at how you create one:

1. Open the table that will contain the multi-valued field in Datasheet view.
2. Click the Datasheet tab.
3. Select Lookup Column from the Fields & Columns group. The Lookup Wizard appears (see Figure 1.69).
4. Click to designate whether you want the lookup column to look up the values in a table or a query, or whether you will type the values that you want. For this example, opt to look up the values in a table or query and click Next.

5. Select the table that you will use to populate the list (see Figure 1.70). Click Next.

6. Select the field(s) that you want to include in your lookup (see Figure 1.71). To select each field, you must click it and then click the greater than button (>). Click Next.

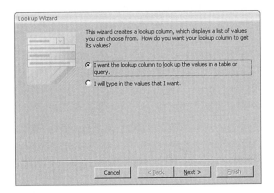

FIGURE 1.69   The Lookup Wizard assists with the process of creating a multi-value field.

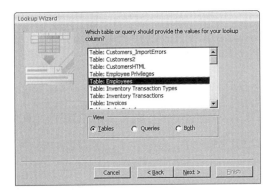

FIGURE 1.70   Select the table that you will use to populate the list.

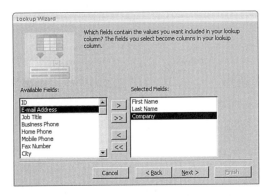

FIGURE 1.71   Select the fields that you want to include in your lookup.

7. Designate the sort order for the items in the list (see Figure 1.72). Click Next.

8. Designate the width of each column (see Figure 1.73). Click Next.

9. In the last step of the wizard, Access prompts whether you want to allow multiple values in the lookup (see Figure 1.74). Select the Allow Multiple Values check box and click Finish. The resulting drop-down appears in Figure 1.75.

10. Save the table.

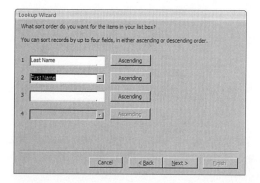

FIGURE 1.72   Designate the sort order for the items in the list.

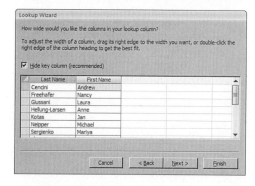

FIGURE 1.73   Designate the width of each column.

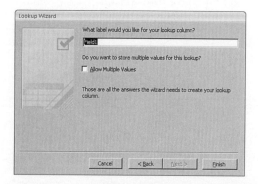

FIGURE 1.74   Click to select the Allow Multiple Values check box.

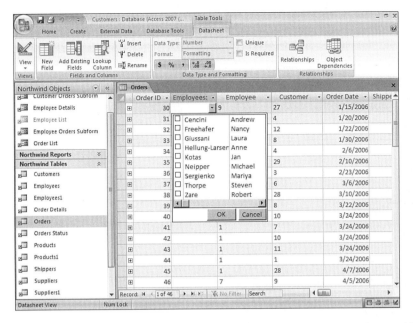

FIGURE 1.75   The completed multi-valued field enables you to select multiple items from the list.

Exploring the Effect of Multi-valued Fields on Queries

There are a couple of issues that you need to know about multi-valued fields when working with queries. To illustrate these items, follow these steps:

1. Open a database and click the Create tab.

2. Select Query Design from the Other group. The Show Table dialog box appears.

3. Select the table containing the multi-valued field and click Add.

4. Click Close to close the Show Table dialog box. Your screen should appear as shown in Figure 1.76.

5. Click and drag the desired fields to the query grid. Make sure you select the multi-valued field.

6. Click Run in the Results group. The results appear as in Figure 1.77. Notice that the multi-valued field appears with all the selected items in one column, separated by commas.

As an alternative, you can see the Employees field expanded so that each Employee value appears on a separate row. To do this, simply change the field row to read [Employees:].Value (see Figure 1.78). The Value property causes Access to display the multi-valued field in expanded form so that each value appears in a separate row (see Figure 1.79). Notice that for each order, the EmployeeID associated with that order appears on a different row in the query result.

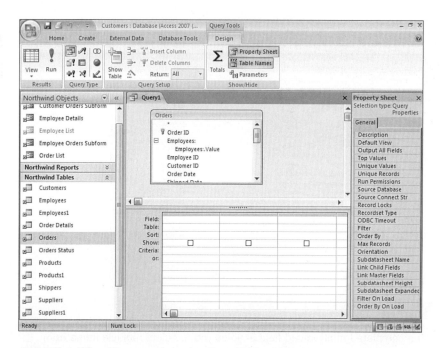

FIGURE 1.76   After you close the Show Table dialog box, Access places you in Design view of the query.

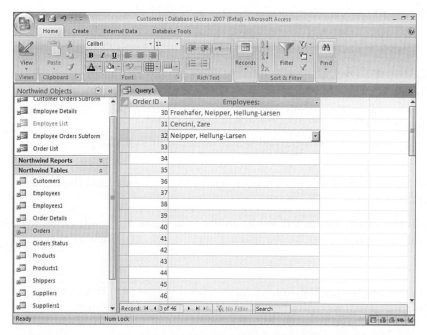

FIGURE 1.77   The results appear with all the selected items in one column.

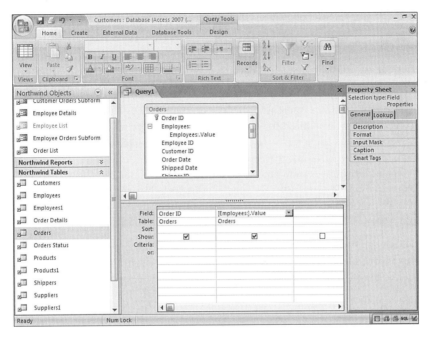

FIGURE 1.78   Change the field row to read [Employees:].Value.

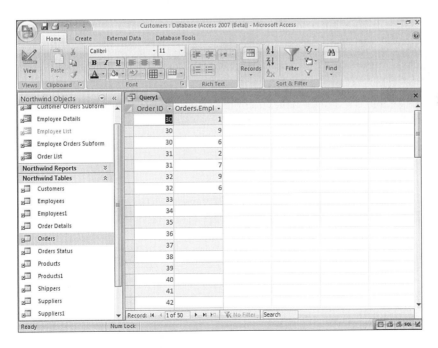

FIGURE 1.79   Each employee appears in a different row for each order.

Practical Examples: The Application Design for a Computer Consulting Firm

Consider a hypothetical computer consulting firm that wishes to track its time and billing with an Access application. First, look at the application from a design perspective.

The system will track client contacts and the projects associated with those clients. It will enable the users to record all hours billed to, and expenses associated with, each client and project. It will also let users track pertinent information about each employee or subcontractor. I have based the tables in the system on the tables produced by the Database Wizard. I modified them somewhat and changed their names to follow the Reddick naming conventions. Twenty-one tables will be included in the system. You will build some of these tables in Chapter 2. You can find all of them in the application databases on the sample code CD-ROM:

- ▶ tblClients—This table contains all the pertinent information about each client; it's related to tblProjects, the table that will track the information about each project associated with a client.

- ▶ tblClientAddresses—This table contains all addresses for each client; it's related to tblClients and tblAddressTypes.

- ▶ tblAddressTypes—This table is a lookup table. It contains all valid address types for a client; it's related to tblClientAddresses.

- ▶ tblClientPhones—This table contains all phone numbers for each client; it's related to tblClients and tblPhoneTypes.

- ▶ tblPhoneTypes—This table is a lookup table. It contains all valid phone types for a client; it's related to tblClientPhones.

- ▶ tblTerms—This table is a lookup table. It contains all valid payment terms for a client; it's related to tblClients.

- ▶ tblContactType—This table is a lookup table. It contains all valid contact types for a client; it's related to tblClients.

- ▶ tblProjects—This table holds all the pertinent information about each project; it's related to several other tables: tblClients, tblPayments, tblEmployees, tblTimeCardHours, and tblTimeCardExpenses.

- ▶ tblTimeCardHours—This table is used to track the hours associated with each project and employee; it's related to tblProjects, tblTimeCards, and tblWorkCodes.

- ▶ tblPayments—This table is used to track all payments associated with a particular project; it's related to tblProjects and tblPaymentMethods.

- ▶ tblTimeCardExpenses—This table is used to track the expenses associated with each project and employee; it's related to tblProjects, tblTimeCards, and tblExpenseCodes.

- ▶ tblEmployees—This table is used to track employee information; it's related to tblTimeCards and tblProjects.

- ▶ **tblTimeCards**—This table is used to track each employee's hours; it's actually a bridge between the many-to-many relationship between Employees and Time Card Expenses, as well as between Employees and Time Card Hours. It's also related to **tblEmployees**, **tblTimeCardHours**, and **tblTimeCardExpenses**.

- ▶ **tblExpenseCodes**—This table is a lookup table for valid expense codes; it's related to **tblTimeCardExpenses**.

- ▶ **tblWorkCodes**—This table is a lookup table for valid work codes; it's related to **tblTimeCardHours**.

- ▶ **tblPaymentMethods**—This table is a lookup table for valid payment methods; it's related to **tblPayments**.

- ▶ **tblCorrespondence**—This table is used to track the correspondence related to a project; it's related to **tblProjects** and **tblCorrespondenceTypes**.

- ▶ **tblCorrespondenceTypes**—This table is a lookup table for valid correspondence types; it's related to **tblCorrespondence**.

- ▶ **tblCompanyInfo**—This table is a system table. It is used to store information about the company. You can find this information on forms and reports throughout the system.

- ▶ **tblErrorLog**—This table is a system table. You use it to store runtime errors that occur.

- ▶ **tblErrors**—This table is a system table. You use it to store valid error codes and descriptions.

The relationships among the tables are covered in more detail in Chapter 3, but they're also shown in Figure 1.80.

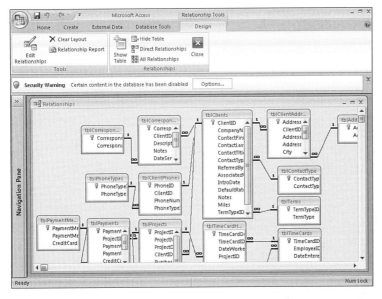

FIGURE 1.80   Here are the relationships among tables in the time and billing system.

Summary

Before you learn about the practical aspects of Access development, you need to understand what Access is and how it fits into the application development world. Access is an extremely powerful product with a variety of uses; you can find Access applications on everything from home PCs to the desks of many corporate PC users going against enterprisewide client/server databases.

After you understand what Access is and what it does, you're ready to learn about its many objects. Access applications are made up of tables, queries, forms, reports, macros, modules, ribbons, relationships, and other objects. When designed properly, an Access application effectively combines these objects to give the user a powerful, robust, and useful application.

CHAPTER 2

What Every Developer Needs to Know About Databases and Tables

Why This Chapter Is Important

You might find it is useful to think of table design as similar to the process of building a foundation for your house. Just as a house with a faulty foundation will fall over, an application with a poor table design will be difficult to build, maintain, and use. This chapter covers all the ins and outs of table design in Access 2007. After reading this chapter, you will be ready to build the other components of your application, knowing that the tables you design provide the application with a strong foundation.

Creating a New Database

In generic terms, a database stores a collection of information. Access databases are composed of tables, queries, forms, reports, data access pages, macros, and modules. Each table within a database should contain information about a particular subject. You use queries to extract specific information from one or more tables. The forms and reports provide a means of displaying your data. Finally, macros and modules allow you to build an integrated application.

When you are building an Access application, the first step you must take is to perform the necessary analysis and design steps. The section in Chapter 1 titled "How Do I Get Started Developing an Access Application?" covers these initial steps. After you have a design document in place, you are ready to build the Access database. You can complete this process by basing your database on a template or by building the database yourself from the ground up. The text that follows covers both of these options.

Creating a Database Using a Template

Getting started working with Microsoft Access is easy using the new database templates. Each template is a different type of application, complete with the necessary tables, relationships, queries, forms, reports, and macros. In addition to the predefined templates that ship with Microsoft Office Access 2007, templates are also available on Microsoft Office Online. There, you can download the latest revisions to existing templates, as well as any new templates that Microsoft has created. The following categories of templates are available (see Figure 2.1):

▶ Business

▶ Education

▶ Personal

▶ Sample

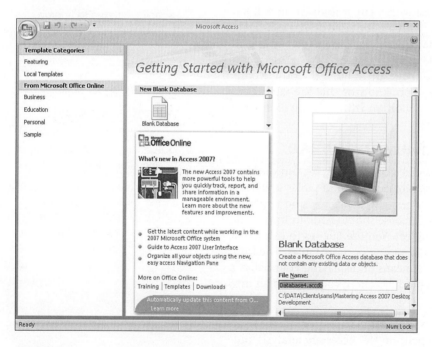

FIGURE 2.1   You can select the appropriate template category.

Building a Database Based on a Template

Here are the steps you take to build a new database based on a template:

1. Click the Microsoft Office button and select New. Your screen should appear as in Figure 2.1.

2. Click to select the category of template that you want to create. For example, in Figure 2.2, Business is selected. All the appropriate templates appear.

3. Click to select the specific template that you want to use. Sales Pipeline is selected in Figure 2.3.

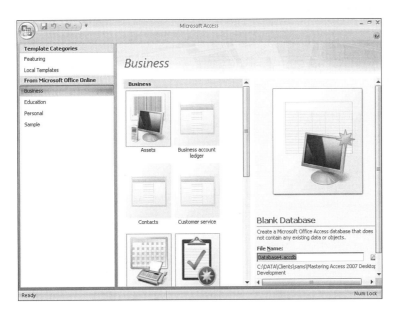

FIGURE 2.2   When you select a category of template, the appropriate templates appear.

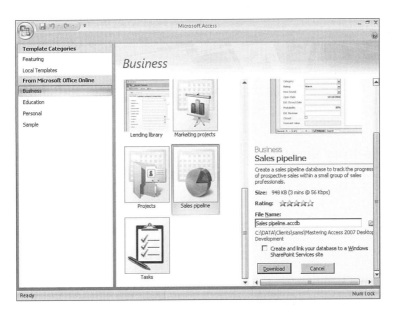

FIGURE 2.3   The Sales Pipeline template is available under the Business templates.

4. Select the name and location of the new database. Notice that the database will have the new file format (.accdb).

5. Click Download if the database is available on the Internet or click Create if the template is available locally.

6. If you click Download, Access will download the template.

7. The new database appears, as shown in Figure 2.4.

8. You can now begin working with the database just as you would work with any database.

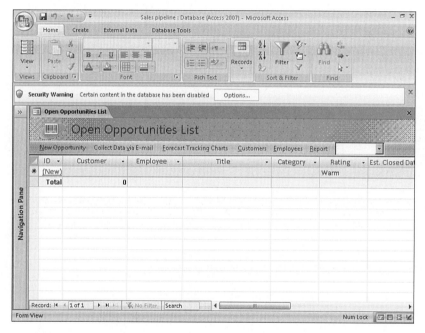

FIGURE 2.4   The new database appears with the Open Opportunities List open.

Creating a Database from Scratch

When none of the available databases that the templates generate give you what you need, you will have to create your own database. To create a new database from scratch, follow these steps:

1. Click the Microsoft Office button and select New.

2. Enter a filename for the new database in the File Name box on the right side of the screen.

3. Click the Browse icon to select a drive or folder where you will place the database.

4. Click OK to close the browse window.

5. Click the Create button.

Access creates a new blank database.

Database filenames have the following rules:

▶ Database names can contain up to 255 characters.

▶ Database names can contain spaces, but you should avoid special characters such as asterisks, semicolons, commas, and so on.

▶ Access will assign the extension .accdb to the databases that you create.

Building a New Table

You can add a new table to an Access 2007 database in several ways: by building the table from a spreadsheet-like format, designing the table from scratch, using a table template, importing the table from another source, or linking to an external table. This chapter discusses the process of building a table using a spreadsheet-like format, designing a table from scratch, and using a table template; importing and linking are covered extensively throughout this book.

NOTE

Access 2007 natively supports the Access 2000, Access 2002, and Access 2003 file formats so that you can read and write to Access 2000, Access 2002, and Access 2003 databases without converting the file format. It is important to note that if you choose one of the earlier file formats, not all functionality will be available to you.

Designing a Table from Scratch

Designing tables from scratch offers flexibility and encourages good design principles. This approach is almost always the best choice when you are creating a custom business solution. To design a table from scratch, click to select the Create tab and then select Table Design. The Table Design view window, pictured in Figure 2.5, appears. Follow these steps:

1. Define each field in the table by typing its name in the Field Name column.

2. Tab to the Data Type column. Select the default field type, which is Text, or use the drop-down combo box to select another field type. You can find details on which field type is appropriate for your data in the "Selecting the Appropriate Field Type for Your Data" section of this chapter. If you use the Field Builder, it sets a data type value for you that you can modify.

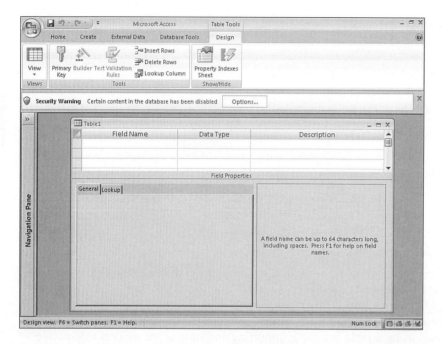

FIGURE 2.5   The Table Design view window enables you to create a table from scratch.

3. Tab to the Description column. What you type in this column appears on the status bar when the user is entering data into the field. This column is also great for documenting what data is actually stored in the field.

4. Continue entering fields. If you need to insert a field between two existing fields, click the Insert Rows button on the ribbon. Access inserts the new field above the field you were on. To delete a field, select it and click the Delete Rows button.

5. To save your work, click the Save tool on the Quick Access toolbar. The Save As dialog box, shown in Figure 2.6, appears. Enter a table name and click OK. A dialog box appears, recommending that you establish a primary key. Every table should have a primary key. The section of this chapter titled "Using the All-Important Primary Key" discusses the details of primary keys.

FIGURE 2.6   Use the Save As dialog box to name a table.

The naming conventions for table names are similar to those for field names, except that the standard for table names is that they should begin with the tag tbl. Chapter 1, "Access as a Development Tool," and Appendix A, "Naming Conventions," (available for download at www.samspublishing.com) cover the details of naming conventions.

Field names can be up to 64 characters long. For practical reasons, you should try to limit them to 10–15 characters—enough to describe the field without making the name difficult to type.

Field names can include any combination of letters, numbers, spaces, and other characters, excluding periods, exclamation points, accents, and brackets. I recommend that you stick to letters. Spaces in field names can be inconvenient when you're building queries, modules, and other database objects. Don't be concerned that your users will see the field names without the spaces. The Caption property of a field, discussed later in this chapter, allows you to designate the text that Access displays for your users.

Field names cannot begin with leading spaces. As mentioned, field names shouldn't contain spaces, so this convention shouldn't be a problem. Field names also cannot include ASCII control characters (ASCII values 0 through 31).

Try not to duplicate property names, keywords, function names, or the names of other Access objects when naming your fields. Although your code might work in some circumstances, you'll get unpredictable results in others.

To make a potential move to the client/server platform as painless as possible, you should be aware that not all field types are supported by every back-end database. Furthermore, most back-end databases impose stricter limits than Access does on the length of field names and the characters that are valid in field names. To reduce the number of problems you'll encounter if you migrate your tables to a back-end database server, you should consider these issues when you're naming the fields in your Access tables.

Adding descriptions to your table, query, form, report, macro, and module objects goes a long way toward making your application self-documenting. This information helps you, or anyone who modifies your application, to perform any required maintenance on the application's objects. Chapter 29, "Documenting Your Application," covers the details of documenting your application.

TIP

It is important to be aware how the field names you select affect the potential for upsizing your tables to a client/server database. Database servers often have much more stringent rules than Access does regarding the naming of fields. For example, most back ends do not allow spaces in field names. Furthermore, most back ends limit the length of object names to 30 characters or fewer. If you create Access field names that cannot be upsized and later need to move your data to a back-end database server, you will increase the amount of work involved in the upsizing process. The reason is that you must modify any queries, forms, reports, macros, and modules that use the invalid field names to reference the new field names when you move your tables to a back-end database server.

Selecting the Appropriate Field Type for Your Data

The data type you select for each field can greatly affect the performance and functionality of your application. Several factors can influence your choice of data type for each field in your table:

▶ The type of data that's stored in the field

▶ Whether the field's contents need to be included in calculations

▶ Whether you need to sort the data in the field

▶ The way you want to sort the data in the field

▶ How important storage space is to you

The type of data you need to store in a field has the biggest influence on which data type you select. For example, if you need to store numbers beginning with leading zeros, you can't select a Number field because Access ignores leading zeros entered into a Number field. This rule affects data such as ZIP codes (some begin with leading zeros) and department codes.

> **NOTE**
>
> If it is unimportant that leading zeros are stored in a field, and you simply need them to appear on forms and reports, you can accomplish this by using the Format property of the field. The "Working with Field Properties" section of this chapter covers the Format property.

If the contents of a field need to be included in calculations, you must select a Number or Currency data type. You can't perform calculations on the contents of fields defined with the other data types. The only exception to this rule is the Date field, which can be included in date/time calculations.

You also must consider whether you will sort or index the data in a field. You cannot sort by OLE, Attachment, and Hyperlink fields, so don't select these field types if you must sort or index the data in the field. Furthermore, you must think about the *way* you want to sort the data. For example, in a Text field, Access would sort a set of numbers in the order of their left most character, then the second character from the left, and so on (that is, 1, 10, 100, 2, 20, 200) because Access sorts data in the Text field in a standard ASCII sequence. On the other hand, Access would sort the numbers in a Number or Currency field in ascending value order (that is, 1, 2, 10, 20, 100, 200). You might think you would never want data sorted in a standard ASCII sequence, but sometimes it makes sense to sort certain information, such as department codes, in this fashion. Access 2007 enables you to sort or group based on a Memo field, but it performs the sorting or grouping based only on the first 255 characters. Finally, you should consider how important disk space is to you. Each field type takes up a different amount of storage space on your hard disk, which could be a factor when you're selecting a data type for a field.

Ten field types are available in Access: Text, Memo, Number, Date/Time, Currency, AutoNumber, Yes/No, OLE Object, Attachment, and Hyperlink. Table 2.1 summarizes the appropriate uses for each field type and the amount of storage space each type needs.

TABLE 2.1   Appropriate Uses and Storage Space for Access Field Types

Field Type	Appropriate Uses	Storage Space
Text	Data containing text, a combination of text and numbers, or numbers that you don't need to include in calculations. Examples are names, addresses, department codes, and phone numbers.	Based on what's actually stored in the field; ranges from 0 to 255 bytes.
Memo	Long text and numeric strings. Examples are notes and descriptions.	Ranges from 0 to 65,536 bytes.
Number	Data that's included in calculations (excluding money). Examples are ages, codes (such as employee ID), or payment methods.	1, 2, 4, or 8 bytes, depending on the field size selected (or 16 bytes for replication ID).
Date/Time	Dates and times. Examples are date ordered and birth date.	8 bytes.
Currency	Currency values. Examples are amount due and price.	8 bytes.
AutoNumber	Unique sequential or random numbers. Examples are invoice numbers and project numbers.	4 bytes (16 bytes for replication ID).
Yes/No	Fields that contain one of two values (yes/no, true/false). Sample uses are indicating bills paid and tenure status.	1 bit.
OLE Object	Objects such as Word documents or Excel.	0 bytes to 1 gigabyte, depending on what's stored within the field spreadsheets. Examples are employee reviews and budgets.
Attachment	Images, spreadsheet files, documents, charts, and other types of supported files.	Varies depending on what's stored within the field.
Hyperlink	Text, or a combination of text and numbers, stored as text and used as a hyperlink for a web address (URL) or a UNC path. Examples are web pages or network files.	0 to 2,048 bytes for each of the three parts that compose the address (up to 64,000 characters total).
Lookup Wizard	Used to create a field that allows the user to select a value from another table or from a list of values via a combo box that the wizard helps to define for you.	4 bytes generally required; it needs the same storage size as the primary key for the lookup field.

NOTE

The `Hyperlink` field type contains a hyperlink object. The hyperlink object consists of three parts. The first part is called the *display text*; it's the text that appears in the field or control. The second part is the actual *file path* (UNC) or *page* (URL) the field is referring to. The third part is the *subaddress*, a location within the file or page.

The most difficult part of selecting a field type is in knowing which type is best in each situation. The following detailed descriptions of each field type and when you should use them should help you with this process.

`Text` **Fields: The Most Common Field Type**

Most fields are `Text` fields. Many developers don't realize that it's best to use `Text` fields for any numbers not used in calculations. Examples are phone numbers, part numbers, and ZIP codes. Although the default size for a `Text` field is 50 characters, you can store up to 255 characters in a `Text` field. Because Access allocates disk space dynamically, a large field size doesn't use hard disk space, but you can improve performance if you allocate the smallest field size possible. You use the `FieldSize` property to control the maximum number of characters allowed in a `Text` field.

`Memo` **Fields: For Those Long Notes and Comments**

`Memo` fields can store up to 65,536 characters of text, which can hold up to 16 pages of text for each record. `Memo` fields are excellent for any types of notes you want to store with table data. Remember, you can sort by a `Memo` field under Access 2007.

`Number` **Fields: For When You Need to Calculate++**

You use `Number` fields to store data that you must include in calculations. If you must include currency amounts in calculations, or if your calculations require the highest degree of accuracy, you should use a `Currency` field rather than a `Number` field. The `Number` field is actually several types of fields in one because Access 2007 offers seven sizes of numeric fields. `Byte` can store integers from 0–255, `Integer` can hold whole numbers from –32768 through 32767, and `Long Integer` can hold whole numbers ranging from less than –2 billion to just over 2 billion. Although all three of these sizes offer excellent performance, each type requires an increasingly larger amount of storage space. Two of the other numeric field sizes, `Single` and `Double`, offer floating decimal points and, therefore, much slower performance. `Single` can hold fractional numbers to seven significant digits; `Double` extends the precision to 14 significant digits. `Decimal` is a numeric data type introduced with Access 2002. The `Decimal` data type allows storage of very large numbers and provides decimal precision up to 28 digits! The final size, `Replication ID`, supplies a unique identifier required by the data synchronization process (available with the `.MDB` file format).

`Date/Time` **Fields: Tracking When Things Happened**

You use the `Date/Time` field type to store valid dates and times. `Date/Time` fields allow you to perform date calculations and make sure dates and times are always sorted properly. Access actually stores the date or time internally as an 8-byte floating-point number. It represents time as a fraction of a day.

2

> **NOTE**
>
> Access reflects in your data any date and time settings you establish in the Windows Control Panel. For example, if you modify the Short Date style in Regional Settings within the Control Panel, your forms, reports, and datasheets will immediately reflect those changes.

Currency **Fields: Storing Money**

The Currency field type is a special type of number field you use when you are storing currency values in a table. Currency fields prevent rounding off data during calculations. They hold 15 digits of whole dollars, plus accuracy to the hundredths of a cent. Although very accurate, this type of field is quite slow to process.

> **NOTE**
>
> Access reflects in your data any changes to the currency format made in the Windows Control Panel. Of course, Access doesn't automatically perform any actual conversion of currency amounts. As with dates, if you modify the currency symbol in Regional Settings within the Control Panel, your forms, reports, and datasheets will immediately reflect those changes.

AutoNumber **Fields: For Unique Record Identifiers**

Access automatically generates AutoNumber field values when the user adds a record. In earlier versions of Access, counter values had to be sequential. The AutoNumber field type in Access 2007 can be either sequential or random. The random assignment is useful when several users are adding records offline because it's unlikely that Access will assign the same random value to two records. A special type of AutoNumber field is a Replication ID. This randomly produced unique number helps with the replication process (available with the .MDB file format) by generating unique identifiers used to synchronize database replicas.

You should note a few important points about sequential AutoNumber fields. If a user deletes a record from a table, its unique number is lost forever. Likewise, if a user adds a record and cancels the action, the unique counter value for that record is lost forever. If this behavior is unacceptable, you can generate your own counter values.

> **TIP**
>
> As with field names, if you plan to upsize your Access database to a client/server database, you must be cognizant of the field types that you select. For example, Access exports AutoNumber fields as Long Integers. Because some non-Microsoft database servers do not support autonumbering, you have to create an insert trigger on the server that provides the next key value. You also can achieve autonumbering by using form-level events, but this is not desirable because the database engine will not enforce the numbering if other applications access the data. If you are upsizing to Microsoft SQL Server, the Upsizing Wizard for Access 2007 converts all AutoNumber fields to Identity fields (the SQL Server equivalent of AutoNumber).

Yes/No **Fields: When One of Two Answers Is Correct**

You should use Yes/No fields to store a logical true or false. What's actually stored in the field is -1 for Yes, 0 for No, or Null for no specific choice. The display format for the field determines what the user actually sees (normally Yes/No, True/False, On/Off, or a third option—Null—if you set the TripleState property of the associated control on a form to True). Yes/No fields work efficiently for any data that can have only a true or false value. They not only limit the user to valid choices, but they also take up only one bit of storage space.

OLE Object **Fields: The Place to Store Just About Anything**

Microsoft designed OLE Object fields to hold data from any object linking and embedding (OLE) server application registered in Windows, including spreadsheets, word processing documents, sound, and video. There are many business uses for OLE Object fields, such as storing resumes, employee reviews, budgets, or videos. However, in many cases, it is more efficient to use a Hyperlink field to store a link to the document rather than store the document itself in an OLE Object field.

Attachment **Fields: Storing Several Files in a Single Field**

Using the attachment field type, you can store multiple attachments in a single field. Those attachments can even be of various types. For example, you can use an Excel spreadsheet and a Word document in a single field. Attachment fields are meant to replace their predecessor, OLE Object fields. With OLE Object fields, Access stored the bitmap of the object in the Access database. This caused database bloat. Access stores the data in Attachment fields much more efficiently.

There are additional benefits of Attachment fields. For example, Access renders image files and displays the program icon associated with other file types. If a field contains a photo, spreadsheet, and Word document, Access will display the image and will present application icons for the other objects. Access compresses the objects as it stores them, unless those files are compressed natively. Finally, you can manipulate attachments programmatically!

There are also some other things about Attachment fields that you should be aware of. You can attach a maximum of 2GB of data per database, and each attachment must be less than 256MB in size. You must use the Attachments dialog box (see Figure 2.7) to add, edit, and manage attachments, unless you manage them programmatically.

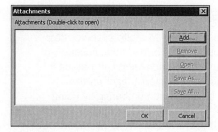

FIGURE 2.7   You use the Attachments dialog box to manage your attachments.

Hyperlink **Fields: Your Link to the Internet**

You use `Hyperlink` fields to store uniform resource locator addresses (URLs), which are links to web pages on the Internet or on an intranet, or Universal Naming Convention paths (UNCs), which are links to a file location path. Access breaks the `Hyperlink` field type into three parts:

- What the user sees
- The URL or UNC
- A subaddress, such as a range name or bookmark

After the user places an entry in a `Hyperlink` field, the entry serves as a direct link to the file or page it's referring to. I cover the `Hyperlink` field type in more detail later in this chapter, in the section "Using Access Tables with the Internet."

Working with Field Properties

After you have added fields to your table, you need to customize their properties. Field properties let you control how Access stores data as well as what data the user can enter into the field. The available properties differ depending on which field type you select. You will find the most comprehensive list of properties under the `Text` field type (see Figure 2.8). The following sections describe each field property.

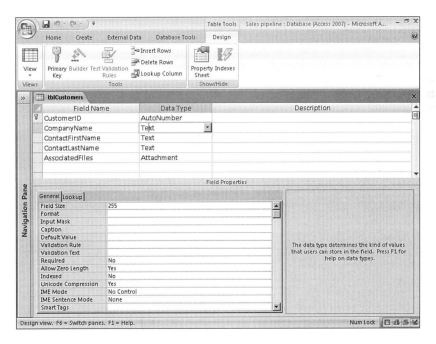

FIGURE 2.8   Field properties available for a `Text` field.

Field Size: Limiting What's Entered into a Field

The first property is `Field Size`, available for `Text` and `Number` fields only. As mentioned previously, it's best to set the `Field Size` property to the smallest value possible. For `Number` fields, a small size means lower storage requirements and faster performance.

Build a table with the following fields and types:

> CompanyID: `AutoNumber`
>
> CompanyName: `Text`
>
> State: `Text`
>
> PhoneNumber: `Text`
>
> ContactDate: `Date/Time`
>
> CreditLimit: `Currency`

1. To set the `Field Size` property of the `State` field to two characters, click anywhere in the field and then type **2** in the `Field Size` property.

2. Switch to Datasheet view. Access prompts you to save the table. Name it **tblCustomers**. Because you have not assigned a primary key, Access prompts you to do so. When you try to enter data into the `State` field, notice that you can enter only two characters.

NOTE

You can find this example, and all others in this chapter, in the `CHAP2TryIt.ACCDB` file included on the book's sample code CD-ROM. Refer to this file if you want to verify that your table structures are correct.

Format: Determining How Data Is Displayed

The second property is `Format`, available for all but `OLE Object` fields and Attachment fields. It allows you to specify how Access displays your data. Access lets you select from predefined formats or create your own custom formats. The available formats differ, depending on the field's data type. For example, with Access you can select from a variety of `Date/Time` formats, including `Short Date` (7/7/07); `Long Date` (Saturday, July 7, 2007); `Short Time` (7:17); and `Long Time` (7:17:11AM). The formats for a `Currency` field include `Currency` ($1,767.25); `Fixed` (1767.25); and `Standard` (1,767.25).

Set the `Format` property of the `ContactDate` field to `Medium Date`. Switch to Datasheet view and enter some dates in different formats, such as 07/04/07 and July 4, 2007. Notice that, no matter how you enter the dates, as soon as you tab away from the field, they appear in the format *dd-mmm-yyyy* as 04-Jul-07.

NOTE

The behavior of the Short Date and Long Date formats is dictated by the Regional Options designated in the Control Panel.

TIP

Access 2007 supports Multiple Undo and Multiple Redo actions. You can undo and redo multiple actions in Design view for Microsoft Database (MDB) tables and queries, ACCDB forms, reports, data access pages, macros, and modules. This feature allows you to roll forward or roll back your changes in Design view in a similar fashion to working with documents under Microsoft Word or Excel.

TIP

The shortcut keys Ctrl+>, Ctrl+. (period), Ctrl+<, and Ctrl+, (comma) allow you to easily toggle between the various table views. Ctrl+> and Ctrl+. (period) take you to the next view. Ctrl+< and Ctrl+, (comma) take you to the previous view.

Input Mask: Determining What Data Goes into a Field

Another important property is Input Mask, available for Text, Number, Date/Time, and Currency fields. The Format property affects how Access displays data, but the Input Mask property controls what data Access stores in a field. You can use the Input Mask property to control, on a character-by-character basis, what type of character (numeric, alphanumeric, and so on) Access can store and whether Access requires a particular character. The Input Mask Wizard, shown in Figure 2.9, helps you create commonly used input masks for Text and Date fields only. To access the Input Mask Wizard, click the button to the right of the Input Mask field.

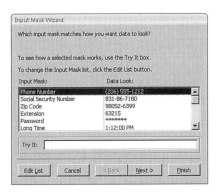

FIGURE 2.9   The Input Mask Wizard helps you enter an input mask.

> **NOTE**
>
> The Input Mask Wizard is available only if you selected the Additional Wizards compo-nent during setup. If you did not, Access prompts you to install the option on the fly the first time you use it.

For example, the input mask `000-00-0000;;_` (converted to `000\-00\-0000;;_` as soon as you tab away from the property) forces the entry of a valid Social Security number. Everything that precedes the first semicolon designates the actual mask. The zeros force the entry of the digits `0` through `9`. The dashes are literals that appear within the control as the user enters data. The character you enter between the first and second semicolon determines whether Access stores the literal characters (the dashes in this case) in the field. If you enter a `0` in this position, Access stores the literal characters in the field; if you enter a `1` or leave this position blank, Access does not store the literal characters. The final position (after the second semicolon) indicates what character Access displays to indicate the space where the user types the next character (in this case, the underscore).

Here's a more detailed example: In the mask `\(999") "000\-0000;;_`, the first backslash causes the character that follows it (the open parenthesis) to display as a literal. The three nines allow the user to enter optional numbers or spaces. Access displays the close paren-thesis and space within the quotation marks as literals. The first three zeros require values `0` through `9`. Access displays the dash that follows the next backslash as a literal. It then requires that the user enter four additional numbers. The two semicolons have nothing between them, so Access does not store the literal characters in the field. The second semicolon is followed by an underscore, so Access displays an underscore to indicate the space where the user types the next character.

Use the Input Mask Wizard to add a mask for the `PhoneNumber` field, which you should have set up as a `Text` field. The steps are as follows:

1. Click anywhere in the `PhoneNumber` field and then click the `Input Mask` property.

2. Click the ellipsis to the right of the `Input Mask` property.

3. Select `Phone Number` from the list of available masks and choose not to store the literal characters in the field when the wizard asks "How do you want to store the data?"

4. Switch to Datasheet view and enter a phone number. Notice how your cursor skips over the literal characters. Try leaving the area code blank; Access should allow you to do this.

5. Now try to enter a letter in any position. Access should prohibit you from doing this.

6. Try to leave any character from the seven-digit phone number blank. Access shouldn't let you do this, either.

> **TIP**
>
> When you use an input mask, the user is always in Overtype mode. This behavior is a feature of the product and is not a feature that you can alter.

Caption: **A Great Timesaver**

The next available property is Caption. The text placed in this property becomes the caption for fields in Datasheet view. Access also uses the contents of the Caption property as the caption for the attached label added to data-bound controls when you add them to forms and reports. The Caption property becomes important whenever you name your fields without spaces. Whatever is in the Caption property overrides the field name for use in Datasheet view, on forms, and on reports.

> **NOTE**
>
> The term *data-bound control* refers to a control that is bound to a field in a table or query. The term *attached label* refers to the label attached to a data-bound control.

> **TIP**
>
> It's important to set the Caption property for fields *before* you build any forms or reports that use them. When you produce a form or report, Access looks at the current caption. If you add or modify the caption at a later time, Access does not modify captions for that field on existing forms and reports.

Default Value: **Saving Data Entry Time**

Another important property is the Default Value property, used to specify the default value that Access will place in the field when the user adds new records to the table. Default values, which can be either text or expressions, can save the data entry person a lot of time. However, Access in no way uses them to validate what the user enters into a field.

> **TIP**
>
> Access automatically carries default values into any queries and forms containing the field. Unlike what happens with the Caption property, this occurs whether you created the default value before or after you created the query or form.

> **TIP**
>
> If you plan to upsize your Access database to a client/server database, you must be aware that default values are not always moved to the server, even if the server supports them. You can set up default values directly on the server, but these values

do *not* automatically appear when the user adds new records to the table unless the user saves the record without adding data to the field containing the default value. As in autonumbering, you can implement default values at the form level, with the same drawbacks. If you use the Upsizing Wizard for Access 2007 to move the data to Microsoft SQL Server, Access exports default values to your server database if it can convert them to a constant value or to T-SQL (Transact SQL).

Enter the following default values for the State, ContactDate, and CreditLimit fields:

State: CA

ContactDate: =Date()

CreditLimit: 1000

Switch to Datasheet view and add a new record. Notice that default values appear for the State, ContactDate, and CreditLimit fields. You can override these defaults, if you want.

NOTE

Date() is a built-in Visual Basic for Applications (VBA) function that returns the current date. When used as a default value for a field, Access enters the current date into the field when the user adds a new row to the table.

Validation Rule: Controlling What the User Enters in a Field

The Default Value property suggests a value to the user, but the Validation Rule property actually limits what the user can place in the field. The user cannot violate validation rules; the database engine strictly enforces them. As with the Default Value property, this property can contain either text or a valid Access expression, but you cannot include user-defined functions in the Validation Rule property. You also can't include references to forms, queries, or tables in the Validation Rule property.

TIP

If you set the Validation Rule property but not the Validation Text property (covered in the next section), Access automatically displays a standard error message whenever the user violates the validation rule. To display a custom message, you must enter your message text in the Validation Text property.

TIP

If you plan to upsize your Access database to a database server, you should be aware that you cannot always easily export validation rules to the server. You must sometimes re-create them using triggers on the server. No Access-defined error messages are displayed when a server validation rule is violated. Your application should be coded to provide the appropriate error messages. You can also perform validation rules at the form level, but they are not enforced if the data is accessed by other means. If you use the Upsizing Wizard for Access 2007 to move the data to Microsoft SQL Server, the wizard exports the validation rules to the server database.

Add the following validation rules to the fields in your table. (Access will place quotation marks around the state abbreviations as soon as you tab away from the property.)

> State: `In (CA, AZ, NY, MA, UT)`
>
> ContactDate: `<= Date()`
>
> CreditLimit: `Between 0 And 5000`

1. Switch to Datasheet view. If the table already contains data, when you save your changes, the message shown in Figure 2.10 appears.

NOTE

In this example, the expression `<= Date()` is used to limit the value entered into the field to a date that is on or before the current date. Because the `Date()` expression always returns the current date, the validation rule applies whether the user is adding a new row or is modifying an existing row.

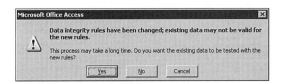

FIGURE 2.10   The message box asking whether you want to validate existing data.

If you select Yes, Access tries to validate all existing data using the new rules. If any errors are found, you're notified that errors occurred, but you aren't informed of the offending records (see Figure 2.11). You have to build a query to find all the records violating the new rules.

If you select No, Access doesn't try to validate your existing data, and you aren't warned of any problems.

FIGURE 2.11   A warning that all data did not validate successfully.

2. After you have entered Datasheet view, try to enter an invalid state in the `State` field; you should see the message box displayed in Figure 2.12. As you can see, this isn't the friendliest message, which is why you should create a custom message by using the `Validation Text` property.

FIGURE 2.12   The message displayed when a validation rule is violated, and no validation text has been entered.

TIP

Validation rules entered at a table level are automatically applied to forms and queries built from the table. This occurs whether the rule was entered before or after the query or form was built. If you create a validation rule for a field, Access won't allow `Null` values to be entered in the field, which means the field can't be left blank. If you want to allow the field to be left `Null`, you must add the `Null` value to the validation expression:

```
In (CA, AZ, NY, MA, UT) or Is Null
```

Validation Text: **Providing Error Messages to the User**

Use the `Validation Text` property to specify the error message users see when they violate the validation rule. The `Validation Text` property must contain text; expressions aren't valid in this property.

Add the following to the `Validation Text` properties of the `State`, `ContactDate`, and `CreditLimit` fields:

State: `The State Must Be CA, AZ, NY, MA, or UT`

ContactDate: `The Contact Date Must Be On or Before Today`

CreditLimit: `The Credit Limit Must Be Between 0 and 5000`

Try entering invalid values for each of the three fields and observe the error messages.

Required: **Making the User Enter a Value**

The `Required` property is very important: It determines whether you require that a value be entered into a field. This property is useful for foreign key fields, when you want to make sure data is entered into the field. It's also useful for any field containing information that's needed for business reasons (company name, for example).

NOTE

A *foreign key field* is a field that is looked up in another table. For example, in the case of a Customers table and an Orders table, both might contain a CustomerID field. In the Customers table, the CustomerID is the primary key field. In the Orders table, the CustomerID is the foreign key field because its value is looked up in the Customers table.

Set the Required property of the CompanyName and PhoneNumber fields to Yes. Switch to Datasheet view and try to add a new record, leaving the CompanyName and PhoneNumber fields blank. Make sure you enter a value for at least one of the other fields in the record. When you try to move off the record, the error message shown in Figure 2.13 appears.

FIGURE 2.13   A message appears when you leave blank a field that has the Required property set to Yes.

Allow Zero Length: **Accommodating Situations with Nonexistent Data**

The Allow Zero Length property is similar to the Required property. Use it to determine whether you allow the user to enter a zero-length string (""). A zero-length string isn't the same as a Null (which represents the absence of an entry); a zero-length string indicates that the data doesn't exist for that particular field. For example, a foreign employee might not have a Social Security number. When you enter a zero-length string, the data entry person can indicate that the Social Security number doesn't exist.

Add a new field called ContactName and set its Required property to Yes. Try to add a new record and enter two quotation marks ("") in the ContactName field. You should not get an error message because, in Access 2007, the Allow Zero Length property defaults to Yes. Your zero-length string will appear blank when you move off the field. Return to the Design view of the table. Change the setting for the Allow Zero Length property to No. Go back to Datasheet view and once again enter two quotation marks in the ContactName field. This time you should not be successful. You should get the error message shown in Figure 2.14.

FIGURE 2.14   The result of entering "" when the Allow Zero Length property is set to No.

CAUTION

In previous versions of Access, the default setting for the `Allow Zero Length` property was No. Under Access 2002, Access 2003, and Access 2007, Microsoft has changed this default setting to `Yes`. Pay close attention to this default behavior, especially if you're accustomed to working with prior releases of the product.

TIP

Don't forget that if you want to cancel changes to the current field, press Esc once. To abandon all changes to a record, press Esc twice.

TIP

The `Required` and `Allow Zero Length` properties interact with each other. If the `Required` property is set to `Yes` and the `Allow Zero Length` property is set to `No`, you're being as strict as possible with your users. Not only must they enter a value, but that value can't be a zero-length string.

If the `Required` property is set to `Yes` and the `Allow Zero Length` property is set to `Yes`, you're requiring users to enter a value, but that value can be a zero-length string. However, if the `Required` property is set to `No` and the `Allow Zero Length` property is set to `No`, you're allowing users to leave the field `Null` (blank) but not allowing them to enter a zero-length string.

Finally, if you set the `Required` property to `No` and the `Allow Zero Length` property to `Yes`, you're being as lenient as possible with your users. In this case, they can leave the field `Null` or enter a zero-length string.

Indexed: **Speeding Up Searches**

You use *indexes* to improve performance when the user searches a field. Although it's generally best to include too many indexes rather than too few, indexes do have downsides (see the next Tip). A general rule is to provide indexes for all fields regularly used in searching and sorting, and as criteria for queries.

Set the `Indexed` property of the `CompanyName`, `ContactName`, and `State` fields to `Yes – (Duplicates OK)`. Click the Indexes button in the Show/Hide group on the Design tab of the ribbon. Your screen should look like the one in Figure 2.15.

To create non-primary-key, multifield indexes, you must use the Indexes window. You create an index with one name and more than one field. See Figure 2.15, which shows an index called `StateByCredit` that's based on the combination of the `CreditLimit` and `State` fields. Notice that only the first field in the index has an index name. The second field, `State`, appears on the line below the first field but doesn't have an index name.

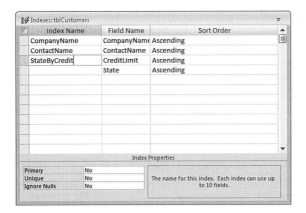

FIGURE 2.15   The Indexes window shows you all the indexes defined for a table.

Indexes speed up searching, sorting, and grouping data. The downside is that they take up hard disk space and slow down the process of editing, adding, and deleting data. Although the benefits of indexing outweigh the detriments in most cases, you should not index every field in each table. Create indexes only for fields, or combinations of fields, on which the user will search or sort. Do not create indexes for fields that contain highly repetitive data, such as a field that can contain only two different values. Finally, never index Yes/No fields. They are only 1 bit in storage size; furthermore, they apply to the previous rule in that they can take on only one of two values. For these reasons, indexes offer no benefits with Yes/No fields.

TIP

Indexes are equally important on a database server. When you are upsizing an Access database to a non-Microsoft server, no indexes are created. You must re-create all indexes on the back-end database server. If your database server is running Microsoft SQL Server, you can use the Access Upsizing Wizard for Access 2007 to upsize your Access database. This tool creates indexes for server tables in the place where the indexes exist in your Access tables.

Unicode Compression: **Compressing Your Data**

Another important property is Unicode Compression. The Unicode Compression property applies to Text and Memo fields only. You use this property to designate whether you want the data in the field to be compressed using Unicode compression. Prior to Access 2000, data was stored in the double-byte character set (DBCS) format, which was designed to store character data for certain languages such as Chinese. With Access 2000 and higher, all character data is stored in the Unicode 2-byte representation format. Although this format requires more space for each character (2 bytes, rather than 1 byte), the Unicode Compression property allows the data to be compressed, if possible. If the character set being used allows compression and the Unicode Compression property is set to Yes, the data in the column is stored in a compressed format.

Using the All-Important Primary Key

The most important index in a table is called the Primary Key index; it ensures unique-ness of the fields that make up the index and also gives the table a default order. You must set a primary key for the fields on the "one" side of a one-to-many relationship. To create a Primary Key index, select the fields you want to establish as the primary key and then click the Primary Key button on the ribbon.

Figure 2.16 shows the `tblCustomers` table with a Primary Key index based on the `CompanyID` field. Notice that the Index Name of the field designated as the primary key of the table is called `PrimaryKey`. Note that the `Primary` and `Unique` properties for this index are both set to `Yes (True)`.

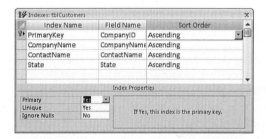

FIGURE 2.16   A Primary Key index based on the `CompanyID` field.

Working with the Lookup Feature

Using the Lookup Wizard, you can instruct a field to look up its values in another table or query or from a fixed list of values. You can also display the list of valid values in a combo or list box. A lookup is generally created from the foreign key (the "many" side) to the primary key (the "one" side) of a one-to-many relationship.

You can invoke the Lookup Wizard by selecting Lookup Wizard from the list of data types for the field. The first wizard dialog box asks whether you want to look up the values in a table or query or whether you want to input the values (see Figure 2.17). I recommend that you always look up the values in a table or query; this makes your application easier to maintain. The second wizard dialog box asks you to indicate the table or query used to look up the values (see Figure 2.18). Select a table or query and click Next to open the third wizard dialog box. This step of the Lookup Wizard asks you which field in the table or query will be used for the lookup (see Figure 2.19). The fourth step of the Lookup Wizard asks you the sort order you want for your list. The fifth step, shown in Figure 2.20, gives you the opportunity to control the width of the columns in your combo or list box.

TIP

To work through the preceding example, you can use the `Chap2.ACCMDB` sample data-base file. All the lookup tables have already been added to the sample database.

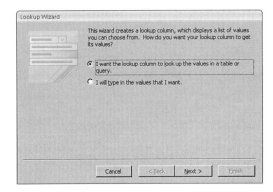

FIGURE 2.17   The first step of the Lookup Wizard asks you for the source of the values.

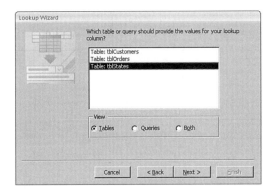

FIGURE 2.18   In the second step of the Lookup Wizard, you select the table or query whose data will appear in the drop-down.

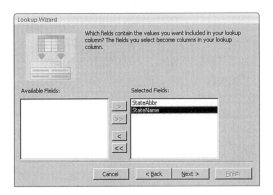

FIGURE 2.19   In the third step of the Lookup Wizard, you designate the field that Access will use for the lookup.

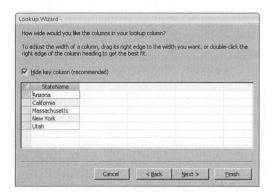

FIGURE 2.20   In the fifth step of the Lookup Wizard, you can adjust the column widths.

NOTE

If you select more than one field for your lookup and one is a key column, such as an ID, the Hide Key Column check box appears. You should leave this box checked; it automatically hides the key column in the lookup, even though the result will be bound to the key field.

Finally, the wizard lets you specify a title for your lookup column. When you click Finish, Access will prompt you to save the table, and the wizard will fill in all the appropriate properties; they appear on the Lookup tab of the field (see Figure 2.21). The Display Control property is set to Combo Box, indicating that the valid values will be displayed in a combo box. This occurs whether the user is in Datasheet view or in a form. The Row Source Type indicates that the source for the combo box is a table or query, and the Row Source shows the actual SQL Select statement used to populate the combo box. Other properties show the column in the combo box that is bound to data, the number of columns in the combo box, the width of the combo box, and the width of each column in the combo box. These properties are covered in more detail in Chapter 5, "What Every Developer Needs to Know About Forms." You can modify the SQL statement for the combo box later, if necessary.

NOTE

In my opinion, the lookup feature is more of a hindrance than a help. After you invoke the lookup feature, you and your users will no longer have easy access to the under-lying numeric values stored in the foreign key field. You will see only the lookup value displayed in the combo box. This makes troubleshooting application problems very difficult.

The main advantage of the lookup feature is that it facilitates the process of building forms by automatically adding a combo box to a form whenever a field with a lookup is placed on a form. Personally, I find it so easy to build a combo box on a form that I do not find the lookup feature to be much of a timesaver. After evaluating the pros and cons of this user-related feature, I opted to eliminate it from the applications that I build.

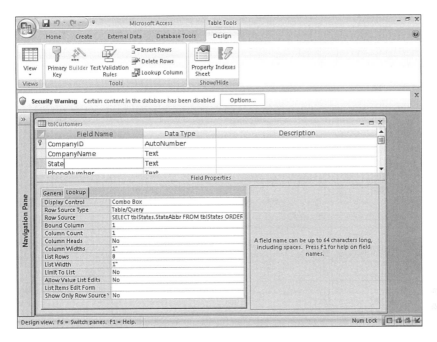

FIGURE 2.21   The field properties set by the Lookup Wizard.

Working with Table Properties

In addition to field properties, you can specify properties that apply to a table as a whole. To access the table properties, click the Property Sheet button on the ribbon while in a table's Design view. The available table properties are shown in Figure 2.22. The Description property is used mainly for documentation purposes. The Default View property designates the view in which the table appears when the user first opens it. The Validation Rule property specifies validations that must occur at a record level, instead of a field level. For example, credit limits might differ depending on what state a customer is in. In that case, what's entered in one field depends on the value in another field. When you enter a table-level validation rule, it doesn't matter in what order the user enters the data. A table-level validation rule ensures that the proper dependency between fields is enforced. The validation rule might look something like this:

```
[State] In ("CA","NY") And [CreditLimit]<=2500 Or _
    [State] In ("MA","AZ") And [CreditLimit]<=3500 Or _
    [State] Not In ("CA", "NY", "MA", "AZ")
```

This validation rule requires a credit limit of $2,500 or less for applicants in California and New York and a limit of $3,500 or less for applicants in Massachusetts and Arizona, but it doesn't specify a credit limit for residents of any other states. Table-level validation rules can't be in conflict with field-level validation rules.

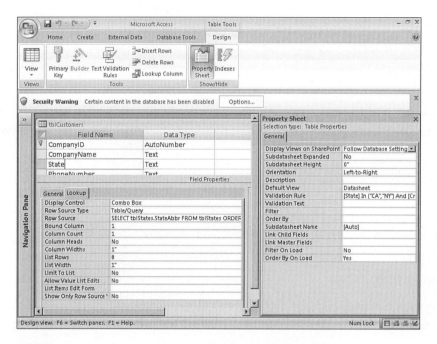

FIGURE 2.22   Viewing the available table properties.

The `Validation Text` property determines the message that appears when the user violates the validation rule. If this property is left blank, a default message appears.

You use the `Filter` property to indicate a subset of records that appear in a datasheet, form, or query. You use the `Order By` property to specify a default order for the records. The `Filter` and `Order By` properties aren't generally applied as properties of a table.

The `Subdatasheet Name` property identifies the name of a table used as a drill-down. If this property is set to `Auto`, the drill-down table is automatically detected based on relationships established in the database. The `Link Child Fields` and `Link Master Fields` properties are implemented to designate the fields that are used to link the current table with the table specified in the `Subdatasheet Name` property. These properties should be left blank when `Auto` is selected for the `Subdatasheet Name`. You use the `Subdatasheet Height` property to specify the maximum height of the subdatasheet and the `Subdatasheet Expanded` property to designate whether the subdatasheet is automatically displayed in an expanded state.

The `Orientation` property determines the layout direction for the table when it is displayed. The default setting for USA English is obviously `Left-to-Right`. This property is language-specific, and the `Right-to-Left` setting is available only if you are using a language version of Microsoft Access that supports right-to-left language displays. Arabic and Hebrew are examples of right-to-left languages. By installing the Microsoft Office Multilanguage Pack and the Microsoft Office Proofing Tools for a specific language, and by enabling the specific right-to-left language under the Microsoft Office Language Settings, you can also turn on right-to-left support.

Using Indexes to Improve Performance

As previously mentioned, indexes can help you improve your application's performance. You should create indexes on any fields you sort, group, join, or set criteria for, unless those fields contain highly repetitive data. Queries can greatly benefit from indexes, especially when indexes are created for fields included in your criteria, fields used to order the query, and fields used to join two tables that are not permanently related but are joined in a query. In fact, you should always create indexes for fields on both sides of a join. If your users are using the Find dialog box, indexes can help reduce the search time. Remember, the downsides to indexes are the disk space they require and the amount of time it takes to update them when adding, deleting, and updating records. You should always perform benchmarks with your own applications, but you will probably find indexes helpful in many situations.

> **NOTE**
>
> When you establish a relationship between two tables, an index for the table on the "many" side of the relationship (the foreign key field) is automatically created. For example, if you relate `tblOrders` to `tblCustomers` based on the `CustomerID` field, an internal index is automatically created for the `CustomerID` field in the `tblOrders` table. You therefore don't need to explicitly create a foreign key index. Relationships are covered in Chapter 3, "Relationships: Your Key to Data Integrity."

Using Access Tables with the Internet

Microsoft has made it easier to develop Internet-aware applications by including the `Hyperlink` field type and by allowing users to save table data as HTML. The `Hyperlink` field type lets your users easily store UNC or URL addresses within their tables. The ability to save table data as HTML makes it easy for you or your users to publish table data on an Internet or intranet site. The sections that follow cover these features.

The `Hyperlink` Field Type

When you use the `Hyperlink` field type, your users can store a different UNC or URL address for each record in the table. Although you can type a different UNC or URL address directly into a field, it's much easier to enter the address by using the Insert Hyperlink dialog box (see Figure 2.23). Here, users can graphically browse hyperlink addresses and subaddresses, and the address is entered automatically when they exit the dialog box. To invoke the Insert Hyperlink dialog box, right-click the `Hyperlink` field and then select Hyperlink, Edit Hyperlink.

The Text to Display text box is used to enter the text the user will see when viewing the field data in Datasheet view, in a form, or on a report. The hyperlink can be to any of the following:

- ▶ An existing file or web page
- ▶ Another object in the current database
- ▶ A new data access page
- ▶ An email address

FIGURE 2.23   With the Insert Hyperlink dialog box, users can select or create a hyperlink object for the field.

To select an existing file or web page, click the appropriate Link To icon and either type the file or web page name, or select it from the list of Recent Files, Browsed Pages, or the Current Folder. The Browse for File button is used to browse for an existing file, and the Browse the Web button is used to browse for an existing web page.

To link to an object in the current database, click the appropriate Link To icon. Click a plus (+) sign to expand the list of tables, queries, forms, reports, pages, macros, or modules. Then click the database object to which you want to link.

To link to a new data access page that you create, click the appropriate Link To icon. Enter the name of the new page and designate whether you want to edit the new page now or later.

To designate an email address you want to link to, click the appropriate Link To icon. Enter the email address and subject, or select from the list of recently used email addresses.

After all the required information has been entered, the link is established, and the hyperlink is entered in the field. If a UNC was entered, clicking the hyperlink invokes the application associated with the file. The selected file is opened, and the user is placed in the part of the document designated in the subaddress. If a URL is entered, and the user is logged on to the Internet or connected to her company's intranet, she is taken directly to the designated page. If the user isn't currently connected to the Internet or an intranet, the Connect To dialog box appears, allowing her to log on to the appropriate network.

Saving Table Data as HTML

Table data can be easily saved as HTML so that it can be published on an Internet or intranet site. You can save a file as HTML by using the File, Export menu item. The steps are as follows:

1. Click within the Navigation Pane to select the table you want to export.

2. Click to select the External Data tab.

3. Click the More drop-down in the Export group.

4. Select HTML Document from the drop-down menu. The Export – HTML Document dialog box appears (see Figure 2.24).

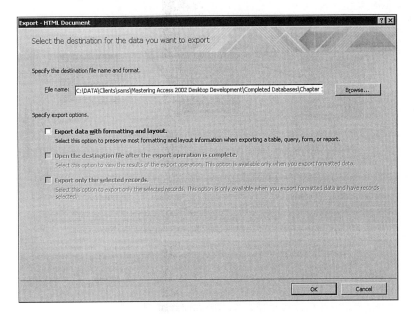

FIGURE 2.24   The Export – HTML Document dialog box allows you to select the name and location for the exported file.

5. Click Browse to select a name and location for the .htm file. The File Save dialog box appears.

6. Provide a filename and location and then click Save. Access returns you to the Export – HTML Document dialog box.

7. Specify the export options as desired.

8. Click OK. The HTML Output Options dialog box appears. Here, you can select an HTML template and designate the type of encoding that you want to use for the file.

9. Click OK. If you opted to open the destination file after the export operation is complete, the exported document appears in your browser (see Figure 2.25). Figure 2.26 displays the underlying HTML that you can edit using any HTML editor.

10. The final step of the wizard asks if you want to save your export steps. If you do, click the Save Export Steps check box.

11. Click Close to complete the process.

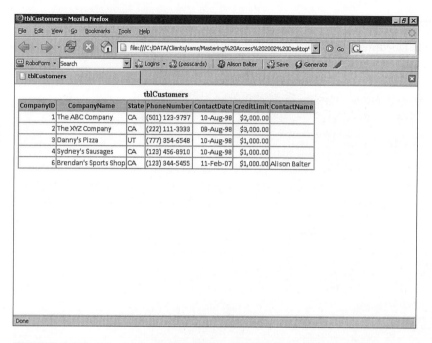

FIGURE 2.25   Viewing an HTML document in a browser after a table was saved as HTML.

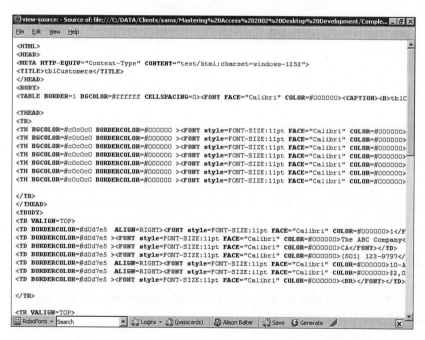

FIGURE 2.26   Viewing the source HTML for the exported document.

NOTE

Building applications for the Internet is covered extensively in *Alison Balter's Mastering Access 2002 Enterprise Development*.

Saving Table Data as XML

Access 2007 allows you to export your data to XML and to import data from XML. Using either code or the Access user interface to export XML data, you can generate data (XML), schema (XSD), and presentation (XSL) files. Although in-depth coverage of Access and XML is included in *Alison Balter's Mastering Access 2002 Enterprise Development*, this section provides you with basic information about the import and export processes. To export a table to XML, follow these steps:

1. Select the table you want to export.

2. Click to select the External Data tab.

3. Click the More drop-down in the Export group.

4. Select XML File from the drop-down menu. The Export – XML Document dialog box appears.

5. Click Browse to select a name and location for the `.xml` file. The File Save dialog box appears.

6. Provide a filename and location and then click Save. Access returns you to the Export – XML Document dialog box.

7. Click OK. The Export XML dialog box appears. Here, you designate whether you want to export data, schema of the data, and the presentation of your data (see Figure 2.27).

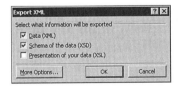

FIGURE 2.27   The Export XML dialog box allows you to specify what XML documents you want to generate as part of the export process.

8. Click OK. Access generates the appropriate files.

9. The final step of the wizard asks if you want to save your export steps. If you do, click the Save Export Steps check box.

Figure 2.28 displays the underlying XML that you can edit using any XML editor.

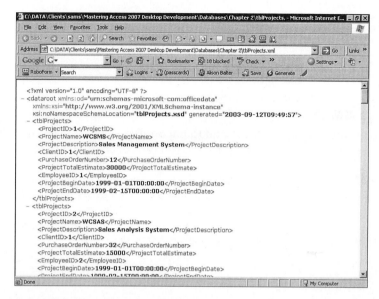

FIGURE 2.28   Viewing the XML generated when you save a table as XML.

Just as you can export data to XML, you can import XML data into Access. To import XML data into an Access table, follow these steps:

1. Click to select the External Data tab.

2. Click the Import XML file button in the Import group.

3. Click Browse to select the file you want to import and click Import. The File Open dialog box appears.

4. Select the file you want to import and click Open. Access returns you to the Get External Data – XML File dialog box.

5. Click OK to perform the import. The Import XML dialog box appears (see Figure 2.29).

FIGURE 2.29   The Import XML dialog box allows you to designate options used for the import process.

6. Indicate whether you want to import the structure only, the structure and data, or append data to existing table(s).

7. Click OK to continue. Access completes the import process.

Viewing Object Dependencies

Sometimes you will need to know what objects depend on a particular table. Here's how this process works:

1. Click to open the Navigation Pane drop-down and select Tables and Related Views. The first time you perform this task for a database, a dialog box appears, prompting you to update object dependency information for the database (see Figure 2.30). After you click OK, Access updates the dependency information for the database and displays each table along with the objects that depend on it (see Figure 2.31).

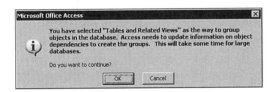

FIGURE 2.30   The first time you attempt to display object dependencies within a database, Access prompts you to update dependency information for that database.

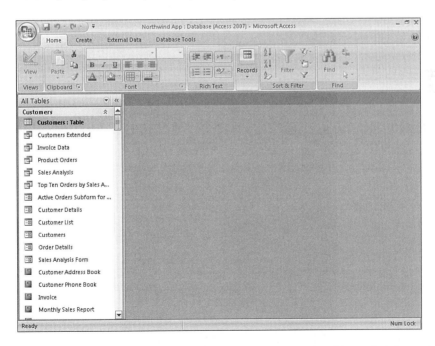

FIGURE 2.31   Access displays each table, along with the objects that depend on it.

2. By default, the Object Dependencies window shows you the objects that depend on the selected object. You can click the Objects That I Depend On button to view the objects that the selected object depends on.

3. You can click the node of an item to drill down to additional dependencies. Because we have not established relationships between the tables, and this database contains no queries, forms, or reports that are based on the tables in the database, no dependencies yet exist. If you practice this exercise on the Northwind database, you will find the results to be much more interesting.

4. Close the Object Dependencies window when you are finished viewing and working with object dependencies.

Examining Database Specifications and Limitations

Databases have a number of specifications and limitations that you should be aware of. Fortunately, you will generally not find them too restricting. They are listed in Table 2.2.

TABLE 2.2   Table Specifications and Limitations

Item	Limitation
Number of objects in a database	32,768
Number of modules in a database (includes all `Has Module=Yes`)	1,000
Number of characters in an object name	64
Number of characters in a password	20
Number of characters in a username or group name	20
Number of concurrent users	255

Examining Table Specifications and Limitations

Tables have a number of specifications and limitations as well. Although you will generally not find them restricting, you should keep them in mind. They are listed in Table 2.3.

TABLE 2.3   Table Specifications and Limitations

Item	Limitation
Number of characters in a table name	64
Number of characters in a field name	64
Number of fields in a table	255
Number of open tables	2048; the actual number is less because of tables opened internally by Microsoft Access

TABLE 2.3   Continued

Item	Limitation
Table size	2 gigabytes minus the space needed for system objects
Number of characters in a `Text` field	255
Number of characters in a `Memo` field	65,535 when entering data through the user interface; 1 gigabyte of character storage when entering data programmatically
Size of an `OLE Object` field	1 gigabyte
Number of indexes in a table	32
Number of fields in an index	10
Number of characters in a validation message	255
Number of characters in a validation rule	2,048
Number of characters in a table or field description	255
Number of characters in a record (excluding `Memo` and `OLE Object` fields)	2,000
Number of characters in a field property setting	255

You also can save table data under the XML format.

Practical Examples: Designing the Tables Needed for a Computer Consulting Firm's Time and Billing Application

Create a new database and try designing a few of the tables needed by a computer consulting firm's time and billing application. You will build tblClients and tblProjects tables. The main table for the application, tblClients, will be used to track the key information about each client. The second table, tblProjects, will hold all the key information users need to store for the projects they're working on for each client. Table 2.4 shows the field names, data types, and sizes for each field in tblClients. You should include indexes for all fields except Notes. Table 2.5 shows the properties that need to be set for these fields. Table 2.6 shows the fields, data types, and sizes for the fields in tblProjects, and Table 2.7 shows the properties that need to be set for these fields. You should include indexes for all fields except ProjectDescription.

TABLE 2.4   Field Names, Data Types, and Sizes for the Fields in tblClients

Field Name	Data Type	Size
ClientID	AutoNumber	Long Integer (Stored as 4)
CompanyName	Text	50
ContactFirstName	Text	30

TABLE 2.4   Continued

Field Name	Data Type	Size
ContactLastName	Text	50
ContactTitle	Text	50
ContactTypeID	Number	Long Integer (Stored as 4)
ReferredBy	Text	30
AssociatedWith	Text	30
IntroDate	Date/Time	Stored as 8
DefaultRate	Currency	Stored as 8
Notes	Memo	—
Miles	Number	Long Integer (Stored as 4)
TermTypeID	Number	Long Integer (Stored as 4)
HomePage	Hyperlink	—

TABLE 2.5   Properties That Need to Be Set for the Fields in tblClients

Field Name	Property	Value
ClientID	Caption	Client ID
ClientID	Set as primary key	—
CompanyName	Caption	Company Name
CompanyName	Required	Yes
ContactFirstName	Caption	Contact First Name
ContactLastName	Caption	Contact Last Name
ContactTitle	Caption	Contact Title
ContactTypeID	Caption	Contact Type ID
ReferredBy	Caption	Referred By
AssociatedWith	Caption	Associated With
IntroDate	Input Mask	99/99/0000
IntroDate	Caption Default Value	Intro DateIntroDate=Date()
IntroDate	Validation Rule	<=Date()
IntroDate	Validation Text	Date Entered Must Be On Or Before Today
IntroDate	Required	Yes
DefaultRate	Caption	Default Rate
DefaultRate	Default Value	125
DefaultRate	Validation Rule	Between 75 and 150
DefaultRate	Validation Text	Rate Must Be Between 75 and 150
DefaultRate	Format	Currency
Miles	Validation Rule	>=0
Miles	Validation Text	Miles Must Be Greater Than or Equal to Zero

TABLE 2.5   Continued

Field Name	Property	Value
TermTypeID	Caption	Term Type ID
HomePage	Caption	Home Page

TABLE 2.6   Field Names, Data Types, and Sizes for the Fields in `tblProjects`

Field Name	Data Type	Size
ProjectID	AutoNumber	Long Integer (Stored as 4)
ProjectName	Text	50
ProjectDescription	Memo	—
ClientID	Number	Long Integer (Stored as 4)
PurchaseOrderNumber	Text	30
ProjectTotalEstimate	Currency	8
EmployeeID	Number	Long Integer (Stored as 4)
ProjectBeginDate	Date/Time	Stored as 8
ProjectEndDate	Date/Time	Stored as 8

TABLE 2.7   Properties That Need to Be Set for the Fields in `tblProjects`

Field Name	Property	Value
ProjectID	Caption	Project ID
ProjectID	Set as primary key	—
ProjectName	Caption	Project Name
ProjectName	Required	Yes
ProjectDescription	Caption	Project Description
ClientID	Caption	Client ID
ClientID	Default Value	Remove default value of 0
ClientID	Required	Yes
PurchaseOrderNumber	Caption	Purchase Order Number
ProjectTotalEstimate	Caption	Project Total Estimate
ProjectTotalEstimate	Format	Currency
EmployeeID	Caption	Employee ID
ProjectBeginDate	Input Mask	99/99/0000
ProjectBeginDate	Caption	Project Begin
DateProjectEndDate	Input Mask	99/99/0000
ProjectEndDate	Caption	Project End Date

The rest of the tables needed by the time and billing application are listed in Appendix B, "Table Structures," which is downloadable at www.samspublishing.com. The finished table structures can be found in CHAP2.ACCDB. You can find this file, and all files referred to in this book, on the book's sample code CD-ROM.

Summary

Tables are the foundation for your application. A poorly designed table structure can
render an otherwise well-designed application useless. This chapter began by walking you
through several methods for creating tables. It then discussed theoretical issues, such as
selecting the correct field type and effectively using field properties. Each property, and its
intended use, was discussed in detail. Finally, table properties and indexes were covered.
After reading this chapter, you should be ready to harness the many features that the
Access table designer has to offer.

CHAPTER 3

Relationships: Your Key to Data Integrity

Why This Chapter Is Important

A *relationship* exists between two tables when one or more key fields from one table are matched to one or more key fields in another table. The fields in both tables usually have the same name, data type, and size. Relationships are a necessary by-product of the data normalization process. *Data normalization*, which was introduced in Chapter 1, "Access as a Development Tool," and is covered in additional detail in this chapter, is the process of eliminating duplicate information from your system by splitting information into several tables, each containing a unique value (primary key). Although data normalization brings many benefits, you need to relate your application's tables to each other so that your users can view the data in the system as a single entity. After you define relationships between tables, you can build queries, forms, and reports that combine information from multiple tables. In this way, you can reap all the benefits of data normalization while ensuring that your system provides users with all the information they need.

Introduction to Relational Database Design

Many people believe Access is such a simple product to use that database design is something they don't need to worry about. I couldn't disagree more! Just as a house without a foundation will fall over, a database with poorly designed tables and relationships will fail to meet the needs of its users.

The History of Relational Database Design

Dr. E. F. Codd first introduced formal relational database design in 1969 while he was at IBM. Relational theory, which is based on set theory, applies to both databases and database applications. Codd developed 12 rules that determine how well an application and its data adhere to the relational model. Since Codd first conceived these 12 rules, the number of rules has expanded into the hundreds. (Don't worry; you need to learn only a few of them!)

You should be happy to learn that, although not perfect as an application development environment, Microsoft Access measures up quite well as a relational database system.

Goals of Relational Database Design

The number one goal of relational database design is to, as closely as possible, develop a database that models some real-world system. This involves breaking the real-world system into tables and fields and determining how the tables relate to each other. Although on the surface this task might appear to be trivial, it can be an extremely cumbersome process to translate a real-world system into tables and fields.

A properly designed database has many benefits. The processes of adding, editing, deleting, and retrieving table data are greatly facilitated by a properly designed database. In addition, reports are easier to build. Most importantly, the database becomes easy to modify and maintain.

Rules of Relational Database Design

To adhere to the relational model, tables must follow certain rules. These rules determine what is stored in tables and how the tables are related.

The Rules of Tables

Each table in a system must store data about a single entity. An entity usually represents a real-life object or event. Examples of objects are customers, employees, and inventory items. Examples of events include orders, appointments, and doctor visits.

The Rules of Uniqueness and Keys

Tables are composed of rows and columns. To adhere to the relational model, each table must contain a unique identifier. Without a unique identifier, it becomes programmatically impossible to uniquely address a row. You guarantee uniqueness in a table by designating a *primary key*, which is a single column or a set of columns that uniquely identifies a row in a table.

Each column or set of columns in a table that contains unique values is considered a *candidate key*. One candidate key becomes the *primary key*. The remaining candidate keys become *alternate keys*. A primary key made up of one column is considered a *simple key*. A primary key comprising multiple columns is considered a *composite key*.

It is generally a good idea to pick a primary key that is

▶ Minimal (has as few columns as possible)

▶ Stable (rarely changes)

▶ Simple (is familiar to the user)

Following these rules greatly improves the performance and maintainability of your database application, particularly if you are dealing with large volumes of data.

Consider the example of an employee table. An employee table is generally composed of employee-related fields such as Social Security number, first name, last name, hire date, salary, and so on. The combination of the first name and the last name fields could be considered a primary key. This choice might work, until the company hires two employees with the same name. Although the first and last names could be combined with additional fields to constitute uniqueness (for example, hire date), this would violate the rule of keeping the primary key minimal. Furthermore, an employee might get married and change her last name. This violates the rule of keeping a primary key stable.

Using a name as the primary key violates the principle of stability. The Social Security number might be a valid choice, but a foreign employee might not have a Social Security number. This is a case in which a derived, rather than a natural, primary key is appropriate. A *derived key* is an artificial key that you create. A *natural key* is one that is already part of the database.

In examples such as this, I suggest adding `EmployeeID` as an `AutoNumber` field. Although the field would violate the rule of simplicity (because an employee number is meaningless to the user), it is both small and stable. Because it is numeric, it is also efficient to process. In fact, I use `AutoNumber` fields (an `Identity` field in SQL Server) as primary keys for most of the tables that I build.

The Rules of Foreign Keys and Domains

A *foreign key* in one table is the field that relates to the primary key in a second table. For example, the `CustomerID` is the primary key in the `Customers` table. It is the foreign key in the `Orders` table.

A *domain* is a pool of values from which columns are drawn. A simple example of a domain is the specific data range of employee hire dates. In the case of the `Orders` table, the domain of the `CustomerID` column is the range of values for the `CustomerID` in the `Customers` table.

Normalization and Normal Forms

Some of the most difficult decisions that you face as a developer are what tables to create and what fields to place in each table, as well as how to relate the tables that you create. *Normalization* is the process of applying a series of rules to ensure that your database achieves optimal structure. *Normal forms* are a progression of these rules. Each successive normal form achieves a better database design than the previous form did. Although there are several levels of normal forms, it is generally sufficient to apply only the first three levels of normal forms. The following sections describe the first three levels of normal forms.

First Normal Form

To achieve first normal form, all columns in a table must be atomic. This means, for example, that you cannot store first names and last names in the same field. The reason for this rule is that data becomes very difficult to manipulate and retrieve if multiple groups are stored in a single field. Using the full name as an example, it would become impossible to sort by first name or last name independently if both groups were stored in the same field. Furthermore, you or the user must perform extra work to extract just the first name or the last name from the field.

Another requirement for first normal form is that the table must not contain repeating values. An example of repeating values is a scenario in which the Item1, Quantity1, Item2, Quantity2, Item3, and Quantity3 fields are all found within the Orders table (see Figure 3.1). This design introduces several problems. What if the user wants to add a fourth item to the order? Furthermore, finding the total ordered for a product requires searching several columns. In fact, all numeric and statistical calculations on the table become extremely cumbersome. The alternative, shown in Figure 3.2, achieves first normal form. Notice that each item ordered is located in a separate row.

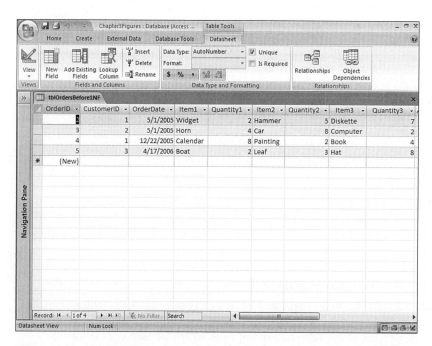

FIGURE 3.1   This table contains repeating groups. Repeating groups make it difficult to summarize and manipulate table data.

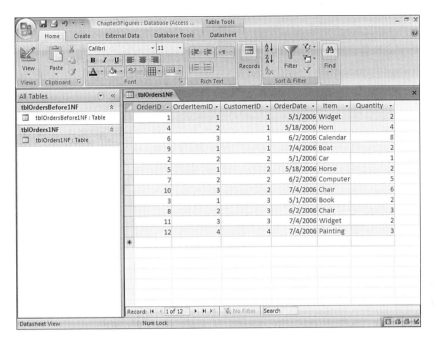

FIGURE 3.2   This table achieves first normal form. Notice that all fields are atomic and that the table contains no repeating groups.

Second Normal Form

To achieve second normal form, all non-key columns must be fully dependent on the primary key. In other words, each table must store data about only one subject. Notice the table shown in Figure 3.2. It includes information about the order (OrderID, CustomerID, and OrderDate) and information about the items the customer is ordering (Item and Quantity). To achieve second normal form, you must break this data into two tables: an order table and an order detail table. The process of breaking the data into two tables is called *decomposition*. It is considered to be *non-loss* decomposition because no data is lost during the decomposition process. After you separate the data into two tables, you can easily bring the data back together by joining the two tables in a query. Figure 3.3 shows the data separated into two tables. These two tables achieve second normal form.

Third Normal Form

To attain third normal form, a table must meet all the requirements for first and second normal form, and all non-key columns must be mutually independent. This means that you must eliminate any calculations, and you must break out data into lookup tables.

An example of a calculation stored in a table is the product of price multiplied by quantity. Instead of storing the result of this calculation in the table, you would generate the calculation in a query, or in the control source of a control on a form or a report.

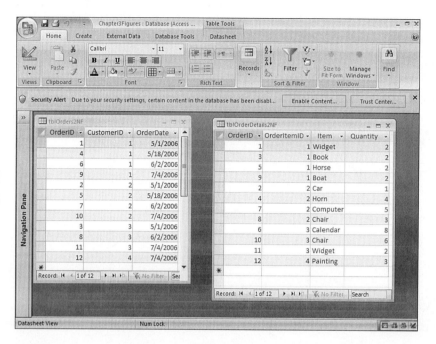

FIGURE 3.3   These tables achieve second normal form. The fields in each table pertain to the primary key of the table.

The example in Figure 3.3 does not achieve third normal form because the description of the inventory items is stored in the order details table. If the description changes, all rows with that inventory item need to be modified. The order detail table, shown in Figure 3.4, shows the item descriptions broken into an inventory table. This design achieves third normal form. All fields are mutually independent. You can modify the description of an inventory item in one place.

Denormalization—Purposely Violating the Rules

Although the developer's goal is normalization, often it makes sense to deviate from normal forms. We refer to this process as *denormalization*. The primary reason for applying denormalization is to enhance performance.

An example of when denormalization might be the preferred tactic could involve an open invoices table and a summarized accounting table. It might be impractical to calculate summarized accounting information for a customer when we need it. Instead, you can maintain the summary calculations in a summarized accounting table so that you can easily retrieve them as needed. Although the upside of this scenario is improved performance, the downside is that you must update the summary table whenever you make changes to the open invoices. This imposes a definite trade-off between performance and maintainability. You must decide whether the trade-off is worthwhile.

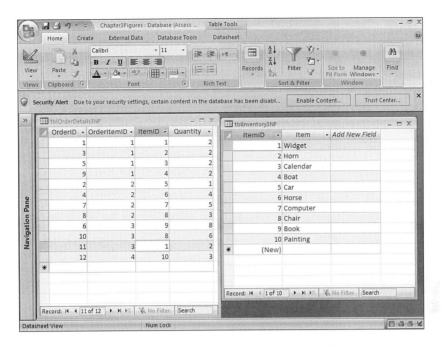

FIGURE 3.4   The table on the right achieves third normal form. The description of the inventory items has been moved to an inventory table, and the `ItemID` is stored in the order details table.

If you decide to denormalize, document your decision. Make sure that you make the necessary application adjustments to ensure that you properly maintain the denormalized fields. Finally, test to ensure that the denormalization process actually improves performance.

Integrity Rules

Although integrity rules are not part of normal forms, they are definitely part of the database design process. Integrity rules are broken into two categories. They include overall integrity rules and database-specific integrity rules.

Overall Rules

The two types of overall integrity rules are *referential integrity rule*s and *entity integrity rules*. Referential integrity rules dictate that a database does not contain orphan foreign key values. This means that

▶ Child rows cannot be added for parent rows that do not exist. In other words, an order cannot be added for a nonexistent customer.

▶ A primary key value cannot be modified if the value is used as a foreign key in a child table. This means that a `CustomerID` in the customers table cannot be changed if the orders table contains rows with that `CustomerID`.

▶ A parent row cannot be deleted if child rows are found with that foreign key value. For example, a customer cannot be deleted if the customer has orders in the order table.

Entity integrity dictates that the primary key value cannot be `Null`. This rule applies not only to single-column primary keys, but also to multi-column primary keys. In fact, in a multi-column primary key, no field in the primary key can be `Null`. This makes sense because, if any part of the primary key can be `Null`, the primary key can no longer act as a unique identifier for the row. Fortunately, the Access Database Engine (Access 2007's new version of the JET database engine, available with the new ACCDB file format) does not allow a field in a primary key to be `Null`.

Database-Specific Rules

The other set of rules applied to a database are not applicable to all databases but are, instead, dictated by business rules that apply to a specific application. Database-specific rules are as important as overall integrity rules. They ensure that only valid data is entered into a database. An example of a database-specific integrity rule is that the delivery date for an order must fall after the order date.

Examining the Types of Relationships

Three types of relationships can exist between tables in a database: one-to-many, one-to-one, and many-to-many. Setting up the proper type of relationship between two tables in your database is imperative. The right type of relationship between two tables ensures

▶ Data integrity

▶ Optimal performance

▶ Ease of use in designing system objects

The reasons behind these benefits are covered throughout this chapter. Before you can understand the benefits of relationships, though, you must understand the types of relationships available.

One-to-Many

A one-to-many relationship is by far the most common type of relationship. In a *one-to-many relationship*, a record in one table can have many related records in another table. A common example is a relationship set up between a `Customers` table and an `Orders` table. For each customer in the `Customers` table, you want to have more than one order in the `Orders` table. On the other hand, each order in the `Orders` table can belong to only one customer. The `Customers` table is on the *one side* of the relationship, and the `Orders` table is on the *many side*. For you to implement this relationship, the field joining the two tables on the one side of the relationship must be unique.

In the Customers and Orders tables example, the CustomerID field that joins the two tables must be unique within the Customers table. If more than one customer in the Customers table has the same customer ID, it is not clear which customer belongs to an order in the Orders table. For this reason, the field that joins the two tables on the one side of the one-to-many relationship must be a primary key or have a unique index. In almost all cases, the field relating the two tables is the primary key of the table on the one side of the relationship. The field relating the two tables on the many side of the relationship is the foreign key.

One-to-One

In a one-to-one relationship, each record in the table on the one side of the relationship can have only one matching record in the table on the many side of the relationship. This relationship is not common and is used only in special circumstances. Usually, if you have set up a one-to-one relationship, you should have combined the fields from both tables into one table. The following are the most common reasons why you should create a one-to-one relationship:

▸ The number of fields required for a table exceeds the number of fields allowed in an Access table.

▸ Several fields in a table are required for only a subset of records in the table.

The maximum number of fields allowed in an Access table is 255. There are very few reasons why a table should ever have more than 255 fields. In fact, before you even get close to 255 fields, you should take a close look at the design of your system. On the rare occasion when having more than 255 fields is appropriate, you can simulate a single table by moving some of the fields to a second table and creating a one-to-one relationship between the two tables.

The other situation in which you would want to define one-to-one relationships is when you will use certain fields in a table for only a relatively small subset of records. An example is an Employee table and a Vesting table. Certain fields are required only for employees who are vested. If only a small percentage of a company's employees are vested, it is not efficient, in terms of performance or disk space, to place all the fields containing information about vesting in the Employee table. This is especially true if the vesting information requires a large volume of fields. By breaking the information into two tables and creating a one-to-one relationship between them, you can reduce disk-space requirements and improve performance. This improvement is particularly pronounced if the Employee table is large.

Many-to-Many

In a *many-to-many relationship*, records in both tables have matching records in the other table. You cannot directly define a many-to-many relationship in Access; you must develop this type of relationship by adding a table called a *junction table*. You relate the junction table to each of the two tables in one-to-many relationships. An example is an

Orders table and a Products table. Each order probably will contain multiple products, and each product is found on many different orders. The solution is to create a third table called OrderDetails. You relate the OrderDetails table to the Orders table in a one-to-many relationship based on the OrderID field. You relate it to the Products table in a one-to-many relationship based on the ProductID field.

Establishing Relationships in Access

You use the Relationships window to establish relationships between Access tables, as shown in Figure 3.5. To open the Relationships window, click to select the Database Tools tab on the ribbon, and then select the Relationships tool in the Show/Hide group. If you have not established any relationships, the Show Table dialog box appears. The Show Table dialog box allows you to add tables to the Relationships window.

Looking at the Relationships window, you can see the types of relationships that exist for each table. All the one-to-many and one-to-one relationships defined in a database are represented with a join line. If you enforce referential integrity between the tables involved in a one-to-many relationship, the join line between the tables appears with the number *1* on the one side of the relationship and with an infinity symbol (∞) on the many side of the relationship. One-to-one relationships appear with a 1 on both ends of the join lines.

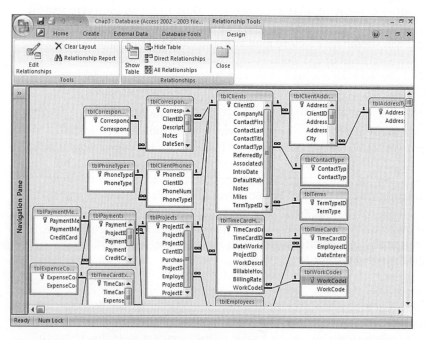

FIGURE 3.5   The Relationships window enables you to view, add, modify, and remove relationships between tables.

Establishing a Relationship Between Two Tables

To establish a relationship between two tables, follow these six steps:

1. Open the Relationships window.

2. If you're opening the Relationships window of a particular database for the first time, the Show Table dialog box appears (see Figure 3.6). Select each table you want to relate and click Add.

FIGURE 3.6   The Show Table dialog box enables you to select the tables you want to relate.

3. If you have already established relationships in the current database, the Relationships window appears. If the tables you want to include in the relationship do not appear, click the Show Table button in the Relationships group on the ribbon. To add the desired tables to the Relationships window, select a table and then click Add. Repeat this process for each table you want to add. To select multiple tables at once, press Shift while clicking to select contiguous tables or press Ctrl while clicking to select noncontiguous tables; then click Add. Click Close when you are finished.

4. Click and drag the field from one table to the matching field in the other table. The Edit Relationships dialog box appears, as shown in Figure 3.7.

5. Determine whether you want to establish referential integrity and whether you want to cascade update related fields or cascade delete related records by enabling the appropriate check boxes. The section later in this chapter titled "Establishing Referential Integrity" covers these topics.

6. Click Create.

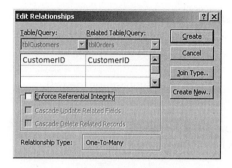

FIGURE 3.7   The Edit Relationships dialog box enables you to view and modify the relationships between the tables in a database.

Looking at Guidelines for Establishing Relationships

You must remember a few important points when establishing relationships. If you are not aware of these important gotchas, you could find yourself in some pretty hairy situations:

▶ It is important to understand the correlation between the Relationships window and the actual relationships you have established within the database. The Relationships window lets you view and modify the existing relationships. When you establish relationships, Access creates the relationships the moment you click Create. You can delete the tables from the Relationships window (by selecting them and pressing Delete), but the relationships still exist. (The "Modifying an Existing Relationship" section, which appears later in this chapter, covers the process of permanently removing relationships.) The Relationships window provides a visual blueprint of the relationships that you have established. If you modify the layout of the window by moving tables around, or by adding tables to or removing them from the window, Access prompts you to save the layout after you close the Relationships window. Access is not asking whether you want to save the relationships you have established; it is simply asking whether you want to save the visual layout of the window.

▶ When you are adding tables to the Relationships window using the Show Tables dialog box, it is easy to accidentally add the same table to the window many times. The reason is that the tables you are adding can hide behind the Show Tables dialog box, or they can appear below the portion of the Relationships window that you are viewing. If this occurs, you'll see multiple occurrences of the same table when you close the Show Tables dialog box. Access gives each occurrence of the table a different alias. You must remove the extra occurrences.

▶ You also can add queries to the Relationships window by using the Show Tables dialog box. Although rarely used, this approach might be useful if you regularly include the same queries within other queries and want to permanently establish a relationship between them.

▶ If you remove tables from the Relationships window (this does not delete the relationships) and you want to once again show all relationships that exist in the database, click All Relationships in the Relationships group on the Design tab. These processes show all existing relationships.

▶ To delete a relationship, select the join line and click Delete.

Create a new database and add a table called `tblCustomers`, another called `tblOrders`, and a third called `tblOrderDetails`. The tables should have the following fields:

tblCustomers: CustomerID, CompanyName, Address, City, State, ZipCode

tblOrders: OrderID, CustomerID, OrderDate, ShipVIA

tblOrderDetails: OrderID, LineNumber, ItemID, Quantity, Price

1. In the `tblCustomers` table, make the `CustomerID` field a `Text` field. Designate the `CustomerID` field as the primary key. Set the size of the field to 5. Make all other fields `Text` fields with their default properties.

2. In the `tblOrders` table, set `OrderID` to the `AutoNumber` field type. Make the `OrderID` the primary key field. Make the `CustomerID` field a `Text` field with a field size of 5. Set the field type of the `OrderDate` field to `Date/Time`, and the field type of the `ShipVIA` field to `Number` with a size of `Long Integer`.

3. In the `tblOrderDetails` table, set the field type of the `OrderID` field to `Number` and make sure that the size is `Long Integer`. Set the field type of the `LineNumber` field to `Number` with a size of `Long Integer`. You should base the primary key of the table on the combination of the `OrderID` and `LineNumber` fields. The `ItemID` and `Quantity` fields should be the `Number` type with a size of `Long Integer`. The `Price` field should be the `Currency` type.

4. To open the Relationships window, click the Relationships button in the Show/Hide group of the Database Tools tab. With the `tblCustomers` table in the Show Table dialog box selected, hold down your Shift key and click to select the `tblOrders` table. Click Add. All three tables should appear in the Relationships window. Click Close. Click and drag from the `CustomerID` field in the `tblCustomers` table to the `CustomerID` field in the `tblOrders` table. After the Edit Relationships dialog box appears, click Create. Repeat the process, clicking and dragging the `OrderID` field from the `tblOrders` table to the `OrderID` field in the `tblOrderDetails` table.

NOTE

You can find this example, and all examples included in this chapter, in the `Chap3TryIt.ACCDB` file included with the sample code on the accompanying CD-ROM.

Modifying an Existing Relationship

Modifying an existing relationship is easy. Access gives you the capability to delete an existing relationship or to simply modify the nature of the relationship. To permanently remove a relationship between two tables, follow these three steps:

1. Click to select the Database Tools tab and then click to select the Relationships tool in the Show/Hide group on the ribbon.

2. Click the line joining the two tables whose relationship you want to delete.

3. Press Delete. Access prompts you to verify your actions. Click Yes.

You often will want to modify the nature of a relationship rather than remove it. To modify a relationship, follow these four steps:

1. Click to select the Database Tools tab, and then click to select the Relationships tool in the Show/Hide group on the ribbon.

2. Double-click the line joining the two tables whose relationship you want to modify.

3. Make the required changes.

4. Click OK. All the normal rules regarding the establishment of relationships will apply.

Establishing Referential Integrity

As you can see, establishing a relationship is quite easy. Establishing the right kind of relationship is a little more difficult. When you attempt to establish a relationship between two tables, Access makes some decisions based on a few predefined factors:

▶ Access establishes a one-to-many relationship if one of the related fields is a primary key or has a unique index.

▶ Access establishes a one-to-one relationship if both the related fields are primary keys or have unique indexes.

▶ Access creates an indeterminate relationship if neither of the related fields is a primary key and neither has a unique index. You cannot establish referential integrity in this case.

As covered earlier in the chapter, *referential integrity* consists of a series of rules that the Access Database Engine applies to ensure that it properly maintains the relationships between tables. At the most basic level, referential integrity rules prevent the creation of orphan records in the table on the many side of the one-to-many relationship. After a relationship is established between a Customers table and an Orders table, for example, all orders in the Orders table must be related to a particular customer in the Customers table. Before you can establish referential integrity between two tables, the following conditions must be met:

▶ The matching field on the one side of the relationship must be a Primary Key field or must have a unique index.

▶ The matching fields must have the same data types (for linking purposes, AutoNumber fields match Long Integer fields). With the exception of Text fields, they also must have the same size. Number fields on both sides of the relationship must have the same size (Long Integer, for example).

▶ Both tables must be part of the same Access database.

▶ Both tables must be stored in the proprietary Access file (.ACCDB) format. (They cannot be external tables from other sources.)

▶ The database containing the two tables must be open.

▶ Existing data within the two tables cannot violate referential integrity rules. All orders in the Orders table must relate to existing customers in the Customers table, for example.

CAUTION

Although Text fields involved in a relationship do not have to be the same size, it is prudent to make them the same size. Otherwise, you will degrade performance as well as risk the chance of unpredictable results when creating queries based on the two tables.

After you establish referential integrity between two tables, the Access Database Engine applies the following rules:

▶ You cannot enter a value in the foreign key of the related table that does not exist in the primary key of the primary table. For example, you cannot enter a value in the CustomerID field of the Orders table that does not exist in the CustomerID field of the Customers table.

▶ You cannot delete a record from the primary table if corresponding records exist in the related table. For example, you cannot delete a customer from the Customers table if related records exist in the Orders table (records with the same value in the CustomerID field).

▶ You cannot change the value of a primary key on the one side of a relationship if corresponding records exist in the related table. For example, you cannot change the value in the CustomerID field of the Customers table if corresponding orders exist in the Orders table.

If you attempt to violate any of the preceding three rules and you have enforced referential integrity between the tables, Access displays an appropriate error message, as shown in Figure 3.8.

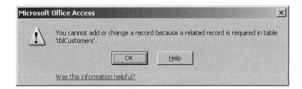

FIGURE 3.8   An error message when attempting to add an order for a customer who doesn't exist.

The Access Database Engine's default behavior is to prohibit the deletion of parent records that have associated child records and to prohibit the change of a primary key value of a parent record when that parent has associated child records. You can override these restrictions by using the three check boxes available in the Edit Relationships dialog box when you establish or modify a relationship.

The following example enforces referential integrity between the tblCustomers table and the tblOrders table. It illustrates how this affects the process of adding and deleting records:

1. To open the Relationships window, click to select the Database Tools tab and then click the Relationships tool in the Show/Hide group. Double-click the join line between tblCustomers and tblOrders. Enable the Enforce Referential Integrity check box. Click OK. Repeat the process for the relationship between tblOrders and tblOrderDetails.

2. Go into tblCustomers and add a couple of records. Take note of the customer IDs. Go into tblOrders. Add a couple of records, taking care to assign customer IDs of customers who exist in the tblCustomers table. Now try to add an order for a customer whose customer ID does not exist in tblCustomers. You should get an error message.

3. Attempt to delete a customer from tblCustomers who does not have any orders. You should get a warning message, but Access should allow you to complete the process. Now try to delete a customer who does have orders. The Access Database Engine should prohibit you from deleting the customer. Attempt to change the customer ID of a customer who has orders. You should not be able to do this.

Cascade Update Related Fields

The Cascade Update Related Fields option is available only if you have established referential integrity between the tables. With this option selected, the user can change the primary key value of the record on the one side of the relationship. When the user tries to modify the field joining the two tables on the one side of the relationship, the Access Database Engine cascades the change down to the foreign key field on the many side of the relationship. This technique is useful if the primary key field is modifiable. For example, a purchase number on a purchase order master record might be updatable.

If the user modifies the purchase order number of the parent record, you would want to cascade the change to the associated detail records in the purchase order detail table.

> **NOTE**
>
> You do not need to select the Cascade Update Related Fields option when the related field on the one side of the relationship is an AutoNumber field. You can never modify an AutoNumber field. The Cascade Update Related Fields option has no effect on AutoNumber fields.

> **CAUTION**
>
> You can easily introduce a loophole into your system accidentally. If you create a one-to-many relationship between two tables but forget to set the Required property of the foreign key field to Yes, you allow the addition of orphan records. Figure 3.9 illustrates this point. I added an order to tblOrders without entering a customer ID. This record is an orphan record because no records in tblCustomers have a customer ID of Null. To eliminate the problem, set the Required property of the foreign key field to Yes.

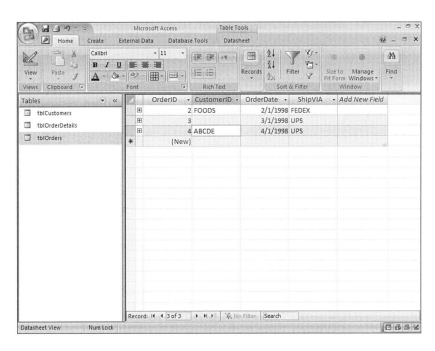

FIGURE 3.9   An orphan record with Null in the foreign key field.

Cascade Delete Related Records

The Cascade Delete Related Records option is available only if you have established referential integrity between the tables. With this option selected, the user can delete a record on the one side of a one-to-many relationship, even if related records exist in the table on the many side of the relationship. A user can delete a customer even if the customer has existing orders, for example. The Access Database Engine maintains referential integrity between the tables because it automatically deletes all related records in the child table.

If you attempt to delete a record from the table on the one side of a one-to-many relationship and no related records exist in the table on the many side of the relationship, you get the usual warning message, as shown in Figure 3.10. On the other hand, if you attempt to delete a record from the table on the one side of a one-to-many relationship and related records exist in the child table, Access warns you that you are about to delete the record from the parent table, as well as any related records in the child table (see Figure 3.11).

FIGURE 3.10   A message that appears after the user attempts to delete a parent record without related child records.

FIGURE 3.11   A message that appears after the user attempts to delete a parent record with related child records.

TIP

The Cascade Delete Related Records option is not always appropriate. It is an excellent feature, but you should use it prudently. Although it is usually appropriate to cascade delete from a `tblOrders` table to a `tblOrderDetails` table, for example, it generally is not appropriate to cascade delete from a `tblCustomers` table to a `tblOrders` table. The reason is that you generally do not want to delete all your order history from the `tblOrders` table if for some reason you want to delete a customer. Deleting the order history causes important information, such as your profit and loss history, to change. Therefore, it is appropriate to prohibit this type of deletion and handle the customer in some other way, such as marking him as inactive or archiving his data. On the other hand, if you delete an order because the customer canceled it, you probably want to remove the corresponding order detail information as well. In this case, the Cascade Delete Related Records option is appropriate. You need to make the most prudent decision in each situation, based on business needs. The important point is to carefully consider the implications of each option before making your decision.

With the Cascade Update feature enabled, you are able to update the primary key value of a record that has associated child records. With the Cascade Delete feature enabled, you can delete a parent record that has associated child records. This exercise illustrates the use of Cascade Update and Cascade Delete:

1. Modify the relationship between `tblCustomers` and `tblOrders`. Enable the Cascade Update Related Fields check box. Modify the relationship between `tblOrders` and `tblOrderDetails`. Enable the Cascade Delete Related Records check box. You do not need to enable Cascade Update Related Fields because the `OrderID` field in `tblOrders` is an `AutoNumber` field.

2. Attempt to delete a customer who has orders. The Access Database Engine should still prohibit you from doing deleting because you did not enable Cascade Delete Related Records. Change the customer ID in `tblCustomers` of a customer who has orders. The Access Database Engine should allow this change. Take a look at the `tblOrders` table. The Access Database Engine should have updated the customer ID of all corresponding records in the table to reflect the change in the parent record.

3. Add some order details to the `tblOrderDetails` table. Try to delete any order that has details within the `tblOrderDetails` table. You should receive a warning, but the Access Database Engine should allow you to complete the process.

Looking at the Benefits of Relationships

The primary benefit of relationships is the data integrity they provide. Without the establishment of relationships, users are free to add records to child tables without regard to entering required parent information. After referential integrity is established, you can enable Cascade Update Related Fields or Cascade Delete Related Records, as appropriate, which will save you quite a bit of code in maintaining the integrity of the data in your system. Most relational database management systems require that you write the code to delete related records when the user deletes a parent record or to update the foreign key in related records when the user modifies the primary key of the parent. By enabling the Cascade Update and Cascade Delete check boxes, you are sheltered from having to write a single line of code to perform these tasks when they are appropriate.

NOTE

SQL Server 2000 and SQL Server 2005 offer Cascade Update and Cascade Delete features similar to those found in Microsoft Access. This means that you no longer need to write your own T-SQL statements when it is appropriate to implement Cascade Update and Delete functionality.

Access automatically carries relationships into your queries. This means that each time you build a new query, Access automatically establishes the relationships between the tables within the query, based on the relationships you have set up in the Relationships window. Furthermore, each time you build a form or report, Access uses relationships between the tables included on the form or report to assist with the design process. Whether you delete or update data using a datasheet or a form, all referential integrity rules automatically apply, even if you establish the relationship after you build the form.

Examining Indexes and Relationships

The field that joins two tables on the one side of a one-to-many relationship must be a primary key field or must have a unique index so that the Access Database Engine can maintain referential integrity. If the index on the one side of the relationship is not unique, there is no way to determine to which parent a child record belongs.

In Access 2007, you do not need to create an index for the field on the many side of the relationship. Access 2007 will create an internal index for you. If you do create an index on the many side of the relationship, make sure that you set the index to Yes (Duplicates OK); otherwise, you will have a one-to-one, rather than a one-to-many, relationship.

Practical Examples: Establishing the Relationships Between the Tables Included in the Time and Billing Database

In this example, you'll establish some of the relationships you need to set up for the tables included in a hypothetical time and billing database. If you would like to build the relationships yourself, open the database that you created in Chapter 2, "What Every Developer Needs to Know About Databases and Tables."

▶ tblClients to tblProjects—You need to relate tblClients and tblProjects in a one-to-many relationship based on the ClientID field. You must enforce referential integrity to ensure that the user cannot add projects for nonexistent clients. There is no need to set Cascade Update Related Fields because the client ID that relates the two tables is an AutoNumber field in tblClients. You do not want to enable Cascade Delete Related Records because you do not want billing information to change if the user deletes a client. Instead, you want to prohibit the deletion of clients who have projects by establishing referential integrity between the two tables.

▶ tblProjects to tblPayments—You need to relate tblProjects and tblPayments in a one-to-many relationship based on the ProjectID field. You must enforce referential integrity to ensure that the user cannot add payments for nonexistent projects. There is no need to set Cascade Update Related Fields because the ProjectID that relates the two tables is an AutoNumber field in tblProjects. You do not want to enable Cascade Delete Related Records because you do not want payment information to change if the user deletes a client. Prohibit the deletion of clients who have payments by establishing referential integrity between the two tables.

▶ `tblProjects` to `tblTimeCardHours`—You need to relate `tblProjects` and `tblTimeCardHours` in a one-to-many relationship based on the `ProjectID` field. You must enforce referential integrity to ensure that the user cannot add hours for nonexistent projects. There is no need to set Cascade Update Related Fields because the `ProjectID` that relates the two tables is an `AutoNumber` field in `tblProjects`. Enable Cascade Delete Related Records so that the Access Database Engine deletes the associated hours if the user deletes a project.

▶ `tblProjects` to `tblTimeCardExpenses`—You need to relate `tblProjects` and `tblTimeCardExpenses` in a one-to-many relationship based on the `ProjectID` field. You must enforce referential integrity to ensure that the user cannot add expenses for nonexistent projects. There is no need to set Cascade Update Related Fields because the `ProjectID` that relates the two tables is an `AutoNumber` field in `tblProjects`. Enable Cascade Delete Related Records so that the Access Database Engine deletes expenses if the user deletes a project.

▶ `tblEmployees` to `tblTimeCards`—You need to relate `tblEmployees` and `tblTimeCards` in a one-to-many relationship based on the `EmployeeID` field. You must enforce referential integrity to ensure that the user cannot add time cards for nonexistent employees. There is no need to set Cascade Update Related Fields because the `EmployeeID` that relates the two tables is an `AutoNumber` field in `tblEmployees`. You do not want to enable Cascade Delete Related Records because, if the user deletes an employee, you do not want the Access Database Engine to delete all the employee's time cards.

▶ `tblEmployees` to `tblProjects`—You need to relate `tblEmployees` and `tblProjects` in a one-to-many relationship based on the `EmployeeID` field. You must enforce referential integrity to ensure that the user cannot assign projects to nonexistent employees. There is no need to set Cascade Update Related Fields because the employee ID that relates the two tables is an `AutoNumber` field in `tblEmployees`. You do not want to enable Cascade Delete Related Records because, if the user deletes an employee, you do not want the Access Database Engine to delete all the employee's projects, which is generally not desirable.

▶ `tblTimeCards` to `tblTimeCardHours`—You need to relate `tblTimeCards` and `tblTimeCardHours` in a one-to-many relationship based on the `TimeCardID` field. You must enforce referential integrity to ensure that the user cannot add time card hours for nonexistent time cards. There is no need to set Cascade Update Related Fields because the time card ID that relates the two tables is an `AutoNumber` field in `tblTimeCards`. You do want to enable Cascade Delete Related Records because, if the user deletes a time card, you want the Access Database Engine to delete the corresponding hours.

▶ `tblTimeCards` to `tblTimeCardExpenses`—You need to relate `tblTimeCards` and `tblTimeCardExpenses` in a one-to-many relationship based on the `TimeCardID` field. You must enforce referential integrity to ensure that the user cannot add time card expenses for nonexistent time cards. There is no need to set Cascade Update Related

Fields because the time card ID that relates the two tables is an `AutoNumber` field in `tblTimeCards`. You do want to enable Cascade Delete Related Records because, if the user deletes a time card, you want the Access Database Engine to delete the corresponding expenses.

▶ `tblExpenseCodes` to `tblTimeCardExpenses`—You need to relate `tblExpenseCodes` and `tblTimeCardExpenses` in a one-to-many relationship based on the `ExpenseCodeID` field. You must enforce referential integrity to ensure that the user cannot add time card expenses with nonexistent expense codes. There is no need to set Cascade Update Related Fields because the expense code ID that relates the two tables is an `AutoNumber` field in `tblExpenseCodes`. You do not want to enable Cascade Delete Related Records because, if the user deletes an expense code, you do not want the Access Database Engine to delete the corresponding expenses.

▶ `tblWorkCodes` to `tblTimeCardHours`—You need to relate `tblWorkCodes` and `tblTimeCardHours` in a one-to-many relationship based on the `WorkCodeID` field. You must enforce referential integrity to ensure that the user cannot add time card hours with invalid work codes. There is no need to set Cascade Update Related Fields because the work code ID that relates the two tables is an `AutoNumber` field in `tblWorkCodes`. You do not want to enable Cascade Delete Related Records because, if the user deletes a work code, you do not want the Access Database Engine to delete the corresponding hours.

▶ `tblPaymentMethods` to `tblPayments`—You need to relate `tblPaymentMethods` and `tblPayments` in a one-to-many relationship based on the `PaymentMethodID` field. You must enforce referential integrity to ensure that the user cannot add payments with an invalid payment method. There is no need to set Cascade Update Related Fields because the `PaymentMethodID` that relates the two tables is an `AutoNumber` field in `tblPaymentMethods`. You do not want to enable Cascade Delete Related Records because, if the user deletes a payment method, you do not want the Access Database Engine to delete the corresponding payments.

Summary

Relationships enable you to normalize your database. Using relationships, you can divide your data into separate tables, once again combining the data at runtime. This chapter began by explaining relational database design principles. It described the types of relationships that you can define. It then covered the details of establishing and modifying relationships between tables and described all the important aspects of establishing relationships.

The capability to easily establish and maintain referential integrity between tables is an important strength of Microsoft Access. This chapter described the referential integrity options and highlighted when each option is appropriate. Finally, this chapter summarized the benefits of relationships.

CHAPTER 4

What Every Developer Needs to Know About Query Basics

Why This Chapter Is Important

Although tables act as the ultimate foundation for any application that you build, queries are very important as well. Most of the forms and reports that act as the user interface for your application are based on queries. An understanding of queries, what they are, and when and how to use them is imperative for your success as an Access application developer. This chapter teaches you the basics of working with queries. After reading this chapter, you will know how to build queries, add tables and fields to the queries that you create, sort the query output, and apply criteria to limit the data that appears in the query output. You will also be familiar with tips and tricks and important "gotchas" of working with queries.

What Is a Query, and When Should You Use One?

Microsoft Access offers several different types of queries. This chapter focuses on the most basic type of query, the Select query. A Select query is a stored question about the data stored in your database's tables. Select queries are the foundation of much of what you do in Access. They underlie most of your forms and reports, allowing you to view the data you want, when you want. You use a simple Select query to define the tables and fields whose data you want to view and also to specify the criteria to limit the data that the query's output displays. A Select query is a query of a table or tables that just displays data; it doesn't modify data in any way. You use more advanced `Select` queries to summarize data, supply the results of calculations, or cross-tabulate your data. You can use Action queries to add, edit, or delete data from your tables, based on selected criteria, but this chapter covers `Select` queries. Chapter 12, "Advanced Query Techniques," covers other types of queries.

Everything You Need to Know About Query Basics

Creating a basic query is easy because Microsoft has provided a user-friendly, drag-and-drop interface. There are two ways to start a new query in Access 2007. The first way is to select the Create tab and then click to select the Query Wizard button in the Other group. The New Query dialog box appears (see Figure 4.1). The Simple Query Wizard walks you through the steps for creating a basic query. The other wizards help you create three specific types of queries: Crosstab, Find Duplicates, or Find Unmatched. The second method is to click to select the Create tab and then click to select the Query Design button in the Other group. The Show Table dialog box appears (see Figure 4.2). This dialog box lets you select which tables and queries you want to include in the query.

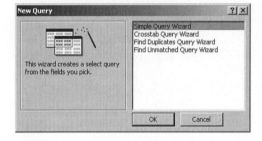

FIGURE 4.1   Use the New Query dialog box to select a wizard for the query you want to create.

FIGURE 4.2   When you click to select the Query Design icon in the Other group of the Create tab, the Show Table dialog box appears.

Adding Tables to Your Query

As mentioned previously, if you select Query Design rather than one of the wizards, the Show Table dialog box appears (see Figure 4.2). In this dialog box, you can select the tables or queries that supply data to your query. Access doesn't care whether you select tables or queries as the foundation for your queries. You can select them by double-clicking on the name of the table or query you want to add or by clicking on the table or query and then clicking Add. You can select multiple tables or queries by using the Shift key to select a contiguous range of tables or queries, or the Ctrl key to select noncontiguous tables or queries. When you have selected the tables or queries you want, click Add and then click Close. This brings you to the Query Design window shown in Figure 4.3.

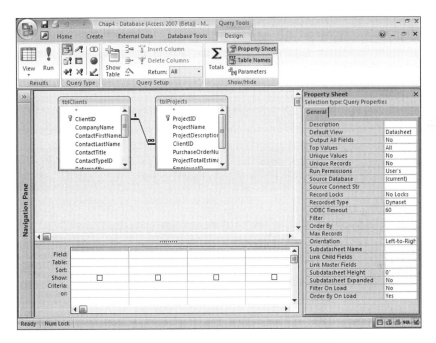

FIGURE 4.3   The Query Design window presents an easy-to-use (and learn) query design grid.

Adding Fields to Your Query

You're now ready to select the fields you want to include in the query. The query shown in Figure 4.3 is based on the `tblClients` table and the `tblProjects` table included in the `CHAP4.ACCDB` database on the sample code CD-ROM. Notice that the query window is divided into two sections. The top half of the window shows the tables or queries that underlie the query you're designing; the bottom half shows any fields that will be included in the query output. You can add a field to the query design grid on the bottom half of the query window in several ways:

▶ Double-click the name of the field you want to add.

▶ Click and drag a single field from the table in the top half of the query window to the query design grid below.

▶ Select multiple fields at the same time by using your Shift key (for a contiguous range of fields) or your Ctrl key (for a noncontiguous range). You can double-click the title bar of the field list to select all fields and then click and drag any one of the selected fields to the query design grid.

TIP

You can double-click the asterisk to include all fields within the table in the query result. Although this "trick" is handy, in that changes to the table structure magically affect the query's output, I believe that it is dangerous. When the asterisk is selected, all table fields are included in the query result, regardless of whether they are needed. Including all these fields can cause major performance problems in a LAN, WAN, or client/server application.

Create a database based on the Northwind 2007 template database that comes with Access (see Figure 4.4). If you want to prevent the Startup form from appearing, hold down your Shift key as you click the Create button and until the database opens. Click to select the Create tab. Select Query Design from the Other group. The Show Table dialog box appears. Add the Customers table to the query and close the Show Table dialog.

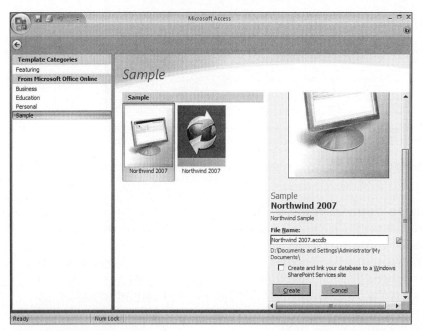

FIGURE 4.4   Create a database based on the Northwind 2007 template database that comes with Access.

Follow these steps to select eight fields from the Customers table:

1. Click the ID field.

2. Hold down your Shift key and click the Job Title field. This should select the ID, Company, First Name, Last Name, E-mail Address, and Job Title fields.

3. Scroll down the list of fields, using the vertical scrollbar, until the Country/Region field is visible.

4. Hold down your Ctrl key and click the Home Phone field.

5. With the Ctrl key still held down, click the Country/Region field. All eight fields should now be selected.

Click and drag any of the selected fields from the table on the top half of the query window to the query design grid on the bottom. All eight fields should appear in the query design grid (see Figure 4.5). You might need to use the horizontal scrollbar to view some of the fields on the right.

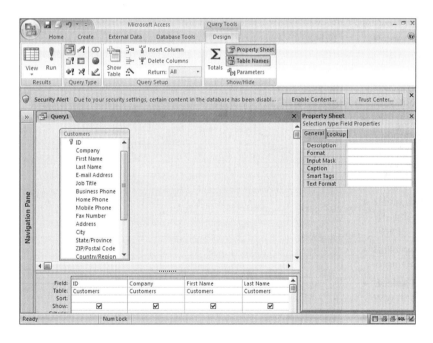

FIGURE 4.5   After you add fields to the query, they appear on the query design grid.

TIP

The easiest way to run a query is to click the Run button on the ribbon (which looks like an exclamation point). You can click the View button to run a query, but this method works only for Select queries, not for Action queries. The View button has a special meaning for Action queries (explained in Chapter 12). Clicking Run is preferable because you don't have to worry about what type of query you're running. After running a Select query, you should see what looks like a datasheet, with only the fields you selected. To return to the query's design, click the View button.

TIP

Introduced with Access 2002 are shortcut keys that allow you to easily toggle between the various query views: Ctrl+>, Ctrl+.(period), Ctrl+<, and Ctrl,(comma). Ctrl+> and Ctrl+.(period) take you to the next view; Ctrl+< and Ctrl,(comma) take you to the previous view.

Removing a Field from the Query Design Grid

To remove a field from the query design grid, follow these steps:

1. Find the field you want to remove.

2. Click the small horizontal gray button (column selector) immediately above the name of the field. The entire column of the query design grid should become black (see Figure 4.6).

3. Press the Delete key or click Delete Columns in the Query Setup group of the Design tab.

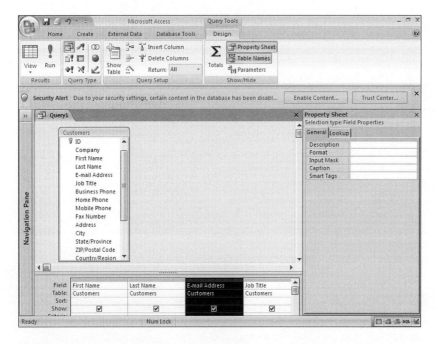

FIGURE 4.6   Removing a field from the query design grid.

Assume that you have decided to remove the Region field from the query design grid. Use the horizontal scrollbar to see the Country/Region field on the query design grid, and then do the following:

1. Click the column selector immediately above the Country/Region field. The entire column of the query design grid should become black, and the cursor turns into a downward-pointing arrow.

2. Press the Delete key to remove the Country/Region field from the query design grid.

Inserting a Field After the Query Is Built

The process for inserting a field after a query is built differs, depending on where you want to insert the new field. If you want to insert it after the existing fields, the easiest method is to double-click the name of the field you want to add. If you prefer to insert the new field between two existing fields, the best approach is to click and drag the field you want to add, dropping it onto the field you want to appear to the right of the inserted field.

To insert the Business Phone field between the Job Title and Home Phone fields, click and drag the Business Phone field from the table until it's on top of the Home Phone field. This technique inserts the field in the correct place. To run the query, click Run on the ribbon.

Moving a Field to a Different Location on the Query Design Grid

Although the user can move a column while in a query's Datasheet view, sometimes you want to permanently alter the position of a field in the query output. You can do this as a convenience to the user or, more importantly, because you will use the query as a foundation for forms and reports. The order of the fields in the query becomes the default order of the fields on any forms and reports you build using any of the wizards. You can save yourself quite a bit of time by ordering your queries effectively.

To move a single column, follow these steps:

1. Select a column while in the query's Design view by clicking its column selector (the button immediately above the field name).

2. Click the selected column a second time and then drag it to a new location on the query design grid.

Follow these steps to move more than one column at a time:

1. Drag across the column selectors of the columns you want to move.

2. Click any of the selected columns a second time and then drag them to a new location on the query design grid.

Move the First Name and Last Name fields so that they appear before the Company field. Do this by clicking and dragging from the column selector for First Name to the column selector for Last Name. Both columns should be selected. Click again on the column selector for either column and then click and drag until the thick black line jumps to the left of the Company field.

> **NOTE**
>
> Moving a column in the Datasheet view doesn't modify the query's underlying design. If you move a column in Datasheet view, subsequent reordering in the Design view isn't reflected in the Datasheet view. In other words, Design view and Datasheet view are no longer synchronized, and you must reorder both by hand. This actually serves as an advantage in most cases. As you will learn later, if you want to sort by the Country/Region field and then by the Company field, the Country/Region field must appear to the left of the Company field in the design of the query. If you want the Company field to appear to the left of the Country/Region field in the query's result, you must make that change in Datasheet view. The fact that Access maintains the order of the columns separately in both views allows you to easily accomplish both objectives.

Saving and Naming Your Query

To save your query at any time, click the Save button on the Quick Access toolbar. If the query is a new one, Access prompts you to name your query. Query names should begin with the tag qry so that you can easily recognize and identify them as queries. It's important to understand that, when you save a query, you're saving only the query's definition, not the actual query result.

Return to the design of the query. To save your work, click Save on the Quick Access toolbar that appears to the right of the Microsoft Access button. When prompted for a name, call the query **qryCustomers**.

Ordering Your Query Result

When you run a new query, notice that the query output appears in no particular order, but generally, you want to order it. You can do this by using the Sort row of the query design grid.

To order your query result, follow these steps:

1. In Design view, click within the query design grid in the Sort cell of the column you want to sort (see Figure 4.7).

2. Use the drop-down combo box to select an ascending or descending sort.

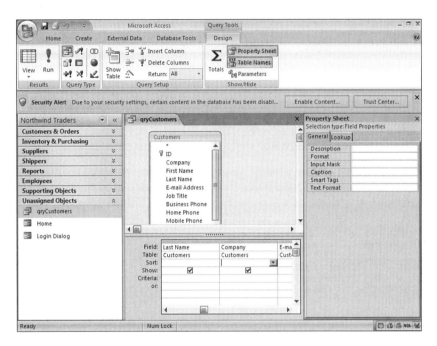

FIGURE 4.7   Changing the order of the query result.

To sort in ascending order by the Company field, follow these steps:

1. In Design view, click in the Sort row of the query design grid for the Company field.

2. Open the Sort drop-down combo box.

3. Select Ascending.

4. Run your query and view the results. Your records should now be ordered by the Company field.

5. If you want to return to the query's design, click View on the toolbar.

Sorting by More Than One Field

Quite often, you want to sort your query output by more than one field. The columns you want to sort must be placed in order from left to right on the query design grid, with the column you want to act as the primary sort on the far left and the secondary, tertiary, and any additional sorts following to the right. If you want the columns to appear in a different order in the query output, you must move them manually in Datasheet view after you run the query.

Sort the query output by the Country/Region field and, within individual country groupings, by the Last Name and First Name fields. Because sorting always occurs from left to right, you must place the Country/Region field before the LastName and FirstName fields. Therefore, you must move the Country/Region field. Follow these steps:

1. Select the `Country/Region` field from the query design grid by clicking the thin gray button above the `Country/Region` column.

2. After you have selected the `Country/Region` field, move your mouse back to the thin gray button and click and drag to the left of the `First Name` and `Last Name` fields. A thick gray line should appear to the left of the `First Name` field.

3. Release the mouse button.

4. Select the `Last Name` field from the query design grid by clicking the thin gray button above the `Last Name` column.

5. After you have selected the `Last Name` field, move your mouse back to the thin gray button and click and drag to the left of the `First Name` field. A thick gray line should appear to the left of the `First Name` field.

6. Release the mouse button.

7. Change the sort of the `Country/Region` field to Ascending.

8. Change the sort of the `Last Name` field to Ascending.

9. Change the sort of the `First Name` field to Ascending.

10. Run the query. The records should be ordered by country/region and, within the country grouping, by last name and first name.

Refining Your Query with Criteria

So far, you have learned how to select the fields you want and how to indicate the sort order for your query output. One of the important features of queries is the capability to limit your output by selection criteria. Access allows you to combine criteria by using any of several operators to limit the criteria for one or more fields. The operators and their meanings are covered in Table 4.1.

TABLE 4.1   Access Operators and Their Meanings

Operator	Meaning	Example	Result
=	Equal to	="Sales"	Finds only those records with "Sales" as the field value
<	Less than	<100	Finds all records with values less than 100 in that field
<=	Less than or equal to	<=100	Finds all records with values less than or equal to 100 in that field
>	Greater than	>100	Finds all records with values greater than 100 in that field
>=	Greater than or equal to	>=100	Finds all records with values greater than or equal to 100 in that field

TABLE 4.1   Continued

Operator	Meaning	Example	Result
<>	Not equal to	<>"Sales"	Finds all records with values other than Sales in the field
And	Both conditions must be true	Created by adding criteria on the same line of the query design grid to more than one field	Finds all records where the conditions in both fields are true
Or	Either condition can be true	"CA" or "NY" or "UT"	Finds all records with the value of "CA", "NY", or "UT" in the field
Like	Compares a string expression to a pattern	Like "Sales*"	Finds all records with the value of "Sales" at the beginning of the field
Between	Finds a range of values	Between 5 and 10	Finds all records with the values of 5–10 (inclusive) in the field
In	Determines if the value is in the string	In("CA", "NY","UT")	Finds all records with the value of "CA", "NY", or "UT" in the field
Not	Same as not equal to	Not "Sales"	Finds all records with values other than Sales in the field
Is Null	Finds Nulls	Is Null	Finds all records where no data has been entered in the field
Is Not Null	Finds all records not Null	Is Not Null	Finds all records where data has been entered in the field

---

NOTE

The asterisk (*) is a wildcard. Used in the example "Like Sales*", it will return all records that begin with Sales and are followed by any remaining characters.

Criteria entered for two fields on a single line of the query design grid are considered an And, which means that both conditions need to be true for the record to appear in the query output. Entries made on separate lines of the query design grid are considered an Or, which means that either condition can be true for the record to be included in the query output. Take a look at the example in Figure 4.8; this query would output all records in which the Job Title field begins with either Marketing or Owner, regardless of the last name. It outputs the records in which the Job Title field begins with Sales only for the customers whose last names begin with the letters *M* through *R* inclusive.

Design a query to find all the sales agents in Brazil or France. The criteria you build should look like those in Figure 4.9.

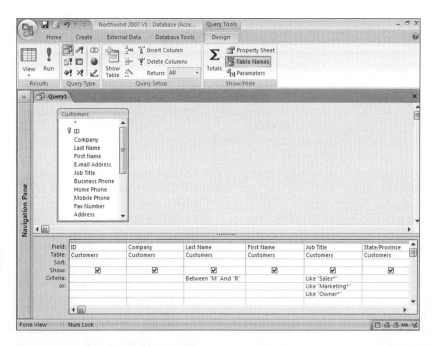

FIGURE 4.8   Adding And and Or conditions to a query.

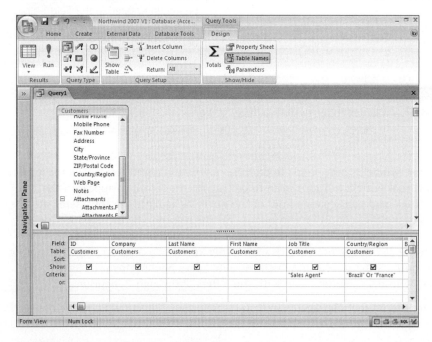

FIGURE 4.9   The criteria to select sales agents whose country is either Brazil or France.

1. Notice that the criterion for the Country/Region field is "Brazil" Or "France" because you want both Brazil and France to appear in the query output. The criterion for the Job Title field is "Sales Agent". Because the criteria for both the Country/Region and Job Title fields are entered on the same line of the query design grid, both must be true for the record to appear in the query output. In other words, the customer must be in either Brazil or France and must also be a sales agent.

2. Modify the query so that you can output all the customers for whom the job title begins with Sales. Try changing the criteria for the Job Title field to Sales. Notice that no records appear in the query output because no contact titles are just Sales. You must enter "Like Sales*" for the criteria. Now you get the Sales Agents, Sales Associates, Sales Managers, and so on. You still don't see the Assistant Sales Agents because their titles don't begin with Sales. Try changing the criteria to "Like *Sales*". Now all the Assistant Sales Agents appear.

Working with Dates in Criteria

Access gives you significant power for adding date functions and expressions to your query criteria. Using these criteria, you can find all records in a certain month, on a specific weekday, or between two dates. Table 4.2 lists several examples.

TABLE 4.2   Sample Date Criteria

Expression	Meaning	Example	Result
Date()	Current date	Date()	Records with the current date within a field
Day(Date)	The day of a date	Day ([OrderDate])=1	Records with the order date on the first day of the month
Month(Date)	The month of a date	Month ([OrderDate])=1	Records with the order date in January
Year(Date)	The year of a date	Year ([OrderDate])=2007	Records with the order date in 2007
Weekday(Date)	The weekday of a date	Weekday ([OrderDate])=2	Records with the order date on a Monday
Between Date And Date	A range of dates	Between #1/1/2007# and #12/31/2007#	All records in 2007
DatePart (Interval, Date)	A specific part of a date	DatePart ("q", [OrderDate])=2	All records in the second quarter

The Weekday(Date, [FirstDayOfWeek]) function works based on your locale and how your system defines the first day of the week. Weekday() used without the optional

FirstDayOfWeek argument defaults to vbSunday as the first day. A value of 0 defaults the FirstDayOfWeek to the system definition. Other values can be set also.

Figure 4.10 illustrates the use of a date function. Notice that DatePart("q",[Order Date]) is entered as the expression, and the value of 2 is entered for the criteria. Year([Order Date)] is entered as another expression, with the number 2007 as the criteria. Therefore, this query outputs all records in which the order date is in the second quarter of 2007.

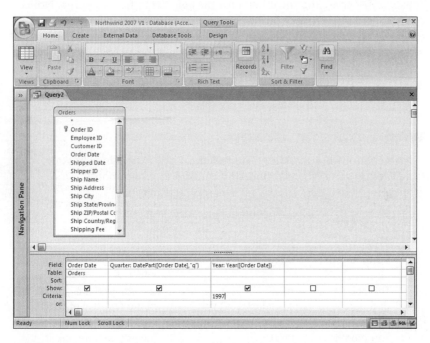

FIGURE 4.10   Using the DatePart() and Year() functions in a query.

Understanding How You Can Update Query Results

If you haven't realized it yet, you can usually update the results of your query. This means that if you modify the data in the query output, the data in the tables underlying the query is permanently modified.

Build a query based on the Customers table. Add the ID, Company, Address, City, and Country/Region fields to the query design grid; then run the query. Change the address of a particular customer and make a note of the customer ID of the customer whose address you changed. Make sure you move off the record so that Access writes the change to disk. Close the query, open the actual table in Datasheet view, and find the record whose address you modified. Notice that the change you made was written to the original table; the reason is that a query result is a dynamic set of records that maintains a link back to the original data. You get this result whether you're on a standalone machine or on a network.

> **CAUTION**
>
> Understanding how Access updates query results is essential; otherwise, you might mistakenly update table data without even realizing you did so. Updating multitable queries is covered later in this chapter in the sections "Pitfalls of Multitable Queries" and "Row Fix-Up in Multitable Queries."

Building Queries Based on Multiple Tables

If you have properly normalized your table data, you probably want to bring the data from your tables back together by using queries. Fortunately, you can do this quite easily with Access queries.

The query in Figure 4.11 joins the Customers, Orders, and Order Details tables, pulling fields from each. Notice that the ID and Company fields are selected from the Customers table, the Order ID and Order Date from the Orders table, and the Unit Price and Quantity from the Order Details table. After running this query, you should see the results shown in Figure 4.12. By creating a multitable query, you can look at data from related tables, along with the data from the Order Details table.

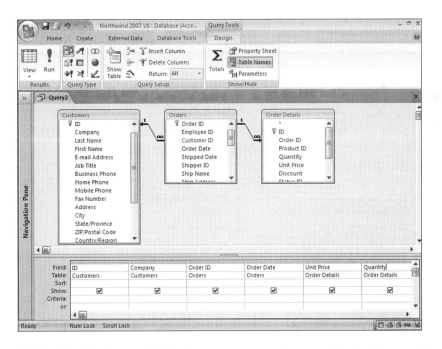

FIGURE 4.11   A query joining the Customers, Orders, and Order Details tables.

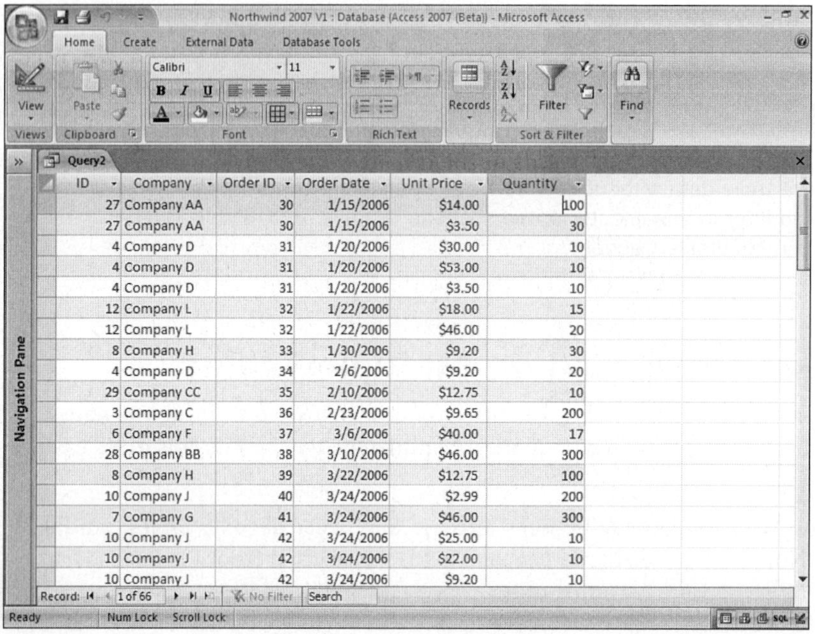

FIGURE 4.12   The results of querying multiple tables.

Build a query that combines information from the Customers, Orders, and Order Details tables. To do this, build a new query by following these steps:

1. Click to select the Create tab.

2. Click Query Design in the Other group. The Show Table dialog box appears.

3. From the Show Table dialog box, select Customers, Orders, and Order Details by holding down the Ctrl key and clicking on each table name. Then select Add.

4. Click Close.

5. Some of the tables included in the query might be hiding below. If so, scroll down using the vertical scrollbar to view any tables that aren't visible. Notice the join lines between the tables; they're based on the relationships set up in the Relationships window.

6. Select the following fields from each table:

    Customers: Country/Region, City

    Orders: Order Date

    Order Details: Unit Price, Quantity

7. Sort by Country/Region and then City in ascending order. Your finished query design should look like the one in Figure 4.13.

8. Run the query. Data from all three tables should be included in the query output.

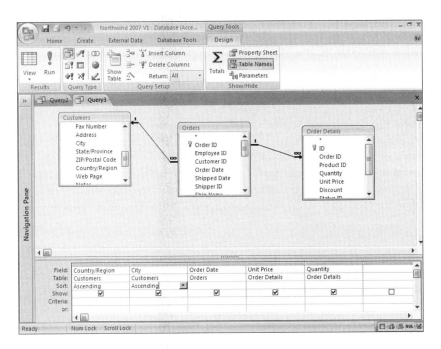

FIGURE 4.13   The query design from the example.

> **NOTE**
>
> To remove a table from a query, click anywhere on the table in the top half of the query design grid and press the Delete key. You can add tables to the query at any time by clicking the Show Table button on the ribbon. If you prefer, you can select the Navigation Pane and then click and drag tables directly from the Navigation Pane to the top half of the query design grid.

Pitfalls of Multitable Queries

You should be aware of some pitfalls of multitable queries; they involve updating as well as which records you see in the query output.

Remember that you can't update certain fields in a multitable query. These are the join fields on the "one" side of a one-to-many relationship (unless the Cascade Update Referential Integrity feature has been activated). You also can't update the join field on the "many" side of a relationship after you've updated data on the "one" side. More importantly, which fields can be updated, and the consequences of updating them, might surprise you. If you update the fields on the "one" side of a one-to-many relationship, you must be aware of that change's impact. You're actually updating that record in the original table on the "one" side of the relationship; several records on the "many" side of the relationship will be affected.

> **NOTE**
>
> For more information about referential integrity, refer to Chapter 3, "Relationships: Your Key to Data Integrity."

For example, Figure 4.14 shows the result of a query based on the Customers, Orders, and Order Details tables. I have changed "Company AA" to "Business AA" on a specific record of my query output. You might expect this change to affect only that specific order detail item. Pressing the down-arrow key to move off the record shows that all records associated with Company AA have been changed (see Figure 4.15). This happened because all the orders for Company AA were actually getting their information from one record in the Customers table—the record for ID 27. This is the record I modified while viewing the query result.

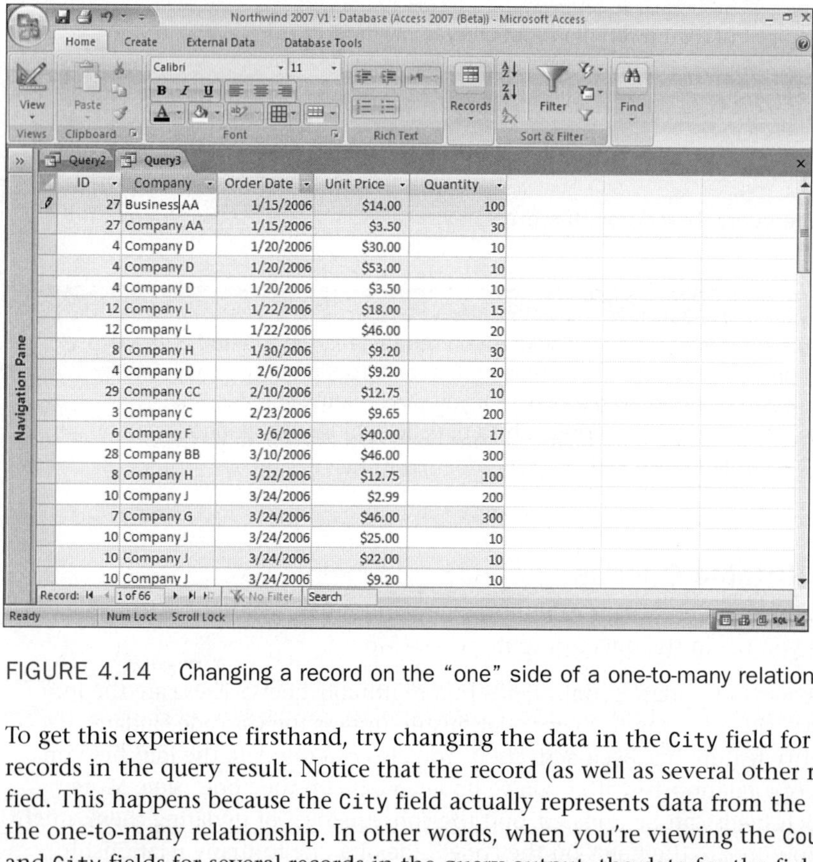

FIGURE 4.14   Changing a record on the "one" side of a one-to-many relationship.

To get this experience firsthand, try changing the data in the City field for one of the records in the query result. Notice that the record (as well as several other records) is modified. This happens because the City field actually represents data from the "one" side of the one-to-many relationship. In other words, when you're viewing the Country/Region and City fields for several records in the query output, the data for the fields might originate from one record. The same goes for the Order Date field because it's also on the "one" side of a one-to-many relationship. The only field in the query output that can't be modified is TotalPrice, a calculated field. Practice modifying the data in the query result and then returning to the original table and noticing which data has changed.

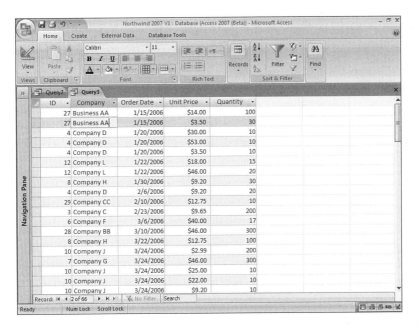

FIGURE 4.15   The result of changing a record on the "one" side of a one-to-many relationship. Notice that the Company Name field has been updated for all records with 27 as the ID.

The second pitfall of multitable queries is figuring out which records result from such a query. So far, you have learned how to build only inner joins. Join types are covered in detail in Chapter 12, but for now, it's important to understand that the query output contains all customers, regardless if they have orders, and all orders, regardless if they have order detail. This means that not all customers and all orders are listed. In Chapter 12, you'll learn how to build queries in which you can list only customers who have orders. You'll also learn how to list only the customers without orders.

Row Fix-Up in Multitable Queries

The Row Fix-Up feature is automatically available to you in Access. As you fill in key values on the "many" side of a one-to-many relationship in a multitable query, the nonkey values are automatically looked up in the parent table. Most database developers refer to this as *enforced referential integrity*. A foreign key must first exist on the "one" side of the query to be entered successfully on the "many" side. As you can imagine, you don't want to be able to add an order to your database for a nonexistent customer.

For example, the query in Figure 4.16 is based on the Customers and Orders tables. The fields included in the query are Customer ID from the Orders table; Company, Address, and City from the Customers table; and Order ID from the Orders table. If the Customer ID associated with an order is changed, the Company, Address, and City are looked up from the Customers table and immediately displayed in the query result. Notice in Figure 4.17 how the information for Business AA is displayed in the query result. Figure 4.18 shows that the Company, Address, and City change automatically when the Customer ID is changed to Company AA. Don't be confused by the combo box used to select the customer ID. The presence of the combo box within the query is a result of Access's auto-lookup feature, covered in Chapter 2, "What Every Developer Needs to Know About Databases and Tables." The customer ID associated with a particular order is actually being modified in the query. If the user adds a new record to the query, Access fills in the customer information as soon as the user selects the customer ID associated with the order.

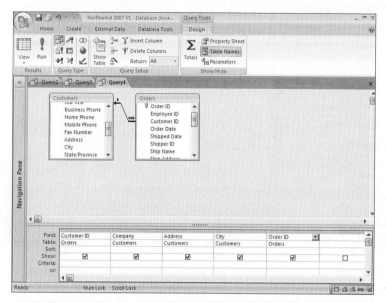

FIGURE 4.16   This query illustrates the use of Row Fix-Up in a query with multiple tables.

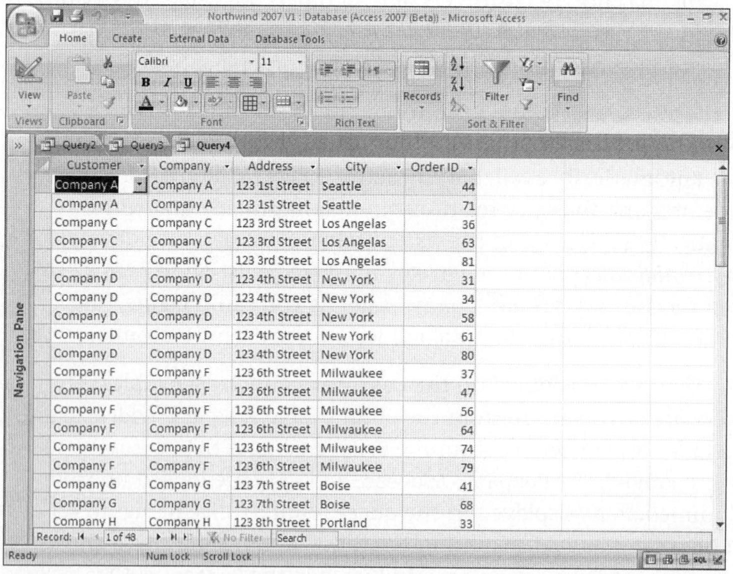

FIGURE 4.17   The query result before selecting another customer ID.

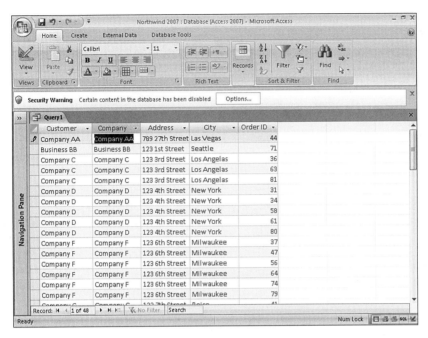

FIGURE 4.18   The result of an auto-lookup after the customer ID is changed. The information on the "one" side of the relationship is "fixed up" to display information for the appropriate customer.

Creating Calculated Fields

One of the rules of data normalization is that the results of calculations shouldn't be included in your database. You can output the results of calculations by building those calculations into your queries, and you can display the results of the calculations on forms and reports by making the query the foundation for a form or report. You can also add controls to your forms and reports containing the calculations you want. In certain cases, this can improve performance. (This topic is covered in more depth in Chapter 16, "Debugging: Your Key to Successful Development.")

The columns of your query result can hold the result of any valid expression, including the result of a user-defined function. This makes your queries extremely powerful. For example, you can enter the following expression:

```
Left([First Name],1) & "." & Left([Last Name],1) & "."
```

This expression would give you the first character of the first name followed by a period, the first character of the last name, and another period. An even simpler expression would be this one:

```
[Unit Price]*[Quantity]
```

This calculation would simply take the Unit Price field and multiply it by the Quantity field. In both cases, Access would automatically name the resulting expression. For example, the calculation that results from concatenating the first and last initials is shown in Figure 4.19. Notice that in the figure, the expression has been given a name (often referred to as an *alias*). To give the expression a name, such as Initials, you must enter it as follows:

```
Initials:Left([First Name],1) & "." & Left([Last Name],1) & "."
```

The text preceding the colon is the name of the expression—in this case, Initials. If you don't explicitly give your expression a name, it defaults to Expr1.

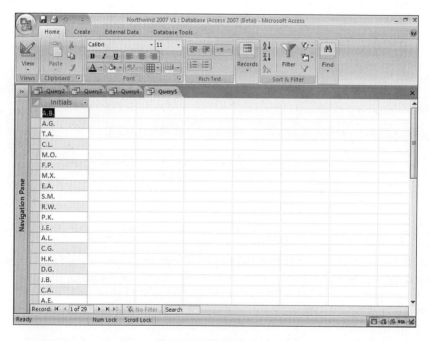

FIGURE 4.19   The result of the expression Initials:Left([FirstName],1) & "." & Left([LastName],1) & "." in the query.

Follow these steps to add a calculation that shows the unit price multiplied by the quantity:

1. Scroll to the right on the query design grid until you can see a blank column.

2. Click in the Field row for the new column.

3. Type **Total Price:[Unit Price]*Quantity**. (These fields come from the Order Details table.) If you want to see more easily what you're typing, press Shift+F2 (Zoom). The dialog box shown in Figure 4.20 appears. (Access will supply the space after the colon and the square brackets around the field names if you omit them.)

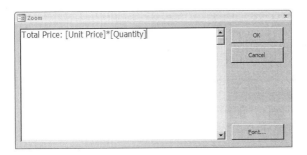

FIGURE 4.20   Expanding the field with the Zoom function (Shift+F2).

4. Click OK to close the Zoom window.

5. Run the query. The total price should appear in the far-right column of the query output. The query output should look like the one in Figure 4.21.

> **NOTE**
>
> You can enter any valid expression in the Field row of your query design grid. Notice that field names included in an expression are automatically surrounded by square brackets, unless your field name has spaces. If a field name includes any spaces, you must enclose the field name in brackets; otherwise, your query won't run properly. This is just one of the many reasons why field and table names shouldn't contain spaces.

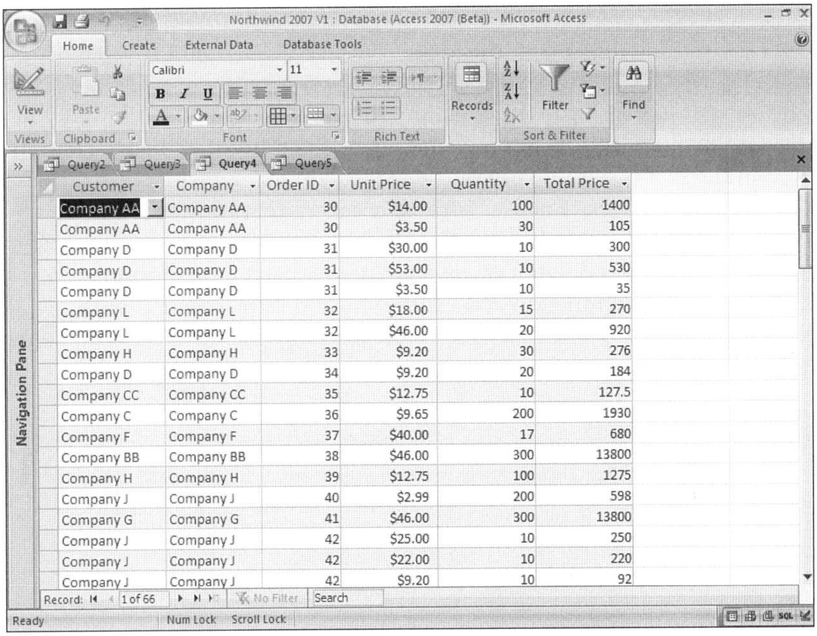

FIGURE 4.21   The result of the total price calculation.

Getting Help from the Expression Builder

The Expression Builder is a helpful tool for building expressions in your queries, as well as in many other situations in Access. To invoke the Expression Builder, click in the Field cell of your query design grid and then click Builder on the Ribbon (see Figure 4.22). Notice that the Expression Builder is divided into three columns. The first column shows the objects in the database. After selecting an element in the left column, select the elements you want to paste from the middle and right columns.

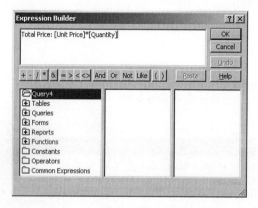

FIGURE 4.22   The Expression Builder makes it easier for you to create expressions in your query.

The example in Figure 4.23 shows Functions selected in the left column. Within Functions, both user-defined and built-in functions are listed; here, the Functions object is expanded with Built-In Functions selected. In the center column, Date/Time is selected. After you select Date/Time, all the built-in date and time functions appear in the right column. If you double-click a particular function—in this case, the DatePart function—the function and its parameters are placed in the text box at the top of the Expression Builder window. Notice that the DatePart function has four parameters: interval, date, firstweekday, and firstweek. If you know what needs to go into each of these parameters, you can simply replace the parameter placemarkers with your own values. If you need more information, you can invoke help on the selected function and learn more about the required parameters. In Figure 4.24, two parameters are filled in: the interval and the name of the field being evaluated. After you click OK, the expression is placed in the Field cell of the query.

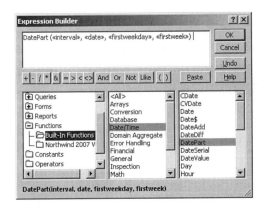

FIGURE 4.23   The Expression Builder with the DatePart function selected and pasted in the expression box.

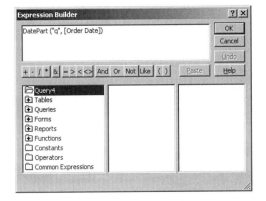

FIGURE 4.24   A function pasted by Expression Builder with the parameters updated with appropriate values.

Summarizing Data with Totals Queries

By using Totals queries, you can easily summarize numeric data. You can use Totals queries to calculate the Sum, Average, Count, Minimum, Maximum, and other types of summary calculations for the data in your query result. These queries let you calculate one value for all the records in your query result or group the calculations as desired. For example, you could determine the total sales for every record in the query result, as shown in Figure 4.25, or you could output the total sales by country and city (see Figure 4.26). You could also calculate the total, average, minimum, and maximum sales amounts for all customers in the United States. The possibilities are endless.

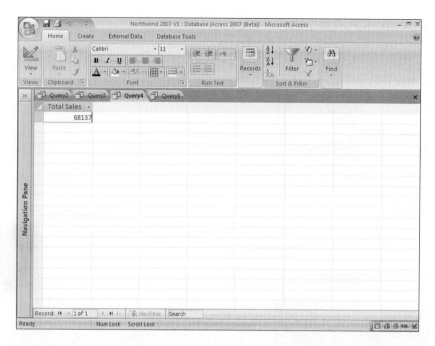

FIGURE 4.25   Total sales for every record in the query result.

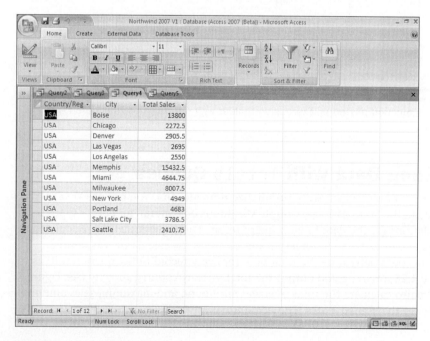

FIGURE 4.26   Total sales by country and city.

To create a `Totals` query, follow these steps:

1. Add to the query design grid the fields or expressions you want to summarize. It's important that you add the fields in the order in which you want them grouped. For example, Figure 4.27 shows a query grouped by country and then city.

2. Click Totals on the ribbon to add a Total row to the query. By default, each field in the query has `Group By` in the Total row.

3. Click in the Total row on the query design grid.

4. Open the combo box and choose the calculation you want (see Figure 4.27).

5. Leave `Group By` in the Total cell of any fields you want to group by, as shown in Figure 4.27. Remember to place the fields in the order in which you want them grouped. For example, if you want the records grouped by country and then by sales representative, you must place the `Country/Region` field to the left of the `Employee ID` field on the query design grid. On the other hand, if you want records grouped by `Employee ID` and then by country, you must place the `Employee ID` field to the left of the `Country` field on the query design grid.

6. Add the criteria you want to the query.

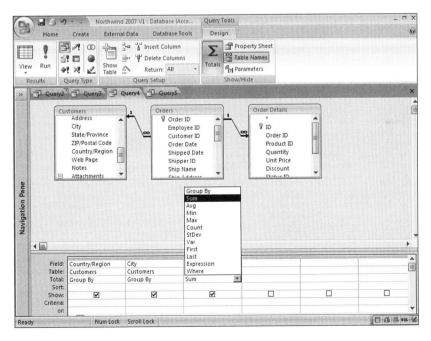

FIGURE 4.27   Selecting the type of calculation for the Total row from a drop-down list.

Figure 4.28 shows the design of a query that finds the total, average, maximum, and number of sales by country and city; Figure 4.29 shows the results of running the query. As you can see, `Totals` queries can give you valuable information.

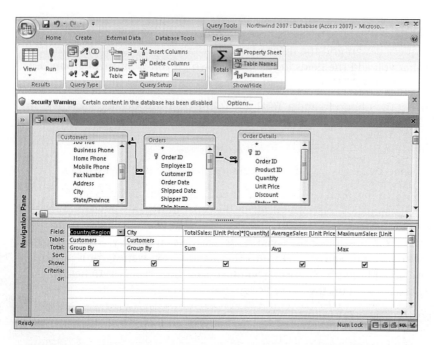

FIGURE 4.28   A query that finds the total, average, maximum, and number of sales by country and city.

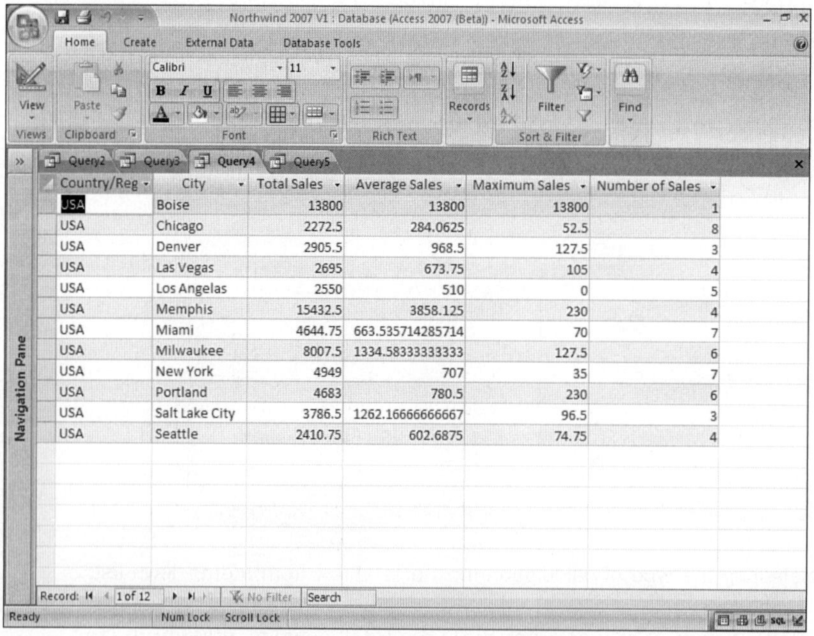

Country/Reg ▾	City ▾	Total Sales ▾	Average Sales ▾	Maximum Sales ▾	Number of Sales ▾
USA	Boise	13800	13800	13800	1
USA	Chicago	2272.5	284.0625	52.5	8
USA	Denver	2905.5	968.5	127.5	3
USA	Las Vegas	2695	673.75	105	4
USA	Los Angelas	2550	510	0	5
USA	Memphis	15432.5	3858.125	230	4
USA	Miami	4644.75	663.535714285714	70	7
USA	Milwaukee	8007.5	1334.58333333333	127.5	6
USA	New York	4949	707	35	7
USA	Portland	4683	780.5	230	6
USA	Salt Lake City	3786.5	1262.16666666667	96.5	3
USA	Seattle	2410.75	602.6875	74.75	4

FIGURE 4.29   The results of running a query with many aggregate functions.

If you save this query and reopen it, you'll see that Access has made some changes to its design. The Total cell for the Sum is changed to Expression, and the Field cell is changed to the following:

```
TotalSales: Sum([Unit Price]*[Quantity])
```

If you look at the Total cell for the Avg, it's also changed to Expression. The Field cell is changed to the following:

```
AverageSales: Avg([Unit Price]*[Quantity])
```

Access modifies the query in this way when it determines that you're using an aggregate function on an expression having more than one field. You can enter the expression either way. Access stores and resolves the expression as noted.

Modify the query to show the total sales by country, city, and order date. Before you continue, save your query as **qryCustomerOrderInfo** and then close it. With the list of queries visible, click qryCustomerOrderInfo. Right-click the query and select Copy from the context-sensitive menu. Right-click the query again and select Paste. Access should prompt you for the name of the new query. Type **qryCustomerOrderSummary** and click OK. Right-click qryCustomerOrderSummary and select Design from the context-sensitive menu. Delete both the Unit Price and Quantity fields from the query output. To turn your query into a Totals query, follow these steps:

1. Click Totals on the Design tab of the ribbon. Notice that an extra line, called the Total line, is added to the query design grid; this line says Group By for all fields.

2. Group by country, city, and order date but total by the total price (the calculated field). Click the Total row for the Total Price field and use the drop-down list to select Sum (refer to Figure 4.27).

3. Run the query. Your result should be grouped and sorted by country, city, and order date, with a total for each unique combination of the three fields.

4. Return to the query's design and remove the order date from the query design grid.

5. Rerun the query. Notice that now you're summarizing the query by country and city.

6. Change the Total row to Avg. Now you're seeing the average price times quantity for each combination of country and city. Change it back to Sum and save the query.

As you can see, Totals queries are both powerful and flexible. You can't edit their output, but you can use them to view the sum, minimum, maximum, average, and count of the total price, all at the same time. You can easily modify how you're viewing this information—by country, country and city, and so on—all at the click of your mouse.

Excluding Fields from the Output

At times, you need to include a column in your query that you don't want displayed in the query output; this is often the case with columns used solely for criteria. Figure 4.30 shows an example. If you run this query, you get the total, average, count, and maximum sales grouped by both country and order date. However, you want to group only by country and use the order date only as criteria. Therefore, you need to set the Total row of the query to Where, as shown in Figure 4.31. The column used in Where has been excluded from the query result. You can easily determine this by noting that the check box in the Show row of the Order Date column is unchecked.

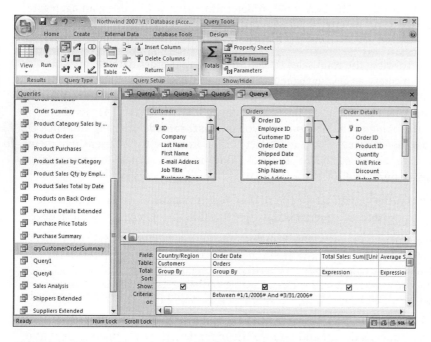

FIGURE 4.30   A query with criteria for the order date, before excluding fields from the query output.

Understanding Nulls and Query Results

Null values in your table's fields can noticeably affect query results. A Null value is different from a zero or a zero-length string, which indicates that the data doesn't exist for a particular field; a field contains a Null value when no value has yet been stored in the field. (As discussed in Chapter 2, you enter a zero-length string in a field by typing two quotation marks.)

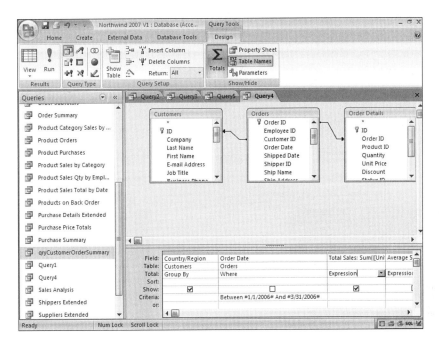

FIGURE 4.31   The Total row of the Order Date field is set to Where, excluding the field from the query result.

Null values can affect the results of multitable queries, queries including aggregate functions (Totals queries), and queries with calculations. Null values can also affect the result of aggregate queries. For example, if you perform a count on a field containing Null values, the Access Database Engine includes in the count only records having non-Null values in that field. If you want to get an accurate count, it's best to perform the count on a primary key field or some other field that can't have Null values.

Probably the most insidious problem with Nulls happens when you include them in calculations. Including a Null value in a calculation containing a numeric operator (+, -, /, *, and so on) results in a Null value. In Figure 4.32, for example, notice that the query includes a calculation that adds the values in the Parts and Labor fields. These fields have been set to have no default value and, therefore, contain Nulls unless something has been explicitly entered into them. Running the query gives you the results shown in Figure 4.33. Notice that all the records having Nulls in either the Parts or Labor fields contain a Null in the result.

The solution to this problem is constructing an expression that converts the Null values to zero. The expression looks like this:

```
TotalCost: NZ([Parts])+NZ([Labor])
```

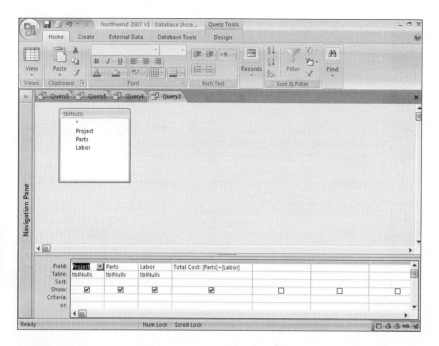

FIGURE 4.32   The Design view of a query that propagates Nulls in the query result.

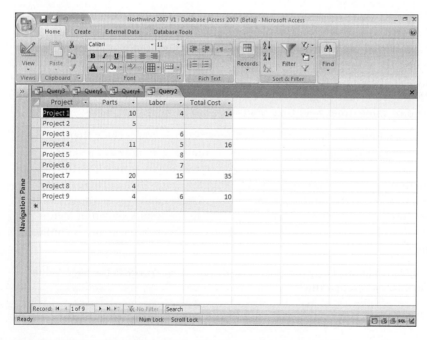

FIGURE 4.33   The result of running a query illustrating Nulls.

The NZ() function determines whether the Parts field contains a Null value. If the Parts field contains a Null value, the expression converts it to a zero and includes it in the calculation; otherwise, the expression uses the field's value in the calculation. The same expression is used to evaluate the Labor field. The result of the modified query is shown in Figure 4.34.

CAUTION

Nulls really cause trouble when the results of one query containing Nulls are used in another query; a snowball effect occurs. You can easily miss the problem and output reports with inaccurate results. Using the NZ() function eliminates this kind of problem. You can use the NZ() function to replace the Null values with zeros or zero-length strings. Be careful when doing this, though, because this function might affect other parts of your query that use this value for another calculation. Also, be sure to use any function in a query on the top level of the query tree only because functions at lower levels might hinder query performance. A *query tree* refers to the fact that a query can be based on other queries. Placing the criteria at the top of the query tree means that, if queries are based on other queries, the criteria should be placed in the highest-level queries.

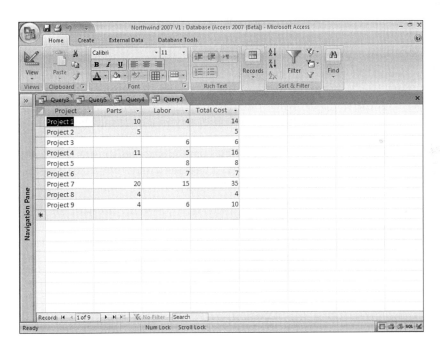

FIGURE 4.34   The query with an expression to convert Nulls to zero.

Refining Your Queries with Field, Field List, and Query Properties

You can use field and query properties to refine and control the behavior and appearance of the columns in your query and of the query itself. Here's how:

1. Click in a field to select the field, click in a field list to select the field list, or click in the Query Design window anywhere outside a field or the field list to select the query.

2. Click Property Sheet on the Design tab of the ribbon.

3. Modify the desired property.

> **NOTE**
>
> If you click a field within the query design grid that has its Show check box cleared, only the query properties will display when you bring up the property sheet for that field, not the field properties. If you mark the Show check box with the property sheet open, the field properties will then display.

Field Properties: Changing the Behavior of a Field

The properties of a field in your query include the Description, Format, Input Mask, and Caption of the column. The Description property documents the use of the field and controls what appears on the status bar when the user is in that column in the query result. The Format property is the same as the Format property in a table's field; it controls the display of the field in the query result. The Input Mask property, like its table counterpart, actually controls how the user enters and modifies data in the query result. The Caption property in the query does the same thing as a Caption property of a field: It sets the caption for the column in Datasheet view and the default label for forms and reports.

You might be wondering how the properties of the fields in a query interact with the same properties of a table. For example, how does the Caption property of a table's field interact with the Caption property of the same field in a query? All properties of a table's field are automatically inherited in your queries. Properties explicitly modified in the query override those same properties of a table's fields. Any objects based on the query inherit the properties of the query, not those of the original table.

> **NOTE**
>
> In the case of the Input Mask property, it is important that the Input Mask of the query not be in conflict with the Input Mask of the table. You can use the Input Mask of the query to further restrict the Input Mask of the table, but not to override it. If the query's Input Mask conflicts with the table's Input Mask, the user will not be able to enter data into the table.

Field List Properties: Changing the Properties of the Field List

Field List properties specify attributes of each table participating in the query. The two Field List properties are Alias and Source. The Alias property is used most often when the same table is used more than once in the same query. This is done in self-joins, covered in Chapter 12. The Source property specifies a connection string or database name when you're dealing with external tables that aren't linked to the current database.

Query Properties: Changing the Behavior of the Overall Query

Microsoft offers many properties, shown in Figure 4.35, that allow you to affect the behavior of the overall query. Some of the properties are discussed here; the rest are covered as applicable throughout this book.

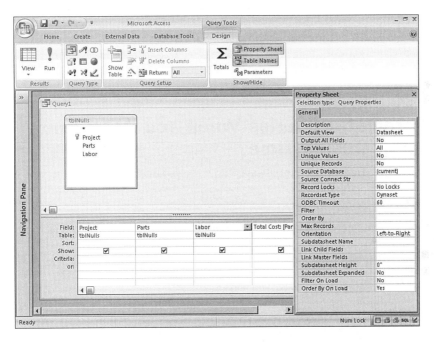

FIGURE 4.35   Query properties that affect the behavior of a given query.

The Description property documents what the query does. The Default View property was introduced with Access 2002. This property determines which view will display by default whenever the query is run. Datasheet is the default setting; PivotTable or PivotChart are the other two Default View settings that are available. Output All Fields shows all the fields in the query results, regardless of the contents of the Show check box in each field. Top Values lets you specify the top *x* number or *x* percent of values in the query result. The Unique Values and Unique Records properties are used to determine whether only unique values or unique records are displayed in the query's output. (These properties are also covered in detail in Chapter 12.)

Several other more advanced properties exist. The `Run Permissions` property has to do with user-level security and is covered in *Mastering Microsoft Office Access 2003*. `Source Database`, `Source Connect String`, `ODBC Timeout`, and `Max Records` all have to do with client/server issues and are covered in *Alison Balter's Mastering Access 2002 Enterprise Development*. The `Record Locks` property concerns multiuser issues and is also covered in *Alison Balter's Mastering Access 2002 Enterprise Development*. The `Recordset Type` property determines whether updates can be made to the query output. By default, this is set to the Dynaset type, allowing updates to the underlying data. `Filter` displays a subset that you determine, rather than the full result of the query. `Order By` determines the sort order of the query. The `Orientation` property determines whether the visual layout of the fields is left-to-right or right-to-left. The `Subdatasheet Name` property allows you to specify the name of the table or query that will appear as a subdatasheet within the current query. After you set the `Subdatasheet Name` property, the `Link Child Fields` and `Link Master Fields` properties designate the fields from the child and parent tables or queries that are used to link the current query to its subdatasheet. Finally, the `Subdatasheet Height` property sets the maximum height for a subdatasheet, and the `Subdatasheet Expanded` property determines whether the subdatasheet automatically appears in an expanded state.

Building Parameter Queries When You Don't Know the Criteria at Design Time

You, or your application's users, might not always know the parameters for query output when designing the query. Parameter queries let you specify different criteria at runtime so that you don't have to modify the query each time you want to change the criteria.

For example, say you have a query, like the one shown in Figure 4.36, for which you want users to specify the date range of the data they want to view each time they run the query. The following clause has been entered as the criterion for the `Order Date` field:

```
Between [Enter Starting Date] And [Enter Ending Date]
```

This criterion causes two dialog boxes to appear when the user runs the query. The first one, shown in Figure 4.37, prompts the user with the criterion text in the first set of brackets (refer to Figure 4.36). The text the user types is substituted for the bracketed text. A second dialog box appears, prompting the user for whatever is in the second set of brackets. The user's response is used as the criterion for that query.

Add a parameter to the query `qryCustomerOrderSummary` so that you can view only `Total Price` summaries within a specific range. Go to the criteria for `Total Price` and type **Between [Please Enter Starting Value] and [Please Enter Ending Value]**. This allows you to view all the records in which the total price is within a specific range. The bracketed text is replaced by actual values when the user runs the query. Click OK and run the query. You're then prompted to enter both a starting and an ending value.

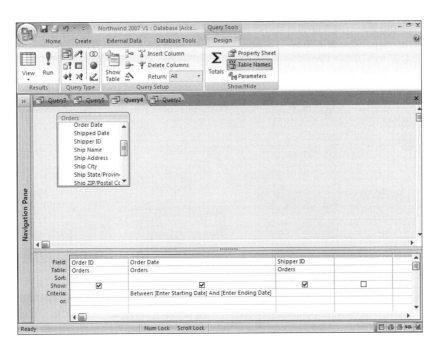

FIGURE 4.36 This parameter query prompts for a starting date and an ending date.

FIGURE 4.37 This dialog box appears when the parameter query is run.

To make sure Access understands what type of data should be placed in these parameters, you must define the parameters. Do this by selecting Parameters from the Query menu to open the Query Parameters window. Another way to display the Query Parameters window is to right-click a gray area in the top half of the query design grid; then select Parameters from the ribbon while on the Design tab.

The text that appears within the brackets for each parameter must be entered in the Parameter field of the Query Parameters dialog box. The type of data in the brackets must be defined in the Data Type column. Figure 4.38 shows an example of a completed Query Parameters dialog box.

You can easily create parameters for as many fields as you want, and you add parameters just as you would add more criteria. For example, the query shown in Figure 4.39 has parameters for the Job Title, City, and Country/Region fields in the Employees table from the Northwind database. Notice that all the criteria are on one line of the query design grid, which means that all the parameters entered must be satisfied for the records to appear in the output. The criterion for the title is [Please Enter a Job Title]. This means that the records in the result must match the title entered when the query is run. The criterion for the City field is [Please Enter a City]. Only records with a city matching the city entered will appear in the result when the query is run. Finally, the criterion for the Country/Region field is [Please Enter a Country or Region]. This means that only records with the country or region entered when the query is run will appear in the output.

The criteria for a query can also be the result of a function; this technique is covered in Chapter 12.

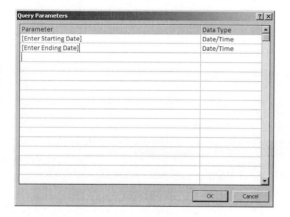

FIGURE 4.38   This completed Query Parameters dialog box declares two date parameters.

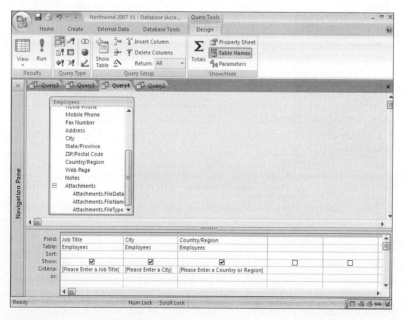

FIGURE 4.39   The Query Design window showing a query with parameters for three fields.

NOTE

Parameter queries offer significant flexibility; they allow the user to enter specific criteria at runtime. What's typed in the Query Parameters dialog box must exactly match what's typed within the brackets; otherwise, Access prompts the user with additional dialog boxes.

TIP

You can add as many parameters as you like to a query, but the user might become bothered if too many dialog boxes appear. Instead, build a custom form that feeds the `Parameter` query. This technique is covered in Chapter 11, "Advanced Report Techniques."

Adding Smart Tags to Your Queries

You use smart tags to perform tasks that you would usually open other applications to perform. For example, you can use smart tags to schedule an appointment, email a letter, or add an Outlook contact, all based on data stored in an Access table or found in an Access query result. Taking things a step further, you can even determine the weather or get the latest news on each city that appears in the result of an Access query!

Adding a Smart Tag to a Query

Adding a smart tag to an Access query is extremely simple. Here are the steps involved:

1. Create a new query or open an existing query in Design view.

2. Select the field on which you want to base the smart tag. For example, if you want to use the smart tag to schedule an appointment, you would probably want to select the contact name field.

3. Show the Field properties for the field and click within the `Smart Tags` property (see Figure 4.40).

4. Click the Build button (the ellipsis). The Smart Tags dialog box appears (see Figure 4.41).

5. Click to select the smart tag you want to add. For example, to send mail, schedule a meeting, open an existing contact, and add new contacts, select Person Name.

6. Click OK. A smart tag appears in the `Smart Tags` property (see Figure 4.42).

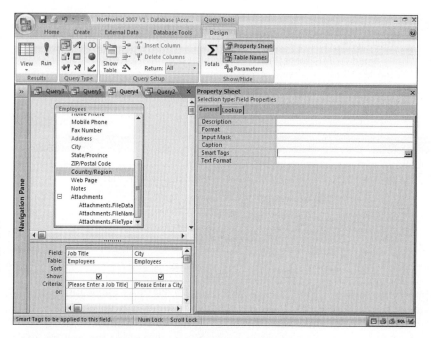

FIGURE 4.40   The Field Properties window with the Smart Tags property selected.

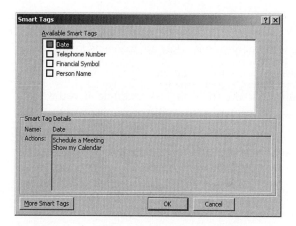

FIGURE 4.41   The Smart Tags dialog box allows you to select the smart tag you want to add.

Using a Smart Tag

After you have added a smart tag to a query, you will notice smart tag action buttons when you run the query (see Figure 4.43). Click the action button for a particular cell in the query result to see the actions available for that smart tag. In Figure 4.44, you can see that the Person Name smart tag has the Schedule a Meeting and Show my Calendar menu items associated with it. Figure 4.45 shows the result of selecting the Schedule a Meeting menu item.

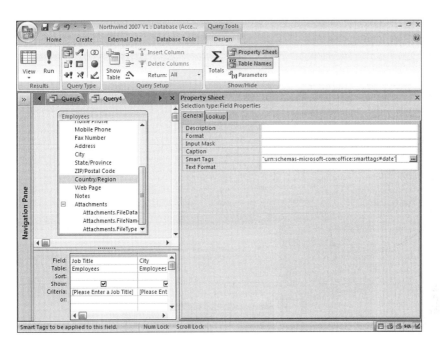

FIGURE 4.42   After you click OK, a smart tag appears in the Smart Tags property.

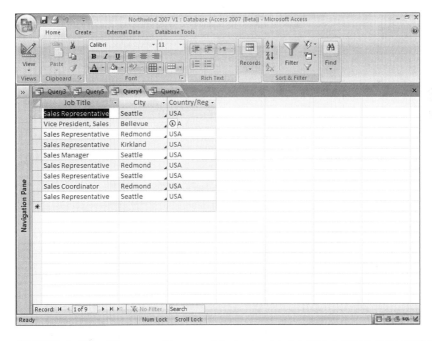

FIGURE 4.43   After you add a smart tag, smart tag action buttons appear when you run the query.

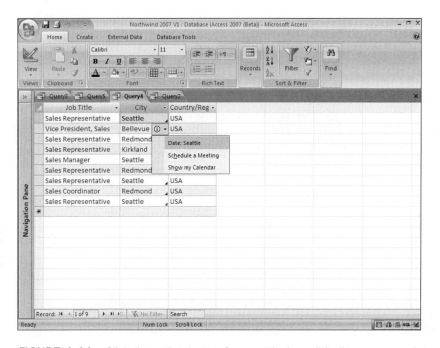

FIGURE 4.44   Click the action button for a particular cell in the query result to see the actions available for that smart tag.

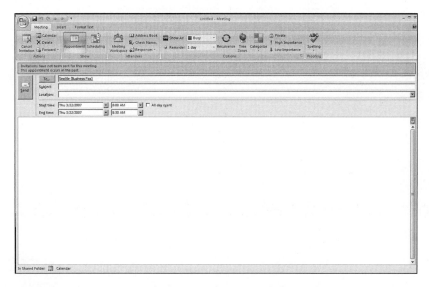

FIGURE 4.45   After you select the Schedule a Meeting menu item, a new appointment appears.

Creating a Pivot Table or Pivot Chart from a Query

Pivot tables and pivot charts provide great ways for you to summarize detailed data stored in your Access Database Engine and SQL Server databases. Pivot tables present your data in a spreadsheet-like format, whereas pivot charts automatically render pivot table views as line, bar, or area charts. Access 2002 introduced two views for queries: PivotTable and PivotChart.

Creating the Query to Display in PivotTable or PivotChart View

You must build a query that is appropriate to display in PivotTable or PivotChart view. Queries that lend themselves to be displayed in PivotTable or PivotChart view provide many ways for the user to manipulate his data. An example of such a query is one that contains information about country, city, salesperson, sales, and date of sale. You could determine sales by city and salesperson for each month, or you could determine sales in each country for each salesperson during the year 2006. As you can see, the idea of pivot tables is to let you slice and dice the data in any way you need to at a given moment in time.

For this example, create the following query within the Northwind database:

1. Create a new query in Design view.

2. Add the `Customers`, `Orders`, `Products`, `Order Details`, and `Employees` tables to the query.

3. Add the `Country/Region` and `City` fields from the `Customers` table.

4. Add an expression: **SalesPerson:Employees![Last Name] & ", " & Employees![First Name]**.

5. Add the `Order Date` from the `Orders` table.

6. Add the `Product Name` from the `Products` table.

7. Add an expression: **Total:[Order Details]!UnitPrice * [Order Details]!Quantity**.

You now have a query on which you can base your pivot table.

> **NOTE**
>
> When you are adding tables to the query, some may be joined with outer joins. You must change these joins to inner joins for the query to run properly. Chapter 12 covers the process of converting the outer joins to inner joins.

Displaying the Query in PivotTable View

To switch to PivotTable view, click to select the Design tab and then open the View drop-down on the ribbon. Select PivotTable View from the drop-down. The empty PivotTable view appears, and the Access ribbon changes to include the PivotTable tab (see Figure 4.46).

FIGURE 4.46   When you switch to PivotTable view, the empty PivotTable view appears and the Access toolbar changes to the PivotTable toolbar.

The PivotTable Field List window also appears. You will add four types of fields to your pivot table. They include the following:

- **Column fields**—Often hold date fields; generally hold information with the fewest number of data items.

- **Row fields**—One or more fields that display data by attributes.

- **Totals or Detail fields**—The crosstab data itself. These are the numeric values that make up the meat of the pivot table.

- **Filter fields**—One or more *optional* fields that restrict that data appearing in the columns, rows, or both.

To display your initial pivot table, take the following steps:

1. Drag the Country/Region field so that it appears as a Row field.

2. Drag the City field so that it appears as a second Row field to the right of the Country field.

3. Drag and drop the `Order Date By Month` field so that it appears as a `Column` field.

4. Drag and drop the `Total` field so that it appears as a `Detail` field. The resulting pivot table appears as shown in Figure 4.47.

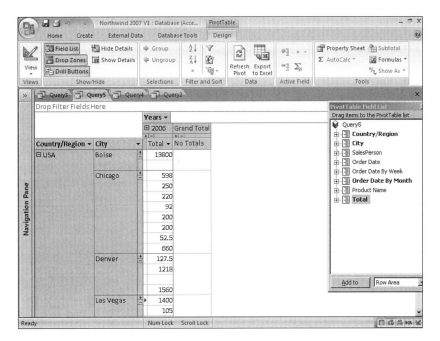

FIGURE 4.47   The pivot table that appears after dragging and dropping the `Total` so that it appears as a `Detail` field.

Displaying Summarized Data

Including all the detail data may be much more information than you need. You can alter the query design to show only summary information. Here's how it works:

1. Switch to Design view.

2. Click the Totals button on the Design tab of the ribbon.

3. Group by all fields except the data field and any fields that you are using for a filter.

4. Change the Total cell for any fields you are filtering by to Where.

5. Change the Total cell for the data field to Sum. The resulting query appears as shown in Figure 4.48.

6. Run the query to verify the design (see Figure 4.49).

7. Return to PivotTable view.

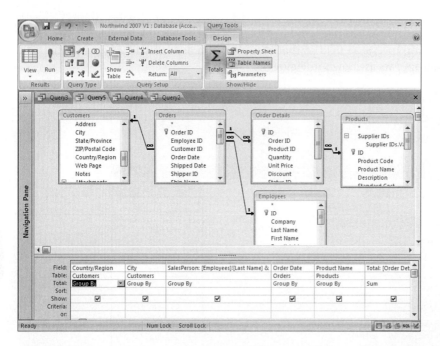

FIGURE 4.48   The query that appears after changing the Total cell for the data field to Sum.

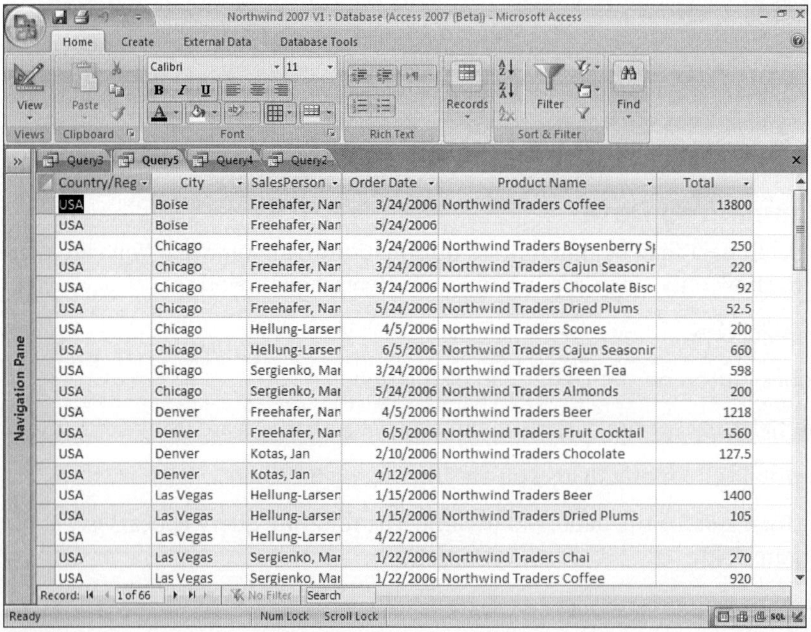

FIGURE 4.49   The underlying query after modifying it to summarize the data.

8. To add grand totals, click any one of the Total buttons to select all three columns and then click the AutoCalc button on the Design tab of the ribbon.

9. Select the desired calculation from the drop-down.

10. With the columns still selected, right-click and select Hide Details.

11. Observe the summarized data (see Figure 4.50).

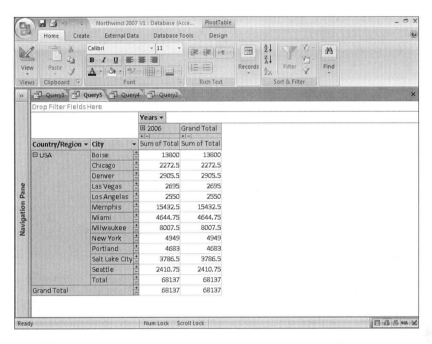

FIGURE 4.50   The PivotTable view after modifying the underlying query to summarize the data.

Filtering Pivot Table Data

By default, Access includes all data in the pivot table. You can filter the pivot table to display only selected values for a row or column. For example, you can filter to display data for only sales in specific countries. Here's how it works:

1. Make sure that you have expanded the pivot table display to include the detail for the data on which you want to filter (see the next section, "Using Drill-Down").

2. Click the arrow of the field button to filter. The list contains an item for each field value (see Figure 4.51).

3. Click the (All) check box to deselect all fields.

4. Click to select the field values that you want to include in the output.

5. Click OK to close the list and apply the filter.

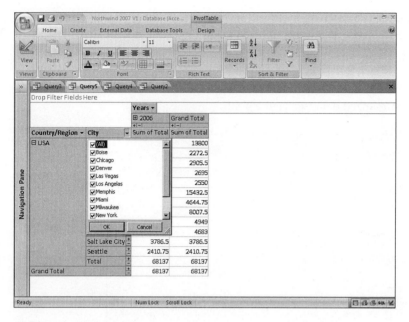

FIGURE 4.51   The list contains an item for each field value.

Using Drill-Down

Generally, the initial pivot table contains an excessive amount of detail. Here's how you can modify the amount of detail to show summary information only:

1. Switch to Design view.

2. Click the Totals button on the Design tab of the ribbon to eliminate the data grouping.

3. Return to PivotTable view. The Total or Details Fields drop zone is empty because you changed the structure of the query.

4. Click the Field List button to display the PivotTable Field List.

5. Expand the Totals item.

6. Right-click the Sum of Total item and select Delete, which clears the data from the cells.

7. Drag the Years button outside the window to remove the columns for the years, leaving an empty No Totals column.

8. Click Show Details and then drag the No Totals column outside the window. At this point, the Column Fields and Totals or Detail Fields drop zones are empty.

9. Drag the Total column to the Columns drop zone.

10. Click the Show Details button and then the Hide Details button. You will see the data expand and collapse.

Exchanging Axes

If you are viewing Year across the top and Country down the side, and you decide to view Year across the side and Country across the top, simply drag and drop their name buttons to switch the positions in which they appear. You can also easily drag new items to the pivot table from the PivotTable list at any time or remove them from the pivot table entirely.

Switching to PivotChart View

When you define a PivotTable view, you automatically generate a PivotChart view. You will see how evident this is by using the View tool to switch to PivotChart view. The results appear as shown in Figure 4.52. You can use Ribbon buttons to add legends and to modify the chart type.

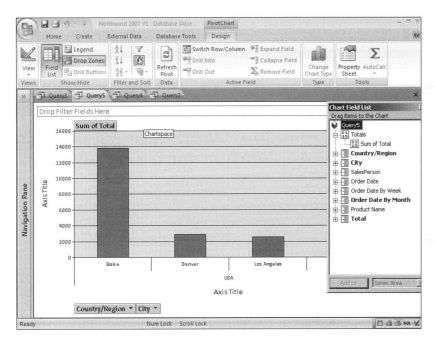

FIGURE 4.52   The PivotChart view shows the pivot table as a chart.

Understanding Query Specifications and Limitations

Queries have a number of specifications and limitations that you should be aware of. Fortunately, you will generally not find them too restricting. They are listed in Table 4.3.

TABLE 4.3   Query Specifications and Limitations

Item	Limitation
Number of enforced relationships	32 per table minus the number of indexes that are on the table for fields or combinations of fields that are not involved in relationships
Number of tables in a query	32
Number of fields in a recordset	255
Recordset size	1GB
Sort limit	255 characters in one or more fields
Number of levels of nested queries	50
Number of characters in a cell of the query design grid	1024
Number of characters for a parameter in a parameter query	255
Number of Ands in a WHERE or HAVING clause	99
Number of characters in an SQL statement	Approximately 64,000

Practical Examples: Building Queries Needed by the Time and Billing Application for a Computer Consulting Firm

Build a query based on tblTimeCardHours. This query gives you the total billing amount by project for a specific date range. The query's design is shown in Figure 4.53. Notice that this is a Totals query that groups by project and totals by using the following expression:

```
BillAmount: Sum([BillableHours]*[BillingRate])
```

The DateWorked field is used as the Where clause for the query with this criteria:

```
Between [Enter Start Date] And [Enter End Date]
```

The two parameters of the criteria are declared in the Query Parameters dialog box (see Figure 4.54). Save this query as **qryBillAmountByProject**.

The second query is based on tblClients, tblProjects, and tblTimeCardHours. This query gives you the total billing amount by client for a specific date range. The query's design is shown in Figure 4.54. This query is a Totals query that groups by the company name from the tblClients table and totals by using the following expression:

```
BillAmount: Sum([BillableHours]*[BillingRate])
```

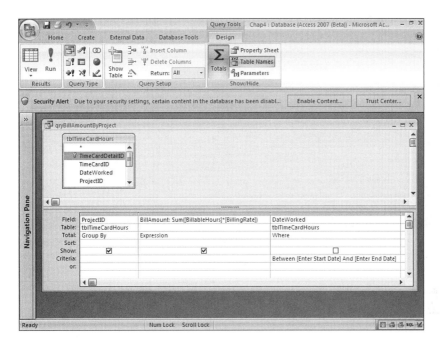

FIGURE 4.53   The design of the `qryBillAmountByProject` query.

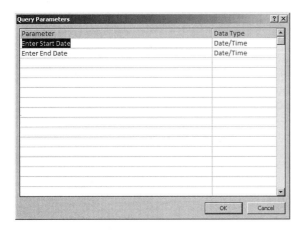

FIGURE 4.54   The Query Parameters window for `qryBillAmountByProject`.

As with the first query, the `DateWorked` field is used as the `Where` clause for the query, and the parameters are defined in the Query Parameters dialog box. Save this query as **qryBillAmountByClient**.

These queries are included on the sample CD-ROM in a database called `CHAP4.ACCDB`. Of course, if this were a completed application, you would build many other queries.

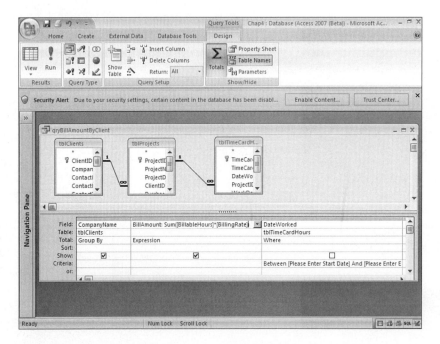

FIGURE 4.55   The design of the qryBillAmountByClient query.

Summary

This chapter covered the foundations of perhaps the most important function of a database: getting data from the database and into a usable form. You learned about the Select query used to retrieve data from a table, how to retrieve data from multiple tables, and how to use functions in your queries to make them more powerful by synthesizing data. In later chapters, you will extend your abilities with Action queries and queries based on other queries (also known as *nested queries*).

CHAPTER 5

What Every Developer Needs to Know About Forms

Why This Chapter Is Important

Most Access applications are centered on forms. Forms are used to collect and display information, navigate about the application, and more. This chapter covers all the basics of creating and working with forms. We'll begin by looking at the various uses of forms. Then we'll delve into the wealth of form and control properties. You'll learn the differences between bound, unbound, and calculated controls and when it is appropriate to use each. You'll also learn important form techniques, such as how to create forms based on data from more than one table and when you should populate forms with a query result rather than a table or embedded Structured Query Language (SQL) statement.

Understanding the Uses of Forms

Developers often think that forms exist solely for the purpose of data entry. To the contrary, forms serve many different purposes in Access 2007:

▶ **Data entry**—Displaying and editing data

▶ **Application flow**—Navigating through your application

▶ **Custom dialog boxes**—Providing messages to your users

▶ **Printing information**—Providing hard copies of data entry information

Probably the most common use of an Access form is as a vehicle for displaying and editing existing data or for adding new data. Fortunately, Access offers many features that allow you to build forms that ease data entry for your users. Access also makes it easy for you to design forms that let your users view and modify data, view data but not modify it, or add new records only.

Although not everyone immediately thinks of an Access form as a means of navigating through an application, forms are quite strong in this area. Figure 5.1 shows a form created with the Switchboard Manager in Access 2007; Figure 5.2 shows a form containing links that allow you to navigate about your application. Although the Switchboard Manager makes designing a switchboard form simple, you will find any type of switchboard easy to develop. You can be creative with switchboard forms by designing forms that are both useful and exciting. Switchboard forms are covered in detail in Chapter 10, "Advanced Form Techniques."

You can also use Access to create custom dialog boxes used to display information or retrieve information from your users. The custom dialog box shown in Figure 5.3 gets the information needed to run a report. The user must fill in the required information before he can proceed.

Another strength of Access is its capability to produce professional-looking printed forms. With many other products, print a data entry form is difficult; sometimes you need to re-create the entire form as a report. In Access, printing a form is simply a matter of clicking a button that has a little code written behind it. You have the option of creating a report that displays the information your user is entering or of printing the form itself.

FIGURE 5.1   A form created with the Switchboard Manager.

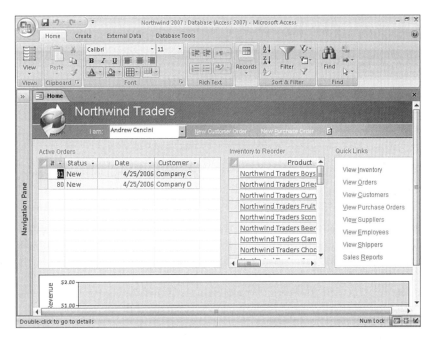

FIGURE 5.2   A form containing links to database objects.

FIGURE 5.3   A custom dialog box that lets the user specify criteria for a report.

Access offers many styles of forms. You can display the data in a form one record at a time, or you can let the user view several records at once. You can display forms *modally*, meaning that the user must respond to and close the form before continuing, or you can display them so that the user can move through the open forms at will. The important point to remember is that there are many uses and styles of forms. You will learn about them throughout this chapter, in Chapter 10, and throughout the book. As you read this chapter, remember that your forms are limited only by your imagination.

Examining the Anatomy of a Form

Access forms are composed of a few different sections; each one has its own function and behavior. The three main sections of an Access form are

▶ Header

▶ Detail

▶ Footer

The Detail section of a form is the main section; it's the one used to display the data of the table or query underlying the form. As you will see, the Detail section can take on many different looks. It's quite flexible and robust.

The Header and Footer sections of the form are used to display information that doesn't change from record to record. You will often place command buttons that control the form—such as one used to let users view all the projects associated with a particular client—in a form's header or footer. Controls can also be used to help the user navigate around the records associated with the form. In the example shown in Figure 5.4, the user can select from a valid list of clients. After the user selects a client from the combo box, the user is moved to the appropriate record.

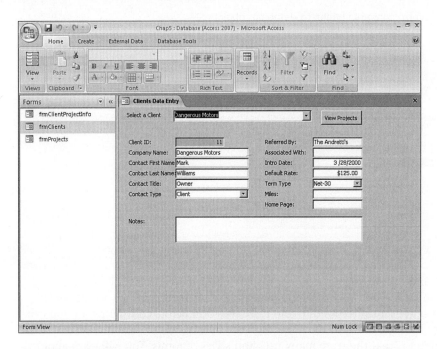

FIGURE 5.4   Record navigation using a combo box placed in the form header.

Creating a New Form

You can create a new form in several ways. The most common way is to first use the Navigation Pane to select the table or query on which you want to base the form and then select the Form button in the Forms group on the Create tab. Access creates a form based on the table or query and places you in Layout view of that form. (See the section of this chapter "Working in Layout View.") There are several other methods that you can use to create a form (see Figure 5.5). These methods include creating a split form, a multiple item form, a pivot chart, a blank form, a form using a Form Wizard, a datasheet, a modal dialog box, and a pivot table. Before we look at the other methods of creating a form, let's look at creating a form using the Form Wizard. Even the most experienced developers use the Form Wizard to perform certain tasks.

Creating a Form with the Form Wizard

To create a form with the Form Wizard, click to expand the More Forms drop-down in the Forms group on the Create tab (see Figure 5.5). First, the Form Wizard prompts you for the name of the table or query you want to use as the form's foundation. Whether you're creating a form with the Form Wizard or from Design view, it's generally better to base a form on a query or on an embedded SQL statement (a query stored as part of a form). Doing so offers better performance (unless your form requires all fields and all records), allows for more flexibility, and lets you create a form based on data from several tables.

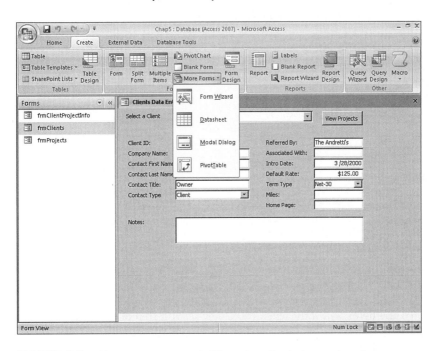

FIGURE 5.5   You can use several different methods to create a form.

Figure 5.6 shows the Tables/Queries drop-down list. You can see that all the tables are listed, and if you scroll down, you can see that the tables are followed by all the queries. After you select a particular table or query, Access displays its fields in the list box on the left (see Figure 5.7). To select the fields you want to include on the form, double-click the name of the field or click on the field and then click the > button. In the example shown in Figure 5.7, several fields have been selected from the qryClients query.

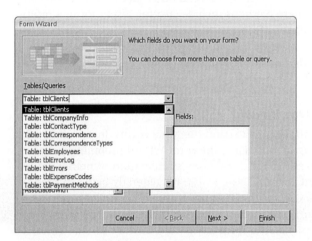

FIGURE 5.6   A list of tables and queries available for use in the Form Wizard.

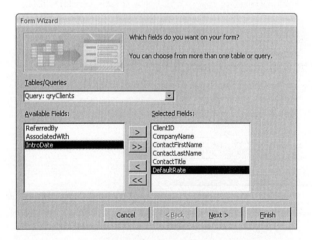

FIGURE 5.7   Selected fields from qryClients.

After you've selected the fields you want, click Next. The second step of the Form Wizard allows you to specify the layout for the form you're designing. You can select from Columnar, Tabular, Datasheet, or Justified; the most common choice is Columnar. Click Next after selecting a form layout.

In the third step of the Form Wizard, you can select a style for your form from several predefined styles (see Figure 5.8). Although you can modify all the properties set by the wizard in Design view after the form has been created, to save time, it's best to select the appropriate style now. Click Next after selecting a style.

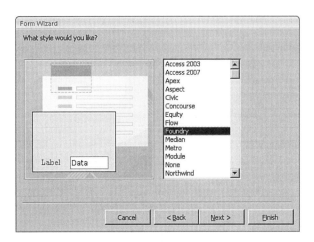

FIGURE 5.8   Selecting a form style.

In the final step of the Form Wizard, supply a title for your form. (If you just accept the default, the form will have the same name as the underlying table or query, which could be confusing.) Unfortunately, the form's title becomes the name of the form as well. For this reason, type the text you want to use as the name of the form. If you want to follow standard naming conventions, you should begin the name of the form with the tag frm. You can worry about changing the title in Design view of the form. This last step of the Form Wizard also lets you specify whether you want to view the results of your work or open the form in Design view. It's usually best to view the results and then modify the form's design after you have taken a peek at what the Form Wizard has done.

TIP

Appendix A, "Naming Conventions," (available for download at www.samspublishing.com) has a complete list of standard naming conventions that you can refer to when you have questions about the proper names to give an object.

TIP

Another way to start the Form Wizard is to use the Navigation Pane to first select the table or query on which you want to base the form. You then click the Create tab and select Form Wizard from the More Forms drop-down. You won't have to use the Tables/Queries drop-down list to select a table or query. The table or query you selected before invoking the wizard is automatically selected for you.

Creating a Form from Design View

Although the Form Wizards are both powerful and useful, in many cases you'll prefer building a form from scratch, especially if you're building a form that's not bound to data. To create a form without using a wizard, click to select the Create tab. Then click the Form Design button in the Forms group. The Form Design window appears (see Figure 5.9).

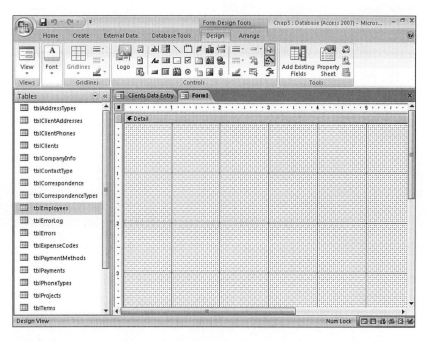

FIGURE 5.9   Use the Form Design window to build and customize a form.

Working with the Form Design Window

You can use the Form Design window to build and customize a form. Using this window, you can add objects to a form and customize them by using the property sheet. You can also build and customize a form using Layout View. The section of this chapter titled "Working in Layout View" covers this process in detail. Microsoft has supplied many form and control properties. After gaining a command of these properties, you can customize the look and feel of your forms.

Understanding and Working with the Form Design Tools

Even the best developer needs the right tools for the job. Fortunately, Microsoft has given you tools to help you build exciting and useful forms. The Form Design window includes the Ribbon and the actual form you're designing. Other tools are available to help you with the design process, including the Field List window and property sheet.

Two additional tabs appear when you're in a form's Design view: the Design tab and the Arrange tab. The Design tab has buttons you use to switch views, add controls, add fields, and work with control and form properties. As its name implies, the Arrange tab contains tools that allow you to control the layout of controls on the form. It contains tools used for control alignment, control layering, control sizing, and more.

Toggling the Tools to Get What You Want

A few windows are available to help you with the design process when you're in a form's Design view. If you don't have a high-resolution monitor, you'll probably find it annoying to have all the windows open at once. In fact, with all the windows open at once on a low-resolution monitor, the form is likely to get buried underneath all the windows. This is why Microsoft has made each window open and close in a toggle-switch–like fashion. The Design tab has buttons for the Field List window and property sheet, and each of these toolbar buttons is a toggle. Clicking once on the button opens the appropriate window; clicking a second time closes it. Furthermore, you can show or hide the Navigation Pane.

Figure 5.10 shows a form with the Field List window, Navigation Pane, and property sheet open. Although you can size each of these windows however you like, the design environment in this low-resolution display is rather cluttered with all these windows open. One of the tricks in working with Access is in knowing when it's appropriate to have each set of tools available. The goal is to have the right windows open at the right time as often as possible.

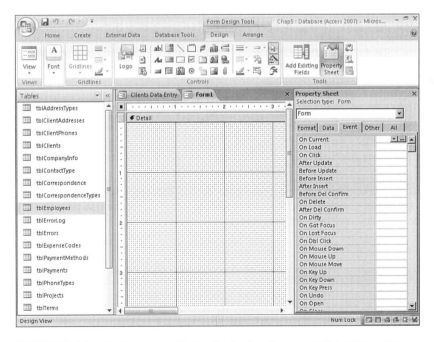

FIGURE 5.10   Design view with the Navigation Pane and Field List visible.

NOTE

You can close the Field List window and property sheet by using the toolbar buttons. In addition, you can close them by using the Close button on each window. You can hide the Navigation Page using the collapse button.

TIP

Access 2007 offers some handy shortcut keystrokes for working with forms and form properties. In Design view, the F4 key displays the property sheet. When you are working with a property sheet in Design view, pressing Shift+F7 will shift the focus to the Form Design window while maintaining the focus on the selected control. You can toggle among all available views for a form (Design, Datasheet, Form, Layout, PivotTable, PivotChart) by pressing Ctrl+> or Ctrl+. (period). You can toggle among the different views in the reverse order using Ctrl+< or Ctrl+, (comma). These shortcut keys are also supported for changing between available views of tables, queries, reports, pages, views, and stored procedures.

Adding Fields to the Form

You can easily add fields to a form by using the Field List window, which contains all the fields that are part of the form's record source. The *record source* for the form is the table, query, or embedded SQL statement that underlies the form. For example, in Figure 5.10, the form's record source is qryClients. The fields listed in the Field List pane are the fields that are part of the query. To add fields to a form, use these two steps:

1. Make sure the Field List window is visible. If it isn't, click the Add Existing Fields button on the ribbon.

2. Locate the field you want to add to the form; then click and drag the field from the field list to the place on the form where you want it to appear. The location you select becomes the upper-left corner of the text box, and the attached label appears to the left of where you dropped the control.

NOTE

A *control* is an object that you add to a form or report. Types of controls include text boxes, combo boxes, list boxes, and check boxes.

NOTE

To add multiple fields to a form at the same time, select several qryClients fields from the field list. Use the Ctrl key to select noncontiguous fields or the Shift key to select contiguous fields. For example, hold down your Ctrl key and click on three noncontiguous fields. Each field will be selected. Next, click a field, hold down your Shift key, and click another field. All fields between the two fields will be selected. If you want to select all fields, double-click the field list title bar. Click and drag any one of the selected fields to the form, and all of them will be added to the form at once.

Selecting, Moving, Aligning, and Sizing Form Objects

You must know several important tricks of the trade when selecting, moving, aligning, and sizing form objects. These tips will save you hours of frustration and wasted time.

Selecting Form Objects

The easiest way to select a single object on a form is to click it. After you have selected the object, you can move it, size it, or change any of its properties. Selecting multiple objects is a bit trickier, but you can do it in several ways. Different methods are more efficient in different situations. To select multiple objects, you can hold down the Shift key and click each object you want to select. Each selected object is surrounded by selection handles, indicating that it has been selected.

Figure 5.11 shows a form with four selected objects; it's important to understand which objects are actually selected. The ClientID text box, Company Name label and text box, and Contact First Name label are all selected; however, the Client ID label, ContactFirstName, and Contract Last Name label and associated text box aren't selected. If you look closely at the figure, you can see that the selected objects are completely surrounded by selection handles. The Client ID label and ContactFirstName text box each has just a single selection handle because each is attached to objects that are selected. If you change any properties of the selected objects, the Client ID label and ContactFirstName text box will be unaffected.

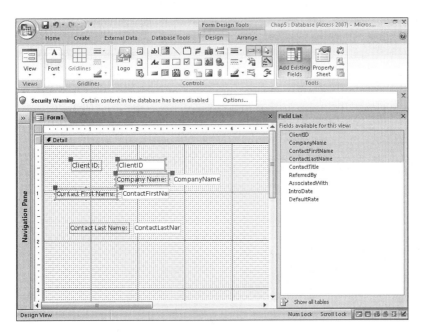

FIGURE 5.11   Selecting objects on a form.

You can also select objects by lassoing them. Objects to be lassoed must be located adjacent to one another on the form. Place your mouse pointer on a blank area of the form (not over any objects) and then click and drag your mouse pointer. You can see a thin line around the objects your mouse pointer is encircling. When you let go, any objects that were within the lasso, including those only partially surrounded, are selected. If you want to deselect any of these objects to exclude them, hold down your Shift key and click the object(s) you want to deselect.

One of my favorite ways to select multiple objects is to use the horizontal and vertical rulers that appear at the edges of the Form Design window. Click and drag within the ruler. Notice that as you click and drag on the vertical ruler, two horizontal lines appear, indicating which objects are selected. As you click and drag across the horizontal ruler, two vertical lines appear, indicating the selection area. When you let go of your mouse, any objects within the lines are selected. As with the process of lassoing, to remove any objects from the selection, hold down your Shift key and click on the object(s) you want to deselect.

Moving Things Around

To move a single control with its attached label, you don't need to select it first. Place your mouse over the object and click and drag. An outline appears, indicating the object's new location. When the object reaches the position you want, release the mouse button. The attached label automatically moves with its corresponding control.

To move more than one object at a time, you must first select the objects you want to move. Select the objects using one of the methods outlined in the preceding section. Place your mouse pointer over any of the selected objects and click and drag. An outline appears, indicating the proposed new position for the objects. Release the mouse button when you have reached the position you want for the objects.

Sometimes you want to move a control independent of its attached label, which requires a special technique. If you click to select a control, such as a text box, and then you click and drag, both the control and the attached label move as a unit, and the relationship between them is maintained. If you place your mouse pointer over the larger handle in the upper-left corner of the object and click and drag here, the control moves independently of its attached label, and the relationship between the objects changes.

Aligning Objects to One Another

Access makes it easy to align objects. Figure 5.12 shows several objects that aren't aligned. Notice that the attached labels of three of the objects are selected. If you align the attached labels, the controls (in this case, text boxes) remain in their original positions. If you select the text boxes as well, they will try to align with the attached labels. Because Access doesn't allow the objects to overlap, the text boxes end up immediately next to their attached labels. To left-align any objects (even objects of different types), select the objects you want to align and then click to select the Arrange tab. Click Align Left in the Control Alignment group. The selected objects are then aligned (see Figure 5.13). You can align the left, right, top, or bottom edges of any objects on a form.

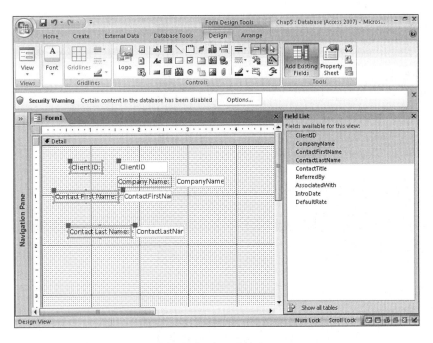

FIGURE 5.12   The form before aligning objects.

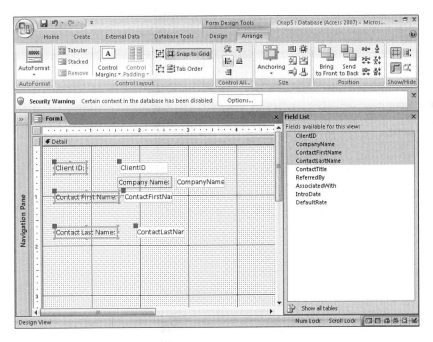

FIGURE 5.13   The form after aligning objects.

> **NOTE**
>
> Don't confuse the Control Alignment feature with the Align tools (Align Left, Center, Align Right) on the Home tab. The Control Alignment feature aligns objects one to the other, but the Align tools on the Home tab provide justification for the text inside an object.

Snap to Grid

The Snap to Grid feature determines whether objects snap to the gridlines on the form as you move and size them. This feature is found on the Arrange tab. If you turn off this feature (it's a toggle), objects can be moved and sized without regard for the gridlines.

> **TIP**
>
> I prefer to leave the Snap to Grid feature on at all times. I use a special trick to temporarily deactivate the feature when needed: I hold down my Ctrl key as I click and drag to move objects. The Snap to Grid setting is then ignored.

Power Sizing Techniques

Just as there are several ways to move objects, you have several options for sizing objects. When you select an object, you can use each handle, except for the handle in the upper-left corner of the object, to size the object. The handles at the top and bottom of the object allow you to change the object's height, and the handles at the left and right of the object let you change the object's width. You can use the handles in the upper-right, lower-right, and lower-left corners of the object to change the width and height of the object simultaneously. To size an object, place your mouse pointer over a sizing handle, click, and drag. You can select several objects and size them all at once. Each of the selected objects increases or decreases in size by the same amount; their relative sizes stay intact.

Access offers several powerful methods of sizing multiple objects, found on the Arrange tab:

- **To Fit**—Sizes the selected objects to fit the text within them
- **To Grid**—Sizes the selected objects to the nearest gridlines
- **To Tallest**—Sizes the selected objects to the height of the tallest object in the selection
- **To Shortest**—Sizes the selected objects to the height of the shortest object in the selection
- **To Widest**—Sizes the selected objects to the width of the widest object in the selection
- **To Narrowest**—Sizes the selected objects to the width of the narrowest object in the selection

Probably the most confusing of the options is To Fit. This option is somewhat deceiving because it doesn't perfectly size text boxes to the text within them. In today's world of proportional fonts, you can't perfectly size a text box to the largest possible entry it contains. Generally, however, you can visually size text boxes to a sensible height and width. Use the field's `Size` property to limit what's typed in the text box. If the entry is too large to fit in the allocated space, the user can scroll to view the additional text. As the following Tip indicates, the To Fit option is much more appropriate for labels than it is for text boxes.

TIP

To quickly size a label to fit the text within it, select the label and then double-click any of its sizing handles, except the sizing handle in the upper-left corner of the label.

Controlling Object Spacing

Access gives you excellent tools for spacing the objects on your form an equal distance from one another. Notice in Figure 5.14 that the `ClientID`, `CompanyName`, `ContactFirstName`, and `ContactLastName` text boxes aren't equally spaced vertically from one another. To make the vertical distance between selected objects equal, choose the Make Vertical Spacing Equal tool in the Position group of the Arrange tab. In Figure 5.15, you can see the result of using this command on the selected objects in Figure 5.14.

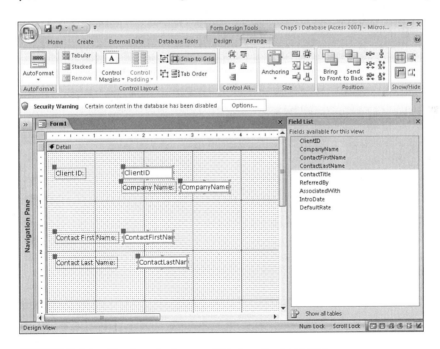

FIGURE 5.14   The form before modifying vertical spacing.

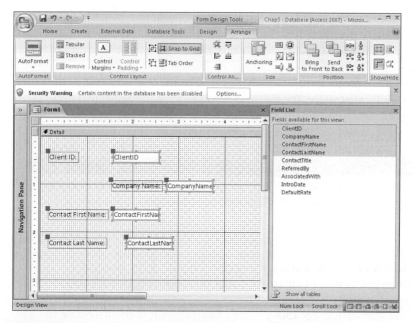

FIGURE 5.15   The form after modifying vertical spacing.

You can make the horizontal distance between objects equal by using the Make Horizontal Spacing Equal tool in the Position group of the Arrange tab. Other related commands that are useful are Increase Vertical Spacing, Increase Horizontal Spacing, Decrease Vertical Spacing, and Decrease Horizontal Spacing, all available in the Position group on the Arrange tab. These commands maintain the relationship between objects while proportionally increasing or decreasing the distance between them.

Modifying Object Tab Order

The tab order for the objects on a form is determined by the order in which you add the objects to the form. However, this order isn't necessarily appropriate for the user. You might need to modify the tab order of the objects on the form. To do so, select Tab Order from the Control Layout group of the Arrange tab. This opens the Tab Order dialog box, shown in Figure 5.16. This dialog box offers two options. Use the Auto Order button to tell Access to set the tab order based on each object's location in a section on the form. However, if you want to customize the order of the objects, click and drag the gray buttons to the left of the object names listed under the Custom Order heading to specify the objects' tab order.

NOTE

You must set the tab order for the objects in each section of the form (that is, Header, Detail, or Footer) separately. To do this, select the appropriate section from the Tab Order dialog box and then set the order of the objects in the section. If your selected form doesn't have a header or footer, the Form Header and Form Footer sections are unavailable.

FIGURE 5.16   Use the Tab Order dialog box to select the tab order of the objects in each section of a form.

Working in Layout View

After you use Quick Create to create a form, Access leaves you in Layout view for that form (see Figure 5.17). Using Layout view, you can work with a form and immediately see the results of your efforts. In other words, instead of having to switch back and forth between Design view and Form view, you can remain in Layout view and look at your live data as you are modifying the design of the form. Most design changes are supported in Layout view.

> **NOTE**
>
> When you use Quick Create to create a form based on a query, Access automatically names the form with the same name as the query *and* creates a header containing a label with the query name. You should rename the form to begin with frm and change the caption of the label to a more appropriate caption.

The following are some examples of design changes:

- ▶ Dragging a field from the new Field List window onto the new form
- ▶ Using the property sheet to change most properties
- ▶ Working with grouped controls
- ▶ Removing fields from the form
- ▶ Adding formatting to the form objects

> **NOTE**
>
> You can easily switch between views using the View drop-down in the Views group of the Design tab.

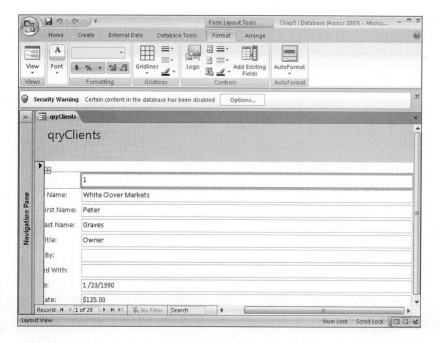

FIGURE 5.17   In Layout view, you can work with a form and immediately see the results of your efforts.

Layout view is even supported with the new stacked and tabular layouts. If you prefer to work in Design view, it is still available to you.

Using Stacked and Tabular Layouts

Forms and reports often contain tabular information, such as a row that contains all the fields for a customer. Using Access 2007, you can group these controls so that you can easily manipulate them as a unit. You can even create a layout with objects from different sections of the form! Using a layout, you can

- ▶ Move or resize the layout

- ▶ Apply formatting to the layout

- ▶ Move controls within the layout

- ▶ Add columns to the layout

- ▶ Remove columns from the layout

There are two types of layouts: tabular and stacked. With a tabular layout, the controls are arranged like a spreadsheet in rows and columns (see Figure 5.18). The labels appear at the top of the layout. Tabular layouts always span two sections because the labels are in one section and the controls are in another.

With a stacked layout, the controls are arranged vertically, as you would see them on a paper form (see Figure 5.19). A label appears to the left of each control. Stacked layouts are always contained within a single section of the form.

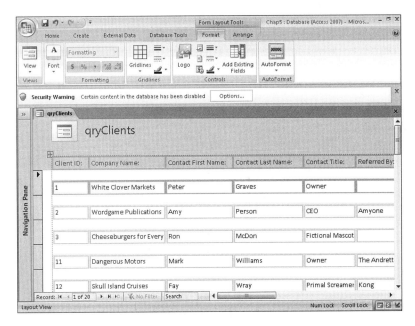

FIGURE 5.18   A tabular layout is arranged like a spreadsheet.

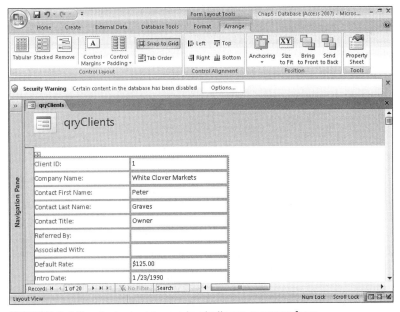

FIGURE 5.19   A stacked layout is similar to a paper form.

You can have multiple layouts on one form, and you can have both a tabular and a stacked layout on the same form. Layouts are saved with the form so that you can use them each time you are working in Layout view or Design view. The following sections go into the details of how to create and work with a layout.

Creating a Layout

Access automatically creates a stacked control layout if you use Quick Create to create the form or if you create a blank form and then drag a field from the Field List window onto the form. Creating your own layout is easy. Here's how:

1. Use the Shift key to select the controls that you want to include in the layout.

2. Click the Arrange tab (see Figure 5.20). Notice in the figure that on the active form the controls are arranged with the labels immediately above the field controls.

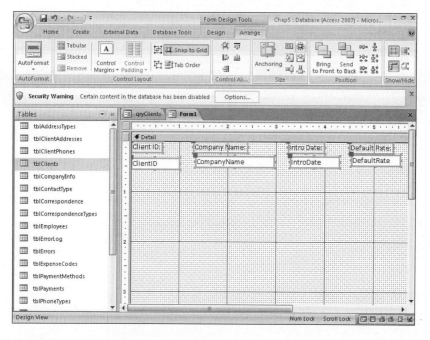

FIGURE 5.20   Before you create the layout, the active form has controls arranged with the labels immediately above the field controls.

3. Select Tabular or Stacked in the Control Layout group. Access creates the layout. If you select Tabular, the result appears as shown in Figure 5.21. Note that the labels now appear in a form header. If you select Stacked, the result appears as shown in Figure 5.22. In this case, there is no form header.

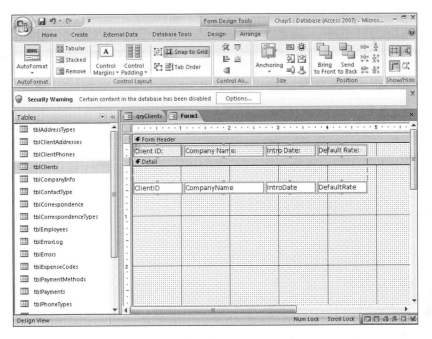

FIGURE 5.21   The tabular form appears with the labels contained in the form header.

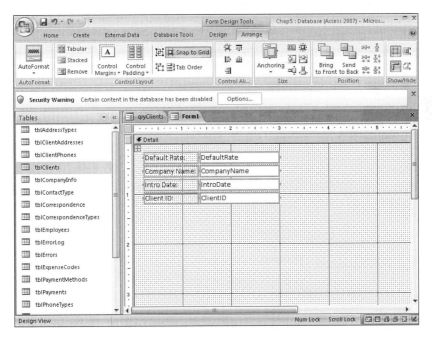

FIGURE 5.22   The stacked form appears with the controls stacked one above the other.

Moving and Resizing a Form Layout

After you have created a layout, you can easily move and resize it. Whether you are in Layout view or Design view, an orange selector appears in the upper-left corner of the layout. To move a layout, simply click to select the layout and then click and drag it to the appropriate place on the form. Notice in Figure 5.23 that the layout appears in two places. The first version of the layout designates the original position, and the second version of the layout shows the new position of the layout if you stop dragging it with the mouse. To size a layout, you must also click to select it. Use any sizing handle to click and drag to resize the layout. An outline appears designating the new size of the layout (see Figure 5.24). When you release the mouse button, the resizing process will be complete.

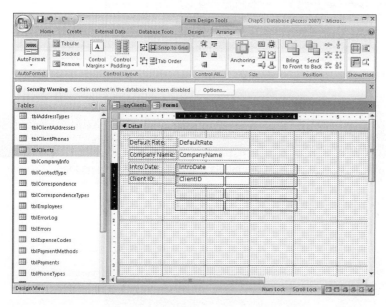

FIGURE 5.23   You can see the proposed new position for the layout.

Formatting a Form Layout

Whenever you want to apply formatting to all the controls in a layout, simply select the layout and then apply the necessary formatting. All controls within the layout are affected by the change. For example, if you select a layout and modify the font, the font will change for all controls within the layout.

Moving Controls Within a Form Layout

After you have created a layout, you might want to move a column within it. This simple process takes four steps:

1. Select the appropriate control within the layout (the control that you want to move).

2. Hover your mouse pointer over the control. Be sure the mouse pointer does not appear as a sizing handle.

3. Click and drag the control to its new location. Notice that a horizontal or vertical bar appears as you drag the control, indicating its new location (see Figure 5.25).

4. Release the mouse button. The control appears in its new location.

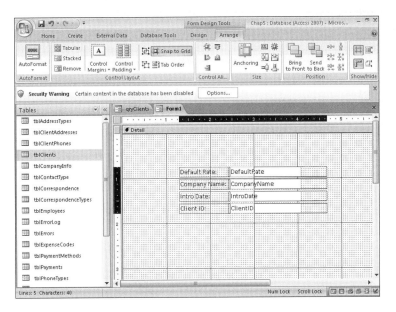

FIGURE 5.24   You can see the proposed new size for the layout.

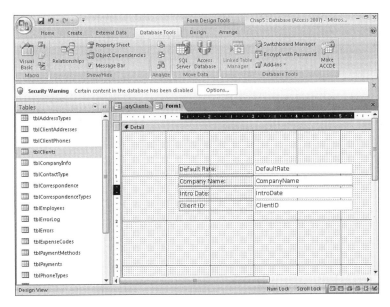

FIGURE 5.25   The horizontal bar indicates the new location for the layout.

Adding Columns to a Form Layout

Sometimes you will want to add a field from the Field List window to the layout. The process is quite simple: Select the field in the Field List window and drag it over the layout. A horizontal or vertical bar appears, indicating where the field will be placed when you release the mouse button.

In another situation, you might want to add existing controls on the form to your layout. This process differs depending on whether you are in Design view or Layout view. If the form is open in Design view, follow these steps:

1. Click to select the first control that you want to add to the control layout.

2. Hold down the Shift key and click to select any additional controls that you want to include in the layout. These fields can even be in other layouts.

3. If the form is open in Design view, simply drag the selected fields to the layout. A horizontal or vertical bar appears, indicating where the fields will be placed when you release the mouse button.

If the form is open in Layout view, here are the steps involved:

1. Click to select the first control that you want to add to the control layout.

2. Hold down the Shift key and click to select any additional controls that you want to include in the layout. These fields can even be in other layouts.

3. Click to select the Arrange tab (see Figure 5.26).

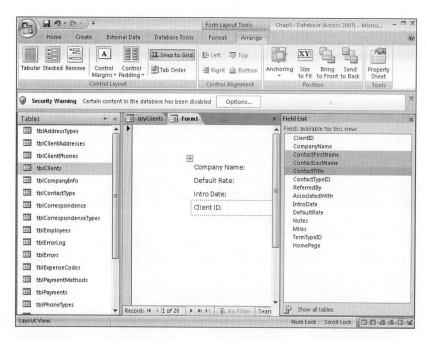

FIGURE 5.26   The Arrange tab provides features applicable to a layout.

4. Select the type of layout to which you are adding the controls (Tabular or Stacked). Access creates a new layout and adds the selected controls to it.

5. Drag the new layout to the existing layout. A horizontal or vertical bar indicates where the fields will be placed when you release the mouse button. The layout with the added fields appears as shown in Figure 5.27.

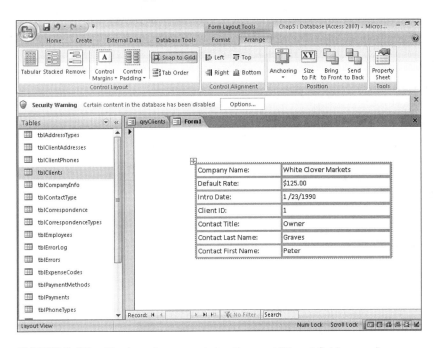

FIGURE 5.27   The layout now contains three additional fields.

Removing Columns from a Form Layout
Removing columns from a layout requires these steps:

1. Click to select the columns that you want to remove from the layout.

2. Right-click one of the controls that you want to remove and select Layout, Remove (see Figure 5.28). Access removes the field from the layout but does *not* remove it from the form. The control can now be moved, formatted, and in other ways manipulated independent of the controls in the layout.

Switching Between a Stacked and a Tabular Layout
Access 2007 makes it easy to switch been a stacked and a tabular layout. Here are the steps involved:

1. Select the control layout by clicking the orange layout selector at the top-left corner of the layout. This action selects all the objects in the layout.

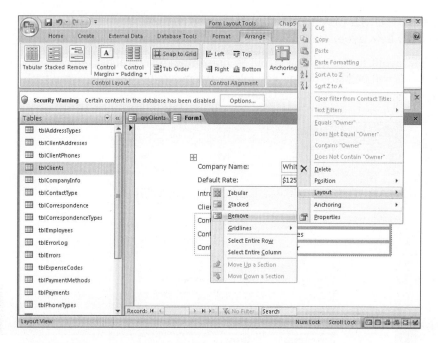

FIGURE 5.28   Removing a field from the layout does not remove it from the form.

2. On the Arrange tab, select the appropriate layout from the Control Layout group. As an alternative, you can right-click the control layout, select Layout, and then click to select the layout that you want. In either case, Access rearranges the controls into the selected layout type.

Splitting One Control Layout into Two Form Layouts

Sometimes you may want to split a single control layout into two layouts. Here's how this procedure works:

1. Use the Shift key to select the controls that you want to move to the new layout.

2. On the Arrange tab, select the appropriate layout for the selected controls (Tabular or Stacked). As an alternative, you can right-click the selected controls and then select Layout. You are given the option of selecting the layout that you want.

Removing a Form Layout

If you no longer want to work with controls as a layout, you can remove the layout entirely. This technique does not remove any of the controls but instead treats each control entirely as a separate object. To remove a layout, follow these steps:

1. Use the orange layout selector to select the entire layout.

2. Right-click and select Layout, Remove (see Figure 5.29). As an alternative, you can simply click the Remove button within the Control Layout group on the Layout tab. In either case, Access removes the layout, and the orange layout selector is no longer available.

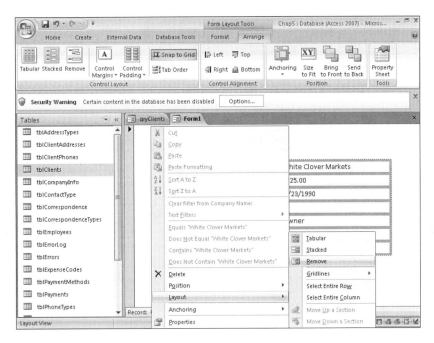

FIGURE 5.29   When you remove the layout, the layout selector is no longer available.

Getting to Know Split Forms

Access 2007 provides a new type of form called the *split form*. A split form allows you to view your data in both Form view and Datasheet view simultaneously. Without your having to write a single line of code, a split form automatically ties both views to the same data source. Access keeps the two views synchronized at all times. In fact, when you select a field on one part of the form, Access automatically selects the same field on the other part of the form. Figure 5.30 provides an example of a split form. Notice that the company information appears in Datasheet view at the top of the form and in Form view on the bottom of the form. Creating a split form requires just three steps:

1. Open the table or query on which you want to base the form in Datasheet view, *or* click to select the appropriate table or query in the Navigation Pane.

2. Click the Create tab.

3. Select the Split Form tool from the Forms group. Access creates the form and displays it in Layout view.

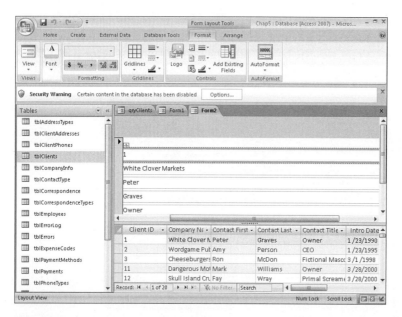

FIGURE 5.30   A split form enables you to view your data in Datasheet and Form view at the same time.

You should be aware of some properties when working with split forms. They all appear on the property sheet of the form (see Figure 5.31). They are listed here, along with their functionality:

▶ **Split Form Orientation**—Use this property to determine whether the datasheet will be on the top, bottom, left, or right side of the Form view section of the form.

▶ **Split Form Splitter Bar**—When this property is set to Yes, Access displays a splitter bar between the two sections of the form.

▶ **Save Splitter Bar Position**—This property determines whether Access saves the position of the splitter bar.

▶ **Split Form Size**—Use this property to designate the size of the form portion of the split form.

▶ **Split Form Printing**—Use this property to determine whether the Datasheet or Form view will print when you send the form to the printer.

Using Alternating Background Colors for a Form

Access 2007 enables you to alternate the background color on datasheets, continuous forms, and reports. You can select any color that you'd like for the shading. The process requires the following steps:

1. Switch to Design view of the form.

2. Right-click the Detail section of the form and select Fill/Back Color (see Figure 5.32).

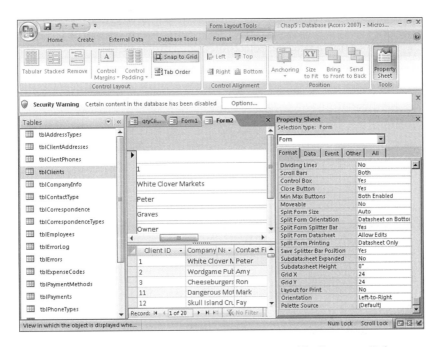

FIGURE 5.31   Several form properties pertain specifically to a split form.

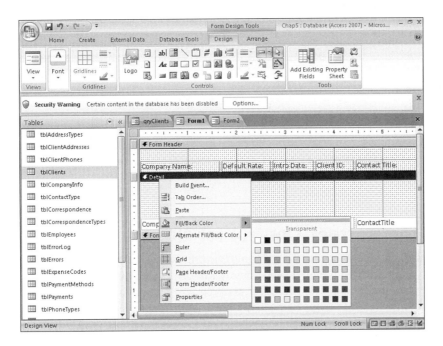

FIGURE 5.32   You must designate the Fill/Back Color and Alternate Fill/Back Color for the Detail section of the form.

3. Select the appropriate color for the back color.

4. Right-click the Detail section again and select Alternate Fill/Back Color.

5. Select the appropriate color for the alternate back color.

6. Switch to Form view. Your form should appear as shown in Figure 5.33.

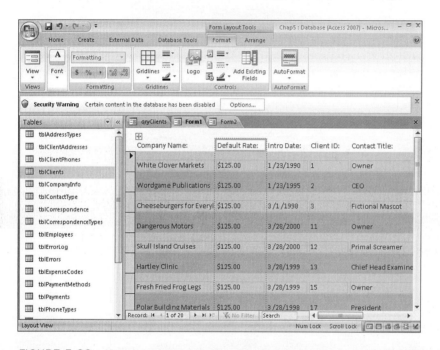

FIGURE 5.33   Your completed form should appear with alternating background colors.

> **NOTE**
>
> The controls on the form must have a back color of transparent; otherwise, you will be unable to see the alternating background colors.

Selecting the Correct Control for the Job

Windows programming in general, and Access programming in particular, isn't limited to just writing code. Your ability to design a user-friendly interface can make or break the success of your application. Access and the Windows programming environment offer a variety of controls, and each one is appropriate in different situations. The following sections discuss each type of control, outlining when and how it should be used.

Labels

You generally use labels to display information to your users. Attached labels are automatically added to your form when you add other controls, such as text boxes, combo boxes, and so on, and they can be deleted or modified as necessary. Their default captions are based on the Caption property of the field that underlies the control they're attached to. If nothing has been entered into a field's Caption property, the field name is used for the label's caption.

The Label tool, found on the Design tab of the ribbon, can be used to add any text to the form. Click the Label tool and then click and drag the label to place it on the form. Labels are often used to provide a description of the form or to supply instructions to users. Labels can be customized by modifying their font, size, color, and so on. Although developers can use Visual Basic for Applications (VBA) code to modify label properties at runtime, users don't have this ability.

> **TIP**
>
> Sometimes attached labels become detached from their associated text boxes. This means that the label will no longer move, size, and become selected with the text box that it applies to. To reassociate the label with the text box, press Ctrl+X to cut the label, click to select the text box, and then press Ctrl+V to paste.
>
> If you purposely want to disassociate a label from its attached control, simply cut the label and then paste it back on the form *without* selecting the control that it was attached to. This technique allows you to perform tasks such as hiding the control without hiding the label.

Text Boxes

Text boxes are used to get information from the user. Bound text boxes display and retrieve field information stored in a table; unbound text boxes gather information from the user that's not related to a specific field in a specific record. For example, a text box can be used to gather information about report criteria from a user.

Text boxes are automatically added to a form when you click and drag a field from the field list to the form. The Display control for the field must be set to Text Box. (The Display control is the default control type for an object; this default is set in the design of the underlying table.) Another way to add a text box is to select the Text Box tool from the Design tab of the ribbon and then click and drag to place the text box on the form. This process adds an unbound text box to the form. If you want to bind the text box to data, you must set its Control Source property.

Combo Boxes

Combo boxes allow a user to select from a list of appropriate choices. Access offers several easy ways to add a combo box to a form. If a field's Display Control property has been set to Combo Box, a combo box is automatically added to a form when the field is added. The combo box automatically knows the source of its data as well as all its other important properties.

If a field's Display Control property hasn't been set to Combo Box, the easiest way to add a combo box to a form is to use the Control Wizard. When selected, the Use Control Wizards tool helps you add combo boxes, list boxes, option groups, and subforms to your forms. Although all the properties set by the Combo Box Wizard can be set manually, using the wizard saves both time and energy. If you want the Combo Box Wizard to be launched when you add a combo box to the form, make sure the Control Wizards tool in the Controls group on the Design tab of the ribbon has been clicked (switched on) before you add the combo box.

Select the Combo Box tool on the Design tab of the ribbon and then click and drag to place the combo box on the form. This launches the Combo Box Wizard; its first step is shown in Figure 5.34. You're offered three sources for the combo box's data. Use the first option if your combo box will select the data that's stored in a field, such as the state associated with a particular client. I rarely, if ever, use the second option, which requires that you type the values for the combo box. Populating a combo box this way makes it difficult to maintain. Every time you want to add an entry to the combo box, your application must be modified. The third, and final, option is appropriate when you want the combo box to be used as a tool to search for a specific record. For example, a combo box can be placed in the form's header to display a list of valid customers. After selecting a customer, the user is then moved to the appropriate record. This option is available only when the form is bound to a record source.

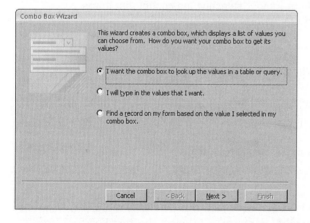

FIGURE 5.34   The first step of the Combo Box Wizard: selecting the source of the data.

In the second step of the Combo Box Wizard, you select a table or query to populate the combo box. For optimal performance, you should select a query. In the third step, you select the fields that appear in your combo box (see Figure 5.35). The combo box being built in the example will be used to select the contact type associated with a particular client. Although the ContactType field will be the only field visible in the combo box, ContactTypeID and ContactType should both be selected because ContactTypeID is a necessary element of the combo box. After a contact type has been selected from the combo box, the ContactTypeID associated with the Contact Type will be stored in the ContactTypeID field of the tblClients table.

The fourth step allows you to select a sort order for your list (see Figure 5.36). The fifth step lets you specify the width of each field in the combo box. Notice in Figure 5.37 that Access recommends that the key column, `ContactTypeID`, be hidden. The idea is that the user will see the meaningful English description while Access worries about storing the appropriate key value in the record.

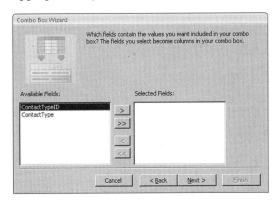

FIGURE 5.35   The third step of the Combo Box Wizard: selecting fields.

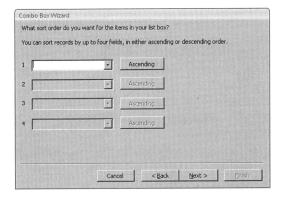

FIGURE 5.36   The fourth step of the Combo Box Wizard: setting the sort order.

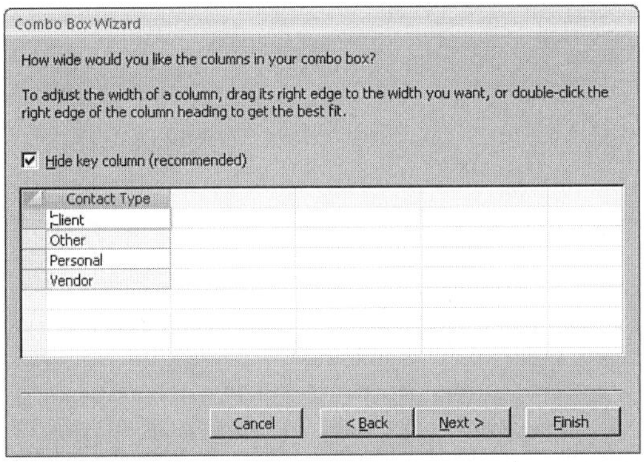

FIGURE 5.37   The fifth step of the Combo Box Wizard: setting column widths.

In the wizard's sixth step, you are asked to designate a field in the combo box that uniquely identifies the row (see Figure 5.38). Select a field and click Next. In the wizard's seventh step, specify whether you want Access to simply remember the selected value or store it in a particular field in a table. In the example shown in Figure 5.39, the selected combo box value will be stored in the `ContactTypeID` field of the `tblClients` table.

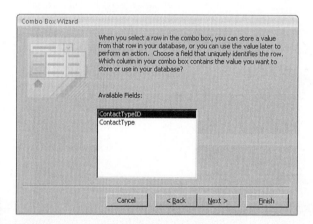

FIGURE 5.38   The sixth step of the Combo Box Wizard: indicating the field in the combo box that uniquely identifies each row.

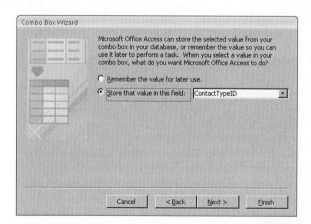

FIGURE 5.39   The seventh step of the Combo Box Wizard: indicating where the selected value will be stored.

The eighth and final step of the Combo Box Wizard prompts for the text that will become the attached label for the combo box. Clicking the Finish button completes the process, building the combo box and filling in all its properties with the appropriate values.

Although the Combo Box Wizard is a helpful tool, you need to understand the properties it sets. Figure 5.40 shows the property sheet for a combo box. Many of the combo box properties are covered in other chapters, but take a moment to go over the properties set by the Combo Box Wizard in this example.

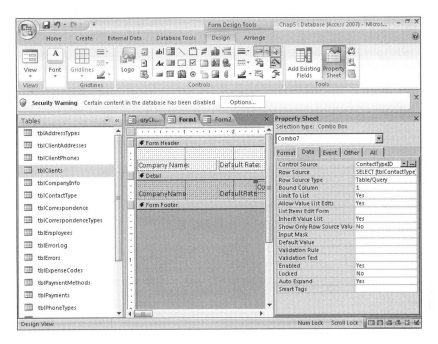

FIGURE 5.40   Properties of a combo box, showing that the `ContactTypeID` field has been selected as the control source for the Combo7 combo box.

The `Control Source` property indicates the field in which the selected entry is stored. In Figure 5.40, the selected entry will be stored in the `ContactTypeID` field of the `tblClients` table. The `Row Source Type` property specifies whether the source used to populate the combo box is a table/query, value list, or field list. In the example, the `Row Source Type` is `Table/Query`. The Row Source is the name of the actual table or query used to populate the combo box. In the example, the Row Source is `tblContactType`. The `Column Count` property, found on the Format tab, designates how many columns are in the combo box, and the `Column Widths` property (also found on the Format tab) indicates the width of each column. In the example, the width of the first column is 1. Finally, the `Bound Column` property is used to specify which column in the combo box is being used to store data in the `Control Source`. In the example, this is column 1.

Combo boxes are powerful controls, but you need to know many of their other features to leverage their power. Chapter 10 covers the advanced aspects of combo boxes.

List Boxes

List boxes are similar to combo boxes but differ from them in three major ways:

- ▶ They consume more screen space.

- ▶ They allow you to select only from the list that's displayed. This means you can't type new values into a list box (as you can with a combo box).

- ▶ They can be configured to let you select multiple items.

As with a combo box, the Display Control property of a field can be set to List Box, and a list box will be added to the form when the field is clicked and dragged from the field list to the form.

The List Box Wizard is almost identical to the Combo Box Wizard. After you run the List Box Wizard, the list box properties affected by the wizard are the same as the combo box properties. Advanced list box techniques are covered in Chapter 10.

Check Boxes

Check boxes enable you to limit your user to entering one of two values, such as Yes/No, True/False, or On/Off. You can add a check box to a form in several ways:

- ▶ Set the Display Control property of the underlying field to Check Box; then click and drag the field from the field list to the form.

- ▶ Click the Check Box tool on the Design tab of the ribbon; then click and drag a field from the field list to the form. This method adds a check box to the form even if the Display Control property of the underlying field isn't a check box.

- ▶ Click the Check Box tool in the Design tab of the ribbon; then click and drag to add a check box to the form. The check box you have added will be unbound. To bind the check box to data, you must set the control's Control Source property.

TIP

Use the Triple state property of a check box to add a third value, Null, to the possible choices for the check box value.

Option and Toggle Buttons

You can use option buttons and toggle buttons alone or as part of an option group. You can use an option button or toggle button alone to display a True/False value, but this isn't a standard use of an option or toggle button. (Check boxes are standard for this purpose.) As part of an option group, option buttons and toggle buttons force the user to select from a mutually exclusive set of options, such as choosing from American Express, MasterCard, Visa, or Discover for a payment type. This use of option buttons and toggle buttons is covered in the next section, "Option Groups."

The difference between option buttons and toggle buttons is in their appearance. Personally, I find toggle buttons confusing to users. I find that option buttons provide a much more intuitive interface.

Option Groups

Option groups allow the user to select from a mutually exclusive set of options. They can include check boxes, toggle buttons, or option buttons, but the most common implementation of an option group is option buttons.

The easiest way to add an option group to a form is to use the Option Group Wizard. Make sure the Control Wizards button on the Design tab of the ribbon is selected, click Option Group on the Design tab of the ribbon, and then click and drag to add the option group to the form. This launches the Option Group Wizard.

The first step of the Option Group Wizard, shown in Figure 5.41, allows you to type the text associated with each item in the option group. The second step gives you the option of selecting a default choice for the option group. This choice comes into effect when the user adds a new record to the table underlying the form. The third step of the wizard lets you select values associated with each option button (see Figure 5.42). The text displayed with the option button isn't stored in the record; instead, the underlying numeric value is stored in the record. In Figure 5.42, the number 1 is stored in the field if Client is selected.

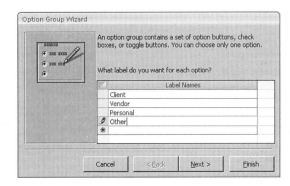

FIGURE 5.41   The first step of the Option Group Wizard: adding text to options.

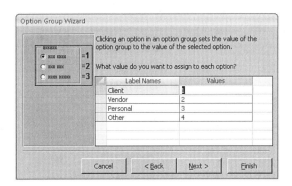

FIGURE 5.42   The third step of the Option Group Wizard: selecting values for options.

The fourth step of the Option Group Wizard asks whether you want to remember the option group value for later use or store the value in a field. In Figure 5.43, the option group value is stored in the ContactTypeID field. In the fifth step, you can select from a variety of styles for the option group buttons, including option buttons, check boxes, and toggle buttons. You can also select from etched, flat, raised, shadowed, or sunken effects for your buttons. The wizard lets you preview each option. The sixth and final step of the wizard allows you to add an appropriate caption to the option group. The completed group of option buttons is shown in Figure 5.44.

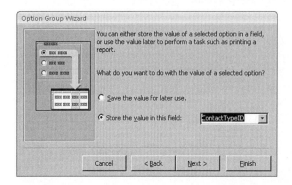

FIGURE 5.43   The fourth step of the Option Group Wizard: tying the group to data.

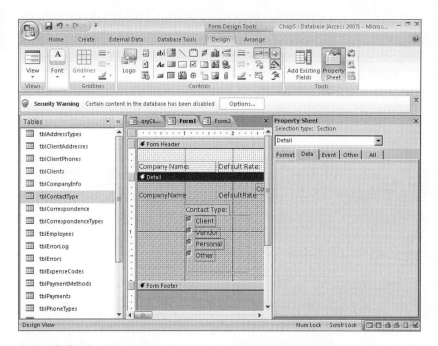

FIGURE 5.44   The results of running the Option Group Wizard.

You need to understand that the Option Group Wizard sets properties of the frame, the option buttons within the frame, and the labels attached to the option buttons. The properties of the frame are shown in Figure 5.45. The control source of the frame and the default value of the option group are set by the Option Group Wizard. Each option button is assigned a value, and the caption of the attached labels associated with each button is set.

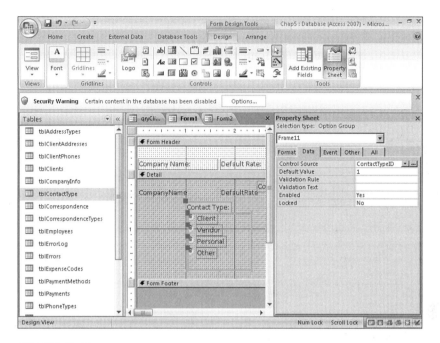

FIGURE 5.45   An option group frame, showing the properties of the selected button.

Control Morphing

When you build a form, you might not always choose the best type of control to display each field on the form, or you might make what you think is the best choice for the control, only to find out later that it wasn't exactly what your user had in mind. In Access, you can easily *morph*, or convert, the type of control into another type. For example, you can morph a list box into a combo box, a text box into a combo box, or a combo box into a text box.

Morphing a Text Box into a Combo Box

One of the most common types of conversions is from a text box into a combo box. To morph a text box into a combo box, right-click on the text box. Choose Change To and then select Combo Box. The types of controls available depend on the type of control you're morphing. For example, a text box can be converted into a label, list box, or combo box (see Figure 5.46).

After morphing a text box into a combo box, you modify the appropriate control properties. The Row Source, Bound Column, Column Count, and Column Widths properties need to be filled in. For the row source, you must select the appropriate table or query. If you select a table and then click the ellipsis, you are prompted to create a query based on the table. After selecting Yes, you can build a query containing only the fields you want to include in the combo box. You're then ready to select the bound column, which is used to store data in the underlying table. For example, the user might select the name of a project that a payment is being applied to, but the `ProjectID` will be stored in the `Payments` table. Set the column count to the number of columns selected in the underlying query; the column widths can be set so that the key column is hidden.

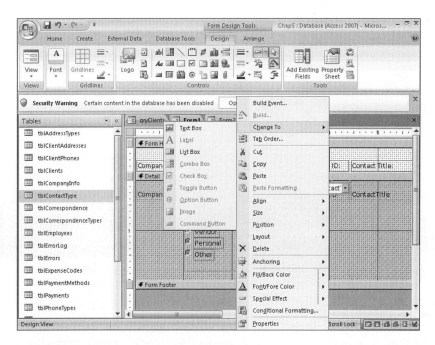

FIGURE 5.46   Morphing a text box.

Morphing a Combo Box into a List Box

Morphing a combo box into a list box is a much simpler process than morphing a text box into a combo box or a list box because combo boxes and list boxes share so many properties. To morph a combo box into a list box, simply right-click on the combo box and choose Change To, List Box.

Conditional Formatting

Conditional formatting displays data meeting specified criteria differently than it displays data meeting other criteria. For example, you can display sales higher than a certain amount in one color and sales less than that amount in another color. To conditionally format data displayed within a control, follow these steps:

1. While in Layout view, select the control you want to conditionally format.

2. On the Format tab, open up the Font drop-down and select Conditional. The Conditional Formatting dialog box appears.

3. Select Field Value Is, Expression Is, or Field Has Focus from the first combo box.

4. Select the appropriate operator from the second combo box.

5. Enter the values you are testing for in the text boxes that appear on the right.

6. Select the special formatting (bold, italic, background color, and so on) that you want to apply when the conditional criteria are met.

7. Click Add to add additional formats.

8. Click OK to apply the conditional formatting.

Determining Which Form Properties Are Available and Why You Should Use Them

Forms have many properties that can be used to affect their look and behavior. The properties are broken down into categories: Format, Data, Event, and Other.

To view a form's properties, you must select the form. To do this, click the Form Selector (the small gray button at the intersection of the horizontal and vertical rulers).

Working with the Property Sheet

After you have selected a form, click the Properties button on the toolbar to view its properties. The property sheet, shown in Figure 5.47, consists of five tabs: Format, Data, Event, Other, and All. Many developers prefer to view all properties at once on the All tab, but a form can have a total of 119 properties! Instead of viewing all 119 properties at once, try viewing the properties by category. The Format category includes all the physical attributes of the form—in other words, the ones that affect the form's appearance (such as background color, for example). The Data category includes all the properties of the data that the form is bound to, such as the form's underlying record source. The Event category contains all the Windows events to which a form can respond. For example, you can write code that executes in response to the form being loaded, becoming active, displaying a different record, and so on. The Other category holds a few properties that don't fit into the other three categories.

Working with the Important Form Properties

As mentioned, forms have 67 properties and 52 events associated with them. Event properties are covered in Chapter 10. The following sections cover the Format, Data, and Other properties of forms.

Format Properties of a Form

The Format properties of a form affect its physical appearance. Forms have 39 Format properties. Many of them are described here.

▶ Caption—Sets the text that appears on the form's title bar. This property can be customized at runtime. For example, you could include the name of the current user or specify the name of the client for whom an invoice is being generated.

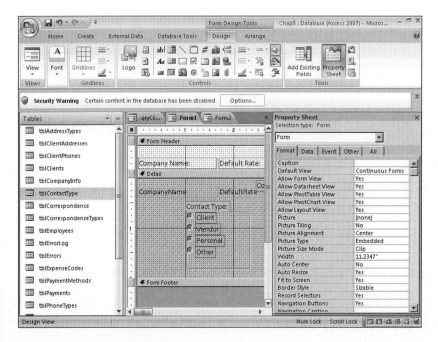

FIGURE 5.47   Viewing the Format properties of a form.

▶ Default View—Allows you to select from 5 available options:

  ▶ Single Form—Allows you to view only one record at a time.

  ▶ Continuous Forms—Displays as many records as will fit within the form window at one time, each presented as the detail section of a single form.

  ▶ Datasheet—Displays the records in a spreadsheet-like format, with the rows representing records and the columns representing fields.

  ▶ Split Form — Displays the records in both a Single form and Datasheet view at the same time. You can easily move from record to record in the datasheet portion of the form. As you move from record to record in the datasheet, the detail of the record appears in the Single form section of the form.

  ▶ PivotTable—Displays the records in a Microsoft Excel–type pivot table format.

  ▶ PivotChart—Displays the records in a Microsoft Excel–type pivot chart format.

The selected option becomes the default view for the form.

▶ Allow Form View—Prior to Access 2002, Access forms had a property called Views Allowed. The Views Allowed property determined whether the user was allowed to switch from Form view to Datasheet view, or vice versa. The Default View property determined the initial default display mode for the form, but Views Allowed determined whether the user was permitted to switch out of the default view.

In Access 2002, Microsoft separated out each type of view as an additional property for the form. `Allow Form View` specifies whether the user is permitted to switch to the Form view of a form.

▶ `Allow Datasheet View`—Determines whether the user is permitted to switch to the Datasheet view of a form.

▶ `Allow PivotTable View`—Determines whether the user is allowed to switch to the PivotTable view of a form.

▶ `Allow PivotChart View`—Determines whether the user is allowed to switch to the PivotChart view of a form.

▶ `Allow Layout View`—Determines whether the user is allowed to switch to the Layout view of a form.

▶ `Picture`, `Picture Type`, `Picture Size Mode`, `Picture Alignment`, and `Picture Tiling`—The `Picture` properties let you select and customize the attributes of a bitmap used as the background for a form.

▶ `Width`—Used to specify the form's width. This option is most often set graphically by clicking and dragging to select an appropriate size for the form. You might want to set this property manually when you want more than one form to be the same size.

▶ `Auto Center`—Specifies whether you want the form to automatically be centered within the Application window whenever it's opened.

▶ `Auto Resize`—Determines whether the form is automatically sized to display a complete record.

▶ `Fit to Screen`—Determines whether Access reduces the width of the form to the width of the screen.

▶ `Border Style`—The `Border Style` property is far more powerful than its name implies. The options for the `Border Style` property are `None`, `Thin`, `Sizable`, and `Dialog`. The border style is often set to `None` for splash screens, which means the form has no border. A `Thin` border is not resizable; the Size command isn't available in the Control menu. This setting is a good choice for pop-up forms, which remain on top even when other forms are given the focus. A `Sizable` border is standard for most forms. It includes all the standard options in the Control menu. A `Dialog` border looks like a `Thin` border. A form with a border style of `Dialog` can't be maximized, minimized, or resized. After the border style of a form is set to `Dialog`, the Maximize, Minimize, and Resize options aren't available in the form's Control menu. The `Dialog` border is often used along with the `Pop Up` and `Modal` properties to create custom dialog boxes.

▶ `Record Selectors`—Determines whether the record selectors appear. A record selector is the gray bar to the left of a record in Form view, or the gray box to the left of each record in Datasheet view. It's used to select a record to be copied or deleted. If you give the user a custom menu, you can opt to remove the record selector to make sure the user copies or deletes records using only the features specifically built in to your application.

▶ Navigation Buttons—Determines whether the navigation buttons are visible. Navigation buttons are the controls that appear at the bottom of a form; they allow the user to move from record to record within the form. You should set this property to No for any dialog forms. You might want to set it to No for data entry forms, too, and add your own ribbon that enhances or limits the standard buttons' functionality. For example, in a client/server environment, you might not want to give users the capability to move to the first or last record because that type of record movement can be inefficient in a client/server architecture.

▶ Navigation Caption—Allows you to specify a custom navigation caption.

▶ Dividing Lines—Indicates whether you want a line to appear between records when the default view of the form is set to Continuous Forms. It also determines whether dividing lines are placed between the form's sections (header, detail, and footer).

▶ Scroll Bars—Determines whether scrollbars appear if the controls on the form don't fit within the form's display area. You can select from vertical and horizontal scrollbars, neither vertical nor horizontal, just vertical, or just horizontal.

▶ Control Box—Determines whether a form has a Control menu. You should use this option sparingly. One of your responsibilities as an Access programmer is to make your applications comply with Windows standards. If you look at the Windows programs you use, you'll find very few forms without Control menu boxes. This should tell you something about how to design your own applications.

▶ Close Button—Determines whether the user can close the form by using the Control menu or double-clicking the Control icon. If you set the value of this property to No, you must give your user another way to close the form; otherwise, the user might have to reboot her computer to close your application.

▶ Min Max Buttons—Indicates whether the form has minimize and maximize buttons. The available options are None, Min Enabled, Max Enabled, and Both Enabled. If you remove one or both buttons, the appropriate options also become unavailable in the Control menu. The Min Max property is ignored for forms with a border style of None or Dialog. As with the Control Box property, I rarely use this property. To make my applications comply with Windows standards, I set the Border Style property and then inherit the standard attributes for each border style.

▶ Moveable—Determines whether the user can move the form window around the screen by clicking and dragging the form by its title bar.

▶ Split Form Size—Indicates the size of the form part of the Split Form.

▶ Split Form Orientation—Determines whether the Split view is oriented horizontally or vertically.

▶ Split Form Splitter Bar—Indicates whether the Splitter bar appears.

- ▶ `Split Form Datasheet`—Determines whether the datasheet portion of the Split form is read-only or is editable.

- ▶ `Split Form Printing`—Indicates whether the form or the datasheet will print.

- ▶ `Save Splitter Bar Position`—Determines whether Access saves the Splitter bar position from session to session.

- ▶ `Subdatasheet Expanded`—Allows you to designate whether a subdatasheet is initially displayed in an expanded format. When this property is set to `False`, the subdatasheet appears collapsed. When it is set to `True`, the subdatasheet appears in an expanded format.

- ▶ `Subdatasheet Height`—Indicates the maximum height of the subdatasheet.

- ▶ `Grid X, Grid Y`—Allow you to modify the spacing of the horizontal and vertical lines that appear in the form when in Design view. By setting these properties, you can affect how precisely you place objects on the form when the Snap to Grid option is active.

- ▶ `Layout for Print`—Specifies whether screen or printer fonts are used on the form. If you want to optimize the form for printing rather than display, set this property to Yes.

- ▶ `Orientation`—Allows you to take advantage of language-specific versions of Microsoft Access, such as Arabic. This property can be set to support right-to-left display features for language-specific editions of Access.

- ▶ `Palette Source`—Determines the source for selecting colors for a form.

Data Properties of a Form

The 13 Data properties of a form are used to control the source for the form's data, the actions the user can take on the data in the form, and the way the data in the form is locked in a multiuser environment.

- ▶ `Record Source`—Indicates the Table, Stored Query, or SQL statement on which the form's records are based. After you have selected a record source for a form, the controls on the form can be bound to the fields in the record source.

> **NOTE**
>
> The Field List window is unavailable until the record source of the form has been set.

> **TIP**
>
> The record source of a form can be changed at runtime. Because of this aspect of the `Record Source` property, you can create generic, reusable forms for many situations.

▶ `Recordset Type`—Gives you three options: `Dynaset`, `Dynaset (Inconsistent Updates)`, and `Snapshot`. Each offers different performance and updating capability. The `Dynaset` option creates a fully updateable recordset. The only exceptions to this rule involve records or fields that can't be updated for some other reason. An example is a form based on a query involving a one-to-many relationship. The join field on the one side of the relationship can be updated only if the Cascade Update Related Records feature has been enabled. The `Dynaset (Inconsistent Updates)` option allows all tables and bound data to be edited. This might result in inconsistent updating of data in the tables involved in the query. The `Snapshot` option doesn't allow updating.

▶ `Fetch Defaults`—Allows you to specify whether defaults for bound fields underlying the form are retrieved when new records are added. When this property, introduced in Access 2002, is set to `No`, default values are not retrieved. When it is set to `Yes`, default values are retrieved.

▶ `Filter`—Allows you to automatically load a stored filter along with the form. I prefer to base a form on a query that limits the data displayed on the form. The query can be passed parameters at runtime to customize exactly what data is displayed.

▶ `Filter On Load`—Determines whether Access applies the filter when the form loads.

▶ `Order By`—Specifies in what order the records on a form appear. This property can be modified at runtime.

▶ `Order By on Load`—Determines whether Access applies the Order By when the form loads.

▶ `Data Entry`—Determines whether users can only add records within a form. Set this property to `Yes` if you don't want your users to view or modify existing records but want them to be able to add new records.

▶ `Allow Edits, Allow Deletions, Allow Additions`—Let you specify whether the user can edit data, delete records, or add records from within the form.

▶ `Allow Filters`—Controls whether records can be filtered at runtime. When this option is set to `No`, all filtering options become disabled to the user.

▶ `Record Locks`—Specifies the locking mechanism to be used for the data underlying the form's recordset. Three options are available. The `No Locks` option—the least restrictive locking mechanism—provides *optimistic locking*; that is, Access doesn't try to lock the record until the user moves off it. This option can lead to potential conflicts when two users simultaneously make changes to the same record. The `All Records` option locks all records underlying the form the entire time the form is open. This is the most restrictive option and should be used only when it's necessary for the form's user to make sure other users can view, but not modify, the form's underlying recordset. The `Edited Record` option locks a 4KB page of records as soon as a user starts editing the data in the form. This option provides *pessimistic locking*. Although it averts conflicts by prohibiting two users from modifying a record at the same time, it can lead to potential locking conflicts. These three locking options are covered in detail in *Alison Balter's Mastering Access 2002 Enterprise Development*.

Other Properties of a Form

Additional properties of a form, although quite powerful, do not fit neatly into any of the other property categories. Microsoft places these properties under the Other properties of the form. They are listed here:

- ▶ Pop Up—Indicates whether the form always remains on top of other windows. This property is often set to Yes, along with the Modal property, for custom dialog boxes.

- ▶ Modal—Indicates whether focus can be removed from a form while it's open. When the Modal property is set to Yes, the form must be closed before the user can continue working with the application. As mentioned, this property is used with the Pop Up property to create custom dialog boxes.

- ▶ Display on SharePoint Site—Determines whether the form will be displayed on the SharePoint site.

- ▶ Cycle—Controls the behavior of the Tab key in the form. The options are All Records, Current Record, and Current Page. When the Cycle property is set to All Records, the user moves to the next record on a form when she presses Tab from the last control on the previous record. With Current Record, the user is moved from the last control on a form to the first control on the same record. The Current Page option refers only to multipage forms; when the Cycle property is set to Current Page, the user tabs from the last control on the page to the first control on the same page. All three options are affected by the tab order of the objects on the form.

- ▶ Ribbon Name—Specifies the ribbon to apply when the form opens. Chapter 23, "Working with and Customizing Ribbons," covers ribbons.

- ▶ Shortcut Menu, Shortcut Menu Bar—The Shortcut Menu property indicates whether a shortcut menu is displayed when the user clicks with the right mouse button over an object on the form. The Shortcut Menu Bar property lets you associate a custom menu with a control on the form or with the form itself. As with a standard menu bar, a shortcut menu bar is created by choosing Toolbars from the View menu and then selecting Customize. Shortcut menus are covered in Chapter 10.

- ▶ Help File, Help Context id—Enable you to associate a specific Help file and topic with a form.

- ▶ Has Module—Determines whether the form has a class module. If no code is associated with your form, setting this property to No can noticeably decrease load time and improve your form's performance while decreasing the database's size.

5

▶ `Fast Laser Printing`—Determines whether lines and rectangles print along with the form. When this property is set to `Yes`, you'll notice a definite improvement when printing the form to a laser printer.

▶ `Tag`—The `Tag` property is an extra property used to store miscellaneous information about the form. This property is often set and monitored at runtime to store necessary information about the form. You could use the `Tag` property to add a tag to each of several forms that should be unloaded as a group.

▶ Use Default Paper Size—The Use Default Paper Size property is used to determine if when printed, the form prints using the default paper size setting.

Determining Which Control Properties Are Available and Why You Should Use Them

Available control properties vary quite a bit, depending on the type of control that's been selected. The more common properties are covered in the following sections; individual properties are covered throughout the book as they apply to a specific topic.

Format Properties of a Control

The Format properties of a control affect the appearance of the control. They include the following:

▶ `Format`—Determines how the data in the control is displayed. A control's format is automatically inherited from its underlying data source. This property is used in three situations:

  ▶ When the `Format` property is not set for the underlying field

  ▶ When you want to override the existing `Format` setting for the field

  ▶ When you want to apply a format to an unbound control

You can select from a multitude of predefined values for a control's format, or you can create a custom format. I often modify this property at runtime to vary the format of a control depending on a certain condition. For example, the format for a Visa card number is different from the format for an ATM card number.

▶ `Decimal Places`—Specifies how many decimal places you want to appear in the control. This property is used with the `Format` property to determine the control's appearance.

▶ `Visible`—Indicates whether a control is visible. This property can be toggled at runtime, depending on specific circumstances. For example, a question on the form might apply only to records in which the gender is set to `Female`; if the gender is set to `Male`, the question shouldn't be visible.

▶ `Show Date Picker`—Determines whether Access displays the Date Picker for date fields.

► Left, Top, Width, Height—Enable you to set the control's position and size.

► Back Style, Back Color—You can set the Back Style property to Normal or Transparent, as well as to numerous other settings. When it is set to Transparent, the form's background color shows through the control. This is often the preferred setting for an option group. The control's Back Color property specifies the background color (as opposed to text color) for the control.

CAUTION

If the Back Style property of a control is set to Transparent, the control's back color is ignored.

► Border Style, Border Color, Border Width—Affect the look, color, and thickness of a control's border. The border style options are Transparent, Solid, Dashes, Short Dashes, Dots, Sparse Dots, Dash Dot, and Dash Dot Dot. The Border Color property specifies the color of the border; you can select from a variety of colors. The Border Width property can be set to one of several point sizes.

CAUTION

If the Border Style of a control is set to Transparent, the control's border color and border width are ignored.

► Special Effect—Adds 3D effects to a control. The options for this property are Flat, Raised, Sunken, Etched, Shadowed, and Chiseled. Each of these effects gives the control a different look.

► Scroll Bars—Determines whether scrollbars appear when the data in the control doesn't fit within the control's size. The options are None and Vertical. I often set the Scroll Bars property to Vertical when the control is used to display data from a Memo field. The scrollbar makes it easier for the user to work with a potentially large volume of data in the Memo field.

► Fore Color, Font Name, Font Size, Font Weight, Font Italic, Font Underline— Control the appearance of the text in a control. As their names imply, these properties let you select the color, font, size, and thickness of the text and determine whether the text is italicized or underlined. These properties can be modified in response to a runtime event, such as modifying a control's text color if the value in that control exceeds a certain amount. The Font Weight selections generally exceed what is actually available for a particular font and printer; normally, you have a choice of only Regular and Bold in whatever value you select for this property.

► Text Align—Affects how the data is aligned *within* a control. The Text Align property is often confused with the capability to align controls.

▶ `Line Spacing`—Enables you to determine the spacing between lines of text in a multiline control. This property is most commonly used with a text box based on a memo field.

▶ `Is Hyperlink`—Formats the data in the control as a hyperlink, when set to `Yes`. If the data in the control is a relevant link (that is, `http:\\microsoft.com`), the data will function as a hyperlink.

▶ `Display as Hyperlink`—Allows you to control when Access displays the control text as a hyperlink.

▶ `Caption`—Allows you to specify information helpful to the user. This property is available for labels, command buttons, and toggle buttons.

▶ `Hyperlink Address`—Contains a string used to specify the UNC (path to a file) or URL (web page address) associated with the control. The `Hyperlink Address` property is available only for command buttons, images, and unattached labels. When the form is active and the cursor is placed over the control, clicking the control displays the specified object or web page.

▶ `Hyperlink SubAddress`—Contains a string used to represent a location in the document specified in the `Hyperlink Address` property. Like the `Hyperlink Address` property, the `Hyperlink SubAddress` property is available only for command buttons, images, and unattached labels.

▶ `Display When`—Allows you to send certain controls on the form only to the screen or only to the printer. The three options are `Always`, `Print Only`, or `Screen Only`. An example of the use of the `Display When` property is a label containing instructions. You might want the instructions to appear on the screen but not on the printout.

▶ `Can Grow, Can Shrink`—Apply only to the form's printed version. The `Can Grow` property, when set to `Yes`, expands the control when printing so that all the data in the control fits on the printout. When you set the `Can Shrink` property to `Yes` and no data has been entered, the control shrinks so that blank lines won't be printed.

▶ `Gridline Style Top, Bottom, Left, and Right`—Determines the style of the control's gridlines.

▶ `Gridline Color`—Determines the color of the control's gridlines.

▶ `Gridline Width Top, Bottom, Left, and Right`—Determines the width of the control's gridlines.

▶ `Left Margin, Top Margin, Right Margin, Bottom Margin`—Determine how far the text appears from the left, top, right, and bottom of the control. They are particularly useful with controls such as text boxes based on memo fields, which are generally large controls.

▶ `Top, Bottom, Left, and Right Padding`—Determines the amount of space between the gridline and the text.

▶ `Horizontal` and `Vertical Anchor`—Determines how the control is anchored (left, right, top, bottom) when the form grows horizontally or vertically.

▶ `Can Grow`/`Can Shrink`—Indicates whether the control can grow or shrink vertically, based on the volume of text, when the form prints.

▶ `Reading Order`—Allows you to specify the reading order for text in a control. The `Reading Order` property was introduced with Access 2002. This feature is available only if you are using a version of Microsoft Office that supports right-to-left features.

▶ `Scroll Bar Align`—Allows you to place the vertical scrollbars in the appropriate left-to-right or right-to-left position. If you select the System option, the position of the scrollbar is based on the selected user interface language. The scrollbar is placed on the right for left-to-right languages and on the left for right-to-left languages. If you select Left or Right, the scrollbar is placed on the left or right side of the control, respectively. The `Scroll Bar Align` property is another language-related property introduced with Access 2002.

▶ `Numerical Shapes`—Allows you to designate whether numeric shapes are displayed in the Arabic or Hindi style. The available choices for this property are `System`, `Arabic`, `National`, and `Context`. `System` bases the `Numerical Shapes` on the operating system. `Arabic` and `National` use the Arabic and Hindi styles, respectively. `Context` bases the numerical style on the text adjacent to the control. The `Numerical Shapes` property was introduced with Access 2002.

▶ `Keyboard Language`—Allows you to override the keyboard language currently in use. This means that when a specific control receives the focus, the language specified in this property becomes the keyboard language in effect while typing data into the control. The `Keyboard Language` property was introduced with Access 2002.

Data Properties of a Control

The Data properties of a control all have to do with the data underlying the control. They include the following:

▶ `Control Source`—Specifies the field from the record source that's associated with a particular control. A control source can also be any valid Access expression.

▶ `Text Format`—Allows you to apply rich formatting to the text in the control if set to HTML. If set to Plain text, Access stores only text within the control and you cannot apply formatting to the text.

▶ `Input Mask`—Affects what data can be entered into the control, whereas the `Format` and `Decimal Places` properties affect the appearance of a control. The input mask of the field underlying the control is automatically inherited into the control. If no input mask is entered as a field property, the input mask can be entered directly in the form. If the input mask of the field is entered, the input mask of the associated control on a form can be used to further restrict what is entered into that field via the form.

NOTE

If a control's Format property and Input Mask property are different, the Format property affects the display of the data in the control until the control gets focus. After the control gets focus, the Input Mask property prevails.

▶ Default Value—Determines the value assigned to new records entered in the form. You can set this property within the field properties. A default value set at the field level is automatically inherited into the form. The default value set for the control overrides the default value set at the field level.

▶ Validation Rule, Validation Text—Perform the same functions for a control as they do for a field.

CAUTION

Because the validation rule is enforced at the database engine level, the validation rule set for a control can't be in conflict with the validation rule set for the field to which the control is bound. If the two rules conflict, the user can't enter data into the control.

▶ Filter Lookup—Indicates whether you want the values associated with a bound text box to appear in the Filter By Form window.

▶ Enabled—Determines whether you allow a control to get focus. If this property is set to No, the control appears dimmed.

▶ Locked—Determines whether the user can modify the data in the control. When the Locked property is set to Yes, the control can get focus but can't be edited. The Enabled and Locked properties of a control interact with one another. Table 5.1 summarizes their interactions.

TABLE 5.1   How the Enabled and Locked Properties Interact

Enabled	Locked	Effect
Yes	Yes	The control can get focus; its data can be copied but not modified.
Yes	No	The control can get focus, and its data can be edited.
No	Yes	The control can't get focus.
No	No	The control can't get focus; its data appears dimmed.

Other Properties of a Control

The Other properties of a control are properties that do not fit neatly into any other category. They include the following:

▶ Name—Allows you to name the control. This name is used when you refer to the control in code and is also displayed in various drop-down lists that show all the controls on a form. Naming your controls is important because named controls improve your code's readability and make working with Access forms and other objects easier. The naming conventions for controls are shown in Appendix A.

▶ `Datasheet Caption`—Determines the caption that Access uses for the column header when the form displays in datasheet view.

▶ `Enter Key Behavior`—Determines whether the Enter key causes the cursor to move to the next control or adds a new line in the current control. This setting is often changed for text boxes used to display the contents of `Memo` fields.

▶ `ControlTip Text`—Specifies the ToolTip associated with a control. The ToolTip automatically appears when the user places the mouse pointer over the control and leaves it there for a moment.

▶ `Tab Index`—Sets the tab order for the control. I generally set the `Tab Index` property by using View, Tab Order rather than by setting the value directly in the control's `Tab Index` property.

▶ `Tab Stop`—Determines whether the Tab key can be used to enter a control. It's appropriate to set this property to `No` for controls whose values rarely get modified. The user can always opt to click in the control when necessary.

▶ `Status Bar Text`—Specifies the text that appears in the status bar when the control gets focus. This property setting overrides the `Description` property that can be set in a table's design.

▶ `Shortcut Menu Bar`—Attaches a specific menu to a control. The menu bar appears when the user right-clicks the control.

▶ `Help Context Id`—Designates the Help topic associated with a particular control.

▶ `Auto Tab`—Automatically advances the cursor to the next control when the last character of an input mask has been entered, when this property is set to `Yes`. Some users like this option, and others find it annoying, especially if they must tab out of some fields but not others.

▶ `Vertical`—Enables you to control whether the text in the control is displayed horizontally or vertically. The default is `No`, or horizontal. When `Yes` (vertical display) is selected, the text within the control is rotated 90 degrees.

▶ `Allow AutoCorrect`—Specifies whether the AutoCorrect feature is available in the control. The AutoCorrect feature automatically corrects common spelling errors and typos.

▶ `Default`—Applies to a command button or ActiveX control and specifies whether the control is the default button on a form.

▶ `Cancel`—Applies to a command button or ActiveX control. It indicates that you want the control's code to execute when the Esc key is pressed while the form is active.

▶ `Auto Repeat`—Specifies whether you want an event procedure or macro to execute repeatedly while its command button is being pressed.

▶ `IME Hold`, `IME Mode`, `IME Sentence Mode`—Allows you to designate the settings in effect when an Input Method Editor (IME) is used. The IME properties were introduced with Access 2002. IME is a program that converts keystrokes into East Asian character sets.

▶ `Tag`—An extra property you can use to store information about a control. Your imagination determines how you use this property. The `Tag` property can be read and modified at runtime.

Understanding Bound, Unbound, and Calculated Controls

There are important differences between bound and unbound controls. *Unbound controls* display information to the user or gather information from the user that's not going to be stored in your database. Here are some examples of unbound controls:

▶ A label providing instructions to the user

▶ A logo placed on a form

▶ A combo or text box placed on a form so that the user can enter report criteria

▶ A rectangle placed on the form to logically group several controls

Bound controls are used to display and modify information stored in a database table. A bound control automatically appears in the form specified in its `Display Control` property; the control automatically inherits many of the attributes assigned to the field that the control is bound to.

> **NOTE**
>
> The `Display Control` property is set in the design of the underlying table. Located on the Lookup tab of the Table Design window, it determines the default control type that is used when a control is added to a form or report.

A *calculated control* is a special type of control that displays the results of an expression. The data in a calculated control can't be modified by the user. The control's value automatically changes as the values in its expression are changed. For example, the Sales Total changes as the Price or Quantity is changed.

Using Expressions to Enhance Your Forms

As mentioned previously, a control can contain any valid expression as its control source. When you enter an expression as a control source, you must precede the expression with an equal sign. You can manually type the control source, or you can use the Expression Builder to make the process easier.

To add an expression to a control source, start by adding an unbound control to the form. To use the Expression Builder, click the control's Control Source property and then click the ellipsis. The Expression Builder appears (see Figure 5.48). In the list box on the left, select the type of object you want to include in the expression. The middle and right list boxes let you select the specific element you want to paste into your expression. The Expression Builder is useful when you're not familiar with the specific syntax required for the expression. You can also enter an expression directly into the text box for the Control Source property. To view the expression more easily, you can use the Zoom feature (Shift+F2). The Zoom dialog box for the control source is pictured in Figure 5.49; the expression shown in the figure evaluates the PaymentAmt. If the PaymentAmt is greater than or equal to 1,000, the message Big Hitter is displayed; otherwise, nothing is displayed.

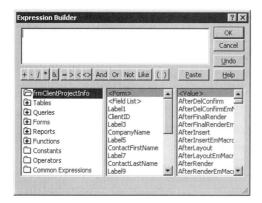

FIGURE 5.48   The Expression Builder helps you add an expression as a control's control source.

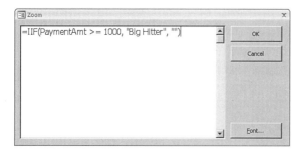

FIGURE 5.49   The Zoom dialog box for a control source.

Using the Command Button Wizards: Programming Without Typing

With the Command Button Wizard, you can quickly and easily add functionality to your forms. It writes the code to perform more than 28 commonly required tasks. The tasks are separated into record navigation, record operations, form operations, report operations, application operations, and other miscellaneous tasks. The Command Button Wizard is automatically invoked when you add a command button with the Control Wizards tool selected. The first step of the Command Button Wizard is shown in Figure 5.50; here, you specify the category of activity and specific action you want the command button to perform. The subsequent wizard steps vary, depending on the category and action you select.

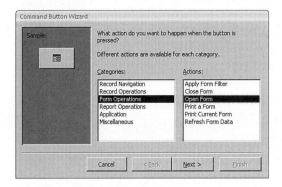

FIGURE 5.50   The first step of the Command Button Wizard.

Figure 5.51 shows the second step of the Command Button Wizard when the Form Operations category and Open Form action are selected in the first step. This step asks which form you want to open. After selecting a form and clicking Next, you're asked whether you want Access to open the form and find specific data to display, or whether you want the form to be opened and all records displayed. If you indicate that you want only specific records displayed, the dialog box shown in Figure 5.52 appears. This dialog box asks you to select fields relating the two forms. In the next step of the wizard, select text or a picture for the button. The final step of the wizard asks you to name the button.

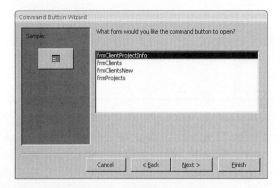

FIGURE 5.51   The Command Button Wizard requesting the name of a form to open.

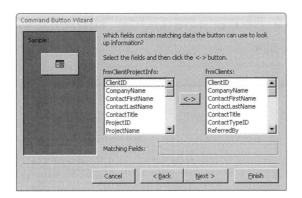

FIGURE 5.52   The Command Button Wizard asking for the fields that relate to each form.

What's surprising about the Command Button Wizard is how much it varies depending on the features you select. It allows you to add somewhat sophisticated functionality to your application without writing a single line of code. The Command Button Wizard generates a macro similar to that shown in Figure 5.53; it will make a lot more sense after you read Chapter 7, "What Are Macros, and When Do You Need Them?" The advantage to the macro generated by the Command Button Wizard is that you can fully modify it after it's written; this means that you can have Access do some of the dirty work for you and then customize the work to your liking.

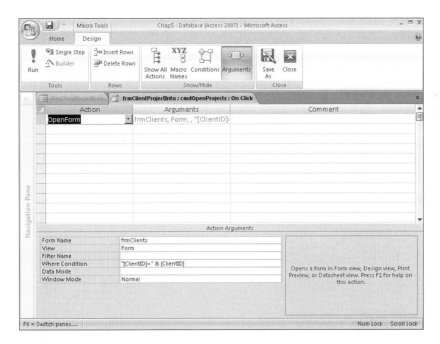

FIGURE 5.53   The macro generated from the Command Button Wizard.

Building Forms Based on More Than One Table

Many forms are based on data from more than one table. A form, for example, that shows a customer at the top and the orders associated with that customer at the bottom is considered a one-to-many form. Forms can also be based on a query that joins more than one table. Instead of seeing a one-to-many relationship in such a form, you see the two tables displayed as one, with each record on the "many" side of the relationship appearing with its parent's data.

Creating One-to-Many Forms

There are several ways to create one-to-many forms. As with many other types of forms, you can use a wizard to help you or build the form from scratch. Because all the methods for creating a form are helpful to users and developers alike, the available options are covered in the following sections.

Building a One-to-Many Form by Using the Form Wizard

Building a one-to-many form by using the Form Wizard is a 10-step process:

1. Use the More Forms drop-down on the Create tab to select Form Wizard.

2. Use the Tables/Queries drop-down list to select the table or query that will appear on the "one" side of the relationship.

3. Select the fields you want to include from the "one" side of the relationship.

4. Use the Tables/Queries drop-down list to select the table or query that will appear on the "many" side of the relationship.

5. Select the fields you want to include from the "many" side of the relationship.

6. Click Next.

7. Select whether you want the parent form to appear with subforms or the child forms to appear as linked forms (see Figure 5.54). Click Next.

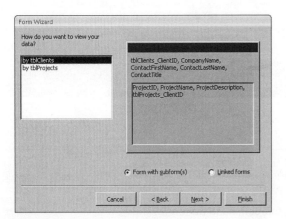

FIGURE 5.54   The Form Wizard creating a one-to-many form.

8. If you select the Subform option, indicate whether you want the subform to appear in a tabular format, as a datasheet, as a pivot table, or as a pivot chart. (This option is not available if you selected Linked Forms in step 7.) Click Next.

9. Select a style for the form; then click Next.

10. Name both the form and the subform and click Finish.

The result is a main form that contains a subform. An example is shown in Figure 5.55.

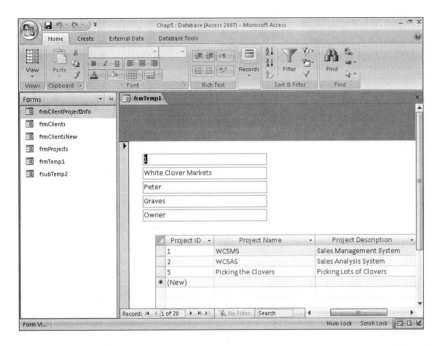

FIGURE 5.55   The result of creating a one-to-many form with the Form Wizard.

Building a One-to-Many Form with the SubForm/SubReport Wizard

You can also create a one-to-many form by building the parent form and then adding a SubForm/SubReport control, which is found in the Controls group on the Design tab of the Ribbon. If you want to use the SubForm/SubReport Wizard, make sure that the Control Wizards tool is selected before you add the SubForm/SubReport control to the main form. Then follow these steps:

1. Click to select the SubForm/SubReport control.

2. Click and drag to place the SubForm/SubReport control on the main form; this invokes the SubForm/SubReport Wizard.

3. Indicate whether you want to use an existing form as the subform or build a new subform from an existing table or query.

4. If you select Use Existing Tables and Queries, the next step of the SubForm/ SubReport Wizard prompts you to select a table or query and which fields you want to include from it (see Figure 5.56). Select the fields; then click Next.

5. The next step of the SubForm/SubReport Wizard allows you to define which fields in the main form link to which fields in the subform. You can select from the suggested relationships or define your own (see Figure 5.57). Select the appropriate relationship and click Next.

6. Name the subform and click Finish.

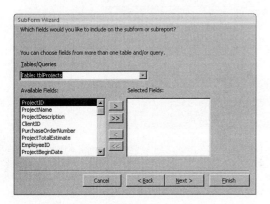

FIGURE 5.56   Selecting fields to include in the subform.

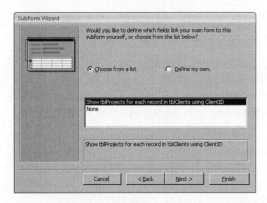

FIGURE 5.57   Defining the relationship between the main form and the subform.

The resulting form should look similar to the form created with the Form Wizard. Creating a one-to-many form this way is simply an alternative to using the Form Wizard.

TIP

Another way to add a subform to a main form is to click and drag a form from the Database window onto the main form. Access then tries to identify the relationship between the two forms.

Working with Subforms

After you have added a subform, you need to understand how to work with it. To begin, familiarize yourself with a few properties of a Subform control:

- ▶ `Source Object`—The name of the form that's being displayed in the control

- ▶ `Link Child Fields`—The fields from the child form that link the child form to the master form

- ▶ `Link Master Fields`—The fields from the master form that link the child form to the master form

You should also understand how to make changes to the subform. One option is to open the subform in a separate window (as you would open any other form). After you close and save the form, all the changes automatically appear in the parent form. The other choice is to modify the subform from within the main form. With the main form open, the subform is visible. Any changes made to the design of the subform from within the main form are permanent.

The default view of the subform is Datasheet or Continuous Forms, depending on how you added the subform and what options you selected. If you want to modify the default view, simply change the subform's `Default View` property.

5

NOTE

When the subform is displayed in Datasheet view, the order of the fields in the subform has no bearing on the datasheet that appears in the main form. The order of the columns in the datasheet depends on the tab order of the fields in the subform. You must therefore modify the tab order of the fields in the subform to change the order of the fields in the resulting datasheet.

TIP

Access 2003 made it easier to work with subforms and subreports in Design view. Scrolling was improved so that it's easier to design subforms and subreports. In addition, you can open subforms in their own separate Design view window by right-clicking the subform and selecting Subform in New Window. Alternatively, instead of right-clicking the subform, you can select the subform and then click to select Subform in New Window from the Tools group on the Design tab of the ribbon.

Basing Forms on Queries: The Why and How

One strategy when building forms is to base them on queries; by doing this, you generally get optimal performance and flexibility. Instead of bringing all fields and all records over the network, you bring only the fields and records you need. The benefits are even more pronounced in a client/server environment where the query is run on the server. Even in an environment where data is stored in the proprietary Access file format (.accdb) on a file server, a form based on a stored query can take better advantage of Access's indexing and paging features. By basing a form on a query, you also have more control over which records are included in the form and in what order they appear. Finally, you can base a form on a query containing a one-to-many join, viewing parent and child information as if it were one record. Notice in Figure 5.58 that the client and project information appear on one form as if they were one record.

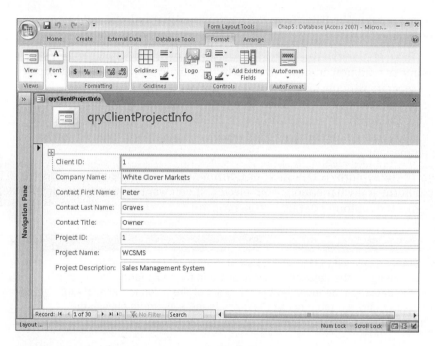

FIGURE 5.58   A form based on a one-to-many query.

Embedding SQL Statements Versus Stored Queries

In earlier versions of Access, stored queries offered better performance than embedded SQL statements. The reason is that, when a query is saved, Access compiles the query and creates a query plan, which has information on the best way to execute the query based on available indexes and the volume of data. In earlier versions of Access, if a form was based on an embedded SQL statement, the SQL statement was compiled and optimized each time the form was opened. With Access 2000 and higher, embedded SQL statements are compiled just like stored queries. You might ask whether, with Access 2007, it is better to base a query on a stored query or on a SQL statement. My personal preference is as follows: If I plan to use the same or a similar query with multiple forms and reports, I build a query and base multiple forms and reports on that query. This keeps me from having to duplicate my efforts in building the query. If I have a query that is unique to the form, I build it as an embedded SQL statement. This eliminates the extra "clutter" of the query in the database container.

> **NOTE**
>
> A query plan can sometimes be inaccurate because it optimizes the query based on the amount of data in the underlying tables. If the amount of data in the tables underlying a form changes significantly, you need to rebuild the query plan. You can do this by opening, running, and saving the query or by compacting the database. Chapter 30, "Maintaining Your Application," covers the process of compacting your databases.

Connecting Access Forms and the Internet

Microsoft has made it easier to develop Internet-aware applications by adding hyperlinks to forms and allowing you to save an Access form as HTML or XML. These features are covered in the following sections.

Adding a Hyperlink to a Form

Hyperlinks can be added to unattached labels (labels not attached to a text box or other object), command buttons, and image controls. Once added, they let the user jump to a document (UNC) or web page (URL) simply by clicking the control containing the hyperlink. To add a hyperlink to a label, command button, or image control, follow these steps:

1. Click to select the control.

2. View the control's properties.

3. Select the Format tab of the property sheet.

4. Click in the Hyperlink Address property.

5. Click the build button (the ellipsis) to open the Insert Hyperlink dialog box (see Figure 5.59).

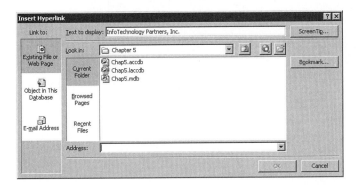

FIGURE 5.59   Establishing a link to a file or URL by using the Insert Hyperlink dialog box.

6. With Existing File or Web Page selected as the Link To option, you can enter a file path or URL in the text box or click Current Folder to locate a file or web page in the current folder. You can also click to insert hyperlinks to browsed pages or recent files. With Object in This Database selected as the Link To option, you can link to an object in the current database (see Figure 5.60). Select E-Mail Address to link to an email address.

7. Click OK to finish the process. The contents of the Link to File or URL combo box become the Hyperlink Address, and the object name becomes the Hyperlink SubAddress (see Figure 5.61).

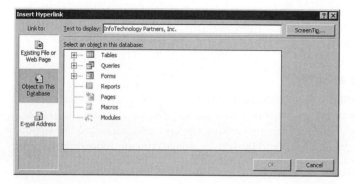

FIGURE 5.60   Setting the location within an Access database for your hyperlink.

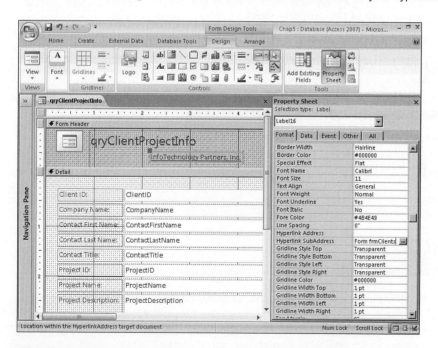

FIGURE 5.61   Hyperlink address and subaddress defined for a label control.

5

TIP

Using a hyperlink address to open an object in an Access database, instead of using the `Click` event of the command button and VBA code, allows you to remove the class module associated with the form (if that is the only procedure you need for the form), thereby optimizing the form's performance.

Saving a Form as HTML

You can save forms as HTML documents in one of two ways. The first method is to save a form as HTML by selecting the form in the Navigation Pane and then selecting HTML Document from the More drop-down in the Export group on the External Data tab. (You can also right-click the form in the database Navigation Pane and select Export, HTML Document.) The Export – HTML Document dialog appears. Click Browse to designate the location for the exported document. If you want the system's default browser to load after the HTML document is saved, click Open the Destination File After the Export Operation Is Complete. Click OK. The HTML Output Options dialog box appears. If desired, click Browse to locate an HTML template file. Click OK to close the dialog box. Only the datasheet associated with the form is saved as HTML; the format of the form itself isn't saved.

Saving a Form as XML

You can also save forms as XML by selecting the form within the Navigation Pane (or by having the form open and in focus) and clicking XML File from the More drop-down from the Export group on the External Data tab. Browse to select a name and location for the exported document. Click OK to continue. Access can generate three files: `filename.xml`, `filename.xsd`, and `filename.xsl`. The `.xml` file contains the actual data. The `.xsd` file contains the schema, or structure, of the data. The `.xsl` file is the stylesheet for displaying the XML data.

Adding Smart Tags to Your Forms

You use smart tags to perform tasks such as scheduling appointments, emailing letters, and adding Outlook contacts, all based on data displayed on an Access form. You can even determine the weather or get the latest news on each city that appears on an Access form!

Adding a Smart Tag to a Form

Adding a smart tag to an Access form involves these steps:

1. Create a new form or open an existing form in Design view.

2. Select the control on which you want to base the smart tag. For example, if you want to use the smart tag to schedule an appointment, you would probably want to select a control bound to the Contact Name field.

3. Show the Data properties for the control and click within the `Smart Tags` property (see Figure 5.62).

4. Click the Build button (the ellipsis). The Smart Tags dialog box appears (see Figure 5.63).

5. Click to select the smart tag you want to add. For example, to send mail, schedule a meeting, open an existing contact, and add new contacts, select Person Name.

6. Click OK. A smart tag appears in the `Smart Tags` property (see Figure 5.64).

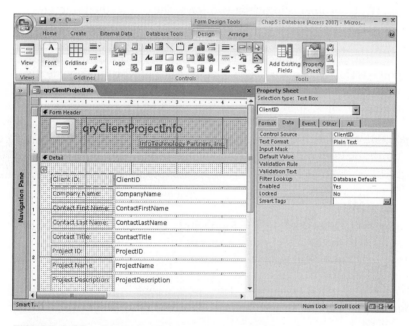

FIGURE 5.62   The Data tab of the property sheet with the `Smart Tags` property selected.

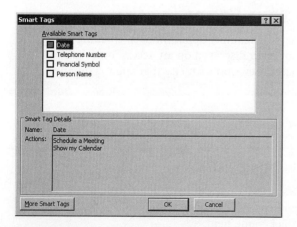

FIGURE 5.63   The Smart Tags dialog box allows you to select the smart tag you want to add.

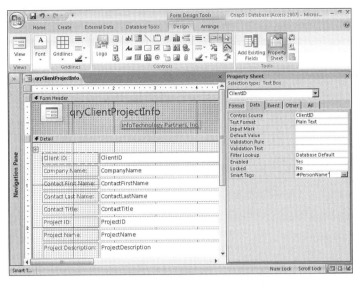

FIGURE 5.64   After you click OK, a smart tag appears in the Smart Tags property.

Using a Smart Tag

After you have added a smart tag to a control, you will notice smart tag action buttons when you view the form in Form view (see Figure 5.65). Click the action button for a particular record to see the actions available for that smart tag. In Figure 5.66, you can see that the Person Name smart tag has the Send Mail, Schedule a Meeting, Open Contact, and Add to Contacts menu items all associated with it. If, for example, you select the Schedule a Meeting menu item, Microsoft Outlook launches and a new meeting appears.

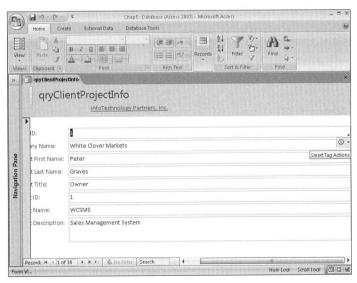

FIGURE 5.65   After you add a smart tag, smart tag action buttons appear when you display the form in Form view.

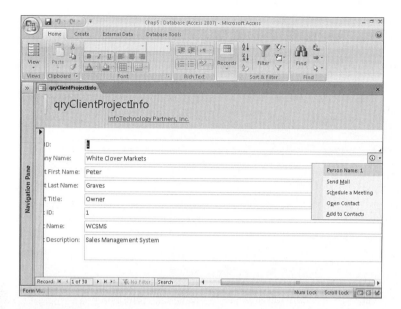

FIGURE 5.66   Click the Action button for a particular control on the form to see the actions available for that smart tag.

Creating a Pivot Table or Pivot Chart from a Form

Pivot tables and pivot charts provide great ways for you to summarize detailed data stored in your Access Database Engine and SQL Server databases. Pivot tables present your data in a spreadsheet-like format, whereas pivot charts automatically render pivot table views as line, bar, or area charts. Access 2002 and Access 2003 provided two new views for forms: PivotTable and PivotChart.

Creating the Form to Display in PivotTable or PivotChart View

You first must build a form that is appropriate to display in PivotTable or PivotChart view. Forms that lend themselves to be displayed in PivotTable or PivotChart view provide many ways for users to manipulate their data. An example of such a form is one that contains information about country, city, salesperson, sales, and date of sale. You could determine sales by city and salesperson for each month, or you could determine sales in each country for each salesperson during the year 2006. As you can see, the idea of pivot tables is to let you slice and dice the data in any way you need to at a given moment in time.

For this example, create the following query within the Northwind database. Then use the Autoform feature to base a form on the query:

1. Create a new query in Design view.

2. Add the `Customers`, `Orders`, `Products`, `Order Details`, and `Employees` tables to the query.

3. Add the `Country/Region` and `City` fields from the `Customers` table.

4. Add an expression: `SalesPerson:Employees!LastName & ", " & Employees!FirstName`.

5. Add the `Order Date` from the `Orders` table.

6. Add the `Product Name` from the `Products` table.

7. Add an expression: `Total:[Order Details]![Unit Price] * [Order Details]!Quantity`.

8. Double-click the join line between the `Customers` and `Orders` tables and select option 1. Click OK to close the dialog. This changes the type of join between the tables to an inner join. Chapter 10 covers join types in detail.

9. Double-click the join line between the Orders and Order Details tables and select option 1. Click OK to close the dialog.

10. Close and save the query as `qryPivotTable`.

11. Select the query in the Navigation Pane.

12. Select PivotTable from the More Forms drop-down on the Create tab.

You now have the foundation for your pivot table (see Figure 5.67).

Displaying the Form in PivotTable View

Once you are in PivotTable view, notice that the empty PivotTable view appears and the ribbon contains a Design tab with the tools appropriate for working with a pivot table (see Figure 5.67).

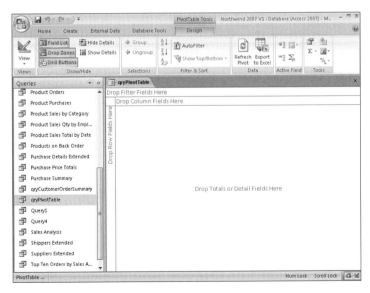

FIGURE 5.67   The Design tab contains tools necessary to work with a pivot table.

Included on the Design tab is the Field List button. There are four types of fields that you will add to your pivot table. They include the following:

▶ **Column fields**—Often hold date fields; generally hold information with the fewest number of data items.

▶ **Row fields**—One or more fields that display data by attributes.

▶ **Totals or Detail fields**—The crosstab data itself. These are the numeric values that make up the meat of the pivot table.

▶ **Filter fields**—One or more *optional* fields that restrict that data appearing in the columns, rows, or both.

To display the initial pivot table, take the following steps:

1. Click Field List on the Design tab to display the PivotTable Field List.

2. Drag the Country/Region field so that it appears as a Row field.

3. Drag the City field so that it appears as a second Row field to the right of the Country/Region field.

4. Drag and drop the Order Date By Month field so that it appears as a Column field.

5. Drag and drop the Total field so that it appears as a Detail field. The resulting pivot table appears as shown in Figure 5.68.

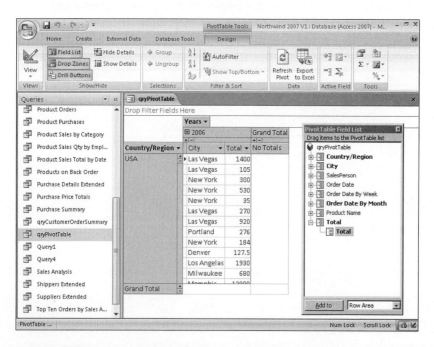

FIGURE 5.68   The pivot table that appears after dragging and dropping the Total field so that it appears as a Detail field.

Displaying Summarized Data

Including all the detail data might be much more detail than you need. You can alter the query design to show only summary information. Here's how this procedure works:

1. Switch to Design view.

2. Select the Data tab of the property sheet.

3. Click the Build button for the Record Source property. This places you in Design view of the query underlying the form.

4. Click the Totals tool on the ribbon.

5. Group by all fields except the data field and any fields that you are using for a filter.

6. Change the Total cell for any fields you are filtering by to Where.

7. Change the Total cell for the data field to sum. The resulting query appears as shown in Figure 5.69.

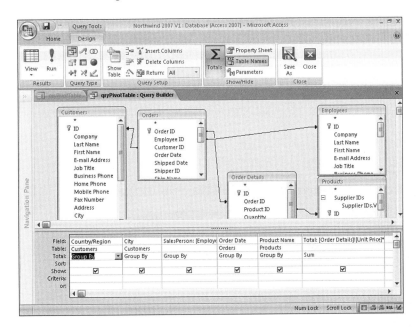

FIGURE 5.69   The query that appears after changing the Total cell for the data field to sum.

8. Run the query to verify the design (see Figure 5.70).

9. Return to PivotTable view.

10. To add grand totals, click the Total button to select it, select the AutoCalc drop-down from the Tools group, and then select Sum.

11. With the columns still selected, right-click and select Hide Details.

12. Observe the summarized data (see Figure 5.71).

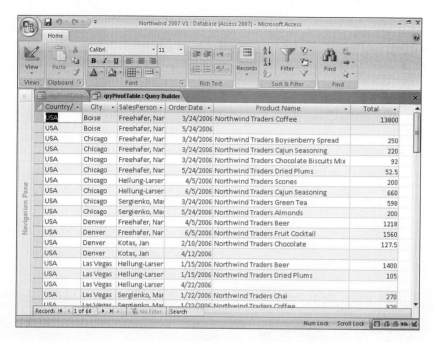

FIGURE 5.70   The underlying query after modifying it to summarize the data.

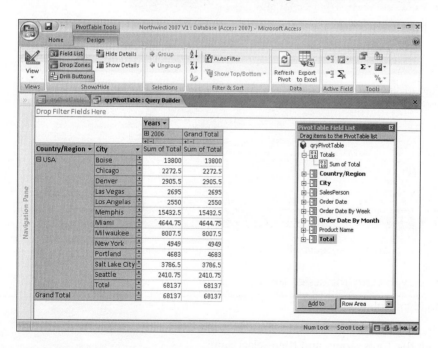

FIGURE 5.71   PivotTable view after modifying the underlying query to summarize the data.

Filtering Pivot Table Data

By default, Access includes all data in the pivot table. You can filter the pivot table to display only selected values for a row or column. For example, you can filter to display data for only sales in specific countries. Here's how this procedure works:

1. Make sure that you have expanded the PivotTable display to include the detail for the data on which you want to filter. (See the following section on using drill-down.)

2. Click the arrow of the field button to filter. The list contains an item for each field value (see Figure 5.72).

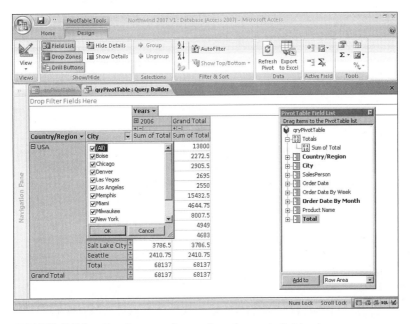

FIGURE 5.72   The list contains an item for each field value.

3. Click the (All) check box to deselect all fields.

4. Click to select the field values that you want to include in the output.

5. Click OK to close the list and apply the filter.

Using Drill-Down

Generally, the initial pivot table contains an excessive amount of detail. Here's how you can modify the amount of detail to show summary information only:

1. Switch to Design view.

2. Click the Totals button in the Show/Hide group to eliminate the data grouping.

3. Return to PivotTable view. The Total or Details Fields drop zone is empty because you changed the structure of the query.

4. Click the Field List button to display the PivotTable Field List.

5. Expand the Total item.

6. Right-click the Sum of Total item and select Remove, which clears the data from the cells.

7. Drag the Years button outside the window to remove the columns for the years, leaving an empty No Totals column.

8. Click Show Details in the Show/Hide group and then drag the No Totals column outside the window. At this point, the Column Fields and Totals or Detail Fields drop zones are empty.

9. Drag the Total column to the Columns drop zone.

10. Click the Show Details button and then the Hide Details button. You will see the data expand and collapse.

Exchanging Axes

If you are viewing Year across the top and Country down the side, and you decide to view Year across the side and Country across the top, simply drag and drop their name buttons to switch the positions in which they appear. You can also easily drag new items to the pivot table from the PivotTable list at any time or remove them from the pivot table entirely.

Switching to PivotChart View

When you define a PivotTable view, you automatically generate a PivotChart view. You will see how evident this is by using the View tool to switch to PivotChart view. You can use ribbon buttons to add legends and modify the chart type.

Examining Form Specifications and Limitations

Forms have a number of specifications and limitations that you should be aware of. Fortunately, you will generally not find them too restricting. They are listed in Table 5.2.

TABLE 5.2   Form Specifications and Limitations

Item	Limitation
Number of characters in a label	2,028
Number of characters in a text box	65,535
Form width	22 in.
Section height	22 in.
Height of all sections plus section headers	200 in.
Number of nested forms	7
Number of controls and sections you can add	754
Number of characters in the SQL statement that serves as the RowSource	32,750

Practical Examples: Designing Forms for Your Application

Several forms are required by the hypothetical time and billing application. I recommend that you build them yourself. They are somewhat complex. If you prefer, you can review the completed forms in CHAP5.ACCDB, rather than build them yourself. They are called frmClients and frmProjects.

Designing the Clients Form

Here are the steps involved in creating the Clients form:

1. Click to select the Create tab and then click Form Design.

2. Activate the Data tab of the property sheet. Select the Record Source property and select tblClients as the Record Source. Although you will modify this form later in the book to be based on a query, for now it is based directly on the tblClients table.

3. Click to select the Add Existing Fields tool in the Tools group on the Design tab.

4. Select the CompanyName, ContactFirstName, ContactLastName, ContactTitle, ReferredBy, AssociatedWith, DefaultRate, Miles, and HomePage fields from the field list. Drag and drop them to the form so that they appear as shown in Figure 5.73.

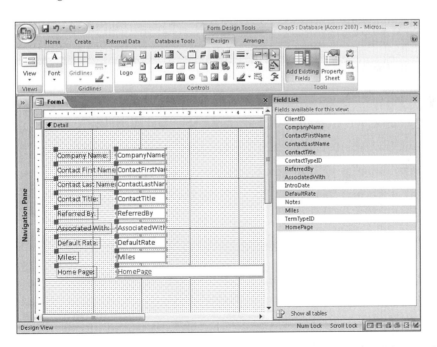

FIGURE 5.73   The frmClients form allows you to select and work with a particular client.

The next step is to add a combo box that allows the user to select the appropriate contact type for the client. The easiest way to accomplish the task is to use the Control Wizards:

1. Make sure that the Control Wizards tool is selected.

2. Click to select a combo box from the Controls group. Then click and drag to add the combo box to the appropriate location in the detail section of the form. The Combo Box Wizard launches.

3. Select I Want the Combo Box to Look Up the Values in a Table or Query. Click Next.

4. Select the `tblContactType` table from the list of available tables and click Next.

5. Select both the `ContactTypeID` and the `ContactType` fields and click Next.

6. Indicate that you want to sort by `ContactType`. Click Next.

7. Leave the Key column hidden, and size the `ContactType` column, if desired. Click Next.

8. Select Store That Value in This Field. Select `ContactTypeID` from the combo box and click Next.

9. Enter **Contact Type** as the text to appear within the label and click Finish.

You can add another combo box to the form, allowing the user to designate the terms for the client, with the following steps:

1. Make sure that the Control Wizards tool is selected.

2. Click to select a combo box from the Controls group on the Design tab of the ribbon; then click and drag to add it to the appropriate location in the detail section of the form. The Combo Box Wizard launches.

3. Select I Want the Combo Box to Look Up the Values in a Table or Query. Click Next.

4. Select the `tblTerms` table from the list of available tables and click Next.

5. Select both the `TermTypeID` and the `TermType` fields and click Next.

8. Indicate that you want to sort the records by `TermType` and click Next.

9. Hide the key column and click Next.

10. Store the value in the `TermTypeID` field and click Next.

11. Enter **Term Type** as the text to appear within the label and click Finish.

Take the following steps to refine the look and feel of the form:

1. Use the appropriate tools to size and align the objects to appear as shown in Figure 5.74.

2. Rename the objects per the naming conventions found in Appendix A (`txt` for text boxes, `cbo` for combo boxes, and so on).

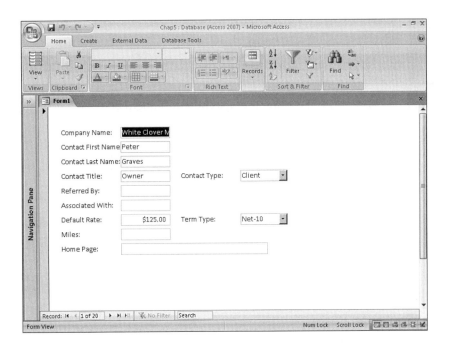

FIGURE 5.74   The objects should appear as shown here.

3. Set the Dividing Line, Navigation Buttons, and Record Selector properties of the form to No. Set the Auto Center property to Yes.

4. Select Tab Order from the Controls Layout group on the Arrange tab and set the tab order of the controls as appropriate.

5. Set the Caption property of the form to Client Data Entry.

6. Because the txtClientID is bound to an AutoNumber field, it is best to set its Locked property to Yes, its Tab Stop property to No, and its Back Color property to the same color as the background of the form.

You have now built the foundation for the form.

The next step is to add a combo box to the form that allows the user to select the client whose data she wants to view:

1. Select Form Header/Footer from the Show/Hide group on the Arrange tab.

2. Expand the header to make it large enough to hold the combo box and a command button that navigates to the frmProjects form.

3. Make sure that the Control Wizards tool is selected.

4. Click to select a combo box from the Controls group on the Design tab; then click and drag to add it to the header section of the form. The Combo Box Wizard launches.

5. Select Find a Record on My Form Based on a Value I Selected in My Combo Box. Click Next.

6. Select the `ClientID`, `CompanyName`, `ContactFirstName`, and `ContactLastName` fields as the Selected fields and click Next.

7. Size the columns as appropriate (keeping the Key column hidden) and click Next.

8. Type **Select a Company** as the text for the label and click Finish.

9. Click the Data tab of the property sheet. Select the `Row Source` property and click the ellipsis to launch the Query Builder.

10. Change the Sort Order to sort the combo box entries by `CompanyName`, `ContactFirstName`, and `ContactLastName`.

11. Close the Query Builder window and choose Yes, you want to save changes made to the SQL statement and update the property.

12. Run the form and make sure that the combo box functions properly.

Designing the Projects Form

The next step is to design the Projects form, which is pictured in Figure 5.75. The form is easily created with the Form Wizard and then customized.

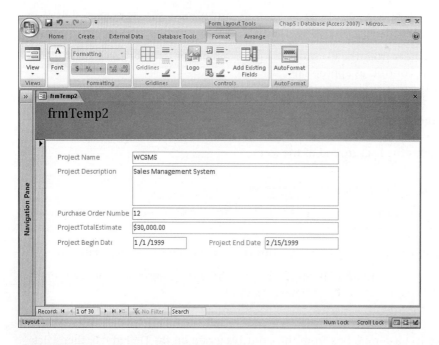

FIGURE 5.75   The `frmClients` form allows you to select and work with projects associated with a particular client.

Here are the steps involved in designing the Projects form:

1. Select the Create tab.

2. Select Form Wizard from the More Forms drop-down.

3. Select `tblProjects` from the Tables/Queries drop-down. This record source is modified in Chapter 10.

4. Click to select all fields and click Next.

5. Select Columnar from the list of layouts and click Next.

6. Select a style of your choice and click Next.

7. Title the form **frmProjects** and click Finish.

8. Switch to the Form Design view. Delete the `ProjectID` and `EmployeeID` text boxes and the `ClientID` combo box. Move and size the form objects so that the form appears as shown in Figure 5.75.

A combo box must be added for the `EmployeeID`:

1. Make sure that the Control Wizards tool is selected.

2. Click to select a combo box from the Controls tab of the Design tab on the ribbon; then click and drag to add it to the appropriate location in the detail section of the form. The Combo Box Wizard launches.

3. Select I Want the Combo Box to Look Up the Values in a Table or Query. Click Next.

4. Select the `tblEmployees` table from the list of available tables and click Next.

5. Select the `EmployeeID`, `LastName`, and `FirstName` fields and click Next.

6. Indicate that you want the data sorted by Last Name and then First Name and click Next.

7. Leave the Key column hidden, and size the `LastName` and `FirstName` columns, if desired. Click Next.

8. Select Store That Value in This Field. Select `EmployeeID` from the combo box and click Next.

9. Enter **Employee** as the text to appear within the label and click Finish.

Take the following steps to refine the look and feel of the form:

1. Rename the objects per the naming conventions found in Appendix A (`txt` for text boxes, `cbo` for combo boxes, and so on). Appendix A is available for download at www.samspublishing.com.

2. Set the `Dividing Line` and `Record Selector` properties of the form to `No`.

3. Select Tab Order from the Controls Layout group on the Arrange tab of the ribbon and set the tab order of the controls as appropriate.

4. Set the `Caption` property of the form to `Project Information`.

Adding a Command Button That Links the Clients and Projects Forms

The final step is to tie the Clients form to the Projects form. The Command Wizard will help to accomplish the task:

1. Return to the `frmClients` form in Design view.

2. Make sure the Control Wizards toolbar button is active.

3. Click to select a command button and then click and drag to place it within the Header section of the `frmClients` form. The Command Button Wizard launches.

4. Click Form Operations within the list of categories.

5. Click Open Form within the list of Actions and click Next.

6. Select `frmProjects` as the name of the form you would like the command button to open. Click Next.

7. Click Open Form and Find Specific Data to Display. Click Next.

8. Click to select the `ClientID` field from the `frmClients` form and the `ClientID` field from the `frmProjects` form. Click the <-> button to designate that the fields are joined. Click Next to continue.

9. Select a picture or enter text for the caption of the command button.

10. Enter the name for the command button. Don't forget to use proper naming conventions (for example, **cmdShowProjects**). Click Finish.

11. Switch from Design view to Form view and test the command button. The `frmProjects` form should load, displaying projects for the currently selected client.

Summary

Microsoft Access gives you rich, powerful tools you can use to build even the most sophisticated form. This chapter featured an overview of what Access forms are capable of and explained the many options you have for creating a new form.

Regardless of how a form has been created, you need to know how to modify all the attributes of a form and its controls. This chapter showed you how to work with form objects, modifying both their appearance and how they're tied to data. Control types and their properties were discussed in detail, and all the properties of the form itself were covered. Using the techniques in this chapter, you can control both the appearance and functionality of a form and its objects.

CHAPTER 6

What Every Developer Needs to Know About Reports

Why This Chapter Is Important

Although forms provide an excellent means for data entry, reports are the primary output device in Access. You can preview reports on the screen, output them to a printer, display them in a browser, and more! Reports are relatively easy to create and are extremely powerful. This chapter covers the basics of creating and working with reports. After reading this chapter, you'll be familiar with the types of reports available. You'll learn how to build reports with and without a wizard and how to manipulate the reports that you build. You will understand the report and control properties available and when it is appropriate to use each. You'll also be familiar with many important report techniques.

Examining Types of Reports Available

The reporting engine of Microsoft Access is very powerful, with a wealth of features. Many types of reports are available in Access 2007:

▶ Detail reports

▶ Summary reports

▶ Cross-tabulation reports

▶ Reports containing graphics and charts

▶ Reports containing forms

▶ Reports containing labels

▶ Reports including any combination of the preceding

Detail Reports

A Detail report supplies an entry for each record included in the report. As you can see in Figure 6.1, there's an entry for each order in the Customers table. The report's detail is grouped by the first character of the customer's last name.

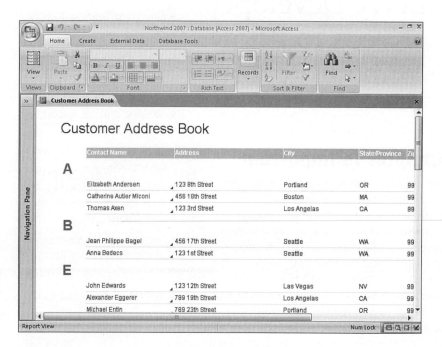

FIGURE 6.1   An example of a Detail report.

Summary Reports

A Summary report gives you summary data for all the records included in the report. In Figure 6.2, only total sales by product for the month of June are displayed in the report. The underlying detail records that compose the summary data aren't displayed in the report. The report itself contains only programmatically calculated controls in its Detail section. The remainder of the controls are placed in report Group Headers and Footers that are grouped on the month and year of the order. Because only programmatically calculated controls are found in the report's Detail section, Access prints summary information only.

Cross-Tabulation Reports

Cross-tabulation reports display summarized data grouped by one set of information on the left side of the report and another set across the top. The report shown in Figure 6.3 shows total sales by product name and employee. The report is based on a crosstab query and is generated using a fair amount of Visual Basic for Applications (VBA) code. This code is required because each time the report is run, a different number of employees might need to be displayed in the report's columns. In other words, the number of columns needed might be different each time the user runs the report. This report and the techniques needed to produce it are covered in Chapter 11, "Advanced Report Techniques."

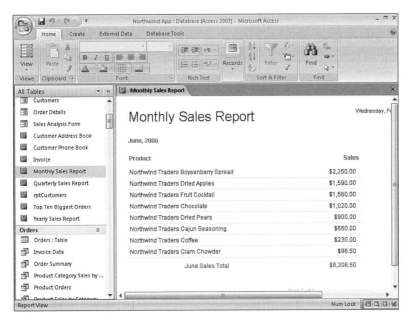

FIGURE 6.2   An example of a Summary report.

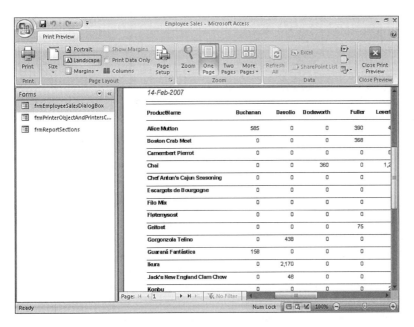

FIGURE 6.3   An example of a cross-tabulation report.

NOTE

You can find this report in the Chap11EX.accdb sample databases, covered in Chapter 11.

Reports with Graphics and Charts

Although the statement "A picture paints a thousand words" is a cliché, it's also quite true; research proves that you retain data much better when it's displayed as pictures rather than numbers. Fortunately, Access makes including graphics and charts in your reports quite easy. As you can see in Figure 6.4, you can design a report that contains one or more charts. The report in Figure 6.4 shows the sales by product for the month. The main report is grouped by order date and product category. The chart totals product sales by product category, displaying the information graphically.

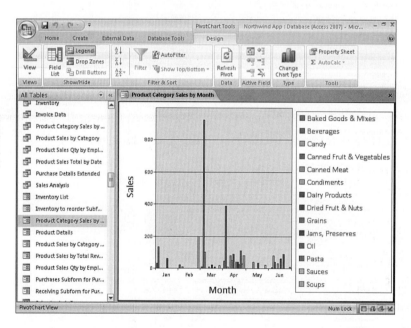

FIGURE 6.4   An example of a report with a chart.

Reports with Forms

Users often need a report that looks like a printed form. The Access Report Builder, with its many graphical tools, allows you to quickly produce reports that emulate the most elegant data entry form. The report shown in Figure 6.5 produces an invoice for a customer. The report is based on a query that draws information from the Customers, Orders, Order Details, Products, Employees Extended, and Shippers tables. The report's Filter property is filled in, limiting the data that appears on the report to a particular order in the Orders table. Using graphics, color, fonts, shading, and other special effects gives the report a professional look.

Reports with Labels

Creating mailing labels in Access 2007 is easy using the Label Wizard. Mailing labels are simply a special type of report with a page setup indicating the number of labels across the page and the size of each label. An example of a mailing label report created by using the Label Wizard is shown in Figure 6.6. This report is based on the Customers table but could have just as easily been based on a query that limits the mailing labels produced.

FIGURE 6.5   An example of a report containing a form.

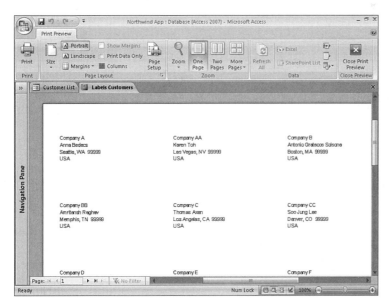

FIGURE 6.6   An example of a report containing mailing labels.

Understanding the Anatomy of a Report

Reports can have many parts. These parts are referred to as *sections* of the report. A new report is automatically made up of the following three sections, shown in Figure 6.7:

▶ Page Header section

▶ Detail section

▶ Page Footer section

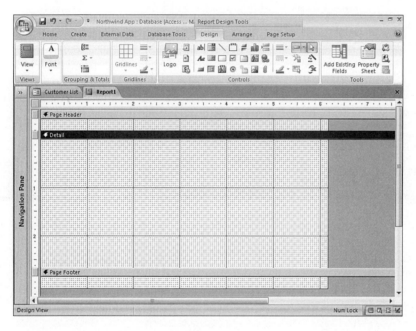

FIGURE 6.7   Sections of a report.

The Detail section is the main section of the report; it's used to display the detailed data of the table or query underlying the report. Certain reports, such as Summary reports, have nothing in the Detail section. Instead, Summary reports contain data in Group Headers and Footers (discussed at the end of this section).

The Page Header is the portion that automatically prints at the top of every page of the report. It often includes information such as the report's title. The Page Footer automatically prints at the bottom of every page of the report and usually contains information such as the page number and date. Each report can have only one Page Header and one Page Footer.

In addition to the three sections automatically added to every report, a report can have the following sections:

▶ Report Header

▶ Report Footer

- ▶ Group Headers
- ▶ Group Footers

A Report Header is a section that prints once, at the beginning of the report; the Report Footer prints once, at the end of the report. Each Access report can have only one Report Header and one Report Footer. You will often use the Report Header to create a cover sheet for the report. It can include graphics or other fancy effects, adding a professional look to a report. The most common use of the Report Footer is for grand totals, but it can also include any other summary information for the report.

In addition to Report and Page Headers and Footers, an Access report can have up to 10 Group Headers and Footers. Report groupings separate data logically and physically. The Group Header prints before the detail for the group, and the Group Footer prints after the detail for the group. For example, you can group customer sales by country and city, printing the name of the country or city for each related group of records. If you total the sales for each country and city, you can place the country and city names in the country and city Group Headers and the totals in the country and city Group Footers.

Creating a New Report

You can create a new report in several ways; the most common is to select the Create tab and then click Report Wizard from the Reports group. You can create reports from scratch by using Design view; you can also create them with Quick Create. Access also sports a Label Wizard, which helps quite a bit when you need to print labels. The Report Wizards are so powerful that I use one of them to build the initial foundation for almost every report I create.

Creating a Report with the Report Wizard

To create a report with the Report Wizard, click to select the Create tab. Next, select Report Wizard from the Reports group. This launches the Report Wizard. The first step is to select the table or query that will supply data to the report. I prefer to base my reports on queries or on embedded Structured Query Language (SQL) statements (a query stored as part of a report). This approach generally improves performance because it returns as small a dataset as possible. In a client/server environment, this is particularly pronounced because the query is usually run on the server, and only the results are sent over the network wire. Basing reports on queries also enhances your ability to produce reports based on varying criteria.

After you have selected a table or query, you can select the fields you want to include in the report. The fields included in the selected table or query are displayed in the list box on the left. To add fields to the report, double-click the name of the field you want to add or click the field name and click the > button. In the example in Figure 6.8, five fields have been selected from the tblClients table.

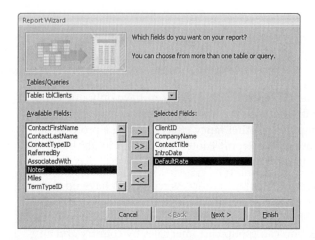

FIGURE 6.8   The first step of the Report Wizard: table/field selection.

After you have selected a table or query and the fields you want to include on the report, click Next. The wizard prompts you to add group levels, which add report groupings, to the report. Add group levels if you need to visually separate groups of data or include summary calculations (subtotals) in your report. Report groupings are covered later in this chapter. If your report doesn't require groupings, click Next.

In the third step of the Report Wizard, you choose sorting levels for your report. Because the order of a query underlying a report is overridden by any sort order designated in the report, it's a good idea to designate a sort order for the report. You can add up to four sorting levels with the wizard. In the example shown in Figure 6.9, the report is sorted by the ClientID field. After you select the fields you want to sort on and whether you wish to sort in ascending or descending order, click Next.

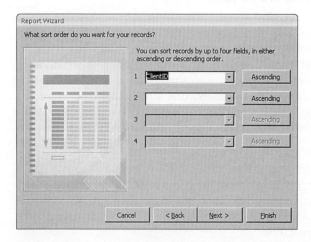

FIGURE 6.9   The third step of the Report Wizard: sorting report data.

In the fourth step of the Report Wizard, you decide on the report's layout and orientation. The layout options vary depending on what selections you made in the wizard's previous steps. The orientation can be Portrait or Landscape. This step of the Report Wizard also allows you to specify whether you want Access to adjust the width of each field so that all the fields fit on each page. After you supply Access with this information, click Next.

You choose a style for your report in the Report Wizard's fifth step. There are quite a few choices available. You can preview each look before you make a decision. Any of the style attributes applied by the Report Wizard, as well as other report attributes defined by the wizard, can be modified in Report Design view any time after the wizard has produced the report. After you have selected a style, click Next.

The final step of the Report Wizard prompts you for the report's title. Access uses this title as both the name and the caption for the report. I supply a standard Access report name and modify the caption after the Report Wizard has finished its process. You're then given the opportunity to preview the report or modify the report's design. If you opt to modify the report's design, you're placed in Design view (see Figure 6.10). You can then preview the report at any time. You can optionally mark the check box Display Help on Working with the Report to have Access display the help window and list the associated report topics.

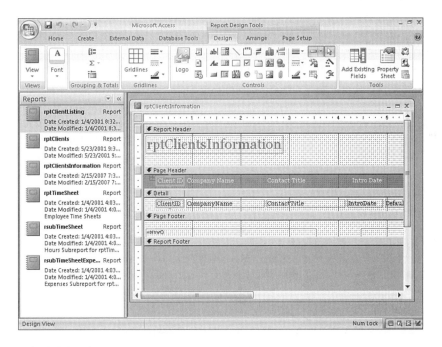

FIGURE 6.10   Design view of a completed report.

Creating a Report from Design View

Although you usually start most of your reports by using a Report Wizard, you should understand how to create a new report from Design view. To create a report without using a wizard, click the Report Design button in the Reports group of the Create tab. The Report Design window appears. You must then set the Record Source of the report to the table or query upon which you want the report to be based.

Working with the Report Design Window

You use the Report Design window to build and modify a report. Using this window, you can add objects to a report and modify their properties. Microsoft provides numerous Report, Report Grouping, and Control properties. By modifying these properties, you can create reports with diverse looks and functionality.

Understanding the Report Design Tools

To help you design reports, several report design tools are available, including the Ribbon, Property Sheet, Field List, and Sorting and Grouping windows. Three tabs are also available to make developing and customizing your reports easier: Design, Arrange, and Page Setup. The Design tab contains tools that allow you to group and total your report, add controls to your report, add existing fields to the report, and view and modify the property sheet associated with the report. The Arrange tab is specifically designed to help you customize the look of your report. It includes tools for applying an AutoFormat to a report, aligning and positioning control on the report, and sizing report objects.

The Properties, Toolbox, Field List, and Sorting and Grouping windows are all designed as toggles. This means that buttons on the Report Design toolbar alternately hide and show these valuable windows. If you have a high-resolution monitor (or multiple monitors), you might want to leave the windows open at all times. If you have a low-resolution monitor, you need to get a feel for when it's most effective for each window to be opened or closed.

Adding Fields to the Report

You can most easily add fields to a report by using the Field List window. With the Field List window open (see Figure 6.11), click and drag a field from the field list onto the appropriate section of the report. You can add several fields at one time, just as you can do with forms. Use the Ctrl key to select noncontiguous fields, use the Shift key to select contiguous fields, or double-click the field list's title bar to select all the fields; then click and drag them to the report as a unit.

CAUTION

One problem with adding fields to a report is that both the fields and the attached labels are placed in the same section of the report. This means that, if you click and drag fields from the Field List window to the Detail section of the report, both the fields and the attached labels appear in the Detail section. If you're creating a tabular report, this isn't acceptable, so you must cut the attached labels and paste them into the report's Page Header section.

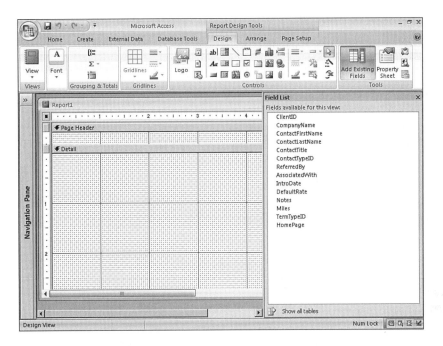

FIGURE 6.11   Design view of a completed report.

Selecting, Moving, Aligning, and Sizing Report Objects

Microsoft Access offers several techniques to help you select, move, align, and size report objects. Different techniques are effective in different situations. Experience will tell you which technique you should use and when. The steps for selecting, moving, aligning, and sizing report objects are quite similar to performing the same tasks with form objects. The techniques are covered briefly in this chapter; for a more detailed explanation of each technique, refer to Chapter 5, "What Every Developer Needs to Know About Forms."

Selecting Report Objects

To select a single report object, click it; selection handles appear around the selected object. After you select the object, you can modify any of its attributes (properties), or you can size, move, or align it.

To select multiple objects so that you can manipulate them as a unit, use one of the following techniques:

- Hold down the Shift key as you click multiple objects. Each object you click is then added to the selection.

- Place your mouse pointer in a blank area of the report. Click and drag to lasso the objects you want to select. When you let go of the mouse, any object even partially within the lasso is selected.

► Click and drag within the horizontal or vertical ruler. As you click and drag, lines appear indicating the potential selection area. When you release the mouse, all objects within the lines are selected.

Make sure you understand which objects are actually selected; attached labels can cause some confusion. Figure 6.12 shows a report with four objects selected: the Client ID and Intro Date labels and the CompanyName and DefaultRate text boxes. The Company Name and Default Rate labels and the ClientID and IntroDate text boxes are *not* selected. If you were to modify the properties of the selected objects, those controls would be unaffected.

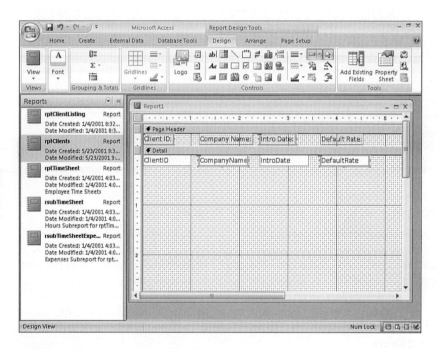

FIGURE 6.12   Selecting objects in an Access report.

Moving Objects Around

If you want to move a single control along with its attached label, click the object and drag it to a new location. The object and the attached label move as a unit. To move multiple objects, use one of the methods explained in the preceding section to select the objects you want to move. After you select the objects, click and drag any of them; the selected objects and their attached labels move as a unit.

Moving an object without its attached label is a trickier process. When placed over the center or border of a selected object (not on a sizing handle), the mouse pointer looks like a hand with all five fingers pointing upward. This indicates that the selected object and its attached label move as a unit, maintaining their relationship to one another. However, if you place your mouse pointer directly over the selection handle in the object's upper-left corner, the mouse pointer looks like a cross-bar. This indicates that the object and the attached label move independently of one another so that you can alter the distance between them.

Aligning Objects with One Another

To align objects with one another, you must select them first. Click the Arrange tab. Then select the appropriate button in the Control Alignment group. The selected objects will align in relation to each other.

> **CAUTION**
>
> Watch out for a few "gotchas" when you're aligning report objects: If you select several text boxes and their attached labels and align them, Access tries to align the left sides of the text boxes with the left sides of the labels. To avoid this problem, you have to align the text boxes separately from their attached labels.
>
> During the alignment process, Access never overlaps objects. For this reason, if the objects you're aligning don't fit, Access can't align them. For example, if you try to align the bottom of several objects horizontally and they don't fit across the report, Access aligns only the objects that fit on the line.

Using Snap to Grid

The Snap to Grid feature is a toggle found on the Arrange tab. When you select Snap to Grid, all objects that you're moving or sizing snap to the report's gridlines. To temporarily disable the Snap to Grid feature, hold down your Ctrl key while sizing or moving an object.

Using Power-Sizing Techniques

Access offers many techniques to help you size report objects. A selected object has eight sizing handles, and you can use all of them, except for the upper-left handle, to size the object. Using the upper-left handle moves the object independently of an object it is attached to (that is, it moves an attached label independently of the text box it is attached to). Simply click and drag one of the sizing handles. If you select multiple objects, Access sizes them by the same amount.

The tools found in the Size group on the Arrange tab can also help you size objects. The Size group has six options: To Fit, To Grid, To Tallest, To Shortest, To Widest, and To Narrowest. These options are discussed in detail in Chapter 5.

> **TIP**
>
> Access offers a great trick that can help size labels to fit. Simply double-click any sizing handle, and the object is automatically sized to fit the text within it.

Controlling Object Spacing

Access also makes it easy for you to control object spacing. You can make both the horizontal and vertical distances between selected objects equal. Select the objects, click to select the Arrange tab, and then use the appropriate tool in the Position group to achieve the desired effect. You can also maintain the relative relationship between selected objects while increasing or decreasing the space between them. Once again, to do this, use the appropriate tool in the Position group.

Selecting the Correct Control for the Job

Reports usually contain labels, text boxes, lines, rectangles, image controls, and bound and unbound object frames. You use the other controls for reports that emulate data entry forms. The different controls you can place on a report, as well as their uses, are discussed briefly in the following sections.

Labels

You use labels to display information to your users. They're commonly used as report headings, column headings, or group headings for your report. Although you can modify the text they display at runtime by using VBA code, you can't directly bind them to data.

To add a label to a report, select the Label tool on the ribbon; then click and drag to place the label on the report.

Text Boxes

You use text boxes to display field information or the result of an expression. Text boxes are used throughout a report's different sections. For example, in a Page Header, a text box might contain an expression showing the date range that's the criterion for the report. In a Group Header, a text box might be used to display a heading for the group. The possibilities are endless because a text box can hold any valid expression.

To add a text box to a report, select the Text Box tool from the ribbon. Click and drag the text box to place it on the report. You can also add a text box to a report by dragging a field from the field list to a report. This works as long as the field's Display control property is a text box.

Lines

You can use lines to visually separate objects on your report. For example, you can place a line at the bottom of a section or underneath a subtotal. To add a line to a report, click the Line tool to select it; then click and drag to place the line on your report. When added, the line has several properties that you can modify to customize its look.

TIP

To make sure that the line you draw is perfectly straight, hold down the Shift key while you click and drag to draw the line.

Rectangles

You can use rectangles to visually group items that logically belong together on the report. You can also use them to make certain controls on your report stand out. I often draw rectangles around important subtotal or grand total information that I want to make sure that the report's reader notices.

To add a rectangle to a report, select the Rectangle tool from the ribbon; then click and drag to place the rectangle on the report.

> **CAUTION**
>
> The rectangle might obscure objects that have already been added to the report. To rectify this problem, you can set the rectangle's Back Style property to Transparent. This setting is fine unless you want the rectangle to have a background color. If so, choose Send to Back on the Arrange tab to layer the objects so that the rectangle lies behind the other objects on the report.

Bound Object Frames

Bound object frames let you display the data in object linking and embedding (OLE) fields, which contain objects from other applications, such as pictures, spreadsheets, and word processing documents.

To add a bound object frame to a report, click the Bound Object Frame tool in the Ribbon; then click and drag the frame onto the report. Set the Control Source property of the frame to the appropriate field. You can also add a bound object frame to a report by dragging and dropping an OLE field from the field list onto the report.

Unbound Object Frames

You can use unbound object frames to add logos and other pictures to a report. Unlike bound object frames, however, they aren't tied to underlying data.

To add an unbound object frame to a report, click the Unbound Object Frame tool in the Controls group on the Design tab of the ribbon. Click and drag the object frame to place it on the report. This opens the Insert Object dialog box, shown in Figure 6.13, which you use to create a new OLE object or insert an existing OLE object from a file on disk. If you click Create from File, the Insert Object dialog box changes to look like Figure 6.14. Click Browse and locate the file you want to include in the report. The Insert Object dialog box gives you the option of linking to or embedding an OLE object. If you select Link, a reference is created to the OLE object. Only the bitmap of the object is stored in the report, and the report continues to refer to the original file on disk. If you don't select Link, the object you select is copied and embedded in the report and becomes part of the Access ACCDB file; no link to the original object is maintained.

Using an image control rather than an unbound object frame is usually preferable for static information like a logo because the image control requires fewer resources than an unbound object frame does. Image controls are covered in the next section.

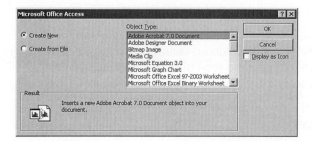

FIGURE 6.13   Use the Insert Object dialog box to insert a new or existing object into an unbound object frame.

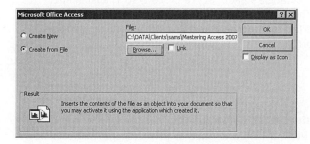

FIGURE 6.14   The Insert Object dialog box with Create from File selected.

Image Controls

Image controls are your best option for displaying static images, such as logos, on a report (see Figure 6.15). You can modify an unbound object after it is placed on a report, but you can't open the object application and modify an image when it's placed on a report. This limitation, however, means far fewer resources are needed, so performance improves noticeably.

Other Controls

As mentioned in a previous section, it's standard to include mostly labels and text boxes on your reports, but you can add other controls when appropriate. To add any other type of control, click to select the control; then click and drag to place it on the report.

What Report Properties Are Available, and Why Should You Use Them?

Reports have many different properties that you can modify to change how the report looks and performs. Like Form properties, Report properties are divided into categories: Format, Data, Event, and Other. To view a report's properties, first select the report, rather than a section of the report, in one of two ways:

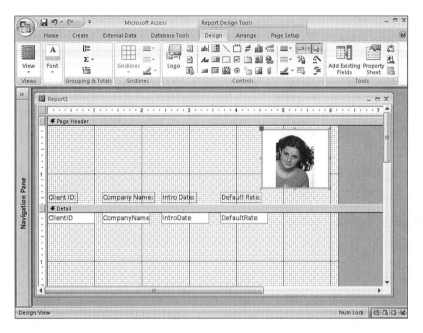

FIGURE 6.15   A report with an image control.

► Click the Report Selector, which is the small gray button at the intersection of the horizontal and vertical rulers.

► Select Report from the drop-down in the property sheet.

After you have selected a report, you can view and modify its properties.

Working with the Property Sheet

When you select the report, the property sheet shows all the properties associated with the report. To select the report and open the property sheet at the same time, double-click the Report Selector. A report has numerous properties available on the property sheet (additional properties are available only from code) broken down into the appropriate categories in the property sheet. Forty of the properties relate to the report's format, data, and other special properties; the remaining properties relate to the events that occur when a report is run. The format, data, and other properties are covered here, and the event properties are covered in Chapter 11.

The Report's Format Properties

A report has the following Format properties for changing the report's physical appearance:

► Caption—The Caption property of the report is the text that appears in the Report window's title bar when the user is previewing the report. You can modify it at runtime to customize it for a particular situation.

▶ Default View—The `Default View` property of the report determines whether a report automatically opens in Report view or Print Preview.

▶ Allow Report View—The `Allow Report View` property of the report determines whether a user can switch to Report view. The `Allow Layout View` property of the report determines whether a user can switch to Layout view.

▶ Auto Resize—The `Auto Resize` property was introduced with Access 2002. This setting determines whether a report is resized automatically to display all the data on the report.

▶ Auto Center—The `Auto Center` property was introduced with Access 2002. You use the `Auto Center` property to designate whether you want the Report window to automatically be centered on the screen.

▶ Fit to Page—The `Fit to Page` property of the report determines whether the report will expand to fit a page.

▶ Page Header, Page Footer—The `Page Header` and `Page Footer` properties determine on what pages these sections appear. The options are `All Pages`, `Not with Rpt Hdr`, `Not with Rpt Ftr`, and `Not with Rpt Hdr/Ftr`. Because you might not want the Page Header or Page Footer to print on the Report Header or Report Footer pages, these properties give you control over where those sections print.

▶ Grp Keep Together—In Access, you can keep a group of data together on the same page by using the `Grp Keep Together` property. The `Per Page` option forces the group of data to remain on the same page, and the `Per Column` option forces the group of data to remain within a column. A *group of data* refers to all the data within a report grouping (for example, all the customers in a city).

▶ Border Style—The `Border Style` property was introduced with Access 2002 reports. Like its form counterpart, it is far more powerful than its name implies. The options for the `Border Style` property are `None`, `Thin`, `Sizable`, and `Dialog`. A border style set to `None` means the report has no border. A `Thin` border is not resizable; the Size command isn't available in the Control menu. This setting is a good choice for pop-up reports, which remain on top even when other forms or reports are given the focus. A `Sizable` border is standard for most reports. It includes all the standard options in the Control menu. A `Dialog` border looks like a `Thin` border. A report with a border style of `Dialog` can't be maximized, minimized, or resized. After the border style of a report is set to `Dialog`, the Maximize, Minimize, and Resize options aren't available in the report's Control menu.

▶ Control Box—The `Control Box` property was introduced with Access 2002 as well. This property lets you specify whether the Report window under print preview has the Control menu available. The Control menu, which you activate by clicking the icon in the upper-left corner of a window, displays options for manipulating the window—Restore, Move, Size, Minimize, Maximize, and Close.

▶ Min Max Buttons—The `Min Max Buttons` property was also introduced with Access 2002. This property lets you specify whether the Minimize and/or Maximize options should be available from the Control menu for the Report window in Print Preview mode. You can select from None, Min Enabled, Max Enabled, or Both Enabled.

▶ Close Button—The Close Button property was also introduced with Access 2002. This setting specifies whether to enable or disable the Close button on the Print Preview window.

▶ Width—The Width property specifies the width of the report sections.

▶ Picture, Picture Type, Picture Size Mode, Picture Alignment, Picture Tiling, and Picture Pages—The background of a report can be a picture. The Picture properties determine what picture is used as a background for the report and what attributes are applied to it.

▶ Show Page Margins—The Show Page Margins property determines whether the margins appear in Report view.

▶ Grid X/Grid Y—The Grid X and Grid Y properties determine the density of the gridlines in the Report Design window. The number shown is the number of sub-divisions per unit of measure.

▶ Layout for Print—The Layout for Print property specifies whether screen or printer fonts are used in the report. If you want to optimize reports for preview, select No; if you want to optimize reports for the printer, select Yes. This option is not as important if you select TrueType fonts because TrueType fonts usually print equally well to the screen and printer.

▶ Palette Source—The Palette Source property determines the source for the report's selectable color.

▶ Orientation—The Orientation property enables you to take advantage of language-specific versions of Microsoft Access, such as Arabic. You can set this property to support right-to-left display features for these language-specific editions of Access.

▶ Moveable—The Moveable property determines whether the user can move the Report window around the screen by clicking and dragging the report by its title bar.

The Report's Data Properties

A report has the following six Data properties used to supply information about the data underlying the report:

▶ Record Source—Specifies the table or query whose data underlies the report. You can modify the record source of a report at runtime. This aspect of the Record Source property makes it easy for you to create generic reports that use different record sources in different situations.

▶ Filter—Allows you to open the report with a specific filter set. I usually prefer to base a report on a query rather than apply a filter to it. At other times, it's more appropriate to base the report on a query but then apply and remove a filter as required, based on the report's runtime conditions.

▸ `Filter On Load`—Determines whether a report filter is applied. If the value of this property is set to `No`, the `Filter` property of the report is ignored.

▸ `Order By`—Determines how the records in a report are sorted when the report is opened.

▸ `Allow Filters`—Determines whether the user will be able to filter report data.

▸ `Order By On Load`—Determines whether the sort is applied when the report first loads.

The Other Report Properties

A report has 16 Other properties; these miscellaneous properties, explained here, allow you to control other important aspects of the report:

▸ `Record Locks`—Determines whether the tables used in producing the report are locked while the report is being run. The two values for this property are `No Locks` and `All Records`. `No Locks` is the default value; it means that no records in the tables underlying the report are locked while the report is being run. Users can modify the underlying data as the report is run, which can be disastrous when running sophisticated reports. Users can change the data in the report as the report is being run, which would make figures for totals and percent of totals invalid. Although the `All Records` option for this property locks all records in all tables included in the report (thereby preventing data entry while the report is being run), it might be a necessary evil for producing an accurate report.

▸ `Display on SharePoint Site`—Determines whether the report will appear on the SharePoint site.

▸ `Date Grouping`—Determines how grouping of dates occurs in your report. The `US Defaults` option means that Access uses United States' defaults for report groupings; therefore, Sunday is the first day of the week, the first week begins January 1, and so on. The `Use System Settings` option means that date groupings are based on the locale set in the Control Panel's Regional and Language Options rather than on U.S. defaults.

▸ `Pop Up`—Determines whether the report's print preview window opens as a pop-up window. Within Microsoft Access, pop-up windows always remain on top of other open windows.

▸ `Modal`—Instructs Access to open the Report window in a modal or modeless state. The default is `No`, meaning that the window will not be opened as modal. A modal window retains the application program's focus until the window receives the appropriate user input that it requires.

▸ `Menu Bar`—Allows you to associate a custom menu bar with the report that's visible when the user is previewing the report. Adding a custom menu to your report lets you control what the user can do while the report is active.

▶ Toolbar—Lets you associate a custom toolbar with the report that's visible when the user is previewing the report.

▶ Shortcut Menu Bar—Determines what shortcut menu is associated with the report while the report is being previewed. The shortcut menu bar appears when the user clicks the right mouse button over the Preview window.

▶ Ribbon Name—Designates the ribbon that appears when the report is the active object.

▶ Fast Laser Printing—Determines whether lines and rectangles are replaced with text character lines when you print a report with a laser printer. If fast printing is your objective and you're using a laser printer, you should set this property to Yes.

▶ Use Default Paper Size—Determines whether the report follows the default paper size.

▶ Cycle—Determines how the Tab key cycles. This feature is more applicable to forms than it is to reports.

▶ Help File, Help Context Id—Let you associate a help file and help topic with the report.

▶ Tag—Stores information defined by the user at either design time or runtime. The Tag property is Microsoft Access's way of giving you an extra property. Access makes no use of this property; if you don't take advantage of it, it will never be used.

▶ Has Module—Determines whether the report contains an associated class module. If no code will be included in the report, eliminating the class module can both improve performance and reduce the size of the application database. A report without a class module is considered a "lightweight object," which loads and displays faster than an object with an associated class module.

CAUTION

A couple of the Has Module property's behaviors deserve special attention. When a report is created, the default value for the Has Module property is No. Access automatically sets the Has Module property to Yes as soon as you try to view a report's module. If you set the Has Module property of an existing report to No, Access asks if you want to proceed. If you confirm the change, Access deletes the object's class module and all the code it contains!

What Control Properties Are Available, and Why Should You Use Them?

Just as reports have properties, so do controls. You can change most control properties at design time or at runtime, allowing you to easily build flexibility into your reports. For example, certain controls are visible only when specific conditions are true.

The Control's Format Properties

You can modify several formatting properties of the selected objects using the ribbon. If you prefer, you can set all the properties in the property sheet. The following are most of the Format properties of a report control:

▶ Format—Determines how the data in the control is displayed. This property is automatically inherited from the underlying field. If you want the control's format on the report to differ from the underlying field's format, you must set the Format property of the control.

▶ Caption—Specifies the text displayed for labels and command buttons. A caption is a string containing up to 2,048 characters.

▶ Hyperlink Address—Is a string representing the path to a UNC (network path) or URL (web page). The Hyperlink control, command buttons, image controls, and labels all contain the Hyperlink Address property.

▶ Hyperlink SubAddress—Is a string representing a location within the document specified in the Hyperlink Address property. The Hyperlink control, command buttons, image controls, and labels all contain the Hyperlink SubAddress property.

▶ Decimal Places—Defines the number of decimal places displayed for numeric values.

▶ Visible—Determines whether a control is visible. In many cases, you will want to toggle the visibility of a control in response to different situations.

▶ Hide Duplicates—Hides duplicate data values in a report's Detail section. Duplicate data values occur when one or more consecutive records in a report contain the same value in one or more fields.

▶ Can Grow, Can Shrink—Allows a control to expand vertically to accommodate all the data in it when the Can Grow property is set to Yes. The Can Shrink property eliminates blank lines when no data exists in a field for a particular record. For example, if you have a second address line on a mailing label, but there's no data in the Address2 field, you don't want a blank line to appear on the mailing label.

▶ Left, Top, Width, Height—Set the size and position of the controls on a report.

▶ Back Style, Back Color—Enables you to set the Back Style property to Normal or Transparent. When this property is set to Transparent, the color of the report shows through to the control. When it is set to Normal, the control's Back Color property determines the object's color.

▶ Special Effect—Adds 3D effects to a control.

▶ Border Style, Border Color, Border Width—Set the physical attributes of a control's border.

▶ Fore Color—Sets the color of the text within the control.

▶ Font Color, Font Name, Font Size, Font Weight, Font Italic, Font Underline—Affect the appearance of the text within the control, unlike the border properties, which affect the control's border.

▶ Text Align—Sets the alignment of the text within the control. It can be set to Left, Center, Right, or Distribute. When set to Distribute, text is justified.

▶ Reading Order—Determines the visual order in which characters, words, and groups of words are displayed. This property is often used with language-specific editions of Microsoft Access, where the reading order needs to be changed. The default setting is Context; Left-to-Right and Right-to-Left are the other available settings.

▶ Scroll Bar Align—Specifies the visual placement of the control's vertical scrollbars and buttons. This property also works in conjunction with language-specific versions of Access to determine scrollbar placement in either the right-to-left or left-to-right direction. The default setting is System, which lets the operating system determine the scrollbar alignment.

▶ Numeral Shapes—Determines the format for displaying numeric characters. This property also works in conjunction with language-specific versions of Access to determine the type of numeric character to display. The default setting is System, which lets the operating system determine the numeric character display format. The other settings include Arabic, National, and Context.

▶ Left Margin, Top Margin, Right Margin, Bottom Margin—Determine how far the text within the control prints from the left, top, right, and bottom of the control. These properties are particularly useful for large controls containing a lot of text, such as a memo or an invoice.

▶ Line Spacing—Controls the spacing between lines of text within a control. The Line Spacing property is designated in inches.

▶ Gridline Styles, Color, and Width—Determine the style of the top, bottom, left, and right gridline, as well as the gridline color and width.

▶ Top, Bottom, Left, and Right Padding—Determine the amount of space between the gridline and the text within the control.

▶ Is Hyperlink—Determines whether the text within the control is displayed as a hyperlink. If the Is Hyperlink property is set to Yes, and the text within the control is a relevant link, the text will serve as a hyperlink. (This property is useful only if you save the report in HTML format.)

▶ Display as Hyperlink—Determines whether the data in a text box displays on the screen only, always (regardless of whether it is a hyperlink), or only if it is a hyperlink.

The Control's Data Properties

The Data properties of a control specify information about the data underlying a particular report control.

▶ Control Source—Specifies the field in the report's record source that's used to populate the control. A control source can also be a valid expression.

▶ Input Mask—Assigns specific formatting to any data that is entered into a particular control. For example, you could use Input Mask !(999) 000-0000 to format the data entered as a phone number.

▶ Text Format—Determines whether Access stores your text as plain text or as rich text.

▶ Running Sum—Calculates a record-by-record or group-by-group total. The Running Sum property, which is unique to reports, is quite powerful. It can be set to No, Over Group, or Over All. When it is set to Over Group, the value of the text box accumulates from record to record within the group but is reset each time the group value changes. An example is a report that shows deposit amounts for each state with a running sum for the amount deposited within the state. Each time the state changes, the amount deposited is set to zero. When it is set to Over All, the sum continues to accumulate over the entire report.

The Other Control Properties

The Other properties of a control designate properties that don't fit into any other category, such as the following:

▶ Name—The Name property gives you an easy and self-documenting way to refer to the control in VBA code and in many other situations. You should name all your controls. Naming conventions for report controls are the same as those for form controls. Refer to Appendix A, "Naming Conventions," which is available for download at www.samspublishing.com, for more detailed information.

▶ Vertical—The Vertical property is used to determine whether the text within the control is displayed vertically. The default value for this property is No.

▶ Tag—Like the Tag property of a form, the Tag property of a control gives you a user-defined slot for the control. You can place any extra information in the Tag property.

CAUTION

A common mistake many developers make is giving controls names that conflict with Access names. This type of error is very difficult to track down. Make sure you use distinctive names for both fields and controls. Furthermore, don't give a control the same name as the name of a field within its expression. For example, the expression =ClientName & Title shouldn't have the name ClientName; that would cause an #error# message when the report is run. Finally, don't give a control the same name as its control source. Access gives bound controls the same name as their fields, so you need to change them to avoid problems. Following these simple warnings will spare you a lot of grief!

Inserting Page Breaks

Page breaks can be set to occur before, within, or at the end of a section. The way you set each type of page break is quite different. To set a page break within a section, you must use the Insert or Remove Page Break tool on the Design tab of the ribbon. After you click this tool, click the report where you want the page break to occur. To set a page break before or after a section, set the Force New Page property of the section to Before Section, After Section, or Before & After. The Force New Page property applies to Group Headers, Group Footers, and the report's Detail section.

> **CAUTION**
>
> Be careful not to place a page break within a control on the report. The page break will occur in the middle of the control's data.

Using Unbound, Bound, and Calculated Controls

You can place three types of controls on a report: Unbound, Bound, and Calculated. Unbound controls, such as logos placed on reports, aren't tied to data. Bound controls are tied to data within a field of the table or query underlying the report. Calculated controls contain valid expressions; they can hold anything from a page number to a sophisticated financial calculation. Most complex reports have a rich combination of Unbound, Bound, and Calculated controls.

Using Expressions to Enhance Your Reports

Calculated controls use expressions as their control sources. To create a Calculated control, you must first add an Unbound control to the report. You must precede expressions with an equal sign (=); an example of a report expression is =Sum([BillableHours]). This expression, if placed in the Report Footer, totals the contents of the BillableHours control for all detail records in the report. You can build an expression by typing it directly into the control source or by using the Expression Builder, covered in Chapter 5.

Building Reports Based on More Than One Table

The majority of reports you create will probably be based on data from more than one table. The reason is that a properly normalized database usually requires that you bring table data back together to give your users valuable information. For example, a report that combines data from a Customers table, an Orders table, an Order Details table, and a Product table can supply the following information:

▸ **Customer information**—Company name and address

▸ **Order information**—Order date and shipping method

▸ **Order detail information**—Quantity ordered and price

▸ **Product table**—Product description

You can base a multitable report directly on the tables whose data it displays or on a query that has already joined the tables, providing a flat table structure.

Creating One-to-Many Reports

You can create one-to-many reports by using a Report Wizard, or you can build reports from scratch. Different situations require different techniques, some of which are covered in the following sections.

Building a One-to-Many Report with the Report Wizard

Building a one-to-many report with the Report Wizard is quite easy; just follow these steps:

1. Click to select the Create tab and then select the Report Wizard tool in the Reports group. The Report Wizard launches.

2. Use the Tables/Queries drop-down list to select the first table or query whose data will appear on the report.

3. Select the fields you want to include from that table.

4. Select each additional table or query you want to include on the report, selecting the fields you need from each. Click Next.

5. Step 2 of the Report Wizard offers a suggested layout for your data (see Figure 6.16). You can accept Access's suggestion, or you can choose from any of the available layout options. After you choose a layout, click Next.

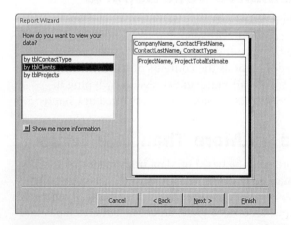

FIGURE 6.16   Step 2 of the Report Wizard: selecting a layout.

6. Step 3 of the Report Wizard asks whether you want to add any grouping levels. Grouping levels can be used to visually separate data and to provide subtotals. In the example in Figure 6.17, the report is grouped by ContactType. After you select grouping levels, click Next.

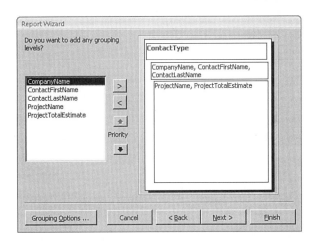

FIGURE 6.17   Step 3 of the Report Wizard: selecting groupings.

7. Step 4 of the Report Wizard lets you select how you want the records in the report's Detail section to be sorted (see Figure 6.18). This step of the wizard also allows you to specify any summary calculations you want to perform on the data (see Figure 6.19). Click the Summary Options button to specify the summary calculations. Using the button, you can even opt to include the percent of total calculations. Make your selection and click OK to close the Summary Options dialog.

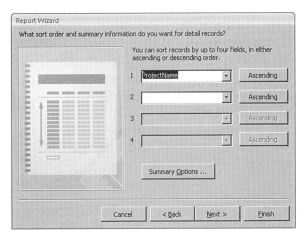

FIGURE 6.18   Step 4 of the Report Wizard: selecting a sort order.

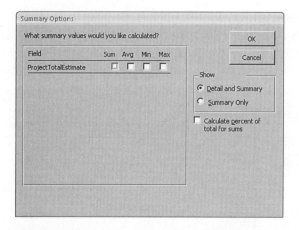

FIGURE 6.19   Adding summary calculations.

8. In step 5 of the Report Wizard, you select the layout and orientation of your report. Layout options include Stepped, Blocked, Outline 1, Outline 2, Align Left 1, and Align Left 2. Click Next to continue.

9. Step 6 of the Report Wizard lets you select from predefined styles for your report. You can preview each style to see what it looks like. Click Next to continue.

10. In step 7 of the Report Wizard, you select a title for your report. The title also becomes the name for the report. I like to select an appropriate name and change the title after the wizard is finished. The final step also allows you to determine whether you want to immediately preview the report or to see the report's design first. Click Finish after making your selection.

The report created in the preceding example is shown in Figure 6.20. Notice that the report is sorted and grouped by ContactType and CompanyName. The report's data is in order by ProjectName within a CompanyName grouping.

This method of creating a one-to-many report is by far the easiest. In fact, the "background join" technology that the wizards use when they allow you to pick fields from multiple tables—figuring out how to build the complex queries needed for the report or form—is one of Access's strong points. It's a huge timesaver and helps hide unnecessary complexity from you as you build a report. Although you should take advantage of this feature, it's important that, as a developer, you know what's happening under the covers. The following two sections give you this necessary knowledge.

Building a Report Based on a One-to-Many Query
Another popular method of building a one-to-many report is to use a one-to-many query. A one-to-many report built in this way is constructed as though it were based on the data within a single table. First, you build the query that will underlie the report (see Figure 6.21).

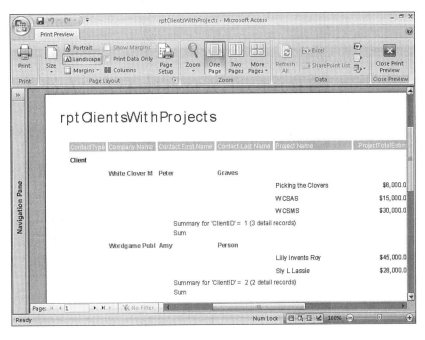

FIGURE 6.20   A completed one-to-many report.

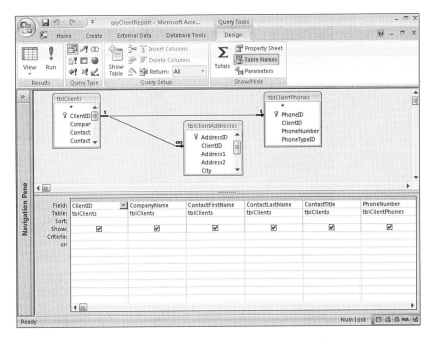

FIGURE 6.21   An example of a query underlying a one-to-many report.

After you have finished the query, you can select it rather than select each individual table (as done in the preceding section). After you select the query, you use the same process to create the report as you used for the previous report.

Building a One-to-Many Report with the Subreport Wizard

You can also create a one-to-many report by building the parent report and then adding a SubForm/SubReport control. This is often the method used to create reports such as invoices that show the report's data in a one-to-many relationship rather than in a denormalized format (as shown in Figure 6.20). If you want to use the SubForm/SubReport Wizard, you must make sure that you select the Control Wizards tool before you add the SubForm/SubReport control to the main report. Here is the process:

1. Click to select the SubForm/SubReport control tool.

2. Click and drag to place the SubForm/SubReport control on the main report. You will usually place the SubForm/SubReport control in the report's Detail section. After you place the SubForm/SubReport control on the report, the SubForm/SubReport Wizard is invoked.

3. Indicate whether you want the subreport to be based on an existing report or form or you want to build a new subreport based on a query or table (see Figure 6.22). Click Next.

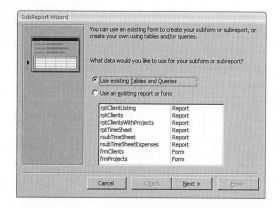

FIGURE 6.22   The SubForm/SubReport Wizard: indicating whether you want to base the subreport on an existing report or on a query or table.

4. If you select a table or query, you have to select the table or query on which the subreport will be based. You can then select the fields you want to include on the subreport (see Figure 6.23). You can even select fields from more than one table or query. When you're finished, click Next.

5. The next step of the SubForm/SubReport Wizard suggests a relationship between the main report and the subreport (see Figure 6.24). You can accept the selected relationship, or you can define your own. When you're finished, click Next.

6. The final step of the SubReport Wizard asks you to name the subreport. To follow standards, the name should begin with the prefix *rsub*. Click Finish when you're finished.

As you can see in Figure 6.25, the one-to-many relationship between two tables is clearly highlighted by this type of report. In the example, each customer is listed. All the detail records reflecting the projects for each customer are listed immediately following each customer's data.

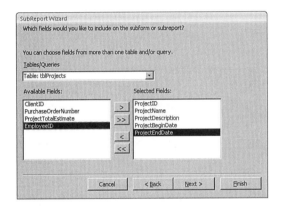

FIGURE 6.23   The SubForm/SubReport Wizard: indicating the fields that you want to include in the subreport.

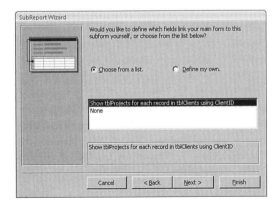

FIGURE 6.24   The SubForm/SubReport Wizard: identifying the relationship.

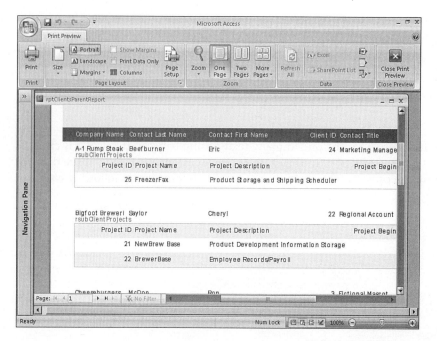

FIGURE 6.25 A completed one-to-many report created with the SubForm/SubReport Wizard.

Working with Subreports

When a subreport has been added to a report, it's important to understand what properties have been set by the SubReport Wizard so that you can modify the SubReport control, if needed. You should become familiar with a few properties of a subreport:

▶ Source Object—Enables you to indicate the name of the report or other object that's being displayed within the control.

▶ Link Child Fields—Enables you to indicate the fields from the child report that link the child report to the master report.

▶ Link Master Fields—Enables you to indicate the fields from the master report that link the master report to the child report.

▶ Can Grow—Determines whether the control can expand vertically to accommodate data in the subreport.

▶ Can Shrink—Determines whether the control can shrink to eliminate blank lines when no data is found in the subreport.

You should not only know how to work with the properties of a SubReport object but also be able to easily modify the subreport from within the main report. You can always modify the subreport by selecting it within the list of reports in the Navigation Pane. To do this, click the report you want to modify; then click Design. You can also modify a subreport by selecting its objects directly within the parent report.

> **TIP**
>
> Access 2007 makes it easy to work with subforms and subreports in Design view. Scrolling has been improved so that it's easier to design subforms and subreports. In addition, you can open a subreport in its own separate Design view window by right-clicking the subreport and selecting Subreport in New Window. Alternatively, instead of right-clicking the subreport, you can select the subreport and then click Subreport in New Window on the Design tab of the ribbon.

Working with Sorting and Grouping

As opposed to sorting within forms, sorting the data within a report isn't determined by the underlying query. In fact, the underlying query affects the report's sort order only when no sort order has been specified for the report. Any sort order specified in the query is completely overwritten by the report's sort order, which is determined by the report's Sorting and Grouping window (see Figure 6.26). The sorting and grouping of the report is affected by what options you select when you run a Report Wizard. You can use the Sorting and Grouping window to add, remove, or modify sorting and grouping options for the report. Sorting simply affects the order of the records on the report. Grouping adds Group Headers and Footers to the report.

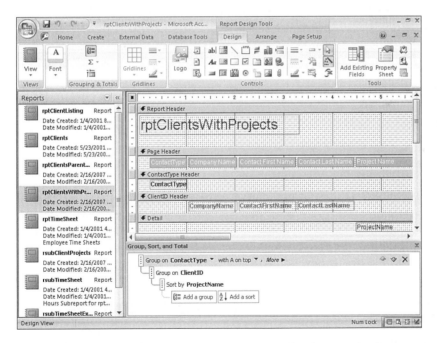

FIGURE 6.26   The Sorting and Grouping window, showing grouping by contact type and ClientID.

Adding Sorting or Grouping

Often, you want to add sorting or grouping to a report. To do so, follow these four steps:

1. Click the Group and Sort tool, found in the Grouping & Totals group on the Design tab. The Group, Sort, and Total window appears.

2. Click the Add a Group tool within the Group, Sort, and Total window. All the fields found on the report appear in a list box (see Figure 6.27).

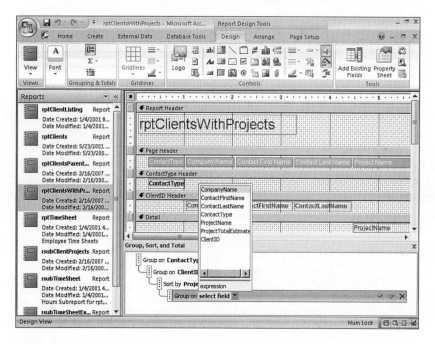

FIGURE 6.27   Inserting a grouping level.

3. Select a field in the list.

4. Click the More button to view additional grouping options (see Figure 6.28). They include whether you want to sort from smallest to largest or largest to smallest; whether you want to group by the entire value or by a portion of it; whether you want totals for the grouping level; whether you want a header section, a footer section, or both; and finally how you want the data grouped on a page.

> **NOTE**
>
> To remove a sorting or grouping that you have added, click to select the Group on or Sort by expression that you want to delete. Click the X found to the right of the selection band. Access warns you that any controls in the Group Header or Footer will be deleted (see Figure 6.29). Click Yes if you want to complete the process.

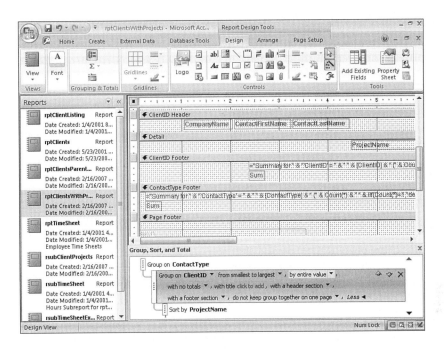

FIGURE 6.28   When you click More, you can determine the specifics of the grouping.

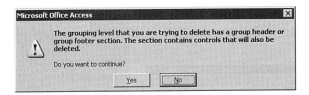

FIGURE 6.29   When you delete a group, Access deletes the Group Header and Footer associated with that group.

> **NOTE**
>
> To sort the report data within a group, click the Add a Sort button. As with the Add a Group button, Access displays a list of available fields. After you make your selection, Access adds that sort to the report.

What Are Group Header and Footer Properties, and Why Should You Use Them?

Each Group Header and Footer has its own properties that determine the behavior of the Group Header or Footer:

▶ Force New Page—The Force New Page property can be set to None, Before Section, After Section, or Before & After. When it is set to None, no page break occurs either before or after the report section. If it is set to `Before Section`, a page break occurs before the report section prints; if it is set to `After Section`, a page break occurs after the report section prints. When this property is set to `Before & After`, a page break occurs before the report section prints as well as after it prints.

▶ New Row or Col—The `New Row or Col` property determines whether a column break occurs whenever the report section prints. This property applies only to multi-column reports. The choices are `None`, `Before Section`, `After Section`, and `Before & After`. Like the `Force New Page` property, this property determines whether the column break occurs before the report section prints, after it prints, or before and after, or whether it's affected by the report section break at all.

▶ Keep Together—The `Keep Together` property specifies whether you want Access to try to keep an entire report section together on one page. If this property is set to `Yes`, Access starts printing the section at the top of the next page if it can't print the entire section on the current page. When this property is set to `No`, Access prints as much of the section as possible on the current page, inserting each page break as necessary. If a section exceeds the page length, Access starts printing the section on a new page and continues printing it on the following page.

▶ Visible—The `Visible` property indicates whether the section is visible. It's common to hide the visibility of a particular report section at runtime in response to different situations. You can easily do this by changing the value of the report section's `Visible` property with VBA code, usually on the `Format` event.

▶ Can Grow, Can Shrink—The `Can Grow` property determines whether the section stretches vertically to accommodate the data in it. The `Can Shrink` property specifies whether you want the section to shrink vertically, eliminating blank lines.

▶ Repeat Section—The `Repeat Section` property is a valuable property because it lets you specify whether the group header is repeated on subsequent pages if a report section needs more than one page to print.

Improving Performance and Reusability by Basing Reports on Stored Queries or Embedded SQL Statements

Basing your Access reports on stored queries offers you two major benefits:

▶ The query underlying the report can be used by other forms and reports.

▶ Sophisticated calculations need to be built only once; they don't need to be re-created for each report (or form).

With earlier versions of Access, reports based on stored queries opened faster than reports based on embedded SQL statements. The reason is that, when you build and save a query, Access compiles and creates a query plan. This query plan is a plan of execution that's based on the amount of data in the query's tables as well as all the indexes available in each table. In earlier versions of Access, if you ran a report based on an embedded SQL statement, the query was compiled, and the query plan was built at runtime, slowing the query's execution. With Access 2002, Access 2003, and Access 2007, query plans are built for embedded SQL statements when the form or report is saved. Query plans are stored with the associated form or report.

So what are the benefits of basing a report on a stored query instead of an embedded SQL statement? Often, you want to build several reports and forms all based on the same information. An embedded SQL statement can't be shared by multiple database objects. At the very least, you must copy the embedded SQL statement for each form and report you build. Basing reports and forms on stored queries eliminates this problem. You build the query once and modify it once if changes need to be made to it. Many forms and reports can all use the same query (including its criteria, expressions, and so on).

Reports often contain complex expressions. If a particular expression is used in only one report, nothing is lost by building the expression into the embedded SQL statement. On the other hand, many complex expressions are used in multiple reports and forms. By building these expressions into queries on which the reports and forms are based, you have to create the expression only one time.

TIP

You can easily save an embedded SQL statement as a query. This allows you to use the Report Wizard to build a report using several tables; you can then save the resulting SQL statement as a query. With the report open in Design view, bring up the property sheet. Click the Data tab, click on the Record Source property, and then click the ellipsis. The embedded SQL statement appears as a query. Click Save As on the Design tab of the ribbon, enter a name for the query, and click OK. Close the Query window, indicating that you want to update the Record Source property. Your query is now based on a stored query instead of an embedded SQL statement.

Although you can see that basing reports on stored queries offers several benefits, it has its downside as well. If your database contains numerous reports, the database container becomes cluttered with a large number of queries that underlie those reports. Furthermore, queries and the expressions within them are often very specific to a particular report. If that is the case, you should opt for embedded SQL statements rather than stored queries.

Using Access Reports and the Internet

Microsoft makes it easy to develop Internet-aware applications by adding hyperlinks to reports and by allowing you to save an Access report as an HTML document. These features are covered in the following sections.

Adding a Hyperlink to a Report

You can add hyperlinks to reports in the form of labels. When added, they serve as a direct link to a UNC or URL. To add a hyperlink to a report, follow these steps:

1. With the report open in Design view, add a label to the report.

2. Set the `Hyperlink Address` property to the UNC or URL you want to link to. The easiest way to do this is to click in the `Hyperlink Address` property; then click the ellipsis to open the Insert Hyperlink dialog box.

3. With Existing File or Web Page selected as the Link To, you can enter a file path or URL in the text box or click Current Folder to locate a file or web page in the current folder. You can also click to insert hyperlinks to Browsed Pages or Recent Files. With Object in This Database selected as the Link To, you can link to an object in the current database.

4. If you want to enter a `Hyperlink SubAddress`, click Bookmark. The Hyperlink SubAddress can be a range name, bookmark, slide number, or any other recognized location in the document specified in the Link to File or URL combo box.

5. Click OK. The `Hyperlink Address` and `Hyperlink SubAddress` properties are filled in with the information supplied in the Insert Hyperlink dialog box.

The `Hyperlink Address` and `Hyperlink SubAddress` properties apply when the report is in Report view (not Print Preview). They also come into play only when a report is saved as HTML and viewed in a web browser, such as Internet Explorer 7.0. Saving a report as an HTML document is covered in the following section.

> **NOTE**
>
> Attached labels (those associated with a text box) do not have `HyperLink Address` or `HyperLink SubAddress` properties.

Saving a Report as HTML

To save a report as HTML, right-click the report in the Navigation Pane and select HTML Document from the More drop-down on the External Data tab of the ribbon. The Export – HTML Document dialog box appears. Pick a location and name for the file and whether you want to open the destination file after the export completes. Then click OK. Designate the HTML Output Options. Click OK when you are finished. The document is saved as HTML and assigned the name and location you specified.

Saving a Report as XML

To save a report as XML, right-click the report in the Navigation Pane and select XML File. The Export – XML File dialog box appears. Pick a location and name for the file. Then click OK. Designate the Export XML Options. Click OK when you are finished. The document is saved as XML and assigned the name and location you specified. Saving reports as XML is covered in detail in *Alison Balter's Mastering Access 2002 Enterprise Development.*

Understanding Report Specifications and Limitations

Reports have a number of specifications and limitations that you should be aware of, and Table 6.1 lists them. Fortunately, you will generally not find them too restricting.

TABLE 6.1   Report Specifications and Limitations

Item	Limitation
Number of characters in a label	2,028
Number of characters in a text box	65,535
Report width	22 in.
Section height	22 in.
Height of all sections plus section headers	200 in.
Number of nested reports	7
Number of fields or expressions you can sort or group on	10
Number of headers and footers	1 report header/footer; 1 page header/footer; 10 group headers/footers
Number of printed pages	65,536
Number of controls and sections you can add	754
Number of characters in the SQL statement that serves as the RowSource	32,750

Practical Examples: Building Reports Needed for Your Application

The sample application requires several reports. A couple of the simpler ones are built here.

Designing the rptClientListing Report

The rptClientListing report lists all the clients in the tblClients table. The report includes the company name, contact name, intro date, default rate, and term type of each customer. The report is grouped by contact type and sorted by company name. It provides the average default rate by contact type and overall.

The rptClientListing report is based on a query called qryClientListing, which is shown in Figure 6.30. The query includes the CompanyName, IntroDate, and DefaultRate fields from the tblClients table. It joins the tblClients table to the tblContactType table to obtain the ContactType field from tblContactType and joins the tblClients table to the tblTerms table to obtain the TermType field from the tblTerms table. It also includes an expression called ContactName that concatenates the ContactFirstName and ContactLastName fields. The expression looks like this:

ContactName: [ContactFirstName] & " " & [ContactLastName]

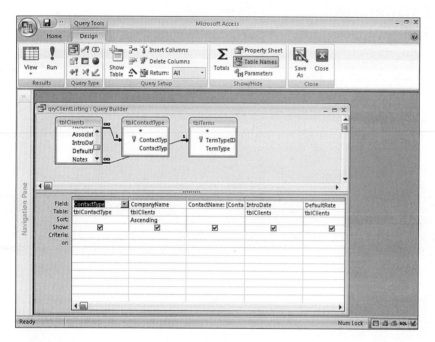

FIGURE 6.30   The qryClientListing query—a foundation for the rptClientListing report.

To build the report, follow these steps:

1. Click the Report Wizard tool in the Reports group on the Create tab.

2. Use the drop-down list to select the qryClientListing query (see Figure 6.31).

3. Click the >> button to designate that you want to include all the fields in the query within the report. Click Next.

4. Indicate that you want to view your data by tblContactType. Click Next.

5. Do not add any grouping to the report. Click Next.

6. Use the drop-down list to select CompanyName as the sort field (see Figure 6.32).

7. Click Summary Options and click the Avg check box to add the average default rate to the report. Click OK to close the Summary Options dialog box and click Next to proceed to the next step of the wizard.

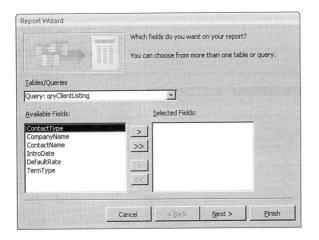

FIGURE 6.31   Selecting the qryClientListing query.

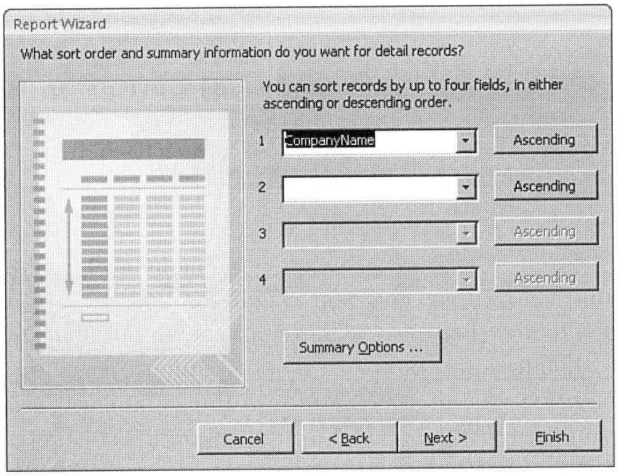

FIGURE 6.32   Selecting CompanyName as the sort field.

8. Select Landscape for the Orientation and click Next.

9. Select a style for the report and click Next.

10. Give the report the title rptClientListing; then click Finish.

11. The completed report should look like Figure 6.33. Click Design to open the report in Design view. Notice that both the name and title of the report are rptClientListing (see Figure 6.34). Modify the title of the report so that it reads Client Listing by Contact Type and Company Name.

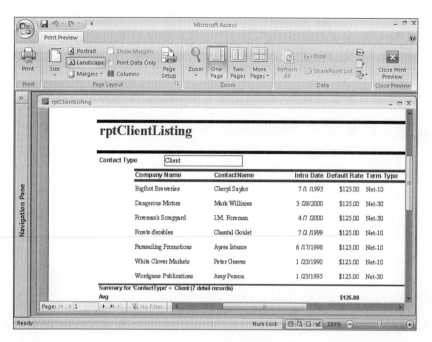

FIGURE 6.33   A preview of the completed report.

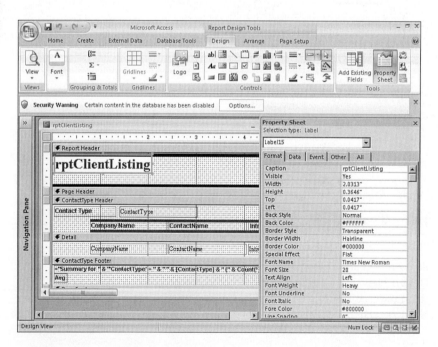

FIGURE 6.34   Changing the report title.

Designing the `rptTimeSheet` Report

The `rptTimeSheet` report is much more complex than the `rptClientListing` report. It includes two subreports: `rsubTimeSheet` and `rsubTimeSheetExpenses`.

The `rptTimeSheet` report is shown in Figure 6.35. It's based on a query called `qryTimeSheet` (see Figure 6.36). It contains fields from both `tblTimeCards` and `tblEmployees`.

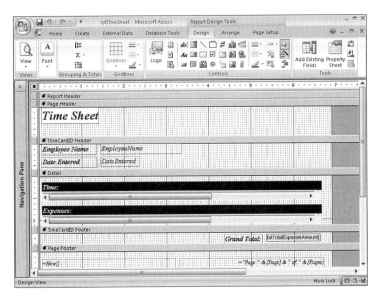

FIGURE 6.35   The `rptTimeSheet` report in Design view.

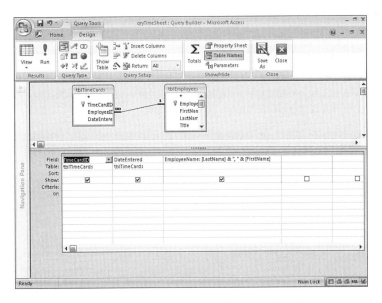

FIGURE 6.36   The `qryTimeSheet` query in Design view.

The rptTimeSheet report has a Page Header that includes the title of the report, but nothing else is found within the Page Header. The TimeCardID header contains the EmployeeName and DateEntered from the qryTimeSheet query. The report's Detail section contains the two subreports rsubTimeSheet and rsubTimeSheetExpenses. The TimeCardID footer has a text box that contains the grand total of hours and expenses. The expression within the text box is

```
=[rsubTimeSheet].[Report]![txtTotalHourlyBillings]+[rsubTimeSheetExpenses]._
[Report]![txtTotalExpenseAmount]
```

The easiest way to build the expression is to use the Expression Builder.

The Page Footer holds two expressions, one for the date and another for the page number. They look like this:

```
=Now()
="Page " & [Page] & " of " & [Pages]
```

The rsubTimeSheet report is based on qrySubTimeSheet; this query contains the following fields from the tblProjects and tblTimeCardHours tables:

```
tblProjects: ProjectName
tblTimeCardsHours: TimeCardID, TimeCardDetailID, DateWorked, WorkDescription,_
BillableHours, BillingRate, and the expression HourlyBillings:_
 [tblTimeCardHours].[BillingRate]*[BillableHours]
```

The design of rsubTimeSheet is shown in Figure 6.37. This subreport can easily be built from a wizard. Select all fields except TimeCardID and TimeCardDetailID from qrySubTimeSheets. View the data by tblTimeCardHours. Don't add any groupings and don't sort the report. When you're finished with the wizard, modify the design of the report. Remove the caption from the Report Header and move everything from the Page Header to the Report Header. Collapse the Page Header, remove everything from the Page Footer, and add a Report Footer with the expression =Sum([HourlyBillings]).

Change the format of the HourlyBillings and the TotalHourlyBillings controls to Currency. Use the Sorting and Grouping window to sort by TimeCardID and TimeCardDetailID.

The rsubTimeSheetExpenses report is based on qrySubTimeSheetExpense, which contains the following fields from the tblProjects, tblExpenseCodes, and tblTimeCardExpenses tables:

```
tblProjects: ProjectName
tblTimeCardsExpenses: TimeCardID, TimeCardExpenseID, ExpenseDate,
ExpenseDescription, and ExpenseAmount
tblExpenseCodes: ExpenseCode
```

The design of rsubTimeSheetExpenses is shown in Figure 6.38. This subreport can easily be built from a wizard. Select all fields except TimeCardID and TimeCardExpenseID from qrySubTimeSheetExpense. View the data by tblTimeCardExpenses. Don't add any groupings and don't sort the report. When you're finished with the wizard, modify the design of the report. Remove the caption from the Report Header and move everything from the Page Header to the Report Header. Collapse the Page Header, remove everything from the Page Footer, and add a Report Footer with the expression =Sum(ExpenseAmount).

Change the format of the ExpenseAmount and the TotalExpenseAmount controls to Currency and use the Sorting and Grouping window to sort by TimeCardID and TimeCardExpenseID.

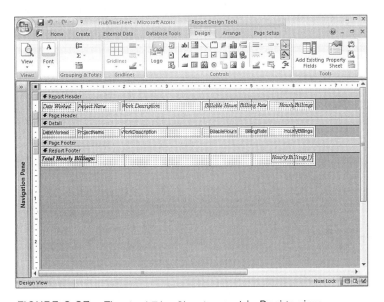

FIGURE 6.37   The rsubTimeSheet report in Design view.

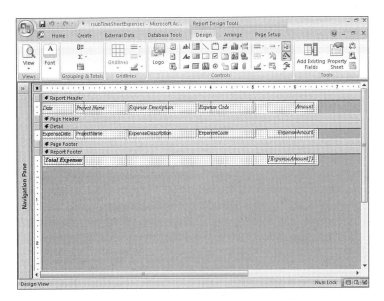

FIGURE 6.38   The rsubTimeSheetExpenses report in Design view.

Summary

Reports give you valuable information about the data stored in your database. Many types of reports can be built in Access 2007, including Detail reports, Summary reports, reports that look like printed forms, and reports containing graphs and other objects. Access offers many properties for customizing the look and behavior of each report to fit your users' needs. Understanding how to work with each property is integral to the success of your application-development projects. For more information about reports and their use, refer to Chapter 11.

CHAPTER 7

What Are Macros, and When Do You Need Them?

Why This Chapter Is Important

Although you may not prefer to use macros to develop the routines that control your applications, macros in Access 2007 play a major role in the development process. Available in Microsoft Office Access 2007 are *embedded* macros. Rather than appearing in the Navigation Pane as a separate object, an embedded macro is part of the object to which it is associated. When you modify an embedded macro, it does not affect any other macros or objects in the database. Because you can prevent embedded macros from performing certain potentially unsafe operations, they are trusted. In addition to their other benefits, using Access 2007 macros can often help you get started with developing applications—because these macros can be converted to VBA code. This means you can develop part of your application using macros, convert the macros to VBA code, and then continue developing your application. Although I don't recommend this approach for serious developers, it offers a great jump-start for those new to Access or Windows development in general.

Learning the Basics of Creating and Running a Macro

To create a macro, click to select the Create tab. Then select Macro from the Other group. The Macro Design window shown in Figure 7.1 appears. In this window, you can build a program by adding macro actions, arguments, names, and conditions to the macro.

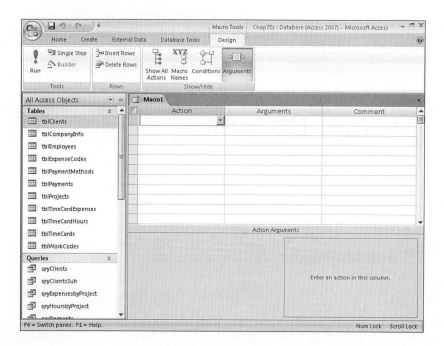

FIGURE 7.1   The Macro Design window, showing the macro Action, Arguments, and Comment columns.

Macro *actions* are like programming commands or functions. They instruct Access to take a specific action, for example, to open a form. Macro *arguments* are like parameters to a command or function; they give Access specifics on the selected action. For example, if the macro action instructs Access to open a form, the arguments for that action tell Access which form should be opened and how it should be opened (Form, Design, or Datasheet view or Print Preview). Macro *names* are like subroutines, and several subroutines can be included in one Access macro. Each of these routines is identified by its macro name. Macro *conditions* allow you to determine when a specific macro action will execute. For example, you might want one form to open in one situation and a second form to open in another situation.

Macro Actions

As mentioned, macro actions instruct Access to perform a task. You can add a macro action to the Macro Design window in several ways. One method is to click in a cell in the Macro Action column and then click to open the drop-down list. A list of all the macro actions appears, as in Figure 7.2. Select the one you want from the list, and it's instantly added to the macro. Use this method of selecting a macro action if you aren't sure of the macro action's name and want to browse the available actions.

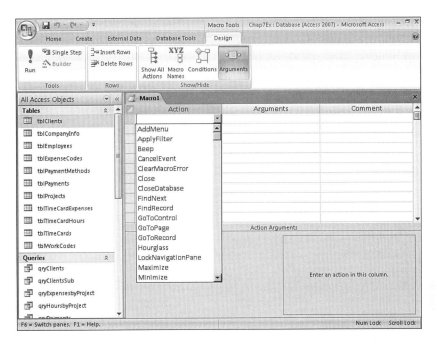

FIGURE 7.2   The Macro Action drop-down list, showing all the available macro actions.

After you have been working with macros for a while, you will know which actions you want to select. Rather than open the drop-down list and scroll through the entire list of actions, you can click a cell in the Action column and then start typing the name of the macro action you want to add. Access will find the first macro action beginning with the character(s) you type.

The OpenTable, OpenQuery, OpenForm, OpenReport, and OpenModule actions are used to open a table, query, form, report, or module, respectively. You can fill in all these actions and associated arguments quite easily with a drag-and-drop technique:

1. Scroll through the Navigation Pane until you see the object that you want to add to the macro.

2. Click and drag the object you want to open over to the Macro Design window. The appropriate action and arguments are automatically filled in. Figure 7.3 shows the effects of dragging and dropping the frmClients form onto the Macro Design window.

Dragging and dropping a table, query, form, report, or module onto the Macro Design window saves you time because all the macro action arguments are automatically filled in for you. Notice in Figure 7.3 that six action arguments are associated with the OpenForm action: Form Name, View, Filter Name, Where Condition, Data Mode, and Window Mode.

Three of the arguments for the `OpenForm` action have been filled in: the name of the form (`frmClients`), the view (Form), and the window mode (Normal). Macro action arguments are covered more thoroughly in the next section.

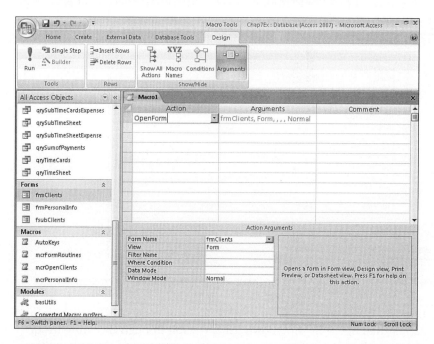

FIGURE 7.3   The Macro Design window after the `frmClients` form was dragged and dropped on it.

Action Arguments

As mentioned, macro action arguments are like command or function parameters; they give Access specific instructions on how to execute the selected macro action. The available arguments differ depending on what macro action has been selected. Some macro action arguments force you to select from a drop-down list of appropriate choices; others allow you to enter a valid Access expression. Macro action arguments are automatically filled in when you click and drag a Table, Query, Form, Report, or Module object to the Macro Design window. In all other situations, you must supply Access with the arguments required to properly execute a macro action. To specify a macro action argument, follow these five steps:

1. Select a macro action.

2. Press the F6 function key to jump down to the first macro action argument for the selected macro action.

3. If the macro action argument requires selecting from a list of valid choices, click to open the drop-down list of available choices for the first macro action argument associated with the selected macro action. Figure 7.4 shows all the available choices for the Form Name argument associated with the OpenForm action. Because the selected argument is Form Name, the names of all the forms included in the database are displayed in the drop-down list.

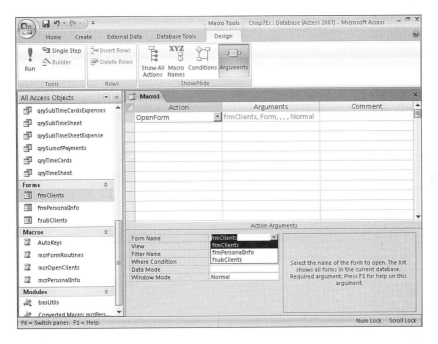

FIGURE 7.4   Available choices for Form Name argument.

4. If the macro action argument requires entering a valid expression, you can type the argument into the appropriate text box or get help from the Expression Builder. Take a look at the Where Condition argument of the OpenForm action, for example. After you click in the Where Condition text box, an ellipsis appears. If you click on the ellipsis, the Expression Builder dialog box is invoked, as shown in Figure 7.5.

5. To build an appropriate expression, select a database object from the list box on the left; then select a specific element from the center and right list boxes. Click Paste to paste the element into the text box. In Figure 7.5, the currently selected database object is Built-in Functions, and the currently selected elements are Date/Time and Date. Click OK to close the Expression Builder. The completed expression appears as shown in Figure 7.6.

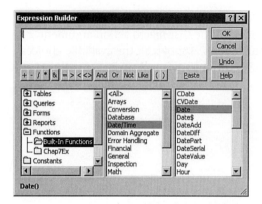

FIGURE 7.5   The Expression Builder dialog box allows you to easily add complex expressions to your macros.

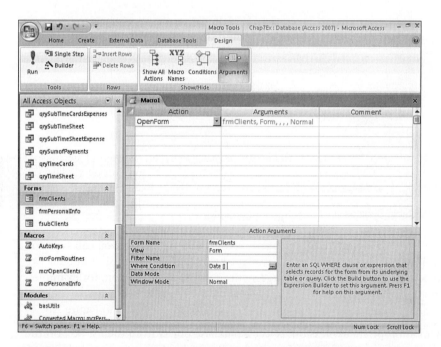

FIGURE 7.6   The completed expression for the Where argument of the OpenForm action.

Remember that each macro action has different macro action arguments. Some of the arguments associated with a particular macro action are required, and others are optional. If you need help on a particular macro action argument, click in the argument and Access gives you a short description of that argument. If you need more help, press F1 to see Help for the macro action and all its arguments, as shown in Figure 7.7.

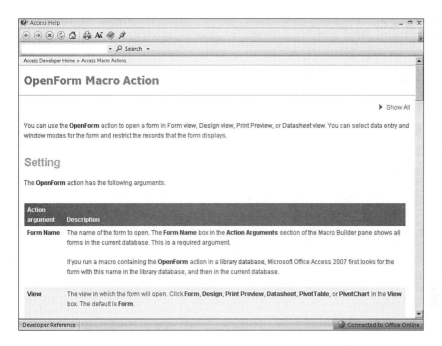

FIGURE 7.7   Help on the `OpenForm` action.

Macro Names

Macro names are like subroutines; they allow you to place more than one routine in a macro. This means you can create many macro routines without having to create several separate macros. You should include macros that perform related functions within one particular macro. For example, you might build a macro that contains all the routines required for form handling and another that has all the routines needed for report handling.

Only two steps are needed to add macro names to a macro:

1. Click the Macro Names in the Show/Hide group on the Design tab. The Macro Name column appears, as in Figure 7.8.

2. Add macro names to each macro subroutine. Figure 7.9 shows a macro with three subroutines: `OpenFrmClients`, `OpenFrmTimeCards`, and `CloseAnyForm`. The `OpenFrmClients` subroutine opens the `frmClients` form, showing all the clients added in the past 30 days. The `OpenFrmTimeCards` subroutine opens the `frmTimeCards` form, and the `CloseAnyForm` subroutine displays a message to the user and then closes the active form.

NOTE

The Macro Name column is a toggle. You can hide it and show it at will, without losing the information in the column.

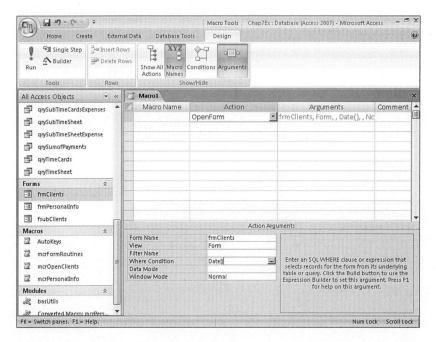

FIGURE 7.8   The Macro Name column allows you to create subroutines within a macro.

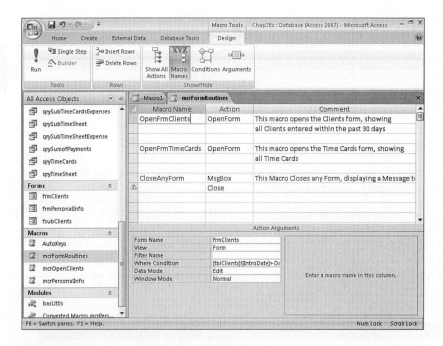

FIGURE 7.9   A macro with three subroutines.

Macro Conditions

At times, you want a macro action to execute only when a certain condition is true. Fortunately, Access allows you to specify the conditions under which a macro action executes:

1. Click the Conditions tool in the Show/Hide group of the Design tab. The Condition column appears, as in Figure 7.10.

2. Add the conditions you want to each macro action.

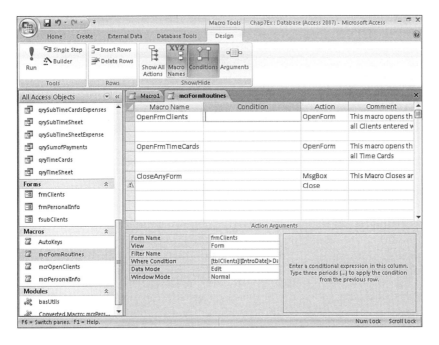

FIGURE 7.10   You can designate the condition under which a macro action executes in the Condition column of a macro.

The macro pictured in Figure 7.11 evaluates information entered on a form. The CheckBirthDate subroutine evaluates the date entered in the txtBirthDate text box. Here's the expression entered in the first condition:

```
DateDiff("yyyy",[Forms]![frmPersonalInfo]![txtBirthDate],Date()) Between 25 And 49
```

This expression uses the DateDiff function to determine the difference between the date entered in the txtBirthDate text box and the current date. If the difference between the two dates is between 25 and 49 years, a message box is displayed indicating that the person is over a quarter century old.

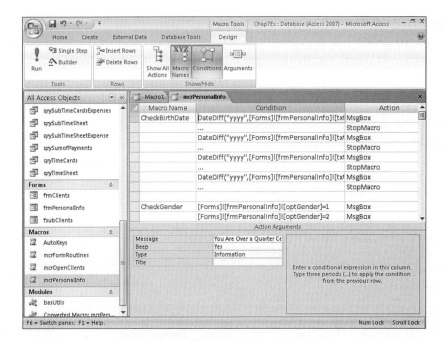

FIGURE 7.11   An example of a macro containing conditions.

The ellipsis on the second line of the CheckBirthDate subroutine indicates to Access that the macro action should be executed only if the condition entered on the previous line is true. In this case, if the condition is true, the macro is terminated.

If the first condition isn't satisfied, the macro continues evaluating each condition in the subroutine. The CheckBirthDate subroutine displays an age-specific message for each person 25 years of age and older. If the person is younger than 25, none of the conditions is met, and no message is displayed.

The CheckGender subroutine works a little bit differently. It evaluates the value of the optGender option group. One of the first two lines of the subroutine execute, depending on whether the first or second option button is selected. The third line of the subroutine executes regardless of the Option Group value because no ellipsis is entered in the macro action's Condition column. If no ellipsis is found on any line of the subroutine, the macro action executes unconditionally. If an ellipsis were placed before the line, the macro action would execute only if the value of OptGender was 2.

Running an Access Macro

You have learned quite a bit about macros but haven't yet learned how to execute them. This process varies depending on what you're trying to do. You can run a macro from the Macro Design window or by double-clicking the macro in the Macros Group of the

Navigation Pane, triggered from a Form or Report event, or invoked by selecting a custom ribbon button. The first three methods are covered in the following sections, but invoking a macro from a custom ribbon is covered in Chapter 23, "Working with and Customizing Ribbons."

Running a Macro from the Macro Design Window

A macro can be executed easily from the Macro Design window. Running a macro without subroutines is simple: Just click Run in the Tools group of the Design tab. Each line of the macro is executed unless conditions have been placed on specific macro actions. After you click the Run button of mcrOpenClients (shown in Figure 7.12), the frmClients form is opened.

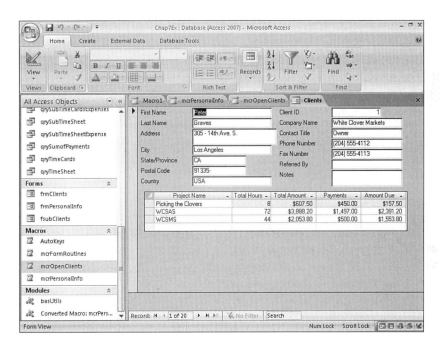

FIGURE 7.12   Running a macro from the Macro Design window.

From Macro Design view, you can run only the first subroutine in a macro. To run a macro with subroutines, click Run from the Tools group on the Design page to execute the first subroutine in the macro. As soon as the second macro name is encountered, the macro execution terminates. The section "Triggering a Macro from a Form or Report Event," later in this chapter, explains how to execute subroutines other than the first one in a macro.

Running a Macro from the Macros Group of the Navigation Pane

To run a macro from the Macros group of the Navigation Pane, follow these two steps:

1. Scroll down to the Macros group in the Navigation Pane. If the Macros group does not appear in the Navigation Pane, you will need to select All Access Objects from the Navigation Pane drop-down and then expand the Macros group.

2. Double-click on the name of the macro you want to execute, or right-click the macro and select Run.

> **NOTE**
>
> If the macro you execute contains macro names, only the macro actions with the first subroutine are executed.

Triggering a Macro from a Form or Report Event

Chapter 9, "Objects, Properties, Methods, and Events Explained," introduces the concept of executing code in response to an event. Here, you learn how to associate a macro with a command button.

The form in Figure 7.13 illustrates how to associate a macro with the Click event of a form's command button. Four steps are needed to associate a macro with a Form or Report event:

1. Select the object you want to associate the event with. In the example, the cmdCheckGender command button is selected.

2. Open the property sheet and click the Event tab.

3. Click the event you want the macro to execute in response to. In the example, the Click event of the command button is selected.

4. Use the drop-down list to select the name of the macro you want to execute. If the macro has macro names, make sure you select the correct macro name subroutine. In the example, the macro mcrPersonalInfo and the macro name CheckGender have been selected. Notice the period between the name of the macro and the name of the macro name subroutine. The period is used to differentiate the macro group (mcrPersonalInfo, in this case) from the macro name (CheckGender, in this example).

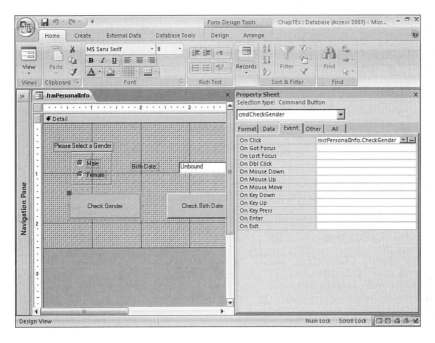

FIGURE 7.13   Associating a macro with a Form or Report event.

Try It: Building a Macro

To practice the techniques you have learned, build the macro shown in Figure 7.11.

1. Click the Create tab and then select Macro from the Macro drop-down in the Other group.

2. Click New.

3. Click the Macro Names and Conditions buttons on the Macro Design toolbar to show both the Macro Name and Condition columns of the Macro Design window.

4. Enter all the macro names, actions, arguments, and conditions shown in Table 7.1.

5. Save and name the macro **mcrPersonalInfo**.

6. Build a form.

7. Add an option group with two option buttons. Set one of their Text properties to Male and the other to Female; then set one of their values to 1 and the other to 2. Name the option group **optGender**.

8. Add a text box for the birth date. Set the Format and Input Mask properties to Short Date. Name the text box **txtBirthDate**.

9. Add two command buttons to the form. Name the first button **cmdCheckGender** and set its Text property to Check Gender, and name the second button **cmdCheckBirthDate** and set its Text property to Check Birth Date. Set the Click event of the first command button to mcrPersonalInfo.CheckGender and the second command button to mcrPersonalInfo.CheckBirthDate.

10. Save the form as **frmPersonalInfo**.
11. Test the macros by clicking each of the command buttons after selecting a gender and entering a birth date.

TABLE 7.1   The mcrPersonalInfo Macro

Macro Name	Macro Condition	Macro Action	Argument	Value
CheckBirthDate	DateDiff("yyyy", [Forms]! [frmPersonalInfo]! [txtBirthDate], Date()) Between 25 And 49	MsgBox	Message	You Are Over a Quarter Century Old
			Type	Information
	...	StopMacro		
	DateDiff("yyyy", [Forms]! [frmPersonalInfo]! [txtBirthDate],Date()) Between 50 And 74	MsgBox	Message	You Are Over a Half Century Old
			Type	Information
	...	StopMacro		
	DateDiff("yyyy", [Forms]! [frmPersonalInfo]! [txtBirthDate],Date()) Between 75 And 99	MsgBox	Message	You Are Over Three Quarters of a Century Old
			Type	Warning
	...	StopMacro		
	DateDiff("yyyy", [Forms]! [frmPersonalInfo]! [txtBirthDate], Date())>100	MsgBox	Message	You Are Over a Century Old!!
			Type	Warning
	...	StopMacro		
CheckGender	[Forms]! [frmPersonalInfo]! [optGender]=1	MsgBox	Message	You Are Male
			Type	Information
	[Forms]! [frmPersonalInfo]! [optGender]=2	MsgBox	Message	You Are Female
			Type	Information
		MsgBox	Message	Thank You for the Information

Modifying an Existing Macro

You have learned how to create a macro, add macro actions and their associated arguments, create macro subroutines by adding macro names, and conditionally execute the actions in the macro by adding macro conditions. However, after you have created a macro, you might want to modify it. First, you must enter Design view for the macro:

1. Select the Macros group on the Navigation Pane.

2. Select the macro you want to modify.

3. Right-click and select Design View.

When the design of the macro appears, you're then ready to insert new lines, delete existing lines, move the macro actions around, or copy macro actions to the macro you're modifying or to another macro.

Inserting New Macro Actions

To insert a macro action, follow these steps:

1. Click on the line above where you want the macro action to be inserted.

2. Press your Insert key or click Insert Rows in the Rows group on the Design tab. A new line is inserted in the macro at the cursor.

To insert multiple macro actions, follow these steps:

1. Place your cursor on the line above where you want the new macro action lines to be inserted.

2. Click and drag on the Macro Action Selector (the gray box to the left of the macro's Action column) to select the same number of Macro Action Selectors as the number of macro actions you want to insert.

3. Press the Insert key or click Insert Rows in the Rows group on the Design tab. All the new macro lines are inserted above the macro actions that were selected.

Deleting Macro Actions

Follow these steps to delete a macro action:

1. Click on the Macro Action Selector of the macro action you want to delete.

2. Press the Delete key or click Delete Rows in the Rows group on the Design tab.

Follow these steps to delete multiple macro actions:

1. Click and drag to select the Macro Action Selectors of all the macro actions you want to delete. All the macro actions should be surrounded by a box, as in Figure 7.14.

2. Press the Delete key or click Delete Rows in the Rows group on the Design tab.

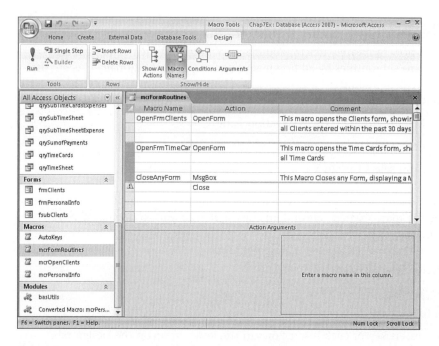

FIGURE 7.14   Selecting and deleting macro actions.

Moving Macro Actions

You can move macro actions in a few ways, including dragging and dropping and cutting and pasting. To move macro actions by dragging and dropping, follow these steps:

1. Click and drag to select the macro action(s) you want to move.

2. Release the mouse button.

3. Place your mouse cursor over the Macro Action Selector of any of the selected macro actions.

4. Click and drag. A line appears, indicating where the selected macro actions will be moved.

5. Release the mouse button.

TIP

If you accidentally drag and drop the selected macro actions to an incorrect place, use the Undo button on the Quick Access toolbar to reverse your action.

To move macro actions by cutting and pasting, follow these steps:

1. Click and drag to select the Macro Action Selectors of the macro actions you want to move.

2. Click Cut in the Clipboard group on the Home tab or press Ctrl+X.

3. Click in the line above where you want the cut macro actions to be inserted. Don't click the Macro Action Selector.

4. Click Paste in the Clipboard group on the Design tab. The macro actions you cut are inserted at the cursor.

CAUTION

Don't click the Macro Action Selector of the row where you want to insert the cut macro actions unless you want to overwrite the macro action you have selected. If you don't click to select the Macro Action Selectors, the cut lines are inserted into the macro without overwriting any other macro actions; if you click to select Macro Action Selectors, existing macro actions are overwritten.

Copying Macro Actions

Macro actions can be copied within a macro or to another macro. Follow these steps to copy macro actions within a macro:

1. Click and drag to select the Macro Action Selectors of the macro actions you want to copy.

2. Click Copy in the Clipboard group on the Home tab or press Ctrl+C.

3. Click in the line above where you want the copied macro actions to be inserted. Don't click on any Macro Action Selectors unless you want to overwrite existing macro actions. (See the Caution preceding this section.)

4. Click Paste in the Clipboard group on the Home tab. The macro actions you copied are inserted at the cursor.

Follow these steps to copy macro actions to another macro:

1. Click and drag to select the Macro Action Selectors of the macro actions you want to copy.

2. Click Copy in the Clipboard group on the Home tab or press Ctrl+C.

3. Open the macro that will include the copied actions.

4. Click in the line above where you want the copied macro actions to be inserted.

5. Click Paste. The macro actions you copied are inserted at the cursor.

Creating an Embedded Macro

Creating an embedded macro is similar to creating a standard macro. The main difference is that the macro is embedded in the object with which it is associated and does not appear in the list of macros in the Navigation Pane. Here's how to create an embedded macro:

1. In Design view, click to select the object to which you want to associate the macro (for example, a command button).

2. Open the property sheet, as shown in Figure 7.15.

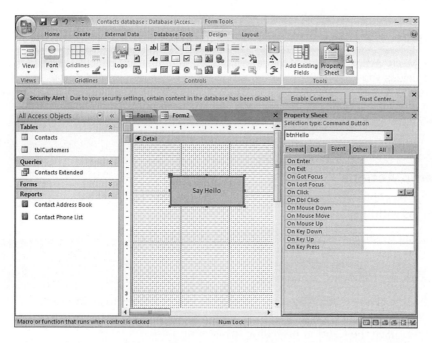

FIGURE 7.15   Use the property sheet to associate a macro with the event of an object.

3. Click the Event tab of the property sheet.

4. Click within the event to which you want to associate the embedded macro. In Figure 7.15, the On Click event is selected.

5. Click the build button (the ellipse). The Choose Builder dialog box appears (see Figure 7.16).

6. Select Macro Builder and click OK. A Macro Design window appears, as in Figure 7.17. Notice in Figure 7.17 that the Macro tab is labeled btnHello: On Click, indicating that the macro is associated with the On Click event of btnHello.

FIGURE 7.16   The Choose Builder dialog box enables you to specify that you want to build a macro.

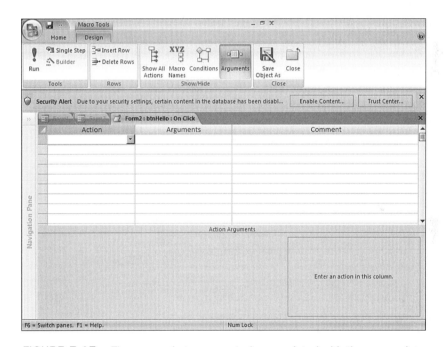

FIGURE 7.17   The macro that you create is associated with the appropriate event of the designated object.

7. Enter the macro commands as you would for any macro, as shown in Figure 7.18.

8. Close the Macro Design window. Access prompts you to save changes to the macro and update the property, as in Figure 7.19.

9. Click Yes to save your changes and close the dialog box. You have now created the embedded macro.

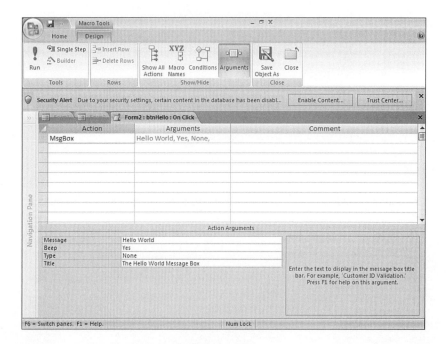

FIGURE 7.18   Your macro commands appear just like macros in earlier versions of Access.

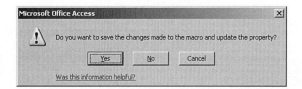

FIGURE 7.19   If you save your changes, Access embeds the macro in the object.

What New Features Are Available in Macros?

There are two main major improvements to Access 2007 macros. The first is the introduction of error handling, and the second is the introduction of variables. Notice the OnError macro action in Figure 7.20. The example branches to a macro named ErrorHandler in the case of an error. Unlike previous versions of Access, where error handling in macros was virtually nonexistent, the new OnError macro action provides similar error handling to that of VBA code.

Another exciting addition to Access 2007 macros is the introduction of variables. The new SetTempVar macro action enables you to create a variable and assign it a value. Figure 7.21 provides an example. Notice in the figure that the macro uses the SetTempVar action to create a variable called CurrentDate and assign it the value returned from the built-in Date() function.

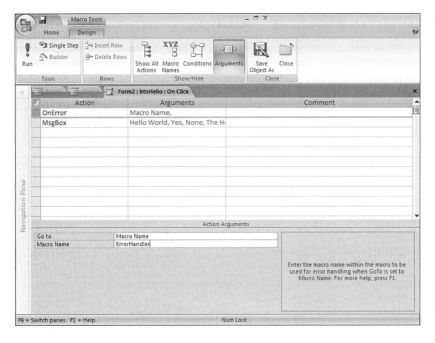

FIGURE 7.20   The OnError macro action provides similar error handling to that of VBA code.

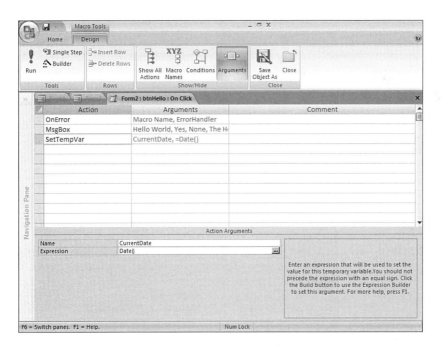

FIGURE 7.21   You use the SetTempVar action to create a temporary variable in a Microsoft Office Access 2007 macro.

Documenting Your Macro: Adding Comments

Just as it's useful to document any program, it's also useful to document what you're trying to do in your macro. These comments can be used when you or others are trying to modify your macro later. They can also be used as documentation because they print when you print the macro.

To add a comment to a macro, click in the Comment column of the macro and begin to type. Figure 7.22 shows a macro with comments. As you can see in Figure 7.23, these comments appear in the printed macro.

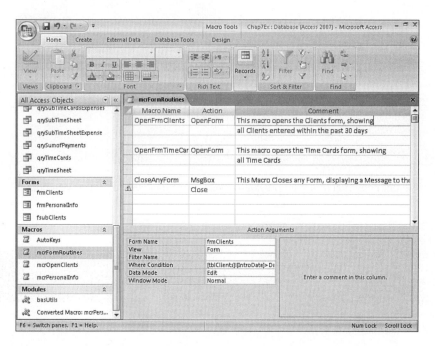

FIGURE 7.22   Adding comments to a macro.

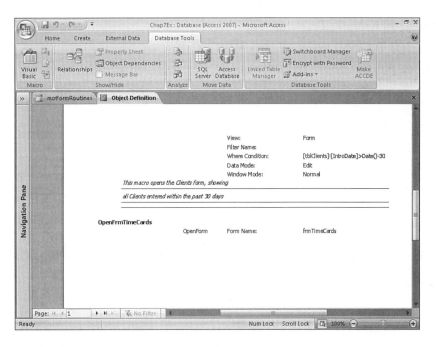

FIGURE 7.23   Comments included in the printed macro.

Testing a Macro

Although Access doesn't offer very sophisticated tools for testing and debugging your macros, it does give you a method for stepping through each line of a macro:

1. Open the macro in Design view.

2. Click Single Step in the Tools group of the Design tab.

3. To execute the macro, click Run. The first line of the macro is executed, and the Macro Single Step dialog box appears, showing you the Macro Name, Condition, Action Name, and Arguments, as in Figure 7.24. In the figure, the Macro Name is mcrPersonalInfo, the Condition evaluates to False, and the Action Name is MsgBox. The MsgBox arguments are You Are Over a Quarter Century Old, Yes, and Information.

4. To continue stepping through the macro, click the Step button on the Macro Single Step dialog box. If you want to halt the execution of the macro without proceeding, click the Stop All Macros button. To continue normal execution of the macro without stepping, click the Continue button.

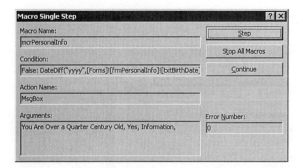

FIGURE 7.24   In the Macro Single Step dialog box, you can view the macro name, condition, action name, and arguments for the current step of the macro.

Try It: Stepping Through a Macro

Learning about stepping through a macro is easiest when you experience it firsthand. To begin, open the `mcrPersonalInfo` macro that you created in the previous Try It example in Design view. Click the Single Step button in the Tools group of the Design tab. Run the `frmPersonalInfo` form, also created in the previous example. Select a gender and type in a birth date. Click the Check Gender command button; this should invoke the Macro Single Step dialog box. Step through the macro one step at a time. View the Macro Name, Condition, Action Name, and Arguments for each step. Change the gender and run the macro again. Carefully observe how this affects the macro's execution.

Now click the Check Birth Date command button. Step through the macro one step at a time, viewing whether the condition evaluates to `True` or `False`. After the macro ends, try entering a different value for the birth date. Step through the macro again and carefully observe whether the condition evaluates to `True` or `False` for each step.

As you can see, although Microsoft supplies some tools to help you debug your macro, you will probably agree that they are limited compared to the tools available with the VBA debugger. (See Chapter 16, "Debugging: Your Key to Successful Development.") That's one reason why many developers prefer to develop applications by using VBA code.

NOTE

The Single Step button in the Tools group of the Design tab is a toggle. After you activate Step Mode, it's activated for all macros in the current database and all other databases until you either turn off the toggle or exit Access. This behavior can be quite surprising if you don't expect it. You might have invoked Step Mode in another database quite a bit earlier in the day, only to remember that you forgot to click the toggle button when some other macro unexpectedly goes into Step Mode.

Determining When You Should Use Macros and When You Shouldn't

Macros aren't always the best tools for creating code that controls industrial-strength applications because they're limited in some functionality. Access macros are limited in the following ways:

▶ You can't create user-defined functions by using macros.

▶ Access macros don't allow you to pass parameters.

▶ Access macros provide no method of processing table records one at a time.

▶ When using Access macros, you can't use object linking and embedding automation to communicate with other applications.

▶ Debugging Access macros is more difficult than debugging VBA code.

▶ Transaction processing can't be done with Access macros.

▶ You can't call Windows API functions by using Access macros.

▶ Access macros don't allow you to create database objects at runtime.

Converting a Macro to VBA Code

Sometimes you will create a macro, later to discover that you want to convert it to VBA code. Fortunately, Access 2007 comes to the rescue. You can easily convert an Access macro to VBA code; after the macro has been converted to VBA code, the code can be modified just like any VBA module. Follow these six steps to convert an Access macro to VBA code:

1. Open the macro you want to convert in Design view.

2. Click the Microsoft Office Access button and select Save As, Save Object As.

3. Click the As drop-down and select Module, as shown in Figure 7.25.

4. Click OK; this opens the Convert Macro dialog box, as shown in Figure 7.26.

5. Indicate whether you want to add error handling and comments to the generated code; then click Convert.

6. After you get an indication that the conversion is finished, click OK. Access places you in the Visual Basic Editor (VBE).

7. The converted macro appears under the list of modules with `Converted Macro:` followed by the name of the macro. Click Design to view the results of the conversion.

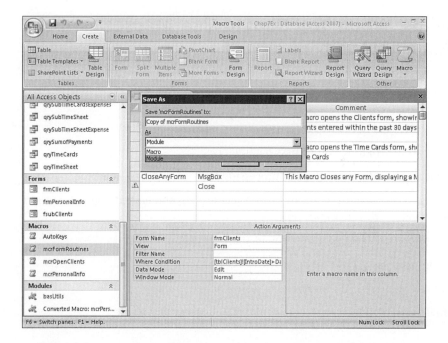

FIGURE 7.25   The macro Save As dialog box allows you to save a macro as a Visual Basic module.

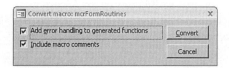

FIGURE 7.26   Use the Convert Macro dialog box to indicate whether error handling and comments will be added to the Visual Basic module.

Figure 7.27 shows a macro that's been converted into distinct subroutines, one for each macro name. The macro is complete with logic, comments, and error handling. All macro conditions are converted into If...Else...End If statements, and all the macro comments are converted into VBA comments. Basic error-handling routines are automatically added to the code.

CAUTION

When you convert a macro to a Visual Basic module, the original macro remains untouched. Furthermore, all the objects in your application will still call the macro. To effectively use the macro conversion options, you must find all the places where the macro was called and replace the macro references with calls to the VBA function.

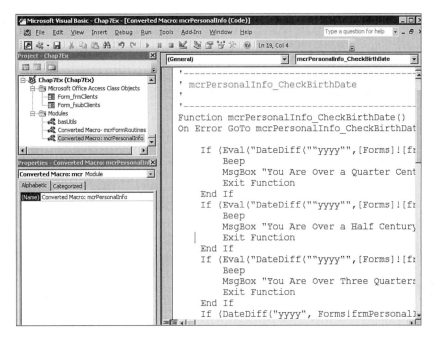

FIGURE 7.27   A converted macro as a module.

Creating an AutoExec Macro

With Access 2007, you can use either an AutoExec macro or Startup options to determine what occurs when a database is opened. Using an AutoExec macro to launch the processing of your application is certainly a viable option.

Creating an AutoExec macro is quite simple; it's just a normal macro saved with the name AutoExec. An AutoExec macro usually performs tasks such as hiding or minimizing the Navigation Pane and opening a Startup form or switchboard. The macro shown in Figure 7.28 hides the Navigation Pane, displays a welcome message, and opens the frmClients form.

TIP

When you're opening your own database to make changes or additions to the application, you probably won't want the AutoExec macro to execute. To prevent it from executing, hold down your Shift key as you open the database.

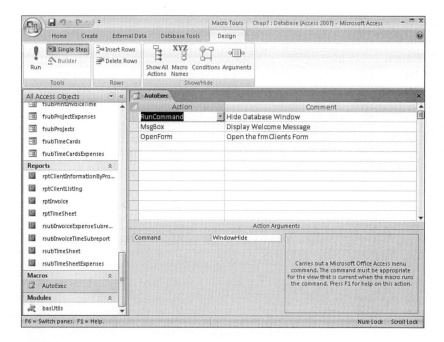

FIGURE 7.28   An example of an AutoExec macro.

Using the DoCmd Object

Most macro commands can be performed in VBA code by using the DoCmd object. The macro action becomes a method of the DoCmd object, and the arguments associated with each macro action become the arguments of the method. For example, the following method of the DoCmd object is used to open a form:

```
DoCmd.OpenForm "frmClients", acNormal, "", "[tblClients]![IntroDate]>Date()-30", _
            acEdit, acNormal
```

The OpenForm method of the DoCmd object that opens the form appears as the first argument to the method. The second argument indicates the view in which the form is opened. The third and fourth arguments specify a filter and Where condition, respectively. The fifth argument of the OpenForm method specifies the Data mode for the form (Add, Edit, or Read Only). The sixth argument indicates the Window mode (Normal, Hidden, Minimized, or Dialog).

Notice the intrinsic constants used for the OpenForm arguments; they help make the code more readable. You can find them in the Help for each DoCmd method.

Practical Examples: Adding an AutoExec **Macro to the Time and Billing Application**

In Chapter 10, "Advanced Form Techniques," you will learn how to add a switchboard to your application. For now, you'll build an AutoExec macro that acts as the launching point for your application. The macro will start the application by hiding the Navigation Pane, displaying a message to the user, and opening the frmClients form.

Build the macro shown in Figure 7.28. Start by opening a new macro in Design view. Set the first action of the macro to RunCommand and then set the DatabaseCommand argument to WindowHide. This will hide the Navigation Pane when it's run. Set the second action of the macro to MsgBox and set the message to Welcome to the Client Billing Application. Set Beep to No, the Type to Information, and the Title to Welcome. The final action of the macro opens the frmClients form. Set the action to OpenForm and set the FormName to frmClients. Leave the rest of the arguments at their default values.

Close and reopen the database. The AutoExec macro should automatically execute when the database is opened. Close the database and open it again, holding down the Shift key to prevent the macro from executing.

Summary

Many end users try to develop entire applications by using macros. Although this is possible, you will generally want to use a combination of macros and modules to build your applications.

New to Microsoft Office Access 2007 are embedded macros. You associate these macros with a specific event. Also new to Microsoft Office Access 2007 are the capability to add error handling to a macro and the capability to include variables in a macro. These three new features make macros a much more viable choice for application development.

CHAPTER **8**

VBA: An Introduction

Why This Chapter Is Important

The Visual Basic for Applications (VBA) language is at the heart of every application that you write. It is your key to taking Access beyond the world of wizards into a world where anything is possible. This chapter introduces you to the VBA language. It serves as a foundation for the remainder of the book. After reading this chapter, you will be familiar with the development environment. You will know how to declare variables, use control structures, pass and return parameters, work with built-in functions, and more.

VBA Explained

VBA is the development language for Microsoft Access 2007. It offers a consistent language for application development in the Microsoft Office suite. The core language, its constructs, and the environment are the same in Microsoft Access 2007, Microsoft Visual Basic 6.0 and earlier, Microsoft Excel, Microsoft Word, Microsoft Outlook (for application-wide programming), and Microsoft Project. What differs among these environments are the built-in objects specific to each application. For example, Access has a `CurrentProject` object, but Excel has a `Workbook` object. Each application's objects have appropriate properties (attributes) and methods (actions)—and, in some cases, events—associated with them. This chapter gives you an overview of the VBA language and its constructs.

Unlike macros in Word or Excel, Access macros are not subprocedures in modules; instead, they are a different type of database object, with their own interface. Because of this, you can't use Access macros to learn to program in VBA, as you can by recording a Word or Excel macro and then examining its VBA code. You can write some Access 2007 applications by using macros. Although macros are okay for relatively basic application development, you will do most serious Access development by using the VBA language. Unlike macros, VBA enables you to do the following:

▶ Work with complex logic structures (case statements, loops, and so on)

▶ Take advantage of functions and actions not available in macros

▶ Loop through and perform actions on recordsets

▶ Perform transaction processing

▶ Create database objects programmatically and work with them

▶ Create libraries of user-defined functions

▶ Call Windows API functions

▶ Perform complex object linking and embedding (OLE) automation commands

The VBA language enables you to use complex logic structures. Macros let you perform only simple If…Then…Else logic, but the VBA language offers a wealth of logic and looping constructs, which are covered later in this chapter.

If you try to develop an application using only macros, you can't take advantage of many of the rich features available in the VBA language. In addition, many of the actions available in both macros and modules can be performed much more efficiently with VBA code.

Complex Access applications often require you to loop through a recordset, performing some action on each member of the set. There's no way to do this using Access macros. However, with the VBA language and ActiveX Data Objects (ADO), you can add, delete, update, and manipulate data. Chapter 15, "What Are ActiveX Data Objects, and Why Are They Important?" covers the details of ADO.

When manipulating sets of records, you want to ensure that all processing finishes successfully before the Access Database Engine permanently updates your data. Macros don't enable you to protect your data with transaction processing. Using the BeginTrans, CommitTrans, and Rollback methods, you can make sure that the Access Database Engine updates your data only if all parts of a transaction finish successfully. Transaction processing, if done properly, can substantially improve your application's performance because no data is written to disk until the process is finished. Transaction processing and its benefits are covered in *Alison Balter's Mastering Access 2002 Enterprise Development*.

With Access macros, you can't create or modify database objects at runtime. Using VBA, you can create databases, tables, queries, and other database objects; you can also modify existing objects. There are many practical applications of this capability to create or modify database objects (discussed in more detail in Chapter 15). When users are able to build queries on the fly, for example, you might want to give them the capability to design a query by using a front-end form that you provide. You can also enable users to store the query so that they can run it again later.

VBA also makes it easier for you to write code libraries of reusable functions, design and debug complex processes, and even write your own add-ins. If you're developing even moderately complex applications, you want to be able to create generic function libraries that can be used with all your Access applications. Doing this using macros is extremely difficult, if not impossible.

Many powerful functions not available within the VBA language are available as part of Windows itself. The Windows API (Application Programming Interface) refers to the nearly 1,000 Windows functions that Microsoft exposes for use by Access programmers. You can't take advantage of these functions from an Access macro. However, by using VBA code, you can declare and call these functions, improving both the performance and functionality of your applications. Chapter 25, "Exploiting the Power of the Windows API," covers the Windows API.

Both DDE and Automation technology enable you to communicate between your Access applications and other applications. Although DDE is an older technology than Automation, it's still used to communicate with a few applications that don't support Automation. Automation is used to control Automation server applications, such as Excel and Project, and their objects (all Microsoft Office applications are Automation servers). Automation is covered in Chapter 24, "Automation: Communicating with Other Applications."

Although macros in Microsoft Office Access 2007 are significantly more powerful than macros in previous versions of Access (see Chapter 7, "What Are Macros, and When Do You Need Them?"), it is best to use a combination of *both* macros and VBA for developing complex solutions. If you would ever like to convert a macro to VBA code, a Save As menu option is available when saving an existing macro.

What Are Access Class Modules, Standard Modules, Form Modules, and Report Modules?

VBA code is written in units called *subroutines* and *functions* that are stored in modules. Microsoft Access modules are either Standard modules or Class modules. *Standard modules* are created by clicking to select the Database Tools tab and then selecting the Visual Basic button from the Macro group. Access takes you to the Access Visual Basic Editor (VBE). Finally, select Insert, Module from the VBE menu. *Class modules* can be standalone objects or can be associated with a form or report. To create a standalone Class module, you choose the Class Module command from the VBE Insert menu. In addition, whenever you add code behind a form or report, Microsoft Access creates a Class module associated with that form or report that contains the code you create.

Modules specific to a form or report are generally called *Form* and *Report Class modules*, and their code is often referred to as *Code Behind Forms (CBF)*. CBF is created and stored in that form or report and triggered from events occurring within it.

A *subroutine* (or *subprocedure*) is a routine that responds to an event or performs some action. An *event procedure* is a special type of subroutine that automatically executes in response to an event such as a mouse click on a command button or the loading of a form. A *function* is a special type of routine because it can return a value; a subroutine can't return a value. Like a subroutine, a function can be triggered from an event.

Where Is VBA Code Written?

You write all VBA code in the Visual Basic Editor, also known as the VBE. Access places you in the VBE anytime you select Visual Basic from the Macro group on the Database Tools tab or press Alt+F11. Figure 8.1 shows the Visual Basic Editor. The VBE environment in Microsoft Access is consistent with the editor interfaces in other Microsoft Office products. The VBE is a separate window from that of Microsoft Access and comprises a menu bar, toolbar, Project window, Properties window, Immediate window, Locals window, Watch window, Object Browser, and Code windows. The various components of the VBE are discussed as appropriate in this chapter and throughout the book.

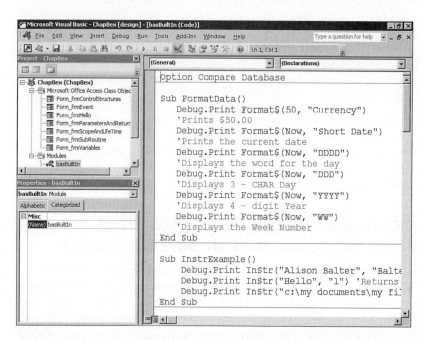

FIGURE 8.1   The Visual Basic Editor (VBE).

The Anatomy of a Module

Whether you're dealing with a Standard module or a Class module, all modules contain a General Declarations section (see Figure 8.2). As the name implies, this is the place you can declare variables and constants that you want to be visible to all the functions and subroutines in the module. You can also set options in this section. These variables are referred to as *module-level* or *private variables*. You can also declare public variables in the General Declarations section of a module. *Public variables* can be seen and modified by any function or procedure in any module in the database.

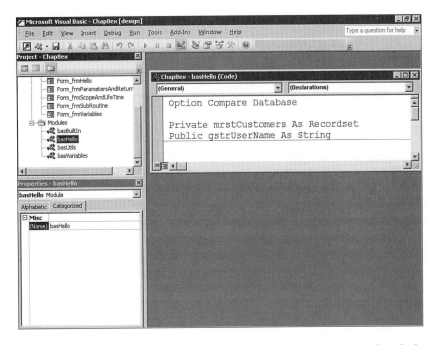

FIGURE 8.2 The General Declarations section of a module is used to declare private and public variables.

A module is also made up of user-defined subroutines and functions. Figure 8.3 shows a subroutine called SayHello. Notice the drop-down list in the upper-left portion of the window titled Chap8Ex—basHello (Code). This is referred to as the Object drop-down list. Subroutines and functions are sometimes associated with a specific object, such as a form or a control within a form. This is the place where such an association is noted. In this case, the subroutine named SayHello is not associated with any object, so the Object drop-down list contains (General).

Option Explicit

Option Explicit is a statement that you can include in the General Declarations section of any module, including the Class module of a form, or report. When you use Option Explicit, you must declare all variables in that module before you use them; otherwise, an error saying that a variable is undefined will occur when you compile the module. If Access encounters an undeclared variable when it compiles a module without Option Explicit, VBA will simply treat it as a new variable and continue without warning. At first glance, you might think that, because Option Explicit can cause compiler errors that would otherwise not occur, it might be better to avoid the use of this option. However, just the opposite is true. You should use Option Explicit in every module, without exception. For example, look at the following code:

```
intAmount = 2
intTotal = intAmont * 2
```

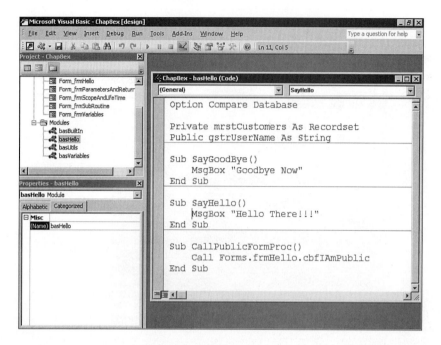

FIGURE 8.3   An example of a user-defined subroutine called SayHello.

Clearly, the intent of this code is to multiply the value contained in the variable
intAmount, in this case 2, by 2. Notice, however, that the variable name is misspelled on
the second line. If you have not set Option Explicit, VBA views intAmont as a new variable and simply continues its processing. The variable intTotal will be set to 0 instead of
4, and no error indication will be given at all. You can totally avoid this kind of result by
using Option Explicit.

TIP

In earlier versions of Access, you had the option of globally instructing Access to insert
the Option Explicit statement in all new modules. In Access 2007, the default
setting is to insert the Option Explicit statement in all new modules. To review this
setting in Access 2007, with the VBE active, choose Tools, Options. Under the Editor
tab, click Require Variable Declaration (see Figure 8.4). It's important that you place
the Option Explicit statement in all your modules, so make sure this option is set
to True. Option Explicit will save you hours of debugging and prevent your cell
phone from ringing after you distribute your application to your users.

In addition to a General Declarations section and user-defined procedures, forms, and
reports, Class modules also contain event procedures that are associated with a particular
object on a form. Notice in Figure 8.5 that the Object drop-down list says cmdHello. This
is the name of the object whose event routines you are viewing. The drop-down list on

the right shows all the events that you can code for a command button; each of these events creates a separate event routine. You will have the opportunity to write many event routines as you read through this book.

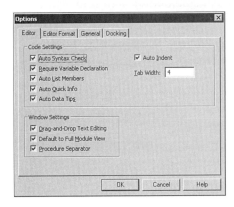

FIGURE 8.4   Use the Options dialog box in the VBE to indicate that you want VBA to require variable declaration.

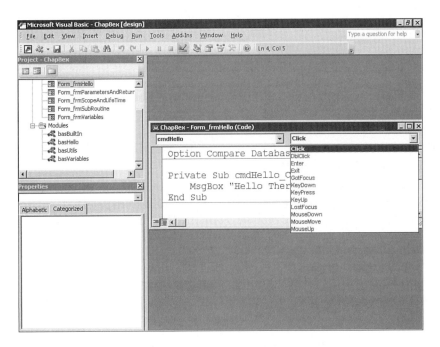

FIGURE 8.5   An event procedure for the Click event of the cmdHello command button.

Creating Event Procedures

Access automatically creates event procedures when you write event code for an object. For example, Access automatically creates the routine Private Sub cmdHello_Click when you place code in the Click event of the cmdHello command button, shown in Figure 8.5. To get to the event code of an object, follow these steps:

1. Click on the object in Design view and click the Property Sheet button on the toolbar, or right-click on the object and choose Properties from the context-sensitive menu.

2. Click on the Event properties tab.

3. Select the event for which you want to write code (for example, the On Click event).

4. Select [Event Procedure] from the drop-down list.

5. Click on the ellipsis button, which places you in the VBE within the event code for that object.

You are now ready to write code that will execute when that event occurs for the selected object.

> **NOTE**
>
> As discussed at the beginning of this chapter, the VBE opens in a separate window. It provides a programming environment consistent with that of all the other Microsoft Office applications. Modules added in the VBE will not appear in the database container until you save them within the VBE.

Creating Functions and Subroutines

You can also create your own procedures that aren't tied to a particular object or event. Depending on how and where you declare them, you can call them from anywhere in your application or from a particular Code module, Form module, or Report module.

Creating a User-Defined Routine in a Code Module

Whereas event routines are tied to a specific event that occurs for an object, user-defined routines are not associated with a particular event or a particular object. Here are the steps that you can take to create a user-defined routine:

1. Click to select the Create tab.

2. Open the Macro drop-down in the Other group and select Module (see Figure 8.6). The VBE appears, and Access places you in a new module.

3. Select Procedure from the Insert menu. The Add Procedure dialog box shown in Figure 8.7 appears.

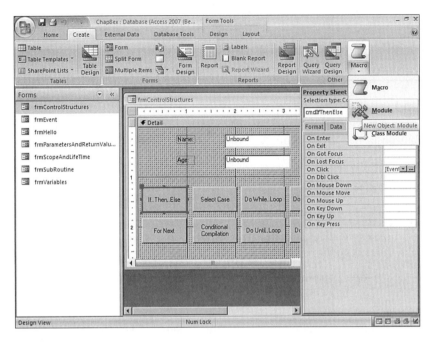

FIGURE 8.6   You use the Macro drop-down in the Other group to insert a new module.

FIGURE 8.7   In the Add Procedure dialog box, you specify the name, type, and scope of the procedure you're creating.

4. Type the name of the procedure.

5. Select Sub, Function, or Property as the Type of procedure.

6. To make the procedure available to your entire application, select Public as the Scope (Scope is covered later in this chapter in the section "Scope and Lifetime of Procedures"); to make the procedure private to this module, select Private.

7. Finally, indicate whether you want all the variables in the procedure to be static. (Static variables are discussed in this chapter under "Scope and Lifetime of Variables: Exposing Your Variables as Little as Possible.") Then click OK.

Access creates a user-defined routine. Your cursor is placed within the routine, and you can now write the code that encompasses the body of the routine.

Creating a User-Defined Routine in a Form or Report Class Module

Just as you can create a user-defined routine in a Code module, you can also create a user-defined routine in a Form or Report Class module. Here's the process:

1. While in Design view of a form or report, click to select the Design tab. Select the View Code button in the Tools group. Access places you in the VBE.

2. Choose Procedure from the Insert menu to open the Insert Procedure dialog box.

3. Type the name of the procedure.

4. Select Sub, Function, or Property as the Type of procedure.

5. To make the procedure available to your entire application, select Public as the Scope; to make the procedure private to this module, select Private.

6. Finally, indicate whether you want all the variables in the procedure to be static. When you're finished, click OK.

Access places a user-defined procedure within your Form or Report Class module. You are now ready to write the code that executes when another procedure calls the user-defined procedure.

> **TIP**
>
> Whether you're creating a procedure in a Standard module or a Class module, you're now ready to enter the code for your procedure. A great shortcut for creating a procedure is to type directly in the Code window the name of the new procedure, preceded by its designation as either a Sub or a Function. Example: **Sub *Whatever*** or **Function *Whatever***. This creates a new subroutine or function as soon as you press Enter.

Calling Event and User-Defined Procedures

Event procedures are automatically called when an event occurs for an object. For example, when a user clicks a command button, the Click event code for that command button executes.

The standard method for calling user-defined procedures is to use the Call keyword—Call SayHello, for example. You can also call the same procedure without using the Call keyword: SayHello.

> **NOTE**
>
> The Call keyword works only with subroutines, not with functions.

Although not required, using the `Call` keyword makes the statement self-documenting and easier to read. You can call a user-defined procedure from an event routine or from another user-defined procedure or function.

Scope and Lifetime of Procedures

You can declare the scope of a procedure as public or private. A procedure's scope determines how widely you can call it from other procedures. In addition to a procedure's scope, the placement of a procedure can noticeably affect your application's functionality and performance.

Another attribute of a procedure has to do with the lifetime of any variables that you declare within the procedure. By default, the variables you declare within a procedure have a *lifetime;* that is, they have value and meaning only while the procedure is executing. When the procedure completes execution, the variables that it declared are destroyed. You can alter this default lifetime by using the `Static` keyword.

Public Procedures

You can call a public procedure placed in a code module from anywhere in the application. Procedures declared in a module are automatically public. This means that, unless you specify otherwise, you can call procedures that you place in any code module from anywhere within your application.

You might think that two public procedures can't have the same name. Although this was true in earlier versions of Access, it isn't true in Access 2000 and later. If two public procedures share a name, the procedure that calls them must explicitly state which of the two routines it's calling. This is illustrated by the following code snippet found in `frmHello`'s Class module in the sample database, `CHAP8EX.ACCDB`:

```
Private Sub cmdSayGoodBye_Click()
    Call basUtils.SayGoodBye
End Sub
```

> **NOTE**
>
> Unless noted otherwise, this code, and all the sample code in this chapter, is found in `CHAP8EX.ACCDB` on the sample code CD-ROM.

You can find the `SayGoodBye` routine in two Access code modules; however, the prefix `basUtils` indicates that the routine you want to execute is in the Standard module named `basUtils`.

Procedures declared in Form or Report Class modules are also automatically public, so you can call them from anywhere within the application. The procedure called `cbfIAmPublic`, shown in Figure 8.8, is found in the form called `frmHello`. The only requirement for this procedure to be called from outside the form is that the form containing the procedure must be open in Form view. You can call the `cbfIAmPublic` procedure from anywhere within the application by using the following syntax (found in the Standard module basHello):

```
Sub CallPublicFormProc()
    Call Forms.frmHello.cbfIAmPublic
End Sub
```

> **TIP**
>
> Although all procedures (except event procedures) are by default public, you should use the `Public` keyword to show that the procedure is visible to any subroutine or function in the database.

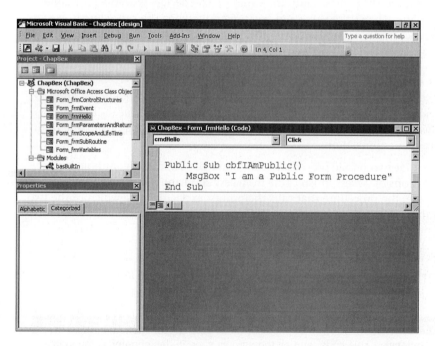

FIGURE 8.8   A public form procedure is visible to any subroutine or function in the database.

Private Procedures

As mentioned, all user-defined procedures are automatically public. If you want a procedure declared in a module to have the scope of that module only, meaning that you can call it only from another routine within the module, you must explicitly declare it as private (see Figure 8.9).

The procedure shown in Figure 8.9, called `IAmPrivate`, is private. You can call it only from other procedures in the Standard basUtils module.

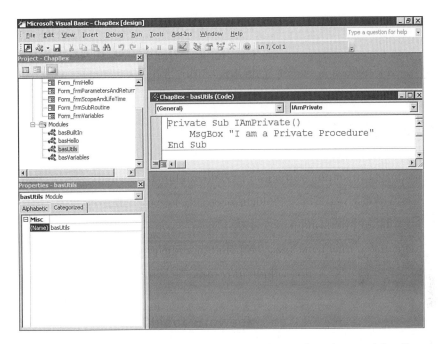

FIGURE 8.9   A private procedure is visible only to subroutines and functions in the `basUtils` module.

Scope Precedence

Private procedures always take precedence over public procedures. If a private procedure in one module has the same name as a public procedure declared in *another* module, the private procedure's code is executed if it's called by any routine in the module where it was declared. Naming conflicts don't occur between public and private procedures (unless you declare a public and private variable with the same name in the same module).

> **TIP**
>
> Developers often wonder where to place code: in Form or Report Class modules, or in Standard modules? There are pros and cons to each method. Placing code in Standard modules means that you can easily call the code from anywhere in your application, without loading a specific form or report. Public routines placed in Standard modules can also be called from other databases. For this reason, Standard modules are a great place to put generic routines that you want readily available as part of a library.
>
> Access 2000, Access 2002, Access 2003, and Access 2007 load modules on a demand-only basis, which means that procedures no longer take up memory unless they're being used. This is especially true if you plan your modules carefully (see Chapter 18, "Optimizing Your Application"). Regardless of when Access loads the code, an advantage of placing code behind forms and reports (rather than within modules) is that the form or report is self-contained and, therefore, portable. You can import the

form or report into any other database, and it still operates as expected. This object-oriented approach means that the form requires nothing from the outside world.

As you can see, there are pluses and minuses to each method. As a general rule, if a routine is specific to a particular form or report, place that routine in the form or report; if it's widely used, place it in a module.

Static Procedures

If a procedure is declared as static, all the variables declared in the procedure maintain their values between calls to the procedure. This is an alternative to explicitly declaring each variable in the procedure as static. Here's an example of a static procedure, found in basVariables:

```
Static Sub IncrementThem()
    Dim intCounter1 As Integer
    Dim intCounter2 As Integer
    Dim intCounter3 As Integer
    intCounter1 = intCounter1 + 1
    intCounter2 = intCounter2 + 1
    intCounter3 = intCounter3 + 1
    MsgBox intCounter1 & " - " & intCounter2 & " - " & intCounter3
End Sub
```

Ordinarily, each variable in this procedure would be reinitialized to zero each time the procedure is run. This means that all 1s would appear in the message box each time you run the procedure. Because the procedure is declared as static, the variables in it retain their values from call to call. That means that each time you run the procedure, the values in the message box increase. This behavior should become much clearer after the discussion of variables later in this chapter.

Working with Variables

You must consider many issues when creating VBA variables. The way that you declare a variable determines its scope, its lifetime, and more. The following topics will help you better understand declaring variables in VBA.

Declaring Variables

There are several ways to declare variables in VBA. For example, you could simply declare x=10. With this method of variable declaration, you really aren't declaring your variables at all; you're essentially declaring them as you use them. This method is quite dangerous. It lends itself to typos and other problems. If you follow the practice recommended previously—of always using the Option Explicit statement—Access will not allow you to declare variables in this manner.

You could also type **Dim intCounter**; the `Dim` statement declares the variable. The only problem with this method is that you haven't declared the type of the variable to the compiler, so it's declared as a variant variable.

Another common mistake is declaring multiple variables on the same line, as in this example:

```
Dim intCounter, intAge, intWeight As Integer
```

In this line, only the last variable is explicitly declared as an integer variable. The other variables are implicitly declared as variants. If you're going to declare multiple variables on one line, make sure each variable is specifically declared, as in the following example:

```
Dim intCounter As Integer, intAge As Integer, intWeight As Integer
```

The most efficient and bug-proof way to declare your variables is to strong-type them to the compiler and declare only one variable per line of code, as in this example:

```
Dim intCounter As Integer
Dim strName As String
```

As you can see, strong-typing declares the name of the variable as well as the type of data it can contain. This type of declaration enables the compiler to catch errors, such as storing a string in an integer variable, before your program runs. If implemented properly, this method can also reduce the resources needed to run your programs by selecting the smallest practical data type for each variable.

> **NOTE**
>
> You should try to avoid using variants whenever possible. Besides requiring a significant amount of storage space, variants are also slow because they must be resolved by the compiler at runtime. However, certain situations warrant using a variant. One example is when you want the variable to contain different types of data at different times. Another case occurs when you want to be able to differentiate between an empty variable (one that hasn't been initialized) and a variable that has a zero or a zero-length string. Also, variant variables are the only type of variable that can hold the special value of `Null`. Empty and `Null` values are covered in Chapter 13, "Advanced VBA Techniques."

VBA Data Types

VBA offers several data types for variables. Table 8.1 shows a list of the available data types, the standard for naming them, the amount of storage space they require, the data they can store, and their default values.

TABLE 8.1   Data Types and Naming Conventions

Data Type	Naming Conv Example	Storage of Data	Range	Default Value
Byte	bytValue	1 byte	0 to 255	0
Boolean	boolAnswer	2 bytes	True or False	False
Integer	intCounter	2 bytes	–32768 to 32767	0
Long Integer	lngAmount	4 bytes	–2,147,483,648 to 2,147,483,647	0
Single	sngAmount	4 bytes	–3.402823E38 to –1.401298E-45 for negative values; from 1.401298E-45 to 3.402823E38 for positive values	0
Double	dblValue	8 bytes	–1.79769313486231E308 to –4.94065645841247E-324 for negative values; from 4.94065645841247E-324 to 1.79769313486232E308 for positive values	0
Currency	curSalary	8 bytes	–922,337,203,685,477.5808 to 922,337,203,685,477.5807	0
Date	dtmStartDate	8 bytes	1/1/100 to 12/31/9999	12/30/1899
Object Reference	objExcel	4 bytes	Any object	N/A
String	strName	varies	Up to 65,526 characters	" "
Variant	varData	varies	Can contain any of the other data types except Fixed String	Empty
User-Defined Data Type	typEmp	varies	Based on Elements	N/A

Scope and Lifetime of Variables: Exposing Your Variables as Little as Possible

You have read about the different types of variables available in VBA. Like procedures, variables also have a scope. A variable can be declared as local, private (Module), or public in scope. You should try to use local variables in your code because they're shielded from being accidentally modified by other routines.

Variables also have an attribute referred to as their lifetime. The *lifetime* of a variable reflects the time during which the variable actually exists and, therefore, the time during which its value is retained. In the following sections, we take a closer look at how to set the scope and lifetime of variables.

Local Variables

Local variables are available only in the procedure where they are declared. Consider this example (not included in Chap8ex):

```
Private Sub cmdOkay_Click
  Dim strAnimal As String
  strAnimal = "Dog"
  Call ChangeAnimal
  Debug.Print strAnimal 'Still Dog
End Sub

Private Sub ChangeAnimal
  strAnimal = "Cat"
End Sub
```

This code can behave in one of three ways. If Option Explicit is in effect, meaning that all variables must be declared before they're used, this code generates a compiler error. If the Option Explicit statement isn't used, strAnimal is changed to Cat only within the context of the subroutine ChangeAnimal. If the Dim strAnimal As String statement is moved to the General Declarations section of the module, the variable's value is changed to "Cat".

> **NOTE**
>
> Notice the Debug.Print statement in the cmdOkay_Click event routine shown previously. The expression that follows the Debug.Print statement is printed in the Immediate window. The Immediate window is a tool that helps you to troubleshoot your applications. You can invoke the Immediate window from almost anywhere within your application. The easiest way to activate the Immediate window is with the Ctrl+G keystroke combination. You are placed in the VBE within the Immediate window. You can then view the expressions that were printed to the Immediate window. The Immediate window is discussed in detail in Chapter 16, "Debugging: Your Key to Successful Development."

Static Variables: A Special Type of Local Variable

The following examples illustrate the difference between local and static variables. Local variables are reinitialized each time the code is called. You can run the following procedure by opening the form named frmScopeAndLifeTime and clicking the Local Age button. Notice that each time you run the procedure, the numeral 1 is displayed in the txtNewAge text box.

```
Private Sub cmdLocalAge_Click()
  Dim intAge As Integer
  intAge = intAge + 1
  Me.txtNewAge.Value = intAge
End Sub
```

Each time this code runs, the `Dim` statement reinitializes `intAge` to zero. This is quite different from the following code, which illustrates the use of a static variable:

```
Private Sub cmdStaticAge_Click()
  Static sintAge As Integer
  sintAge = sintAge + 1
  Me.txtNewAge.Value = sintAge
End Sub
```

Each time this code executes, the variable called `sintAge` is incremented, and its value is retained. You can test this by opening on the accompanying CD-ROM the form named `frmScopeAndLifeTime` and clicking the Static Age button.

Private Variables

So far, this discussion has been limited to variables that have scope within a single procedure. Private (module-level) variables can be seen by any routine in the module they were declared in, but not from other modules. Thus, they are private to the module. You declare private variables by placing a `Private` statement, such as the following, in the General Declarations section of a form, report, or Access module:

```
[General Declarations]
Option Explicit
Private mintAge As Integer
```

You can change the value of a variable declared as private from any subroutine or function within that module. For example, the following subroutine increments the value of the private variable `mintAge` by 1. You can run this code by opening the form named `frmScopeAndLifeTime` on the accompanying CD-ROM and clicking the Module Age button.

```
Private Sub cmdModuleAge_Click()
  mintAge = mintAge + 1
  Me.txtNewAge.Value = mintAge
End Sub
```

Notice the naming convention of using the letter m to prefix the name of the variable, which denotes the variable as a private module-level variable. You should use private declarations only for variables that need to be seen by multiple procedures in the same module. Aim for making most of your variables local to make your code modular and more bulletproof.

Public Variables

You can access public variables from any VBA code in your application. They're usually limited to things such as login IDs, environment settings, and other variables that must be seen by your entire application. You can place declarations of public variables in the General Declarations section of a module. The declaration of a public variable looks like this:

```
Option Explicit
Public gintAge As Integer
```

Notice the prefix g (a relic of the old Global variables), the proper prefix for a public variable declared in a Standard module. This standard is used because public variables declared in a Standard module are visible not only to the module they were declared in, but also to other modules. The following code, placed in the Click event of the cmdPublic command button, increments the public variable gintAge by 1. You can run this code by opening the form frmScopeAndLifeTime and clicking the Public Age button.

```
Private Sub cmdPublicAge_Click()
  gintAge = gintAge + 1
  Me.txtNewAge.Value = gintAge
End Sub
```

Adding Comments to Your Code

You add comments, which have been color-coded since the release of Access 97 (prior to Access 97 they were the same color as the programming code), to modules by using an apostrophe ('). You can also use the keyword Rem, but the apostrophe is generally preferred. You can place the apostrophe at the beginning of the line of code or anywhere within it. Anything following the apostrophe is considered a comment. Figure 8.10 shows code containing comments.

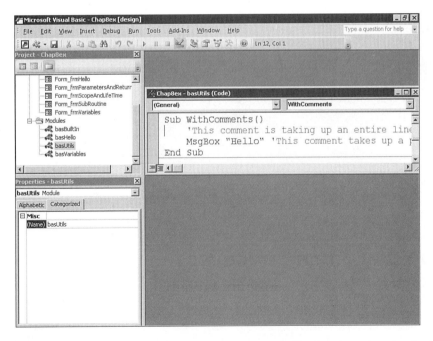

FIGURE 8.10   Code containing comments that clarify what the subroutine is doing.

> **TIP**
>
> Many people ask if it is possible to comment several lines of code at once. Although not easily discoverable, the process is quite simple. Within the VBE, right-click any toolbar or menu bar and display the Edit toolbar. Click the Comment Block tool on the Edit toolbar. To uncomment the block of code, click the Uncomment Block tool.

Using the Line Continuation Character

Access Basic code, used in Access 2.0, didn't have a line continuation character. Therefore, you had to scroll a lot, as well as pull out a bag of tricks to simulate continuing a line of code. With VBA, Access 97 and higher solve this problem: The line continuation character is an underscore. Figure 8.11 illustrates the use of this character.

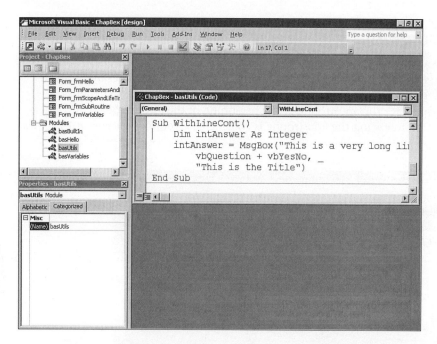

FIGURE 8.11   The line continuation character is used to improve the readability of a long line of code.

Using the VBA Control Structures

VBA gives the developer several different constructs for looping and decision processing. The most commonly used ones are covered in the following sections and are found in the form called frmControlStructures.

If...Then...Else

The `If...Then...Else` construct evaluates whether a condition is `True`. In the following example, anything between `If` and `Else` will occur if the statement evaluates to `True`, and any code between `Else` and `End If` will be executed if the statement evaluates to `False`. The `Else` is optional.

```
Private Sub cmdIfThenElse_Click()
 If IsNull(Me.txtName.Value) or IsNull(Me.txtAge.Value) Then
    MsgBox "Name or Age is Blank"
  Else
    MsgBox "Your Name Is " & Me.txtName.Value _
        & " And Your Age Is " & Me.txtAge.Value
  End If
End Sub
```

This code tests whether the text box called `txtName` or the text box `txtAge` contains a `Null`. A different message is displayed depending on whether one of the text boxes contains a `Null` value.

One-line `If` statements are also permitted; they look like this:

```
If IsNull(Me.txtvalue.Value) Then MsgBox "You must enter a value"
```

However, this format for an `If` statement isn't recommended because it reduces readability.

Another useful form of an `If` statement is `ElseIf`, which enables you to evaluate an unlimited number of conditions in one `If` statement. The following code gives you an example: (This example is not included in `CHAP8EX`.)

```
Sub MultipleIfs(intNumber As Integer)
   If intNumber = 1 Then
      MsgBox "You entered a one"
   ElseIf intNumber = 2 Then
      MsgBox "You entered a two"
   ElseIf intNumber >= 3 And intNumber <= 10 Then
      MsgBox "You entered a number between 3 and 10"
   Else
      MsgBox "You entered some other number"
   End If
End Sub
```

The conditions in an `If` statement are evaluated in the order in which they appear. For this reason, it's best to place the most common conditions first. After a condition is met, execution continues immediately after `End If`. If no conditions are met, and there's no `Else` statement, execution will also continue immediately after `End If`.

> **NOTE**
>
> If multiple conditions exist, using a `Select Case` statement, described later in this chapter, is almost always preferable to using an `If` statement. `Case` statements generally make your code easier to read and maintain.

The Immediate `If` (`IIf`)

An Immediate `If` (`IIf`) is a variation of an `If` statement. It's actually a built-in function that returns one of two values, depending on whether the condition being tested is true or false. Here's an example: (This code is not included in `CHAP8EX`.)

```
Function EvalSales(curSales As Currency) As String
   EvalSales = IIf(curSales >= 100000, "Great Job", "Keep Plugging")
End Function
```

This function evaluates the curSales parameter to see whether its value is greater than or equal to $100,000. If it is, the function returns the string "Great Job"; otherwise, the function returns the string "Keep Plugging".

> **CAUTION**
>
> Both the `True` and `False` portions of the `IIf` are evaluated, so if there's a problem with either part of the expression (for example, a divide-by-zero condition), an error occurs.

The `IIf` function is most often used in a calculated control on a form or report, or to create a new field in a query. Probably the most common example is an `IIf` expression that determines whether the value of a control is `IsNull`. If the value is `IsNull`, you can have the expression return a zero or an empty string; otherwise, you can have the expression return the value in the control. The following expression, for example, evaluates the value of a control on a form:

```
=IIf(IsNull(Forms!frmOrders.txtFreight.Value),0,_
   Forms!frmOrders.txtFreight.Value)
```

This expression displays either a zero or the value for freight in the control called txtFreight.

> **NOTE**
>
> Although the `IIf` function can be used to handle `Null`s, the built-in `NZ` function is a more efficient solution to this problem and avoids the inherent pitfalls of `IIf`.

> **CAUTION**
>
> The `IIf` function is rather slow. It is best to avoid using it whenever possible by replacing it with a properly formed `If...Then...Else` block.

The Conditional `If`: **Conditional Compilation**

Conditional compilation enables you to selectively execute blocks of code. This feature is useful in several situations:

▶ When you want certain blocks of code to execute in the demo version of your product and other blocks to execute in your product's retail version

▶ When you're distributing your application in different countries and want certain blocks of code to apply to some countries but not to others

▶ When you want certain blocks of code to execute only during the testing of your application

Conditional compilation is done by using the #If...Then...#Else directive, as shown here and found under the Conditional Compilation command button on the frmControlStructures form:

```
Sub cmdConditionalCompilation_Click()
    #If Language = "Spanish" Then
        MsgBox "Hola, Que Tal?"
    #Else
        MsgBox "Hello, How Are You?"
    #End If
End Sub
```

> **NOTE**
>
> The difference between conditional compilation and standard If..Then..Else logic is that conditional compilation is performed at compile time. Only the appropriate line(s) of code is placed in the compiled code. This improves performance if similar logic is needed throughout the application.

You can declare the compiler constant, in this case, Language, in one of two places: in a module's General Declarations section or in the Project Properties dialog box. A compiler constant declared in the General Declarations section of a module looks like this:

```
#Const Language = "Spanish"
```

The disadvantage of this constant is that you can't declare it as public. It isn't possible to create public compiler constants by using the #Const directive. This means that any compiler constants declared in a module's Declarations section can be used only within that module. The major advantage of declaring this type of compiler constant is that it can contain a string. For example, the compiler constant Language, defined in the preceding paragraph, is given the value "Spanish".

Public compiler constants can be declared by modifying the Project Properties. Because they are public in scope, compiler constants declared in the Project Properties can be referred to from anywhere in your application. The major limitation on compiler directives set up in Project Properties is that they can contain only integers. For example, you would have to enter `Language = 1`.

To define compiler constants using the Project Properties dialog box, right-click within the Project window and select *projectx* Properties, where *projectx* is the name of the project you are working with. You can now enter the values you need into the text box labeled Conditional Compilation Arguments. You can enter several arguments by separating them with a colon, such as `Language = 1 : Version = 2`.

With the compiler directive `Language=1`, the code would look like this:

```
Sub ConditionalIf()
    #If Language = 1 Then
        MsgBox "Hola, Que Tal?"
    #Else
        MsgBox "Hello, How Are You?"
    #End If
End Sub
```

> **NOTE**
>
> For this code to execute properly, you must remove the constant declaration from the previous example.

Notice that `ConditionalIf` now evaluates the constant `Language` against the integer of 1.

It's important to understand that using conditional constants isn't the same as using regular constants or variables with the standard `If…Then…Else` construct. Regular constants or variables are evaluated at runtime, which requires processing time each occasion the application is run. Conditional constants and conditional `If…Then…Else` statements control which sections of code are actually compiled. All resolution is completed at compile time; this eliminates the need for unnecessary processing at runtime.

Select Case

Rather than using multiple `If…Then…Else` statements, using a `Select Case` statement is often much clearer, as shown here. This `Select Case` statement is found under the Select Case command button of the `frmControlStructures` form.

```
Private Sub cmdCase_Click()
    Dim intAge As Integer
    intAge = Nz(Me.txtAge.Value, 0)      Select Case intAge
        Case 0
          MsgBox "You Must Enter a Number"
        Case 1 To 18
          MsgBox "You Are Just a Kid"
        Case 19, 20, 21
```

```
        MsgBox "You are Almost an Adult"
      Case 22 to 40
        MsgBox "Good Deal"
      Case Is > 40
        MsgBox "Getting Up There!"
      Case Else
        MsgBox "You Entered an Invalid Number"
    End Select
End Sub
```

This subroutine first uses the Nz function to convert a Null or empty value in the txtAge control to 0; otherwise, the value in txtAge is stored in intAge. The Select Case statement then evaluates intAge. If the value is 0, the code displays a message box with You Must Enter a Number. If the value is between 1 and 18 inclusive, the code displays a message box saying You Are Just a Kid. If the user enters 19, 20, or 21, the code displays the message You are Almost an Adult. If the user enters a value between 22 and 40 inclusive, the code displays the message Good Deal. If the user enters a value greater than 40, the code displays the message Getting Up There!; otherwise, the user gets a message indicating that she entered an invalid number.

Looping

Several looping structures are available in VBA; most are discussed in this section. Take a look at the following example of a looping structure (found under the Do While…Loop command button of the frmControlStructures form):

```
Sub cmdDoWhileLoop_Click()

    Do While Nz(Me.txtAge.Value)< 35

        Me.txtAge.Value = Nz(Me.txtAge.Value) + 1
    Loop
End Sub
```

In this structure, if the value in the txtAge text box is greater than or equal to 35, the code in the loop is not executed. If you want the code to execute unconditionally at least one time, you need to use the following construct (found under the Do…Loop While command button of the frmControlStructures form):

```
Sub cmdDoLoopWhile_Click()

    Do

        Me.txtAge = Nz(Me.txtAge.Value) + 1
    Loop While Nz(Me.txtAge.Value) < 35
End Sub
```

This code will execute one time, even if the value in the `txtAge` text box is set to 35. The `Do While…Loop` in the previous example evaluates before the code is executed, so it doesn't ensure code execution. The `Do…Loop While` is evaluated at the end of the loop and therefore guarantees execution.

Alternatives to the `Do While…Loop` and the `Do…Loop While` are `Do Until…Loop` and `Do…Loop Until`. `Do Until…Loop` (found under the `Do Until…Loop` command button of the `frmControlStructures` form) works like this:

```
Sub cmdDoUntil_Click()

   Do Until Nz(Me.txtAge.Value) = 35

      Me.txtAge.Value = Nz(Me.txtAge.Value) + 1
   Loop
End Sub
```

This loop continues to execute until the value in the `txtAge` text box becomes equal to 35. The `Do…Loop Until` construct (found under the `Do…Loop Until` command button of the `frmControlStructures` form) is another variation:

```
Sub cmdLoopUntil_Click()

   Do

      Me.txtAge.Value = Nz(Me.txtAge.Value) + 1
   Loop Until Nz(Me.txtAge.Value) = 35
End Sub
```

As with the `Do…Loop While` construct, the `Do…Loop Until` construct doesn't evaluate the condition until the end of the loop, so the code in the loop is guaranteed to execute at least once.

TIP

As covered in Chapter 18, it is not a good idea to reference a control over and over again in a loop. Notice that, in the looping examples, the `txtAge` control is referenced each time through the loop. This was done to keep the examples simple. To eliminate the performance problem associated with this technique, use the code that follows (found under the `cmdEfficient` command button on the `frmControlStructures` form):

```
Private Sub cmdEfficient_Click()
    Dim intCounter As Integer
    intCounter = Nz(Me.txtAge.Value)
    Do While intCounter < 35
       intCounter = intCounter + 1
    Loop
    Me.txtAge.Value = intCounter
End Sub
```

> **CAUTION**
>
> With any of the looping constructs, it's easy to unintentionally cause a loop to execute endlessly, as is shown in this example and can also be illustrated with the code samples shown previously. (This code is not included in CHAP8EX.)
>
> ```
> Sub EndlessLoop()
>     Dim intCounter As Integer
>     intCounter = 5
>     Do
>         Debug.Print intCounter
>         intCounter = intCounter + 1
>     Loop Until intCounter = 5
> End Sub
> ```
>
> This code snippet sets `intCounter` equal to 5. The code in the loop increments `intCounter` and then tests to see whether `intCounter` equals 5. If it doesn't, the code in the loop executes another time. Because `intCounter` will never become equal to 5 (it starts at 6 within the Do loop), the loop executes endlessly. You need to use Ctrl+Break to exit the loop; however, Ctrl+Break doesn't work in Access's runtime version.

For…Next

The `For...Next` construct is used when you have an exact number of iterations you want to perform. It looks like this and is found under the For…Next command button of the `frmControlStructures` form:

```
Sub cmdForNext_Click()
    Dim intCounter As Integer
    For intCounter = 1 To 5
        Me.txtAge.Value = Nz(Me.txtAge.Value) + 1
    Next intCounter
End Sub
```

Note that `intCounter` is self-incrementing. The start value and the stop value can both be variables. A For…Next construct can also be given a step value, as shown in the following. (The counter is incremented by the value of `Step` each time the loop is processed.)

```
Sub ForNextStep()
' Note that this code is not in database Chap8ex.mdb
    Dim intCounter As Integer
    For intCounter = 1 To 5 Step 2
        Me.txtAge.Value = Nz(Me.txtAge.Value) + 1
    Next intCounter
End Sub
```

With...End With

The With...End With statement executes a series of statements on a single object or user-defined type. Here's an example (found under the With...End With command button of the frmControlStructures form:

```
Private Sub cmdWithEndWith_Click()
    With Me.txtAge
        .BackColor = 16777088
        .ForeColor = 16711680
        .Value = "Hello World"
        .FontName = "Arial"
    End With
End Sub
```

This code performs four operations on the txtAge text box, found on the form it's run on. The code modifies the BackColor, ForeColor, Value, and FontName properties of the txtAge text box.

> **TIP**
>
> The With...End With statement offers two main benefits. The first is simply less typing: You don't need to repeat the object name for each action you want to perform on the object. The more important benefit involves performance. Because the object is referred to once rather than multiple times, this code runs much more efficiently. The benefits are even more pronounced when the With...End With construct is found in a loop.

For Each...Next

The For Each...Next statement executes a group of statements on each member of an array or collection. The following example (found under the For Each...Next command button of the frmControlStructures form) illustrates the use of this powerful construct:

```
Private Sub cmdForEachNext_Click()

    Dim ctl As Control
    For Each ctl In Controls
        ctl.FontSize = 8
    Next ctl
End Sub
```

This code loops through each control on the form, modifying the FontSize property of each control.

As in the following example, the With...End With construct is often used along with the For Each...Next construct:

```
Private Sub cmdForEachWith_Click()
    Dim ctl As Control
    For Each ctl In Controls
        With ctl
            .ForeColor = 16711680
            .FontName = "Arial"
            .FontSize = 14
        End With
    Next ctl

End Sub
```

This code loops through each control on a form; the ForeColor, FontName, and FontSize properties of each control on the form are modified.

CAUTION

Before you put all this good information to use, remember that no error handling has been implemented in the code yet. If one of the controls on the form in the example doesn't have a ForeColor, FontName, or FontSize property, the code would cause an error. In Chapter 9, "Objects, Properties, Methods, and Events Explained," you will learn how to determine the type of an object before you perform a command on it. Knowing the type of an object before you try to modify its properties can help you prevent errors.

Passing Parameters and Returning Values

Both subroutines and functions can receive arguments (parameters), but subroutines can return values only when you use the ByRef keyword. The following subroutine (found under the Pass Parameters command button of the frmParametersAndReturnValues form) receives two parameters: txtFirst and txtLast. It then displays a message box with the first character of each of the parameters that was passed.

```
Private Sub cmdPassParameters_Click()
    Call Initials(Nz(Me.txtFirstName.Value), Nz(Me.txtLastName.Value))
End Sub

Sub Initials(strFirst As String, strLast As String)
' This procedure can be found by selecting General in
' the Object drop-down list in the VBE window
    MsgBox "Your Initials Are: " & Left$(strFirst, 1) _
        & Left$(strLast, 1)
End Sub
```

Notice that the values in the controls txtFirstName and txtLastName from the current form (represented by the Me keyword) are passed to the subroutine called Initials. The parameters are received as strFirst and strLast. The code displays the first left character of each parameter in the message box.

The preceding code simply passes values and then operates on those values. This next example (found under the Return Values command button of the frmParametersAndReturnValues form) uses a function to return a value:

```
Private Sub cmdReturnValues_Click()
    Dim strInitials As String
    strInitials = ReturnInit(Nz(Me.txtFirstName.Value), _
        Nz(Me.txtLastName.Value))
    MsgBox "Your initials are: " & strInitials
End Sub


Function ReturnInit(strFName As String, strLName As String) As String
' This procedure can be found by selecting General in
' the Object drop-down list in the VBE window
    ReturnInit = Left$(strFName, 1) & Left(strLName, 1)
End Function
```

Notice that this example calls the function ReturnInit, sending values contained in the two text boxes as parameters. The function sets ReturnInit (the name of the function) equal to the first two characters of the strings. This returns the value to the calling routine (cmdReturnValues _Click) and sets strInitials equal to the return value.

> **NOTE**
>
> Notice that the function ReturnInit is set to receive two string parameters. You know this because of the As String keywords that follow each parameter. The function is also set to return a string. You know this because the keyword As String follows the list of the parameters, outside the parentheses. If you don't explicitly state that the function should return a particular type of data, it returns a variant.

Executing Procedures from the Module Window

You can easily test procedures from the Module window in Access 2007. Simply click anywhere inside the procedure you want to execute, and then press the F5 key or click the Run Sub/UserForm button on the toolbar. The procedure you're in will execute as though you had called it from code or from the Immediate pane of the Debug window.

The DoCmd Object: Performing Macro Actions

The Access environment is rich with objects that have built-in properties and methods. By using VBA code, you can modify the properties and execute the methods. One of the objects available in Access is the DoCmd object, used to execute macro actions in Visual Basic procedures. The macro actions are executed as methods of the DoCmd object. The syntax looks like this:

```
DoCmd.ActionName [arguments]
```

Here's a practical example:

```
DoCmd.OpenReport strReportName, acViewPreview
```

The OpenReport method is a method of the DoCmd object; it runs a report. The first two parameters that the OpenReport method receives are the name of the report you want to run and the view in which you want the report to appear (Preview, Normal, or Design). The name of the report and the view are both arguments of the OpenReport method.

Most macro actions have corresponding DoCmd methods that you can find in Help, but some don't. They are AddMenu, MsgBox, RunApp, RunCode, SendKeys, SetValue, StopAllMacros, and StopMacro. The SendKeys method is the only one that has any significance to you as a VBA programmer. The remaining macro actions either have no application to VBA code, or you can perform them more efficiently by using VBA functions and commands. The VBA language includes a MsgBox function, for example, that's far more robust than its macro action counterpart.

Many of the DoCmd methods have optional parameters. If you don't supply an argument, its default value is assumed. You can use commas as place markers to designate the position of missing arguments, as shown here:

```
DoCmd.OpenForm "frmOrders", , ,"[OrderAmount] > 1000"
```

The OpenForm method of the DoCmd object receives seven parameters; the last six parameters are optional. In the example, two parameters are explicitly specified. The first is the name of the form ("FrmOrders"), a required parameter. The second and third parameters have been omitted, meaning that you're accepting their default values. The commas, used as place markers for the second and third parameters, are necessary because one of the parameters following them is explicitly designated. The fourth parameter is the Where condition for the form, which has been designated as the record in which the OrderAmount is greater than 1,000. The remaining parameters haven't been referred to, so default values are used for them.

If you prefer, you can use named parameters to designate the parameters that you are passing. Named parameters, covered later in this chapter, can greatly simplify the preceding syntax. With named parameters, you don't need to place the arguments in a particular order, and you don't need to worry about counting commas. The preceding syntax can be changed to the following:

```
DoCmd.OpenForm FormName:="frmOrders", WhereCondition:=
"[OrderAmount] > 1000"
```

Working with Built-In Functions

VBA has a rich and comprehensive function library as well as tools to assist in their use.

Built-In Functions

Some of the more commonly used VBA functions and examples are listed in the following sections. On some rainy day, go through the online Help to become familiar with the rest.

> **NOTE**
>
> The following examples are located in basBuiltIn in the CHAP8EX database.

Format

The Format function formats expressions in the style specified. The first parameter is the expression you want to format; the second is the type of format you want to apply. Here's an example of using the Format function:

```
Sub FormatData()
    Debug.Print Format$(50, "Currency")
    'Prints $50.00
    Debug.Print Format$(Now, "Short Date")
    'Prints the current date
    Debug.Print Format$(Now, "DDDD")
    'Displays the word for the day
    Debug.Print Format$(Now, "DDD")
    'Displays 3 - CHAR Day
    Debug.Print Format$(Now, "YYYY")
    'Displays 4 - digit Year
    Debug.Print Format$(Now, "WW")
    'Displays the Week Number
End Sub
```

Instr

The Instr function returns the position where one string begins within another string:

```
Sub InstrExample()
  Debug.Print InStr("Alison Balter", "Balter") 'Returns 8
  Debug.Print InStr("Hello", "l") 'Returns 3
  Debug.Print InStr("c:\my documents\my file.txt", "\") 'Returns 3
End Sub
```

InStrRev

InStrRev begins searching at the end of a string and returns the position where one string is found within another string:

```
Sub InstrRevExample()
    Debug.Print InStrRev("c:\my documents\my file.txt", "\") 'Returns 16
End Sub
```

Notice that the InStr function returns 3 as the starting position for the backslash character within "c:\my documents\my file.txt", whereas the InStrRev function returns 16 as
the starting position for the backslash character in the same string. The reason is that
InStr starts searching at the beginning of the string, continuing until it finds a match,
whereas InStrRev begins searching at the end of the string, continuing until it finds a
match.

Left
Left returns the leftmost number of characters in a string:

```
Sub LeftExample()
  Debug.Print Left$("Hello World", 7) 'Prints Hello W
End Sub
```

Right
Right returns the rightmost number of characters in a string:

```
Sub RightExample()
 Debug.Print Right$("Hello World", 7) 'Prints o World
End Sub
```

Mid
Mid returns a substring of a specified number of characters in a string. This example starts
at the fourth character and returns five characters:

```
Sub MidExample()
    Debug.Print Mid$("Hello World", 4, 5) ''Prints lo Wo
End Sub
```

UCase
UCase returns a string that is all uppercase:

```
Sub UCaseExample()
    Debug.Print UCase$("Hello World") 'Prints HELLO WORLD
End Sub
```

DatePart
DatePart returns the specified part of a date:

```
Sub DatePartExample()
    Debug.Print DatePart("YYYY", Now)
    'Prints the Year
    Debug.Print DatePart("M", Now)
```

```
    'Prints the Month Number
    Debug.Print DatePart("Q", Now)
    'Prints the Quarter Number
    Debug.Print DatePart("Y", Now)
    'Prints the Day of the Year
    Debug.Print DatePart("WW", Now)
    'Prints the Week of the Year
End Sub
```

DateDiff

DateDiff returns the interval of time between two dates:

```
Sub DateDiffExample()
  Debug.Print DateDiff("d", Now, "12/31/2010")
  ''Days until 12/31/2010
  Debug.Print DateDiff("m", Now, "12/31/2010")
  ''Months until 12/31/2010
  Debug.Print DateDiff("yyyy", Now, "12/31/2010")
  ''Years until 12/31/2010
  Debug.Print DateDiff("q", Now, "12/31/2010")
  ''Quarters until 12/31/2010
End Sub
```

DateAdd

DateAdd returns the result of adding or subtracting a specified period of time to a date:

```
Sub DateAddExample()
    Debug.Print DateAdd("d", 3, Now)
    'Today plus 3 days
    Debug.Print DateAdd("m", 3, Now)
    'Today plus 3 months
    Debug.Print DateAdd("yyyy", 3, Now)
    'Today plus 3 years
    Debug.Print DateAdd("q", 3, Now)
    'Today plus 3 quarters
    Debug.Print DateAdd("ww", 3, Now)
    'Today plus 3 weeks
    Debug.Print DateAdd("ww", -3, Now)
    'Today minus 3 weeks
End Sub
```

Replace

Replace replaces one string with another:

```
Sub ReplaceExample()
    Debug.Print Replace("Say Hello if you want to", "hello", "bye")
    'Returns Say bye if you want to
```

```
    Debug.Print Replace("This gets rid of all of the spaces", " ", "")
    'Returns Thisgetsridofallofthespaces
End Sub
```

StrRev
StrRev reverses the order of text in a string:

```
Sub StrReverseExample()
    Debug.Print StrReverse("This string looks very funny when reversed!")
    'Returns !desrever nehw ynnuf yrev skool gnirts sihT
End Sub
```

MonthName
MonthName returns the text string associated with a month number:

```
Sub MonthNameExample()
    Debug.Print MonthName(7)
    'Returns July
    Debug.Print MonthName(11)
    'Returns November
End Sub
```

Functions Made Easy with the Object Browser

With the Object Browser, you can view members of an ActiveX component's type library. In plain English, the Object Browser enables you to easily browse through a component's methods, properties, and constants. You can also copy information and add it to your code. It even adds a method's parameters for you. The following steps let you browse among the available methods, copy the method you want, and paste it into your code:

1. With the VBE active, select View, Object Browser from the menu (note that the menu line also shows an icon that you can use from the toolbar), or press F2 to open the Object Browser window (see Figure 8.12).

8

FIGURE 8.12   The Object Browser showing all the classes in the CHAP8EX database and all the members in the basUtils module.

2. The Object Browser window is divided into two parts: the upper part of the window and the lower part. The drop-down list at the upper left of the window is used to filter the items to be displayed in the lower part of the window. Use this drop-down list to select the project or library whose classes and members you want to view in the lower part of the window.

3. In the lower portion of the window, select the class from the left list box, which lists Class modules, templates for new objects, standard modules, and modules containing subroutines and functions.

4. Select a related property, method, event, constant, function, or statement from the Members Of list box. In Figure 8.12, the basUtils module is selected from the list box on the left. Notice that the subroutines and functions included in basUtils appear in the list box on the right.

5. Click the Copy to Clipboard button (third from the right in the upper toolbar within the Object Browser window) to copy the function name and its parameters to the Clipboard so that you can easily paste it into your code.

The example in Figure 8.12 shows choosing a user-defined function selected from a module in a database, but you can also select any built-in function. Figure 8.13 shows an example in which the DatePart function is selected from the VBA library. The Object Browser exposes all libraries referred to by the database and is covered in more detail in Chapters 9 and 24.

FIGURE 8.13   The Object Browser with the VBA library selected.

Working with Constants

A *constant* is a meaningful name given to a meaningless number or string. Constants can be used only for values that don't change at runtime. A tax rate or commission rate, for example, might be constant throughout your application. There are three types of constants in Access:

▶ Symbolic

▶ Intrinsic

▶ System defined

Symbolic constants, created by using the Const keyword, are used to improve the readability of your code and make code maintenance easier. Instead of referring to the number .0875 every time you want to refer to the tax rate, you can refer to the constant mccurTaxRate. If the tax rate changes, and you need to modify the value in your code, you'll make the change in only one place. Furthermore, unlike the number .0875, the name mccurTaxRate is self-documenting.

Intrinsic constants are built into Microsoft Access; they are part of the language itself. As an Access programmer, you can use constants supplied by Microsoft Access, Visual Basic, Data Access Objects (DAO), and ADO. You can also use constants provided by any object libraries you're using in your application.

There are only three system-defined constants—True, False, and Null—and they are available to all applications on your computer.

Working with Symbolic Constants

As mentioned, you declare a symbolic constant by using the Const keyword. You can declare a constant in a subroutine or function, or in the General section of a Form or Report module. You can strong-type constants in Access 2000 and later. The declaration and use of a private constant looks like this:

```
Private Const TAXRATE As Currency = .0875
```

This code, when placed in a module's Declarations section, creates a private constant called TAXRATE and sets it equal to .0875. Here's how you use the constant in code:

```
Function TotalAmount(curSaleAmount As Currency)
   TotalAmount = curSaleAmount * TAXRATE
End Function
```

This routine multiplies the curSaleAmount, received as a parameter, by the constant TAXRATE. It returns the result of the calculation by setting the function name equal to the product of the two values. The advantage of the constant in this example is that the code is more readable than TotalAmount = curSaleAmount * .0875 would be.

Scoping Symbolic Constants

Just as regular variables have scope, user-defined constants have scope. In the preceding example, you created a private constant. The following statement, when placed in a module's General Declarations section, creates a public constant:

```
Public Const TAXRATE As Currency = .0875
```

Because this constant is declared as public, you can access it from any subroutine or function (including event routines) in your entire application. To better understand the benefits of a public constant, consider a case in which you have many functions and subroutines all making reference to the constant TAXRATE. Imagine what would happen if the tax rate were to change. If you hadn't used a constant, you would need to search your entire application, replacing the old tax rate with the new tax rate. However, because your public constant is declared in one place, you can easily go in and modify the one line of code where this constant is declared.

By definition, the values of constants cannot be modified at runtime. If you try to modify the value of a constant, you get this VBA compiler error:

```
Assignment to constant not permitted
```

Figure 8.14 illustrates this message box. You can see that an attempt is made to modify the value of the constant TAXRATE, which results in a compile error.

FIGURE 8.14   Trying to modify the value of a constant.

If you need to change the value at runtime, you should consider storing the value in a table instead of declaring it as a constant. You can read the value into a variable when the application loads and then modify the variable if needed. If you choose, you can write the new value back to the table.

Working with Intrinsic Constants

Microsoft Access declares a number of intrinsic constants that you can use in Code, Form, and Report modules. Because they're reserved by Microsoft Access, you can't modify their values or reuse their names; however, you can use them at any time without declaring them.

You should use intrinsic constants whenever possible in your code. Besides making your code more readable, they make your code more portable to future releases of Microsoft Access. Microsoft might change the value associated with a constant, but Microsoft isn't likely to change the constant's name. All intrinsic constants appear in the Object Browser; to activate it, simply click the Object Browser tool on the Visual Basic toolbar. To view the constants that are part of the Access library, select Access from the Object Browser's Project/Library drop-down list. Click Constants in the Classes list box, and a list of those constants is displayed in the Members Of 'Constants' list box (see Figure 8.15).

In the list shown in Figure 8.15, all VBA constants are prefixed with *vb*, all Data Access Object constants are prefixed with *db*, and all constants that are part of the Access language are prefixed with *ac*. To view the Visual Basic language constants, select VBA from the Project/Library drop-down list and Constants from the Classes list box. If the project you are working with has a reference to the ADO library, you can view these constants by selecting ADODB from the Project/Library drop-down list. Click <globals>. A list of the ADODB constants appears. (These constants have the prefix *ad*.)

FIGURE 8.15   Using the Object Browser to view intrinsic constants.

Another way to view constants is within the context of the parameter you're working with in the Code window. Right-click the name of a parameter and select List Constants to display the constants associated with the parameter.

Working with the Visual Basic Editor Tools

Effectively using the tips and tricks of the trade, many of which are highlighted in this chapter, can save you hours of time. These tricks help you to navigate around the coding environment, as well as to modify your code quickly and easily. They include the capability to easily zoom to a user-defined procedure, search and replace within modules, get help on VBA functions and commands, and split the Code window so that two procedures can be viewed simultaneously.

Access 2007 offers a very rich development environment. It includes several features that make coding easier and more pleasant for you. These features include the capability to do the following:

▶ List properties and methods

▶ List constants

▶ Get quick information on a command or function

▶ Get parameter information

▶ Enable Access to finish a word for you

▶ Get a definition of a function

All these features that help you with coding are available with a right-click when you place your cursor within the Module window.

List Properties and Methods

With the List Properties and Methods feature, you can view all the objects, properties, and methods available for the current object. To invoke this feature, right-click after the name of the object and select List Properties, Methods. (You can also press Ctrl+J.) The applicable objects, properties, and methods appear in a list box (see Figure 8.16). To find the appropriate object, property, or method in the list, use one of these methods:

▶ Begin typing the name of the object, property, or method.

▶ Use the up- and down-arrow keys to move through the list.

▶ Scroll through the list and select your choice.

Use one of these methods to insert your selection:

▶ Double-click the entry.

▶ Click to select the entry. Then press Tab to insert, or Enter to insert and move to the next line.

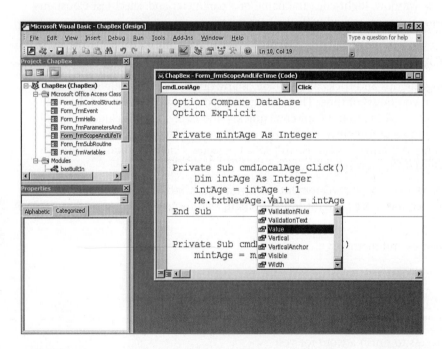

FIGURE 8.16   A list of properties and methods for the TextBox object.

TIP

The Auto List Members option, available on the Editor tab of the Options dialog box, causes the List Properties and Methods feature, as well as the List Constants feature, to be invoked automatically each time you type the name of an object or property.

List Constants

The List Constants feature, which is part of IntelliSense, opens a drop-down list displaying valid constants for a property you have typed and for functions with arguments that are constants. It works in a similar manner to the List Properties and Methods feature. To invoke it, right-click after the name of the property or argument (in cases in which multiple arguments are available, the previous argument must be delimited with a comma) and select List Constants (or press Ctrl+Shift+J). A list of valid constants appears (see Figure 8.17). You can use any of the methods listed in the preceding section to select the constant you want.

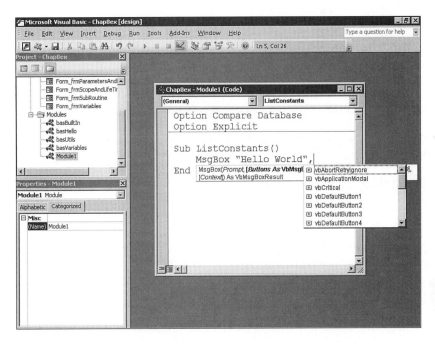

FIGURE 8.17   A list of constants for the vbMsgBoxStyle parameter.

Quick Info

The Quick Info feature gives you the full syntax for a function, statement, procedure, method, or variable. To use this feature, right-click after the name of the function, statement, procedure, method, or variable, and then select Quick Info (or press Ctrl+I). A tip appears, showing the valid syntax for the item (see Figure 8.18). As you type each parameter in the item, it's displayed in boldface type until you type the comma that delineates it from the next parameter.

TIP

The Auto Quick Info option, available in the Options dialog box, causes the Quick Info feature to be invoked automatically each time you type the name of an object or property.

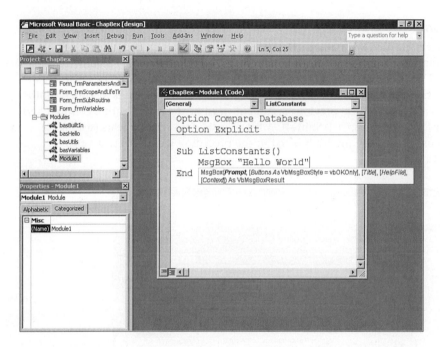

FIGURE 8.18   The syntax for the `MsgBox` function.

Parameter Info

The Parameter Info feature gives you information about the parameters of a function, statement, or method. To use this feature, after the delimiter that denotes the end of the function, statement, or method name, right-click and select Parameter Info (or press Ctrl+Shift+I). A pop-up list appears with information about the parameters of the function or statement. This list doesn't close until you enter all the required parameters, you complete the function without any optional parameters, or you press the Esc key.

> **NOTE**
>
> The Parameter Info feature supplies information about the initial function only. If parameters of a function are themselves functions, you must use Quick Info to find information about the embedded functions.

Complete Word

The Complete Word feature completes a word you're typing. To use this feature, you must first type enough characters for Visual Basic to recognize the word you want. Next, right-click and select Complete Word (or press Ctrl+Spacebar). Visual Basic then finishes the word you're typing.

Definition

The Definition feature shows the place in the Code window where the selected variable or procedure is defined. To get a definition of a variable or procedure, right-click in the name of the variable or procedure of interest, and select Definition (or press Shift+F2). Your cursor is moved to the module and location where the variable or procedure was defined.

As you become more proficient with VBA, you can create libraries of VBA functions and subroutines. When you're viewing a call to a particular subroutine or function, you often want to view the code behind that function. Fortunately, VBA gives you a quick and easy way to navigate from procedure to procedure. Assume that the following code appears in your application:

```
Private Sub cmdOkay_Click()
    Dim intAgeInTen As Integer
    If IsNull(Me.txtNameValue) Or IsNull(Me.txtAge.Value) Then
        MsgBox "You must fill in name and age"
        Exit Sub
    Else
        MsgBox "Your Name Is: " & Me.txtName.Value & " _
        and Your Age Is: " & Nz(Me.txtAge.Value)
        Call EvaluateAge(Nz(Me.txtAge.Value))
        intAgeInTen = AgePlus10(Fix(Val(Me.txtAge.Value)))
        MsgBox "In 10 Years You Will Be " & intAgeInTen
    End If
End Sub
```

If you want to quickly jump to the procedure called EvaluateAge, all you need to do is place your cursor anywhere within the name, EvaluateAge, and then press Shift+F2. This procedure immediately moves you to the EvaluateAge procedure. Ctrl+Shift+F2 takes you back to the routine you came from (in this case, cmdOkay_Click). This procedure works for both functions and subroutines.

TIP

If you prefer, you can right-click the name of the routine you want to jump to and select Definition. To return to the original procedure, right-click again and select Last Position.

NOTE

If the definition is in a referenced library, the Object Browser is invoked, and the definition is displayed.

Mysteries of the Coding Environment Solved

If you're a developer who's new to VBA, you might be confused by the VBE. We will begin by talking about the Code window. The Code window has two combo boxes, shown in Figure 8.19. The combo box on the left lists objects. For a form or report, the list includes all its objects; for a standard module, which has no objects, only (General) appears.

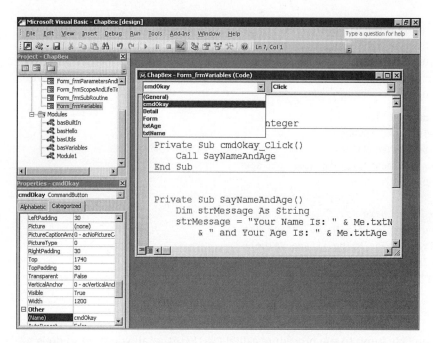

FIGURE 8.19   The Code window with the Object combo box open.

The combo box on the right lists all the event procedures associated with a particular object. Figure 8.20 shows all the event procedures associated with a command button. Notice that the Click event is the only one that appears in bold because it's the only event procedure that has been coded.

The Project Window

The Project window, shown in Figure 8.21, enables you to easily maneuver between the modules behind the objects within your database. The elements of your project are displayed hierarchically in a tree view within the Project window. All elements of the project are divided into Microsoft Access Classes and Modules. All Form, Report, and Class modules are found within the Microsoft Access Classes. All Standard modules are found within Modules. To view the code behind an object, simply double-click the object within the Project window. To view the object, such as a form, single-click the name of the form in the Project window and then click the View Object tool (the second icon from the left on the Project window toolbar). You are returned to Microsoft Access with the selected object active.

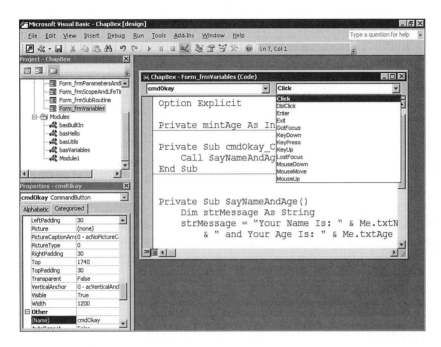

FIGURE 8.20   The Code window with the Procedure combo box open.

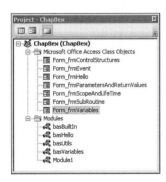

FIGURE 8.21   The Project window showing all the classes and modules contained within the Chap8Ex project.

NOTE

You can also right-click the object and then select View Code (the left icon on the Project window toolbar) to view the code or View Object to view the object. The context-sensitive menu also enables you to insert modules and Class modules, to import and export files, to print the selected object, and to view the database properties. These features are covered in Chapter 13.

The Properties Window

The Properties window, pictured in Figure 8.22, enables you to view and modify object properties from within the VBE. At the top of the Properties window is a combo box that allows you to select the object whose properties you want to modify. The objects listed in the combo box include the parent object selected in the Project window (for example, the form) and the objects contained within the parent object (for example, the controls). After an object is selected, its properties can be modified within the list of properties. The properties can be viewed either alphabetically or categorically. In the example, the command button cmdOK is selected. The properties of the command button are shown by category.

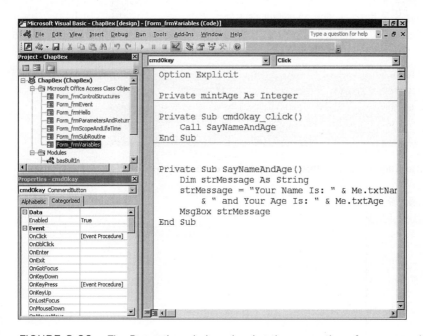

FIGURE 8.22   The Properties window showing the properties of a command button displayed categorically.

The View Microsoft Access Tool

If at any time you want to return to the Access application environment, simply click the View Microsoft Access icon (the left icon) on the toolbar. You can then return to the VBE by using the taskbar or using one of the methods covered earlier in this chapter.

Find and Replace

Often, you name a variable only to decide later that you want to change the name. VBA comes with an excellent find-and-replace feature to help you with this change. You can simply search for data, or you can search for a value and replace it with some other value. To invoke the Find dialog box, shown in Figure 8.23, choose Edit, Find or press Ctrl+F.

FIGURE 8.23   The Find dialog box is set up to search for `strMessage` in the current module.

Type the text you want to find in the Find What text box. Notice that you can search in the Current Procedure, Current Module, Current Project, or Selected Text. The option Find Whole Word Only doesn't find the text if it's part of another piece of text. For example, if you check Find Whole Word Only and then search for *Count*, VBA doesn't find *Counter*. Other options include toggles for case sensitivity and pattern matching.

You can also use the Replace dialog box to search for text and replace it with another piece of text (see Figure 8.24). You can invoke this dialog box by selecting Edit, Replace from the menu or by pressing Ctrl+H (or Alt+E, E). It offers all the features of the Find dialog box but also enables you to enter Replace With text. In addition, you can select Replace or Replace All. Replace asks for confirmation before each replacement, but Replace All replaces text without this prompt. I recommend that you take the time to confirm each replacement because it's all too easy to miscalculate the pervasive effects of a global find-and-replace.

FIGURE 8.24   The Replace dialog box is set to find `strMessage` and replace it with `strNewMessage` in the current project.

Help

A very useful but underutilized feature of VBA is the ability to get context-sensitive help while coding. With your cursor placed anywhere in a VBA command or function, press the F1 key to get context-sensitive help on that command or function. Most of the help topics let you view practical examples of the function or command within code. Figure 8.25 shows help on the `With...End With` construct. Notice that the Help window includes the syntax for the command, a detailed description of each parameter included in the command, and remarks about using the command. If you scroll down, examples of the construct appear that you can copy and place into a module (see Figure 8.26). This feature is a great way to learn about the various parts of the VBA language.

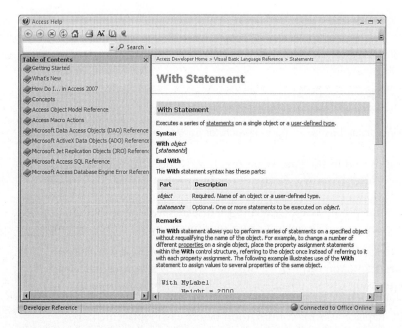

FIGURE 8.25   Help on With...End With.

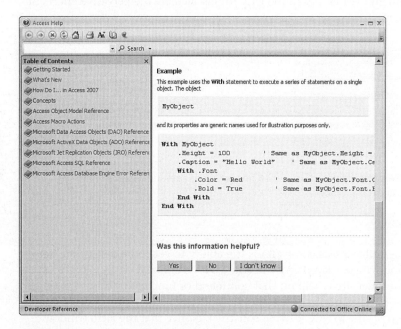

FIGURE 8.26   An example of With...End With.

Splitting the Code Window

You can split the VBA Code window so that you can look at two routines in the same module at the same time. This option is useful if you're trying to solve a problem involving two procedures or event routines in a large module. To split your Code window, as shown in Figure 8.27, choose Window, Split.

Notice the splitter. Place your mouse cursor on the gray splitter button just above the Code window's vertical scrollbar. By clicking and dragging, you can size each half of the window. The window can be split into only two parts. After you have split it, you can use the Object and Procedure drop-down lists to navigate to the procedure of your choice. The drop-down lists will work for either of the two panes of the split window, depending on which pane was last selected.

> **NOTE**
>
> You can only view routines in the same module in a particular Code window, but several Code windows can be open at the same time. Each time you open an Access, Form, or Report module, Access places you in a different window. You can then size, move, and split each module.

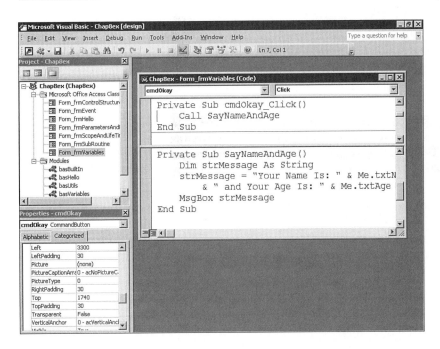

FIGURE 8.27   A split Code window lets you view two routines.

Using Bookmarks to Save Your Place

The Access 2007 coding environment enables you to create place markers called *bookmarks* so that you can easily return to key locations in your modules. To add a bookmark, right-click on the line of code where you will place the bookmark and choose Toggle, Bookmark, or choose Bookmarks, Toggle Bookmark from the Edit menu. You can add as many bookmarks as you like.

To navigate between bookmarks, choose Edit, Bookmarks, Next Bookmark, or Edit, Bookmarks, Previous Bookmark. A bookmark is a toggle. To remove one, you simply choose Toggle, Bookmark from the shortcut menu or Bookmarks, Toggle Bookmark from the Edit menu. If you want to clear all bookmarks, choose Edit, Bookmarks, Clear All Bookmarks. Bookmarks are not saved when you close the database.

> **NOTE**
>
> Do not confuse the bookmarks discussed in this section with recordset bookmarks. Recordset bookmarks are covered in Chapter 15.

Customizing the VBE

Access 2007 provides Access programmers with significant opportunity to customize the look and behavior of the VBE. To view and customize the environment options, choose Tools, Options with the VBE active. Figure 8.28 shows the Options dialog box; its different aspects are discussed in detail in the following sections.

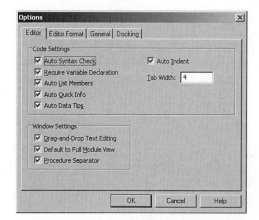

FIGURE 8.28   The Options dialog box.

Coding Options—The Editor Tab

The coding options available to you are found under the Editor tab of the Options dialog box. They include Auto Indent, Tab Width, Auto Syntax Check, Require Variable Declaration, Auto List Members, Auto Quick Info, and Auto Data Tips.

The Auto Indent feature invokes the automatic indenting of successive lines of code. This means that when you indent one line, all other lines are indented to the same position until you specify otherwise. I recommend that you use this feature.

The Tab Width feature determines the number of characters that Access indents each line. It's important that you do not change this number in the middle of a project; otherwise, different parts of the program will be indented differently.

The Auto Syntax Check feature determines whether Access performs a syntax check each time you press Enter after typing a single line of code. Many developers find this option annoying. It's not uncommon to type a line of code and notice a typo in a previous line of code. You want to rectify the error before you forget, so you move off the incomplete line of code you're typing, only to get an error message that your syntax is incorrect. I recommend that you turn off this feature.

The Require Variable Declaration option is a must. If this option is turned on, all variables must be declared before they are used. This important feature, when set, places the Option Explicit line in the Declarations section of every module you create. You're then forced to declare all variables before they're used. The compiler identifies many innocent typos at compile time, rather than by your users at runtime. I strongly recommend that you use this feature.

The Auto List Members option determines whether the List Properties/Methods and List Constants features are automatically invoked as you type code in the Code window. They help you in your coding endeavors by presenting a valid list of properties, methods, and constants. I recommend that you use these features. For more about these features, see Chapter 9.

The Auto Quick Info feature determines whether the syntax of a procedure or method is automatically displayed. If this option is selected, the syntax information is displayed as soon as you type a procedure or method name followed by a space, period, or opening parenthesis. I recommend that you use this feature.

The Auto Data Tips feature is used when you're debugging. It displays the current value of a selected value when you place your mouse pointer over the variable in Break mode. I recommend that you use this feature. This feature is discussed in Chapter 16.

Code Color, Fonts, and Sizes—The Editor Format Tab

In Access 2007, you can customize code colors, fonts, and sizes within the coding environment. You can also specify the foreground and background colors for the Code window text, selection text, syntax error text, comment text, keyword text, and more. You can select from any of the Windows fonts and sizes for the text in the Code window. For a more readable Code window, select the FixedSys font.

General Options—The General Tab

The General tab contains miscellaneous options that affect the behavior of the development environment. For example, the Show Grid option determines whether a form grid is displayed, and the Grid Units are used to designate the granularity of the gridlines. The other options on this tab are discussed in Chapter 13.

Docking Options—The Docking Tab

The Docking tab enables you to specify whether the windows within the VBE are dockable. A window is said to be *dockable* if you can lock it alongside and dock it to another window. It is not dockable when you can move it anywhere and leave it there. The windows you can dock include the Immediate, Locals, Watch, Project, Properties, and Object Browser windows.

CAUTION

All the customization options that have been discussed apply to the entire Access environment. This means that, when set, they affect all your databases.

Practical Examples: Using Event Routines, User-Defined Functions, and Subroutines

The CHAP8.ACCDB database includes two forms: frmClients and frmProjects. The frmClients form contains two command buttons. The first command button is used to save changes to the underlying record source (the tblClients table). The code looks like this:

```
Private Sub cmdSave_Click()
    'Save changes to the client record
    DoCmd.RunCommand acCmdSaveRecord
End Sub
```

The code, placed under the cmdSave command button on the frmClients form, executes the RunCommand method of the DoCmd object. The acCmdSaveRecord intrinsic constant, when used as a parameter to the RunCommand method, causes changes made to the form to be saved to the underlying data source.

The second command button is used to undo changes made to the current record. The code looks like this:

```
Private Sub cmdUndo_Click()
    'Undo changes
    DoCmd.RunCommand acCmdUndo
End Sub
```

This code is found under the cmdUndo button on the frmClients form. It executes the RunCommand method of the DoCmd object. The acCmdUndo intrinsic constant, when used as a parameter to the RunCommand method, undoes changes made to the form.

The code originally located under the cmdViewProjects was generated by the command button wizard (as covered in Chapter 5, "What Every Developer Needs to Know About Forms"). It looked like this:

```
Private Sub cmd_Click()
On Error GoTo Err_cmd_Click

    Dim stDocName As String
    Dim stLinkCriteria As String

    stDocName = "frmProjects"

    stLinkCriteria = "[ClientID]=" & Me![txtClientID]
    DoCmd.OpenForm stDocName, , , stLinkCriteria

Exit_cmd_Click:
    Exit Sub

Err_cmd_Click:
    MsgBox Err.Description
    Resume Exit_cmd_Click

End Sub
```

The code first declared two variables: one for the name of the form to be opened and the other to hold the criteria used to open the form. It then assigned a value to the stDocName variable as well as to the stLinkCriteria variable. Finally, it used the OpenForm method of the DoCmd object to open the frmProjects form, passing the value in stLinkCriteria as the WHERE clause for the OpenForm method. This wizard-generated code is inefficient. It uses variables that are not necessary. More importantly, it is difficult to read. To eliminate both problems, the code is changed as follows:

```
Private Sub cmdViewProjects_Click()
On Error GoTo Err_cmdViewProjects_Click

    DoCmd.OpenForm FormName:="frmProjects", _
        WhereCondition:="[ClientID]=" & Me![txtClientID]

Exit_cmdViewProjects_Click:
    Exit Sub

Err_cmdViewProjects_Click:
    MsgBox Err.Description
    Resume Exit_cmdViewProjects_Click
End Sub
```

Although the RecordSource appears to be the entire tblProjects table, this is not the case. The key to the solution is found in the frmProjects form. The code in the Open event of the frmProjects form looks like this:

```
Private Sub Form_Open(Cancel As Integer)
    If Not IsLoaded("frmClients") Then
        MsgBox "You must load this form from the Projects form", _
            vbCritical, "Warning"
        Cancel = True
    End If
End Sub
```

This code first uses a user-defined function called IsLoaded to determine whether the frmClients form is loaded. (The mechanics of the IsLoaded function are discussed in the following text.) The function returns True if the frmClients form is loaded, and False if it is not. If the frmClients form is not loaded, a message is displayed to the user, and the loading of the frmProjects form is canceled. If the frmClients form is loaded, the RecordSource property of the frmProjects form is determined by the WHERE clause passed as part of the OpenForm method. Even in a client/server environment, Access sends *only* the appropriate project records over the network wire.

The IsLoaded function looks like this:

```
Public Function IsLoaded(strFormName As String) As Boolean
    Const FORMOPEN = -1
    Const FORMCLOSED = 0

    If SysCmd(acSysCmdGetObjectState, acForm, strFormName) <> FORMCLOSED Then
        IsLoaded = True
    Else
        IsLoaded = False
    End If

    'IsLoaded = SysCmd(acSysCmdGetObjectState, acForm, strFormName)
End Function
```

The function declares two user-defined constants. These constants are intended to make the function more readable. The built-in SysCmd function is used to determine whether the form whose name is received as a parameter is loaded. The SysCmd function, when passed the intrinsic constant acSysCmdGetObjectState as the first argument and acForm as the second argument, attempts to determine the state of the form whose name is passed as the third argument. The IsLoaded function returns True to its caller if the form is loaded, and False if it is not. An alternative to this function is the following:

```
Public Function IsLoaded(strFormName As String) As Boolean
    IsLoaded = SysCmd(acSysCmdGetObjectState, acForm, strFormName)
End Function
```

This function is much shorter and more efficient but is less readable. It simply places the return value from the SysCmd directly into the return value for the function.

In addition to the save and undo that are included in the `frmClients` form, this version of the `frmProjects` form contains one other routine. The `BeforeUpdate` event of the form, covered in Chapter 10, "Advanced Form Techniques," executes before the data underlying the form is updated. The code in the `BeforeUpdate` event of the `frmProjects` form looks like this:

```
Private Sub Form_BeforeUpdate(Cancel As Integer)
    If Me.txtProjectBeginDate.Value > _
        Me.txtProjectEndDate.Value Then
        MsgBox "Project Start Date Must Precede " & _
            "Project End Date"
        Cancel = True
    End If
End Sub
```

This code tests to see whether the project begin date falls after the project end date. If so, a message is displayed to the user, and the update is canceled.

Summary

A strong knowledge of the VBA language is imperative for the Access developer. This chapter has covered all the basics of the VBA language. You have learned the differences between Code, Form, and Report modules and how to effectively use each. You have also learned the difference between event procedures and user-defined subroutines and functions. To get the most mileage out of your subroutines and functions, you have learned how to pass parameters to, and receive return values from, procedures.

Variables are used throughout your application code. Declaring each variable with the proper scope and lifetime helps make your application bulletproof and easy to maintain. Furthermore, selecting an appropriate variable type ensures that the minimal amount of memory is consumed and that your application code protects itself. Effectively using control structures and built-in functions gives you the power, flexibility, and functionality required by even the most complex of applications. Finally, a strong command of the VBE is imperative to a successful development experience!

8

CHAPTER 9

Objects, Properties, Methods, and Events Explained

Why This Chapter Is Important

Objects, properties, methods, and events are at the heart of all programming that you do within Microsoft Access. Without a strong foundation in objects, properties, methods, and events and how you should use them, your efforts at Access and Visual Basic for Applications (VBA) programming will fail. This chapter introduces you to Access's object model. You will not only become familiar with Access's objects, properties, methods, and events and how to manipulate them, but you will also learn concepts that will carry throughout the book and throughout your Access and VBA programming career.

NOTE

Most of the examples in this chapter are included in the Chap9Ex database located on the sample code CD-ROM.

Understanding Objects, Properties, Events, and Methods

Many people, especially those accustomed to a procedural language, don't understand the concept of objects, properties, methods, and events. As mentioned earlier, you need a thorough knowledge of Access's objects, their properties, the methods associated with them, and the events that each object can respond to if you want to be a productive and successful Access programmer.

What Exactly Are Objects?

Objects are all the things that make up your database. They include tables, queries, forms, reports, macros, and modules, as well as the components of those objects. For example, a `Table` object contains `Field` and `Index` objects. A `Form` object contains various controls (text boxes, combo boxes, list boxes, and so on). Each object in the database has specific properties that determine its appearance or behavior. Each object also has specific methods, which are actions that it can take.

What Exactly Are Properties?

A *property* is an attribute of an object, and each object has many properties. Often, different types of objects share the same properties; at other times, an object's properties are specific to that particular object. Forms, combo boxes, and text boxes all have `Width` properties, for example, but a form has a `RecordSource` property that the combo box and text box don't have.

You can set most properties at design time and modify them at runtime; however, you can't modify some properties at runtime, and you can't access others at design time. (You can only modify them at runtime.) Access's built-in Help for each property tells you one of the following:

► You can set this property in the object's property sheet, a macro, or Visual Basic.

► You can set this property only in Design view.

► You can access this property by using Visual Basic or a macro.

Each of these descriptions indicates when you can modify the property.

As a developer, you set the values of many objects' properties at design time; the ones you set at design time are the starting values at runtime. Much of the VBA code you write modifies the values of these properties at runtime in response to different situations. For example, suppose that a text box has a `Visible` property. Let's take a look at an example. If a client is paying for something by cash, you might not want the text box for the credit card number to be visible. If he's paying by credit card, you might want to set the `Visible` property of the text box with the credit card number to `True`. This is just one of the many things you can do to modify the value of an object's property at runtime in response to an event or action that has occurred.

You might wonder how you can determine all the properties associated with a particular object (both those that can be modified at design time and those that can be modified at runtime). Of course, to view the properties that can be set at design time, you can select the object and then view its property sheet. Viewing all the properties available in Access 2007 is actually quite easy to do; just invoke Help by clicking the Help button (?). Click Macros and programmability in the Table of Contents, and then click Properties. Your screen will appear as in Figure 9.1. Scroll down and notice that one of the available properties is the `OnNotInList` property. If you click the link, help appears on the `OnNotInList` property (see Figure 9.2). You can also use the Object Browser to quickly and easily view all properties associated with an object.

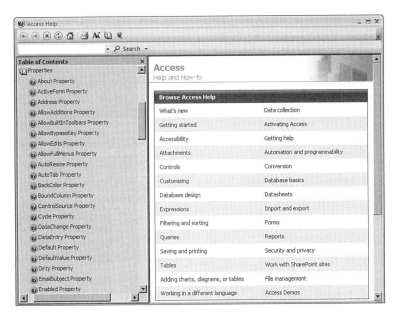

FIGURE 9.1   Viewing properties in the Table of Contents.

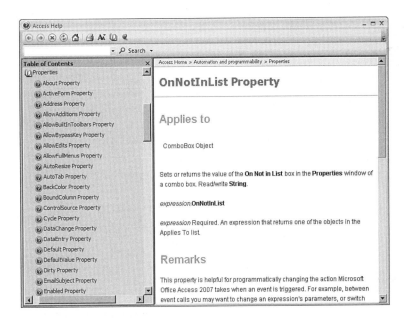

FIGURE 9.2   Help on the OnNotInList property.

What Exactly Are Events?

Windows is an event-driven operating system; in other words, the operating system responds to many events that are triggered by actions that the user takes and by the operating system itself. Access exposes many of these events through its Object Model. An *event* in an Access application is something your application can respond to. Events include mouse movements, changes to data, a form opening, a record being added, and much more. Users initiate events, as does your application code. It's up to you to determine what happens in response to the events that are occurring. You respond to events by using macros or VBA code. Each Access object responds to different events. If you want to find out all the events associated with a particular object, take the following steps:

1. Select the object (for example, a text box).

2. Open the property sheet.

3. Click the Event tab, as shown in Figure 9.3.

4. Scroll through the available list of events.

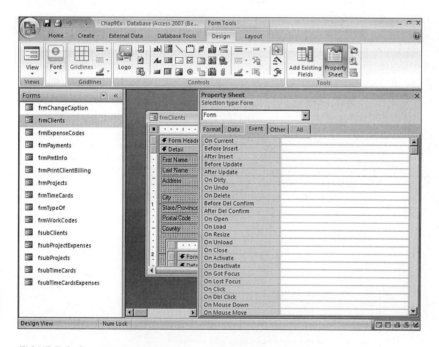

FIGURE 9.3   The list of events associated with a text box.

What Exactly Are Methods?

Methods are actions that an object takes on itself. As with properties and events, different objects have different methods associated with them. A method is like a function or subroutine, except that it's specific to the object it applies to. For example, a form has a GoToPage method that doesn't apply to a text box or most other objects.

Using the Object Browser to Learn About Access's Objects

The Object Browser is a powerful tool that can help you learn about and work with the objects that are part of both Access 2007 and the Microsoft Windows environment. The Object Browser displays information about Microsoft Access and other objects and can help you with coding by showing you all the properties and methods associated with a particular object.

Access objects are complex; they have many properties and methods. The Object Browser helps you to understand and use objects, properties, and methods by doing the following:

▶ Displaying the types of objects available

▶ Allowing you to quickly navigate between application procedures

▶ Displaying the properties and methods associated with a particular object

▶ Finding and pasting code into your application

How to Use the Object Browser

The Object Browser can easily be invoked from the Visual Basic Editor. You can click the Object Browser button on the toolbar, press F2, or choose View, Object Browser. The window shown in Figure 9.4 appears.

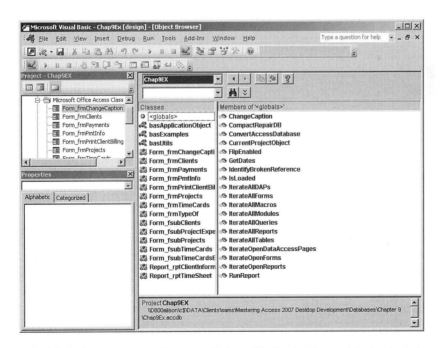

FIGURE 9.4   The Object Browser window with the database object selected.

The Object Browser displays two levels of information about the selected library or database. With the Chap9Ex database open, select Chap9Ex.accdb from the Project/Library drop-down (the top drop-down), and your screen will look similar to Figure 9.4. The Classes list box displays all modules, including Form and Report modules, in the database. The Members Of list box displays any procedures that have been defined in the selected module. Notice the basUtils module, which is part of the Chap9Ex.accdb database. Looking at the list box on the right, you can see the procedures (subroutines and functions) included in the basUtils module. You can click to select each Form and Report module in the list box on the left and view the associated methods and properties in the list box on the right.

You can use the Project/Library drop-down list to select a different object library (provided you have set a reference to it). The Classes list box displays the types of objects available in the selected library or database. Just as with the Access object library, the Members Of list box displays the methods, properties, and data elements defined for the selected object (see Figure 9.5). You can even add other libraries to the Library drop-down list by referring to other type libraries. This method is covered in Chapter 24, "Automation: Communicating with Other Applications."

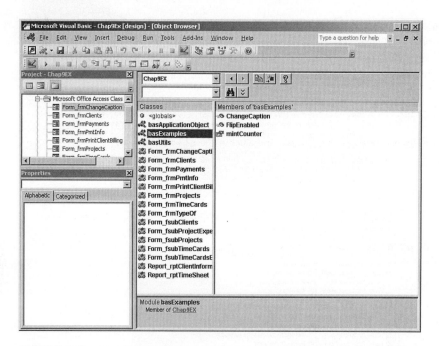

FIGURE 9.5   The Object Browser window with the application object selected.

Pasting Code Templates into a Procedure

After you have located the method or property you're interested in, you have the option of pasting it into your application. With the method or property selected, simply click the

Copy to Clipboard button in the Object Browser; then paste it in the appropriate module. If you want to get more information about a particular method or property, click the Help button in the Object Browser or press F1.

Referring to Objects

Access objects are categorized into *collections*, which are groupings of objects of the same type. The Forms collection, for example, is a grouping of all the open forms in a database. Each form has a Controls collection that includes all the controls on that form. Each control is an object, and you must refer to an object through the collection to which it belongs. For example, you refer to a form through the Forms collection. VBA offers three ways to refer to an object; if you want to refer to the frmProjects form, for example, you can choose from the following options:

▶ Forms.frmProjects (or Forms!frmProjects)

▶ Forms("frmProjects")

▶ Forms(0)

Referring to the form as Forms(0) assumes that frmProjects was the first form opened. However, you need to understand that although Access assigns an element number as it loads each form, this element number changes as Access loads and unloads forms at runtime. For example, the third form that's loaded can initially be referred to as element two, but if the second form is unloaded, that third form becomes element one. In other words, you can't rely on the element number assigned to a form; that number is a moving target.

You must refer to a control on a form first through the Forms collection and then through the specific form. The reference looks like this:

```
Forms.frmProjects.txtClientID
```

In this example, Forms is the name of the collection, frmProjects is the name of the specific form, and txtClientID is the name of a control on the frmProjects form. If this code is found in the Code module of frmProjects, it could be rewritten like this:

```
Me.txtClientID
```

Me refers to the current form or report. It's generic because the code could be copied to any form having a txtClientID control, and it would still run properly. Referring to a control on a report is similar to referring to a control on a form. Here's an example:

```
Reports.rptTimeSheet.txtHoursBilled
```

This example refers to the txtHoursBilled text box on the rptTimeSheet report, part of the Reports collection. After you know how to refer to an object, you're ready to write code that modifies its properties and executes its methods.

6

Working with Properties and Methods

To modify an object's properties and execute its methods, you must refer to the object and then supply an appropriate property or method, as shown in this example:

```
Forms.frmHello.cmdHello.Visible = False
```

This line of code refers to the Visible property of cmdHello, found in the frmHello form, which is in the Forms collection. Notice that you must identify the object name frmHello as being associated with the Forms collection. If you want to change the Caption property of frmHello to say "Hello World", you would use the following code:

```
Forms.frmHello.Caption = "Hello World"
```

Telling the Difference Between Properties and Methods

You might be confused about whether you're looking at an object's property or method, but there are a couple of quick ways to tell. You will always use a property in some type of an expression. For example, you might be setting a property equal to some value:

```
Forms.frmClients.txtAddress.Visible = False
```

Here, you're changing the Visible property of the txtAddress text box on the frmClients form from True to False. You also might retrieve the value of a property and place it in a variable:

```
strFirstName = Forms.frmClients.txtFirstName.Value
```

You also might use the value of a property in an expression, as in the following example:

```
MsgBox Forms.frmClients.txtFirstName.Value
```

The pattern here is that you will always use a property somewhere in an expression. You can set it equal to something, or something can be set equal to its value, or it's otherwise used in an expression.

A method, however, is an action that an object takes on itself. The syntax for a method is Object.Method. A method isn't set equal to something; however, you frequently create an object variable and then set it by invoking a method. A method looks like this:

```
Forms.frmHello.txtHelloWorld.SetFocus
```

In this example, the text box called txtHelloWorld executes its SetFocus method.

A method that returns an object variable looks like this:

```
Dim cbr As CommandBar
Set cbr = CommandBars.Add("MyNewCommandBar")
```

In this example, the `CommandBars` collection's `Add` method is used to set the value of the `CommandBar` object variable named `cbr`. For more information, see the section "Declaring and Assigning Object Variables," later in this chapter.

Using a Bang Versus a Period

Many people are confused about when to use a bang (!) and when to use a period. You can use a bang whenever you're separating an object from its collection, as shown in these two examples:

```
Forms!frmClients
```

```
Forms!frmClients!txtClientID
```

In the first example, `frmClients` is part of the `Forms` collection. In the second example, `txtClientID` is part of the `Controls` collection of the `frmClients` form.

In most cases, you can also use a period to separate an object from its collection. The reason is that the expression `Me!txtClientID` is actually a shortcut to the complete reference `Me.Controls!txtClientID`. Because `Controls` is the default collection for a form, you can omit `Controls` from the statement. You can abbreviate the expression to `Me.txtClientID`. The advantage of using the period over the bang is that the period provides you with IntelliSense. To test this, create a form and add a control called `txtFirstName`. Go to the code behind the form, and try typing **Me!**. Notice that IntelliSense is not invoked. Next, type **Me.** and watch as IntelliSense is invoked. IntelliSense facilitates the development process by providing a list box containing valid properties, methods, constants, and so on, as appropriate.

> **NOTE**
>
> IntelliSense is a tool that helps you when writing programming code. It provides you with auto-completion when writing your programming code.

In addition to separating an object from its collection, the period is also used to separate an object from a property or method. The code looks like this:

```
Forms.frmClients.RecordSource = "tblClients"
```

```
Forms.frmClients.txtClientID.Visible = False
```

The first example sets the `RecordSource` property of `frmClients` to `tblClients`, and the second example sets the `Visible` property of the `txtClientID` on the `frmClients` form to `False`.

Default Properties

Each object has a default property, and if you're working with an object's default property, you don't have to explicitly refer to it in code. Take a look at the following two code samples:

```
Forms.frmHello.txtHello.Value = "Hello World"
```

```
Forms.frmHello.txtHello = "Hello World"
```

The Value property is the default property of a text box, so you don't need to explicitly refer to it in code. However, I prefer to explicitly state the property; it is a practice that contributes to the code's readability and keeps novice Access programmers who work with my code from having to guess which property I'm changing.

Declaring and Assigning Object Variables

Object variables are variables that reference an object of a specific type, such as databases, recordsets, forms, controls, and even objects created in other applications. They allow you to create shortcut references to objects and pass objects to subroutines and functions. You can use them to streamline code by using short names to refer to objects with long names and to optimize code by supplying a direct pointer to a particular object.

First, you must declare an object variable; then you assign—or *point*—the object variable to a particular object, as shown in the following code:

```
Private Sub cmdChangeCaption_Click()
    'Declare a CommandButton object
    Dim cmdAny As CommandButton
    'Point the CommandButton object at the cmdHello Command button
    Set cmdAny = Me.cmdHello
    'Change the Caption of the control referenced by the cmdAny variable
    cmdAny.Caption = "Hello"
End Sub
```

This code creates an object variable called cmdAny of the type CommandButton. You then use the Set statement to point your CommandButton object variable toward the cmdHello object on the current form, using the Me keyword. Finally, you modify the caption of the cmdAny object variable. Because an object variable is a reference to the original object, you're actually changing the caption of the cmdHello command button.

Object Variables Versus Regular Variables

The difference between object variables and regular variables is illustrated by the following code:

```
Dim intVar1 As Integer
Dim intVar2 As Integer
```

```
intVar1 = 5
intVar2 = intVar1
intVar1 = 10
Debug.Print intVar1 'Prints 10
Debug.Print intVar2 'Prints 5
```

This code uses ordinary variables. When you dimension these variables, each one is assigned a separate memory location. Although `intVar2` is initially assigned the value of `intVar1`, changing the value of `intVar1` has no effect on `intVar2`. This differs from the following code, which uses an object variable:

```
Private Sub Command5_Click()
    Dim ctlText As TextBox
    Set ctlText = Forms.frmSales.txtProductID
    ctlText.Text = "New Text"
    Debug.Print Forms.frmSales.txtProductID.Text 'Prints New Text
End Sub
```

This routine creates an object variable called `ctlText` of type `TextBox`. It then associates the object variable with `Forms.frmSales.txtProductID`. Next, it modifies the `Text` property of the object variable. Because the object variable is actually pointing to the text box on the form, the `Debug.Print` statement prints the new text value.

Generic Versus Specific Object Variables

Access supports the use of generic object variables, including `Application`, `Control`, `Form`, and `Report`. Generic object variables can be used to refer to any object of that generic type:

```
Private Sub ChangeVisible_Click()
    Dim ctlAny As Control
    Set ctlAny = Me.txtCustomerID
    ctlAny.Visible = False
End Sub
```

In this example, `ctlAny` can be used to point to any control. Compare that to the following code:

```
Private Sub cmdChangeVisible_Click()
    Dim txtAny As TextBox
    Set txtAny = Me.txtCustomerID
    txtAny.Visible = False
End Sub
```

Here, your object variable can be used only to point to a text box.

6

Cleaning Up After Yourself

When you're finished working with an object variable, you should set its value to Nothing. As used in the following example, this statement frees up all memory and system resources associated with the object:

```
Set frmNew = Nothing
```

Understanding the Differences Between Objects and Collections

Many people get confused about the differences between an object and a collection. Think of an object as a member of a collection. For example, frmHello is a form that's a member of the Forms collection; cmdHello, a command button on frmHello, is a member of the Controls collection of frmHello. Sometimes you want to manipulate a specific object, but other times you want to manipulate a collection of objects.

Manipulating a Single Object

You have already learned quite a bit about manipulating a single object, such as setting the Enabled property of a text box:

```
Me.txtCustomerID.Enabled = False
```

This line of code affects only one text box and only one of its properties. However, when you're manipulating a single object, you might want to affect several properties at the same time. In that case, it's most efficient to use the With...End With construct, explained in the following section.

One method you can use to modify several properties of an object is to modify the value of each property, one at a time:

```
Me.txtCustomerID.Enabled = False
Me.txtCustomerID.SpecialEffect = 1
Me.txtCustomerID.FontSize = 16
Me.txtCustomerID.FontWeight = 700
```

Contrast this with the following code:

```
With Me.txtCustomerID
    .Enabled = False
    .SpecialEffect = 1
    .FontSize = 16
    .FontWeight = 700
End With
```

This code uses the With...End With statement to assign multiple properties to an object. In addition to improving the readability of your code, the With...End With construct results in a slight increase in performance.

Manipulating a Collection of Objects

A *collection* is like an array of objects. What makes the array special is that it's defined and maintained by Access. Every collection in Microsoft Access is an object, each with its own properties and methods. The VBA language makes it easy for you to manipulate Access's collections of objects; you simply use the For Each…Next construct, which performs the same command on multiple objects.

In the "Determining the Type of a Control" section later in this chapter, you learn how to loop through the collection of controls on a form, performing actions on all the command buttons. This illustrates a practical use of a collection. In the following example, you loop through all the open forms, changing the caption of each form:

```
Sub FormCaptions()
    Dim frm As Form
    For Each frm In Forms
        frm.Caption = frm.Caption & " - " & CurrentUser
    Next frm
End Sub
```

This routine uses the For Each…Next construct to loop through each form in the Forms collection, setting the caption of each form to the form's caption concatenated with the current username. As you travel through the loop, the code frm.Caption refers to each member of the Forms collection.

Passing Objects to Subroutines and Functions

Just as you can pass a string or a number to a subroutine or function, you can also pass an object to a subroutine or function. The code, found in the basExamples module in the Chap9Ex database, looks like this:

```
Sub ChangeCaption(frmAny as Form)
    'Change the caption property of the form received
    'to what was already in the caption property,
    'concatenated with a colon and the name of the current user
    frmAny.Caption = frmAny.Caption & ": " & CurrentUser
End Sub
```

The ChangeCaption routine receives a reference to a form as a parameter. The caption of the form referenced by the procedure is modified to include the name of the current user. The ChangeCaption routine is called like this:

```
Private Sub cmdChangeCaption_Click()
    'Call the ChangeCaption routine, passing a reference to the current form
    Call ChangeCaption(Me)
End Sub
```

In this example, the click event of the cmdChangeCaption command button calls the ChangeCaption routine, sending a reference to the form that the command button is contained within. You will find this code in the frmChangeCaption form.

Determining the Type of a Control

When writing generic code, you might need to determine the type of a control. For example, you might want to loop through all the controls on a form and flip the Enabled property of all the command buttons. To do this, use the ControlType property of a control. Here's an example of how it's used. (You can find this in Chap9Ex.accdb in the module called basExamples.)

```
Sub FlipEnabled(frmAny As Form, ctlAny As Control)
    'Declare a control object variable
    Dim ctl As Control
    'Loop through the Controls collection using the For..Each Construct
    ctlAny.Enabled = True
    ctlAny.SetFocus
    For Each ctl In frmAny.Controls
        'Evaluate the type of the control
        If ctl.ControlType = acCommandButton Then
            'Make sure that we don't try to disable the command button _
            that invoked this routine
            If ctl.Name <> ctlAny.Name Then
                ctl.Enabled = Not ctl.Enabled
            End If
        End If
    Next ctl
End Sub
```

The FlipEnabled procedure is called from the frmTypeOf form. Each command button on the form (Add, Edit, Delete, and so on) sends the form and the name of a control to the FlipEnabled routine. The control that it sends is the one that you want to receive the focus after the routine executes. In the example that follows, the code sends the cmdSave command button to the FlipEnabled routine. The FlipEnabled routine sets focus to the Save button:

```
Private Sub cmdAdd_Click()
    'Call the FlipEnabled routine, passing references to the current form,
    'and to the cmdSave command button on the current form
    Call FlipEnabled(Me, Me.cmdSave)
End Sub
```

The FlipEnabled routine receives the form and control as parameters. It begins by enabling the command button that was passed to it and setting focus to it. The FlipEnabled routine then uses the VBA construct For...Each to loop through all the controls on a form. The For...Each construct repeats a group of statements for each object in an array or collection—in this case, the Controls collection. The code evaluates each control on the form to determine whether it's a command button. If it is, and it isn't the command button that was passed to the routine, the routine flips the control's Enabled property. The following VBA intrinsic controls are used when evaluating the ControlType property of a control:

Intrinsic Constant	Type of Control
acLabel	Label
acRectangle	Rectangle
acLine	Line
acImage	Image
acCommandButton	Command button
acOptionButton	Option button
acCheckBox	Check box
acOptionGroup	Option group
acBoundObjectFrame	Bound object frame
acTextBox	Text box
acListBox	List box
acComboBox	Combo box
acSubform	Subform/subreport
acObjectFrame	Unbound object frame or chart
acPageBreak	Page break
acPage	Page
acCustomControl	ActiveX (custom) control
acToggleButton	Toggle button
acTabCtl	Tab

Using Special Properties That Refer to Objects

VBA offers the convenience of performing actions on the active control, the active form, and other specially recognized objects. The following is a list of special properties that refer to objects in the Access Object Model:

▶ The ActiveControl property refers to the control that has focus on a screen object, form, or report.

▶ The ActiveForm property refers to the form that has focus.

▶ The ActiveReport property refers to the report that has focus.

▶ The `Form` property refers to the form that a subform is contained in or to the form itself.

▶ `Me` refers to the form or report where code is currently executing.

▶ `Module` refers to the module of a form or report.

▶ The `Parent` property refers to the form, report, or control that contains a control.

▶ `PreviousControl` refers to the control that had focus immediately before the `ActiveControl`.

▶ `RecordsetClone` refers to a clone of the form's underlying recordset.

▶ The `Report` property refers to the report that a subform is contained in or to the report itself.

▶ The `Section` property refers to the section in a form or report where a particular control is located.

The following example using the `Screen.ActiveForm` property shows how a subroutine can change the caption of the active form:

```
Sub ChangeCaption()
    Screen.ActiveForm.Caption = Screen.ActiveForm.Caption & _
        " - " & CurrentUser()
End Sub
```

This subroutine modifies the caption of the active form, appending the value of the `CurrentUser` property onto the end of the existing caption.

Understanding Access's Object Model

Now that I've discussed the concept of objects, properties, methods, and events in a general sense, I'm going to switch the discussion to the objects that are natively part of Microsoft Access. Databases are composed of objects, such as the tables, queries, forms, reports, macros, and modules that appear in the Navigation Pane. They also include the controls (text boxes, list boxes, and so on) on a form or report. The key to successful programming lies in your ability to manipulate the database objects using VBA code at runtime. It's also very useful to be able to add, modify, and remove application objects at runtime.

The `Application` Object

At the top of the Access Object Model, you will find the `Application` object, which refers to the active Access application. It contains all of Access's other objects and collections, including the `Forms` collection, the `Reports` collection, the `DataAccessPages` collection, the `Modules` collection, the `CurrentData` object, the `CurrentProject` object, the `CodeProject` object, the `CodeData` object, the `Screen` object, and the `DoCmd` object. You can use the `Application` object to modify the properties of, or execute commands on, the Access application itself, such as specifying whether Access's built-in toolbars are available while the application is running.

Application **Object Properties**

The `Application` object has a rich list of properties. An important property introduced with Access 2002 is the `BrokenReference` property. You use this property to determine whether any broken references exist within the current project. The property is equal to `True` if broken references exist, and `False` if no broken references are identified. The property eliminates the need to iterate through each reference, determining whether any references are broken. The following code returns the value of the `BrokenReference` property:

```
Public Function IdentifyBrokenReference() As Boolean
    'Return whether or not broken references are identified
    'within the current project
    IdentifyBrokenReference = Application.BrokenReference
End Function
```

Application **Object Methods**

Just as the `Application` object has a rich list of properties, it also has a rich list of methods. Another important method introduced with Access 2002 is the `CompactRepair` method, which allows you to programmatically compact and repair a database, without declaring ActiveX Data Objects (ADO) objects. The code looks like this:

```
Sub CompactRepairDB()
    Dim strFilePath As String

    'Store path of current database in a variable
    strFilePath = CurrentProject.Path

    'If destination database exists, delete it
    If Len(Dir(strFilePath & "\Chap8Small.mdb")) Then
        Kill strFilePath & "\Chap8Small.mdb"
    End If

    'Use the CompactRepair method of the Application object
    'to compact and repair the database
    Application.CompactRepair strFilePath & "\Chap9Big.accdb", _
        strFilePath & "\Chap9Small.accdb", True

End Sub
```

This code uses the `Path` property of the `CurrentProject` object to extract the path of the current project and place it into a string variable. Covered later in this chapter, the `CurrentProject` object returns a reference to the current database project. The code uses the `Dir` function to evaluate whether the database called `Chap9Small.accdb` exists. If it does, the code uses the `Kill` command to delete the file. Finally, the code uses the `CompactRepair` method to compact the `Chap9Big.accdb` file into `Chap9Small.accdb`.

Another important method introduced with Access 2002 is the `ConvertAccessProject` method. This method allows you to programmatically convert an Access database from one version of Access to another. Here's an example:

```
Sub ConvertAccessDatabase()
    Dim strFilePath As String

    'Store current file path into variable
    strFilePath = CurrentProject.Path

    'Delete destination database if it exists
    If Len(Dir(strFilePath & "\Chap9V2007.accdb")) Then
        Kill strFilePath & "\Chap9V2007.accdb"
    End If

    'Convert source database to Access 2007 file format
    Application.ConvertAccessProject strFilePath & "\Chap9Ex.mdb", _
        strFilePath & "\Chap9V2007.accdb", _
        DestinationFileFormat:=acFileFormatAccess2007
End Sub
```

This code first places the path associated with the current project into a variable called `strFilePath`. Next, it determines whether a file called `Chap9V2007.mdb` exists. If such a file does exist, it deletes the file. Finally, the code uses the `ConvertAccessProject` method of the `Application` object to convert an Access 2003 database called `Chap9Ex.mdb` to the Access 2007 file format. The destination file is called `Chap9V2007.accdb`. Different constants are used for the `DestinationFileFormat` parameter to designate conversion of the source file to different versions of Access.

The `Forms` **Collection**

The `Forms` collection contains all the currently open forms in the database. Using the `Forms` collection, you can perform an action, such as changing the color, on each open form.

> **NOTE**
>
> The `Forms` collection isn't the same as the list of all forms in the database; that list is part of the `CurrentProject` object discussed later in this chapter.

The code that follows iterates through the `Forms` collection, printing the name of each form. It is found in the `basApplicationObject` module within the `Chap9Ex` database. It begins by establishing a form object variable. It then uses the `For Each…Next` construct to loop through each form in the Forms collection (the collection of open forms), printing its name. Before running the code, open a few forms. Run the code and then take a look in the Immediate window. Close a couple of the forms and rerun the code. The list of forms displayed in the Immediate window should change.

```
Sub IterateOpenForms()
    'Declare a form object variable
    Dim frm As Form
    'Use the form object variable to point at each form in the Forms collection
    For Each frm In Forms
        'Print the name of the referenced form to the Immediate window
        Debug.Print frm.Name
    Next frm
End Sub
```

> **NOTE**
>
> The Immediate window and its uses are covered in Chapter 16, "Debugging: Your Key to Successful Development." You can easily invoke it using the Ctrl+G keystroke combination.

> **NOTE**
>
> Notice that you do not need to refer to Application.Forms. The reason is that the Application object is always assumed when writing VBA code within Access.

The Reports **Collection**

Just as the Forms collection contains all the currently open forms, the Reports collection contains all the currently open reports. Using the Reports collection, you can perform an action on each open report.

The code that follows iterates through the Reports collection, printing the name of each open report. It is found in basApplicationObject. It begins by establishing a report object variable. It then uses the For Each…Next construct to loop through each report in the Reports collection (the collection of reports open in print preview), printing its name.

```
Sub IterateOpenReports()
    'Declare a report object variable
    Dim rpt As Report
    'Use the report object variable to point at each report in the Reports
collection
    For Each rpt In Reports
        'Print the name of the referenced report to the Immediate window
        Debug.Print rpt.Name
    Next rpt
End Sub
```

The Modules Collection

The Modules collection contains all the standard and class modules that are open. All open modules are included in the Modules collection, regardless of whether they're compiled and whether they contain code that's currently running.

The CurrentProject Object

The CurrentProject object returns a reference to the current project. The CurrentProject object contains properties such as Name, Path, and Connection. It contains the following collections: AllDataAccessPages, AllForms, AllMacros, AllModules, and AllReports. You can use these collections to iterate through all the data access pages, forms, macros, modules, and reports stored in the database. These collections differ from the DataAccessPages, Forms, Macros, Modules, and Reports collections in that they refer to all objects stored in the current project, rather than to just the open objects.

The following code retrieves the Name and Path properties of the current project. It uses the With...End With construct to retrieve the properties of the CurrentProject object:

```
Sub CurrentProjectObject()
    With CurrentProject
        Debug.Print .Name
        Debug.Print .Path
    End With
End Sub
```

The AllForms Collection

As previously mentioned, the CurrentProject object contains collections that refer to the various objects in your database. The following code iterates through the AllForms collection of the CurrentProject, printing the name of each form:

```
Sub IterateAllForms()

    Dim vnt As Variant
    'Loop through each form in the current project,
    'printing the name of each form to the Immediate window
    With CurrentProject
        For Each vnt In .AllForms
            Debug.Print vnt.Name
        Next vnt
    End With
End Sub
```

> **NOTE**
>
> You might easily confuse the AllForms collection of the CurrentProject object with the Forms collection. The AllForms collection of the CurrentProject object comprises all the saved forms that are part of the database; the Forms collection

comprises only the forms currently running in memory. If you want to see a list of all the forms that make up a database, you must use the `AllForms` collection of the `CurrentProject` object. However, if you want to change the caption of all the open forms, you must use the `Forms` collection.

The `AllReports` Collection

The `AllReports` collection allows you to loop through all reports in the current project. The example that follows prints the name of each report stored in the database referenced by the `CurrentProject` object:

```
Sub IterateAllReports()
    'Declare iteration variable
    Dim vnt As Variant
    'Loop through each report in the current project,
    'printing the name of each report to the Immediate window
    With CurrentProject
        For Each vnt In .AllReports
            Debug.Print vnt.Name
        Next vnt
    End With
End Sub
```

The `AllMacros` Collection

The `AllMacros` collection allows you to iterate through all macros stored in the current project. The example that follows prints the name of each macro stored in the database referenced by the `CurrentProject` object:

```
Sub IterateAllMacros()
    'Declare iteration variable
    Dim vnt As Variant
    'Loop through each macro in the current project,
    'printing the name of each macro to the Immediate window
    With CurrentProject
        For Each vnt In .AllMacros
            Debug.Print vnt.Name
        Next vnt
    End With
End Sub
```

The `AllModules` Collection

The `AllModules` collection is another collection associated with the `CurrentProject` object. The code that follows iterates through all modules located in the database referenced by the `CurrentProject` object. The name of each module is printed to the Immediate window.

```
Sub IterateAllModules()
    'Declare iteration variable
    Dim vnt As Variant
    'Loop through each module in the current project,
    'printing the name of each module to the Immediate window
    With CurrentProject
        For Each vnt In .AllModules
            Debug.Print vnt.Name
        Next vnt
    End With
End Sub
```

The CurrentData Object

Whereas you use the CurrentProject object to access and manipulate the application
components of your database, you use the CurrentData object to reference the
data elements of the database. The CurrentData object contains six collections:
AllDatabaseDiagrams, AllQueries, AllStoredProcedures, AllTables, AllViews, and
AllFunctions. You use these collections to iterate through and manipulate all the data-
base diagrams, queries, stored procedures, views, and functions stored in the database.
The sections that follow cover the AllTables and AllQueries collections. The
AllDatabaseDiagrams, AllStoredProcedures, AllViews, and AllFunctions collections
are available only in Access Data Projects and are discussed in detail in *Alison Balter's
Mastering Access 2002 Enterprise Development*.

The AllTables Collection

The AllTables collection is used to iterate through all tables in the database referenced by
the CurrentData object, as shown in the following code. It prints the name of each table
in the database.

```
Sub IterateAllTables()
    'Declare looping variable
    Dim vnt As Variant
    'Loop through each table in the database
    'referenced by the CurrentData object
    With CurrentData
        For Each vnt In .AllTables
            'Print the name of the table
            Debug.Print vnt.Name
        Next vnt
    End With
End Sub
```

The AllQueries Collection

You use the AllQueries collection to iterate through all queries located in the database referenced by the CurrentData object. The following example loops through all queries in the database referenced by the CurrentData object. The name of each query is printed to the Immediate window.

```
Sub IterateAllQueries()
    'Declare looping variable
    Dim vnt As Variant
    'Loop through each query in the database
    'referenced by the CurrentData object
    With CurrentData
        For Each vnt In .AllQueries
            'Print the name of the table
            Debug.Print vnt.Name
        Next vnt
    End With
End Sub
```

The CodeProject Object

You use the CodeProject object when your database implements code libraries. It is similar to the CurrentProject object but is used to reference the properties and collections stored within the library database. Chapter 26, "Creating Your Own Libraries," covers library databases.

The CodeData Object

Just as the CodeProject object is used to reference the application objects stored within a library database, the CodeData object is used to reference the data elements of a code library. These elements include the database diagrams, queries, stored procedures, tables, views, and functions stored within the library.

The Screen Object

You can use the Screen object to refer to the form, datasheet, report, data access page, or control that has the focus. The Screen object contains properties that refer to the active form, active report, active control, and previous control. Using these properties, you can manipulate the currently active form, report, or control, as well as the control that was active just before the current control. If you try to refer to the Screen object when no form or report is active, a runtime error occurs.

The DoCmd Object

The DoCmd object is used to perform macro commands or Access actions from VBA code; it's followed by a period and the name of an action. Most of the DoCmd actions—the

OpenQuery action, for example—also require arguments. The OpenQuery action is used to execute an Access query. It receives the following arguments:

▶ **Query Name**—The name of the query you want to execute

▶ **View**—Datasheet, Design, or Print preview

▶ **Data Mode**—Add, edit, or read-only

Here's an example of the OpenQuery action of the DoCmd object:

```
DoCmd.OpenQuery "qryCustomers", acViewNormal, acReadOnly
```

The OpenQuery action is performed by the DoCmd object. The first argument, the query name, is "qryCustomers". This is the name of the query that's opened in Datasheet view (rather than Design view or Print preview). It's opened in read-only mode, meaning the resulting data can't be modified.

Taking Advantage of Additional Useful Properties

In addition to the properties already discussed, two other properties are worth mentioning. They are the DateCreated and DateModified properties. They are available for *all* Access objects. Here's an example that shows the use of these properties with the AllTables collection:

```
Public Sub GetDates()
    'Declare looping variable
    Dim vnt As Variant
    'Loop through each table in the database
    'referenced by the CurrentData object
    With CurrentData
        For Each vnt In .AllTables
            'Print the name, date created, and the date
            'the table was last modified
            Debug.Print vnt.Name & ", " & _
                vnt.DateCreated & ", " & _
                vnt.DateModified
        Next vnt
    End With
End Sub
```

This code loops through each table stored in the database referenced by the CurrentData object. The name, creation date, and last modification data are all printed to the Immediate window.

Practical Examples: Working with Objects

Most applications use objects throughout. The example that follows applies the technique you learned to enable and disable command buttons in response to the user making changes to the data on the frmClients form, located in Chap9Ex.mdb on the sample code CD-ROM.

Enabling and Disabling Command Buttons

When a user is in the middle of modifying form data, there's really no need for her to use other parts of the application. It makes sense to disable other features until the user has opted to save the changes to the Client data. The clean form begins with the View Projects command button enabled and the Save and Cancel buttons disabled. The KeyPreview property of the form is set to Yes so that the form previews all keystrokes before the individual controls process them. In the example, the KeyDown event of the form is used to respond to the user "dirtying" the form. It executes whenever the user types ANSI characters while the form has the focus. The KeyDown event of the form (discussed in detail in Chapter 10, "Advanced Form Techniques") looks like this:

```
Private Sub Form_KeyDown(KeyCode As Integer, Shift As Integer)
    'If the Save command button is not already enabled
    If Not cmdSave.Enabled Then

        'If a relevant key was pressed
        If ImportantKey(KeyCode, Shift) Then

            'Flip the command buttons on the form,
            'setting focus to the active control
            Call FlipEnabled(Me, Screen.ActiveControl)

            'Disable the cboSelectClient combo box
            Me.cboSelectClient.Enabled = False

        End If

    'If the Save button is already enabled (form is dirty)
    'ignore the PageUp and PageDown keys
    Else
        If KeyCode = vbKeyPageDown Or _
         KeyCode = vbKeyPageUp Then
         KeyCode = 0
        End If
    End If
End Sub
```

6

The KeyDown event automatically receives the code of the key that was pressed, whether Shift, Alt, or Ctrl was pressed along with that key. The event routine checks to determine whether the Save button is already enabled. If it is, there's no reason to continue; the Enabled property of the command buttons has already been flipped. If Save isn't already enabled, the ImportantKey function (discussed in detail later) is called. It receives the key that was pressed, despite whether Shift, Alt, or Ctrl was used.

The ImportantKey evaluates the key that was pressed to determine whether a keystroke is modifying the data. If it is, the function returns True. Otherwise, it returns False. If ImportantKey returns True, the FlipEnabled routine is executed. FlipEnabled flips the enabled property of the command buttons on the form so that Save and Cancel are enabled, and View Projects is disabled.

If the value returned from the ImportantKey function is True, the enabled property cboSelectClient combo is set to False. If you fail to prevent movement to other records while the form is dirty, Access automatically saves the user's changes when the user navigates to another record. Furthermore, the enabled state of the command buttons still reflects a dirty state of the form.

Finally, if Save is already enabled, you know that the form is in a dirty state. If that is the case, it is not appropriate for the user to be able to move to another record using the PageUp and PageDown keys. If the cmdSave command button is enabled, and the key pressed is PageUp or PageDown, the keystroke is ignored.

Now that you understand the role of the KeyDown event of the form, take a look at the functions that underlie its functionality. The ImportantKey function looks like this:

```
Function ImportantKey(KeyCode, Shift)
    'Set return value to false
    ImportantKey = False

    'If Alt key was pressed, exit function
    If Shift = acAltMask Then
        Exit Function
    End If

    'If Delete, Backspace, or a typeable character was pressed
    If KeyCode = vbKeyDelete Or KeyCode = vbKeyBack Or (KeyCode > 31 _
        And KeyCode < 256) Then
        'If the typeable character was NOT a right, left, up,
        'or down arrow, page up, or page down, return True
        If KeyCode = vbKeyRight Or KeyCode = vbKeyLeft Or _
            KeyCode = vbKeyUp Or KeyCode = vbKeyDown Or _
            KeyCode = vbKeyPageUp Or KeyCode = vbKeyPageDown Then

        Else
            ImportantKey = True
        End If
    End If
End Function
```

This generic function, found in basUtils, sets its default return value to False. It tests to see whether the user pressed the Alt key. If so, the user was accessing a menu or accelerator key, which means that there's no reason to flip the command buttons. The function is exited. If the user didn't press the Alt key, the key that was pressed is evaluated. If the Delete key, Backspace key, or any key with an ANSI value between 31 and 256 was pressed (excluding the left-, right-, up-, and down-arrow keys, and PageUp or PageDown), True is returned from this function. The KeyDown event of the form then calls the FlipEnabled routine. It looks like this:

```
Sub FlipEnabled(frmAny As Form, ctlAny As Control)
    'Declare a control object variable
    Dim ctl As Control

    'If the type of control received as a parameter
    'is a command button, enable it and set focus to it
    ctlAny.Enabled = True
    ctlAny.SetFocus

    'Loop through each control in the controls collection
    'of the form that was received as a parameter
    For Each ctl In frmAny.Controls

        'If the type of the control is a command button
        'and the name of the control does not match the
        'name of the control received as a parameter
        'flip the enabled property of the control
        If ctl.ControlType = acCommandButton Then
            If ctl.Name <> ctlAny.Name Then
                ctl.Enabled = Not ctl.Enabled
            End If
        End If
    Next ctl
End Sub
```

This generic routine, also found in basUtils, flips the Enabled property of every command button in the form, except the one that was passed to the routine as the second parameter. The FlipEnabled routine receives a form and a control as parameters. It begins by creating a control object variable; then it enables the control that was passed as a parameter and sets focus to it. The routine then loops through every control on the form that was passed to it. It tests to see whether each control is a command button. If it finds a command button, and the name of the command button isn't the same as the name of the control that was passed to it, it flips the Enabled property of the command button. The idea is this: When the user clicks Save, you can't immediately disable the Save button because it still has focus. You must first enable a selected control (the one that was passed to the routine) and set focus to the enabled control. After the control is enabled, you don't want to disable it again, so you need to eliminate it from the processing loop.

Objects, Properties, Methods, and Events Explained

Remember that as long as the `cmdSave` command button is enabled, the PageUp and PageDown keys are ignored. This is an important step because it is imperative that the user not be able to move from record to record while editing the form data.

You need a way to flip the command buttons back the other way when editing is complete. The `Click` event of the Save button contains the following code:

```
Private Sub cmdSave_Click()
    'Save changes to the client record
    DoCmd.RunCommand acCmdSaveRecord

    'Enable client selection combo
    Me.cboSelectClient.Enabled = True

    'Call routine to disable save and cancel and
    'enable view projects
    Call FlipEnabled(Me, Me.cboSelectClient)
End Sub
```

This code saves the current record and enables the `cboSelectClient` control. It then calls the `FlipEnabled` routine, passing a reference to the `cboSelectClient` control as a parameter. The `FlipEnabled` routine flips the command buttons back to their original state.

The form contains a cancel command button with a similar routine. It looks like this:

```
Private Sub cmdUndo_Click()
    'Undo changes
    DoCmd.RunCommand acCmdUndo

    'Enable client selection combo
    Me.cboSelectClient.Enabled = True

    'Call routine to disable save and cancel and
    'enable view projects
    Call FlipEnabled(Me, Me.cboSelectClient)

End Sub
```

This code undoes changes to the current record. It enables the `cboSelectClient` control and calls the `FlipEnabled` routine to once again disable Save and Cancel and enable View Projects.

Summary

The ability to successfully work with objects and understand their properties, methods, and events is fundamental to your success as an Access programmer. In this chapter, you learned about various objects, properties, methods, and events. You learned how to set properties at design time and change their values in response to events that occur at runtime. You also learned how to pass forms and other objects to subroutines and functions to make the VBA language extremely robust and flexible.

Advanced Form Techniques

Why This Chapter Is Important

Given Access's graphical environment, your development efforts are often centered on forms. Therefore, you must understand all the Form and Control events and know which event you should code to perform each task. You should also know what types of forms are available and how you can get the look and behavior you want in them.

Often, you won't need to design your own form because you can make use of one of the built-in dialog boxes that are part of the Visual Basic for Applications (VBA) language. Whatever types of forms you create, you should take advantage of all the tricks and tips of the trade covered throughout this chapter.

What Are the Form Events, and When Do You Use Them?

Microsoft Access *traps* (responds to) for over 30 Form events (excluding those specifically related to pivot tables), each of which has a distinct purpose. Access also traps events for Form sections and controls. The following sections cover the Form events and when you should use them.

Current

A form's Current event is one of the more commonly coded events. It happens each time focus moves from one record to another. The Current event is a great place to put code that you want to execute whenever the user displays a record. For example, you might want the cursor to move to the contact first name control if the user moves to a new client. The following code is placed in the Current event of the frmClients form that's part of the hypothetical time and billing application that you've been building in the previous chapters:

```
Private Sub Form_Current()
    'If user is on a new record,
    'move the focus to the Contact First Name control
    If Me.NewRecord Then
        Me.txtContactFirstName.SetFocus
    End If
End Sub
```

This code moves focus to the txtContactFirstName control if the txtClientID control of the record that the user is moving to happens to be Null; this happens if the user is adding a new record.

BeforeInsert

The BeforeInsert event occurs when the first character is typed in a new record but before the new record is actually created. If the user is typing in a text or combo box, the BeforeInsert event occurs even before the Change event of the text or combo box. The frmProjects form of the time and billing application has an example of a practical use of the BeforeInsert event:

```
Private Sub Form_BeforeInsert(Cancel As Integer)
On Error GoTo Err_Form_BeforeInsert
    'Set the ClientID to the ClientID on the Clients form
    Me.ClientID = Forms.frmClients.txtClientID

Exit_Form_BeforeInsert:
    Exit Sub

Err_Form_BeforeInsert:
    MsgBox Err.Description
    Resume Exit_Form_BeforeInsert
End Sub
```

The frmProjects form is always called from the frmClients form. The BeforeInsert event of frmProjects sets the value of the txtClientID text box equal to the value of the txtClientID text box on frmClients.

AfterInsert

The AfterInsert event occurs after the record has actually been inserted. You can use it to requery a recordset after a new record is added.

> **NOTE**
>
> Here's the order of form events when a user begins to type data into a new record:
>
> ```
> BeforeInsert->BeforeUpdate->AfterUpdate->AfterInsert
> ```
>
> The `BeforeInsert` event occurs when the user types the first character, the `BeforeUpdate` event happens when the user updates the record, the `AfterUpdate` event takes place when the record is updated, and the `AfterInsert` event occurs when the record that's being updated is a new record.

BeforeUpdate

The `BeforeUpdate` event runs before a record is updated. It occurs when the user tries to move to a different record (even a record on a subform) or when the Records, Save Record command is executed. You can use the `BeforeUpdate` event to cancel the update process when you want to perform complex validations. When a user adds a record, the `BeforeUpdate` event occurs after the `BeforeInsert` event. The `frmClients` form in the `CHAP10EX` sample database provides an example of using a `BeforeUpdate` event:

```
Private Sub Form_BeforeUpdate(Cancel As Integer)

    'If the Contact FirstName, LastName, Company, or
    'Phone Number is left blank, display a message
    'and cancel the update
    If IsNull(Me.txtContactFirstName) Or _
        IsNull(Me.txtContactLastName) Or _
        IsNull(Me.txtCompanyName) Or _
        IsNull(Me.txtPhoneNumber) Then
        MsgBox "The Contact First Name, " & vbCrLf & _
            "Contact Last Name, " & vbCrLf & _
            "Company Name, " & vbCrLf & _
            "And Contact Phone Must All Be Entered", _
            vbCritical, _
            "Canceling Update"
        Me.txtContactFirstName.SetFocus
        Cancel = True
    End If
End Sub
```

This code determines whether the first name, last name, company name, or phone number contains `Null`. If any of these fields contains `Null`, the code displays a message, and the `Cancel` parameter is set to `True`, canceling the update process. As a convenience to the user, focus is placed in the `txtFirstName` control.

10

AfterUpdate

The `AfterUpdate` event occurs after the changed data in a record is updated. You might use this event to requery combo boxes on related forms or perhaps to log record changes. Here's an example:

```
Private Sub Form_AfterUpdate()
    Me.cboSelectProduct.Requery
End Sub
```

This code requeries the `cboSelectProduct` combo box after the user updates the current record.

Dirty

The `Dirty` event occurs when the contents of the form, or of the text portion of a combo box, change. It also occurs when you programmatically change the `Text` property of a control. Here's an example:

```
Private Sub Form_Dirty(Cancel As Integer)
    'Flip the Enabled properties of the appropriate
    'command buttons
    Call FlipEnabled(Me, ActiveControl)

    'Hide the form navigation buttons
    Me.NavigationButtons = False
End Sub
```

This code, located in the `frmClients` form of the time and billing application, calls `FlipEnabled` to flip the command buttons on the form. This has the effect of enabling the Save and Cancel command buttons and disabling the other command buttons on the form. The code also removes the navigation buttons, prohibiting the user from moving to other records while the data is in a "dirty" state.

Undo

The `Undo` event executes before changes to a row are undone. The `Undo` event initiates when the user clicks the Undo button on the Quick Access toolbar, presses the Esc key, or executes code that attempts to undo changes to the row. If you cancel the `Undo` event, the changes to the row are not undone. Here's an example:

```
Private Sub Form_Undo(Cancel As Integer)

    'Ask user if he meant to undo changes
    If MsgBox("You Have Attempted to Undo Changes " & _
        "to the Current Row.  Would You Like to Proceed " & _
        "with the Undo Process?", _
        vbYesNo) = vbYes Then
```

```
        'If he responds yes, proceed with the undo
        Cancel = False

    Else

        'If he responds no, cancel the undo
        Cancel = True
    End If

End Sub
```

This code, located in the `frmProjects` form of the time and billing application, displays a message to the user, asking him if he really wants to undo his changes. If he responds Yes, the Undo process proceeds. If he responds No, the Undo process is canceled.

Delete

The `Delete` event occurs when a user tries to delete a record but before the record is removed from the table. This is a great way to place code that allows deleting a record only under certain circumstances. If the `Delete` event is canceled, the `BeforeDelConfirm` and `AfterDelConfirm` events (covered next) never execute, and the record is never deleted.

> **TIP**
>
> When the user deletes multiple records, the `Delete` event happens after each record is deleted. This allows you to evaluate a condition for each record and decide whether to delete each record.

BeforeDelConfirm

The `BeforeDelConfirm` event takes place after the `Delete` event but before the Delete Confirm dialog box is displayed. If you cancel the `BeforeDelConfirm` event, the record being deleted is restored from the delete buffer, and the Delete Confirm dialog box is never displayed.

AfterDelConfirm

The `AfterDelConfirm` event occurs after the record is deleted or when the deletion is canceled. If the code does not cancel the `BeforeDelConfirm` event, the `AfterDelConfirm` event takes place after Access displays the Confirmation dialog box.

Open

The `Open` event occurs when a form is opened but before the first record is displayed. With this event, you can control exactly what happens when the form first opens. The `Open` event of the time and billing application's `frmProjects` form looks like this:

10

```
Private Sub Form_Open(Cancel As Integer)
    'If the Clients form is not loaded,
    'display a message to the user and
    'do not load the form
    If Not IsLoaded("frmClients") Then
        MsgBox "Open the Projects form using the Projects " & _
            "button on the Clients form."
        Cancel = True
    End If
End Sub
```

This code checks to make sure the frmClients form is loaded. If it isn't, it displays a message box and sets the Cancel parameter to True, which prohibits the form from loading.

Load

The Load event happens when a form opens, and the first record is displayed; it occurs after the Open event. A form's Open event can cancel the loading of a form, but the Load event can't. The following routine is placed in the Load event of the time and billing application's frmExpenseCodes form:

```
Private Sub Form_Load()
    'If the form is opened in Data Entry mode
    'and the OpenArgs property is not null,
    'set the txtExpenseCode text box equal to
    'the value of the opening arguments
    If Me.DataEntry _
        And Not (IsNull(Me.OpenArgs)) Then
        Me.txtExpenseCode = Me.OpenArgs
    End If
End Sub
```

This routine looks at the string that's passed as an opening argument to the form. If the OpenArgs string is not Null, and the form is opened in Data Entry mode, the txtExpenseCode text box is set equal to the opening argument. In essence, this code allows the form to be used for two purposes. If the user opens the form from the database container, no special processing occurs. On the other hand, if the user opens the form from the fsubTimeCardsExpenses subform, the form is opened in Data Entry mode, and the expense code that the user specified is placed in the txtExpenseCode text box.

Resize

The Resize event takes place when a form is opened or whenever the form's size changes.

Unload

The Unload event happens when a form is closed but before Access removes the form from the screen. It's triggered when the user closes the form, quits the application by choosing End Task from the task list or quits Windows, or when your code closes the form. You can place code that makes sure it's okay to unload the form in the Unload event, and you can also use the Unload event to place any code you want executed whenever the form is unloaded. Here's an example:

```
Private Sub Form_Unload(Cancel As Integer)
    'Determine if the form is dirty
    If Me.cmdSave.Enabled Then

        'If form is dirty, ask user if he wants to save
        Select Case MsgBox("Do You Want To Save?", _
            vbYesNoCancel + vbCritical, _
            "Please Respond")

            'If user responds yes, save record and allow unload
            Case vbYes
                DoCmd.RunCommand Command:=acCmdSaveRecord
                Cancel = False

            'If user responds no, undo changes to record and
            'allow unload
            Case vbNo
                On Error Resume Next
                DoCmd.RunCommand Command:=acCmdUndo
                Cancel = False

            'If user clicks Cancel, cancel unloading of form
            Case vbCancel
                Cancel = True
        End Select
    End If
End Sub
```

This code is in the Unload event of the frmClients form from the time and billing application. It checks whether the Save button is enabled. If it is, the form is in a dirty state. The user is prompted as to whether she wants to save changes to the record. If she responds yes, the code saves the data, and the form is unloaded. If she responds no, the code cancels changes to the record, and the form is unloaded. Finally, if she opts to cancel, the value of the Cancel parameter is set to False, and the form is not unloaded.

10

Close

The Close event occurs *after* the Unload event, when a form is closed and removed from the screen. Remember, you can cancel the Unload event but not the Close event.

The following code is located in the Close event of the frmClients form that's part of the time and billing database:

```
Private Sub Form_Close()
    'If the frmProjects form is loaded,
    'unload it
    If IsLoaded("frmProjects") Then
        DoCmd.Close acForm, "frmProjects"
    End If
End Sub
```

When the frmClients form is closed, the code tests whether the frmProjects form is open. If it is, the code closes it.

Activate

The Activate event takes place when the form gets focus and becomes the active window. It's triggered when the form opens, when a user clicks on the form or one of its controls, and when the SetFocus method is applied by using VBA code. The following code, found in the Activate event of the time and billing application's frmClients form, requeries the fsubClients subform whenever the frmClients main form activates:

```
Private Sub Form_Activate()
    'Requery form when it becomes active
    'This ensures that changes made in the Projects form
    'are immediately reflected in the Clients form
    Me.fsubClients.Requery
End Sub
```

Deactivate

The Deactivate event occurs when the form loses focus, which happens when a table, query, form, report, macro, module, or the Navigation Pane becomes active. However, the Deactivate event isn't triggered when a dialog box, pop-up form, or another application becomes active.

GotFocus

The GotFocus event happens when a form gets focus, but only if there are no visible, enabled controls on the form. This event is rarely used for a form.

LostFocus

The LostFocus event occurs when a form loses focus, but only if there are no visible, enabled controls on the form. This event, too, is rarely used for a form.

Click

The Click event takes place when the user clicks on a blank area of the form, on a disabled control on the form, or on the form's record selector.

DblClick

The DblClick event happens when the user double-clicks on a blank area of the form, on a disabled control on the form, or on the form's record selector.

MouseDown

The MouseDown event occurs when the user clicks on a blank area of the form, on a disabled control on the form, or on the form's record selector. However, it happens *before* the Click event fires. You can use it to determine which mouse button was pressed.

MouseMove

The MouseMove event takes place when the user moves the mouse over a blank area of the form, over a disabled control on the form, or over the form's record selector. It's generated continuously as the mouse pointer moves over the form. The MouseMove event occurs *before* the Click event fires.

MouseUp

The MouseUp event occurs when the user releases the mouse button. Like the MouseDown event, it happens before the Click event fires. You can use the MouseUp event to determine which mouse button was pressed.

KeyDown

The KeyDown event happens if there are no controls on the form or if the form's KeyPreview property is set to Yes. If the latter condition is true, all keyboard events are previewed by the form and occur for the control that has focus. If the user presses and holds down a key, the KeyDown event occurs repeatedly until the user releases the key. Here's an example:

```
Private Sub Form_KeyDown(KeyCode As Integer, Shift As Integer)
    'If the form is dirty and the user presses page up or
    'page down, ignore the keystroke
    If Me.Dirty Then
        If KeyCode = vbKeyPageDown Or _
```

10

```
            KeyCode = vbKeyPageUp Then
            KeyCode = 0
        End If
    End If
End Sub
```

This code, found in the `frmClients` form that is part of the time and billing application, tests to see if the form is in a dirty state. If it is, and the user presses the Page Down or Page Up key, Access ignores the keystroke. This prevents the user from moving to other records without first clicking the Save or Cancel command buttons.

KeyUp

Like the `KeyDown` event, the `KeyUp` event occurs if there are no controls on the form, or if the form's `KeyPreview` property is set to `Yes`. The `KeyUp` event takes place only once, though, regardless of how long the user presses the key. You can cancel the keystroke by setting `KeyCode` to 0.

KeyPress

The `KeyPress` event occurs when the user presses and releases a key or key combination that corresponds to an ANSI code. It takes place if there are no controls on the form, or if the form's `KeyPreview` property is set to `Yes`. You can cancel the keystroke by setting `KeyCode` to `0`.

Error

The `Error` event triggers whenever an error happens while the user is in the form. Access Database Engine errors are trapped, but Visual Basic errors aren't. You can use this event to suppress the standard error messages. You must handle Visual Basic errors using standard `On Error` techniques. Both the `Error` event and handling Visual Basic errors are covered in Chapter 17, "Error Handling: Preparing for the Inevitable."

Filter

The Filter event takes place whenever the user selects the Filter By Form or Advanced Filter/Sort options. You can use this event to remove the previous filter, enter default settings for the filter, invoke your own custom filter window, or prevent certain controls from being available in the Filter By Form window. The later section "Taking Advantage of Built-In, Form-Filtering Features" covers filters in detail.

ApplyFilter

The `ApplyFilter` event occurs when the user selects the Apply Filter/Sort, Filter By Selection, or Remove Filter/Sort options. It also takes place when the user closes the Advanced Filter/Sort window or the Filter By Form window. You can use this event to make sure that the applied filter is correct, to change the form's display before the filter is applied, or to undo any changes you made when the Filter event occurred. The later section "Taking Advantage of Built-In, Form-Filtering Features" covers filters in detail.

Timer

The Timer event and a form's TimerInterval property work hand in hand. You can set the TimerInterval property to any value between 0 and 2,147,483,647. The value used determines the frequency, expressed in milliseconds, at which the Timer event will occur. For example, if the TimerInterval property is set to 0, the Timer event will not occur at all; if set to 5000 (5000 milliseconds), the Timer event will occur every five seconds. The following example uses the Timer event to alternate the visibility of a label on the form. This produces a flashing effect. The TimerInterval property can be initially set to any valid value other than 0 but will be reduced by 50 milliseconds each time the code executes. This has the effect of making the control flash faster and faster. The Timer events continue to occur until the TimerInterval property is finally reduced to 0.

```
Private Sub Form_Timer()
'If Label1 is visible, hide it; otherwise, show it
If Me.Label2.Visible = True Then
    Me.Label2.Visible = False
Else
    Me.Label2.Visible = True
End If


'Decrement the timer interval, causing the
'label to flash more quickly
Me.TimerInterval = Me.TimerInterval - 50


'Once the timer interval becomes zero,
'make the label visible
If Me.TimerInterval = 0 Then
    Me.Label2.Visible = True
End If
End Sub
```

Understanding the Sequence of Form Events

One of the mysteries of events is the order in which they occur. One of the best ways to figure this out is to place Debug.Print statements in the events you want to learn about. This technique is covered in Chapter 16, "Debugging: Your Key to Successful Development." Keep in mind that event order isn't an exact science; it's nearly impossible to guess when events will happen in all situations. It's helpful, though, to understand the basic order in which certain events do take place.

What Happens When a Form Is Opened?

When a user opens a form, the following events occur:

```
Open->Load->Resize->Activate->Current
```

10

After these Form events take place, the Enter and GotFocus events of the first control occur. Remember that the Open event provides the only opportunity to cancel opening the form.

What Happens When a Form Is Closed?

When a user closes a form, the following events take place:

```
Unload->Deactivate->Close
```

Before these events occur, the Exit and LostFocus events of the active control trigger.

What Happens When a Form Is Sized?

When a user resizes a form, what happens depends on whether the form is minimized, restored, or maximized. When the form minimizes, here's what happens:

```
Resize->Deactivate
```

When a user restores a minimized form, these events take place:

```
Activate->Resize
```

When a user maximizes a form or restores a maximized form, just the Resize event occurs.

What Happens When Focus Shifts from One Form to Another?

When a user moves from one form to another, the Deactivate event occurs for the first form; then the Activate event occurs for the second form. Remember that the Deactivate event doesn't take place if focus moves to a dialog box, a pop-up form, or another application.

What Happens When Keys Are Pressed?

When a user types a character, and the form's KeyPreview property is set to True, the following events occur:

```
KeyDown->KeyPress->Dirty->KeyUp
```

If you trap the KeyDown event and set the KeyCode to 0, the remaining events never happen. The KeyPress event captures only ANSI keystrokes. This event is the easiest to deal with. However, you must handle the KeyDown and KeyUp events when you need to trap for non-ANSI characters, such as Shift, Alt, and Ctrl.

What Happens When Mouse Actions Take Place?

When a user clicks the mouse button, the following events occur:

```
MouseDown->MouseUp->Click
```

What Are the Section and Control Events, and When Do You Use Them?

Sections have only five events: Click, DblClick, MouseDown, MouseMove, and MouseUp. These events rarely play significant roles in your application.

Each control type has its own set of events to which it responds. Many events are common to most controls, but others are specific to certain controls. Furthermore, some controls respond to very few events. The following sections cover most of the Control events and the controls they apply to.

BeforeUpdate

The BeforeUpdate event applies to text boxes, option groups, combo boxes, list boxes, and bound object frames. It occurs before changed data in the control updates. You can find the following code example in the BeforeUpdate event of the txtProjectTotalBillingEstimate control on the frmProjects form in the sample database:

```
Private Sub txtProjectTotalBillingEstimate_BeforeUpdate(Cancel As Integer)
    'If project total billings are less than or equal to zero
    'display a message to the user and cancel the update
    If Me.txtProjectTotalBillingEstimate <= 0 Then
        MsgBox "Project Total Billings Must Be Greater Than " & _
            "or Equal to Zero", vbCritical, "Canceling Update"
        Cancel = True
    End If

End Sub
```

This code tests whether the value of the CustomerID control is less than or equal to zero. If it is, the code displays a message box, and the Update event is canceled.

AfterUpdate

The AfterUpdate event applies to text boxes, option groups, combo boxes, list boxes, and bound object frames. It occurs after changed data in the control updates. The following code example is from the AfterUpdate event of the txtBeginDate control on the frmPrintInvoice form found in the time and billing database:

```
Private Sub txtBeginDate_AfterUpdate()
    'Requery the subforms when the begin
    'date changes
    Me.fsubPrintInvoiceTime.Requery
    Me.fsubPrintInvoiceExpenses.Requery
End Sub
```

10

This code requeries both the `fsubPrintInvoiceTime` subform and the `fsubPrintInvoiceExpenses` subform when the `txtBeginDate` control updates. This ensures that the subforms display the time and expenses appropriate for the selected date range.

Updated

The `Updated` event applies to a bound object frame only. It occurs when the object linking and embedding (OLE) object's data is modified.

Change

The `Change` event applies to text and combo boxes and takes place when data in the control changes. For a text box, this event occurs when the user types a character; for a combo box, it happens when a user types a character or selects a value from the list. You use this event when you want to trap for something happening on a character-by-character basis.

NotInList

The `NotInList` event applies only to a combo box and happens when a user enters a value in the text box portion of the combo box that's not in the combo box list. By using this event, you can allow the user to add a new value to the combo box list. For this event to be triggered, the `LimitToList` property must be set to `Yes`. Here's an example from the time and billing application's `frmPayments` form:

```
Private Sub cboPaymentMethodID_NotInList _
    'If payment method is not in the list,
    'ask user if he wants to add it
    If MsgBox("Payment Method Not Found, Add?", _
        vbYesNo + vbQuestion, _
        "Please Respond") = vbYes Then

        'If he responds yes, open the frmPaymentMethods form
        'in Add mode, passing in the new payment method
        DoCmd.OpenForm "frmPaymentMethods", _
            Datamode:=acFormAdd, _
            WindowMode:=acDialog, _
            OpenArgs:=NewData

        'If form is still loaded, unload it
        If IsLoaded("frmPaymentMethods") Then
            Response = acDataErrAdded
            DoCmd.Close acForm, "frmPaymentMethods"

        'If the user cancels the add, redisplay the existing options
        Else
```

```
            Response = acDataErrContinue
        End If
    Else
        'If the user responds no, redisplay the existing options
        Response = acDataErrContinue
    End If

End Sub
```

This code executes when a user enters a payment method that's not in the cboPaymentMethodID combo box. It asks the user if he wants to add the entry. If he responds yes, the frmPaymentMethods form displays. Otherwise, the user must select another entry from the combo box. The NotInList event is covered in more detail later in the "Handling the NotInList Event" section.

Enter

The Enter event applies to text boxes, option groups, combo boxes, list boxes, command buttons, object frames, and subforms. It occurs *before* a control gets focus from another control on the same form and *before* the GotFocus event. Here's an example from the time and billing application's frmTimeCards form:

```
Private Sub fsubTimeCards_Enter()
    'If the user clicks to enter time cards, and the EmployeeID
    'is Null, display a message and set focus back to the
    'cboEmployeeID combo box
    If IsNull(Me.EmployeeID) Then
        MsgBox "Enter employee before entering time or expenses."
        Me.cboEmployeeID.SetFocus
    End If
End Sub
```

When the user moves into the fsubTimeCards subform control, its Enter event tests whether the EmployeeID has been entered on the main form. If it hasn't, a message box displays, and focus is moved to the cboEmployeeID control on the main form.

Exit

The Exit event applies to text boxes, option groups, combo boxes, list boxes, command buttons, object frames, and subforms. It occurs just before the LostFocus event.

GotFocus

The GotFocus event applies to text boxes, toggle buttons, option buttons, check boxes, combo boxes, list boxes, and command buttons. It takes place when focus moves to a control in response to a user action or when the SetFocus, SelectObject, GoToRecord, GoToControl, or GoToPage method is issued in code. Controls can get focus only if they're visible and enabled.

10

LostFocus

The LostFocus event applies to text boxes, toggle buttons, option buttons, check boxes, combo boxes, list boxes, and command buttons. It occurs when focus moves away from a control in response to a user action or when your code issues the SetFocus, SelectObject, GoToRecord, GoToControl, or GoToPage methods.

> **NOTE**
>
> The difference between GotFocus/LostFocus and Enter/Exit lies in when they occur. If focus is lost (moved to another form) or returned to the current form, the control's GotFocus and LostFocus events are triggered. The Enter and Exit events don't take place when the form loses or regains focus. Finally, it is important to note that none of these events take place when the user makes menu selections or clicks ribbon buttons.

Click

The Click event applies to labels, text boxes, option groups, combo boxes, list boxes, command buttons, and object frames. It occurs when a user presses and then releases a mouse button over a control. Here's an example from the time and billing application's frmProjects form:

```
Private Sub cmdToggleView_Click()
    'If the caption of the control is View Expenses,
    'hide the Projects subform and show the Project Expenses subform
    'Change caption of command button to View Hours
    If Me.cmdToggleView.Caption = "&View Expenses" Then
        Me.fsubProjects.Visible = False
        Me.fsubProjectExpenses.Visible = True
        Me.cmdToggleView.Caption = "&View Hours"
    'If the caption of the control is View Hours,
    'hide the Project Expenses subform and show the Project subform
    'Change caption of command button to View Expenses
    Else
        Me.fsubProjectExpenses.Visible = False
        Me.fsubProjects.Visible = True
        Me.cmdToggleView.Caption = "&View Expenses"
    End If
End Sub
```

This code checks the caption of the cmdToggleView command button. If the caption reads "&View Expenses" (with the ampersand indicating a hotkey), the fsubProjects subform is hidden, the fsubProjectExpenses subform is made visible, and the caption of the cmdToggleView command button is modified to read "&View Hours". Otherwise, the fsubProjectExpenses subform is hidden, the fsubProjects subform is made visible, and the caption of the cmdToggleView command button is modified to read "&View Expenses".

NOTE

The Click event is triggered when the user clicks the mouse over an object, as well as in the following situations:

▶ When the user presses the spacebar while a command button has focus

▶ When the user presses the Enter key and a command button's Default property is set to Yes

▶ When the user presses the Escape key and a command button's Cancel property is set to Yes

▶ When an accelerator key for a command button is used

DblClick

The DblClick event applies to labels, text boxes, option groups, combo boxes, list boxes, command buttons, and object frames. It occurs when a user presses and then releases the left mouse button twice over a control. Here's an example from the time and billing application's fsubTimeCards form:

```
Private Sub cboWorkCodeID_DblClick(Cancel As Integer)
Dim strWorkCode As String

On Error GoTo Err_cboWorkCodeID_DblClick

    'If the cboWorkCodeID is Null, set the
    'strWorkCode variable to a zero-length string
    'otherwise set it to the text in the combo box
    If IsNull(Me.cboWorkCodeID.Text) Then
        strWorkCode = ""
    Else
        strWorkCode = Me.cboWorkCodeID.Text
    End If

    'If the cboWorkCodeID is Null, set the
    'Text property to a zero-length string
    If IsNull(Me.cboWorkCodeID) Then
        Me.cboWorkCodeID.Text = ""
    Else

        'Otherwise, set the cboWorkCodeID
        'combo box to Null
        Me.cboWorkCodeID = Null
    End If

    'Open the frmWorkCodes form modally
    DoCmd.OpenForm "frmWorkCodes", _
```

10

```
            DataMode:=acFormAdd, _
            WindowMode:=acDialog, _
            OpenArgs:=strWorkCode

    'After the form is closed, requery the combo box
    Me.cboWorkCodeID.Requery

    'Set the text of the combo box to the value added
    Me.cboWorkCodeID.Text = strWorkCode

Exit_cboWorkCodeID_DblClick:
    Exit Sub

Err_cboWorkCodeID_DblClick:

    MsgBox Err.Description
    Resume Exit_cboWorkCodeID_DblClick
End Sub
```

In this example, the code evaluates the cboWorkCodeID combo box control to see whether it's Null. If it is, the text of the combo box is set to a zero-length string. Otherwise, a long integer variable is set equal to the combo box value, and the combo box value is set to Null. The frmWorkCodes form is opened modally. When it's closed, the cboWorkCodeID combo box is requeried. If the long integer variable doesn't contain a zero, the combo box value is set equal to the long integer value.

MouseDown

The MouseDown event applies to labels, text boxes, option groups, combo boxes, list boxes, command buttons, and object frames. It takes place when a user presses the mouse button over a control, *before* the Click event fires.

MouseMove

The MouseMove event applies to labels, text boxes, option groups, combo boxes, list boxes, command buttons, and object frames. It occurs as a user moves the mouse over a control.

MouseUp

The MouseUp event applies to labels, text boxes, option groups, combo boxes, list boxes, command buttons, and object frames. It occurs when a user releases the mouse over a control, *before* the Click event fires.

KeyDown

The KeyDown event applies to text boxes, toggle buttons, option buttons, check boxes, combo boxes, list boxes, and bound object frames. It happens when a user presses a key while within a control; the event occurs repeatedly until the user releases the key. You can cancel it by setting `KeyCode` equal to 0.

KeyUp

The `KeyUp` event applies to text boxes, toggle buttons, option buttons, check boxes, combo boxes, list boxes, and bound object frames. It occurs when a user releases a key within a control. It occurs only once, no matter how long the user presses a key.

KeyPress

The `KeyPress` event applies to text boxes, toggle buttons, option buttons, check boxes, combo boxes, list boxes, and bound object frames. It occurs when a user presses and releases an ANSI key while the control has focus. You can cancel it by setting `KeyCode` equal to `0`.

Understanding the Sequence of Control Events

Just as Form events take place in a certain sequence when the form is opened, activated, and so on, Control events occur in a specific sequence. You need to understand this sequence to write the event code for a control.

What Happens When Focus Is Moved to or from a Control?

When focus is moved to a control, the following events occur:

```
Enter->GotFocus
```

If focus is moving to a control as the form is opened, the Form and Control events take place in the following sequence:

```
Open(form)->Activate(form)->Current(form)->Enter(control)_
GotFocus(control)
```

When focus leaves a control, the following events occur:

```
Exit->LostFocus
```

When focus leaves the control because the form is closing, the following events happen:

```
Exit(control)->LostFocus(control)->Unload(form)->Deactivate(form)_
Close(form)
```

What Happens When the Data in a Control Is Updated?

When you change data in a control and then move focus to another control, the following events occur:

```
BeforeUpdate->AfterUpdate->Exit->LostFocus
```

10

After every character that's typed in a text or combo box, the following events take place before focus is moved to another control:

KeyDown->KeyPress->Change->KeyUp

For a combo box, if the NotInList event is triggered, it occurs after the KeyUp event.

Referring to Me

The Me keyword is like an implicitly declared variable; it's available to every procedure in a Form or Report module. Using Me is a great way to write generic code in a form or report. You can change the name of the form or report, and the code will be unaffected. Here's an example:

```
Me.RecordSource = "qryProjects"
```

This code changes the RecordSource property of the current form or report to qryProjects.

It's also useful to pass Me (the current form or report) to a generic procedure in a module, as shown in the following example:

```
Call ChangeCaption(Me)
```

The ChangeCaption procedure looks like this:

```
Sub ChangeCaption(frmAny As Form)
   If IsNull(frmAny.Caption) Then
      frmAny.Caption = "Form For - " & CurrentUser
   Else
      frmAny.Caption = frmAny.Caption & " - " & CurrentUser
   End If
End Sub
```

The ChangeCaption procedure in a Code module receives any form as a parameter. It evaluates the caption of the form that was passed to it. If the caption is Null, ChangeCaption sets the caption to "Form For -", concatenated with the user's name. Otherwise, it takes the existing caption of the form passed to it and appends the user's name.

What Types of Forms Can I Create, and When Are They Appropriate?

You can design a variety of forms with Microsoft Access. By working with the properties available in Access's form designer, you can create forms with many different looks and types of functionality. This chapter covers all the major categories of forms, but remember that you can create your own forms. Of course, don't forget to maintain consistency with the standards for Windows applications.

Single Forms: Viewing One Record at a Time

One of the most common types of forms, the Single form, allows you to view one record at a time. The Single form shown in Figure 10.1, for example, lets the user view one customer record and then move to other records as needed.

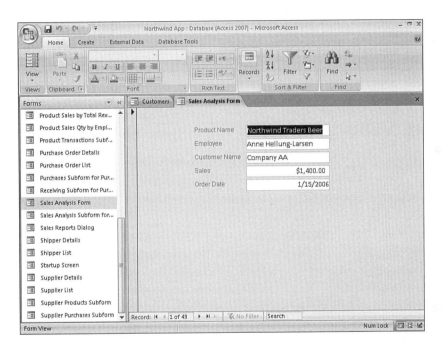

FIGURE 10.1   A Single form.

Creating a Single form is easy: Simply set the form's Default View property to Single Form (see Figure 10.2).

Continuous Forms: Viewing Multiple Records at a Time

Often, the user wants to be able to view multiple records at a time, which requires creating a Continuous form, like the one shown in Figure 10.3. To do this, just set the Default View property to Continuous Forms.

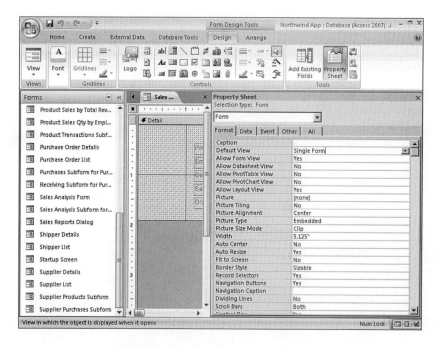

FIGURE 10.2   Setting the form's Default View property.

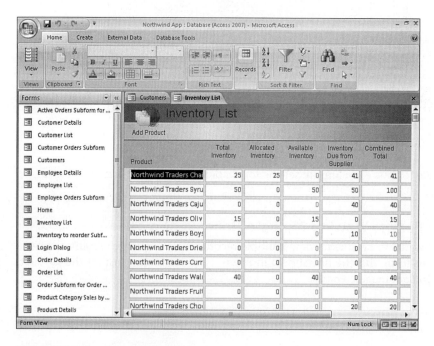

FIGURE 10.3   A Continuous form.

A subform is a common use for a Continuous form; generally, you should show multiple records in a subform. The records displayed in the subform are all the records that relate to the record displayed in the main form. Figure 10.4 shows a subform, with its Default View property set to Continuous Forms. The subform shows all the products relating to a specific supplier.

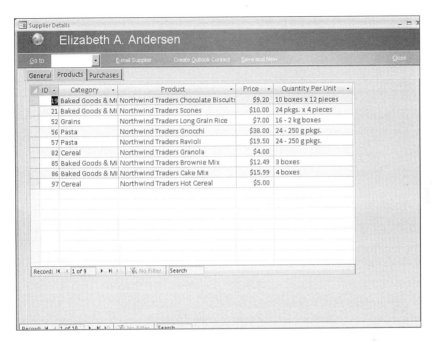

FIGURE 10.4   A form containing a Continuous subform.

Multipage Forms: Finding Solutions When Everything Doesn't Fit on One Screen

Scarcity of screen real estate is a never-ending problem, but a multipage form can be a good solution. Figures 10.5 and 10.6 show the two pages of a multipage Employees form. When looking at the form in Design view, you can see a Page Break control placed just at the 3½-inch mark on the form (see Figure 10.7). To insert a Page Break control, select it from the Controls group of the Design tab and then click and drag to place it on the form.

10

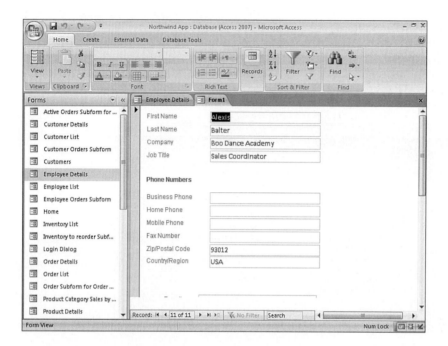

FIGURE 10.5   The first page of a multipage form.

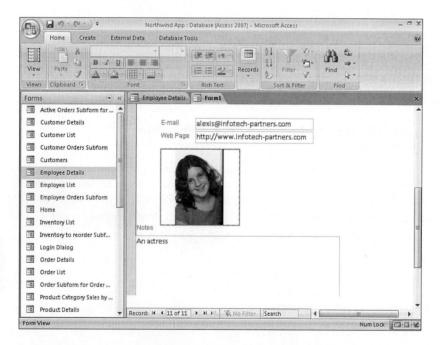

FIGURE 10.6   The second page of a multipage form.

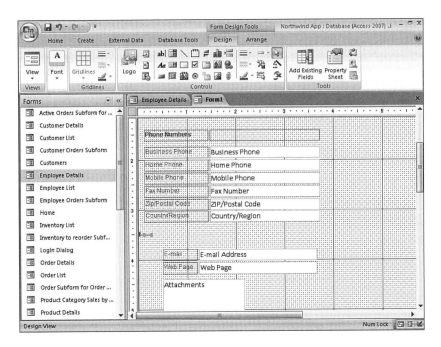

FIGURE 10.7   A multipage form in Design view, showing a Page Break control just before the 3½ -inch mark on the form.

When creating a multipage form, remember a few important steps:

▶ Set the `Default View` property of the form to `Single Form`.

▶ Set the `Scrollbars` property of the form to `Neither` or `Horizontal Only`.

▶ Set the `Auto Resize` property of the form to `No`.

▶ Place the Page Break control exactly halfway down the form's Detail section if you want the form to have two pages. If you want more pages, divide the total height of the Detail section by the number of pages and place Page Break controls at the appropriate positions on the form.

▶ Size the Form window to fit exactly one page of the form.

Tabbed Forms: Conserving Screen Real Estate

A tabbed form is an alternative to a multipage form. Access 2007 includes a built-in Tab control that allows you to easily group sets of controls. A tabbed form could, for example, show customers on one tab, orders for a selected customer on another tab, and order detail items for the selected order on a third tab.

The form shown in Figure 10.8 uses a Tab control. This form, called Employee Details, is included in the Northwind database. It shows an employee's general information on one tab and his orders on the second tab. No code is needed to build the example.

10

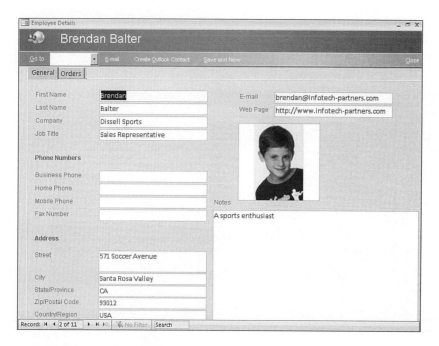

FIGURE 10.8   A tabbed form.

Adding a Tab Control and Manipulating Its Pages

To add a Tab control to a form, simply select it from the Controls group on the Design tab and drag and drop it onto the form. By default, two tab pages appear. To add more tabs, right-click the control and select Insert Page. To remove tabs, right-click the page you want to remove and select Delete Page. To change the order of pages, right-click any page and select Page Order.

Adding Controls to the Pages of a Tab Control

You can add controls to each tab just as you would add them directly to the form. Remember to select a tab by clicking it before you add the controls. If you don't select a specific tab, the controls you add will appear on every tab.

Modifying the Tab Order of Controls

The controls on each page have their own tab order. To modify their tab order, right-click the page and select Tab Order. You can then reorder the controls in whatever way you want.

Changing the Properties of the Tab Control

To change the properties of the Tab control, click to select it rather than a specific page. You can tell whether you've selected the Tab control because the words Tab Control appear in the upper-left corner of the title bar of the property sheet. A Tab control's properties include its name, whether it is visible, the text font on the tabs, and more (see Figure 10.9).

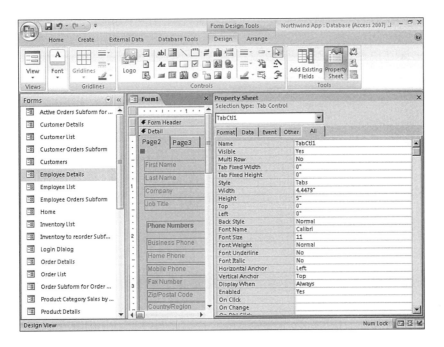

FIGURE 10.9   Viewing properties of a Tab control.

Changing the Properties of Each Page

To change the properties of each page, select a specific page of the Tab control. You can tell whether you've selected a specific page because the word Page is displayed in the upper-left corner of the title bar of the property page. Here, you can select a name for the page, the page's caption, a picture for the page's background, and more (see Figure 10.10).

Switchboard Forms: Controlling Your Application

Using a Switchboard form is a great way to control your application. A Switchboard form is simply a form with command buttons that allow you to navigate to other Switchboard forms or to the forms and reports that make up your system.

Figure 10.11 shows a Switchboard form. It lets a user work with different components of the database. What differentiates a Switchboard form from other forms is that its purpose is limited to navigating through the application. It usually has a border style of Dialog, and it has no scrollbars, record selectors, or navigation buttons. Other than these characteristics, a Switchboard form is a normal form. There are many styles of Navigation forms; which one you use depends on your users' needs.

10

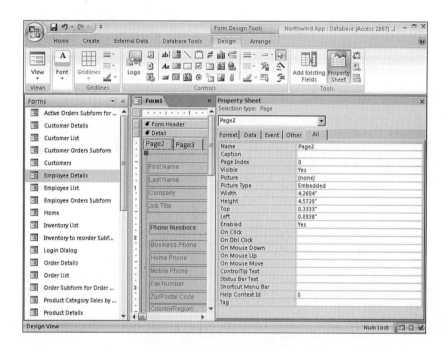

FIGURE 10.10   Viewing properties of a Tab page.

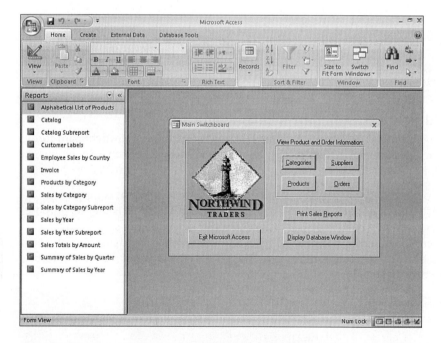

FIGURE 10.11   An example of a Switchboard form.

Splash Screen Forms: Creating a Professional Opening to Your Application

Splash screens add professional polish to your applications and give your users something to look at while your programming code is setting up the application. Just follow these steps to create a Splash Screen form:

1. Create a new form.

2. Set the Scrollbars property to Neither, the Record Selectors property to No, the Navigation Buttons property to No, the Auto Resize property to Yes, the Auto Center property to Yes, and the Border Style to None.

3. Make the form pop-up and modal by setting the Pop Up and Modal properties of the form to Yes.

4. Add a picture to the form and set the picture's properties.

5. Add any text you want on the form.

6. Set the form's timer interval property to the number of seconds you want the splash screen to be displayed.

7. Code the form's Timer event for DoCmd.Close.

8. Code the form's Unload event to open your main Switchboard form.

Because the Timer event of the Splash Screen form closes the form after the amount of time specified in the timer interval, the Splash Screen form unloads itself. While it's unloading, it loads a Switchboard form. The Splash Screen form included in CHAP10EX.ACCDB is called frmSplash. When it unloads, it opens the frmSwitchboard form.

You can implement a Splash Screen form in many other ways. For example, you can call a Splash Screen form from a Startup form; its Open event simply needs to open the Splash Screen form. The problem with this method is that if your application loads and unloads the Switchboard while the application is running, the Splash Screen is displayed again.

> **TIP**
>
> You can also display a splash screen by including a bitmap file with the same name as your database (ACCDB) in the same directory as the database file. When the application is loaded, the splash screen is displayed for a couple of seconds. The only disadvantage to this method is that you have less control over when, and how long, the splash screen is displayed.

10

Dialog Forms: Gathering Information

Dialog forms are typically used to gather information from the user. What makes them Dialog forms is that they're *modal*, meaning that the user can't go ahead with the application until the form is handled. You generally use Dialog forms when you must get specific information from your user before your application can continue processing. A custom Dialog form is simply a regular form that has a `Dialog` border style and has its `Modal` property set to `Yes`. Remember to give users a way to close the form; otherwise, they might close your modal form with the famous "Three-Finger Salute" (Ctrl+Alt+Del) or, even worse, by using the PC's Reset button. The `frmArchivePayments` form in `CHAP10EX.ACCDB` is a custom Dialog form.

TIP

Although opening a form with its `BorderStyle` property set to `Dialog` and its `Modal` property set to `Yes` will prevent the user from clicking outside the form (thereby continuing the application), it does not halt the execution of the code that opened the form. Suppose the intent is to open a Dialog form to gather parameters for a report and then open a report based on those parameters. In this case, the `OpenForm` method used to open the form must include the `acDialog` option in its `Windowmode` argument. Otherwise, the code will continue after the `OpenForm` method and open the report before the parameters are collected from the user.

Using Built-In Dialog Boxes

Access comes with two built-in dialog boxes: the standard Windows message box and the input box. The `FileDialog` object introduced with Access 2002 gives you access to other commonly used dialog boxes.

Message Boxes

A message box is a predefined dialog box that you can incorporate into your applications; however, you can customize it by using parameters. The VBA language has a `MsgBox` statement, which just displays a message, and a `MsgBox` function, which can display a message and return a value based on the user's response.

The message box in the VBA language is the same message box that is standard in most Windows applications, so most Windows users are already familiar with it. Rather than create your own dialog boxes to get standard responses from your users, you can use an existing, standard interface.

The `MsgBox` Function

The `MsgBox` function receives five parameters. The first parameter is the message that you want to display. The second is a numeric value indicating which buttons and icons you want to display. Tables 10.1 and 10.2 list the values that you can numerically add to create the second parameter. You can substitute the intrinsic constants in the table for the numeric values, if you want.

TABLE 10.1   Values Indicating the Buttons That a Message Box Can Display

Buttons	Value	Intrinsic Constant
OK button only	0	vbOKOnly
OK and Cancel	1	vbOKCancel
Abort, Retry, and Ignore	2	vbAbortRetryIgnore
Yes, No, and Cancel	3	vbYesNoCancel
Yes and No	4	vbYesNo
Retry and Cancel	5	vbRetryCancel

You must numerically add the values in Table 10.1 to one of the values in Table 10.2 if you want to include an icon other than the dialog box's default icon.

TABLE 10.2   Values Indicating the Icons That a Message Box Can Display

Icon	Value	Intrinsic Constant
Critical (Stop Sign)	16	vbCritical
Warning Query (Question)	32	vbQuestion
Warning Exclamation (!)	48	vbExclamation
Information (I)	64	vbInformation

MsgBox's third parameter is the message box's title. Its fourth and fifth parameters are the Help file and context ID that you want available if the user selects Help while the dialog box is displayed. The MsgBox function syntax looks like this:

```
MsgBox "This is a Message", vbInformation, "This is a Title"
```

This example displays the message "This is a Message" and the information icon. The title for the message box is "This is a Title". The message box also has an OK button that's used to close the dialog box.

The MsgBox function is normally used to display just an OK button, but it can also be used to allow a user to select from a variety of standard button combinations. When used in this way, it returns a value indicating which button the user selected.

In the following example, the message box displays Yes, No, and Cancel buttons:

```
Sub MessageBoxFunction()
    Dim intAnswer As Integer
    intAnswer = MsgBox("Are You Sure?", vbYesNoCancel + vbQuestion, _
        "Please Respond")
End Sub
```

This message box also displays the Question icon (see Figure 10.12). The Function call returns a value stored in the Integer variable intAnswer.

10

FIGURE 10.12   The dialog box displayed by the MsgBox function.

After you have placed the return value into a variable, you can easily introduce logic into your program to respond to the user's selection, as shown in this example:

```
Sub MessageBoxAnswer()
    Dim intAnswer As Integer
    intAnswer = MsgBox("Are You Sure?", vbYesNoCancel + vbQuestion, _
        "Please Respond")
    Select Case intAnswer
        Case vbYes
            MsgBox "I'm Glad You are Sure!!"
        Case vbNo
            MsgBox "Why Aren't You Sure??"
        Case vbCancel
            MsgBox "You Coward! You Bailed Out!!"
    End Select
End Sub
```

This code evaluates the user's response and displays a message based on her answer. Of course, in a real-life situation, the code in the Case statements would be more practical. Table 10.3 lists the values returned from the MsgBox function, depending on which button the user selected.

TABLE 10.3   Values Returned from the MsgBox Function

Response	Value	Intrinsic Constant
OK	1	vbOK
Cancel	2	vbCancel
Abort	3	vbAbort
Retry	4	vbRetry
Ignore	5	vbIgnore
Yes	6	vbYes
No	7	vbNo

Input Boxes

The InputBox function displays a dialog box containing a simple text box. It returns the text that the user typed in the text box and looks like this:

```
Sub InputBoxExample()
   Dim strName As String
   strName = InputBox("What is Your Name?", _
                 "This is the Title", "This is the Default")
   MsgBox "You Entered " & strName
End Sub
```

This subroutine displays the input box shown in Figure 10.13. Notice that the first parameter is the message, the second is the title, and the third is the default value. The second and third parameters are optional.

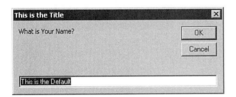

FIGURE 10.13   An example of using the InputBox function to gather information.

The FileDialog **Object**

The FileDialog object was introduced with Access 2002. This object allows you to easily display the common dialog boxes previously available only by using the Common Dialog ActiveX control. Here's an example of how FileDialog works:

```
Sub SaveDialog()

    'Declare a FileDialog object
    Dim dlgSaveAs As FileDialog

    'Instantiate the FileDialog object
    'indicating that it will act as a File SaveAs dialog
    Set dlgSaveAs = Application.FileDialog( _
        DialogType:=msoFileDialogSaveAs)

    'Display the dialog
    dlgSaveAs.Show

    'Display the specified filename in a message box
    MsgBox dlgSaveAs.SelectedItems(1)

End Sub
```

The code in the example declares a FileDialog object. It instantiates the object, setting its type to a File Save As dialog box. It shows the dialog box and then displays the first selected file in a message box. Here's another example:

10

```
Sub OpenDialog()
    'Declare a FileDialog object
    Dim dlgOpen As FileDialog

    'Instantiate the FileDialog object, setting its
    'type to a File Open dialog
    Set dlgOpen = Application.FileDialog( _
        DialogType:=msoFileDialogOpen)

    With dlgOpen

        'Allow multiple selections in the dialog
        .AllowMultiSelect = True

        'Display the dialog
        .Show
    End With

    'Display the first file selected in the dialog
    MsgBox dlgOpen.SelectedItems(1)
End Sub
```

This code once again declares a `FileDialog` object. When the code instantiates the object, it designates the dialog box type as a File Open dialog box. It sets the `AllowMultiSelect` property of the dialog box to allow multiple selections in the dialog box. It displays the dialog box and then displays the first selected file in a message box.

Taking Advantage of Built-In, Form-Filtering Features

Access has several form-filtering features that are part of the user interface. You can opt to include these features in your application, omit them from your application entirely, or control their behavior. For your application to control their behavior, it needs to respond to the Filter event, which it does by detecting when a filter is placed on the data in the form. When it has detected a filter, the code in the Filter event executes.

Sometimes you might want to alter the standard behavior of a filter command. You might want to display a special message to a user, for example, or take a specific action in your code. You might also want your application to respond to a Filter event because you want to alter the form's display before the filter is applied. For example, if a certain filter is in place, you might want to hide or disable certain fields. When the filter is removed, you could then return the form's appearance to normal.

Fortunately, Access not only lets you know that the Filter event occurred, but it also lets you know how the filter was invoked. Armed with this information, you can intercept and change the filtering behavior as needed.

When a user chooses Filter By Form or Advanced Filter/Sort, the `FilterType` parameter is filled with a value that indicates how the filter was invoked. If the user invokes the filter by selecting Filter By Form, the `FilterType` parameter equals the constant `acFilterByForm`; however, if she selects Advanced Filter/Sort, the `FilterType` parameter equals the constant `acFilterAdvanced`. The following code demonstrates how to use these constants:

```
Private Sub Form_Filter(Cancel As Integer, FilterType As Integer)
    Select Case FilterType
        Case acFilterByForm
            MsgBox "You Just Selected Filter By Form"
        Case acFilterAdvanced
            MsgBox "You Are Not Allowed to Select Advanced Filter/Sort"
            Cancel = True
    End Select
End Sub
```

This code, placed in the form's Filter event, evaluates the filter type. If the user selected Filter By Form, the code displays a message box, and the filtering proceeds as usual. However, if the user selected Advanced Filter/Sort, she's told she can't do this, and the filter process is canceled.

You can not only check how the filter was invoked, but you can also intercept the process when the filter is applied. You do this by placing code in the form's `ApplyFilter` event, as shown in this example:

```
Private Sub Form_ApplyFilter(Cancel As Integer, ApplyType As Integer)
    Dim intAnswer As Integer
    If ApplyType = acApplyFilter Then
        intAnswer = MsgBox("You just selected the criteria: " & _
                    Chr(13) & Chr(10) & Me.Filter & _
                    Chr(13) & Chr(10) & "Are You Sure You Wish " & __
                    to Proceed?", vbYesNo + vbQuestion)
        If intAnswer = vbNo Then
            Cancel = True
        End If
    End If
End Sub
```

This code evaluates the value of the `ApplyType` parameter. If it's equal to the constant `acApplyFilter`, a message box is displayed, verifying that the user wants to apply the filter. If the user responds Yes, the filter is applied; otherwise, the filter is canceled.

10

Including Objects from Other Applications: Linking Versus Embedding

Microsoft Access is an ActiveX client application, meaning that it can contain objects from other applications. All versions of Access subsequent to Access 97 are also ActiveX server applications. Using Access as an ActiveX server is covered in Chapter 24, "Automation: Communicating with Other Applications." Access's capability to control other applications with programming code is also covered in Chapter 24. In the following sections, you learn how to link to and embed objects in your Access forms.

Bound OLE Objects

Bound OLE objects are tied to the data in an OLE field within a table in your database. An example is the Picture field that's part of the Categories table in the Northwind database. The field type of the Categories table that supports multimedia data is of the OLE Object field type. This means that each record in the table can contain a unique OLE object. The Categories form contains a bound OLE control, whose control source is the Picture field from the Categories table.

If you double-click the picture associated with a category, you can edit the OLE object in-place. The picture associated with the category is actually embedded in the Categories table. This means that the data associated with the OLE object is stored as part of the Access database (ACCDB) file, within the Categories table. Embedded objects, if they support the OLE 2.0 standard, can be modified in-place. This Microsoft feature is called *In-Place activation*.

To insert a new object, take the following steps:

1. Move to the record that will contain the OLE object.

2. Right-click the OLE Object control and select Insert Object to open the Insert Object dialog box.

3. Select an object type. Select Create New if you want to create an embedded object or select Create from File if you want to link to or embed an existing file.

4. If you select Create from File, the Insert Object dialog box changes to look like the one shown in Figure 10.14.

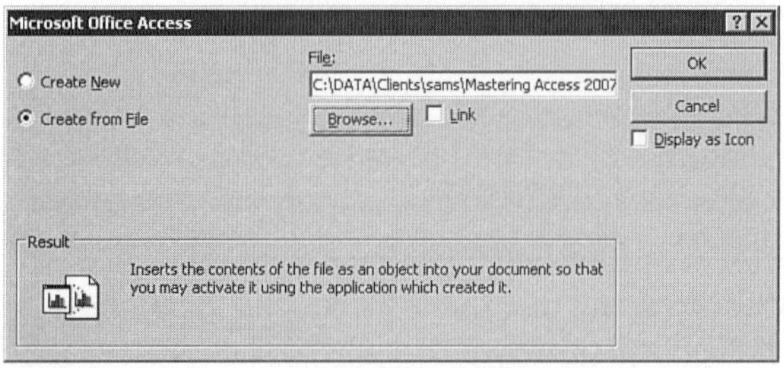

FIGURE 10.14   The Insert Object dialog box as it appears when you select Create from File.

5. Select Link if you want to link to the existing file. Don't check Link if you want to embed the existing file. If you link to the file, the Access table will have a reference to the file as well as to the presentation data (a bitmap) for the object. If you embed the file, Access copies the original file, placing the copy in the Access table.

6. Click Browse and select the file you want to link to or embed.

7. Click OK.

Access returns you to the record that you were working with, and you can continue working with that record or move to another record.

If you double-click a linked object, you launch its source application; you don't get In-Place activation (see Figure 10.15).

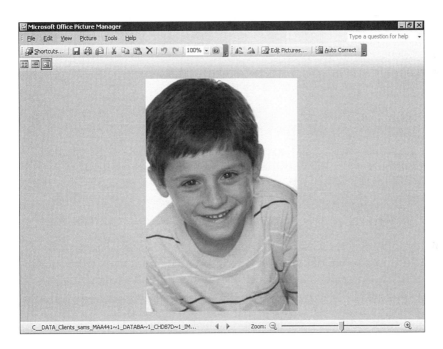

FIGURE 10.15   Editing a linked object.

Unbound OLE Objects

Unbound OLE objects aren't stored in your database. Instead, they are part of the form they were created in. Like bound OLE objects, unbound OLE objects can be linked or embedded. You create an unbound OLE object by adding an unbound object frame to the form.

10

Using OpenArgs

The OpenArgs property gives you a way to pass information to a form as it's being opened. The OpenArgs argument of the OpenForm method is used to populate a form's OpenArgs property at runtime. It works like this:

```
DoCmd.OpenForm "frmPaymentMethods", _
          Datamode:=acFormAdd, _
          WindowMode:=acDialog, _
          OpenArgs:=NewData
```

This code is found in the time and billing application's frmPayments form. It opens the frmPaymentMethods form when a new method of payment is added to the cboPaymentMethodID combo box. It sends the frmPaymentMethods form an OpenArg of whatever data is added to the combo box. The Load event of the frmPaymentMethods form looks like this:

```
Private Sub Form_Load()
    If Not IsNull(Me.OpenArgs) Then
        Me.txtPaymentMethod.Value = Me.OpenArgs
    End If
End Sub
```

This code sets the txtPaymentMethod text box value to the value passed as the opening argument. This occurs only when the frmPaymentMethods form is opened from the frmPayments form.

Switching a Form's RecordSource

Many developers don't realize how easy it is to switch a form's RecordSource property at runtime. This is a great way to use the same form to display data from more than one table or query containing the same fields. It's also a great way to limit the data that's displayed in a form at a particular moment. Using the technique of altering a form's RecordSource property at runtime, as shown in Listing 10.1, you can dramatically improve performance, especially for a client/server application. This example is found in the frmShowSales form of the CHAP10EX database (see Figure 10.16).

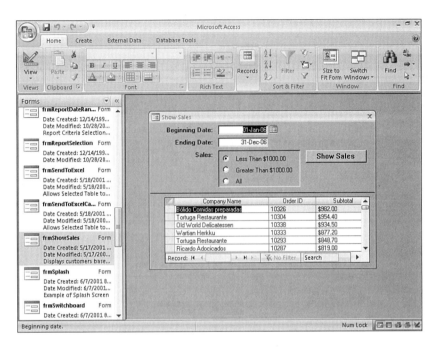

FIGURE 10.16   Changing the RecordSource property of a form at runtime.

LISTING 10.1   Altering a Form's RecordSource at Runtime

```
Private Sub cmdShowSales_Click()

    'Check to see that Ending Date is later than Beginning Date.
    If Me.txtEndingDate < Me.txtBeginningDate Then
        MsgBox "The Ending Date must be later than the Beginning Date."
        txtBeginningDate.SetFocus
        Exit Sub
    End If

    'Create an SQL statement using search criteria entered by user and
    'set RecordSource property of ShowSalesSubform.

    Dim strSQL As String
    Dim strRestrict As String
    Dim lngX As Long

    lngX = Me.optSales.Value
    strRestrict = ShowSalesValue(lngX)
```

10

LISTING 10.1   Continued

```
'Create SELECT statement.
strSQL = "SELECT DISTINCTROW tblCustomers.CompanyName,_" & )
  "qryOrderSubtotals.OrderID, "
strSQL = strSQL & "qryOrderSubtotals.Subtotal ," & _
    "tblOrders.ShippedDate "
strSQL = strSQL & "FROM tblCustomers INNER JOIN " & __
  "(qryOrderSubtotals INNER JOIN tblOrders ON "
strSQL = strSQL & "qryOrderSubtotals.OrderID = " & _
    "tblOrders.OrderID) ON "
strSQL = strSQL & "tblCustomers.CustomerID = tblOrders.CustomerID "
strSQL = strSQL & "WHERE (tblOrders.ShippedDate _" & _
"Between Forms!frmShowSales!txtBeginningDate "
strSQL = strSQL & "And Forms!frmShowSales!txtEndingDate) "
strSQL = strSQL & "And " & strRestrict
strSQL = strSQL & " ORDER BY qryOrderSubtotals.Subtotal DESC;"

'Set RecordSource property of ShowSalesSubform.
Me.fsubShowSales.Form.RecordSource = strSQL

'If no records match criteria, reset subform's
'RecordSource property,
'display message, and move focus to BeginningDate text box.
If Me.fsubShowSales.Form.RecordsetClone.RecordCount = 0 Then
    Me.fsubShowSales.Form.RecordSource = _
    "SELECT CompanyName FROM tblCustomers WHERE False;"
    MsgBox "No records match the criteria you entered.", _
     vbExclamation, "No Records Found"
    Me.txtBeginningDate.SetFocus
Else
    'Enable control in Detail section.
    EnableControls Me, acDetail, True
    'Move insertion point to ShowSalesSubform.
    Me.fsubShowSales!txtCompanyName.SetFocus
End If

End Sub

Private Function ShowSalesValue(lngOptionGroupValue As Long) As String

    'Return value selected in Sales option group.

    'Define constants for option group values.
    Const conSalesUnder1000 = 1
```

LISTING 10.1   Continued

```
    Const conSalesOver1000 = 2
    Const conAllSales = 3

    'Create restriction based on value of option group.
    Select Case lngOptionGroupValue
        Case conSalesUnder1000:
            ShowSalesValue = "qryOrderSubtotals.Subtotal < 1000"
        Case conSalesOver1000:
            ShowSalesValue = "qryOrderSubtotals.Subtotal >= 1000"
        Case Else
            ShowSalesValue = "qryOrderSubtotals.Subtotal = True"
    End Select
End Function
```

Listing 10.1 begins by storing the value of the optSales option group on the frmShowSales main form into a Long Integer variable. It calls the ShowSalesValue function, which declares three constants; then it evaluates the parameter that was passed to it (the Long Integer variable containing the option group value). Based on this value, it builds a selection string for the subtotal value. This selection string becomes part of the SQL statement used for the subform's record source and limits the range of sales values displayed on the subform.

The ShowSales routine builds a string containing a SQL statement, which selects all required fields from the tblCustomers table and qryOrderSubtotals query. It builds a WHERE clause that includes the txtBeginningDate and txtEndingDate from the main form as well as the string returned from the ShowSalesValue function.

After the SQL statement has been built, the RecordSource property of the fsubShowSales subform control is set equal to the SQL statement. The RecordCount property of the RecordsetClone (the form's underlying recordset) is evaluated to determine whether any records meet the criteria specified in the RecordSource. If the record count is zero, no records are displayed in the subform, and the user is warned that no records met the criteria. However, if records are found, the form's Detail section is enabled, and focus is moved to the subform.

Learning Power Combo Box and List Box Techniques

Combo and list boxes are very powerful. Being able to properly respond to a combo box's NotInList event, to populate a combo box by using code, and to select multiple entries in a list box are essential skills of an experienced Access programmer. They're covered in detail in the following sections.

10

Handling the NotInList Event

As previously discussed, the NotInList event occurs when a user types a value in the text box portion of a combo box that's not found in the combo box list. This event takes place only if the LimitToList property of the combo box is set to True. It's up to you whether you respond to this event.

You might want to respond with something other than the default error message when the LimitToList property is set to True and the user tries to add an entry. For example, if a user is entering an order and she enters the name of a new customer, you could react by displaying a message box asking whether she really wants to add the new customer. If the user responds affirmatively, you can display a customer form.

After you have set the LimitToList property to True, any code you place in the NotInList event is executed whenever the user tries to type an entry that's not found in the combo box. The following is an example:

```
Private Sub cboPaymentMethodID_NotInList(NewData As String, _
    Response As Integer)
    'If payment method is not in the list,
    'ask user if he wants to add it
    If MsgBox("Payment Method Not Found, Add?", _
        vbYesNo + vbQuestion, _
        "Please Respond") = vbYes Then

        'If he responds yes, open the frmPaymentMethods form
        'in add mode, passing in the new payment method
        DoCmd.OpenForm "frmPaymentMethods", _
            DataMode:=acFormAdd, _
            WindowMode:=acDialog, _
            OpenArgs:=NewData

        'If form is still loaded, unload it
        If IsLoaded("frmPaymentMethods") Then
            Response = acDataErrAdded
            DoCmd.Close acForm, "frmPaymentMethods"

        'If the user responds no,
        Else
            Response = acDataErrContinue
        End If
    Else
        Response = acDataErrContinue
    End If

End Sub
```

When you place this code in the NotInList event procedure of your combo box, it displays a message asking the user whether she wants to add the payment method. If the user responds No, she is returned to the form without the standard error message being displayed, but she still must enter a valid value in the combo box. If the user responds Yes, she is placed in the frmPaymentMethods form, ready to add the payment method whose name she typed.

The NotInList event procedure accepts a response argument, which is where you can tell VBA what to do *after* your code executes. Any one of the following three constants can be placed in the response argument:

- ▶ acDataErrAdded—This constant is used if your code adds the new value into the record source for the combo box. This code requeries the combo box, adding the new value to the list.

- ▶ acDataErrDisplay—This constant is used if you want VBA to display the default error message.

- ▶ acDataErrContinue—This constant is used if you want to suppress VBA's error message, using your own instead. Access still requires that a valid entry be placed in the combo box.

Working with a Pop-Up Form

The NotInList technique just described employs the pop-up form. When the user opts to add the new payment method, the frmPaymentMethods form displays modally. This halts execution of the code in the form that loads the frmPaymentMethods form (in this case, the frmPayments form). The frmPaymentMethods form is considered a pop-up form because the form is modal, it uses information from the frmPayments form, and the frmPayments form reacts according to whether the OK or Cancel button is selected. The code in the Load event of the frmPaymentMethods form in the time and billing database appears as follows:

```
Private Sub Form_Load()
    Me.txtPaymentMethod.Value = Me.OpenArgs
End Sub
```

This code uses the information received as an opening argument to populate the txtPaymentMethod text box. No further code executes until the user clicks either the OK or the Cancel command button. If the user clicks the OK button, the following code executes:

```
Private Sub cmdOK_Click()
    Me.Visible = False
End Sub
```

10

Notice that the preceding code hides, rather than closes, the `frmPaymentMethods` form. If the user clicks the Cancel button, this code executes:

```
Private Sub cmdCancel_Click()
    DoCmd.RunCommand acCmdUndo
    DoCmd.Close
End Sub
```

The code under the Cancel button first undoes the changes that the user made. It then closes the `frmPaymentMethods` form. Once back in the `NotInList` event of the `cboPaymentMethod` combo box on the `frmPayments` form, the following code executes:

```
If IsLoaded("frmPaymentMethods") Then
        Response = acDataErrAdded
        DoCmd.Close acForm, "frmPaymentMethods"
Else
        Response = acDataErrContinue
End If
```

The code evaluates whether the `frmPaymentMethods` form is still loaded. If it is, the user must have clicked OK. The `Response` parameter is set to `acDataErrAdded`, designating that the new entry has been added to the combo box and to the underlying data source. The code then closes the `frmPaymentMethods` form.

If the `frmPaymentMethods` form is not loaded, the user must have clicked Cancel. The user is returned to the combo box where he must select another combo box entry. In summary, the steps are as follows:

1. Open the pop-up form modally (with the `WindowMode` parameter equal to `acDialog`).

2. Pass an `OpenArgs` parameter, if desired.

3. When control returns to the original form, check to see whether the pop-up form is still loaded.

4. If the pop-up form is still open, use its information and then close it.

Adding Items to a Combo Box or List Box at Runtime

Prior to Access 2002, it was very difficult to add and remove items from list boxes and combo boxes at runtime. Access 2002, Access 2003, and Access 2007 list boxes and combo boxes support two powerful methods that make it easier to programmatically manipulate these boxes at runtime. The `AddItem` method allows you to easily add items to a list box or a combo box. The `RemoveItem` method allows you to remove items from a combo box or a list box. Here's an example:

```
Private Sub Form_Load()
    Dim obj As AccessObject

    'Loop through all tables in the current database
    'adding the name of each table to the list box
    For Each obj In CurrentData.AllTables
        Me.lstTables.AddItem obj.Name
    Next obj

    'Loop through all queries in the current database
    'adding the name of each query to the list box
    For Each obj In CurrentData.AllQueries
        Me.lstTables.AddItem obj.Name
    Next obj
End Sub
```

This code is found in the frmSendToExcel form that's part of the CHAP10EX database. It loops through all tables in the database, adding the name of each table to the lstTables list box. It then loops through each query in the database, once again adding each to the list box.

Handling Multiple Selections in a List Box

List boxes have a Multiselect property. When set to True, this property lets the user select multiple elements from the list box. Your code can then evaluate which elements are selected and perform some action based on the selected elements. The frmReportSelection form, found in the CHAP10EX database, illustrates the use of a multiselect list box. The code under the Click event of the Run Reports button looks like that shown in Listing 10.2.

LISTING 10.2   Evaluating Which Items Are Selected in the Multiselect List Box

```
Private Sub cmdRunReports_Click()
    Dim varItem As Variant
    Dim lst As ListBox

    Set lst = Me.lstReports
    'Single select is 0, Simple multiselect is 1,
    'and extended multiselect is 2.
    If lst.MultiSelect > 0 Then
        'Loop through all the elements
        'of the ItemsSelected collection, and use
        'the Column array to retrieve the
        'associated value.
        If lst.ItemsSelected.Count > 0 Then
            For Each varItem In lst.ItemsSelected
```

10

LISTING 10.2   Continued

```
              DoCmd.OpenReport lst.ItemData(varItem), acViewPreview
         Next varItem
      End If
   End If

End Sub
```

This code first checks to ensure that the list box is a multiselect list box. If it is, and at least one report is selected, the code loops through all the selected items in the list box. It prints each report that is selected.

Learning Power Subform Techniques

Many new Access developers don't know the ins and outs of creating and modifying a subform and referring to subform controls, so here are some important points you should know when working with subforms:

▶ The easiest way to add a subform to a main form is to open the main form and then drag and drop the subform onto the main form.

▶ The subform control's LinkChildFields and LinkMasterFields properties determine which fields in the main form link to which fields in the subform. A single field name, or a list of fields separated by semicolons, can be entered into these properties. When they are properly set, these properties make sure all records in the child form relate to the currently displayed record in the parent form.

Referring to Subform Controls

Many developers don't know how to properly refer to subform controls. You must refer to any objects on the subform through the subform control on the main form, as shown in this example:

```
Forms.frmCustomer.fsubOrders
```

This example refers to the fsubOrders control on the frmCustomer form. If you want to refer to a specific control on the fsubOrders subform, you can then point at its controls collection. Here's an example:

```
Forms.frmCustomer.fsubOrders!txtOrderID
```

You can also refer to the control on the subform implicitly, as shown in this example:

```
Forms!frmCustomer!subOrders!txtOrderID
```

Both of these methods refer to the `txtOrderID` control on the form in the `fsubOrder` control on the `frmCustomer` form. To change a property of this control, you would extend the syntax to look like this:

```
Forms.frmCustomer.fsubOrders!txtOrderID.Enabled = False
```

This code sets the `Enabled` property of the `txtOrderID` control on the form in the `fsubOrders` control to `False`.

Using Automatic Error Checking

In Access 2007, you can enable automatic error checking of forms. Error checking not only points out errors in a form but also provides suggestions for correcting them.

To activate error checking, click to select the Microsoft Access button and then click Access Options. Click to select the Object Designers tab (see Figure 10.17). Click the Enable Error Checking check box within the Error checking group of options to enable error checking. After you enable error checking, indicators appear on your form, letting you know that something is wrong (see Figure 10.18). You then click the indicator, and an explanation and suggestions appear for correcting the error (see Figure 10.19).

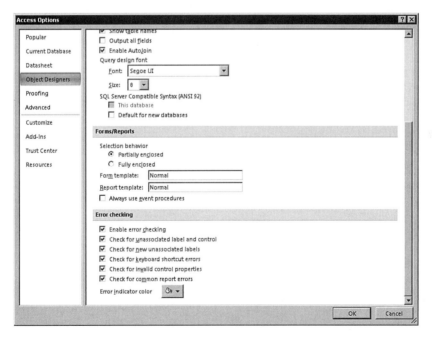

FIGURE 10.17   You can activate error checking from the Object Designers tab of the Access Options dialog box.

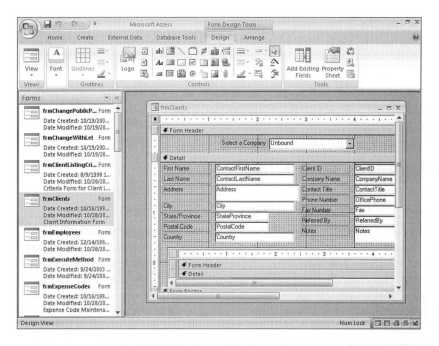

FIGURE 10.18 Indicators appear on your form, letting you know that something is wrong.

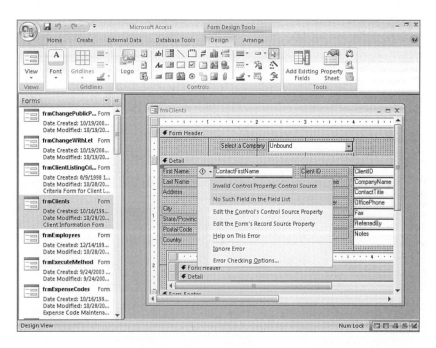

FIGURE 10.19 A menu appears, providing you with an explanation and suggestions for correcting the error.

The error checker will identify several categories of errors. They are shown in Table 10.4.

TABLE 10.4   Categories of Errors Identified by the Error Checker

Category	Description
Unassociated label and control	You select a label and a control (for example, a label and a text box) that are not associated with one another.
New unassociated labels	You add a label that is not associated with another control.
Keyboard shortcut errors	You select a control with an invalid shortcut key associated with it (that is, duplicate shortcut key or space as a shortcut key).
Invalid control properties	The string in the control source is not valid. The reason for this error might be that it is not a valid field name or that the control source refers to itself. It can also be that the expression does not begin with an equal sign or that the option value in an option group is not unique.

If Access identifies several errors for the same control, the error indicator remains until all errors are corrected. If you choose to ignore an error, simply select the Ignore Error option on the Error Checking Options menu. This will clear the error indicator until you close and open the form again. Remember that via the Access Options, you can turn off error checking entirely (although I find this feature to be extremely valuable).

Viewing Object Dependencies

Microsoft added a wonderful feature to Access 2003. It enables you to view information about object dependencies. Here's how it works:

1. To invoke the Object Dependency feature, select Tables and Related Views from the Navigation Pane drop-down. The first time you perform this task for a database, a dialog box appears, prompting you to update object dependency information for the database (see Figure 10.20). After you click OK, Access updates the dependency information for the database and displays the object dependencies within the Navigation Pane (see Figure 10.21). In Figure 10.21, you can see all the objects that depend on the Categories table.

10

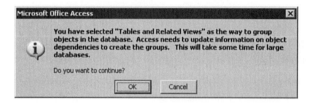

FIGURE 10.20 The first time you attempt to display object dependencies within a database, Access prompts you to update dependency information for that database.

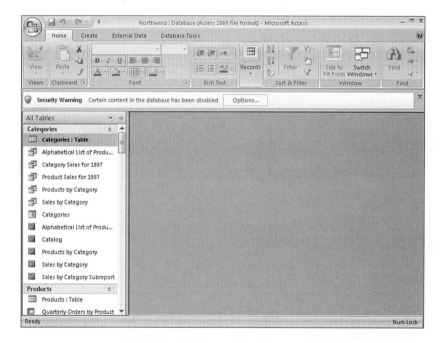

FIGURE 10.21 The Navigation Pane shows you the objects that depend on the selected object.

Using AutoCorrect Options

The AutoCorrect feature minimizes the problems that occur when you rename tables, fields, queries, forms, reports, text boxes, or other controls. You enable AutoCorrect on the Current Database tab of the Access Options dialog box (see Figure 10.22).

You can enable AutoCorrect at one of three levels:

▶ **Track Name AutoCorrect Info**—Access simply keeps track of the name changes. It does not fix errors caused by renaming.

▶ **Perform Name AutoCorrect**—Access keeps track of changes and fixes all changes as they are made.

▶ **Log Name Autocorrect Changes**—In addition to tracking changes and fixing errors, this option provides you with a table that logs all changes made to the names of objects.

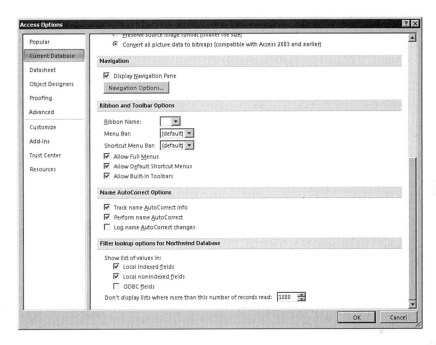

FIGURE 10.22   You enable AutoCorrect on the Current Database tab of the Access Options dialog box.

Propagating Field Properties

When you make a change to an inherited property in a table's Design view, you can opt to propagate that change to the controls on your forms that are bound to that field. Here's how it works:

1. Open the table whose design you want to modify in Design view.

2. Click in the field whose property you want to change.

3. Click in the property whose value you want to change.

4. Change the property and press Enter. If the property that you changed is inheritable, the Property Update Options button appears (see Figure 10.23).

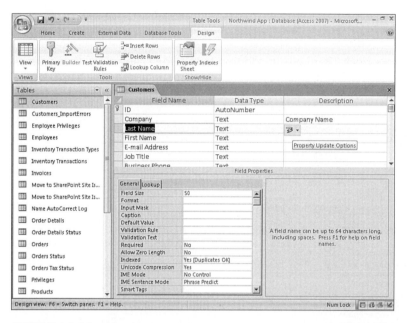

FIGURE 10.23   The Property Update Options button appears for inheritable properties.

5. Open the menu and select Update (see Figure 10.24). The Update Properties dialog box appears (see Figure 10.25). Select the forms and reports that contain the controls that you want to update. Click Yes to complete the process.

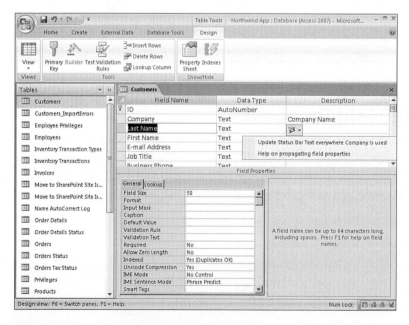

Figure 10.24   Open the menu and select Update.

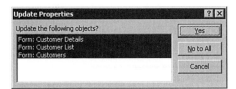

FIGURE 10.25   The Update Properties dialog box allows you to select the forms and reports that you want to update.

Synchronizing a Form with Its Underlying Recordset

You use a form's `RecordsetClone` property to refer to its underlying recordset. You can manipulate this recordset independently of what's currently being displayed on the form. Here's an example:

```
Private Sub cboCompany_AfterUpdate()
    'Create a recordset based on the recordset underlying the form
    Dim rst As DAO.Recordset
    Set rst = Me.RecordsetClone

    'Search for the client selected in the combo box
    rst.FindFirst "ClientID = " & cboCompany.Value

    'If the client is not found, display an error message
    'If the client is found, move the bookmark of the form
    'to the bookmark in the underlying recordset
    If rst.NoMatch Then
       MsgBox "Client Not Found"
    Else
       Me.Bookmark = rst.Bookmark
    End If
```

This code creates an object variable that points at the form's `RecordsetClone`. The recordset object variable can then be substituted for `Me.RecordsetClone` because it references the form's underlying recordset. The example then uses the object variable to execute the `FindFirst` method. It searches for a record in the form's underlying recordset whose `ClientID` is equal to the current combo box value. If a match is found, the form's bookmark is synchronized with the bookmark of the form's underlying recordset.

The `RecordsetClone` property allows you to navigate or operate on a form's records independently of the form. This capability is often useful when you want to manipulate the data behind the form without affecting the appearance of the form. On the other hand, when you use the `Recordset` property of the form, the act of changing which record is current in the recordset returned by the form's `Recordset` property also sets the current record of the form. Here's an example:

```
Private Sub cboSelectEmployee_AfterUpdate()
    'Find the employee selected in the combo box
    Me.Recordset.FindFirst "EmployeeID = " _
        & Me.cboSelectEmployee

    'If employee not found, display a message
    If Me.Recordset.EOF Then
        MsgBox "Employee Not Found"
    End If
End Sub
```

Notice that you do not need to set the `Bookmark` property of the form equal to the `Bookmark` property of the recordset. They are one and the same.

Creating `Custom` Properties and Methods

Forms and reports are *Class modules*, which means they act as templates for objects you create instances of at runtime. Public procedures of a form and report become `Custom` properties and methods of the form object at runtime. Using VBA code, you can set the values of a form's `Custom` properties and execute its methods.

Creating `Custom` Properties

You can create `Custom` properties of a form or report in one of two ways:

- ▶ Create `Public` variables in the form or report.
- ▶ Create `PropertyLet` and `PropertyGet` routines.

Creating and Using a `Public` Variable as a Form Property

The following steps are used to create and access a `Custom` form or report property based on a `Public` variable. The example is included in `CHAP10EX.ACCDB` in the forms `frmPublicProperties` and `frmChangePublicProperty`.

1. Begin by creating the form that will contain the `Custom` property (`Public` variable).

2. Place a `Public` variable in the General Declarations section of the form or report (see Figure 10.26).

3. Place code in the form or report that accesses the `Public` variable. The code in Figure 10.26 creates a `Public` variable called `CustomCaption`. The code behind the `Click` event of the `cmdChangeCaption` command button sets the form's (`frmPublicProperties`) `Caption` property equal to the value of the `Public` variable.

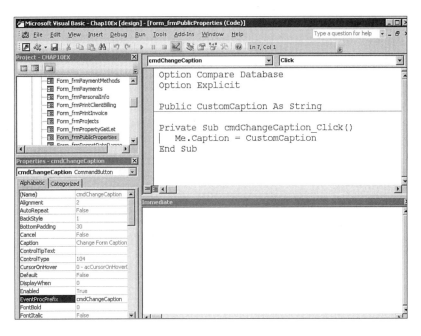

FIGURE 10.26   Creating a `Public` variable in the General Declarations section of a Class module.

4. Create a form, report, or module that modifies the value of the `Custom` property. Figure 10.27 shows a form called `frmChangePublicProperty`.

5. Add the code that modifies the value of the `Custom` property. The code behind the `ChangeCaption` button, as shown in Figure 10.26, modifies the value of the `Custom` property called `CustomCaption` that's found on the `frmPublicProperties` form.

To test the `Custom` property created in the preceding example, run the `frmPublicProperties` form, which is in the `CHAP10EX.MDB` database on the sample code CD-ROM. Click the Change Form Caption command button. Nothing happens because the value of the `Custom` property hasn't been set. Open the `frmChangePublicProperty` form and click the Change Form Property command button. Return to `frmPublicProperties` and again click the Change Form Caption command button. The form's caption should now change.

Close the `frmPublicProperties` form and try clicking the Change Form Property command button. A runtime error occurs, indicating that the form you're referring to is not open. You can eliminate the error by placing the following code in the `Click` event of `cmdPublicFormProperty`:

```
Private Sub cmdPublicFormProperty_Click()
    Form_frmPublicProperties.CustomCaption = _
         "This is a Custom Caption"
    Forms_frmPublicProperties.Visible = True
End Sub
```

This code modifies the value of the `Public` property by using the syntax `Form_FormName.Property`. If the form isn't loaded, this syntax loads the form but leaves it hidden. The next command sets the form's `Visible` property to `True`.

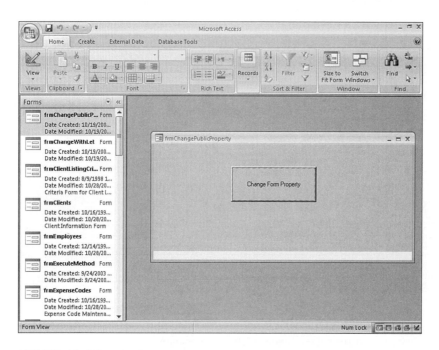

FIGURE 10.27   Viewing the `frmChangePublicProperty` form.

Creating and Using Custom **Properties with** PropertyLet **and** PropertyGet **Routines**
A `PropertyLet` routine is a special type of subroutine that automatically executes whenever the property's value is changed. A `PropertyGet` routine is another special subroutine that automatically executes whenever the value of the `Custom` property is retrieved. Instead of using a `Public` variable to create a property, you insert two special routines: `PropertyLet` and `PropertyGet`. This example is found in `CHAP10EX.ACCDB` in the `frmPropertyGetLet` and `frmChangeWithLet` forms. To insert the `PropertyLet` and `PropertyGet` routines, follow these steps:

1. Choose Insert, Procedure. The dialog box shown in Figure 10.28 appears.

2. Type the name of the procedure in the Name text box.

3. Select Property from the Type option buttons.

4. Select Public as the Scope so that the property is visible outside the form.

5. Click OK. The `PropertyGet` and `PropertyLet` subroutines are inserted in the module (see Figure 10.29).

FIGURE 10.28   Starting a new procedure with the Add Procedure dialog box.

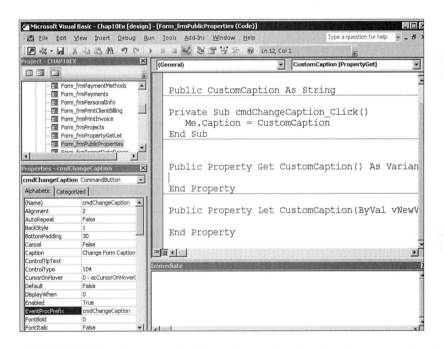

FIGURE 10.29   The PropertyGet and PropertyLet subroutines inserted in the module.

Notice that the Click event code for the cmdChangeCaption command button hasn't changed. The PropertyLet routine, which automatically executes whenever the value of the CustomCaption property is changed, takes the uppercase value of what it's being sent and places it in a Private variable called mstrCustomCaption. The PropertyGet routine takes the value of the Private variable and returns it to whoever asked for the value of the property. The following code is placed in the form called frmChangeWithLet:

10

```
Private Sub cmdPublicFormProperty_Click()
    Form_frmPropertyGetLet.CustomCaption = "This is a Custom Caption"
    Forms!frmPropertyGetLet.Visible = True
End Sub
```

This routine tries to set the value of the Custom property called CustomCaption to the value "This is a Custom Caption". Because the property's value is being changed, the PropertyLet routine in frmPropertyGetLet is automatically executed. It looks like this:

```
Public Property Let CustomCaption(ByVal CustomCaption As String)
    mstrCustomCaption = UCase$(CustomCaption)
End Property
```

The PropertyLet routine receives the value "This is a Custom Caption" as a parameter. It uses the UCase function to manipulate the value it was passed and convert it to uppercase. It then places the manipulated value into a Private variable called mstrCustomCaption. The PropertyGet routine isn't executed until the user clicks the cmdChangeCaption button in the frmPropertyGetLet form. The Click event of cmdChangeCaption looks like this:

```
Private Sub cmdChangeCaption_Click()
    Me.Caption = CustomCaption
End Sub
```

Because this routine needs to retrieve the value of the Custom property CustomCaption, the PropertyGet routine automatically executes:

```
Public Property Get CustomCaption() As String
    CustomCaption = mstrCustomCaption
End Property
```

The PropertyGet routine takes the value of the Private variable, set by the PropertyLet routine, and returns it as the value of the property.

You might wonder why this method is preferable to declaring a Public variable. Using the UCase function within PropertyLet should illustrate why. Whenever you expose a Public variable, you can't do much to validate or manipulate the value you receive. The PropertyLet routine gives you the opportunity to validate and manipulate the value to which the property is being set. By placing the manipulated value in a Private variable and then retrieving the Private variable's value when the property is returned, you gain full control over what happens internally to the property.

NOTE

This section provides an introduction to custom properties and methods. You can find a comprehensive discussion of custom classes, properties, and methods in Chapter 14, "Exploiting the Power of Class Modules."

Creating Custom Methods

Custom methods are simply Public functions and subroutines placed in a Form module or a Report module. As you will see, they can be called by using the Object.Method syntax. Here are the steps involved in creating a Custom method; they are found in CHAP10EX.ACCDB in the forms frmMethods and frmExecuteMethod:

1. Open the form or report that will contain the Custom method.

2. Create a Public function or subroutine (see Figure 10.30).

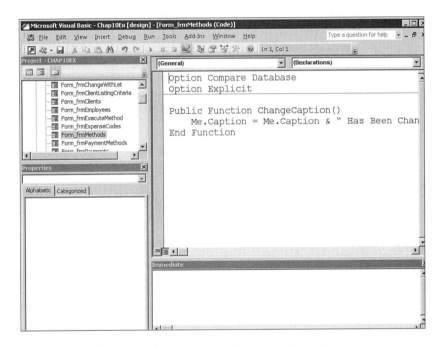

FIGURE 10.30   Using the custom method ChangeCaption.

3. Open the Form module, Report module, or Code module that executes the Custom method.

4. Use the Object.Method syntax to invoke the Custom method (see Figure 10.31).

Figure 10.30 shows the Custom method ChangeCaption found in the frmMethods form. The method changes the form's caption. Figure 10.31 shows the Click event of cmdExecuteMethod found in the frmExecuteMethod form. It issues the ChangeCaption method of the frmMethods form and then sets the form's Visible property to True.

10

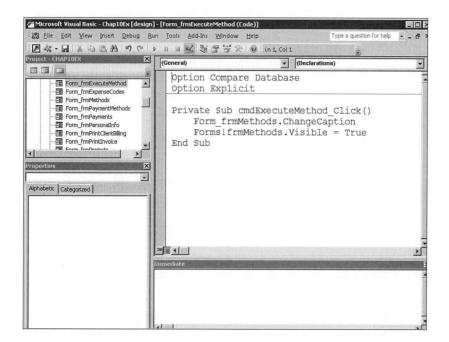

FIGURE 10.31   The Click event code behind the Execute Method button.

Practical Examples: Applying Advanced Techniques to Your Application

You can use many examples in this chapter in all the applications that you build. To polish your application, build a startup form that displays a splash screen and then performs some setup functions. The CHAP10EX.ACCDB file contains these examples.

Getting Things Going with a Startup Form

The frmSwitchboard form is responsible both for displaying the splash screen and for performing the necessary setup code. The code in the Load event of the frmSwitchboard form looks like this:

```
Private Sub Form_Load()
    DoCmd.Hourglass True
    DoCmd.OpenForm "frmSplash"
    Call GetCompanyInfo
    DoCmd.Hourglass False
End Sub
```

The Form_Load event first invokes an hourglass. It then opens the frmSplash form. Next, it calls the GetCompanyInfo routine to fill in the CompanyInfo type structure that is eventually used throughout the application. (Type structures are covered in Chapter 13, "Advanced VBA Techniques.") Finally, Form_Load turns off the hourglass.

Building a Splash Screen

The splash screen, shown in Figure 10.32, is called frmSplash. Its timer interval is set to 3,000 milliseconds (3 seconds), and its Timer event looks like this:

```
Private Sub Form_Timer()
    DoCmd.Close acForm, Me.Name
End Sub
```

FIGURE 10.32   Using an existing form as a splash screen.

The Timer event unloads the form. The frmSplash Pop-up property is set to Yes, and its border is set to None. Record selectors and navigation buttons have been removed.

Summary

Forms are the centerpiece of most Access applications, so it's vital that you are able to fully harness their power and flexibility. This chapter showed you how to work with Form and Control events. You saw many examples illustrating when and how to leverage the event routines associated with forms and specific controls. You also learned about the types of forms available, their uses in your applications, and how you can build them. Finally, you learned several power techniques that will help you develop complex forms.

10

Advanced Report Techniques

Why This Chapter Is Important

Chapter 6, "What Every Developer Needs to Know About Reports," covers all the basics of report design. Reports are an integral part of almost every application, so fortunately for you, the Access 2007 report design tool is very powerful. Although it's easy to create most reports, as you mature as an Access developer, you'll probably want to learn the intricacies of Access report design. This chapter covers report events, advanced techniques, and tips and tricks of the trade.

Events Available for Reports and When to Use Them

Although report events aren't as plentiful as form events, the report events you can trap for allow you to control what happens as your report runs. The following sections discuss report events, and the section "Events Available for Report Sections and When to Use Them" covers events specific to report sections.

The Open Event

The Open event is the first event that occurs in a report, before the report begins printing or displaying. In fact, it happens even before the query underlying the report is run. Listing 11.1 provides an example of using the Open event.

LISTING 11.1   The Open Event

```
Private Sub Report_Open(Cancel As Integer)
    'Ignore an error if it occurs
    On Error Resume Next

    'Open the report criteria form
    DoCmd.OpenForm "frmReportDateRange", _
        WindowMode:=acDialog, _
        OpenArgs:="rptProjectBillingsbyWorkCode"

    'If the criteria form is not loaded, display an error
    'message and cancel the printing of the report
    '(the form will not be loaded if the user clicks Cancel)
    If Not IsLoaded("frmReportDateRange") Then
        MsgBox "Criteria Form Not Successfully Loaded, " & _
            "Canceling Report"
        Cancel = True
    End If
End Sub
```

You can find this code in rptProjectBillingsByWorkCode in CHAP11.ACCDB on the sample code CD-ROM. It tries to open the frmReportDateRange form, the criteria form that supplies the parameters for the query underlying the report. The code cancels the report if it is unable to load the form.

The Close Event

The Close event occurs as the report is closing, before the Deactivate event occurs. Listing 11.2 illustrates the use of the Close event.

LISTING 11.2   The Close Event

```
Private Sub Report_Close()
    'Close criteria form as report is closing
    DoCmd.Close acForm, "frmReportDateRange"
End Sub
```

You can find this code in the rptProjectBillingsByWorkCode report in CHAP11.ACCDB on the sample code CD-ROM. It closes the criteria form frmReportDateRange when the report is closing, in case the form is still open.

The NoData Event

If no records meet the criteria of the recordset underlying a report's RecordSource, the report prints without data and displays #Error in the report's Detail section. To eliminate this problem, you can code the NoData event of the report, which executes when no records meet the criteria specified in the report's RecordSource (see Listing 11.3).

LISTING 11.3   The NoData Event

```
Private Sub Report_NoData(Cancel As Integer)
    'Display a message and cancel processing
    MsgBox "There is no data for this report. Canceling report..."
    Cancel = True
End Sub
```

You can find this code in the NoData event of rptProjectBillingsByWorkCode in
CHAP11.ACCDB on the sample code CD-ROM. In case no data is returned by the report's
underlying recordset, a message is displayed to the user, and Cancel is set equal to True.
This exits the report without running it.

The Page Event

The Page event gives you the opportunity to do something immediately before the
formatted page is sent to the printer. For example, the Page event can be used to place a
border around a page, as shown in Listing 11.4.

LISTING 11.4   The Page Event

```
Private Sub Report_Page()
    'Draw a red line starting in the upper-left corner
    'and going to the lower-right corner
    Me.Line (0, 0)-(Me.ScaleWidth - 30, Me.ScaleHeight - 30), _
        RGB(255, 0, 0), B
End Sub
```

You will find this code in the rptTimeSheet report, in CHAP11.ACCDB. It draws a red line
on the report, starting in the upper-left corner and going to the lower-right corner. It uses
the ScaleWidth and ScaleHeight properties to determine where the lower-right corner of
the report's printable area is. The B in the third parameter creates a rectangle by using the
coordinates as opposite corners of the rectangle.

The Error Event

If an Access Database Engine error occurs when the report is formatting or printing, the
Error event is triggered. This error usually occurs if there's no RecordSource for the report
or if someone else has exclusive use over the report's RecordSource. Listing 11.5 provides
an example.

LISTING 11.5   The Error Event

```
Private Sub Report_Error(DataErr As Integer, Response As Integer)
    'If Data Source Not Found error occurs, display message
    'To test this, rename qryTimeSheet
    If DataErr = 2580 Then
```

LISTING 11.5   Continued

```
        MsgBox "Record Source Not Available for this Report"
        Response = acDataErrContinue
    End If
End Sub
```

NOTE

> If you have Name Autocorrect turned on, the process of renaming the query will not
> cause the desired error to occur.

This code responds to a DataErr of 2580, which means that the report's RecordSource
isn't available. A custom message is displayed to the user, and the Access error is
suppressed.

Order of Events for Reports

Understanding the order of events for reports is important. When the user opens a report,
previews it, and then closes it, the following sequence of events occurs:

```
Open->Activate->Close->Deactivate
```

When the user switches to another report or to a form, the following sequence occurs:

```
Deactivate(Current Report)->Activate(Form or Report)
```

NOTE

> The Deactivate event doesn't occur when the user switches to a dialog box, to a
> form whose PopUp property is set to Yes, or to a window of another application.

Events Available for Report Sections and When to Use Them

Just as the report itself has events, so does each section of the report. The three section
events are the Format event, Print event, and Retreat event, covered in the following
sections.

The Format Event

The Format event happens after Access has selected the data to be included in a report
section but before it formats or prints the data. With the Format event, you can affect the
layout of the section or calculate the results of data in the section, before the section actually prints. Listing 11.6 shows an example.

LISTING 11.6   Using the Format Event to Affect the Report Layout

```
Private Sub DetailSection_Format(Cancel As Integer, FormatCount As Integer)

    'Determine whether to print detail record or "Continued on Next Page..."

    'Show Continued text box if at maximum number of
    'detail records for page.
    If (Me.txtRow = Me.txtOrderPage * (Me.txtRowsPerPage - 1) + 1) _
        And Me.txtRow <> Me.txtRowCount Then
        Me.txtContinued.Visible = True
    End If

    'Show page break and hide controls in detail record.
    With Me
        If .txtContinued.Visible Then
            .txtDetailPageBreak.Visible = True
            .txtProductID.Visible = False
            .txtProductName.Visible = False
            .txtQuantity.Visible = False
            .txtUnitPrice.Visible = False
            .txtDiscount.Visible = False
            .txtExtendedPrice.Visible = False

            'Increase value in Order Page.
            .NextRecord = False
            .txtOrderPage = Me.txtOrderPage + 1
        Else
            'Increase row count if detail record is printed.
            .txtRow = Me.txtRow + 1
        End If
    End With

End Sub
```

This code is found in the rptInvoice report included in the CHAP11EX.ACCDB database found on your sample code CD-ROM. The report has controls that track how many rows of detail records should be printed on each page. If the maximum number of rows has been reached, a control with the text Continued on Next Page... is visible. If the control is visible, the page break control is also made visible, and all the controls that display the detail for the report are hidden. The report is kept from advancing to the next record.

Another example of the Format event is found in the Page Header of the rptEmployeeSales report, found in the CHAP11EX.ACCDB database. Because the report is an unbound report whose controls are populated by using Visual Basic for Applications (VBA) code at runtime, the report needs to determine what's placed in the report header. This varies depending on the result of the crosstab query on which the report is based. The code is shown in Listing 11.7.

LISTING 11.7   Using the Format Event to Populate Unbound Controls at Runtime

```
Private Sub PageHeader0_Format(Cancel As Integer, FormatCount As Integer)

    Dim intX As Integer

    'Put column headings into text boxes in page header.
    For intX = 1 To mintColumnCount
        Me("Head" + Format(intX)) = mrstReport(intX - 1).Name
    Next intX

    'Make next available text box Totals heading.
    Me("Head" + Format(mintColumnCount + 1)) = "Totals"

    'Hide unused text boxes in page header.
    For intX = (mintColumnCount + 2) To conTotalColumns
        Me("Head" + Format(intX)).Visible = False
    Next intX
End Sub
```

The code loops through each column of the recordset that results from executing the crosstab query (in the Open event of the report). The code populates the controls in the report's Page Header with the name of each column in the query result. The final column header is set equal to Totals. Finally, any remaining (extra) text boxes are hidden. This is one of several examples in the chapter that covers the Format event.

NOTE

The example in Listing 11.7 and several other examples in this chapter use an ActiveX Data Objects (ADO) recordset. ADO is covered in Chapter 15, "What Are ActiveX Data Objects, and Why Are They Important?" If you are unfamiliar with ADO, you might want to review Chapter 15 before reviewing the examples.

TIP

By placing logic in the Format event of a report's Detail section, you can control what happens as each line of the Detail section is printed.

The Print Event

The code in the Print event executes when the data formats to print in the section but before it's actually printed. The Print event occurs at the following times for different sections of the report:

▶ **Detail Section**—Just before the data is printed.

▶ **Group Headers**—Just before the Group Header is printed; the Group Header's Print event has access to both the Group Header and the first row of data in the group.

▶ **Group Footers**—Just before the Group Footer is printed; the Print event of the Group Footer has access to both the Group Footer and the last row of data in the group.

Listing 11.8 is in the Print event of the rptEmployeeSales report's Detail section; this report is included in the CHAP11EX.ACCDB database and is called from frmEmployeeSalesDialogBox.

LISTING 11.8   Using the Print Event to Calculate Column and Row Totals

```
Private Sub Detail1_Print(Cancel As Integer, PrintCount As Integer)

    Dim intX As Integer
    Dim lngRowTotal As Long

    'If PrintCount is 1, initialize rowTotal variable.
    'Add to column totals.
    If Me.PrintCount = 1 Then
        lngRowTotal = 0

        For intX = 2 To mintColumnCount
            'Starting at column 2 (first text box with crosstab value),
            'compute total for current row in Detail section.
            lngRowTotal = lngRowTotal + Me("Col" + Format(intX))
            'Add crosstab value to total for current column.
            mlngRgColumnTotal(intX) = mlngRgColumnTotal(intX) + _
                Me("Col" + Format(intX))
        Next intX

        'Place row total in text box in Detail section.
        Me("Col" + Format(mintColumnCount + 1)) = lngRowTotal
        'Add row total for current row to grand total.
        mlngReportTotal = mlngReportTotal + lngRowTotal
    End If
End Sub
```

The code begins by evaluating the PrintCount property. If it's equal to 1, meaning this is the first time the Print event has occurred for the Detail section, the row total is set equal to 0. The code then loops through each control in the section, accumulating totals for each column of the report and a total for the row. After the loop has been exited, the routine places the row total in the appropriate control and adds the row total to the report's grand total. The report's Detail section is now ready to be printed.

NOTE

Many people are confused about when to place code in the Format event and when to place code in the Print event. If you're doing something that doesn't affect the page layout, you should use the Print event. However, if you're doing something that affects the report's physical appearance (the layout), use the Format event.

The Retreat Event

Sometimes Access needs to move back to a previous section when printing, such as when a group's Keep Together property is set to With First Detail or Whole in the Property Sheet. Access needs to format the Group Header and the first detail record or, in the case of Whole, the entire group. It then determines whether it can fit the section on the current page. It retreats from the two sections and then formats and prints them; a Retreat event occurs for each section. Here's an example of the Retreat event for a report's Detail section:

```
Private Sub Detail1_Retreat()

    'Always back up to previous record when detail section retreats.
    mrstReport.MovePrevious

End Sub
```

This code is placed in the Retreat event of the rptEmployeeSales report that's part of CHAP11EX.ACCDB. Because the report is unbound, it needs to return to the previous record in the recordset whenever the Retreat event occurs.

CAUTION

Whenever you're working with an unbound report, you need to be careful that the record pointer remains synchronized with the report. For example, if the record pointer has been advanced and the Retreat event occurs, the record pointer must be moved back to the previous record.

Order of Section Events

Just as report events have an order, report sections also have an order of events. All the Format and Print events for each section happen after the report's Open and Activate events, but before the report's Close and Deactivate events. The sequence looks like this:

```
Open(Report)->Activate(Report)->Format(Report Section)->
Print(Report Section)->Close(Report)->Deactivate(Report)
```

Programmatically Manipulating Report Sections

You create and manipulate report sections not only at design time, but also at runtime. You must first open the report in Design view. You use the DoCmd object to add a report header and footer or a page header and footer. The code is shown in Listing 11.9.

LISTING 11.9   Using the DoCmd Object to Programmatically Add Sections to Reports at Runtime

```
Private Sub cmdAddHeadersFooters_Click()
    'Open rptAny in Design view
    DoCmd.OpenReport "rptAny", acViewDesign

    'Add a report header and footer
    DoCmd.RunCommand acCmdReportHdrFtr

    'Add a page header and footer
    DoCmd.RunCommand acCmdPageHdrFtr
End Sub
```

You can also add section headers and footers. The code in Listing 11.10 illustrates the process. It is found in frmReportSections on the sample code CD-ROM.

LISTING 11.10   Adding Sections to Reports at Runtime

```
Private Sub cmdAddSections_Click()
    Dim boolSuccess As Boolean

    'Use the CreateGroupLevel function to create a grouping
    'based on the City field in the report rptAny
    boolSuccess = CreateGroupLevel("rptAny", "City", True, True)
End Sub
```

Note that the CreateGroupLevel function receives four parameters. The first is the name of the report you want to affect. The second is an expression designating the expression on which the grouping is based. The third parameter allows you to specify whether you want the group to have a group header, and the final parameter lets you designate whether you want to include a group footer.

Taking Advantage of Special Report Properties

Several report properties are available only at runtime. They let you refine your report's processing significantly. These properties are covered in the sections that follow. The later section "Incorporating Practical Applications of Report Events and Properties" provides examples of these properties.

MoveLayout

The MoveLayout property indicates to Access whether it should move to the next printing location on the page. When you set the property to False, the printing position is not advanced.

NextRecord

The NextRecord property specifies whether a section should advance to the next record. By setting this property to False, you suppress advancing to the next record.

PrintSection

The PrintSection property indicates whether the section is printed. By setting this property to False, you can suppress printing the section.

Interaction of MoveLayout, NextRecord, and PrintSection

By using the MoveLayout, NextRecord, and PrintSection properties in combination, you can determine exactly where, how, and whether data is printed. Table 11.1 illustrates this point.

TABLE 11.1   Interaction of MoveLayout, NextRecord, and PrintSection

MoveLayout	NextRecord	PrintSection	**Effect**
True	True	True	Move to the next position, get the next record, and print the data.
True	False	True	Move to the next position, remain on the same record, and print the data.
True	True	False	Move to the next position, get the next record, and don't print the data. This has the effect of skipping a record and leaving a blank space.
True	False	False	Move to the next position, remain on the same record, and don't print. This causes a blank space to appear without moving to the next record.
False	True	True	Remain in the same position, get the next record, and print the data. This has the effect of overlaying one record on another.
False	False	True	Not allowed.
False	True	False	Remain in the same position, get the next record, and refrain from printing. This has the effect of skipping a record without leaving a blank space.
False	False	False	Not allowed.

FormatCount

The FormatCount property evaluates the number of times the Format event has occurred for the report's current section. The Format event happens more than once whenever the Retreat event occurs. By checking the FormatCount property, you can make sure that complex code placed in the Format event is executed only once.

PrintCount

The PrintCount property identifies the number of times the Print event has occurred for the report's current section. The Print event happens more than once whenever the Retreat event occurs. By checking the value of the PrintCount property, you can make sure that logic in the Print event is executed only once.

HasContinued

The HasContinued property determines whether part of the current section is printed on a previous page. You can use this property to hide or show certain report controls (for example, Continued From...), depending on whether the section is continued.

WillContinue

The WillContinue property determines whether the current section continues on another page. You can use this property as you do the HasContinued property to hide or display certain controls when a section continues on another page.

Controlling the Printer

Prior to Access 2002, there was no easy way to programmatically control the printer in the applications that you built. Unlike other aspects of Access in which Microsoft provided you with objects, properties, methods, and events that you could easily manipulate, programmatically controlling the printer in versions prior to Access 2002 involved rolling up your sleeves and talking at a low level to operating system objects.

Fortunately, Access 2002 introduced a new Printer object and a Printers collection. The Printer object greatly facilitates the process of programmatically manipulating a printer. The Printers collection allows you to loop through all the Printer objects and perform a task.

The Printer Object

The Printers collection consists of individual Printer objects. You use a Printer object to control each printer in the Printers collection. Listing 11.11 provides an example of the Printer object.

LISTING 11.11   The Printer Object

```
Private Sub cmdPrinterObject_Click()
    'Declare a Printer object
    Dim prt As Printer

    'Point the Printer object at the first printer in
    'the Printers collection
    Set prt = Printers(0)

    'Display properties of the printer
    MsgBox "Device Name: " & prt.DeviceName & vbCrLf & _
        "Port: " & prt.Port & vbCrLf & _
        "Color Mode: " & prt.ColorMode & vbCrLf & _
        "Copies: " & prt.Copies
End Sub
```

Listing 11.11 begins by instantiating a `Printer` object. It points the `Printer` object at the first printer in the `Printers` collection. It then retrieves the `DeviceName`, `Port`, `ColorMode`, and `Copies` properties of the printer. These are four of the many properties included for the `Printer` object. Other properties include `LeftMargin`, `RightMargin`, `TopMargin`, `BottomMargin`, `Orientation`, and `PrintQuality`. Most properties of the `Printer` object are read/write. This means that you can programmatically manipulate the properties at runtime, easily controlling the behavior of the printer.

The `Printers` Collection

Using the `Printers` collection, you can loop through all the printers available for a user, programmatically manipulating each one. Listing 11.12 provides an example. It is found in `frmPrinterObjectAndPrintersCollection` on the sample code CD-ROM.

LISTING 11.12   The Printers Collection

```
Private Sub cmdPrintersCollection_Click()
    'Declare a Printer object
    Dim prt As Printer

    Dim strPrinterInfo As String

    'Loop through each printer in the user's
    'Printers collection
    For Each prt In Printers

        'Retrieve properties of the printer
        strPrinterInfo = strPrinterInfo & vbCrLf & _
            "Device Name: " & prt.DeviceName & "; " & _
```

LISTING 11.12   Continued

```
            "Port: " & prt.Port & "; "
    Next prt

    'Display the properties of all printers in a
    'message box
    MsgBox strPrinterInfo
End Sub
```

Using Automatic Error Checking

In Access 2007, you can enable automatic error checking of reports. Error checking not only points out errors in a report but also provides suggestions for correcting them.

To activate error checking, click the Microsoft Office Access button and then select Access Options. Click to select the Object Designers tab (see Figure 11.1). Click the Enable Error Checking check box to enable error checking. After you enable error checking, indicators appear on your report, letting you know that something is wrong (see Figure 11.2). You then click the indicator, and an explanation along with suggestions for correcting the error appear (see Figure 11.3).

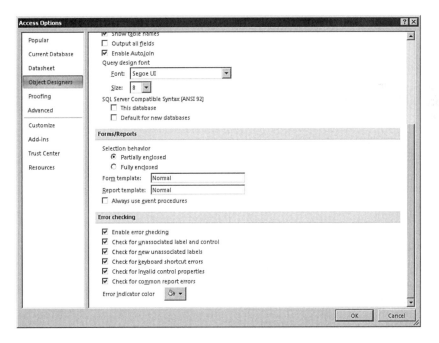

FIGURE 11.1   You can activate error checking from the Object Designers tab of the Access Options dialog box.

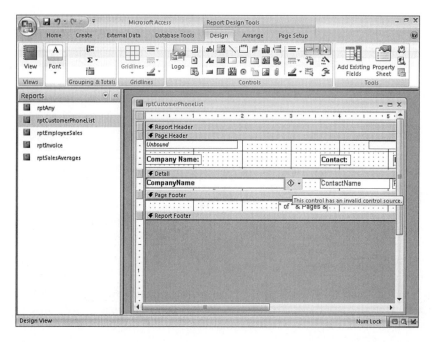

FIGURE 11.2   Indicators appear on your report, letting you know that something is wrong.

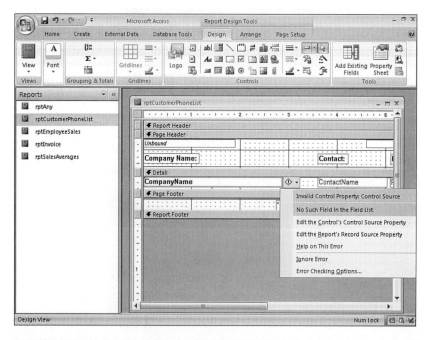

FIGURE 11.3   A menu appears, providing you with an explanation and suggestions for correcting the error.

The error checker will identify several categories of errors, which are described in Table 11.2.

TABLE 11.2   Categories of Errors Identified by the Error Checker

Category	Description
Unassociated label and control	You select a label and a control (for example, a label and a text box) that are not associated with one another.
New unassociated labels	You add a label that is not associated with another control.
Invalid control properties	The string in the control source is not valid. The problem could be that it is not a valid field name or that the control source refers to itself. It can also be that the expression does not begin with an equal sign or that the option value in an option group is not unique.
Other common errors	The report has an invalid sorting or grouping definition or is wider than the selected paper size.

If Access identifies several errors for the same control, the error indicator remains until all errors are corrected. If you choose to ignore an error, simply select the Ignore Error option on the Error Checking Options menu. This will clear the error indicator until you close and open the report again. Remember that you can turn off error checking entirely via Access Options (although I find this feature to be extremely valuable).

Propagating Field Properties

When you make a change to an inherited property in a table's Design view, you can opt to propagate that change to the controls on your reports that are bound to that field. Here's how it works:

1. Open the table whose design you want to modify in Design view.

2. Click in the field whose property you want to change.

3. Click in the property whose value you want to change.

4. Change the property and press Enter. If the property that you changed is inheritable, the Property Update Options button appears (see Figure 11.4).

5. Open the menu and select Update (see Figure 11.5). The Update Properties dialog box appears (see Figure 11.6). Select the forms and reports that contain the controls that you want to update. Click Yes to complete the process.

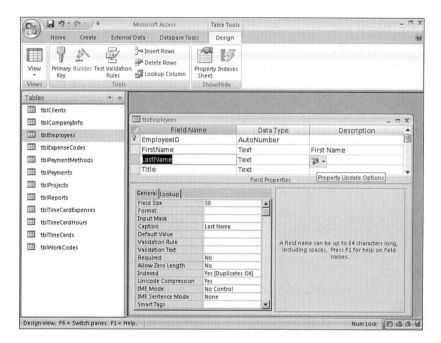

FIGURE 11.4   The Property Update Options button appears for inheritable properties.

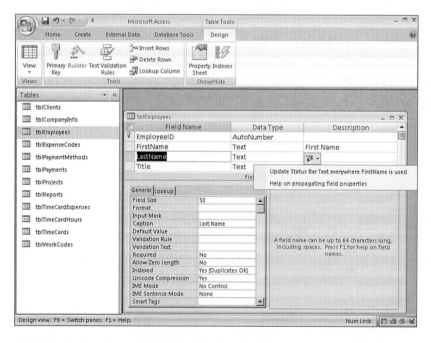

FIGURE 11.5   Open the menu and select Update.

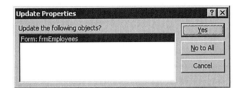

FIGURE 11.6   The Update Properties dialog box allows you to select the forms and reports that you want to update.

Incorporating Practical Applications of Report Events and Properties

When developing reports, you should make sure that you can use the report in as many situations as possible—that you build as much flexibility into the report as you can. Instead of managing several similar reports, making changes to each one whenever something changes, you can manage one report that handles different situations. Using the events and properties covered in this chapter will help you do just that. This might involve changing the report's RecordSource at runtime; using the same report to print summary data, detail data, or both; changing the print position; or even running a report based on a crosstab query with unbound controls. All these aspects of report design are covered in the following sections.

Changing a Report's RecordSource

Often you might want to change a report's RecordSource at runtime. By doing this, you can allow your users to alter the conditions for your report and transparently modify the query on which the report is based. The rptClientListing report in CHAP11.ACCDB contains the code in Listing 11.13 in its Open event.

LISTING 11.13   An Example of Using the Report Open Event to Modify a Report's RecordSource

```
Private Sub Report_Open(Cancel As Integer)
    On Error Resume Next

    'Open the report criteria form
    DoCmd.OpenForm "frmClientListingCriteria", WindowMode:=acDialog

    'Ensure that the form is loaded
    If Not IsLoaded("frmClientListingCriteria") Then
        MsgBox "Criteria form not successfully loaded, " & _
        "Canceling Report"
        Cancel = True
    Else

        'Evaluate which option button was selected
```

LISTING 11.13   Continued

```
        'Set the RecordSource property as appropriate
        Select Case Forms!frmClientListingCriteria.optCriteria.Value
            Case 1
                Me.RecordSource = "qryClientListingCity"
            Case 2
                Me.RecordSource = "qryClientListingStateProv"
            Case 3
                Me.RecordSource = "qryClientListing"
        End Select
    End If
End Sub
```

This code begins by opening the frmClientListingCriteria form, if it isn't already loaded. It loads the form modally and waits for the user to select the report criteria (see Figure 11.7). After the user clicks to preview the report, the form sets its own Visible property to False. This causes execution to continue in the report but leaves the form in memory so that its controls can be accessed with VBA code. The code evaluates the value of the form's optCriteria option button. Depending on which option button is selected, the report's RecordSource property is set to the appropriate query. The following code is placed in the Close event of the report:

```
Private Sub Report_Close()
    DoCmd.Close acForm, "frmClientListingCriteria"
End Sub
```

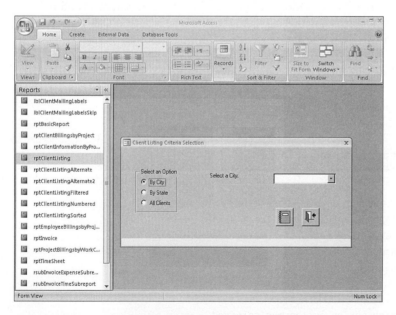

FIGURE 11.7   The criteria selection used to determine the RecordSource.

This code closes the criteria form as the report is closing. The `frmClientListingCriteria` form has some code that's important to the processing of the report. It's found in the `AfterUpdate` event of the `optCriteria` option group (see Listing 11.14).

LISTING 11.14   The `AfterUpdate` Event of the `optCriteria` Option Group

```
Private Sub optCriteria_AfterUpdate()
    'Evaluate which option button is selected
    'Hide and show combo boxes as appropriate

    Select Case optCriteria.Value
        Case 1
            Me.cboCity.Visible = True
            Me.cboStateProv.Visible = False
        Case 2
            Me.cboStateProv.Visible = True
            Me.cboCity.Visible = False
        Case 3
            Me.cboCity.Visible = False
            Me.cboStateProv.Visible = False
    End Select
End Sub
```

This code evaluates the value of the option group. It hides and shows the visibility of the `cboCity` and `cboStateProv` combo boxes, depending on which option button the user selects. The `cboCity` and `cboStateProv` combo boxes are then used as appropriate criteria for the queries that underlie the `rptClientListing` report.

The example shown in Listing 11.13 uses three stored queries to accomplish the task of switching the report's record source. An alternative to this technique is to programmatically set the `RecordSource` property of the report to the appropriate SQL statement. This technique is illustrated in Listing 11.15 and is found in `rptClientListingAlternate` on the sample code CD-ROM.

LISTING 11.15   Using the `Report Open` Event to Modify a Report's `RecordSource` to the Appropriate SQL Statement

```
On Error Resume Next

'Open the report criteria form
DoCmd.OpenForm "frmClientListingCriteria", WindowMode:=acDialog

'Ensure that the form is loaded
If Not IsLoaded("frmClientListingCriteria") Then
    MsgBox "Criteria form not successfully loaded, " & _
    "Canceling Report"
    Cancel = True
```

LISTING 11.15   Continued

```
Else

    'Evaluate which option button was selected
    'Set the RecordSource property as appropriate
    Select Case Forms!frmClientListingCriteria.optCriteria.Value
        Case 1
            Me.RecordSource = "SELECT DISTINCTROW " & _
            "tblClients.CompanyName, " & _
            "ContactFirstName & ' ' & ContactLastName AS ContactName, " & _
            "tblClients.City, tblClients.StateProvince, " & _
            "tblClients.OfficePhone, tblClients.Fax " & _
            "FROM tblClients " & _
            "WHERE tblClients.City = '" & _
            Forms!frmClientListingCriteria.cboCity.Value & _
            "' ORDER BY tblClients.CompanyName;"
        Case 2
            Me.RecordSource = "SELECT DISTINCTROW " & _
            "tblClients.CompanyName, " & _
            "ContactFirstName & ' ' & ContactLastName AS ContactName, " & _
            "tblClients.City, tblClients.StateProvince, " & _
            "tblClients.OfficePhone, tblClients.Fax " & _
            "FROM tblClients " & _
            "WHERE tblClients.StateProvince = '" & _
            Forms!frmClientListingCriteria.cboStateProv.Value & _
            "' ORDER BY tblClients.CompanyName;"
        Case 3
            Me.RecordSource = "SELECT DISTINCTROW " & _
            "tblClients.CompanyName, " & _
            "ContactFirstName & ' ' & ContactLastName AS ContactName, " & _
            "tblClients.City, tblClients.StateProvince, " & _
            "tblClients.OfficePhone, tblClients.Fax " & _
            "FROM tblClients " & _
            "ORDER BY tblClients.CompanyName;"
    End Select
End If
```

This example programmatically builds a SQL statement based on the option selected on the criteria form. It uses the cboCity and cboStateProv combo boxes to build the WHERE clause in the appropriate SQL strings.

Listing 11.16 shows my favorite alternative. It is somewhat of a compromise between the first two alternatives. You will find the code in frmClientListingCriteriaAlternate. Unlike in the previous two examples, the criteria form drives this entire example. In other words, you will not find *any* code behind the report. Listing 11.16 looks like this.

LISTING 11.16   The Code Behind the `frmClientListingCriteriaAlternate` Form

```
Private Sub cmdPreview_Click()
    Dim strWhere As String

    Select Case Me.optPrint
        Case 1
            strWhere = "City='" & Me.cboCity & "'"
            DoCmd.OpenReport _
                "rptClientListingAlternate2", acViewPreview, _
                WhereCondition:=strWhere
        Case 2
            strWhere = "StateProvince='" & Me.cboStateProv & "'"
            DoCmd.OpenReport _
                "rptClientListingAlternate2", acViewPreview, _
                WhereCondition:=strWhere
        Case 3
            DoCmd.OpenReport _
                "rptClientListingAlternate2", acViewPreview
    End Select
End Sub
```

The code begins by determining which option button the user selected. Based on which option button the user selected, the code enters the appropriate branch of the Case statement to build the necessary Where clause. The code uses the Where clause as the WhereCondition parameter of the OpenReport method of the DoCmd object. The RecordSource of the report is always the same. It is the WhereCondition parameter that differentiates the data that appears in the report.

Working with Report Filters

The Filter and FilterOn properties allow you to set a report filter and to turn it on and off. Three possible scenarios can apply:

- No filter is in effect.
- The Filter property is set but is not in effect because the FilterOn property is set to False.
- The filter is in effect. This requires that the Filter property is set, and the FilterOn property is set to True.

You can set filtering properties either at design time or at runtime. This solution provides *another* alternative to the example provided in Listing 11.13. With this alternative, the RecordSource of the report is fixed. The Filter and FilterOn properties are used to display the appropriate data. Listing 11.17 provides an example. You can find the code in rptClientListingFiltered on the sample code CD-ROM.

LISTING 11.17   Using the `Filter` and `FilterOn` Properties

```
Private Sub Report_Open(Cancel As Integer)
    On Error Resume Next

    'Open the report criteria form
    DoCmd.OpenForm "frmClientListingCriteria", WindowMode:=acDialog

    'Ensure that the form is loaded
    If Not IsLoaded("frmClientListingCriteria") Then
        MsgBox "Criteria form not successfully loaded, " & _
        "Canceling Report"
        Cancel = True
    Else

        'Evaluate which option button was selected
        'Set the Filter and FilterOn properties as appropriate
        Select Case Forms!frmClientListingCriteria.optCriteria.Value
            Case 1
                Me.Filter = "City = '" & _
                    Forms!frmClientListingCriteria.cboCity & "'"
                Me.FilterOn = True
            Case 2
                Me.Filter = "StateProvince = '" & _
                    Forms!frmClientListingCriteria.cboStateProv & "'"
                Me.FilterOn = True
            Case 3
                Me.FilterOn = False
        End Select
    End If
End Sub
```

In this example, the `RecordSource` property of the report is the `qryClients` query. The query returns clients in all cities and all states. The example uses the `Open` event of the report to filter the data to the appropriate city or state.

> **CAUTION**
>
> Listings 11.13, 11.15, and 11.16 are much more efficient than the code in Listing 11.17. In a client/server environment, such as Microsoft SQL Server, with the code in Listings 11.13, 11.15, and 11.16, only the requested data comes over the network wire. For example, only data for the requested city comes over the wire. On the other hand, the `Filter` property is applied *after* the data comes over the wire. This means that, in the example, all clients come over the wire, and the filter for the requested `City` or `State` is applied at the workstation.

Working with the Report Sort Order

The OrderBy and OrderByOn properties are similar to the Filter and FilterOn properties. They allow you to apply a sort order to the report. As with filters, three scenarios apply:

- ▶ No sort is in effect.

- ▶ The OrderBy property is set but is not in effect because the OrderByOn property is set to False.

- ▶ The order is in effect. This requires that the OrderBy property is set, and the OrderByOn property is set to True.

You can set ordering properties either at design time or at runtime. The OrderBy and OrderByOn properties are used to determine the sort order of the report and whether the sort is in effect. Listing 11.18 provides an example. You can find the code in rptClientListingSorted on the sample code CD-ROM.

LISTING 11.18   Using the Report Open Event to Modify the Sort Order of a Report

```
Private Sub Report_Open(Cancel As Integer)
    On Error Resume Next

    'Open the report sort order form
    DoCmd.OpenForm "frmClientListingSortOrder", WindowMode:=acDialog

    'Ensure that the form is loaded
    If Not IsLoaded("frmClientListingSortOrder") Then
        MsgBox "Criteria form not successfully loaded, " & _
        "Canceling Report"
        Cancel = True
    Else

        'Evaluate which option button was selected
        'Set the OrderBy and OrderByOn properties as appropriate
        Select Case Forms!frmClientListingSortOrder.optCriteria.Value
            Case 1
                Me.OrderBy = "City, CompanyName"
                Me.OrderByOn = True
            Case 2
                Me.OrderBy = "StateProvince, CompanyName"
                Me.OrderByOn = True
            Case 3
                Me.OrderBy = "CompanyName"
                Me.OrderByOn = True
        End Select
    End If
End Sub
```

The code appears in the Open event of the report. It evaluates which option button the user selected on the frmClientListingSortOrder form. It then sets the OrderBy property as appropriate and sets the OrderByOn property to True so that the OrderBy property takes effect.

> **CAUTION**
>
> The OrderBy property *augments,* rather than replaces, the existing sort order of the report. If the OrderBy property is in conflict with the sort order of the report, the OrderBy property is ignored. For example, if the sort order in the Sorting and Grouping window is set to CompanyName and the OrderBy property is set to City combined with CompanyName, the OrderBy property is ignored.

Using the Same Report to Display Summary, Detail, or Both

Many programmers create three reports for their users: one that displays summary only, one that displays detail only, and another that displays both. Creating all these reports is unnecessary. Because you can hide and display report sections as necessary at runtime, you can create one report that meets all three needs. The rptClientBillingsByProject report included in the CHAP11.ACCDB database illustrates this point. Place the code shown in Listing 11.19 in the report's Open event.

LISTING 11.19   Using the Report Open Event to Hide and Show Report Sections as Appropriate

```
Private Sub Report_Open(Cancel As Integer)
    'Load the report criteria form
    DoCmd.OpenForm "frmReportDateRange", _
        WindowMode:=acDialog, _
        OpenArgs:="rptClientBillingsbyProject"

    'Ensure that the form is loaded
    If Not IsLoaded("frmReportDateRange") Then
        Cancel = True
    Else

        'Evaluate which option button is selected
        Select Case Forms!frmReportDateRange!optDetailLevel.Value

            'Modify caption and hide and show detail section and summary
            'section as appropriate
            Case 1
                Me.Caption = Me.Caption & " - Summary Only"
                Me.lblTitle.Caption = Me.lblTitle.Caption & " - Summary Only"
                Me.Detail.Visible = False
            Case 2
                Me.Caption = Me.Caption & " - Detail Only"
```

LISTING 11.19   Continued

```
            Me.lblTitle.Caption = Me.lblTitle.Caption & " - Detail Only"
            Me.GroupHeader0.Visible = False
            Me.GroupFooter1.Visible = False
            Me.txtCompanyNameDet.Visible = True
        Case 3
            Me.Caption = Me.Caption & " - Summary and Detail"
            Me.lblTitle.Caption = Me.lblTitle.Caption & " - Summary and Detail"
            Me.txtCompanyNameDet.Visible = False
    End Select
  End If
End Sub
```

The code begins by opening frmReportDateRange included in CHAP11.ACCDB (see Figure 11.8). The form has an option group asking users whether they want a Summary report, Detail report, or a report that contains both Summary and Detail. If the user selects Summary, the caption of the Report window and the lblTitle label are modified, and the Visible property of the Detail section is set to False. If the user selects Detail Only, the captions of the Report window and the lblTitle label are modified, and the Visible property of the Group Header and Footer sections is set to False. A control in the Detail section containing the company name is made visible. The CompanyName control is visible in the Detail section when the Detail Only report is printed, but it's invisible when the Summary and Detail report is printed. When Both is selected as the level of detail, no sections are hidden. The captions of the Report window and the lblTitle label are modified, and the CompanyName control is hidden.

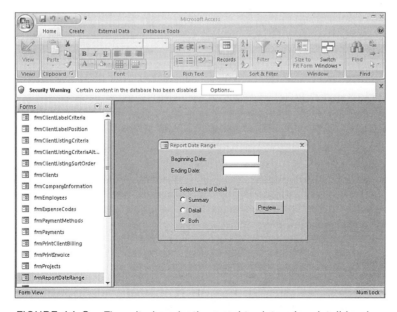

FIGURE 11.8   The criteria selection used to determine detail level.

The code behind the form's Preview button looks like that shown in Listing 11.20.

LISTING 11.20   Code That Validates the Date Range Entered by the User

```
Private Sub cmdPreview_Click()
    'Ensure that both the begin date and end date are populated
    'If not, display a message and set focus to the begin date
    If IsNull(Me.txtBeginDate) Or IsNull(Me.txtEndDate) Then
        MsgBox "You must enter both beginning and ending dates."
        Me.txtBeginDate.SetFocus

    'If begin date and end date are populated, ensure that
    'begin date is before end date
    Else
        If Me.txtBeginDate > Me.txtEndDate Then
            MsgBox "Ending date must be greater than Beginning date."
            Me.txtBeginDate.SetFocus

        'If all validations succeed, hide form, allowing report to print
        Else
            Me.Visible = False
        End If
    End If
End Sub
```

This code makes sure that both the beginning date and the ending date are filled in and that the beginning date comes before the ending date. If both of these rules are fulfilled, the code sets the Visible property of the form to False. Otherwise, the code displays an appropriate error message.

Numbering Report Items

Many people are unaware how simple it is to number the items on a report. Figure 11.9 provides an example of a numbered report. This report is called rptClientListingNumbered and is located on the sample code CD-ROM. The process of creating such a report is extremely simple. Figure 11.10 shows the Data properties of the txtNumbering text box. The Control Source property allows you to set the starting number for a report. The Running Sum property allows you to determine when the numbering is reset to the starting value. The Control Source property of the text box is set to =1, and the Running Sum property is set to Over All. The combination of these two properties causes the report to begin numbering with the number 1 and to continue the numbering throughout the report. Setting the Running Sum property to Over Group causes the numbering to reset itself at the beginning of each report grouping.

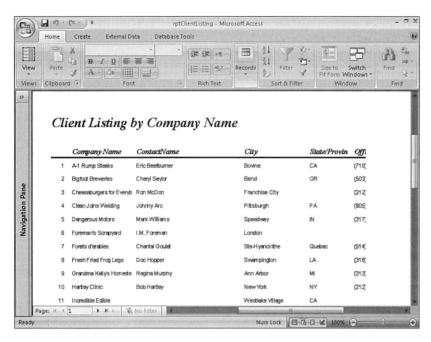

FIGURE 11.9   You can add numbering to items on a report easily.

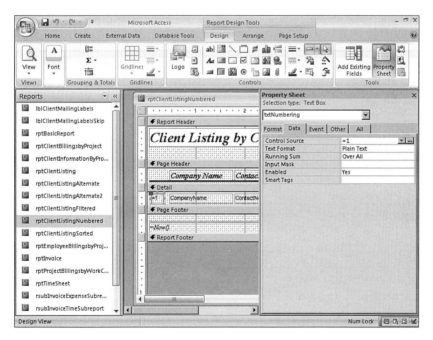

FIGURE 11.10   The Control Source property and the Running Sum property.

Printing Multiple Labels

Many times, users want to print multiple copies of the same label. The report's
MoveLayout, NextRecord, PrintSection, and PrintCount properties help us to accomplish
the task. The form shown in Figure 11.11 is called frmClientLabelCriteria and is found
in CHAP11.ACCDB. It asks users to select a company and the number of labels they want to
print for that company. The code for the Print Labels command button looks like that
shown in Listing 11.21.

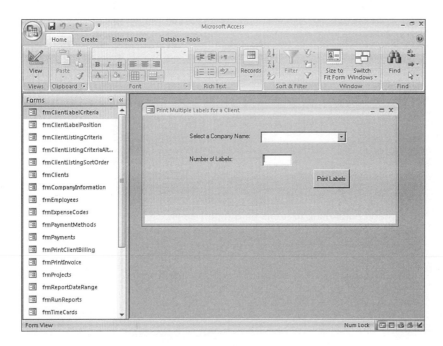

FIGURE 11.11   The criteria selection used to specify the company name and number of
labels to print.

LISTING 11.21   Code That Prints the lblClientMailingLabels Report for the Selected
Company

```
Sub cmdPrintLabels_Click()
On Error GoTo Err_cmdPrintLabels_Click

    'Run the mailing labels, showing only those
    'rows where the company name matches
    'the company selected in the combo box
    DoCmd.OpenReport "lblClientMailingLabels", _
        View:=acPreview, _
        WhereCondition:="CompanyName = '" & _
            Me.cboCompanyName.Value & "'"
```

LISTING 11.21   Continued

```
Exit_cmdPrintLabels_Click:
    Exit Sub

Err_cmdPrintLabels_Click:
    MsgBox Err.Description
    Resume Exit_cmdPrintLabels_Click

End Sub
```

Notice that the routine uses the company name selected from the combo box as a criterion to run the lblClientMailingLabels report. The Open event of lblClientMailingLabels is shown in Listing 11.22.

LISTING 11.22   The Open Event of lblClientMailingLabels

```
Private Sub Report_Open(Cancel As Integer)
    'Ensure that the criteria form is loaded
    'If not, display message and cancel report
    If Not IsLoaded("frmClientLabelCriteria") Then
        MsgBox "You Must Run This Report From Label Criteria Form"
        Cancel = True
    End If
End Sub
```

This code tests to make sure the frmClientLabelCriteria form is open. If it's not, the code displays a message and cancels the report. The Detail section's Print event, which compares the requested number of labels with the number of labels printed, is the key to the whole process (see Listing 11.23).

LISTING 11.23   The Code in the Print Event

```
Private Sub Detail_Print(Cancel As Integer, PrintCount As Integer)
    'If the number of times the detail section has been printed is
    'less than the number of labels that has been printed,
    'cancel movement to the next row
    If PrintCount < _
        Forms!frmClientLabelCriteria!txtNumberOfLabels Then
        Me.NextRecord = False
    End If
End Sub
```

This code compares the PrintCount property to the number of labels the user wants to print. As long as the PrintCount is less than the number of labels requested, the record pointer is not advanced. This causes multiple labels to be printed for the same record.

Determining Where a Label Prints

Users often want to print several copies of the same label, but they might also want to print mailing labels in a specific position on the page. Users generally do this so that they can begin the print process on the first unused label. The frmClientLabelPosition form from CHAP11.ACCDB lets the user specify the first label location on which to print by designating the number of labels that the user wants to skip (see Figure 11.12). The Open event of lblClientMailLabelsSkip is shown in Listing 11.24.

LISTING 11.24   The Code in the Open Event of lblClientMailLabelsSkip

```
Private Sub Report_Open(Cancel As Integer)
    'Ensure that the criteria form is loaded
    'If not, display message and cancel printing
    If Not IsLoaded("frmClientLabelPosition") Then
        MsgBox "You Must Run This Report From Label Criteria Form"
        Cancel = True
    Else
        mboolFirstLabel = True
    End If
End Sub
```

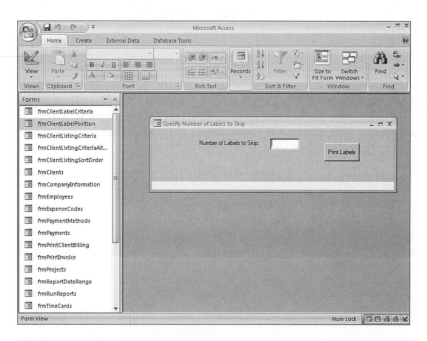

FIGURE 11.12   The criteria selection used to indicate the number of labels to skip.

The code tests to make sure that the frmClientLabelPosition form is loaded. It also sets a private variable, mboolFirstLabel, equal to True. The Detail section's Print event, which suppresses printing until the correct number of labels is skipped, is shown in Listing 11.25.

LISTING 11.25   The Detail Print Event

```
Private Sub Detail_Print(Cancel As Integer, PrintCount As Integer)
    'Check to see if the number of times the detail section was
    'visited is less than the number of labels to skip AND
    'that the mboolFirstLabel flag is true
    If PrintCount <= _
        Forms!frmClientLabelPosition.txtLabelsToSkip _
        And mboolFirstLabel = True Then

        'Do not move to the next record and do not print anything
        Me.NextRecord = False
        Me.PrintSection = False
    Else
        'Allow printing and turn mboolFirstLabel flag to false
        mboolFirstLabel = False
    End If
End Sub
```

This routine checks to see whether the PrintCount property of the report is less than or equal to the number of the labels to skip. It also checks to make sure that the mboolFirstLabel variable is equal to True. If both conditions are True, the report doesn't move to the next record and doesn't print anything. The print position is advanced. When the PrintCount becomes greater than the number of labels to skip, the mboolFirstLabel variable is set to False and printing proceeds as usual. If mboolFirstLabel is not set to False, the designated number of labels is skipped between each record. One additional event makes all this work—the Format event of the Report Header:

```
Private Sub ReportHeader_Format(Cancel As Integer, FormatCount As Integer)
    'Set the mboolFirstLabel flag to True when the header
    'formats for the first time
    mboolFirstLabel = True
End Sub
```

The ReportHeader Format event sets mboolFirstLabel back to True. You must include this step in case the user previews and then prints the labels. If the mboolFirstLabel variable is not reset to True, the selected number of labels isn't skipped on the printout because the condition that skips the labels is never met.

Building a Report from a Crosstab Query

Basing a report on the results of a crosstab query is difficult because its number of columns usually varies. Look at the example shown in Figure 11.13. Notice that the employee names appear across the top of the report as column headings, and the products are listed down the side of the report. This report is based on the crosstab query called qxtabEmployeeSales, part of the CHAP11.ACCDB database found on the sample code CD-ROM (see Figure 11.14). The problem is that the number of employees—and, therefore, column headings—can vary. This report is coded to handle such an eventuality.

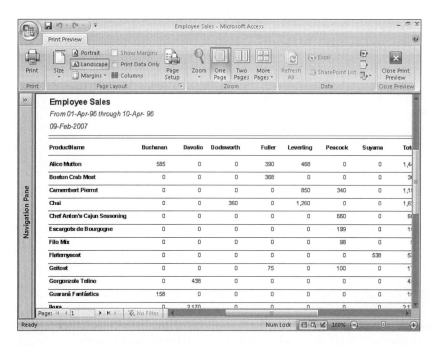

FIGURE 11.13   A report based on a crosstab query.

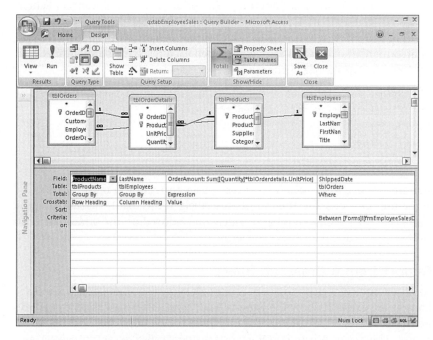

FIGURE 11.14   A crosstab query underlying a report.

When the rptEmployeeSales (located in CHAP11EX.ACCDB) report runs, its Open event executes (see Listing 11.26).

LISTING 11.26   Code That Obtains Criteria Information for the Report and Then Builds a Recordset That Underlies the Report

```
Private Sub Report_Open(Cancel As Integer)

    'frmEmployeeSalesDialogBox form.

    Dim intX As Integer
    Dim db As DAO.Database
    Dim qdf As DAO.QueryDef
    Dim frm As Form

    Set db = CurrentDb

    'Cancel printing if frmEmployeeSalesDialogBox form isn't loaded.
    If Not (IsLoaded("frmEmployeeSalesDialogBox")) Then
        Cancel = True
        MsgBox "To preview or print this report, you must open " _
        & "EmployeeSalesDialogBox in Form view.", vbExclamation, _
        "Must Open Dialog Box"
        Exit Sub
    End If

    Set frm = Forms!frmEmployeeSalesDialogBox

    'Point at the qxtabEmployeeSales query.
    Set qdf = db.QueryDefs("qxtabEmployeeSales")

    'Set parameters for query based on values entered
    'in EmployeeSalesDialogBox form.
    qdf.Parameters("Forms!frmEmployeeSalesDialogBox!txtBeginningDate") _
        = frm!txtBeginningDate
    qdf.Parameters("Forms!frmEmployeeSalesDialogBox!txtEndingDate") _
        = frm!txtEndingDate

    'Open Recordset object.
    Set mrstReport = qdf.OpenRecordset

    'Set a variable to hold number of columns in Crosstab query.
    mintColumnCount = mrstReport.Fields.Count

End Sub
```

The Open event points a database object variable to the current database. It then checks to make sure the criteria form, frmEmployeeSalesDialogBox, is open. This form supplies the criteria for the qxtabEmployeeSales query that underlies the report. It opens the qxtabEmployeeSales query definition and passes it the parameters from the frmEmployeeSalesDialogBox criteria form. Next, it opens a recordset based on the query definition, using the criteria found on the frmEmployeeSalesDialogBox form. The number of columns returned from the crosstab query is very important. The code stores this number in a Private variable called mintColumnCount and uses it throughout the remaining functions to determine how many columns to fill with data.

> **NOTE**
>
> This book focuses on the use of ADO (ActiveX Data Objects) rather than DAO (Data Access Objects). You might wonder why this example uses DAO rather than ADO. The query that underlies this example is a crosstab query. The ADO command object does not recognize crosstab queries. It was therefore necessary to use DAO in this example. If you need more information about DAO, see *Alison Balter's Mastering Access 2003 Desktop Development*.

Next, the Report Header Format event occurs. It moves to the first record in the record-set created during the Open event (see Listing 11.27). It also calls the InitVars routine shown in Listing 11.28.

LISTING 11.27   The Report Header Format Routine

```
Private Sub ReportHeader3_Format(Cancel As Integer, _
FormatCount As Integer)

    'Move to first record in recordset at beginning of report
    'or when report is restarted. (A report is restarted when
    'you print a report from Print Preview window, or when you return
    'to a previous page while previewing.)
    mrstReport.MoveFirst

    'Initialize variables.
    Call InitVars

End Sub
```

The InitVars routine initializes some variables used in the report.

LISTING 11.28   The InitVars Routine

```
Private Sub InitVars()

    Dim intX As Integer
```

LISTING 11.28   Continued

```
    'Initialize lngReportTotal variable.
    mlngReportTotal = 0

    'Initialize array that stores column totals.
    For intX = 1 To conTotalColumns
        mlngRgColumnTotal(intX) = 0
    Next intX

End Sub
```

The `mlngReportTotal` variable is used for the report grand total (all products, all salespeople), and the `mlngRgColumnTotal` array contains the total for each salesperson. After the `Report Header Format` event occurs, the `Page Header Format` event takes place (see Listing 11.29.)

LISTING 11.29   The Code in the `Page Header Format` Event That Inserts the Appropriate Column Headings and Hides the Appropriate Controls

```
Private Sub PageHeader0_Format(Cancel As Integer, FormatCount As Integer)

    Dim intX As Integer

    'Put column headings into text boxes in page header.
    For intX = 1 To mintColumnCount
        Me("Head" + Format$(intX)) = mrstReport(intX - 1).Name
    Next intX

    'Make next available text box Totals heading.
    Me("Head" + Format$(mintColumnCount + 1)) = "Totals"

    'Hide unused text boxes in page header.
    For intX = (mintColumnCount + 2) To conTotalColumns
        Me("Head" + Format$(intX)).Visible = False
    Next intX
End Sub
```

The `PageHeader Format` event uses the names of the fields in the query results as column headings for the report. This essential routine is "smart" because, after it fills in all the column headings, it hides all the extra controls on the report.

Next, the `Detail Section Format` event, shown is Listing 11.30, occurs.

LISTING 11.30   The Code in the `Detail Section Format` Event That Inserts Data from the Current Row into the Report and Hides the Appropriate Controls

```
Private Sub DetailSection1_Format(Cancel As Integer, FormatCount As Integer)
 'Place values in text boxes and hide unused text boxes.

    Dim intX As Integer
    'Verify that not at end of recordset.
    If Not mrstReport.EOF Then
      'If FormatCount is 1, place values from recordset into text boxes
      'in Detail section.
      If Me.FormatCount = 1 Then
          For intX = 1 To mintColumnCount
              'Convert Null values to 0.
              Me("Col" + Format(intX)) = xtabCnulls(mrstReport(intX - 1))
          Next intX

          'Hide unused text boxes in Detail section.
          For intX = mintColumnCount + 2 To conTotalColumns
              Me("Col" + Format(intX)).Visible = False
          Next intX

          'Move to next record in recordset.
          mrstReport.MoveNext
        End If
    End If


End Sub
```

The `Detail Section Format` event checks the recordset's `EOF` property to determine whether the last record in the query has already been read. If not, the section's `FormatCount` property is tested to see whether it's equal to 1. If so, each column in the current record of the recordset is read. The code fills each control in the Detail section with data from a column in the recordset, and any unused text boxes in the report's Detail section are hidden. Finally, the code moves to the next record in the recordset, readying the report to print the next line of detail. The `xtabCnulls` function, which converts `Null` values into zeros, is called each time the recordset underlying the report is read:

```
Private Function xtabCnulls(varX As Variant)

    'Test if a value is null.
    xtabCnulls = Nz(varX,0)


End Function
```

The xtabCnulls function evaluates each value sent to it to check whether the value is Null. If so, it returns zero from the function; otherwise, it returns the value passed to the function.

After the code executes the Detail Section Format event, it executes the Detail Section Print event (shown in Listing 11.31).

LISTING 11.31   The Code in the Detail Section Print Event That Accumulates Column Totals and Prints Row Totals

```
Private Sub Detail1_Print(Cancel As Integer, PrintCount As Integer)

    Dim intX As Integer
    Dim lngRowTotal As Long

    'If PrintCount is 1, initialize rowTotal variable.
    'Add to column totals.
    If Me.PrintCount = 1 Then
        lngRowTotal = 0

        For intX = 2 To mintColumnCount
            'Starting at column 2 (first text box with crosstab value),
            'compute total for current row in Detail section.
            lngRowTotal = lngRowTotal + Me("Col" + Format(intX))
            'Add crosstab value to total for current column.
            mlngRgColumnTotal(intX) = mlngRgColumnTotal(intX) + _
                Me("Col" + Format(intX))
        Next intX

        'Place row total in text box in Detail section.
        Me("Col" + Format(mintColumnCount + 1)) = lngRowTotal
        'Add row total for current row to grand total.
        mlngReportTotal = mlngReportTotal + lngRowTotal
    End If
End Sub
```

The Detail Section Print event generates the row total value, placing it in the last column of the report, accumulating column totals, and accumulating the mlngReportTotal value, which is the grand total for all columns and rows. It does this by making sure the PrintCount of the section is 1. If so, it resets the lngRowTotal variable to 0. Starting at column 2 (column 1 contains the product name), it begins accumulating a row total by looking at each control in the row, adding its value to lngRowTotal. As it traverses each column in the row, it also adds the value in each column to the appropriate element of the mlngRgColumnTotal private array, which maintains all the column totals for the report. It prints the row total and adds the row total to the report's grand total.

When the `Retreat` event occurs, the following code executes:

```
Private Sub Detail1_Retreat()

    'Always back up to previous record when Detail section retreats.
    mrstReport.MovePrevious

End Sub
```

This code forces the record pointer to move back to the previous record in the recordset. Finally, the report footer prints, which causes the `Report Footer Print` event to execute. In turn, this event prints the grand totals and hides the appropriate controls (see Listing 11.32).

LISTING 11.32   The Code in the `Report Footer Print` Event

```
Private Sub ReportFooter4_Print(Cancel As Integer, PrintCount As Integer)

    Dim intX As Integer

    'Place column totals in text boxes in report footer.
    'Start at column 2 (first text box with crosstab value).
    For intX = 2 To mintColumnCount
        Me("Tot" + Format(intX)) = mlngRgColumnTotal(intX)
    Next intX

    'Place grand total in text box in report footer.
    Me("Tot" + Format(mintColumnCount + 1)) = mlngReportTotal

    'Hide unused text boxes in report footer.
    For intX = mintColumnCount + 2 To conTotalColumns
        Me("Tot" + Format(intX)).Visible = False
    Next intX
End Sub
```

The `Report Footer Print` event loops through each control in the footer, populating each control with the appropriate element of the `mlngRgColumnTotal` array. This gives you the column totals for the report. Finally, the grand total is printed in the next available column. Any extra text boxes are hidden from display.

Printing the First and Last Page Entries in the Page Header

Another useful technique is printing the first and last entries from a page in the report's header. The `rptCustomerPhoneList` report, found in the `CHAP11EX.ACCDB` database located on the sample code CD-ROM, illustrates this (see Figure 11.15). The code for this report relies on Access making two passes through the report. During the first pass, a variable called `gboolLastPage` is equal to `False`. The `gboolLastPage` variable becomes `True` only when the `Report Footer Format` event is executed at the end of the first pass through the report. Keep this in mind as you review the code behind the report.

> **NOTE**
>
> To view the desired results, make sure that you click Options and enable code to run; also make sure you view this report in Print Preview mode.

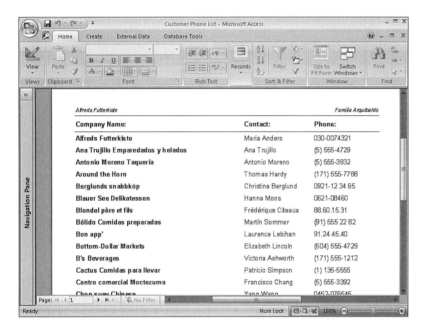

FIGURE 11.15   The first and last entry printed in the report header.

The first routine that affects the report processing is the `Page Header Format` event routine shown in Listing 11.33.

LISTING 11.33   The Code in the `Page Header Format` Event That Updates the Appropriate Text Boxes with the First and Last Entries on the Page

```
Private Sub PageHeader0_Format(Cancel As Integer, FormatCount As Integer)

    'During second pass, fill in FirstEntry and LastEntry text boxes.
    If gboolLastPage = True Then
        Reports!rptCustomerPhoneList.txtFirstEntry = _
            Reports!rptCustomerPhoneList.txtCompanyName
        Reports!rptCustomerPhoneList.txtLastEntry = _
            gstrLast(Reports!rptCustomerPhoneList.Page)
    End If

End Sub
```

The `Page Header Format` routine tests to see whether the `gboolLastPage` variable is equal to `True`. During the first pass through the report, the `gboolLastPage` variable is equal to `False`. During the second pass, the `txtFirstEntry` and `txtLastEntry` text boxes (both of which appear in the report's header) are populated with data. The `txtFirstEntry` text box is filled with the value in the `txtCompanyName` control of the current record (the first record on the page), and the `txtLastEntry` text box is populated with the appropriate element number from the `CustomerPhoneList` array. Each element of the `CustomerPhoneList` array is populated by the `Format` event of the Page Footer for that page during the first pass through the report.

Next, the `Page Footer Format` event, which populates the array with the last entry on a page, is executed (see Listing 11.34).

LISTING 11.34   The Code in the `Page Footer Format` Event

```
Private Sub PageFooter2_Format(Cancel As Integer, FormatCount As Integer)

    'During first pass, increase size of array and enter last record on
    'page into array.
    If Not gboolLastPage Then
        ReDim Preserve gstrLast(Reports!rptCustomerPhoneList.Page + 1)
        gstrLast(Reports!rptCustomerPhoneList.Page) = _
            Reports!rptCustomerPhoneList.txtCompanyName
    End If

End Sub
```

The `Page Footer Format` event determines whether the `gboolLastPage` variable is equal to `False`. If so (which it is during the first pass through the report), the code redimensions the `gstrLast` array to add an element. The value from the `txtCompanyName` control of the last record on the page is stored in the new element of the `gstrLast` array. This value eventually appears in the Page Header of that page as the last company name that appears on the page. Finally, the `Report Footer Format` event executes, as shown in Listing 11.35. This event inserts data from the last row in the recordset into the last element of the array.

LISTING 11.35   The Code in the `Report Footer Format` Event

```
Private Sub ReportFooter4_Format(Cancel As Integer, _
FormatCount As Integer)

    Dim rst As ADODB.Recordset
    Set rst = New ADODB.Recordset

    'Set flag after first pass has been completed.
    gboolLastPage = True
```

LISTING 11.35   Continued

```
'Open recordset for report.
rst.Open "tblCustomers", CurrentProject.Connection, adOpenStatic

'Move to last record in recordset.
rst.MoveLast

'Enter last record into array.
ReDim Preserve gstrLast(Reports!rptCustomerPhoneList.Page + 1)
gstrLast(Reports!rptCustomerPhoneList.Page) = rst!CompanyName
```

End Sub

The `Report Footer` routine sets the `gboolLastPage` variable equal to `True` and opens a recordset based on the `Customers` table. This is the recordset on which the report is based. It moves to the last record in the recordset and adds the `CompanyName` value from the recordset's last record in an additional element of the array.

Now the first pass of the report has finished. As the user moves to each page of the report during a print preview, or as each page is printed to the printer, the `Format` event executes for the Page Header. The company name from the first record on the page is placed in the `txtFirstEntry` control, and the appropriate element from the `gstrLast` array is placed in the `txtLastEntry` control.

Creating a Multifact Crosstab Report

By nature, crosstab queries are limited because they don't allow you to place multiple rows of data in the result. For example, you can't display months as column headings and then show the minimum, average, and maximum sales for each employee as row headings. The `rptSalesAverages` report, found in the `CHAP11EX` database and shown in Figure 11.16, solves this problem.

NOTE

Run this report for the year of 2006 to get results similar to those in the figure.

Each time the `Format` event of the Page Header executes, the variable `mboolPrintWhat` is reset to `False`:

```
Private Sub PageHeader1_Format(Cancel As Integer, FormatCount As Integer)

    'At top of page, initialize mboolPrintWhat variable to False
    mboolPrintWhat = False
```

End Sub

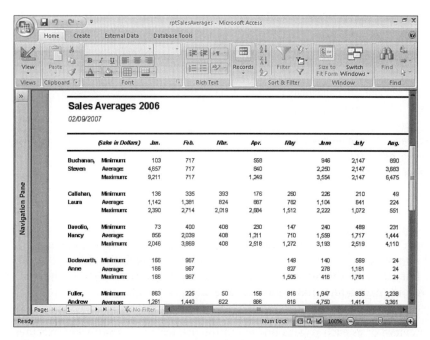

FIGURE 11.16   An example of a multifact crosstab report.

After the `Page Header Format` event executes, the `Group Header Format` event launches, as shown in Listing 11.36.

LISTING 11.36   The Code in the `Group Header Format` Event Used to Hide and Show the Appropriate Controls

```
Private Sub GroupHeader2_Format(Cancel As Integer, _
FormatCount As Integer)


    'Print SalespersonLastName and FirstName text boxes,
    'hide Minimum, Average, and Maximum labels,
    'set mboolPrintWhat variable to True, and don't advance to next record.
    With Me
        If mboolPrintWhat = False Then
            .txtSalespersonLastName.Visible = True
            .txtFirstName.Visible = True
            .lblMinimum.Visible = False
            .lblAverage.Visible = False
            .lblMaximum.Visible = False
            mboolPrintWhat = True
            .NextRecord = False


        'Hide SalespersonLastName and FirstName text boxes,
```

LISTING 11.36   Continued

```
        'print Minimum, Average, and Maximum labels,
        'and set mboolPrintWhat variable to False
        Else
            .txtSalespersonLastName.Visible = False
            .txtFirstName.Visible = False
            .lblMinimum.Visible = True
            .lblAverage.Visible = True
            .lblMaximum.Visible = True
            mboolPrintWhat = False
        End If
    End With
End Sub
```

The first time the `Format` event for the `LastName` Group Header (`GroupHeader2`) executes, the value of the `mboolPrintWhat` variable is equal to `False`. The `txtSalesPersonLastName` and the `txtFirstName` controls are made visible, and the `lblMinimum`, `lblAverage`, and `lblMaximum` controls are hidden. The `mboolPrintWhat` variable is set to `True`, and movement to the next record is suppressed by setting the value of the `NextRecord` property to `False`.

The second time the `Format` event for the `LastName` Group Header executes, the code hides the `txtSalespersonLastName` and `txtFirstName` controls. The code makes the `lblMinimum`, `lblAverage`, and `lblMaximum` controls visible and sets the value of the `mboolPrintWhat` variable to `False`.

The only other code for the report, shown in Listing 11.37, is in the `Format` event of the Shipped Date Header (`GroupHeader3`).

LISTING 11.37   The Code in the Group Header Format Event Used to Determine When Printing Occurs

```
Private Sub GroupHeader3_Format(Cancel As Integer, _
FormatCount As Integer)
    'Print data in correct column.

    'Don't advance to next record or print next section.
    If Me.Left < Me.txtLeftMargin + _
        (Month(Me.txtShippedDate) + 1) _
        * Me.txtColumnWidth Then
        Me.NextRecord = False
        Me.PrintSection = False
    End If
End Sub
```

This code compares the report's Left property to the result of an expression. The Left property is the amount that the current section is offset from the page's left edge. This number is compared to the value in the txtLeftMargin control added to the current month plus one, and then it's multiplied by the value in the txtColumnWidth control. If this expression evaluates to True, the code sets the NextRecord and PrintSection properties of the report to False. This causes the printer to move to the next printing position but to remain on the same record and not print anything, which forces a blank space in the report. You might wonder what the complicated expression is all about. Simply put, it's an algorithm that makes sure printing occurs and that Access moves to the next record only when the data is ready to print.

Practical Examples: Practicing What You Learned

I use the techniques covered in this section in many of the applications that I distribute to my users. The report that you'll build here could be included in the hypothetical time and billing application. It covers generic techniques that you can use in any application that you build.

One report not covered in the chapter is the rptEmployeeBillingsByProject report. This report has the following code in its NoData event:

```
Private Sub Report_NoData(Cancel As Integer)
    'If there is no data in the RecordSource underlying the report,
    'display a message and cancel printing
    MsgBox "There is no data for this report. Canceling report..."
    Cancel = True
End Sub
```

If there's no data in the report's RecordSource, a message box is displayed, and the report is canceled. The Open event of the report looks like this:

```
Private Sub Report_Open(Cancel As Integer)
    'Open the criteria form
    DoCmd.OpenForm "frmReportDateRange", _
        WindowMode:=acDialog, _
        OpenArgs:="Employee Billings by Project"

    'If the criteria form is not loaded, cancel printing
    If Not IsLoaded("frmReportDateRange") Then
        Cancel = True
    End If
End Sub
```

The report's Open event opens a form called frmReportDateRange (see Figure 11.17). This form is required because it supplies criteria to the query underlying the report. If the form isn't loaded successfully, the report is canceled.

FIGURE 11.17   A criteria selection form.

NOTE

You must open this form by running the rptEmployeeBillingsbyProject report. The report will open the form and then will apply the designated criteria. Also, don't forget to click Options and enable code to run.

Finally, the report's Close event looks like this:

```
Private Sub Report_Close()
    'Close the criteria form when the report closes
    DoCmd.Close acForm, "frmReportDateRange"
End Sub
```

The report cleans up after itself by closing the criteria form.

Summary

To take full advantage of what the Access reporting tool has to offer, you must understand—and be able to work with—report and section events. This chapter described the report and section events, giving you detailed examples of when to use each event.

In addition to the report events, several special properties are available to you only at runtime. By manipulating these properties, you can have more control over your reports' behavior. After covering the report and section events, this chapter covered the properties you can manipulate only at runtime. Examples highlighted the appropriate use of each property.

There are many tips and tricks of the trade that help you do things you might otherwise think are impossible to accomplish. This chapter gave you several practical examples of these tips and tricks, making it easy for you to use them in your own application development.

CHAPTER 12

Advanced Query Techniques

Why This Chapter Is Important

You learned the basics of query design in Chapter 4, "What Every Developer Needs to Know About Query Basics," but Access has a wealth of query capabilities. In addition to the relatively simple Select queries covered in Chapter 4, you can create crosstab queries, union queries, self-join queries, and many other complex selection queries. You can also easily build Access queries that modify information, rather than retrieve it. This chapter covers these topics and the more advanced aspects of query design.

Using Action Queries

With action queries, you can easily modify data without writing code. In fact, using action queries is often a more efficient method than using code. Four types of action queries are available: update, delete, append, and make table. You use update queries to modify data in a table, delete queries to remove records from a table, append queries to add records to an existing table, and make table queries to create an entirely new table. Each type of query and its appropriate uses are explained in the following sections.

Update Queries

You use update queries to modify all records or any records meeting specific criteria. You can use an update query to modify the data in one field or several fields (or even tables) at one time (for example, a query that increases the salary of everyone in California by 10%). As mentioned,

using update queries is usually more efficient than performing the same task with Visual
Basic for Applications (VBA) code, so update queries are considered a respectable way to
modify table data.

To build an update query, follow these steps:

1. Click the Query Design tool in the Other group on the Create tab. The Show Table
   dialog box appears.

2. In the Show Table dialog box, select the tables or queries that will participate in the
   update query and click Add. Click Close when you're ready to continue.

3. Click Update in the Query Type group on the Design tab.

4. Add fields to the query that will either be used for criteria or be updated as a result
   of the query. In Figure 12.1, StateProvince has been added to the query grid
   because it will be used as a criterion for the update. DefaultRate has been included
   because it's the field that's being updated.

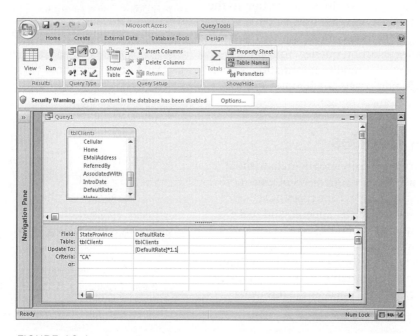

FIGURE 12.1   An update query that increases the DefaultRate for all clients in California.

5. Add any further criteria, if you want. In Figure 12.1, the criterion for StateProvince
   has been set to CA.

6. Add the appropriate Update expression. In Figure 12.1, the DefaultRate is being
   increased by 10%.

7. Click Run on the ribbon. The message box shown in Figure 12.2 appears. Click Yes
   to continue. The Access Database Engine updates all records meeting the selected
   criteria.

FIGURE 12.2   The confirmation message you see when running an update query.

You should name Access update queries with the prefix qupd. To adhere to standard naming conventions, you should give each type of action query a prefix indicating what type of query it is. Table 12.1 lists all the proper prefixes for action queries.

TABLE 12.1   Naming Prefixes for Action Queries

Type of Query	Prefix	Example
Update	qupd	qupdDefaultRate
Delete	qdel	qdelOldTimeCards
Append	qapp	qappArchiveTimeCards
Make Table	qmak	qmakTempSales

NOTE

Access displays each type of action query in the Database window with a distinctive icon.

All Access queries are stored as Structured Query Language (SQL) statements. (Access SQL is discussed later in this chapter in the "Understanding SQL" section.) You can display the SQL for a query by selecting SQL view from the View drop-down on the Design tab. The SQL behind an Access update query looks like this:

```
UPDATE tblClients SET tblClients.
    DefaultRate = [DefaultRate]*1.1
        WHERE (((tblClients.StateProvince)="CA"));
```

CAUTION

The actions taken by an update query, as well as by all action queries, can't be reversed. You must exercise extreme caution when running any action query.

CAUTION

Remember that if you have turned on the Cascade Update Related Fields Referential Integrity setting and the update query modifies a primary key field, the Access Database Engine updates the foreign key of all corresponding records in related tables. If you have not turned on the Cascade Update Related Fields option and refer-ential integrity is being enforced, the update query doesn't allow the offending records to be modified.

Delete Queries

Rather than simply modify table data, delete queries permanently remove from a table any records meeting specific criteria; they're often used to remove old records. You might want to delete all orders from the previous year, for example.

To build a delete query, follow these steps:

1. While in a query's Design view, select Delete from the Query Type group on the Design tab.

2. Add the criteria you want to the query grid. The query shown in Figure 12.3 deletes all time cards more than 365 days old.

3. Click Run on the ribbon. The message box shown in Figure 12.4 appears.

4. Click Yes to permanently remove the records from the table.

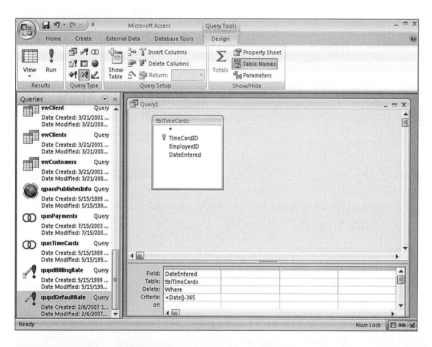

FIGURE 12.3   A delete query used to delete all time cards entered more than a year ago.

FIGURE 12.4   The delete query confirmation message box.

The SQL behind a delete query looks like this:

```
DELETE tblTimeCards.DateEntered
    FROM tblTimeCards
    WHERE (((tblTimeCards.DateEntered)<Date()-365));
```

NOTE

Viewing the results of an action query is often useful before you actually change the records included in the criteria. To view the records affected by the action query, click the Datasheet View button on the ribbon before you select Run. All records that will be affected by the action query appear in Datasheet view. If necessary, you can temporarily add key fields to the query to get more information about these records.

CAUTION

Remember that if you have turned on the Cascade Delete Related Records Referential Integrity setting, the Access Database Engine deletes all corresponding records in related tables. If you have not turned on the Cascade Delete Related Records option and you are enforcing referential integrity, the delete query doesn't allow the offending records to be deleted. If you want to delete the records on the one side of the relationship, you must first delete all the related records on the many side.

Append Queries

With append queries, you can add records to an existing table. This is often done during an archive process. First, you append the records to be archived to the history table by using an append query. Next, you remove them from the master table by using a delete query.

To build an append query, follow these steps:

1. While in Design view of a query, select Append from the Query Type group on the Design tab. The dialog box shown in Figure 12.5 appears.

FIGURE 12.5   Identifying the table to which data will be appended and the database containing that table.

2. Select the table to which you want the data appended.

3. Drag all the fields whose data you want included in the second table to the query grid. If the field names in the two tables match, Access automatically matches the field names in the source table to the corresponding field names in the destination table (see Figure 12.6). If the field names in the two tables don't match, you need to explicitly designate which fields in the source table match which fields in the destination table.

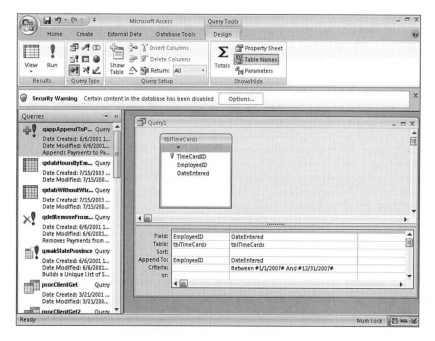

FIGURE 12.6 An append query that appends the EmployeeID and DateEntered of all employees entered in the year 2007 to another table.

4. Enter any criteria in the query grid. Notice in Figure 12.6 that all records with a DateEntered in 2007 are appended to the destination table.

5. To run the query, click Run on the ribbon. The message box shown in Figure 12.7 appears.

6. Click Yes to finish the process.

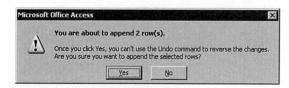

FIGURE 12.7 The append query confirmation message box.

The SQL behind an append query looks like this:

```
INSERT INTO tblTimeCardsArchive ( TimeCardID, EmployeeID, DateEntered )
    SELECT tblTimeCards.TimeCardID, tblTimeCards.EmployeeID,
    tblTimeCards.DateEntered
    FROM tblTimeCards
    WHERE (((tblTimeCards.DateEntered) Between #1/1/2007# And #12/31/2007#));
```

Append queries don't allow you to introduce any primary key violations. If you're appending any records that duplicate a primary key value, the message box shown in Figure 12.8 appears. If you go ahead with the append process, only those records without primary key violations are appended to the destination table.

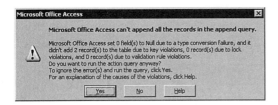

FIGURE 12.8   The warning message you see when an append query and conversion, primary key, lock, or validation rule violation occurs.

Make Table Queries

An append query adds records to an existing table, but a make table query creates a new table, which is often a temporary table used for intermediary processing. You will often create a temporary table to freeze data while a user runs a report. By building temporary tables and running the report from those tables, you make sure users can't modify the data underlying the report during the reporting process. Another common use of a make table query is to supply a subset of fields or records to a user.

To build a make table query, follow these steps:

1. While in the query's Design view, select Make Table from the Query Type group on the Design tab. The dialog box shown in Figure 12.9 appears.

FIGURE 12.9   Enter a name for the new table and select which database to place it in.

2. Enter the name of the new table and click OK.

3. Move all the fields you want included in the new table to the query grid. The result of an expression is often included in the new table (see Figure 12.10).

4. Add the criteria you want to the query grid.

5. Click Run on the ribbon to run the query. The message shown in Figure 12.11 appears.

6. Click Yes to finish the process.

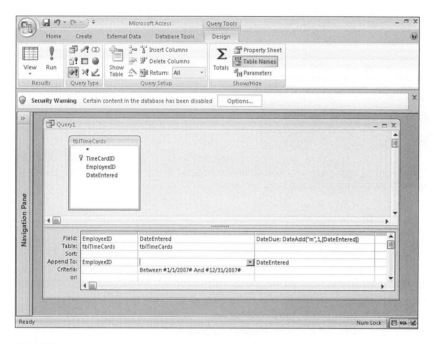

FIGURE 12.10   Add an expression to a make table query.

FIGURE 12.11   The make table query confirmation message box.

If you try to run the same make table query more than one time, the table with the same name as the table you're creating is permanently deleted (see the warning message in Figure 12.12).

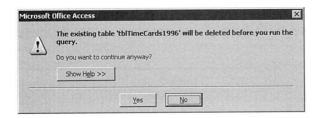

FIGURE 12.12   The make table query warning message displayed when a table already exists with the same name as the table to be created.

The SQL for a make table query looks like this:

```
SELECT tblTimeCards.TimeCardID, tblTimeCards.EmployeeID,
    tblTimeCards.DateEntered
    INTO tblOldTimeCards
    FROM tblTimeCards
    WHERE (((tblTimeCards.DateEntered) Between #1/1/2007# And #12/31/2007#));
```

Using Action Queries Versus Processing Records with Code

As mentioned previously, action queries can be far more efficient than VBA code. Look at this example:

```
Sub ModifyRate()
    Dim rst As ADODB.Recordset

    Set rst = New ADODB.Recordset

    With rst
        .CursorType = adOpenKeyset
        .LockType = adLockOptimistic
        .Open "tblEmployees", CurrentProject.Connection

        Do Until .EOF
            !BillingRate = !BillingRate + 1
            .Update
            .MoveNext
        Loop
    End With
End Sub
```

This subroutine uses ActiveX Data Objects (ADO) code to loop through tblEmployees. It increases the billing rate by 1. Compare the ModifyRate subroutine to the following code:

```
Sub RunActionQuery()
    DoCmd.OpenQuery "qupdBillingRate"
End Sub
```

As you can see, the RunActionQuery subroutine is much easier to code. The qupdBillingRate query, shown in Figure 12.13, performs the same tasks as the ModifyRate subroutine. In most cases, the action query runs more efficiently.

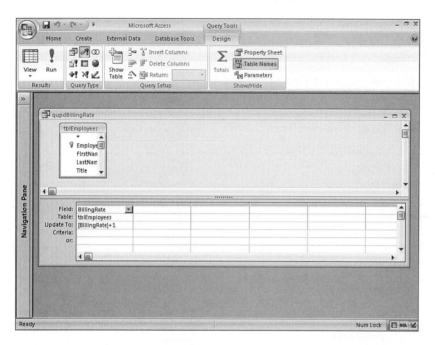

FIGURE 12.13   The qupdBillingRate query increments the BillingRate by 1.

NOTE

An alternative to the two techniques shown previously is to use ADO code (rather than the DoCmd object) to execute an action query. This technique is covered in detail in Chapter 15, "What Are ActiveX Data Objects, and Why Are They Important?"

Viewing Special Query Properties

Access 2007 queries have several properties that can dramatically change their behavior. To look up a query's properties, right-click on a blank area in the top half of the Query window and select Properties to open the Property Sheet (see Figure 12.14). Chapter 4 discusses many of these properties. The following sections cover the Unique Values, Unique Records, and Top Values properties.

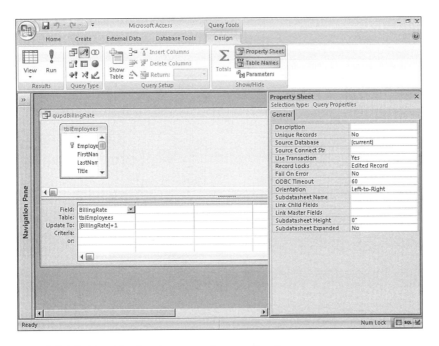

FIGURE 12.14   Viewing the general properties for a query.

Unique Values **Property**

When set to Yes, the Unique Values property causes the query output to contain no duplicates for the combination of fields you include in it. Figure 12.15, for example, shows a query that includes the Country and City fields from tblClients. The Unique Values property in this example is set to No, its default value. Notice that many combinations of countries and cities appear more than once. This happens whenever more than one client is found in a particular country and city. Compare this with Figure 12.16, in which the Unique Values property is set to Yes. Each combination of country and city appears only once.

Unique Records **Property**

In Access 2000 and later, the default value for the Unique Records property is No. Setting it to Yes causes the DISTINCTROW statement to be included in the SQL statement underlying the query. When set to Yes, the Unique Records property denotes that the Access Database Engine includes only unique rows in the recordset underlying the query in the query result—and not just unique rows based on the fields in the query result. The Unique Records property applies only to multitable queries; the Access Database Engine ignores it for queries that include only one table.

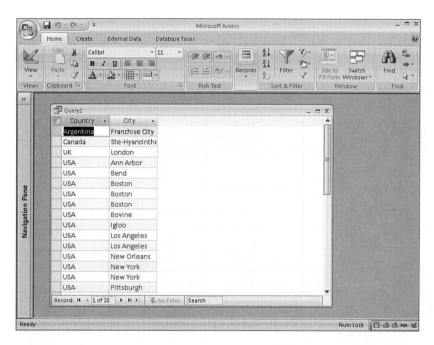

FIGURE 12.15   A query with the Unique Values property set to No.

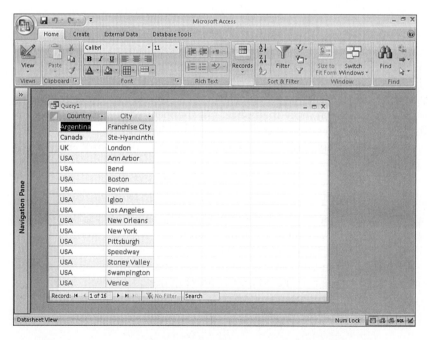

FIGURE 12.16   A query with the Unique Values property set to Yes.

Top Values **Property**

The Top Values property enables you to specify a certain percentage or a specific number of records that the user wants to view in the query result. For example, you can build a query that outputs the country/city combinations with the top 10 sales amounts. You can also build a query that shows the country/city combinations whose sales rank in the top 50%. You can specify the Top Values property in a few different ways. Here are two examples:

▶ Click the Top Values combo box on the ribbon and choose from the predefined list of choices (this combo box is not available for certain field types).

▶ Type a number or a number with a percent sign directly into the Top Values property in the Query Properties window, or select one of the predefined entries from the drop-down list for the property.

Figure 12.17 illustrates the design of a query showing the companies with the top 25% of sales. This Total query summarizes the result of the BillableHours multiplied by the BillingRate for each company. Notice that the Top Values property is set to 25%. The output of the query is sorted in descending order by the result of the BillableAmount calculation (see Figure 12.18). If the SaleAmount field were sorted in ascending order, the bottom 10% of the sales amount would be displayed in the query result. Remember that the field(s) you want to use to determine the top values must appear as the left-most field(s) in the query's sort order.

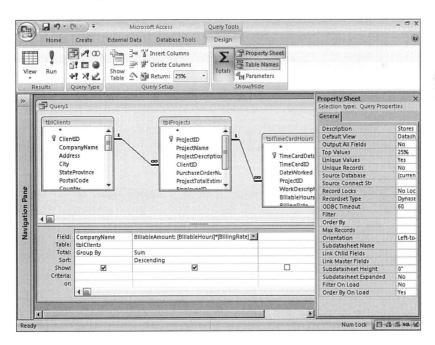

FIGURE 12.17   A Total query that retrieves the top 25% of the billable amounts.

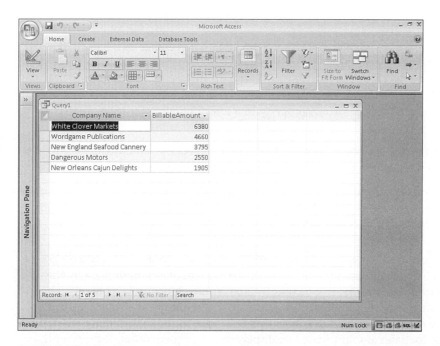

FIGURE 12.18   The result of a Total query showing the top 25% of the billable amounts.

NOTE

You might be surprised to discover that the Top Values property doesn't always seem to accurately display the correct number of records in the query result. The Access Database Engine returns all records with values that match the value in the last record as part of the query result. In a table with 100 records, for example, the query asks for the top 10 values. Twelve records will appear in the query result if the 10th, 11th, and 12th records all have the same value in the field being used to determine the top value.

Optimizing Queries

The Access Database Engine includes an Optimizer that looks at how long it takes to perform each task needed to produce the required query results. It then produces a plan for the shortest path to get the results that you want. This plan is based on several statistics:

- ▶ The amount of data in each table included in the query

- ▶ How many data pages are in each table

- ▶ The location of each table included in the query

- ▶ What indexes are available in each table

- ▶ Which indexes are unique

Understanding the Query Compilation Process

The statistics just listed are updated whenever the query is compiled. For a query to be compiled, it must be flagged as needing to be compiled. The flag can be any of the following occurrences:

- ▶ Changes are saved to the query.
- ▶ Changes are saved to any tables underlying a query.
- ▶ The database is compacted.

After the Access Database Engine flags a query as needing to be compiled, it isn't compiled until the next time the query is run. During compiling, which takes 1–4 seconds, all statistics are updated, and a new optimization or Query Plan is produced.

> **NOTE**
>
> Because a Query Plan is based on the number of records in each table included in the query, you should open and save your queries each time the volume of data in a table changes significantly. This is especially true when you're moving your query from a test environment to a production environment. If you test your application with a few records in each table and the table's production data soon grows to thousands of records, your query will be optimized for only a few records and won't run efficiently. I handle this problem by compacting the production database on a regular basis.

Analyzing a Query's Performance

When you're analyzing the time it takes for a particular query to run, it's important to time two tasks:

- ▶ How long it takes for the first screen of data to display
- ▶ How long it takes to get the last record in the query result

The first measurement is fairly obvious; it measures the amount of time it takes from the moment the Run button is clicked on the ribbon until the first screen of data is displayed. The second measurement is a little less obvious; it involves waiting until the N value in Record 1 of N displays at the bottom of the query result. The two measurements might be the same, if the query returns only a small number of records. The Access Database Engine decides whether it's more efficient to run the query and then display the query results, or to display partial query results while the query continues to run in the background.

> **TIP**
>
> The Performance Analyzer can analyze your queries to determine whether additional indexes will improve query performance. It's important to run the Performance Analyzer with the same volume of data that will be present in the production version of your

tables. The Performance Analyzer is covered in Chapter 18, "Optimizing Your Application."

Steps You Can Take to Improve a Query's Performance

You can take many steps to improve a query's performance. They include, but aren't limited to, the following techniques:

- Index fields on both sides of a join. If you establish a permanent relationship between two tables, the foreign key index is automatically created for you.

- Add to the query grid only the fields you actually need in the query results. If a field is required for criteria, but it doesn't need to appear in the query result, clear the Show check box on the query grid.

- Add indexes for any fields that you are using in the sort order of the query result.

- Always index on fields used in the criteria of the query.

- Compact the database often. During compacting, Access tries to reorganize a table's records so that they reside in adjacent database pages, ordered by the table's primary key. The Access Database Engine rebuilds the query plans, based on the current amount of data. These side effects of the compacting process improve performance when the Access Database Engine is scanning the table during a query.

- When running a multitable query, test to see whether the query runs faster with the criteria placed on the "one" side or the "many" side of the join.

- Avoid adding criteria to calculated or nonindexed fields.

- Select the smallest field types possible for each field. For example, create a Long Integer CustID field instead of specifying the CompanyName field as the primary key for the table.

- Avoid calculated fields in nested queries. It's always preferable to add calculations to the higher-level queries.

- Instead of including all expressions in the query, consider placing some expressions in the control source of form and report controls. If you do this, the expression will need to be repeated and maintained on each form and report.

- Use make table queries to build tables out of query results based on tables that rarely change. In a State table, for example, instead of displaying a unique list of states based on all the states currently included in the Customer table, build a separate State table and use that in your queries.

- When using Like in the query criteria, try to place the asterisk at the end of the character string rather than at the beginning. When you place the asterisk at the end of a string, as in Like Th*, an index can be used to improve query performance. If you place the asterisk at the beginning of a string, as in Like *Sr, the Access Database Engine cannot use any indexes.

▶ Use Count(*) rather than Count([*fieldname*]) when counting how many records meet a particular set of criteria. Count(*) simply tallies up the total number of records, but Count([*fieldname*]) actually checks to see whether the value is Null, which would exclude the record from the total computation. Furthermore, as mentioned in the next section on Rushmore technology, the Count(*) function is highly optimized by Rushmore.

▶ Use Group By as little as possible. When possible, use First instead. For example, if you're totaling sales information by order date and order number, you can use First for the order date and group by order number. The reason is that all records for a given order number automatically occur on the same order date.

▶ Use Rushmore technology to speed query performance whenever possible. Rushmore technology—a data-access technology "borrowed" from Microsoft's FoxPro PC database engine—improves the performance of certain queries. The following section discusses Rushmore technology.

One of the most important lessons to learn about the tips listed here is that you shouldn't follow them blindly. Query optimization is an art, not a science. What helps in some situations might actually do harm in others, so it's important to perform benchmarks with your actual system and data.

Rushmore Technology

Rushmore is a data-access technology that can help improve processing queries. You can use Rushmore technology only when you include certain types of expressions in the query criteria. It won't automatically speed up all your queries. You must construct a query in a certain way for the query to benefit from Rushmore.

Rushmore can optimize a query with an expression and a comparison operator as the criteria for an Indexed field. The comparison operator must be <, >, =, <=, >=, <>, Between, Like, or In.

The expression can be any valid expression, including constants, functions, and fields from other tables. Here are some examples of expressions that Rushmore can optimize:

```
[Age] > 50
[OrderDate] Between #1/1/2007# And #12/31/2007#
[State] = "CA"
```

Rushmore can also optimize queries that include complex expressions combining the And and Or operators. If Rushmore can optimize both expressions, the query will be fully optimized. However, if Rushmore can optimize only one expression and you combine the expressions with an And, the query will be partially optimized. If Rushmore can fully optimize only one expression and you combine the expressions with an Or, the query won't be optimized.

Important Notes About Rushmore

You should remember a few important concepts about Rushmore:

▶ Queries containing the Not operator can't be optimized.

▶ The Count(*) function is highly optimized by Rushmore.

▶ Descending indexes cannot be used by Rushmore unless the expression is =.

▶ Queries on Open Database Connectivity (ODBC) data sources can't use Rushmore.

▶ Rushmore can use multi-field indexes only when the criteria are in the order of the index. For example, if an index exists for the LastName field in combination with the FirstName field, the index can be used to search on LastName or on a combination of LastName and FirstName, but it can't be used in an expression based on the FirstName field.

Using Crosstab Queries

A crosstab query summarizes query results by displaying one field in a table down the left side of the datasheet and additional facts across the top of the datasheet. A crosstab query can, for example, summarize the dollars sold by a salesperson to each company. You can place the name of each company in the query output's left-most column, and you can display each salesperson across the top. The dollars sold appear in the appropriate cell of the query output (see Figure 12.19).

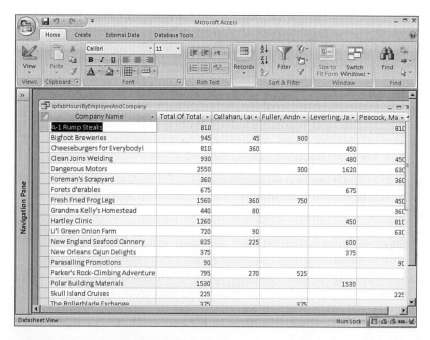

FIGURE 12.19   An example of a crosstab query that shows the dollars sold to each company by salesperson.

`Crosstab` queries are probably one of the most complex and difficult queries to create. For this reason, Microsoft offers a Crosstab Query Wizard. The following sections explain the methods for creating a `crosstab` query with and without the Crosstab Query Wizard.

Creating a Crosstab Query with the Crosstab Query Wizard

Follow these steps to design a `crosstab` query with the Crosstab Query Wizard:

1. Select Query Wizard from the Other group on the Create tab.

2. Select Crosstab Query Wizard and click OK.

3. Select the table or query that will act as a foundation for the query (see Figure 12-20). If you want to include fields from more than one table in the query, you'll need to base the `crosstab` query on another query that has the tables and fields you want. Click Next.

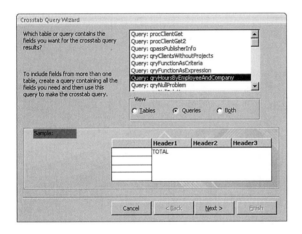

FIGURE 12.20   The first step of the wizard asks you to select a table or query on which you want to base the crosstab query.

4. Select the fields whose values you want to use as the row headings for the query output. In Figure 12.21, the `CompanyName` field is selected as the row heading. Click Next.

5. Select the field whose values you want to use as the column headings for the query output. In Figure 12.22, the `Employee` field is selected as the column heading. Click Next.

6. The Crosstab Query Wizard asks you to specify what field stores the number you want to use to calculate the value for each column and row intersection. In Figure 12.23, the `Total` field is totaled for each company and employee. Click Next.

7. Specify a name for your query. When you're done, click Finish.

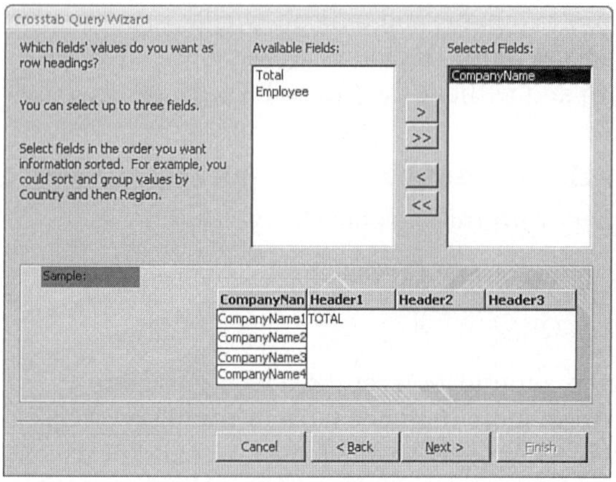

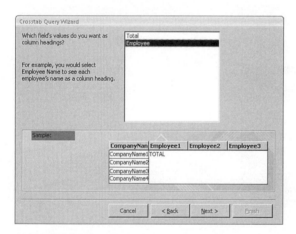

FIGURE 12.21   Specifying the rows of a crosstab query.

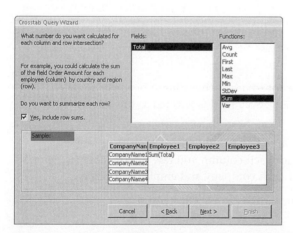

FIGURE 12.22   Specifying the columns of a crosstab query.

FIGURE 12.23   Specifying the field you want the crosstab query to use for calculating.

Figure 12.24 shows a completed crosstab query in Design view; take a look at several important attributes. Notice the Crosstab row of the query grid. The CompanyName field is specified as the row heading and is used as Group By columns for the query. The Employee field is included as a column heading; it is also used as a Group By for the query.

The Total is specified as a value. The Total cell for the column indicates that this field will be summed (as opposed to being counted, averaged, and so on).

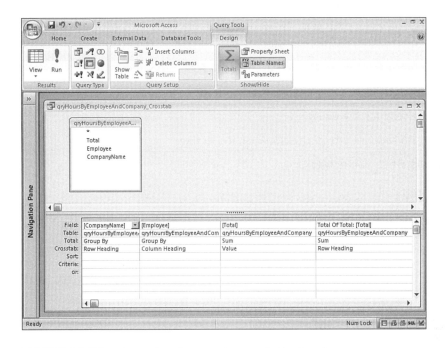

FIGURE 12.24   A completed crosstab query in Design view.

Notice the column labeled Total of Total. This column displays the total of all the columns in the query. It's identical to the column containing the value except for the alias in the field name and the fact that the Crosstab cell is set to Row Heading rather than Value.

Creating a Crosstab Query Without the Crosstab Query Wizard

Although you can create many of your crosstab queries by using the Crosstab Query Wizard, you should know how to build one without the wizard. This knowledge lets you modify existing crosstab queries and gain ultimate control over creating new queries.

To build a crosstab query without using the Crosstab Query Wizard, follow these steps:

1. Click Query Design in the Other group on the Create tab.

2. Select the table or query that will be included in the query grid. Click Add to add the table or query. Click Close.

3. Select Crosstab from the Query Type group on the Design tab.

4. Add to the query grid the fields you want to include in the query output.

5. Click the Crosstab row of each field you want to include as a row heading. Select Row Heading from the drop-down list.

6. Click the Crosstab row of the field you want to include as a column heading. Select Column Heading from the drop-down list.

7. Click the Crosstab row of the field whose values you want to cross-tabulate. Select Value from the Crosstab drop-down list.

8. Select the appropriate aggregate function from the Total drop-down list.

9. Add any date intervals or other expressions you want to include.

10. Specify any criteria for the query.

11. Change the sort order of any of the columns, if you like.

12. Run the query when you're ready.

Figure 12.25 shows a query in which the column heading is set to the month of the ProjectBeginDate field; the row heading is set to the EmployeeName field. The sum of the ProjectTotalEstimate field is the value for the query. The ProjectBeginDate is also included in the query grid as a WHERE clause for the query. Figure 12.26 shows the results of running the query.

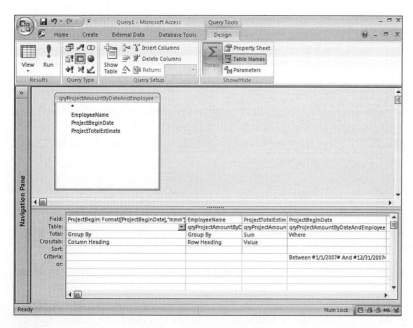

FIGURE 12.25   A crosstab query, designed without a wizard, showing the project total estimate by employee and month.

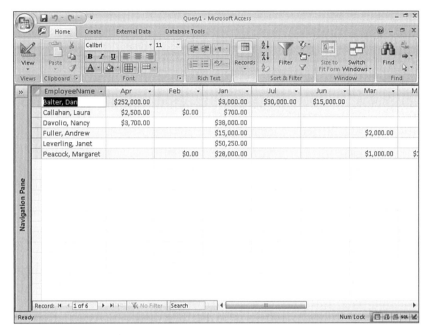

FIGURE 12.26   The result of running the crosstab query shown in Figure 12.25.

Creating Fixed Column Headings

If you don't use fixed column headings, all the columns are included in the query output in alphabetical order. For example, if you include month names in the query result, they appear as Apr, Aug, Dec, Feb, and so on. By using fixed column headings, you tell Access the order in which each column appears in the query result. You can specify column headings by setting the query's Column Headings property (see Figure 12.27).

> **NOTE**
>
> All fixed column headings must match the underlying data exactly; otherwise, information will be omitted inadvertently from the query result. For example, if the column heading for the month of June was accidentally entered as June and the data output by the format statement included data for the month of Jun, all June data would be omitted from the query output.

Important Notes About Crosstab Queries

Regardless of how crosstab queries are created, you should be aware of some special caveats when working with them:

▶ You can select only one value and one column heading for a crosstab query, but you can select multiple row headings.

▶ The results of a crosstab query can't be updated.

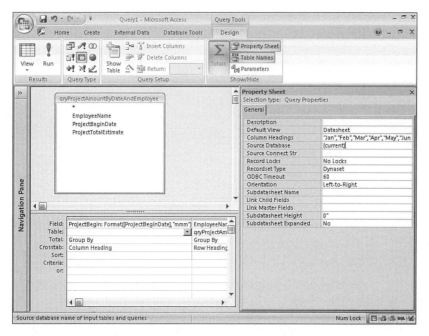

FIGURE 12.27   A query's Column Headings property.

▶ You can't define criteria on the Value field. If you do, you get the error message You can't specify criteria on the same field for which you enter a Value in the Crosstab row. If you must specify criteria for the Value field, you must first build another query that includes your selection criteria and base the crosstab query on the first query.

▶ All parameters used in a crosstab query must be explicitly declared in the Query Parameters dialog box.

TIP

Pivot tables, introduced with Access 2002, have all the functionality of crosstab queries and then some! Consider replacing crosstab queries with Select queries stored in PivotTable view.

Establishing Outer Joins

You use outer joins when you want the records on the one side of a one-to-many relationship to be included in the query result, regardless of whether there are matching records in the table on the many side. With a Customers table and an Orders table, for example, users often want to include only customers with orders in the query output. An inner join (the default join type) does this. In other situations, users want all customers to be included in the query result, whether or not they have orders. This is when an outer join is necessary.

> **NOTE**
>
> In Access, there are two types of outer joins: left outer joins and right outer joins. A *left outer join* occurs when all records on the "one" side of a one-to-many relationship are included in the query result, regardless of whether any records exist on the "many" side. A *right outer join* means all records on the "many" side of a one-to-many relationship are included in the query result, regardless of whether there are any records on the "one" side. A right outer join should never occur if you are enforcing referential integrity.

To establish an outer join, you must modify the join between the tables included in the query:

1. Double-click the line joining the tables in the query grid.

2. The Join Properties window appears (see Figure 12.28). Select the type of join you want to create. To create a left outer join between the tables, select Option 2 (Option 3 if you want to create a right outer join). Notice in Figure 12.28 that the description is Include ALL Records from `tblClients` and Only Those Records from `tblProjects` Where the Joined Fields Are Equal.

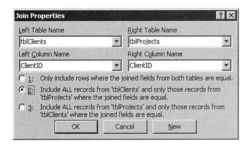

FIGURE 12.28   Establishing a left outer join.

3. Click OK to accept the join. An outer join should be established between the tables. Notice that the line joining the two tables now has an arrow pointing to the many side of the join.

The SQL statement produced when a left outer join is established looks like this:

```
SELECT DISTINCTROW tblClients.ClientID, tblClients.CompanyName
FROM tblClients
LEFT JOIN tblProjects ON tblClients.ClientID = tblProjects.ClientID;
```

A left outer join can also be used to identify all the records on the "one" side of a join that don't have corresponding records on the "many" side. To do this, simply enter Is Null as the criterion for any required field on the "many" side of the join. A common solution is to place the criterion on the foreign key field. In the query shown in Figure 12.29, only clients without projects are displayed in the query result.

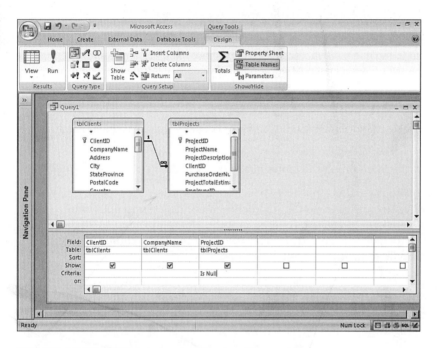

FIGURE 12.29   A query showing clients without projects.

Establishing Self-Joins

A self-join enables you to join a table to itself. This is often done so that information in a single table can appear to exist in two separate tables. A classic example is seen with employees and supervisors. Two fields are included in the Employees table: One field includes the EmployeeID of the employee being described in the record, and the other field specifies the EmployeeID of the employee's supervisor. If you want to see a list of employee names and the names of their supervisors, you'll need to use a self-join.

To build a self-join query, follow these steps:

1. Click the Query Design button in the Other group on the Create tab.

2. From the Show Tables dialog box, add the table to be used in the self-join to the query grid two times. Click Close. Notice that the second instance of the table appears with an underscore and the number 1.

3. To change the alias of the second table, right-click on top of the table in the query grid and select Properties. Change the Alias property as desired. In Figure 12.30, the alias has been changed to Supervisors.

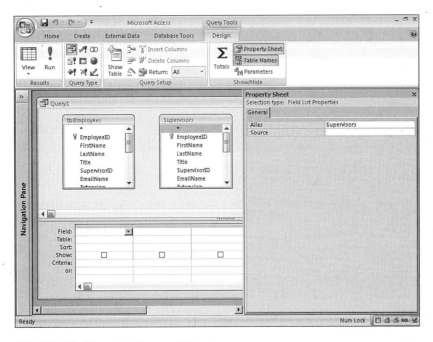

FIGURE 12.30   Building a self-join.

4. To establish a join between the table and its alias, click and drag from the field in one table that corresponds to the field in the aliased table. In Figure 12.31, the SupervisorID field of the tblEmployees table has been joined with the EmployeeID field from the aliased table.

5. Drag the appropriate fields to the query grid. In Figure 12.31, the FirstName and LastName fields are included from the tblEmployees table. The SupervisorName expression (a concatenation of the supervisor's first and last names) is supplied from the copy of the table with the Supervisors alias.

TIP

You can permanently define self-relationships in the Relationships window. You will often do this so that you can establish referential integrity between two fields in the same table. In the example of employees and supervisors, you can establish a perma-nent relationship with referential integrity to make sure supervisor ID numbers aren't entered with employee ID numbers that don't exist.

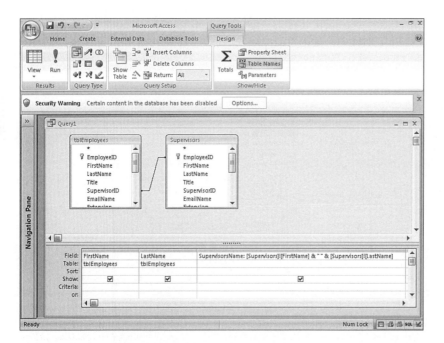

FIGURE 12.31   Establishing a self-join between the table and its alias.

NOTE

To learn more about referential integrity, see Chapter 3, "Relationships: Your Key to Data Integrity."

Understanding SQL

Access SQL is the language that underlies Access queries, so you need to understand a little bit about it, where it came from, and how it works. Access SQL enables you to construct queries without using the Access Query By Example (QBE) grid. This is necessary, for example, if you must build a SQL statement on the fly in response to user interaction with your application. Furthermore, certain operations supported by Access SQL aren't supported by the graphical QBE grid. You must build these SQL statements in the Query Builder's SQL view. In addition, many times you will want to build the record source for a form or report on the fly. In those situations, you must have command of the SQL language. Finally, you will want to use SQL statements in your ADO code. For all these reasons, learning SQL is a valuable skill.

What Is SQL, and Where Did It Come From?

SQL is a standard from which many different dialects have emerged. It was developed at an IBM research laboratory in the early 1970s and first formally described in a research paper released in 1974 at an Association for Computing Machinery meeting. Jet 4.0, the version of the Jet Engine provided with Access 2000 and above, has two modes: One supports Access SQL, and the other supports SQL-92. The Access Database Engine, included with Access 2007, also supports the SQL-92 extensions. The SQL-92 extensions are not available from the user interface. They can only be accessed using ADO. They are covered in a later section of this chapter, "Understanding Jet 4.0 ANSI-92 Extensions."

What Do You Need to Know About SQL?

At the very least, you need to understand SQL's basic constructs, which enable you to select, update, delete, and append data by using SQL commands and syntax. Access SQL is made up of very few verbs. The sections that follow cover the most commonly used verbs.

SQL Syntax

SQL is easy to learn. When retrieving data, you simply build a SELECT statement. SELECT statements are composed of clauses that determine the specifics of how the data is selected. When they're executed, SELECT statements select rows of data and return them as a recordset.

> **NOTE**
>
> In the examples that follow, keywords appear in uppercase. Values that you supply appear italicized. Optional parts of the statement appear in square brackets. Curly braces, combined with vertical bars, indicate a choice. Finally, ellipses are used to indicate a repeating sequence.

The SELECT Statement

The SELECT statement is at the heart of the SQL language. It is used to retrieve data from one or more tables. Its basic syntax is

```
SELECT column-list FROM table-list WHERE where-clause ORDER BY order-by-clause
```

The SELECT Clause

The SELECT clause specifies what columns you want to retrieve from the table whose data is being returned to the recordset. The basic syntax for a SELECT clause is

```
SELECT column-list
```

The simplest SELECT clause looks like this:

```
SELECT *
```

This SELECT clause retrieves all columns from a table. Here's another example that retrieves only the ClientID and CompanyName columns from a table:

```
SELECT ClientID, CompanyName
```

You not only can include columns that exist in your table, but also can include expressions in a SELECT clause. Here's an example:

```
SELECT ClientID, City & ", " & State & "  " & PostalCode AS Address
```

This SELECT clause retrieves the ClientID column as well as an alias called Address, which includes an expression that concatenates the City, State, and PostalCode columns.

The FROM **Clause**

The FROM clause specifies the tables or queries from which the records should be selected. It can include an alias you use to refer to the table. The FROM clause looks like this:

```
FROM table-list [AS alias]
```

Here's an example of a basic FROM clause:

```
FROM tblClients AS Clients
```

In this case, the name of the table is tblClients, and the alias is Clients. If you combine the SELECT clause with the FROM clause, the SQL statement looks like this:

```
SELECT ClientID, CompanyName FROM tblClients
```

This SELECT statement retrieves the ClientID and CompanyName columns from the tblClients table.

Just as you can alias the fields included in a SELECT clause, you can also alias the tables included in the FROM clause. The alias is used to shorten the name, to simplify a cryptic name, and to perform a variety of other functions. Here's an example:

```
SELECT ClientID, CompanyName FROM tblClients AS Customers
```

This SQL statement selects the ClientID and CompanyName fields from the tblClients table, aliasing the tblClients table as Customers.

The WHERE **Clause**

The WHERE clause limits the records retrieved by the SELECT statement. You must follow several rules when building a WHERE clause. The text strings that you are searching for must be enclosed in quotation marks. Dates must be surrounded by pound (#) signs. Finally, you must include the keyword LIKE when using wildcard characters. A WHERE clause can include up to 40 columns combined by the keywords AND and OR. The syntax for a WHERE clause looks like this:

```
WHERE expression1 [{AND|OR} expression2 [...]]
```

A simple WHERE clause looks like this:

```
WHERE Country = "USA"
```

Using an AND to further limit the criteria, the WHERE clause looks like this:

```
WHERE Country = "USA" AND ContactTitle Like "Sales*"
```

This WHERE clause limits the records returned to those in which the country is equal to USA and the ContactTitle begins with Sales. Using an OR, the SELECT statement looks like this:

```
WHERE Country = "USA" OR Country = "Canada"
```

This WHERE clause returns all records in which the country is equal to either USA or Canada. Compare that with the following example:

```
WHERE Country = "USA" OR ContactTitle Like "Sales*"
```

This WHERE clause returns all records in which the Country is equal to USA or the ContactTitle begins with Sales. For example, if the ContactTitle for the salespeople in China begins with Sales, the names of those salespeople will be returned from this WHERE clause. The WHERE clause combined with the SELECT and FROM clauses looks like this:

```
SELECT ClientID, CompanyName FROM tblClients
    WHERE Country = "USA" OR Country = "Canada"
```

> **NOTE**
>
> Although Access SQL uses quotation marks to surround text values you're searching for, the ANSI-92 standard dictates that apostrophes (single quotation marks) must be used to delimit text values.

The ORDER BY Clause

The ORDER BY clause determines the order in which the returned rows are sorted. It's an optional clause, and it looks like this:

```
ORDER BY column1 [{ASC|DESC}], column2 [{ASC|DESC}] [,...]]
```

Here's an example:

```
ORDER BY ClientID
```

The ORDER BY clause can include more than one field:

```
ORDER BY Country, ClientID
```

When more than one field is specified, the leftmost field is used as the primary level of sort. Any additional fields are the lower sort levels. Combined with the rest of the SELECT statement, the ORDER BY clause looks like this:

```
SELECT ClientID, CompanyName FROM tblClients
    WHERE Country = "USA" OR Country = "Canada"
    ORDER BY ClientID
```

The ORDER BY clause allows you to determine whether the sorted output appears in ascending or descending order. By default, output appears in ascending order. To switch to descending order, use the optional keyword DESC. Here's an example:

```
SELECT ClientID, CompanyName FROM tblClients ORDER BY ClientID DESC
```

This example selects the ClientID and CompanyName fields from the tblClients table, ordering the output in descending order by the ClientID field.

The JOIN Clause

Often you'll need to build SELECT statements that retrieve data from more than one table. When building a SELECT statement based on more than one table, you must join the tables with a JOIN clause. The JOIN clause differs depending on whether you join the tables with an INNER JOIN, a LEFT OUTER JOIN, or a RIGHT OUTER JOIN.

The SQL-89 and SQL-92 syntax for joins differs. The basic SQL-89 syntax is

```
SELECT column-list FROM table1, table2 WHERE table1.column1 = table2.column2
```

The SQL-92 syntax is preferred because it separates the join from the WHERE clause. It is

```
SELECT column-list FROM table1 {INNER|LEFT [OUTER]|RIGHT [OUTER]} JOIN table2
    ON table1.column1 = table2.column2
```

Note that the keyword OUTER is optional.

Here's an example of a simple INNER JOIN:

```
SELECT DISTINCTROW tblClients.ClientID,
    tblClients.CompanyName, tblProjects.ProjectName,
    tblProjects.ProjectDescription
    FROM tblClients
    INNER JOIN tblProjects ON tblClients.ClientID = tblProjects.ClientID
```

Notice that four columns are returned in the query result. Two columns are from tblClients and two are from tblProjects. The SELECT statement uses an INNER JOIN from tblClients to tblProjects based on the ClientID field. This means that only clients who have projects are displayed in the query result. Compare this with the following SELECT statement:

```
SELECT DISTINCTROW tblClients.ClientID,
    tblClients.CompanyName, tblProjects.ProjectName,
    tblProjects.ProjectDescription
    FROM tblClients
    LEFT JOIN tblProjects ON tblClients.ClientID = tblProjects.ClientID
```

This SELECT statement joins the two tables using a LEFT JOIN from tblClients to tblProjects based on the ClientID field. All clients are included in the resulting records, whether or not they have projects.

> **NOTE**
>
> The word OUTER is assumed in the LEFT JOIN clause used when building a left outer join.

Sometimes you will need to join more than two tables in a SQL statement. When you need to do this, the ANSI-92 syntax is

```
FROM table1 JOIN table2 ON condition1 JOIN table3 ON condition2
```

The following example joins the tblClients, tblProjects, and tblPayments tables:

```
SELECT tblClients.ClientID, tblClients.CompanyName,
    tblProjects.ProjectName, tblPayments.PaymentAmount
    FROM (tblClients
    INNER JOIN tblProjects
    ON tblClients.ClientID = tblProjects.ClientID)
    INNER JOIN tblPayments
    ON tblProjects.ProjectID = tblPayments.ProjectID
```

In the example, the order of the joins is unimportant. The exception to this is when inner and outer joins are combined. When combining inner and outer joins, the Access Database Engine applies two specific rules. First, the nonpreserved table in an outer join cannot participate in an inner join. The nonpreserved table is the one whose rows might not appear. In the case of a left outer join from tblClients to tblProjects, the tblProjects table is considered the nonpreserved table. It therefore cannot participate in an inner join with tblPayments. The second rule is that the nonpreserved table in an outer join cannot participate with another nonpreserved table in another outer join.

Self-Joins

Self-joins were covered earlier in this chapter. The SQL syntax required to create them is similar to a standard join and is covered here:

```
SELECT tblEmployees![FirstName] & " " & tblEmployees![LastName] AS EmployeeName,
    tblSupervisors![FirstName] & " " & tblSupervisors![LastName] AS SupervisorName
    FROM tblEmployees
    INNER JOIN tblEmployees
    AS tblSupervisors
    ON tblEmployees.SupervisorID = tblSupervisors.EmployeeID
```

Notice that the tblEmployees table is joined to an alias of the tblEmployees table that is referred to as tblSupervisors. The SupervisorID from the tblEmployees table is joined

with the `EmployeeID` field from the `tblSupervisors` alias. The fields included in the
output are the `FirstName` and `LastName` from the `tblEmployees` table and the `FirstName`
and `LastName` from the alias of the `tblEmployees` table.

Non-Equi Joins

So far, all the joins that we have covered involve situations in which the value of a field
in one table is equal to the value of the field in the other table. You can create non-equi
joins in which the >, >=, <, <=, <>, or `Between` operator is used to join two tables. Here's an
example:

```
SELECT tblClients.CompanyName, tblProjects.ProjectName
    FROM tblClients
    INNER JOIN tblProjects
    ON tblClients.ClientID = tblProjects.ClientID
    AND tblProjects.ProjectBeginDate >=  tblClients.IntroDate
```

This example returns only the rows from `tblProjects` where the `ProjectBeginDate` is on
or after the `IntroDate` stored in the `tblClients` table.

ALL, DISTINCTROW, and DISTINCT Clauses

The `ALL` clause of a `SELECT` statement means that all rows meeting the `WHERE` clause are
included in the query result. When the `DISTINCT` keyword is used, Access eliminates
duplicate rows, based on the fields included in the query result. This is the same as setting
the `Unique Values` property to `Yes` in the graphical QBE grid. When the `DISTINCTROW`
keyword is used, Access eliminates any duplicate rows based on all columns of all tables
included in the query (whether they appear in the query result or not). This is the same
as setting the `Unique Records` property to `Yes` in the graphical QBE grid. These keywords
in the `SELECT` clause look like this:

```
SELECT [{ALL|DISTINCT|DISTINCT ROW}] column-list
```

The TOP Predicate

The `Top Values` property, available via the user interface, is covered in the "Viewing
Special Query Properties" section, earlier in this chapter. The keyword `TOP` is used to
implement this feature in SQL. The syntax looks like this:

```
SELECT [{ALL|DISTINCT|DISTINCTROW}] [TOP n [PERCENT]] column-list
```

The example that follows extracts the five clients whose `IntroDate` field is most recent:

```
SELECT TOP 5 tblClients.ClientID, tblClients.CompanyName, tblClients.IntroDate
    FROM tblClients
    ORDER BY tblClients.IntroDate DESC
```

The GROUP BY **Clause**

The GROUP BY clause is used to calculate summary statistics; it's created when you build a Totals query by using the graphical QBE grid. The syntax of the GROUP BY clause is

```
GROUP BY group-by-expression1 [,group-by-expression2 [,...]]
```

The GROUP BY clause is used to dictate the fields on which the query result is grouped. When multiple fields are included in a GROUP BY clause, they are grouped from left to right. The output is automatically ordered by the fields designated in the GROUP BY clause. In the following example, the SELECT statement returns the country, city, and total freight for each country/city combination. The results are displayed in order by country and city:

```
SELECT DISTINCTROW tblCustomers.Country, tblCustomers.City,
    Sum(tblOrders.Freight) AS SumOfFreight
    FROM tblCustomers
    INNER JOIN tblOrders ON tblCustomers.CustomerID = tblOrders.CustomerID
    GROUP BY tblCustomers.Country, tblCustomers.City
```

The GROUP BY clause indicates that detail for the selected records isn't displayed. Instead, the fields indicated in the GROUP BY clause are displayed uniquely. One of the fields in the SELECT statement must include an aggregate function. This result of the aggregate function is displayed along with the fields specified in the GROUP BY clause.

The HAVING **Clause**

A HAVING clause is similar to a WHERE clause, but it differs in one major respect: It's applied after the data is summarized rather than before. In other words, the WHERE clause is used to determine which rows are grouped. The HAVING clause determines which groups are included in the output. A HAVING clause looks like this:

```
HAVING expression1 [{AND|OR} expression2[...]]
```

In the following example, the criterion > 1000 will be applied after the aggregate function SUM is applied to the grouping:

```
SELECT DISTINCTROW tblCustomers.Country, tblCustomers.City,
    Sum(tblOrders.Freight) AS SumOfFreight
    FROM tblCustomers
    INNER JOIN tblOrders ON tblCustomers.CustomerID = tblOrders.CustomerID
    GROUP BY tblCustomers.Country, tblCustomers.City
    HAVING (((Sum(tblOrders.Freight))>1000))
```

Applying What You Have Learned

You can practice entering and working with SQL statements in two places:

▶ In a query's SQL View window

▶ In VBA code

In the following sections, you look at both of these techniques.

Using the Graphical QBE Grid as a Two-Way Tool

A great place to practice writing SQL statements is in the SQL View window of a query. It works like this:

1. Start by building a new query.

2. Add a couple of fields and maybe even some criteria.

3. Use the View drop-down list in the Results group of the Design tab to select SQL view.

4. Try changing the SQL statement, using what you have learned in this chapter.

5. Use the View drop-down list in the Results group of the Design tab to select Design view. As long as you haven't violated any Access SQL syntax rules, you can easily switch to the query's Design view and see the graphical result of your changes. If you've introduced any syntax errors into the SQL statement, an error occurs when you try to return to the query's Design view.

Including SQL Statements in VBA Code

You can also execute SQL statements directly from VBA code. You can run a SQL statement from VBA code in two ways:

▶ You can build a temporary query and execute it.

▶ You can open a recordset with the SQL statement as the foundation for the recordset.

The VBA language enables you to build a query on the fly, execute it, and never store it. The code looks like this:

```
Sub CreateTempQuery()
    Dim cmd As ADODB.Command
    Dim rst As ADODB.Recordset

    Set cmd = New ADODB.Command
    With cmd
        .ActiveConnection = CurrentProject.Connection
        .CommandText = "Select ProjectID, ProjectName from " & _
            "tblProjects Where ProjectTotalEstimate > 30000"
        .CommandType = adCmdText
        .Prepared = True
        Set rst = .Execute
    End With

    Do Until rst.EOF
```

```
        Debug.Print rst!ProjectID, rst!ProjectName
        rst.MoveNext
    Loop

End Sub
```

Working with recordsets is covered extensively in Chapter 15. For now, you need to understand that this code creates a temporary query definition using a SQL statement. In this example, the query definition is never added to the database. Instead, the SQL statement is executed but never stored.

A SQL statement can also be provided as part of the recordset's Open method. The code looks like this:

```
Sub OpenRWithSQL()
    Dim rst As ADODB.Recordset

    Set rst = New ADODB.Recordset

    rst.Open "Select ProjectId, ProjectName from " & _
        "tblProjects Where ProjectTotalEstimate > 30000", _
        CurrentProject.Connection

    Do Until rst.EOF
        Debug.Print rst!ProjectID, rst!ProjectName
        rst.MoveNext
    Loop
End Sub
```

Again, this code is discussed more thoroughly in Chapter 15. Notice that the Open method of the recordset object receives two parameters: The first is a SELECT statement, and the second is the Connection object.

Building Union Queries

A union query enables you to combine data from two tables with similar structures; data from each table is included in the output. For example, suppose you have a tblTimeCards table containing active time cards and a tblTimeCardsArchive table containing archived time cards. The problem occurs when you want to build a report that combines data from both tables. To do this, you must build a union query as the record source for the report. The syntax for a union query is

```
Select-statement1 UNION [ALL]
  Select-statement2 [UNION [ALL]
  SelectStatement3] [...]
```

Here's an example:

```
SELECT FirstName, LastName, Department, Salary
    FROM tblEmployees
    UNION ALL SELECT FirstName, LastName, Department, Salary
    FROM tblSummerEmployees
```

This example combines data from the tblEmployees table with data from the tblSummerEmployees table, preserving duplicate rows, if there are any.

The ALL Keyword

Notice the keyword ALL in the previous SQL statement. By default, Access eliminates all duplicate records from the query result. This means that if an employee is found in both the tblEmployees and tblSummerEmployees tables, he appears only once in the query result. Including the keyword ALL causes any duplicate rows to display.

Sorting the Query Results

When sorting the results of a union query, you must include the ORDER BY clause at the end of the SQL statement. Here's an example:

```
SELECT FirstName, LastName, Department, Salary
    FROM tblEmployees
    UNION ALL SELECT FirstName, LastName, Department, Salary
    FROM tblSummerEmployees
    ORDER BY Salary
```

This example combines data from the tblEmployees table with data from the tblSummerEmployees table, preserving duplicate rows, if there are any. It orders the results by the Salary field (combining the data from both tables).

If the column names that you are sorting by differ in the tables included in the union query, you must use the column name from the first table.

Using the Graphical QBE to Create a Union Query

You can use the graphical QBE to create a union query. The process is as follows:

1. Click Query Design in the Other group on the Create tab.

2. Click Close from the Show Tables dialog box without selecting a table.

3. Choose Union Query in the Query Type group on the Design tab. A SQL window appears.

4. Type in the SQL UNION clause. Notice that you can't switch back to the query's Design view (see Figure 12.32).

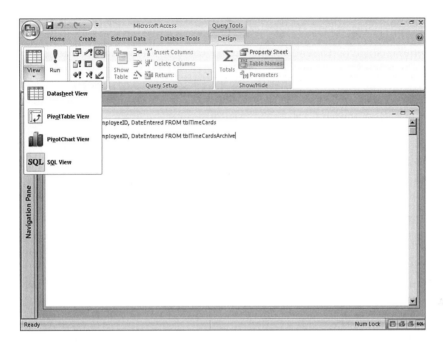

FIGURE 12.32   An example of a union query that combines `tblTimeCards` with `tblTimeCardsArchive`.

5. Click the Run button on the ribbon to execute the query.

CAUTION

If you build a query and then designate the query as an `SQL Specific` query, you lose *everything* that you did prior to the switch. There is *no* warning, and Undo is not available!

Important Notes about Union Queries

It is important to note that the result of a union query is not updateable. Furthermore, the fields in each `SELECT` statement are matched only by position. This means that you can get strange results by accidentally listing the `FirstName` field followed by the `LastName` field in the first `SELECT` statement, and the `LastName` field followed by the `FirstName` field in the second `SELECT` statement. Each `SELECT` statement included in a union query must contain the same number of columns. Finally, each column in the first SELECT statement much have the same data type as the corresponding column in the second SELECT statement.

Using Pass-Through Queries

Pass-Through queries enable you to send uninterpreted SQL statements to your back-end database when you're using something other than the Access Database Engine. These uninterpreted statements are in the SQL that's specific to your particular back end. Although the Access Database Engine sees these SQL statements, it makes no attempt to parse or modify them. Pass-Through queries are used in several situations:

▶ The action you want to take is supported by your back-end database server but not by Access SQL or ODBC SQL.

▶ Access or the ODBC driver is doing a poor job parsing the SQL statement and sending it in an optimized form to the back-end database.

▶ You want to execute a stored procedure on the back-end database server.

▶ You want to make sure the SQL statement is executed on the server.

▶ You want to join data from more than one table residing on the database server. If you execute the join without a Pass-Through query, the join is done in the memory of the user's PC after all the required data has been sent over the network.

Although Pass-Through queries offer many advantages, they aren't a panacea. They do have a few disadvantages:

▶ Because you're sending SQL statements specific to your particular database server, you must write the statement in the "dialect" of SQL used by the database server. For example, in writing a Pass-Through query to access SQL Server data, you must write the SQL statement in T-SQL. When writing a Pass-Through query to access Oracle data, you must write the SQL statement in PL-SQL. This means that you'll need to rewrite all the SQL statements if you switch to another back end.

▶ The results returned from a Pass-Through query can't be updated.

▶ The Access Database Engine does no syntax checking of the query before passing it on to the back end.

Now that you know all the advantages and disadvantages of Pass-Through queries, you can learn how to build one:

1. Click Query Design in the Other group on the Create tab.

2. Click Close from the Show Tables dialog box without selecting a table.

3. Choose Pass-Through Query in the Query Type group on the Design tab to open the SQL Design window.

4. Type in the SQL statement in the dialect of your back-end database server.

5. View the Query Properties window and enter an ODBC connect string (see Figure 12.33).

6. Click the Run button on the ribbon to run the query.

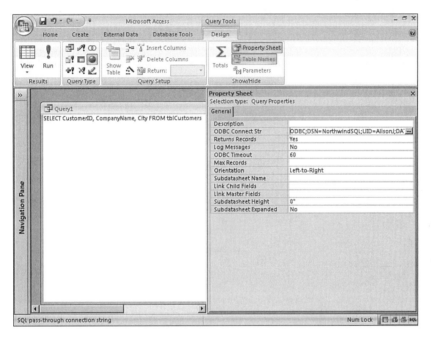

FIGURE 12.33   A SQL Pass-Through query that selects specific fields from the Sales table, which resides in the PublisherInfo data source.

Examining the Propagation of Nulls and Query Results

Null values can wreak havoc with your query results because they propagate. Look at the query in Figure 12.34. Notice that when parts and labor are added, and either the Parts field or the Labor field contains a Null, the result of adding the two fields is Null. In Figure 12.35, the problem is rectified. Figure 12.36 shows the design of the query that eliminates the propagation of the Nulls. Notice the expression that adds the two values:

```
TotalPrice: Nz([Parts]) + Nz([Labor])
```

This expression uses the Nz function to convert the Null values to 0 before the two field values are added together.

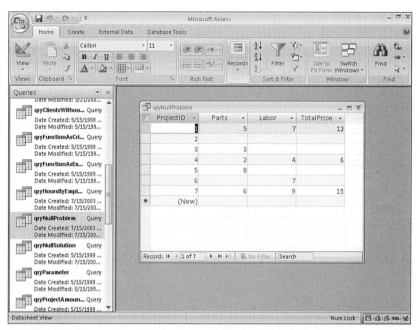

FIGURE 12.34   An example that shows the propagation of Nulls in a query result.

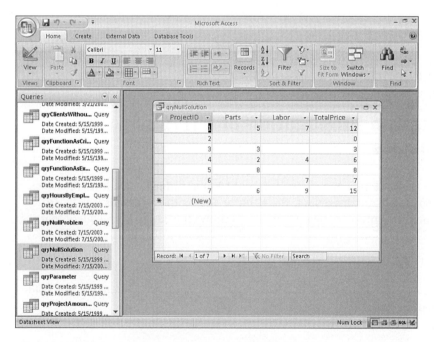

FIGURE 12.35   An example that shows Nulls eliminated from the query result.

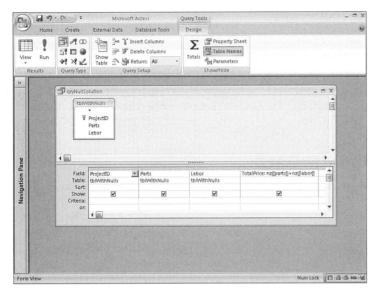

FIGURE 12.36   A solution to eliminate propagation of `Null`s.

Running Subqueries

Subqueries allow you to embed one `SELECT` statement within another. By placing a subquery in a query's criteria, you can base one query on the result of another. Figure 12.37 shows an example. The query pictured finds all the clients without projects.

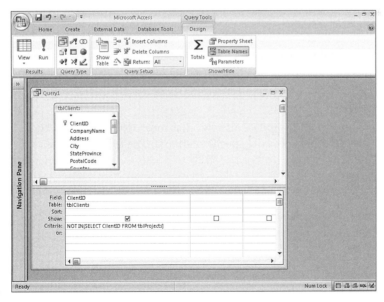

FIGURE 12.37   A query containing a subquery.

The SQL statement looks like this:

```
SELECT DISTINCTROW tblClients.ClientID,
    tblClients.CompanyName FROM tblClients
    WHERE tblClients.ClientID Not In (Select ClientID from tblProjects)
```

This query first runs the SELECT statement SELECT ClientID from tblProjects. It uses the result as criteria for the first query.

Using SQL to Update Data

SQL can be used not only to retrieve data, but to update it as well. This concept was introduced in the section "Using Action Queries," which focused on the SQL statements behind the action queries.

The UPDATE Statement

The UPDATE statement is used to modify the data in one or more columns of a table. The syntax for the UPDATE statement is

```
UPDATE table/query
    SET column1=expression1 [,column2=expression2] [,...]
    [WHERE criteria]
```

The WHERE clause in the UPDATE statement is used to limit the rows that are updated. The following is an example of an UPDATE statement:

```
UPDATE tblClients
    SET tblClients.DefaultRate = [DefaultRate]*1.1
    WHERE tblClients.DefaultRate<=125
```

This statement updates the DefaultRate column of the tblClients table, increasing it by 10% for any clients that have a default rate less than or equal to 125.

The DELETE Statement

Whereas the UPDATE statement is used to update all rows that meet specific criteria, the DELETE statement deletes all rows that meet the specified criteria. The syntax for the DELETE statement is

```
DELETE FROM table [WHERE criteria]
```

As with the UPDATE statement, the WHERE clause is used to limit the rows that are deleted. The following is an example of the use of a DELETE statement:

```
DELETE tblClients.*, tblClients.DefaultRate
    FROM tblClients
    WHERE tblClients.DefaultRate<=125
```

This statement deletes all clients from the tblClients table whose DefaultRate field is less than or equal to 125.

The INSERT INTO Statement

The INSERT INTO statement is used to copy rows from one table to another. The syntax for the INSERT INTO statement is

```
INSERT INTO target-table select-statement [WHERE criteria]
```

Once again, the optional WHERE clause is used to limit the rows that are copied. Here's an example:

```
INSERT INTO tblCheapClients
    (ClientID, CompanyName, ContactFirstName,
    ContactLastName, ContactTitle, DefaultRate )
    SELECT tblClients.ClientID, tblClients.CompanyName,
    tblClients.ContactFirstName,
    tblClients.ContactLastName, tblClients.ContactTitle, tblClients.DefaultRate
    FROM tblClients
    WHERE tblClients.DefaultRate<=125
```

This statement inserts the ClientID, CompanyName, ContactFirstName, ContactLastName, ContactTitle, and DefaultRate fields into the corresponding fields in the tblCheapClients table for any clients whose DefaultRate field is less than or equal to 125.

The SELECT INTO Statement

Whereas the INSERT INTO statement inserts data into an existing table, the SELECT INTO statement inserts data into a new table. The syntax looks like this:

```
SELECT column1 [,column2 [,...]] INTO new-table
    FROM table-list
    [WHERE where-clause]
    [ORDER BY orderby-clause]
```

The WHERE clause is used to determine which rows in the source table are inserted into the destination table. The ORDER BY clause is used to designate the order of the rows in the destination table. Here's an example:

```
SELECT tblClients.ClientID, tblClients.CompanyName,
    tblClients.ContactFirstName, tblClients.ContactLastName,
    tblClients.ContactTitle, tblClients.DefaultRate
    INTO tblCheapClients
    FROM tblClients
    WHERE tblClients.DefaultRate<=125
```

This statement inserts data from the selected fields in the tblClients table into a new table called tblCheapClients. Only the clients whose DefaultRate field is less than or equal to 125 are inserted.

Using SQL for Data Definition

Access 2007 offers two methods of programmatically defining and modifying objects. You can use either ActiveX Data Object Extensions for DDL and Security (ADOX) or Data Definition Language (DDL). DDL is covered in this chapter. ADOX is introduced in Chapter 15.

The CREATE TABLE Statement

As its name implies, the CREATE TABLE statement is used to create a new table. The syntax is

```
CREATE TABLE table-name
    (column1 type1 [(size1)] [CONSTRAINT column-constraint1]
    [,column2 type2 [(size2)] [CONSTRAINT column-constraint2]
    [,...]]
    [CONSTRAINT table-constraint1 [,table-constraint2 [,]]])
```

You must designate the type of data for each column included in the table. When defining a text field, you can also specify the size parameter. Notice that constraints are available at the table level and at the field level. Here's an example of a CREATE TABLE statement:

```
CREATE TABLE tblCustomers
    (CustomerID LONG, CompanyName TEXT (50), IntroDate DATETIME)
```

This example creates a table named tblCustomers. The table will contain three fields: CustomerID (Long), CompanyName (Text), and IntroDate (DateTime).

The CONSTRAINT clause allows you to create primary and foreign keys. It looks like this:

```
CONSTRAINT name {PRIMARY KEY|UNIQUE|REFERENCES foreign-table [foreign-column]}
```

Here's an example:

```
CREATE TABLE tblCustomers
    (CustomerID LONG CONSTRAINT CustomerID PRIMARY KEY,
    CompanyName TEXT (50), IntroDate DATETIME)
```

The example creates a primary key index based on the CustomerID field.

The CREATE INDEX Statement

The CREATE INDEX statement is used to add an index to an existing table. It is supported in Access but is not part of the ANSI standard. It looks like this:

```
CREATE [UNIQUE] INDEX index-name
    ON table-name (column1 [,column2 [,...]])
    [WITH {PRIMARY|DISALLOW NULL|IGNORE NULL}]
```

Here's an example:

```
CREATE INDEX  CompanyName
    ON tblCustomers (CompanyName)
```

The example creates an index called `CompanyName`, based on the `CompanyName` field.

The ALTER TABLE **Statement**

The `ALTER TABLE` statement is used to modify the structure of an existing table. The syntax has four forms. The first form looks like this:

```
ALTER TABLE table-name ADD [COLUMN] column-name datatype [(size)]
[CONSTRAINT column-constraint]
```

This form of the `ALTER TABLE` statement adds a column to an existing table. Here's an example:

```
ALTER TABLE tblCustomers ADD ContactName Text 50
```

The second form uses the following syntax to delete a column from an existing table:

```
ALTER TABLE table-name DROP [COLUMN] column-name
```

Here's an example:

```
ALTER TABLE tblCustomers DROP COLUMN ContactName
```

The third form uses the `ALTER TABLE` statement to add a constraint to an existing column. The syntax is

```
ALTER TABLE table-name ADD CONSTRAINT constraint
```

Here's an example:

```
ALTER TABLE tblCustomers ADD CONSTRAINT CompanyName UNIQUE (CompanyName)
```

Finally, the fourth form drops a constraint from an existing column:

```
ALTER TABLE table-name DROP CONSTRAINT index
```

Here's an example:

```
ALTER TABLE tblCustomers DROP CONSTRAINT CompanyName
```

The DROP INDEX **Statement**

The `DROP INDEX` statement is used to remove an index from a table. The syntax is as follows:

```
DROP INDEX index ON table-name
```

Here's an example:

```
DROP INDEX CompanyName ON tblCustomers
```

The DROP TABLE Statement

The DROP TABLE statement is used to remove a table from the database. The syntax is

```
DROP TABLE table-name
```

Here's an example:

```
DROP TABLE  tblCustomers
```

Using the Result of a Function as the Criteria for a Query

Many people are unaware that the result of a function can serve as an expression in a query or as a parameter to a query. The query shown in Figure 12.38 evaluates the result of a function called Initials. The return value from the function is evaluated with criteria to determine whether the employee is included in the query result. The Initials function shown here (it's also in the basUtils module of CHAP12EX.ACCDB, found on the sample code CD-ROM) receives two strings and returns the first character of each string followed by a period:

```
Function Initials(strFirstName As String, _
     strLastName As String) As String
   Initials = Left(strFirstName, 1) & "." & _
     Left(strLastName, 1) & "."
End Function
```

The return value from a function can also be used as the criteria for a query (see Figure 12.39). The query in the figure uses a function called HighlyPaid to determine which records appear in the query result. Here's what the HighlyPaid function looks like. (It's also in the basUtils module of CHAP12EX.ACCDB, found on the sample code CD-ROM.)

```
Function HighlyPaid(strTitle) As Currency
   Dim curHighRate As Currency
   Select Case strTitle
     Case "Sr. Programmer"
        curHighRate = 60
     Case "Systems Analyst"
        curHighRate = 80
     Case "Project Manager"
        curHighRate = 100
     Case Else
        curHighRate = 50
   End Select
```

```
    HighlyPaid = curHighRate
End Function
```

The function receives the employee's title as a parameter. It then evaluates the title and returns a threshold value to the query that's used as the criterion for the query's Billing Rate column.

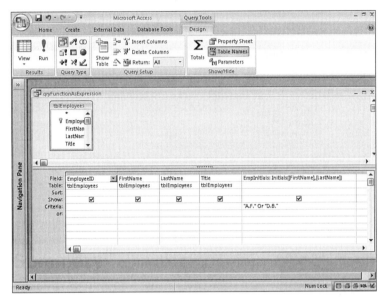

FIGURE 12.38   A query that uses the result of a function as an expression.

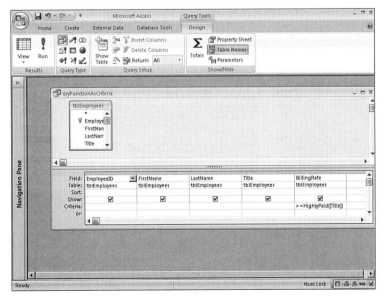

FIGURE 12.39   A query that uses the result of a function as criteria.

Passing Parameter Query Values from a Form

The biggest frustration with Parameter queries occurs when multiple parameters are required to run a query. The user is confronted with multiple dialog boxes, one for each parameter in the query. The following steps explain how to build a Parameter query that receives its parameter values from a form:

1. Create a new unbound form.

2. Add text boxes or other controls to accept the criteria for each parameter added to your query.

3. Name each control so that you can readily identify the data it contains.

4. Add a command button to the form and instruct it to call the Parameter query (see Figure 12.40).

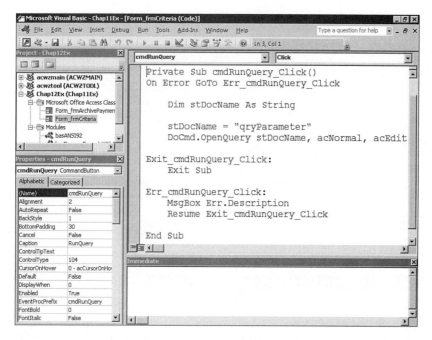

FIGURE 12.40   The Click event code of the command button that calls the Parameter query.

5. Save the form.

6. Create the query and add the parameters to it. Each parameter should refer to a control on the form (see Figure 12.41).

7. Right-click the top half of the Query Design grid and select Parameters. Define a data type for each parameter in the Query Parameters dialog box (see Figure 12.42).

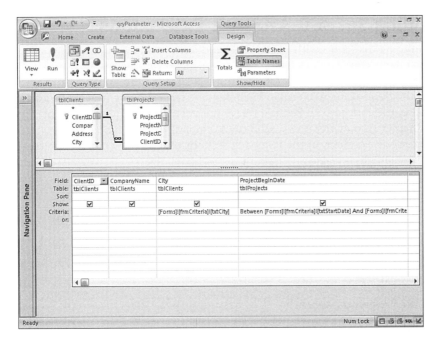

FIGURE 12.41   Parameters that refer to controls on a form.

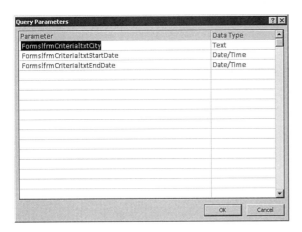

FIGURE 12.42   The Query Parameters dialog box lets you select the data type for each parameter in the query.

8. Save and close the query.

9. Fill in the values on the criteria form and click the command button to execute the query. It should execute successfully.

Understanding Jet 4.0 ANSI-92 Extensions

Jet 4.0, the version of Jet that ships with Access 2000 and later, includes expanded support for the ANSI-92 standard. The Access Database Engine, included with Access 2007, supports these same features. Although these extensions are not available via the Access user interface, you can tap into them using ADO code. The following sections cover the extensions and the functionality they afford you. Because I have not yet covered ADO, you might want to refer to Chapter 15 to better understand the examples. For now, you need to understand that the code examples in the following sections use the ADO `Command` object to execute SQL statements that create and manipulate database objects.

Table Extensions

Six table extensions are included with the Access Database Engine. These extensions enable you to

- ▶ Create defaults
- ▶ Create check constraints
- ▶ Set up cascading referential integrity
- ▶ Control fast foreign keys
- ▶ Implement Unicode string compression
- ▶ Better control autonumber fields

Creating Defaults

The `DEFAULT` keyword can be used with the `CREATE TABLE` statement. The syntax is

```
DEFAULT (value)
```

Here's an example:

```
Sub CreateDefault()
    Dim cmd As ADODB.Command
    Set cmd = New ADODB.Command

    cmd.ActiveConnection = CurrentProject.Connection
    cmd.CommandText = "CREATE TABLE tblCustomers " & _
        "(CustomerID LONG CONSTRAINT CustomerID PRIMARY KEY, " & _
        "CompanyName TEXT (50), IntroDate DATETIME, " & _
        "CreditLimit CURRENCY DEFAULT 5000)"
    cmd.Execute
End Sub
```

Notice first that ADO is used to execute the SQL statement. The reason is that the `DEFAULT` keyword is not accessible via the use interface. The `CreditLimit` field includes a `DEFAULT` clause that sets the default value of the field to `5000`.

Creating Check Constraints

The CHECK keyword can be used with the CREATE TABLE statement. It allows you to add business rules for a table. Unlike field- and table-level validation rules that are available via the user interface, check constraints can span tables. The syntax for a check constraint is

```
[CONSTRAINT [name]] CHECK (search_condition)
```

Here's an example:

```
Sub CreateCheckConstraint()
    Dim cmd As ADODB.Command
    Set cmd = New ADODB.Command

    cmd.ActiveConnection = CurrentProject.Connection
    cmd.CommandText = "CREATE TABLE tblCustomers " & _
        "(CustomerID LONG CONSTRAINT CustomerID PRIMARY KEY, " & _
        "CompanyName TEXT (50), IntroDate DATETIME, " & _
        "CONSTRAINT IntroDateCheck CHECK (IntroDate <= Date()), " & _
        "CreditLimit CURRENCY DEFAULT 5000)"
    cmd.Execute
End Sub
```

This example creates a check constraint on the IntroDate field that limits the value entered in the field to a date on or before today's date.

Implementing Cascading Referential Integrity

The ANSI-92 extensions can also be used to establish cascading referential integrity. The syntax is

```
CONSTRAINT name FOREIGN KEY (column1 [,column2 [,...]])
REFERENCES foreign-table [(foreign-column1 [, foreign-column2 [,...]])]
[ON UPDATE {NO ACTION|CASCADE}]
[ON DELETE {NO ACTION|CASCADE}]
```

Without the CASCADE options, the primary key field cannot be updated if the row has child records, and the row on the "one" side of the one-to-many relationship cannot be deleted if it has children.

Controlling Fast Foreign Keys

Whenever you join two tables in a one-to-many relationship, Access automatically creates an index on the foreign key field (the "many" side of the relationship). This is generally a good thing. It is bad only if the foreign key contains a lot of Nulls. In that case, the index serves only to degrade performance rather than improve it. Fortunately, using the Jet 4.0 or the Access Database Engine ANSI-92 extensions and the NO INDEX keywords, you can create the foreign key without the index. Here's the syntax:

```
CONSTRAINT name FOREIGN KEY NO INDEX (column1 [,column2 [,...]])
REFERENCES foreign-table [(foreign-column1 [, foreign-column2 [,...]])]
```

```
[ON UPDATE {NO ACTION|CASCADE}]
[ON DELETE {NO ACTION|CASCADE}]
```

Implementing Unicode String Compression

Just as you can implement Unicode string compression using the user interface, you can also implement it in code. The syntax is

```
Column string-data-type [(length)] WITH COMPRESSION
```

Controlling Autonumber Fields

Using the Jet 4.0 or the Microsoft Access Database ANSI-92 extensions, you can change both the autonumber seed and increment. The syntax is

```
Column AUTOINCREMENT (seed, increment)
```

Here's an example:

```
Sub CreateAutonumber()
    Dim cmd As ADODB.Command
    Set cmd = New ADODB.Command

    cmd.ActiveConnection = CurrentProject.Connection
    cmd.CommandText = "CREATE TABLE tblCustomers " & _
        "(CustomerID AUTOINCREMENT (100000,1), " & _
        "CompanyName TEXT (50), IntroDate DATETIME, " & _
        "CreditLimit CURRENCY DEFAULT 5000)"
    cmd.Execute
End Sub
```

The code creates an auto-increment field called CustomerID. The starting value is 100000. The field increments by 1. In addition to the added support for seed value and increment value, the Jet 4.0 or Access Database Engine ANSI-92 extensions allow you to retrieve the last-assigned autonumber value. Here's how it works:

```
Sub LastAutonumber()
    Dim cmd As ADODB.Command
    Dim rst As ADODB.Recordset
    Set cmd = New ADODB.Command
    Set rst = New ADODB.Recordset

    cmd.ActiveConnection = CurrentProject.Connection
    cmd.CommandText = "INSERT INTO tblCustomers " & _
        "(CompanyName, IntroDate, CreditLimit) " & _
        "VALUES ('Test Company', #1/1/2007#, 100) "
    cmd.Execute
```

```
    rst.ActiveConnection = CurrentProject.Connection
    rst.Open ("SELECT @@Identity as LastCustomer FROM tblCustomers")
    MsgBox rst("LastCustomer")
End Sub
```

The code first inserts a row into the tblCustomers table. It then opens a recordset and retrieves the @@Identity value. As with SQL Server, this @@Identity variable contains the value of the last assigned autonumber.

View and Stored Procedures Extensions

The Jet 4.0 or Access Database Engine ANSI-92 extensions allow you to create views and stored procedures similar to those found in SQL Server. Essentially, these views and stored procedures are Access queries that are repackaged to behave like their SQL Server counterparts. Although stored as queries, the views and stored procedures that you create are not visible via the user interface. You can execute them just like saved queries. The syntax to create a view looks like this:

```
CREATE VIEW view-name [(field1 [(,field2 [,...]])])] AS select-statement
```

Here's an example:

```
Sub CreateView()
    Dim cmd As ADODB.Command
    Set cmd = New ADODB.Command

    cmd.ActiveConnection = CurrentProject.Connection
    cmd.CommandText = "CREATE VIEW vwClients " & _
        "AS SELECT ClientID, CompanyName " & _
        "FROM tblClients"
    cmd.Execute
End Sub
```

As covered in Chapter 15, use the following code to execute the view:

```
Sub ExecuteView()
    Dim rst As ADODB.Recordset
    Set rst = New ADODB.Recordset

    rst.ActiveConnection = CurrentProject.Connection
    rst.CursorType = adOpenStatic
    rst.Open "vwClients"
    MsgBox rst.RecordCount
End Sub
```

The syntax to create a stored procedure is

```
CREATE PROC[EDURE] procedure [(param1 datatype1 [,param2 datatype2 [,...]])]_
AS sql-statement
```

Here's an example:

```
Sub CreateStoredProc()
    Dim cmd As ADODB.Command
    Set cmd = New ADODB.Command

    cmd.ActiveConnection = CurrentProject.Connection
    cmd.CommandText = "CREATE PROCEDURE procClientGet " & _
        "(ClientID long) " & _
        "AS SELECT ClientID, CompanyName " & _
        "FROM tblClients " & _
        "WHERE ClientID = ClientID"
    cmd.Execute
End Sub
```

Use the EXECUTE statement, as shown in the following code, to execute the stored procedure:

```
Sub ExecuteStoredProc()
    Dim rst As ADODB.Recordset
    Dim cmd As Command
    Set cmd = New ADODB.Command

    cmd.ActiveConnection = CurrentProject.Connection
    cmd.CommandText = "EXECUTE procClientGet 1"
    Set rst = cmd.Execute
    MsgBox rst("CompanyName")
End Sub
```

Transaction Extensions

Using Jet 4.0 or Access Database Engine ANSI-92 security extensions, you can create trans-actions that span an ADO connection. These extensions are intended to augment, rather than replace, ADO transactions. You use BEGIN TRANSACTION to start a transaction, COMMIT TRANSACTION to commit a transaction, and ROLLBACK [TRANSACTION] to cancel a transac-tion. Transactions are covered in detail in *Alison Balter's Mastering Access 2002 Enterprise Development*.

Practical Examples: Applying These Techniques in Your Application

The following sections provide several practical applications of the advanced techniques learned in this chapter.

> **NOTE**
>
> The examples shown in the following sections are included in the CHAP12EX.ACCDB database on the sample code CD-ROM.

Archiving Payments

After a while, you might need to archive some of the data in the tblPayment table. Two queries archive the payment data. The first, called qappAppendToPaymentArchive, is an append query that sends all data in a specified date range to an archive table called tblPaymentsArchive (see Figure 12.43). The second query, called qdelRemoveFromPayments, is a delete query that deletes all the data archived from the tblPayments table (see Figure 12.44). The archiving is run from a form called frmArchivePayments, where the date range can be specified by the user at runtime (see Figure 12.45).

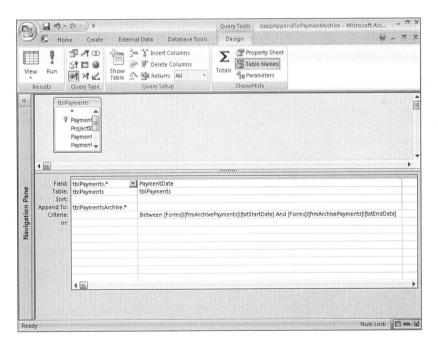

FIGURE 12.43   The append query qappAppendToPaymentArchive.

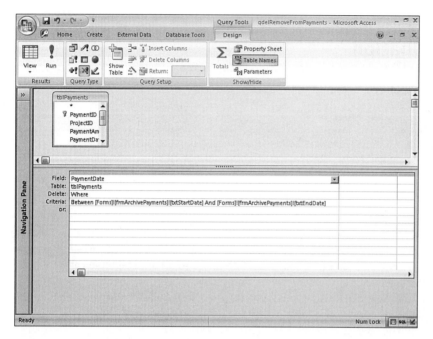

FIGURE 12.44   The delete query qdelRemoveFromPayments.

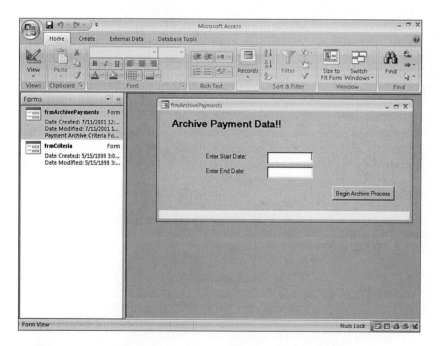

FIGURE 12.45   The form that supplies criteria for the archive process.

Showing All Payments

At times, you might want to combine data from both tables. To do this, you'll need to create a union query that joins `tblPayments` to `tblPaymentsArchive`. The query's design is shown in Figure 12.46.

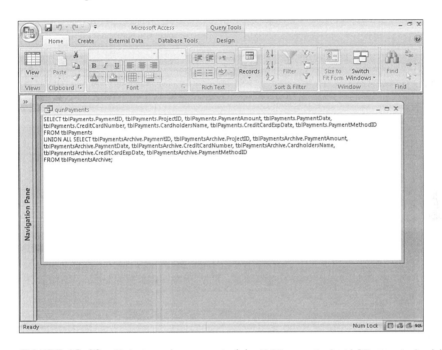

FIGURE 12.46   Using a union query to join `tblPayments` to `tblPaymentsArchive`.

Creating a State Table

Because you'll regularly be looking up the states and provinces, you need to build a unique list of all the states and provinces in which your clients are currently located. The query needed to do this is shown in Figure 12.47. The query uses the `tblClients` table to come up with all the unique values for the `StateProvince` field. Here, you use a make table query that takes the unique list of values and outputs it to a `tblStateProvince` table.

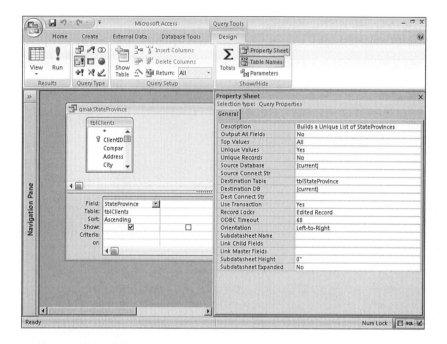

FIGURE 12.47   A make table query that creates a `tblStateProvince` table.

Summary

As you can see, Microsoft gives you a sophisticated query builder for constructing complex and powerful queries. Action queries let you modify table data without writing code; you can use these queries to add, edit, or delete table data. The `Unique Values` and `Top Values` properties of a query offer you flexibility in determining exactly what data is returned in your query result.

You can do many things to improve your queries' efficiency. A little attention to the details covered in this chapter can give you dramatic improvements in your application's performance.

Other special types of queries covered in this chapter include crosstab queries, outer joins, and self-joins. Whatever you can't do by using the graphical QBE grid, you can accomplish by typing the required SQL statement directly into the SQL View window. In this window, you can type Access SQL statements or use SQL Pass-Through to type SQL statements in the SQL dialect that's specific to your back-end database. After you harness the power of the SQL language, you can perform powerful tasks such as modifying the record source of a form or report at runtime.

CHAPTER 13

Advanced VBA Techniques

Why This Chapter Is Important

The Visual Basic for Applications (VBA) language is extremely rich and comprehensive. I cover VBA throughout this book as it applies to different topics, but this chapter focuses on some advanced application development techniques. These topics include user-defined types, arrays, advanced function techniques, and VBA compilation options. Mastering these topics will help to ensure your success as a VBA programmer.

What Are User-Defined Types, and Why Would You Use Them?

A user-defined type, known as a *struct* or *record*, allows you to create a variable containing several pieces of information. You will often use user-defined types to hold information from one or more records in memory. You can also use them to hold related information that you would otherwise store in several unrelated variables. Because you can instruct each element of a user-defined type to hold a particular type of data, you can define each element in the type to correspond to the type of data stored in a specific field of a table. A user-defined type might look like this:

```
Public Type TimeCardInfo
    TimeCardDetailID As Long
    TimeCardID As Long
    DateWorked As Date
    ProjectID As Long
    WorkDescription As String * 255
```

```
    BillableHours As Double
    BillingRate As Currency
    WorkCodeID As Long
End Type
```

This user-defined type stores time-card information for an employee. Notice that the code explicitly declares the type of data stored in each element. The code declares the element containing the string WorkDescription with a length of 255. User-defined types make code cleaner by storing related data as a unit. A user-defined type exists only in memory and is, therefore, temporary. It's excellent for information that needs to be temporarily tracked at runtime. Because it's in memory, it can be quickly and efficiently read from and written to.

> **NOTE**
>
> The code snippets shown in the previous example are located in the basDataHandling module on the sample code CD-ROM that accompanies this book. They are in the database called CHAP13EX.ACCDB.

Declaring a User-Defined Type

You declare a user-defined type by using a Type statement that must be placed in the module's Declarations section. You can declare types as Public or Private within a standard module. You can use types in Form and Report modules, but you cannot declare them there.

Creating a Type Variable

A Type variable is an instance of the type in memory; you must declare it before you can use the type. To declare a Type variable, create a Local, Private, Module-Level, or Public variable based on the type. Depending on where you place this declaration and how you declare it (using keywords Dim, Private, or Public), you determine its scope. The same rules for any other kind of variable apply to Type variables. The Dim statement in the code that follows creates a variable called mtypTimeCardData. If you place this Dim statement in the module's General section, it's visible to all routines in that module (notice the m, indicating that it is declared at the module level). If you place it in a subroutine or function, it's local to that particular routine:

```
Dim mtypTimeCardData As TimeCardInfo
```

> **NOTE**
>
> For more information on the scoping and visibility of variables, see Chapter 8, "VBA: An Introduction."

Storing Information from a Record in a Form into a Type **Variable**

After you have declared a Type variable, you can store data in each of its elements. The following code in the frmTimeCardHours form stores information from the form into a Type variable called mtypTimeCardData. The code declares the Type variable as a Private variable in the General Declarations section of the form. The code declares the Type structure in basDataHandling:

```
Private Sub cmdWriteToType_Click()

    'Retrieve control values and place them in the type structure
    mtypTimeCardData.TimeCardDetailID = Me.txtTimeCardDetailID
    mtypTimeCardData.TimeCardID = Me.txtTimeCardID
    mtypTimeCardData.DateWorked = Me.txtDateWorked
    mtypTimeCardData.ProjectID = Me.cboProjectID
    mtypTimeCardData.WorkDescription = Me.txtWorkDescription
    mtypTimeCardData.BillableHours = Me.txtBillableHours
    mtypTimeCardData.BillingRate = Me.txtBillingRate
    mtypTimeCardData.WorkCodeID = Me.cboWorkCodeID
End Sub
```

> **NOTE**
>
> You can find the code for this chapter in the CHAP13EX.ACCDB database on the book's sample code CD-ROM.

The advantage of this code is that, rather than creating eight variables to store these eight pieces of related information, it creates one variable with eight elements. This method keeps things nice and neat.

Retrieving Information from the Elements of a Type **Variable**

To retrieve information from your Type variable, simply refer to its name, followed by a period, and then the name of the element. The following code displays a message box containing all the time card hour information:

```
Private Sub cmdDisplayFromType_Click()
    'Retrieve information from the type structure
    MsgBox "Timecard Detail ID Is " & _
    mtypTimeCardData.TimeCardDetailID & _
Chr(13) & _
        "Timecard ID Is " & mtypTimeCardData.TimeCardID & Chr(13) & _
        "Date Worked Is " & mtypTimeCardData.DateWorked & Chr(13) & _
        "Project ID Is " & mtypTimeCardData.ProjectID & Chr(13) & _
        "Work Description Is " & _
        Trim(mtypTimeCardData.WorkDescription) & _
Chr(13) & _
```

```
        "Billable Hours Is " & mtypTimeCardData.BillableHours & Chr(13) & _
        "Billing Rate Is " & mtypTimeCardData.BillingRate & Chr(13) & _
        "Workcode ID Is " & mtypTimeCardData.WorkCodeID
End Sub
```

> **NOTE**
>
> In Chapter 17, "Error Handling: Preparing for the Inevitable," an exercise shows a user-defined type used to hold pertinent error information. The example replaces the user-defined type with properties of a custom error class. Although user-defined types are still useful and are, in fact, necessary for many Windows API function calls, custom class modules have replaced much of their functionality.

Working with Constants

A *constant* is a meaningful name given to a number or string. You can use constants only for values that don't change at runtime. A tax rate or commission rate, for example, might be constant throughout your application. There are three types of constants in Access:

- ▶ Symbolic
- ▶ Intrinsic
- ▶ System-defined

Symbolic constants, created by using the Const keyword, improve the readability of your code and make code maintenance easier. Instead of referring to the number .0875 every time you want to refer to the tax rate, for instance, you can refer to the constant MTAXRATE (M indicating that it is a module-level constant). If the tax rate changes and you need to modify the value in your code, you'll make the change in only one place. Furthermore, unlike the number .0875, the name MTAXRATE is self-documenting.

Intrinsic constants are built into Microsoft Access; they are part of the language itself. As an Access programmer, you can use constants supplied by Microsoft Access, Visual Basic, and ActiveX Data Objects (ADO). You can also use constants provided by any object libraries you're using in your application.

Only three system-defined constants are available to all applications on your computer: True, False, and Null.

Defining Your Own Constants

As mentioned previously, you declare a symbolic constant by using the Const keyword. You can declare a constant in a subroutine or function, or in the General section of a Form, Report, or Class module. You can *strong-type* constants, meaning that you can declare them with a data type. There are several naming conventions for constants. One of them is to use a suitable scoping prefix, the letter c to indicate that you're working with a constant rather than a variable, and then the appropriate tag for the data type. The declaration and use of a `Private` constant in the previous tax-rate example would look like this:

```
Private Const mccurTaxRate As Currency = .0877
```

I prefer using a scoping prefix and typing the name of the constant in all uppercase. Following this convention, the example given previously is changed to appear as follows:

```
Private Const MTAXRATE as Currency = .0877
```

This code, when placed in a module's Declarations section, creates a `Private` constant called MTAXRATE and sets it equal to `.0875`. Here's how the constant is used in code:

```
Function TotalAmount(curSaleAmount As Currency)
    TotalAmount = curSaleAmount * MTAXRATE
End Function
```

This routine multiplies the `curSaleAmount`, received as a parameter, by the constant MTAXRATE. It returns the result of the calculation by setting the function name equal to the product of the two values. The advantage of the constant in this example is that the code is more readable than `TotalAmount = curSaleAmount * .0877` would be.

Scoping Symbolic Constants

Just as regular variables have scope, user-defined constants have scope. In the preceding example, you created a `Private` constant. The following statement, when placed in a module's Declarations section, creates a `Public` constant:

```
Public Const GTAXRATE As Currency = 0.0877
```

Because this constant is declared as `Public`, it can be accessed from any subroutine or function (including event routines) in your entire application. To better understand the benefits of a `Public` constant, suppose that you have many functions and subroutines, all referencing the constant GTAXRATE. Imagine what would happen if the tax rate were to change. If you hadn't used a constant, you would need to search your entire application, replacing the old tax rate with the new tax rate. However, because you declared your `Public` constant in one place, you can easily go in and modify the one line of code where you declared this constant.

By definition, you cannot modify the values of constants at runtime. If you try to modify the value of a constant, you get this VBA compiler error:

```
Compile error: Assignment to constant not permitted
```

Figure 13.1 illustrates this message box. You can see that an attempt was made to modify the value of the constant called GTAXRATE, which resulted in a compile error.

FIGURE 13.1   An error message resulting from trying to modify the value of a constant.

If you must change the value at runtime, you should consider storing the value in a table rather than declaring it as a constant. You can read the value into a variable when the application loads and then modify the variable if needed. If you choose, you can write the new value back to the table.

Working with Intrinsic Constants

Microsoft Access declares a number of intrinsic constants that you can use in Code, Form, and Report modules. Because they're reserved by Microsoft Access, you can't modify their values or reuse their names; however, you can use them at any time without declaring them.

You should use intrinsic constants whenever possible in your code. Besides making your code more readable, they make your code more portable to future releases of Microsoft Access. Microsoft might change the value associated with a constant, but it isn't likely to change the constant's name. All intrinsic constants appear in the Object Browser; to activate it, simply click the Object Browser tool on the Visual Basic toolbar while in the Visual Basic Editor (VBE). To view the constants that are part of the VBA language, select VBA from the Object Browser's Project/Library drop-down list. Click Constants in the Classes list box, and a list of those constants is displayed in the Members of 'Constants' list box (see Figure 13.2).

All VBA constants are prefixed with vb; all ActiveX Data Object constants, with ad; all Data Access Object (DAO) constants, with db; and all constants that are part of the Access language, with ac. In Figure 13.2, all the constant names begin with vb. To view the Access language constants, select Access from the Project/Library drop-down list and Constants from the Classes list box. To view the ActiveX Data Object constants, select ADODB from the Project/Library drop-down list. The constants are categorized by their function into various classes (for example, LockTypeEnum and ExecuteOptionEnum). Select the appropriate class from the Classes list box, and its members appear in the Members Of list box.

Another way to view constants is within the context of the parameter you're working with in the Code window. Right-click after the name of a parameter and select List Constants to display the constants associated with the parameter. This feature is covered in detail in Chapter 8 in the section titled "VBA: An Introduction."

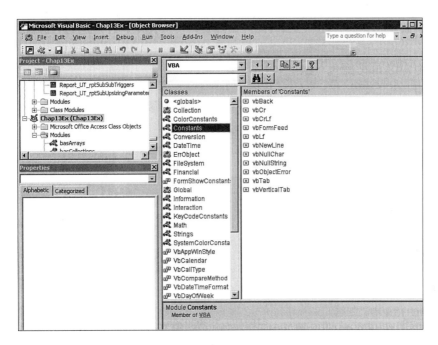

FIGURE 13.2   Using the Object Browser to view intrinsic constants.

Working with Arrays

An *array* is a series of variables referred to by the same name. You differentiate each element of the array by using a unique index number, but all the elements must be of the same data type. Arrays help make coding more efficient. It's easy to loop through each element of an array, performing some process on each element. Arrays have a lower bound, which is zero by default, and an upper bound, and array elements must be contiguous.

The scope of an array can be Public, Module, or Local. As with other variables, the scope depends on where the array is declared and whether the Public, Private, or Dim keyword is used.

Declaring and Working with Fixed Arrays

When declaring a *fixed array*, you give VBA the upper bound and the type of data that it will contain. The following code creates an array that holds six string variables:

```
Dim astrNames(5) As String
```

Fixed means that you cannot alter this array's size at runtime. The following code gives an example of how you can loop through the array:

```vba
Sub FixedArray()
    'Declare an array of six elements
    Dim astrNames(5) As String
    Dim intCounter As Integer

    'Populate the first four elements of the array
    astrNames(0) = "Dan"
    astrNames(1) = "Alexis"
    astrNames(2) = "Brendan"
    astrNames(3) = "Zachary"

    'Use a For...Next loop to loop through the
    'elements of the array
    For intCounter = 0 To UBound(astrNames)
        Debug.Print astrNames(intCounter)
    Next intCounter
End Sub
```

This code starts by storing values into the first four elements of a six-element array. It then loops through each element of the array, printing the contents. Notice that the For...Next loop starts at zero and goes until the upper bound of the array, which is (5). Because the array is made up of strings, the last two elements of the array contain zero-length strings. If the array were composed of integers, the last two elements would contain zeros.

Another way to traverse the array is to use the For Each...Next construct. Your code would look like this:

```vba
Sub ArrayWith()
    'Declare an array of six elements
    Dim astrNames(5) As String
    Dim intCounter As Integer
    Dim vntAny As Variant

    'Populate the first four elements of the array
    astrNames(0) = "Dan"
    astrNames(1) = "Alexis"
    astrNames(2) = "Brendan"
    astrNames(3) = "Zachary"

    'Use a For...Each loop to loop through the
    'elements of the array
    For Each vntAny In astrNames
        Debug.Print vntAny
    Next vntAny
End Sub
```

This code declares a `Variant` variable called `vntAny`. Instead of using a loop with `Ubound` as the upper delimiter to traverse the array, the example uses the `For Each...Next` construct.

> **NOTE**
>
> Many people do not like the fact that, by default, the elements of an array are zero-based. Fortunately, the VBA language allows you to declare both the lower bound and the upper bound of any array. The syntax looks like this:
>
> ```
> Dir astrNames(1 to 6)
> ```

Declaring and Working with Dynamic Arrays

Often, you don't know how many elements your array needs to contain. In this case, you should consider declaring a *dynamic array*, which you can resize at runtime. Using this type of array can make your code more efficient because VBA preallocates memory for all elements of a fixed array, regardless of whether you store data in each of the elements. However, if you aren't sure how many elements your array will contain, preallocating a huge amount of memory can be quite inefficient.

To create a dynamic array, you declare it without assigning an upper bound. You do this by omitting the number between the parentheses when declaring the array, as shown in this example:

```
Sub DynamicArray()
    'Declare a dynamic array
    Dim astrNames() As String
    Dim intCounter As Integer
    Dim vntAny As Variant

    'Resize the array to hold two elements
    ReDim astrNames(1)

    'Populate the two elements
    astrNames(0) = "Dan"
    astrNames(1) = "Alexis"

    'Use a For...Each loop to loop through the
    'elements of the array
    For Each vntAny In astrNames
        Debug.Print vntAny
    Next vntAny
End Sub
```

However, there's a potential problem when you try to resize the array:

```
Sub ResizeDynamic()
    'Declare a dynamic array
    Dim astrNames() As String
    Dim intCounter As Integer
    Dim vntAny As Variant

    'Resize the array to hold two elements
    ReDim astrNames(1)

    'Populate the two elements
    astrNames(0) = "Dan"
    astrNames(1) = "Alexis"

    'Resize the array to hold four elements
    ReDim astrNames(3)

    'Populate the last two elements
    astrNames(2) = "Brendan"
    astrNames(3) = "Zachary"

    'Use a For..Each loop to loop through the
    'elements of the array
    For Each vntAny In astrNames
        Debug.Print vntAny
    Next vntAny
End Sub
```

You might expect that all four elements will contain data. Instead, the ReDim statement reinitializes all the elements, and only elements 2 and 3 contain values. You can avoid this problem by using the Preserve keyword. The following code behaves quite differently:

```
Sub ResizePreserve()
    'Declare a dynamic array
    Dim astrNames() As String
    Dim intCounter As Integer
    Dim vntAny As Variant

    'Resize the array to hold two elements
    ReDim astrNames(1)

    'Populate the two elements
    astrNames(0) = "Dan"
    astrNames(1) = "Alexis"
```

```
    'Resize the array to hold four elements
    ReDim Preserve astrNames(3)

    'Populate the last two elements
    astrNames(2) = "Brendan"
    astrNames(3) = "Zachary"

    'Use a For...Each loop to loop through the
    'elements of the array
    For Each vntAny In astrNames
        Debug.Print vntAny
    Next vntAny
End Sub
```

In this example, all values already stored in the array are preserved. The Preserve keyword brings its own difficulties, though. It can temporarily require huge volumes of memory because, during the ReDim process, VBA creates a copy of the original array. All the values from the original array are copied to a new array. The original array is removed from memory when the process is complete. The Preserve keyword can cause problems if you're dealing with very large arrays in a limited memory situation.

> **TIP**
>
> Each type of array complements the other's drawbacks. As a VBA developer, you have the flexibility of choosing the right type of array for each situation. Fixed arrays are the way to go when the number of elements doesn't vary widely. Dynamic arrays should be used when the number varies widely, and you're sure you have enough memory to resize even the largest possible arrays.

Passing Arrays as Parameters

Many people are unaware that you can pass an array as a parameter to a function or subroutine. The following code provides an example:

```
Sub PassArray()
    'Declare a six-element array
    Dim astrNames(5) As String
    Dim intCounter As Integer

    'Call the FillNames function, passing a reference
    'to the array
    Call FillNames(astrNames)

    'Use a For...Next loop to loop through the
    'elements of the array
```

```
    For intCounter = 0 To UBound(astrNames)
        Debug.Print astrNames(intCounter)
    Next intCounter
End Sub
```

The code begins by declaring a fixed array called astrNames. The code calls the FillNames routine. It receives the array as a parameter and then populates all its elements. The PassArray routine is then able to loop through all the elements of the array that was passed, displaying information from each element. The FillNames routine looks like this:

```
Sub FillNames(varNameList As Variant)
    'Populate the elements of the array
    varNameList(0) = "Alison"
    varNameList(1) = "Dan"
    varNameList(2) = "Alexis"
    varNameList(3) = "Brendan"
    varNameList(4) = "Zachary"
    varNameList(5) = "Sonia"
End Sub
```

Notice that the routine receives the array as a variant variable. It then populates each element of the array.

Understanding Advanced Function Techniques

The advanced function techniques covered in the following sections allow you to get the most out of the procedures you build. First, you learn the difference between passing your parameters by reference and passing them by value, and see that the default method of passing parameters isn't always the most prudent method.

Next, you learn how to work with optional parameters, which help you build flexibility into your functions. Whereas optional parameters allow you to omit parameters, named parameters help you to add readability to your code. Named parameters also shelter you from having to worry about the order in which the parameters must appear. After reading these sections, you will be able to build much more robust and easy-to-use functions.

Passing by Reference Versus Passing by Value

By default, parameters in Access are passed *by reference*. This means that a memory reference to the variable being passed is received by the function. This process is best illustrated by an example:

```
Sub PassByRef()
    'Declare string variables
    Dim strFirstName As String
    Dim strLastName As String
```

```
    'Assign values to the string variables
    strFirstName = "Alison"
    strLastName = "Balter"

    'Call a subroutine that receives the two variables as
    'parameters by reference
    Call FuncByRef(strFirstName, strLastName)

    'Print the changed values of the variables
    Debug.Print strFirstName
    Debug.Print strLastName
End Sub


Sub FuncByRef(strFirstParm As String, strSecondParm As String)
    'Modify the values of the parameters
    strFirstParm = "Bill"
    strSecondParm = "Gates"
End Sub
```

You might be surprised that the Debug.Print statements found in the subroutine
PassByRef print "Bill" and "Gates". The reason is that strFirstParm is actually a reference to the same location in memory as strFirstName, and strSecondParm is a reference
to the same location in memory as strLastName. This code violates the concepts of *black-
box processing*, in which a variable can't be changed by any routine other than the one it
was declared in. The following code eliminates this problem:

```
Sub PassByVal()
    'Declare the string variables
    Dim strFirstName As String
    Dim strLastName As String

    'Assign values to the string variables
    strFirstName = "Alison"
    strLastName = "Balter"

    'Call a subroutine that receives the two variables as
    'parameters by value
    Call FuncByVal(strFirstName, strLastName)

    'Print the unchanged values of the variables
    Debug.Print strFirstName
    Debug.Print strLastName
End Sub
```

13

```
Sub FuncByVal(ByVal strFirstParm As String, _
ByVal strSecondParm As String)
    'Change the values of the parameters
    'Since they are received by value,
    'the original variables are unchanged
    strFirstParm = "Bill"
    strSecondParm = "Gates"
End Sub
```

This `FuncByVal` subroutine receives the parameters *by value*. This means that the code passes only the values in `strFirstName` and `strLastName` to the `FuncByVal` routine. The `strFirstName` and `strLastName` variables, therefore, can't be modified by the `FuncByVal` subroutine. The `Debug.Print` statements print `"Alison"` and `"Balter"`.

The following example illustrates a great reason why you might want to pass a parameter by reference:

```
Sub GoodPassByRef()
    'Declare variables
    Dim blnSuccess As Boolean
    Dim strName As String

    'Set the value of the string variable
    strName = "Microsoft"

    'Set the boolean variable equal to the value
    'returned from the GoodFunc function
    blnSuccess = GoodFunc(strName)

    'Print the value of the boolean variable
    Debug.Print blnSuccess
End Sub


Function GoodFunc(strName As String)
    'Evaluate the length of the value received
    'as a parameter
    'Convert to uppercase and return true if not zero-length
    'Return false if zero-length
    If Len(strName) Then
        strName = UCase$(strName)
        GoodFunc = True
    Else
        GoodFunc = False
    End If
End Function
```

In essence, the `GoodFunc` function needs to return two values. Not only does the function need to return the uppercase version of the string passed to it, but it also needs to return a success code. Because a function can return only one value, you need to be able to modify the value of `strName` within the function. As long as you're aware of what you're doing and why you're doing it, there's no problem with passing a parameter by reference.

> **TIP**
>
> I use a special technique to help readers of my code see whether I'm passing parameters by reference or by value. When passing parameters by reference, I refer to the parameters by the same name in both the calling routine and the actual procedure that I'm calling. On the other hand, when passing parameters by value, I refer to the parameters by different names in the calling routine and in the procedure that's being called.

After reading this section, you might ask yourself whether it is better to pass parameters by reference or by value. Although in terms of black-box processing it is better to pass by value, code that involves parameters passed by reference actually executes more quickly than those passed by value. As long as you and the programmers that you work with are aware of the potential problems with passing parameters by reference, in general, in VBA, I feel that it is better to pass parameters by reference.

Optional Parameters: Building Flexibility into Functions

The VBA language allows you to use optional parameters. In other words, you don't need to know how many parameters will be passed. The `ReturnInit` function in the following code receives the last two parameters as optional; it then evaluates whether the parameters are missing and responds accordingly:

```
Function ReturnInit(ByVal strFName As String, _
      Optional ByVal strMI, Optional ByVal strLName)
   'If strMI parameter is not received, prompt user for value
   If IsMissing(strMI) Then
      strMI = InputBox("Enter Middle Initial")
   End If


   'If strLName parameter is not received, prompt user for value
   If IsMissing(strLName) Then
      strLName = InputBox("Enter Last Name")
   End If

   'Return concatenation of last name, first name,
   'and middle initial
   ReturnInit = strLName & "," & strFName & " " & strMI
End Function
```

This function could be called as follows:

```
strName = ReturnInit("Bill",,"Gates")
```

As you can see, the second parameter is missing. Instead of causing a compiler error, this code compiles and runs successfully. The IsMissing function, built into Access, determines whether a parameter has been passed. After identifying missing parameters, you must decide how to handle the situation in code. In the example, the function prompts for the missing information, but here are some other possible choices:

▶ Insert default values when parameters are missing.

▶ Accommodate for the missing parameters in your code.

Listing 13.1 and Listing 13.2 illustrate how to carry out these two alternatives.

LISTING 13.1   Inserting Default Values When Parameters Are Missing

```
Function ReturnInit2(ByVal strFName As String, _
      Optional ByVal strMI, Optional ByVal strLName)
   'If middle initial is not received, set it to "A"
   If IsMissing(strMI) Then
       strMI = "A"
   End If

   'If last name is not received, set it to "Roman"
   If IsMissing(strLName) Then
       strLName = "Roman"
   End If

   'Return concatenation of last name, first name,
   'and middle initial
   ReturnInit2 = strLName & "," & strFName & " " & strMI
End Function
```

This example uses a default value of "A" for the middle initial and a default last name of "Roman". Now look at Listing 13.2, which illustrates another method of handling missing parameters.

LISTING 13.2   Accommodating for Missing Parameters in Your Code

```
Function ReturnInit3(ByVal strFName As String, _
      Optional ByVal strMI, Optional ByVal strLName)
   Dim strResult As String

   'If middle initial and last name are missing,
   'return first name
   If IsMissing(strMI) And IsMissing(strLName) Then
```

LISTING 13.2   Continued

```
        ReturnInit3 = strFName

    'If only the middle initial is missing
    'return last name and first name
    ElseIf IsMissing(strMI) Then
        ReturnInit3 = strLName & ", " & strFName

    'If only the last name is missing
    'return first name and middle initial
    ElseIf IsMissing(strLName) Then
        ReturnInit3 = strFName & " " & strMI

    'Otherwise (If nothing is missing),
    'return last name, first name, and middle initial
    Else
        ReturnInit3 = strLName & "," & strFName & " " & strMI
    End If
End Function
```

This example manipulates the return value, depending on which parameters it receives. If neither optional parameter is passed, just the first name displays. If the first name and middle initial are passed, the return value contains the first name followed by the middle initial. If the first name and last name are passed, the return value contains the last name, a comma, and the first name. If all three parameters are passed, the function returns the last name, a comma, a space, and the first name.

You can easily modify the declaration of the ReturnInit3 function shown in Listing 13.2 to provide default values for each optional parameter. The following declaration illustrates this:

```
Function ReturnInit4(Optional ByVal strFName As String = "Alison", _
        Optional ByVal strMI As String = "J", _
        Optional ByVal strLName As String = "Balter")
```

ReturnInit4 has three optional parameters. The declaration assigns a default value to each parameter. The function uses the default value if the calling routine does not supply the parameter.

> **NOTE**
>
> The IsMissing function works only with parameters that have a data type of Variant. The reason is that the IsMissing function returns True only if the value of the parameter is empty. If the parameter is numeric (for example, an integer), you will need to test for zero. If the parameter is a string, you will need to test for a zero-length string ("") or against the VBA constant vbNullString.

Named Parameters: Eliminate the Need to Count Commas

In all the examples you've seen so far, the parameters of a procedure have been supplied positionally. Named parameters allow you to supply parameters without regard for their position, which is particularly useful in procedures that receive optional parameters. Take a look at this example:

```
strName = ReturnInit3("Bill",,"Gates")
```

Because the second parameter isn't supplied, and the parameters are passed positionally, a comma must be used as a placemarker for the optional parameter. This requirement can become unwieldy when you're dealing with several optional parameters. The following example greatly simplifies the process of passing the parameters and also better documents what's happening:

```
strName = ReturnInit3(strFName:= "Bill",strLName:= "Gates")
```

As shown in the following example, when you pass parameters by name, the order that the parameters appear doesn't even matter:

```
strName = ReturnInit3(strLName:= "Gates",strFName:="Bill")
```

This call to the ReturnInit3 function yields the same results as the call to the function in the previous example.

> **NOTE**
>
> When you use named parameters, each parameter name must be exactly the same as the name of the parameter in the function being called. Besides requiring intimate knowledge of the function being called, this method of specifying parameters has one important disadvantage: If the author of the function modifies a parameter's name, all routines that use the named parameter will fail when calling the function.

Recursive Procedures

A *recursive procedure* is one that calls itself. If a procedure calls itself over and over again, it will eventually render an error because it runs out of stack space. Here's an example:

```
Function Recursive(lngSomeVal)
    'Return value based on another call to the function
    Recursive = Recursive(lngSomeVal)
End Function
```

There are practical reasons why you might want to call a function recursively. Here's an example:

```
Function GetFactorial(intValue as Integer) as Double
    'If value passed is less than or equal to one, we're done
    If intValue <= 1 Then
        GetFactorial = 1

    'If value passed is greater than one,
    'call function again with decremented value
    'and multiply by value
    Else
        GetFactorial = GetFactorial(intValue - 1) * intValue
    End If
End Function
```

13

The code receives an input parameter (for example, 5). The value is evaluated to see whether it is less than or equal to 1. If it is, the function is exited. If the value is greater than 1, the function is called again but is passed the previous input parameter minus 1 (for example, 4). The return value from the function is multiplied by the original parameter value (for example, 4*5). The function calls itself over and over again until the value that it passes to itself is 2 minus 1 (1), and the function is exited. In the example where 5 is passed to the function, it multiplies 5*4*3*2*1, resulting in 120, the factorial of 5.

Using Parameter Arrays

Using a parameter array, you can easily pass a variable number of arguments to a procedure. Here's an example:

```
Sub GetAverageSalary(strDepartment As String, _
    ParamArray currSalaries() As Variant)

    Dim sngTotalSalary As Single
    Dim sngAverageSalary As Single
    Dim intCounter As Integer

    'Loop through the elements of the array,
    'adding up all of the salaries
    For intCounter = 0 To UBound(currSalaries())
        sngTotalSalary = sngTotalSalary + currSalaries(intCounter)
    Next intCounter

    'Divide the total salary by the number of salaries in the array
    sngAverageSalary = sngTotalSalary / (UBound(currSalaries()) + 1)

    'Display the department and the average salary in a message box
    MsgBox strDepartment & " has an average salary of " & _
        sngAverageSalary
End Sub
```

The routine is called like this:

```
Call GetAverageSalary("Accounting", 60000, 20000, 30000, 25000, 80000)
```

The beauty of the `ParamArray` keyword is that you can pass a variable number of parameters to the procedure. In the example, a department name and a variable number of salaries are passed to the `GetAverageSalary` procedure. The procedure loops through all the salaries that it receives in the parameter array, adding them together. It then divides the total by the number of salaries contained in the array.

Working with `Empty` and `Null`

`Empty` and `Null` are values that can exist only for `Variant` variables. They're different from one another and different from zero or a zero-length string. At times, you need to know whether the value stored in a variable is zero, a zero-length string, `Empty`, or `Null`. You can make this differentiation only with `Variant` variables.

Working with `Empty`

`Variant` variables are initialized to the value of `Empty`. Often, you need to know whether a value has been stored in a `Variant` variable. If a `Variant` has never been assigned a value, its value is `Empty`. As mentioned, the `Empty` value is not the same as zero, `Null`, or a zero-length string.

Your ability to test for `Empty` in a runtime environment is important. You can do this by using the `IsEmpty` function, which determines whether a variable has the `Empty` value. The following example tests a `String` variable for the `Empty` value:

```
Sub StringVar()
    Dim strName As String
    Debug.Print IsEmpty(strName) 'Prints False
    Debug.Print strName = "" 'Prints True
End Sub
```

The `Debug.Print` statement prints `False`. This variable is equal to a zero-length string because the variable is initialized as a `String` variable. All `String` variables are initialized to a zero-length string. The next example tests a `Variant` variable to see whether it has the `Empty` value:

```
Sub EmptyVar()
    Dim vntName As Variant
    Debug.Print IsEmpty(vntName) 'Prints True
    vntName = ""
    Debug.Print IsEmpty(vntName) 'Prints False
    vntName = Empty
    Debug.Print IsEmpty(vntName) 'Prints True
End Sub
```

A `Variant` variable loses its `Empty` value when any value has been stored in it, including zero, `Null`, or a zero-length string. It can become `Empty` again only by storing the keyword `Empty` in the variable.

Working with `Null`

`Null` is a special value that indicates unknown or missing data. `Null` is not the same as `Empty`; in addition, one `Null` value is not equal to another one. `Variant` variables can contain the special value called `Null`.

Often, you need to know whether specific fields or controls have never been initialized. Uninitialized fields and controls have a default value of `Null`. By testing for `Null`, you can make sure fields and controls contain values.

If you want to make sure that all fields and controls in your application have data, you need to test for `Null`s. You can do this by using the `IsNull` function:

```
Sub NullVar()
    Dim vntName As Variant
    Debug.Print IsEmpty(vntName) 'Prints True
    Debug.Print IsNull(vntName) 'Prints False
    vntName = Null
    Debug.Print IsNull(vntName) 'Prints True
End Sub
```

Notice that `vntName` is equal to `Null` only after you explicitly store the value of `Null` in it. It's important to know not only how variables and `Null` values interact, but also how to test for `Null` within a field in your database. A field contains a `Null` if data hasn't yet been entered in the field, and the field has no default value. In queries, you can test for the criteria `"Is Null"` to find all the records in which a particular field contains a `Null` value. When dealing with recordsets (covered in Chapter 15, "What Are ActiveX Data Objects, and Why Are They Important?"), you can also use the `IsNull` function to test for a `Null` value in a field. Here's an example:

```
Sub LoopProjects()
    Dim rst As ADODB.Recordset
    Set rst = New ADODB.Recordset

    'Open a recordset based on the Projects table
    rst.Open "tblProjects", CurrentProject.Connection

    'Loop through all of the records in the recordset
    Do Until rst.EOF

        'Print the ProjectID and the ProjectName
        Debug.Print rst!ProjectID, rst!ProjectName
```

13

```
        'If the ProjectBeginDate field is null,
        'display a message to the user
        If IsNull(rst!ProjectBeginDate) Then
            Debug.Print "Project Begin Date Contains No Value!!"
        End If

        'Move to the next row in the recordset
        rst.MoveNext
    Loop
End Sub
```

Alternatively, you could use the more compact Nz function to detect Nulls and print a special message:

```
Sub LoopProjects2()
    Dim rst As ADODB.Recordset
    Set rst = New ADODB.Recordset

    'Open a recordset based on the Projects table
    rst.Open "tblProjects", CurrentProject.Connection

    'Loop through all of the rows in the recordset
    Do Until rst.EOF

        'Print the ProjectID and the ProjectName
        Debug.Print rst!ProjectID, rst!ProjectName

        'Print the ProjectBeginDate, or a message if
        'the ProjectBeginDate is null
        Debug.Print Nz(rst!ProjectBeginDate, _
            "Project Begin Date Contains No Value!!")
        rst.MoveNext
    Loop
End Sub
```

Chapter 15 covers all the concepts of recordset handling. For now, you need to understand only that this code loops through each record in tblProjects. It uses the IsNull function to evaluate whether the ProjectBeginDate field contains a Null value. If the field does contain a Null, the code prints a warning message to the Immediate window. Here is another example:

```
Private Sub Form_Current()

    Dim ctl as Control
```

```
'Loop through each control in the form's
'Controls collection
For Each ctl In Controls

    'If the control is a TextBox
    If TypeOf ctl Is TextBox Then

        'If the value in the control is null,
        'change the BackColor property to cyan
        If IsNull(ctl.Value) Then
            ctl.BackColor = vbCyan

        'If the value in the control is not null
        'change the BackColor property to white
        Else
            ctl.BackColor = vbWhite
        End If
    End If
Next ctl
End Sub
```

The code in this example (found in the `frmProjects` form in `CHAP13EX.ACCDB`) loops through every control on the current form. If the control is a text box, the routine checks to see whether the value in the text box is `Null`. If it is, the `BackColor` property of the text box is set to `Cyan`; otherwise, it's set to `White`. If the control is not a text box, the code ignores it and moves to the next control.

You should know about some idiosyncrasies of `Null`:

▸ Expressions involving `Null` always result in `Null`. (See the next example.)

▸ A function that's passed a `Null` usually returns a `Null`.

▸ `Null` values propagate through built-in functions that return variants.

The following example shows how `Null` values are propagated:

```
Sub PropNulls()
    Dim rst As ADODB.Recordset
    Set rst = New ADODB.Recordset

    'Open a recordset based on the Projects table
    rst.Open "tblProjects", CurrentProject.Connection

    'Loop through the recordset
    Do Until rst.EOF
```

```
        'Print the ProjectID and the value of the
        'ProjectBeginDate plus one
        Debug.Print rst!ProjectID, rst!ProjectBeginDate + 1

        'Move to the next row
        rst.MoveNext
    Loop
End Sub
```

Figure 13.3 illustrates the effects of running this routine on a table in which the first and third records contain Null values. Notice that the result of the calculation is Null for those records because the Null propagated within those records.

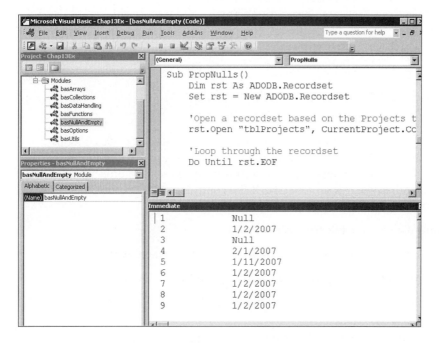

FIGURE 13.3   The result of running the PropNulls routine.

Notice the difference from the previous example if the value in the field is Empty:

```
Sub EmptyVersusNull()
    Dim rst As ADODB.Recordset
    Set rst = New ADODB.Recordset

    'Open a recordset based on the Projects table
    rst.Open "tblProjects", CurrentProject.Connection
```

```
    'Loop through the recordset
    Do Until rst.EOF

        'Print the ProjectID and the PurchaseOrderNumber
        'combined with the word "Hello"
        Debug.Print rst!ProjectID, rst!PurchaseOrderNumber + "Hello"

        'Move to the next row
        rst.MoveNext
    Loop
End Sub
```

In this example, the `tblProjects` table has many records. The `PurchaseOrderNumber` for the first record contains a `Null`; for the third record, it contains an `Empty`. Notice the different effects of the two values, as shown in Figure 13.4.

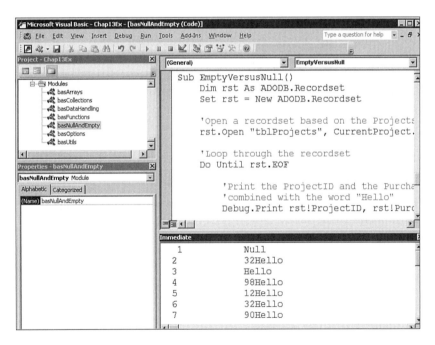

FIGURE 13.4   The result of running the `EmptyVersusNull` routine shows the propagation of the `Null` value.

Looking at Figure 13.4, you can see that `Null` printed for the first record, and `Hello` printed for the third record.

The `EmptyVersusNull` routine uses a numeric operator (+). As discussed, the effect of `Null` used in a calculation is a resulting `Null`. In text strings, you can use an ampersand (&)

instead of a plus (+) to eliminate this problem. Figure 13.5 illustrates the same code with an ampersand to concatenate rather than add. You can see that no Null values result from the concatenation.

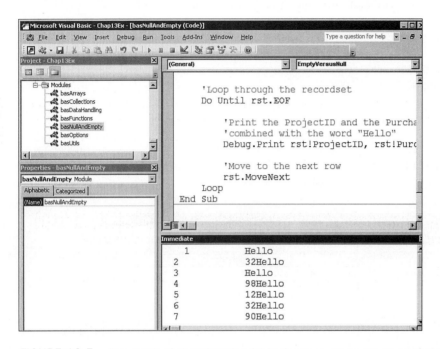

FIGURE 13.5   The result of changing plus (+) in the EmptyVersusNull routine to an ampersand (&).

It's common to create a generic routine that receives any value, tests to see whether it's Null, and returns a non-Null value. An example is the CvNulls function:

```
Function CvNulls(vntVar1 As Variant, vntVar2 As Variant) _
     As Variant
   'If first variable is null, return the second variable
   'otherwise, return the first variable
   CvNulls = IIf(IsNull(vntVar1), vntVar2, vntVar1)
End Function
```

You would call this routine as follows:

```
Sub TestForNull(vntSalary As Variant, vntCommission As Variant)
   'Add the result of calling the CVNulls function,
   'passing the salary and zero to the
   'result of calling the CVNulls function
```

```
    'passing the commission and zero
    curTotal = CvNulls(vntSalary, 0) + CvNulls(vntCommission, 0)

    'Display the total of salary plus commission
    MsgBox curTotal
End Sub
```

The `TestForNull` routine receives two parameters: `salary` and `commission`. It adds the two values to determine the total of salaries plus commissions. Ordinarily, if the value of either parameter is `Null`, the expression results in `Null`. The code eliminates the problem with the `CvNulls` function, which also receives two parameters. The first parameter is the variable being tested for `Null`; the second is the value you want the function to return if the first parameter is determined to be `Null`. The routine combines the `Immediate If` (`IIf`) function and the `IsNull` function to evaluate the first parameter and return the appropriate value.

> **NOTE**
>
> If you simply want to substitute a value for a `Null`, you can use the built-in function NZ instead of a user-defined function. The user-defined function offers more functionality, when necessary.

Creating and Working with Custom Collections

Earlier in this chapter, I discussed the problems associated with arrays. If you are unsure of the number of elements that the array will contain, fixed arrays can take up large amounts of memory unnecessarily. On the other hand, the resizing of dynamic arrays is rather inefficient. Finally, all the elements of an array must be contiguous, and the arbitrary identifier for the array element is meaningless. The answer—custom collections. Custom collections can contain values and objects. You can easily add items to, and remove items from, a collection. VBA identifies each element in the collection by a meaningful unique key.

In summary, custom collections are similar to arrays, but they offer several advantages:

- ▶ Collections are dynamically allocated. They take up memory based only on what's in them at a given time. This is different from arrays, whose size you must either predefine or redimension at runtime. When you redimension an array, Access actually makes a copy of the array in memory, taking up substantial resources. By using custom collections, you can avoid this consumption of extra resources.

- ▶ A collection always knows how many elements it has, and you can easily add and remove elements.

- ▶ Each element of a collection can contain a different type of data.

- ▶ You can add elements into any element of a collection.

NOTE

You can find the code examples in this section in the `basCollections` module of the `CHAP13EX.ACCDB` database.

Creating a Custom Collection

You create a collection using a `Collection` object. After you declare the `Collection` object, you can add items to the collection. The code necessary to create a custom collection looks like this:

```
Dim colNames as Collection
```

Adding Items to a Custom Collection

You use the `Add` method of the `Collection` object to add items to a custom collection. The `Add` method receives a value or object reference as its first parameter and a unique key to that element of the collection as its second parameter. The `Add` method appears as follows:

```
colNames.Add "Alexis", "Alexis"
```

The code shown previously adds the name `Alexis` to a collection called `colNames`. The key to the item in the collection is the name `Alexis`. In the following code example, the collection `colNames` is first declared and instantiated. The code then adds several names to the custom collection `colNames`:

```
Sub AddToCollection()
    'Declare a Collection object
    Dim colNames As Collection

    'Instantiate the Collection object
    Set colNames = New Collection

    'Add items to the collection
    colNames.Add "Alison", "Alison"
    colNames.Add "Dan", "Dan"
    colNames.Add "Alexis", "Alexis"
    colNames.Add "Brendan", "Brendan"
    colNames.Add "Sonia", "Sonia"
    colNames.Add "Sue", "Sue"
End Sub
```

CAUTION

Unlike almost every other array or collection in VBA, custom collections are one-based rather than zero-based. This means that the element numbers begin with one rather than zero. This is a big change if you're used to thinking of arrays and collections as always zero-based.

Accessing an Item in a Custom Collection

After you have added items to a collection, you use the `Item` method to access them via either their ordinal position or the key designated when you added them. Accessing an item in a collection using the ordinal position looks like this:

```
Debug.Print colNames.Item(1)
```

Because the `Item` method is the default method of the `Collection` object, you can shorten the code to this:

```
Debug.Print colNames(1)
```

I usually prefer to refer to an item in a collection using its unique key. The code appears as follows:

```
Debug.Print colNames("Alexis")
```

Removing Items from a Custom Collection

You use the `Remove` method of the `Collection` object to remove items from a collection. The syntax looks like this:

```
colNames.Remove 2
```

The preceding syntax would remove the second element of the collection. Using the key, you can change the code to this:

```
colNames.Remove "Sonia"
```

You can easily remove all the elements of a collection in two ways:

```
Set colNames = New Collection
```

or

```
Set colNames = Nothing
```

Iterating Through the Elements of a Custom Collection

You use the For...Each loop to iterate through the items in a collection. The code looks like this:

```
Sub IterateCollection()
    'Declare a Collection object
    Dim colNames As Collection

    'Declare a variant variable for looping
    'through the collection
    Dim varItem As Variant

    'Instantiate the Collection object
    Set colNames = New Collection

    colNames.Add "Alison", "Alison"
    colNames.Add "Dan", "Dan"
    colNames.Add "Alexis", "Alexis"
    colNames.Add "Brendan", "Brendan"
    colNames.Add "Sonia", "Sonia"
    colNames.Add "Sue", "Sue"

    'Use the variant variable and a For..Each
    'loop to loop through each element in
    'the collection, printing its value
    For Each varItem In colNames
        Debug.Print colNames(varItem)
    Next varItem
End Sub
```

Notice that in addition to the declaration of the Collection variable, the code declares a Variant variable. The code uses the Variant variable in the For...Each loop to loop through each item in the collection. The Variant variable is the subscript within the For...Each loop for accessing a particular item within the collection.

Handling Files with Low-Level File Handling

On occasion, you need to write data to or read data from a text file. This is often referred to as *low-level file handling*. Three types of file access exist: sequential, random, and binary. This text covers only sequential access. You use sequential access to read and write to a text file, such as an error log. You use the Open keyword to open a text file. You use the Input # keyword to read data. Likewise, you use the Write # keyword to write data. Finally, you use the Close keyword to close the file. The subroutine LogErrorText provides a practical example of why you may need to use this technique. It writes error information to a text file. Here's how it works:

```
Sub LogErrorText()
    Dim intFile As Integer

    'Store a free file handle into a variable
    intFile = FreeFile

    'Open a file named ErrorLog.txt in the current directory
    'using the file handle obtained above
    Open CurDir & "\ErrorLog.Txt" For Append Shared As intFile

    'Write the error information to the file
    Write #intFile, "LogErrorDemo", Now, Err, Error, CurrentUser()

    'Close the file
    Close intFile
End Sub
```

The code uses the FreeFile function to locate a free file handle. The Open keyword opens a file with the name ErrorLog.txt located in the current directory. The code opens the file in shared mode and for append, using the file handle returned by the FreeFile function. The code then uses the Write # keyword to write error information to the text file. Finally, the Close keyword closes the text file.

> **NOTE**
>
> This example is taken from Chapter 15. The sample code is located in the
> CHAP15EX.ACCDB database.

Understanding and Effectively Using Compilation Options

Microsoft Access gives you a few alternatives for compilation. Understanding them can help you to decide whether compilation speed or trapping compilation errors is more important to you.

Compile on Demand

By default, VBA compiles your code only when the code in the module changes or when a procedure in one module is called by another module. Although this default setting can dramatically speed the compilation process, it can leave you wondering whether you have a hidden time bomb lurking somewhere in your application.

Here's a typical scenario: You open a form, make some simple changes, save the changes, and close the form. You repeat this process for a few additional forms. You also open a couple of modules to make some equally simple changes. During the testing process, you forget to test one or more of the forms and one or more of the modules. With the Compile On Demand option set to True (its default value), you won't identify the errors until your users access the offending code!

To disable the Compile On Demand feature, choose Tools, Options from the VBE. Click the General tab and remove the check from Compile On Demand. You might notice some degradation in performance each time your code compiles, but this is time well spent.

Importing and Exporting Code Modules

The Access 2007 VBE allows you to import code or form modules into and export code modules from a database. To export a form or code module, take the following steps:

1. Activate the VBE.

2. Within the Project Explorer window, right-click the object you want to export.

3. Select Export File. The Export File dialog box appears (see Figure 13.6).

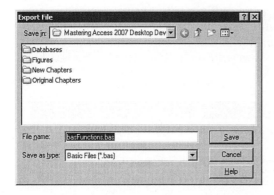

FIGURE 13.6   The Export File dialog box allows you to export a VBA module.

4. Select a location and name for the exported file and then click Save.

When you export a module, it is exported as an ASCII text file. You can import the text file into another Microsoft Access database, into any other Microsoft Office product (for example, Microsoft Excel), or into a Visual Basic project.

> **NOTE**
>
> If you export a Form module from the VBE, Access exports only the Class module behind the form. It does not export any visual aspects of the form.

Just as you can export a text file, you can import a text file. Consequently, you can add an existing module or form to a project. Access copies the file and imports it into the database. It does not affect the original file. To import a file into your Access database, follow these steps:

1. Activate the VBE.

2. Within the Project Explorer window, right-click and select Import File. The Import File dialog box appears (see Figure 13.7).

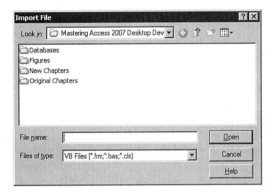

FIGURE 13.7   The Import File dialog box allows you to import a text file into your database.

3. Locate and select the file you want to import and then click Open.

Working with Project Properties

Every database project has user-definable properties. They include the following:

► The project name

► A description of the project

► The name of the help file associated with the project

► The help context ID associated with the project

► Conditional compilation arguments

► A password associated with the project

To view or modify project properties, follow these steps:

1. Activate the VBE.

2. Select Tools, <i>project name</i> Properties. The Project Properties dialog box appears (see Figure 13.8).

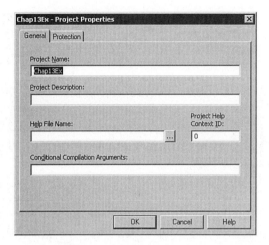

FIGURE 13.8   The Project Properties dialog box.

3. Click the General tab, where you can designate or change any of the general project properties.

4. Click the Protection tab, where you can specify a password for the VBA project.

5. Click OK to close the dialog box, accepting the options you have set. You must close the database and reopen it for any security options to take effect.

The Protection option deserves special attention. If you click to select Lock Project for Viewing, the VBA project cannot be viewed or edited by someone who does not have the correct password. If you do not select Lock Project for Viewing, anyone can view the VBA project, but only someone with the correct password can change the project properties.

Practical Examples: Putting Advanced Techniques to Use

The examples in the following sections put into practice all that you have learned throughout this chapter. Concepts covered include the use of Null, intrinsic constants, and type structures.

Examples of Null, the DoCmd Object, and Intrinsic Constants

The following event routine illustrates how you could view all the projects associated with the selected client. It illustrates the importance of the ability to work with Null values and intrinsic constants:

```
Private Sub cmdViewProjects_Click()
On Error GoTo Err_cmdViewProjects_Click
```

```
'Evaluate the ClientID text box to determine if it is null
'If it is null, display a message to the user
'Otherwise, save the current record and open the
'projects form (which is set up to only show projects
'related to the selected client)
If IsNull(Me.txtClientID.Value) Then
    MsgBox "You Must Enter Client Information Before " & _
        "Viewing the Projects Form"
Else
    DoCmd.RunCommand acCmdSaveRecord
    DoCmd.OpenForm FormName:="frmProjects"
End If

Exit_cmdViewProjects_Click:
    Exit Sub

Err_cmdViewProjects_Click:
    MsgBox Err.Description
    Resume Exit_cmdViewProjects_Click

End Sub
```

The routine first invokes error handling (discussed in Chapter 17) and then uses the IsNull function to test whether the user has entered a ClientID. The IsNull function returns True if the value in the txtClientID control is Null. If it is, the code displays an error message. If the txtClientID control contains a non-Null value, the code performs two methods on the DoCmd object.

The first method performed on the DoCmd object is the RunCommand method. This method receives the constant associated with the name of the menu command you want to execute. The use of intrinsic constants makes this code more readable, and the RunCommand method makes it much easier to call menu commands from code. The second method performed on the DoCmd object is OpenForm, which opens the frmProjects form. The code programmatically sets the RecordSource property of the frmProjects form to a query that displays only projects associated with the currently selected customer.

An Example of Using a Type Structure

If many parts of an application require the same information that is stored in a specific table, reading the data from this table each time the application needs it would be inefficient. A much more efficient approach would be to read this data once, when the application loads, and store it in a type structure. Because it remains in memory at all times, you can efficiently retrieve it whenever needed. The type structure is defined, and a Public Type variable based on the type structure is declared in a module's Declarations section. It looks like this:

```
Type CompanyInfo
    SetUpID As Long
    CompanyName As String * 50
    Address As String * 255
    City As String * 50
    StateProvince As String * 20
    PostalCode As String * 20
    Country As String * 50
    PhoneNumber As String * 30
    FaxNumber As String * 30
    DefaultPaymentTerms As String * 255
    DefaultInvoiceDescription As String
End Type
Public typCompanyInfo As CompanyInfo
```

You must build a subroutine that is invoked when your startup form is first loaded. This routine populates all the elements of the type structure. The routine looks like this:

```
Sub GetCompanyInfo()

    Dim strSubName As String
    Dim rst As ADODB.Recordset

    'Instantiate and open a recordset
    'based on the tblCompanyInfo table
    Set rst = New ADODB.Recordset
    rst.ActiveConnection = CurrentProject.Connection
    rst.Open "Select * from tblCompanyInfo", Options:=adCmdText

    'Populate the elements of the type structure
    'with data from the table
    With typCompanyInfo
        .SetUpID = rst!SetUpID
        .CompanyName = rst!CompanyName
        .Address = rst!Address
        .City = rst!City
        .StateProvince = rst!StateOrProvince
        .PostalCode = rst!PostalCode
        .Country = rst!Country
        .PhoneNumber = rst!PhoneNumber
        .FaxNumber = rst!PhoneNumber
    End With

    'Close the recordset and destroy the object
    rst.Close
    Set rst = Nothing
End Sub
```

Don't be concerned with the recordset handling included in this routine. Instead, notice that the code loads the value from each field in the first (and only) record of the tblCompanyInfo table into the elements of the Global Type variable. Here's an example of how the code uses the Type variable:

```
Sub PopulateControls()
    'Populate the text boxes on the report
    'with data from the type structure
    txtCompanyName.Value = Trim(typCompanyInfo.CompanyName)
    txtAddress.Value = Trim(typCompanyInfo.Address)
    txtCityStateZip.Value = Trim(typCompanyInfo.City) & ", " & _
        Trim(typCompanyInfo.StateProvince) & _
        "   " & Format(Trim(typCompanyInfo.PostalCode), "!&&&&&-&&&&")
    txtPhoneFax.Value = "PHONE: " & _
        Format(Trim(typCompanyInfo.PhoneNumber), "(&&&)&&&-&&&&") & _
        "     FAX: " & _
        Format(Trim(typCompanyInfo.FaxNumber), "(&&&)&&&-&&&&")
End Sub
```

This routine populates four different controls on a form with the company information retrieved from the elements of the Global Type variable.

Summary

As an Access developer, you spend much of your time writing VBA code. Knowing the tricks and tips of the trade and understanding the more advanced aspects of the language will save you much time and help you streamline your application code.

This chapter showed you tricks and tips you can use to effectively navigate the VBA environment. It delved into more advanced aspects of the VBA language, such as user-defined types, constants, and arrays. You have seen the important difference between passing parameters by reference and passing them by value, and learned about other advanced function techniques, such as optional and named parameters. Other important topics covered in this chapter included collections, Empty versus Null, and compilation options. Understanding these valuable aspects of the VBA language will help you get the most out of the code you write.

13

Exploiting the Power of Class Modules

Why This Chapter Is Important

Access 2007 offers two types of modules: Standard modules and Class modules. A Class module is similar to a Code module. The subroutines and functions in the Class module become the methods of the class. The Property Let and Property Get routines become the properties of the class, and the Class module's name becomes the name of the custom object. A Class module is a great way to encapsulate related functions into a portable, self-contained object. Class modules can help you simplify the process of performing the following tasks:

▶ Manipulating databases and recordsets

▶ Calling Windows API functions

▶ Performing low-level, file-handling tasks

▶ Accessing and modifying the Registry

If you regularly open databases and recordsets and traverse those recordsets by using code, you might decide that you want to simplify these tasks. By building Class modules, you can more easily access table data.

Object Orientation—An Introduction

The world of object orientation is exciting, but it requires a new way of thinking about things. Access Office 2007 is object-based rather than object-oriented. So, what exactly is the difference? The definitions of the following terms should help you differentiate between these two concepts:

- ▶ **Class**—A template for an object

- ▶ **Object**—An instance of a class

- ▶ **Instantiation**—The process of creating an object based on a class

- ▶ **Polymorphism**—The state of being multifaced; using the same method and property names with different objects, the properties and methods of which are implemented differently for different objects

- ▶ **Subclassing**—Building one class based on another

- ▶ **Inheritance**—In object-oriented programming, the ability of newly created subclasses to take on the behavior of their parent classes

Visual Basic for Applications (VBA), and therefore Access, supports the creation of custom classes and the instantiation of objects based on those classes. Polymorphism can also be simulated by using the same property and method names within different classes. VBA does not fully support subclassing and inheritance. With the exception of a keyword called `Implements`, classes cannot be based on other classes and, therefore, cannot elicit the behavior of other classes. True polymorphism can exist only when child classes inherit the properties and methods of their parents. The `Implements` keyword gets you close but does not fully exhibit the behavior of polymorphism.

To make sure that you understand the terms, let's use an analogy. Imagine that you are going to bake some cookies. The cookie cutter is the class, the template for a cookie object. When you use the cookie cutter to create an actual cookie, you instantiate the cookie class to create a cookie object. The cookie has some properties, such as a powdered sugar property, and some methods, such as the bake method. A ham class is a template for a ham object. The ham class also has a bake method. The "code" behind the bake method of the cookie object and the bake method of the ham object is different. This is polymorphism (being multifaced) in action. If VBA were fully object-oriented, the cookie class and the ham class would have been derived from the same parent. When you would change the code of the parent, the changes would automatically be seen in the children. Now that you are familiar with some object-oriented terms and concepts, take a look at how custom classes work in VBA.

Creating and Using a Class Module

You can insert a Class module in one of three ways:

- ▶ Click to select the Create tab of the Ribbon. Open up the Macro drop-down in the Other group and select Class Module.

- ▶ With the Visual Basic Editor active, select Insert, Class Module.

- ▶ With the Visual Basic Editor active, right-click the project within the Project Explorer window and select Insert, Class Module from the pop-up menu.

After being inserted, a Class module looks like a Standard Code module (see Figure 14.1). The differences lie in how the variables and procedures in the Class module are accessed, as well as in the behavior of the Class module.

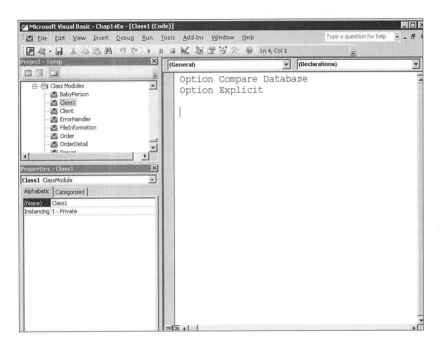

FIGURE 14.1   A new Class module.

Adding Properties

The most basic way to add a property to a Class module is to use a `Public` variable. For example, the following code shows the declaration of two `Public` variables: `FirstName` and `LastName`. After you add them to a class, VBA considers them properties of the class.

```
Public FirstName as String
Public LastName as String
```

Adding Methods

A function or subroutine placed within a Class module is considered a method of the class. The `Speak` subroutine that follows acts as a method of the `PublicPerson` class. It accesses the `FirstName` and `LastName` properties of the class, displaying them in a message box.

```
Public Function Speak()
    Speak = FirstName & " " & LastName
End Function
```

Instantiating and Using the Class

To utilize the code within a class, you must instantiate an object based on that class. To do that, you first declare an object based on the class. You then instantiate the object by using a Set statement. You can then access the properties and methods of the object. The code looks like this:

```
Sub SingleInstance()
    'Declare and instantiate a Person object
    Dim oPerson As Person
    Set oPerson = New Person

    'Set the first name and last name
    'properties of the Person object
    oPerson.FirstName = "Alison"
    oPerson.LastName = "Balter"

    'Display the return value from the Speak
    'method in a message box
    MsgBox oPerson.Speak
End Sub
```

The code begins by declaring a Person object. The code uses a Set statement to create an instance of the Person object. The code then sets the FirstName and LastName properties of the instance to Alison and Balter, respectively. The code then executes the Speak method of the object. It returns the concatenated name, which is displayed in a message box.

Property Let and Get—Adding Properties the Right Way

Public variables, when used as properties, have the following major disadvantages:

- ▶ Using Public variables, you cannot create properties that are read-only or write-only.
- ▶ You cannot validate what goes into Public variables.
- ▶ You cannot manipulate the value as the Public variable is set.
- ▶ You cannot track changes to Public variables.

For these reasons, it is prudent to use property procedures rather than Public variables. With property procedures, you can create custom runtime properties of user-defined objects. After you have defined custom properties, you can use Property Let and Get to assign values to and retrieve values from custom properties. Custom properties give you more flexibility in creating your applications; you can create reusable objects that expose properties to other objects.

Custom properties are `Public` by default and are placed in Class, Form, or Report modules, making them visible to other modules in the current database. They aren't visible to other databases.

The `Property Let` routine defines a property procedure that assigns a value to a user-defined object's property. Using `Property Let` is similar to assigning a value to a `Public` variable, but a `Public` variable can be written to from anywhere in the database, with little or no control over what's written to it. With a `Property Let` routine, you can control exactly what happens when a value is assigned to the property. Here's an example:

```
Public Property Let FirstName(ByVal strNewValue As String)
    mstrFirstName = UCase(strNewValue)
End Property
```

You might be thinking this code looks just like a subroutine, and you're somewhat correct. It's a special type of subroutine that executes automatically in response to the change in a custom property's value. The example receives the value that the property is changed to as `strNewValue`. The code stores the uppercase version of the value in the `Private` variable `mstrFirstName`. The following line of code causes the code in the `Property Let` to execute:

```
FirstName = "Alison"
```

`Property Let` sets the value of a custom property, but `Property Get` defines a property procedure that retrieves a value from a user-defined object's property. This example illustrates how `Property Get` is used:

```
Public Property Get FirstName() As String
    FirstName = mstrFirstName
End Property
```

The `Property Get` routine automatically executes whenever the code tries to retrieve the value of the property. The value stored in the `Private` variable `mstrFirstName` is returned from the `Property Get` procedure. This routine can be executed by retrieving the property from anywhere in the database. The following line of code causes the code in the `Property Get` to execute:

```
MsgBox FirstName
```

The code that follows shows the declaration of the two `Private` variables `mstrFirstName` and `mstrLastName`. The `Property Let` for `FirstName` and the `Property Let` for `LastName` store values into these two `Private` variables. The `Property Get` for `FirstName` and the `Property Get` for `LastName` retrieve the values stored in the `Private` variables.

```
Private mstrFirstName As String
Private mstrLastName As String
```

```
Public Property Get FirstName() As String
    FirstName = mstrFirstName
End Property

Public Property Let FirstName(ByVal strNewValue As String)
    mstrFirstName = UCase(strNewValue)
End Property

Public Property Get LastName() As String
    LastName = mstrLastName
End Property

Public Property Let LastName(ByVal strNewValue As String)
    mstrLastName = UCase(strNewValue)
End Property
```

Unlike with `Public` variables, you have significant control over a property created with `Property Let` and `Property Get` routines. To create a read-only property, include only a `Property Get`. To create a write-only property, include only a `Property Let`. If you want a read/write property, include both the `Property Get` and `Property Let` routines.

Setting Values with `Property Set`

Whereas a `Property Let` stores a value in a property, a `Property Set` stores a reference to an object in a property. It looks like this:

```
Private mobjCustomer as Customer

Public Property Set GoodCustomer(objCustomer as Customer)
    Set mobjCustomer = objCustomer
End Property
```

`Property Set` and its uses are covered in more detail in the later section "Building Hierarchies of Classes."

Creating Multiple Class Instances

One of the advantages of Class modules is that you can create multiple instances of the class. Each instance maintains its own variables and executes its own code. This is illustrated in the following code:

```
Sub MultipleInstance()
    'Declare both class objects
    Dim oPerson1 As Person
    Dim oPerson2 As Person
```

```
    'Instantiate both class objects
    Set oPerson1 = New Person
    Set oPerson2 = New Person

    'Set the first name and last name
    'properties of the oPerson1 object
    oPerson1.FirstName = "Alison"
    oPerson1.LastName = "Balter"

    'Display the return value from the Speak
    'method of the first instance in a message box
    MsgBox oPerson1.Speak

    'Set the first name and last name
    'properties of the oPerson2 object
    oPerson2.FirstName = "Dan"
    oPerson2.LastName = "Balter"

    'Display the return value from the Speak
    'method of the second instance in a message box
    MsgBox oPerson2.Speak

End Sub
```

The code creates two instances of the Person class. The first is referred to as oPerson1 and the second as oPerson2. The code sets the FirstName property of oPerson1 to Alison and the LastName property of oPerson1 to Balter. The code sets the FirstName property of oPerson2 to Dan and the LastName property of oPerson2 to Balter. The Speak method returns the name of the correct person, which the code displays in a message box.

Adding Code to the Initialize and Terminate Events

The Initialize and Terminate events are the two built-in events that execute for a class object. The Initialize event executes as the class is instantiated, and the Terminate event executes as the class is destroyed.

Initialize

You generally use the Initialize event to perform tasks such as establishing a connection to a database and initializing variables. The following is an example of the use of the Initialize event:

```
Private Sub Class_Initialize()
    FirstName = "Alison"
    LastName = "Balter"
End Sub
```

In this example, the code sets the default values of the FirstName and LastName properties of the class to Alison and Balter, respectively.

Terminate

You generally use the Terminate event to perform the class's cleanup tasks. An example is closing a recordset used by the class. The following is an example of the use of the Terminate event:

```
Private Sub Class_Terminate()
    rstCustomer.Close
    Set rstCustomer = Nothing
End Sub
```

This code closes the recordset and destroys the recordset object variable. It provides an example of cleanup code that you would place in your own application.

Working with Enumerated Types

By now, you should be quite familiar with IntelliSense and its benefits. One benefit is that when you type the name of a property or a method whose value should be set to one of a set of constants, the list of appropriate constants automatically appears. For example, when you use the OpenForm method of the DoCmd object, a list of six intrinsic constants appears for the View parameter. Using enumerated types, you can benefit from this behavior with your own custom properties and methods.

Here's how enumerated types work: For the custom PersonType property, imagine that only four values are appropriate: Client, PersonalContact, Vendor, and Other. Using an enumerated type, you can easily set it up so that the four appropriate types appear in a list whenever you set the PersonType property of the class. Use the Enum keyword to define an enumerated type:

```
'Enumeration for PersonType
Public Enum PersonTypeList
    Client
    PersonalContact
    Vendor
    Other
End Enum
```

To use the enumerated type with the property, you must include it in the definition of the Property Get and Property Let routines:

```
Public Property Get PersonType() As PersonTypeList
    'Retrieve the PersonType property
    PersonType = mlngPersonType
End Property
```

```
Public Property Let PersonType(ByVal lngPersonType As PersonTypeList)
    'Set the PersonType property
    mlngPersonType = lngPersonType
End Property
```

Whenever you attempt to set the value of the PersonType property of the class, the list of valid types automatically appears (see Figure 14.2).

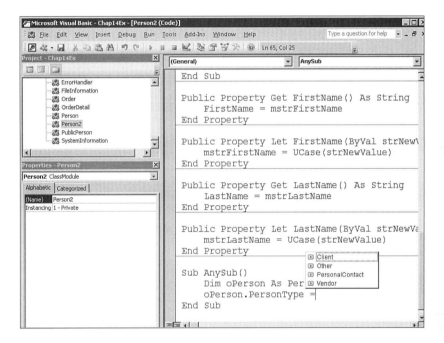

FIGURE 14.2   The list of types appears after you define an enumerated type for the PersonType property of the class.

Notice that the code uses a long integer to store the person type. The reason is that VBA limits *all* enumerated type constants to long integer values. Furthermore, you might wonder what values are stored in the variable when you use each constant. Unless directed otherwise, VBA assigns the first item in the list the value 0 (zero). It assigns each subsequent item in the list the next value (1, 2, 3, and so on). In this example, VBA assigns 0 to the Client, 1 to the PersonalContact, 2 to the Vendor, and 3 to Other. If you wish to control the long integer value assigned to each item in the list, simply set the constant equal to a value:

```
Public Enum PersonTypeList2
    Client = 10
    PersonalContact = 5
    Vendor = 2
    Other = 999
End Enum
```

One additional aspect of enumerated types is worth noting. The process of defining an enumerated type does not ensure that only valid values are used for the property or method. Although IntelliSense provides a list of the constants included in the enumerated type, any value can be entered.

Building Hierarchies of Classes

You commonly emulate real-life relationships between objects in the classes that you build. This necessitates the building of a class hierarchy. The relationships that you build between classes make up an object model. For example, you might have a Client class that has multiple Order objects associated with it. Each Order object can then have multiple Order Detail objects associated with it.

To relate one class to another, place a declaration of the child class in the General Declarations section of the parent. For example, the Order class contains the following declaration:

```
Public OrderDetail as OrderDetail
```

The Initialize event of the Order class contains the code that instantiates the OrderDetail class:

```
Private Sub Class_Initialize()
    Set OrderDetail = New OrderDetail
End Sub
```

When you instantiate the Order class (the parent class), the code automatically instantiates the child class. You can then set the properties and execute the methods of the child class. Here's an example:

```
Sub CreateOrder()
    'Declare and instantiate the Order object
    Dim objOrder As Order
    Set objOrder = New Order

    'Set properties of the child class (OrderDetail)
    With objOrder.OrderDetail
        .ItemNumber = 5
        .OrderNumber = 1
        .Quantity = 3
    End With
End Sub
```

Notice that the code declares and instantiates an Order object. It then uses a With statement to point at the OrderDetail object instantiated in the Initialize event of the Order class. It sets the ItemNumber, OrderNumber, and Quantity properties of the OrderDetail object.

This example shows how to have one child associated with a parent. The section titled "Using a Collection to Manipulate Multiple Instances of the `FileInformation` Class" shows how to use a `Custom` collection to emulate a one-to-many relationship with classes.

Adding a `Parent` Property to Classes

Many Microsoft-generated objects have a `Parent` property. This property generally provides a reference back to the parent of an object in a hierarchy. You can emulate this behavior in your own classes. Place this code in the child class:

```
Private mobjParent As Order

Public Property Get Parent() As Order
    'Return the pointer stored in mobjParent
    Set Parent = mobjParent
End Property

Public Property Set Parent(ByVal objParent As Order)
    If mobjParent Is Nothing Then
        Set mobjParent = objParent
    End If
End Property
```

Code in the `Initialize` event of the parent class sets the `Parent` property of the child class. The code looks like this:

```
Private Sub Class_Initialize()
    Set OrderDetail = New OrderDetail
    Set OrderDetail.Parent = Me
End Sub
```

After the `Initialize` event of the `Order` class sets the `Parent` property of the `OrderDetail` class, the `Property Set` for the `Parent` property of the `OrderDetail` class executes. If the `mobjParent` variable is `Nothing`, a `Set` statement points the `mobjParent` variable at the reference to the parent class (`Set OrderDetail.Parent = Me`). Notice that the `Set` statement executes only if `mobjParent` is `Nothing`. This renders the property as write-once. The following code illustrates how the `Parent` property is used:

```
Sub FindParentsName()
    'Declare and instantiate the Order object
    Dim objOrder As Order
    Set objOrder = New Order

    'Retrieve Name property of the parent
    MsgBox objOrder.OrderDetail.Parent.Name
End Sub
```

This code declares and instantiates the `Order` object. The `Initialize` event of the `Order` object instantiates the `OrderDetail` object and sends it a reference to the `Order` object. The code retrieves the `Name` property of the `Parent` object and displays it in a message box.

Using the `Implements` Keyword

Using the `Implements` keyword, you can share interfaces between classes. This means that one class can inherit the properties and methods of one or more other classes. The process is quite simple. All you need to do is place the following in the General Declarations section of the class that derives from another class:

```
Implements Person
```

After you place this code in the General Declarations section of the `BabyPerson` class, it allows you to select the `Person` class from the Objects drop-down. The property and method names of the `Person` class will then appear in the Procedure drop-down. You must write code for each property and method. In other words, the interface of the `Person` class is inherited, but its code is not. You can add properties and methods to the derived class (`BabyPerson`), just as you would in any class.

Working with Custom Collections

In addition to the collections built into the Access and other object libraries, you can create custom collections. Custom collections are similar to arrays, but they offer several advantages:

▶ Collections are dynamically allocated. They take up memory based only on what's in them at a given time. This is different from arrays, whose size must be either predefined or redimensioned at runtime. When you redimension an array, Access actually makes a copy of the array in memory, taking up substantial resources. By using custom collections, you can avoid that.

▶ A collection always knows how many elements it has, and elements can easily be added and removed.

▶ Each element of a collection can contain a different type of data.

▶ Elements can be added into any element of a collection.

Although collections are very powerful and provide several advantages, it is important that you be aware of their disadvantages, which are as follows:

▶ Every item in a collection is stored as a variant.

▶ Although the capability to store a different type of data in each element of a collection can be an advantage, it can also be a disadvantage. If you attempt to treat each item in the collection the same (for example, by accessing the same property in each element of the collection), your code might render an error.

You might wonder why collections are covered in this section. A common use of collections is to house instances of custom objects. An example of such a use is covered in the section of this chapter titled "Using a Collection to Manipulate Multiple Instances of the FileInformation Class."

Creating a Custom Collection

Defining a custom collection is easy: Simply use the Dim keyword to create an object of the type Collection, as shown here:

```
Dim colSports As New Collection
```

The Dim statement tells the compiler you want to declare a variable, and the As New keywords indicate that you're creating a new instance of something. Specifically, you're creating a new instance of a Collection object. In the following sections, look at how you can add items to and remove items from a custom collection.

Adding Items to a Custom Collection

The Add method adds a new item to a custom collection. It looks like this:

```
colSports.Add "Basketball"
```

This line of code adds the text "Basketball" to the colSports collection. The Add method has three optional arguments: Key, Before, and After. Key is a string name you can use to uniquely identify an element; the Before and After arguments enable you to specify where in the collection the new item will be placed. Here's an example:

```
Sub NewCollection()
    Dim colSports As New Collection
    colSports.Add "Basketball"
    colSports.Add "Skiing"
    colSports.Add "Skating", Before:=1
    colSports.Add "Hockey", After:=2
End Sub
```

This code creates a new collection called colSports and adds two consecutive elements to the collection: Basketball and Skiing. It then adds Skating before Basketball. Skating becomes Element 1 and Basketball becomes Element 2. Finally, it adds Hockey after Element 2 (Basketball).

CAUTION

Unlike almost every other array or collection in VBA, custom collections are one-based rather than zero-based. This means that the first element is numbered one (rather than zero), the second element is numbered two, and so on. This is a big change if you're accustomed to thinking of arrays and collections as being only zero-based.

14

Looping Through the Elements of a Custom Collection

Just as you can loop through built-in collections, you can also loop through a custom collection. The code looks like this:

```
Sub LoopThroughCollection()
    Dim colSports As New Collection
    Dim varSport As Variant
    colSports.Add "Basketball"
    colSports.Add "Skiing"
    colSports.Add "Skating", Before:=1
    colSports.Add "Hockey", After:=2
    For Each varSport In colSports
        Debug.Print varSport
    Next varSport
End Sub
```

This code uses a `For Each...Next` loop to loop through each element of `colSports`. Notice that the routine declares a variant variable as the type of object in the collection. This is done so that different types of values can be stored in each object in the collection.

Referencing Items in a Custom Collection

When you add an item to a collection, you can specify a custom key for the object. This way, you can easily return to the item in the collection whenever necessary. The following code illustrates how to specify a custom key:

```
Sub CustomKey()
    Dim colSports As New Collection
    colSports.Add "Basketball", "B"
    colSports.Add "Skiing", "S1"
    colSports.Add "Skating", "S2"
    colSports.Add "Hockey", "H"
    Debug.Print colSports.Item("S1")
End Sub
```

This code adds several items to the `colSports` collection. As the code adds each item, it assigns the item a unique key. You can easily access each item in the collection by using its unique key. You will often use the `Item` method when adding several instances of a form, such as a Customer form to a collection. The customer ID of each customer is added as the unique key for each form in the collection. This unique identifier enables you to readily return to a specific instance of the Customer form.

Removing Items from a Custom Collection

Removing items from a custom collection is just as easy as adding them. You use the `Remove` method, which looks like this:

```
Sub RemoveElements()
   Dim colSports As New Collection
   colSports.Add "Basketball"
   colSports.Add "Skiing"
   colSports.Add "Skating"
   colSports.Add "Hockey"
   colSports.Remove 2
End Sub
```

This routine removes Element 2 (Skiing) from the collection.

Adding Your Own Events

Just as you can add custom properties and methods to the classes that you build, you can also add custom events. You will often use custom events to return information back to the application code that uses them. For example, if an error occurs in the Class module, it is prudent to raise an event to the user of the class, notifying it that the error occurred. Error handling is one of the *many* uses of a custom event. To declare a custom event, place a Public Event statement in the General Declarations section of the Class module:

```
Public Event Speaking(strNameSaid As String)
```

This statement declares a Speaking event that passes a string up to its caller. After you have declared an event, you must then raise it in the appropriate place in the class code. You raise an event with the RaiseEvent command. Realize that custom events mean nothing to Access or to the operating system. In other words, they are not triggered by something that the operating system responds to. Instead, you generate them with the code that you write, in the places in your application where you deem appropriate. Although you can declare an event only once, you can raise it as many times as you like. The following is an example of raising the Speaking event from the Speak method of the class:

```
Public Function Speak()
    Dim strNameSaid As String
    Speak = mstrFirstName & " " & mstrLastName
    strNameSaid = mstrLastName & ", " & mstrFirstName
    RaiseEvent Speaking(strNameSaid)
End Function
```

In this example, the Speak method raises the Speaking event. It passes the concatenation of the last name and first name spoken back to the caller.

After you have raised an event, you need to respond to it in some other part of your application. You can only respond to events in Class modules (form, report, or stand-alone). You must first create an object variable that is responsible for reporting the events of the class to your application:

```
Private WithEvents mobjPerson As Person2
```

You can then select the class from the Objects drop-down and the event from the Procedures drop-down. The code that follows responds to the Speaking event, displaying what was said in a message box:

```
Private Sub mobjPerson_Speaking(strNameSaid As String)
    MsgBox strNameSaid
End Sub
```

Practical Examples: Using Class Modules

If you want to best understand how to benefit from the use of Class modules, it is beneficial to see them in action. This chapter covers three examples. The first shows the use of a file information class. Each instance of the class is used to house information about a particular file. The second illustrates how the use of a customer class facilitates the process of dealing with customer data. The third is a system information class. It retrieves and then provides information about the computer system. An additional example of the use of Class modules is found in Chapter 17, "Error Handling: Preparing for the Inevitable." It shows how a custom error class facilitates the process of implementing error handling within your application.

The FileInformation Class

A common application requirement is to be able to extract the drive, path, or short filename from a complete filename. Although you can obtain these pieces of information using a Standard Code module and functions, placing the functions in a Class module makes them easier to work with. The FileInformation class contained in the Chap14Ex sample database contains four properties: FullFileName, Drive, Path, and Name. The user of the class sets the FullFileName property. It contains the complete filename and path of the file whose parts the user wants to extract. The Drive, Path, and Name properties of the class contain the drive, path, and name of the file specified in the FullFileName property. Listing 14.1 shows the Property Let and Property Get procedures, as well as the Private variables associated with these properties.

LISTING 14.1   The Property Declarations for the FileInformation Class

```
Private mstrFullFileName As String
Private mstrDrive As String
Private mstrPath As String
Private mstrName As String

Public Property Get FullFileName() As String
    FullFileName = mstrFullFileName
End Property

Public Property Let FullFileName(ByVal strFileName As String)
    Call GetDrive(strFileName)
```

LISTING 14.1   Continued

```
   Call GetPath(strFileName)
   Call GetName(strFileName)
End Property

Public Property Get Drive() As String
   Drive = mstrDrive
End Property

Public Property Get Path() As String
   Path = mstrPath
End Property

Public Property Get Name() As String
   Name = mstrName
End Property
```

Notice that the Drive, Path, and Name properties have no associated Property Let routines. The reason is that these properties are read-only properties from outside the class. When the code sets the FullFileName property, it executes the GetDrive, GetPath, and GetName routines. Each of these routines populates the appropriate Private variables so that they can be retrieved in the Property Get routines. Listing 14.2 shows the GetDrive, GetPath, and GetName routines.

LISTING 14.2   The GetDrive, GetPath, and GetName Routines

```
Private Sub GetDrive(ByVal strFile As String)
    'Everything before the : is the drive
    mstrDrive = Left(strFile, _
        InStr(strFile, ":"))
End Sub

Private Sub GetPath(ByVal strFile As String)
    'Everything up until the last backslash
    'is the path
    mstrPath = _
        Mid(strFile, 1, InStrRev(strFile, "\"))
End Sub

Private Sub GetName(strFile)
    'Everything after the last backslash
    'is the name
    mstrName = _
        Mid(strFile, InStrRev(strFile, "\") + 1)
End Sub
```

The GetDrive routine extracts the characters to the left of the colon, including the colon, thereby extracting the drive. The GetPath routine locates the last backslash in the file-name. The string to the left of the last backslash contains the pathname. Finally, the GetName routine extracts everything to the right of the last backslash.

Note that the GetDrive, GetPath, and GetName routines are private to the Class module. This means that their code cannot be executed from outside the Class module. The code shown in Listing 14.3 illustrates how the code within the Class module is used.

LISTING 14.3   Using the FileInformation Class

```
Private Sub cmdGetFileInfo_Click()
    'Declare a FileInformation object
    Dim objFile As FileInformation

    'If the txtFullFileName text box is null,
    'display a message and bail out
    If IsNull(Me.txtFullFileName.Value) Then
        MsgBox "File Name Must Be Entered"

    'If the filename is entered, instantiate the
    'FileInformation class
    Else
        Set objFile = New FileInformation
        With objFile

            'Set the FullFileName property of the class
            'this causes the Drive, Path, and Name properties
            'to be populated
            .FullFileName = Me.txtFullFileName

            'Extract the values of the Drive, Path, and Name
            'properties and display them in text boxes
            Me.txtDrive = .Drive
            Me.txtPath = .Path
            Me.txtName = .Name
        End With
    End If
End Sub
```

This code, found in the frmFileInformation form in CHAP14EX, declares a FileInformation variable. As long as the user has entered a filename, the code instanti-ates an instance of the FileInformation class. It sets the FullFileName property equal to the value contained in the txtFullFileName text box. This causes the GetDrive, GetPath, and `GetName` routines to execute, thereby populating the `Private` variables contained within the class. The code then retrieves the `Drive`, `Path`, and `Name` property values and places them in text boxes on the form.

Using a Collection to Manipulate Multiple Instances of the `FileInformation` **Class**
The idea of using a collection to manipulate multiple instances of a class was discussed in the "Working with Custom Collections" section of this chapter. It is illustrated in Listing 14.4.

LISTING 14.4   Using a Collection to Manipulate Multiple Instances of the `FileInformation`
Class

```
Sub FileInfoCollection(strDirName As String)
    'Declare a Collection object
    Dim colFiles As Collection

    'Declare a FileInformation object
    Dim objFileInfo As FileInformation

    Dim strFile As String
    Dim vntFile As Variant

    'Instantiate the Collection object
    Set colFiles = New Collection

    'Return the first file that meets the file spec
    strFile = Dir(strDirName)

    'Loop as long as files meet the file spec
    Do Until Len(strFile) = 0

        'Instantiate a FileInformation object
        Set objFileInfo = New FileInformation

        'Set its FullFileName property
        objFileInfo.FullFileName = strDirName & strFile

        'Add that instance of the FileInformation class
        'to the Collection object
        colFiles.Add objFileInfo

        'Find the next file that meets the criteria
        strFile = Dir()

    Loop
```

14

LISTING 14.4   Continued

```
    'Loop through the collection, extracting the Drive,
    'Path, and Name properties
    For Each vntFile In colFiles
        Debug.Print vntFile.Drive, vntFile.Path, vntFile.Name
    Next vntFile

End Sub
```

The code receives a directory path (including a trailing backslash) as a parameter. It creates and instantiates a Collection object. It then executes the Dir function, which retrieves the name of the first file in the specified directory. As long as it finds at least one file, it executes the code within the Do Until loop. The code creates an instance of the FileInformation class. The FullFileName property of the instance is then set equal to the directory name concatenated with the filename. The most important line of code in the routine is then executed, adding the instance of the FileInformation class to the collection. This enables the instance to persist. The code calls the Dir function to retrieve the name of the next file in the specified directory, and the process is repeated until no additional filenames are located.

After the code adds all the instances of the FileInformation class to the collection, it uses the For...Each loop to iterate through all items in the collection. It retrieves the Drive, Path, and Name properties of each item in the collection and prints them to the Debug window. Notice that the code uses a variant variable to iterate through the elements of the Collection object.

NOTE

Although this example requires the use of a variant variable, you should use variant variables only when absolutely necessary (as in this example). This is because variant variables take up more memory and process more slowly than other variable types such as String, Int, or Double.

The Data Access Class

Building a data access class greatly facilitates the process of dealing with data, particularly when the data within a table is accessed from numerous forms or numerous databases. By encapsulating the data access activities into a Class module, you can better ensure that all the forms and applications treat the data consistently. Each field within the table becomes a property of the class. This is illustrated by the private declarations and Property Let and Property Get routines shown in Listing 14.5.

LISTING 14.5   The Private Variables and Property Let and Property Get Routines Used
by the Data Access Class

```
Private mlngClientID As Long
Private mstrCompanyName As String
Private mstrAddress As String
Private mstrCity As String
Private mconn As ADODB.Connection
Private mrst As ADODB.Recordset
Private mboolAddFlag As Boolean

Public Property Get ClientID() As Long
    ClientID = mlngClientID
End Property

Public Property Get CompanyName() As String
    CompanyName = mstrCompanyName
End Property

Public Property Let CompanyName(ByVal strCompanyName As String)
    mstrCompanyName = strCompanyName
End Property

Public Property Get Address() As String
    Address = mstrAddress
End Property

Public Property Let Address(ByVal strAddress As String)
    mstrAddress = strAddress
End Property

Public Property Get City() As String
    City = mstrCity
End Property

Public Property Let City(ByVal strCity As String)
    mstrCity = strCity
End Property

Public Property Get AddFlag() As Boolean
    AddFlag = mboolAddFlag
End Property

Public Property Let AddFlag(ByVal boolAddFlag As Boolean)
    mboolAddFlag = boolAddFlag
End Property
```

14

The `Initialize` event of the class, shown in Listing 14.6, is responsible for establishing a connection with the database and opening a recordset based on the data in the `tblClients` table. This example uses the ActiveX Data Object (ADO) object library. ADO is covered in detail in Chapter 15, "What Are ActiveX Data Objects, and Why Are They Important?" For now, it's only important to understand the basics. The example sets the `LockType` of the recordset to `adLockOptimistic` and the `CursorType` of the recordset to `adOpenDynamic`. The combination of these two property settings renders the recordset's data updateable.

LISTING 14.6   The `Initialize` Event of the Client Class

```
Private Sub Class_Initialize()
    'Instantiate the Recordset object
    Set mrst = New ADODB.Recordset

    'Set the LockType and CursorType of the
    'recordset to render it updateable
    mrst.LockType = adLockOptimistic
    mrst.CursorType = adOpenDynamic

    'Open a recordset based on the tblClients table,
    'utilizing the connection associated with the current project
    mrst.Open "tblClients", _
        CurrentProject.Connection, _
        Options:=adCmdTable

    'Call the Scatter routine to populate the controls on the form
    'with the first row from the recordset
    Call Scatter
End Sub
```

After the code opens the recordset, the contents of the first record in the recordset must be available as properties of the class. This is necessary so that the contents of the first record can be displayed in the `frmClients` form. The `Scatter` method, shown in Listing 14.7, accomplishes this task.

LISTING 14.7   The `Scatter` Method of the Client Class

```
Public Sub Scatter()
    'Take the field values from the current row
    'and place them into private variables
    With mrst
        mlngClientID = !ClientID
        mstrCompanyName = !CompanyName
        mstrAddress = !Address
        mstrCity = !City
    End With
End Sub
```

The Scatter method simply takes the contents of the fields in the current record (in this case, the first record) and stores them in Private variables that are accessed by the Property Get and Property Let routines within the class. The variables are then used by the Form_Load event of the frmClients form, shown in Listing 14.8.

LISTING 14.8   The Form_Load Routine of the frmClients Form

```
Private Sub Form_Load()
    'Instantiate the Client Class
    Set mobjClients = New Client

    'Grab the values out of the class
    'properties to populate the text boxes
    With mobjClients
        Me.txtClientID = .ClientID
        Me.txtCompanyName = .CompanyName
        Me.txtAddress = .Address
        Me.txtCity = .City
    End With
End Sub
```

The Form_Load event instantiates the Client class, causing the Initialize event of the class to execute. The Scatter method of the class executes, and then the code populates the text boxes on the form with the contents of the ClientID, CompanyName, Address, and City properties of the class. The frmClient form, populated with data from the first record in the tblClients table, is shown in Figure 14.3.

After the code displays the first record, the user can opt to move to the next record in the recordset. Listing 14.9 shows the Click event of the cmdNext command button on the frmClients form, which calls the MoveNext method of the class and then displays the contents of the class's properties.

Listing 14.9   The Click Event of the cmdNext Command Button

```
Private Sub cmdNext_Click()
    With mobjClients
        'Execute the MoveNext method of the class
        .MoveNext

        'Populate the text boxes with the
        'property values of the class
        Me.txtClientID = .ClientID
        Me.txtCompanyName = .CompanyName
        Me.txtAddress = .Address
        Me.txtCity = .City
    End With
End Sub
```

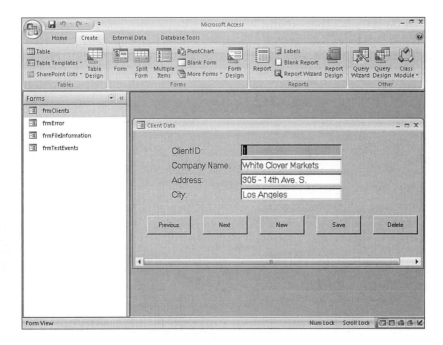

FIGURE 14.3   The frmClients form is used to display and manipulate data in the
tblClients table.

The cmdNext Click event calls the MoveNext method of the class. The MoveNext method is
responsible for moving forward from record to record within the class. It uses the module-
level recordset object set in the Initialize event of the class. This method is shown in
Listing 14.10.

LISTING 14.10   The MoveNext Method of the Client Class

```
Public Sub MoveNext()
    With mrst
        'Determine if at end of file
        If Not .EOF Then

            'If not at EOF, move next
            .MoveNext

            'Evaluate to see if movement
            'caused us to be at EOF
            'If so, move back to the last row
            If .EOF Then
                .MoveLast
            End If
        End If
```

LISTING 14.10   Continued

```
        'Once on the correct row,
        'call Scatter routine to populate the properties
        Call Scatter
    End With
End Sub
```

The MoveNext method first tests to see whether the end of the recordset has been reached. If not, the MoveNext method is used to move to the next record in the recordset. If the end of the recordset is encountered, the code moves back to the last record. The Scatter method is called to update the values of the module-level variables. The cmdNext Click event then retrieves these values via the Property Get routines, to update the data displayed on the form.

The cmdPrevious Click event of the frmClients form is similar to the cmdNext Click event. In Listing 14.11, it calls the MovePrevious method of the class and then displays the contents of the class's properties.

LISTING 14.11   The Click Event of the cmdPrevious Command Button

```
Private Sub cmdPrevious_Click()
    With mobjClients
        'Execute the MovePrevious method of the class
        .MovePrevious

        'Populate the text boxes with the
        'property values of the class
        Me.txtClientID = .ClientID
        Me.txtCompanyName = .CompanyName
        Me.txtAddress = .Address
        Me.txtCity = .City
    End With
End Sub
```

The Click event of the cmdPrevious command button first calls the MovePrevious method of the class. The MovePrevious method of the class is similar to the MoveNext method. In Listing 14.12, it moves to and displays the previous record in the recordset.

LISTING 14.12   The MovePrevious Method

```
Public Sub MovePrevious()
    With mrst
        'Determine if at Beginning of file
        If Not .BOF Then
```

LISTING 14.12   Continued

```
            'If not at BOF, move next
            .MovePrevious

            'Evaluate to see if movement
            'caused us to be at BOF
            'If so, move back to the first row
            If .BOF Then
                .MoveFirst
            End If
        End If

        'Once on the correct row,
        'call Scatter routine to populate the properties
        Call Scatter
    End With
End Sub
```

The MovePrevious method first tests to see whether the record pointer is before the first record in the recordset. If not, the MovePrevious method moves to the previous record in the recordset. If it encounters the beginning of the recordset, the code moves forward to the first record. The code calls the Scatter method to update the values of the module-level variables. These variables are then retrieved by the Property Get routines initiated by the Click event of the cmdPrevious command button.

The Client class enables the user to edit the data in the underlying recordset. The user simply enters data into the form's unbound text boxes. After entering the data, the user clicks Save. The Click event of the cmdSave command button saves the form's data to the underlying recordset, as shown in Listing 14.13.

LISTING 14.13   The Click Event of the cmdSave Command Button

```
Private Sub cmdSave_Click()
    'Ensure that the txtCompany text box is populated
    If IsNull(Me.txtCompanyName.Value) Or _
        Len(Me.txtCompanyName.Value) = 0 Then
        MsgBox "Company Name Must be Filled In Before Proceeding"

    Else

        'If txtCompany text box is populated,
        'populate the properties of the class
        'with values in the text boxes
        With mobjClients
            .CompanyName = Me.txtCompanyName
```

LISTING 14.13   Continued

```
            .Address = Me.txtAddress
            .City = Me.txtCity

            'Execute the Save method of the class to write
            'the record to disk
            .Save

            'Reset the Add Flag
            .AddFlag = False

            'Populate the txtClientId text box with the
            'ClientID assigned by the Add method
            Me.txtClientID = .ClientID
        End With
    End If
End Sub
```

The code in the `Click` event of the `cmdSave` command button first sets all the properties of the class to the corresponding text box values. It then executes the `Save` method of the class (see Listing 14.15).

Before you look at the `Save` method, it is important to explore the code under the `Click` event of the `cmdNew` command button (see Listing 14.14). It's very simple: It clears the text boxes on the form, readying them for the entry of the new data. It then sets the value of the `AddFlag` to `True`.

LISTING 14.14   The `Click` Event of the `cmdNew` Command Button

```
Private Sub cmdNew_Click()
    'Clear the text box values
    Me.txtClientID = ""
    Me.txtCompanyName = ""
    Me.txtAddress = ""
    Me.txtCity = ""

    'Set the Add flag
    mobjClients.AddFlag = True
End Sub
```

In the case of either an edit or an add, the code in the `Save` method of the class actually writes the data from the new record to disk. This code is shown in Listing 14.15.

LISTING 14.15   The Save Method of the Class

```
Public Sub Save()
    'If add flag is true, call AddNew routine
    'otherwise, call Edit routine
    If mboolAddFlag Then
        Call AddNew
    Else
        Call Edit
    End If
End Sub
```

The Save method of the class first determines whether the user is adding or editing data. This is determined by evaluating the mboolAddFlag. The code sets the mboolAddFlag to True when the user clicks the Add button. When the user is editing, the value of the variable is False. If the user is adding the record, the code executes the private routine called AddNew, which appears in Listing 14.16.

LISTING 14.16   The AddNew Method of the Class

```
Private Sub AddNew()
    With mrst
        'Add a new row to the recordset,
        'populating it with values from the
        'class properties
        .AddNew
            !CompanyName = mstrCompanyName
            !Address = mstrAddress
            !City = mstrCity
        .Update

        'Set the ClientID property equal
        'to the ClientID of the inserted row
        mlngClientID = !ClientID
End Sub
```

The AddNew method of the class uses the AddNew method of an ADO recordset to populate a new record with the values contained in the Private variables. The Update method of the recordset object writes the new data to disk. When the Update method executes, the value of the AutoNumber field is assigned and stored in the variable called mlngClientID. This variable is retrieved in the Click event of cmdSave so that the txtClientID text box contains the appropriate value.

Whereas the AddNew method of the class adds the record in the recordset, the Edit method of the class updates the data in an existing record. This method is shown in Listing 14.17.

LISTING 14.17   The Edit Method of the Class

```
Private Sub Edit()
    'Edit the current row, setting the field
    'values equal to the values in the
    'class properties
    With mrst
        !CompanyName = mstrCompanyName
        !Address = mstrAddress
        !City = mstrCity
        .Update
    End With
End Sub
```

The Edit method uses the Update method of the ADO recordset to take the values in the module-level variables and write them to disk.

The last data task associated with the cmdClients form provides the user with the capability to delete a record from the recordset. The code behind the Click event of the cmdDelete command button appears in Listing 14.18.

LISTING 14.18   The Click Event of the cmdDelete Command Button

```
Private Sub cmdDelete_Click()
    With mobjClients
        'Execute the Delete method of the class
        .Delete

        'Populate the controls on the form with
        'the property values of the class
        Me.txtClientID = .ClientID
        Me.txtCompanyName = .CompanyName
        Me.txtAddress = .Address
        Me.txtCity = .City
    End With
End Sub
```

This code executes the Delete method of the class, shown in Listing 14.19. It uses the Delete method of an ADO recordset to delete the current record from the recordset. After the deletion, the record pointer is sitting on the deleted record. The MoveNext method of the class moves the record pointer to the next valid record. The Click event of the cmdDelete command button then populates the text boxes on the form with the values of the record that the MoveNext method moved to.

LISTING 14.19   The Delete Method of the Class

```
Public Sub Delete()
    With mrst
        'Delete the current row
        .Delete

        'Move off the deleted row
        Call MoveNext
    End With
End Sub
```

The SystemInformation Class

The process of obtaining system information, such as the amount of free drive space, is usually a somewhat tedious and difficult process. This information is generally available only through the Windows API, covered in Chapter 25, "Exploiting the Power of the Windows API." The execution of Windows API functions is best left to more advanced developers. So how can a junior developer access this important information? If the senior developer encapsulates the complex functionality of the Windows API calls in a Class module, the junior developer can obtain the system information as properties of the class.

The class called SystemInformation is responsible for obtaining information about the hardware, operating system, and system resources. To obtain this information, the Declare statements, type structure declarations, and constant declarations are included in the General Declarations section of the Class module (see Listing 14.20).

LISTING 14.20   The Private Variables and Type Structures Required by the SystemInformation Class

```
Private Declare Sub GlobalMemoryStatus _
    Lib "Kernel32" (lpBuffer As MEMORYSTATUS)
Private mlngTotalMemory As Long
Private mlngAvailableMemory As Long
Private mstrOSVersion As String
Private msngOSBuild As Single
Private mstrOSPlatform As String
Private mlngProcessor As Long

Private Type MEMORYSTATUS
    dwLength As Long
    dwMemoryLoad As Long
    dwTotalPhys As Long
    dwAvailPhys As Long
    dwTotalPageFile As Long
    dwAvailPageFile As Long
```

LISTING 14.20   Continued

```
   dwTotalVirtual As Long
   dwAvailVirtual As Long
End Type

Private Declare Function GetVersionEx Lib "Kernel32" _
    Alias "GetVersionExA" (lpOSInfo As OSVERSIONINFO) As Boolean

Private Type OSVERSIONINFO
   dwOSVersionInfoSize As Long
   dwMajorVersion As Long
   dwMinorVersion As Long
   dwBuildNumber As Long
   dwPlatformId As Long
   strReserved As String * 128
End Type

Private Declare Sub GetSystemInfo Lib "Kernel32" _
 (lpSystemInfo As SYSTEM_INFO)

Private Type SYSTEM_INFO
   dwOemID As Long
   dwPageSize As Long
   lpMinimumApplicationAddress As Long
   lpMaximumApplicationAddress As Long
   dwActiveProcessorMask As Long
   dwNumberOrProcessors As Long
   dwProcessorType As Long
   dwAllocationGranularity As Long
   dwReserved As Long
End Type
```

The SystemInformation class contains six read-only properties: TotalMemory, AvailableMemory, OSVersion, OSBuild, OSPlatform, and Processor. These properties are set within the class and cannot be modified from outside the class. The Property Get functions for the six properties are shown in Listing 14.21.

LISTING 14.21   The Property Get Routines Required by the SystemInformation Class

```
Public Property Get TotalMemory() As Long
    TotalMemory = mlngTotalMemory
End Property

Public Property Get AvailableMemory() As Long
    AvailableMemory = mlngAvailableMemory
```

LISTING 14.21   Continued

```
End Property

Public Property Get OSVersion() As String
    OSVersion = mstrOSVersion
End Property

Public Property Get OSBuild() As Single
    OSBuild = msngOSBuild
End Property

Public Property Get OSPlatform() As String
    OSPlatform = mstrOSPlatform
End Property

Public Property Get Processor() As Long
    Processor = mlngProcessor
End Property
```

All the work is done in the `Initialize` event of the class. When the class is instantiated, the `Initialize` event executes all the Windows API functions necessary to obtain the required system information. The `Initialize` event of the class is shown in Listing 14.22.

LISTING 14.22   The Initialize Event of the SystemInformation Class

```
Private Sub Class_Initialize()
    'Get Free Memory
    Dim MS As MEMORYSTATUS
    MS.dwLength = Len(MS)
    GlobalMemoryStatus MS

    mlngTotalMemory = Format(MS.dwTotalPhys, "Standard")
    mlngAvailableMemory = Format(MS.dwAvailPhys, "Standard")

    'Get Version Information
    Dim OSInfo As OSVERSIONINFO
    OSInfo.dwOSVersionInfoSize = Len(OSInfo)
    If GetVersionEx(OSInfo) Then
        mstrOSVersion = OSInfo.dwMajorVersion & "." & _
            OSInfo.dwMinorVersion
        msngOSBuild = OSInfo.dwBuildNumber And &HFFFF&
    End If
```

LISTING 14.22 Continued

```
'Get System Information
Dim SI As SYSTEM_INFO
 GetSystemInfo SI
mlngProcessor = SI.dwProcessorType
```

End Sub

The `GlobalMemoryStatus` Windows API function populates the `TotalMemory` and `AvailableMemory` properties. The `GetVersionEX` function is used to set the `OSVersion`, `OSBuild`, and `OSPlatform` properties. Finally, the `GetSystemInfo` function populates the `Processor` property.

Summary

In this chapter, you learned how to implement your application's subroutines and functions as methods of Class modules. In doing so, you discovered how complex activities can be encapsulated into Class modules, greatly simplifying the implementation of their functionality. After exploring the basics of object orientation and Class modules, you saw several practical examples of classes in action. They included a file information class, a data access class, and a system information class. The possible practical application of classes within the business environment is limited only by your imagination!

14

CHAPTER 15

What Are ActiveX Data Objects, and Why Are They Important?

Why This Chapter Is Important

ActiveX Data Objects (ADO) are used to create, modify, and remove Jet Engine, Access Database Engine, SQL Server, or other open database connectivity (ODBC) objects via code. They give you the flexibility to move beyond the user interface to manipulate data stored in the Jet Engine, Access Database Engine, and other formats. Some of the many tasks that you can perform with ADO include the following:

- ▶ Analyzing the structure of an existing database
- ▶ Adding or modifying tables and queries
- ▶ Creating new databases
- ▶ Changing the underlying definitions for queries by modifying the SQL on which the query is based
- ▶ Traversing through sets of records
- ▶ Administrating security
- ▶ Modifying table data

Examining the ADO Model

Figure 15.1 shows an overview of the Microsoft ADO model. Unlike the DAO model, the ADO object model is not hierarchical.

IN THIS CHAPTER

- ▶ Why This Chapter Is Important
- ▶ Examining the ADO Model
- ▶ Understanding ADO Recordset Types
- ▶ Working with ADO Recordset Properties and Methods
- ▶ Modifying Table Data Using ADO Code
- ▶ Creating and Modifying Database Objects Using ADO Code
- ▶ Practical Examples: Applying These Techniques to Your Application

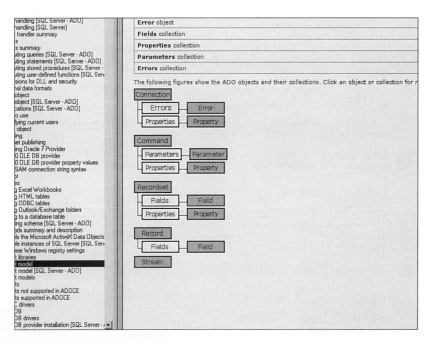

FIGURE 15.1   The ADO object model.

The Connection Object

The Connection object defines a session for a user for a data source. Although the ADO object model is not considered to be hierarchical, the Connection object is considered the highest-level ADO object. After you have established a Connection object, you can use it with multiple recordsets. This improves performance and greatly simplifies your programming code.

You must declare a Connection object before you use it. The declaration looks like this:

```
Dim cnn as ADODB.Connection
```

> **NOTE**
>
> Notice that the declaration specifies ADODB.Connection rather than just Connection. This process is called *disambiguation*. The process of disambiguating a reference ensures that you create the correct type of object. For example, both the ADO and DAO object libraries have Recordset objects. By disambiguating the reference, you explicitly designate the type of Recordset object you want to create. If you do not disambiguate the reference, the object library with priority in Tools, References is assumed.

> **NOTE**
>
> Listing 15.1 and most of the code in this chapter is located in the Chap15Ex.accdb file included with this book's CD-ROM.

After you have declared the `Connection` object, you must instantiate a new `Connection` object. The code looks like this:

```
Set cnn = New ADODB.Connection
```

The `Connection` must then be opened. The `Open` method of the `Connection` object receives a connection string, and optionally a user ID, password, and options as a parameter. The following is an example of the simplest use of the `Open` method:

```
cnn.Open "Provider=Microsoft.ACE.OLEDB.12.0;" & _
    "Persist Security Info=False;" & _
    "User ID=Admin;" & _
    "Data Source=" & CurrentProject.Path & _
        "\Chap15Ex.accddb;"
```

The connection string contains three pieces of information:

- ▶ The OLEDB provider that you want to use (in this case, the Access Database Engine)

- ▶ Standard ADO connection properties (for example, `User ID`)

- ▶ Provider-specific connection properties

If you want to programmatically manipulate an `MDB` file (Access 2003 and earlier), you use the Jet Engine. Your connection string will look like this:

```
cnn.Open "Provider=Microsoft.Jet.OLEDB.4.0;" & _
    "Persist Security Info=False;" & _
    "User ID=Admin;" & _
    "Data Source=" & CurrentProject.Path & _
        "\Chap15Ex.mdb;"
```

Notice that the example uses the Jet provider and provides a connection string for an `MDB` file.

Table 15.1 lists the most commonly used connection string properties used by the Jet and Access Database Engine OLEDB providers.

TABLE 15.1   Connection String Properties Used by the Jet and Access Database Engine OLEDB Provider

Property Name	Description
`ACE.OLEDB:Database Locking Mode`	Can be set to 0 for page-locking and 1 for row-locking
`ACE.OLEDB:Database Password`	Used to designate the password for a password-protected database (database security rather than user-level security)
`ACE.OLEDB:System Database`	Used to designate the full path and filename to the system database (when user-level security is used)

TABLE 15.1   Continued

Property Name	Description
ACE.OLEDB:Lock Delay	Used to indicate the number of milliseconds to wait before attempting to acquire a lock after the previous attempt has failed
ACE.OLEDB:Lock Retry	Used to designate how many times an attempt to access a locked page is repeated

The complete routine required to establish a connection appears in Listing 15.1.

LISTING 15.1   Creating a Connection Object

```
Sub CreateConnection()
    'Declare and instantiate the connection
    Dim cnn As ADODB.Connection
    Set cnn = New ADODB.Connection

    'Open the connection
    cnn.Open "Provider=Microsoft.ACE.OLEDB.12.0;" & _
    "Persist Security Info=False;" & _
    "User ID=Admin;" & _
    "Data Source=" & CurrentProject.Path & _
        "\Chap15Ex2.accdb;"

    'Close the connection
    cnn.Close

    'Destroy the Connection object
    Set cnn = Nothing
End Sub
```

TIP

All the examples in this chapter first declare a variable using the keyword Dim and then instantiate it using the keyword Set. You can remove the Set statement by specifying the New keyword in the Dim statement. For example, you could use

```
Dim rst as New ADODB.Recordset
```

Although this approach works, it is not considered desirable. The reason is that you have little control over when the object is placed in memory. For example, if the variable is public, Access places it in memory the moment anything in the module is referenced. Separating the Dim and Set statements allows you to declare the variable wherever you like and place it in memory when you need to.

Creating a connection in a client/server environment is similar to creating a connection with an Access database. The code appears in Listing 15.2.

LISTING 15.2   Creating a SQL Server Connection Object with SQL Server Security

```
Sub CreateConnection()
    'Declare and instantiate the connection
    Dim cnn As ADODB.Connection
    Set cnn = New ADODB.Connection

    'Open the connection
    cnn.Open "Provider=SQLOLEDB.1;" & _
            "Data Source=(local); Initial Catalog=NorthWind;" & _
            "User ID=sa;PWD="

    'Close the connection
    cnn.Close

    'Destroy the connection object
    Set cnn = Nothing
End Sub
```

As you can see, the difference lies in the connection string. This example used SQL Server security to connect to the database. The example in Listing 15.3 uses NT Integrated Security.

LISTING 15.3   Creating a SQL Server Connection Object with Integrated Security

```
Sub CreateConnectionIntegrated()
    'Declare and instantiate the connection
    Dim cnn As ADODB.Connection
    Set cnn = New ADODB.Connection

    'Open the connection
    cnn.Open "Provider=SQLOLEDB.1;" & _
            "Data Source=(local); Initial Catalog=NorthWind;" & _
            "Integrated Security=SSPI"

    'Close the connection
    cnn.Close

    'Destroy the connection object
    Set cnn = Nothing
End Sub
```

Notice that this example sets integrated security equal to SSPI. This causes the Access Database Engine to use NT Integrated Security to connect to the SQL Server database.

The Recordset Object

A Recordset object is used to look at records as a group. A Recordset object refers to the set of rows returned from a request for data. As with a Connection object, to use a Recordset object, you must first declare it. The code looks like this:

```
Dim rst as ADODB.Recordset
```

After you have declared the Recordset object, you must instantiate it. The code looks like this:

```
Set rst = New ADODB.Recordset
```

As with a Connection object, you use the Open method to point the Recordset object to a set of records. The code looks like this:

```
rst.Open "Select * From tblClients", CurrentProject.Connection
```

The first parameter of the Open method is the source of the data. The source can be a table name, a SQL statement, a stored procedure name, a Command object variable name, or the filename of a persisted recordset. In the example, the source is a SQL Select statement.

The second parameter of the Open method must be either a valid connection string or the name of a Connection object. In the example, the Connection property of the CurrentProject object returns a reference to a copy of the connection associated with the current project. The reference supplies the connection for the Recordset object. The completed code appears in Listing 15.4.

LISTING 15.4   Creating a Recordset Using a Connection String

```
Sub CreateRecordset1()
    'Declare and instantiate the recordset
    Dim rst As ADODB.Recordset
    Set rst = New ADODB.Recordset

    'Open the recordset
    rst.Open "Select * From tblClients", CurrentProject.Connection

    'Print its contents
    Debug.Print rst.GetString

    'Close and destroy the recordset
    rst.Close
    Set rst = Nothing
End Sub
```

Notice that after you open the recordset, the code prints the result of the GetString method of the Recordset object to the Immediate window. The GetString method of the

Recordset object builds a string based on the data contained in the recordset. For now, this is a simple way of verifying that your code works as expected. Also note that the code uses the Close method of the Recordset object to close the recordset. The Close method, when applied to either a Connection object or to a Recordset object, has the effect of freeing the associated system resources. The Close method does *not* eliminate the object from memory. Setting the Recordset object equal to Nothing eliminates the object from memory.

Although this syntax works quite well, I prefer to set the parameters of the Open method as properties of the Recordset object, before the Open method is issued. You will see that this makes your code much more readable as you add parameters to the Open method. The code appears in Listing 15.5.

LISTING 15.5   Creating a Recordset Using the ActiveConnection Property

```
Sub CreateRecordset2()
    'Declare and instantiate the recordset
    Dim rst As ADODB.Recordset
    Set rst = New ADODB.Recordset

    'Set the connection of the recordset to the connection
    'associated with the current project
    rst.ActiveConnection = CurrentProject.Connection

    'Open the recordset and print its contents
    rst.Open "Select * From tblClients"
    Debug.Print rst.GetString

    'Close and destroy the recordset object
    rst.Close
    Set rst = Nothing
End Sub
```

Finally, you can use a Connection object, rather than a copy of the Connection object associated with the CurrentProject object, to provide a connection for the recordset. In fact, you can use the same Connection object for multiple recordsets. The code appears in Listing 15.6.

LISTING 15.6   Creating a Recordset Using a Connection Object

```
Sub CreateRecordset3()
    'Declare and instantiate one Connection object
    'and two Recordset objects
    Dim cnn As ADODB.Connection
    Dim rst1 As ADODB.Recordset
    Dim rst2 As ADODB.Recordset
```

LISTING 15.6   Continued

```
Set cnn = New ADODB.Connection
Set rst1 = New ADODB.Recordset
Set rst2 = New ADODB.Recordset

'Point the Connection object
'to the connection associated with the CurrentProject object
Set cnn = CurrentProject.Connection

'Utilize the connection just opened as the connection for
'two different recordsets
rst1.ActiveConnection = cnn
rst1.Open "Select * From tblClients"
rst2.ActiveConnection = cnn
rst2.Open "Select * From tblPayments"

'Retrieve data out of the recordsets
Debug.Print rst1.GetString
Debug.Print rst2.GetString

'Close the recordsets and the connection and destroy the objects
rst1.Close
rst2.Close
cnn.Close

Set rst1 = Nothing
Set rst2 = Nothing
Set cnn = Nothing

End Sub
```

Notice that both rst1 and rst2 use the same Connection object.

The Command Object

The ADO Command object represents a query, SQL statement, or stored procedure that is executed against a data source. Although not always necessary, a Command object is particularly useful when executing parameterized queries and stored procedures. Just as with the Connection object and the Recordset object, you must declare a Command object before you use it:

```
Dim cmd as ADODB.Command
```

Next, you must instantiate the Command object:

```
Set cmd = New ADODB.Command
```

After you instantiate the `Command` object, you must set its `ActiveConnection` property and its `CommandText` property. As with a `Recordset` object, the `ActiveConnection` property can be either a connection string or a reference to a `Connection` object. The `CommandText` property is the SQL statement or stored procedure used by the `Command` object. The `ActiveConnection` and the `CommandText` properties look like this:

```
cmd.ActiveConnection = CurrentProject.Connection
cmd.CommandText = "tblClients"
```

The completed code appears in Listing 15.7.

LISTING 15.7   Using a Command Object

```
Sub CommandObject()
    'Declare a Recordset and a Command object
    Dim rst As ADODB.Recordset
    Dim cmd As ADODB.Command

    'Instantiate the Command object
    Set cmd = New ADODB.Command

    'Designate where the data comes from
    cmd.CommandText = "Select * from tblClients"

    'Establish the connection information
    cmd.ActiveConnection = CurrentProject.Connection

    'Use the Execute method to return a result set
    'into the recordset object
    Set rst = cmd.Execute

    'Display the resulting data
    Debug.Print rst.GetString

    'Close the recordset and destroy the objects
    rst.Close

    Set cmd = Nothing
End Sub
```

This example instantiates the `Command` object. It sets the `CommandText` property to a SQL `Select` statement and points the `ActiveConnection` property to the connection associated with the current database. It uses the `Execute` method of the `Command` object to return the results of the SQL statement into the `Recordset` object.

Understanding ADO Recordset Types

Three parameters of the `Open` method of a `Recordset` object affect the type of recordset that is created. They are the `CursorType`, the `LockType`, and the `Options` parameters. These parameters combine to determine the types of movements that you can execute within a recordset, when changes that other users make to data underlying the recordset will be seen, and whether the recordset's data can be updated.

The `CursorType` Parameter

By default, when you open a recordset, the `CursorType` parameter is set to `adOpenForwardOnly`. This means that you can only move forward through the records in the recordset. You will not see additions, edits, or deletions that other users make. Furthermore, many properties and methods, such as the `RecordCount` property and the `MovePrevious` method, are unavailable. Listing 15.8 illustrates this.

LISTING 15.8   The `RecordCount` Property Is Not Supported with a Forward-Only Recordset

```
Sub ForwardOnlyRecordset()

    'Declare and instantiate a Recordset object
    Dim rst As ADODB.Recordset
    Set rst = New ADODB.Recordset

    'Establish a connection and open a forward-only recordset
    rst.ActiveConnection = CurrentProject.Connection
    rst.Open "Select * from tblClients"

    'Attempt to retrieve the record count
    Debug.Print rst.RecordCount

    'Close and destroy the recordset*
    rst.Close
    Set rst = Nothing


End Sub
```

The value -1 displays in the Immediate window because the forward-only recordset does not support the `RecordCount` property. Because you did not explicitly designate the cursor type, a forward-only recordset was created.

Three other values are available for the `CursorType`. They are `adOpenStatic`, `adOpenKeyset`, and `adOpenDynamic`. The `adOpenStatic` option allows forward and backward movement through the records in the recordset, but changes that other users make to the underlying data are not seen by the recordset. The `adOpenKeyset` option offers everything from the `adOpenStatic` option, but in addition, edits that other users make are seen by the recordset. Finally, with the adOpenDynamic option, additions, edits, and deletions made by other users are seen by the recordset. Table 15.2 illustrates each of these options in further detail.

TABLE 15.2   Valid Choices for the CursorType Parameter

Value	Description
adOpenForwardOnly	Copies a set of records as the recordset is created. Therefore, it doesn't show changes made by other users. This is the fastest type of cursor but allows only forward movement through the recordset.
adOpenStatic	Copies a set of records as the recordset is created. Supports bookmarks and allows forward and backward movement through the recordset. Doesn't show changes made by other users. This is the only type of recordset allowed when using client-side cursors.
adOpenKeyset	Provides a set of pointers back to the original data. Supports bookmarks. Shows changes made by other users. Does not show new records and provides no access to deleted rows.
adOpenDynamic	Provides access to a set of records. Shows all changes, including additions and deletions, made by other users.

15

You can set the CursorType property of the recordset in one of two ways. You can set it as a parameter of the Open method or as a property of the Recordset object. Listing 15.9 illustrates the first method.

LISTING 15.9   Supplying the CursorType as a Parameter of the Open Method

```
Sub StaticRecordset1()
    'Declare and instantiate a Recordset object
    Dim rst As ADODB.Recordset
    Set rst = New ADODB.Recordset

    'Establish a connection and open a static recordset
    rst.ActiveConnection = CurrentProject.Connection
    rst.Open "Select * from tblClients", _
        CursorType:=adOpenStatic

    'Retrieve the record count
    Debug.Print rst.RecordCount

    rst.Close
    Set rst = Nothing



End Sub
```

Notice that, in Listing 15.9, the CursorType appears as a parameter of the Open method. Contrast Listing 15.9 with Listing 15.10.

LISTING 15.10   Supplying the `CursorType` as a Property of the `Recordset` Object

```
Sub StaticRecordset2()
    'Declare and instantiate a Recordset object
    Dim rst As ADODB.Recordset
    Set rst = New ADODB.Recordset

    'Set the ActiveConnection and CursorType properties
    'of the recordset
    rst.ActiveConnection = CurrentProject.Connection
    rst.CursorType = adOpenStatic

    'Open the recordset
    rst.Open "Select * from tblClients"

    'Retrieve the record count
    Debug.Print rst.RecordCount

    rst.Close
    Set rst = Nothing

End Sub
```

In Listing 15.10, the `CursorType` is set as a property of the `Recordset` object, prior to the execution of the `Open` method. Separating the properties from the `Open` method improves the readability of the code.

The `LockType` Parameter

Although the `CursorType` property of a `Recordset` object determines how movements can occur within the recordset and whether other users' changes are seen, the `CursorType` in no way affects the updateability of the recordset's data. In fact, when you open a recordset, you open it as read-only by default. It is only by changing the `LockType` property that you can make the recordset updateable.

The options for lock type are `adLockReadOnly`, `adLockPessimistic`, `adLockOptimistic`, and `adLockBatchOptimistic`. The default, `adLockReadOnly`, does not allow changes to the recordset. The other options all provide updateability for the recordset's data. The difference is when the records are locked. With the `adLockPessimistic` option, locking occurs as soon as the editing process begins. With the `adLockOptimistic` option, the record is locked when you issue the `Update` method. Finally, with the `adLockBatchOptimistic` option, you can postpone locking until you update a batch of records. All these options are discussed in extensive detail in *Alison Balter's Mastering Access 2002 Enterprise Development*.

As with the `CursorType` property, you can set the `LockType` property as a parameter of the `Open` method or as a property of the `Recordset` object. Listing 15.11 shows the configuration of the lock type as a property of the `Recordset` object.

LISTING 15.11   Configuration of LockType as a Property of the Recordset Object

```
Sub OptimisticRecordset()
    'Declare and instantiate a Recordset object
    Dim rst As ADODB.Recordset
    Set rst = New ADODB.Recordset

    'Set the ActiveConnection, CursorType, and
    'LockType properties of the recordset
    rst.ActiveConnection = CurrentProject.Connection
    rst.CursorType = adOpenStatic
    rst.LockType = adLockOptimistic

    'Open the recordset
    rst.Open "Select * from tblClients"

    'Modify the contents of the city field
    rst("City") = "Westlake Village"
    rst.Update
    Debug.Print rst("City")

    rst.Close
    Set rst = Nothing

End Sub
```

In Listing 15.11, the LockType property is set to adLockOptimistic. The record is locked when the Update method of the Recordset object is issued.

NOTE

Listing 15.11 references the field name in the format rst("City"). You can use any one of four syntactical constructs to reference a member of a collection. They include the following:

```
Collection("Name")
Collection(VariableName)
Collection!Name
Collection(Ordinal)
```

You might wonder which is best. Although all are valid, I most prefer the Collection("Name") and Collection(VariableName) methods. I like the fact that the syntax is the same whether you are supplying a string or a variable. Furthermore, the same syntax works with Active Server Pages (ASP). The bang (!) does not work with ADO .NET, and you cannot rely on the ordinal position because it changes based on the order of the fields in a select, for other reasons as well. One of the only instances when you must use a bang is when you are supplying a parameter for a query. Besides that, I use the Collection("Name") syntax in the ADO code that I write.

The Options **Parameter**

The Options parameter determines how the provider should evaluate the source argument. The valid choices are illustrated in Table 15.3.

TABLE 15.3   Valid Choices for the Options Parameter

Value	Description
adCmdText	The provider evaluates the source as a command.
adCmdTable	A SQL query is generated to return all rows from the table named in the source.
adCmdTableDirect	The provider returns all rows in the table named in the source.
adCmdStoredProc	The provider evaluates the source as a stored procedure.
adCmdUnknown	The type of command in the source is unknown.
adCmdFile	The source is evaluated as a persisted recordset.
adAsyncExecute	The source is executed asynchronously.
adAsyncFetch	The initial quantity specified in the Initial Fetch Size property is fetched.
adAsyncFetchNonBlocking	The main thread never blocks when fetching.

The default for the Options parameter is adCmdUnknown. If you do not explicitly specify the Options parameter, the provider attempts to evaluate it while the code is running, which degrades performance. It is therefore important to specify the parameter. Listing 15.12 illustrates the use of the Options parameter of the Open method.

LISTING 15.12   The Options Parameter of the Open Method

```
Sub OptionsParameter()
    'Declare and instantiate a Recordset object
    Dim rst As ADODB.Recordset
    Set rst = New ADODB.Recordset

    'Set the ActiveConnection, CursorType, and
    'LockType properties of the recordset
    rst.ActiveConnection = CurrentProject.Connection
    rst.CursorType = adOpenStatic
    rst.LockType = adLockOptimistic

    'Open the recordset, designating that the source
    'is a command
    rst.Open "Select * from tblClients", _
        Options:=adCmdText

    'Modify the contents of the city field
    rst("City") = "Westlake Village"
```

LISTING 15.12   Continued

```
    rst.Update
    Debug.Print rst("City")

    rst.Close
    Set rst = Nothing
```

End Sub

In Listing 15.12, the Options parameter is set to adCmdText. This causes the source to be evaluated as a SQL command.

Consistent Versus Inconsistent Updates

When a recordset is based on data from more than one table, the Access Database Engine automatically allows you to make changes to the foreign key field. For example, if a recordset is based on data from the Customers table and the Orders table, you are able to make changes to the CustomerID in the Orders table. This is referred to as a *consistent update*. At times, you might want to make changes to the primary key field. This could result in a violation of referential integrity and is therefore referred to as an *inconsistent update*.

If you've established referential integrity and have designated that you want to cascade updates, consistent and inconsistent updates yield the same results. On the other hand, without cascade updates activated, a change to the primary key field causes referential integrity to be violated.

Listing 15.13 shows you how to open a recordset with inconsistent updates.

LISTING 15.13   Opening a Recordset with Inconsistent Updates

```
Sub InconsistentUpdates()
    'Declare and instantiate a Recordset object
    Dim rst As ADODB.Recordset
    Set rst = New ADODB.Recordset

    'Set the ActiveConnection, CursorType, and
    'LockType properties of the recordset
    rst.ActiveConnection = CurrentProject.Connection
    rst.CursorType = adOpenStatic
    rst.LockType = adLockOptimistic

    'Open the recordset, designating that the source
    'is a SQL statement based on more than one table
    rst.Properties("Jet OLEDB:Inconsistent") = True
```

15

LISTING 15.13   Continued

```
    rst.Open Source:="Select * from tblClients " & _
        "INNER JOIN tblProjects " & _
        "ON tblClients.ClientID = tblProjects.ClientID", _
        Options:=adCmdText

    'Modify the contents of the foreign key field
    rst("tblProjects.ClientID") = 1
    rst.Update
    Debug.Print rst("tblProjects.ClientID")

    rst.Close
    Set rst = Nothing

End Sub
```

Notice that this code sets the Jet OLEDB:Inconsistent property prior to the Open method of the recordset. This causes the recordset to be opened so that you can use inconsistent updates if you want.

> **NOTE**
>
> Very few providers support inconsistent updates. In fact, the Jet Provider and Access Database Engine Provider are two of the few providers that support this feature.

Selecting a Cursor Location

A *cursor* refers to the set of rows or row pointers that are returned when you open a recordset. With DAO, the location of the cursor was not an issue. On the other hand, ADO supports two cursor locations. As its name implies, the client manages a client-side cursor. The server manages a server-side cursor.

If you are using the Jet Engine or the Access Database Engine, the client machine always manages the cursor because the Jet Engine and the Access Database Engine run only on the client machine. You might think this means that you should always designate a client-side cursor when working with the Jet Engine and the Access Database Engine. Actually, the opposite is true. If you designate a client-side cursor when working with the Jet Engine or the Access Database Engine, the data is cached twice on the client machine. When a client-side cursor is specified, the Microsoft Cursor Service for OLEDB requests all the data from the OLEDB provider and then caches it and presents it to the application as a static recordset. For this reason, when working with the Jet Engine or the Access Database Engine, you should designate a client-side cursor only when you want to take advantage of functionality provided only by a client-side cursor.

Listing 15.14 illustrates how to designate the cursor location.

LISTING 15.14   Designating the Cursor Location

```
Sub CursorLocation()
    'Declare and instantiate a Recordset object
    Dim rst As ADODB.Recordset
    Set rst = New ADODB.Recordset

    'Set the ActiveConnection, CursorType,
    'LockType, and CursorLocation properties of the recordset
    rst.ActiveConnection = CurrentProject.Connection
    rst.CursorType = adOpenStatic
    rst.LockType = adLockOptimistic
    rst.CursorLocation = adUseServer

    'Open the recordset, designating that the source
    'is a SQL statement
    rst.Open Source:="Select * from tblClients ", _
        Options:=adCmdText

    'Modify the contents of the city field
    rst("City") = "New City"
    rst.Update
    Debug.Print rst("City")

    rst.Close
    Set rst = Nothing

End Sub
```

This example designates a server-side cursor.

Working with the Supports **Method**

Depending on which CursorType, LockType, CursorLocation, and Provider are used to open a recordset, the functionality of the recordset varies. The Supports method of a recordset determines which features a particular recordset supports. It returns a Boolean value designating whether the selected feature is supported. Listing 15.15 provides an example.

LISTING 15.15   The Supports Method of the Recordset Object

```
Sub SupportsMethod()
    'Declare and instantiate a Recordset object
    Dim rst As ADODB.Recordset
    Set rst = New ADODB.Recordset
```

LISTING 15.15   Continued

```
'Set the ActiveConnection, CursorType,
'LockType, and CursorLocation properties of the recordset
rst.ActiveConnection = CurrentProject.Connection
rst.CursorType = adOpenStatic
rst.LockType = adLockOptimistic
rst.CursorLocation = adUseServer

'Open the recordset, designating that the source
'is a SQL statement
rst.Open Source:="Select * from tblClients ", _
    Options:=adCmdText

'Determine whether the recordset supports certain features
Debug.Print "Bookmark " & rst.Supports(adBookmark)
Debug.Print "Update Batch " & rst.Supports(adUpdateBatch)
Debug.Print "Move Previous " & rst.Supports(adMovePrevious)
Debug.Print "Seek " & rst.Supports(adSeek)
rst.Close
Set rst = Nothing

End Sub
```

Working with ADO Recordset Properties and Methods

The ADO Recordset object is rich with properties and methods. These properties and methods allow you to move through a recordset; sort, filter, and find data; as well as update data contained with the recordset. The sections that follow cover the most commonly used properties and methods.

Examining Record-Movement Methods

When you have a Recordset object variable set, you probably want to manipulate the data in the recordset. Table 15.4 shows several methods you can use to traverse through the records in a recordset.

TABLE 15.4   Methods for Moving Through the Records in a Recordset

Method	Moves
MoveFirst	To the first record in a recordset
MoveLast	To the last record in a recordset
MovePrevious	To the previous record in a recordset
MoveNext	To the next record in a recordset

Listing 15.16 shows an example of using the record-movement methods on a `Recordset` object.

LISTING 15.16   Using the `RecordsetMovements()` Methods on a `Recordset` Object

```
Sub RecordsetMovements()
    Dim rst As ADODB.Recordset
    Set rst = New ADODB.Recordset

    'Establish the connection and cursor type and open
    'the recordset
    rst.ActiveConnection = CurrentProject.Connection
    rst.CursorType = adOpenStatic
    rst.Open "Select * from tblProjects"

    'Print the ProjectID of the first row
    Debug.Print rst("ProjectID")

    'Move to the next row and print the ProjectID
    rst.MoveNext
    Debug.Print rst("ProjectID")

    'Move to the last row and print the ProjectID
    rst.MoveLast
    Debug.Print rst("ProjectID")

    'Move to the previous row and print the ProjectID
    rst.MovePrevious
    Debug.Print rst("ProjectID")

    'Move to the first row and print the ProjectID
    rst.MoveFirst
    Debug.Print rst("ProjectID")

    rst.Close
    Set rst = Nothing
End Sub
```

This code opens a recordset based on the `tblProjects` table. When the recordset is open, the `ProjectID` of the first record is printed to the Immediate window. The `MoveNext` method of the `Recordset` object is used to move to the next record in the recordset. The `ProjectID` of the record is printed. The `MoveLast` method of the `Recordset` object is used to move to the last record in the recordset. Once again, the `ProjectID` is printed. The `MovePrevious` method moves the record pointer back one record, and the `ProjectID` is

15

printed again. Finally, the `MoveFirst` method moves the record pointer to the first record, and the `ProjectID` is printed. The code closes the recordset and destroys the `Recordset` object.

Detecting the Limits of a Recordset

Before you begin to traverse through recordsets, you must understand two recordset properties: `BOF` and `EOF`. The names of these properties are outdated acronyms that stand for *beginning of file* and *end of file*, respectively. They determine whether you have reached the limits of your recordset. The `BOF` property is `True` when the record pointer is before the first record, and the `EOF` property is `True` when the record pointer is after the last record.

You commonly will use the `EOF` property when moving forward through your recordset with the `MoveNext` method. This property becomes `True` when your most recent `MoveNext` has moved you beyond the bounds of the recordset. Similarly, `BOF` is most useful when using the `MovePrevious` method.

You must keep in mind some important characteristics of the `BOF` and `EOF` properties:

▶ If a recordset contains no records, both the `BOF` and `EOF` properties evaluate to `True`.

▶ When you open a recordset containing at least one record, the `BOF` and `EOF` properties are set to `False`.

▶ If the record pointer is on the first record in the recordset and you issue the `MovePrevious` method, the `BOF` property is set to `True`. If you attempt to use `MovePrevious` again, a runtime error occurs.

▶ If the record pointer is on the last record in the recordset and you issue the `MoveNext` method, the `EOF` property is set to `True`. If you attempt to use `MoveNext` again, a runtime error occurs.

▶ When the `BOF` and `EOF` properties are set to `True`, they remain `True` until you move to a valid record.

▶ When the only record in a recordset is deleted, the `BOF` and `EOF` properties remain `False` until you attempt to move to another record.

Listing 15.17 shows an example of using the `EOF` property to determine the bounds of a recordset.

LISTING 15.17   Using the `EOF` Property to Determine the Bounds of a Recordset

```
Sub DetermineLimits()
    'Declare and instantiate a Recordset object
    Dim rst As ADODB.Recordset
    Set rst = New ADODB.Recordset

    'Establish the connection and cursor type and open
    'the recordset
```

LISTING 15.17   Continued

```
    rst.ActiveConnection = CurrentProject.Connection
    rst.CursorType = adOpenStatic
    rst.Open "Select * from tblProjects"

    'Loop through the recordset, printing the
    'ClientID of each row
    Do Until rst.EOF
        Debug.Print rst("ClientID")
        rst.MoveNext
    Loop

    rst.Close
End Sub
```

In Listing 15.17, a recordset is opened based on `tblProjects`. The `EOF` property is evaluated. As long as the `EOF` property equals `False`, the code prints the contents of the `ClientID` field and advances the record pointer to the next record in the recordset.

Counting the Number of Records in a Recordset

The `RecordCount` property returns the number of rows in the recordset. Not all types of recordsets and providers support the `RecordCount` property. If the `RecordCount` property is not supported, no error occurs. Instead, the `RecordCount` is `-1`. Listing 15.18 provides an example.

LISTING 15.18   A Recordset That Does Not Support the `RecordCount` Property

```
Sub CountRecordsBad()
    'Declare and instantiate a recordset
    Dim rst As ADODB.Recordset
    Set rst = New ADODB.Recordset

    'Establish the connection and open a
    'forward-only cursor
    rst.ActiveConnection = CurrentProject.Connection
    rst.Open "Select * from tblProjects"

    'Print the RecordCount property
    Debug.Print rst.RecordCount   'Prints -1

    rst.Close
    Set rst = Nothing
End Sub
```

15

Because the default CursorType is adOpenForwardOnly, and a forward-only cursor does not support the RecordCount property, -1 prints to the Immediate window. Listing 15.19 rectifies this problem.

LISTING 15.19   A Recordset That Supports the RecordCount Property

```
Sub CountRecordsGood()
    'Declare and instantiate a recordset
    Dim rst As ADODB.Recordset
    Set rst = New ADODB.Recordset

    'Establish the connection and cursor type and open
    'the recordset
    rst.ActiveConnection = CurrentProject.Connection
    rst.CursorType = adOpenStatic
    rst.Open "Select * from tblProjects"

    'Print the RecordCount property
    Debug.Print rst.RecordCount   'Prints Record count

    rst.Close
    Set rst = Nothing

End Sub
```

Notice that the CursorType is set to adOpenStatic. Because the RecordCount property is supported with static cursors, the correct number of records is printed to the Immediate window.

> **NOTE**
>
> If you are accustomed to the DAO RecordCount property, you might be surprised by the ADO RecordCount property. The DAO RecordCount returns only the number of *visited* records in the recordset. This means that, in using DAO, you must move to the last record in the recordset to obtain an accurate record count. Although this step is unnecessary when using ADO, it is important to note that attempting to retrieve the RecordCount property might result in severe performance degradation. Whether obtaining the RecordCount degrades performance depends on the particular database provider.

One of the important uses of the RecordCount property is to determine whether a recordset contains any rows. Listing 15.20 illustrates this important use of the RecordCount property.

LISTING 15.20   Checking to See Whether Records Are Returned in a Recordset

```
Sub CheckARecordset()
    'Declare and instantiate the recordset
    Dim rst As ADODB.Recordset
```

LISTING 15.20   Continued

```
    Set rst = New ADODB.Recordset

    'Establish the connection and cursor type and open
    'the recordset
    rst.ActiveConnection = CurrentProject.Connection
    rst.CursorType = adOpenStatic
    rst.Open "Select * from tblEmpty"

    'Call a routine to determine if the recordset contains
    'any records
    If Not AreThereRecords(rst) Then
      MsgBox "Recordset Empty...Unable to Proceed"
    End If

    rst.Close
    Set rst = Nothing
End Sub

Function AreThereRecords(rstAny As ADODB.Recordset) As Boolean
    'Return whether or not there are any rows
    AreThereRecords = rstAny.RecordCount
End Function
```

The CheckARecordset routine opens a recordset based on a table called tblEmpty, which contains no data. The CheckARecordset routine calls the AreThereRecords function, passing a reference to the recordset. The AreThereRecords function evaluates the RecordCount property of the recordset that it is passed. It returns False if the RecordCount is zero and True if the RecordCount is nonzero.

Sorting, Filtering, and Finding Records

Sometimes you need to sort, filter, or find data within an existing recordset. The Sort property, Filter property, and Find method of the Recordset object allow you to accomplish these tasks. The sections that follow cover these properties and this method.

Sorting a Recordset

The Sort property of the Recordset object allows you to sort data in an existing recordset. Listing 15.21 illustrates its use.

LISTING 15.21   The Sort Property of the Recordset Object

```
Sub SortRecordset()
    Dim intCounter As Integer

    'Declare and instantiate a recordset
```

LISTING 15.21   Continued

```
    Dim rst As ADODB.Recordset
    Set rst = New ADODB.Recordset

    'Establish the connection and cursor location and open
    'the recordset
    rst.ActiveConnection = CurrentProject.Connection
    rst.CursorLocation = adUseClient
    rst.Open "Select * from tblTimeCardHours"

    'Loop through the recordset, printing
    'the contents of the DateWorked field
    Debug.Print "NOT Sorted!!!"
    Do Until rst.EOF
        Debug.Print rst("DateWorked")
        rst.MoveNext
    Loop

    'Sort the recordset and then loop through
    'it, printing the contents of the DateWorked field
    Debug.Print "Now Sorted!!!"
    rst.Sort = "[DateWorked]"
    Do Until rst.EOF
        Debug.Print rst("DateWorked")
        rst.MoveNext
    Loop

    rst.Close
    Set rst = Nothing
End Sub
```

This code begins by opening a recordset based on the tblTimeCardHours table. The code prints the records in the recordset in their "natural" order. Next, the Sort property of the Recordset object sorts the data by the DateWorked field. Notice that the Sort property is set equal to a field. If you want to sort by more than one field, you must separate the field names with commas. When the records are once again printed, they appear in order by the DateWorked field.

NOTE

If you want to sort in descending order, the field name must be followed by a space and then the keyword DESC.

Filtering a Recordset

Sometimes you might want to select a subset of the data returned in a recordset. The Filter property helps you to accomplish this task. Its use is illustrated in Listing 15.22.

LISTING 15.22   The Filter Property of the Recordset Object

```
Sub FilterRecordset()
    'Declare and instantiate a recordset
    Dim rst As ADODB.Recordset
    Set rst = New ADODB.Recordset

    'Establish the connection, cursor type,
    'and lock type, and open the recordset
    rst.ActiveConnection = CurrentProject.Connection
    rst.CursorType = adOpenKeyset
    rst.LockType = adLockOptimistic
    rst.Open "Select * from tblTimeCardHours"

    'Loop through the recordset, printing the contents of
    'the DateWorked field
    Debug.Print "Without Filter"
    Do Until rst.EOF
        Debug.Print rst("DateWorked")
        rst.MoveNext
    Loop

    'Filter the recordset and then loop through it, printing the
    'contents of the DateWorked field
    rst.Filter = "DateWorked >= #1/1/2007# and DateWorked <= #1/5/2007#"
    Debug.Print "With Filter"
    Do Until rst.EOF
        Debug.Print rst("DateWorked")
        rst.MoveNext
    Loop

    rst.Close
    Set rst = Nothing
End Sub
```

15

This example opens a recordset based on tblTimeCardHours. The code prints the records without a filter applied. The Filter property is then set to limit the data to only those records with a DateWorked value between 1/1/2007 and 1/5/2007. The code prints the records in the recordset again.

NOTE

It is inefficient to build a large recordset and to then filter only those records that you need. If you know that you need only records meeting specific criteria, you should build a recordset using those criteria. The difference in performance can be profound, particularly when dealing with client/server data. In summary, you should use the `Filter` property only when you are initially dealing with a larger set of records and then need to perform an operation on a subset of the records.

TIP

To return to the complete recordset after a filter has been applied, set the `Filter` property to a zero-length string (`""`) or to the `vbNullString` constant.

Finding a Specific Record in a Recordset

The `Find` method allows you to locate a particular record in the recordset. It is different from the `Filter` property in that all records in the recordset remain available. Listing 15.23 illustrates the use of the `Find` method.

LISTING 15.23   The Find Method of a Recordset Object

```
Sub FindProject(lngValue As Long)
    Dim strSQL As String

    'Declare and instantiate a recordset
    Dim rst As ADODB.Recordset
    Set rst = New ADODB.Recordset

    'Establish the connection and cursor type,
    'and open the recordset
    rst.ActiveConnection = CurrentProject.Connection
    rst.CursorType = adOpenStatic
    rst.Open "Select * from tblProjects"

    'Attempt to find a specific project
    strSQL = "[ProjectID] = " & lngValue
    rst.Find strSQL

    'Determine if the specified project was found
    If rst.EOF Then
        MsgBox lngValue & " Not Found"
    Else
        MsgBox lngValue & " Found"
    End If
```

LISTING 15.23   Continued

```
        rst.Close
        Set rst = Nothing
End Sub
```

> **TIP**
>
> Because the `FindProject` routine is found in more than one module, the routine must be executed as follows:
>
> ```
> Call basADORecordsets.FindProject(1)
> ```
>
> Preceding the name of the routine with the name of the module removes the ambiguity as to which `FindProject` routine to execute.

Listing 15.23 opens a recordset based on all the records in the `tblProjects` table. The `Find` method is used to locate the first record where the `ProjectID` is equal to a specific value. If the record is not found, the `EOF` property of the `Recordset` object is `True`.

> **NOTE**
>
> Unlike its DAO counterpart, ADO does not support the `FindFirst`, `FindNext`, `FindPrevious`, and `FindLast` methods. The default use of the `Find` method locates the *next* record that meets the specified criteria. This means that, if the record pointer is not at the top of the recordset, records meeting the specified criteria might not be located. The `SkipRows`, `SearchDirection`, and `Start` parameters of the `Find` method modify this default behavior. The `SkipRows` parameter allows you to specify the offset from the current row where the search begins. The `SearchDirection` parameter allows you to designate whether you want the search to proceed forward or backward from the current row. Finally, the `Start` parameter determines the starting position for the search.

Working with Variables in Strings

When using the `Find` method or when building a SQL statement in code, you must be cognizant of the delimiters to use. No delimiters are necessary when working with numeric values. For example:

```
Select * FROM tblClients WHERE ClientID = 1
```

You must use a pound symbol (#) when delimiting dates for Microsoft Access, like this:

```
Select * FROM tblClients WHERE IntroDate = #12/31/2007#
```

> **CAUTION**
>
> If your back-end database is Microsoft SQL Server, you must use an apostrophe to delimit dates.

15

The process of delimiting strings is somewhat more difficult than it initially seems. The basic process is to surround the string with apostrophes:

```
Select * FROM tblClients WHERE City = 'Oak Park'
```

This approach works unless there is an apostrophe in the string. Listing 15.24 provides the solution.

LISTING 15.24   Handling Apostrophes Within Strings

```
Sub DelimitString()

    Dim strCompanyName As String
    'Declare and instantiate a Recordset object
    Dim rst As ADODB.Recordset
    Set rst = New ADODB.Recordset

    'Ask for the company to locate
    strCompanyName = InputBox("Please Enter a Company")

    'Set the ActiveConnection, CursorType,
    'LockType, and CursorLocation properties of the recordset
    rst.ActiveConnection = CurrentProject.Connection
    rst.CursorType = adOpenStatic
    rst.LockType = adLockOptimistic
    rst.CursorLocation = adUseServer

    'Open the recordset, designating that the source
    'is a SQL statement
    rst.Open Source:="Select * from tblClients " & _
    "WHERE CompanyName = " & ReplaceApostrophe(strCompanyName), _
        Options:=adCmdText

    'Display a message as to whether the selected company
    'was found
    If rst.EOF Then
        MsgBox strCompanyName & " NOT Found!"
    Else
        MsgBox rst("ClientID")
    End If

    rst.Close
    Set rst = Nothing

End Sub
Public Function ReplaceApostrophe(strCompanyName As String) As String
```

LISTING 15.24   Continued

```
    'Surround text with apostrophes and replace any
    'apostrophes in the string with two apostrophes
    ReplaceApostrophe = "'" & _
        Replace(strCompanyName, "'", "''") & "'"
End Function
```

This code passes the string to a user-defined function called `ReplaceApostrophe`, which surrounds the string with apostrophes. If any apostrophes are found within the string, they are replaced with two apostrophes.

Using the `AbsolutePosition` **Property**

The `AbsolutePosition` property of the `Recordset` object sets or returns the ordinal position of the current row in the recordset. Its use is illustrated in Listing 15.25.

LISTING 15.25   The `AbsolutePosition` Property of a `Recordset` Object

```
Sub FindPosition(lngValue As Long)
    Dim strSQL As String

    'Declare and instantiate a recordset
    Dim rst As ADODB.Recordset
    Set rst = New ADODB.Recordset

    'Establish the connection and cursor type,
    'and open the recordset
    rst.ActiveConnection = CurrentProject.Connection
    rst.CursorType = adOpenStatic
    rst.Open "Select * from tblProjects"

    'Attempt to find a specific project
    strSQL = "[ProjectID] = " & lngValue
    rst.Find strSQL

    'If record is found, print its position
    If rst.EOF Then
        MsgBox lngValue & " Not Found"
    Else
        Debug.Print rst.AbsolutePosition
    End If

    rst.Close
    Set rst = Nothing

End Sub
```

In this example, the Find method is used to locate a project with a specific ProjectID. If the project is found, the ordinal position of the record that is located is printed to the Immediate window.

Using the Bookmark **Property**

The Bookmark property of a Recordset object returns a variant variable that acts as a unique identifier for that particular record in the recordset. You can use the Bookmark property to save the current position and then quickly and easily return to it at any time. Listing 15.26 illustrates the use of a bookmark.

LISTING 15.26   The Bookmark Property of a Recordset Object

```
Sub UseBookmark()
    Dim strSQL As String
    Dim vntPosition As Variant

    'Instantiate and declare a recordset
    Dim rst As ADODB.Recordset
    Set rst = New ADODB.Recordset

    'Establish the connection and cursor type,
    'and open the recordset
    rst.ActiveConnection = CurrentProject.Connection
    rst.CursorType = adOpenStatic
    rst.Open "Select * from tblProjects"

    'Store bookmark in a variant variable
    vntPosition = rst.Bookmark

    'Perform some operation
    'on the records in the recordset
    Do Until rst.EOF
        Debug.Print rst("ProjectID")
        rst.MoveNext
    Loop

    'Return to the bookmarked record by setting
    'the Bookmark property of the recordset to the
    'value stored in the variant variable
    rst.Bookmark = vntPosition
    Debug.Print rst("ProjectID")

    rst.Close
    Set rst = Nothing


End Sub
```

In this example, a unique identifier to the current record is stored in a variant variable. The code then loops through the remainder of the records in the recordset. When it is done, it sets the `Bookmark` property of the `Recordset` object equal to the unique identifier stored in the variant variable.

> **CAUTION**
>
> Not all recordsets support bookmarks. Whether a recordset supports bookmarks depends on the provider as well as the type of recordset created.

Running Parameter Queries

You will not always know the criteria for a recordset at design time. Fortunately, ADO allows you to supply parameters to the `CommandText` property of the `Command` object. Listing 15.27 provides an example.

LISTING 15.27   Running a Parameter Query

```
Sub RunParameterQuery(datStart As Date, datEnd As Date)
    'Declare Command and Recordset objects
    Dim cmd As ADODB.Command
    Dim rst As ADODB.Recordset

    'Instantiate the Command object
    Set cmd = New ADODB.Command

    'Establish the connection, command text,
    'and command type of the Command object
    cmd.ActiveConnection = CurrentProject.Connection
    cmd.CommandText = "Select * from tblTimeCardHours " & _
        "Where DateWorked Between ? and ?"
    cmd.CommandType = adCmdText

    'Use the Execute method of the Command object to
    'return results into the recordset object; notice that
    'an array is passed to the Parameters parameter of
    'the Command object
    Set rst = cmd.Execute(Parameters:=Array(datStart, datEnd))

    'Loop through the resulting recordset, printing the
    'contents of the TimeCardID and DateWorked fields
    Do Until rst.EOF
        Debug.Print rst("TimeCardID"), rst("DateWorked")
        rst.MoveNext
    Loop
```

LISTING 15.27   Continued

```
    rst.Close
    Set rst = Nothing
    Set cmd = Nothing

End Sub
```

Notice that in this example, the `CommandText` property contains two question marks. Each of these is considered a parameter. The parameters are supplied when the `Execute` method of the `Command` object is used. Notice that the `Parameters` argument of the `Execute` method receives an array containing the parameter values. Note that unless you specify `basADORecordsets.RunParameterQuery`, you get an "ambiguous name detected" error.

Refreshing Recordset Data

You can use two methods to refresh the data in a recordset: `Requery` and `Resync`. The `Requery` method is roughly equivalent to once again opening the recordset. The `Requery` method forces the OLEDB provider to perform all the steps it performed when first creating the recordset. New rows are added to the recordset, changes to data made by other users are reflected in the recordset, and deleted rows are removed from the recordset. The `Requery` method requires significant resources to execute. The `Resync` method is much more efficient. It updates the recordset to reflect changes made by other users. It does not show added rows or remove deleted rows from the recordset.

Working with Persisting Recordsets

Using ADO, recordsets can not only exist in memory, but they can also be written to disk. A recordset written to disk is referred to as a *persisted recordset*. Listing 15.28 illustrates how to persist a recordset to disk.

LISTING 15.28   Persisting a Recordset

```
Sub PersistRecordset()

    Dim strFileName As String

    'Prompt user for filename and path
    strFileName = InputBox("Please Enter Filename and Path")

    'Declare and instantiate a Recordset object
    Dim rst As ADODB.Recordset
    Set rst = New ADODB.Recordset

    'Set the ActiveConnection, CursorType,
    'and LockType properties of the recordset
    rst.ActiveConnection = CurrentProject.Connection
```

LISTING 15.27   Continued

```
    rst.CursorType = adOpenStatic
    rst.LockType = adLockOptimistic

    'Open the recordset, designating that the source
    'is a SQL statement
    rst.Open Source:="Select * from tblClients ", _
        Options:=adCmdText

    'Destroy existing file with that name
    On Error Resume Next
    Kill strFileName

    'Save the recordset
    rst.Save strFileName, adPersistADTG

    rst.Close
    Set rst = Nothing

End Sub
```

Notice that the Save method of the Recordset object is used to persist the recordset to disk. The Format parameter of the Save method allows you to designate whether you want to save the recordset in the Microsoft proprietary Advanced Data Tablegram (ADTG) format or whether you want to save the recordset as XML. Listing 15.29 shows you how to read a persisted recordset.

LISTING 15.29   Reading a Persisted Recordset

```
Sub ReadPersistedRecordset()
    Dim strFileName As String

    'Prompt user for filename and path to read
    strFileName = InputBox("Please Enter Filename and Path")

    'Ensure that the selected file exists
    If Len(Dir(strFileName)) = 0 Then
        MsgBox "File Not Found"
        Exit Sub
    End If

    'Declare and instantiate a Recordset object
    Dim rst As ADODB.Recordset
    Set rst = New ADODB.Recordset
```

LISTING 15.29   Continued

```
    'Set the ActiveConnection, CursorType,
    'and LockType properties of the recordset
    rst.ActiveConnection = CurrentProject.Connection
    rst.CursorType = adOpenStatic
    rst.LockType = adLockOptimistic

    'Open the recordset, designating that the source
    'is a SQL statement
    rst.Open Source:=strFileName, _
        Options:=adCmdFile

    'Loop through the recordset, printing ClientIDs
    Do Until rst.EOF
        Debug.Print rst("ClientID")
        rst.MoveNext
    Loop

    rst.Close
    Set rst = Nothing

End Sub
```

After prompting the user for a filename, the code ensures that the designated file is found. It then opens a recordset, using the file as the source argument. The `adCmdFile` constant is used for the `Options` parameter of the `Open` method. The `adCmdFile` value notifies ADO that the source is a persisted recordset.

Modifying Table Data Using ADO Code

So far, this chapter has covered only the process of retrieving data from a recordset. It is common that you might need to update the data in a recordset. The sections that follow show you how to change data one record at a time, update a batch of records, delete records, and add records.

Changing Record Data One Record at a Time

You can loop through a recordset, modifying all the records in the recordset. Listing 15.30 shows this technique.

LISTING 15.30   Modifying One Record at a Time

```
Sub IncreaseEstimate()

    Dim rst As ADODB.Recordset
    Set rst = New ADODB.Recordset
```

LISTING 15.30   Continued

```
    Dim strSQL As String
    Dim lngUpdated As Long

    'Establish the connection, cursor type,
    'and lock type, and open the recordset
    rst.ActiveConnection = CurrentProject.Connection
    rst.CursorType = adOpenDynamic
    rst.LockType = adLockOptimistic
    rst.Open ("Select * from tblProjectsChange")

    strSQL = "ProjectTotalEstimate < 30000"
    lngUpdated = 0

    'Find the first row meeting the designated criteria
    rst.Find strSQL

    'Loop through the recordset, locating all rows meeting
    'the designated criteria, increasing the ProjecTotalEstimate
    'field by 10%
    Do Until rst.EOF
        lngUpdated = lngUpdated + 1
        rst("ProjectTotalEstimate") = rst("ProjectTotalEstimate") * 1.1
        rst.Update
        rst.Find strSQL, 1, adSearchForward
    Loop

    'Print how many rows are updated
    Debug.Print lngUpdated & " Records Updated"

    rst.Close
    Set rst = Nothing

End Sub
```

The code in Listing 15.30 opens a recordset based on all the records in the tblProjectsChange table. It locates the first record where the ProjectTotalEstimate is less than 30,000. The ProjectTotalEstimate is increased by 10%, and the record is updated. The code locates the next record that meets the specified criteria. The code repeats the process until it locates all records meeting the specified criteria.

This code is very inefficient from several standpoints. The first problem is that it opens a recordset based on all the records in the tblProjectsChange table, when only those with a ProjectTotalEstimate less than 30,000 needed to be updated. A more efficient approach is to open a recordset containing only those records that you need to update. Listing 15.31 illustrates this technique.

LISTING 15.31   Improving the Process of Modifying One Record at a Time

```
Sub IncreaseEstimateImproved()

    'Declare and instantiate a recordset
    Dim rst As ADODB.Recordset
    Set rst = New ADODB.Recordset

    Dim lngUpdated As Long

    'Establish the connection, cursor type,
    'and lock type, and open the recordset
    rst.ActiveConnection = CurrentProject.Connection
    rst.CursorType = adOpenDynamic
    rst.LockType = adLockOptimistic
    rst.Open ("Select * from tblProjectsChange " & _
        "WHERE ProjectTotalEstimate < 30000")

    'Loop through the recordset, locating all rows meeting
    'the designated criteria, increasing the ProjecTotalEstimate
    'field by 10%
    Do Until rst.EOF
        lngUpdated = lngUpdated + 1
        rst("ProjectTotalEstimate") = rst("ProjectTotalEstimate") * 1.1
        rst.Update
        rst.MoveNext
    Loop

    'Print how many rows are updated
    Debug.Print lngUpdated & " Records Updated"

    rst.Close
    Set rst = Nothing

End Sub
```

Furthermore, it would be more efficient to simply execute an action query that performs the update. This technique is covered in the section that follows.

> **CAUTION**
>
> If you're accustomed to DAO, you might be quite surprised by the behavior of ADO. Whereas DAO requires that the Edit method be used before field values are assigned, no Edit method is used with ADO. Furthermore, if you forget to issue the Update method on a DAO recordset, the record is not updated. On the other hand, with ADO, the Update method is implied. The update occurs automatically as soon as the record pointer is moved. These behavior differences can lead to big surprises!

Performing Batch Updates

If you use a client-side cursor, along with a static or keyset cursor, you can take advantage of batch updates. Using batch updates, all changes you make to a recordset are sent to the underlying OLEDB provider as a batch. The process is illustrated in Listing 15.32.

LISTING 15.32   Performing Batch Updates

```
Sub BatchUpdates()
    'Declare and instantiate a recordset
    Dim rst As ADODB.Recordset
    Set rst = New ADODB.Recordset

    Dim strSQL As String
    Dim lngUpdated As Long

    'Establish the connection, cursor type, cursor
    'location, and lock type, and open the recordset
    rst.ActiveConnection = CurrentProject.Connection
    rst.CursorType = adOpenKeyset
    rst.CursorLocation = adUseClient
    rst.LockType = adLockBatchOptimistic
    rst.Open ("Select * from tblProjectsChange")

    strSQL = "ProjectTotalEstimate < 30000"
    lngUpdated = 0

    'Find the first row meeting the designated criteria
    rst.Find strSQL

    'Loop through the recordset, locating all rows meeting
    'the designated criteria, increasing the ProjecTotalEstimate
    'field by 10%
    Do Until rst.EOF
        lngUpdated = lngUpdated + 1
        rst("ProjectTotalEstimate") = rst("ProjectTotalEstimate") * 1.1
        rst.Find strSQL, 1, adSearchForward
    Loop

    'Send all changes to the provider
    rst.UpdateBatch

    'Print how many rows are updated
    Debug.Print lngUpdated & " Records Updated"

    rst.Close
    Set rst = Nothing

End Sub
```

15

In this example, the `CursorLocation` property of the recordset is set to `adUseClient`, the `CursorType` is set to `adOpenKeyset`, and the `LockType` is set to `adLockBatchOptimistic`. Notice that the `Update` method is not included in the `Do Until` loop. Instead, the `UpdateBatch` method is used to send all the changes to the server at once.

Making Bulk Changes

As mentioned in the preceding section, it is inefficient to open a recordset and then update each record individually. A much more efficient approach is to execute an action query. Listing 15.33 illustrates this process.

LISTING 15.33   Making Bulk Changes to the Records in a Recordset

```
Sub RunUpdateQuery()
    'Declare and instantiate a Connection object
    Dim cnn As ADODB.Connection
    Set cnn = New ADODB.Connection

    'Establish the connection and execute an action query
    Set cnn = CurrentProject.Connection
    cnn.Execute "qryIncreaseTotalEstimate"
    cnn.Close

End Sub
```

In Listing 15.33, the `Execute` method of the `Connection` object executes a stored query called `qryIncreaseTotalEstimate`. Any criteria contained within the query are applied.

You might be wondering how you can update data stored in a SQL Server database. One method is to call a stored procedure located in the SQL Server database. The code in Listing 15.34 illustrates an example.

> **NOTE**
>
> The three listings that follow all require SQL Server 2000 or SQL Server 2005. You must build the stored procedures used by Listing 15.34 and Listing 15.36. Finally, you must have the copy of Northwind that ships with SQL Server 2000 to run the examples. (Otherwise the field names will be inaccurate.) Of course, you could modify the field names that the code references to update any table in any database.

LISTING 15.34   Using a Stored Procedure to Make Bulk Changes to Data in a SQL Server Database

```
Sub RunUpdateQuery()
    'Declare and instantiate a Connection object
    Dim cnn As ADODB.Connection
    Set cnn = New ADODB.Connection
```

LISTING 15.34   Continued

```
'Establish the connection and execute a stored procedure
cnn.Open "Provider=SQLOLEDB.1;" & _
        "Data Source=(local); Initial Catalog=NorthWind;" & _
        "Integrated Security=SSPI"
cnn.Execute "procIncreaseTotalEstimate"
cnn.Close
```

End Sub

The example in Listing 15.34 executes a SQL Server procedure called procIncreaseTotalEstimate. Notice that the example does not receive parameters. The example in Listing 15.35 uses a Command object to execute a SQL statement containing parameters.

LISTING 15.35   Executing a SQL Statement Containing Parameters

```
Public Sub UpdateWithSQL()

        'Declare necessary variables
        Dim cmd As New ADODB.Command
        Dim conn As ADODB.Connection
        Dim prm As ADODB.Parameter
        Dim strConn As String
        Dim strSQL As String

        'Build a connection string
         strConn = "Provider=SQLOLEDB.1;" & _
            "Data Source=(local); Initial Catalog=NorthWind;" & _
            "Integrated Security=SSPI"

        'Open the connection
        Set conn = New ADODB.Connection
        conn.Open strConn

        'Instantiate the SqlCommand object
        Set cmd = New ADODB.Command

        'Set the CommandText property
        cmd.CommandText = "UPDATE Orders " & _
            "SET OrderDate = OrderDate, " & _
            "ShipVia = ShipVia, " & _
            "Freight = Freight " & _
            "WHERE OrderID = OrderID"
```

15

LISTING 15.35   Continued

```
'Designate the CommandType
cmd.CommandType = adCmdText

'Set the Connection property of the SqlCommand
cmd.ActiveConnection = conn

'Add parameters and set their values
'NOTE THAT THE ORDER DOESN'T MATTER!
Set prm = cmd.CreateParameter("OrderID", adInteger, adParamInput)
cmd.Parameters.Append prm
cmd.Parameters("OrderID").Value = 1

Set prm = cmd.CreateParameter("OrderDate", adDate, adParamInput)
cmd.Parameters.Append prm
cmd.Parameters("OrderDate").Value = "1/1/2007"

Set prm = cmd.CreateParameter("ShipVia", adInteger, adParamInput)
cmd.Parameters.Append prm
cmd.Parameters("ShipVia").Value = 2

Set prm = cmd.CreateParameter("Freight", adCurrency, adParamInput)
cmd.Parameters.Append prm
cmd.Parameters("Freight").Value = "10.5"

'Execute the Update statement
cmd.Execute

'Close the connection
conn.Close

End Sub
```

The example begins by building a connection string. It then instantiates and opens a connection. It instantiates a Command object and sets its CommandText property to an UPDATE statement. Next it sets the CommandType and ActiveConnection properties of the command object. It appends four parameters to the Command object, and finally uses the Execute method of the Command object to update data in the Orders table. Although the example sets the parameter values to fixed values, it could instead take the values from variables or from text boxes on a form. In addition, the example could execute a stored procedure stored in the SQL Server database. This alternative code appears in Listing 15.36.

LISTING 15.36   Executing a Stored Procedure Containing Parameters

```
Public Sub UpdateWithStoredProcedure()

        'Declare necessary variables
        Dim cmd As New ADODB.Command
        Dim conn As ADODB.Connection
        Dim prm As ADODB.Parameter
        Dim strConn As String
        Dim strSQL As String

        'Build a connection string
         strConn = "Provider=SQLOLEDB.1;" & _
            "Data Source=(local); Initial Catalog=NorthWind;" & _
            "Integrated Security=SSPI"

        'Open the connection
        Set conn = New ADODB.Connection
        conn.Open strConn

        'Instantiate the SqlCommand object
        Set cmd = New ADODB.Command

        'Set the CommandText property
        cmd.CommandText = "procOrderUpdate"

        'Designate the CommandType
        cmd.CommandType = adCmdStoredProc

        'Set the Connection property of the SqlCommand
        cmd.ActiveConnection = conn

        'Add parameters and set their values
        'NOTE THAT THE ORDER DOESN'T MATTER!
        Set prm = cmd.CreateParameter("OrderID", adInteger, adParamInput)
        cmd.Parameters.Append prm
        cmd.Parameters("OrderID").Value = 1

        Set prm = cmd.CreateParameter("OrderDate", adDate, adParamInput)
        cmd.Parameters.Append prm
        cmd.Parameters("OrderDate").Value = "1/1/2007"

        Set prm = cmd.CreateParameter("ShipVia", adInteger, adParamInput)
        cmd.Parameters.Append prm
        cmd.Parameters("ShipVia").Value = 2
```

15

LISTING 15.36   Continued

```
        Set prm = cmd.CreateParameter("Freight", adCurrency, adParamInput)
        cmd.Parameters.Append prm
        cmd.Parameters("Freight").Value = "10.5"

        'Execute the Stored Procedure
        cmd.Execute

        'Close the connection
        conn.Close
    End Sub
```

This example is quite similar to the example in Listing 15.35. There are two main differences between the two examples. The first difference is the value of the CommandType property designated in each example. Whereas Listing 15.35 sets the CommandType property of the Command object to acCmdText, Listing 15.36 sets it to acCmdStoredProc, indicating that the text in the CommandText property is the name of a stored procedure. The second difference is that the text in the CommandText property is a SQL statement in Listing 15.35, but it is the name of a stored procedure in Listing 15.36. The stored procedure looks like this:

```
CREATE PROCEDURE [dbo].[ProcOrderUpdate] @OrderID int,
@OrderDate DateTime, @ShipVia int, @Freight money
AS
UPDATE Orders
    SET OrderDate = @OrderDate,
        ShipVia = @ShipVia,
        Freight = @Freight
WHERE OrderID = @OrderID
```

Notice that it declares four parameters and then uses the parameter values passed to it to update the OrderDate, ShipVisa, and Freight fields.

Deleting an Existing Record

You can use ADO code to delete a record in a recordset. The code appears in Listing 15.37. Note that it must be called using basADORecordset.DeleteCusts.

LISTING 15.37   Deleting an Existing Record

```
Sub DeleteCusts(lngProjEst As Long)

    Dim intCounter as Integer

    'Declare and instantiate a recordset
    Dim rst As ADODB.Recordset
```

LISTING 15.37   Continued

```
Set rst = New ADODB.Recordset

'Establish the connection, cursor type,
'and lock type, and open the recordset
rst.ActiveConnection = CurrentProject.Connection
rst.CursorType = adOpenDynamic
rst.LockType = adLockOptimistic
rst.Open "Select * from tblProjectsChange"

intCounter = 0

'Loop through the recordset, deleting all projects
'with an estimate lower than the specified amount
Do Until rst.EOF
    If rst("ProjectTotalEstimate") < lngProjEst Then
        rst.Delete
        intCounter = intCounter + 1
    End If
    If Not rst.EOF Then
        rst.MoveNext
    End If
Loop

'Designate how many customers were deleted
Debug.Print intCounter & " Customers Deleted"

rst.Close
Set rst = Nothing

End Sub
```

In Listing 15.37, a recordset is opened, based on all the records in the `tblProjectsChange` table. The code loops through all the records in the recordset. If the `ProjectTotalEstimate` is less than the value passed as a parameter to the routine, the `Delete` method of the `Recordset` object removes the record from the recordset.

As previously discussed, this example is very inefficient. You should either build a recordset containing only the records you want to delete or use an action query to accomplish the task.

TIP

If you are using a provider that supports stored procedures, it is most efficient to add, edit, and delete data using a stored procedure. Stored procedures execute on the server, sending no data over the network wire.

Adding a New Record

You can not only edit and delete data using ADO, but also add records as well. Listing 15.38 illustrates this process.

LISTING 15.38   Adding a New Record to a Recordset

```
Private Sub cmdAddADO_Click()
    Dim rst As ADODB.Recordset

    'Ensure that the project name and ClientID are entered
    If IsNull(Me.txtProjectName) Or _
        IsNull(Me.cboClientID) Then

        MsgBox "The Project Name and Client Must be Filled In"

    Else

        'Instantiate a recordset
        Set rst = New ADODB.Recordset

        'Set the connection, cursor type, and lock type,
        'and open the recordset
        With rst
            .ActiveConnection = CurrentProject.Connection
            .CursorType = adOpenKeyset
            .LockType = adLockOptimistic
            .Open "Select * from tblProjectsChange Where ProjectID = 0"

            'Add a new row to the recordset, populating its values with
            'the controls on the form
            .AddNew
                !ProjectName = Me.txtProjectName
                !ProjectDescription = Me.txtProjectDescription
                !ClientID = Me.cboClientID
            .Update

            'Populate the txtProjectID text box with the
            'autonumber value assigned to the new row
            Me.txtProjectID = !ProjectID
        End With

    End If

End Sub
```

This code, an event procedure for a command button on frmUnbound, begins by setting the CursorType property of the recordset to adOpenKeyset and the LockType property to adLockOptimistic. The AddNew method creates a buffer for a new record. All the field values are assigned, based on values in the text boxes on the form. The Update method writes the data to disk. Because the ProjectID field is an Autonumber field, the txtProjectID text box must be updated to reflect the Autonumber value that was assigned.

> **CAUTION**
>
> With the DAO example, included on the sample code CD-ROM, you are not placed on the new record after it is added. With ADO, you are moved to the new record when you issue the Update method.

Creating and Modifying Database Objects Using ADO Code

Although most of the time you will design your database structure before you deploy your application, sometimes you will need to design or modify database objects at runtime. Fortunately, you can accomplish these tasks using ADO code. The following sections cover adding and removing tables, modifying relationships, and building queries, all using ADO code. These are only a few of the tasks that you can accomplish.

Adding a Table Using Code

Adding a table using ADO code is relatively easy. Listing 15.39 provides an example.

LISTING 15.39   Adding a Table

```
Sub CreateTable()
   Dim tdf As ADOX.Table
   Dim idx As ADOX.Index

    'Declare and instantiate a Catalog object
    Dim cat As ADOX.Catalog
    Set cat = New ADOX.Catalog

    'Establish a connection
    cat.ActiveConnection = CurrentProject.Connection

    ' Instantiate a Table object
    Set tdf = New ADOX.Table

    ' Name the table and add fields to it
    With tdf
        .Name = "tblFoods"
```

LISTING 15.39   Continued

```
        Set .ParentCatalog = cat
        .Columns.Append "FoodID", adInteger
        .Columns("FoodID").Properties("AutoIncrement") = True
        .Columns.Append "Description", adWChar
        .Columns.Append "Calories", adInteger
    End With

    'Append the table to the Tables collection
    cat.Tables.Append tdf

    'Instantiate an Index object
    Set idx = New ADOX.Index

   'Set properties of the index
    With idx
        .Name = "PrimaryKey"
        .Columns.Append "FoodID"
        .PrimaryKey = True
        .Unique = True
    End With

    'Add the index to the Indexes collection
    'of the table
    tdf.Indexes.Append idx

    Set idx = Nothing
    Set cat = Nothing



End Sub
```

Listing 15.39 begins by instantiating an ADOX table object. It sets the Name and ParentCatalog properties of the Table object. Then it uses the Append method of the Columns collection of the table to append each field to the table. After all the columns are appended, it uses the Append method of the Tables collection of the Catalog object to append the Table object to the database.

After the table is appended to the Catalog, you can add indexes to the table. An Index object is instantiated. The Name property of the index is set. Next, the Append method of the Columns object of the Index adds a column to the Index. The PrimaryKey and Unique properties of the index are both set to True. Finally, the Index object is appended to the Indexes collection of the Table object.

> **CAUTION**
>
> When you are running code that appends an object, an error occurs if the object already exists. You must either include error handling in your routine to handle this eventuality or delete the existing instance of the object before appending the new object.

Removing a Table Using Code

Sometimes you need to remove a table from a database. Fortunately, this task is easily accomplished using ADO code. Listing 15.40 illustrates the process.

LISTING 15.40   Removing a Table

```
Sub DeleteTable()
    'Ignore error if it occurs
    On Error Resume Next

    'Declare and instantiate a Catalog object
    Dim cat As ADOX.Catalog
    Set cat = New ADOX.Catalog

    'Establish the connection for the Catalog object
    cat.ActiveConnection = CurrentProject.Connection

    'Delete a table from the Tables collection
    cat.Tables.Delete "tblFoods"

End Sub
```

First, this code declares and instantiates a Catalog object. Then it uses the Delete method of the Tables collection of the Catalog object to remove the table from the database.

Establishing Relationships Using Code

If your application adds new tables to a database, you might need to establish relationships between those tables, as demonstrated in Listing 15.41.

LISTING 15.41   Establishing a Relationship

```
Sub CreateRelation()
    Dim tbl As ADOX.Table
    Dim fk As ADOX.Key

    'Declare and instantiate a Catalog object
    Dim cat As ADOX.Catalog
```

LISTING 15.41   Continued

```
    Set cat = New ADOX.Catalog

    'Establish a connection
    cat.ActiveConnection = CurrentProject.Connection

    'Point the Table object at the tblPeople table
    Set tbl = cat.Tables("tblPeople")

    'Instantiate a Key object
    Set fk = New ADOX.Key

    'Set properties of the Key object to relate the
    'tblPeople table to the tblFoods table
    With fk
        .Name = "PeopleFood"
        .Type = adKeyForeign
        .RelatedTable = "tblFoods"
        .Columns.Append "FoodID"
        .Columns("FoodID").RelatedColumn = "FoodID"
    End With

    'Append the Key object to the Keys collection of
    'the tblPeople table
    tbl.Keys.Append fk

    Set cat = Nothing
    Set tbl = Nothing
    Set fk = Nothing
End Sub
```

This code begins by pointing a Table object at the foreign key table in the relationship. The code instantiates a Key object. It sets the Name property of the Key object. Next, it establishes the Type property of the Key object. It sets the RelatedTable property equal to the name of the primary key table involved in the relationship. The Append method of the Columns collection of the Key object appends the foreign key field to the Key object. Then the RelatedColumn property of the column is set equal to the name of the primary key field. Finally, the code appends the Key object to the Keys collection of the Table object.

Creating a Query Using Code

At times, you will want to build a query on the fly and permanently store it in the database. Listing 15.42 illustrates this process.

LISTING 15.42   Creating a Query

```
Sub CreateQuery()
    Dim cmd As ADODB.Command
    Dim strSQL As String

    'Declare and instantiate a Catalog object
    Dim cat As ADOX.Catalog
    Set cat = New ADOX.Catalog

    'Establish a connection
    cat.ActiveConnection = CurrentProject.Connection

    'Instantiate a Command object and set its
    'CommandText property
    Set cmd = New ADODB.Command
    cmd.CommandText = "Select * From tblClients Where State='CA'"

    'Append the Command object to the Views collection
    'of the Catalog object
    cat.Views.Append "qryCAClients", cmd
    cat.Views.Refresh

    Set cat = Nothing
    Set cmd = Nothing

End Sub
```

This code begins by creating and instantiating a `Catalog` object and a `Command` object. It sets the `CommandText` property of the `Command` object equal to the SQL statement that underlies the query. The `Append` method of the `Views` collection of the `Catalog` object appends the `Command` object to a query with the specified name. Finally, the code refreshes the `Views` collection of the `Catalog` object.

Practical Examples: Applying These Techniques to Your Application

The potential applications for the methodologies learned in this chapter are endless. The sections that follow explore just a few of the ways you can apply these techniques. The examples here are located in `Chap15Ex.accdb`.

Using Recordset Methods on a Data-Entry Form

At times, you might want to disable the default record movement and add, edit, or delete functionality from a form and code all the functionality yourself. You might want to perform these actions if you are going against client/server data and want to execute additional control over the data-entry environment. You also might want to use these techniques when you are developing applications for both the Access and Visual Basic environments and are striving for maximum code compatibility. Regardless of your reasons for using the following techniques, it is a good idea to know how to assign a Recordset object to a form and then use the form's underlying recordset to display and modify data.

Figure 15.2 shows a form in which the navigation buttons and record selectors have been removed. The form contains six command buttons: Move Previous (<), Move Next (>), Add, Delete, Find, and Exit. All the buttons use the recordset underlying the form to move from record to record in the form and modify the data contained within the form.

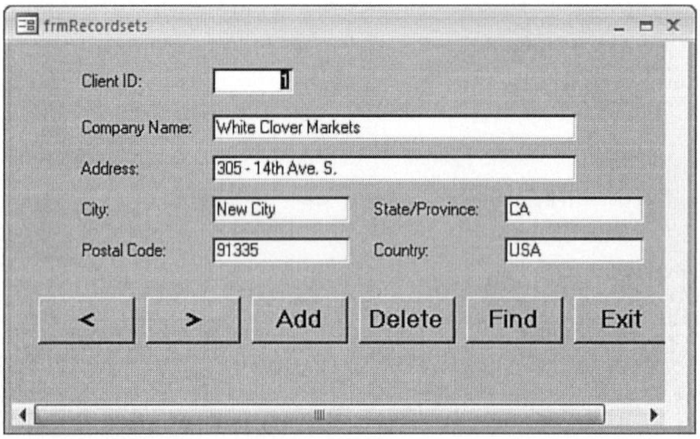

FIGURE 15.2   The frmRecordsets form.

The RecordSource property of the form is not set. The Load event of the form is responsible for assigning a Recordset object to the form. Listing 15.43 shows the Load event of the form.

LISTING 15.43   The Load Event Assigning a Recordset Object to the Form

```
Private Sub Form_Load()
    'Declare and instantiate a recordset
    Dim rst As ADODB.Recordset
    Set rst = New ADODB.Recordset

    'Establish the Connection, Cursor Type, Cursor
    'Location, and Lock Type and open the recordset
    rst.ActiveConnection = CurrentProject.Connection
    rst.CursorType = adOpenKeyset
    rst.CursorLocation = adUseClient
    rst.LockType = adLockOptimistic
    rst.Open "Select * from tblClients", Options:=adCmdText

    'Set the form's recordset to the recordset just created
    Set Me.Recordset = rst
End Sub
```

The code begins by declaring and instantiating an ADODB `Recordset` object. It then sets four properties of the `Recordset` object: the `ActiveConnection`, the `CursorType`, the `Cursor Location`, and the `LockType`. The `Open` method is used to open a recordset, based on the `tblClients` table. Finally, a `Set` statement is used to assign the recordset to the recordset underlying the form.

> **NOTE**
>
> When an ADO recordset is assigned to a form, and the form is based on Jet Engine or Access Database Engine data, the form is rendered read-only. If an ADO recordset is assigned to a form based on SQL data, the form is rendered read/write. If you want to render a form based on Access Database Engine data as read/write, you must set the `CursorLocation` property of the `Recordset` object to `adUseClient`.

Listing 15.44 shows the code for the Move Previous button.

LISTING 15.44   Code for the Move Previous Button

```
Private Sub cmdPrevious_Click()
    'Move to the previous record in the recordset
    Me.Recordset.MovePrevious

    'If at BOF, move to the next record
    If Me.Recordset.BOF Then
        Me.Recordset.MoveNext
        MsgBox "Already at First Record!!"
    End If

    'Set the bookmark of the form to the bookmark
    'of the recordset underlying the form
    Me.Bookmark = Me.Recordset.Bookmark
End Sub
```

This routine performs the `MovePrevious` method on the `Recordset` property of the form. If the `BOF` property becomes `True`, indicating that the record pointer is before the first valid record, the `MoveNext` method is performed on the `Recordset` property of the form to return the record pointer to the first record in the recordset. Finally, the bookmark of the form is synchronized with the bookmark of the `Recordset` property. Listing 15.45 shows the code for the Move Next button.

LISTING 15.45   Code for the Move Next Button

```
Private Sub cmdNext_Click()
    'Move to the next record in the recordset
    Me.Recordset.MoveNext

    'If at EOF, move to the previous record
```

15

LISTING 15.45   Continued

```
    If Me.Recordset.EOF Then
        Me.Recordset.MovePrevious
        MsgBox "Already at Last Record!!"
    End If

    'Set the bookmark of the form to the bookmark
    'of the recordset underlying the form
    Me.Bookmark = Me.Recordset.Bookmark
End Sub
```

The code for the Add button is a little tricky, as Listing 15.46 shows.

LISTING 15.46   Code for the Add Button

```
Private Sub cmdAdd_Click()
    'Add a new row to the recordset
    Me.Recordset.AddNew
    Me.Recordset("CompanyName") = "New Company"
    Me.Recordset.Update

    'Move to the row that was added
    Me.Bookmark = Me.Recordset.Bookmark
End Sub
```

The AddNew method is performed on the Recordset property of the form. This method creates a buffer in memory that is ready to accept the new data. When the Update method is issued, the record pointer is moved to the new record. Because the CompanyName field is a required field, you must populate it with data before issuing the Update method on the Recordset property.

By setting the bookmark of the form to the Bookmark property of the recordset, you synchronize the form with the new record. In a production environment, you would want to clear out all the text boxes and force the user to save or cancel before the AddNew or Update methods are issued.

The process of deleting a record is quite simple, as Listing 15.47 shows.

LISTING 15.47   Deleting a Record

```
Private Sub cmdDelete_Click()
    'Ask user if he really wants to delete the row
    intAnswer = MsgBox("Are You Sure???", _
        vbYesNo + vbQuestion, _
        "Delete Current Record?")
```

LISTING 15.47   Continued

```
        'If he responds yes, delete the row and
        'move to the next row
        If intAnswer = vbYes Then
            Me.Recordset.Delete
            Call cmdNext_Click
            Me.Refresh
        End If
End Sub
```

CAUTION

Because the tblClients table is linked to the tblProjects table, the process of deleting a client will render an error if that client has associated projects. This must be handled using standard error handling techniques.

This code verifies that the user actually wants to delete the record and then issues the Delete method on the Recordset property of the form. Because the current record no longer is valid, the code calls the Click event of the cmdNext button.

The last piece of code involved in the form is the code for the Find button, as shown in Listing 15.48.

LISTING 15.48   Code for the Find Button

```
Private Sub cmdFind_Click()
    Dim strClientID As String
    Dim varBookmark As Variant

    'Store the bookmark of the current record
    varBookmark = Me.Recordset.Bookmark

    'Attempt to locate another client
    strClientID = InputBox("Enter Client ID of Client You Want to Locate")
    Me.Recordset.Find "ClientID = " & strClientID, Start:=1

    'If client not found, display a message and return to
    'the original record
    If Me.Recordset.EOF Then
        MsgBox "Client ID " & strClientID & " Not Found!!"
        Me.Recordset.Bookmark = varBookmark

    'If client found, synchronize the form with the
    'underlying recordset
```

15

```
    Else
        Me.Bookmark = Me.Recordset.Bookmark
    End If
End Sub
```

This routine begins by storing the bookmark of the current record to a Variant variable. Users are prompted for the client ID they want to locate, and then the Find method is issued on the Recordset property of the form. If the EOF property is True, the user is warned, and the bookmark of the recordset is set to the value within the Variant variable, returning the record pointer to the position it was in prior to the search. If the client ID is found, the bookmark of the form is synchronized with the bookmark of the Recordset property.

Summary

In this chapter, you learned how to manipulate recordsets via code. The chapter began by contrasting ActiveX Data Objects with Data Access Objects. It continued by introducing you to the ADO model. It explored the different types of ADO recordsets available, highlighting why you would want to use each type.

Next, you learned how to manipulate recordsets using code. The capability to manipulate recordsets behind the scenes is an important aspect of the VBA language. It frees you from the user interface and enables you to control what is going on programmatically. Finally, you learned how to create and modify database objects using code. This is important if the application you are creating requires you to create or modify tables, queries, or other objects at runtime.

PART II

What to Do When Things Don't Go as Planned

IN THIS PART

CHAPTER 16

Debugging: Your Key to Successful Development

Why This Chapter Is Important

A good programmer is not necessarily one who can get things right the first time. To be fully effective as a Visual Basic for Applications (VBA) programmer, you need to master the art of *debugging*—the process of troubleshooting your application. Debugging involves locating and identifying problem areas within your code and is a mandatory step in the application-development process. Fortunately, the Access 2007 Visual Basic Editor (VBE) provides excellent tools to help you with the debugging process. Using the Access 2007 debugging tools, you can step through your code, setting watchpoints and breakpoints as needed.

Using the VBA debugging tools is significantly more efficient than taking random stabs at fixes to your application. A strong command of the Access 2007 debugging tools can save you hours of trial and error. In fact, it can be the difference between a successfully completed application-development process and one that continues indefinitely with problems left unsolved.

Avoiding Bugs

The best way to deal with bugs is to avoid them in the first place. Proper coding techniques can really aid you in this process. Using the `Option Explicit` statement, strong-typing, naming standards, and tight scoping can help you eliminate bugs in your code.

Option Explicit

Option Explicit requires that you declare all your variables before you use them. Including Option Explicit in each Form, Code, and Report module helps the VBA compiler find typos in the names of variables.

As discussed in detail in Chapter 8, "VBA: An Introduction," the Option Explicit statement is a command that you can manually insert into the General Declarations section of any Code, Form, or Report module. If you prefer, you can have Access automatically insert the Option Explicit statement. To accomplish this, select Require Variable Declaration from the Editor tab after choosing Tools, Options from within the Visual Basic Editor. After you select that setting, Access inserts an Option Explicit statement in the General Declarations section of all new modules. This setting does not affect existing modules.

Strong-Typing

Chapter 8 covers the process of strong-typing your variables. *Strong-typing* a variable means indicating at declaration time the type of data you will store in a variable. For example, Dim intCounter As Integer initializes a variable that contains integers. If elsewhere in your code you assign a character string to intCounter, the compiler will catch the error.

Naming Standards

Naming standards can also go a long way toward helping you eliminate errors. The careful naming of variables makes your code easier to read and makes the intended use of the variable more obvious. Problem code tends to stand out when you have judiciously followed naming conventions. Chapter 1, "Access as a Development Tool," covers naming standards. Appendix A, "Naming Conventions," which is available for download at www.samspublishing.com, covers the details of naming standards.

Variable Scoping

Finally, giving your variables the narrowest scope possible reduces the chances of one piece of code accidentally overwriting a variable within another piece of code. You should use local variables whenever possible. Use module-level and global variables only when it is necessary to see the value of a variable from multiple subroutines or multiple modules. For more information about the issues surrounding variable scoping, see Chapter 8.

Bugs Happen!

Unfortunately, no matter what you do to prevent problems and errors, they still creep into your code. Probably the most insidious type of error is a logic error. A *logic error* is sneaky because it escapes the compiler; your code compiles but simply does not execute as planned. This type of error might become apparent when you receive a runtime error or when you don't get the results you expected. In these cases, the debugger comes to the rescue.

Harnessing the Power of the Immediate Window

The Immediate window serves several purposes. It provides you with a great way to test VBA and user-defined functions, it enables you to inquire about and change the values of variables while your code is running, and it enables you to view the results of Debug.Print statements. To open the Immediate window while in the Visual Basic Editor, do one of three things:

- ▶ Click the Immediate window tool on the Debug toolbar.

- ▶ Choose View, Immediate window.

- ▶ Press Ctrl+G.

NOTE

An advantage of pressing Ctrl+G is that this keystroke combination invokes the Immediate window without a Code window being active. You can click the Immediate window toolbar button or choose View, Immediate window only from within the VBE.

Figure 16.1 shows the Immediate window.

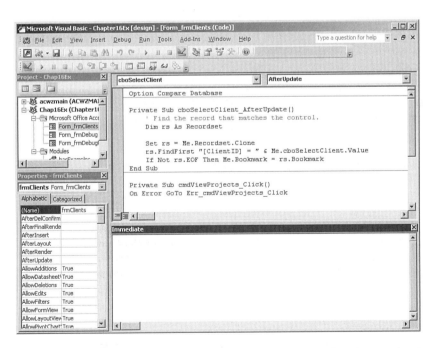

FIGURE 16.1   The Immediate window enables you to test functions and to inquire about and change the values of variables.

> **NOTE**
>
> The Debug tools are available on a separate toolbar. To show the Debug toolbar, right-click any toolbar or menu bar and select Debug from the list of available toolbars.

Testing Values of Variables and Properties

The Immediate window enables you to test the values of variables and properties as your code executes. This feature can be quite enlightening as to what is actually happening within your code.

To practice with the Immediate window, you do not even need to be executing code. To invoke the Immediate window while in a form, report, or module, press Ctrl+G. To see how this works, follow these steps:

1. Run the `frmClients` form from the `CHAP16EX.ACCDB` database on the accompanying CD-ROM.

2. Press Ctrl+G to open and activate the Immediate window. Access places you in the VBE within the Immediate window.

3. Type **`?Forms!frmClients.txtClientID.Value`** and press Enter. The client ID of the current client appears on the next line.

4. Type **`?Forms!frmClients.txtCompanyName.Visible`** and press Enter. The word `True` appears on the next line, indicating that the control is visible.

5. Type **`?Forms!frmClients.txtContactTitle.BackColor`** and press Enter. The number associated with the `BackColor` of the Contact Title text box appears on the next line.

Your screen should look like the one shown in Figure 16.2. You can continue to request the values of properties or variables within your VBA code.

Setting Values of Variables and Properties

You can not only display things in the Immediate window, but you also can use the Immediate window to modify the values of variables and controls as your code executes. This feature becomes even more valuable when you realize that you can re-execute code within a procedure after changing the value of a variable. Here's how this process works:

1. Invoke the Immediate window, if necessary. Remember that you can do this by pressing Ctrl+G.

2. Type **`Forms!frmClients.txtContactTitle.Value = "Hello"`** in the Immediate window. Press Enter. The contact title of the current record changes to `Hello`.

3. Type **`Forms!frmClients.txtIntroDate.Visible = False`**. Press Enter. Access hides the `txtIntroDate` control on the `frmClients` form.

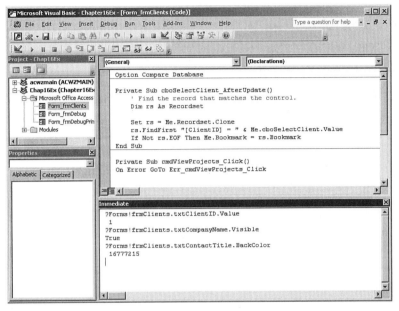

FIGURE 16.2   Use the Immediate window to test the values of properties.

4. Type **Forms!frmClients.txtClientID.BackColor = 123456**. Press Enter. The background color of the txtClientID control on the frmClients form turns green. The Immediate window and your form now look like those shown in Figures 16.3 and 16.4, respectively.

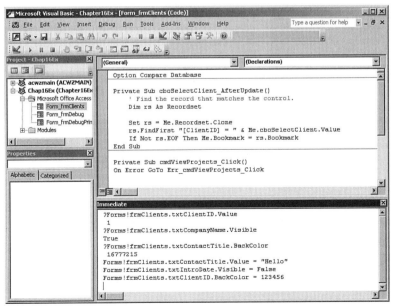

FIGURE 16.3   Set the values of properties using the Immediate window.

16

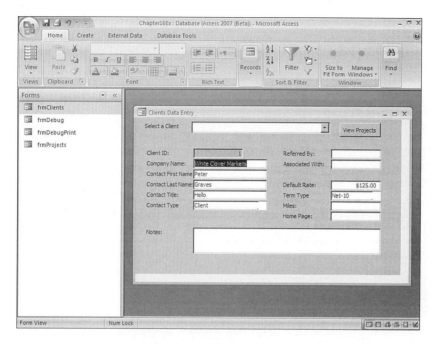

FIGURE 16.4   The results of using the Immediate window to set the values of properties are shown here.

The Immediate window is an extremely valuable testing and debugging tool. The examples here barely begin to illustrate its power and flexibility.

> **CAUTION**
>
> Changes you make to data while working in the Immediate window are permanent. On the other hand, Access does not save changes you make to the properties of controls or the values of variables with the form or report.
>
> Some people think that data changes made in the Immediate window are not permanent. In other words, if you modify the last name of a customer, they believe that the change will not be permanent (but, of course, it is). Other people think that if they change the BackColor property of a control, the change will persist in the design environment (but, of course, it won't).

Clearing the Immediate Window

The Immediate window displays the last 200 lines of output. As you add additional lines of code to the Immediate window, older lines disappear. When you exit completely from Access, it clears the Immediate window. If you want to clear the Immediate window at any other time, follow these three steps:

1. With the Immediate window active, press Ctrl+Home to go to the top of the Immediate window.

2. Hold down your Shift key and press Ctrl+End to go to the last statement in the Immediate window.

3. Press Delete.

Practicing with the Built-In Functions

In addition to being able to test and set the values of properties and variables using the Immediate window, you can test any VBA function. To do so, type the function and its arguments in the Immediate window, preceded by a question mark. This code returns the month of the current date, for example:

```
?datepart("m",date)
```

This code tells you the date one month after today's date:

```
?dateadd("m",1,date)
```

This code tells you how many days exist between the current date and the end of the millennium:

```
?datediff("d",date(),#12/31/2999#)
```

Executing Subroutines, Functions, and Methods

In addition to enabling you to test any VBA function, the Immediate window lets you test any user-defined subroutine, function, or method. This is a great way to debug your user-defined procedures. To see how this works, follow these steps:

1. Open the basExamples module found in the CHAP16EX.ACCDB database on the accompanying CD-ROM.

2. Invoke the Immediate window if it is not already visible.

3. Type **?ReturnInitsFunc("Bill","Gates")**. This calls the user-defined function ReturnInitsFunc, sending "Bill" as the first parameter and "Gates" as the second parameter. The value B.G. appears in the Immediate window. This is the return value from the function.

4. Type **Call ReturnInitsSub("Bill","Gates")**. This calls the user-defined subroutine ReturnInitsSub, sending "Bill" as the first parameter and "Gates" as the second parameter. The value B.G. appears in a message box.

Notice the difference between how you call a function and how you call a subroutine. Because the function returns a value, you must call it using a question mark. On the other hand, when calling a subroutine, you use the Call keyword.

16

NOTE

You also can call a subroutine from the Immediate window by using this syntax:

`RoutineName Parameter1, Parameter2, ....`

Notice that, when you omit the `Call` keyword, you do not need to enclose the parameters in parentheses.

Printing to the Immediate Window at Runtime

The capability to print to the Immediate window is useful because you can test what is happening as your code executes without having to suspend code execution. It also is valuable to be able to print something to a window when you are testing, without interfering with the user-interface aspect of your code. You can test a form without being interrupted and then go back and view the values of variables and so on. Here's how the process works:

1. Type **Call LoopThroughCollection** in the Immediate window. This calls the user-defined subroutine `LoopThroughCollection`. The values `Skating`, `Basketball`, `Hockey`, and `Skiing` appear. The routine prints these values to the Immediate window.

2. Open the `frmDebugPrint` form in Form view.

3. Press Tab to move from the First Name field to the Last Name field.

4. Press Tab to move back to the First Name field.

5. Type your first name.

6. Open the Immediate window. Notice that the routine sent all the statements to the Immediate window (see Figure 16.5). I coded these `Debug.Print` statements in all the appropriate form and control events.

NOTE

Although it is good practice to remove `Debug.Print` statements after you have completed the debugging process, you can safely deploy your applications without removing them. Your users will never know that the statements are in your code unless they view the Immediate window. The `Debug.Print` statements result in only a minor degradation in performance.

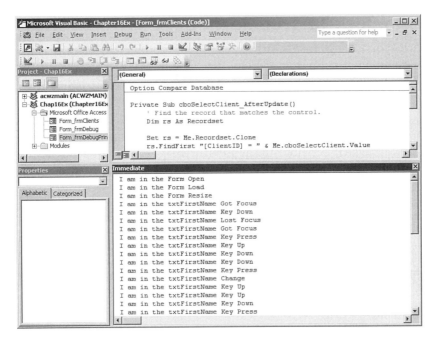

FIGURE 16.5   Use `Debug.Print` statements to print values to the Immediate window.

Invoking the Debugger

You can invoke the Access debugger in several ways:

▶ Place a breakpoint in your code.

▶ Place a watch in your code.

▶ Press Ctrl+Break while the code is running.

▶ Insert a `Stop` statement in your code.

A *breakpoint* is an unconditional point at which you want to suspend code execution. It is temporary because it is in effect only while the database is open. In other words, Access does not save breakpoints with the database.

A *watch* is a condition under which you want to suspend code execution. You might want to suspend code execution when a `counter` variable reaches a specific value, for example. A watch also is temporary; Access removes it after you close the database.

A `Stop` statement is permanent. In fact, if you forget to remove `Stop` statements from your code, your application stops execution while the user is running it.

Using Breakpoints to Troubleshoot

As mentioned, a breakpoint is a point at which Access will unconditionally halt the execution of code. You can set multiple breakpoints in your code. You can add and remove breakpoints as your code executes.

A breakpoint enables you to halt your code execution at a suspicious area of code. This way, you can examine everything that is going on at that point in your code execution. By strategically placing breakpoints in your code, you quickly can execute sections of code that you already debugged, stopping only at problem areas.

To set a breakpoint, follow these steps:

1. Place your cursor on the line of code where you want to invoke the debugger.

2. You can insert a breakpoint in one of four ways:

   ▶ Press your F9 function key.

   ▶ Click in the gray margin area to the left of the line of the code that will contain the breakpoint.

   ▶ Click the Toggle Breakpoint button on the Debug toolbar.

   ▶ Choose Debug, Toggle Breakpoint.

   The line of code containing the breakpoint appears in a different color, and a dot appears, indicating the breakpoint.

3. Run the form, report, or module containing the breakpoint. VBA suspends execution just before executing the line of code where you placed the breakpoint. The statement that is about to execute appears in a contrasting color. (The default is yellow.)

Now that you have suspended your code, you can step through it one line at a time, change the value of variables, and view your call stack, among other things.

Keep in mind that a breakpoint is actually a toggle. If you want to remove a breakpoint, click in the gray margin area, press F9, or click Toggle Breakpoint on the Debug toolbar. Access removes breakpoints when you close the database, when you open another database, or when you exit Access.

The easiest way to get to know the debugger is to actually use it. The following example gives you hands-on experience in setting and stopping code execution at a breakpoint. The example is developed further later in the chapter.

Start by creating a form called frmDebug that contains a command button called cmdDebug. Give the button the caption Start Debug Process. Place the following code in the Click event of the command button:

```
Sub cmdDebug_Click ()
    Call Func1
End Sub
```

Create a module called basFuncs. Enter three functions into the module:

```
Sub Func1 ()
   Dim intTemp As Integer

   intTemp = 10
   Debug.Print "We Are Now In Func1()"
   Debug.Print intTemp
   Call Func2
End Sub

Sub Func2 ()
   Dim strName As String

   strName = "Bill Gates"
   Debug.Print "We Are Now In Func2()"
   Debug.Print strName
   Call Func3

End Sub

Sub Func3 ()
   Debug.Print "We Are Now In Func3()"
   MsgBox "Hi There From The Func3() Sub Procedure"
End Sub
```

Now you should debug. Start by placing a breakpoint within the Click event of cmdDebug on the line called Call Func1. Here are the steps:

1. Click anywhere on the line of code that says Call Func1.

2. Click in the gray margin area, press the F9 function key, click the Toggle Breakpoint button on the Debug toolbar, or choose Debug, Toggle Breakpoint. The line with the breakpoint turns a different color (red by default).

3. Go into Form view and click the Start Debug Process button. Access suspends execution just before executing the line where you placed the breakpoint. VBA displays the line that reads Call Func1 in a different color (by default, yellow), indicating that it is about to execute that line (see Figure 16.6).

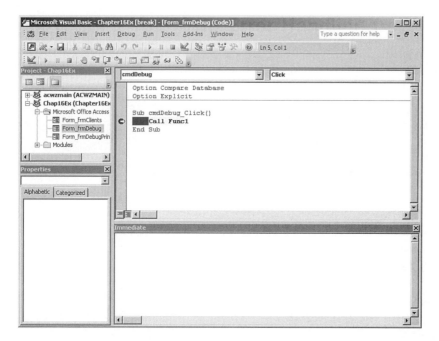

FIGURE 16.6   Code execution is halted at a breakpoint.

Stepping Through Code

Access 2007 gives you three main options for stepping through your code. Each one is slightly different. The Step Into option enables you to step through each line of code within a subroutine or function, whereas the Step Over option executes a procedure without stepping through each line of code within it. The Step Out option runs all code in nested procedures and then returns you to the procedure that called the line of code you are on. Knowing the right option to use to solve a particular problem is an acquired skill that comes with continued development experience.

Using Step Into

When you reach a breakpoint, you can continue executing your code one line at a time or continue execution until you reach another breakpoint. To step through your code one line at a time, click Step Into on the Debug toolbar, press F8, or choose Debug, Step Into.

The following example illustrates the process of stepping through your code, printing the values of variables to the Immediate window, and modifying the values of variables using the Immediate window.

You can continue the debug process from the breakpoint you set in the previous example. Step two times (press F8). You should find yourself within Func1, about to execute the line of code intTemp = 10 (see Figure 16.7). Notice that VBA did not stop on the line Dim intTemp As Integer. The debugger does not stop on variable declarations.

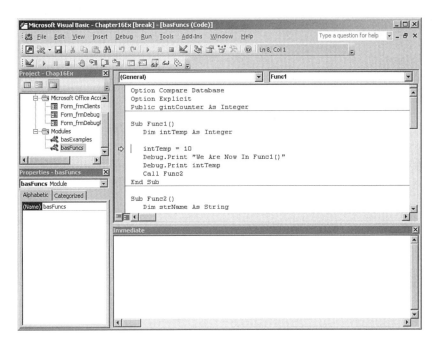

FIGURE 16.7   The Immediate window is halted within Func1.

The code is about to print the Debug statements to the Immediate window. Take a look by opening the Immediate window. None of your code has printed anything to the Immediate window yet. Press F8 (step) three more times until you have executed the line Debug.Print intTemp. Your screen should look like Figure 16.8. Notice the results of the Debug.Print statements.

Now that you have seen how you can display variables and the results of expressions to the Immediate window, take a look at how you can use the Immediate window to modify values of variables and controls. Start by changing the value of intTemp. Click the Immediate window and type **intTemp = 50**. When you press Enter, you actually modify the value of intTemp. Type **?intTemp**, and you'll see that Access echoes back the value of 50. You also can see the value of intTemp in the Locals window. Notice in Figure 16.9 that the intTemp variable appears along with its value and type.

Executing Until You Reach the Next Breakpoint

Suppose that you have reached a breakpoint, but you realize that your problem is farther down in the code execution. In fact, the problem is actually in a different function. You might not want to continue to move one step at a time down to the offending function. Use the Procedure drop-down menu to locate the questionable function, and then set a breakpoint on the line where you want to continue stepping. You now are ready to continue code execution until Access reaches this line. To do this, click Continue on the Debug toolbar, press F5, or choose Run, Continue. Your code continues to execute, stopping at the next breakpoint. To see how this works, continue the Debug process with the next example.

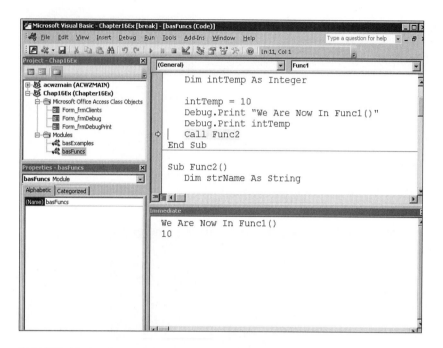

FIGURE 16.8   The Immediate window shows entries generated by `Debug.Print` statements.

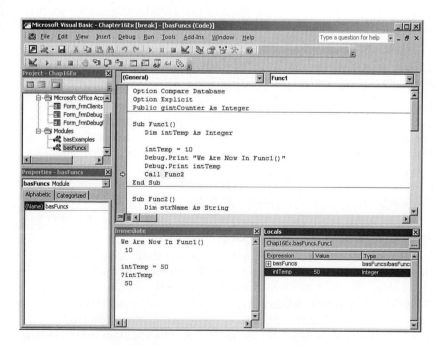

FIGURE 16.9   Here are the Immediate and Locals windows after modifying the value of `intTemp`.

You also can opt to resume code execution to the point at which your cursor is located. To do this, select Run to Cursor from the Debug menu, or press Ctrl+F8.

Suppose that you realize your problem might be in Func3. You do not want to continue to move one step at a time down to Func3. No problem. Use the Procedure drop-down menu to view Func3, as shown in Figure 16.10. Set a breakpoint on the line that reads Debug.Print "We Are Now In Func3()". You are ready to continue code execution until Access reaches this line. Click Continue on the Debug toolbar, press F5, or choose Run, Continue. Your code continues to execute, stopping on the breakpoint you just set. Press F5 again. The code finishes executing. Return to the Form View window.

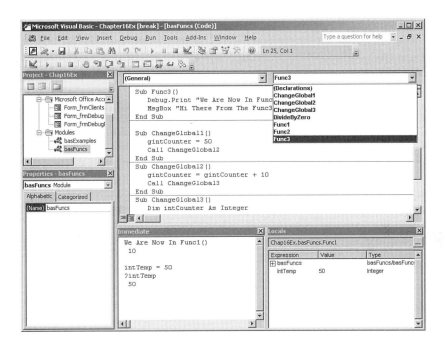

FIGURE 16.10   Use the Procedure drop-down menu to view another function.

Using Step Over

Sometimes you already have a subroutine fully tested and debugged. You want to continue stepping through the routine that you are in, but you don't want to watch the execution of subroutines. In this case, you use Step Over. To step over a subroutine or function, click Step Over on the Debug toolbar, press Shift+F8, or choose Debug, Step Over. The code within the subroutine or function you are stepping over executes, but you do not step through it. To experiment with the Step Over feature, follow the next example.

Click the open form and click the Start Debug Process button one more time. Because you did not remove the existing breakpoints, Access places you on the line of code that reads Call Func1. Select Clear All Breakpoints from the Debug menu or use the Ctrl+Shift+F9 keystroke combination to remove all breakpoints. Step (press F8) five times until you are about to execute the line Call Func2. Suppose that you have tested Func2 and Func3 and know that they are not the cause of the problems in your code. With Func2 highlighted as the next line Access will execute, click Step Over on the toolbar. Notice that Access executes Func2 and Func3, but that you now are ready to continue stepping in Func1. In this case, Access places you on the End Sub line immediately following the call to Func2.

Using Step Out

You use the Step Out feature to step out of the procedure you are in and to return to the procedure that called the line of code you are on. You use this feature when you have accidentally stepped into a procedure that you realize you have fully tested. You want to execute all the code called by the procedure you are in and then step out to the calling procedure so that you can continue with the debugging process. To test how this works, follow this example.

1. Place a breakpoint on the call to Func2.

2. Click the Reset button on the toolbar to halt code execution.

3. Activate the frmDebug form and click the Start Debug Process command button.

4. Step once to place yourself in the first line of Func2.

5. Suppose that you realize you just stepped one step too far. You really intended to step over Func2 and all the procedures it calls. No problem! Click the Step Out button to step out of Func2 and return to the line following the line of code that called Func2. In this case, you should find yourself on the End Sub statement of Func1.

Setting the Next Statement to Execute

After you have stepped through your code, watched the logical flow, and modified some variables, you might want to re-execute the code beginning at a prior statement. The easiest way to do this is to click and drag the yellow arrow in the margin to the statement on which you want to continue execution. If you prefer, you can click anywhere in the line of code where you want to commence execution and then choose Debug, Set Next Statement. Regardless of the method you chose, notice that the contrasting color (usually yellow)—indicating the next line of code that Access will execute—is now placed over that statement. You then can step through the code by pressing F8, or you can continue normal code execution by pressing F5. Access enables you to set the next line it will execute within a procedure only. You can use this feature to re-execute lines of code or to skip over a problematic line of code.

The following example walks you through the process of changing the value of a variable and then re-executing code after you have changed the value.

The preceding example left you at the last line of code (the `End Sub` statement) within `Func1`. Now you want to change the value of `intTemp` and re-execute everything:

1. Go to the Immediate window and type `intTemp = 100`.

2. You need to set the next statement to print on the line that reads `Debug.Print "We Are Now in Func1()"`. To do this, click and drag the yellow arrow from the `End Sub` statement to the `Debug.Print "We Are Now In Func1()"` line. Notice the contrasting color (yellow), indicating that that is the next statement of code Access will execute.

3. Press F8 (step) two times. The code now executes with `intTemp` set to `100`. Observe the Immediate window again. Notice how the results have changed.

Using the Call Stack Window

You have learned how to set breakpoints, step through and over code, use the Immediate window, set the next line to be executed, and continue to run until you reach the next breakpoint. When you reach a breakpoint, it often is important to see which functions the code called to bring you to this point. In this case, the Calls feature can help.

To bring up the Call Stack window, click the Call Stack button on the toolbar or choose View, Call Stack. The window in Figure 16.11 appears. If you want to see the line of code that called a particular function or subroutine, double-click that particular function or click the function and then click Show. Although Access does not move your execution point to the calling function or subroutine, you are able to view the code within the procedure. If you want to continue your code execution, press F8. You move back to the procedure through which you were stepping, and the next line of code executes. If you press F5, your code executes until it reaches another breakpoint or watch. If you want to return to where you were without executing additional lines of code, choose Debug, Show Next Statement.

Figure 16.11   You can view the stack with the Call Stack window.

To test this process, perform the next example:

1. Click the Reset button to stop your code execution if you are still in Break mode.

2. Remove the breakpoint on the call to `Func2`.

3. Move to the procedure called `Func3` in `basFuncs`. Set a breakpoint on the line `Debug.Print "We Are Now in Func3()"`.

4. Run the `frmDebug` form and click the command button. Access places you in `Func3` on the line where you set the breakpoint.

5. Bring up the Call Stack window by clicking the Call Stack button on the toolbar. If you want to see the line of code that called `Func2` from `Func1`, double-click `Func1`. Although Access does not move your execution point to `Func1`, you are able to view the code within the procedure. To return to the next line of code to execute, choose Debug, Show Next Statement.

6. Press F5, and the rest of your code executes.

Working with the Locals Window

The Locals window enables you to see all the variables on the current stack frame and to view and modify their values. To access the Locals pane, click Locals Window on the toolbar, or select Locals Window from the View menu. Three columns appear: Expression, Value, and Type. The Expression column shows you the variables, user-defined types, arrays, and other objects visible within the current procedure. The Value column displays the current value of a variable or expression. The Type column tells you what type of data a variable contains. The Locals windows displays variables that contain hierarchical information—arrays, for example—with an Expand/Collapse button.

The information contained within the Locals window is dynamic. Access automatically updates it as it executes your code and as you move from routine to routine. Figure 16.12 illustrates how you can use the Locals window to view the variables available with the `Func2` subroutine. To try this example yourself, remove all existing breakpoints. Place a breakpoint in `Func2` on the line of code that reads `Debug.Print strName`. Click Reset if you are still executing code, and click the Start Debug Process command button to execute code until the breakpoint. Click the Locals Window button on the Debug toolbar. Click the plus sign to view the contents of the public variable `gintCounter`.

> **NOTE**
>
> You can change the value of a variable in the Locals window, but you cannot change its name or type.

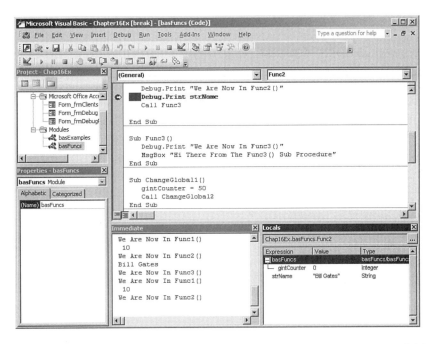

FIGURE 16.12   You can use the Locals window to view the variables available within a subroutine.

Working with Watch Expressions

Sometimes it is not enough to use the Immediate window to test the value of an expression or variable. You might want to keep a constant eye on the expression's value. To do so, you can set a watch expression. After you add a watch expression, it appears in the Watch window. As you'll see, you can create several types of watches.

Using Auto Data Tips

The quickest and easiest way to view the value contained within a variable is to use Auto Data Tips, which is an option for working with modules. This feature is available only when your code is in Break mode. While in Break mode, simply move your mouse pointer over the variable or expression whose value you want to check. A tip appears with the current value. To set the Auto Data Tips option from the VBE, choose Tools, Options, click the Editor tab, and check the option for Auto Data Tips, which is under the Code Settings options.

Using a Quick Watch

A *quick watch* is the most basic type of watch. To add a quick watch, highlight the name of the variable or expression you want to watch and click the Quick Watch button on the toolbar. The Quick Watch dialog box, shown in Figure 16.13, appears. You can click Add to add the expression as a permanent watch or choose Cancel to view the current value without adding it as a watch. If you click Add, the Watches window appears, like the one in Figure 16.14. The next section discusses this window in more detail.

FIGURE 16.13   The Quick Watch dialog box enables you to quickly view the value of a variable or add an expression as a permanent watch.

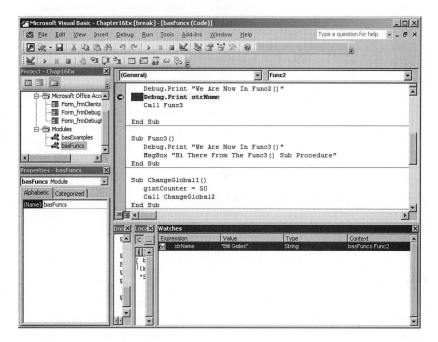

FIGURE 16.14   You can add a watch expression in the Watches window.

Adding a Watch Expression

As you saw, you can add a watch expression using a quick watch. Adding a watch this way does not give you full control over the nature of the watch, however. If you need more control over the watch, you must choose Debug, Add Watch. The Add Watch dialog box appears, as shown in Figure 16.15.

> ## TIP
>
> If you add a quick watch or add a watch by choosing Debug, Add Watch, you easily can customize the specifics of the watch by clicking with the right mouse button over the watch in the Watches window. Then select Edit Watch.
>
> A quick way to add a watch to the Watches window is to click and drag a variable or expression from a Code module into the Watches window. Access adds the watch with default settings.

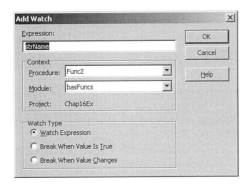

FIGURE 16.15   The Add Watch dialog box enables you to easily designate all the specifics of a watch expression.

In the Expression text box, enter a variable, property, function call, or any other valid expression. It is important to select the procedure and module in which you want to watch the expression. Next, indicate whether you want to simply watch the value of the expression in the Immediate window, break when the expression becomes True, or break whenever the value of the expression changes. The sections that follow cover the two latter options.

The next example walks you through the process of adding a watch and viewing the watch variable as you step through your code. It illustrates how a variable goes in and out of scope and changes value during code execution.

1. To begin, stop code execution if your code is running and remove any breakpoints you have set.

2. Click within the strName variable in Func2.

3. Right-click and choose Add Watch.

4. Click OK to accept the Func2 procedure as the context for the variable and basFuncs as the module for the variable.

5. Set a breakpoint on the line strName = "Bill Gates".

6. Run the frmDebug form and click the command button. View the Watches window and notice that strName has the value of a zero-length string.

7. Step one time and notice that strName is equal to Bill Gates.

8. Step three more times. Notice that, although you are in the Func3 routine, strName still has the value Bill Gates. The reason is that the variable is still in memory in the context of basFuncs.Func2.

9. Step four more times until you are back on the End Sub statement of Func2. The strName variable is still in context.

10. Step one more time. The strName variable is finally out of context because you have completed the execution of Func2.

Editing a Watch Expression

After you add a watch, you might want to edit the nature of the watch or remove it entirely. You use the Edit Watch dialog box to edit or delete a watch expression. Follow these steps:

1. Activate the Watches window.

2. Select the expression you want to edit.

3. Choose Debug, Edit Watch, or right-click and choose Edit Watch. The dialog box in Figure 16.16 appears.

4. Make changes to the watch or click Delete to remove it.

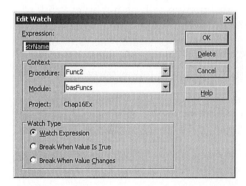

FIGURE 16.16   You can use the Edit Watch dialog box to modify the specifics of a watch after you add it.

Breaking When an Expression Is True

A powerful aspect of a watch expression is that you can break whenever an expression becomes True. You can break whenever a Public variable reaches a specific value, for example. You might want to do this when a Public or Private variable somehow is being changed, and you want to find out where. Consider the following code, located in the basFuncs module of CHAP16EX.ACCDB:

```
Sub ChangeGlobal1()
   gintCounter = 50
   Call ChangeGlobal2
End Sub

Sub ChangeGlobal2()
   gintCounter = gintCounter + 10
   Call ChangeGlobal3
End Sub

Sub ChangeGlobal3()
   Dim intCounter As Integer
   For intCounter = 1 To 10
      gintCounter = gintCounter + intCounter
   Next intCounter
End Sub
```

You might find that gintCounter somehow is reaching a number greater than 100, and you are not sure how. To solve the problem, add the watch shown in Figure 16.17. Notice that the expression you are testing for is gintCounter > 100. You have set the breakpoint to break the code whenever the expression becomes True. To test the code, type **ChangeGlobal1** in the Immediate window and press Enter. The code should break in the ChangeGlobal3 routine, indicating that this routine is the culprit.

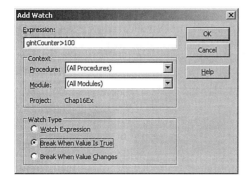

FIGURE 16.17   This watch will cause the code execution to break whenever the expression is True.

Breaking When an Expression Changes

Instead of breaking when an expression becomes True, you might want to break whenever the value of the expression changes. This is a great way to identify the place where something is mysteriously modifying the value of a variable. Like Break When Value Is True, the Break When Value Changes option is great for tracking down problems with

Public and Private variables. Notice the watch being set in Figure 16.18. It is in the context of all procedures within all modules. It is set to break whenever the value of gintCounter changes. If you execute the ChangeGlobal1 routine, you'll find that the code halts execution within ChangeGlobal1 immediately after the code sets the value of gintCounter to 50. If you press F5 to continue execution, the code halts within ChangeGlobal2 immediately after it increments the value of gintCounter by 10. In other words, every time the code modifies the value of gintCounter, the code execution breaks.

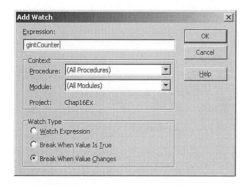

FIGURE 16.18   This watch will cause code execution to break whenever the value of an expression changes.

Continuing Execution After a Runtime Error

As you are testing, you often discover runtime errors that are quite easy to fix. When a runtime error occurs, a dialog box similar to the one shown in Figure 16.19 appears.

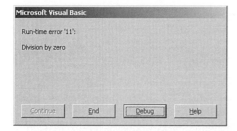

FIGURE 16.19   You can fix runtime errors from the Runtime Error dialog box.

If you click Debug, Access places you in the Code window on the line that generated the error. After rectifying the problem, click the Continue button on the toolbar, or choose Run, Continue.

Figure 16.20 shows a divide-by-zero error, for example, after the user clicked Debug from the Runtime Error dialog box. The Locals window in the figure shows that the programmer set the value of int2 to 20. Code execution now can continue without error.

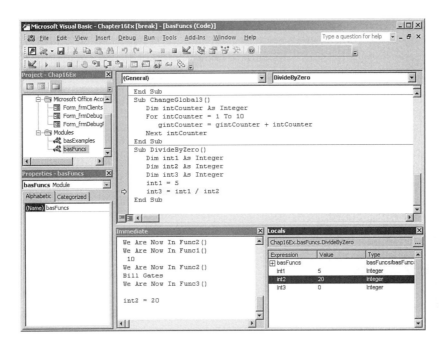

FIGURE 16.20   Here is the Debug mode after a divide-by-zero error.

Often, after an error occurs, VBA displays a message giving you the option of resetting your code. If you opt to reset your code, all variables (including Publics and Statics) lose their values. You also can click Reset on the toolbar. You must decide whether it is better to proceed with your variables already set or to reset the variables and then proceed.

NOTE

The General tab of the Options dialog box allows you to configure how VBA error handling and the debugger interact. Chapter 17, "Error Handling: Preparing for the Inevitable," covers the options available to you.

Looking at Gotchas with the Immediate Window

Although the Access debugger is excellent, the debugging process itself is wrought with an array of potential problems, as follows:

▶ The debugging process can interrupt code execution, especially when forms are involved. When this occurs, the best bet is to place Debug.Print statements in your code and examine what happens after the code executes.

▶ Along the lines of the preceding problem, it is difficult to debug code where you have coded the GotFocus and LostFocus events. Moving to the VBE triggers the

LostFocus event of the control. Returning to the form causes Access to trigger the GotFocus event of the control. Once again, a great solution is Debug.Print. You also might consider writing information to an error log for perusal after the code executes.

▶ Code that uses Screen.ActiveForm and Screen.ActiveControl wreaks havoc on the debugging process. When the VBE is active, there is no active form and no active control. Avoiding these lines in your code wherever possible alleviates this problem.

▶ Finally, be aware that resetting code can cause problems. If you are modifying environmental settings, you are left with whatever environmental settings your application code changed. If you continue execution after the error without resetting, all sorts of other problems can occur. It is a good idea to code a special utility routine that resets your environment.

Using Assertions

You use assertions to ensure that, if the user encounters a certain state, your code invokes the debugger. The following code, found in basExamples, is an example:

```
Sub Assertion()
    Dim intAge As Integer
    intAge = InputBox("Please Enter Your Age")
    Debug.Assert (intAge >= 0)
    MsgBox "You are " & intAge
End Sub
```

This example sets the value of a variable called intAge equal to the value entered into an Input Box. The Debug.Assert statement "asserts" that the value entered is greater than or equal to zero. If it is, code execution proceeds as expected. If the assertion is *incorrect*, the code invokes the debugger.

It is a good idea to include a comment as to why an assertion might fail. By doing this, you will facilitate the process of responding to the situation when it occurs. Also, it is important to realize that, if you deploy your application with Debug.Assert statements intact, you will receive a technical support call when an assertion fails, and your code places the user in the debugger without warning!

Debugging Tips

The following tips will make your life much easier when debugging:

▶ Before starting to debug, be clear about what the problem is. Make sure that you get all the necessary information from the user as to what he did to generate the problem. Without this vital information, you can spend countless hours trying to reproduce the problem rather than solve it.

▶ Make changes one line of code at a time. I have seen many hot-shot developers attempt to change multiple lines of code simultaneously. Instead of correcting the problem they initially set out to solve, they generate a multitude of additional problems.

▶ Talk out the problem with other developers. Sometimes the process of simply verbalizing the problem can be enough to help you to figure it out. If verbalizing the problem doesn't provide you with the answer, the person that you are verbalizing to might know the answer.

▶ When all else fails, take a break. Many times I have stayed up into the wee hours of the night, attempting to solve a problem. After finally giving up, I surrender and go to bed. It's amazing how many times I solve the "unsolvable" problem from the night before while in the shower the next morning!

Practical Examples: Debugging Real Applications

As you develop your own applications, use the techniques you learned to help solve any problems you encounter. For now, use the debugger to step through and learn more about the debugging process with one of the routines found in the sample database.

Summary

If programming were a perfect science, there would be no reason to use a debugger. Given the reality of the challenges of programming, a thorough understanding of the use of the debugger is imperative. Fortunately, the Access 2007 VBE provides an excellent tool to assist in the debugging process.

This chapter began by showing you how you can reduce the chance of bugs within your application in the first place. It then taught you how to use the Immediate window to test and change the values of variables and properties. You learned how to use watches and breakpoints, as well as how to view the call stack. All these techniques help make the process of testing and debugging your application a pleasant experience.

Error Handling: Preparing for the Inevitable

Why This Chapter Is Important

Errors happen, even in the absence of programmer error. You need to protect your programs and your data from the adverse effects of errors by practicing error handling.

Error handling (also known as *error trapping*) is the process of intercepting the Access Database Engine's or Visual Basic for Applications' (VBA's) response to an error. It enables the developer to determine the severity of an error and to take the appropriate action in response. This chapter shows you the techniques required to successfully implement error handling within your applications.

Implementing Error Handling

Without error handling, the user of your application is forced to exit abruptly from your application code. Consider the example in Listing 17.1.

The Click event behind the command button calls the routine TestError1, passing it the values from two text boxes. TestError1 accepts those parameters and attempts to divide the first parameter by the second parameter. If the second parameter is equal to 0, a runtime error occurs. Because no error handling is in effect, the program terminates.

LISTING 17.1   An Example of Code Without Error Handling

```
Private Sub cmdNoErrorHandler_Click()
    'Call TestError1, passing the values in the txtValue1
    'and txtValue2 text boxes
    Call TestError1(Me.txtValue1.Value, Me.txtValue2.Value)
End Sub


Sub TestError1(Numerator As Integer, Denominator As Integer)
    'Divide the value received as the first parameter
    'by the value received as the second parameter
    Debug.Print Numerator / Denominator
    'If successful, display a message to the user
    MsgBox "I am in Test Error"
End Sub
```

Figure 17.1 shows the error message that the user receives. As you can see, the choices are Continue, End, Debug, and Help. If users click Debug, the module window appears, and they are placed in Debug mode on the line of code causing the error. Clicking Continue (this button is not always available) tells Access to ignore the error and continue with the execution of the program. End terminates execution of the programming code. If the application is running with the runtime version of Access, it shuts down, and users are returned to Windows. If users click Help, VBA Help attempts to give them some information about the error that occurred. With error handling in effect, you can attempt to handle the error in a more appropriate way whenever possible.

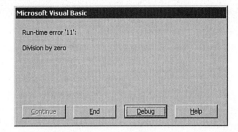

FIGURE 17.1   The default error handling message.

You can add error-handling code to the error event procedure of a form or report. You can also add it to any VBA subroutine, function, or event routine. You can easily modify the code in Listing 17.1 to handle the error gracefully. The code in Listing 17.2 shows a simple error-handling routine.

LISTING 17.2   A Simple Error-Handling Routine

```
Sub TestError2(Numerator As Integer, Denominator As Integer)
On Error GoTo TestError2_Err
    'Divide the value received as the first parameter
    'by the value received as the second parameter
    Debug.Print Numerator / Denominator
    'If successful, display a message to the user
    MsgBox "I am in Test Error"

    Exit Sub

TestError2_Err:
    'If a divide by zero (error 11) occurs, display an
    'appropriate message to the user
    If Err = 11 Then
        MsgBox "Variable 2 Cannot Be a Zero", , "Custom Error Handler"
    End If
    Exit Sub

End Sub
```

The routine now invokes error handling. If a divide-by-zero error occurs, a message box alerts the user to the problem, as Figure 17.2 shows.

> **NOTE**
>
> This code is located in the basError module, which is in the CHAP17EX.ACCDB database on the accompanying CD-ROM.

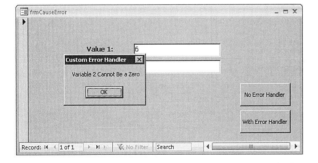

FIGURE 17.2   A custom error handler message.

Using On Error Statements

On Error statements activate error handling. Each routine must contain its own On Error statement if you want that routine to do its own error handling. Otherwise, the VBA compiler cascades error handling up the call stack (the series of routines that executed to get you to this point in code). If the VBA compiler does not find any On Error statements in the call stack, it invokes its own error handling.

Suppose that Func1 calls Func2, and Func2 calls Func3. Only Func1 contains error handling. An error occurs in Func3. Func3 passes control up to Func2. Func2 has no error handling, so it passes control up to Func1. Func1 handles the error. Needless to say, the error handler found in Func1 is not necessarily appropriate to handle the error that occurred in Func3.

Using an On Error statement, you can cause the application to branch to error-handling code, resume code execution on the line immediately following the error, or attempt to re-execute the problematic line of code.

The On Error GoTo Statement

The statement On Error GoTo <label> tells VBA that, from this point forward in the subroutine or function, if an error occurs, it should jump to the label specified in the statement. This is the most common form of error handling.

The label specified in the On Error statement must be located in the current procedure. Listing 17.3 shows a simple example of error handling.

LISTING 17.3   An Example of Error Handling Using the On Error GoTo Statement

```
Sub SimpleErrorHandler(iVar1 As Integer, iVar2 As Integer)
    'Invoke error handling
    On Error GoTo SimpleErrorHandler_Err

    'Declare a variable to hold the result
    Dim sngResult As Single
    'Divide the first parameter received by the
    'second parameter received
    sngResult = iVar1 / iVar2

    'Exit the subroutine if all went as planned
    Exit Sub

SimpleErrorHandler_Err:
    'If an error occurs, display a message and exit
    'the subroutine
    MsgBox "Oops!"
    Exit Sub

End Sub
```

> **NOTE**
>
> The example in Listing 17.3 differs from the code on the CD-ROM and will be modified in the next section.

You can learn some important points from this simple routine. The routine receives two integer values. It then invokes the error handler. When an error occurs, execution continues at the label. Notice that this routine contains two `Exit Sub` statements. If you remove the first `Exit Sub` statement, the code falls through to the label regardless of whether an error occurred. The `Exit Sub` statement at the bottom gracefully exits the procedure, setting the error code back to 0.

Including the Error Number and Description in the Error Handler

The error-handling code in Listing 17.3 did not give a very descriptive message to users. The `Description` and `Number` properties of the `Err` object give users more meaningful error messages. The `Err` object is covered in detail later in this chapter in the section "Using the Err Object." For now, take a look at the `Description` and `Number` properties to see how you can use them to enhance an error-handling routine. To display the error number and description, you must modify the error-handling code to look like this:

```
SimpleErrorHandler_Err:
    'If an error occurs, display a message and exit
    'the subroutine
    MsgBox "Error #" & Err.Number & ": " & Err.Description
    Exit Sub
```

This time, instead of hard-coding the error message, you display the error number and VBA's internal error string. Figure 17.3 shows the resulting error message. You can find the `SimpleErrorHandler` routine and all the following examples in the `basError` module of the `CHAP17EX.ACCDB` database.

Microsoft Office Access

Error #11: Division by zero

OK

FIGURE 17.3   An error message with an error number and error string.

Using `On Error GoTo 0`

You use `On Error GoTo 0` for two purposes:

▶ When you want Access to return to its default error handler

▶ When you have other error handling in a routine but want Access to return to the calling routine when a specific condition occurs

Generally, you don't want Access to return to its default error handler. You might do this only if you are unable to handle the error, or if you are in the testing phase and not yet ready to implement your own error handler.

The reason you want Access to return the error to a higher-level routine is much clearer. You do this if you want to *centralize* the error handling, meaning that one routine may call several others. Instead of placing error-handling code in each routine that is called, placing the error handling in the calling routine is appropriate in certain situations.

The On Error Resume Next Statement

On Error Resume Next continues program execution on the line immediately following the error. This construct is generally used when it is acceptable to ignore an error and continue code execution. Listing 17.4 shows an example of such a situation.

LISTING 17.4   Ignoring an Error and Continuing Execution

```
Sub TestResumeNext()
    'Instruct VBA to continue on the next line if an error
    'occurs
    On Error Resume Next

    'Attempt to delete a file
    Kill "AnyFile"

    'If no error occurred, do nothing. Otherwise, display
    'a message with the description of the error that occurred
    If Err.Number = 0 Then
    Else
        MsgBox "We Didn't Die, But the Error Was: " & Err.Description
    End If
End Sub
```

You use the Kill statement to delete a file from disk. If the specified file is not found, an error results. You delete the file only if it exists, so you are not concerned about an error. On Error Resume Next is appropriate in this situation because resuming execution after the offending line of code does no harm. The example illustrates that, although code execution proceeds, the properties of the error object are still set.

Using Resume Statements

While you are in your error-handling code, you can use the Resume, Resume Next, and Resume <LineLabel> statements to specify how you want VBA to respond to the error. Resume attempts to re-execute the offending line of code, Resume Next resumes execution after the offending line of code, and Resume <LineLabel> continues execution at a specified line label. The following sections cover these statements in detail.

The Resume **Statement**

The Resume statement resumes code execution on the line of code that caused the error. You must use this statement with extreme care because it can throw the code into an unrecoverable endless loop. Listing 17.5 shows an example of an inappropriate use of the Resume statement.

LISTING 17.5   Using Resume Inappropriately

```
Function BadResume(strFileName As String)
    'Invoke error handling
    On Error GoTo BadResume_Err
    Dim strFile As String

    'Perform the Dir function to determine if
    'the file passed as a parameter exists
    strFile = Dir(strFileName)

    'If the file doesn't exist, return False
    'Otherwise, return True
    If strFile = "" Then
      BadResume = False
    Else
      BadResume = True
    End If

    'Exit the function if all goes well
    Exit Function

BadResume_Err:
    'Display an error message with the
    'description of the error that occurred
    MsgBox Error.Description

    'Attempt to re-execute the offending line of code
    Resume
End Function
```

This function is passed a filename. The Dir function searches for a file with that name and returns True or False, depending on whether the specified file is found. The problem occurs when the drive requested is not available or does not exist. This code throws the computer into an endless loop. To remedy the problem, you should modify your code to look like the code in Listing 17.6.

Listing 17.6   Using Resume Conditionally Based on User Feedback

```
Function GoodResume(strFileName As String)
    'Invoke error handling
    On Error GoTo GoodResume_Err
    Dim strFile As String

    'Perform the Dir function to determine if
    'the file passed as a parameter exists
    strFile = Dir(strFileName)

    'If the file doesn't exist, return False
    'Otherwise, return True
    If strFile = "" Then
      GoodResume = False
    Else
      GoodResume = True
    End If

    'Exit the function if all goes well
    Exit Function

GoodResume_Err:
    Dim intAnswer As Integer

    'Ask user if they want to try again
    intAnswer = MsgBox(Error & ", Would You Like to Try Again?", vbYesNo)

    'If they respond yes, attempt to re-execute the offending line
    'of code. Otherwise, exit the function
    If intAnswer = vbYes Then
        Resume
    Else
        Exit Function
    End If
End Function
```

In this example, the error handler enables the user to decide whether to try again. The Resume occurs only if the user's response is affirmative.

The Resume Next Statement

Just as you can invoke error handling using an On Error Resume Next statement, you can place a Resume Next statement in your error handler, as Listing 17.7 shows.

LISTING 17.7   Placing a Resume Next Statement in Your Error Handler

```
Sub TestResumeNextInError()

    'Invoke error handling
    On Error GoTo TestResumeNextInError_Err

    'Attempt to delete a file
    Kill "AnyFile"

    'If no error occurred, do nothing. Otherwise, display
    'a message with the description of the error that occurred
    If Err.Number = 0 Then
    Else
        MsgBox "We Didn't Die, But the Error Was: " & Err.Description
    End If

    Exit Sub

TestResumeNextInError_Err:
    'Reset error information and resume execution on the
    'line of code following the line on which the error cocured
    Resume Next
End Sub
```

In this example, the code is instructed to go to the label called
TestResumeNextInError_Err when an error occurs. The TestResumeNextInError_Err label
issues a Resume Next statement. This statement clears the error and causes execution to
continue on the line after the line on which the error occurred. The message box therefore never displays.

> **NOTE**
>
> Note the difference between On Error Resume Next and Resume Next. You place On
> Error Resume Next in the body of the routine. It causes code execution to continue
> on the line of code following the line that caused the error. It does *not* reset error
> information.
>
> You place Resume Next *within* the error handler. It also causes code execution to
> continue on the line of code following the line that caused the error. It *does* reset the
> error information.

The Resume <LineLabel> Statement

The Resume <LineLabel> statement enables you to specify a line of code where you want
code execution to continue after an error occurs. Using this statement is a great way to

eliminate the two `Exit Sub` or `Exit Function` statements required by the error-handling routines you have looked at so far. Listing 17.8 shows an example.

LISTING 17.8   Using the `Resume <LineLabel>` Statement to Specify Where Execution Continues After an Error Occurs

```
Sub TestResumeLineLabel(intVar1 As Integer, intVar2 As Integer)
    'Invoke error handling
    On Error GoTo TestResumeLineLabel_Err

    Dim sngResult As Single
    'Divide the value received as the first parameter
    'by the value received as the second parameter
    sngResult = intVar1 / intVar2

TestResumeLineLabel_Exit:
    'Exit subroutine
    Exit Sub

TestResumeLineLabel_Err:
    'If an error occurs, display message with the error
    'number and description
    MsgBox "Error #" & Err.Number & ": " & Err.Description

    'Resume execution at the TestResumeLineLabel_Exit label
    Resume TestResumeLineLabel_Exit

End Sub
```

Notice that this routine contains only one `Exit Sub` statement. If no error occurs, Access drops through the `TestResumeLineLabel_Exit` label to the `Exit Sub` statement. If an error *does* occur, the code in the `TestResumeLineLabel_Err` label executes. Notice that the last line of the error label resumes execution at the `TestResumeLineLabel_Exit` label.

This method of resolving an error is useful because any code required to execute as the routine is exited can be written in one place. Object variables might need to be set equal to `Nothing` as the routine is exited, for example. You can place these lines of code in the exit routine.

Clearing an Error

When an error occurs, the `Err` object remains set with the error information until one of the following clears the error:

▶ Resume, Resume Next, or Resume `<LineLabel>`

▶ Exit Sub, Exit Function, or Exit Property

▶ End Sub, End Function, or End Property

▶ Any Goto statement

▶ Explicitly using the Clear method on the Err object

Until the error is somehow cleared, all the information remains set in the Err object. After the error is cleared, no information is found in the Err object.

Examining the Cascading Error Effect

As mentioned earlier in the section "Using On Error Statements," if Access does not find error handling in a particular subroutine or function, it looks up the call stack for a previous error handler. Listing 17.9 shows an example of this process.

LISTING 17.9   Looking Up the Call Stack for a Previous Error Handler

```
Sub Func1()

    'Invoke error handling
    On Error GoTo Func1_Err

    'Print to the Immediate window
    Debug.Print "I am in Function 1"

    'Execute the Func2 routine
    Call Func2

    'Print to the Immediate window
    Debug.Print "I am back in Function 1"

    'Exit the subroutine
    Exit Sub

Func1_Err:
    'Display a message to the user,
    'indicating that an error occurred
    MsgBox "Error in Func1"

    'Resume execution
    Resume Next
End Sub

Sub Func2()
    'No error handling in this routine!
    'Print to the Immediate window
    Debug.Print "I am in Func2"
```

17

LISTING 17.9   Continued

```
    'Execute Func3
    Call Func3

    'Print to the Immediate window
    Debug.Print "I am still in Func2"
End Sub

Sub Func3()
    'No error in this routine either!
    Dim sngAnswer As Single

    'Print to the Immediate window
    Debug.Print "I am in Func3"

    'Oops, an error occurred
    sngAnswer = 5 / 0

    'This line of code will never execute
    Debug.Print "I am still in Func3"
End Sub
```

In this situation, the error occurs in Func3. Because Func3 does not have its own error handling, it refers back to Func2. Func2 does not have error handling either, so Func2 relinquishes control to Func1. VBA executes the error code in Func1. The real problem occurs because of the Resume Next statement. The application continues executing within Func1 on the Debug.Print "I am back in Function 1" statement. This type of error handling is dangerous and confusing. Therefore, it is best to develop a generic error-handling routine that is accessed throughout your application. The creation of a generic error handler is discussed in the section "Creating a Generic Error Handler."

Using the Err Object

The Err object contains information about the most recent error that occurred. As with all Access objects, it has its own built-in properties and methods. Table 17.1 lists the properties of the Err object.

TABLE 17.1   Properties of the Err Object

Property	Description
Description	Description of the error that occurred
HelpContext	Context ID for the Help file
HelpFile	Path and filename of the Help file
LastDllError	Last error that occurred in a 32-bit dynamic link library (DLL)

TABLE 17.1   Continued

Property	Description
Number	Number of the error that was set
Source	System in which the error occurred (which is extremely useful when you are using object linking and embedding [OLE] automation to control another application, such as Excel)

The `Err` object has only two methods: `Clear` and `Raise`. The `Clear` method enables you to clear an error condition explicitly. This method is used primarily when you write code that uses the `On Error Resume Next` statement. This statement does not clear the error condition. Remember that there is no reason to issue the `Clear` method explicitly with any type of `Resume`, `Exit Sub`, `Exit Function`, `Exit Property`, `On Error GoTo`, or `End Sub` statement. The `Clear` method is implicitly issued when these constructs are used. The `Raise` method of the `Err` object is covered in the next section.

Raising an Error

You use the `Raise` method of the error object in these situations:

- ▶ When you want to generate an error on purpose (for example, in testing)

- ▶ When you want to generate a user-defined error

- ▶ When no code in the error routine handles the current error, and you want to allow other parts of the call stack to attempt to handle the error

- ▶ When you want to nest an error handler

Using the `Raise` method to generate an error on purpose and creating a user-defined error are both complicated and important enough that they require special attention. They are covered in the following sections.

Generating an Error on Purpose

Many times during testing, you want to generate an error so that you can check your own error handling. Instead of figuring out how to cause the error condition, you can use the `Raise` method of the `Err` object to accomplish this task, as Listing 17.10 shows.

LISTING 17.10   Raising an Error

```
Sub TestRaiseError()
    'Invoke error handling
    On Error GoTo TestRaiseError_Err

    Dim sngResult As String

    'Raise a divide-by-zero error
```

LISTING 17.10   Continued

```
    Err.Raise 11

    'Exit the subroutine
    Exit Sub

TestRaiseError_Err:
    'Display a message with the error number and description
    MsgBox "Error #" & Err.Number & ": " & Err.Description

    'Exit the subroutine
    Exit Sub

End Sub
```

This code invokes an error 11 (divide-by-zero error).

Creating User-Defined Errors

Another important use of the `Raise` method of the `Err` object is the generation of a custom error condition. This method is useful when you want to *force* an error in response to something that the user did. For example, assume that the user must enter five characters into an unbound text box. Entering only two characters would not generate an Access error. Instead of handling this *user-generated* error in some other manner, you can raise the error and have your standard error handler respond to the error condition. Because the `Raise` method enables you to set all the properties of the `Err` object, you can create a user-defined error complete with a number, description, source, and so on, as shown in Listing 17.11.

LISTING 17.11   Creating a User-Defined Error

```
Sub TestCustomError()
    'Invoke error handling
    On Error GoTo TestCustomError_Err
    Dim strName As String

    'Prompt the user to enter their name
    strName = InputBox("Please Enter Your Name")

    'If the length of the name is less than five
    'characters, raise an error number 11111
    If Len(strName) < 5 Then
        Err.Raise Number:=11111, _
                Description:="Length of Name is Too Short"
    Else
        MsgBox "You Entered " & strName
```

LISTING 17.11   Continued

```
    End If

    Exit Sub

TestCustomError_Err:
    'Display a message with the error number
    'and description
    MsgBox "Error # " & Err.Number & _
        " - " & Err.Description
    Exit Sub
End Sub
```

Although this example is simple, Listing 17.11 illustrates an important use of generating user-defined errors. The code tests to see whether the value entered has fewer than five characters. If it does, the code generates a user-defined error message (number 11111). The routine drops into the normal error-handling routine. The section "Creating a Generic Error Handler," later in this chapter, explores how to put together a generic error handler. When you pass user-defined errors through your generic error handler, all errors—user-defined or not—are handled in the same way.

Using the Errors Collection

The Errors collection is part of Access's Database Engine. It stores the most recent set of DAO errors that have occurred. This capability is important when you are dealing with DAO (Data Access Objects) and ODBC (Open Database Connectivity), in which one operation can result in multiple errors. If you are concerned with each error generated by one operation, you need to look at the Errors collection. Each error object in the Errors collection contains information about an error that occurred. If you want to view the errors stored in the Errors collection, you must loop through it, viewing the properties of each Err object. Listing 17.12 shows the code you can use to accomplish this task.

LISTING 17.12   Viewing the Errors Stored in the Errors Collection

```
Sub TestErrorsCollection()
    'Invoke error handling
    On Error GoTo TestErrorsCollection_Err

    'Declare a DAO database object
    Dim db As DAO.Database

    'Point the database object at the database
    'referenced by the CurrentDB object
    Set db = CurrentDb
```

LISTING 17.12   Continued

```
    'Attempt to execute a query that doesn't exist
    db.Execute ("qryNonExistent")

    Exit Sub

TestErrorsCollection_Err:

    Dim ErrorDescrip As DAO.Error

    'Loop through the Errors collection,
    'sending the error number and description to
    'the Immediate window
    For Each ErrorDescrip In Errors
        Debug.Print ErrorDescrip.Number
        Debug.Print ErrorDescrip.Description
    Next ErrorDescrip
    Exit Sub
End Sub
```

This routine loops through each `Error` object in the `Errors` collection, printing the description of each error contained in the collection.

Creating a Generic Error Handler

A *generic* error handler can be called from every procedure in your application to respond to any type of error.

A generic error handler prevents you from having to write specific error handling in each of your subroutines and functions. Using such an error handler enables you to invoke error handling throughout your application in the most efficient manner possible.

You can take many approaches to create a generic error handler. It should give users information about the error, enable users to print this information, and log the information to a file. You might even want to email this information to yourself or to someone else in charge of maintaining the database.

The `On Error` routine (in this case, the label `AnySub_Err`) of every procedure that performs error handling should look like the error-handling routine contained in the subroutine in Listing 17.13.

LISTING 17.13   A Generic Error Handler for All Your Functions and Subroutines

```
Sub AnySub()
'Declare constant with the name of the routine
Const SUBNAME As String = "AnySub"
```

LISTING 17.13   Continued

```
'Invoke error handling
On Error GoTo AnySub_Err

    'Beginning of any routine
    MsgBox "This is the rest of your code...."

    'Oops! Something causes an error!
    Err.Raise 11

    'Code after the error
    MsgBox "We are Past the Error!!"

AnySub_Exit:
    'Generic exit point for routine
    Exit Sub

AnySub_Err:
    Dim intAction As Integer

    'Call generic error handler, passing it the error
    'number and description, as well as the module name
    'and subroutine name
    intAction = ErrorHandler(lngErrorNum:=Err.Number, _
                strErrorDescription:=Err.Description, _
                strModuleName:=MODULENAME, _
                strRoutineName:=SUBNAME)

    'Evaluate return value to determine what action to take
    Select Case intAction
        Case ERR_CONTINUE
            Resume Next
        Case ERR_RETRY
            Resume
        Case ERR_EXIT
            Resume AnySub_Exit
        Case ERR_QUIT
            Quit
    End Select
End Sub
```

This error-handling routine in AnySub creates an Integer variable that holds the return value from the error system. The intAction variable holds an appropriate response to the error that occurred. The error routine calls the generic error-handling function

ErrorHandler, passing it the error number (Err.Number), a description of the error (Err.Description), the name of the module containing the error, and the name of the subroutine or function containing the error. The name of the module is stored in a Private constant called MODULENAME. The Private constant is declared in the General section of the module and needs to be created for every module you make. The name of the subroutine or function is stored in a local constant called SUBNAME. With this approach, you create a local constant and assign it the name of the sub at the beginning of each procedure. This approach requires upkeep because procedure names can change, and you need to remember to change your string. Unfortunately, because the VBA environment does not expose the subroutine and module names to you when an error occurs, this sort of brute force is necessary if you want your error handler to track the subroutine and module. When the code returns from the ErrorHandler function, a return value is placed in the intAction variable. This return value is used to determine the fate of the routine.

Now that you have seen how to implement error handling in your procedures, look at the function that's called when an error occurs, as shown in Listing 17.14.

LISTING 17.14   A Type Structure Declaration to Be Used for Generic Error Handling

```
'Type structure used to hold error information
Type typErrors
    lngErrorNum As Long
    strMessage As String
    strModule As String
    strRoutine As String
    strUserName As String
    datDateTime As Variant
End Type

'Declaration of public type structure variable
Public gtypError As typErrors

'Constants used by global error handler
Public Const ERR_CONTINUE = 0  'Resume Next
Public Const ERR_RETRY = 1 'Resume
Public Const ERR_QUIT = 2   'End
Public Const ERR_EXIT = 3   'Exit Sub or Func
```

This code is placed in the General section of basHandleErrors. The type structure declared holds all the pertinent information about the error. A *type structure* is a special kind of variable made up of various parts, each of which stores a different piece of information. (Type structures are covered in Chapter 13, "Advanced VBA Techniques.")

In Listing 17.14, the public variable gtypError holds all the information from the type structure. The constants are used to help determine the fate of the application after an error occurs. Listing 17.15 shows the ErrorHandler function.

LISTING 17.15   Using the ErrorHandler Function

```
Function ErrorHandler(lngErrorNum As Long, _
                strErrorDescription As String, _
                strModuleName As String, _
                strRoutineName As String) As Integer

    Dim strUserInfo As String
    Dim strErrorInfo As String

    'Populate elements of the type structure variable
    'with information about the error that occurred
    gtypError.lngErrorNum = lngErrorNum
    gtypError.strMessage = strErrorDescription
    gtypError.strModule = strModuleName
    gtypError.strRoutine = strRoutineName
    gtypError.strUserName = CurrentUser()
    gtypError.datDateTime = Now

    'Log the error
    Call LogError

    'E-mail the error
    strUserInfo = gtypError.strUserName & _
        " Date: " & gtypError.datDateTime
    strErrorInfo = "Module: " & gtypError.strModule & vbCrLf & _
        "Routine: " & gtypError.strRoutine & vbCrLf & _
        "Error Number: " & gtypError.lngErrorNum & vbCrLf & _
        "Error Message: " & gtypError.strMessage
    Call MailError(strUserInfo, strErrorInfo)

    'Locate the error number in tblErrors to
    'determine how you should respond to the error
    Dim rst As adodb.Recordset
    Set rst = New adodb.Recordset
    rst.Open "Select Response from tblErrors Where ErrorNum = " & lngErrorNum, _
        CurrentProject.Connection, adOpenStatic

    'If the error number that occurred is not found
    'in tblErrors, display the error form and return
    'ERR_QUIT to the problem routine
    If rst.EOF Then
        DoCmd.OpenForm "frmError", WindowMode:=acDialog, _
            OpenArgs:="ErrorHandler"
        ErrorHandler = ERR_QUIT
```

17

LISTING 17.15   Continued

```
    'If the error is in tblErrors, evaluate the contents of
    'the Response field. Respond appropriately, displaying the appropriate
    'form and returning the appropriate value to the offending routine
    Else
        Select Case rst!Response
            Case ERR_QUIT
                DoCmd.OpenForm "frmError", WindowMode:=acDialog, _
                    OpenArgs:="Critical Error:  Application will Terminate"
                ErrorHandler = ERR_QUIT
            Case ERR_RETRY
                ErrorHandler = ERR_RETRY
            Case ERR_EXIT
                DoCmd.OpenForm "frmError", WindowMode:=acDialog, _
                    OpenArgs:="Severe Error:  Processing Did Not Complete"
                ErrorHandler = ERR_EXIT
            Case ERR_CONTINUE
                ErrorHandler = ERR_CONTINUE
        End Select
    End If

End Function
```

The ErrorHandler function receives the error number, error description, module name, and subroutine or function name as parameters. It then fills in the gtypError type structure with the information that it was passed, as well as the current user and date. Next, it calls a routine that logs the error into an Access table. The routine looks up the severity of the error code in an Access table called tblErrors to decide the most appropriate way to handle the error. If it does not find the error code in the error table, the code displays an error form, and it sends a return value to the calling function, indicating that application execution is to be terminated. If it finds the error code in the tblErrors table and determines it to be critical or severe, the code displays an error form before it returns control to the calling routine. In any case, the code returns a severity code for the error to the calling function. The following section discusses the details involved in each step of the process.

Logging the Error

The LogError routine is responsible for logging all the error information into an Access table. Because users often decide not to print the error form or provide you with inaccurate information about what was happening when the error occurred (or neglect to tell you about the error), it is important that you log each error so that you can review the error log at any time. You can log errors to a text file or to a data table. This section shows you both methods of logging your errors. Start with logging your errors to a table, as shown in Listing 17.16 with the LogError routine.

LISTING 17.16   Using the LogError Routine

```
Sub LogError()

    'Declare a Connection object
    Dim cnn As adodb.Connection
    Dim strSQL As String

    'Point the Connection object at the connection
    'associated with the current project
    Set cnn = CurrentProject.Connection

    'Build a SQL statement that inserts error information
    'into the tblErrorLog table
    strSQL = "INSERT INTO tblErrorLog ( ErrorDate, ErrorTime, " & _
    UserName, ErrorNum, ErrorString, ModuleName, RoutineName) "
    strSQL = strSQL & "Select #" & gtypError.datDateTime & "#, #" _
                        & gtypError.datDateTime & "#, '" _
                        & gtypError.strUserName & "', " _
                        & gtypError.lngErrorNum & ", '" _
                        & gtypError.strMessage & "', '" _
                        & gtypError.strModule & "', '" _
                        & gtypError.strRoutine & "'"

    'Execute the SQL statement
    cnn.Execute strSQL, , adExecuteNoRecords

End Sub
```

This routine uses the Execute method of the ADO Connection object to add a record to your error table. The record contains all the information from the structure called gtypError. The code logs the information to a table called tblErrorLog. Figure 17.4 shows the structure of this table.

The alternative error-logging method is to write the information to a textual error log file, as shown in Listing 17.17.

LISTING 17.17   Writing Information to a Textual Error Log File

```
Sub LogErrorText()
    Dim intFile As Integer

    'Store a free file handle into a variable
    intFile = FreeFile

    'Open a file named ErrorLog.txt in the current directory
    'using the file handle obtained above
```

LISTING 17.17   Continued

```
    Open CurDir & "\ErrorLog.Txt" For Append Shared As intFile

    'Write the error information to the file
    Write #intFile, "LogErrorDemo", Now, Err, Error, CurrentUser()

    'Close the file
    Close intFile
End Sub
```

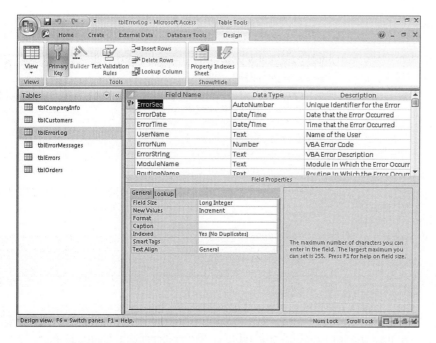

FIGURE 17.4   The structure of the `tblErrorLog` table.

This code uses low-level file functions to open and write to an ASCII text file. The code writes all the pertinent information about the error to this text file. The routine then uses the `Close` command to close the text file. The potential advantage of this routine is that, if the problem is with the database (for example, the network is down), the error-logging process still succeeds.

Determining the Appropriate Response to an Error

After the code logs the error, you are ready to determine the best way to respond to the error. By making your error system data-driven, you can handle each error a little differently. Figure 17.5 shows the structure of the `tblErrors` table. This table should contain a list of all the error numbers you want to trap. It contains three fields: `ErrorNum`,

`ErrorDescription`, and `Response`. When an error occurs, the `ErrorHandler` function searches for a record with a value in the `ErrorNum` field that matches the number of the error that occurred.

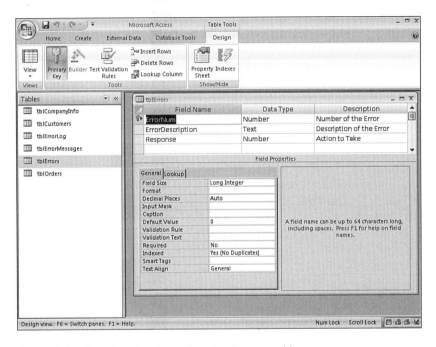

FIGURE 17.5   The structure of the `tblErrors` table.

The `ErrorHandler` function, as shown in Listing 17.15, uses the code in Listing 17.18 to locate the error code in the `tblErrors` table.

LISTING 17.18   Locating the Error Code in the `tblErrors` Table

```
'Locate the error number in tblErrors to
'determine how you should respond to the error
Dim rst As adodb.Recordset
Set rst = New adodb.Recordset
rst.Open "Select Response from tblErrors Where ErrorNum = " & lngErrorNum, _
    CurrentProject.Connection, adOpenStatic

'If the error number that occurred is not found
'in tblErrors, display the error form and return
'ERR_QUIT to the problem routine
If rst.EOF Then
    DoCmd.OpenForm "frmError", WindowMode:=acDialog, _
        OpenArgs:="ErrorHandler"
    ErrorHandler = ERR_QUIT
```

LISTING 17.18   Continued

```
'If the error is in tblErrors, evaluate the contents of
'the Response field. Respond appropriately, displaying the appropriate
'form and returning the appropriate value to the offending routine
Else
    Select Case rst!Response
        Case ERR_QUIT
            DoCmd.OpenForm "frmError", WindowMode:=acDialog, _
                OpenArgs:="Critical Error:  Application will Terminate"
            ErrorHandler = ERR_QUIT
        Case ERR_RETRY
            ErrorHandler = ERR_RETRY
        Case ERR_EXIT
            DoCmd.OpenForm "frmError", WindowMode:=acDialog, _
                OpenArgs:="Severe Error:  Processing Did Not Complete"
            ErrorHandler = ERR_EXIT
        Case ERR_CONTINUE
            ErrorHandler = ERR_CONTINUE
    End Select
End If
```

The part of the ErrorHandler function shown in Listing 17.18 creates an ADO Recordset object variable. It opens a recordset using a Select statement, which in turn searches a table called tblErrors. If a match is found, the code uses the Response column to determine the response to the error. Notice in Listing 17.18 that, if the error number is not found in tblErrors, default error handling occurs, which means that the code handles all other errors as a group. (This is my default error handling, not Access's.) If the error number is found, the code evaluates the Response field and takes the appropriate action (via the Case statement). If it is not found, the code opens the frmError form, and the ERR_QUIT constant value is returned from the ErrorHandler function. When using this method, you need to add to the table only specific errors that you want to trap.

If the error number is found in tblErrors, the code evaluates the Response field from the recordset. If the Response field contains the constant value ERR_QUIT or ERR_EXIT, the frmError form appears before the code returns the constant value to the offending function or subroutine. If the Response field contains the constant value for ERR_RETRY or ERR_CONTINUE, the code returns the constant value without displaying the frmError form.

NOTE

The tblErrors table is included in CHAP17EX.ACCDB on the sample code CD-ROM. To take full advantage of this table, you must add all the errors you want to trap, along with the actions you want the error handler to take when a particular error occurs.

Listing 17.19 shows how the code uses the return value from the ErrorHandler function.

LISTING 17.19   Using the Return Value from the ErrorHandler Function

```
Sub AnySub()
'Declare constant with the name of the routine
Const SUBNAME As String = "AnySub"

'Invoke error handling
On Error GoTo AnySub_Err

    'Beginning of any routine
    MsgBox "This is the rest of your code...."

    'Oops! Something causes an error!
    Err.Raise 11

    'Code after the error
    MsgBox "We are Past the Error!!"

AnySub_Exit:
    'Generic exit point for routine
    Exit Sub

AnySub_Err:
    Dim intAction As Integer

    'Call generic error handler, passing it the error
    'number and description, as well as the module name
    'and subroutine name
    intAction = ErrorHandler(lngErrorNum:=Err.Number, _
                strErrorDescription:=Err.Description, _
                strModuleName:=MODULENAME, _
                strRoutineName:=SUBNAME)

    'Evaluate return value to determine what action to take
    Select Case intAction
        Case ERR_CONTINUE
            Resume Next
        Case ERR_RETRY
            Resume
        Case ERR_EXIT
            Resume AnySub_Exit
        Case ERR_QUIT
            Quit
    End Select
End Sub
```

17

In Listing 17.19, the AnySub routine generates an error 11 (divide-by-zero error). Because tblErrors contains the number 3 in the Response column and the ERR_CONTINUE constant is equal to 3, the error form displays, and the AnySub routine exits with an Exit Sub statement.

> **NOTE**
>
> To test what happens when the error code is not found in the tblErrors table, run the SubWithUnknownError routine found in basError. To test what happens when the code returns the ERR_CONTINUE code, execute the SubWithContinue routine.

Emailing the Error

Whereas the LogError routine is responsible for logging the error to a database, the MailError routine, shown in Listing 17.20, is responsible for mailing the error information to a key system administrator.

LISTING 17.20   The MailError Routine

```
Sub MailError(strUserInfo As String, _
    strErrorInfo As String)

    'Declare necessary variables
    Dim objCurrentMessage As Outlook.MailItem
    Dim objNamespace As Outlook.NameSpace
    Dim objMessage As Outlook.MAPIFolder

    'Get reference to a namespace variable
    Set objNamespace = GetOutlook()

    'Use GetDefaultFolder method of the NameSpace object
    'to get a reference to a MAPIFolder object
    Set objMessage = objNamespace.GetDefaultFolder(olFolderOutbox)

    'Use the Add method of the Items collection
    'of the MAPIFolder object to add a mail item
    With objMessage.Items.Add(olMailItem)
        'Set properties of the mail item
        .To = "guru@somecompany.com"
        .Subject = strUserInfo
        .Body = strErrorInfo
        'Save the mail item as a draft
        .Save
    End With
End Sub
```

The `MailError` routine receives user and error information from the calling routine. It instantiates Outlook `MailItem`, `NameSpace`, and `MAPIFolder` objects. It then points the `NameSpace` object at the namespace returned from the `GetOutlook` function. The `GetOutlook` function appears in Listing 17.21.

LISTING 17.21   The GetOutlook Function

```
Function GetOutlook() As Outlook.NameSpace
    Dim objOutlook As New Outlook.Application
    Dim objNamespace As Outlook.NameSpace
    Dim strProfile As String
    Dim strPassword As String

    strProfile = "alison"
    strPassword = "mypassword"

    'Use the GetNamespace method of the Outlook
    'Application object to get a pointer to a
    'MAPI namespace
    Set objNamespace = objOutlook.GetNamespace("MAPI")

    'Use the Logon method of the NameSpace object
    'to Logon to the namespace
    Call objNamespace.Logon(strProfile, _
        strPassword, False, True)

    'Return a reference to the namespace
    Set GetOutlook = objNamespace
End Function
```

The `GetOutlook` function declares an Outlook `NameSpace` object and an Outlook `Application` object. It uses the `GetNamespace` method of the Outlook `Application` object to obtain a reference to a `MAPI` namespace. It then uses the `Logon` method of the namespace to log on to the namespace, using a given profile name and password. You will need to change the values of `strProfile` and `strPassword` to a valid profile name and password for this code to run properly on your machine. Finally, this code returns a reference to the namespace that it created.

After the `MailError` routine has a reference to a MAPI namespace, it can use that reference to point to the Outbox. The code uses the `Add` method of the `Items` collection of the Outbox to add a mail item to the Outbox. The code then sets the appropriate properties (such as `To`, `Subject`, and so on) to the appropriate pieces of the error information. Finally, the code can either save the message as a draft or else send it so that it's immediately sent to the administrator and appears in the Sent Items folder of the sender.

NOTE

Listing 17.21 requires that you know the username and profile of the user sending the email. You could provide a dialog box where the user can enter this information each time an error occurs, or this could be part of the initial logon to the system. I generally recommend that this be integrated as part of the initial logon so that the user does not have to take extra steps each time an error occurs.

Creating an Error Form

The code in the error form's Load event calls two subroutines: GetSystemInfo and GetErrorInfo, as shown here:

```
Private Sub Form_Load()

    Dim objSys as SystemInformation
    Set objSys = New SystemInformation

    'Call routine to obtain system information
    Call GetSysInfo(Me)

    'Call routine to obtain error information
    Call GetErrorInfo(Me)

    'If FormCaption property contains a value, use the
    'value as the caption for the form
    If Not IsNull(Me.OpenArgs) Then
        Me.lblAction.Caption = Me.OpenArgs
    End If
End Sub
```

The first subroutine is called GetSysInfo. It performs several Windows Application Programming Interface (API) calls to fill in the system information on your form. This code is shown in Listing 17.22 and is discussed in Chapter 25, "Exploiting the Power of the Windows API."

LISTING 17.22   Getting System Information Through Code

```
Sub GetSysInfo(frmAny As Form)

    'Get Free Memory
    Dim MS As MEMORYSTATUS
    MS.dwLength = Len(MS)
    GlobalMemoryStatus MS

    frmAny.lblMemoryTotal.Caption = Format(MS.dwTotalPhys, "Standard")
    frmAny.lblMemoryAvail.Caption = Format(MS.dwAvailPhys, "Standard")
```

LISTING 17.22   Continued

```
    'Get version information
    Dim OSInfo As OSVERSIONINFO
    OSInfo.dwOSVersionInfoSize = Len(OSInfo)
    If GetVersionEx(OSInfo) Then
        frmAny.lblOSVersion.Caption = & _
        OSInfo.dwMajorVersion & "." & OSInfo.& _
        dwMinorVersion
        frmAny.lblBuild.Caption = OSInfo.dwBuildNumber And &HFFFF&
    End If

    'Get system information
    Dim SI As SYSTEM_INFO
     GetSystemInfo SI
    frmAny.lblProcessor.Caption = SI.dwProcessorType
```

End Sub

These API calls require the Declare statements and constants shown in Listing 17.23. You will find them in a module called basAPI.

LISTING 17.23   Declaring Windows API Calls

```
'Declarations required by WinAPI Calls
Option Compare Database
Option Explicit

Private Declare Sub GlobalMemoryStatus Lib "Kernel32" _
(lpBuffer As MEMORYSTATUS)

Private Type MEMORYSTATUS
    dwLength As Long
    dwMemoryLoad As Long
    dwTotalPhys As Long
    dwAvailPhys As Long
    dwTotalPageFile As Long
    dwAvailPageFile As Long
    dwTotalVirtual As Long
    dwAvailVirtual As Long
End Type

Private Declare Function GetVersionEx Lib "Kernel32" _
  Alias "GetVersionExA" (lpOSInfo As OSVERSIONINFO) As Boolean
```

17

LISTING 17.23   Continued

```
Type OSVERSIONINFO
   dwOSVersionInfoSize As Long
   dwMajorVersion As Long
   dwMinorVersion As Long
   dwBuildNumber As Long
   dwPlatformId As Long
   strReserved As String * 128
End Type

Private Declare Sub GetSystemInfo Lib "Kernel32" _
  (lpSystemInfo As SYSTEM_INFO)

Private Type SYSTEM_INFO
   dwOemID As Long
   dwPageSize As Long
   lpMinimumApplicationAddress As Long
   lpMaximumApplicationAddress As Long
   dwActiveProcessorMask As Long
   dwNumberOfProcessors As Long
   dwProcessorType As Long
   dwAllocationGranularity As Long
   dwReserved As Long
End Type
```

The second subroutine, GetErrorInfo, fills in the labels on the error form with all the information from your structure, as shown in Listing 17.24.

LISTING 17.24   Using the GetErrorInfo Subroutine

```
Sub GetErrorInfo(frmAny As Form)
    'Populate form controls with error information
    'contained in the type variable
    frmAny.lblErrorNumber.Caption = gtypError.lngErrorNum
    frmAny.lblErrorString.Caption = gtypError.strMessage
    frmAny.lblUserName.Caption = gtypError.strUserName
    frmAny.lblDateTime.Caption = Format(gtypError.datDateTime, "c")
    frmAny.lblModuleName.Caption = gtypError.strModule
    frmAny.lblRoutineName.Caption = gtypError.strRoutine
End Sub
```

Finally, the disposition of the error, sent as an OpenArg from the ErrorHandler function, is displayed in a label on the form. Figure 17.6 shows the error form.

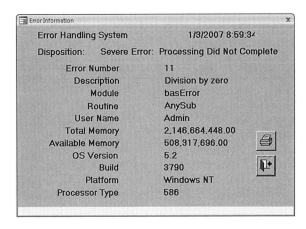

FIGURE 17.6   The `frmErrors` form displays important information about the error that occurred.

Printing the Error Form

Users often are not very accurate in describing an error and the corresponding error message. It's therefore important to give them the capability to print their error message. The code in Listing 17.25 prints your error form. You will find it behind the `Click` event of the Print button on the error form.

LISTING 17.25   Printing an Error Form

```
Sub cmdPrint_Click()
On Error GoTo Err_cmdPrint_Click

    'Use the PrintOut method to print the form
    DoCmd.PrintOut

Exit_cmdPrint_Click:
    Exit Sub

Err_cmdPrint_Click:
    MsgBox Err.Description
    Resume Exit_cmdPrint_Click

End Sub
```

17

Preventing Your Own Error Handling from Being Invoked

When you are testing your application, you do not want to trigger your own error handling. Instead, you want to activate VBA's own error handling. The trick is in the Options dialog box of the Visual Basic Editor (VBE). Choose Tools, Options and click the General tab. Enable the option Break on All Errors located in the Error Trapping section. As long as this option is set, your error handling is ignored, and Access's default error handling is invoked. Using this setting, you can turn error handling on and off from one central location.

Other settings for error trapping are Break in Class Module and Break on Unhandled Errors (the default). With the latter setting, handled errors do not cause the application to enter Break mode. Unhandled errors do cause the project to enter Break mode and place you, or the user, on the line of code that invoked the error handler. The Break in Class Module option causes *only* unhandled errors in a *Class module* to invoke Break mode.

Creating a Call Stack

While in the debugger, you can easily view the call stack. Unfortunately, the call stack information cannot be accessed programmatically when an error occurs. If you want to keep track of the sequence of procedures that brought you to the error condition, you must do it yourself. The code in Listing 17.26 shows three routines. Func1 calls Func2, and then Func2 calls Func3. Func3 renders an error.

LISTING 17.26   Routines That Call One Another

```
Sub Func1()

    'Invoke error handling
    On Error GoTo Func1_Err

    'Put routine in call stack
    ERH_PushStack_TSB ("Func1")

    'Print to the Immediate window
    Debug.Print "I am in Function 1"

    'Execute the Func2 routine
    Call Func2

    'Print to the Immediate window
    Debug.Print "I am back in Function 1"

Func1_Exit:
```

LISTING 17.26   Continued

```
    'Pop error stack
    ERH_PopStack_TSB

    'Exit the subroutine
    Exit Sub

Func1_Err:
    'Display a message to the user,
    'indicating that an error occurred
    MsgBox "Error in Func1"

    'Resume execution
    Resume Func1_Exit
End Sub

Sub Func2()
    'Put routine in call stack
    ERH_PushStack_TSB ("Func2")

    On Error GoTo Func2_Err

    Debug.Print "I am in Func2"

    'Execute Func3
    Call Func3

    'Print to the Immediate window
    Debug.Print "I am still in Func2"

Func2_Exit:

    'Pop error stack
    ERH_PopStack_TSB

    'Exit the subroutine
    Exit Sub

Func2_Err:
    'Display a message to the user,
    'indicating that an error occurred
    MsgBox "Error in Func1"

    'Resume execution
    Resume Func2_Exit

End Sub
```

17

LISTING 17.26   Continued

```
Sub Func3()
    Dim sngAnswer As Single

    'Put routine in call stack
    ERH_PushStack_TSB ("Func3")

    On Error GoTo Func3_Err

    'Print to the Immediate window
    Debug.Print "I am in Func3"

    'Oops, an error occurred
    sngAnswer = 5 / 0

    'This line of code will never execute
    Debug.Print "I am still in Func3"

Func3_Exit:

    'Pop error stack
    ERH_PopStack_TSB

    'Exit the subroutine
    Exit Sub

Func3_Err:
    Dim intCounter As Integer
    Dim strCallStack As String

    For intCounter = LBound(gaERH_Stack_TSB) To UBound(gaERH_Stack_TSB)
        If Len(gaERH_Stack_TSB(intCounter)) Then
            strCallStack = strCallStack & _
                gaERH_Stack_TSB(intCounter) & vbCrLf
        End If
    Next intCounter

    MsgBox Err.Number & ": " & Err.Description & _
        vbCrLf & strCallStack

    Resume Func3_Exit
End Sub
```

Notice that at the beginning of each routine, the `ERH_PushStack_TSB` subroutine is called, pushing the error into the stack, as shown in Listing 17.27.

LISTING 17.27   The `ERH_PushStack_TSB` Function

```
Sub ERH_PushStack_TSB(strProc As String)
  ' Comments  : Pushes the supplied procedure name onto the error handling stack
  ' Parameters: strProc - name of the currently executing procedure
  ' Returns   : Nothing
  '
  gintERH_Pointer_TSB = gintERH_Pointer_TSB + 1

  If gintERH_Pointer_TSB <= ERH_MAXITEMS_TSB Then
    gaERH_Stack_TSB(gintERH_Pointer_TSB) = strProc
  Else
    gaERH_Stack_TSB(gintERH_Pointer_TSB + 2) = strProc
  End If

End Sub
```

The code adds the name of the procedure to the `gaERH Stack_TSB` array. The `ERH_PopStack_TSB` subroutine, shown in Listing 17.28, is executed in the exit code for each procedure and removes the error from the stack.

LISTING 17.28   The `ERH_PopStack_TSB` Function

```
Sub ERH_PopStack_TSB()
  ' Comments  : Pops the current procedure name off the error handling stack
  ' Parameters: None
  ' Returns   : Nothing
  '
  If gintERH_Pointer_TSB <= ERH_MAXITEMS_TSB Then
    gaERH_Stack_TSB(gintERH_Pointer_TSB) = ""
  End If

  gintERH_Pointer_TSB = gintERH_Pointer_TSB - 1

  If gintERH_Pointer_TSB < 0 Then
    gintERH_Pointer_TSB = 0
  End If

End Sub
```

The `ERH_PopStack_TSB` subroutine removes the text in the largest array element.

As the code goes in and out of routines, it adds entries to and removes entries from the array. Because the array is Public, you can review its contents at any time. Notice in Func3 in Listing 17.26 that the error handler iterates through the array, pulling out the error information.

Building a Custom Error Handler Class

Implementing error handling within an application can be tedious, especially if you attempt to place specific error-handling logic in each routine you write. Although implementing a generic error handler does not mandate the use of a Class module, using a Class module greatly facilitates the process of implementing error handling within your applications. Listing 17.29 illustrates this point.

LISTING 17.29   An Example of an Access Subroutine

```
Sub AnySub2()
'Declare constant with the name of the routine
Const SUBNAME As String = "AnySub"

'Invoke error handling
On Error GoTo AnySub2_Err

    'Beginning of any routine
    MsgBox "This is the rest of your code...."

    'Oops! Something causes an error!
    Err.Raise 11

    'Code after the error
    MsgBox "We are Past the Error!!"

AnySub2_Exit:
    'Generic exit point for routine
    Exit Sub

AnySub2_Err:
    Dim intAction As Integer

    'Instantiate the error handler class
    Set gobjErrorHandler = New ErrorHandler

    'Execute the ErrorProcess method,
    'passing the error information
    intAction = gobjErrorHandler.ErrorProcess(ModuleName, _
        SUBNAME, Err.Number, Err.Description)
```

LISTING 17.29   Continued

```
    'Evaluate return value to determine what action to take
    Select Case intAction
        Case ERR_CONTINUE
            Resume Next
        Case ERR_RETRY
            Resume
        Case ERR_EXIT
            Resume AnySub2_Exit
        Case ERR_QUIT
            Quit
    End Select
End Sub
```

When an error occurs, your code instantiates the ErrorHandler class. The Initialize event of the class executes, as shown in Listing 17.30.

LISTING 17.30   The Initialize Event of the ErrorHandler Class

```
Private Sub Class_Initialize()
    'Place username into private variable
    mstrUsername = CurrentUser

    'Place current date and time into private variable
    mdatDateTime = Now
End Sub
```

The Initialize event of the class sets the module-level variables mstrUserName and mdatDateTime equal to the CurrentUser and the current date and time, respectively. The Username and DateTime properties of the class use these variables.

The code then executes the ErrorProcess method of the ErrorHandler class, which logs the error and then takes appropriate action in response to the error. It appears in Listing 17.31.

LISTING 17.31   The ErrorProcess Method of the ErrorHandler Class

```
Public Function ErrorProcess(strRoutine As String, _
    strModule As String, _
    lngErrorNumber As Long, _
    strErrorMessage As String) As Integer

    'Store error information into module-level variables
    mstrRoutine = strRoutine
    mstrModule = strModule
```

17

LISTING 17.31   Continued

```
    mlngErrorNumber = lngErrorNumber
    mstrErrorMessage = strErrorMessage

    'Log error
    Call LogError

    'Locate the error number in tblErrors to
    'determine how you should respond to the error
    Dim rst As ADODB.Recordset
    Set rst = New ADODB.Recordset
    rst.Open "Select Response from tblErrors " & _
    Where ErrorNum = " & lngErrorNumber, _
        CurrentProject.Connection, adOpenStatic

    'If the error number that occurred is not found
    'in tblErrors, display the error form and return
    'ERR_QUIT to the problem routine
    If rst.EOF Then
        DoCmd.OpenForm "frmError2", WindowMode:=acDialog, _
            OpenArgs:="ErrorHandler"
        ErrorProcess = ERR_QUIT

    'If the error is in tblErrors, evaluate the contents of
    'the Response field. Respond appropriately, displaying the appropriate
    'form and returning the appropriate value to the offending routine
    Else
        Select Case rst!Response
            Case ERR_QUIT
                DoCmd.OpenForm "frmError2", WindowMode:=acDialog, _
                    OpenArgs:="Critical Error:  Application will Terminate"
                ErrorProcess = ERR_QUIT
            Case ERR_RETRY
                ErrorProcess = ERR_RETRY
            Case ERR_EXIT
                DoCmd.OpenForm "frmError2", WindowMode:=acDialog, _
                    OpenArgs:="Severe Error:  Processing Did Not Complete"
                ErrorProcess = ERR_EXIT
            Case ERR_CONTINUE
                ErrorProcess = ERR_CONTINUE
        End Select
    End If

End Function
```

The routine first sets the `ModuleName`, `Routine`, `ErrorMessage`, and `ErrorNumber` variables within the class to the values of the parameters passed to the `ErrorProcess` method. The `Property Get` routines for the `ModuleName`, `Routine`, `ErrorMessage`, and `ErrorNumber` properties, which are responsible for manipulating error information, appear in Listing 17.32. Because you want the properties to be set via only the `ErrorProcess` method, no `Property Let` routines exist.

LISTING 17.32   The Property Get Routines of the Class

```
Public Property Get ModuleName() As String
    ModuleName = mstrModule
End Property


Public Property Get Routine() As String
    Routine = mstrRoutine
End Property


Public Property Get ErrorMessage() As String
    ErrorMessage = mstrErrorMessage
End Property


Public Property Get ErrorNumber() As Integer
    ErrorNumber = mlngErrorNumber
End Property


Public Property Get UserName() As String
    UserName = mstrUsername
End Property


Public Property Get DateTime() As Date
    DateTime = mdatDateTime
End Property
```

As you can see, the `Property Get` routines retrieve the values from their associated module-level variables.

Next, the function calls a routine that logs the error that occurred. This `LogError` routine is shown in Listing 17.33. The `LogError` routine uses ADO code to add a record to the `tblErrorLog` table. The record contains all the information about the error that occurred. Notice that the error information is retrieved from the module-level variables populated by the `ErrorHandler` class's `ErrorProcess` method.

LISTING 17.33   The LogError Subroutine

```
Sub LogError()

    'Declare a Connection object
    Dim cnn As ADODB.Connection
    Dim strSQL As String

    'Point the Connection object at the connection
    'associated with the current project
    Set cnn = CurrentProject.Connection

    'Build a SQL statement that inserts error information
    'into the tblErrorLog table
    strSQL = "INSERT INTO tblErrorLog ( ErrorDate, ErrorTime, UserName, _
    ErrorNum, ErrorString, ModuleName, RoutineName) "
    strSQL = strSQL & "Select #" & Me.DateTime & "#, #" _
                            & Me.DateTime & "#, '" _
                            & Me.UserName & "', " _
                            & Me.ErrorNumber & ", '" _
                            & Me.ErrorMessage & "', '" _
                            & Me.ModuleName & "', '" _
                            & Me.Routine & "'"

    'Execute the SQL statement
    cnn.Execute strSQL, , adExecuteNoRecords

End Sub
```

After the error is logged, the number of the error that occurred is looked up in the tblErrors table. If it is not found in the tblErrors table, a form is displayed, containing all the critical information about the error that occurred. The value contained in the constant ERR_QUIT is returned from the ErrorHandler function. If the error number is found in the tblErrors table, the value contained in the Response field is evaluated. If it is the value contained in the constant ERR_QUIT, the frmError form is displayed, and the value in the constant ERR_QUIT is returned from the ErrorHandler method. If the Response field contains the value of the ERR_RETRY constant, that value is returned from the method, without the frmError form being displayed. If the Response field contains the value associated with the ERR_EXIT constant, the frmError form is displayed, and the ERR_EXIT value is returned from the ErrorHandler method. Finally, if the value in the Response field is the value associated with the ERR_CONTINUE constant, no error information is displayed, and the ERR_CONTINUE value is returned from the ErrorHandler method.

All the code contained in the ErrorHandler class is similar to that contained in the basErrorHandler module. The code has been modified so that it is implemented using properties and methods of a Class object.

The other code that is changed to use classes is the code behind the error form. Listing 17.34 shows the Load event of the error form, modified to call methods of the appropriate classes.

LISTING 17.34   The Form_Load Event of the Error Form

```
Private Sub Form_Load()

    Dim objSys As SystemInformation
    Set objSys = New SystemInformation

    'Call routine to obtain system information
    Call objSys.GetSysInfo(Me)

    'Call routine to obtain error information
    Call gobjErrorHandler.GetErrorInfo(Me)

    'If FormCaption property contains a value, use the
    'value as the caption for the form
    If Not IsNull(Me.OpenArgs) Then
        Me.lblAction.Caption = Me.OpenArgs
    End If
End Sub
```

Notice that instead of calling the GetSysInfo and GetErrorInfo functions, the Load event executes the GetSysInfo method of the SystemInformation object and the GetErrorInfo method of the ErrorHandler object.

The GetSystemInfo function and associated declarations were moved to a SystemInformation class. No other changes were made to the code.

The GetErrorInfo function was moved to the ErrorHandler class and modified to retrieve properties of the class, as shown in Listing 17.35.

LISTING 17.35   The GetErrorInfo Method of the ErrorHandler Class Retrieving Properties of the Class

```
Sub GetErrorInfo(frmAny As Form)
    'Populate form controls with error information
    'contained in the type variable
    frmAny.lblErrorNumber.Caption = Me.ErrorNumber
    frmAny.lblErrorString.Caption = Me.ErrorMessage
    frmAny.lblUserName.Caption = Me.UserName
    frmAny.lblDateTime.Caption = Format(Me.DateTime, "c")
    frmAny.lblModuleName.Caption = Me.ModuleName
    frmAny.lblRoutineName.Caption = Me.Routine
End Sub
```

17

Notice that instead of using a type structure, the code references its own properties. The `Private` variables associated with these properties were set by the `ErrorProcess` method of the class.

Working with Error Events

Every form and report contains an error event procedure. This event is triggered by any interface or Access Database Engine error. It is not triggered by a programming error made by the Access developer.

Errors often occur in the interface of a form or report, as well as in the Access Database Engine. A user might try to enter an order for a customer who doesn't exist, for example. Instead of displaying Access's default error message, you might want to intercept and handle the error in a particular way.

After an error occurs within a form, its error event is triggered. In Listing 17.36, you can see Sub `Form_Error`. It contains two parameters. The first parameter is the number of the error. The second is the way you want to respond to the error. The error number is an Access-generated number.

This code, which is located in the `frmOrders` form in the `CHAP17EX.ACCDB` database, tests to see whether a referential integrity error has occurred. If it has, a message box asks whether the user wants to add the customer. If the user answers `Yes`, the customer form is displayed.

LISTING 17.36   Viewing Sub `Form_Error` from the Form `frmOrders`

```
Private Sub Form_Error(DataErr As Integer, Response As Integer)
    Dim intAnswer As Integer
    If DataErr = 3201 Then  'Referential Integrity Error
        intAnswer = MsgBox("Customer Does Not Exist..." & _ _
                "Would You Like to Add Them Now?", vbYesNo)
        If intAnswer = vbYes Then
            DoCmd.OpenForm "frmCustomer", , , , acAdd, acDialog
        End If
    End If
    Response = acDataErrContinue
End Sub
```

> **CAUTION**
>
> Be aware that the code in Listing 17.36 only traps referential integrity errors. It does not handle any other error.

The `Response = acDataErrContinue` line is very important. It instructs Access to continue the code execution without displaying the standard error message. The other option for `Response` is `AcDataErrDisplay`. It tells Access to display the default error message.

Creating a List of Error Codes and Descriptions

Many people ask me how to create a list of error numbers and descriptions. The code in Listing 17.37 creates a table of all the errors that can occur in your VBA code, with a description of what each error number means. You can copy this code into any module and run it.

LISTING 17.37   Code That Creates a Table of Errors and Descriptions

```
Sub CreateErrorsTable()
    Dim cnn As ADODB.Connection
    Dim rst As New ADODB.Recordset
    Dim lngCode As Long
    Const conAppObjectError = "Application-defined or object-defined error"

    Set cnn = CurrentProject.Connection
    ' Open recordset on Errors table.
    rst.Open "tblErrorMessages", cnn, adOpenStatic, adLockOptimistic
    ' Loop through first 10000 Visual Basic error codes.
    For lngCode = 1 To 10000
        On Error Resume Next
        ' Raise each error.
        Err.Raise lngCode
        DoCmd.Hourglass True
        ' Skip error codes that generate application or object-defined errors.
        If Err.Description <> conAppObjectError Then
            ' Add each error code and string to Errors table.
            rst.AddNew
            rst!ErrorCode = Err.Number
            rst!ErrorString = Err.Description
            rst.Update
        End If
        ' Clear Err object.
        Err.Clear
    Next lngCode
    ' Close recordset.
    rst.Close
    DoCmd.Hourglass False
    MsgBox "Errors table created."
End Sub
```

The code opens a recordset based on the tblErrorMessages table. It loops through from 1 to 10000, raising an error with each number. Each time through the loop, it appends the error number and the associated error description to the tblErrorMessages table.

17

Practical Examples: Incorporating Error Handling

Error-handling code should be added throughout the applications that you build. The following example shows you how to incorporate a generic error handler into your applications.

Assume that your application contains a routine called GetCompanyInfo. This routine reads all the company information from the tblCompanyInfo table. The information is read from the public class instance as needed, while the application is running. This routine, like any routine, has the potential for error. The original routine has been modified to incorporate the generic error handler, as shown in Listing 17.38.

LISTING 17.38   Incorporating the Generic Error Handler into Your Code

```
Sub GetCompanyInfo()
    Dim strSubName As String
    Dim rst As ADODB.Recordset

    'Declare constant with the name of the routine
    Const SUBNAME As String = "GetCompanyInfo"

    'Invoke error handling
    On Error GoTo GetCompanyInfo_Err

    'Instantiate the CompanyInformation class
    Set gobjCompanyInfo = New CompanyInformation
    Set rst = New ADODB.Recordset

    'Open a recordset based on the tblCompanyInfo table
    rst.Open "tblCompanyInfo", CurrentProject.Connection

    'Populate the properties of the public class instance
    'with values from the tblCompanyInfo table
    With gobjCompanyInfo
        .SetupID = rst!SetupID
        .CompanyName = rst!CompanyName
        .Address = rst!Address
        .City = rst!City
        .StateProvince = rst!StateProvince
        .PostalCode = rst!PostalCode
        .Country = rst!Country
        .PhoneNumber = rst!PhoneNumber
        .FaxNumber = rst!PhoneNumber
    End With

    rst.Close
```

LISTING 17.38   Continued

```
GetCompanyInfo_Exit:
    'Generic exit point for routine
    Exit Sub

GetCompanyInfo_Err:
    Dim intAction As Integer

    'Instantiate the error handler class
    Set gobjErrorHandler = New ErrorHandler

    'Execute the ErrorProcess method,
    'passing the error information
    intAction = gobjErrorHandler.ErrorProcess(ModuleName, _
        SUBNAME, Err.Number, Err.Description)

    'Evaluate return value to determine what action to take
    Select Case intAction
        Case ERR_CONTINUE
            Resume Next
        Case ERR_RETRY
            Resume
        Case ERR_EXIT
            Resume GetCompanyInfo_Exit
        Case ERR_QUIT
            Quit
    End Select
End Sub
```

Notice the On Error GoTo statement at the beginning of the routine, and that the local constant SUBNAME is declared and set equal to GetCompanyInfo. The generic error handler uses the value in the constant to display the routine within which the error occurred. The error handler GetCompanyInfo_Err instantiates the ErrorHandler class. It executes the ErrorProcess method of the class and then evaluates its return value.

Summary

In this chapter, you learned the alternatives for handling errors in your Access applications. This chapter covered how you can use the error event to trap for application and Access Database Engine errors in forms and reports. You also learned how to use the On Error statement. Finally, you learned how to build a generic error system. Regardless of the amount of testing done on an application, errors will occur. It is important that you properly trap for those errors.

CHAPTER 18

Optimizing Your Application

Why This Chapter Is Important

In a world where it can be difficult for hardware to keep up with software, it is important to do everything you can to improve the performance of your application. This chapter helps you optimize your application's speed and reduce its memory and hard disk space requirements.

Introducing Optimization

Optimization is the process of reviewing your operating environment, Visual Basic for Applications (VBA) code, application objects, and data structures to ensure that they are providing optimum performance. In a nutshell, optimization is the process of making your application leaner and meaner.

Users become frustrated when an application runs slowly. In fact, if a user is not warned about a slow process, he will often reboot or shut down the power on the machine while a process is running. This can have dire results on the integrity of the data.

TIP

If you want to help reduce the chance of users rebooting the computer during a lengthy process, it's generally a good idea to provide them with some sort of indication that a process will take awhile. You can do this by using a message box that appears before processing begins or by providing a status bar or progress meter that shows the progress of the task being completed.

You can take many steps to optimize an application's performance, ranging from using a front-end tool such as the Performance Analyzer, to fastidiously adhering to certain coding techniques. This chapter highlights the major steps you can take to optimize the performance of your applications.

Modifying Hardware and Software Configurations

The Access *environment* refers to the combination of hardware and software configurations under which Microsoft Access runs. These environmental settings can greatly affect the performance of an Access application.

The easiest way to improve an application's performance is to upgrade its hardware and software configuration. This form of optimization requires no direct intervention from the developer. Plus, a side benefit of most of the environmental changes you can make is that any improvements made to the environment are beneficial to users in all their Windows applications.

Improving the environment involves more than just adding some RAM. It also can mean optimally configuring the operating system and the Access application.

Hardware, Hardware, More Hardware, Please!

The bottom line is that Windows XP, Windows Server 2003, Windows Vista, and Access 2007 all crave hardware—the more, the better. The faster your users' machines are, and the more memory they have, the better your applications will run. Obtaining additional hardware might not be the least expensive solution, but it certainly is the quickest and easiest thing you can do to improve the performance of your application. You can make a number of changes to your system's hardware to improve your application's performance, as the next sections illustrate.

RAM, RAM—That's All I Need!

Memory is what Access craves most, whether you are running under the full version of Microsoft Access or using the runtime version of the product. Microsoft Access *requires* 256MB of RAM just to run, and Microsoft *recommends* additional RAM if possible. Microsoft considers these minimums to be the standard operating environment for Access. Microsoft recommends additional RAM for each application that your users are running simultaneously with Access 2007. Put in a straightforward way, the more RAM you and the users of your application have, the better. A great environment for Access 2007 is 2GB or more of RAM. In fact, if every one of your users has at least 2GB of RAM, you can stop reading this chapter, because everything else covered here is going to provide you with minor benefits compared to adding more RAM. If you are like most of us, though (meaning that not every one of your users has a machine running at 1GHz with 2GB of RAM or more), read on.

> **NOTE**
>
> Developers should have a bare minimum of 1GB of RAM installed on their machines. Remember that this is a minimum! Most developers agree that 2GB of RAM or more is ideal if you intend to do any serious development work, especially if you plan to develop client/server or Internet/intranet applications.

Defragment Your User's Hard Disk

As your computer writes information to disk, it attempts to find contiguous space on which to place data files. As the hard disk fills up, the computer places files in fragmented pieces on the hard disk. Each time your application attempts to read data and programs, it must locate the information scattered over the disk. This is a time-consuming process. Therefore, it's helpful to defragment the hard disk on which the application and data tables are stored using a utility such as the Disk Defragmenter that ships with Windows XP, Windows 2003, and Windows Vista.

Compact Your Database

Just as the operating system fragments your files over time, Access itself introduces its own form of fragmentation. Each time you add and modify data, your database grows. When you delete data or objects within your database, it does not shrink. Instead, Access leaves empty pages available in which it will place new data. The problem is that these empty pages are not necessarily filled with data. You can free the empty space using the Compact utility, which is included in the Microsoft Access software. The Compact utility frees this excess space and attempts to make all data pages contiguous. You should compact your database frequently, especially if records or database objects (for example, forms and reports) are regularly added and deleted. You can access the Compact utility by clicking the Microsoft Access button and selecting Manage, Compact and Repair Database.

Tune Virtual Memory: Tweak the Paging File

Although Windows XP, Windows Server 2003, and Windows Vista attempt to manage virtual memory on their own, you might find it useful to provide them with some additional advice. To modify the physical location of the paging file, right-click My Computer, and choose Properties. The System Properties dialog box appears. Click the Advanced tab (see Figure 18.1). Then click Settings under the Performance options. The Performance Options dialog box appears. Click the Advanced tab (see Figure 18.2). Click the Change button under Virtual Memory. The Virtual Memory dialog box appears (see Figure 18.3). In this dialog box, you can modify all the settings for the paging file. It might be useful to move the paging file to a faster disk drive or to a drive connected to a separate controller card. Any changes you make might adversely affect performance. It is important that you evaluate whether any changes you make will help the situation—or perhaps make things worse! In general, it is advisable to let Windows dynamically manage the size of the paging file unless the system is running very low on disk space.

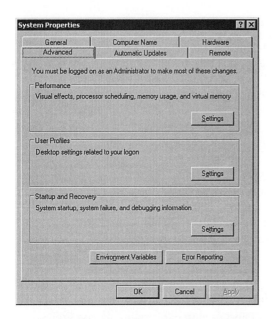

FIGURE 18.1   The Advanced tab of the System Properties dialog box.

> **TIP**
>
> If Access 2007 or Windows is running on a compressed drive, you can improve perfor-
> mance by moving the paging file to an uncompressed drive. If possible, the paging file
> should be located on a drive or partition solely dedicated to the paging file, or on a
> drive or partition that is accessed rarely by other applications. This helps to ensure
> that the entire paging file remains in a contiguous location on a disk.

Run Access and Your Application Locally

In Chapter 22, "Developing Multiuser and Enterprise Applications," you will learn that it is
best to install both the Access software and your application objects on each user's local
machine. You should store only the data tables on a network file server. Otherwise, you
will be sending dynamic link libraries (DLLs), object linking and embedding (OLE) objects,
help files, type libraries, executables, and database objects all over the network wire.

> **TIP**
>
> One viable option is to run Access 2007 using Windows 2003 Terminal Services. In
> this scenario, Access is installed on a powerful server machine running Windows 2003
> Terminal Services. Workstations connect to the terminal server using the Terminal
> Services Client utility. No data travels over the network wire. Each user becomes a
> session running on the server machine. All processing is done on the server machine.
> Keystrokes and mouse movements are sent from the client machine to the server,
> which processes them and sends a screen image back to the client.

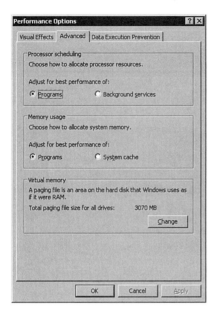

FIGURE 18.2   The Advanced tab of the Performance Options dialog box.

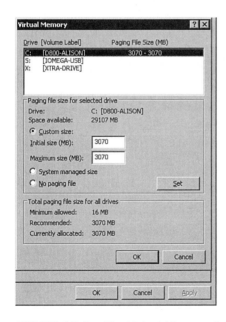

FIGURE 18.3   The Virtual Memory dialog box allows you to change paging file settings.

Do Everything You Can to Make Windows Itself Faster

I am always amused that the users with the slowest machines and the least memory have the most accessories running. These accessories include multimedia, fancy wallpapers, and other nifty utilities. If performance is a problem, you might try to see whether eliminating some of the frivolous niceties improves the performance of your application. If it does, encourage the user to eliminate the frills, get more memory, or accept your application's performance. Furthermore, if you are finished using other applications, such as Microsoft Excel, close them. This frees up system memory for Access.

If you have Windows XP, a tip to make it run faster is to shut down and restart on a regular basis. Memory tends to become fragmented, making applications run more slowly. Although I can go weeks or months in Windows 2003 Server without rebooting, I find it beneficial to reboot my Windows XP machine once a week.

Change Access's Software Settings

In addition to the more obvious measures just outlined, some minor software tweaking can go a long way toward improving performance. Adjusting several settings in the Windows Registry can dramatically improve performance. All these changes involve the Registry's ISAM section. The properties you might want to change include `MaxBufferSize` and `ReadAheadPages`. Both of these settings determine how the Jet Engine uses memory.

`MaxBufferSize` controls the maximum size of the Jet Engine's internal cache. By default, it is set to optimize performance on most machines. It does this by reading data in 2KB pages, placing the data in a memory cache. The data in the cache is readily available to forms, reports, tables, and queries. Lowering the value for `MaxBufferSize` frees memory for other tasks. Lowering the value might be helpful on a machine with a minimum memory configuration.

`ReadAheadPages` controls the number of 4KB data pages that the Jet Engine reads ahead when performing sequential page reads. This number can range from 0 to 31, with the default at 16. The higher this number is, the more efficient Access is at reading ahead so that data is available when you need it. The lower this number is, the more memory is freed up for other tasks.

As you configure any of these settings, remember that what is good for one machine is not necessarily good for the next. The settings for each machine must be optimized with its unique hardware configuration in mind.

What Is the Access Database Engine?

Introduced with Access 2007 is the *Access Database Engine*. This is the new name for *Jet*. It includes functionality required for the new Access 2007 feature set. This engine provides the functionality necessary for the integration with Microsoft Windows SharePoint Servers 3.0. It also allows for integration with Microsoft Office Outlook 2007. Finally, this new database engine allows you to create multivalued lookup fields.

Letting the Performance Analyzer Determine Problem Areas

You can make many changes to improve the performance of an application. Most of them require significant attention and expertise on your part. The Performance Analyzer is a tool that does some of that work for you. This tool analyzes the design of an Access application to suggest techniques you can use to improve the application's performance. Many of the techniques that the Performance Analyzer suggests can be implemented automatically.

To use the Performance Analyzer, click to select the Database Tools tab. Then select the Analyze Performance tool found in the Analyze group. The dialog box in Figure 18.4 appears.

FIGURE 18.4   The Performance Analyzer dialog box.

Select the individual tables, queries, forms, reports, macros, modules, and relationships that you want the Performance Analyzer to scrutinize. If you want Access to analyze the relationships, you must click the Current Database tab and then select Relationships. Make all your selections and click OK. When the Performance Analyzer completes the analysis process, the second part of the Performance Analyzer dialog box appears, as shown in Figure 18.5. This window provides you with a list of suggested improvements to the selected objects. The results are broken down into Recommendations, Suggestions, Ideas, and Fixed (meaning items that were automatically fixed). Suggested improvements will include enhancements such as the addition of an index or the conversion of an OLE object. After analyzing the CHAP18EX database included on the sample CD-ROM, for example, the Performance Analyzer suggested that Option Explicit be added to the basBenchMarks module.

18

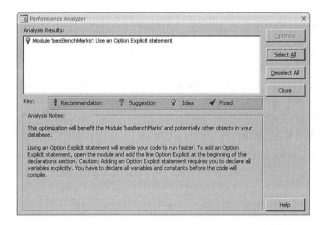

FIGURE 18.5   The second part of the Performance Analyzer dialog box.

Designing Tables to Optimize Performance

Now that you have seen the changes you can make to your environment to improve performance, take a look at the changes you can make to your data structures to optimize performance. Such changes include eliminating redundant data, using indexes, selecting appropriate field data types, and using various query techniques.

Tweaking the data structure is imperative for good performance. No matter what else you do, poor data design can dramatically degrade the performance of your application. All other optimization attempts are futile without proper attention to this area.

You can spend days and days optimizing your data. You must carefully think through and analyze these data changes. You will often make data changes over time as you or your users identify problems. Such changes can include those in the following sections.

Why Be Normal?

In essence, "be normal" means normalize your tables—that is, consolidate common data in related tables. Processing the same data that appears in multiple places can significantly slow down your application. This slowdown is the result of both the volume of data that is generated, as well as the need to update all copies of the data whenever the data changes. Suppose a company address appears in both the Customers table and the Orders table. If the company address changes, it must be changed in both the Customers table and in the Orders table. This information should be included only in the Customers table. Queries should be used to combine the address and order data when needed.

I Thought You Just Told Me to Normalize

When it comes to performance, unfortunately, there are no hard-and-fast rules. Although most of the time you gain performance by normalizing your data structure, denormalizing your structure can help at times. This generally is the case when you find yourself creating a particular join over and over again. Another example is an accounting application in which you need to be able to readily see the total amount that a customer owes. Instead of evaluating all the open invoices each time you move to a customer record, you can store the total amount that the customer owes on the customer record. Of course, this requires that you update the summarized figure whenever the customer is billed or makes a payment. In summary, you can try denormalizing the data to see whether dramatic performance improvements result. Remember that denormalization has definite downsides regarding data integrity and maintenance.

Index, Index, Index!

It is amazing how far an index can go toward improving performance. You should include any fields or combination of fields on which you search in an index. You should create indexes for all columns used in query joins, searches, and sorts. You should create primary key indexes rather than unique indexes, and unique indexes rather than nonunique indexes. It is not necessary to create an index for the foreign key field in a one-to-many relationship. Access automatically creates the index when you establish the relationship. Furthermore, there is no benefit to creating an index on a field containing highly repetitive data. An example is a state field in a customer table where all the customers are located in one of two states. Although you can overuse indexes, when you use them properly, the performance improvements rendered by indexes are profound.

> **CAUTION**
>
> Although indexes can dramatically improve performance, you should not create an index for every field in a table. Indexes do have their downside. Besides taking up disk space, they also slow down the process of adding, editing, and deleting data.

> **TIP**
>
> In a multiple-field index, index on as few fields as possible. Searching through multiple-field indexes can dramatically degrade performance.

> **NOTE**
>
> Client/server optimization strategies are covered in detail in *Alison Balter's Mastering Access 2002 Enterprise Development*.

18

Select the Correct Data Type

When defining a field, select the shortest data type available for the storage of the data. If you will be storing a code between 1 and 10 within the field, for example, there is no reason to select Double for a numeric field. Although Double would work, it would require unnecessary storage space as well as unnecessary processing time. On the other hand, make sure that you always leave room for growth of your data. For example, many people often select Integer, not realizing that they should have selected Long Integer.

Designing Database Objects to Improve Performance

There are many things that you can do to make queries, modules, forms, and reports run more efficiently. The sections that follow cover each of these objects in detail.

Optimizing the Performance of Your Queries

Optimizing your queries requires a great deal of practice and experimentation. Some queries involving a one-to-many relationship run more efficiently if you place the criteria on the "one" side of the relationship, for example. Others run more efficiently if you place the criteria on the "many" side. Understanding some basics can go a long way toward improving the performance of your queries and your application as a whole, as listed in the following:

▶ Include as few columns in the resultset as possible. This limits the data returned to the client if you ever convert your application to a client/server environment.

▶ Try to reduce the number of complex expressions contained in the query. Although including a complex expression in a query eliminates the need to build the expression into each form and report, the performance benefits gained sometimes are worth the trouble.

▶ Use the `Between` operator rather than greater than (>) and less than (<) operators. The Access Database Engine is able to process `Between` more efficiently.

▶ Group `Totals` queries by the field that is in the same table you are totaling. In other words, if you are totaling cost multiplied by price for each order in the `Order Detail` table, group by the order ID within the `Order Detail` table, not by the order ID within the `Orders` table. This reduces the number of rows that the Access Database Engine must process when running the query.

Now that you have seen what you can do with the design of your queries to improve performance, take a look at a couple of simple techniques you can use to improve the performance of your queries.

A simple but often neglected method of optimizing queries is to deliver your queries compiled. A query compiles when you open it in Datasheet view and then simply close it. If you modify a query and then save it, it is not compiled until the query runs. The Access Database Engine compiles all queries when you compact a database. Delivering precompiled queries ensures that they run as quickly as possible. It is therefore a good idea to compact a database before you distribute it to your users.

Finally, it is important that you compile your queries using the same amount of data that your application will contain. The reason is that the Access Database Engine's Query

Optimizer optimizes the query differently, depending on the amount of data it finds. If you build a query using 100 records that will run on a live table containing 100,000 records, the query will not be optimized properly. You must rerun and resave your query using the correct quantity of data if you want the query to be optimized properly, or you must compact the database after the live data has been entered.

Making Coding Changes to Improve Performance

No matter what you do to optimize the operating system environment and improve your data design, poor code can continue to bog you down. A properly optimized application is optimized in terms of the environment, data design, and code. Just as poor table design can degrade performance, poor coding techniques also can have a dramatic negative effect on performance. Changes to your code include eliminating variants and dead code, using built-in collections, and using specific object types. An important code-related optimization is to deliver your modules precompiled.

The following changes and techniques can aid in the improvement of performance. It is important to recognize that any one change won't make much of a difference. However, an accumulation of all the changes, especially where code is being re-executed in a loop, can make a significant impact on your application's performance.

Eliminate Variants and Use the Smallest Data Type Possible

Variant variables are the slowest for the operating system to process; they carry a lot of overhead because the compiler resolves them at runtime. Remember that this statement declares a variant type of variable:

```
Dim intCounter
```

To strong-type this variable as an integer, for example, you must modify your code to look like this:

```
Dim intCounter As Integer
```

Not only should you strong-type your variables, but you also should use the smallest data type possible. Remember that data types such as Boolean, Byte, Integer, and Long are the smallest and therefore the fastest to resolve. They are followed by Single, Double, Currency, and (finally) Variant. Of course, if you must store very large numbers with decimal points in a variable, you cannot pick Single. Just keep in mind that it is wise to select the smallest data type appropriate for the use of the variable. Listing 18.1 provides code that illustrates the difference between using a variant and a long integer.

LISTING 18.1   Data Type Benchmark Illustrating the Effect of Data Type on Performance

```
Private Sub cmdVariantBenchMark_Click()
    Dim vntAny
    Dim intCounter As Long
    Dim dblStartTime As Double
    Dim dblTime1 As Double
```

18

LISTING 18.1   Continued

```
    Dim dblTime2 As Double

    'Execute loop with variant
    dblStartTime = Timer

    Do Until vntAny = 500000
        vntAny = vntAny + 1
    Loop

    dblTime1 = Timer - dblStartTime

    'Execute loop with integer
    dblStartTime = Timer

    Do Until intCounter = 500000
        intCounter = intCounter + 1
    Loop

    dblTime2 = Timer - dblStartTime

    'Display time and percent differences
    Me.txtSlow = dblTime1
    Me.txtOptimized = dblTime2
    Me.txtPercent = (1 - (dblTime1 / dblTime2)) * 100

End Sub
```

The code, found in the form frmBenchmark in the CHAP18EX.ACCDB sample database, loops using a variant and then a long integer. The example displays the amount of time required to execute each loop, along with the percent difference between the two techniques.

Use Specific Object Types

Just as using the General variant data type is inefficient, using generic object variables also is inefficient. The reason is that the compiler needs to evaluate their type at runtime. The MakeItBold subroutine uses a generic object variable, as shown in Listing 18.2.

LISTING 18.2   The MakeItBold Subroutine

```
Private Sub cmdMakeBold_Click()
    Call MakeItBold(Screen.PreviousControl)
End Sub

Sub MakeItBold(ctlAny As Control)
    ctlAny.FontBold = True
End Sub
```

> **NOTE**
>
> The code in Listing 18.2 is overly simplified. It contains no error handling. The control passed as `Screen.PreviousControl` could be any type of control. The type of control received by the `MakeItBold` routine might not have a `FontBold` property, in which case an error occurs. It is therefore important for either one or both of these routines to contain proper error handling.

On the other hand, the `SpecificBold` subroutine uses a specific object variable, as Listing 18.3 shows.

LISTING 18.3   The `SpecificBold` Subroutine

```
Private Sub cmdSpecificBold_Click()
    Call SpecificBold(Screen.PreviousControl)
End Sub

Sub SpecificBold(txtAny As TextBox)
    txtAny.FontBold = True
End Sub
```

The difference is that the `SpecificBold` routine expects to receive only text boxes. It does not need to resolve the type of object it receives and therefore is more efficient.

This code is contained in the `CHAP18EX.ACCDB` database on the accompanying CD-ROM. You can find the example in the form called `frmObjVar`.

The best way to truly compare using a specific control versus a generic control is to benchmark the techniques, as shown in Listing 18.4.

LISTING 18.4   Object Type Benchmark Compares Using a Specific Control and a Generic Control

```
Private Sub cmdObjectTypes_Click()
    Dim intCounter As Long
    Dim dblStartTime As Double
    Dim dblTime1 As Double
    Dim dblTime2 As Double

    'Execute loop with generic control
    dblStartTime = Timer

    For intCounter = 1 To 5000
        Call MakeItBold(Me.txtOptimized)
    Next intCounter

    dblTime1 = Timer - dblStartTime
```

18

LISTING 18.4   Continued

```
    'Execute loop with specific control
    dblStartTime = Timer

    For intCounter = 1 To 5000
        Call SpecificBold(Me.txtOptimized)
    Next intCounter

    dblTime2 = Timer - dblStartTime

    'Display time and percent differences
    Me.txtSlow = dblTime1
    Me.txtOptimized = dblTime2
    Me.txtPercent = (1 - (dblTime1 / dblTime2)) * 100


End Sub
```

The code, found in the form called frmBenchmark, passes a text box to two different routines. The first routine receives any control as a parameter. The second routine receives only text boxes as a parameter. The benchmarks prove that routines that use specific object types take less time and are therefore more efficient.

Use Inline Code
There is a tendency to call out to procedures for everything. These calls are good from a maintenance standpoint, but not from an efficiency standpoint. Each time VBA calls out to a procedure, it takes additional time to locate and execute the procedure. This is particularly evident when the procedure is called numerous times. The alternative is to use inline code. Executing inline code is more efficient than calling out to procedures because Access does not need to locate the code. The downside of inline code is that it is more difficult to maintain. You must decide how important maintainability is compared to speed.

Listing 18.5 shows the same code called as a routine and executed inline. The benchmark shows that the inline code executes much more quickly.

LISTING 18.5   Inline Code Benchmark

```
Private Sub cmdInLine_Click()
    Dim dblAny As Double
    Dim intCounter As Long
    Dim dblStartTime As Double
    Dim dblTime1 As Double
    Dim dblTime2 As Double
```

LISTING 18.5   Continued

```
    'Execute loop calling out to procedure
    dblStartTime = Timer

    For intCounter = 1 To 500000
        Call SmallRoutine
    Next intCounter

    dblTime1 = Timer - dblStartTime

    'Execute loop with inline code
    dblStartTime = Timer

    For intCounter = 1 To 500000
        dblAny = 5 / 3
    Next intCounter

    dblTime2 = Timer - dblStartTime

    'Display time and percent differences
    Me.txtSlow = dblTime1
    Me.txtOptimized = dblTime2
    Me.txtPercent = (1 - (dblTime1 / dblTime2)) * 100
End Sub

Private Sub SmallRoutine()
    Dim dblAny As Double
    dblAny = 5 / 3
End Sub
```

Toggle Booleans Using Not

This code is very inefficient:

```
If bFlag = True Then
  bFlag = False
Else
    bFlag = True
End If
```

You should modify it to look like this:

```
bFlag = Not bFlag
```

Besides requiring fewer lines of code, this expression evaluates much more quickly at
runtime. Listing 18.6 proves that toggling the Boolean variable is a much more efficient

approach to the problem than having to test each condition separately. You can find this code in the form called `frmBenchmark` on the CD-ROM accompanying this book.

LISTING 18.6   Toggling Boolean Benchmark

```
Private Sub cmdBooleans_Click()
    Dim boolAny As Boolean
    Dim intCounter As Long
    Dim dblStartTime As Double
    Dim dblTime1 As Double
    Dim dblTime2 As Double

    'Execute loop with If statement
    dblStartTime = Timer

    For intCounter = 1 To 1000000
        If boolAny = True Then
            boolAny = False
        Else
            boolAny = True
        End If
    Next intCounter

    dblTime1 = Timer - dblStartTime

    'Execute loop toggling Boolean
    dblStartTime = Timer

    For intCounter = 1 To 1000000
        boolAny = Not boolAny
    Next intCounter

    dblTime2 = Timer - dblStartTime

    'Display time and percent differences
    Me.txtSlow = dblTime1
    Me.txtOptimized = dblTime2
    Me.txtPercent = (1 - (dblTime1 / dblTime2)) * 100

End Sub
```

Use the Built-In Collections
The built-in collections are available whether or not you use them. By using `For Each...Next` and a collection of objects, you can write efficient code, as shown in Listing 18.7.

LISTING 18.7   Using For Each...Next

```
Sub FormCaption()
    Dim frm As Form
    For Each frm In Forms
        frm.Caption = frm.Caption & " - " & CurrentUser()
    Next
End Sub
```

In this example, you use the Forms collection to quickly and efficiently loop through each form, changing the caption on its title bar. The code shown in Listing 18.8 illustrates the use of the Forms collection, as well as an alternative method of accomplishing the same task.

LISTING 18.8   For Each...Next Benchmark

```
Private Sub cmdCollections_Click()
    Dim frm As Form
    Dim intNumForms As Integer
    Dim intLoop As Integer
    Dim intCounter As Long
    Dim dblStartTime As Double
    Dim dblTime1 As Double
    Dim dblTime2 As Double

    'Execute loop with For Next
    dblStartTime = Timer

    For intCounter = 1 To 500
        intNumForms = Forms.Count - 1
        For intLoop = 0 To intNumForms
            Forms(intLoop).Caption = "Hello"
        Next intLoop
    Next intCounter

    dblTime1 = Timer - dblStartTime

    'Execute loop with For Each
    dblStartTime = Timer

    For intCounter = 1 To 500
        For Each frm In Forms
            frm.Caption = "Hello"
        Next frm
    Next intCounter
```

18

818   CHAPTER 18   Optimizing Your Application

LISTING 18.8   Continued

```
    dblTime2 = Timer - dblStartTime

    'Display time and percent differences
    Me.txtSlow = dblTime1
    Me.txtOptimized = dblTime2
    Me.txtPercent = (1 - (dblTime1 / dblTime2)) * 100
End Sub
```

Without the For Each..Next loop, you must use a variable to loop through the forms. Notice that the code sets intNumForms equal to the number of forms in the Forms collection minus one. The loop goes from zero to the value stored in intNumForms, changing the caption of the specified form. Although the performance gains realized by using the Forms collection are not dramatic, the Forms collection technique is much simpler to implement.

Use the Len Function

Using the Len function (as shown in Listing 18.9) is more efficient than testing for a zero-length string (as shown in Listing 18.10).

LISTING 18.9   Using the Len Function

```
Sub SayNameLen(strName As String)
    If Len(strName) Then
        MsgBox strName
    End If
End Sub
```

LISTING 18.10   Testing for a Zero-Length String

```
Sub SayNameZero(strName As String)
    If strName <> "" Then
        MsgBox strName
    End If
End Sub
```

Listing 18.9 is easier for VBA to evaluate and therefore runs more quickly and efficiently. This point is emphasized by the code shown in Listing 18.11 (located in the form frmBenchmark). The code shows two loops. One uses the Len function, and the other does not. The benchmark proves that the routine that uses the Len function executes more quickly.

LISTING 18.11   Len Benchmark

```
Private Sub cmdLen_Click()
    Dim dblStartTime As Double
    Dim dblTime1 As Double
    Dim dblTime2 As Double
    Dim strTextBoxValue As String

    strTextBoxValue = Me.txtOptimized

    'Execute loop with zero-length string
    dblStartTime = Timer

    For intCounter = 1 To 500000
        If strTextBoxValue <> "" Then
        End If
    Next intCounter

    dblTime1 = Timer - dblStartTime

    'Execute loop with Len
    dblStartTime = Timer

    For intCounter = 1 To 500000
        If Len(strTextBoxValue) Then
        End If
    Next intCounter

    dblTime2 = Timer - dblStartTime

    'Display time and percent differences
    Me.txtSlow = dblTime1
    Me.txtOptimized = dblTime2
    Me.txtPercent = (1 - (dblTime1 / dblTime2)) * 100

End Sub
```

Use True **and** False **Instead of** 0
This example is similar to the preceding one. It is better to evaluate for True and False (as shown in Listing 18.12) instead of 0 (as shown in Listing 18.13).

18

LISTING 18.12   Evaluating for True and False

```
Sub SaySalaryTrue(lngSalary As Long)
    If lngSalary Then
        MsgBox "Salary is " & lngSalary
    End If
End Sub
```

LISTING 18.13   Evaluating for 0

```
Sub SaySalaryZero(lngSalary As Long)
    If lngSalary <> 0 Then
        MsgBox "Salary is " & lngSalary
    End If
End Sub
```

The code in Listing 18.12 runs more efficiently. The benchmark shown in Listing 18.14 provides an example. The lngSalary variable is evaluated against zero in the top loop. The bottom loop tests lngSalary against True. The second loop runs more quickly.

LISTING 18.14   True/False Benchmark

```
Private Sub cmdTrueFalse_Click()

    On Error Resume Next

    Dim intCounter As Long
    Dim lngSalary As Long
    Dim dblStartTime As Double
    Dim dblTime1 As Double
    Dim dblTime2 As Double

    'Execute loop with zero
    dblStartTime = Timer

    For intCounter = 1 To 500000
        If lngSalary <> 0 Then
        End If
    Next intCounter

    dblTime1 = Timer - dblStartTime

    'Execute loop with True/False
    dblStartTime = Timer
```

LISTING 18.14   Continued

```
    For intCounter = 1 To 500000
        If lngSalary Then
        End If
    Next intCounter


    dblTime2 = Timer - dblStartTime


    'Display time and percent differences
    Me.txtSlow = dblTime1
    Me.txtOptimized = dblTime2
    Me.txtPercent = (1 - (dblTime1 / dblTime2)) * 100


End Sub
```

Eliminate Unused Dim and Declare Statements

As you modify your subroutines and functions, you often declare a variable and then
never use it. Each Dim statement takes up memory, whether or not you are using it.
Furthermore, Declare statements, which you use to call external library functions,
also take up memory and resources. You should remove these statements if you are not
using them.

Eliminate Unused Code

Most programmers experiment with various alternatives for accomplishing a task. These
experiments often involve creating numerous test subroutines and functions. The
problem is that most people do not remove this code when they are done with it. This
dead code is loaded with your application and therefore takes up memory and resources.
Several third-party tools are available that can help you find both dead code and variable
declarations.

Use Variables to Refer to Properties, Controls, and Data Access Objects

If you are going to repeatedly refer to an object, you should declare an object and refer to
the object variable rather than the actual control, as shown in Listing 18.15.

LISTING 18.15   Declaring an Object and Referring to the Object Variable

```
Forms!frmAny.txtHello.FontBold = True
Forms!frmAny.txtHello.Enabled = True
Forms!frmAny.txtHello.Left = 1
Forms!frmAny.txtHello.Top = 1
```

This is a scaled-down example, but if numerous properties are being changed, or if this
code is being called recursively, an object variable can make the code more efficient, as
Listing 18.16 shows.

18

LISTING 18.16   Using an Object Variable to Make Your Code More Efficient

```
Private Sub cmdChangeObject_Click()
    Dim txt As TextBox
    Set txt = Forms!frmHello.txtHello1
    txt.FontBold = True
    txt.Enabled = True
    txt.Left = 100
    txt.Top = 100
End Sub
```

The benchmark shown in Listing 18.17 contains two loops. The first loop sets four prop-erties of the same control, explicitly referencing the control as each property is set. The second loop uses an object variable to accomplish the same task. The difference in perfor-mance between the two loops is somewhat dramatic.

LISTING 18.17   Object Variable Benchmark

```
Private Sub cmdObjectVariable_Click()
    Dim intCounter As Long
    Dim dblStartTime As Double
    Dim dblTime1 As Double
    Dim dblTime2 As Double

    'Execute loop without object variable
    dblStartTime = Timer

    For intCounter = 1 To 1000
        Forms.frmBenchMark.txtOptimized.FontBold = True
        Forms.frmBenchMark.txtOptimized.Enabled = True
        Forms.frmBenchMark.txtOptimized.Locked = False
        Forms.frmBenchMark.txtOptimized.BackStyle = vbNormal
    Next intCounter

    dblTime1 = Timer - dblStartTime

    'Execute loop with object variable
    dblStartTime = Timer

    For intCounter = 1 To 1000
        Dim txt As TextBox
        Set txt = Forms.frmBenchMark.txtOptimized
        txt.FontBold = True
        txt.Enabled = True
        txt.Locked = False
```

LISTING 18.17   Continued

```
        txt.BackStyle = vbNormal
    Next intCounter

    dblTime2 = Timer - dblStartTime

    'Display time and percent differences
    Me.txtSlow = dblTime1
    Me.txtOptimized = dblTime2
    Me.txtPercent = (1 - (dblTime1 / dblTime2)) * 100


End Sub
```

Use With...End With

Another way to optimize the code in the preceding example is to use a With...End With
construct, as shown in Listing 18.18.

LISTING 18.18   Using With...End With

```
Private Sub cmdChangeObjectWith_Click()
    With Forms!frmHello.txtHello2
        .FontBold = True
        .Enabled = True
        .Left = 100
        .Top = 100
    End With
End Sub
```

The code in Listing 18.19 shows two different loops. The first loop explicitly references
the text box four different times to set four different properties. The second loop uses a
With statement to reference the same control and set the four properties. The code in the
second loop executes much more efficiently.

LISTING 18.19   Object Variable Resolution Benchmark

```
Private Sub cmdWith_Click()
    Dim intCounter As Long
    Dim dblStartTime As Double
    Dim dblTime1 As Double
    Dim dblTime2 As Double

    'Execute loop without With statement
    dblStartTime = Timer
```

LISTING 18.19   Continued

```
    For intCounter = 1 To 1000
        Forms.frmBenchMark.txtOptimized.FontBold = True
        Forms.frmBenchMark.txtOptimized.Enabled = True
        Forms.frmBenchMark.txtOptimized.Locked = False
        Forms.frmBenchMark.txtOptimized.BackStyle = vbNormal
    Next intCounter

    dblTime1 = Timer - dblStartTime

    'Execute loop with With statement
    dblStartTime = Timer

    For intCounter = 1 To 1000
        With Forms.frmBenchMark.txtOptimized
            .FontBold = True
            .Enabled = True
            .Locked = False
            .BackStyle = vbNormal
        End With
    Next intCounter

    dblTime2 = Timer - dblStartTime

    'Display time and percent differences
    Me.txtSlow = dblTime1
    Me.txtOptimized = dblTime2
    Me.txtPercent = (1 - (dblTime1 / dblTime2)) * 100

End Sub
```

Resolve Variables Outside a Loop

Although both the object variable reference and the With statement significantly improve performance, Listings 18.17 and 18.19 can be further improved by resolving the object variable outside the loop whenever possible. Listing 18.20 provides an example.

LISTING 18.20   Resolving the Object Variable Outside the Loop

```
Private Sub cmdVariable_Click()
    Dim txtAny As TextBox
    Dim intCounter As Long
    Dim dblStartTime As Double
    Dim dblTime1 As Double
    Dim dblTime2 As Double
```

LISTING 18.20   Continued

```
'Execute loop without object resolution
dblStartTime = Timer

For intCounter = 1 To 1000
    Forms.frmBenchmark.txtOptimized.FontBold = True
    Forms.frmBenchmark.txtOptimized.Enabled = True
    Forms.frmBenchmark.txtOptimized.Locked = False
    Forms.frmBenchmark.txtOptimized.BackStyle = vbNormal
Next intCounter

dblTime1 = Timer - dblStartTime

'Execute loop with object resolution
dblStartTime = Timer

Set txtAny = Forms.frmBenchmark.txtOptimized
For intCounter = 1 To 1000
    With txtAny
        .FontBold = True
        .Enabled = True
        .Locked = False
        .BackStyle = vbNormal
    End With
Next intCounter

dblTime2 = Timer - dblStartTime

'Display time and percent differences
Me.txtSlow = dblTime1
Me.txtOptimized = dblTime2
Me.txtPercent = (1 - (dblTime1 / dblTime2)) * 100
End Sub
```

Notice that the object variable is resolved outside the loop. This loop executes significantly faster than the loops in Listings 18.17 and 18.19.

Use the Me Keyword

The preceding example uses Forms!frmHello.txtHello to refer to a control on the current form. It is more efficient to refer to the control as Me.txtHello because VBA searches only in the local name space. Although this makes your code more efficient, the downside is that the Me keyword works only within form, report, and class modules. It won't work within standard code modules. This means that you cannot include the Me keyword in generic functions that are accessed by all your forms.

Use Dynamic Arrays

Array elements take up memory, whether or not you use them. It's therefore sometimes preferable to use dynamic arrays. You can increase the size of a dynamic array as necessary. If you want to reclaim the space used by all the elements of the array, you can use the Erase keyword, as in this example:

```
Erase aNames
```

If you want to reclaim some of the space being used by the array without destroying data in the elements you want to retain, use Redim Preserve:

```
Redim Preserve aNames(5)
```

This statement sizes the array to six elements (it's zero-based). Data within those six elements is retained.

> **CAUTION**
>
> You must be careful when using dynamic arrays with Redim Preserve. When you resize an array using Redim Preserve, the entire array is copied in memory. If you are running in a low-memory environment, this can mean that virtual disk space is used, which slows performance—or worse than that, the application can fail if both physical and virtual memory are exhausted.

Use Constants When They Are Available

Constants improve both readability and performance. A constant's value is resolved after compilation. The value that the constant represents is written to code. A normal variable has to be resolved as the code is running because VBA needs to obtain the current value of the variable.

Use Bookmarks

A bookmark provides you with the most rapid access to a record. If you are planning to return to a record, set a variable equal to that record's bookmark, making it easy to return to that record at any time. Listing 18.21 shows an example that uses a bookmark.

LISTING 18.21   Using a Bookmark

```
Sub BookMarkIt()
    Dim rst As ADODB.Recordset
    Set rst = New ADODB.Recordset

    Dim varBM As Variant

    rst.Open "tblProjects", CurrentProject.Connection, adOpenStatic
    varBM = rst.Bookmark
    Do Until rst.EOF
```

LISTING 18.21   Continued

```
        Debug.Print rst!ProjectID
        rst.MoveNext
    Loop
    rst.Bookmark = varBM
    Debug.Print rst!ProjectID
End Sub
```

You can find this code in basOptimize of CHAP18EX.ACCDB. The code stores the bookmark in a variable until the Do...Until loop executes. Then the code sets the recordset's bookmark equal to the value contained within the variable.

Set Object Variables Equal to Nothing

Object variables take up memory and associated resources. Their value should be set to Nothing when you are finished using them. For example:

```
Set oObj = Nothing
```

Setting variables this way conserves memory and resources.

Use Action Queries Instead of Looping Through Recordsets

Besides being easier to code, executing a stored query is much more efficient than looping through a recordset, performing some action on each record. Listing 18.22 shows an example that loops through a recordset.

LISTING 18.22   Looping Through a Recordset

```
Sub LoopThrough()
    Dim rst As ADODB.Recordset
    Set rst = New ADODB.Recordset

    rst.Open "tblProjects", CurrentProject.Connection, adOpenDynamic, _
    adLockOptimistic
    Do Until rst.EOF
        rst!ProjectTotalEstimate = rst!ProjectTotalEstimate + 1
        rst.UPDATE
        rst.MoveNext
    Loop
End Sub
```

This code, which is located in basOptimize of CHAP18EX.ACCDB, loops through a recordset, adding 1 to each project's total estimate. Contrast this with the code in Listing 18.23.

LISTING 18.23   Executing a Stored Query

```
Sub ExecuteQuery()
    Dim adoCat As ADOX.Catalog
    Dim cmd As ADODB.Command
    Set adoCat = New ADOX.Catalog
    Set cmd = New ADODB.Command

    Set adoCat.ActiveConnection = CurrentProject.Connection
    Set cmd = adoCat.Procedures("qupdLowerEstimate").Command
    cmd.Execute

End Sub
```

This code uses a command object to execute a stored query called qupdLowerEstimate. The query runs much more efficiently than the Do...Until loop shown in Listing 18.22.

> **NOTE**
>
> The most efficient method to update records is to use a stored procedure. You can use stored procedures with a client/server database engine such as Microsoft SQL Server. This issue is covered in detail in *Alison Balter's Mastering Access 2002 Enterprise Development*.

Deliver Your Application with the Modules Compiled

Applications run slower when they are not compiled. Forms and reports load slower, and the application requires more memory. If you deliver your application with all the modules compiled, they do not need to be compiled on the user's machine before they run.

To easily recompile all modules, choose Debug, Compile with the Visual Basic Editor (VBE) active. This command opens and compiles all code in the application, including the code behind forms and reports. It then saves the modules in the compiled state, preserving the compiled state of the application.

Retain the Compiled State

Don't bother choosing the Debug, Compile command if you plan to make additional changes to the application. An application becomes decompiled whenever you modify the application's controls, forms, reports, or modules. Even something as simple as changing a single line of code causes the application to lose its compiled state. It's therefore important to choose the Debug, Compile command immediately before you distribute the application.

CAUTION

Renaming a database file causes the code contained in the database to decompile. It's therefore important to always choose the Compile command after renaming a database.

Distribute Your Application as an ACCDE

The process of creating an ACCDE file compiles all modules, removes editable source code, and compacts the destination database. All Visual Basic code will run but cannot be viewed or edited. This improves performance, reduces the size of the database, and protects your intellectual property. Memory use also is improved.

Organize Your Modules

VBA code theoretically can be placed in any module within your application. The problem is that the compiler does not load a module until you call a function within it. After you call a single procedure in a module, the compiler loads the entire module into memory. Furthermore, if a single variable within a module is used, the compiler loads the entire module into memory. As you might imagine, if you design your application without much thought, every module in your application will be loaded.

If you place similar routines in one module, that module will be loaded, and others will not. This means that if people are using only part of the functionality of your application, they will never be loading other code modules. This conserves memory and therefore optimizes your application.

Designing Forms and Reports to Improve Performance

You can do several things to forms and reports to improve your application's performance. They include techniques to quickly load the forms and reports, tips and tricks regarding OLE objects, and special coding techniques that apply only to forms and reports.

Designing Forms

Because forms are your main interface to your user, making them as efficient as possible can go a long way toward improving the user's perception of your application's performance. Additionally, many of the form techniques are extremely easy to implement.

Form-optimization techniques can be categorized in two ways: those that make the forms load more quickly and those that enable you to more efficiently manipulate objects within the form.

The larger a form and the more controls and objects you have placed on it, the less efficient that form is. Make sure that controls on the form do not overlap. It also is extremely beneficial to group form data onto logical pages. Grouping is especially important if your users have insufficient video RAM. Objects on subsequent pages should not be populated until the user moves to that page.

18

Forms and their controls should be based on saved queries or embedded SQL statements. Include only fields required by the form in the form's underlying query. Avoid using `Select *` queries; because Access is so efficient at internally optimizing the manipulation of query results, this improves the performance of your forms. To further take advantage of the power of queries, reduce the number of records that the query returns, loading only the records you need at a particular time.

If you will use a form solely to add new records, set the `DataEntry` property of the form to `Yes` so that it opens to a blank record. This step is necessary because, otherwise, Access must read all records to display the blank record at the end of the recordset.

Avoid bitmaps and other graphics objects if possible. If you must display an image, it is important to remember that OLE objects take far more resources than images. If an OLE bitmapped object does not need to be changed, convert it to an image. To accomplish this, right-click the object and choose Change To, Image.

Avoid the use of subforms whenever possible. Access treats a subform as a separate form. It therefore takes up significant memory. Make sure that all fields in a subform that are either linked to the main form or used for criteria are indexed. Make sure that only necessary fields are included in the record source of the subform. If the data in the subform does not need to be edited, set its `AllowEdits`, `AllowAdditions`, and `AllowDeletions` properties to `No` or set its `RecordsetType` property to `Snapshot`.

Make sure that the `RowSource` for a combo box includes only the columns needed for the combo box. Index on the first field that appears in the combo box. This technique has a dramatic effect on the speed at which a user can move to an element of the combo box. Also, whenever possible, make the first visible field of a combo box a text field. Access converts numeric fields to text as it searches through the combo box to find a matching value. Finally, don't base list boxes or combo boxes on linked data if that data rarely, if ever, changes. Instead, make the static table local, updating it whenever necessary.

As a general rule regarding the performance of forms, place all database objects, except data, on each user's machine. This way, you eliminate the need for Access to constantly pull object definitions over the network.

Close forms that no longer are being used. This action is necessary because open forms take up memory and resources, degrading performance.

Another tip that can help you dramatically improve the performance of your forms is to use the default formatting and properties for as many controls as possible. By doing this, you significantly improve performance because only the form and control properties that differ from the default properties are saved with the form.

> **TIP**
>
> If most controls have a set of properties that are different from those of the default control for the form, you should change the default control and then add controls based on the default. Access saves only the properties of the default control and does not need to store the properties for each control placed on the form. Taking this step can result in dramatic performance improvements. Changing the default control is covered in Chapter 10, "Advanced Form Techniques."

Finally, eliminate the code module from forms that don't need it. A form without a code module loads more quickly and occupies less disk space. You can still call function procedures from an event property using an expression, or you can navigate about your application from the form using hyperlinks. You can remove the module associated with a form by setting the HasModule property to No.

Designing Reports

Many of the report-optimization techniques are the same as the form-optimization techniques. Reducing the number of controls, avoiding overlapping controls, basing reports on queries, avoiding OLE objects, and converting unbound object frames that display graphics to image controls are all techniques that improve the performance of reports as well as forms.

You can use a few additional techniques to specifically improve the performance of reports. Eliminate any unnecessary sorting and grouping expressions, and index all fields on which you sort or group. Base subreports on queries rather than on tables, and include only necessary fields in the queries. Make sure that the queries underlying the report are optimized and that you index all fields in the subreport that are linked to the main report.

A special technique that you can use to improve the performance of reports involves the No Data event and the HasData property. The No Data event is fired when a report is opened, and no data is returned by the record source of the report. The HasData property is used to determine whether a report is bound to an empty recordset. If the HasData property of a subreport is False, you can hide the subreport, thereby improving performance.

Practical Examples: Improving the Performance of Your Applications

To ensure that your applications are optimized, you can take several steps:

▶ Make sure that the database is compacted.

▶ Use the Performance Analyzer to analyze the application and make recommendations for improvement.

▶ Choose Debug, Compile from the VBE before distributing the application.

Summary

The most attractive application can be extremely frustrating to use if its performance is less than acceptable. Because Access itself requires significant resources, you must take the responsibility of making your code as lean and efficient as possible.

This chapter focused on several techniques for improving performance. Probably one of the easiest ways to improve performance is to modify the hardware and software environment within which Access operates. You learned about adding RAM, defragmenting a hard disk, and tuning virtual memory and other settings to dramatically improve the performance of your applications. You also looked at using the Performance Analyzer to quickly and easily identify problem areas in your application. Finally, the chapter focused on data-design fundamentals, coding techniques, and techniques to optimize forms and reports.

By following the guidelines covered in this chapter, you can help ensure that you are not inadvertently introducing bottlenecks into your application. Although any one of the suggestions included in this chapter might not make a difference by itself, the combined effects of these performance enhancements can be quite dramatic.

PART III

Developing Multiuser and Enterprise Applications

IN THIS PART

A Strategy to Developing Access Applications

Why This Chapter Is Important

You should know about several tricks of the trade that can save you a lot of time in the development process and help ensure that your applications are as optimized as possible for performance. This chapter addresses these strategies. You should keep all the topics covered in this chapter in mind when developing your Access applications. When reading this chapter, think of the general strategy outlined rather than the details of each topic. I cover each topic in depth in other chapters of the book.

Splitting Databases into Tables and Other Objects

When earlier versions of Access ran in a multiuser environment, it was imperative that you placed the system's tables in one database and the rest of the system objects in another database. With the advent of replication, you could either split the tables from the other objects or use replication to deploy design changes without compromising live data. Access 2000, Access 2002, and Access 2003 took this a step further with the Access Data Project (ADP), in which Access stores tables, views, stored procedures, and data diagrams in a SQL Server database or the SQL Server 2000 Desktop Engine (formerly the Microsoft Database Engine, or MSDE). Access stored forms, reports, macros, and modules in the ADP file.

Access 2007 creates an entirely new scenario. The new Access file format (.accdb) does not support replication. The ADP file is supported for backward compatibility only. Therefore, splitting tables from other system objects is a viable solution. For simplicity, I'll refer to the database containing the tables as the Table database and the database with the other objects as the Application database. Linking from the Application database to the Table database connects the two databases. This strategy enhances

▶ Maintainability

▶ Performance

▶ Scalability

Assume for a moment that you distribute your application as one ACCDB file. Your users work with your application for a week or two, writing down all problems and changes. It's time for you to make modifications to your application. Meanwhile, the users have entered live data into the application for two weeks. You make a copy of the database (which includes the live data) and make all the fixes and changes. This process takes a week. You're ready to install your copy of the database on the network. Now what? The users of the application have been adding, editing, and deleting records all week. You are left with the task of integrating your application changes with the users' data.

The simplest solution is to split the database objects so that the tables containing your data are in one ACCDB file, and the rest of your database objects (your application) are in a second ACCDB file. When you're ready to install the changes, all you need to do is copy the Application database to the file server. You can then install the new Application database on each client machine from the file server. In this way, users can run new copies of the application from their machines. The database containing your data tables will remain intact and be unaffected by the process. (Of course, this is possible only if you finalize your table structure before splitting the database.)

The second benefit of splitting the database objects is performance. Your Table database obviously needs to reside on the network file server so that the users can share the data; however, there's no good reason why the users need to share the other database components. Access gives you optimal performance if you store the Application database on each local machine. This method also significantly reduces network traffic, and it decreases the chance of database corruption. If you store the Application database on the file server, Access will need to send the application objects and code over the network each time the user opens an object in the database. If you store the Application database on each local machine, Access needs to send only the data over the network. The only complication to this scenario is that each time you update the Application database, you will need to redistribute it to the users. Even on an already overtaxed network, this is a small inconvenience compared to the performance benefits your users will gain from this structural split.

The third benefit of splitting tables from the other database objects is scalability. Because you have already linked the tables, you can easily change from a link to a table stored in Access's own proprietary format to any database that supports ODBC (such as Microsoft

SQL Server). This capability gives you quick-and-dirty access to client/server databases. If you have already thought through your system's design with linked tables in mind, the transition will be that much easier. Don't be fooled, though, by how easy this process sounds. Many issues associated with using Access as a front end to client/server data go far beyond simply linking to the external tables. This chapter and Chapter 22, "Developing Multiuser and Enterprise Applications," cover some of these issues. *Alison Balter's Mastering Access 2002 Enterprise Development* covers client/server development techniques in extensive detail.

> **TIP**
>
> You should store a few special types of tables in the Application database rather than the Table database. You should store tables that rarely change in the Application database on each user's local machine. For example, a State table rarely, if ever, changes, but your application continually accesses it to populate combo boxes, participate in queries, and so on. Placing the State table on each local machine therefore improves performance and reduces network traffic. You should place lookup tables containing localized information, such as department codes, in the Application database.
>
> You should also place temporary tables on each local machine; this is more a necessity than an option. If two users are running the same process at the same time and that process uses temporary tables, a conflict occurs when one user overwrites the other's temporary tables. Placing temporary tables on each local machine improves performance and eliminates the chance of potentially disastrous conflicts.

> **NOTE**
>
> I split all the applications I build into two databases. However, you might notice when looking at the sample databases in this book that, until you reach Chapter 20, "Using External Data," none of the chapters show databases split in the manner I recommend. The reason is that, until you learn all you need to know about splitting database objects, I don't think it's helpful to be working with a split sample database. From Chapter 20 on, however, each chapter offers some sample databases split according to the strategy recommended here.

Basing Forms and Reports on Queries or Embedded SQL Statements

You can base the record source for a form or report on a table object, a query object, or a SQL statement. By basing forms and reports on stored queries or embedded SQL statements, you can improve the performance and flexibility of your applications. In most cases, you don't need to display all fields and all records on a form or report. By basing a form or report on a query or embedded SQL statement, you can better limit the data transferred over the network. These benefits are most pronounced in a client/server environment. When you base a form or report on a table object, Access sends a SQL statement that retrieves all fields and all records from the database server. On the other hand, if the record source for the form or report is a query or embedded SQL statement, the server returns to the workstation just the fields and records specified within the query.

An Access 2007 form or report based on a stored query or SQL statement is very efficient. This is the case because when you save a query (or in the case of an embedded SQL statement, the form or report), the Access Database Engine creates a Query Plan. This plan contains information on the most efficient method of executing the query. When you save a query or form or report based on an embedded SQL statement, the Access Database Engine looks at the volume of data and the available indexes, determines the optimal method of executing the query, and stores the method as the Query Plan. The Microsoft Database Engine uses this plan whenever it executes a query underlying a form or report. It is up to you whether you use a stored query or an embedded SQL statement as the foundation for your forms and reports. There are advantages and disadvantages to each method. With a stored query, the upside is that multiple forms and reports can use the same query. The downside is that you have another object to manage in the Navigation Pane. With an embedded SQL statement, the advantage is that the SQL is stored neatly with the form or report that it is associated with. The downside is that if multiple forms and reports share the same SQL statement, you will need to maintain each separately. My rule is that, when I feel that the query will be reused by other forms and reports, I create a query. When I feel that the query is unique to the form or report I am creating, I create an embedded SQL statement.

When you base a form on table data, you can't control the order of the records in the form, nor can you base the form on more than one table. You can't limit the records that the form displays until the user opens the form. If you base a form on a query or an embedded SQL statement, you can control the criteria for the form as well as the default order in which the form displays the records.

Everything just mentioned applies to reports as well, except the order of the records, which you determine by how the report itself is sorted and grouped.

> **TIP**
>
> Many other techniques are available to you when displaying a form based on a large recordset. My favorite involves basing the form on only a single record at a time and changing the form's `RecordSource` property each time the user wants to view a different record. Another technique that I use is to base the form's `RecordSource` property on the value the user selects in a combo box in the Header section of the form. I use the `After_Update` event of the combo box to requery the form. Because the form's `RecordSource` uses the combo box value for criteria, the form displays the desired record. I cover these techniques, and others, in detail in *Alison Balter's Mastering Access 2002 Enterprise Development*.

Preparing an Application for Distribution

You must take some special steps to prepare your application for distribution. Most are steps you'll probably want to take so that your application seems professional to the user. The following are preparations that you should take before distributing your application:

- Base your application around forms.
- Add startup options to your database.
- Secure your application.
- Build error handling into your application.
- Add some level of custom help.
- Build custom ribbons to be associated with your application's forms and reports.

Basing Your Application Around Forms

You should base your application around forms. It should generally begin with a main switchboard that lets the user get to the other components of your application. Or, it can start with a core data entry form around which you base the rest of the application. If you opt to go with an application switchboard, the main switchboard can direct the user to additional switchboards, such as a data entry switchboard, a report switchboard, or a maintenance switchboard. You can build switchboards with a tool called the *Switchboard Manager*. Alternatively, you can design them as custom dialog boxes. Chapter 10, "Advanced Form Techniques," covers building custom dialog boxes. The primary advantage of custom switchboards is the flexibility and freedom they offer.

An alternative to the switchboard approach is to build the application around a core data entry form, such as a contact management application based around a contacts form. The user accesses all other forms and reports that make up the application via a custom ribbon on the contacts form.

Adding Startup Options to Your Database

Regardless of the approach that you take, you designate a form as the starting point for your application by modifying the database's startup options. Here's how:

1. Click the Microsoft Office button and then select Access Options (see Figure 19.1). The Access Options dialog box appears.

2. Click to select Current Database (see Figure 19.2). In this dialog box, you can set options, such as a startup form, an application title, and an icon that appears when the user minimizes your application.

Securing Your Application

As you will learn in the next section, a database isn't secure just because you're running it from a runtime version of Access. If your application doesn't have security, anyone with a full copy of Access can modify it, so securing your database objects is an important step in preparing your application for distribution. Chapter 31, "Database Security Made Easy," covers security.

Access 2000, Access 2002, Access 2003, and Access 2007 also offer you the capability to remove the source code from your applications. This capability protects your intellectual property and improves the performance of your application. Microsoft calls the resulting database an ACCDE.

19

FIGURE 19.1 Click the Microsoft Office button and then select Access Options.

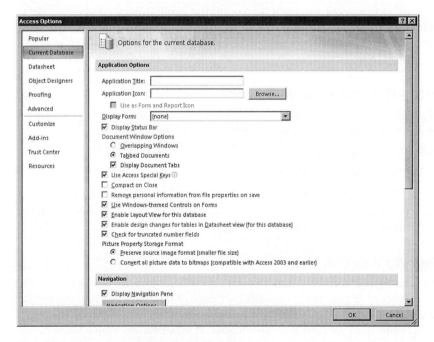

FIGURE 19.2 The Current Database page of the Access Options dialog box lets you control many aspects of your application environment.

Building Error Handling into Your Application

If you don't build error handling into your application and an error occurs while your user runs your application from Access's runtime version, Access will rudely exit the user out of the program. She won't get an appropriate error message and will be left wondering what happened. Hence, it's essential that you add error handling to your application's procedures. Chapter 17, "Error Handling: Preparing for the Inevitable," covers error handling techniques.

Adding Custom Help

In most cases, you want your users to have at least some level of custom help specific to your application. You can use the `ControlTip Text` property of controls and the `Description` property of fields to add the most basic level of help to your application. The `ControlTip Text` property provides a description of a control when a user hovers his mouse pointer over the control. The `Description` property of a field appears on the status bar when a control based on that field has the focus. If you are more ambitious, and if the scope and budget for the application warrant it, you can build a custom help file for your application. To add custom help to your application, you must build a help file; then you can attach parts of it to the application's forms and controls.

Building Custom Ribbons

You should build your own ribbons that you associate with specific forms and reports. Custom ribbons add both polish and functionality to your application.

After you complete these steps, you'll be ready for the final phase of preparing your application for distribution:

- ▶ Test your application by using the `/Runtime` switch.

- ▶ Install your application on a machine that has never run a copy of either the standard or runtime version of Access.

- ▶ Test your application on the machine; make sure it runs as expected.

Begin by testing your application with the `/Runtime` switch. This switch simulates the runtime environment, allowing you to mimic user actions under the runtime version of Access. Taking this step saves you a lot of time and energy. It will find most, if not all, of the problems associated with the runtime version.

After you test your application with the `/Runtime` switch, you must test your application by running the install on a machine that has never contained a copy of either the standard or runtime version of Access. The whole idea is to test your application on a machine containing no Access-related files. This action ensures that you have included all the required files on your setup disks.

19

I suggest that that you use a "ghosting" utility such as Symantec Ghost to create a complete image of your operating system and application drives. Install and fully test your application; make sure you experiment with every feature. After you have completed the testing process, restore the original machine from the Ghost image so that you can use it to test your next installation.

> **TIP**
>
> Symantec Backup Exec System Recovery allows you to restore individual files, selected directories, or entire hard drives as needed. When you create a backup image file, Symantec Backup Exec System Recovery compresses it by up to 70%, greatly reducing transfer times and storage requirements. Among its many other uses, Symantec Backup Exec System Recovery greatly facilitates the testing process by allowing you to easily restore a test machine to its pretesting state.

Using Access as a Front End

If you're planning to use Access as a front end to other databases, you need to consider a few issues. In fact, the whole design methodology of your system will differ depending on whether you plan to store your data in an Access database or on a back-end database server.

In a system where you store your data solely in Access tables, the Access Database Engine supplies all data retrieval and management functions and handles security, data validation, and enforcement of referential integrity.

In a system where Access acts as a front end to client/server data, the server handles the data management functions. It's responsible for retrieving, protecting, and updating data on the back-end database server. In this scenario, the local copy of Access is responsible only for sending requests and getting either data or pointers to data back from the database server. If you're creating an application in which Access acts as a front end, capitalizing on the strengths of both Access and the server can be a challenging endeavor.

Factors You Need to Worry About When Converting to Client/Server

The transition to client/server technology isn't always a smooth one. You need to consider the following factors if you're developing a client/server application or planning to eventually move your application from an Access database to a back-end structured query language (SQL) database server:

▶ Not every back-end database supports all field types that Access supports.

▶ The upsizing process will not convert any security you set up in Access to your back-end database.

- You will have to re-establish many of the validation rules you set up in Access on the back end.

- Not all back ends support referential integrity. Depending on the database that you are upsizing to, the upsizing process might not automatically set up the referential integrity that you established in Access.

- Queries involving joins that could be updated in Access can't always be updated on the back-end server.

This list is just an overview of what you need to think about when moving an application from an Access database with linked tables to a back-end server or when developing an application specifically for a back end. Many of these issues have far-reaching implications. For example, if you set up validation rules and validation text in your application, you will often need to rewrite the rules as triggers on the back end. If the user violates a validation rule that you set up on the back end, you will get a returnable error code. You have to respond to this code by using error handling in your application, displaying the appropriate message to your user. You can't use the `Validation Text` property with your client/server databases.

TIP

The Access 2000, Access 2002, Access 2003, and Access 2007 Upsizing Wizards address most of the transitioning issues covered in this chapter. These tools, included as part of Access 2000, Access 2002, Access 2003, and Access 2007, respectively, automate the migration of data from the native Access data format to Microsoft SQL Server. *Alison Balter's Mastering Access 2002 Enterprise Development* covers the Upsizing Wizard.

Benefits and Costs of Client/Server Technology

With all the issues discussed in the previous section, you might ask, "Why bother with client/server?" In each case, you need to evaluate whether the benefits of client/server technology outweigh its costs. The major benefits include the following:

- Greater control over data integrity

- Increased control over data security

- Increased fault tolerance

- Reduced network traffic

- Improved performance

- Centralized control and management of data

19

These are some of the major expenses:

▶ Increased development costs

▶ Hardware costs for the server machine

▶ Setup costs for the server database

▶ The cost of employing a full- or part-time database administrator (DBA)

These and other issues are covered in more detail in Chapter 22.

Your Options When Using Access as a Front End

Client/server applications are not an all-or-none proposition; there is more than one way to implement them through Access. One option is to use Access as a true front end, which means that you store all data on the server and process all queries on the server. You do this by using pass-through queries and stored procedures, rather than stored Access queries. With pass-through queries, you pass a back-end–specific SQL statement to the back end instead of allowing Access to process it. When you use stored procedures, you store SQL statements on the back end and then execute them using Data Access Objects (DAO) or ActiveX Data Objects (ADO) code. (I cover this scenario briefly in Chapter 22 and in detail in *Alison Balter's Mastering Access 2002 Enterprise Development*.)

To make Access a true front end, you must also disable its natural ability to bind data to forms and reports. Doing so, however, eliminates all the features that make Access a strong product in the first place. Unfortunately, you haven't eliminated all the overhead associated with the functionality you removed. If you want to use unbound forms for most or all of your application, you're better off developing the entire application in a lower-overhead environment, such as Visual Studio .NET.

Another approach is a hybrid method in which you use a combination of linked tables, SQL pass-through queries, stored procedures, unbound forms, and local Access tables. The idea is that you take advantage of Access's features and strong points whenever possible. You use pass-through queries and stored procedures to perform functions that you can accomplish more efficiently by communicating directly to the back end or that aren't available at all with Access SQL. To further improve performance, you can perform many tasks locally and then communicate them to the server as one transaction, after you have completed any initial validation. In addition to the solutions just discussed, you can also download data to Access in bulk so that you can perform additional processing locally. Many possibilities exist, and each is appropriate in different situations. Experience and experimentation are needed to determine the combination of methods that will optimize performance in a given situation.

What Are the Considerations for Migrating to a Client/Server Environment?

The preceding sections have given you an overview of the issues you need to consider when building a client/server application or considering moving to a client/server environment in the future. Chapter 22 provides more detailed information. If you're using Access as a front end, make sure that, as you read through this book, particularly the more advanced chapters, you take special note of any cautions about developing client/server applications. If you want in-depth coverage of client/server development techniques, refer to *Alison Balter's Mastering Access 2002 Enterprise Development*.

Practical Examples: Applying the Strategy to the Computer Consulting Firm Application

The time and billing application for the computer consulting firm introduced in Chapter 1, "Access as a Development Tool," could be composed of two databases: one containing the majority of the tables and the other with the remainder of the database objects, including static and temporary tables. To design the application properly and to make the transition to client/server as smooth as possible, you would develop the application with the idea that you might eventually move the data to a back-end server. You would base the forms and reports that make up the application on stored queries or embedded SQL statements to maximize their flexibility and efficiency. Finally, you would design the application so that it can easily run from Access's runtime version, and you would secure it so that unauthorized users could not access its data and other objects.

Summary

Having a strategy before you begin the application development process is important. This chapter introduced many strategic issues, such as splitting a database into tables and other objects, and using Access as a front end. It also covered converting to a client/server environment, explored the benefits and costs involved in such a conversion, and discussed the different options available to you. The chapter tied these concepts together with an explanation of what you can do to prepare your applications for future growth. The chapter also explained what you need to be concerned about when preparing an application for distribution, including the importance of properly securing your databases.

19

CHAPTER 20

Using External Data

Why This Chapter Is Important

Microsoft Access is capable of interfacing with data from other sources. It can use data from any OLE DB or ODBC data source, as well as data from FoxPro, dBASE, Paradox, Lotus, Excel, and many other sources. In this chapter, you learn how to interface with external data sources, with the user interface, and by using code.

External data is data stored outside the current database. It can refer to data stored in another Microsoft Access database, as well as data stored in a multitude of other file formats—including ISAM, spreadsheet, ASCII, and more. This chapter focuses on accessing data sources other than ODBC and OLE DB. ODBC and OLE DB data sources are discussed briefly in Chapter 22, "Developing Multiuser and Enterprise Applications." They are covered in extensive detail in *Alison Balter's Mastering Access 2002 Enterprise Development*.

Access is an excellent *front-end* product, which means that it provides a powerful and effective means of presenting data—even data from external sources. Data is stored in places other than Access for many reasons. Large databases, for example, can be managed more effectively on a back-end database server such as Microsoft SQL Server. Data is often stored in a FoxPro, dBASE, or Paradox file format because the data is being used by a legacy application written in one of those environments. Text data is often downloaded from a mainframe. Regardless of the reason data is stored in another format, you must understand how to manipulate this external data in your VBA modules. With the capability to access data from other sources, you can create queries, forms, and reports.

When accessing external data, you have three choices: You can import the data into an Access database, access the data by linking to it from your Access database, or open a data source directly. Importing the data is the optimum route (except with ODBC data sources) but isn't always possible. If you can't import external data, you should link to external files because Microsoft Access maintains a lot of information about these linked files. This optimizes performance when manipulating the external files. Sometimes a particular situation warrants accessing the data directly. You therefore should know how to work with linked files, as well as how to open and manipulate files directly.

Importing, Linking, and Opening Files: When and Why

When you import data into an Access table, Access makes a copy of the data and places it in the Access table. After importing the data, Access treats it like any other native Access table. In fact, neither you nor Access has any way of knowing from where the data came. As a result, imported data offers the same performance and flexibility as any other Access table.

Linking to external data is quite different from importing data. Linked data remains in its native format. By establishing a link to the external data, you can build queries, forms, and reports that present the data. After you create a link to external data, the link remains permanently established unless you explicitly remove it. The linked table appears in the database window just like any other Access table, except that its icon is different. In fact, if the data source permits multiuser access, the users of your application can modify the data, as can the users of the applications written in the data source's native database format (such as FoxPro, dBASE, or Paradox). The main difference between a linked and a native table is that you cannot modify the linked table's structure from within Access.

Opening an external table is similar to linking to the table, except that a permanent relationship is not created. When you *link* to an external table, Access maintains connection information from session to session. When you *open* a table, you create a recordset from the table, and Access does not establish a permanent link to the data.

Selecting an Option

It is important that you understand when to import external data, when to link to external data, and when to open an external table directly. You should import external data in either of these circumstances:

▶ You are migrating an existing system into Access.

▶ You want to use external data to run a large volume of queries and reports, and you will not update the data. You want the added performance that native Access data provides.

When you are migrating an existing system to Access and you are ready to permanently migrate test or production data into your application, you import the tables into Access. You might also want to import external data if the data is downloaded from a mainframe into ASCII format on a regular basis, and you want to use the data for reports. Instead of attempting to link to the data and suffering the performance hits associated with such a link, you can import the data each time it is downloaded from the mainframe.

You should link to external data in any of the following circumstances:

▶ The data is used by a legacy application requiring the native file format.

▶ The data resides on an ODBC-compliant database server.

▶ You will access the data on a regular basis (making it prohibitive to keep the data up to date if it is not linked).

Often, you won't have the time or resources to rewrite an application written in FoxPro, Paradox, or some other language. You might be developing additional applications that will share data with the legacy application, or you might want to use the strong querying and reporting capabilities of Access instead of developing queries and reports in the native environment.

By linking to the external data, users of existing applications can continue to work with the applications and their data. Your Access applications can retrieve and modify data without concern of corrupting, or in any other way harming, the data.

If the data resides in an ODBC database such as Microsoft SQL Server, you want to reap the data-retrieval benefits provided by a database server. By linking to the ODBC data source, you can take advantage of Access's ease of use as a front-end tool, while taking advantage of client/server technology.

Finally, if you intend to access data on a regular basis, linking to the external table instead of temporarily opening the table directly provides you with ease of use and performance benefits. After you create the link, in most cases, Access treats the table just like any other Access table.

You should open an external table directly in either of these circumstances:

▶ You rarely need to establish a connection to the external data source.

▶ You have determined that performance actually improves by opening the data source directly.

If you rarely need to access the external data, opening that data directly might be appropriate. Links increase the size of your .ACCDB file. This size increase is not necessary if you rarely will access the data. Furthermore, in certain situations, when accessing Indexed Sequential Access Method (ISAM) data, you might find that opening the table directly provides better performance than linking to it.

Although this chapter covers the process of importing external data, this is essentially a one-time process and doesn't require a lot of discussion. It is important to note, however, that after you import data into an Access table, it no longer is accessed by the application in its native format. The majority of this chapter focuses on linking to or directly opening external data tables.

20

Looking at Supported File Formats

Microsoft Access enables you to import, link to, and open files in these formats:

- ▶ Microsoft Access databases (including previous versions of Jet)
- ▶ ODBC databases
- ▶ SharePoint Lists
- ▶ HTML documents
- ▶ XML documents (import and open only)
- ▶ Microsoft Exchange/Outlook
- ▶ dBASE III, dBASE IV, and dBASE 5.0
- ▶ Paradox 3.*x*, 4.*x*, and 5.*x*
- ▶ Microsoft Excel spreadsheets
- ▶ Lotus WKS, WK1, WK3, and WK4 spreadsheets (import and open only)
- ▶ ASCII text files stored in a tabular format

Importing External Data

The process of importing external data is quite simple. You can import external data by using the user interface or by using VBA code. If you are planning to import the data only once or twice, you should use the user interface. If you are importing data on a regular basis (for example, from a downloaded mainframe file), you should write code that accomplishes the task transparently to the user.

Using the User Interface

To import an external data file using the user interface, follow these steps:

1. Click to select the External Data tab.

2. Select the appropriate import type by clicking the appropriate icon in the Import group. (Note that you can also click Saved Imports to perform an import that you have previously saved.) The dialog box that appears varies depending on the type of data you are importing. Figure 20.1 provides an example.

3. Notice in Figure 20.1 that you can opt to import the source data into a new table in the current database, append a copy of the records to the table, or link to the data source by creating a linked table. For this example, select the first option, Import the Source Data into a New Table in the Current Database.

4. Click Browse to locate the file that you want to import. The File Open dialog box appears.

5. Navigate to the file that you want to import and then click Open. Access returns you to the Get External Data – Excel Spreadsheet dialog box.

6. Click OK. Depending on the type of file you select, the import process finishes, or you see additional dialog boxes. If you select Excel Spreadsheet, for example, the Import Spreadsheet Wizard appears, as shown in Figure 20.2. This wizard walks you through the process of importing spreadsheet data.

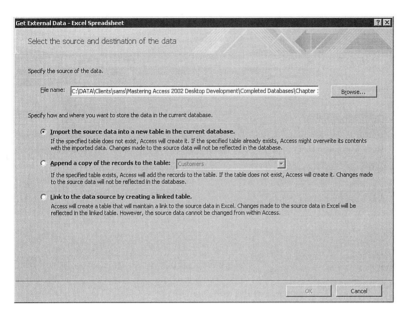

FIGURE 20.1   The import dialog box varies depending on the type of import you are performing.

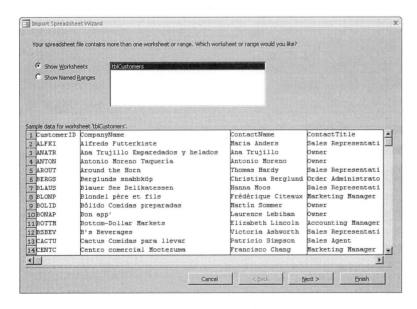

FIGURE 20.2   The Import Spreadsheet Wizard.

CAUTION

If you find that you can't bring a large (4–5MB) text file directly into an Access database, change the text file into an Excel spreadsheet first and then import that file.

Using Code

The DoCmd object has three methods that assist you with importing external data: TransferDatabase, TransferText, and TransferSpreadsheet, each of which I cover in the following sections.

Importing Database Data Using Code

You use the TransferDatabase method of the DoCmd object to import data from a database such as FoxPro, dBASE, Paradox, or another Access database. Listing 20.1, included in basImport, shows an example that uses the TransferDatabase method.

LISTING 20.1   Using the TransferDatabase Method

```
Sub ImportDatabase()
  DoCmd.TransferDatabase _
    TransferType:=acImport, _
    DatabaseType:="dBASE III", _
    DatabaseName:= CurrentProject.Path, _
    ObjectType:=acTable, _
    Source:="Customer", _
    Destination:="tblCustomers", _
    StructureOnly:=False
End Sub
```

NOTE

All the code in this chapter is located in the CHAP20EX.ACCDB file on the sample code CD-ROM.

Table 20.1 lists the arguments for the TransferDatabase method.

TABLE 20.1   TransferDatabase Arguments

Argument	Specifies
TransferType	Type of transfer being performed.
DatabaseType	Type of database being imported.
DatabaseName	Name of the database. If the table is a separate file (as is the case with dBASE, Paradox, and earlier versions of FoxPro), the database name is the name of the directory that contains the table file. Do *not* include a backslash after the name of the directory.

TABLE 20.1   Continued

Argument	Specifies
ObjectType	Type of object you want to import. This argument is ignored for all but Access objects.
Source	Name of the object you are importing. Do *not* include the file extension.
Destination	Name of the imported object.
StructureOnly	Whether you want the structure of the table only or the structure and data.
StoreLogin	Whether you want to save the login ID and password for an ODBC database in the connection string for linked tables.

Importing Text Data Using Code

You use the TransferText method of the DoCmd object to import text from a text file. Listing 20.2 shows an example of this method.

LISTING 20.2   Using the TransferText Method

```
Sub ImportText()
  DoCmd.TransferText _
    TransferType:=acImportDelim, _
    TableName:="tblCustomerText", _
    FileName:=CurrentProject.Path & "\Customer.Txt"
End Sub
```

Table 20.2 lists the arguments for the TransferText method.

TABLE 20.2   TransferText Arguments

Argument	Specifies
TransferType	Type of transfer you want to make
SpecificationName	Name for the set of options that determines how the file is imported
TableName	Name of the Access table that will receive the imported data
FileName	Name of the text file to import from
HTMTableName	Name of the table or list in the HTML file that you want to import or link to
CodePage	A long integer used to indicate the character set of the code page
HasFieldHeadings	Whether the first row of the text file contains field headings

Importing Spreadsheet Data Using Code

You use the TransferSpreadsheet method of the DoCmd object to import data from a spreadsheet file. Listing 20.3 shows an example that uses the TransferSpreadsheet method.

LISTING 20.3   Using the `TransferSpreadsheet` Method

```
Sub ImportSpreadsheet()
  DoCmd.TransferSpreadsheet _
    TransferType:=acImport, _
    SpreadsheetType:=acSpreadsheetTypeExcel12, _
    TableName:="tblCustomerSpread", _
    FileName:=CurrentProject.Path & "\Customer.Xls", _
    HasFieldNames:=True
End Sub
```

Table 20.3 lists the arguments for the `TransferSpreadsheet` method.

TABLE 20.3   `TransferSpreadsheet` Arguments

Argument	Specifies
TransferType	Type of transfer you want to make
SpreadsheetType	Type of spreadsheet to import from
TableName	Name of the Access table that will receive the imported data
FileName	Name of the spreadsheet file to import from
HasFieldNames	Whether the first row of the spreadsheet contains field headings
Range	Range of cells to import

Creating a Link to External Data

If you need to keep the data in its original format but want to treat the data just like any other Access table, linking is the best solution. All the information required to establish and maintain the connection to the remote data source is stored within the linked table definition. You can create links through the user interface and by using code. The following sections cover both alternatives.

One of the most common types of links is a link to another Access table. You create this type of link so that you can place the application objects (queries, forms, reports, macros, and modules) in a local database and so that you can store the tables in another database on a file server. Numerous benefits are associated with such a configuration. Chapter 22 discusses these benefits in more detail.

Using the User Interface

Creating a link using the user interface is very common. If you know what links you want to establish at design time, this is probably the easiest way to establish links to external data. You can establish links using the Database Splitter, or you can establish them manually.

Creating Links Using the Database Splitter

The Database Splitter was designed to split databases that already have been built with all the tables and other database objects in one physical `.ACCDB` database file. It automates the process of moving the data tables to another database.

To use the Database Splitter Wizard, follow these steps:

1. Switch to the Database Tools tab.

2. Click the Access Database button in the Move Data group on the ribbon. The Database Splitter Wizard appears (see Figure 20.3).

3. Click Split Database. The Create Back-End Database dialog box appears (see Figure 20.4). Here, you select a name and location for the database that will contain the table data.

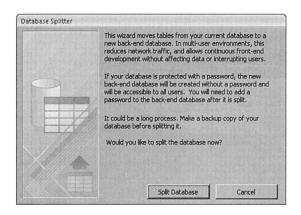

FIGURE 20.3   The Database Splitter Wizard facilitates the process of splitting data into an application and database and a data database.

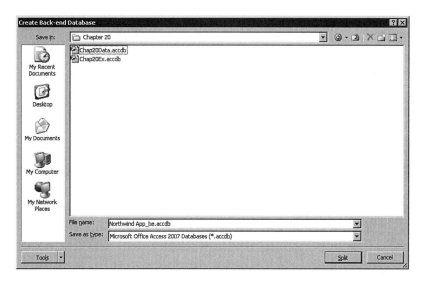

FIGURE 20.4   You use the Create Back-End Database dialog box to indicate the name and location of the database containing the data tables.

4. Make your selection and click Split. You should receive a message that the database successfully split.

5. Click OK to complete the process. If you look in the Navigation Pane, all the tables appear with an arrow, indicating that they are linked (see Figure 20.5).

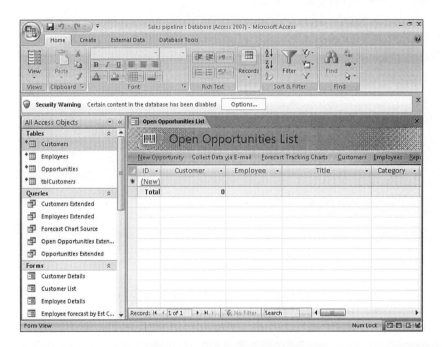

FIGURE 20.5   After you split the database, all tables appear with an arrow, indicating that they are linked.

Creating Links to Access Tables Manually

To create a link to an Access table, follow these steps:

1. Click to select the External Data tab.

2. Click to select the Import Access Database button in the Import group. The Get External Data – Access Database dialog box appears, as shown in Figure 20.6.

3. Browse to locate the database containing the tables that you want to link to. The File Open dialog box appears.

4. Select the database containing the data tables and click Open.

5. Select Link to the Data Source by Creating a Linked Table.

6. Click OK. The Link Tables dialog box appears (see Figure 20.7).

7. Select the tables to which you want to establish a link.

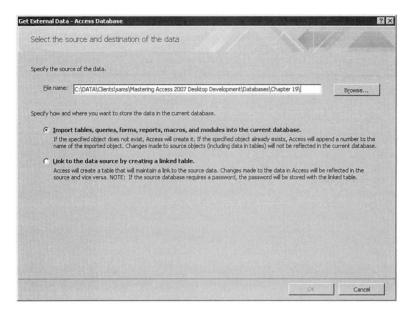

FIGURE 20.6   The Get External Data – Access Database dialog box allows you to designate whether you want to import or link to the Access tables.

FIGURE 20.7   The Link Tables dialog box allows you to select the tables that you want to link to.

8. Click OK. The link process finishes. The Save Import Steps portion of the Get External Data Wizard appears.

9. Click Close to complete the process.

20

Creating Links to Other Types of Tables Manually

The process of creating links to other types of database files is a little different. It works like this:

1. Click to select the External Data tab.

2. Click the appropriate button in the Import group (for example, Excel). The Get External Data – Excel Spreadsheet dialog box appears.

3. Browse to locate the file that you want to link to. The File Open dialog box appears.

4. Select the file that you want to link to and click Open. Access returns you to the Get External Data – Excel Spreadsheet dialog box.

5. Select Link to the Data Source by Creating a Linked Table.

6. Click OK. If you selected Excel Spreadsheet, for example, the Link Spreadsheet Wizard appears.

7. Follow the steps of the wizard. (These steps vary quite a bit depending on the type of file you selected.)

8. Click Finish to complete the process. A dialog box appears, indicating that the process completed successfully. You will see the appropriate icon in the Navigation Pane, indicating the type of file you have linked to (see Figure 20.8).

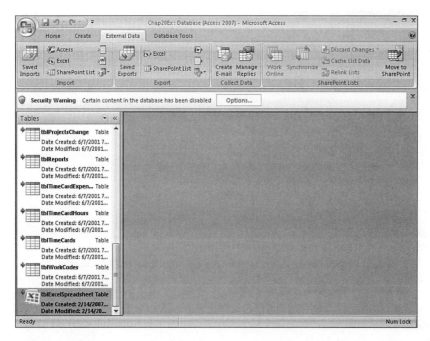

FIGURE 20.8   Notice that the Excel icon appears, indicating that the linked file is an Excel spreadsheet.

Using Code

Creating a link to an external table using code is a six-step process. Here are the steps involved in establishing the link:

1. Create a reference to the Microsoft ADO Extension 2.8 for DDL and Security (ADOX) library.

2. Create a `Catalog` object.

3. Set the `Connection` property of the `Catalog` object to the database that will contain the linked table.

4. Create a new `Table` object.

5. Set properties of the `Table` object.

6. Append the `Table` object to the `Catalog`.

Listing 20.4 shows the code for linking to an external table, which, in this case, exists in another Microsoft Access database.

LISTING 20.4   Linking to an External Table

```
Sub LinkToAccessTableProps()
    Dim cat As ADOX.Catalog
    Dim tbl As ADOX.Table

    'Instantiate a Catalog object
    Set cat = New ADOX.Catalog

    'Set the connection of the Catalog object
    'to the connection associated with the current
    'project
    cat.ActiveConnection = CurrentProject.Connection

    'Instantiate a Table object
    Set tbl = New ADOX.Table

    'Establish the name of the new Table object
    tbl.Name = "tblLinkedTable"

    'Point the catalog of the new table at the
    'catalog object established above
    Set tbl.ParentCatalog = cat

    'Set necessary properties of the new Table object
    tbl.Properties("Jet OLEDB:Create Link") = True
    tbl.Properties("Jet OLEDB:Link Datasource") = _
```

20

LISTING 20.4   Continued

```
        CurrentProject.Path & "\Chap20Data.accdb"
    tbl.Properties("Jet OLEDB:Link Provider String") = ";pwd=password"
    tbl.Properties("Jet OLEDB:Remote Table Name") = "tblClients"


    'Append the new Table object to the tables collection
    'of the Catalog object
    cat.Tables.Append tbl
End Sub
```

In Listing 20.4, a Catalog object is created. The ActiveConnection property of the
Catalog object is pointed at the connection associated with the current database.
Next, a Table object is created. The Name property of the Table object is set equal to
tblLinkedTable. The ParentCatalog property of the Table object is set to point at the
Catalog object. Four properties in the properties collection of the Table object are set to
the appropriate values, and the Table object is appended to the Catalog object. This
process is discussed in further detail in the following sections.

Providing Connection Information

When you link to an external table, you must provide information about the type, name,
and location of the external database. You accomplish this by setting the following properties in the Properties collection of the Table object:

▶ Jet OLEDB:Link Provider String

▶ Jet OLEDB:Remote Table Name

▶ Jet OLEDB:Link Datasource

The following three lines of code illustrate the process of setting the provider string,
name, and location of the source table:

```
tbl.Properties("Jet OLEDB:Link Provider String") = ";pwd=password"
tbl.Properties("Jet OLEDB:Remote Table Name") = "tblClients"
tbl.Properties("Jet OLEDB:Link Datasource") = _
    CurrentProject.Path & "\Chap20Data.accdb"
```

The Jet OLEDB:Link Provider is the ISAM format that will be used for the link. Each
source database type is a different folder in the Windows Registry. The folders are located
in the HKEY_LOCAL_MACHINE\SOFTWARE\Microsoft\Jet\4.0\ISAM Formats section of the
Registry. Valid source database types are as follows:

dBASE	dBASE III, dBASE IV, and dBASE 5.0
Excel	Excel 12.0 and below
HTML	HTML Export and HTML Import
Jet	Jet 2.x, Jet 3.x, Jet 4.x

Lotus	Lotus WK1, Lotus WK3, Lotus WK4, Lotus WJ2, and Lotus WJ3
Exchange	Exchange 4.0
Outlook	Outlook 9.0 through Outlook 12.0
Paradox	Paradox 3.*x*, Paradox 4.*x*, Paradox 5.*x*, and Paradox 7.*x*
SharePoint Team Services	2.0
Text	N/A
Windows SharePoint Services	N/A

The `Jet OLEDB:Link Datasource` must include a fully qualified path to the file. You can specify the path with a drive letter and directory path or by using *universal naming conventions (UNCs)*. For a local database, you must specify the path like this:

```
tbl.Properties("Jet OLEDB:Link Datasource") = "c:\Databases\Chap20Data"
```

For a file server, you can specify the UNC path or the drive letter path. The UNC path looks like this:

```
tbl.Properties("Jet OLEDB:Link Datasource") = _
    "\\FILESERVERNAME\Databases\Chap20Data"
```

In this case, the database called `Chap20Data` is stored on the database's share of a particular file server.

Creating the Link

Listing 20.5 shows how you put all the connection information together to establish a link to an external table.

LISTING 20.5   Establishing a Link to an External Table

```
Sub LinkToDBase(strDirName As String, strTableName As String, _
   strAccessTable)
   Dim cat As ADOX.Catalog
   Dim tbl As ADOX.Table

   'Instantiate a Catalog object
   Set cat = New ADOX.Catalog
   cat.ActiveConnection = CurrentProject.Connection

   'Instantiate a Table object
   Set tbl = New ADOX.Table
   tbl.Name = strAccessTable
   Set tbl.ParentCatalog = cat

   'Set necessary properties of the new Table object
```

20

LISTING 20.5   Continued

```
    tbl.Properties("Jet OLEDB:Create Link") = True
    tbl.Properties("Jet OLEDB:Link Datasource") = strDirName
    tbl.Properties("Jet OLEDB:Link Provider String") = "dBASE III;HDR=NO;IMEX=2;"
    tbl.Properties("Jet OLEDB:Remote Table Name") = strTableName

    'Append the new Table object to the tables collection
    'of the Catalog object
    cat.Tables.Append tbl
End Sub
```

Here is an example of how you call this subroutine:

```
Call LinkToDBase("c:\customer\data","customer","tblCustomers")
```

The `LinkToDBase` subroutine receives three parameters:

▶ The name of the directory in which the dBASE file is stored

▶ The name of the file (the name of the table, without the `.DBF` extension) to which you want to connect

▶ The name of the Access table that you are creating

The subroutine creates two object variables: a `Catalog` object variable and a `Table` object variable. It points the `ActiveConnection` property of the `Catalog` object variable at the connection associated with the current database. Next, it establishes properties of the `Table` object. The Link Datasource is the name of the directory within which the dBASE file is stored. The Link Provider String specifies that the type of table you are linking to is a dBASE III file. The Remote Table Name is the name of the dBASE file that you are linking to. After setting these properties, you are ready to append the table definition to the database.

You have seen how you can link to a dBASE table. Listing 20.6 puts together everything you have learned thus far in this chapter by creating a link to an Access table stored in another database.

LISTING 20.6   Creating a Link to an Access Table Stored in Another Database

```
Sub LinkToAccess(strDBName As String, strTableName As String, _
    strAccessTable)
    Dim cat As ADOX.Catalog
    Dim tbl As ADOX.Table

    'Instantiate a Catalog object
    Set cat = New ADOX.Catalog
```

LISTING 20.6   Continued

```
        'Set the ActiveConnection property of the Catalog object
        'to the connection associated with the current project
        cat.ActiveConnection = CurrentProject.Connection

        'Instantiate a Table object
        Set tbl = New ADOX.Table

        'Set the Name property of the Table object to the name
        'you wish to give to the linked table
        tbl.Name = strAccessTable

        'Set the ParentCatalog property of the Table object
        'to the Catalog object
        Set tbl.ParentCatalog = cat

        'Set all necessary properties of the Table object
        tbl.Properties("Jet OLEDB:Create Link") = True
        tbl.Properties("Jet OLEDB:Link Datasource") = strDBName
        tbl.Properties("Jet OLEDB:Link Provider String") = ";pwd=password"
        tbl.Properties("Jet OLEDB:Remote Table Name") = strTableName

        'Append the Table object to the Tables collection
        'associated with the Catalog object
        cat.Tables.Append tbl
End Sub
```

Notice that the Jet OLEDB Link Provider string no longer specifies the type of database to which you are connecting. Everything else in this routine is the same as the routine that connected to dBASE. Also, notice the parameters passed to this routine:

```
Call LinkToAccess("C:\databases\northwind 2007.accdb","Customers","tblCustomers")
```

The database passed to the routine is an actual Access database (as opposed to a directory), and the table name is the name of the Access table in the other database (instead of the .DBF filename).

> **NOTE**
>
> Whether you link to an external database using the user interface or code, you should always use the UNC path, rather than a drive letter. This ensures that all users with access to the network share are able to see the data, regardless of their drive letter mappings.

20

Opening an External Table

Sometimes you will want to open, rather than link to, an external table. Linking provides ease of use when you are dealing with external tables. After you link to a table, you treat it just like any other Access table. The disadvantage of linking is that it uses ODBC. ODBC is not the most efficient means of interacting with a database for which you have a native OLE DB provider. Therefore, you might want to programmatically open an external table without creating a link to it. Opening an external table is a two-step process:

1. Establish a connection to the external data source.

2. Point a `Recordset` object at the result of executing a SQL statement against the `Connection` object.

Providing Connection Information

The connection information you provide when you open an external table is similar to the information you provide when you link to the table. The connection information is provided as the `ConnectionString` argument of the `Open` method of the `Connection` object. Here's an example:

```
cnn.Open "Provider=sqlodedb;" & _
        "Data Source=(local);" & _
        "Initial Catalog=Pubs;" & _
        "User ID=sa;Password=;"
```

Here, the connection string is to the SQL Server database called `Pubs` on the local machine.

Opening the Table

You point the `Recordset` object at the result of executing a `Select` statement against the `Connection` object:

```
Set rst = cnn.execute("Select * from Authors")
```

Listing 20.7 shows what the entire process looks like in code.

LISTING 20.7   Using the `OpenDatabase` Method

```
Sub OpenExternalSQL(strDBName As String, strTableName As String)
    Dim cnn As ADODB.Connection
    Dim rst As ADODB.Recordset

    'Instantiate Connection and Recordset objects
    Set cnn = New ADODB.Connection
    Set rst = New ADODB.Recordset
```

LISTING 20.7   Continued

```
'Use the Open method of the Connection object to establish
'a connection to the SQL Server database
cnn.Open "Provider=sqloledb;" & _
    "Data Source=(local);" & _
    "Initial Catalog=" & strDBName & ";" & _
    "User Id=sa;Password=; "



'Use the Execute method of the Connection object to execute
'a Select statement and return the result as a Recordset
Set rst = cnn.Execute("Select * from " & strTableName)

'Loop through the resulting recordset,
'printing the value of the first field
Do Until rst.EOF
    Debug.Print rst.Fields(0).Value
    rst.MoveNext
Loop

'Close the connection
cnn.Close
End Sub
```

Listing 20.7 is called with this code:

```
Call OpenExternalSQL("Pubs","authors")
```

Notice that you are not appending a table definition here. Instead, you are creating a temporary recordset that refers to the external data. After you open the external table as a recordset, the code traverses through each record of the table, printing the value of the first field. Of course, after you open the recordset, you can manipulate it in any way you want. The table does not show up as a linked table in the Database window. In fact, when the routine completes and the local variable goes out of scope, the recordset no longer exists.

Now that you have seen how you can link to external tables as well as open them, you are ready to look at how you can refine both of these processes. Refining them involves learning the Windows Registry settings that affect the linking process, learning more about the parameters that are available to you when specifying connection information, learning how to specify passwords, learning how to refresh and remove links, and learning how to create an external table using VBA code.

20

Understanding Windows Registry Settings

Each ISAM driver has a separate key in the Windows Registry. These keys are located in the appropriate ISAM driver in the `HKEY_LOCAL_MACHINE\SOFTWARE\Microsoft\Jet\ 4.0\ISAM Formats` section of the Registry. These keys are used to configure the driver after initialization. As you can see in Figure 20.9, the setup program has created keys for several data sources. If you look at a specific data source (in this case, dBASE III), you can see all the settings that exist for the dBASE driver. The `IndexFilter` is set to `dBASE Index(*.ndx)`, for example. At times, you will need to modify one of the Registry settings to customize the behavior of the ISAM driver; this is covered later in this chapter in the section "Looking at Special Considerations."

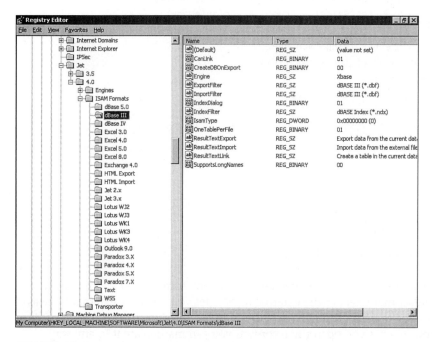

FIGURE 20.9   The Windows Registry with keys for ISAM drivers.

Using the `Jet OLEDB:Link Provider` String

You use the `Jet OLEDB:Link Provider` string when linking to external tables. It includes the source database type, user ID, and password. You must use a semicolon to separate each part of the connection string.

Each source database type has a valid name. This is the name that must be used when accessing that type of data. These database types are found in the Windows Registry under `HKEY_LOCAL_MACHINE\Software\Microsoft\Jet\4.0\ISAM Formats`. You must accurately specify the source database type; otherwise, you cannot access the external data.

The user ID is used whenever a username must be specified to successfully log on to the data source. This is most common when dealing with back-end databases such as Oracle, Sybase, or Microsoft SQL Server. This part of the provider string can be required to log on the user to the system where the source data resides. The `UID` keyword refers to the user ID.

As with the user ID, the password most often is included when dealing with back-end data. It can also be used on other database types that support passwords, such as Paradox, or when linking to an external Access table. The `PWD` keyword is used when specifying the password.

Finally, the dataset name refers to a defined ODBC data source. The `DSN` keyword refers to the dataset name in the connection string. The following is an example of a `Jet OLEDB Link Provider` string:

```
tbl.Properties("Jet OLEDB:Link Provider String") = "ODBC" & _
        ";DATABASE=Pubs" & _
        ";UID=Alison" & _
        ";PWD=MyPass" & _
        ";DSN=PublisherData"
```

In the example, the SQL Server database being accessed is `Pubs`, the user ID is `Alison`, the Password is `MyPass`, and the data source name is `PublisherData`.

Working with Passwords

When working with passwords, you probably won't want to hard-code a password into your application because that defeats the purpose of placing a password on your database. In Listing 20.8, the database's password is included in the code, allowing the link to be made to the secured table without password validation.

LISTING 20.8   Embedding a Database Password in Code

```
Sub LinkToSecured()
    Dim cat As ADOX.Catalog
    Dim tbl As ADOX.Table

    'Instantiate a Catalog object
    Set cat = New ADOX.Catalog

    'Set the ActiveConnection property of the Catalog
    'object to the connection associated with the
    'current project
    cat.ActiveConnection = CurrentProject.Connection

    'Instantiate a Table object
    Set tbl = New ADOX.Table
```

20

LISTING 20.8   Continued

```
    'Set the Name property of the Table object
    tbl.Name = "tblLinkedTable"

    'Associate the ParentCatalog of the Table object
    'with the Catalog object
    Set tbl.ParentCatalog = cat

    'Set properties of the Table object
    tbl.Properties("Jet OLEDB:Create Link") = True
    tbl.Properties("Jet OLEDB:Link Provider String") = "ODBC" & _
        ";DATABASE=Pubs" & _
        ";UID=SA" & _
        ";PWD=" & _
        ";DSN=PublisherData"
    tbl.Properties("Jet OLEDB:Remote Table Name") = "Authors"

    'Append the Table object to the Tables collection
    'associated with the Catalog object
    cat.Tables.Append tbl
End Sub
```

An invalid password results in a message appearing, requiring the user to log on. Unless you are using integrated security to log on to your database server, it is best to require the user to supply the password at runtime. In Listing 20.9, the code prompts the user for a password. The password entered by the user is used as part of the connection string.

LISTING 20.9   Requiring Password Validation

```
Sub ReallySecure()
    Dim cat As ADOX.Catalog
    Dim tbl As ADOX.Table
    Dim strPassword As String

    'Instantiate a Catalog object
    Set cat = New ADOX.Catalog

    'Set the ActiveConnection property of the Catalog
    'object to the connection associated with the
    'current project
    cat.ActiveConnection = CurrentProject.Connection

    Set tbl = New ADOX.Table

    'Set the Name property of the Table object
    tbl.Name = "tblLinkedTable"
```

LISTING 20.9   Continued

```
    'Associate the ParentCatalog of the Table object
    'with the Catalog object
    Set tbl.ParentCatalog = cat

    'Prompt the user for the password
    strPassword = InputBox("Please Enter Your Password", "Database Security!!!")

    'Set properties of the Table object
    tbl.Properties("Jet OLEDB:Create Link") = True
    tbl.Properties("Jet OLEDB:Link Provider String") = "ODBC" & _
        ";DATABASE=Pubs" & _
        ";UID=SA" & _
        ";PWD=" & strPassword & _
        ";DSN=PublisherData"
    tbl.Properties("Jet OLEDB:Remote Table Name") = "Authors"

    'Append the Table object to the Tables collection
    'associated with the Catalog object
    cat.Tables.Append tbl
End Sub
```

Notice that the code retrieves the password from the user and stores it in a variable called
strPassword. This strPassword variable is included in the connection string at runtime.

Refreshing and Removing Links

Refreshing links refers to updating the link to an external table. It is done when the location of an external table has changed. *Removing links* refers to permanently removing a
link to an external table.

Access cannot find external tables if their locations have moved. You need to adjust for
this in your VBA code. Furthermore, sometimes you might want to remove a link to
external data—when you no longer need to use the data or when you have permanently
imported the data into Access.

Updating Links That Have Moved

To refresh a link using VBA code, simply redefine the Jet OLEDB:Link Datasource.
Listing 20.10 shows the code to refresh a link.

LISTING 20.10   Refreshing a Link

```
Sub RefreshLink()
    Dim cat As ADOX.Catalog
    Dim tdf As ADOX.Table
```

LISTING 20.10   Continued

```
        Set cat = New ADOX.Catalog
        Set cat.ActiveConnection = CurrentProject.Connection
        tdf.Properties("Jet OLEDB:Link Datasource") = _
            strNewLocation
End Sub
```

You can modify this routine to prompt the user for the directory containing the data tables, as Listing 20.11 shows.

LISTING 20.11   Prompting the User for the Database Path and Name

```
Sub RefreshLink()
    'Initiate error handling
    On Error GoTo RefreshLink_Err
    Dim cat As ADOX.Catalog
    Dim tdf As ADOX.Table
    Dim strNewLocation As String
    Dim strTemp As String

    'Instantiate a Catalog object
    Set cat = New ADOX.Catalog

    'Set the ActiveConnection property of the Catalog
    'object to the connection associated with the
    'current project
    Set cat.ActiveConnection = CurrentProject.Connection

    'Point the TableDef object at the tblClients table
    Set tdf = cat.Tables("tblClients")

    'Attempt to retrieve the Name property of the table
    strTemp = tdf.Columns(0).Name

    'Exit the routine if all goes well
    Exit Sub

RefreshLink_Err:

    'If an error occurs, prompt the user for the new name
    'and location
    strNewLocation = InputBox("Please Enter Database Path and Name")

    'Set the properties of the TableDef object to the
    'information provided by the user
    tdf.Properties("Jet OLEDB:Link Datasource") = _
        strNewLocation
    Set cat.ActiveConnection = CurrentProject.Connection
```

LISTING 20.11   Continued

```
    Set tdf = cat.Tables("tblClients")

    'Try to grab the name property again
    Resume
End Sub
```

This routine points a `Table` object to the `tblClients` table. It then attempts to access the name of the first column in the table. If an error occurs, an input box prompts the user for the new location of the database. The routine modifies the `Jet OLEDB:Link Datasource` property for the database to incorporate the new location. It then resumes on the offending line of code. You should modify this routine to give the user a way out. `Resume` throws the user into an endless loop if the database is not available. An enhanced routine (see Listing 20.13) is presented later in the "Practical Examples" section of this chapter.

Deleting Links

To remove a link using VBA code, simply execute a `Delete` method of the `Tables` collection of a `Catalog` object connected to the database, as shown in Listing 20.12.

LISTING 20.12   Removing a Link

```
Sub RemoveLink()
    Dim cat As Catalog

    Set cat = New ADOX.Catalog
    cat.ActiveConnection = CurrentProject.Connection

    cat.Tables.Delete ("tblClients")

End Sub
```

Making a Local Table from a Linked Table

Access 2007 gives you the capability to convert a linked table to a local table. The process works like this:

1. Use the Navigation Pane to select the table you want to convert.

2. Click to select the linked table that you want to convert to a local table.

3. Click the Copy button in the Clipboard group on the Home tab.

4. Click the Paste button in the Clipboard group on the Home tab. The Paste Table As dialog box appears (see Figure 20.10).

5. Type a name for the new table.

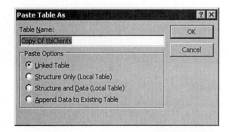

FIGURE 20.10   You use the Paste Table As dialog box to make a local table from a linked table.

6. Select Structure and Data (Local Table) to copy both the structure of the linked table and its data, or select Structure Only (Local Table) to copy only the structure of the linked table.

7. Click OK.

The linked table now appears as a local table within the current database.

Looking at Special Considerations

When you are dealing with different types of external files, various problems and issues arise. If you understand these stumbling blocks before they affect you, you will get a great head start in dealing with them.

dBASE

The major concerns you will have when dealing with dBASE files are deleted records, indexes, data types, and memo fields. When you delete a record from a dBASE table, Access does not remove it from the table. Instead, Access marks it for deletion. You must pack the database (a process in a dBASE table that removes deleted rows) for the records to actually be removed from the table. If records are deleted from a dBASE table using an Access application, the records are not removed. Because you cannot pack a dBASE database from within an Access application, the records still remain in the table. In fact, they are not automatically filtered from the Access table. To filter deleted records so that they cannot be seen within the Access application, you must set the Deleted value in the \HKEY_LOCAL_MACHINE\SOFTWARE\Microsoft\Jet\4.0\Engines\Xbase section of the Registry to 01 (True).

Access can use the dBASE indexes to improve performance. After you link to a dBASE table and select an index, an .INF file is created. This file has the same name as your dBASE database with an .INF extension. It contains information about all the indexes being used. Here's an example of an .INF file:

```
[dBASE III]
NDX1=CUSTID.NDX
UNDX1=CUSTID.NDX
```

dBASE III is the database type identifier. NDX1 is an index number for the first index. The UNDX1 entry specifies a unique index.

The data types available in dBASE files are different from those available in Access files. It is important to understand how the field types are mapped. Table 20.4 shows how each dBASE data type is mapped to a Jet data type.

TABLE 20.4   Mapping of dBASE Data Types

dBASE Data Type	Jet Data Type
Character	Text
Numeric, Float	Double
Logical	Boolean
Date	Date/Time
Memo	Memo
OLE	OLE Object

Finally, make sure that you store the dBASE memo files in the same directory as the table. Otherwise, Access is unable to read the data in the memo file.

Text Data

When you are linking to an ASCII text file, Jet can determine the format of the file directly, or it can use a schema information file, which resides in the same directory as the text file. It always is named SCHEMA.INI, and it contains information about the format of the file, the column names, and the data types. The schema information file is optional for delimited files, but it is required for fixed length files. It is important to understand that ASCII files can never be opened for shared use.

Troubleshooting

Unfortunately, working with external data is not always a smooth process. Many things can go wrong, including connection problems and a lack of temporary disk space.

Connection Problems

Difficulties with accessing external data can be caused by any of the following circumstances:

- ▶ The server on which the external data is stored is down.
- ▶ The user does not have rights to the directory in which the external data is stored.
- ▶ The user does not have rights to the external data source.
- ▶ The external data source was moved.
- ▶ The UNC path or network share name was modified.
- ▶ The connection string is incorrect.
- ▶ The installable ISAM driver has not been installed.

Temp Space

Access requires a significant amount of disk space to run complex queries on large tables. This disk space is required whether the tables are linked tables stored remotely in another format, or they reside on the local machine. The application behaves unpredictably if not enough disk space is available to run the query. It is therefore necessary to make sure that all users have enough disk space to meet the requirements of the queries that are run.

Looking at Performance Considerations and Links

Because your application has to go through an extra translation layer (the installable ISAM), performance is not nearly as good with ISAM files as it is with native Jet data. (The exception to this is using ODBC to connect to SQL Server data.) It's always best to import ISAM data whenever possible. If it's not possible to import the data, you need to accept the performance that linking offers or consider linking the best solution to an otherwise unsolvable problem.

Working with HTML Documents

Access 2007 enables you to import, export, and link to HTML documents. Although working with HTML documents is similar to working with other files types, HTML documents deserve special mention. To import an HTML document, follow these steps:

1. Click to select the External Data tab.

2. Use the More option in the Import group to select HTML Document.

3. Browse to select the document you want to import and click Open. Access returns you to the Get External Data – HTML Document dialog box.

4. Click Import the Source Data into a New Table in the Current Database.

5. Click OK to continue. The Import HTML Wizard appears (see Figure 20.11).

6. The first step of the wizard attempts to parse the HTML document into fields. You can accept what the wizard has done or click Advanced. When you click Advanced, the Import Specification dialog box that appears enables you to designate field names, data types, and indexes for each field and to select any fields you want to eliminate from the imported file (see Figure 20.12). This dialog box also enables you to modify the date order, date delimiter, and more.

7. After you make any required changes to the import specifications, click OK to return to the Import HTML Wizard.

8. If appropriate, click First Row Contains Column headings. Then click Next.

9. Designate a field name, data type, and index for each field, as shown in Figure 20.13. Make any desired changes here and click Next.

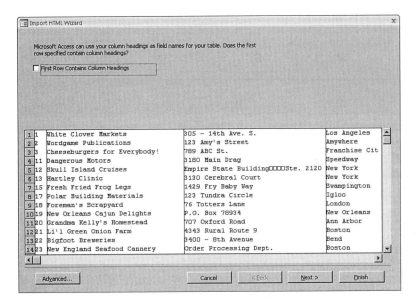

FIGURE 20.11   The Import HTML Wizard allows you to specify the details of the import process.

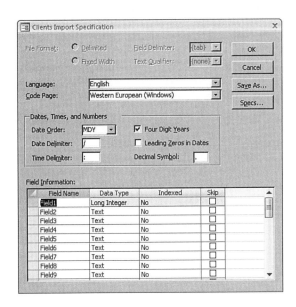

FIGURE 20.12   The Clients Import Specification dialog box enables you to designate the specifics of the import.

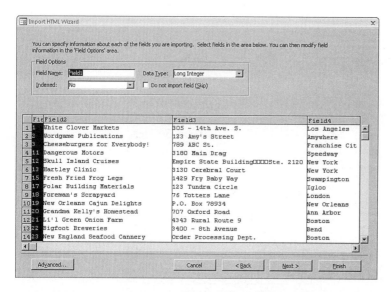

FIGURE 20.13   Customizing the properties of each imported field.

10. The next step of the wizard enables you to indicate that you want Access to add a primary key to the table, that you want to select your own primary key, or that you don't want the imported table to have a primary key (see Figure 20.14). Make your selection and click Next.

11. The final step of the wizard enables you to assign a name to the table. You even can have the wizard analyze the table after importing it. Click Finish after you make your selection.

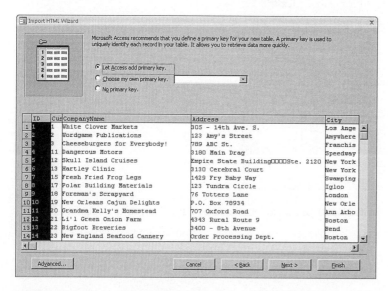

FIGURE 20.14   In this step of the wizard, you can add a primary key to the table.

You can not only import an HTML document, but also link to one. To link to an HTML document, follow these steps:

1. Click to select the External Data tab.

2. Use the More option in the Import group to select HTML Document.

3. Browse to select the document you want to link to and click Open. Access returns you to the Get External Data – HTML Document dialog box.

4. Indicate that you want to link to the data source by creating a linked table.

5. Click OK to continue. The Link HTML Wizard appears.

6. Click the Advanced button to modify any link specifications and return to the first step of the wizard. Click Next to move to the second step of the wizard.

7. Specify information about each field you are linking to. Make any required changes and click Next.

8. Supply a name for the linked table and click Finish.

Although an imported HTML document acts like any other Access table, you can't modify the data in a linked HTML document from within Access. You can use the linked document to create queries, reports, and forms.

Practical Examples: Working with External Data from Within Your Application

It's time to split the data tables from the remainder of the application objects. You can easily accomplish this using the Database Splitter. After you split the tables from the rest of the database objects, you need to write code to refresh links. Both of these topics are covered in the following sections.

Splitting the Database Using the Database Splitter

Begin by using the Database Splitter to separate the tables from the rest of the database objects. You can find the CHAP20EX.ACCDB and CHAP20DATA.ACCDB files included on the sample code CD-ROM. The CHAP20DATA.ACCDB file contains all the tables, and CHAP20EX.ACCDB contains the rest of the database objects.

Refreshing Links

If you distribute your application and all users do not have the same path to the CHAP20DATA.ACCDB file, the application will not load successfully. The LinkTables routine, located in the Switchboard startup form, ensures that the tables are successfully linked, as Listing 20.13 shows.

20

LISTING 20.13   Loading the Application and Checking Table Attachments

```
Sub LinkTables()
    Dim objFileDialog As FileDialog

    On Error GoTo LinkTables_Err:

    DoCmd.Hourglass True

    'Determine if links are ok
    If Not VerifyLink Then

        'If not ok, attempt to relink with expected filename
        If Not ReLink(CurrentProject.FullName, True) Then

            'If still not ok, ask user to locate file
            Set objFileDialog = FileDialog(msoFileDialogOpen)

            With objFileDialog
                .AllowMultiSelect = False
                .Show
            End With

            'Attempt to link to file that user selected
            If Not ReLink(objFileDialog.SelectedItems(1), False) Then

                'If not successful, display a message and quit app
                MsgBox "You Cannot Run This App Without " & _
                    "Locating Data Tables"
                DoCmd.Close acForm, "frmSplash"
                DoCmd.Quit
            End If
        End If
    End If

    DoCmd.Hourglass False
    Exit Sub

LinkTables_Err:
    DoCmd.Hourglass False
    MsgBox "Error # " & Err.Number & ": " & Err.Description
    Exit Sub
End Sub
```

Notice that the VerifyLink routine is called from the LinkTables routine. The VerifyLink routine, which tests to see whether any table links are broken, appears in Listing 20.14.

LISTING 20.14   The VerifyLink Routine

```
Function VerifyLink() As Boolean
    'Verify connection information in linked tables.

    'Declare required variables
    Dim cat As ADOX.Catalog
    Dim tdf As ADOX.Table
    Dim strTemp As String

    'Point Database object variable at the current database
    Set cat = New ADOX.Catalog

    With cat
        Set .ActiveConnection = CurrentProject.Connection

        'Continue if links are broken.
        On Error Resume Next

        'Open one linked table to see if connection
        'information is correct.
        For Each tdf In .Tables
            If tdf.Type = "LINK" Then
                strTemp = tdf.Columns(0).Name
                If Err.Number Then
                    Exit For
                End If
            End If

        Next tdf
    End With

    VerifyLink = (Err.Number = 0)

End Function
```

The routine begins by pointing the ActiveConnection property of the Catalog object to the connection associated with the current database. It then loops through each table in the Tables collection of the Catalog object. If the table is a linked table, it attempts to access the name of the first column in the table. If any of the links are broken, an error occurs, and the For…Each loop is exited. If no error occurs, the function returns True; otherwise, the function returns False.

If the VerifyLink routine returns False, the ReLink routine, which attempts to reestablish the broken links, is called. Listing 20.15 shows the ReLink routine.

20

LISTING 20.15   The ReLink Routine

```
Function ReLink(strDir As String, DefaultData As Boolean) _
    As Boolean

    ' Relink a broken linked Access table.

    Dim cat As ADOX.Catalog
    Dim tdfRelink As ADOX.Table
    Dim oDBInfo As DBInfo
    Dim strPath As String
    Dim strName As String
    Dim intCounter As Integer
    Dim vntStatus As Variant

    'Prepare status bar
    vntStatus = SysCmd(acSysCmdSetStatus, "Updating Links")

    Set cat = New ADOX.Catalog

    'Instantiate database information class
    Set oDBInfo = New DBInfo

    With cat
        .ActiveConnection = CurrentProject.Connection

        'Extract the name and path from the passed database
        oDBInfo.FullName = strDir
        strPath = oDBInfo.FilePathOnly
        strName = Left(oDBInfo.FileName, InStr(oDBInfo.FileName, ".") - 1)

        On Error Resume Next
        'Update progress meter
        Call SysCmd(acSysCmdInitMeter, "Linking Data Tables", .Tables.Count)

        'Loop through each table, attempting to update the link
        For Each tdfRelink In .Tables
            intCounter = intCounter + 1
            Call SysCmd(acSysCmdUpdateMeter, intCounter)
            If .Tables(tdfRelink.Name).Type = "LINK" And _
                Left(tdfRelink.Name, 3) = "tbl" Then
                tdfRelink.Properties("Jet OLEDB:Link Datasource") = _
                strPath & strName & IIf(DefaultData, "Data.Accdb", ".accdb")
            End If
            If Err.Number Then
                Exit For
```

LISTING 20.15   Continued

```
        End If
     Next tdfRelink
   End With

   'Reset the progress meter
   Call SysCmd(acSysCmdRemoveMeter)

   vntStatus = SysCmd(acSysCmdClearStatus)

   ReLink = (Err = 0)
End Function
```

The `ReLink` function receives two parameters. The first parameter is the name of the database the function will attempt to link to. The second parameter is a Boolean variable that designates whether the database is considered the default database.

The function begins by modifying the status bar. It then creates a `Catalog` object and an instance of a custom class called `DBInfo`. Class modules are covered in Chapter 14, "Exploiting the Power of Class Modules." The `ActiveConnection` property of the `Catalog` object is set equal to the `Connection` property of the current project. Next, the `FullName` property of the `DBInfo` class is set equal to the name of the file that is passed as a parameter to the function. The `DBInfo` class extracts the path and the filename from the full filename. Just as with the `VerifyLink` function, the `ReLink` function uses a For...Next loop to loop through all the tables in the database. As it loops through each table, it attempts to establish a link to a database with the name passed as a parameter to the `ReLink` function.

This `ReLink` function is called twice from the `LinkTables` routine, shown in Listing 20.13. The first time it's passed, the `FullName` property of the `CurrentProject` object and the Boolean are `True`, indicating that it will try to locate the table in a database with the same location as the application database. If that attempt is not successful, the `LinkTables` routine uses the `FileDialog` object to display the File Open dialog box, allowing the user to attempt to locate the database. The `ReLink` function is called again, searching for the table in the database selected by the user. If it is still unsuccessful, the routine quits the application.

Summary

The capability to link to external data is one of Access 2007's strongest attributes. It is important that you understand how to link to external data via the user interface and by using VBA code. This chapter taught you how to link to external tables, open external data sources directly, refresh and remove links, and create external tables using VBA code. Many of the techniques covered in this chapter are covered extensively in *Alison Balter's Mastering Access 2002 Enterprise Development*.

20

Access 2007 and SharePoint

Why This Chapter Is Important?

SharePoint Server 2007 offers several benefits in managing data. These benefits include the ability to track versions of data, subscribe to alerts so that you know when another user makes changes to the data, and manage permissions for the site. By integrating SharePoint 2007 and Access 2007, you benefit from these rich collaboration features while utilizing Access's powerful data entry and analysis features.

You can use several different techniques when integrating Access 2007 and SharePoint 2007, including the following:

▶ Exporting selected data to a SharePoint site

▶ Moving an entire database to a SharePoint site

▶ Opening Access forms and reports from a SharePoint site

▶ Creating databases from SharePoint lists

▶ Taking SharePoint lists offline with Access

Although this chapter covers each of these techniques in detail, the sections that follow provide an overview of each topic.

Exporting Selected Data to a SharePoint Site

When you export a table to SharePoint, you make a copy of that table and place it on the SharePoint site as a SharePoint list. Changes made to the Access table do not affect the SharePoint list, and changes made to the SharePoint list do not affect the Access table.

Moving an Entire Database to a SharePoint Site

You can use the Move to SharePoint Site Wizard to move your Access 2007 data to a SharePoint site. During this process, Access removes the tables from the Access database, places them on the SharePoint site, and creates links to the data from within Access. After the tables are on the SharePoint site, people can either work with the tables on the SharePoint site or use the linked tables within Microsoft Access. Because the data is in SharePoint, you can take advantage of the data tracking and permissions benefits of SharePoint.

Opening Access Forms and Reports from a SharePoint Site

After you publish data to a SharePoint site, users can open your Access forms, reports, and datasheets directly from the SharePoint site. The objects appear on the site along with the SharePoint views. When a user selects a given form, report, or datasheet from within SharePoint, Access starts and opens the appropriate object. The user does not have to first open Access to work with the form or report.

Creating Databases from SharePoint Lists

Just as you can create SharePoint lists from Access tables, you can also create Access databases from SharePoint lists. After you create the Access database, you can build forms and reports that you will use to view and update the SharePoint data.

When you import a SharePoint list, you are copying the SharePoint data and creating a new Access table based on the copy. If you make changes to the SharePoint data, those changes do not affect the Access data; and if you make changes to the Access data, the changes do not affect the SharePoint data. When you link to a SharePoint list, the data resides only in SharePoint. Your Access database points at the SharePoint database and reads its data. All changes that you make to the data from within Access are saved to the SharePoint list, and all changes that you make to the data from within SharePoint are reflected in Access. After you have linked to SharePoint lists, you will want to use forms and reports to view and update their data.

Taking SharePoint Lists Offline with Access

Sometimes you will want to work with your SharePoint data when you are disconnected from the network. With one click in Access, you can take your SharePoint lists offline and then synchronize them with the server when you reconnect to the network.

Summary of Benefits of Working with SharePoint

The techniques just covered provide numerous benefits to Access developers and end users. The first has to do with security. Using SharePoint lists *and* Access databases on SharePoint sites, you can apply security settings to groups of users who will access your data. For example, you can assign the appropriate rights to groups so that they can access only the data appropriate for their use. This means that whereas one group has read-only rights to limited items within a list, another group has full editing rights to all items in the list.

21

Another benefit of storing the data in SharePoint is its capability to track and manage versions of data. Using SharePoint as your data store, you can easily determine who modified data and when.

Finally, users can easily view or restore deleted rows. This functionality is available because deleted rows are not actually removed but are instead placed in the Recycle Bin.

The Access 2007 (`accdb`) File Format and SharePoint

It is important to understand that if you want to integrate with SharePoint data from within Access, you not only must use Access 2007 but also must have your database stored in the Access 2007 (`accdb`) file format. There are a few reasons for this. The first is multivalued lookup fields, new to Access 2007 and the `accdb` file format. Multivalued lookup fields enable you to store multiple values in a single field, creating, in effect, a many-to-many relationship within the field. An example is a `SoldBy` field. You can place the names of all the salespeople in a single field and use that field as a lookup for what salesperson is associated with a particular order. Because SharePoint supports multivalued fields, it makes sense for Access to support multivalued fields so that the two can share data.

Another Access 2007 feature important to SharePoint is memo field history tracking. Using memo field history tracking, you can ensure that users can only append to memos, not edit existing memo data. You can then view all those changes. Because SharePoint also enables you to track changes with its versioning feature, adding this feature to Access ensures that you can track changes when linked to data in a SharePoint list.

Exporting Data to a SharePoint Site

If your department or workgroup uses SharePoint to manage its lists, at some time you might need to export some of your Access tables to the SharePoint site. When you export an Access table to SharePoint, you are making a copy of the data. In other words, if you make changes to the data in Access, those changes will not appear in SharePoint; and if you make changes to the data in SharePoint, you will not see the data in Access.

Why Export Data to a SharePoint Site?

There are a few reasons why you might choose to export data to a SharePoint site. Probably the most common reason is that you plan to work with the data in SharePoint, but it currently resides in Access. You can export the data to a SharePoint list and then link to the list from within Access. Linking is covered in the section "Linking to and Importing from SharePoint Lists."

A second reason you might want to export data to a SharePoint site is that you are just getting started with SharePoint and you believe that it might be simpler for your users to work with some of your data if it is stored both in Access and as SharePoint lists. This is due to the ease of use when viewing or editing SharePoint lists within a browser.

Finally, you can use queries to export important results to SharePoint. Users of the SharePoint site can then browse those results from within SharePoint without having to load Access.

How to Export Data to a SharePoint Site

Microsoft Office Access 2007 makes the process of exporting to a SharePoint site quite easy. Here are the steps involved:

1. Open the database containing the table or query that you want to export to SharePoint.

2. Right-click the object that you want to export and select Export, SharePoint List (see Figure 21.1).

   Or

   Select the object that you want to export, click to select the External Data tab, and then select SharePoint List in the Export group (see Figure 21.2).

   In either case, the Export Data to SharePoint List Wizard appears (see Figure 21.3). Note that you can export only tables and query results. The fields and records of the tables and queries in Access become the columns and rows of the SharePoint list.

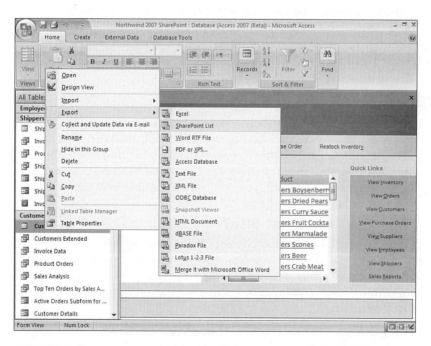

FIGURE 21.1   You can right-click an object to export it to SharePoint.

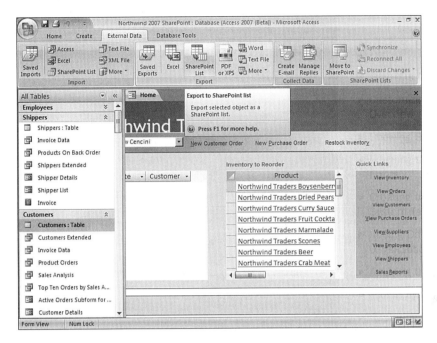

FIGURE 21.2   You can use the External data tab to export an object to SharePoint.

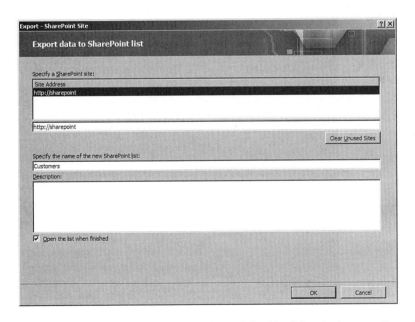

FIGURE 21.3   The Export Data to SharePoint List Wizard takes you through the process of exporting table or query data to SharePoint.

3. Enter the name of the SharePoint site on which you want to place the list. The site address must appear like this:

`http://sharepoint/accounting`

In this example, `sharepoint` is the name of the server, and `accounting` is the name of the specific site on the server where you want to place the list.

4. Ensure that you have appropriate rights to the server. Also, ensure that the name of the list is unique. Access will not allow you to overwrite a list with a list that already exists with that name. Instead, it makes a second copy of the object and adds a suffix to the name (for example, `Customers_1`). Click OK to export the data to SharePoint. The export process places you on the SharePoint Team Site, in the specific site that you designated during the export process. Notice in Figure 21.4 that the copy of the `Orders` table appears on the SharePoint site and is viewed within a browser. You can now manipulate the data in SharePoint.

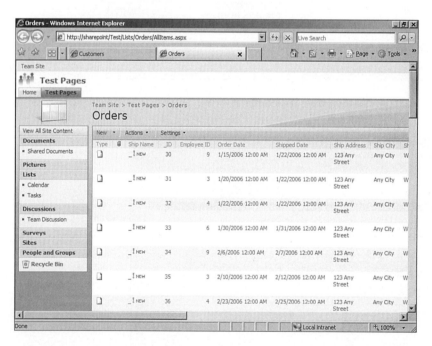

FIGURE 21.4   The `Orders` table appears on the SharePoint site and is viewed within a browser.

Conversion Issues

You should be aware of some conversion issues when exporting your Access tables to SharePoint:

▶ All fields in the table or query, including hidden fields, are exported to SharePoint.

▶ Filter settings are ignored during the export process (use query criteria instead).

▶ Because SharePoint lists support only one attachment column, you must remove all but one attachment column before you export the data to SharePoint. The workaround to this problem is to copy additional attachment columns to other Access objects and then export them to SharePoint lists.

▶ Access exports display values in single-valued lookup fields as drop-down menu choices in the SharePoint list.

▶ If the source column supports multiple values, the wizard creates a Choice field that allows multiple selections in the SharePoint list.

▶ A Choice field in SharePoint can consist of only a single column. If the source lookup field is based on multiple columns, the values of all the columns are combined into a single column.

▶ Only the results of a calculated field in a query are copied to the SharePoint list (not the underlying formula).

▶ When you export a calculated field, the data type selected in the export is dependent on the data type of the formula result.

▶ Access ignores OLE object fields when performing the export.

It is also important to understand how the Windows SharePoint Services data types map to Access data types. Access help provides you with this mapping information. For example, a Text field is converted to a single line of text. The column name, description, required setting, maximum number of characters, and default value mirror their Access counterparts. A Memo field is converted to multiple lines of text. The column name, description, and required properties mirror their Access counterparts. The number of lines to display is set to 5.

After the wizard runs, Access prompts you as to whether you want to save your export steps (see Figure 21.5). If you click Save Export Steps, the wizard prompts you for all the necessary information about the export process (see Figure 21.6). Enter the Save As location, the description, and whether you want to generate an Outlook task that will remind you to complete the operation. Click Save Export to complete the process.

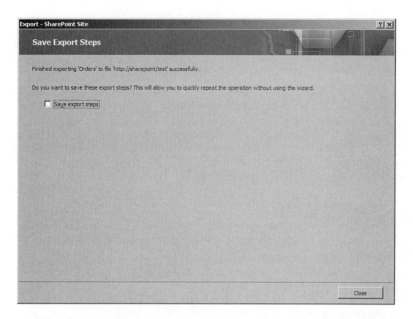

FIGURE 21.5   After you run the wizard, Access prompts you as to whether you want to save the export steps.

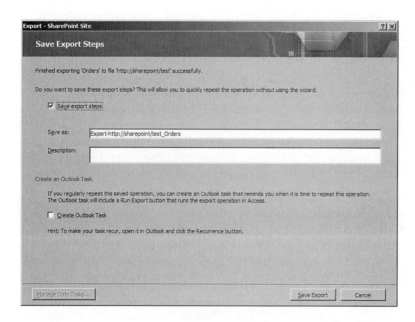

FIGURE 21.6   If you opt to save the export steps, Access prompts you for the appropriate information.

Publishing Data to a SharePoint Site

When you publish data to a SharePoint site, you first copy it to the site and then create links to it from within Access. You can then run your queries, forms, and reports from within Access. The Move to SharePoint Site Wizard assists you with the process of creating the lists in SharePoint, maintaining the relationships between them, and creating links to them within Access. Here's how the wizard works:

1. Click to select the External Data tab.

2. Click the Move to SharePoint button within the SharePoint Lists group. The Move to SharePoint Site Wizard appears (see Figure 21.7).

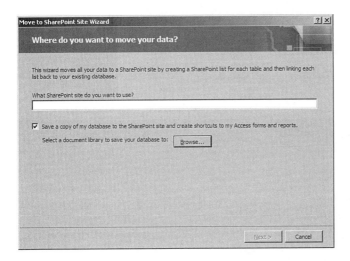

FIGURE 21.7   The Move to SharePoint Site Wizard walks you through the process of moving Access tables to SharePoint lists.

3. Designate the SharePoint site that you want to use (for example, `http://sharepoint/test`).

4. If you plan to run your forms and reports from within Access (rather than from within SharePoint), click Next. It is important to note that you either need to specify a document library (the default) or clear the Save a Copy check box. Otherwise, the Next button will not be available. The process of creating the lists in SharePoint is quite involved and will probably take some time, especially if you have a large number of tables. You can click Stop at any time to abort the process.

5. When the process completes, the wizard should appear as in Figure 21.8. If there are warnings or errors, you should click Show Details. Your screen will then appear as in Figure 21.9. Notice that the details show you the lists the wizard created, where the backup copy of your database is located, and what table contains a log of issues encountered by the wizard.

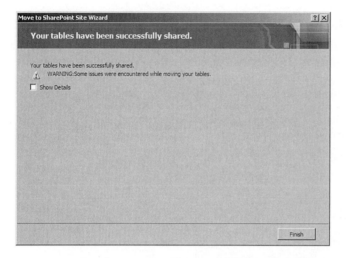

FIGURE 21.8   The wizard provides you with information upon completion.

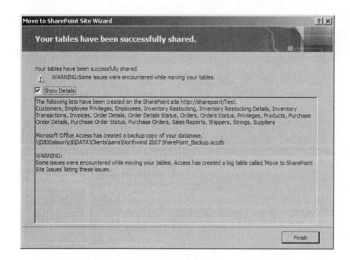

FIGURE 21.9   You can opt to view the details of everything that occurred during the process of creating SharePoint lists.

6. Click Finish to complete the process. Notice that the Access tables appear with links to the SharePoint lists (see Figure 21.10).

It is important that you review the Move to SharePoint Site Issues table. This table lists all issues encountered during the upsizing process. The Move to SharePoint Site Issues table appears in Figure 21.11.

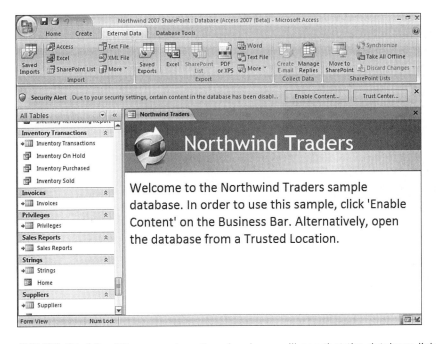

FIGURE 21.10   When you close the wizard, you will see that the database links to all the SharePoint lists.

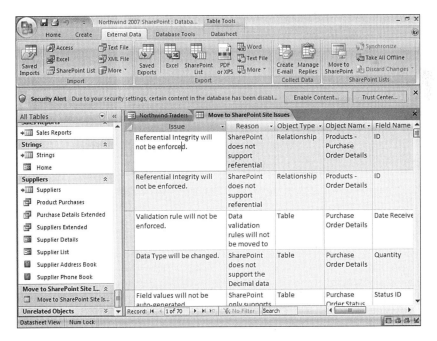

FIGURE 21.11   It is important that you review the Move to SharePoint Site Issues table to determine everything that happened during the upsizing process.

Now that the SharePoint lists are created, you can view and edit list data from within Micro-soft Access (see Figure 21.12). You can also run forms and reports based on that data (see Figures 21.13 and 21.14). You can also edit data directly from the SharePoint site (see Figure 21.15). Because the lists are linked, all changes are reflected both in Access and in SharePoint.

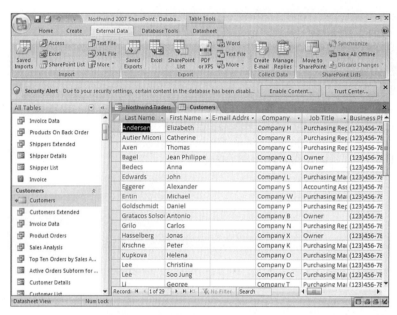

FIGURE 21.12   You can view and edit list data while in Datasheet view.

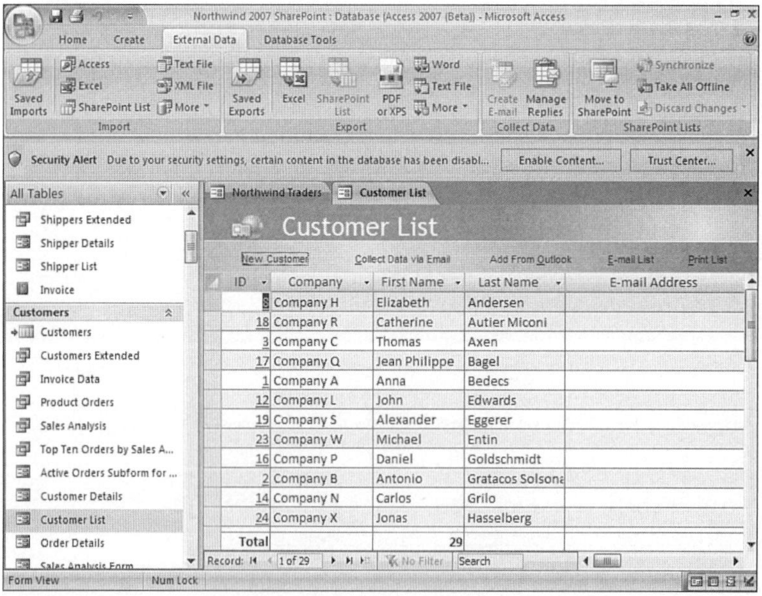

FIGURE 21.13   You can view and edit data using an Access form.

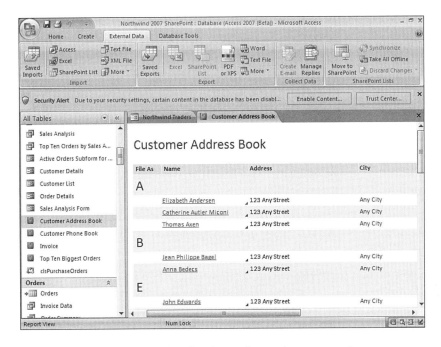

FIGURE 21.14   You can view list data using an Access report.

FIGURE 21.15   You can modify list data via the SharePoint site.

Now that the data is in SharePoint lists, you can fully manage it from the SharePoint site. This means that you can apply various levels of security, manage versions of the data, and retrieve deleted data from the Recycle Bin on the SharePoint site. You can even create alerts so that certain people know when someone has changed the data.

How the Wizard Moves Data to the SharePoint Site

When the wizard runs, it attempts to match each Access table to a template available on the SharePoint site. If it finds a template, it creates the SharePoint list based on that template. If it can't find an appropriate template, it creates a custom list on the SharePoint site. During the process, it creates a backup of your original database and then creates links to the lists on the SharePoint site.

Opening Access Forms and Reports from a SharePoint Site

In the preceding sections, you published data to a SharePoint site. When you ran the wizard, you did not opt to save a copy of the database to the SharePoint site and create shortcuts to Access forms and reports. Instead, you ran all the queries, forms, and reports from within Microsoft Access. In this section, you tell the wizard to save a copy of the database to the SharePoint site and create shortcuts to its forms and reports (see Figure 21.16). To do this, you must select Browse and indicate the location of the document library where you want to save your database (see Figure 21.17). After you have saved your database to the document library, you can easily launch your forms and reports from the SharePoint site. Here are the steps involved:

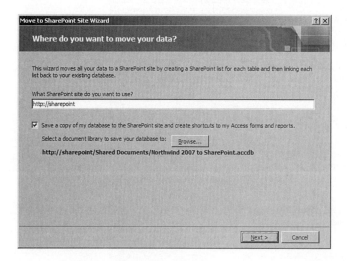

FIGURE 21.16   When you publish data to a SharePoint site, you can opt to create shortcuts to Access forms and reports.

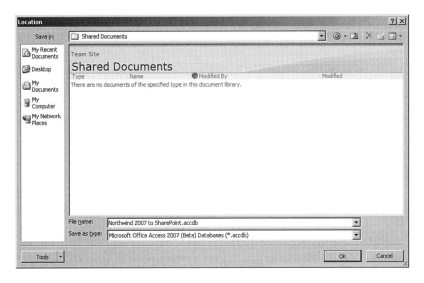

FIGURE 21.17   You must designate the SharePoint library within which you want to save the database.

1. Navigate to the appropriate SharePoint site.

2. Click to expand the lists available on that site (see Figure 21.18).

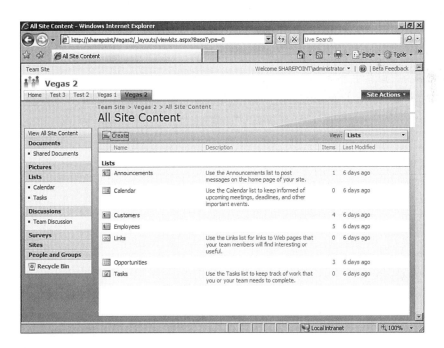

FIGURE 21.18   You must click to expand the lists available on the site.

3. Click the link to open the list that you want to view. The screen appears as in Figure 21.19.

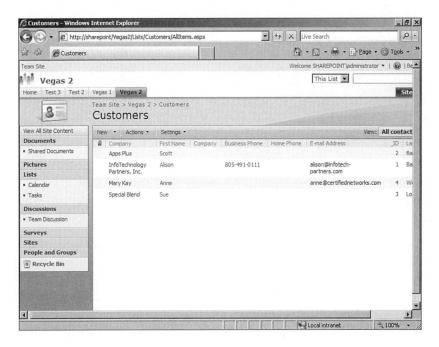

FIGURE 21.19   Click the link to open the list you want to view.

4. Click to open the View drop-down. All the forms and reports associated with that list appear in the drop-down (see Figure 21.20).

5. Click to select the form or report that you want to run. Access launches and displays the form or report (see Figure 21.21).

FIGURE 21.20   The View drop-down displays all the forms and reports associated with a list.

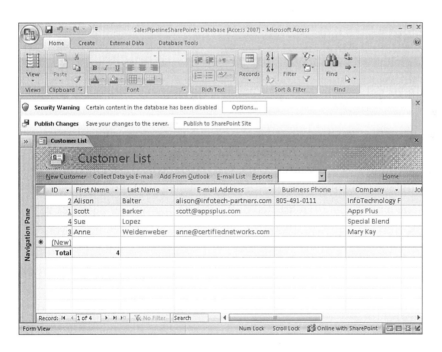

FIGURE 21.21   Access launches and displays the selected form or report.

Linking to and Importing from SharePoint Lists

You can easily create an Access database from existing SharePoint lists. The process is quite simple:

1. Open the database within which you want to place the new tables.

2. Click to select the External Data tab.

3. Select SharePoint List from the Import group. The Get External Data dialog box appears (see Figure 21.22).

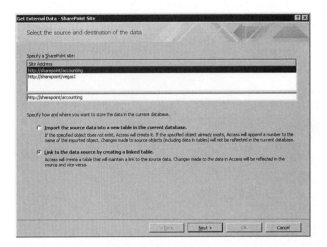

FIGURE 21.22   In the Get External Data dialog box, you can designate whether you want to import or link to the SharePoint data.

4. Designate whether you want to actually import the SharePoint data into the Access database or whether you prefer to create links in the Access database to the SharePoint lists. Realize that if you select the first option, you are simply copying the SharePoint data and are placing the copy of the data within the Access database.

5. Click Next. The Import data from list step of the wizard appears (see Figure 21.23).

6. Click to select the tables that you want to import or link to.

7. Click OK to complete the process.

8. Access prompts you to save the import steps (see Figure 21.24). If you opt to save the import steps, the dialog box in Figure 21.25 appears.

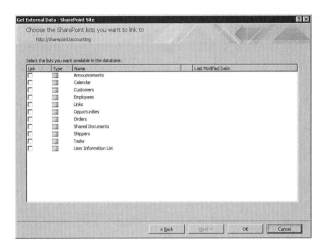

FIGURE 21.23   Select the tables that you want to import or link to.

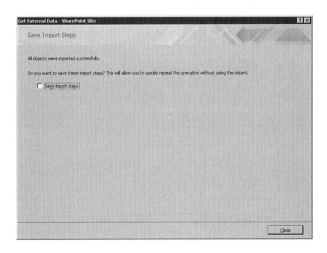

FIGURE 21.24   Access prompts you to save the import steps.

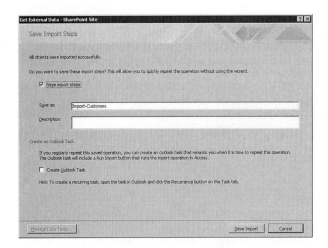

FIGURE 21.25   Access prompts you for information about the import process.

9. Fill in the name for the task, add a description of the task, and designate whether you want to generate an Outlook task that will automatically run at designated times.

10. Click Save Import to complete the process. The resulting database appears as in Figure 21.26. Notice the four tables with links to the SharePoint database.

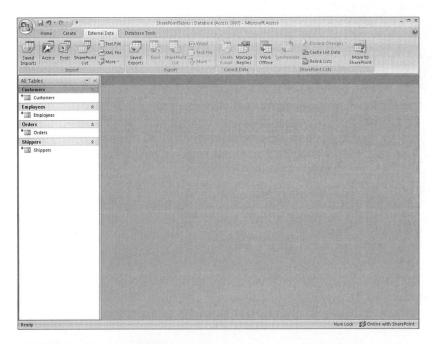

FIGURE 21.26   The linked tables appear in the Access database.

Taking SharePoint Lists Offline with Access

At times, you will want to take your SharePoint lists offline and work with them while you are disconnected from the network. Fortunately, Access 2007 makes this process quite easy. It is important to note that this scenario applies only to Access databases containing links to SharePoint lists, not to imported lists. Here's how you can work with your SharePoint lists offline:

1. Open the database that you want to take offline.

2. Click to select the External Data tab.

3. Click to select Work Offline from the SharePoint Lists group. The icons associated with the linked tables change to appear as in Figure 21.27.

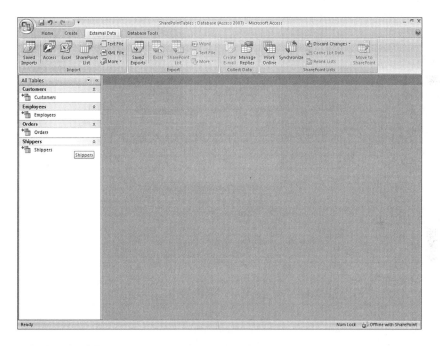

FIGURE 21.27   The icons change to indicate that you are working offline.

Synchronizing Your Changes with SharePoint

Because you are now working on a local copy of the data, changes that you make to the data are not immediately reflected in SharePoint, and changes made in SharePoint are not reflected in the Access database. At some point, you might want to have your changes reflected in SharePoint. You will also want to view the current SharePoint data. This process does not require taking your database back online. Here's how it works:

1. Click to select the External Data tab.

2. Select Synchronize in the SharePoint Lists group. Access will indicate to you that the synchronization process is occurring.

3. If any conflicts occur between the offline database and the SharePoint data, the Resolve Conflicts dialog box appears (see Figure 21.28).

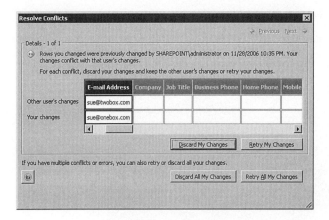

FIGURE 21.28   The Resolve Conflicts dialog box allows you to resolve conflicts between Access and SharePoint data.

4. Resolve any conflicts by opting to either discard your changes or retry your changes.

5. The synchronization process completes, and all changes appear in both the Access copy and the SharePoint copy.

Working Online

At some point, you will be ready to once again work online. Notice that when you are working offline, the ribbon button reads Work Online and is available in the SharePoint Lists group. To work online, just click the Work Online button. The synchronization process completes; and if there are any conflicts, the Resolve Conflicts dialog box appears. When the process completes and all conflicts have been resolved, the link icons return to normal (see Figure 21.29).

Discarding Your Changes

You might decide that you want to discard all the changes that you have made to the data in the Access database. This feature, of course, is appropriate only when you have taken the database offline. Selecting this option in essence rolls back all the changes that you have made to the database since you took it offline. Notice in Figure 21.30 that you can choose either Discard All Changes *or* Discard All Changes and Refresh. If you opt to discard all changes, your changes are eliminated, but you will not see the current data in SharePoint. If you opt to discard all changes and refresh, you eliminate your changes and you will see all changes made to the SharePoint database since you took the database offline.

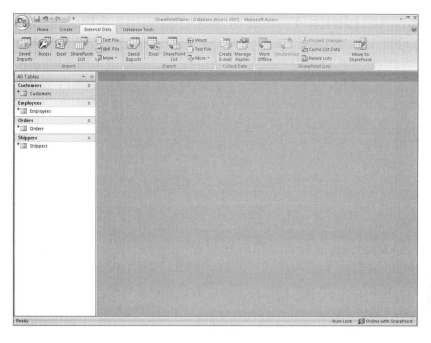

FIGURE 21.29   After you take the database back online, the icons appear in their default state.

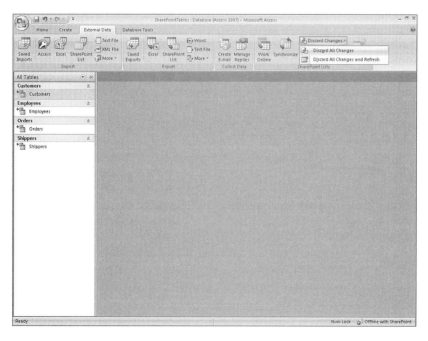

FIGURE 21.30   Access gives you two choices when discarding your changes.

Reestablishing Links When a SharePoint Site Has Been Moved

You or someone else might at some time need to move a SharePoint site to a different location. When this happens, the link from Access to the SharePoint data will be lost. Fortunately, Microsoft Office Access 2007 has a built-in feature that enables you to rectify the link. Here's how it works:

1. Click to select the External Data tab within Microsoft Access 2007.

2. After clicking the Work Online button on the ribbon to take the database back online, click the Relink Lists option in the SharePoint Lists group. The Relink Lists to New Site dialog box appears (see Figure 21.31).

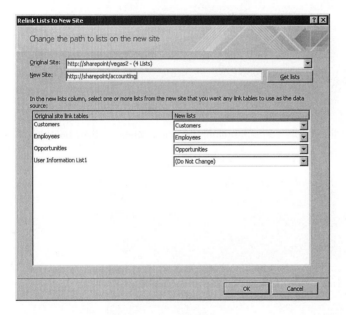

FIGURE 21.31   The Relink Lists to New Site dialog box allows you to designate the new site where the lists reside.

3. Type in the name of the new site that contains the designated lists.

4. Click Get Lists to view the lists available on the designated site. The lists appear in the New Lists column, and Access attempts to map the old list names to the new list names (see Figure 21.32).

5. Click OK to complete the process.

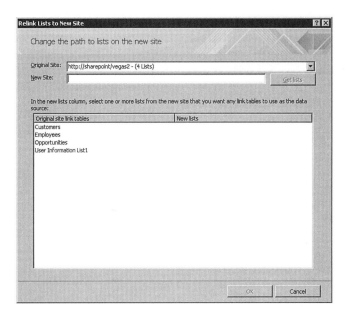

FIGURE 21.32   Access attempts to map the old list names to the new list names.

Summary

Both Access and SharePoint are powerful tools. Used together, they offer the developer or end user several benefits. They accomplish this by allowing you to take advantage of the slick user interface provided by Microsoft Office Access 2007, while taking advantage of the data management provided by SharePoint.

CHAPTER 22

Developing Multiuser and Enterprise Applications

Why This Chapter Is Important

Many people forge right into the application development process with little worry about the scalability of the application. Even a simple application that begins as a single-user application can develop into a multiuser or enterprise-wide application. Unfortunately, the techniques you can get away with in the single-user application can wreak havoc in a network or client/server environment. It is therefore necessary to think about the future when you design any application. Although the initial development process might be more complex, if written properly, the application will survive any growth that it experiences. This chapter focuses on writing applications that transition easily from the single-user environment through the enterprise client/server environment.

Designing Your Application with Multiuser Issues in Mind

When you develop applications that multiple users will access over the network, you must make sure they effectively handle sharing data and other application objects. Many options are available for developers when they design multiuser applications, and this chapter covers the pros and cons of these options.

Multiuser issues revolve around locking data; they include deciding where to store database objects, when to lock data, and how much data to lock. In a multiuser environment, having several users simultaneously trying to modify the same data can cause conflicts. As a developer, you need to handle these conflicts. Otherwise, your users will experience unexplainable errors.

Multiuser Design Strategies

There are many methods for handling concurrent access to data and other application objects by multiple users; each one offers both solutions and limitations. It's important to select the best solution for your particular environment.

Strategies for Installing Access

There are two strategies for installing Access:

▶ Run Access from a file server across a network.

▶ Run a separate copy of Access on each workstation.

The advantages of running Access from a file server are that it

▶ Allows for central administration of the Access software

▶ Potentially reduces the licensing requirements

▶ Allows Access applications to be installed on diskless workstations

▶ Reduces hard disk requirements

File server installations also have *serious* drawbacks, including the following:

▶ Every time the user launches an Access application, the Access EXE, DLLs, and any other files required to run Access are *all* sent over the network wire to the local machine. Obviously, this generates a significant volume of network traffic.

▶ Performance is generally degraded to unacceptable levels.

Because the disadvantages of running Access from a file server are so pronounced, I *strongly* recommend that you install Access, or at least the runtime engine, on each user's machine.

Strategies for Installing Your Application

Just as there are different strategies for installing Access, there are also various strategies for installing your application, such as the following:

▶ Install both the application and data on a file server.

▶ Install the data on the file server and the application on each workstation.

▶ Install the application and the data on a machine running Windows 2003 Terminal Services.

In other words, after you have created an application, you can place the entire application on the network, which means that all the tables, queries, forms, reports, macros, and modules that make up the system reside on the file server. Although this method of shared access keeps everything in the same place, you will see many advantages to placing only the database's data tables on the file server. The remaining objects are placed in a database on each user's machine, and each local application database is linked to the tables on the network. In this way, users share data but not the rest of the application objects.

The advantages of doing this are as follows:

- ▶ Because each user has a copy of the local database objects, load time and network traffic are both reduced.

- ▶ You can easily back up data without having to back up the rest of the application objects.

- ▶ When redistributing new versions of the application, you don't need to worry about overwriting the application's data.

- ▶ You can design multiple applications to use the same centrally located data.

- ▶ Users can add their own objects (such as their own queries) to their local copies of the database.

In addition to storing the queries, forms, reports, macros, and modules that make up the application in a local database, I also recommend that you store the following objects in each local database:

- ▶ Temporary tables

- ▶ Static tables

- ▶ Semistatic tables

Temporary tables should be stored in the database that's on each workstation because, if two users are performing operations that build the same temporary tables, you don't want one user's process to interfere with the other user's process. You can eliminate the potential conflict of one user's temporary tables overwriting the other's by storing all temporary tables in each user's local copy of the database.

You should also place static lookup tables, such as state tables, on each workstation. Because the data doesn't change, maintenance isn't an issue. The benefit is that Access doesn't need to pull that data over the network each time the application needs it.

Semistatic tables—tables that are rarely updated—can also be placed on the local machine. As with static tables, having these tables in a local database means reduced network traffic and better performance, not only for the user needing the data, but also for anyone sharing the same network wire.

The configuration described throughout this section is illustrated in Figure 22.1.

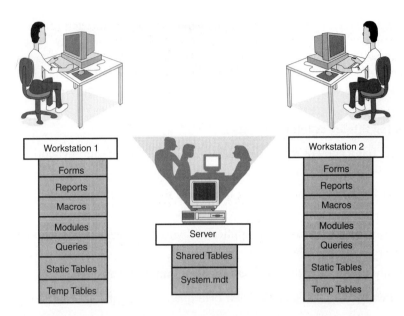

FIGURE 22.1   An example of a configuration with database objects split, storing temporary and static tables locally and shared tables remotely (on the file server).

Terminal Services has emerged as a viable alternative for deployment of an Access application. It addresses both bandwidth and centralization issues. With this option, a Windows 2003 machine runs the Windows 2003 Terminal Services. Client machines then access the server machine using the Terminal Server Client Utility. In this scenario, Access, your application, and the data that it accesses are all installed on the Windows 2003 Server machine. All other machines access the application via user sessions created on the server machine. Keystrokes and mouse events are sent from the client machines to the server machine. The resulting screen image is returned to the client machine. This configuration addresses many of the problems inherent in the two other solutions.

The Basics of Linking to External Data

Chapter 20, "Using External Data," covers linking to external data, including data not stored in another Access database. Two options are available to you:

▶ Design the databases separately from the start.

▶ Include all objects in one database and then split them manually when you're ready to distribute your application.

Chapter 20 covers these two options in detail.

> **CAUTION**
>
> Be aware that when you're distributing an application using linked tables, you must write code to make sure the data tables can be located from each application database on the network. The reason is that Access hard-codes the location of linked tables into the application database. If each user has the same path to the file server, this isn't a problem. However, if the path to the file server varies, you need to write a routine that makes sure the tables can be successfully relinked. If they can't, the routine prompts the user for the data's location. Chapter 20 covers this routine.

Understanding Access's Locking Mechanisms

Although the preceding tips for designing network applications reduce network traffic, they in no way reduce locking conflicts. To protect shared data, Access locks either a record or a page of data as the user edits a record. In this way, multiple users can read the data, but only one user can make changes to it. Data can be locked through a form or through a recordset that isn't bound to a form.

Here are the methods of locking for an Access application:

- ▶ Record locking
- ▶ Page locking
- ▶ Table and Recordset locking
- ▶ Opening an entire database with Exclusive Access

With Record locking, the Access Database Engine locks only the record that the user is editing. With Page locking, the Access Database Engine locks the 4K page with the record being edited. On the other hand, in Table and Recordset locking, the Access Database Engine locks the entire table or recordset with the record being edited. With Database locking, the Access Database Engine locks the entire database, unless the user opening the database has opened it for read-only access. In that case, other users can also open the database for read-only access.

It's important to note that the locking scheme you adhere to depends on the source providing the data. If you're using client/server data, you inherit the locking scheme of the particular back end you're using. If you're manipulating Indexed Sequential Access Method (ISAM) data over a network, you get the type of data locking that the particular ISAM database supports. For example, if you're working with a FoxPro database, you can use Record locking or any other locking scheme that FoxPro supports.

> **NOTE**
>
> Multiuser development and multiuser issues are covered in extensive detail in *Alison Balter's Mastering Access 2002 Enterprise Development*.

Understanding the Client/Server Model

Now that you understand the basics of using Access in a multiuser environment, I am going to take things a step further by discussing client/server applications. One of the hot computing terms of the 21st century, *client/server* refers to distributed processing of information. A client/server model involves the storage of data on database servers dedicated to the tasks of processing data and storing it.

The client/server model introduces a separation of functionalities. The *client*, or front end, is responsible for presenting the data and doing some processing. The *server*, or back end, is responsible for storing, protecting, and performing the bulk of the data processing.

With its tools that assist in the rapid development of queries, forms, and reports, Access provides an excellent front end for the presentation of back-end data.

For years, most information professionals have worked with traditional programming languages to process and maintain data integrity in the application. This means that data validation rules must be embedded in the programming code. Furthermore, these types of applications are record-oriented; that is, all records are read into memory and processed. This scenario has several drawbacks:

▶ If the underlying data structure changes, every application that uses the data structure must be changed.

▶ Data validation rules must be placed in *every* application that accesses a data table.

▶ Presentation, processing, and storage are handled by one program.

▶ Record-oriented processing results in an extraordinary amount of unnecessary network traffic.

Deciding Whether to Use the Client/Server Model

Client/server technology was not as necessary when there was a clear delineation between mainframe applications and personal computer applications. Today, the line of demarcation has blurred. Personal computer applications are taking over many applications that had been relegated to mainframe computers in the past. The problem is that users are still very limited by the bandwidth of network communications. This is one place where client/server technology can really help.

However, many developers are confused about what client/server architecture really is. Some mistakenly believe that an Access ACCDB database file stored on a file server acts as a database server. This is not the case. (In fact, I have participated in many debates in which other developers have insisted that Access itself is a database server application. Well, it's not.) Access is a front-end application that can process data stored on a back end. In this scenario, the Access application runs on the client machine accessing data stored on a database server running software such as Microsoft SQL Server. Access does an excellent job acting as the client-side, front-end software in this scenario. The confusion lies in Access's capability to act as a database server.

The difference lies in the way that data is retrieved when Access is acting as the front end to a database server versus when the data is stored in an Access ACCDB file. Suppose that you have a table with 500,000 records. A user runs a query based on the 500,000-record table stored in an Access database on a file server. Suppose that the user wants to see a list of all the Californians who make more than $75,000 per year. With the data stored on the file server in the Access ACCDB file format, all records would be sent over the network to the workstation, and the query would be performed on the workstation (see Figure 22.2). This results in significant network traffic.

On the other hand, assume that these 500,000 records were stored on a database server such as Microsoft SQL Server. If the user runs the same query, only the names of the Californians who make more than $75,000 per year would be sent over the network. In this scenario, only the specific fields requested would be retrieved (see Figure 22.3).

What does this mean to you? When should you become concerned with client/server technology and what it can offer you? The following sections present some guidelines as to why you might want to upsize from an Access back end to a SQL Server back end.

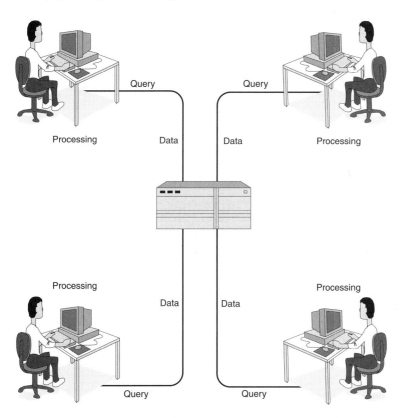

FIGURE 22.2   Access as a front end using data stored in an Access database.

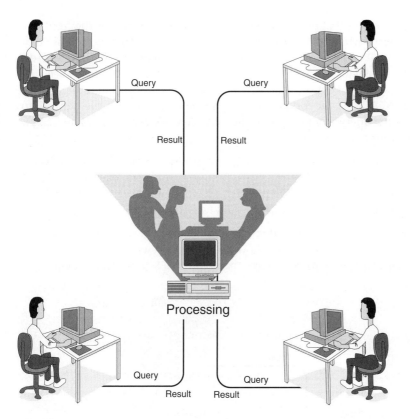

FIGURE 22.3   Access as a front end using a true back end.

Dealing with a Large Volume of Data

As the volume of data in your Access database increases, you will probably notice degra-dation in performance. Many people say that 100MB is the magical number for the maximum size of an Access database, but many back-end database servers can handle databases containing multiple gigabytes of data. Although a maximum size of 100MB for an Access database is a good general guideline, it is *not* a hard-and-fast rule. You might find that the need to upsize occurs when your database is significantly larger or smaller than 100MB. The magic number for you depends on all the factors discussed in the following sections, as well as on how many tables are included in the database. Generally, Access performs better with large volumes of data stored in a single table rather than in multiple tables.

Dealing with a Large Number of Concurrent Users

Just as a large volume of data can be a problem, so can a large number of concurrent users. In fact, more than 10 users concurrently accessing an Access database can degrade perfor-mance. As with the amount of data, this is not a magical number. I have seen applications with fewer than 10 users where performance is awful, and I have seen applications with significantly more than 10 users where performance is acceptable. Performance often depends on how the application is designed, as well as what tasks the users are performing.

Demanding Faster Performance

Certain applications demand better performance than other applications. An Online Transaction Processing (OLTP) system generally requires significantly better performance than a Decision Support System (DSS), for example. Suppose that 100 users are simultaneously taking phone orders. It would not be appropriate for the users of the system to ask their customers to wait 15 seconds between entering each item that is ordered. On the other hand, asking users to wait 60 seconds to process a management report that users run once each month is not a lot to ask (although many will still complain about the wait).

Most back-end database servers can use multithreaded operating systems with multiple processors to handle large volumes of user demand; Access cannot.

Handling Increased Network Traffic

As a file server in an organization experiences increasing demands, the Access application simply might exacerbate an already growing problem. If the application data is moved to a database server, the overall reduced demands on the network might provide all users on the network with better performance, regardless of whether they are using the Access application.

Probably one of the most exaggerated situations I have seen is one in which all the workstations were diskless. Windows and all application software were installed on a file server. All the users were concurrently loading Microsoft Word, Microsoft Excel, and Microsoft PowerPoint over the network. In addition, they had large Access applications with many database objects and large volumes of data. This was all stored on the file server as well. Needless to say, performance was abysmal. You can't expect an already overloaded file server to handle sending large volumes of data over a small bandwidth. The benefits offered by client/server technology can help alleviate this problem.

Implementing Backup and Recovery

The backup and recovery options offered with an Access ACCDB database stored on a file server simply do not rival the options for backup and recovery on a database server. Any database server worth its salt sports very powerful uninterruptible power supplies (UPSs). Many have hot-swappable disk drives with disk mirroring, disk duplexing, or disk striping with parity (RAID Level 5). With disk mirroring and duplexing, data can be written to multiple drives at one time, providing instantaneous backups. Furthermore, some database server tape backup software enables backups to be completed while users are accessing the system. Many offer automatic transaction logging. All these options mean less chance of data loss or downtime. With certain applications, this type of backup and recovery is overkill. With other applications, it is imperative. Although some of what back ends have to offer in backup and recovery can be mimicked by using code and replication, it is nearly impossible to get the same level of protection from an Access database stored on a file server that you can get from a database stored on a database server.

Focusing on Security

Access offers what can be considered the best security for a desktop database. However, it cannot compare with the security provided by most database servers. Database server security often works in conjunction with the network operating system. This is the case, for example, with Microsoft SQL Server 2005 and Windows Server 2003 Enterprise. The user is given no direct rights to the physical database file; it can be accessed only via an Open Database Connectivity (ODBC) data source or an ActiveX Data Objects (ADO) connection. Remember that no matter how much security you place on an Access database, a user can still see or even delete the entire ACCDB file from the network disk.

Offering protection from this potential problem, and others, on a database server is easy. Furthermore, many back-end application database server products offer field-level security not offered within an Access ACCDB file. Finally, many back ends offer integrated security with one logon for both the network and the database.

Sharing Data Among Multiple Front-End Tools

The Access ACCDB file format is proprietary. Very few other products can read data stored in the Access database format. With a back-end database server that supports ODBC, front-end applications can be written in a variety of front-end application software, all concurrently using the same back-end data.

Understanding What It All Means

You must evaluate the specific environment in which your application will run:

- ▶ How many users are there?
- ▶ How much data exists?
- ▶ What is the network traffic already like?
- ▶ What type of performance is required?
- ▶ How disastrous is downtime?
- ▶ How sensitive is the data?
- ▶ What other applications will use the data?

After you answer these and other questions, you can begin to decide whether the benefits of the client/server architecture outweigh the costs involved.

The good news is that it is not an all-or-none decision. Various options are available for client/server applications using Access as a front end. Furthermore, if you design your application with upsizing in mind, moving to client/server technology will not require you to throw out what you have done and start again. In fact, Microsoft provides an upsizing wizard that makes upsizing to a SQL Server database a relatively painless process. How painless depends on numerous factors, including how complex your queries are, whether your queries include Visual Basic for Applications (VBA) functions, and other factors that are covered later in this chapter, and in detail in *Alison Balter's Mastering Access 2002 Enterprise Development.*

Understanding the Roles That Access Plays in the Application Design Model

This section takes a look at the many different roles that Access can take in an application design.

The Front End and Back End as Access ACCDB Files

Earlier in this book, you learned about using Access as both the front end and the back end. The Access database is not acting as a true back end because it is not doing processing. Figure 22.4 shows the architecture in this scenario. The Access application resides on the workstation. Access uses the Access Database Engine to communicate with data stored in an Access ACCDB database file stored on the file server.

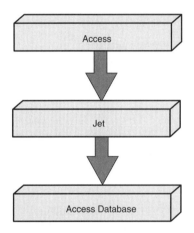

FIGURE 22.4   Access as a front end using an ACCDB file for data storage.

The Front End as an ACCDB File Using Links to Communicate to a Back End

In the second scenario, you can link the back-end tables to the front-end application database (.ACCDB). The process of linking to back-end tables is almost identical to that of linking to tables in other Access databases or to external tables stored in FoxPro, or other database formats. You can also treat the linked tables like any other linked tables. Access uses ODBC to communicate with the back-end tables (see Figure 22.5). Your application sends an Access SQL statement to the Access Database Engine, which translates the statement into ODBC SQL. The Access Database Engine sends this ODBC SQL statement to the ODBC Manager, which locates the correct ODBC driver and passes it the ODBC SQL statement. Supplied by the back-end vendor, the driver translates the statement into the back end's specific dialect. The ODBC Manager sends this now back-end–specific query to the SQL server and to the appropriate database. Although this may seem cumbersome, a properly designed Access front end accessing data stored in a SQL Server database is quite efficient. I have proven this over and over again with enterprise-wide applications written in Microsoft Access.

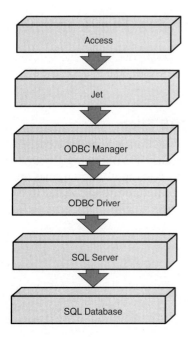

FIGURE 22.5   Access as a front end using links to back-end tables.

The Front End Using SQL Pass-Through to Communicate to a Back End

If a particular query is running inefficiently, you may want to bypass ODBC and go directly against SQL server. Here are a few reasons why a SQL pass-through query may be the best option available in specific situations:

▶ Access SQL might not support some operation that the native query language of the back end supports.

▶ Either the Access Database Engine or the ODBC driver produces a SQL statement that is not optimized for the back end.

▶ You want a process performed in its entirety on the back end.

As an alternative, you can execute a pass-through query written in the syntax specific to the back-end database server. Although the query does pass through the Access Database Engine, the Access Database Engine does not perform any translation on the query. Neither does ODBC. The ODBC Manager sends the query to the ODBC driver, which passes the query to the back end without performing any translation. In other words, exactly what was sent from Access is what is received by the SQL database. Figure 22.6 illustrates this scenario. Notice that the Access Database Engine, the ODBC Manager, and the ODBC driver are not eliminated entirely. They are still there, but they have much less impact on the process than they do with attached tables.

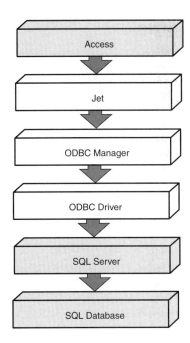

FIGURE 22.6   Access sending a pass-through query to a back-end database.

Pass-through queries are not a panacea, although they are very useful. The results of a pass-through query are not updateable, for example. Furthermore, because pass-through queries are written in the back end's specific SQL dialect, you must rewrite them if you swap out your back end. For these reasons and others, you will generally use pass-through with other solutions.

The Front End Executing Procedures Stored on a Back End

A *stored procedure* is compiled SQL code stored on a back end. You will generally execute it using ADO or Data Access Objects (DAO) code. You can also execute a stored procedure using a pass-through query. Regardless of what you call it, the code within the stored procedure is written in the SQL native to the back end on which it is stored, and the stored procedure is executed in its entirety on the back end. Stored procedures can return results or can simply execute on the back end without returning data.

The Front End as a Microsoft Access Data Project Communicating Directly to a Back End

ADP files were introduced in earlier versions of Access. Although for a while they were considered the technology to use, it turned out that ADP files were the database technology *du jour*. In fact, there is no upgrade path for an ADP file in Access 2007; therefore, using ADP files, you cannot take advantage of the features added to Access 2007.

Learning the Client/Server Buzzwords

People who talk about client/server technology use many terms that are unfamiliar to the average database developer. To get a full appreciation of client/server technology and what it offers, you must have at least a general understanding of the terminology. Table 22.1 lists the most commonly used terms.

TABLE 22.1   Client/Server Terms

Term	Definition
Column	A field.
DDL	A data definition language used to define and describe the database structure.
Foreign key	A value in one table that must be looked up in another table for validation.
Access Database Engine	The native database engine used by Microsoft Access.
ODBC (Open Database Connectivity)	A standard proposed by Microsoft that provides access to a variety of back-end databases through a common interface. In essence, ODBC is a translator.
OLEDB	A standard for connecting to relational and nonrelational data sources.
DAO (Data Access Objects)	A method of manipulating data. It has been replaced by ADO in many databases because it was optimized for accessing Jet databases.
ADO (ActiveX Data Objects)	A COM-based object model that allows you to easily manipulate OLE DB data sources. It is the data access methodology that replaces DAO.
Primary key	A set of fields that uniquely identify a row.
Row	A record.
Schema	A blueprint of the entire database. It includes table definitions, relationships, security, and other important information about the database.
SQL (Structured Query Language)	A type of data manipulation language commonly used to talk to tables residing on a server.
Stored procedures	Compiled SQL statements, such as queries, stored on the database server. They can be called by an application.
Transaction	A set of actions that must be performed on a database. If any one action fails, all the actions are discarded.
Triggers	Pieces of code that execute in response to an action occurring on a table (insert, edit, or delete).

Many books are devoted solely to client/server technology; *Alison Balter's Mastering Access 2002 Enterprise Development* focuses entirely on client/server and Web development using Access 2002. Most magazines targeted at developers contain numerous articles on client/server technology. *Access/VB/SQL Advisor* always offers excellent articles on client/server development. Many of the articles are specifically about client/server connectivity using Access as a front end. *Visual Studio Magazine* often contains useful articles as well. Another excellent source of information is the Microsoft Developer Network CD. Offered by Microsoft as a subscription, it includes numerous articles and white papers on client/server technology, ODBC, and use of Access as a front end to a database server.

Upsizing: What to Worry About

Suppose that your database is using Microsoft Access as both the front end and back end. Although an Access database on a file server might have been sufficient for a while, the need for better performance, enhanced security, or one of the other benefits that a back-end database provides compels your company (or your client's company) to upsize to a client/server architecture. The Access tables already have been created and even contain volumes of data. In this scenario, it might make sense to upsize.

Because all the tables have been designed as Access tables, you must upsize them to the back-end database server. Upsizing involves moving tables from a local Access database (or from any PC database) to a back-end database server that usually runs on UNIX, Windows 2000, and Windows 2003 Server.

Another reason why you might decide to upsize tables from Access to a back-end server is that many developers prefer to design their tables from within the Access environment. Access offers a more user-friendly environment for table creation than most server applications.

Because of the many caveats involved when moving tables from Access to a back end, many people opt to design the tables directly on the back end. If you do design your tables in Access, you can export them to the back end and then link them to your local database, or you can use the Upsizing Wizard to greatly facilitate this process. Regardless of the method that you choose, as you export your tables to the database server, you need to be aware of the issues covered in the following sections.

> **NOTE**
>
> If you are updating to a SQL Server database, most of the concerns regarding upsizing are handled by the Upsizing Wizards included as part of Microsoft Access 2000 and above.

Indexes

When you are exporting a table to a server, no indexes are created. All indexes need to be re-created on the back-end database server. If your database server is running Microsoft SQL Server, you can use the Access 2007 Upsizing Wizard. This wizard will create indexes for server tables in the place where the indexes exist in your Access tables.

AutoNumber Fields

AutoNumber fields are exported as Long integers. Because some database servers do not support autonumbering, you have to create an insert trigger on the server that provides the next key value. You also can achieve autonumbering by using form-level events, but this approach is not desirable. The numbering will not be enforced if other applications access the data. If you are upsizing to Microsoft SQL Server, the Upsizing Wizard for Access 2007 converts all AutoNumber fields to Identity fields.

Default Values

Default values are not automatically moved to the server, even if the server supports them. You can set up default values directly on the server, but these values do *not* automatically appear when new records are added to the table unless the record is saved without data being added to the field containing the default value. As with autonumbering, you can implement default values at the form level, with the same drawbacks. If you use the Upsizing Wizard for Access 2007 to move the data to Microsoft SQL Server, the wizard exports default values to your server database.

Validation Rules

Validation rules are not exported to the server. They must be re-created using triggers on the server. No Access-defined error messages are displayed when a server validation rule is violated. Your application should be coded to provide the appropriate error messages. You also can perform validation rules at the form level, but they are not enforced if the data is accessed by other means. If you use the Upsizing Wizard for Access 2007 to move the data to Microsoft SQL Server, validation rules are exported to the server database where possible.

Relationships

Relationships need to be enforced using server-based triggers. Access's default error messages do not appear when referential integrity is violated. You need to respond to, and code for, these error messages in your application. You can enforce relationships at the form level, but as with other form-level validations, this method of validation does not adequately protect your data. If you use the Upsizing Wizard for Access 2007 to move the data to Microsoft SQL Server, the wizard sets up all relationships and referential integrity that you have set up in your Access database within the server database.

Security

Security features that you have set up in Access do not carry forward to the server. You need to reestablish table security on the server. After you set up security on the server, Access is unaware that the security exists until the Access application attempts to violate the server's security. Then the server returns error codes to the application. You must handle these errors by using code and displaying the appropriate error message to users.

Table and Field Names

Servers often have much more stringent rules than Access does regarding the naming of fields. When you export a table, all characters that are not alphanumeric are converted to underscores. Most back ends do not allow spaces in field names. Furthermore, some back ends limit the length of object names to 30 characters or fewer. If you already have created queries, forms, reports, macros, and modules that use spaces and very long field and table names, these database objects might become unusable when you move your tables to a back-end database server.

Reserved Words

Most back ends have many reserved words. Reserved words are words used by the back end in its own operations. It is important to be aware of the reserved words of your specific back end. It is quite shocking when you upsize a table and find that field names you have been using are reserved words on your database server. If this is the case, you need to rename all the fields in which a conflict occurs. Once again, this means modifying all the queries, forms, reports, macros, and modules that reference the original field names.

Case Sensitivity

Many back-end databases are case sensitive. If this is the case with your back end, you might find that your queries and application code don't process as expected. Queries or code that refer to the field or table name by using the wrong case are not recognized by the back-end database and do not process correctly.

Properties

Most properties cannot be modified on remote tables. Any properties that can be modified are lost upon export, so you need to set them up again when you export the table.

Visual Basic Code

Certain properties and methods that work on Access tables might not work on remote tables. You therefore might need to make some coding changes after you export your tables.

Proactively Preparing for Upsizing

If you set up your tables and code modules with upsizing in mind, you can eliminate many of the pitfalls discussed previously. Despite any of the problems that upsizing can bring, the scalability of Access is one of its stronger points. Sometimes resources are not available to implement client/server technology in the early stages of an application. If you think through the design of the project with the possibility of upsizing in mind, you will be pleased at how relatively easy it is to move to client/server technology when the time is right. With the Access 2007 Upsizing Wizard, which is designed to take an Access application and upsize it to Microsoft SQL Server 2000 or Microsoft SQL Server 2005, the process is relatively simple. The upsizing tools for Access 2007 perform a lot of the work involved in upsizing a database, with just the click of a few buttons.

> **NOTE**
>
> Client/server development and client/server issues are covered in extensive detail in *Alison Balter's Mastering Access 2002 Enterprise Development*.

> **NOTE**
>
> The upsizing wizards available for Access 2000, Access 2002, and Access 2003 are almost identical to the Access 2007 Upsizing Wizard. They therefore afford you the same ease when upsizing from Access to SQL Server.

> **CAUTION**
>
> Although the upsizing tools for Access are excellent, they do have their drawbacks. For example, they do not always map the Access field type to the desired SQL Server field type. For this reason, you can opt not to use the wizards. If, despite their shortcomings, you decide to use the upsizing wizards, make sure that you carefully review both the upsizing report and the structure of each table after the wizard upsizes it.

Using Transaction Processing

Transaction processing refers to the grouping of a series of changes into a single batch. The entire batch of changes is either accepted or rejected as a group. One of the most common implementations of transaction processing is a bank automated teller machine (ATM) transaction. Imagine that you go to the ATM to deposit your paycheck. In the middle of processing, a power outage occurs. Unfortunately, the bank recorded the incoming funds prior to the outage, but the funds had not yet been credited to your account when the power outage occurred. You would not be very pleased with the outcome of this situation. Transaction processing would prevent this scenario from occurring. With transaction processing, the whole process succeeds or fails as a unit.

A group of operations is considered a transaction if it meets the following criteria:

- **It is atomic**—The group of operations should finish as a unit or not at all.
- **It is consistent**—The group of operations, when completed as a unit, retains the consistency of the application.
- **It is isolated**—The group of operations is independent of anything else going on in the system.
- **It is durable**—After the group of operations is committed, the changes persist, even if the system crashes.

If your application contains a group of operations that are atomic and isolated, and if, to maintain the consistency of your application, all changes must persist even if the system crashes, you should place the group of operations in a transaction loop. With Access 2007, the primary benefit of transaction processing is data integrity.

Understanding the Benefits of Transaction Processing

> **NOTE**
>
> This code, and all the code in this chapter, is located in the CHAP22EX.ACCDB database in the basTransactions module on the sample code CD-ROM.

> **NOTE**
>
> Any discussion of Access 2007 covered in this section also applies to Access 2000, Access 2002, and Access 2003.

Access 2007 does its own behind-the-scenes transaction processing. The Access Database Engine does this implicit transaction processing solely to improve the performance of your application. As a processing loop executes, Access buffers and then periodically writes the data to disk. In a multiuser environment, the Access Database Engine (implicitly) commits transactions every 50 milliseconds by default. This period of time is optimized for concurrency rather than performance. If you feel that it is necessary to sacrifice concurrency for performance, you can modify a few Windows Registry settings to achieve the specific outcome you want. The next section covers these settings.

Although implicit transaction processing, along with the modifiable Windows Registry settings, generally gives you better performance than explicit transaction processing, it is not a cut-and-dried situation. Many factors affect the performance benefits gained by both implicit and explicit transaction processing:

- ▶ Amount of free memory
- ▶ Number of columns and rows being updated
- ▶ Size of the rows being updated
- ▶ Network traffic

If you plan to implement explicit transaction processing solely to improve performance, you should make sure that you benchmark performance using both implicit and explicit transactions. It is critical that your application-testing environment be as similar as possible to the production environment in which the application will run.

Modifying the Default Behavior of Transaction Processing

Before you learn how to implement transaction processing, take a look at what you can do to modify the default behavior of the transaction processing built in to Access 2007. Three Registry settings affect implicit transactions in Access 2007: ImplicitCommitSync, ExclusiveAsyncDelay, and SharedAsyncDelay. These keys are located in the \HKEY_LOCAL_MACHINE\SOFTWARE\Microsoft\Jet\4.0\Engines\Jet 4.0 Registry folder.

22

TIP

You can access the Windows Registry using the `RegEdit` utility. To use `RegEdit`, select the Run option from the Start menu and then type **RegEdit**. In Windows Vista, you must locate the `RegEdit` utility and then double-click it to run the utility.

The `ImplicitCommitSync` setting determines whether the system waits for a commit to finish before proceeding with application processing. The default is `No`. This means that the system will proceed without waiting for the commit to finish. You generally won't want to change this setting; using `No` dramatically improves performance. The danger of accepting the value of `No` is that you will increase the amount of time during which the data is vulnerable. Before the data is flushed to disk, the user might turn off the machine, compromising the integrity of the data.

The `ExclusiveAsyncDelay` setting specifies the maximum number of milliseconds that elapse before the Access Database Engine commits an implicit transaction when a database is opened for exclusive use. The default value for this setting is 2000 milliseconds. This setting does not in any way affect databases that are open for shared use.

The `SharedAsyncDelay` setting is similar to the `ExclusiveAsyncDelay` setting. It determines the maximum number of milliseconds that elapse before the Access Database Engine commits an implicit transaction when a database is opened for shared use. The default value for this setting is `50`. The higher this value, the greater the performance benefits reaped from implicit transactions, but also the higher the chances that concurrency problems will result. These concurrency issues are discussed in detail in *Alison Balter's Mastering Access 2002 Enterprise Development*.

In addition to the settings that affect implicit transaction processing in Access 2007, an additional Registry setting affects explicit transaction processing. The `UserCommitSync` setting controls whether explicit transactions are completed synchronously or asynchronously. With the default setting of `Yes`, control doesn't return from a `CommitTrans` statement until the transactions are actually written to disk, resulting in synchronous transactions. When this value is changed to `No`, a series of changes is queued, and control returns before the changes are complete.

You can modify the values of these Registry settings and other Access Database Engine settings by using `Regedit.exe` (the Registry Editor) for Windows Vista, and Windows 2003. Changes to this section of the Registry affect all applications that use the Access Database Engine. If you want to affect only your application, you can export the Microsoft Jet portion of the Registry tree and import it into your application's Registry tree. You then can customize the Registry settings for your application. To force your application to load the appropriate Registry tree, you must set the `INIPath` property of the `DBEngine` object.

A much simpler approach is to set properties of the ADO `Connection` object; you can specify new settings at runtime for all the previously mentioned Registry entries as well as for additional entries. A further advantage of this approach is that it will modify (temporarily) Registry entries for any machine under which your application runs. Any values you change at runtime temporarily override the Registry values that are set, enabling you to easily control and maintain specific settings for each application. This code illustrates how you modify the ExclusiveAsyncDelay and SharedAsyncDelay settings using properties of the Connection object:

```
Sub ChangeOptions()
    Dim cnn As ADODB.Connection
    Set cnn = CurrentProject.Connection

    cnn.Properties("JET OLEDB:Exclusive Async Delay") = 1000
    cnn.Properties("JET OLEDB:Shared Async Delay") = 50
End Sub
```

Implementing Explicit Transaction Processing

Now that you are aware of the settings that affect transaction processing, you are ready to learn how to implement transaction processing. Three methods of the Connection object (covered in Chapter 15, "What Are ActiveX Data Objects, and Why Are They Important?") control transaction processing:

▶ BeginTrans

▶ CommitTrans

▶ RollbackTrans

The BeginTrans method of the Connection object begins the transaction loop. The moment BeginTrans is encountered, Access begins writing all changes to a log file in memory. Unless you issue the CommitTrans method of the Connection object, the Access Database Engine never actually writes the changes to the database file. After the CommitTrans method is issued, the Access Database Engine permanently writes the updates to the database object. If a RollbackTrans method of the Connection object is encountered, the log-in memory is released. Listing 22.2 shows an example of how transaction processing works under Access 2007. Compare this to Listing 22.1.

LISTING 22.2   Transaction Processing in Access 2007 Using BeginTrans, Logging, CommitTrans, and RollbackTrans

```
Sub IncreaseQuantityTrans()
    On Error GoTo IncreaseQuantityTrans_Err
    Dim cnn As ADODB.Connection
    Dim rst As ADODB.Recordset
    Dim boolInTrans As Boolean

    boolInTrans = False
  Set rst = New ADODB.Recordset

    Set cnn = CurrentProject.Connection
```

LISTING 22.2   Continued

```
    rst.ActiveConnection = cnn
    rst.CursorType = adOpenKeyset
    rst.LockType = adLockOptimistic
    rst.Open "Select OrderId, Quantity From tblOrderDetails"

    'Begin the Transaction Loop
    cnn.BeginTrans
        boolInTrans = True
        'Loop through recordset increasing Quantity field by 1
        Do Until rst.EOF
            rst!Quantity = rst!Quantity + 1
            rst.UPDATE
            rst.MoveNext
        Loop
        'Commit the Transaction; Everything went as Planned
    cnn.CommitTrans
    boolInTrans = False

IncreaseQuantityTrans_Exit:
    Set cnn = Nothing
    Set rst = Nothing
    Exit Sub

IncreaseQuantityTrans_Err:
    MsgBox "Error # " & Err.Number & ": " & Err.Description
    'Rollback the Transaction; An Error Occurred
    If boolInTrans Then
        cnn.RollbackTrans
    End If
    Resume IncreaseQuantityTrans_Exit
End Sub
```

This code uses a transaction loop to ensure that everything completes as planned or not at all. Notice that the loop that moves through the recordset, increasing the Quantity field in each record by 1, is placed in a transaction loop. If all processing in the loop completes successfully, the CommitTrans method executes. If the error-handling code is encountered, the RollbackTrans method executes, ensuring that none of the changes are written to disk. The boolInTrans variable is used to determine whether the code is within the transaction loop. This ensures that the error handler performs the rollback only if an error occurs within the transaction loop. If the CommitTrans method or the RollbackTrans method is issued without an open transaction, an error occurs.

Practical Examples: Getting Your Application Ready for an Enterprise Environment

Splitting the application code and data is the first step toward making your application enterprise ready. Consider placing the application data on the network and the application code on each workstation. If you think that the number of users, required security, or volume of data stored in the application warrants client/server technology, consider using one or more of the client/server techniques covered in this chapter. Finally, think about whether any application processes warrant transaction processing. If you feel that client/server technology or transaction processing is a necessary ingredient to your application, learn more about these techniques from a source such as *Alison Balter's Mastering Access 2002 Enterprise Development*.

Summary

Many people think that the transition of a simple Access application to a multiuser or client/server environment is a simple one. I strongly disagree. There are several things to think about when moving an application from a single-user environment to a multiuser environment, and even more things to think about when moving to a client/server environment. The more you think about these potential evolutions when you first design and build your application, the fewer problems you'll have if your application data has to be upsized.

This chapter exposed you to multiuser techniques. It explained client/server technology and when you need it. It also described the various roles that Access plays in the application design model. Finally, you learned about a technique that is important within an enterprise application: transaction processing.

The chapter is intended to be an introduction to these important topics. All the topics in this chapter are covered in detail in *Alison Balter's Mastering Access 2002 Enterprise Development* (which applies to Access 2007 as well).

PART IV

Black Belt Programming

IN THIS PART

Working with and Customizing Ribbons

Why This Chapter Is Important

New to Access 2007, the *ribbon* is the strip across the top of the application window that contains groups of commands. The ribbon in Microsoft Office Access 2007 replaces both menus and toolbars found in earlier versions of Access. As a developer, you might not want the default ribbon to appear in your applications. You may want to hide existing functionality or to add new functionality. You need to understand how to customize the ribbon to be able to accomplish these tasks. Unfortunately, there is no user interface to modify the ribbon. You have to pull up your sleeves and use Extensible Markup Language (XML) to customize the ribbon. This chapter shows you all the tips and tricks that you need to know to add custom ribbons to your overall application and to your forms and reports.

Customizing the Ribbon: An Overview

Using ribbon customization techniques, you can hide existing tabs, add new tabs, add new command groups, and add new commands to a command group. You accomplish all these tasks by using XML. Although there are several places that you can store the XML used to customize the ribbon, the easiest method is to store the XML in a system table in the current database. The steps are as follows:

1. Create a system table named USysRibbons.

2. Add your XML to the table.

3. Specify whether you want the ribbon to display for the entire application or for a specific form or report.

Several steps are involved in creating and applying a custom ribbon. The following is an overview of the steps involved:

1. Show system tables.

2. Enable the display of system errors.

3. Create the USysRibbons table.

4. Add data to the USysRibbons table.

5. Apply the custom ribbon.

6. Hide system objects.

7. Restore the ribbon to its default settings.

8. Add additional groups and controls.

9. Execute a macro from the ribbon.

The sections that follow cover each of these steps in detail.

Showing System Tables

The first step that you should take when creating a new ribbon or modifying the existing ribbon is to show system tables in your database. You accomplish this task by using the Navigation Options. Here's how:

1. Right-click the Navigation Bar at the top of the Navigation Pane and select Navigation Options. The Navigation Options dialog box appears (see Figure 23.1).

2. Click to select the Show System Objects check box found under the Display Options.

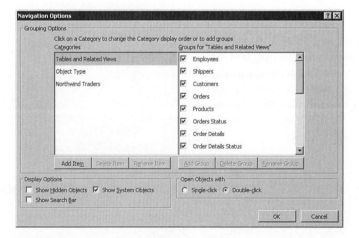

FIGURE 23.1   Using the Navigation Options dialog box, you can opt to show system tables.

3. Click OK to complete the process. The system tables now appear in the Navigation Pane (see Figure 23.2).

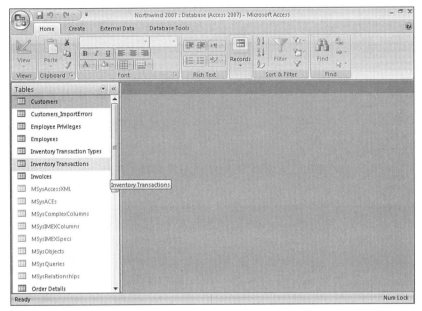

FIGURE 23.2   After you opt to show system tables, they appear in the Navigation Pane.

Enabling the Display of System Errors

The second step when customizing the ribbon is to enable the display of add-in user interface error messages. Here's the process:

1. Click the Microsoft Office button and select Access Options. The Access Options dialog box appears.

2. Click Advanced.

3. Scroll down until you see the General group of commands. Your screen should appear as shown in Figure 23.3.

4. Click the Show Add-In User Interface Errors check box and click OK to complete the process.

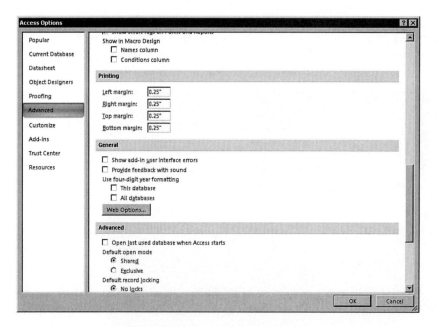

FIGURE 23.3   Select Show Add-In User Interface Errors from the General group.

Creating the USysRibbons Table

The next step is to create the USysRibbons system table. Here are the steps involved:

1. Select Table Design from the Tables group on the Create tab.

2. Add an AutoNumber field called ID that has a field size of Long Integer.

3. Add a Text field called RibbonName that has a field size of 255.

4. Add a Memo field called RibbonXml. The table design appears in Figure 23.4.

5. You can add additional fields, but the designated fields must have the exact name, type, and size as designated in steps 2–4.

6. Designate the ID field as the Primary Key.

7. Click Save on the Quick Access toolbar, and name the table **USysRibbons**.

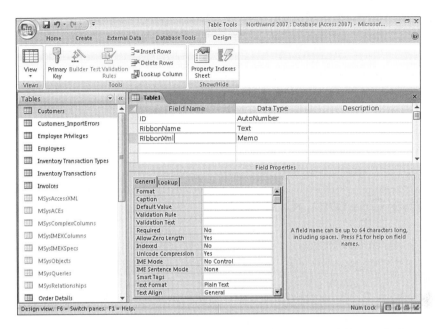

FIGURE 23.4   It is important that you design the custom table exactly the same as in the example.

Adding Data to the USysRibbons Table

You are now ready to add data to the USysRibbons table. Here are the steps involved:

1. Open the USysRibbons table in Datasheet view.

2. Add the XML shown in Listing 23.1.

3. Close the USysRibbons table.

4. Close and reopen the database.

LISTING 23.1   Writing the XML Necessary to Customize the Ribbon

```xml
<customUI xmlns="http://schemas.microsoft.com/office/2006/01/customui">
  <ribbon startFromScratch="false">
    <tabs>
      <tab idMso="TabCreate" visible="false" />
      <tab id="dbCustomTab" label="My New Tab" visible="true">
        <group id="dbCustomGroup" label="My New Group">
          <control idMso="Paste" label="Built-in Paste" enabled="true"/>
        </group>
      </tab>
```

LISTING 23.1   Continued

```
    </tabs>
  </ribbon>
</customUI>
```

The XML first tells Access to display the default tabs. It then designates that the Create tab will be hidden. Next, the XML creates a ribbon tab named My New Tab. It then adds a command group called My Custom Group to the tab. Finally, it adds the Copy command to the group.

Applying the Custom Ribbon

Now that you have created the ribbon code, you are ready to apply the ribbon. You can apply the ribbon to the entire database or to a specific form or report. The sections that follow explain each process in detail.

Applying a Custom Ribbon to the Entire Database

To apply the ribbon to the entire database, follow these steps:

1. Click the Microsoft Office button and then select Access Options. The Access Options dialog box appears.

2. Click Current Database.

3. Scroll down until you see Ribbon and Toolbar Options (see Figure 23.5).

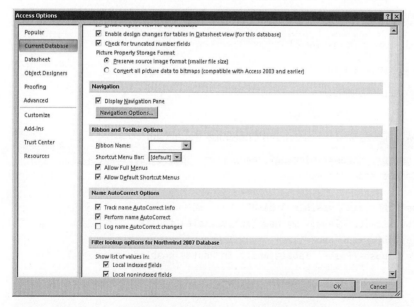

FIGURE 23.5   You must use the Ribbon and Toolbar Options to select your ribbon.

4. Click to open the Ribbon Name drop-down and select your new menu from the list.

5. Click OK to complete the process. A dialog box appears, indicating that you must close and reopen the database for the change to take effect (see Figure 23.6).

FIGURE 23.6   You must close and reopen the database for the change to take effect.

6. Click OK to continue and then close and reopen the database. The Create tab should be hidden, and there should be a tab called My New Tab.

7. Click the My New Tab tab. It should appear as shown in Figure 23.7.

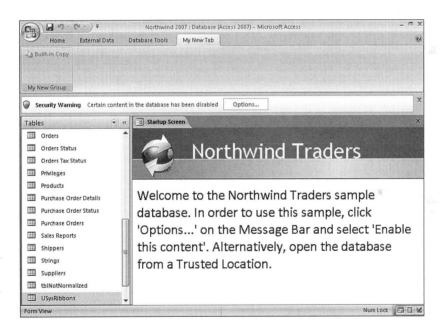

FIGURE 23.7   The ribbon appears with all the custom features that you designated.

Applying a Custom Ribbon to a Form or Report

In the preceding example, you assigned a custom ribbon to a database. Now look at how to assign a custom ribbon to a form or report. Here are the steps involved:

1. In the Navigation Pane, right-click the form or report to which you want to apply a custom ribbon. Select Design View. Access displays the form or report that you selected in Design View.

2. Display the property sheet. (If it is not visible, either press F4 or select the Property Sheet icon on the Design tab.)

3. Make sure that you designate Form or Report in the Property Sheet drop-down.

4. Click the Other tab to select it.

5. Click within the `Ribbon Name` property and open the drop-down to display the available ribbons (see Figure 23.8).

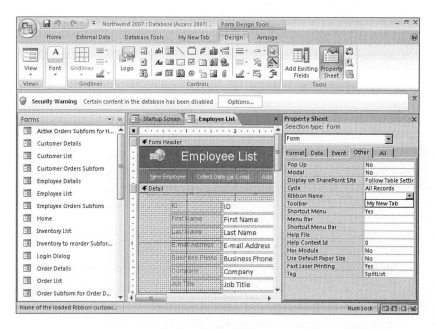

FIGURE 23.8   You must select the ribbon that you want to associate with the form.

6. Select the desired ribbon from the drop-down.

7. Click Save to save your changes and then switch to Form view. Notice that the custom ribbon is associated with the form. After clicking to select the My New Tab tab, your screen should appear as in Figure 23.9.

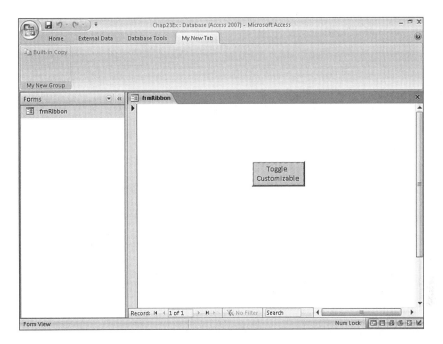

FIGURE 23.9   The custom ribbon is associated with the designated form.

Hiding System Objects

After you have determined that your custom ribbons are working properly, you can once again hide the system objects. To do this, follow these steps:

1. Right-click the Navigation Bar at the top of the Navigation Pane and select Navigation Options. The Navigation Options dialog box appears.

2. Within the Display Options group, click to deselect Show System Objects.

3. Click OK to complete the process.

Restoring the Ribbon to Its Default Settings

Sometimes you will want to restore the ribbon back to its default settings. The process differs depending on whether you have assigned the ribbon to the entire database or to a form or report. Let's start with how to restore a ribbon customized for the entire application:

1. Click the Microsoft Office button and then select Access Options. The Access Options dialog box appears.

2. Click Current Database.

3. Scroll down until you see Ribbon and Toolbar Options.

4. Delete the contents of the Ribbon Name drop-down.

5. Click OK to complete the process. A dialog box appears, indicating that you must close and reopen the database for the change to take effect.

You will sometimes need to return the ribbon associated with a form or report back to the default ribbon. Here's how:

1. In the Navigation Pane, right-click the form or report to which you want to apply the standard ribbon. Select Design View. Access displays the form or report that you selected in Design view.

2. Display the property sheet. (If it is not visible, either press F4 or select the Property Sheet icon on the Design tab.)

3. Make sure that you designate Form or Report in the Property Sheet drop-down.

4. Click the Other tab to select it.

5. Delete the contents of the Ribbon Name property.

6. Save, close, and reopen the form or report. The default ribbon should display.

Adding Additional Groups and Controls

Figure 23.10 shows the new tab further customized. Notice that it now contains two groups, and the first group contains two commands. Listing 23.2 shows in bold the XML modifications necessary to make these changes.

LISTING 23.2   Adding Groups and Commands to the Ribbon

```
<customUI xmlns="http://schemas.microsoft.com/office/2006/01/customui">
  <ribbon startFromScratch="false">
    <tabs>
      <tab idMso="TabCreate" visible="false" />
      <tab id="dbCustomTab" label="My New Tab" visible="true">
        <group id="dbCustomGroup" label="My New Group">
          <control idMso="Copy" label="Built-in Copy" enabled="true"/>

          <control idMso="Paste" label="Built-in Paste" enabled="true"/>
        </group>
        <group id="dbCustomGroup2" label="My Second Group">
          <control idMso="ExportExcel" label="Export to Excel" enabled="true"/>
        </group>
```

LISTING 23.2   Continued

```
        </tab>
      </tabs>
    </ribbon>
</customUI>
```

Notice that the example creates an additional control on the My New Group tab. It also adds a new group containing one control. Figure 23.10 illustrates the result of the changes.

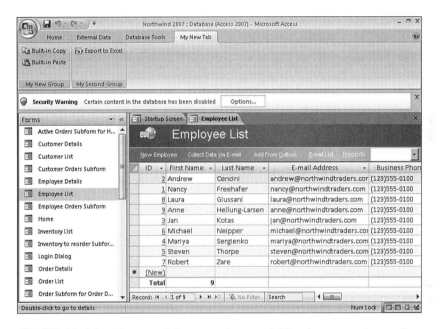

FIGURE 23.10   The new ribbon contains an additional group and control.

You might be wondering where you can find the idMso value associated with a command. The idMso value determines which command Access associates with the button. Here are the steps involved:

1. Click the Microsoft Office button and select Access Options.

2. Click Customize. Your screen will appear as shown in Figure 23.11.

3. Hover your mouse pointer over the item whose idMso value you want to know. The idMso value appears as a ToolTip.

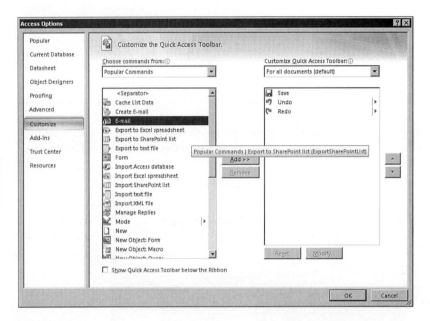

FIGURE 23.11   Adding a ribbon to your Access 2007 application.

Executing a Macro from the Ribbon

You may want to run a macro that you created directly from the ribbon. Listing 23.3 illustrates this simple process.

LISTING 23.3   Executing a Macro from the Ribbon

```
<customUI xmlns="http://schemas.microsoft.com/office/2006/01/customui">
  <ribbon startFromScratch="false">
    <tabs>
      <tab idMso="TabCreate" visible="false" />
      <tab id="dbCustomTab" label="My New Tab" visible="true">
        <group id="dbCustomGroup" label="My New Group">
          <control idMso="Copy" label="Built-in Copy" enabled="true"/>
          <control idMso="Paste" label="Built-in Paste" enabled="true"/>
        </group>
        <group id="dbCustomGroup2" label="My Second Group">
          <control idMso="ExportExcel" label="Export to Excel" enabled="true"/>
          <button id="RunCustomMacro" label="Say Hello" onAction="SayHello"/>
        </group>
      </tab>
    </tabs>
  </ribbon>
</customUI>
```

The code in the example executes the macro named SayHello. The button is named RunCustomMacro, and its label is Say Hello.

Practical Examples: Securing an Access 2007 Database

Practice adding a custom ribbon to one of your databases. Apply the ribbon to the entire database. Then create a second custom ribbon and apply that ribbon to a particular form or report. Finally, add a macro to the ribbon.

Summary

Because ribbons didn't exist in earlier versions of Access, the process of creating them is different from any process in those earlier versions. In this chapter, you learned how to create a system table that contains the XML necessary to create or modify a ribbon. You also learned how to determine when the custom ribbon displays. You learned how to restore the ribbon to its default settings, and finally how to execute macros from the ribbon. All of these techniques are necessary when creating new ribbons or modifying existing ones.

CHAPTER 24

Automation: Communicating with Other Applications

Why This Chapter Is Important

Windows users have come to expect seamless integration between products. They are not concerned with what product you use to develop their application; they just want to accomplish their tasks. Often, Microsoft Word, Microsoft Excel, or some other product is best suited for a particular task that your application must complete. It is your responsibility to pick the best tool for the job. This means that you must know how to communicate from your application directly with that tool.

All this means is that you can no longer learn only about the product and language that you select as your development tool. Instead, you must learn about all the other available applications. Furthermore, you must learn how to communicate with these applications—a challenging but exciting feat.

ActiveX automation is the capability of one application to control another application's objects. This means that your Access application can launch Excel, create or modify a spreadsheet, and print it—all without the user having to directly interact with the Excel application. Many people confuse automation with the process of linking and embedding. OLE 1.0 gave you the capability to create compound documents, meaning that you can embed an Excel spreadsheet in a Word document or link to the Excel spreadsheet from within a Word document. This capability was exciting at the time, and is still quite useful in many situations, but OLE 2.0 (in addition to everything that OLE 1.0 provides) introduced the capability for one application to actually control another application's objects. With Office 97, Microsoft changed the way users refer to OLE. It became known as *automation* and is an industry standard and a feature of the *Component Object Model (COM)*.

Just as you can control other applications using automation, you can control the Access application with other applications, such as Excel or a Visual Basic .NET. This means that you can take advantage of Access's marvelous report writer from your Visual Basic .NET applications. In fact, you can list all the Access reports, allow your user to select one, and then run the report—all from within a Visual Basic .NET Winform.

Defining Some Automation Terms

Before you learn how automation works, you need to understand a few automation terms. Automation requires an automation client and an automation server. The *automation client* application is the one doing the talking. It is the application that is controlling the server application. Because this book is about Access, most of the examples in this chapter show Access as an automation client, meaning that the Access application is controlling the other application (Excel, Word, and so on). The *automation server* application is the application being controlled. It contains the objects being manipulated. Excel is acting as an automation server when Access launches Excel, makes it visible, creates a new worksheet, sends the results of a query to the worksheet, and graphs the spreadsheet data. It is Excel's objects that are being controlled, Excel's properties that are being changed, and Excel's methods that are being executed.

Another important component of automation is a *type library*, which is a dictionary that lists the objects, properties, methods, and events exposed by an automation server application. Type libraries allow the server application's objects, properties, and methods to be syntax checked by the Access compiler. You can also use a type library to get help on another application's objects, properties, and methods from within Access.

An *object model* of an automation server application contains the set of objects that are exposed to automation client applications. The objects within the object model are called *object types*. When you write automation code, you create and manipulate instances of an object type. These instances are called *objects*.

CAUTION

Automation craves RAM—the more, the better! I recommend 1GB of RAM or more for applications that use automation. It's also important to recognize that automation is not lightning fast, even on the slickest of machines.

Declaring an Object Variable to Reference Your Application

Automation requires that you create object variables that reference application objects. After you create an object variable, you can query and change the object's properties as well as execute its methods.

You can learn about an object's properties and methods using its object libraries. An *object library* contains a listing of all the properties and methods that an object exposes. To be able to view foreign objects from within Access, you must first establish a reference to that application. After a reference is established, you can view that object's properties and methods using the Object Browser. You can also view any modules and classes that the parent object exposes.

If you want to register an object, the Visual Basic Editor (VBE) must be active. With the Code window active, choose Tools, References. The References dialog box appears, as shown in Figure 24.1.

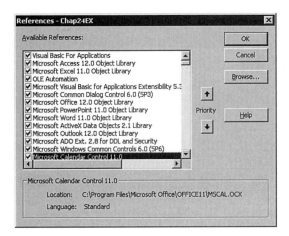

FIGURE 24.1   The References dialog box.

CAUTION

If the Common Dialog control is not installed on your machine or the user's machine, much of the code in this chapter will not run. If that is the case, you must register the common dialog ActiveX control found on the sample code CD-ROM.

Each time you install a program, the Windows Registry is updated. The References dialog box shows you all the objects registered in Windows (see Figure 24.2). If you want to link to one of the available objects from within Access, you must enable the check box to the left of the object name. Then click OK. You can browse that object's properties and methods in the Object Browser, as shown in Figure 24.3. As covered in Chapter 9, "Objects, Properties, Methods, and Events Explained," to access the Object Browser, you can choose View, Object Browser, press F2, or click the Object Browser tool while in the Module window. Notice that in Figure 24.3, the Object Browser displays all the classes that belong to the Excel 12.0 object library. The Range class is selected, and all the members of the Range class are displayed in the list box at the right.

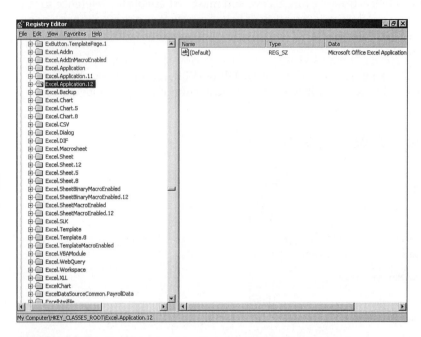

FIGURE 24.2   Registered automation server objects.

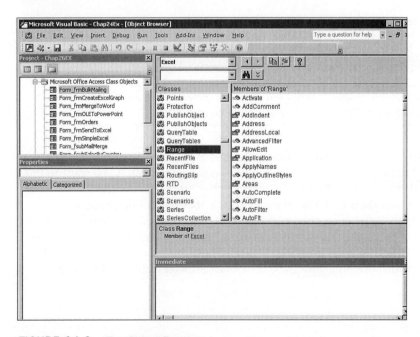

FIGURE 24.3   The Object Browser.

Creating an Automation Object

Before you can talk to an application, you need to know the objects contained within it. You can then use `Dim`, `Private`, or `Public` statements to point to and control various application objects. Each product comes with documentation indicating which objects it supports. You can also view the objects that a product supports by using the Object Browser. After you create an object variable, you can manipulate the object without user intervention.

Declaring an Object Variable

To create an instance of an object, you must first create an object variable that holds a reference to the object. You can do this by using a `Dim` statement:

```
Dim objExcel As New Excel.Application
```

This code creates an object variable pointing to the `Excel` application object. It then creates a new instance of the `Excel` application object. This `Excel` object is part of the Excel application. Visual Basic for Applications (VBA) can control it using the object variable. Unless instructed otherwise, the instance of Excel is invisible. You can make it visible by using this statement:

```
objExcel.Visible = True
```

Alternatively, you can use two statements to declare and instantiate an object. The code looks like this:

```
Dim objExcel as Excel.Application
Set objExcel = New Excel.Application
```

The `Dim` statement declares an object variable that is ready to be associated with a running instance of Excel. The `Set` statement launches Excel and points the object variable at the new instance of Excel. The advantage of this method is that you can better control when the instance of Excel is actually created. If, for example, the declaration is in the General Declarations section of a form, you can place the `Set` statement under a command button that is used to launch Excel.

Manipulating an Automation Object

After you create an instance of an object, you are ready to set its properties and execute its methods. You can talk to the object through the object variable you created. Using this object variable, you can get and set properties and execute methods.

Setting and Retrieving Properties

All the objects you will be talking to through automation have properties. *Properties* are the attributes of the object—the adjectives you use to describe the objects. You can use VBA to inquire about the properties of objects and set the values of these properties. Here are some examples:

```
objExcel.Visible = True
objExcel.Caption = "Hello World"
objExcel.Cells(1, 1).Value = "Here I Am"
```

Each of these examples sets properties of the Excel application object. The first example sets the Visible property of the object to True. The second example sets the Caption of the object to "Hello World". The final example sets the Value property of the Cells object, contained within the Excel object, to the value "Here I Am".

Executing Methods

Properties refer to the attributes of an object, and *methods* refer to the actions you take on the object. Methods are the verbs that apply to a particular object type. Here's an example:

```
objExcel.Workbooks.Add
```

This code uses the Add method to add a workbook to the Excel object.

Using Early Binding Versus Late Binding

Binding is another important automation concept. Two types of binding are available with automation components: early binding and late binding. With early binding, you create a reference to a component's type library. This notifies Access of all the library's objects, properties, methods, and events. With late binding, you instantiate objects at runtime without referencing them at design time. VBA doesn't know anything about the objects that you are creating until runtime.

Most objects that you automate support early binding. You should use early binding whenever possible. Early binding has several benefits. Because each object's properties and methods are resolved at compile time, early binding is faster and more efficient. Furthermore, after you create a reference to a type library, all the library's objects and their properties and methods are available via IntelliSense. Finally, online help is available for any type libraries that you have referenced. This means, for example, if you have referenced Excel's library from Access, the process of placing your cursor on an object, property, or method and pressing F1 displays help for the selected item.

Listing 24.1 provides an example of early binding. This code requires that a reference first be made to the Excel object library.

LISTING 24.1   An Example of Early Binding

```
Sub EarlyBinding()

    'Declare and instantiate an Excel application object
    Dim objExcel As Excel.Application
    Set objExcel = New Excel.Application
```

LISTING 24.1   Continued

```
    'Set properties and execute methods of the object
    With objExcel
        .Visible = True
        .Workbooks.Add
        .Range("A1") = "Hello World"
    End With
End Sub
```

CreateObject **and** GetObject

CreateObject and GetObject are required when you use late binding. Because, with late binding, Access is not aware of the server application and its objects, properties, methods, and events, you cannot use a Dim statement and a Set statement to declare and instanti- ate the server application object. Instead, you must use Dim to declare a generic object variable. You then use a Set statement along with the CreateObject or GetObject func- tion to work with the server object. The CreateObject function launches a new instance of the server object. The GetObject function is similar to CreateObject, but it attempts to reference a running instance of the requested application. Furthermore, unlike the CreateObject function that receives only one argument as a parameter, the GetObject function receives an optional parameter with the name of the document you want to work with.

Listing 24.2 provides an example of CreateObject and late binding.

LISTING 24.2   Using the CreateObject Function to Create a Late-Bound Instance of Excel

```
Sub LateBinding()

    'Declare a generic object variable
    Dim objExcel As Object

    'Point the object variable at an Excel application object
    Set objExcel = CreateObject("Excel.Application")

    'Set properties and execute methods of the object
    With objExcel
        .Visible = True
        .Workbooks.Add
        .Range("A1") = "Hello World"
    End With

End Sub
```

> **NOTE**
>
> Calling `GetObject` doesn't determine whether the object is late- or early-bound. You can declare `Dim objExcel as Excel.Application` using `GetObject`, and the object will be early-bound.

Controlling Excel from Access

Before you attempt to talk to Excel, you must understand its object model. Excel gives you an excellent overview of the `Excel` object model. You can find this model by searching for "object model" in Excel Help. Each object in the model has hypertext links that enable you to obtain specific help on the object, its properties, and its methods.

When using automation, Excel launches as a hidden window with a `Visible` property of `False`. Destroying the `Excel` object variable does not cause Excel to terminate. To make things even more complicated, each time you use the `New` keyword within the `Dim` or `Set` statement, a new instance of Excel is launched. This means that it is possible for numerous hidden copies of Excel to be running on a user's machine, which can lead to serious resource problems. If you want to use a running instance of Excel, you can omit the `New` keyword. This action has its disadvantages as well. Say, for example, that the user of your application has created a large spreadsheet and has not saved it recently. Your application uses an existing instance of Excel, creates a new workbook, prints, and then exits without saving. You might find that your user is very angry about the loss of his important work. For this reason, I have found it preferable to suffer the potential resource costs and create my own instance of Excel. If you want to launch Excel invisibly, do your work, and get out, make sure that you terminate Excel upon completion of your code.

Before you execute code that relies on a running copy of Excel, it is important to ascertain that Excel launched successfully. The function shown in Listing 24.3 attempts to launch Excel. If the launch is successful, `True` is returned from the function. Otherwise, `False` is returned from the function.

LISTING 24.3   The CreateExcelObj Subroutine

```
Function CreateExcelObj() As Boolean
    'Invoke error handling
    On Error GoTo CreateExcelObj_Err

    'Assume a False return value
    CreateExcelObj = False

    'Attempt to launch Excel
    Set gobjExcel = New Excel.Application

    'If Excel launches successfully, return True
    CreateExcelObj = True
```

LISTING 24.3   Continued

```
CreateExcelObj_Exit:
    Exit Function


CreateExcelObj_Err:

    'If an error occurs, display a message and return False
    MsgBox "Couldn't Launch Excel!!", vbCritical, "Warning!!"
    CreateExcelObj = False
    Resume CreateExcelObj_Exit
End Function
```

The routine begins by invoking error handling. It initializes the return value for the function to False. The routine then attempts to launch Excel. If it is successful, the public variable gobjExcel references the running instance of Excel, and the function returns True. If an error occurs, the routine executes the code within the error handler. The code displays a message and sets the return value for the function to False.

NOTE

You can find this code and most other examples used in this chapter in the CHAP24EX.ACCDB database located on your sample code CD-ROM. This routine is located in basUtils.

CAUTION

To take advantage of the exciting world of automation, you must install all automation server applications on the user's machine, and the user must possess a full license to the server applications. In fact, you will be unable to compile and run the examples contained in the sample database for this chapter unless you have the server applications loaded on your development machine.

The CreateExcelObj function is called from the Click event of the cmdFillExcel command button on the frmSimpleExcel form. The application attempts to talk to the Excel object only if the return value of the function is True, indicating that Excel was loaded successfully.

```
Private Sub cmdFillExcel_Click()
    'If Excel is launched successfully,
    'execute the FillCells routine
    If CreateExcelObj() Then
        Call FillCells
    End If
End Sub
```

If Excel launches successfully, the `FillCells` subroutine executes, as shown in Listing 24.4.

LISTING 24.4   The `FillCells` Subroutine

```
Sub FillCells()
    'Declare an Excel Worksheet object
    Dim objWS As Excel.Worksheet

    'Invoke error handling
    On Error GoTo FillCells_Err

    With gobjExcel
        'Add a workbook to the Workbooks collection
        .Workbooks.Add

        'Point the Worksheet object at the active sheet
        Set objWS = gobjExcel.ActiveSheet

        'Set the value of various cells in the sheet
        With objWS
            .Cells(1, 1).Value = "Schedule"
            .Cells(2, 1).Value = "Day"
            .Cells(2, 2).Value = "Tasks"
            .Cells(3, 1).Value = 1
            .Cells(4, 1).Value = 2
        End With

        'Select A3 through A4
        .Range("A3:A4").Select

        'Use the AutoFill method to fill the range of A3
        'through A33 with numeric values
        .Selection.AutoFill gobjExcel.Range("A3:A33")

        'Select cell A1
        .Range("A1").Select

        'Make Excel visible
        .Visible = True
    End With

FillCells_Exit:

    Exit Sub

FillCells_Err:
    'If the Excel object is still set, quit Excel and destroy
```

LISTING 24.4   Continued

```
    'the object variable
    If Not gobjExcel Is Nothing Then
        gobjExcel.Quit
        Set gobjExcel = Nothing
    End If

    Resume FillCells_Exit
End Sub
```

You can find this relatively simple routine in the `frmSimpleExcel` form, which is part of the `CHAP24EX.ACCDB` database file (see Figure 24.4). It begins by using the `Add` method on the `Workbooks` collection of the `Excel` object to add a new workbook to the instance of Excel. It then uses `Set objWS = gobjExcel.ActiveSheet` to provide a shortcut for talking to the active sheet in the new Excel workbook. Using the `objWS` object reference, it modifies the values of several cells. It then uses the `AutoFill` method to quickly fill a range of cells with data. It returns the cursor to cell A1, and the `Excel` object is made visible. You might wonder what the `AutoFill` method is; it automates the process of filling a range of cells with a pattern of data. Figure 24.5 shows the results. I mention this method here not just to tell you what it is, but also to illustrate an important point: You must know the product you are automating and its capabilities. If you are not familiar with the product from a user's perspective, you will find it extremely difficult to work with the product using automation.

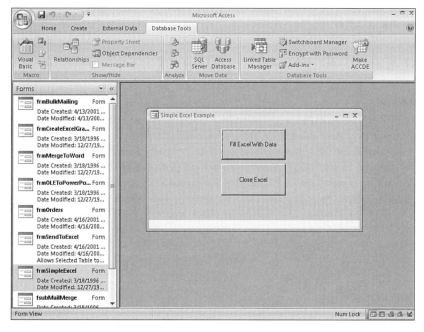

FIGURE 24.4   The form used to launch, communicate with, and close Excel.

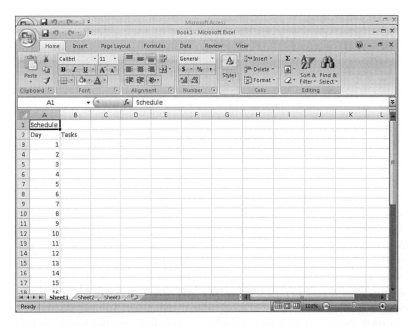

FIGURE 24.5 Using the AutoFill method to populate a range of cells.

> **NOTE**
>
> You must click Options on the Message Bar and select Enable this content for this code to run.

Closing an Excel Automation Object

After the user clicks the Close Excel command button, the CloseExcel subroutine is called, as shown in Listing 24.5. The subroutine first checks to see whether the gobjExcel object variable is still set. If it is, Excel is still running. The DisplayAlerts property of the Excel application object is set to False. This setting ensures that, when the Quit method is executed, Excel will not warn about any unsaved worksheets. This methodology is acceptable because all work was accomplished using a new instance of the Excel application object. If you want to save your work, you should execute the required code before the Quit method is executed.

LISTING 24.5 The CloseExcel Subroutine

```
Sub CloseExcel()

    'Invoke error handling
    On Error GoTo CloseExcel_Err

    'If the Excel object variable is still set,
    'turn off alerts and quit Excel
```

LISTING 24.5   Continued

```
    If Not gobjExcel Is Nothing Then
        gobjExcel.DisplayAlerts = False
        gobjExcel.Quit
    End If

CloseExcel_Exit:
    'Destroy the Excel object variable
    Set gobjExcel = Nothing
    Exit Sub

CloseExcel_Err:
    'Display error message and resume at Exit routine
    MsgBox "Error # " & Err.Number & ": " & Err.Description
    Resume CloseExcel_Exit
End Sub
```

Creating a Graph from Access

Now that you have learned how to talk to Excel, you are ready to learn how to do something a bit more practical. Figure 24.6 shows a form called frmCreateExcelGraph. The form shows the result of a query that groups the result of price multiplied by quantity for each country. The Create Excel Graph command button sends the result of the query to Excel and produces the graph shown in Figure 24.7. (Listing 24.6 shows the code that produces this graph.)

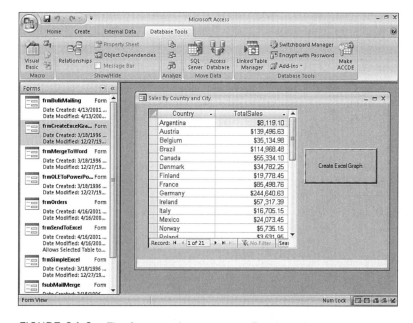

FIGURE 24.6   The form used to create an Excel graph.

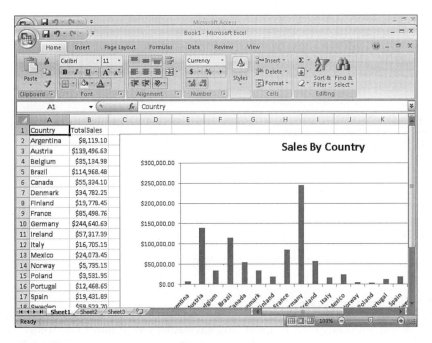

FIGURE 24.7   The result of a query graphed in Excel.

LISTING 24.6   Creating a Graph from Access

```
Private Sub cmdCreateGraph_Click()
    On Error GoTo cmdCreateGraph_Err
    Dim rstData As ADODB.Recordset
    Dim rstCount As ADODB.Recordset
    Dim fld As ADODB.Field
    Dim rng As Excel.Range
    Dim objWS As Excel.Worksheet
    Dim intRowCount As Integer
    Dim intColCount As Integer

    'Display Hourglass
    DoCmd.Hourglass True

    'Instantiate an ADO recordset and set its connection
    Set rstData = New ADODB.Recordset
    rstData.ActiveConnection = CurrentProject.Connection

    'Instantiate a second ADO recordset and set its connection
    Set rstCount = New ADODB.Recordset
    rstCount.ActiveConnection = CurrentProject.Connection

    'Attempt to create Recordset based
```

LISTING 24.6   Continued

```
'on the result of qrySalesByCountry
If CreateRecordset(rstData, rstCount, "qrySalesByCountry") Then

    'If the recordset is created successfully, attempt to launch Excel
    If CreateExcelObj() Then

        'If Excel is launched successfully, add a workbook
        gobjExcel.Workbooks.Add

        'Create a pointer to the Active sheet
        Set objWS = gobjExcel.ActiveSheet
        intRowCount = 1
        intColCount = 1

        'Loop through the Fields collection of the recordset,
        'using field names as column headings
        For Each fld In rstData.Fields
            If fld.Type <> adLongVarBinary Then
                objWS.Cells(1, intColCount).Value = fld.Name
                intColCount = intColCount + 1
            End If
        Next fld

        'Send recordset to Excel
        objWS.Range("A2").CopyFromRecordset rstData, 500

        'Format Data
        With gobjExcel
            .Columns("A:B").Select
            .Columns("A:B").EntireColumn.AutoFit
            .Range("A1").Select
            .ActiveCell.CurrentRegion.Select
            Set rng = .Selection
            .Selection.NumberFormat = "$#,##0.00"

            'Add a Chart object
            .ActiveSheet.ChartObjects.Add(135.75, 14.25, 607.75, 301).Select

            'Run the Chart Wizard
            .ActiveChart.ChartWizard Source:=Range(rng.Address), _
                Gallery:=xlColumn, _
                Format:=6, PlotBy:=xlColumns, CategoryLabels:=1, SeriesLabels _
                :=1, HasLegend:=1, Title:="Sales By Country", CategoryTitle _
                :="", ValueTitle:="", ExtraTitle:=""
```

LISTING 24.6   Continued

```
                'Make Excel Visible
                .Visible = True
            End With
        Else
            'If Excel not launched successfully, display an error message
            MsgBox "Excel Not Successfully Launched"
        End If
    Else
        'If more than 500 records are in result set, display a message
        MsgBox "Too Many Records to Send to Excel"
    End If

cmdCreateGraph_Exit:
    gobjExcel.Visible = True
    Set rstData = Nothing
    Set rstCount = Nothing
    Set fld = Nothing
    Set rng = Nothing
    Set objWS = Nothing

    'Turn hourglass off
    DoCmd.Hourglass False
    Exit Sub

cmdCreateGraph_Err:
    'If an error occurs, display a message and return to
    'common exit routine
    MsgBox "Error # " & Err.Number & ": " & Err.Description
    Resume cmdCreateGraph_Exit
End Sub
```

This routine begins by creating several object variables. It then creates two recordsets and sets the ActiveConnection property of each recordset to the connection associated with the current project. It calls a user-defined function called CreateRecordset, located in the basUtils module. The CreateRecordset function receives three parameters: the two recordset object variables and the name of a query. Listing 24.7 shows the CreateRecordset function.

LISTING 24.7   The CreateRecordset Function

```
Function CreateRecordset(rstData As ADODB.Recordset, _
    rstCount As ADODB.Recordset, _
    strTableName As String)
    On Error GoTo CreateRecordset_Err
```

LISTING 24.7   Continued

```
    'Create recordset that contains count of records in query result
    rstCount.Open "Select Count(*) As NumRecords from " & strTableName

    'If more than 500 records in query result, return false
    'Otherwise, create recordset from query
    If rstCount!NumRecords > 500 Then
        CreateRecordset = False
    Else
        rstData.Open strTableName
        CreateRecordset = True
    End If

CreateRecordset_Exit:
    'Common exit point; destroy the rstCount recordset
    Set rstCount = Nothing
    Exit Function

CreateRecordset_Err:
    'Display error message and resume at common exit point
    MsgBox "Error # " & Err.Number & ": " & Err.Description
    Resume CreateRecordset_Exit
End Function
```

The CreateRecordset function begins by counting how many records are returned by the query name that is passed. If the number of records exceeds 500, the function returns False; otherwise, the function opens a recordset based on the query name that is passed and returns True. This function ensures that only a reasonable number of records are sent to Excel and that a recordset can be opened successfully.

If the CreateRecordset function returns True, the remainder of the code in the Click event of the cmdCreateGraph command button executes. The routine uses the CreateExcelObj function to launch Excel. If Excel is opened successfully, the code creates a new workbook. The routine then loops through each field in the Fields collection of the recordset (the result of the query). The values of the cells in the first row of the worksheet are set equal to the names of the fields in the recordset. Next, the routine uses the CopyFromRecordset method of the Excel Range object to copy the contents of the recordset rstData to cell A2 in the active worksheet. The data from each row is placed in a different row within the spreadsheet. The data from each column in a particular row is placed in the various columns of the worksheet. OLE object fields (adLongVarBinary) are excluded from the process.

After all the data in the recordset is sent to Excel, the routine is ready to create a chart. It moves the cursor to cell A1 and then selects the entire contiguous range of data. It adds a chart object to the worksheet and then uses the Chart Wizard to create a chart. Finally, Excel is made visible so that users can see the fruits of their efforts.

Controlling Word from Access

As you discovered in the preceding section, Excel exposes many objects. You can manipulate each of these objects separately, using Excel's own properties and methods. Prior to Office 97, this was not true for Word, because Word exposed only one object, called `Word.Basic`. Microsoft Word 97, and versions subsequent to it, all sport the Visual Basic for Applications language. These newer versions of Word expose many objects, just as Excel and other Microsoft products do.

Just as with Excel, you can use the `Dim` statement or `Dim as New` statement to launch Word. Like Excel, Word launches as a hidden object. The `Word` application object has a `Visible` property, which makes the `Word` object visible. If you create a `Word` object using automation, Word will not automatically terminate, even if the object variable is destroyed.

Using Word to Generate a Mass Mailing

Figure 24.8 shows the form called `frmMergeToWord`, which shows the results of running a query called `qryMailMerge`. After the user clicks the Merge to Word command button, all the records displayed are sent to a Word mail merge and printed. Figure 24.9 shows an example of the resulting document, and Listing 24.8 shows the code that generated this document.

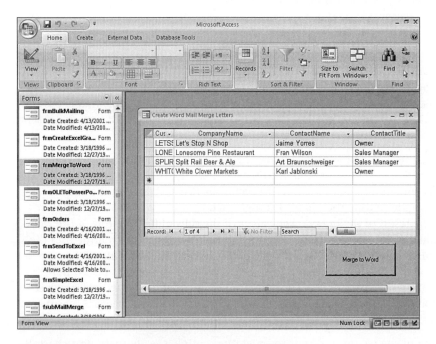

FIGURE 24.8   The data that will be merged to Word.

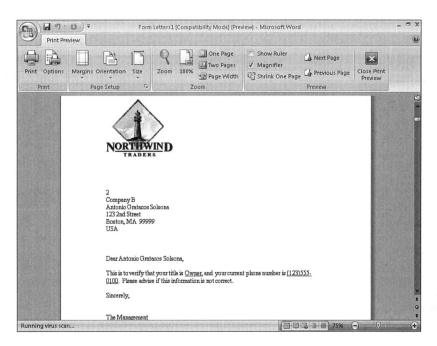

FIGURE 24.9   The result of the mail merge.

LISTING 24.8   Generating a Word Mail Merge Document

```
Private Sub cmdMergeToWord_Click()
    On Error GoTo cmdMergeToWord_Err

    'Turn Hourglass on
    DoCmd.Hourglass True

    'Attempt to create a Word object
    If CreateWordObj() Then

        'If Word object created
        With gobjWord

            'Make Word visible
            .Visible = True

            'Open a document called CustomerLetter in the
            'current folder
            .Documents.Open CurrentProject.Path & _
                "\customerletter.doc"

            'Give the document time to open
            DoEvents
```

LISTING 24.8   Continued

```
            'Use the MailMerge method of the document
            'to perform a mail merge
            With gobjWord.ActiveDocument.MailMerge
                .Destination = wdSendToNewDocument
                .SuppressBlankLines = True
                'For this code to run, you will need to create a
                'data source and then modify the name of the
                'data source below to point at the ODC file.
                .DataSource Name:="c:\documents and settings\" & _
                "alisonj\my documents\my data sources\" _ &
                "Northwind Customers.odc"
                .Execute
            End With

            'Send the result of the merge to the print preview
            'window
            .ActiveDocument.PrintPreview    'Preview

            'Make Word visible
            .Visible = True
        End With
    End If

cmdMergeToWord_Exit:
    'Turn hourglass off
    DoCmd.Hourglass False
    Exit Sub

cmdMergeToWord_Err:
    'Display error message, destroy Word object, and go
    'to common exit routine
    MsgBox "Error # " & Err.Number & ": " & Err.Description
    Set gobjWord = Nothing
    Resume cmdMergeToWord_Exit
End Sub
```

> **NOTE**
>
> The directory names shown in the listing above do not apply to Windows Vista. If you
> are using Windows Vista, you must modify the paths.

The code begins by presenting an hourglass mouse pointer to the user. This helps to
ensure that, if the process takes a while, the user knows that something is happening. It
then calls the CreateWordObj routine to create a Word object. The CreateWordObj routine
is similar to the CreateExcel routine shown earlier in the chapter. The code executes the
Open method on the Documents collection of the Word object. It opens a document called

customerletter in the current folder. The customerletter document already has been set up to do a mail merge. You will need to create an .odc file (from within Word) pointing at the Customers table. The subroutine sets the Destination property of the MailMerge object to a new document. It sets the SuppressBlankLines property to True. Next, it uses the OpenDataSource method to open the datasource indicated in the .odc file. It then executes the mail merge with the Execute method. This merges the contents of the Customers table with the document and creates a new document with the mail-merged letters. The PrintPreview method is executed on the ActiveDocument object so that the merged document is printed. Finally, the Visible property of the Word object is set to True, making Word visible, and the hourglass vanishes.

Using Word to Overcome the Limitations of Access as a Report Writer

Although in most ways Access is a phenomenal report writer, it does have its limitations. For example, you cannot bold or italicize an individual word or phrase within a text box. This is quite limiting if you need to emphasize something such as a past due amount in a dunning letter. When the document I need to produce appears more like a letter than a report, I often think of Microsoft Word. The document pictured in Figure 24.10 produces a letter that provides information to the recipient of an order. The code shown in Listing 24.9 produces the letter based on the information supplied in frmSendConfirmation.

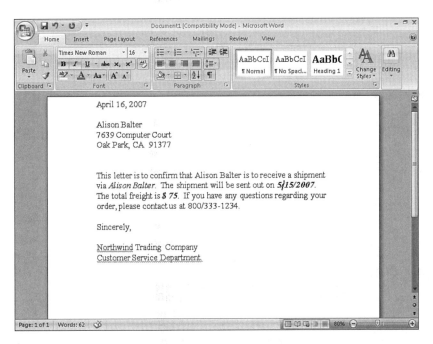

FIGURE 24.10   Order confirmation letter produced in Microsoft Word.

LISTING 24.9   Working with Word Bookmarks

```
Private Sub cmdSendConfirmation_Click()

    Dim objDocument As Word.Document

    'Launch Word
    If CreateWordObj() Then

        'Make Word visible
        gobjWord.Visible = True

        'Point the Document object at a new document
        'based on the Order.dot template
        Set objDocument = gobjWord.Documents.Add _
            (CurrentProject.Path & "\Order.dot")

        'Populate all of the bookmarks with the order information
        With objDocument.Bookmarks
                .Item("CompanyNameAddress").Range.Text = Nz(Me.txtShipName)
                .Item("Address").Range.Text = Nz(Me.txtShipAddress)
                .Item("City").Range.Text = Nz(Me.txtShipCity)
                .Item("Region").Range.Text = Nz(Me.txtShipRegion)
                .Item("PostalCode").Range.Text = Nz(Me.txtShipPostalCode)
                .Item("CompanyName").Range.Text = Nz(Me.txtShipName)
                .Item("Shipper").Range.Text = Nz(Me.txtShipName)
                .Item("ShippedDate").Range.Text = Nz(Me.txtShippedDate)
                .Item("FreightAmount").Range.Text = Nz(Me.txtFreight)

        End With
    End If
End Sub
```

The example first launches Word. It then gets a reference to a new document based on the Order.dot template. After that, it populates bookmarks in the document with values from the currently displayed order.

Controlling PowerPoint from Access

Believe it or not, you can even control PowerPoint using automation. You can create a presentation, print a presentation, or even run a slide show directly from Access.

PowerPoint launches as a hidden window. To make PowerPoint visible, you must set the Visible property of AppWindow to True. Destroying the PowerPoint object variable does not terminate the PowerPoint application.

You can find details of the PowerPoint object model in Microsoft PowerPoint Visual Basic Reference in PowerPoint Help. You should review this object model before attempting to communicate with PowerPoint.

The code shown in Listing 24.10 is located under the `Click` event of the `cmdChangePicture` command button on the `frmOLEToPowerPoint` form, which is shown in Figure 24.11. Figure 24.12 shows the resulting PowerPoint slide.

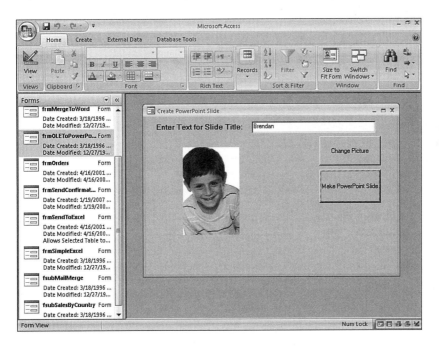

FIGURE 24.11   The form used to create a PowerPoint slide.

LISTING 24.10   Using Select Picture

```
Private Sub cmdChangePicture_Click()
    'Display Open common dialog
    dlgCommon.ShowOpen

    'If the user selected a file, set the SourceDoc
    'property of the OLE control to the selected document
    If Len(dlgCommon.FileName) Then
        imgPicture.Picture = dlgCommon.FileName
        imgPicture.PictureType = 0
    End If
End Sub
```

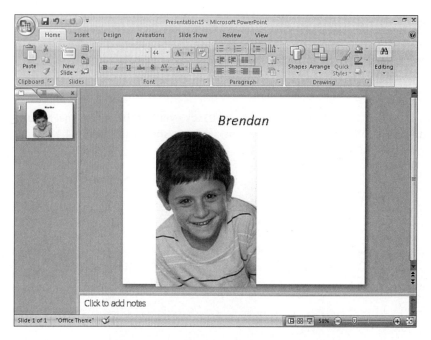

FIGURE 24.12   A PowerPoint slide created using automation.

The code in the `Click` event of `cmdChangePicture` invokes the File Open common dialog box so that the user can select a picture to be added to the slide. The `Filename` property returned from this dialog box is used as the `SourceDoc` property for the automation object. The new picture is then linked to the automation object.

Listing 24.11 shows the routine that creates the PowerPoint slide.

LISTING 24.11   Creating the PowerPoint Slide

```
Private Sub cmdMakePPTSlide_Click()

    Dim objPresentation As PowerPoint.Presentation
    Dim objSlide As PowerPoint.Slide
    Dim strFileName As String

    'Ensure that both the title and the picture are selected
    If IsNull(Me.txtTitle) Or Me.imgPicture.Name = "" Then

        MsgBox "A Title Must Be Entered, and a Picture Selected Before Proceeding"

    Else

        'Create instance of PowerPoint application
        Set mobjPPT = New PowerPoint.Application
```

LISTING 24.11   Continued

```
        'Make instance visible to user
        mobjPPT.Visible = True

        'Add a presentation
        Set objPresentation = mobjPPT.Presentations.Add
        'Add a slide

        Set objSlide = objPresentation.Slides.Add(1, ppLayoutTitleOnly)

        'Change the slide background
        objSlide.Background.Fill.ForeColor.RGB = RGB(255, 100, 100)

        'Modify the slide title
        With objSlide.Shapes.Title.TextFrame.TextRange
            .Text = Me.txtTitle
            .Font.Color.RGB = RGB(0, 0, 255)
            .Font.Italic = True
        End With

        'Add the picture to the slide
        strFileName = imgPicture.Picture
        objSlide.Shapes.AddPicture FileName:=strFileName, _
        Left:=100, Top:=100, _
        LinkToFile:=msoFalse, SaveWithDocument:=msoTrue

    End If

cmdMakePPTSlide_Exit:
    Set objPresentation = Nothing
    Set objSlide = Nothing
    Exit Sub

cmdMakePPTSlide_Err:
    MsgBox "Error # " & Err.Number & ": " & Err.Description
    Resume cmdMakePPTSlide_Exit
End Sub
```

The routine begins by creating an instance of PowerPoint. The code makes the instance
visible. It adds a presentation to the PowerPoint object and then adds a slide to the
presentation. The code modifies the background fill of the slide. It then customizes the
text, color, and italic properties of the title object. Finally, it uses the SourceDoc property
of the olePicture object to create an automation object, which it adds to the slide.

Automating Outlook from Access

Microsoft Outlook is a powerful email client. It is also an excellent tool for both task and contact management. As an application developer, I find many opportunities to automate Outlook from the Access applications that I build. For example, suppose one of my clients sends mass email mailings to selected groups of her customers. I use an Access front end to manipulate customers stored in a SQL Server back end. Included in the front end is a feature that enables the users to generate an email message and then enter the criteria that designates which clients receive the email message. This is one of many examples of how you can integrate the rich features of Access and Outlook.

The form pictured in Figure 24.13 allows the user to select an email template used for a mass mailing. The mailing is sent to all users who meet the criteria entered in a query called qryBulkMail. A more sophisticated example would allow the users to build the query on the fly, using a custom query-by-form. The code that allows the user to select an Outlook email template appears in Listing 24.12.

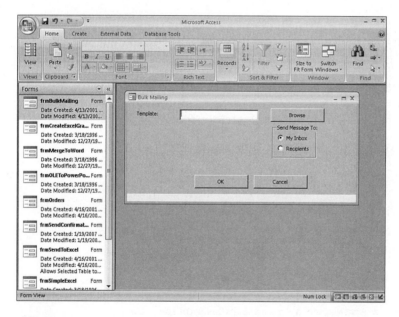

FIGURE 24.13   This form allows the user to select the email template used for a mass mailing.

LISTING 24.12   Selecting the Outlook Template

```
Private Sub cmdBrowse_Click()

    'Filter the Open dialog to Outlook template files
    dlgCommon.Filter = "*.oft"

    'Display the Open dialog
    dlgCommon.ShowOpen
```

LISTING 24.12   Continued

```
    'Populate txtTemplate with the selected file
    Me.txtTemplate = dlgCommon.FileName
End Sub
```

The code first sets the filter of the Common Dialog control to show only files with the
.oft extension. It then displays the Open dialog box. After the user selects a file, the
name and path of the file are placed in the txtTemplate text box. The code required to
send the mailing is shown in Listing 24.13.

LISTING 24.13   Sending the Outlook Message to the Recipients in the qryBulkMail
Resultset

```
Sub CreateMail()
    ' Customize a message for each contact and then send or save the message
    Dim intMessageCount As Integer

    'Declare and instantiate a recordset object
    Dim rst As ADODB.Recordset
    Set rst = New ADODB.Recordset

    'Open a recordset based on the result of qryBulkMail
    rst.Open "qryBulkMail", CurrentProject.Connection
    intMessageCount = 0

    Set mobjOutlook = CreateObject("Outlook.Application")

    ' Loop through the contacts in the open folder
    Do Until rst.EOF
        ' Check that the contact has an email address.
        If rst("EmailAddress") <> "" Then

            'Create a mail item based on the selected template
            Set mobjCurrentMessage = _
            mobjOutlook.CreateItemFromTemplate _
(Me.txtTemplate)

            'Add the email address as the recipient for the message
            mobjCurrentMessage.Recipients.Add rst("EmailAddress")

            'Send the message or save it to the Inbox
            If Me.optSend = 1 Then
                mobjCurrentMessage.Save
            Else
                mobjCurrentMessage.Send
            End If
            intMessageCount = intMessageCount + 1
        End If
        rst.MoveNext
```

LISTING 24.13   Continued

```
Loop

'Write the number of messages created to the worksheet
MsgBox intMessageCount & " Messages Sent"

End Sub
```

First, the code creates a recordset based on qryBulkMail. It then loops through the record-set. As it visits each row in the resultset, it creates an Outlook message based on the designated template. It adds the email address of the current row as a recipient of the email message. It then either saves the message as a draft or immediately sends it to the designated recipient.

Controlling Access from Other Applications

Many times, you will want to control Access from another application. You might want to run an Access report from a Visual Basic or Excel application, for example. Just as you can tap into many of the rich features of other products (such as Excel) from within Access, you can use some of Access's features from within another program. Fortunately, it is extremely easy to control Access from within other applications.

You can find an overview of the Access object model in Access Help. Unless you are very familiar with the Access object model, you should look at this graphical representation of Access's object model before you attempt to use automation to control Access. Access launches with its Visible property set to False. You can change the Visible property of the application object to True to make Access visible.

The form shown in Figure 24.14 is a UserForm associated with an Excel spreadsheet. It is called frmReportSelect and is part of the Excel spreadsheet called RunAccessReports.xls, included on the sample code CD-ROM. The form enables you to select any Access data-base. It displays a list of all reports in the selected database; you can use this list to preview an Access report or print multiple Access reports.

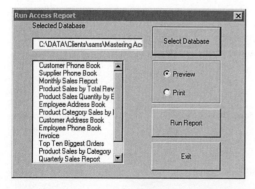

FIGURE 24.14   The UserForm that enables you to print Access reports.

Listing 24.14 shows how this UserForm form accomplishes its work.

LISTING 24.14   Creating a Visual Basic Form to Print Reports

```
Private Sub cmdSelectDatabase_Click()
    'Set the filter property of the Common Dialog control
    dlgCommon.Filter = "*.accdb"

    'Display the open common dialog
    dlgCommon.ShowOpen

    'Ensure that a file was selected
    If dlgCommon.FileName = "" Then
        MsgBox "You Must Select a File to Continue"
    Else

        'Set the text property of the text box to the
        'file selected in the Open dialog
        Me.txtSelectedDB = _
        dlgCommon.FileName

        'Call the ListReports routine
        Call ListReports
    End If
End Sub

Private Sub ListReports()
    On Error GoTo ListReports_Err
    Dim vntReport As Variant

    'If the Access object is not set, instantiate Access
    If mobjAccess Is Nothing Then
        Set mobjAccess = New Access.Application
    End If

    'Open the database selected in the text box
    mobjAccess.OpenCurrentDatabase (Me.txtSelectedDB)

    'Clear the list box
    lstReports.Clear

    'Loop through each report in the AllReports collection
    'of the selected database
    For Each vntReport In mobjAccess.CurrentProject.AllReports
        lstReports.AddItem vntReport.Name
    Next vntReport

ListReports_Exit:
    Exit Sub
```

LISTING 24.14   Continued

```
ListReports_Err:
    MsgBox "Error #" & Err.Number & _
    ": " & Err.Description
    Resume ListReports_Exit
End Sub
```

The cmdSelectDatabase_Click event routine sets the Filter property of the Common
Dialog control to Access database files. The ShowOpen method of the common dialog
control is used to display the File Open dialog box to the user. The ListReports routine
executes after the user selects a file from the dialog box.

The ListReports subprocedure begins by creating an instance of the Access application. It
uses the OpenCurrentDatabase method of the Access object to open the Access database
selected by the user in the File Open common dialog box. It then loops through the
AllReports collection of the CurrentProject object that is associated with the selected
database. It adds the name of each report to the list box.

The routine in Listing 24.15 prints the selected reports.

LISTING 24.15   Creating a New Instance of the Access Application Object

```
Private Sub cmdPrint_Click()
    On Error GoTo cmdPreview_Err
    Dim intCounter As Integer
    Dim intPrintOption As Integer

    'Evaluate whether Print or Preview was selected
    If optPreview.Value = True Then
        intPrintOption = acViewPreview
    ElseIf optPrint.Value = True Then
        intPrintOption = acViewNormal
    End If

    'Make Access visible
    mobjAccess.Visible = True

    'Loop through the list box, printing the
    'selected reports
    For intCounter = 0 To _
        lstReports.ListCount - 1
        If lstReports.Selected(intCounter) Then
            mobjAccess.DoCmd.OpenReport _
            ReportName:=Me.lstReports.List(intCounter), _
            View:=intPrintOption
        End If
```

LISTING 24.16   Continued

```
    Next intCounter

cmdPreview_Exit:
    Exit Sub

cmdPreview_Err:
    MsgBox "Error #" & Err.Number & _
    ": " & Err.Description
    If Not mobjAccess Is Nothing Then
    mobjAccess.Quit
    End If
    Set mobjAccess = Nothing

    Resume cmdPreview_Exit

End Sub
```

The cmdPrint_Click event routine begins by evaluating whether the user selected the print or preview option button. It makes the Access application object visible. The code then loops through the lstReports list box, printing or previewing each selected report. The OpenReport method is used along with the constant acViewPreview or the constant acViewNormal to accomplish this task.

Practical Examples: Using Automation to Extend the Functionality of Your Applications

Many potential applications of automation exist for your applications. One of them is discussed in this section.

The form in Figure 24.15 enables users to select a table or query to send to Excel. The form is called frmSendToExcel.

The Load event of the form is used to add all the table and query names to the list box. The Load event is shown in Listing 24.16. Notice that the function uses the AllTables and AllQueries collections of the current database to populate the list box, excluding all the system tables.

LISTING 24.16   Adding Table and Query Names to the List Box

```
Private Sub Form_Load()
    Dim vntObject As Variant

    'Loop through each table, adding its name
    'to the list box
    For Each vntObject In CurrentData.AllTables
```

LISTING 24.16   Continued

```
        If Left(vntObject.Name, 4) <> "MSys" Then
            Me.lstTables.AddItem vntObject.Name
        End If
    Next vntObject

    'Loop through each query, adding its name to
    'the list box
    For Each vntObject In CurrentData.AllQueries
        Me.lstTables.AddItem vntObject.Name
    Next vntObject
End Sub
```

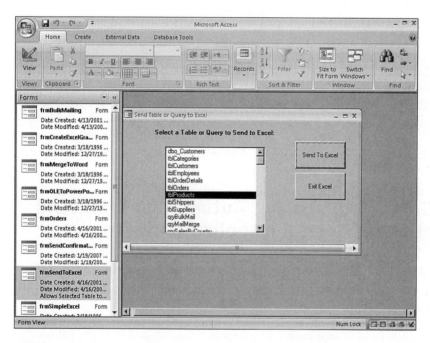

FIGURE 24.15   Exporting a table or query to send to Excel.

The Click event of the cmdSendToExcel command button sends the selected table or query to Excel. Listing 24.17 shows this code.

LISTING 24.17   Sending a Table or Query to Excel

```
Private Sub cmdSendToExcel_Click()
    On Error GoTo cmdSendToExcel_Err
    Dim objWS As Excel.Worksheet
    Dim rstData As ADODB.Recordset
    Dim rstCount As ADODB.Recordset
```

LISTING 24.17   Continued

```
    Dim fld As ADODB.Field
    Dim intColCount As Integer
    Dim intRowCount As Integer

    Set rstData = New ADODB.Recordset
    rstData.ActiveConnection = CurrentProject.Connection
    Set rstCount = New ADODB.Recordset
    rstCount.ActiveConnection = CurrentProject.Connection

    'Invoke hourglass
    DoCmd.Hourglass True

    'Try to create recordset and create Excel Object
    If CreateRecordset(rstData, rstCount, lstTables.Value) Then
        If CreateExcelObj() Then

            'Add a workbook
            gobjExcel.Workbooks.Add

            'Create a reference to the Active sheet
            Set objWS = gobjExcel.ActiveSheet
            intRowCount = 1
            intColCount = 1

            'Loop through the Fields collection
            'Make each field name a column heading in Excel
            For Each fld In rstData.Fields
                If fld.Type <> adLongVarBinary Then
                    objWS.Cells(1, intColCount).Value = fld.Name
                    intColCount = intColCount + 1
                End If
            Next fld

            'Send recordset to Excel
            objWS.Range("A2").CopyFromRecordset rstData, 500
            gobjExcel.Range("A1").Select

            'Set up AutoFilter
            gobjExcel.Selection.AutoFilter
            gobjExcel.Visible = True
        Else
            MsgBox "Excel Not Successfully Launched"
        End If
    Else
        MsgBox "Too Many Records to Send to Excel"
    End If
```

LISTING 24.17   Continued

```
cmdSendToExcel_Exit:
    DoCmd.Hourglass False
    Set objWS = Nothing
    Set rstCount = Nothing
    Set rstData = Nothing
    Set fld = Nothing
    Exit Sub

cmdSendToExcel_Err:
    MsgBox "Error # " & Err.Number & ": " & Err.Description
    Resume cmdSendToExcel_Exit
End Sub
```

The routine begins by creating a recordset object using the CreateRecordSet function shown in Listing 24.18. It then attempts to launch Excel. If it is successful, it loops through the Fields collection of the recordset resulting from the selected table or query. It lists all the field names as column headings in Excel. Next, it uses the CopyFromRecordset method of the range object to copy all the field values to the rows in the Excel worksheet. Finally, it issues the AutoFilter method so that the user easily can manipulate the data in Excel, filtering it as necessary (see Figure 24.16).

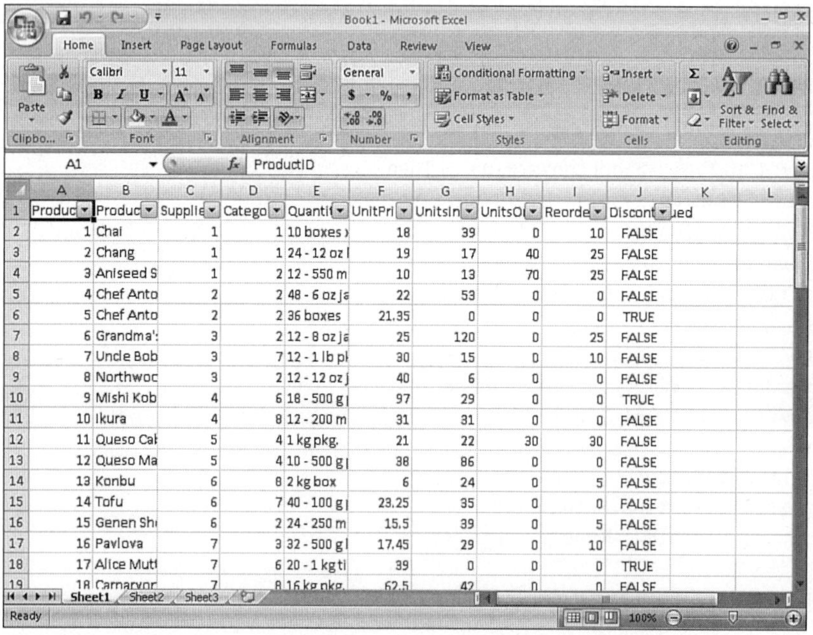

FIGURE 24.16   Using AutoFilter to analyze data sent to Excel.

CAUTION

Although extremely easy to use, the `CopyFromRecordset` method of the range object has one major limitation. If the table or query used to populate the recordset being sent to Excel contains an OLE object field, the method will fail. There are two solutions to this problem. The simplest solution is to always base the recordset sent to Excel on a query. Do not include any OLE object fields in the query. A second solution is to use a less elegant alternative to the `CopyFromRecordset` method. Simply loop through the recordset one record at a time. As each record is visited, send it to the appropriate row and column. Because the first method is easier to code and is more optimized, you should use it wherever possible.

LISTING 24.18   Checking Recordset Size

```
Function CreateRecordset(rstData As ADODB.Recordset, _
    rstCount As ADODB.Recordset, _
    strTableName As String)
    On Error GoTo CreateRecordset_Err

    'Create recordset that contains count of records in query result
    rstCount.Open "Select Count(*) As NumRecords from " & strTableName

    'If more than 500 records in query result, return false
    'Otherwise, create recordset from query
    If rstCount!NumRecords > 500 Then
        CreateRecordset = False
    Else
        rstData.Open strTableName
        CreateRecordset = True
    End If

CreateRecordset_Exit:
    'Common exit point; destroy the rstCount recordset
    Set rstCount = Nothing
    Exit Function

CreateRecordset_Err:
    'Display error message and resume at common exit point
    MsgBox "Error # " & Err.Number & ": " & Err.Description
    Resume CreateRecordset_Exit
End Function
```

This routine, found in `basUtils`, ensures that the recordset is not too large to send to Excel. If the size of the recordset is acceptable, it creates the recordset and returns `True`.

Summary

Automation enables you to control other applications from your Access application, and it enables other programs to control your Access application. This chapter began by providing an overview of automation and why you might want to use it. It discussed creating an object variable to reference the application you are automating. After the ins and outs of the object variable were explained, you saw numerous examples of manipulating automation objects. You looked at detailed code showing automation involving Excel, Word, Outlook, and PowerPoint. Finally, you learned about controlling Access from other applications.

The capability to communicate with other applications has become a prerequisite for successful software development. It is extremely important to be aware of the wealth of tools available. The capability to call on other applications' features is helping to make the world document-centric, rather than application-centric. This means that users can focus on their tasks and not on how they are accomplishing those tasks. Although automation requires significant hardware and also is rather slow, the benefits it provides are often well worth the price.

CHAPTER 25

Exploiting the Power of the Windows API

Why This Chapter Is Important

One of the richest libraries of programming code functions is supplied by Windows itself. This function library commonly is referred to as the *Windows API (Application Programming Interface)*. Fortunately, as a Visual Basic for Applications (VBA) programmer, you can tap into the Windows function library by using these built-in Windows functions in your own VBA modules.

Furthermore, you might discover other *dynamic link libraries (DLLs)* that contain functions that would be useful in your applications. These DLLs also are available to you as long as you are properly licensed to use and distribute them.

A DLL is a library of procedures that applications can link to and use at runtime. Functions contained in the Windows API and other DLLs can provide your applications with significant, added functionality. It is often much more efficient to use an external DLL to accomplish a task than to attempt to write a VBA function to accomplish the same task.

Declaring an External Function to the Compiler

To use a DLL function, you must perform the following steps in order:

1. Declare the function to the VBA compiler.

2. Call the function.

3. Use the return value.

The VBA language is not intrinsically aware of the functions available in external libraries. Declaring a DLL function means making the VBA compiler aware of the name of the function, the library it is located in, the parameters it expects to receive, and the values it expects to return.

If you do not properly declare the library function to the VBA compiler, you receive an error message stating Sub or Function Not Defined. You declare user-defined functions and subroutines written in VBA using Sub or Function keywords. These keywords define the procedures so that VBA can locate the routines when you call them. You declare functions in a DLL in the same way. After you declare a DLL function to the compiler, Access knows where to locate it, and you can use it throughout your application.

You declare an external function to VBA using a Declare statement. You can place Declare statements in the Declarations section of a standard module, a standalone class module, or the class module behind a form or report. A Declare statement placed in a standard module is immediately available to your entire application. If you explicitly declare the Declare statement as private, it is available only to the module in which you declared it. A Declare statement that you place in the General Declarations section of a standalone class module or the class module behind a form or report is available only after you load the form or report or after you instantiate the class. Furthermore, a Declare statement placed in the General Declarations section of a standalone class module or the module behind a form or report can have only private scope.

You can use a Declare statement to declare both subroutines and functions. If the procedure returns a value, you must declare it as a function. If it does not return a value, you must declare it as a subroutine.

A sample Declare statement looks like this:

```
Private Declare Function GetKeyboardType Lib "user32" _
   (ByVal nTypeFlag As Long) As Long
```

This statement declares a function called GetKeyboardType, which is located in the Windows System folder in a DLL file called user32. It receives a long integer parameter by value and returns a long integer. Notice that this function was declared as private.

> **NOTE**
>
> Remember that both the function name and library name are case sensitive. Unless you explicitly include the path as part of the Declare statement, the default system path, the Windows folder, and the Windows System folder are all searched for in the library. Most Windows API functions are contained within the library files user32.dll, gdi32.dll, and kernel32.dll.

> **CAUTION**
>
> Do not include unnecessary `Declare` statements in your applications. Each `Declare` statement consumes memory, whether or not you use the declaration. A large number of unused `Declare` statements can dramatically increase the amount of memory and resources required by your application.

Passing Parameters to DLL Functions

You pass parameters to a DLL function in the same way you pass them to a VBA routine. The only difference is that it is very important that you pass the parameters by reference or by value, as appropriate, and that you always pass the correct data type for each argument. Sending the correct data type means that, if the function expects a long integer value, you shouldn't send a double. Doing so can make your application unstable. The next section covers passing by reference versus passing by value.

Passing by Reference Versus Passing by Value

When you pass a parameter by *reference*, the memory address of the argument is passed to the function. When you pass a parameter by *value*, the actual value of the argument is passed to the function. Unless explicitly told otherwise, VBA passes all parameters by reference. Many library functions expect to receive parameters by value. If such a function is passed a reference to a memory location, it cannot function properly. If you want to pass an argument by value, you must place the `ByVal` keyword in front of the argument in the `Declare` statement. When calling library functions, you must know the types of arguments a function expects to receive and whether the function expects to receive the parameters by reference or by value. Passing an argument by reference rather than by value or passing the incorrect data type for an argument can cause your system to become unstable or can result in the function not working as expected.

Passing String Parameters

String parameters require special handling when being passed to DLL functions. Windows has two ways of storing strings: the BSTR and LPSTR formats. Unless you are dealing with an API call specifically involving object linking and embedding (OLE), the string you are passing to the function is stored in the LPSTR format. DLL functions that receive strings in the LPSTR format cannot change the size of the string they are passed. This means that, if a DLL function is passed a small string that it must fill in with a large value, the function simply overwrites another area of memory with the extra characters. This usually results in a GPF or illegal operation. The following code demonstrates this point and handles the error that is generated:

```
Sub WinSysDir()
    Dim strBuffer As String
    Dim intLength As Integer
    Dim strDirectory As String
```

```
    strBuffer = Space$(160)

    intLength = abGetSystemDirectory(strBuffer, Len(strBuffer))
    strDirectory = Left(strBuffer, intLength)
    MsgBox strDirectory
End Sub
```

> **NOTE**
>
> The code here and most of the code in this chapter is located in CHAP25EX.ACCDB on your sample code CD-ROM.

Notice that the example uses the Space$ function to store 160 spaces in the string variable strBuffer. Actually, the Space$ function returns 160 spaces, followed by a Null character in the strBuffer variable.

The abGetSystemDirectory Windows API function receives two parameters:

▶ The buffer that it will fill with the name of the Windows System folder—in this case, strBuffer.

▶ The length of the buffer that will be filled—in this case, Len(strBuffer). The key here is that the example assumes that the length of the buffer that is passed to the GetSystemDirectoryA function is more than sufficient to hold the path of the Windows System folder.

The GetSystemDirectoryA function fills the buffer and returns the length of the string that it finds. By looking at the left intLength number of characters in the strBuffer variable, you can determine the actual location of the Windows System folder.

> **NOTE**
>
> The abGetSystemDirectory function name is an alias for the real function name, which is GetSystemDirectoryA. To learn more about aliases, refer to the section of this chapter titled "Aliasing a Function."

The Declare statement for the GetSystemDirectoryA function looks like this:

```
Declare Function abGetSystemDirectory _
    Lib "kernel32" _
    Alias "GetSystemDirectoryA"
    (ByVal lpBuffer As String, ByVal nSize As Long) _
    As Long
```

Notice the ByVal keyword that precedes the lpBuffer parameter. Because the ByVal keyword is used, Visual Basic converts the string from BSTR to LPSTR format by adding a Null terminator to the end of the string before passing it to the DLL function. If the

ByVal keyword is omitted, Visual Basic passes a pointer to the function where the string is located in memory. This can cause serious problems, such as database corruption.

CAUTION

Windows API calls are fraught with potential danger. To reduce the chances of data loss or database corruption, always save your work before testing a procedure containing an external function call. If the Access application terminates, at least you won't lose your work. In addition, always make sure that you back up your database. If the Access application terminates and you do not close your database properly, you risk damaging the database. Regularly backing up ensures that if the database becomes corrupted during testing, you can retrieve the last good version from a backup. Fortunately, Access 2007 comes complete with a backup feature that makes it easier than ever to back up your databases.

Aliasing a Function

When you declare a function to VBA, you are given the option to alias it, as in the preceding function. To *alias* means to refer to a function by a substitute name. You might want to alias a Windows API function for several reasons:

▶ A DLL procedure has a name that includes an invalid character.

▶ A DLL procedure name is the same as a VBA keyword.

▶ You want to omit the A required by ANSI versions of the API call.

▶ You want to ensure that you have a unique procedure name in an Access library or application.

▶ You want to call a DLL procedure referenced by an ordinal number.

▶ You want to give your API functions a distinctive prefix to prevent conflicts with API declarations in other modules or add-ins.

The sections that follow further discuss the reasons for aliasing an API function.

Function Calls and Invalid Characters

It is not uncommon for a DLL procedure name to contain a character that is not allowed in VBA code—for example, a DLL procedure that begins with an underscore (_). VBA does not allow a procedure name to begin with an underscore. To use the DLL function, you must alias it, as this example shows:

```
Declare Function LOpen _
    Lib "kernel32" _
    Alias "_lopen" _
    (ByVal lpPathName As String, ByVal ReadWrite As Long) _
    As Long
```

Notice that the Windows API function _lopen begins with an underscore. You can alias the function as LOpen for use in the Access application.

DLL Functions with Duplicate Names

The DLL procedure name you want to use might share the same name as a VBA keyword. You can resolve this conflict only by aliasing the DLL function. The following code aliases a DLL function:

```
Declare Function GetObjectAPI _
    Lib "gdi32" _
    Alias "GetObject" _
    (ByVal hObject As Long, _
    ByVal nCount As Long, _
    lpObject As Any) As Long
```

The GetObject function is part of the Windows API and is also a VBA function. When you alias the function, there is no confusion as to whether you want to call the API or the VBA GetObject function.

Eliminating the A Suffix Required by ANSI

Many API function calls have both ANSI and Unicode versions. The ANSI versions of the functions end with an A. You might want to call the ANSI version of a function but prefer to use the name of the function without the A. You can accomplish this by using an alias, as this code shows:

```
Declare Function FindWindow _
   Lib "user32" Alias "FindWindowA" _
   (ByVal lpClassName As Any, ByVal lpWindowName As String) As Long
```

This Declare statement creates an alias of FindWindow for the ANSI function FindWindowA.

> **NOTE**
>
> *Unicode* is a standard developed by the International Standards Organization (ISO). It was developed to overcome the 256-character limit imposed by the ANSI character standard. The ANSI standard uses only one byte to represent a character, limiting the number of characters to 256. This standard uses two bytes to represent a character, allowing up to 65,536 characters to be represented. Access uses Unicode for string manipulation, which can lead to conversion problems with DLL calls. To overcome this limitation, you always should call the ANSI version of the API function (the version of the function that ends with an A).

Unique Procedure Names in an Access Library or Module

Sometimes you simply want to ensure that a procedure name in a library you are creating is unique, or you might want to ensure that the code you are writing will not conflict with any libraries you are using. Unless you use the Private keyword to declare each procedure, external function declarations are global throughout Access's memory space. This can lead to potential conflicts because Access does not allow multiple declarations of the same external routine. For this reason, you might want to place a unique identifier, such as your initials, at the beginning or end of the function declaration, as in this example:

```
Declare Function ABGetWindowsDirectory Lib "kernel32" _
Alias "GetWindowsDirectoryA" _
(ByVal lpBuffer As String, ByVal nSize As Long) As Long
```

This statement declares the Windows API function `GetWindowsDirectoryA` in the library `kernel32`. The function is aliased as `ABGetWindowsDirectory`. This function was aliased to differentiate it from other calls to the `GetWindowsDirectoryA` function that might share this procedure's scope.

Calling Functions Referenced with Ordinal Numbers

Every DLL procedure can be referenced by an ordinal number in addition to its name. In fact, some DLLs use only ordinal numbers and do not use procedure names at all, requiring you to use ordinal numbers when declaring the procedures. When you declare a function referenced by an ordinal number, you should declare the function with the `Alias` keyword, as in this example:

```
Declare Function GetAppSettings _
    Lib "Utilities" _
    Alias "#47" () As Long
```

This code declares a function with an ordinal number 47 in the library called `Utilities`. You can now refer to it as `GetAppSettings` whenever you call it in VBA code.

Working with Constants and Types

Some DLLs require the use of constants or user-defined types, otherwise known as *structures* or *parameters*. You must place them in the General Declarations section of your module, along with the `Declare` statements you have defined.

Working with Constants

Constants are used by many of the API functions. They provide you with an English-like way of sending required values to an API function. You use the constant as an alias for a specific value. Here's an example:

```
Global Const SM_CXSCREEN = 0
Global Const SM_CYSCREEN = 1
```

You place the constant declarations and function declarations in the General Declarations section of a module. When the `GetSystemMetrics` function is called in the following example, the `SM_CXSCREEN` and `SM_CYSCREEN` constants are passed as arguments to the function:

```
Sub GetScreenInfo()
   MsgBox "Screen Resolution is : " & _
      GetSystemMetrics(SM_CXSCREEN) & _
      " By " & _
      GetSystemMetrics(SM_CYSCREEN)

End Sub
```

When the code in the example passes the `SM_CXSCREEN` constant to the `GetSystemMetrics` function, the function returns the horizontal screen resolution; when the code passes the `SM_CYSCREEN` constant to the function, the code returns the vertical screen resolution.

Working with Types

When working with types, you first must declare the type in the General Declarations section of a module. You then can pass elements of a user-defined type, or you can pass the entire type as a single argument to the API function. The following code shows an example of a `Type` declaration:

```
Type OSVERSIONINFO
   dwOSVersionInfoSize As Long
   dwMajorVersion As Long
   dwMinorVersion As Long
   dwBuildNumber As Long
   dwPlatformId As Long
   strReserved As String * 128
End Type
```

You declare the `Type` structure `OSVERSIONINFO` in the General Declarations section of the module, as shown in Listing 25.1.

LISTING 25.1   Declaring the `Type` Structure `OSVERSIONINFO` in the General Declarations Section of the Module

```
Function GetOSInfo()

   Dim OSInfo As OSVERSIONINFO
   Dim strMajorVersion As String
   Dim strMinorVersion As String
   Dim strBuildNumber As String
   Dim strPlatformId As String

   ' Set the length member before you call GetVersionEx
   OSInfo.dwOSVersionInfoSize = Len(OSInfo)
   If GetVersionEx(OSInfo) Then
       strMajorVersion = OSInfo.dwMajorVersion
       strMinorVersion = OSInfo.dwMinorVersion
```

LISTING 25.1   Continued

```
        strBuildNumber = OSInfo.dwBuildNumber And &HFFFF&
        strPlatformId = OSInfo.dwPlatformId
        MsgBox "The Major Version Is:  " & _
            strMajorVersion & vbCrLf & _

        "The Minor Version Is:  " & strMinorVersion & vbCrLf & _

        "The Build Number Is:  " & strBuildNumber & vbCrLf & _
        "The Platform ID Is:   "
    End If
End Function
```

In this listing, the statement `Dim OSInfo As OSVERSIONIFO` creates a `Type` variable. The entire structure is passed to the `GetVersionEx` function (declared in `basAPICalls`), which fills in the elements of the structure with information about the operating system. The code retrieves and stores this information into variables that it displays in a message box.

Calling DLL Functions: Important Issues

After you declare a procedure, you can call it just like any VBA function. The main issue is that you must ensure that you are passing correct values to the DLL. Otherwise, the bad call can cause your application to shut down without warning. In fact, external library calls are very tricky. You therefore should always save your work before you test the calls.

Most DLLs expect to receive standard C strings. These strings are terminated with a `Null` character. If a DLL expects a `Null`-terminated string, you must pass the string by value. The `ByVal` keyword tells VBA to pass the string as `Null` terminated.

Although you must pass strings by value, they actually are received by reference. The `ByVal` keyword simply means that the string is `Null` terminated. The DLL procedure actually can modify the value of the string, which can cause problems. As discussed in the "Passing String Parameters" section earlier in this chapter, if you do not preallocate space for the procedure to use, it overwrites any memory it can find, including memory currently being used by your application, another application, or even the operating system. You can avoid this problem by making the string argument long enough to accept the longest entry that you think will be placed into the parameter.

Using API Functions

The potential uses for API functions are endless. You can use API functions to modify the System menu, obtain system information, or even switch between running applications. In fact, you can accomplish so many things using API functions that entire books are devoted to the topic. The remainder of this chapter covers several of the common uses of API functions.

Manipulating the Windows Registry

Four built-in VBA functions help you manipulate the Windows Registry. They include
GetAllSettings, GetSetting, SaveSetting, and DeleteSetting. These four functions
allow you to manipulate and work only with a specific branch of the Registry,
HKEY_CURRENT_USER\Software\VB, and VBA program Settings. Sometimes you need to read
from or write to other parts of the Registry. This is one situation in which the Windows
API can really help you out. Using the Windows RegQueryValueEx function, you can
extract information from Registry keys. Using the RegSetValueEx function, you can write
information to the Registry. The declarations for these two functions (found in the
basAPICalls module) look like this:

```
'The RegQueryValueExA function is used to
'read information from the Windows registry

Declare Function RegQueryValueEx _
 Lib "advapi32.dll" Alias "RegQueryValueExA" _
 (ByVal hKey As Long, ByVal lpValueName As String, _
 ByVal lpReserved As Long, lpType As Long, _
 lpData As Any, lpcbData As Long) As Long

'The RegSetValueExA function is used to
'write information to the Windows registry

 Declare Function RegSetValueEx _
 Lib "advapi32.dll" Alias "RegSetValueExA" _
 (ByVal hKey As Long, _
 ByVal lpValueName As String, _
 ByVal Reserved As Long, _
 ByVal dwType As Long, _
 lpData As Any, _
 ByVal cbData As Long) As Long
```

Before you use either function, you must first obtain a handle to the Registry key you
wish to affect. This requires the RegOpenKeyEx function:

```
'The RegOpenKeyExA function is used to
'Return a numeric value that references
'a specific registry key

Declare Function RegOpenKeyEx _
 Lib "advapi32.dll" Alias "RegOpenKeyExA" _
 (ByVal hKey As Long, ByVal lpSubKey As String, _
 ByVal ulOptions As Long, ByVal samDesired As Long, _
 phkResult As Long) As Long
```

Finally, when you are done reading from or saving to the Registry, you must use the `RegCloseKey` function to close the Registry key. The declaration for the `RegCloseKey` function looks like this:

```
'The RegCloseKey function closes the designated
'registry key

Public Declare Function RegCloseKey _
    Lib "advapi32.dll" (ByVal hKey As Long) As Long
```

Listing 25.2 shows how you can use the `RegQueryValueEx` function to read from the Registry.

LISTING 25.2   Using `RegQueryValueEx` to Read Registry Information

```
Private Sub cmdRead_Click()
    Dim strValue As String * 256
    Dim lngRetval As Long
    Dim lngLength As Long
    Dim lngKey As Long

    'Retrieve handle of the registry key
    If RegOpenKeyEx(HKEY_CURRENT_USER, _
        Me.txtKeyName.Value, _
        0, KEY_QUERY_VALUE, lngKey) Then
    End If

    lngLength = 256

    'Retrieve the value of the key
    lngRetval = RegQueryValueEx( _
        lngKey, Me.txtValueName, 0, 0, ByVal strValue, lngLength)
    Me.txtValue = Left(strValue, lngLength)

    'Close the key
    RegCloseKey (lngKey)
End Sub
```

You will find this code in the `frmRegistry` form in the sample database. Notice that the code first retrieves a handle to the requested Registry key. It then uses the `RegQueryValueEx` function to retrieve the designated value from the Registry. After the code is complete, it closes the Registry key. For example, you could request the value `Last User` from the `Software\Microsoft\Office\12.0\Access\Settings` Registry key. The value stored for the `MRU1` setting is displayed in the `txtValue` text box.

25

Listing 25.3 shows how you can use the `RegSetValueEx` function to write to the Registry.

LISTING 25.3   Using `RegSetValueEx` to Write Information to the Registry

```
Private Sub cmdWrite_Click()
    Dim strValue As String
    Dim strKeyName As String
    Dim lngRetval As Long
    Dim lngLength As Long
    Dim lngKey As Long

    'Create string with Key name
    strKeyName = Me.txtKeyName.Value & vbNullString

    'Retrieve handle of the registry key
    If RegOpenKeyEx(HKEY_CURRENT_USER, _
        strKeyName, _
        0, KEY_WRITE, lngKey) Then
    End If

    'Create string with string to store
    strValue = Me.txtValue.Value & vbNullString

    'Create variable with length of string to store
    lngLength = Len(Me.txtValue) + 1

    'Save the value to the key
    lngRetval = RegSetValueEx( _
        lngKey, Me.txtValueName, 0, REG_SZ, _
        ByVal strValue, lngLength)

    'Close the key
    RegCloseKey (lngKey)

End Sub
```

In this listing, the routine first opens a handle to the designated Registry key. It then calls the `RegSetValueEx` function, passing the handle, the value you want to modify, the type of data the key contains, and the new value. Finally, it closes the Registry key.

CAUTION

I generally do not make a practice of writing information to the Windows Registry. If you write to an important Registry key and make a mistake, you can render the Windows operating environment unusable. When you must write to the Windows Registry, do so sparingly and carefully.

> **NOTE**
>
> Listing 25.3 shows you how to write to a Registry key that contains a string. To write to a Registry that expects a DWORD value, you must use the `REG_DWORD` constant rather than the `REG_SZ` constant.

Getting Information About the Operating Environment

By using Windows API calls, you can get volumes of information about the system environment, including the type of hardware on which the application is running, the amount of memory that exists or is available, and the operating system version under which the application is running. It is handy and professional to include system information in your application's Help About box. It also is important to include this system information in your error handling and logging because such information can help you diagnose the problem. This is discussed in Chapter 17, "Error Handling: Preparing for the Inevitable."

Figure 25.1 shows a Custom About dialog box that includes system environment information. This form uses several Windows API calls to get the system information displayed on the form.

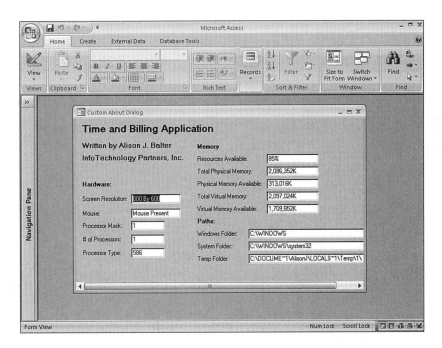

FIGURE 25.1   A Custom About dialog box illustrating the capability to obtain system information from the Windows API.

Before you can call any of the DLL functions required to obtain this information, you must declare all the necessary functions to the compiler. This example accomplishes this in the General Declarations section of the module basUtils. You must also include any constants and type structures used by the DLL calls in the General Declarations section. Listing 25.4 shows what the General Declarations section of basAPICalls looks like.

LISTING 25.4   The General Declarations Section of basAPICalls

```
Option Compare Database
Option Explicit

Public Const MAX_PATH = 160

'The GetVersionEx function gets information about
'the version of the operating system that is currently
'running. The information is filled into the type
'structure OSVERSIONINFO.

Declare Function abGetVersionEx _
    Lib "kernel32" _
    Alias "GetVersionExA" _
    (lpOSInfo As OSVERSIONINFO) As Boolean

Type OSVERSIONINFO
    dwOSVersionInfoSize As Long
    dwMajorVersion As Long
    dwMinorVersion As Long
    dwBuildNumber As Long
    dwPlatformId As Long
    strReserved As String * 128
End Type

'The GetSystemMetrics function utilizes three constants to
'determine whether a mouse is present and to determine
'the width and height of the screen.

Const SM_CXSCREEN = 0
Const SM_CYSCREEN = 1
Const SM_MOUSEPRESENT = 19

Declare Function abGetSystemMetrics _
    Lib "user32" _
    Alias "GetSystemMetrics" _
    (ByVal nIndex As Long) As Long
```

LISTING 25.4   Continued

```
'The GlobalMemoryStatus function retrieves information
'about current available memory. It points to a type
'structure called SYSTEM_INFO, filling in its elements
'with relevant memory information.

Type MEMORYSTATUS
   dwLength As Long
   dwMemoryLoad As Long
   dwTotalPhys As Long
   dwAvailPhys As Long
   dwTotalPageFile As Long
   dwAvailPageFile As Long
   dwTotalVirtual As Long
   dwAvailVirtual As Long
End Type

Declare Sub abGlobalMemoryStatus _
   Lib "kernel32" _
   Alias "GlobalMemoryStatus" _
   (lpBuffer As MEMORYSTATUS)

'The GetSystemInfo function returns information about
'the system. It fills in the type structure SYSTEM_INFO
'with relevant information about the system.

Type SYSTEM_INFO
   dwOemID As Long
   dwPageSize As Long
   lpMinimumApplicationAddress As Long
   lpMaximumApplicationAddress As Long
   dwActiveProcessorMask As Long
   dwNumberOrfProcessors As Long
   dwProcessorType As Long
   dwAllocationGranularity As Long
   dwReserved As Long
End Type

Declare Sub abGetSystemInfo Lib "kernel32" _
   Alias "GetSystemInfo" _
   (lpSystemInfo As SYSTEM_INFO)

'The GetWindowsDirectory function retrieves the name of the
'directory within which Windows is running
```

25

LISTING 25.4   Continued

```
Declare Function abGetWindowsDirectory _
    Lib "kernel32" _
    Alias "GetWindowsDirectoryA" _
    (ByVal lpBuffer As String, _
    ByVal nSize As Long) As Long

'The GetSystemDirectory function retrieves the name of the
'directory in which the Windows system files reside.

Declare Function abGetSystemDirectory _
    Lib "kernel32" _
    Alias "GetSystemDirectoryA" _
    (ByVal lpBuffer As String, _
    ByVal nSize As Long) As Long

'The GetTempPath function retrieves the name of the
'directory where temporary files are stored.

Declare Function abGetTempPath _
    Lib "kernel32" _
    Alias "GetTempPathA" _
    (ByVal nBufferLength As Long, _
    ByVal lpBuffer As String) As Long

'The GetCommandLine function retrieves the command
'line for the current process.

Declare Function abGetCommandLine _
    Lib "kernel32" _
    Alias "GetCommandLineA" () _
    As String

'The GetClassName Function returns the class name
'of a window

Declare Function abGetClassName _
    Lib "user32" _
    Alias "GetClassNameA" _
    (ByVal hwnd As Long, _
    ByVal lpClassName As String, _
    ByVal nMaxCount As Long) _
    As Long
```

LISTING 25.4   Continued

```
'Gets the handle of a parent window

Declare Function abGetParent _
    Lib "user32" _
    Alias "GetParent" _
    (ByVal hwnd As Long) _
    As Long


'The GetWindowText Function gets the title of the
'current window

Declare Function abGetWindowText _
    Lib "user32" _
    Alias "GetWindowTextA" _
    (ByVal hwnd As Long, _
    ByVal lpString As String, _
    ByVal cch As Long) _
    As Long


'The SetWindowText Function modifies the title of the
'current window

Declare Function abSetWindowText _
    Lib "user32" _
    Alias "SetWindowTextA" _
    (ByVal hwnd As Long, _
    ByVal lpString As String) _
    As Long


'The GetDriveType Function returns an integer
'indicating the drive type

Public Const DRIVE_UNKNOWN = 0
Public Const DRIVE_UNAVAILABLE = 1
Public Const DRIVE_REMOVABLE = 2
Public Const DRIVE_FIXED = 3
Public Const DRIVE_REMOTE = 4
Public Const DRIVE_CDROM = 5
Public Const DRIVE_RAMDISK = 6


Declare Function abGetDriveType _
    Lib "kernel32" _
    Alias "GetDriveTypeA" _
    (ByVal nDrive As String) _
    As Long
```

25

LISTING 25.4   Continued

```
'The GetDiskFreeSpace Function determines the amount of
'free space on the active drive

Declare Function abGetDiskFreeSpace _
   Lib "kernel32" _
   Alias "GetDiskFreeSpaceA" _
   (ByVal lpRootPathName As String, _
   lpSectorsPerCluster As Long, _
   lpBytesPerSector As Long, _
   lpNumberOfFreeClusters As Long, _
   lpTotalNumberOfClusters As Long) _
   As Long


'Constants used by RegOpenKeyEx

Public Const KEY_QUERY_VALUE = &H1
Public Const KEY_SET_VALUE = &H2
Public Const READ_CONTROL = &H20000
Public Const STANDARD_RIGHTS_WRITE = (READ_CONTROL)
Public Const SYNCHRONIZE = &H100000
Public Const KEY_CREATE_SUB_KEY = &H4
Public Const KEY_WRITE = ((STANDARD_RIGHTS_WRITE Or KEY_SET_VALUE Or
*KEY_CREATE_SUB_KEY) And (Not SYNCHRONIZE))
Public Const HKEY_CLASSES_ROOT = &H80000000
Public Const HKEY_CURRENT_CONFIG = &H80000005
Public Const HKEY_CURRENT_USER = &H80000001
Public Const HKEY_DYN_DATA = &H80000006
Public Const HKEY_LOCAL_MACHINE = &H80000002
Public Const HKEY_PERFORMANCE_DATA = &H80000004
Public Const HKEY_USERS = &H80000003
Public Const REG_SZ = 1        ' Unicode nul terminated string
Public Const REG_DWORD = 4                    ' 32-bit number


'The RegOpenKeyExA function is used to
'Return a numeric value that references
'a specific registry key

Declare Function RegOpenKeyEx _
 Lib "advapi32.dll" Alias "RegOpenKeyExA" _
 (ByVal hKey As Long, ByVal lpSubKey As String, _
 ByVal ulOptions As Long, ByVal samDesired As Long, _
 phkResult As Long) As Long
```

LISTING 25.4   Continued

```
'The RegQueryValueExA function is used to
'read information from the Windows registry

Declare Function RegQueryValueEx _
 Lib "advapi32.dll" Alias "RegQueryValueExA" _
 (ByVal hKey As Long, ByVal lpValueName As String, _
 ByVal lpReserved As Long, lpType As Long, _
 lpData As Any, lpcbData As Long) As Long

'The RegSetValueExA function is used to
'write information to the Windows registry

 Declare Function RegSetValueEx _
 Lib "advapi32.dll" Alias "RegSetValueExA" _
 (ByVal hKey As Long, _
 ByVal lpValueName As String, _
 ByVal Reserved As Long, _
 ByVal dwType As Long, _
 lpData As Any, _
 ByVal cbData As Long) As Long

'The RegCloseKey function closes the designated
'registry key

Public Declare Function RegCloseKey _
    Lib "advapi32.dll" (ByVal hKey As Long) As Long
```

As you can see, several type structures, constants, and Declare statements are required to obtain all the information that appears on the form. When the form (frmSystemInformation) is opened, all the Windows API functions are called, and the text boxes on the form are filled with the system information. The Open event of the form frmSystemInformation calls a subroutine called GetSysInfo, which is shown in Listing 25.5.

LISTING 25.5   The GetSysInfo Subroutine

```
Sub GetSysInfo(frmAny As Form)
    Dim intMousePresent As Integer
    Dim strBuffer As String
    Dim intLen As Integer
    Dim MS As MEMORYSTATUS
    Dim SI As SYSTEM_INFO
    Dim strCommandLine As String
```

LISTING 25.5   Continued

```
frmAny.txtScreenResolution = abGetSystemMetrics(SM_CXSCREEN) & _
" By " & abGetSystemMetrics(SM_CYSCREEN)
intMousePresent = CBool(abGetSystemMetrics(SM_MOUSEPRESENT))
frmAny.txtMousePresent = IIf(intMousePresent, "Mouse Present", _
"No Mouse Present")

'Set the length member before you call GlobalMemoryStatus
MS.dwLength = Len(MS)
abGlobalMemoryStatus MS
frmAny.txtMemoryLoad = MS.dwMemoryLoad & "%"
frmAny.txtTotalPhysical = Format(Fix(MS.dwTotalPhys / 1024), _
"###,###") & "K"
frmAny.txtAvailablePhysical = Format(Fix(MS.dwAvailPhys / 1024), _
"###,###") & "K"
frmAny.txtTotalVirtual = Format(Fix(MS.dwTotalVirtual / 1024), _
"###,###") & "K"
frmAny.txtAvailableVirtual = Format(Fix(MS.dwAvailVirtual / 1024), _
"###,###") & "K"

abGetSystemInfo SI
frmAny.txtProcessorMask = SI.dwActiveProcessorMask
frmAny.txtNumberOfProcessors = SI.dwNumberOfProcessors
frmAny.txtProcessorType = SI.dwProcessorType


strBuffer = Space(MAX_PATH)
intLen = abGetWindowsDirectory(strBuffer, MAX_PATH)
frmAny.txtWindowsDir = Left(strBuffer, intLen)

strBuffer = Space(MAX_PATH)
intLen = abGetSystemDirectory(strBuffer, MAX_PATH)
frmAny.txtSystemDir = Left(strBuffer, intLen)

strBuffer = Space(MAX_PATH)
intLen = abGetTempPath(MAX_PATH, strBuffer)
frmAny.txtTempDir = Left(strBuffer, intLen)
```

End Sub

Now look at this subroutine in detail. The subroutine calls the function GetSystemMetrics (aliased as abGetSystemMetrics) three times. The first time, it is sent the constant SM_CXSCREEN, and the second time, it is sent the constant SM_CYSCREEN. These calls return the horizontal and vertical screen resolutions. When passed the constant SM_MOUSEPRESENT, the `GetSystemMetrics` function returns a logical `True` or `False`, indicating whether a mouse is present.

The `GlobalMemoryStatus` API call fills in a structure with several pieces of information regarding memory. The code fills the elements of the structure with the memory load, total and available physical memory, and total and available virtual memory.

The `GetSystemInfo` API call also provides you with valuable system information. It fills in a structure with several technical tidbits, including the active processor mask, the number of processors, and the processor type.

Finally, the function calls `GetWindowsDirectory`, `GetSystemDirectory`, and `GetTempPath`. These three functions return the Windows folder, System folder, and temp file path, respectively. Notice that buffer space is preallocated before each call. Because each call returns the length of the folder name retrieved, you then take the characters on the left side of the buffer for the number of characters specified in the return value.

Determining Drive Types and Available Drive Space

Often, you need to determine the types of drives available and the amount of space free on each drive. Fortunately, Windows API functions are available to help you to accomplish these tasks. The `frmListDrives` form lists the type of each drive installed on the system and the amount of free space on each drive, as shown in Figure 25.2. The declarations that are required for the APIs are shown in Listing 25.6.

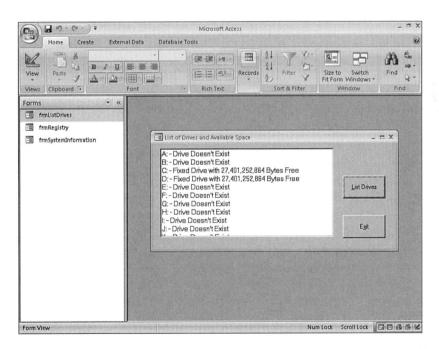

FIGURE 25.2   The `frmListDrives` form showing the type of each drive installed on the system and the amount of free space on each drive.

LISTING 25.6   API Declarations

```
'The GetDriveType Function returns an integer
'indicating the drive type

Public Const DRIVE_UNKNOWN = 0
Public Const DRIVE_UNAVAILABLE = 1
Public Const DRIVE_REMOVABLE = 2
Public Const DRIVE_FIXED = 3
Public Const DRIVE_REMOTE = 4
Public Const DRIVE_CDROM = 5
Public Const DRIVE_RAMDISK = 6

Declare Function abGetDriveType _
    Lib "kernel32" _
    Alias "GetDriveTypeA" _
    (ByVal nDrive As String) _
    As Long

'The GetDiskFreeSpace function determines the amount of
'free space on the active drive

Declare Function abGetDiskFreeSpace _
    Lib "kernel32" _
    Alias "GetDiskFreeSpaceA" _
    (ByVal lpRootPathName As String, _
    lpSectorsPerCluster As Long, _
    lpBytesPerSector As Long, _
    lpNumberOfFreeClusters As Long, _
    lpTotalNumberOfClusters As Long) _
    As Long
```

The Click event of the cmdListDrives command button located on frmListDrives calls a subroutine called GetDriveInfo, sending it the txtDrives text box. Listing 25.7 shows the GetDriveInfo procedure.

LISTING 25.7   The GetDriveInfo Procedure

```
Sub GetDriveInfo(ctlAny As Control)
    Dim intDrive As Integer
    Dim strDriveLetter As String
    Dim strDriveType As String
    Dim strSpaceFree As String

    'Loop through all drives
    For intDrive = 65 To 90 'A through Z
```

LISTING 25.7   Continued

```
      strDriveLetter = (Chr(intDrive) & ":\")
      'Get Drive Type
      strDriveType = TypeOfDrive(strDriveLetter)
      'Get Space Free
      strSpaceFree = NumberOfBytesFree(strDriveLetter)
      ctlAny.Value = _
         ctlAny.Value & _
         Left(strDriveLetter, 2) & _
         " - " & strDriveType & _
         IIf(strDriveType <> "Drive Doesn't Exist", _
            strSpaceFree, "") & _
         vbCrLf
   Next intDrive

End Sub
```

The routine loops through all available drive letters. For each drive letter, the code calls two user-defined functions: TypeOfDrive and NumberOfBytesFree. Listing 25.8 shows the TypeOfDrive function.

LISTING 25.8   The TypeOfDrive Function

```
Function TypeOfDrive(ByVal strDrive As String) As String
   Dim intDriveType As Integer
   Dim strDriveType As String

      intDriveType = abGetDriveType(strDrive)
      Select Case intDriveType
         Case DRIVE_UNKNOWN
            strDriveType = "Type Unknown"
         Case DRIVE_UNAVAILABLE
            strDriveType = "Drive Doesn't Exist"
         Case DRIVE_REMOVABLE
            strDriveType = "Removable Drive"
         Case DRIVE_FIXED
            strDriveType = "Fixed Drive"
         Case DRIVE_REMOTE
            strDriveType = "Network Drive"
         Case DRIVE_CDROM
            strDriveType = "CD-ROM"
         Case DRIVE_RAMDISK
            strDriveType = "RAM Disk"
      End Select
      TypeOfDrive = strDriveType
End Function
```

25

The `TypeOfDrive` function receives a drive letter as a parameter. It calls the Windows API function `GetDriveType` to determine the type of drive whose drive letter was passed to the function. The `GetDriveType` function returns a numeric value that indicates the type of the specified drive. The returned value is evaluated with a case statement, and text representing the drive type is returned from the function.

The `NumberOfBytesFree` function determines how many bytes are free on a particular drive, as shown in Listing 25.9.

LISTING 25.9   The NumberOfBytesFree Function

```
Function NumberOfBytesFree(ByVal strDrive As String) As String
    Dim lngSectors As Long
    Dim lngBytes As Long
    Dim lngFreeClusters As Long
    Dim lngTotalClusters As Long
    Dim intErrNum As Integer

    intErrNum = abGetDiskFreeSpace(strDrive, lngSectors, _
    lngBytes, lngFreeClusters, lngTotalClusters)
    NumberOfBytesFree = " with " & _
            Format((CDbl(lngBytes) * CDbl(lngSectors)) * _
            CDbl(lngFreeClusters), "#,##0") & _
            " Bytes Free"
End Function
```

This function receives a drive letter as a parameter. It then calls the `GetDiskFreeSpace` Windows API function, sending it the drive letter and several long integers. These long integers are filled in with the information required to determine the number of bytes free on the specified drive.

After the code determines the type of drive and number of bytes free, the `GetDriveInfo` procedure concatenates the information with the text contained in a text box on the `frmListDrives` form. If the drive specified is unavailable, the amount of available disk space is not printed.

Practical Examples: Using Windows API Functions in Your Applications

Add an error handler to your application that displays system information. Review all the type structures and function declarations. Also review the function calls. Notice how the return values are used. Make sure that you understand how the Windows API calls make the retrieval of the information included on the system information form possible.

Summary

External libraries, referred to as dynamic link libraries (DLLs), open up the entire Windows API as well as other function libraries to your custom applications. Using external libraries, your applications can harness the power of functions written in other languages, such as C, Delphi, Visual Basic, Visual Basic .NET, or C#. In this chapter, you learned how to declare API functions, type structures, and constants, and how to call Windows API functions. Using the techniques that you learned, you can easily extend beyond the power of Access, harnessing the power of the operating system environment.

CHAPTER 26

Creating Your Own Libraries

Why This Chapter Is Important

As your knowledge of the VBA language expands and you become more proficient as a VBA programmer, you probably will develop functions and subroutines that you would like all your databases to share. Without the use of library databases, the code in each of your databases is an island unto itself. Although you can call the functions and subroutines within your code modules from anywhere in the same database, you cannot call these procedures from a different database.

Without a shared library of code and other standard objects, you will find yourself copying routines and other database objects from one database to the next. All the applications you build can use the library databases that you create. You can distribute your library databases to all your users. A library database is just like any other database; it is simply a collection of procedures and objects that you want to share among numerous databases. The only difference between the library database and other databases is in the way that your application references the database. Instead of opening a library database to use it, you reference it from another database.

Access is highly dependent on library databases. The Table Wizard, Form Wizard, Report Wizard, Database Wizard, Database Splitter, Database Analyzer, and Database Documenter are all examples of tools that reside in library databases. In fact, all the wizards, builders, and menu add-ins you are accustomed to using while developing your applications are contained within library databases.

Chapter 27, "Using Builders and Wizards," covers these tools. This chapter focuses on creating library databases and placing generic functions in a library database to make them available to all your application databases.

Preparing a Database to Be a Library

Creating a library database involves two steps:

1. Writing the functions and creating the objects to be included in the library

2. Loading the database as a library

You begin by creating the generic objects you want to share among your applications. To load the database as a library, you must reference it from another database. The next section covers this process.

Before you can reference a database as a library, you need to think about how to construct the database so that it best serves you as a library. Although a library database is just a normal database, planning the design of the library is integral to its success and usefulness. Improper planning can cause numerous problems, from the need for extra memory to a database malfunction.

Structuring Code Modules for Optimal Performance

Library databases contain the general functions that you use in most of your applications. Because of the way Access loads code modules, you must structure your library databases effectively to achieve optimal performance.

Access 2007 loads code modules only if they are needed. If your code does not call any procedures within a particular module, Access never loads the module into memory. On the other hand, if your code calls a single subroutine or function, or if your code references a public variable, Access loads the entire module. Therefore, it is crucial that you structure your modules to minimize what is loaded into memory, using these techniques:

- Separate frequently used procedures from those that you call infrequently.

- Place in the same module procedures that you use together.

- Place in their own modules procedures that you rarely call.

- If you call the same procedure by routines in more than one module, consider duplicating the routine and placing a copy of it in each module. This method prevents an entire module from loading just because you call a single routine within it.

- Place in the same module procedures within a call tree. This step is necessary because Access looks at the potential call tree when it loads a module. If a procedure in one module calls a procedure from another module, Access loads both modules into memory.

Although you generally want to load as little as possible into memory, the opposite is true for commonly used functions. By placing frequently used procedures in the same module, you ensure that Access loads them into memory so that it can access them quickly when you call them. This improves the performance of your application.

Writing Library Code That Runs

Code that runs perfectly within a normal database might not run as expected when it is part of a library database. A good example is the CurrentDB function. As you have seen throughout this book, the CurrentDB function is a commonly used function that enables you to reference the current database. You would think that the CurrentDB function references the database in which the code is running, but this is actually not the case. It specifically references the database that is active in the user interface. If a library function refers to CurrentDB, it does not refer to itself; instead, it refers to the application database that is calling the library function. If you want to refer to the library database, you must use the CodeDB function. The CodeDB function always refers to the database in which the code is running. You must decide whether CurrentDB or CodeDB is applicable for each situation.

Compiling the Library

Compiling a library database before you distribute it ensures optimal performance. If you do not compile the library code, Access will compile it each time you access it, which significantly degrades the performance of your application. Chapter 18, "Optimizing Your Application," covers the compilation process and its benefits. After you complete all changes to the library database, select Debug, Compile. You must choose this command each time you make changes to the library database.

Creating a Reference

A *reference* is Access's way of locating a library database so that it can use the code in the library. You can establish references in four ways:

- ▶ Create a library reference
- ▶ Create a runtime reference
- ▶ Create an explicit reference
- ▶ Use VBA code

TIP

Much of the text that follows refers to the Windows Registry. You can access the Windows Registry using the RegEdit utility. To use RegEdit, select the Run option from the Start menu and then type **RegEdit**. With Vista, Start does not appear on the Start menu by default. You must add it to the Start menu before running RegEdit.

Creating a Library Reference

You create a library reference by adding the library to the Menu Add-ins section of the Windows Registry, as shown in Figure 26.1. The Menu Add-ins section is located in the HKEY_LOCAL_MACHINE\SOFTWARE\Microsoft\Office\12.0\Access\Menu Add-Ins key. This type of reference is limited because it allows you to invoke the functions of the library database only as an add-in. Chapter 27 covers add-ins in more detail.

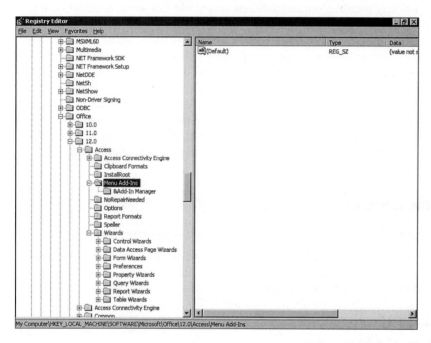

FIGURE 26.1   You create a library reference by adding the library to the Menu Add-ins section of the Windows Registry.

Creating a Runtime Reference

Creating a runtime reference involves establishing a reference to the library at runtime using the Run method of the Application object. This method of creating a reference actually opens the library database and executes the specified function. It uses OLE automation to accomplish this task.

The major advantage of this technique is that Access does not load the library code into memory until it is ready to use it. Furthermore, this technique does not require that Access load additional modules in the call stack into memory unless you explicitly call them. Creating a runtime reference does have a few disadvantages, however. Specifically, the library database must be located in the path specified in the AddInPath key in the Windows Registry. The AddInPath key is located in the HKEY_LOCAL_MACHINE\SOFTWARE\ Microsoft\Office\12.0\Access\Wizards subdirectory of the Windows Registry, as shown in Figure 26.2. If the key does not appear in your registry, you will need to add it.

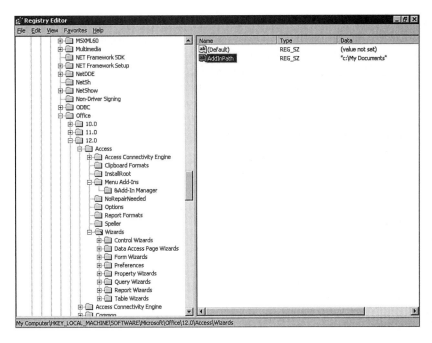

FIGURE 26.2   The AddInPath key is located in the HKEY_LOCAL_MACHINE\SOFTWARE\
Microsoft\Office\12.0\Access\Wizards subdirectory of the Windows Registry.

Calling a Function from a Library at Runtime

The code in Listing 26.1 illustrates how to call a function in a library. Notice that the
example calls the IsLoaded function from the library. You can find this code in the
CHAP26EX.ACCDB database on the sample code CD-ROM.

LISTING 26.1   Calling a Function in a Library

```
Sub AppRun()
   If Application.Run("Chap26Lib.IsLoaded", "frmCustomers") Then
      MsgBox "Customers Form is Loaded"
   Else
      MsgBox "Customers Form is NOT Loaded!!"
   End If
End Sub
```

Listing 26.1 uses the Run method of the Application object to call a function called
IsLoaded, which is located in the CHAP26LIB.ACCDB library. You must reference this file
with an explicit reference (see "Creating an Explicit Reference," later in this chapter), or
you must place the library in the directory you specified in the AddInPath key of the
Windows Registry. Notice the explicit reference to the name of the library in which the
function is located. When using this method of loading a library (without an explicit
reference), you must specify the library name.

Using the LoadOnStartup **Key**

You can add a LoadOnStartup key to the Windows Registry. This key provides a means for Access to load a type library when the user loads the database. A type library is not an actual module, but more of a blueprint of what the module looks like. It displays the functions and constants for a specific module. This feature is helpful because Access can look up functions without having to actually load the module in which you placed the function. Access does not automatically create this key for you. To create the LoadOnStartup key and add an entry to it, follow these steps:

1. Choose Run from the Windows Start menu.

2. Type **RegEdit** and click OK; this launches the Registry Editor.

3. Open the Registry tree until you see HKEY_LOCAL_MACHINE\SOFTWARE\Microsoft\ Office\12.0\Access\Wizards.

4. Click the Wizards entry.

5. Choose Edit, New, Key. The Registry Editor adds a new key.

6. Type **LoadOnStartup** as the name of the new key.

7. With LoadOnStartup selected, choose Edit, New, String Value.

8. Type the full name and path of the library as the name of the new string value.

9. Choose Edit, Modify.

10. Type **rw** for the value.

Figure 26.3 shows an example of a completed entry that references the library in the C:\Libraries folder: CHAP26LIB.ACCDB.

When the user launches Access, Access loads the module and procedure lists of library databases listed under the LoadOnStartup key. When you use the Run method (discussed earlier in the "Creating a Library Reference" section), Access searches for the specified procedure in libraries that you have loaded or referenced. If it does not find the procedure, Access searches any databases listed in the LoadOnStartup key and then locates and loads the required library.

As you can see, the LoadOnStartup key can reap the benefits of Application.Run by using the type library. Access can check the functions without loading the actual module until you reference it explicitly through code.

NOTE

The LoadOnStartup key is not a panacea. Loading the type library when you load Access does slow down the initial load time for your application. Furthermore, Access uses the memory occupied by the type information regardless of whether you ever actually access the library functions. You must decide whether either of these facts is an issue.

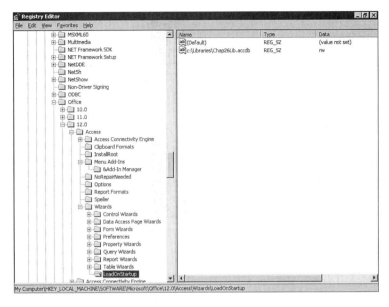

FIGURE 26.3   This completed entry references the library in the `C:\Libraries` folder: `CHAP26LIB.ACCDB`.

Creating an Explicit Reference

The most common type of reference by far is an explicit reference. You can create this type of reference from any code module in the database referencing the library. To create an explicit reference, follow these steps:

1. Click to select the Database Tools tab and select Visual Basic from the Macro group. The VBE appears.

2. Choose Tools, References from the VBE menu. The References dialog box appears, as shown in Figure 26.4.

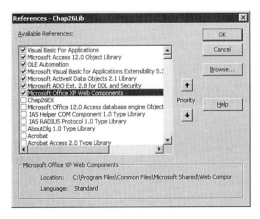

FIGURE 26.4   The References dialog box is the place where you create an explicit reference.

3. Click the Browse button.

4. Select Microsoft Office Access Databases (`*.accdb`) from the Files of Type drop-down.

5. Locate the library database you want to reference.

6. Click Open to close the Add References dialog box.

7. Click OK to close the References dialog box.

When you add a library database to the References dialog box, Access loads the database as a library when you make a call to the library from your code. You can call a library routine just as you would call any subroutine or function. You then can use code in the library database to open forms and other objects stored in the library. Access does not actually load the library database into memory until code in the active application database calls a function or subroutine that is located in the library.

Explicit library references impose a few limitations:

▶ The references you add in a database are available only to that database. Therefore, you must add the library reference to each application database that needs to use the library.

▶ Access stores the explicit path to the reference. This means that, if you move the library, Access will not be able to resolve the reference. Exceptions to this rule are covered later in this section.

When you call a function that is in a library that Access cannot locate, the message shown in Figure 26.5 appears. The References dialog box shows the library is missing, as shown in the sixth line of the Available References list box in Figure 26.6.

Although Access might not be able to find a library database that you have moved, it does its best to resolve library references. By default, Access looks in these places to attempt to resolve a library reference:

▶ The absolute path of the library

▶ The relative path to the library

▶ The current folder

▶ The directory where you installed Access

▶ The Windows path (`Windows` and `Windows\System` folders)

▶ The `PATH` environment variable

▶ The path located in the `RefLibPaths` key of the Windows Registry

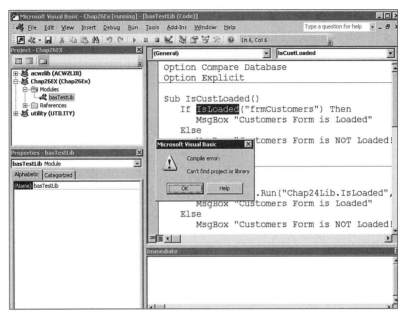

FIGURE 26.5   A warning message indicates that the library database cannot be located.

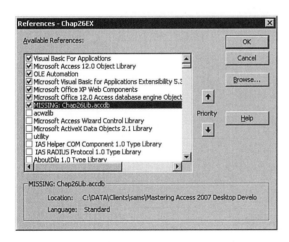

FIGURE 26.6   The References dialog box shows a library flagged as missing.

A couple of these locations require further explanation. If the library is not located in exactly the same location on the user's machine as it is on your machine, Access searches the relative path to the library next. This means that, if you placed the library in the same directory as the database that references it, or in the same relative location, Access will locate the library database. Suppose you have placed your application in C:\AccessApps\ Sales. You have placed the library database in C:\AccessApps\Sales\Libraries. The user installs the application in C:\SalesApp with the library installed in C:\SalesApp\ Libraries. In this case, Access can resolve the reference to the library.

Another trick when dealing with library databases is to use the RefLibPaths key of the Windows Registry. If you create a key called RefLibPaths in the Windows Registry, Access also searches the paths specified under RefLibPaths in an attempt to resolve any references. To use this trick, follow these steps:

1. Create a RefLibPaths key under HKEY_LOCAL_MACHINE\SOFTWARE\Microsoft\ Office\12.0\Access, if it does not already exist.

2. With the key selected, choose Edit, New, String Value.

3. Type the name of the library database as the name of the new string value.

4. Choose Edit, Modify.

5. Type the name of the path containing the library as the value.

6. Repeat steps 2 through 5 for each library you are referencing.

This is a good method to use if you will be distributing an application containing several library databases. You can select a location for the library databases and then reference that location in the Windows Registry. You even can create the Registry entries programmatically by using Windows API calls or the VBA SaveSetting statement. Figure 26.7 shows the RefLibPaths key with an entry for the CHAP26LIB.ACCDB library.

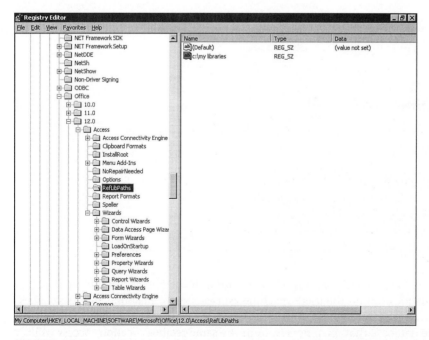

FIGURE 26.7   Access searches the RefLibPaths key of the Windows Registry to resolve any references.

You can use the Packaging Wizard to create the RefLibPaths key in the Windows Registry. This is the easiest way to create the RefLibPaths entry, but it requires that you distribute your application using the Packaging Wizard.

Creating a Reference Using VBA Code

With Access 2000 came the capability to create library references using VBA code. You use the AddFromFile method to accomplish this task. You apply the AddFromFile method to the References collection, which is similar to other collections used within Access and provides a hook to the references associated with a database. The AddFromFile method of the References collection accepts a string as a parameter. The string contains the name of the library reference you are adding. Listing 26.2 shows the code to pass in a library name and then add a reference to it.

LISTING 26.2   Locating and Referencing Libraries in Code

```
Function CreateLibRef(strLibName as String)
    Dim ref As Reference
    On Error GoTo CreateLibRef_Err
    'Create new reference
    Set ref = References.AddFromFile(strLibName)
    CreateLibRef = True
Exit_CreateLibRef:
    Exit Function
CreateLibRef_Err:
    Dim intAnswer As Integer
    Dim strLocation As String
    intAnswer = MsgBox("Library Not Found, Attempt to Locate?", _
        vbYesNo, "Error")
    If intAnswer = vbYes Then
        strLocation = InputBox("Please Enter the Location of the Library")
        Resume
    Else
        CreateLibRef = False
        GoTo Exit_CreateLibRef
    End If

End Function
```

The routine begins by invoking an error handler. A reference object is then set to the result of executing the AddFromFile method on the References collection. If the AddFromFile method executes successfully, Access creates the reference, and the function returns a True condition. Otherwise, the code prompts the user whether he wants to locate the library

26

database. If he responds affirmatively, the code prompts him for the location of the library database and the code attempts once again to establish the reference. If he opts not to supply a location, the routine terminates, returning a `False` condition.

Debugging a Library Database

You can open a library database and test it just like any other database. Although you always should begin testing the library functions this way, it also is important that you give the database a test drive as a library. In other words, after you eliminate any bugs from the database, you should reference it from another database and test it as a library database.

If you need to make changes to a library database while accessing it from another database, you can do so easily by following these steps:

1. Make sure that you have referenced the library database in Tools, References.

2. Click the Object Browser tool from the Module Design window.

3. From the Project/Library drop-down menu, select the library database that contains the code you want to modify (see Figure 26.8).

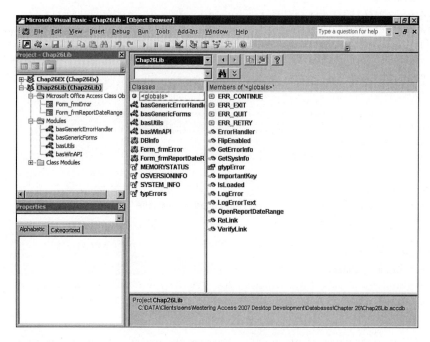

FIGURE 26.8   Use the Object Browser to modify a library database.

4. Select the class you want to modify from the Classes list box.

5. Select the member you want to modify from the Members list box.

6. Click View Definition (the button with the arrow pointing toward the box), or double-click the member whose code you want to view. Access places you in the correct module and procedure of the library database. You can now make changes to the code in the database as required.

Practical Examples: Building a Library for Your Application

Now that you are familiar with library databases and what they offer, try extracting all the generic functions from an application and placing them in a library database. This section presents a step-by-step roadmap for accomplishing this task.

> **NOTE**
>
> This process already has been completed for `CHAP26.ACCDB`. The associated library database is called `CHAP26LIB.ACCDB`. If you want to complete this process as an exercise, copy `CHAP26.ACCDB` and complete the outlined steps.

> **CAUTION**
>
> If the Common Dialog control is not installed on your machine or the user's machine, this example will not work. You will first need to check Tools, References within the IDE. Remove the missing reference to the common dialog control. Next, scroll down and look for the Microsoft Windows Common Controls 6.0 and make sure that you select it. If the Microsoft Windows Common Controls 6.0 is not available, you will need to copy the common dialog control from the sample CD, and register it on your computer. The file that you need to copy is called ComDlg32.ocx. To register it, you select Browse from the Tools, References dialog.

To extract the generic functions from the Time and Billing application and place them in a library database, follow these steps:

1. Create a new database that will become the library database. Import the `basUtils`, `basGenericErrorHandler`, and `basWinAPI` modules as well as the `frmError` form into the library database.

2. Remove two routines from `basUtils` within the library database: `RunReport` and `GetCompanyInfo`. Assume that these routines are specific to the application database and should not be moved to become a part of the library.

3. Choose Debug, Compile to ensure that you do not get compile errors in the library database.

4. Open the application database.

5. Remove `basGenericErrorHandler`, `basWinAPI`, and `frmError` from the application database.

6. Remove six subroutines from basUtils in the application database: IsLoaded, FlipEnabled, ImportantKey, AreTablesAttached, LastOccurrence, and TryAgain.

7. Choose Tools, References to reference the library database.

8. Choose Debug, Compile to ensure that you do not get compile errors in the application database.

9. Test the application to ensure that it runs successfully. To properly check all aspects of the application, you need to introduce an error to test the error-handling routines. Rename the CHAP26DATA.ACCB database to test the linking routines.

You should move one more database element to the library database: the Report Selection Criteria form. This form is generic; therefore, you can use it in many of the applications you create.

Follow these steps to move the frmReportDateRange form to the library database:

1. Open the library database and import the frmReportDateRange form.

2. Create a module called basGenericForms and add the OpenReportDateRange subroutine to the module. Because you cannot open a form in a library database directly, you must create a routine within the library database that opens the form.

3. Open the application database and remove the frmReportDateRange form.

4. Modify the appropriate objects within the application database like this:

```
Sub OpenReportDateRange(strOpenArg As String)
   DoCmd.OpenForm "frmReportDateRange", , , , , acDialog, _
        strOpenArg
End Sub
```

You must modify three reports in the application database to accommodate the movement of the frmReportDateRange form to a library database: rptProjectBillingsByWorkCode, rptClientBillingsByProject, and rptEmployeeBillingsByProject. You must modify the Open event of the rptProjectBillingsByWorkCode report to look like this:

```
Private Sub Report_Open(Cancel As Integer)
    Call OpenReportDateRange("rptProjectBillingsByWorkCode")
    If Not IsLoaded("frmReportDateRange") Then
        Cancel = True
    End If
End Sub
```

Instead of opening the form directly, which would not work because the form is in a library database, you must call the OpenReportDateRange library routine to open the form. The code uses the strOpenArg parameter to the OpenReportDateRange subroutine as the OpenArgs parameter for the frmReportCriteria form. You must make similar changes to the rptClientBillingsByProject and rptEmployeeBillingsByProject reports. You should modify the Open event of the rptClientBillingsByProject report to look like Listing 26.3.

LISTING 26.3   Modifying the Open Event of the rptClientBillingsByProject Report

```
Private Sub Report_Open(Cancel As Integer)
    Call OpenReportDateRange("rptClientBillingsByProject")
    If Not IsLoaded("frmReportDateRange") Then
        Cancel = True
    Else
        Select Case Forms!frmReportDateRange!optDetailLevel.Value
            Case 1
                Me.Caption = Me.Caption & " - Summary Only"
                Me!lblTitle.Caption = Me.lblTitle.Caption & " - _
                  Summary Only"
                Me.Detail.Visible = False
            Case 2
                Me.Caption = Me.Caption & " - Detail Only"
                Me!lblTitle.Caption = Me.lblTitle.Caption & " - _
                  Detail Only"
                Me.GroupHeader0.Visible = False
                Me.GroupFooter1.Visible = False
                Me!CompanyNameDet.Visible = True
            Case 3
                Me.Caption = Me.Caption & " - Summary and Detail"
                Me!lblTitle.Caption = Me.lblTitle.Caption & _
                  " - Summary and Detail"
                Me!CompanyNameDet.Visible = False
        End Select
    End If
End Sub
```

Modify the Open event of the rptEmployeeBillingsByProject report to look like this:

```
Private Sub Report_Open(Cancel As Integer)
    Call OpenReportDateRange("rptEmployeeBillingsByProject")
    If Not IsLoaded("frmReportDateRange") Then
        Cancel = True
    End If
End Sub
```

After you move the generic features of the application to the library database, you can try to build another application database and use the same library features.

26

Summary

Library databases enable you to create libraries of code, forms, reports, and other objects that you will share between multiple databases. Library databases facilitate the application development process by enabling you to easily centralize the development of common code libraries. You also can use these databases to incorporate add-ins, wizards, and builders into your applications and development environment (covered in Chapter 27).

This chapter began by defining a library database and then walked you through all the steps required to prepare a database to become a library database. The chapter discussed the several methods to reference a library database, highlighting the pros and cons of each.

After you reference a library database, the debugging process begins. This chapter highlighted how easy it is to debug a Microsoft Office Access 2007 library database. Finally, it provided you with practical examples of how you can use library databases in your applications.

Library databases can greatly facilitate the application development process, enabling you to easily implement sophisticated functionality in all your applications. Although the process of designing library databases can be intimidating at first, a well-planned library database can shave hours off the application development and maintenance processes.

CHAPTER 27

Using Builders and Wizards

Why This Chapter Is Important

Add-ins are tools that extend the functionality of Access. They enhance the Access environment by making difficult tasks easier, automating repetitive tasks, and adding enhanced functionality. You can design add-ins for yourself or for others in your organization to use. You even might want to distribute add-ins as part of your application so that your users can build their own database objects. If you are really ambitious, you might decide to build an add-in for sale in the Access third-party market.

Microsoft Access supports three types of add-ins: builders, wizards, and menu add-ins. Each has its own advantages and uses. When you begin the process of designing an add-in, you must decide whether it will be a builder, wizard, or menu add-in. This decision affects how you design the add-in as well as how you install it. This chapter defines and shows you how to design and install each type of add-in.

Using Builders

A *builder* is an add-in that helps users construct an expression or another data element. Builders most often are used to help users fill in a property of a database object. Builders generally consist of a single dialog box that appears after the user clicks the ellipsis to the right of the property on the property sheet. An example of a builder is the Expression Builder that appears when users are setting the control source of a text box on a form. Access supports three types of builders:

▶ Property builders

▶ Control builders

▶ Expression builders

Looking at Design Guidelines

When you are designing your own builder, the design should be consistent with that of the builders included in Access. You therefore must learn about the standards for an Access builder. To design builders that are consistent with the built-in builders, keep a few guidelines in mind:

- ▶ Set the AutoCenter property of the Builder form to Yes.

- ▶ Remove record selectors and navigation buttons.

- ▶ Remove scrollbars.

- ▶ Be consistent about the placement of objects on the form. Place the OK and Cancel buttons in the same place in each builder you create, for example.

- ▶ Design the forms as dialog boxes.

Creating a Builder

Now that you are familiar with some general design guidelines for builders, you are ready to design your first builder. What a builder does is completely up to your imagination. For illustration, the following sections begin with a simple builder that prompts users to select the special effect for a text box. Three overall steps are required to create the builder:

1. Write a builder function.

2. Design a builder form.

3. Register the builder.

The following sections go over each of these steps in detail.

Writing a Builder Function

The *builder function* is the function Access calls each time you launch the builder. The function launches the builder form and then returns a value to the appropriate property. Listing 27.1 is an example of a builder function. It is located in CHAP27LIB.ACCDA in the basBuilders module on the accompanying CD-ROM.

LISTING 27.1   Creating a Builder Function

```
Function SpecialEffect(strObject As String, _
          strControl As String, _
          strCurrentValue As String)

   On Error GoTo SpecialEffect_Err

   'Open the special effect form, passing it the special
   'effect currently selected
```

LISTING 27.1   Continued

```
   DoCmd.OpenForm FormName:="frmSpecialEffect", _
                  WindowMode:=acDialog, _
                  OpenArgs:=strCurrentValue

   'If the user selects a special effect and clicks OK, the
   'form remains open but hidden.  Return a value based on
   'which special effect the user selected
   If SysCmd(acSysCmdGetObjectState, acForm, _
           "frmSpecialEffect") = acObjStateOpen Then
      Select Case Forms!frmSpecialEffect.optSpecialEffect.Value
         Case 1
            SpecialEffect = "Flat"
         Case 2
            SpecialEffect = "Raised"
         Case 3
            SpecialEffect = "Sunken"
         Case 4
            SpecialEffect = "Etched"
         Case 5
            SpecialEffect = "Shadowed"
         Case 6
            SpecialEffect = "Chiseled"
      End Select

      'Close the form when done
      DoCmd.Close acForm, "frmSpecialEffect"
   Else

      'If the user clicks Cancel, return the original value
      'for the special effect
      SpecialEffect = strCurrentValue
   End If

SpecialEffect_Exit:
   Exit Function

SpecialEffect_Err:
   MsgBox "Error # " & Err.Number & ": " & Err.Description
   Resume SpecialEffect_Exit
End Function
```

A builder function must receive three preset arguments and must return the value that will become the value for the property being set. The three preset arguments follow:

▶ strObject—The name of the table, query, form, report, or module on which the builder operates

▶ strControl—The name of the control to which the property applies

▶ strCurrentValue—The current property value

Although the names of the arguments are arbitrary, you cannot change their data types, positions, and content. Access automatically fills in the values for the three arguments.

The SpecialEffect function opens the form called frmSpecialEffect in Dialog mode, passing it the current value of the property as the OpenArgs value. Figure 27.1 shows the frmSpecialEffect form.

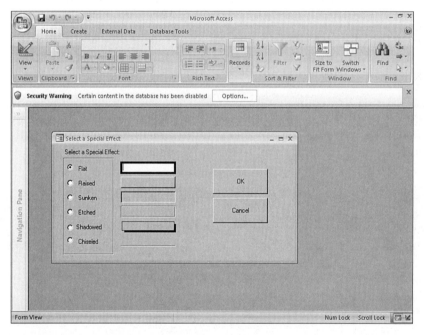

FIGURE 27.1   Here, you see the Special Effect builder form.

The following code is located in the Click event of the cmdOk command button on the form:

```
Private Sub cmdOK_Click()
   Me.Visible = False
End Sub
```

Notice that the code sets the Visible property of the form to False. The code placed behind the cmdCancel command button looks like this:

```
Private Sub cmdCancel_Click()
    DoCmd.Close
End Sub
```

This code closes the `frmSpecialEffect` form.

After the user clicks OK or Cancel, the code within the `SpecialEffect` function continues to execute. The function uses the `SysCmd` function to determine whether the `frmSpecialEffect` form is loaded. You also can use the user-defined `IsLoaded` function to accomplish this task. If the `frmSpecialEffect` form still is loaded, the user must have selected a special effect and clicked OK. Because the form is still open, the function can determine which option button the user selected.

The `Case` statement within the `SpecialEffect` function evaluates the value of the `optSpecialEffect` option group found on the `frmSpecialEffect` form. It sets the return value for the function equal to the appropriate string, depending on the option button that the user of the builder selects. If the user selects the second option button (with a value of 2), for example, the `SpecialEffect` function returns the string `"Raised"`. After the code evaluates the option button value and sets the return value, the code no longer needs the `frmSpecialEffect` form, so the code then closes the form.

If the user chooses Cancel from the `frmSpecialEffect` form, the `SysCmd` function returns `False`, and the code sets the return value of the `SpecialEffect` function equal to `strCurrentValue`, the original property value. In this case, the code does not change the property value.

Designing a Builder Form
Although you have seen the code behind the `Click` event of the OK and Cancel buttons on the `frmSpecialEffect` form, you have not learned about the design of the form or the idea behind this builder. Ordinarily, when you set the `SpecialEffect` property from the Property sheet, no wizard exists to assist with the process. Although the process of setting the `SpecialEffect` property is quite simple, the main problem is that it is difficult to remember exactly what each special effect looks like. I designed the custom special effect builder with this potential problem in mind. It enables users of the builder to see what each special effect looks like before deciding which effect to select.

The properties of the form are quite simple. I set the `Modal` property of the form to `Yes` and removed the record selectors, navigation buttons, and scrollbars. I also set the `AutoCenter` property of the form to `Yes` and included six text boxes on the form. In addition, I set the special effect of each text box to a different style. The form includes an option group. This group has a different value, depending on which option button the user selects. The code sets the `Default` property of the OK command button to `Yes`, making the OK button the default choice. The code sets the `Cancel` property of the Cancel command button to `Yes`, ensuring that if the user presses Esc, the code behind the Cancel button executes. The preceding section showed the code behind the `Click` events of the OK and Cancel buttons. Listing 27.2 shows one more piece of code that enhances this builder.

27

LISTING 27.2   Enhancing the Builder

```
Private Sub Form_Load()
    'Set the value of the Option group
    'To the current value of the property
    Select Case Me.OpenArgs
            Case "Flat"
                Me.optSpecialEffect.Value = 1
            Case "Raised"
                Me.optSpecialEffect.Value = 2
            Case "Sunken"
                Me.optSpecialEffect.Value = 3
            Case "Etched"
                Me.optSpecialEffect.Value = 4
            Case "Shadowed"
                Me.optSpecialEffect.Value = 5
            Case "Chiseled"
                Me.optSpecialEffect.Value = 6
End Select
End Sub
```

I added this subroutine to the Load event of the builder form. It sets the value of the option group to the current value of the property (passed in as an OpenArg).

Although the frmSpecialEffect form is not particularly exciting, it illustrates quite well that you can design a form of any level of complexity to facilitate the process of setting a property value. So far, though, you have not provided an entry point to the builder. If you select the SpecialEffect property, no ellipsis appears. You do not yet have access to the builder.

Registering a Builder

Before you can use a builder, you must register it in one of two ways:

▶ Manually add the required entries to the Windows Registry.

▶ Set up the library database so that the Add-in Manager can create the Windows Registry entries for you.

Manually Adding Entries to the Windows Registry

Adding the required entries to the Windows Registry involves four steps:

1. If no Registry key exists for the property for which you are designing a builder, add the property as a subkey under Property Wizards.

2. Add an additional subkey for the builder.

3. Add four predefined Registry values for the key.

4. Set the proper data value for each value name.

You must create four value names for the subkey. They are Can Edit, Description, Function, and Library. Table 27.1 describes these value names for the Registry subkey.

TABLE 27.1   Values for the Registry Subkey

Value Name	Value Type	Purpose
Can Edit	DWORD	Allows the builder to operate on and modify an existing value
Description	String	Specifies a subkey description that appears in the dialog box, which is invoked automatically if more than one builder exists for a property
Function	String	Name of the builder function
Library	String	Name of the library containing the builder function

Now that you have an overview of the steps involved in the process, you are ready to walk through the steps in detail. The following steps set up the builder called SpecialEffect, which is contained in the library database CHAP27LIB.ACCDA in the folder C:\My Libraries:

1. To invoke the Registry Editor, choose Start, Run from the taskbar. Type **regedit** and click OK. This invokes the Registry Editor. Note that if you are using Vista, you must type **regedit** in the Start Search item on the Start menu.

2. Locate the HKEY_LOCAL_MACHINE\SOFTWARE\Microsoft\Office\12.0\Access\ Wizards\Property Wizards key, as shown in Figure 27.2.

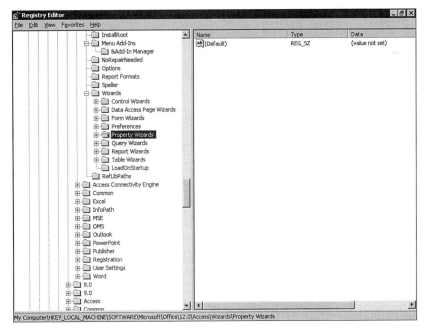

FIGURE 27.2   Use the Registry Editor to navigate to the Property Wizards Registry key.

3. Determine whether a subkey exists with the name of the property for which you are creating a builder (in this case, `SpecialEffect`). If so, skip to step 6.

4. Choose Edit, New, Key.

5. Type the property name as the name for the new key (in this case, **SpecialEffect**).

6. With the new key selected, choose Edit, New, Key again.

7. Type a descriptive name for your builder (in this case, **SpecialEffectBuilder**).

8. Choose Edit, New, DWORD Value.

9. Type **Can Edit** as the value name.

10. Choose Edit, New, String Value.

11. Type **Description** as the value name.

12. Choose Edit, New, String Value.

13. Type **Function** as the value name.

14. Choose Edit, New, String Value.

15. Type **Library** as the value name.

16. Double-click the `Can Edit` value name. The Edit DWORD Value dialog box appears, as shown in Figure 27.3.

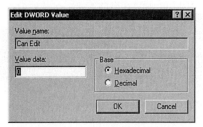

FIGURE 27.3   Double-click the `Can Edit` value name to bring up the Edit DWORD Value dialog box.

17. Enter **1** for Value Data and click OK.

18. Double-click the Description value name. The Edit String dialog box appears, as shown in Figure 27.4.

19. Enter the description you want the user of the builder to see if he has more than one builder assigned to the property (in this case, **Special Effect Builder**). Click OK.

20. Double-click the Function value name. Enter the name of the builder function (in this case, **SpecialEffect**). Click OK.

FIGURE 27.4   The Edit String dialog box appears when you double-click the `Description` value name.

21. Double-click the `Library` value name. Enter the name and location of the library database (in this case, **C:\Libraries\chap27lib.accda**). You do not have to enter the path if the library is located in the Access folder.

Figure 27.5 shows the completed Registry entries. The builder now should be ready to use. To test the builder, you need to exit and relaunch Access. If you successfully created all the Registry entries, you can use the builder. To test the builder, open any database (other than the library database), create a new form, and add a text box. Select Special Effect from the Format tab of the Properties sheet. An ellipsis appears to the right of the Special Effect drop-down arrow, as shown in Figure 27.6. If you click the ellipsis, the builder form appears. Select a special effect and click OK. The special effect you selected now appears in the `SpecialEffect` property.

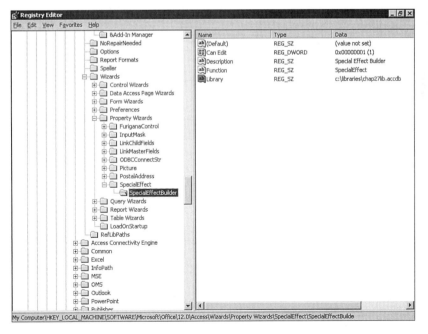

FIGURE 27.5   The completed Registry entries required to add the builder.

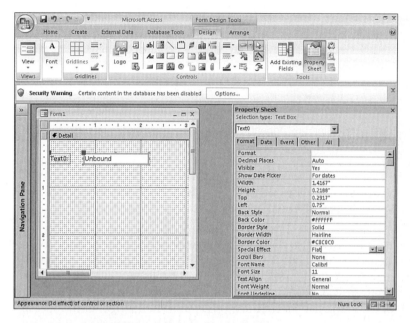

FIGURE 27.6   Using the custom builder.

> **NOTE**
>
> If you do not exactly follow the format for the value names, the message There Is an Invalid Add-in Entry for 'SpecialEffectBuilder' appears, as shown in Figure 27.7. You must correct the Registry entry.

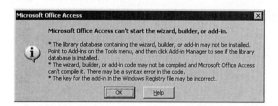

FIGURE 27.7   This error message appears if the Registry entry is invalid.

Automating the Creation of Registry Entries

The alternative to editing the Windows Registry manually is to set up the library database so that the Add-In Manager can create the Registry entries for you. This involves adding a table to the library database. You must call the table USysRegInfo. Follow these steps:

1. Show the system tables. (Access considers tables that begin with USys or MSys system tables and, by default, hides them.) With the library database open, right-click the top of the Navigation Pane and select Navigation Options. The Navigation Options dialog box appears. Click Show System Objects. Click OK. Figure 27.8 shows the database with Tables selected in the Objects list. Notice that the hidden tables appear.

2. Import an existing `USysRegInfo` table by right-clicking within the Navigation Pane and selecting Import, Access Database. Using the Import dialog box, move to the `\Program Files\Microsoft Office 2007\Office12\ACCWIZ` folder and locate the `ACWZMAIN.ACCDE` file. This is a library file that ships with Access. Select the `ACWZMAIN.ACCDE` file and click Open. When you return to the Get External Data dialog box, click OK. The Import Objects dialog box appears, as shown in Figure 27.9.

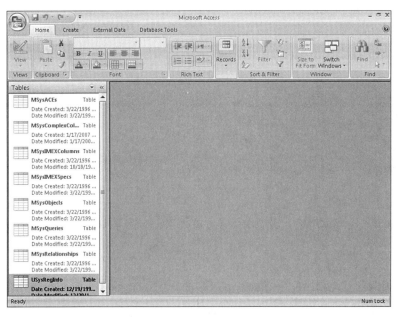

FIGURE 27.8   The Tables tab shows the system objects.

27

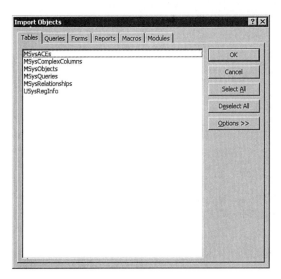

FIGURE 27.9   Using the Import Objects dialog box to add the `USysRegInfo` table to your library database.

3. Locate and select the USysRegInfo table and click OK. Access adds a copy of the USysRegInfo table to your library database. Click Close to complete the process.

4. Double-click to open the USysRegInfo table in the database window.

5. Delete any existing entries in the table.

6. Add specific entries to the USysRegInfo table. Figure 27.10 shows these entries, and Table 27.2 explains them. Close the table.

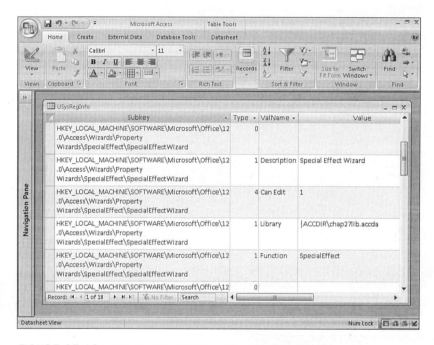

FIGURE 27.10   The completed table with entries for Registry.

TABLE 27.2   The Structure of the USysRegInfo Table

Field Name	Description
SubKey	Name of the subkey value in the Registry where the value you are adding is located
Type	Type of subkey value you are creating (string, binary, or DWORD)
ValName	Value name for the entry
Value	Value associated with the value name

7. Open the database that references the add-in.

8. Click to select the Database Tools tab and then open the Add-Ins drop-down in the Database Tools group. Select Add-In Manager. The Add-In Manager dialog box appears, as shown in Figure 27.11.

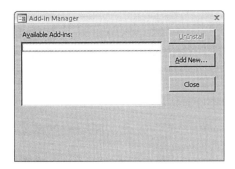

FIGURE 27.11   The Add-in Manager dialog box.

9. Click the Add New button to launch the Open dialog box. Here, you can browse for your add-in or select it from within the default folder.

10. Locate the add-in that you want to add and click Open. Access adds the add-in you select to the Add-in Manager dialog box and selects the add-in for you.

11. Click Close. You now are ready to use the add-in.

Using Wizards

A *wizard* consists of a series of dialog boxes that provide a step-by-step interface for creating a database object. The wizard shields users from the complexities of the process. You probably are familiar with wizards such as the Form Wizard, Report Wizard, and Database Wizard. Access 12 supports the development of several types of custom wizards:

- ▶ Table wizards
- ▶ Query wizards
- ▶ Form wizards
- ▶ Report wizards
- ▶ Data Access Page wizards
- ▶ Property wizards
- ▶ Control wizards

Looking at Design Guidelines

Wizard design guidelines are almost identical to builder design guidelines. The main difference is that a wizard generally presents the user with multiple modal dialog boxes, whereas a builder generally consists of a single modal dialog box. The user must supply information to meet all the data requirements for the wizard before she can close the last dialog box.

Creating a Wizard

NOTE

To successfully create and run the wizard, you must select Options on the Message Bar and indicate that you want to Enable this content.

Creating a wizard is more complex than creating a builder. A wizard generally requires a multipage form and code that creates database objects. Consider a wizard that creates a simple form. The wizard comprises two modal dialog boxes, shown in Figures 27.12 and 27.13. The first dialog box asks the user for a form caption, form name, and message to appear on the new form. The second dialog box enables the user to add OK and Cancel buttons to the form. The multipage form and all the code that enables it to work are in the CHAP27LIB.ACCDA database on the accompanying CD-ROM.

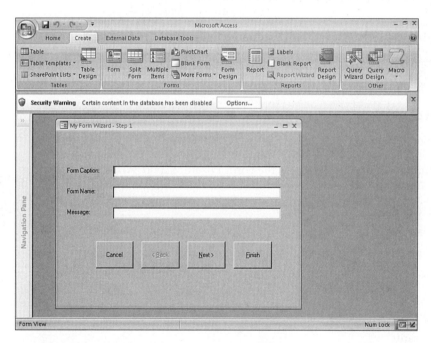

FIGURE 27.12   Step 1 of the custom Form Wizard.

Each page of the wizard contains code to ensure that it operates successfully. I called the form frmGetFormInfo. The first page of this multipage form gives the user the opportunity to choose the next action: Cancel, Next, or Finish. The code for the Cancel button looks like this:

```
Private Sub cmdCancel1_Click()
    DoCmd.Close
End Sub
```

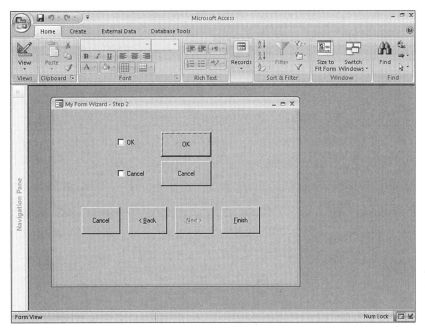

FIGURE 27.13   Step 2 of the custom Form Wizard.

This code closes the wizard form. The code takes no other actions because the user is canceling the process. If the user clicks Next, this code executes:

```
Private Sub cmdNext1_Click()
   DoCmd.GoToPage 2
   Me.Caption = "My Form Wizard - Step 2"
End Sub
```

This code moves to the second page of the form and changes the caption of the form to indicate that the user is on step 2 of the wizard. The code under the Finish button looks like this:

```
Private Sub cmdFinish1_Click()
   If CreateCustomForm() Then
      MsgBox "Form Created Successfully"
      DoCmd.Close
   Else
      MsgBox "Unable to Create Form"
   End If
End Sub
```

This code calls a function called CreateCustomForm, which is responsible for building the actual form. Later in this section, I discuss the details of the CreateCustomForm function.

If the function returns True, the code closes the wizard form and displays a message indicating that the process was successful. Otherwise, the code displays a message indicating that it did not successfully create the form, and the user remains in the wizard. The second page of the form contains similar subroutines. The code under the Back button looks like this:

```
Private Sub cmdBack2_Click()
   DoCmd.GoToPage 1
   Me.Caption = "My Form Wizard - Step 1"
End Sub
```

This code moves back to the first page of the form. If the user chooses Cancel, this code executes:

```
Private Sub cmdCancel2_Click()
   DoCmd.Close
End Sub
```

This code closes the form, taking no further action. If the user clicks Finish, the Click event code of the cmdFinish2 command button executes:

```
Private Sub cmdFinish2_Click()
   Call cmdFinish1_Click
End Sub
```

This code calls the code under the Click event of the cmdFinish1 command button.

The CreateCustomForm function (located in the basWizards module of the library database), as shown in Listing 27.3, contains the code that actually builds the new form.

LISTING 27.3   The CreateCustomForm Function That Builds the Form

```
Function CreateCustomForm() As Boolean

   On Error GoTo CreateCustomForm_Err

   Dim frmNew As Form
   Dim ctlNew As Control

   'Create a new form and set several of its properties
   Set frmNew = CreateForm()
   frmNew.Caption = Forms!frmGetFormInfo.txtFormCaption
   frmNew.RecordSelectors = False
   frmNew.NavigationButtons = False
   frmNew.AutoCenter = True

   'Create a Label control on the new form
```

LISTING 27.3   Continued

```
'Set several of its properties
Set ctlNew = CreateControl(frmNew.Name, acLabel)
ctlNew.Caption = Forms!frmGetFormInfo.txtLabelCaption
ctlNew.Width = 3000
ctlNew.Height = 1000
ctlNew.Top = 1000
ctlNew.Left = 1000

'Evaluate to see if the user requested an OK command button
'If he did, add the command button and set its properties
'Add Click event code for the command button
If Forms!frmGetButtons.chkOK.Value = -1 Then
    Set ctlNew = CreateControl(frmNew.Name, acCommandButton)
    ctlNew.Caption = "OK"
    ctlNew.Width = 1000
    ctlNew.Height = 500
    ctlNew.Top = 1000
    ctlNew.Left = 5000
    ctlNew.Name = "cmdOK"
    ctlNew.Properties("OnClick") = "[Event Procedure]"
    frmNew.Module.InsertText "Sub cmdOK_Click()" & vbCrLf & _
        vbTab & "DoCmd.Close acForm, """ & _
        Forms!frmGetFormInfo.txtFormName & _
        """" & vbCrLf & "End Sub"
End If

'Evaluate to see if the user requested a Cancel command button
'If he did, add the command button and set its properties
'Add Click Event Code for the Command Button
If Forms!frmGetButtons.chkCancel.Value = -1 Then
    Set ctlNew = CreateControl(frmNew.Name, acCommandButton)
    ctlNew.Caption = "Cancel"
    ctlNew.Width = 1000
    ctlNew.Height = 500
    ctlNew.Top = 2000
    ctlNew.Left = 5000
    ctlNew.Name = "cmdCancel"
    ctlNew.Properties("OnClick") = "[Event Procedure]"
    frmNew.Module.InsertText "Sub cmdCancel_Click()" & vbCrLf & _
        vbTab & "MsgBox(""You Canceled!!"")" & vbCrLf & "End Sub"
End If

'If the user entered a form name, save the form
```

27

LISTING 27.3   Continued

```
    If Not IsNull(Forms!frmGetFormInfo.txtFormName) Then
        DoCmd.Save , Forms!frmGetFormInfo.txtFormName
    End If

    'Return True if no errors
    CreateCustomForm = True
    Exit Function

CreateCustomForm_Err:
    MsgBox "Error # " & Err.Number & ": " & Err.Description
    CreateCustomForm = False
    Exit Function
End Function
```

The code first creates both form and control object variables. It sets the form object variable to the return value from the CreateForm function. The CreateForm function creates a new form object. The code sets several properties of the new form object: Caption, RecordSelectors, NavigationButtons, and AutoCenter. Next, the function uses the CreateControl function to create a new label. It calls a reference to the new label ctlNew. The code sets the Caption, Width, Height, Top, and Left properties of the new label. If the user indicated that he wanted an OK button, the code creates a new command button. The code sets the Caption, Width, Height, Top, Left, Name, and Properties properties for the button. The code uses the InsertText method to insert code for the Click event of the command button. If the user requested a Cancel button, the code sets the same properties. Finally, if the user indicated a name for the new form, the code uses the Save method to save the new form object.

> **NOTE**
>
> Access provides several functions for you to create and delete forms, reports, form controls, and report controls. You can use ActiveX Data Object (ADO) code to create, modify, and delete tables and queries. Using the functions and ADO code, you can manipulate database objects any way you want. Chapter 15, "What Are ActiveX Data Objects, and Why Are They Important?" covers ADO code.

Getting the Wizard Ready to Go

As you do with a builder, you need to add a wizard to the Windows Registry before you can use it. You can do this by modifying the Registry directly or by adding entries to the USysRegInfo table. Figure 27.14 shows the completed Registry entry for the custom Form Wizard.

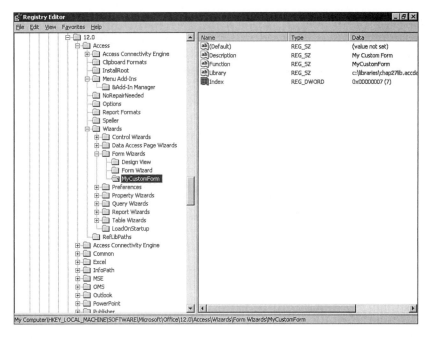

FIGURE 27.14   Registry entries for the custom Form Wizard.

Notice that the function name is `MyCustomForm`. This is the entry point to the wizard. The `Library` key designates the name of the library add-in database containing the entry point function. The `Description` key specifies what appears in the New Object dialog box. Finally, the `Index` key designates the order in which Access displays the wizard in the list in the New Object dialog box. The `MyCustomForm` function, located in the `basWizards` module, simply calls the `frmGetFormInfo` form, initiating the wizard process:

```
Function MyCustomForm(strRecordSource As String) As Variant
    DoCmd.OpenForm FormName:="frmGetFormInfo", WindowMode:=acDialog
End Function
```

Using Menu Add-Ins

A *menu add-in* is a general-purpose tool that enables you to perform a task that generally affects multiple objects or Access itself. The Database Splitter and Database Documenter are examples of menu add-ins. You access menu add-ins through the Add-Ins submenu of the Tools menu.

Looking at Design Guidelines

Menu add-ins are available to the user whenever the Tools menu is available. Menu add-ins are not context sensitive like wizards and builders. Therefore, they should in no way rely on what the user is doing at a particular moment.

27

Creating a Menu Add-In

Creating a menu add-in is just like creating a wizard. The difference is in how you install the add-in. You must register the menu add-in under HKEY_LOCAL_MACHINE\SOFTWARE \Microsoft\Office\12.0\Access\Menu Add-Ins. You can accomplish the registration process by modifying the Registry directly or by using the USysRegInfo table. Figure 27.15 shows the Registry with the correct entries to run the Form Wizard, created earlier in this chapter, as an add-in. Figure 27.16 shows how you can automate the registration process by using the USysRegInfo table. I included three entries in the USysRegInfo table. All three entries designate the proper place in the Registry tree to add the new key. The first entry contains the subkey and a type of zero. The second entry contains the value name Expression and the name of the entry point function as the value. Notice that the expression name is preceded by an equal sign (=) and is followed by parentheses. Access requires the quotation marks within the parentheses because this particular entry-point function requires an argument. The third and final entry contains the value name Library and the name of the library as the value. This is all you need to do to turn a wizard into a menu add-in.

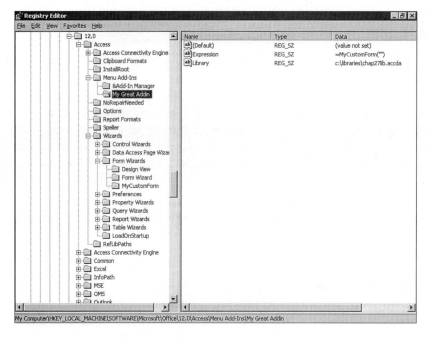

FIGURE 27.15   Registry entries for the menu add-in.

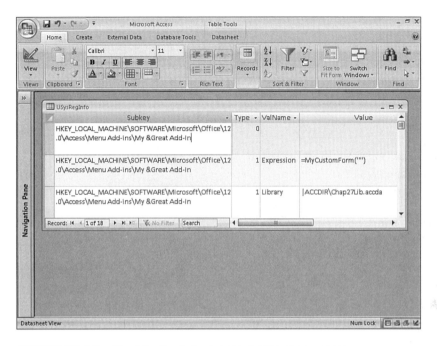

FIGURE 27.16   The USysRegInfo entries for the menu add-in.

Practical Examples: Designing Your Own Add-Ins

The types of builders, wizards, and menu add-ins that you create depend on your specific needs. To reinforce what you have learned, this section includes the step-by-step process for creating a builder to help you add validation text messages. When you invoke the builder, the Choose Builder dialog box shown in Figure 27.17 appears. This dialog box appears because you will design two builders: one that enables the user to select from a list of polite messages and another that enables the user to select from rude messages. If the user selects Polite Validation Text Builder, the dialog box in Figure 27.18 appears. If the user selects Rude Validation Text Builder, the dialog box in Figure 27.19 appears.

FIGURE 27.17   The Choose Builder dialog box.

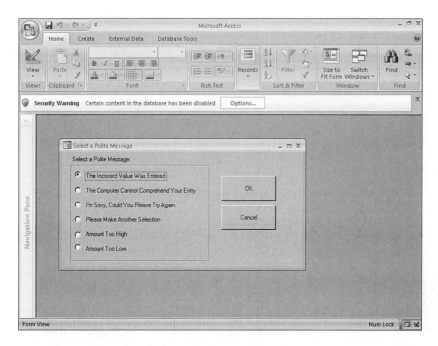

FIGURE 27.18   The polite messages builder.

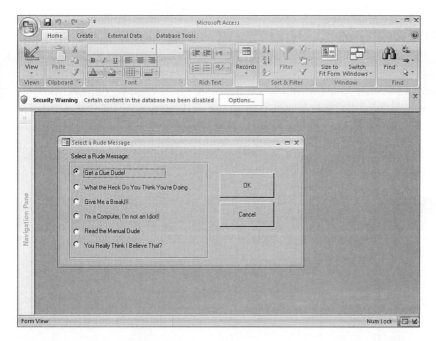

FIGURE 27.19   The rude messages builder.

Listing 27.4 shows the first entry-point function, located in basBuilders.

LISTING 27.4   The First Entry-Point Function

```
Function ValidTextPolite(strObject As String, _
          strControl As String, _
          strCurrentValue As String)

   On Error GoTo ValidTextPolite_Err

   'Open the Builder form
   DoCmd.OpenForm FormName:="frmPolite", _
              WindowMode:=acDialog, _
              OpenArgs:=strCurrentValue

   'If the user selected a message and clicked OK,
   'return the selected text to the caller
   If SysCmd(acSysCmdGetObjectState, acForm, _
          "frmPolite") = acObjStateOpen Then
      Select Case Forms!frmPolite.optPolite.Value
         Case 1
            ValidTextPolite = "The Incorrect Value Was Entered"
         Case 2
            ValidTextPolite = "The Computer Cannot Comprehend Your Entry"
         Case 3
            ValidTextPolite = "I'm Sorry, Could You Please Try Again"
         Case 4
            ValidTextPolite = "Please Make Another Selection"
         Case 5
            ValidTextPolite = "Amount Too High"
         Case 6
            ValidTextPolite = "Amount Too Low"
      End Select

      'Close the form
      DoCmd.Close acForm, "frmPolite"

   'If the user clicked Cancel, return the original value
   Else
      ValidTextPolite = strCurrentValue
   End If

ValidTextPolite_Exit:
   Exit Function

ValidTextPolite_Err:
```

27

LISTING 27.4   Continued

```
    MsgBox "Error # " & Err.Number & ": " & Err.Description
    Resume ValidTextPolite_Exit
End Function
```

The `ValidTextPolite` function shown in Listing 27.4 receives all the parameters required by a builder function. The function opens `frmPolite` modally, passing it the current `ValidationText` property value of the selected control as the `OpenArg`. If the user selects a value from the `frmPolite` form and clicks OK, the code evaluates the selected value and returns the appropriate text from the `ValidTextPolite` function. The return value becomes the validation text of the selected control. Listing 27.5 shows the `Load` event of `frmPolite`.

LISTING 27.5   The Load Event of `frmPolite`

```
Private Sub Form_Load()
    'Set the value of the Option group
    'To the current value of the property
    Select Case Me.OpenArgs
        Case "The Incorrect Value Was Entered"
            Me.optPolite.Value = 1
        Case "The Computer Cannot Comprehend Your Entry"
            Me.optPolite.Value = 2
        Case "I'm Sorry, Could You Please Try Again"
            Me.optPolite.Value = 3
        Case "Please Make Another Selection"
            Me.optPolite.Value = 4
        Case "Amount Too High"
            Me.optPolite.Value = 5
        Case "Amount Too Low"
            Me.optPolite.Value = 6
    End Select

End Sub
```

This code ensures that the value of the option button on the `frmPolite` form reflects the text that the user entered in the `ValidationText` property of the current control. The `ValidTextRude` entry-point function is similar to `ValidTextPolite`. Listing 27.6 shows the `ValidTextRude` entry-point text function; you can find it in `basBuilders` module on the accompanying CD-ROM.

LISTING 27.6   The `ValidTextRude` Entry-Point Function

```
Function ValidTextRude(strObject As String, _
            strControl As String, _
```

LISTING 27.6   Continued

```
                strCurrentValue As String)

    On Error GoTo ValidTextRude_Err

    'Open the Builder form
    DoCmd.OpenForm FormName:="frmRude", _
                    WindowMode:=acDialog, _
                    OpenArgs:=strCurrentValue

    'If the user selected a message and clicked OK,
    'return the selected text to the caller
    If SysCmd(acSysCmdGetObjectState, acForm, _
            "frmRude") = acObjStateOpen Then
        Select Case Forms!frmRude!optRude.Value
            Case 1
                ValidTextRude = "Get a Clue Dude!"
            Case 2
                ValidTextRude = "What the Heck do You Think You're Doing"
            Case 3
                ValidTextRude = "Give Me a Break!!!"
            Case 4
                ValidTextRude = "I'm a Computer, I'm not an Idiot!!"
            Case 5
                ValidTextRude = "Read the Manual Dude"
            Case 6
                ValidTextRude = "You Really Think I Believe That?"
        End Select

        'Close the form
        DoCmd.Close acForm, "frmRude"

    'If the user clicked Cancel, return the original value
    Else
        ValidTextRude = strCurrentValue
    End If

ValidTextRude_Exit:
    Exit Function

ValidTextRude_Err:
    MsgBox "Error # " & Err.Number & ": " & Err.Description
    Resume ValidTextRude_Exit
End Function
```

27

The Load event of frmRude is similar to the Load event of frmPolite, as Listing 27.7 shows.

LISTING 27.7   The Load Event of frmRude

```
Private Sub Form_Load()
    'Set the value of the Option group
    'To the current Value of the property
    Select Case Me.OpenArgs
        Case "Get a Clue Dude!"
            Me.optRude.Value = 1
        Case "What the Heck Do You Think You're Doing"
            Me.optRude.Value = 2
        Case "Give Me a Break!!!"
            Me.optRude.Value = 3
        Case "I'm a Computer, I'm not an Idiot!!"
            Me.optRude.Value = 4
        Case "Read the Manual Dude"
            Me.optRude.Value = 5
        Case "You Really Think I Believe That?"
            Me.optRude.Value = 6
    End Select

End Sub
```

To create the builder, design both forms so that they look like the ones in Figures 27.18 and 27.19. Include code for the Load event of each form as listed previously. The code behind the OK button of each form sets the Visible property of the form to False. The code behind the Cancel button on each form closes the form. Make sure that you name the option groups optPolite and optRude so that the code runs properly for each form. You can place the two entry-point functions, ValidTextPolite and ValidTextRude, in any code module in the library database. The last step involves registering the two builders. The entries in USysRegInfo, shown in Figure 27.20, accomplish the task of registering the builder the first time that the user selects the add-in through the Add-Ins dialog box. You can find this table in the CHAP27LIB.ACCDE database.

> **NOTE**
>
> To complete the process, you must reference the add-in from the database that will use it. Steps 7 through 11, in the section of this chapter titled "Automating the Creation of Registry Entries" covers this process.

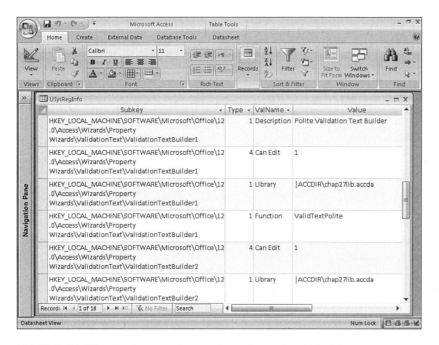

FIGURE 27.20   Registry entries for the polite and rude builders.

Summary

By creating builders, wizards, and add-ins, you can enhance the development environment for yourself and your users. You even can add wizards so that your users can build their own queries, forms, or reports on the fly without a full copy of Access. Your wizard simply needs to prompt the user for the appropriate information and then build the objects to his specifications. What you can do with wizards, builders, and add-ins is limited only by your imagination.

CHAPTER 28

An Introduction to Access and the Internet/Intranet

Why This Chapter Is Important

The Internet is part of our everyday lives. The Internet's penetration into the life of an Access developer is no exception. You can save almost every Access 2007 object as HTML. In this chapter, you'll save tables, query results, forms, and reports, all to HTML. As you'll see, the process is quite simple and produces excellent results.

> **NOTE**
>
> The examples in this chapter are based on the Northwind sample database that you can download from within Microsoft Access.

Saving Database Objects as HTML

Probably one of the most basic but powerful features in Access is the capability to save database objects as Hypertext Markup Language (HTML) documents. You can publish table data, query results, form datasheets, and reports, all as HTML. The following sections cover each of these objects.

Saving Table Data as HTML

When saving table data to HTML, you can store it in the HTML file format so that you can easily publish it on the Web. Just follow these steps:

1. Use the Navigation Pane to select the table that you want to export.

2. Click to select the External Data tab and then open the More drop-down in the Export group.

3. Select HTML Document (see Figure 28.1). The Export – HTML Document dialog box appears (see Figure 28.2).

4. Enter a name and location for the HTML document that you are generating.

5. Indicate if you want to export the document with formatting and layout and whether you want to open the document when the export process is complete.

6. Designate whether you want to export just selected records, and click OK to proceed. The HTML Output Options dialog box appears (see Figure 28.3).

7. Designate a template that you want to use for the outputted document and what type of encoding you want to use.

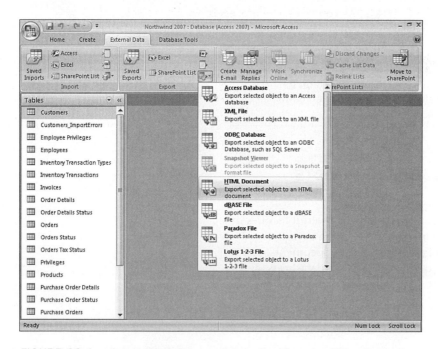

FIGURE 28.1   Select HTML Document from the More drop-down in the Export group.

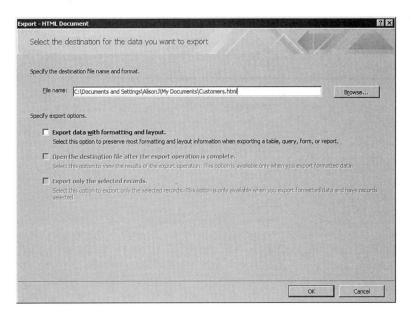

FIGURE 28.2   The Export – HTML dialog box allows you to select options for the export process.

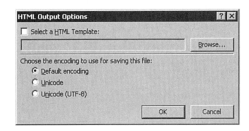

FIGURE 28.3   The HTML Output Options dialog box allows you to designate additional options used during the export process.

8. Click OK to finish the process. Access 2007 generates the HTML file and displays it (see Figure 28.4) if you indicated that you wanted to open the document when the export process was complete. If you'd like, you can view the HTML source (see Figure 28.5).

9. Access prompts you to save the export steps. Indicate your option and click Close to complete the process.

28

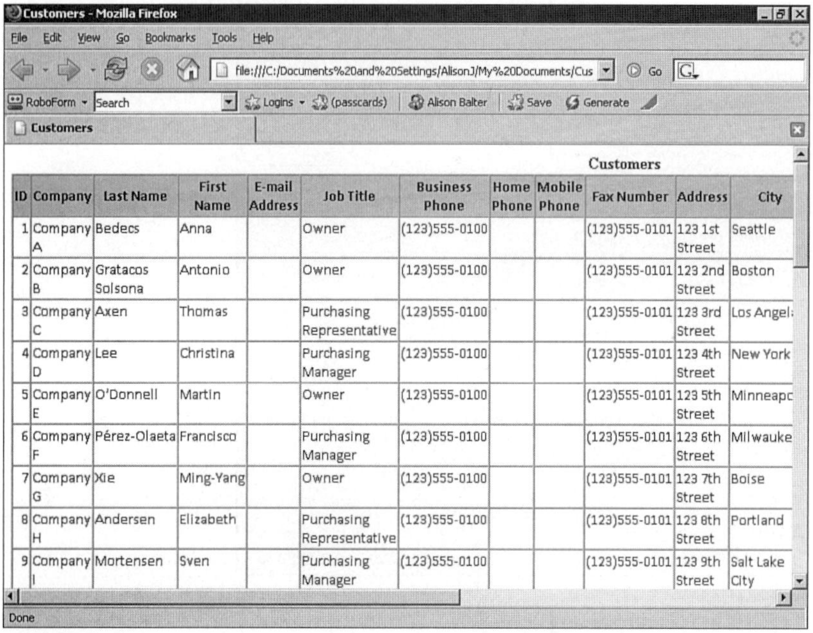

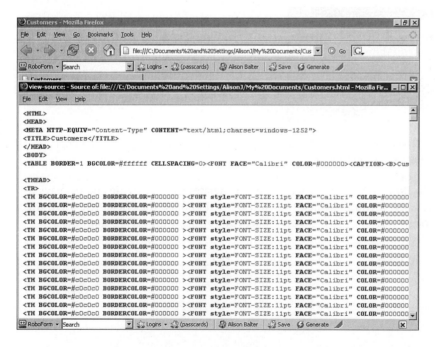

FIGURE 28.4   Access displays the generated document in your browser.

FIGURE 28.5   You can easily view the HTML source associated with the generated web page.

Saving Query Results as HTML

The capability to save query results as HTML means you don't need to save all fields and all records to an HTML file. In fact, you can even save the results of Totals queries and other complex queries as HTML. Saving the result of a query as HTML is similar to saving a table as HTML:

1. Use the Navigation Pane to select the query that you want to export.

2. Click to select the External Data tab, and then open the More drop-down in the Export group.

3. Select HTML Document. The Export – HTML Document dialog box appears.

4. Enter a name and location for the HTML document that you are generating.

5. Indicate if you want to export the document with formatting and layout and whether you want to open the document when the export process is complete.

6. Designate whether you want to export just selected records, and click OK to proceed. The HTML Output Options dialog box appears.

7. Designate a template that you want to use for the outputted document and what type of encoding you want to use.

8. Click OK to finish the process. Access 2007 generates the HTML file and displays it if you indicated that you wanted to open the document when the export process was complete. If you'd like, you can view the HTML source.

9. Access prompts you to save the export steps. Indicate your option and click Close to complete the process.

Access exports the file to HTML so that you can view it from any web browser. You can also view the HTML source.

Saving Forms as HTML

Because an HTML file is a static file, you can save only a form's datasheet as HTML. A static HTML file doesn't change as the data in the database changes; plus, you cannot modify the data in the HTML file. To save a form's datasheet as HTML, follow these steps:

1. Use the Navigation Pane to select the form that you want to export.

2. Click to select the External Data tab, and then open the More drop-down in the Export group.

3. Select HTML document. The Export – HTML Document dialog box appears.

4. Enter a name and location for the HTML document that you are generating.

5. Indicate whether you want to open the document when the export process is complete, and click OK. The HTML Output dialog box appears.

6. Designate a template that you want to use for the outputted document and what type of encoding you want to use.

7. Click OK to finish the process. Access 2007 generates the HTML file and displays it if you indicated that you wanted to open the document when the export process was complete. If you'd like, you can view the HTML source.

8. Access prompts you to save the export steps. Indicate your option, and click Close to complete the process.

Access exports the file to HTML so that you can view it from any web browser. You can also view the HTML source.

Saving Reports as HTML

You can save reports and their formatting as HTML, too, which is an elegant way to publish data on an Internet or intranet site. To publish a report as HTML, just follow these steps:

1. Use the Navigation Pane to select the report that you want to export.

2. Click to select the External Data tab, and then open the More drop-down in the Export group.

3. Select HTML document. The Export – HTML Document dialog box appears.

4. Enter a name and location for the HTML document that you are generating.

5. Indicate whether you want to open the document when the export process is complete, and click OK. The HTML Output dialog box appears.

6. Designate a template that you want to use for the outputted document and what type of encoding you want to use.

7. Click OK to finish the process. Access 2007 generates the HTML file as a nicely formatted report (see Figure 28.6). If you indicated that you wanted to open the document when the export process was complete, Access displays the report. If you'd like, you can view the HTML source.

8. Access prompts you to save the export steps. Indicate your option, and click Close to complete the process.

Access exports the file to HTML so that you can view it from any web browser. You can also view the HTML source. Figure 28.6 shows a report published as HTML. Because this is a multipage report, Access generates several HTML files. Each page of the report is linked, and you can easily navigate from page to page by using the First, Previous, Next, and Last hyperlinks automatically generated during the export process (see Figure 28.7).

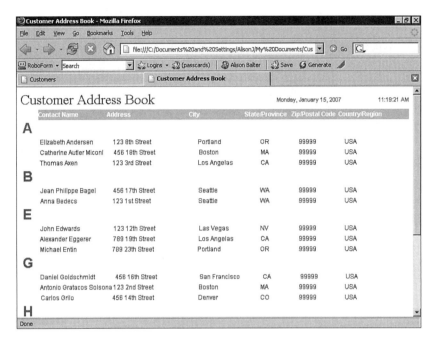

FIGURE 28.6   The report appears as a nicely formatted document.

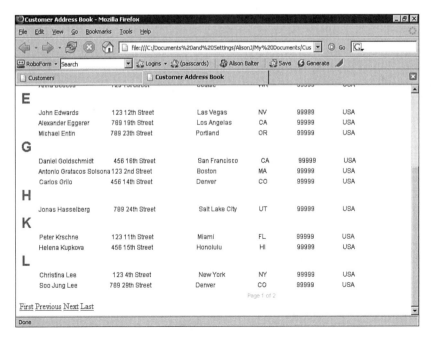

FIGURE 28.7   The export process generates First, Previous, New, and Last hyperlinks, allowing you to navigate between the pages.

Linking to HTML Files

Just as you can link to dBASE tables, Paradox tables, or Open Database Connectivity (ODBC) data sources, you can also link to HTML files by following these steps:

1. Click to select the External Data tab, and then open the More drop-down in the Import group.

2. Select HTML document. The Get External Data – HTML Document dialog box appears (see Figure 28.8).

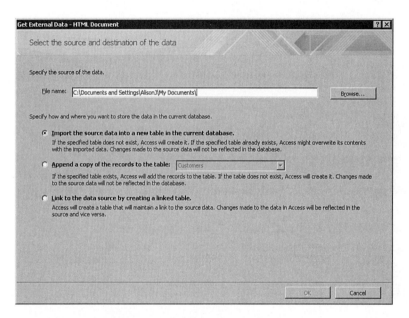

FIGURE 28.8   The Get External Data – HTML dialog box allows you to select options for the import process.

3. Enter a name and location for the HTML document that you are linking to.

4. Indicate whether you want to import the source data into a new table, append it to an existing table, or link to it. In this case, select Link to the Data Source By Creating a Linked Table. Click OK to proceed. The Link HTML Wizard appears (see Figure 28.9).

5. Designate whether the first row contains column headings. If you click Advanced, a plethora of additional options appear (see Figure 28.10). Options include the ability to change field names and data types as well as specifications for dates, times, and numbers. Click OK to close the dialog box and return to the wizard.

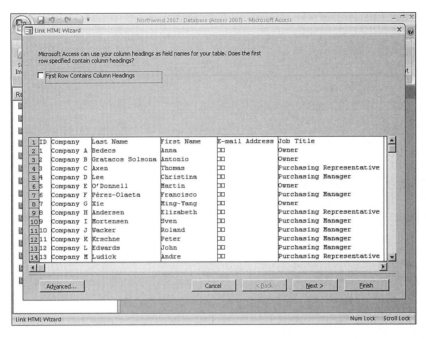

FIGURE 28.9   The Link HTML Wizard allows you to designate the specifics of the linking process.

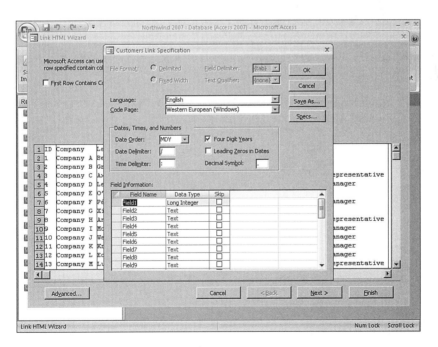

FIGURE 28.10   Using the Advanced dialog box, you can refine the linking options.

6. Click Next. The second step of the wizard appears (see Figure 28.11). Once again, Access gives you the opportunity to modify field types and field names. After you have made any desired changes, click Next to continue. The final step of the wizard appears.

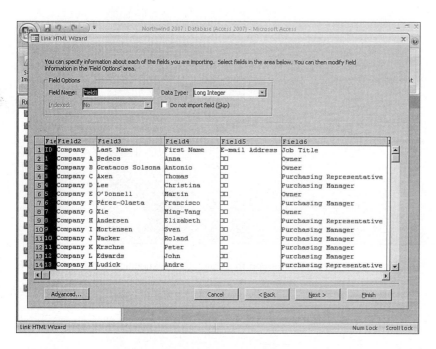

FIGURE 28.11   The second step of the wizard allows you to designate field types and field names that will apply to the new table.

7. Select a name for the linked table, and click Finish. A dialog box appears indicating that the linking process was successful (see Figure 28.12).

8. Click OK to complete the process.

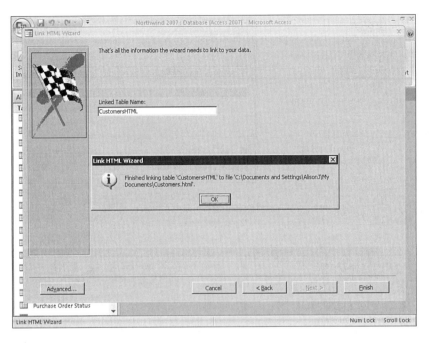

FIGURE 28.12   A dialog box appears indicating the linking process was successful.

Importing HTML Files

You can import the data in an HTML file so that it can be used exactly like any other Access table. Follow these steps to import an HTML file:

1. Click to select the External Data tab, and then open the More drop-down in the Import group.

2. Select HTML document. The Get External Data – HTML Document dialog box appears.

3. Enter a name and location for the HTML document that you are importing. Click OK.

4. Select Import the Source Data into a New Table in the Current Database. Click OK to proceed. The Import HTML Wizard appears.

5. Designate whether the first row contains column headings. If you click Advanced, a plethora of additional options appear. Options include the ability to change field names and data types as well as specifications for dates, times, and numbers. Click OK to close the dialog box and return to the wizard.

28

6. Click Next. The second step of the wizard appears. Once again, Access gives you the opportunity to modify field types and field names. After you have made any desired changes, click Next to continue. The third step of the wizard appears (see Figure 28.13).

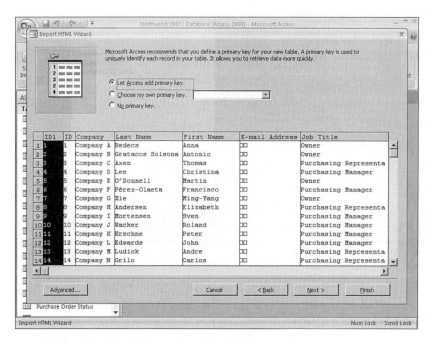

FIGURE 28.13   You can designate whether you want a primary key for your new table.

7. Designate whether you want to set the primary key, let Access set the primary key, or import the table without a primary key. Select your option, and click Next.

8. Select a name for the linked table, and click Finish. A dialog box appears asking whether you want to save your import steps.

9. Click Close to complete the process.

Saving Database Objects as XML

You not only can save database objects as HTML, but you also can save them as XML. XML is another commonly used file format on the Internet. Here's how you save a table as XML:

1. Use the Navigation Pane to select the table that you want to export.

2. Click to select the External Data tab, and then use the More drop-down to select XML File. The Export – XML File dialog box appears (see Figure 28.14).

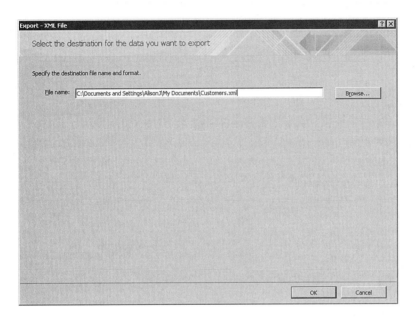

FIGURE 28.14   The Export – XML File dialog box allows you to designate the file and location that you wish to export to.

3. Select a name and location for the new file and click OK.

4. Indicate whether you want to export the data, schema, and presentation of your data. Make your selections, and then click OK.

5. The final step of the wizard appears, prompting you to save your export steps. Click Close to close the dialog.

6. If you browse the XML file that you generated, it will appear as in Figure 28.15.

28

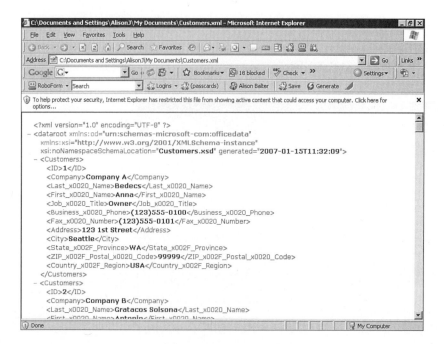

FIGURE 28.15   You can open the generated XML file in your browser.

Importing XML Files

Another option available to you is the ability to import an existing XML document. The process is similar to that used for an HTML document. Just follow these steps:

1. Click to select the External Data tab, and then click the XML button in the Import group. The Get External Data – XML Document dialog box appears.

2. Enter a name and location for the XML document that you are importing. Then click OK. The Import XML dialog box appears (see Figure 28.16).

3. Designate whether you want to import the structure only, import structure and data, or append the XML data to an existing table. Click OK to continue. The wizard asks whether you want to save your import steps.

4. Click Close to close the dialog box. The table should now appear in the Navigation Pane along with the other Access tables.

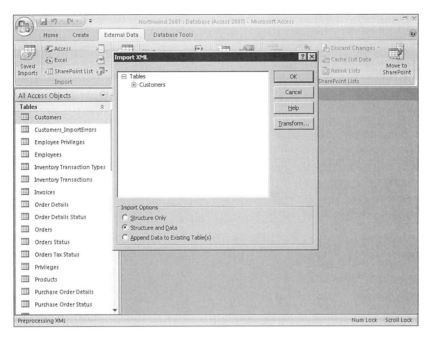

FIGURE 28.16   The Import XML dialog box allows you to designate the specifics of the
import process.

Practical Examples

Practice saving one of your own tables as HTML. Next, save a query, form, and report as
HTML. View the resulting pages in your browser.

Summary

You can easily integrate Access with the Internet or with an intranet. Access enables you
to easily publish database objects to the Web and import HTML data from the Web. In
fact, you can even create dynamic web pages and build forms that display and update live
data directly from a browser! Access 2007 helps bring your data to the continually evolv-
ing IT world; the possibilities are endless!

28

PART V

Adding Polish to Your Application

IN THIS PART

Documenting Your Application

Why This Chapter Is Important

Back in the days of mainframes and very formal centralized management information systems (MIS) departments, documentation was a mandatory requirement for the completion of an application. Today, it seems as though all types of people are developing applications: administrative assistants, CEOs, sales managers, MIS professionals, and so on. To make matters worse, many of us who consider ourselves MIS professionals never received any formal systems training. Finally, the demand to get an application up and running and then to move on to the next application is more prevalent than ever. As a result of all these factors, it seems that documentation has gone by the wayside.

Despite all the reasons why documentation doesn't seem to happen, properly documenting your application is as important today as it was in the mainframe days. Documentation provides you and your users with these benefits:

▶ It makes the system easy for you and others to maintain.

▶ It helps state the purpose and function of each object in the application.

This chapter covers the various ways in which you can document your application objects and code.

Preparing Your Application to Be Self-Documenting

Fortunately, Access ships with an excellent tool to assist you with the process of documenting your database: the Database Documenter. Although you can use this tool without special preparation on your part, a little bit of work as you build the components of your application can go a long way toward enhancing the value of the Database Documenter's output.

Documenting Your Tables

The Database Documenter prints all field and table descriptions that you enter in the design of a table. Figure 29.1 shows a table in Design view. Notice the descriptions for the ClientID and StateProvince fields. These descriptions provide additional information that is not readily obvious from looking at the field names. The Table Properties window also contains a Description property. This Database Documenter includes this property when you print the table's documentation.

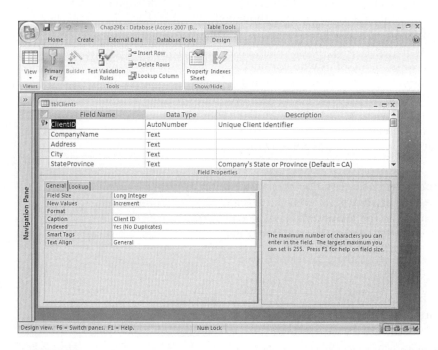

FIGURE 29.1   The descriptions that you include for each field appear in the Database Documenter.

Entering a table description also assists you and the users of your database when you are working with the tables in the database. Figure 9.2 shows the Navigation Pane after I entered table descriptions. The description of each table appears in the Navigation Pane. If the descriptions don't appear, you may need to adjust the View setting to View By Details to see the descriptions.

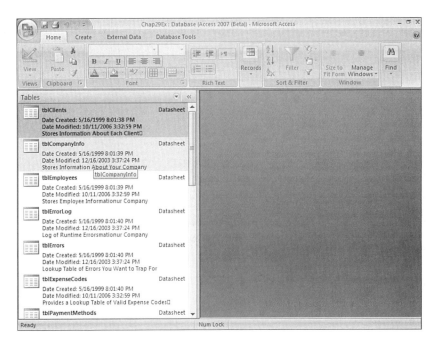

FIGURE 29.2   The description of each table appears in the Navigation Pane.

Documenting Your Queries

Just as you can enhance the output that the Database Documenter provides for tables, you also can enhance the output it provides for queries. Figure 29.3 shows the Query Properties window. I filled in the `Description` property with a detailed description of the purpose of the query. Figure 29.4 shows the description of an individual column in a query. Access includes both the query and field descriptions in the output provided by the Database Documenter.

Documenting Your Forms

Documentation is not limited to table and query objects. A form also has a `Description` property. You cannot access it from the Design view of the form, though. To view or modify the `Description` property of a form, follow these steps:

1. Display the Navigation Pane.

2. Right-click the form for which you want to add a description.

3. Choose View Properties. The Object Properties dialog box appears, as shown in Figure 29.5.

4. Enter a description in the Description text box.

29

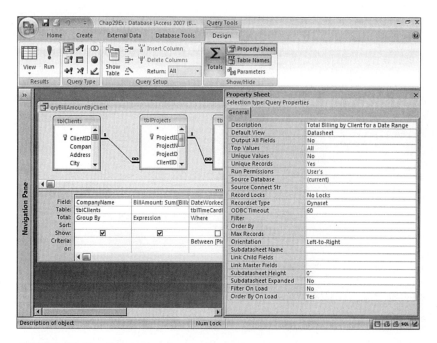

FIGURE 29.3   The Description property shows a detailed description of the purpose of the query.

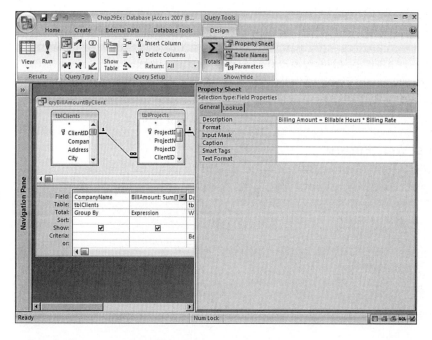

FIGURE 29.4   You can also describe an individual column in a query.

5. Click OK. The description you entered appears in the Navigation Pane, as shown in Figure 29.6, and it also appears in the output from the Database Documenter.

FIGURE 29.5   You can use the Object Properties dialog box to document each object in the database.

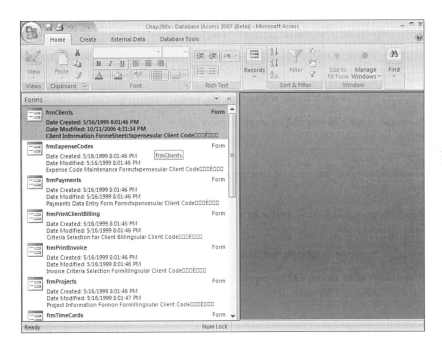

FIGURE 29.6   The Navigation Pane shows a description of a form.

Documenting Your Reports

You document reports in exactly the same manner as forms. Reports have a Description property that you must enter in the Object Properties dialog box. Remember that to access this dialog box, you right-click the object in the Navigation Pane and then choose Properties.

Documenting Your Macros

You can document macros in significantly more detail than forms and reports. You can document each line of the macro, as shown in Figure 29.7. Not only does this provide documentation in the Database Documenter, but macro comments also become code comments when you convert a macro to a Visual Basic module. In addition to documenting each line of a macro, you can add a description to the macro. As with forms and reports, to accomplish this, right-click the macro from the Navigation Pane and choose Properties.

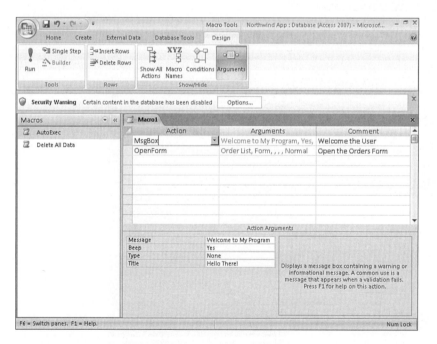

FIGURE 29.7   You can document a macro by including a description of what each line of the macro does.

Documenting Your Modules

I cannot emphasize enough how important it is to document your modules with comments. Of course, you do not need to document every line of code. I document all areas of my code that I feel are not self-explanatory. Comments assist me when I revisit the code to make modifications and enhancements. They also assist anyone who is responsible for maintaining my code. Finally, they provide the user with documentation about what my application is doing. Comments print with your code modules, as shown later in this chapter in the section "Using the Database Documenter." As with the other objects, you can right-click a module to assign a description to it.

Using Database Properties to Document the Overall Database

In addition to enabling you to assign descriptions to the objects in the database, Microsoft Access enables you to document the database as a whole. You do this by filling in the information included in the Database Properties window. To access a database's properties, click the Microsoft Office Access button and select Manage. Choose Database Properties from the Manage cascading menu. The Database Properties dialog box appears, as shown in Figure 29.8. As you can see, it is a tabbed dialog box; tabs include General, Summary, Statistics, Contents, and Custom.

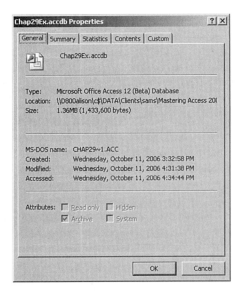

FIGURE 29.8   The Database Properties window shows the General properties of a database.

Descriptions of the tabs in the Database Properties dialog box follow:

▶ **General**—The General tab displays general information about your database. This includes the date the database was created, when it was last modified, when it was last accessed, its location, its size, its MS-DOS name, and its file attributes. You cannot modify any of the information on the General tab.

▶ **Summary**—The Summary tab, shown in Figure 29.9, contains modifiable information that describes the database and what it does. This tab includes the database title, its subject, and comments about the database. It also includes the *hyperlink base*—a base address used for all relative hyperlinks inserted in the database. This can be an Internet address (URL) or a filename path (UNC).

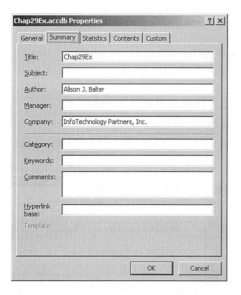

FIGURE 29.9   The Summary tab of the Database Properties dialog box contains modifiable information that describes the database and what it does.

▶ **Statistics**—The Statistics tab contains statistics of the database, such as when it was created, last modified, and last accessed.

▶ **Contents**—The Contents tab, shown in Figure 29.10, includes a list of all the objects contained in the database.

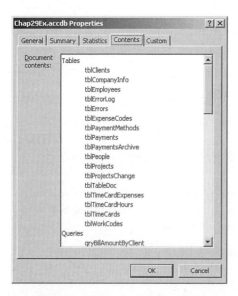

FIGURE 29.10   The Contents tab of the Database Properties dialog box includes a list of all the objects contained in the database.

▶ **Custom**—The Custom tab enables you to define custom properties associated with the database. This capability is useful when you are dealing with a large organization with numerous databases, and you want to be able to search for all the databases containing certain properties.

Using the Database Documenter

The Database Documenter is an elegant tool that is part of the Access application. It enables you to selectively produce varying levels of documentation for each object in your database. To use the Database Documenter, follow these steps:

1. Make sure that a database is open.

2. Click to select the Database Tools tab.

3. Click to select the Database Documenter tool in the Analyze group. The Documenter dialog box appears, as shown in Figure 29.11.

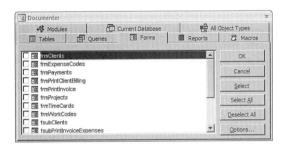

FIGURE 29.11   You can use the Documenter dialog box to designate which objects you want to document.

4. Click the appropriate tab to select the type of object you want to document. To document a table, for example, click the Tables tab.

5. Enable the check box to the left of each object that you want to document. You can click the Select All command button to select all objects shown on a tab.

6. Click the Options button to refine the level of detail provided for each object. Depending on which object type you selected, the Database Documenter displays different options. The next section of this chapter covers Database Documenter options.

7. Repeat steps 4–6 to select all database objects that you want to document.

8. Click OK when you are ready to produce the documentation.

29

TIP

To document all objects in the database, click the All Object Types tab and then click Select All.

CAUTION

Access can produce a very large volume of documentation, particularly if you select numerous objects. For this reason, you should carefully select the objects that you want to document. Make sure that, after you preview the results, you verify that you got what you expected *before* you print volumes of meaningless documentation.

NOTE

To document the properties of the database or the relationships between the tables in the database, click the Current Database tab and select Properties or Relationships.

After you select all the desired objects and options and click OK, the Object Definition window appears. You can use this Print Preview window to view the documentation output for the objects you selected (see Figure 29.12). This Print Preview window is just like any other Print Preview window; you can view each page of the documentation and send the documentation to the printer.

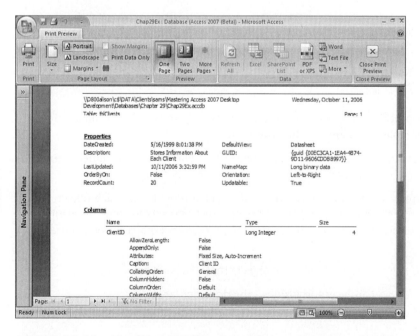

FIGURE 29.12   The Object Definition Print Preview window allows you to view each page of the documentation and send the documentation to the printer.

> **NOTE**
>
> The PDF/XPS option may not appear on your toolbar. It is a downloadable feature that you must obtain from Microsoft's website. You can access it via help under the topic "Enable support for other file formats, such as PDF and XPS."

Using the Documenter Options

By default, the Database Documenter outputs a huge volume of information for each selected object. For example, the Database Documenter documents each control on a form, including every property of the control. You can easily produce 50 pages of documentation for a couple of database objects. Besides being a tremendous waste of paper, this volume of information is overwhelming to review. Fortunately, you can refine the level of detail provided by the Documenter for each category of object you are documenting. Just click the Options button in the Documenter dialog box.

Figure 29.13 shows the table definition options. Notice that you can specify whether you want to print table Properties, Relationships, and Permissions by User and Group. You also can indicate the level of detail you want to display for each field: Nothing; Names, Data Types, and Sizes; or Names, Data Types, Sizes, and Properties. For table indexes, you can opt to include Nothing; Names and Fields; or Names, Fields, and Properties.

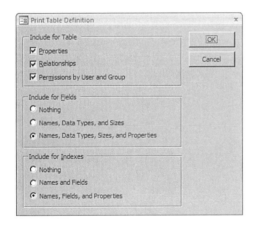

FIGURE 29.13   You can use the Print Table Definition dialog box to designate which aspects of a table's definition Access will document.

If you select the Queries tab in the Documenter dialog box and then click Options, the Print Query Definition dialog box appears, as shown in Figure 29.14. Here, you can select the level of detail the Database Documenter will output for the selected queries. You can choose whether to include Properties, SQL, Parameters, Relationships, and Permissions by User and Group for the query. You also can select the level of detail for each column of the query and for the indexes involved in the query.

FIGURE 29.14   You use the Print Query Definition dialog box to designate which aspects of a query's definition the Database Documenter includes in the output.

The Form and Report options are similar to one another. Figure 29.15 shows the Print Form Definition dialog box. Here, you can specify whether you want to print Properties, Code, and Permissions by User and Group for a form. For each control on the form, you can choose to print Nothing, the Names of the controls, or the Names and Properties of the controls. The Print Report Definition dialog box offers the same options. Both dialog boxes offer a Properties button, used to designate the categories of properties that the Database Documenter prints. You can opt to print Other properties, Event properties, Data properties, or Format properties.

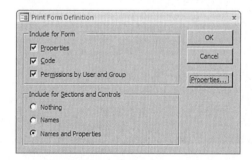

FIGURE 29.15   You use the Print Form Definition dialog box to designate which aspects of a form's definition the Database Documenter includes in the output.

For macros, you can choose whether you want to print macro Properties, Actions and Arguments, or Permissions by User and Group. For modules, you can choose to view Properties, Code, and Permissions by User and Group.

As you can see, the Database Documenter gives you great flexibility in the level of detail it provides. Of course, if you haven't filled in the properties of an object (for example, the description), it does you no good to ask the Documenter to print those properties.

Producing Documentation in Other Formats

After you produce the documentation and it appears in the Object Definition Print Preview window, you can output it to other formats. When the Print Preview window is active, the Print Preview tab appears (see Figure 29.16). The Data group provides you with several options for exporting your report. You can export to a PDF file, XPS file, Word document, Text file, Access database, XML file, Snapshot file, or HTML document! Depending on the option that you select, the next step varies. For example, if you opt to send the file to Microsoft Word, the Export – RTF File dialog box appears (see Figure 29.17). Here, you designate the destination and export options for the file.

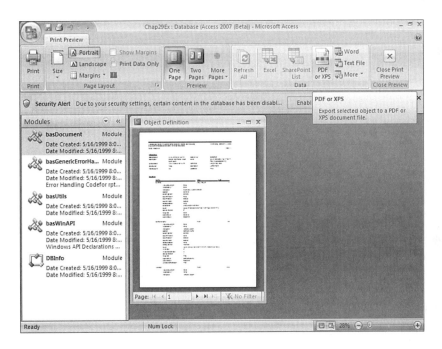

FIGURE 29.16   The Print Preview tab allows you to output your documentation to other formats.

29

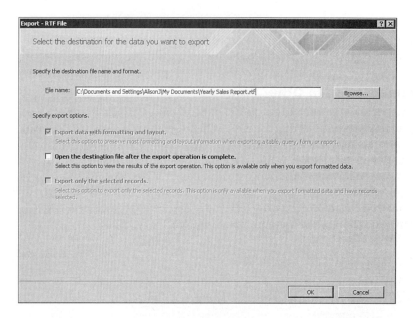

FIGURE 29.17   Using the Export – RTF File dialog box, you can select the export options for Microsoft Word.

Using the Object Dependency Feature

Microsoft added a wonderful feature in Access 2003. It provides the capability to view information about object dependencies. Here's how it works:

1. To invoke the Object Dependency feature, click to select the Database Tools tab.

2. Click Object Dependencies in the Show/Hide group. A message appears indicating that the dependency information needs to be updated before you can view object dependencies (see Figure 29.18).

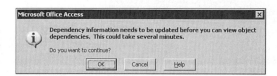

FIGURE 29.18   You must invoke the Track name AutoCorrect info option for dependency information to appear.

3. Click OK to continue. The Object Dependencies pane appears (see Figure 29.19).

4. Click to expand the node for which you want to view object dependencies. In Figure 29.20, you can see all the objects that depend on `tblProjects`.

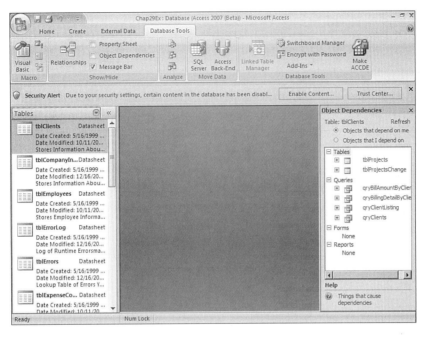

FIGURE 29.19   The Object Dependencies pane allows you to view an object's dependencies.

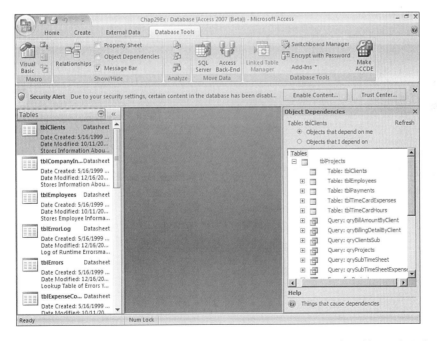

FIGURE 29.20   The Object Dependencies pane shows you the objects that depend on the
selected object, as well as objects that the selected object depends on.

5. By default, the Object Dependencies pane shows you the objects that depend on the selected object. You can click the Objects That I Depend On button to view the objects that the selected object depends on.

6. Using the Object Dependencies pane, you can drill even further down the chain to the objects that depend on those objects.

7. Close the Object Dependencies pane when you are finished viewing and working with object dependencies.

Writing Code to Create Your Own Documentation

Most of the time, the options that the Database Documenter provides are sufficient. At times, you won't like the format that the Database Documenter selects—or, more importantly, you might want to document properties of the database objects not available through the user interface. In these situations, you can choose to enumerate the database objects using code and output them to a custom report format.

Using ADOX (ADO Extensions for DDL and Security), you can enumerate any of the objects in your database. Listing 29.1 shows an example.

LISTING 29.1   Using ADOX to Enumerate the Table Objects in a Database

```
Sub EnumerateTables()

    Dim conn As New Connection
    Dim adoCat As New ADOX.Catalog
    Dim adoTbl As New ADOX.Table
    Dim strSQL As String

    DoCmd.SetWarnings False
    Set conn = CurrentProject.Connection
    adoCat.ActiveConnection = conn

    For Each adoTbl In adoCat.tables
        If adoTbl.Type = "Table" Then
            strSQL = "INSERT INTO tblTableDoc" _
                & "(TableName, DateCreated, LastModified) " _
                & "Values (""" & adoTbl.Name & """, #" _
                & adoTbl.DateCreated & "#, #" _
                & adoTbl.DateModified & "#) "

            conn.Execute strSQL
        End If
    Next adoTbl
    DoCmd.SetWarnings True
End Sub
```

> **NOTE**
>
> For the code in Listing 29.1 to run, you must first set a reference (via Tools, References) to the Microsoft ADO Ext 2.7 for DDL and Security library.

The `EnumerateTables` routine, located in the `basDocument` module of `CHAP29EX.ACCDB` on your sample code CD-ROM, documents various information about the tables in the database. It uses the ADOX catalog and table objects and a `For...Each` loop to loop through all the table definitions in the database. For each table in the database, it determines whether the table's type property is set to `"Table"`, indicating that it is a standard table (as opposed to a system table or a query). It then uses the `Execute` method of the `Connection` object to execute a SQL statement, inserting all the requested information about the table definition into a table called `tblTableDoc`. You can use this table as the foundation for a report. Of course, when you use appropriate `For...Each` loops and properties, along with the `ADOX` object model, you can obtain *any* information about *any* of the objects in the database using the same technique.

Practical Examples: Applying What You Learned

Practice using various options in the Database Documenter for your own applications. As you change the options for each object type, view the output differences. If you are particularly ambitious, try writing some code to enumerate the objects of the database.

Summary

Documentation is a necessary part of the application development process; fortunately, Microsoft Access makes documenting your application easy. This chapter covered the object Description properties Access provides, as well as the extremely powerful Database Documenter. It also covered a feature related to documentation called Object Dependency. Finally, the chapter highlighted how you can create your own documentation using ADOX and custom reports. Using any combination of the techniques covered in the chapter, you can produce complete documentation for all aspects of your application.

Maintaining Your Application

Why This Chapter Is Important

Although you don't need to do too much to maintain an Access database, you must know about a few important techniques that you should use to ensure that you maintain your databases as effectively as possible. The first technique is compacting. *Compacting* a database means removing unused space from a database (`.accdb` or `.mdb` file). The second technique involves backing up your databases. Without a proper backup procedure in place, you are like a circus performer without a safety net. Another useful technique to have at your disposal is the capability to convert a database created in an earlier version of Access to the `.accdb` file format. Finally, it is important that you are able to detect broken references within your database. This chapter covers the compacting process and the ways you can compact. It also covers all the other maintenance techniques available to you within Microsoft Access.

Compacting Your Database

As you and the users of your application work with a database, the database grows in size. To maintain a high state of performance, Access defers the removal of discarded pages from the database until you explicitly compact the database file. This means that as you add data and other objects to the database and remove data and objects from the database, Access does not reclaim the disk space that the deleted objects occupied. This not only results in a very large database file, but it also ultimately degrades performance, as the physical file becomes fragmented on disk. Compacting a database accomplishes the following tasks:

- ▶ Reclaims all space occupied by deleted data and database objects.

- ▶ Reorganizes the database file so that the pages of each table in the database are contiguous. This improves performance because, as the user works with the table, the data in the table is located contiguously on the disk.

- ▶ Resets counter fields so that the next value will be one more than the last *undeleted* counter value. If, while testing, you add many records that you delete just prior to placing the application in production, compacting the database resets all the counter values back to 1.

- ▶ Re-creates the table statistics used by the Access Database Engine when it executes queries and marks all queries so that the Access Database Engine recompiles them the next time they are run. These are two important related benefits of the compacting process. If you have added indexes to a table, or the volume of data in the table has changed dramatically, the query won't execute efficiently. The reason is that the Access Database Engine bases the stored query plan it uses to execute the query on inaccurate information. When you compact the database, the Access Database Engine updates all table statistics and the plan for each query to reflect the current state of the tables in the database.

TIP

Defragmenting the hard drive that a database is stored on before performing the compacting process is a good idea. The defragmentation process ensures that as much contiguous disk space as possible is available for the compacted database.

NOTE

In earlier versions of Access, the repair process was a separate utility from the compacting process. With Access 2000, Access 2002, Access 2003, and Access 2007, there is no longer a separate repair process. The compacting and repair processes both occur when you compact a database. When you open a database in need of repair, Access prompts you to compact it.

To compact a database, you can use one of five techniques:

- ▶ Use commands provided in the user interface.

- ▶ Click an icon you set up for the user.

- ▶ Set up the database so that Access compacts it whenever you close it.

- ▶ Use the `CompactDatabase` method of the `JetEngine` object.

- ▶ Use the `CompactRepair` method of the `Application` object.

Regardless of which method you select for the compacting procedure, the following conditions must be true:

▶ The user performing the procedure must have the rights to open the database exclusively.

▶ The user performing the procedure must have `Modify Design` permission for all tables in the database.

▶ The database must be available for you or the user to open it for exclusive use. This means that no other users can be using the database.

▶ The drive or network share that the database is located on cannot be read-only.

▶ The file attribute of the database cannot be set to read-only.

▶ Enough disk space must be available for both the original database and the compacted version of the database. This is true even if you compact the database to a database by the same name.

CAUTION

Backing up the database before you attempt to compact it is a good idea. It is possible for the compact process to damage the database. Also, do not use the compacting process as a substitute for carefully following backup procedures. The compacting process is not always successful. Nothing is as foolproof as a fastidiously executed routine backup process.

NOTE

If, at any time, Access detects that something has damaged a database, it will prompt you to repair the database. This situation occurs when you attempt to open, compact, encrypt, or decrypt the damaged database. At other times, Access might not detect the damage. Instead, you might suspect that damage has occurred because the database behaves unpredictably. This is the time you should first back up and then perform the compacting process, using one of the methods covered in this chapter.

Using the User Interface

Access provides a fairly straightforward user interface to the compacting operation. To compact a currently open database, click the Microsoft Office Access button and select Manager, Compact and Repair Database. Access closes the database, compacts it, and then reopens it.

To compact a database other than the currently open database, follow these steps:

1. Close the open database.

2. Click to select the Microsoft Office Access button and then choose Manage, Compact and Repair Database. The Database to Compact From dialog box appears, as shown in Figure 30.1.

30

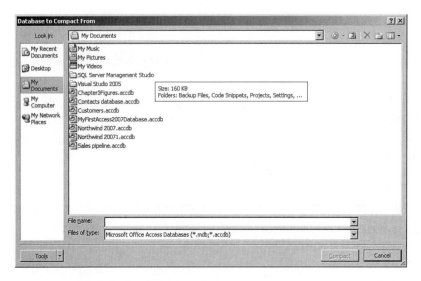

FIGURE 30.1   The Database to Compact From dialog box allows you to select the database you want to compact.

3. Select the database you want to compact and click Compact. The Compact Database Into dialog box appears, as shown in Figure 30.2.

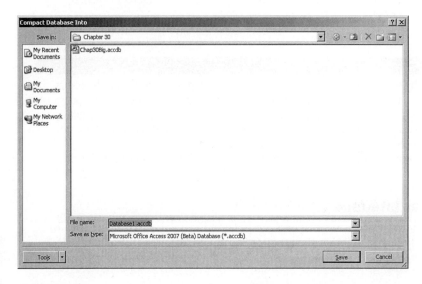

FIGURE 30.2   The Compact Database Into dialog box allows you to select the name for the compacted database.

4. Select the name for the compacted database. This can be the same name as the original database name, or it can be a new name. (If you are compacting a database to the same name, make sure that it is backed up.) Click Save.

5. If you select the same name, Access prompts you to replace the existing file. Click Yes.

Using a Shortcut

To give users a simple way to compact a database, you can create an icon that performs the compacting process. You accomplish this by using the /Compact command-line option, which compacts the database without ever opening it. The shortcut looks like this:

```
c:\Progam Files\Microsoft Office 2007\Office12
\Msaccess.exe c:\Databases\TimeAndBilling.ACCDB /Compact
```

You can follow this syntax with a space and the name of a destination database if you do not want Access to overwrite the current database with the compacted version. If you do not include a path for the destination database, Access places it in the My Documents folder by default.

> **NOTE**
>
> In Vista, the default location for new files is within \Users\UserName\Documents.

To create a shortcut, follow these steps:

1. Open the folder where you have installed your application.

2. Right-click the application (ACCDB) icon for your database.

3. Choose Create Shortcut.

4. Right-click the shortcut you just created.

5. Choose Properties.

6. Click the Shortcut tab.

7. Modify the shortcut to appear with the syntax shown in the previous example.

Compacting Whenever a Database Closes

Using the environmental setting Compact on Close, you can designate that Access will compact specific databases whenever the user closes them. Access compacts a database upon close only if it determines that the compact process will reduce the size by at least 256KB. To set the Compact on Close environmental setting, follow these steps:

1. Open the database that you want to affect. Click the Microsoft Office Access button and select Access Options. The Access Options dialog box appears.

2. Click the Current Database tab of the Access Options dialog box (see Figure 30.3).

3. Click the Compact on Close check box.

30

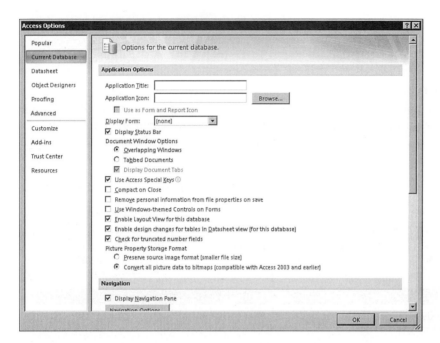

FIGURE 30.3   Select the Current Database tab of the Access Options dialog box.

NOTE

Although set in the Access Options dialog box, because the Compact on Close setting is on the Current Database tab, it applies only to the database that is open when you select the option. This feature allows you to selectively designate which databases Access compacts when the user closes them.

CAUTION

Remember that when you use the Compact on Close option, the database must meet all the conditions ordinarily required for Access to compact a database. For example, if other users are in the database when someone tries to close it, the user trying to close the database receives an error.

Using the CompactDatabase Method of the JetEngine Object

Using the CompactDatabase method, you can compact a database using code. The CompactDatabase method is performed on a member of the Microsoft Jet and Replication Objects (JRO), the JetEngine object. It receives a source connection string and a destination connection string as parameters. The Access Database Engine uses these connection strings to designate the source and destination databases, respectively. The Access Database Engine also uses the `Source Connection` and `Destination Connection` parameters for the following purposes:

▶ To change the locale of the database

▶ To encrypt or decrypt the database

▶ To convert the database from an older Jet version to a new version

▶ To specify the user ID and password

The Locale Identifier property of the `Destination Connection` parameter determines the collating order in which the Access Database Engine sorts the data in the compacted database. You use this option when you are working with a database in which the data is stored in another language, and you want the data to be collated in a particular language.

The Jet OLEDB:Encrypt Database property of the `Destination Connection` parameter specifies whether you want the compacted database to be encrypted. If you do not specify this property, the compacted database will have the same encryption status as the original source database.

The Jet OLEDB:Engine Type property of the `Source Connection` parameter designates the version of the source database to open. The Jet OLEDB:Engine Type property of the `Destination Connection` parameter indicates the version of the new database. If this property is omitted, the version of the source and destination databases is the same.

Finally, the User ID and Password properties of the `Source Connection` parameter enable you to supply the name of the user and the user's password for a database that is password protected.

The following code, contained in the `basCompactDB` module of `Chap30Ex.ACCDB`, compacts and encrypts a database called `Chap30Big.ACCDB`:

```
Sub CompactDB()
    Dim je As New JRO.jetengine
    Dim strFilePath As String

    'Store path of current database in a variable
    strFilePath = Left(CurrentDb.Name, InStrRev(CurrentDb.Name, "\"))

    'If destination database exists, delete it
    If Len(Dir(strFilePath & "Chap30Small.mdb")) Then
        Kill strFilePath & "Chap30Small.mdb"
    End If

    'Use the CompactDatabase method of the JetEngine
    'object to compact the database
    je.CompactDatabase SourceConnection:= _
        "Data Source=" & strFilePath & "Chap30Big.mdb", _
```

30

```
    DestConnection:="Data Source=" & strFilePath & "Chap30Small.mdb; " & _
    "Jet OLEDB:Encrypt Database=True"
```

```
End Sub
```

The code names the compacted database Chap30Small.MDB. The code also encrypts the database during the compacting process.

For this code to execute successfully, remember that you must close the Chap30Big database, and the user running the code must have the right to open the database exclusively. Furthermore, the user must have Modify Design permissions for all tables in the database. Finally, because the JRO JetEngine object performs the CompactDatabase method, you must include a reference to the Microsoft JRO 2.1 Library. Access does not reference this library by default when you create a new Access database. You must use Tools, References to reference it.

NOTE

The CompactDatabase method of the JetEngine object does not work with an Access 2007 database. You need to use the CompactRepair method of the Application object when working with Access 2007 files, and you can use the CompactDB method with databases stored in an earlier file format.

Using the CompactRepair Method of the Application Object

An alternative to the JetEngine object is a method introduced with the Access 2007 Application object. The CompactRepair method simplifies the process shown in the preceding section:

```
Sub CompactDBApp()
    Dim strFilePath As String

    'Store path of current database in a variable
    strFilePath = Left(CurrentDb.Name, InStrRev(CurrentDb.Name, "\"))

    'If destination database exists, delete it
    If Len(Dir(strFilePath & "Chap30Small.accdb")) Then
        Kill strFilePath & "Chap30Small.accdb"
    End If

    'Use the CompactRepair method of the application object
    'to compact and repair the database
    Application.CompactRepair strFilePath & "Chap30Big.accdb", _
        strFilePath & "Chap30Small.accdb", True

End Sub
```

The code, located in `basCompactDB`, declares a string variable. The `Left` and `InstrRev` functions extract the current path from the `Name` property of the `CurrentDB` object. If the designation file is located in the current folder, the code deletes it. The `CompactRepair` method of the `Application` object compacts and repairs the database into the designated destination database. The `CompactRepair` method receives three parameters. The first is the name and location of the source database, the second is the name and location of the destination database, and the third is whether you want Jet to log the operation.

Backing Up Your Database

Introduced with Access 2003 is the capability to back up your database from within Microsoft Access. Here's the process:

1. Open the database that you want to back up.

2. Click the Microsoft Office Access button and select Manage, Back Up Database. The Save As dialog box appears (see Figure 30.4).

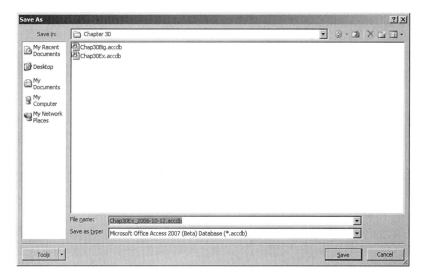

FIGURE 30.4   The Save As dialog box allows you to provide the name and location for the backup database.

3. Supply a filename and location for the database that you are backing up.

4. Click Save. Access creates a backup with the name and location that you designated.

Because the backup process simply creates a copy of the open database in a name and location that you specify, restoring the database involves moving and/or renaming the backup database file to the production location and name. You can then simply open the backup database and continue working as usual.

> **NOTE**
>
> After you have moved or renamed the backup database, you can access it from the Microsoft Office Access button just like any other Access database.

Converting an Access Database

Access 2007 makes it easy to interact with other versions of Access. Access 2007 allows you to open, read, and update Access databases stored in the Access 2000 file format and the Access 2002–2003 file format, without converting the files to the Access 2007 file format. It is important to note that as long as the database is stored in the MDB file format, you will not be able to take full advantage of Microsoft Office Access 2007's rich set of new features.

As mentioned earlier, you can use Access 2000 files and Access 2002–2003 files with Access 2007. If you want to convert an open database stored in the Access 2000 or Access 2002–2003 file format to the Access 2007 file format, take the following steps:

1. Click the Microsoft Office Access button and select Convert (see Figure 30.5). The Convert Database Into dialog box appears.

FIGURE 30.5   The Convert Database option appears after you click the Microsoft Office Access button.

2. Select a location and filename and then click Save to complete the process. Access warns you that the database has been upgraded and cannot be shared with users of Access 2003 or earlier versions (see Figure 30.6).

FIGURE 30.6   Access warns you that you cannot use the ACCDB file with previous versions of Access.

A method introduced with Access 2002 makes it easy to programmatically convert an Access database from one version to another. The code, found in basMaintenance, looks like this:

```
Sub ConvertAccessDatabase()
    Dim strFilePath As String

    'Store current file path into variable
    strFilePath = Left(CurrentDb.Name, InStrRev(CurrentDb.Name, "\"))

    'Delete destination database if it exists
    If Len(Dir(strFilePath & "Chap30V2007.accdb")) Then
        Kill strFilePath & "Chap30V2007.accdb"
    End If

    'Convert source database to Access 2007 file format
    Application.ConvertAccessProject strFilePath & "Chap30Small.mdb", _
        strFilePath & "Chap30V2007.mdb", _
        DestinationFileFormat:=acFileFormatAccess12
End Sub
```

To begin, the code declares a string variable. It uses the built-in Left and InStrRev functions to extract the path associated with the current database and place it in the strFilePath variable. If the destination database exists in the current folder, the code deletes it. The code uses the ConvertAccessProject method of the Application object to convert the Chap30Small.mdb database, located in the current folder and stored in the Access 2002–2003 file format, to the Chap30V2007.ACCDB database, located in the current folder and stored in the Access 2007 file format.

NOTE

Constants exist for the ConvertAccessProject method that allow you to convert to the Access 2007, Access 2002, Access 2000, Access 97, Access 95, and Access 2.0 file formats.

Detecting Broken References

Prior to Access 2002, it was difficult to locate and diagnose broken references. Access 2007 offers BrokenReference, a property of the Application object that rectifies this problem. If broken references exist, the property evaluates to True. If no broken references exist, it evaluates to False. Querying the BrokenReferences property is much more efficient than looping through each reference to determine whether it is intact. The code, found in basMaintenance, looks like this:

```
Sub DetectBrokenReference()
    'Display whether or not database contains a broken reference
    MsgBox Application.BrokenReference
End Sub
```

Practical Examples: Maintaining Your Application

Begin by using the techniques you learned to back up a database. Then practice compacting the database using each of the five methods covered in the chapter. Finally, determine whether your database has any broken references.

Summary

You should perform the compacting process regularly—especially on databases containing your application data. The compacting process provides major benefits in terms of both performance and conservation of disk space. The more activity that occurs on a database, the more frequently you should compact it. Although you should consider the compacting process an important part of the database maintenance process, remember that there is absolutely no substitute for proper backup techniques. This chapter also showed you a feature included in Access 2007 that allows you to back up an open database.

In addition to compacting your database, you need to understand the database conversion options available to you. You can convert databases from one version of Access to another using either the user interface or code. Finally, whereas it was an arduous, time-consuming process to detect broken references prior to Access 2002, the BrokenReference property makes this process much easier, by reporting whether all database references are intact. Using all the techniques covered in this chapter should save you a lot of time and effort in maintaining and working with your databases.

CHAPTER 31

Database Security Made Easy

Why This Chapter Is Important

Security in Microsoft Office Access 2007 is significantly different from that of its predecessors. Without knowledge of how the new security paradigm works, both you and your users will be very surprised at how things have changed. In this chapter, we'll explore all the changes to Microsoft Office Access 2007. After reading this chapter, you will be prepared to successfully deploy Access 2007 applications to your users.

What's New in Access 2007 Security?

Microsoft has completely revamped security in Microsoft Office Access 2007. The User Security model has been completely eliminated in Access 2007, unless you keep your database in the old Access file format (.MDB or .MDE) and that database *already* has user-level security applied. In other words, if you open a database created in an earlier version of Access and that database already has security applied, Access 2007 will support user-level security for that database. If you convert a database created in an earlier version of Access to the Access 2007 file format, Access 2007 will strip all user-level security settings from the database, and Access 2007 security will apply. The following is an overview of the changes to security in Access 2007:

▶ In Microsoft Access 2003, you had to code sign and trust a database before you could view any of its data. With Microsoft Office Access 2007, you can view the data in a database without having to enable Visual Basic for Applications (VBA) code.

▶ With Microsoft Office Access 2007, if you place a database (new or old database format) in a trusted location, those files will open and run without displaying warning messages or asking you to enable disabled content. A *trusted location* is a file folder or network share that you designate as secure. Furthermore, if you open databases created in earlier versions of Access and those databases have been digitally signed, if you have chosen to trust the publisher, those files will run without making trust decisions. VBA code in the signed database will not run until you trust the publisher. If the digital signature becomes invalid, you will once again not be able to run the VBA code.

▶ Microsoft Office Access 2007 includes a new feature called the *Trust Center*. Using the Trust Center, you can set and change security options within Microsoft Access 2007.

▶ In Microsoft Access 2003, you had to deal with a multitude of security messages when you opened a database. Microsoft has greatly simplified this process with Microsoft Office Access 2007. When you open a Microsoft Office Access 2007 database, a message bar appears (see Figure 31.1). You simply click the Options button on the message bar. The Microsoft Office Security Options dialog appears. Click to select Enable this content and then click OK. Access enables all disabled components.

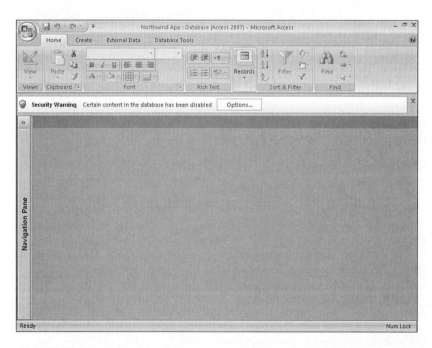

FIGURE 31.1   Using the message bar, you can easily enable disabled components.

▶ In Microsoft Access 2003, you had to apply security certificates to individual database components. In Microsoft Office Access 2007, the process of signing and distributing files is quite easy. All you need to do is to sign the database and then distribute it.

▶ Microsoft Office Access 2007 has a stronger algorithm for encrypting data. The encryption of a database scrambles the data in your tables. This prevents unwanted users from viewing the data in your Access databases using a tool such as a text editor.

▶ With Microsoft Office Access 2007 security, certain macro actions can execute without you or the user having to enable the database. In fact, all embedded macros run even if they contain macro actions that Access would ordinarily disable.

▶ If you open a database in a trusted location, all components of the database run without the need to explicitly trust the database.

▶ If you package, sign, and deploy a database from an earlier version of Access (.MDB or .MDE file), and the database contains a valid digital signature from a trusted publisher whose certificate you have trusted, all components will run without the need to make trust decisions. This is true whether you extract the database to a trusted or an untrusted location. When you package a database that is untrusted or one that contains an invalid digital signature, you will have to choose an option from the message bar to trust the database each time you open it, *unless* you deploy it to a trusted location.

▶ You must enable databases each time you open them if they are untrusted or you place them in an untrusted location.

> **NOTE**
>
> Although Microsoft Office Access 2007 offers an improved security model, if your data requires a higher level of security than what Access provides, you should store your data on a server such as Microsoft SharePoint Services version 3 or SQL Server 2005. Your Access forms and reports can then access the data stored on the server. For more information on integrating Access 2007 with SharePoint services see Chapter 21, "Access 2007 and SharePoint."

What Happened to User-Level Security?

As discussed in the "What's New in Access 2007 Security?" section of this chapter, Microsoft has eliminated user-level security, *unless* you keep your database in the old .MDB file format. If you opt to keep your database in the old file format (.MDB), user-level security will work just as it did in Access 2003. Unfortunately, you will not be able to take advantage of most of the new features available with Access 2007. For example, you will not be able to use rich text in Memo fields. After you convert your database to the Access 2007 file format (.ACCDB), Access strips user-level security from the database, and it will no longer be available to you.

If you do keep your database in the .MDB file format, you need to be aware that, by default, Access disables all potentially unsafe code. You must first trust the database before the code in your database will run.

Trusting a Database

Whether you create your database in the .MDB or .ACCDB format, you will need to trust the database before you can run any code within it. You can opt to trust that database for the current session, or you can trust the database permanently. The text that follows shows what's involved for each scenario.

Trusting a Database for the Current Session

One option is to trust a database while it is open. This process is quite simple. When you open the database, the message bar appears with a security warning that certain content in the database has been disabled (refer to Figure 31.1). After you click the Options button, the Microsoft Office Security Options dialog box appears (see Figure 31.2). Here, either you can opt to enable the content contained in the database, or you can have Access disable the code within the database. If you click Enable This Content, the database is fully functional as long as it is open.

FIGURE 31.2   The Microsoft Office Security Options dialog box allows you to trust a database for the current session.

Trusting a Database Permanently

Sometimes you know a database is safe, and you want to permanently enable its functionality. To do this, you need to create a trusted location. The steps are as follows:

1. Click to open the Microsoft Access button. You don't need to open the database that you want to trust.

2. Click Access Options. The Access Options dialog box appears.

3. Click to select Trust Center. The Access Options dialog box appears, as shown in Figure 31.3.

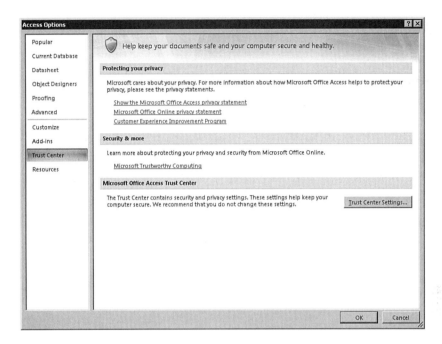

FIGURE 31.3   The Trust Center page of the Access Options dialog box allows you to create a trusted location.

4. Click Trust Center Settings. The Trust Center dialog box appears. Select Trusted Locations on the left side of the dialog box. Your screen appears as shown in Figure 31.4.

5. Click the Add New Location button. The Microsoft Office Trusted Location dialog box appears (see Figure 31.5).

6. Browse to select the location whose content you want to trust.

7. Indicate whether you want to trust subfolders as well.

8. Click OK after making your selections. The Trusted Locations dialog box appears with the new trusted location.

9. To complete the process, you must move the database to the trusted location (unless it is already there). With the database open, click the Microsoft Office button.

10. Select Save As, Access 2007 Database.

11. Navigate to the trusted location and then click Save. When you open any databases in the trusted location, the message bar does not appear.

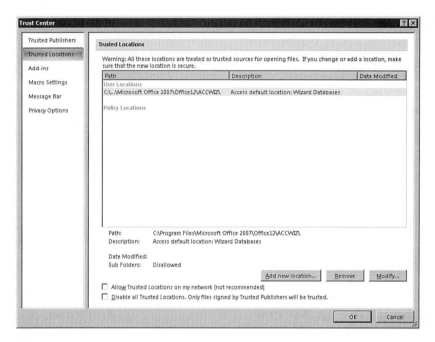

FIGURE 31.4   You use the Trust Center dialog box to add a trusted location.

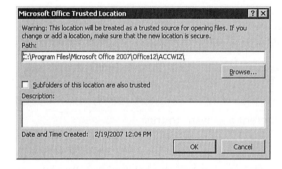

FIGURE 31.5   The Microsoft Office Trusted Location dialog box allows you to designate the specifics of the trusted location.

NOTE

An alternative to steps 9–11 is to close the database and then copy it to the trusted folder.

Using a Database Password to Encrypt an Office Access 2007 Database

The Encryption tool in Microsoft Office Access 2007 replaces two features available in Access 2003: database encryption and the database password. The following are the steps necessary to encrypt an Access 2007 database:

1. Open the database in Exclusive mode. To do this, select Open Exclusive from the Open drop-down in the Open dialog box (see Figure 31.6).

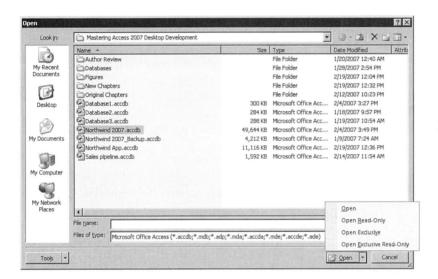

FIGURE 31.6   To encrypt a database, you must open it with the Open Exclusive option.

2. After you have opened the database, switch to the Database Tools tab.

3. Select Encrypt with Password in the Database Tools group. The Set Database Password dialog box appears (see Figure 31.7).

FIGURE 31.7   You use the Set Database Password dialog box to enter a password for the database.

4. Enter and verify the desired password and then click OK. The status bar will inform you that Access is encrypting the database.

5. Close and reopen the database. The Password Required dialog box appears (see Figure 31.8).

6. Enter the password and click OK. The database will now function as usual.

FIGURE 31.8   When you open an encrypted database, Access prompts you for a password.

Removing a Password from a Database

Removing a password from a database is quite simple. Here are the steps involved:

1. Open the database in Exclusive mode.

2. Select the Decrypt Database option in the Database Tools group of the Database Tools tab. The Unset Database Password dialog box appears (see Figure 31.9).

3. Enter the password for the database and click OK. Access removes the database password.

FIGURE 31.9   To remove a password from a database, you must supply the existing password.

Packaging, Signing, and Distributing an Access Database

Access 2007 makes the process of packaging, signing, and distributing an Access database very simple. After you create an .ACCDB or .ACCDE file, you package the file, apply a digital signature to the database, and then distribute the signed package to other users. The process of packaging and signing a database generates an Access Deployment (.ACCDC) file and places it in a designated location. The following are some facts that you should be aware of before you begin the process of packaging, signing, and distributing an Access database:

▶ You can use the new Access 2007 Package-and-Sign feature only on databases stored in the Access 2007 file format (.ACCDB or .ACCDE).

▶ Each package can contain only one database.

▶ When you use the Package-and-Sign feature, Access signs *all* objects in the database (not just code and macros).

▶ The packaging process generates a compressed file that facilitates the process of downloading a package.

Now that you are aware of some of the details applicable to the process, you can take the following steps:

1. Create a self-signed certificate.

2. Create a signed package.

3. Extract and use a signed package.

Creating a Self-Signed Certificate

As outlined in the preceding section, the first step in the process of packaging a database is to create a self-signed certificate. To do that, follow these steps:

1. From the Start menu, select All Programs, Microsoft Office, Microsoft Office Tools, Digital Certificate for VBA Projects. The Create Digital Certificate dialog box appears (see Figure 31.10).

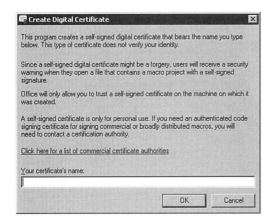

FIGURE 31.10   You use the Create Digital Certificate dialog box to create a new certificate.

2. Enter a name for the new certificate.

3. Click OK. A message appears, indicating that the new certificate was created successfully (see Figure 31.11).

FIGURE 31.11   Access informs you when the certificate is successfully created.

4. Click OK to complete the process.

Creating a Signed Package

Now that you have created a signed certificate, you are ready to create a signed package. Here's how:

1. Open the database that you want to package and sign.

2. Click the Microsoft Office button and then select Publish, Package and Sign (see Figure 31.12). The Select Certificate dialog box appears (see Figure 31.13).

3. Select a digital certificate and click OK. The Create Microsoft Office Access Signed Package dialog box appears (see Figure 31.14).

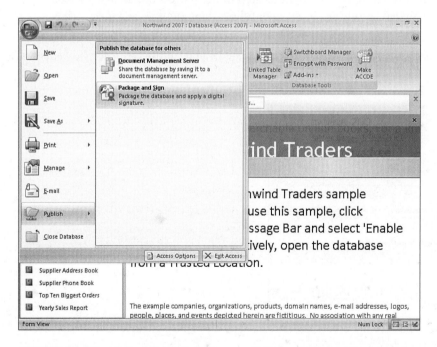

FIGURE 31.12   Select Publish, Package and Sign to create a signed package.

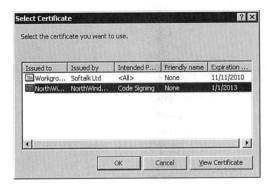

FIGURE 31.13   The Select Certificate dialog box allows you to select a digital certificate.

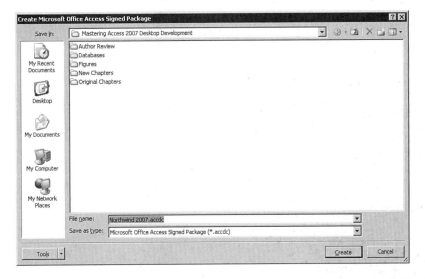

FIGURE 31.14   The Create Microsoft Office Access Signed Package dialog allows you to enter information about the signed package.

4. Supply a name and location for the signed package and then click Create. Access creates the .ACCDC file and places it in the location that you designated.

Extracting and Using a Signed Package

When you are ready to use the packaged database, you extract and use the signed package. Here are the steps involved:

1. With Access open, click the Microsoft Office button and select Open. The Open dialog box appears.

2. From the Files of Type drop-down, select Microsoft Office Access Signed Packages (see Figure 31.15).

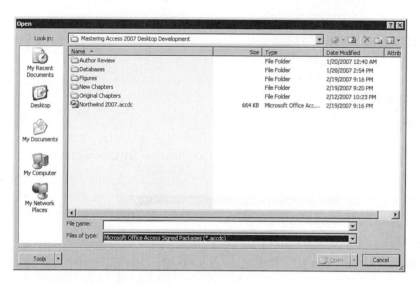

FIGURE 31.15   From the Files of Type drop-down, select Microsoft Office Access Signed Packages.

3. Select the .ACCDC file that you want to extract and click Open. The Microsoft Office Access Security Notice, shown in Figure 31.16, appears.

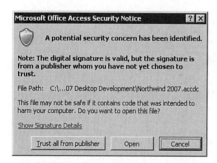

FIGURE 31.16   The Microsoft Office Access Security Notice allows you to designate certificate options.

4. If you want to trust all certificates from the publisher of the database, you can click the appropriate button. If you just want to trust this database, click Open. The Extract Database To dialog box appears.

5. Select a name and location for the extracted database and click Open. Access extracts the database and opens it.

Using the Trust Center

You use the Trust Center to change security and privacy settings in Microsoft Access. Take the following steps to work with the Trust Center:

1. Click the Microsoft Office button and select Access Options.

2. Select Trust Center on the left side of the Access Options dialog box.

3. Click Trust Center Settings. The Trust Center dialog box appears. Here, you can set the various security settings for Microsoft Office Access 2007.

Working with the Message Bar

The message bar provides quite a bit of valuable information. Access displays security alerts, workflow tasks, server document information, and policy messages. The message bar appears by default whenever it is appropriate. You can use the Trust Center to control when the message bar displays (see Figure 31.17). The first option shows all appropriate security messages. The second option hides the message bar in all situations. This feature interacts with the Disable All Macros Without Notification option. If you click Disable All Macros Without Notification, you won't get message bar alerts. If you select Never Show Information About Blocked Content, you will not receive *any* warnings about security issues, regardless of the other settings that you have selected in the Trust Center.

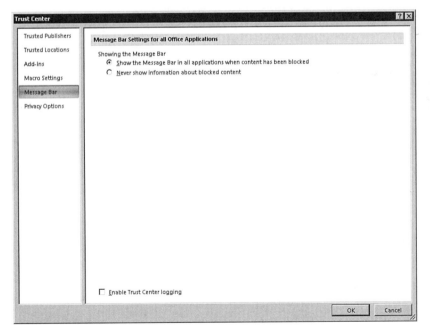

FIGURE 31.17   The message bar options of the Trust Center dialog box allow you to control when the message bar displays.

Using Privacy Settings

A homograph is one of two or more words that are spelled the same but have different meanings or pronunciations. An example is bass, meaning a fish or the lowest voice in a four-part chorus. In Internet terms, a *homograph* is a website that sounds like a well-known website but actually links you to a website that isn't legitimate. Phishers spoof the domain names of banks, credit card issuers, and other companies to gather your personal information. Links in your application can open you and your users up to homograph attacks and phishing schemes. Fortunately, the Trust Center can help to protect you and your users from homograph attacks and phishing schemes.

By default, you get security alerts whenever you have a document open and you click to navigate to a website that has potentially been spoofed. Access also warns you when you attempt to open a file from a website with an address that has a potentially spoofed domain name.

Working with Access Macros and VBA Code

You use macros to automate frequently used tasks. Unfortunately, a hacker can place a virus in an Access database that can propagate to your machine or even your network. For this reason, Access protects you against potentially unsafe macros and VBA code. You use the Macro Settings options in the Trust Center to control how your application reacts to macros (see Figure 31.18).

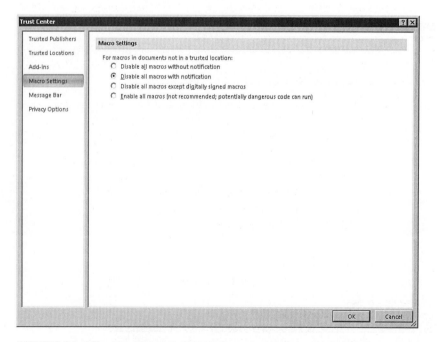

FIGURE 31.18   The Macro Settings allow you to determine what happens when your application contains a macro or VBA code.

If you choose Disable All Macros Without Notification, no macros run. If you want to run macros in a database with this setting in place, you must place any unsigned macros in a trusted location. The Trust Center ignores databases located in a trusted location.

If you choose Disable All Macros with Notification, Access disables macros but provides you with a warning that macros are present. This is the default setting. It's up to you as to whether you want to enable macros in each database. When you enable a macro, it is active only for the current session.

If you choose Disable All Macros Except Digitally Signed Macros, Access disables all macros, except those with a digital signature from a trusted publisher. With this option, Access notifies you that a publisher is not trusted. You are given the option of enabling the signed macros or of trusting the publisher. Access disables all unsigned macros without notification.

If you select the Enable All Macros option, you allow all macros in all databases to run without warning. This option is potentially very dangerous, and you should give some deep thought as to whether you really want to select it.

Security Tips and Tricks

There are certain situations regarding macros that you should know about. The first situation that you should know about is when a macro is not signed. You therefore cannot verify the publisher. Unless you know that the macro was from a trustworthy source, you should not enable the macros. With Microsoft Office Access 2007, you can do anything with a disabled database except run macros and VBA code.

The second situation is when the macro has been digitally signed but the signature has expired. As with the first situation, you should not run the macros contained in the database except if you know that the database is from a trustworthy source.

The next situation is when the macro signature is invalid. As with the preceding two situations, you should not run macros in a database with an invalid signature. In fact, the reason that the signature may not be valid is that someone tampered with it!

Another situation is when the macro signature is not trusted. In this case, the signature is valid, but you haven't yet opted to trust the publisher. When this situation occurs, a security dialog box appears, allowing you to trust all macros provided from the publisher of the database that you are opening. When you select that option, you are adding the publisher to the Trusted Publishers list in the Trust Center.

Working with Trusted Locations

The Trusted Locations portion of the Trust Center appears as shown in Figure 31.19. Using trusted locations, you can eliminate the need to enable the macros in a database each time you open it. You can leave the security settings at the default value, requiring you to enable macros in each of your databases that are not in a trusted location. Macros in any databases placed in a trusted location are automatically enabled, and you won't receive security alerts.

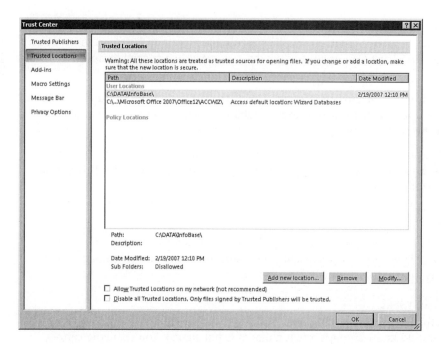

FIGURE 31.19   The Trusted Locations part of the Trust Center allows you to manage the locations of your files.

You can place your databases with macros and VBA code in a directory on your local machine or in a directory on the network. There are a couple of issues you should be aware of with each option. If you store your macros on your local machine, make sure that you use a Microsoft Windows logon password to protect your computer. This will keep people from tampering with your macros or your Access settings. Storing your databases on a network drive is less secure. The reason is that more people have access to them. Do not place your files in a public folder on a network share because they are very susceptible to tampering. Finally, if you opt to store your files on your local machine, do not place them within the Documents or My Documents folders because this will greatly increase your security risk. Instead, place them in a subfolder within the Documents or My Documents folders and make that folder the trusted location.

Creating a Trusted Location

To create a trusted location, you must first go to the Trusted Locations page of the Trust Center. Here's the process.

31

1. Click the Microsoft Office button and select Access Options. The Access Options dialog box appears.

2. Click Trust Center on the left side of the dialog box.

3. Click the Trust Center Settings command button. The Trust Center dialog box appears.

4. Click Trusted Locations on the left side of the dialog box. Your dialog box appears as shown previously in Figure 31.19.

5. Click Add New Location. The Microsoft Office Trusted Location dialog box appears (see Figure 31.20).

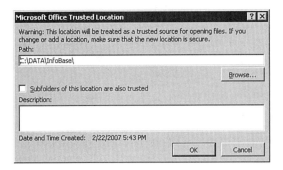

FIGURE 31.20   The Microsoft Office Trusted Location dialog box allows you to add trusted locations.

6. Enter the path for the trusted location and indicate whether you also want to trust subfolders. Finally, you can enter a description of the location that you are adding.

7. Click OK to complete the process. The location that you added appears in the list of trusted locations.

Removing a Trusted Location

Just as you can add a trusted location, you can remove one as well. Here are the steps involved:

1. Click the Microsoft Office button and select Access Options. The Access Options dialog box appears.

2. Click Trust Center on the left side of the dialog box.

3. Click the Trust Center Settings command button. The Trust Center dialog box appears.

4. Click Trusted Locations on the left side of the dialog box.

5. Select the location that you want to remove.

6. Click the Remove button. Access removes the location without warning.

Modifying a Trusted Location

Sometimes you will want to modify the settings associated with a Trusted Location. To do so, follow these steps:

1. Click the Microsoft Office button and select Access Options. The Access Options dialog box appears.

2. Click Trust Center on the left side of the dialog box.

3. Click the Trust Center Settings command button. The Trust Center dialog box appears.

4. Click Trusted Locations on the left side of the dialog box.

5. Select the location that you want to modify.

6. Click the Modify button. The Microsoft Office Trusted Location dialog box appears (the same dialog box that allowed you to add a trusted location).

7. Make the desired changes and click OK to close the dialog box.

Working with Trusted Publishers

Just as you can trust a file location, you can also trust publishers of database files. The Trusted Publishers page of the Trust Center dialog box appears as shown in Figure 31.21. In the figure, you can see the list of trusted publishers. To view a certificate, click the View button. The Certificate dialog box appears. The General tab of the dialog box, pictured in Figure 31.22, shows general information about the certificate. The Details tab, pictured in Figure 31.23, shows additional information about the certificate. The Certification Path tab shows you a tree of levels of certification (see Figure 31.24). If you click one of the levels and then click View Certificate, you will see the certificate associated with another certificate in the certification path.

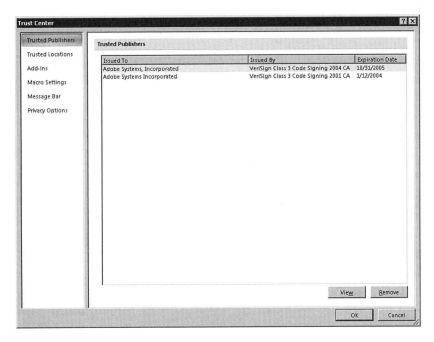

FIGURE 31.21   You use the Trust Center dialog box to view a list of trusted publishers.

FIGURE 31.22   You can easily view the certificate associated with a trusted publisher.

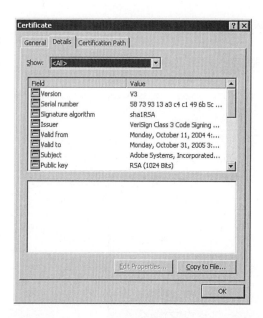

FIGURE 31.23   The Details tab shows additional information about a publisher.

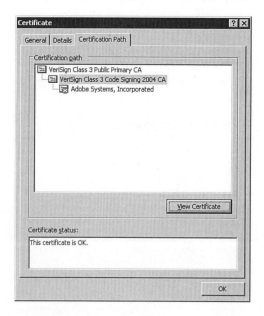

FIGURE 31.24   Using the Certification Path tab, you can see publishers included in the certification process.

Understanding How Databases Behave When Trusted and Untrusted

Unless a database has a digital signature or is located in a trusted location, Access disables several features. The following is a list of differences between a trusted and untrusted database:

- All VBA code is disabled.

- All unsafe expressions (certain formulas and functions in the database) are disabled.

- Unsafe actions in all macros are disabled. Unsafe actions include any functionality that could potentially modify the database or gain access to resources outside the database.

- Action queries, data definition language (DDL) queries, and SQL pass-through queries are all disabled.

- All ActiveX controls are disabled.

Working in Sandbox Mode

By default, when you are working in Access, you are working in Sandbox mode. With Sandbox mode enabled, Access blocks all expressions that it considers unsafe. These expressions include commands such as Kill and Shell that could be used to damage data and files on a computer. Sometimes you will want to execute such commands in a database located in a trusted location or with a valid trust signature. In those situations, you can disable Sandbox mode. Unfortunately, you can make this change only by modifying the Registry.

> **CAUTION**
>
> Modifying the Registry is a dangerous proposition. If you make a mistake when modifying the Registry, you can render your computer unusable. It is therefore important that you carefully back up all important data on your computer *before* you attempt to make the desired changes to the Registry.

To disable Sandbox mode in Windows Vista, follow these steps:

1. Close all running instances of Microsoft Access.

2. Select Start, All Programs, Accessories.

3. Click Run. The Open dialog box appears.

4. Type **regedit** and press Enter. The Registry Editor appears.

5. Expand the HKEY_LOCAL_MACHINE branch of the Registry.

6. Navigate to the key \Software\Microsoft\Office\12.0\Access Connectivity Engine\Engines.

7. In the right pane of the Registry Editor, under Name, double-click SandboxMode. The Edit DWORD Value dialog box appears.

8. Change the Value Data field from 3 to 2 and click OK.

9. Close the Registry Editor.

To disable Sandbox mode in Microsoft Windows XP or Microsoft Windows Server 2003, follow these steps:

1. Close all running instances of Microsoft Access.

2. Select Start, Run. The Open dialog box appears.

3. Type **regedit** and press Enter. The Registry Editor appears (see Figure 31.25).

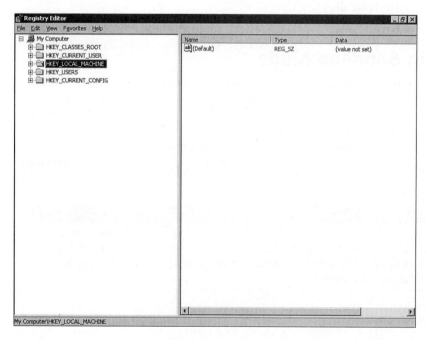

FIGURE 31.25   Using the Registry Editor, you can disable Sandbox mode.

4. Expand the HKEY_LOCAL_MACHINE branch of the Registry.

5. Navigate to the key \Software\Microsoft\Office\12.0\Access Connectivity Engine\Engines.

6. In the right pane of the Registry Editor, under Name, double-click SandboxMode. The Edit DWORD Value dialog box appears (see Figure 31.26).

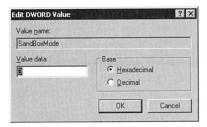

FIGURE 31.26   Change the SandboxMode value from 3 to 2.

7. Change the Value Data field from 3 to 2 and click OK.

8. Close the Registry Editor.

Removing User-Level Security

The only way to remove user-level security while working with Microsoft Office Access 2007 is to convert the .MDB file to an .ACCDB file. The database that you are converting cannot be encrypted, and you must belong to the Admins group of the workgroup used to secure the database.

To convert a database to the .ACCDB file format, take the following steps:

1. Click the Microsoft Office button and select Convert. The Save As dialog box appears.

2. From the Save In list, select a location for the database.

3. Make sure that you set the Save As type to Microsoft Office Access 2007 Database (.ACCDB).

An alternative is to use the Save As command to save an Access database in the .ACCDB format. Here are the steps involved:

1. Click the Microsoft Office button and select Save As, Access 2007 File Format. The Save As dialog box appears.

2. From the Save In list, select a location for the database.

3. Make sure that you set the Save As type to Microsoft Office Access 2007 Database (.ACCDB).

4. Click Save to complete the process.

Enabling or Disabling ActiveX Controls

ActiveX controls are programs that do not run as standalone applications. Instead, ActiveX controls reside within a Microsoft Office file or within a browser such as Internet Explorer. ActiveX controls add rich functionality to your applications. For example, you can use an

ActiveX control to add scheduling features to an Access database. ActiveX controls have full access to your computer. This makes them very powerful. For example, ActiveX controls can access the local file system and can change Registry settings of your operating system. This makes them potentially very dangerous. A hacker can use an ActiveX control to render Windows unusable!

You can take two steps to help ensure that ActiveX controls do not cause harm to your computer. First, as the developer, you can design ActiveX controls with security in mind. Second, you can use the Trust Center to check for two settings before the ActiveX control is loaded. It is important that the *kill bit* on the control is set in the Registry. This prevents controls that have a known exploit from being loaded. If the kill bit is set, Access will not load the control under any circumstances. Another important step is to ensure that the control is marked Safe for Initialization (SFI). The developer marks the control as SFI to verify the safety of the control. If the control is determined to be Unsafe for Initialization (UFI), the Trust Center applies additional restrictions on it. If a database contains VBA code (or macros) *and* ActiveX controls, the Trust Center applies even further restrictions.

If you load a database containing an ActiveX control, you will receive a Security Warning in the message bar. You must click Options and then select Enable This Content before the ActiveX control becomes usable. The exception to this scenario is if the database is either signed or placed in a trusted location. If the kill bit is set, the ActiveX control will not be enabled in either of those situations.

You can use the Trust Center to change ActiveX security settings for all your databases. Here's the process:

1. Click the Microsoft Office button and select Access Options. The Access Options dialog box appears.

2. Click Trust Center on the left side of the dialog box.

3. Click the Trust Center Settings command button. The Trust Center dialog box appears.

4. Click ActiveX Settings. Here, you can disable all ActiveX controls without notification, you can ask to be prompted before enabling Unsafe for UFI controls with additional restrictions and SFI controls with minimal restrictions, you can ask to be prompted before enabling all controls with minimal restrictions, or you can enable all controls without restrictions and without prompting. I do not recommend the final option because it opens you up for significant damage to your computer.

Enabling or Disabling Add-Ins

An add-in increases functionality to an Access application. An example is XML schemas. An add-in extends the capabilities of Microsoft Access. As with ActiveX controls, you can determine how Access handles add-ins. Here's how:

1. Click the Microsoft Office button and select Access Options. The Access Options dialog box appears.

2. Click Trust Center on the left side of the dialog box.

3. Click the Trust Center Settings command button. The Trust Center dialog box appears.

4. Click Add-Ins. The screen appears as shown in Figure 31.27. The first option is Require Application Add-Ins to Be Signed by Trusted Publisher. The second option is Disable Notification for Unsigned Add-Ins. This option becomes available only when you select the first option. Finally, you can choose Disable All Application Add-Ins. It is important to note that this option may significantly impair the functionality of your application.

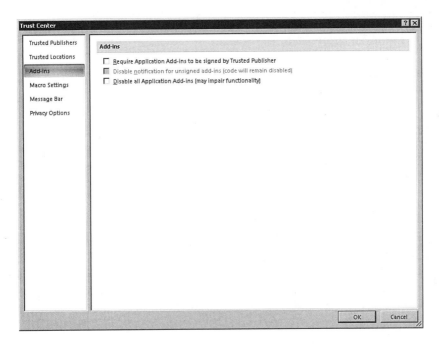

FIGURE 31.27   You can determine how Access reacts to add-ins.

Adding a Trusted Publisher

Earlier in this chapter, you learned how to view and remove Trusted Publishers. In this section, you learn how to add a Trusted Publisher. Before you add a Trusted Publisher, it is important that you understand when you should consider the developer of a database to be a Trusted Publisher. The following criteria should help you out:

▶ The code in the project is signed by the developer with a digital signature.

▶ The digital signature is considered valid.

▶ The digital signature is current. (It hasn't expired.)

▶ The certificate associated with the digital signature was issued by a reputable certificate authority (CA).

▶ The developer who signed the code project is a trusted publisher.

When you open a document containing macros and the document has been signed, one of the choices is Trust All from Publisher (see Figure 31.28). This option appears only if the signature for the document is valid. Simply select Trust All from Publisher, and all future databases published by that publisher will be considered safe.

FIGURE 31.28   You can trust all databases created by a particular publisher.

Practical Examples: Securing an Access 2007 Database

To secure an Access 2007 database, add a database password to an Access 2007 database of your choice. Then test the database to ensure that you can open it properly. Add a digital signature to the database and place it in a trusted location. Notice that you no longer have to enable macros and VBA code. Finally, practice using the Trust Center to work with the message bar, modify privacy settings, work with trusted locations, and work with trusted publishers.

Summary

Security in Access 2007 is dramatically different from that of its predecessors. User-level security is not available with the new .ACCDB file format. Instead, you can add a password to an Access database and encrypt it so that no one can view it with a tool such as a text editor. Whereas macros and VBA code ran without restriction in Access 2003 and lower, they will not run in Access 2007 unless the database has a valid digital signature or is placed in a trusted folder. It is important that you understand the specifics of Microsoft Office Access 2007 security so that your users will be able to properly take advantage of your macros and VBA code.

PART VI

Appendixes

*The following appendixes are available for download
at www.samspublishing.com/title/0672329328.*

IN THIS PART

Index

Symbols

A

custom collections, 648-651

   adding items to, 649

   creating, 649

   deleting items, 650

   looping through, 650

   referencing items, 650

For...Each construct, 413

Forms collection, 418-419

manipulating multiple instances of file
   information class, 655-656

Modules collection, 420

Printer, 504

referencing objects, 407

Reports collection, 419

Column Count property, combo boxes, 223

Column Width property, combo boxes, 223

columns

   adding to forms, 212-213

   client/servers, 922

   queries, selecting, 567

   removing from forms, 213-214

COM (Component Object Model), 950

Combo Box tool, 220

Combo Box Wizard, 220

combo boxes

   adding/removing items at runtime, 474-475

   converting text boxes to, 227-228

   converting to list boxes, 228

   forms, adding, 219-223

   labels, 222

   NotInList event, 472-473

   pop-up forms, 473-474

   properties, 222

Command Button Wizard, 244-245

   inefficient code generation, fixing, 396-398

command buttons

   adding to forms, 244-245

   captions, 290

   enabling and disabling, 425-428

   enabling/disabling, 426-427

hyperlinks, adding, 251

record source, saving changes to, 396

records, undoing changes to, 396

Command object

   ADO object model, 678-679

   declaring, 678

command tabs, ribbons (new features), 30-33

commands

   Add-Ins menu, Add-In Manager, 1038

   adding to ribbons, 944-945

   Debug menu

      Compile, 828

      Set Next Statement, 742-743

   Edit menu, New, 1034

   File menu, Export, 104-109

   Format menu, Change To, 830

   New menu, 1034

   Start menu, Run, 1033

   Tools menu

      Add-Ins, 1038

      Relationships, 124

   VBA, viewing code, 387

   View menu, Object Browser, 405

Comment Block tool (VBE), 364

comments

   adding to macros, 336-337

   VBA, 363-364

CommitTrans method, transaction processing, 929-930

Compact command-line option, 1095

Compact Database Into dialog box, 1094

Compact on Close environmental setting, 1095-1096

Compact utility, 803

CompactDatabase method, JetEngine object, 1096-1098

compacting databases, 803, 1091-1099

   with code, 1096-1099

   Compact on Close environmental setting, 1095-1096

   shortcut icons, creating, 1095

   user interface, 1093-1095

D

domains, 116

drill-down, pivot table data, 184

drivers, ISAM drivers (Windows registry keys), 866

drives, 804

DROP INDEX statement, SQL, 585

DROP TABLE statement, SQL, 586

DSN keyword, 867

DWORD Value command (New menu), 1034

dynamic arrays, 826

   declaring, 607-609

dynamic link libraries. See DLLs

dynasets, tables, 16

E

Edit DWORD Value dialog box, 1034

Edit menu commands, New, 1034

Edit method, data access class, 664-665

Edit Relationships dialog box, 16, 125

Edit String dialog box, 1034

Edit Watch dialog box, 748

editing

   project properties, 631

   Watch expressions, 748

Editor Format Tab, 395

editors, Registry Editor (invoking), 1033

emailing, errors, 780-781

embedded macros, 315

   creating, 332-333

embedded objects, In-Place activation, 466

embedded SQL statements, basing forms/queries on, 837

embedding SQL statements, 250-251

Empty value, Variant variables, 618-619

enabling command buttons, 425-428

encryption, CompactDatabase method,

   Application object, 1098-1099

   JetEngine object, 1096-1098

enforced referential integrity, 155

Enter event, controls, 445

Enter Key Behavior property, controls, 241

entity integrity, 122

entity integrity rules, 121-122

enumerated types, Intellisense and, 644-646

environment, 802

   development, RAM recommendation, 803

environmental settings, Compact on Close, 1095-1096

EOF property (ADO recordsets), 690-691

equal sign (=), query criteria operator, 146

Err object, 766-767

   properties, 766

   Raise method, 767-769

      generating errors, 767-768

      user-defined errors, creating, 768-769

err object-naming prefix, PDF:1133-1134

Error Checker, 479

error descriptions, displaying, 759

Error event

   forms, 440

   reports, 495

error events, 796

error forms, 784

   creating, 782-784

   printing, 785

error handling, 755-757

   call stacks, 765

      creating, 786, 789-790

   cascading error effect, 765-766

   centralizing, 760

   clearing errors, 764

   default error message, 756

   default handler, returning to, 759

   distributing applications, 841

   Err object, 766-767

      properties, 766

      Raise method, 767-769

   error descriptions, displaying, 759

file information class (Class modules), 653-656
  FullFileName property, 652-654
  GetDrive routine, 653-655
  GetName routine, 653-655
  GetPath routine, 653-655
  manipulating instances (collections), 655-656
  property declarations, 652
File menu commands, Export, 104-109
file servers
  applications, installing, 910
  versus client/servers, 9
FileDiaolg object, 463-464
files
  ACCDE files, 829
  ADP files, 56
  dBASE files, 872-873
    mapping dBASE data types, 873
  deleting, from disk, 760
  importing, supported file formats, 850
  INF files, 872
  linking, supported file formats, 850
  low-level file handling, 628-629
  opening, supported file formats, 850
  text files, importing, 630
  WZMAIN80.MDE, importing, 1037
  XML files, importing, 1068-1069
FillCells subroutine, 958
Filter event, forms, 440, 464-465
Filter On Load property, 288
Filter property, 287, 513-514
  forms, 234
  queries, 172
  tables, 102
Filter property (ADO recordsets), 695
filtering
  data, pivot table data, 183
  forms, 464-465
  pivot table data, forms, 261
  recordsets, 695

FilterOn property, 513-514
filters, forms, 234
find and replace feature, VBA, 390-391
Find dialog box, 390
Find method (ADO recordsets), 696-699
finding records in recordsets, 696-699
first normal form, 118
fixed arrays, 605
fld object-naming prefix, 1133-1134
flds object-naming prefix, 1134
FlipEnabled routine, 414-415
fmnu object-naming prefix, 1136
fmsg object-naming prefix, 1136
folders, My Documents, 1095
Font Color property, controls, 291
Font Italic property, controls, 291
Font Name property, controls, 291
Font Size property, controls, 291
Font Underline property, controls, 291
Font Weight property, controls, 291
Footer section, forms, 192
footers, 274. *See also* Page Footers
  adding at runtime (reports), 501
For Each...Next loops, 816-818
For Each...Next, 817
For Each...Next statement, 372-373
For...Each construct, 413
For...Each loops, iterating through collection items, 628
For...Next construct, 371
Force New Page property, reports, 293, 303
Fore Color, 290
foreign key fields, 95
foreign keys, 115-116
  referential integrity and, 121
foreign keys (client/servers), 922
Form and Report Class modules, 347
Form Design toolbar, 196
Form Design window, 196, 198-200, 202-204

H

J

Jet
client/servers, 922
Errors collection, 769-770
Jet Engine
converting databases from old versions, 1096-1098
objects, naming conventions, PDF:1133-1134
queries, optimizing, 553-555
Jet OLEDB Link Datasource, 861
refreshing external links, 869-871
Jet OLEDB Link Provider, 860
Jet OLEDB Link Provider String, 866-867
JOIN clause, SQL, 570-571
join lines (relationships), 124
joining tables, queries, 570-571
joins
outer joins
left outer joins, 563
queries, 562-564
right outer joins, 563
self joins, queries, 564-565
junction tables, 123-124

K

Key argument, Add method, 649
Key command (New menu), 1034
KeyDown event
controls, 448
forms, 439-440
KeyPress event
controls, 449
forms, 440
KeyUp event
controls, 449
forms, 440

keywords
ALL, SQL, 576
ANSI-92 extensions
CHECK, 591
DEFAULT, 590
NO INDEX, 591
As String, 374
ByVal, 987
Close, 628
Const, 381, 602
Dim, custom collections, 649
DSN, 867
Implements, 648
Input #, 628
Me, 450, 825
Open, 628
Preserve, 608-609
Public, 356
PWD, 867
Static, 355
TOP, SQL, 572
UID, 867
Write #, 628
Kill statement, 760

L

Label tool, 219, 282
Label Wizard, 273
labels
associating/disassociating with controls, 219
attached labels, 91
captions, 91, 290
default, 219
combo boxes, 222
forms
adding, 219
controls, 219
sizing, 203

M

O

passing by reference vs. passing by value, 610-613

string parameters, passing, 987, 989

subroutines, 373-374

Parameters dialog box, 588

Parent property, 416

classes, adding to, 647-648

pass-through queries, 578

creating, 578-579

passing objects to subroutines and functions, 413-414

passing parameters, 373-374

by reference vs. by value, 610-613

passing string parameters, 987-989

passwords

using database passwords to encrypt Access 2007 databases, 1109-1110

databases, 867-869

external data, 867-869

removing, 1110

pdbe object-naming prefix, 1134

Performance Analyzer, 807

queries, 553

Performance Analyzer dialog box, 808

period (.), 409

persisting recordsets, 702-704

personal applications, developing, 8

personal error handling, preventing, 786

Picture properties

forms, 231

reports, 287

pivot charts, creating from queries, 179

Pivot Table view

forms

controlling information detail, 261-262

data filtering, 261

displaying, 256-257

summarized data, 259

query displays, 179-183

axes exchange, 185

drill-down, 184

exchanging axes, 185

filtering data, 183

summarized data, 181-183

pivot tables

forms

controlling information detail (Pivot Table view), 261-262

creating from, 256-259

displaying (Pivot Table view), 256-257

filtering data (Pivot Table view), 261

summarized data (Pivot Table view), 259

queries

creating from, 179-183

filtering data, 183

replacing Crosstab queries with, 562

PivotChart view, switching to, 185, 262

PivotCharts, new features, 51

PivotTable view, displaying forms, 257-258

PivotTables, new features, 51

polymorphism, 638

Pop Up, 288

Pop Up property, forms, 235

pop-up forms, 473-474

PowerPoint

controlling from Access, 970-973

slides, 972-973

precedence, procedures, 357-358

prefixes (naming conventions), 1131

Preserve keyword, 608-609

preventing personal error handling, 786

previewing reports, 20

PreviousControl property, 416

Primary Key indexes, creating, 98

primary keys, 117

Append queries, 545

normalization, 25

normalization and, 115

Null values and, 122

Update queries, warnings, 541

primary keys (client/servers), 922

Column Count, combo boxes, 223
Column Width, combo boxes, 223
combo boxes, 222
compared to methods, 408-409
Connection strings, 673
Control, forms, 237, 241-242
control defaults, optimization and, 831
Control Source, combo boxes, 223
controls, 240-242, 290-293
   Allow AutoCorrect, 241
   Auto Repeat, 242
   availability, 236
   Back Color, 290
   Back Style, 290
   Can Grow, 290
   Can Shrink, 290
   Cancel, 241
   ControlTip Text, 241
   Data, 292
   Enter Key Behavior, 241
   Font Color, 291
   Font Italic, 291
   Font Name, 291
   Font Size, 291
   Font Underline, 291
   Font Weight, 291
   Format, 238, 290-291
   Help Context ID, 241
   IME (Input Method Editor), 242
   Name, 240, 292
   Other, 292
   Running Sum, 292
   Scroll Bars, 237
   Special Effect, 237
   Status Bar Text, 241
   Tab Index, 241
   Tab Stop, 241
   Tag, 242, 292
   Vertical, 241
ControlType property, 414-415

custom properties
   adding to classes, 651-652
   creating, 484-488
   PropertyGet routine, 486-488
   PropertyLet routine, 486-488
   Public variables, creating, 484-486
Data properties, form controls, 239-240
databases, documentation, 1081
DateCreated, 424
DateModified, 424
default, 410
Description property
   queries, 171
   query fields, 170
EOF property (ADO recordsets), 690-691
Err object, 766
Field List properties, queries, 171
field properties
   propagating, 481-483, 507-509
   queries, 170
fields
   Default Value, 91
   Input Mask, 90
   Validation Rule, 94
file information class, FullFileName property, 652-654
Filter, 287
   tables, 102
Filter On Load, 288
Filter property
   ADO recordsets, 695
   queries, 172
FilterOn, 513-514
Force New Page, reports, 293
Form, 416
Format properties
   form controls, 236-239
   query fields, 170

runtime errors, 750-751
Set Next Statement command, 742-743
Step Into option, 738-739
Step Out feature, 742
Step Over option, 741-742
Stop statement, 735
Watch expressions, 745-749
watches, 735
external data, 873-874
connection problems, 873
disk space, 874
library databases, 1022-1023
lookup feature, disadvantages of, 100
true/false evaluations, 819-820
Trust Center, 1115
Access macros and VBA code, 1116-1117
message bars, 1115
Trusted Locations, 1117-1119
modifying, 1120
removing, 1119
Trusted Publishers, 1120-1122
trusted databases, 1123
Trusted Locations, 1117-1119
modifying, 1120
removing, 1119
Trusted Publishers, 1120-1122
adding, 1127-1128
trusting
databases
for current sessions, 1106
permanently, 1106-1107
databases, 1106
txt prefix, 1132
Type field (USysRegInfo table), 1038
type libraries, 950
binding, 954
Type statement, 600
type structure declaration, generic error
handlers, 772
type structures
examples, 633-635
system information class, 666-667
Type variables, 600-601

TypeOfDrive, 1007
types, DLLs, 992-993
typing variables, declaring, 359

U

UCase function, 377
UFI (Unsafe for Initialization), 1126
UID keyword, 867
Unassigned Objects group, hiding, 61
unbound controls, 242
Unbound Object Frame tool, 283
unbound object frames, reports, 283-284
unbound OLE objects, 467
UNC (universal naming conventions), 861
hyperlink field type, 87
UNC addresses, tables (Hyperlink field type),
103-104
underlying recordsets, synchronizing forms with,
483-484
underscore (_), line continuation character
(VBA), 364
Undo event, forms, 434
undoing actions, 89
unhiding tables, Relationships window, 14
Unicode, 990
Unicode Compression property (fields), 97
uniform resource locators. See URLs
union queries, 577
creating, 575
graphical QBE, 576-577
sorting results, 576
unique identifiers (tables), 117
Unique Records property, queries, 171, 549
Unique Values property, queries, 171, 548-549
Universal Naming Convention. See UNC
Unload event, forms, 437
Unsafe for Initialization (UFI), 1126
untrusted databases, 1123
Update queries, creating, 539-541
UPDATE statement, SQL, 582
Updated event, controls, 444

V